AUSTRALIA IN THE WAR OF 1939-1945

SERIES ONE
ARMY

VOLUME II
GREECE, CRETE AND SYRIA

AUSTRALIA IN THE WAR OF 1939-1945

SERIES 1 (ARMY)

    I. To Benghazi. *By Gavin Long.**
    II. Greece, Crete and Syria. *By Gavin Long.**
    III. Tobruk and El Alamein. *By Chester Wilmot.*
    IV. The Japanese Thrust. *By Lionel Wigmore.*
    V. South-West Pacific Area—First Year. *By Dudley McCarthy.*
    VI. The New Guinea Offensives. *By David Dexter.*
    VII. The Final Campaigns. *By Gavin Long.*

SERIES 2 (NAVY)

    I. Royal Australian Navy, 1939-42. *By G. Hermon Gill.*
    II. Royal Australian Navy, 1942-45. *By G. Hermon Gill.*

SERIES 3 (AIR)

    I. Royal Australian Air Force, 1939-42. *By Douglas Gillison.*
    II. Air War Against Japan, 1943-45. *By George J. Odgers.*
    III. Air War Against Germany and Italy, 1939-43. *By John Herington.*
    IV. Air Power Over Europe, 1944-45. *By John Herington.*

SERIES 4 (CIVIL)

    I. The Government and the People, 1939-41. *By Paul Hasluck.**
    II. The Government and the People, 1942-45. *By Paul Hasluck.*
    III. War Economy, 1939-42. *By S. J. Butlin.*
    IV. War Economy, 1942-45. *By S. J. Butlin.*
    V. The Role of Science and Technology. *By D. P. Mellor.*

SERIES 5 (MEDICAL)

    I. Clinical Problems of War. *By Allan S. Walker.**
    II. Middle East and Far East. *By Allan S. Walker.**
    III. The Island Campaigns. *By Allan S. Walker.*
    IV. Medical Services of R.A.N. and R.A.A.F. *By Allan S. Walker.*

* Published.

The writers of these volumes have been given full access to official documents, but they and the general editor are alone responsible for the statements and opinions which the volumes contain.

GREECE, CRETE
AND
SYRIA

by

GAVIN LONG

CANBERRA
AUSTRALIAN WAR MEMORIAL

Published by

The Naval & Military Press Ltd
Unit 5 Riverside, Brambleside
Bellbrook Industrial Estate
Uckfield, East Sussex
TN22 1QQ England

Tel: +44 (0)1825 749494

www.naval-military-press.com
www.nmarchive.com

In reprinting in facsimile from the original, any imperfections are inevitably reproduced and the quality may fall short of modern type and cartographic standards.

CONTENTS

		Page
Preface	. . . .	xi
Chronology	. . . .	xiv

Chapter

1	BRITAIN AND GREECE	1
2	THE GERMAN ATTACK OPENS	29
3	THE REARGUARD ACTIONS IN THE FLORINA VALLEY	53
4	THE OLYMPUS-ALIAKMON LINE	72
5	THE CRITICAL DAYS	95
6	THE THERMOPYLAE LINE	131
7	THE EMBARKATION FROM GREECE	160
8	ESCAPES TO CRETE AND TURKEY . . .	185
9	RETROSPECT	191
10	THE PROBLEM OF CRETE	197
11	THE LOSS OF MALEME AIRFIELD . . .	221
12	DEFENCE OF RETIMO	256
13	HERAKLION—DEFENCE AND EMBARKATION .	279
14	RETREAT AND EMBARKATION	295
15	POLITICAL DECISIONS	320
16	THE SYRIAN PLAN	333
17	THE FIRST DAY	345
18	ACROSS THE LITANI	360
19	PRESSING ON: TO SIDON, MERDJAYOUN AND JEZZINE	375
20	THE FRENCH COUNTER-ATTACK . . .	393
21	DAMASCUS FALLS	415
22	MORE ATTACKS ROUND MERDJAYOUN . .	443
23	HARD FIGHTING AT JEZZINE	452
24	PREPARING A FINAL BLOW	467
25	THE BATTLE OF DAMOUR	482
26	ADMINISTERING THE ARMISTICE . . .	515
27	DEBITS AND CREDITS	523
28	ON THE NORTHERN FLANK	530
29	THE END OF A PERIOD	551
	APPENDIX: Abbreviations	563
	INDEX	565

ILLUSTRATIONS

	Page
The Anglo-Greek War Council	18
Mr Anthony Eden and a group of Middle East army and air force leaders	18
Transporting troops to Greece	19
Leave in Athens	50
The headquarters of the 6th Division, south of Olympus	50
Drawing water from a mountain stream east of Servia	50
Piraeus, 6th-7th April	51
Greek and Australian commanding officers at Vevi	51
Greek troops on a mountain road	51
The Aliakmon bridge	82
The crossing of the Aliakmon River	83
At the Aliakmon River	114
Generals Wilson, Blamey and Freyberg	115
An observation post in the Servia Pass	115
Platamon	146
Larisa during an air raid	147
A halt in a train journey during the withdrawal to Thermopylae	147
The crater in the approach to Pharsala bridge	162
Burning trucks south of Lamia	162
Brallos Pass	162
A Henschel 126 reconnaissance plane brought down by Bren gun fire	163
Air attack on the way to Monemvasia	163
On a ship evacuating troops from Greece	163
The sinking of the *Costa Rica*	178
A group of escapers of the 2/2nd Battalion	178
Suda Bay	179
Brigadier G. A. Vasey	210
Heraklion	210
Air attacks on Suda Bay	211
The bombing of Heraklion	226
German transport planes and mountain troops	226
Parachute landings at Suda Bay	227
Above Sfakia	227
Troops from Crete disembarking at Alexandria	322
A group of Australian escapers	322
Ras Naqoura	322
Army and air force leaders in Syria	322
The Iskandaroun crater	323
Bridge construction near Merdjayoun	323
Lieutenant G. B. Connor's party outside Fort Khiam	323

	Page
Major-General A. S. Allen and Brigadiers F. H. Berryman and A. R. Baxter-Cox	323
An artillery post near Merdjayoun	370
Fort Merdjayoun	370
Merdjayoun	371
A captured French sketch	371
The ceremony at Damascus	402
Barada Gorge	402
The Wadi Jezzine	403
Jezzine	466
The "Mad Mile" near Jezzine	467
French mule teams caught by shell fire near Bater	467
The Wadi Damour	498
Stretcher bearers at Damour	498
Khalde	499
Signing of the armistice, Acre, 12th July 1941	514
General Allen and Brigadier J. E. S. Stevens	514
The entry into Beirut	514
Australian ski troops	515
Embarking at Suez	515
On a transport between Suez and Bombay	515

MAPS

	Page
Greece	34
Allied dispositions Greece, 6th April	38
Allied dispositions Vevi, 10th April	66
Dispositions at Pinios, 17th April	106
Dispositions, Suda-Maleme area, 19th May	218
Dispositions, Retimo, 20th May	258
Dispositions, Heraklion, 20th May	282
The Syrian frontiers	339
Merdjayoun	386
Dispositions, Jezzine, 17th June	410
Dispositions, Damour, midnight 6th July	482

SKETCH MAPS

The Greek line in Albania, January 1941	2
The Balkan States and the proposed Allied defence lines	4
The Greek frontiers	10
Allied and Axis dispositions, 6th April	39
Dispositions, morning 9th April	45
The Yugoslav northern frontiers	51
"W" Group dispositions, 11th April	55
Dispositions, Vevi, 12th April	59
The rearguard at Sotir	67
The rearguard at Proasteion	68
The 16th Brigade withdrawal from Veria Pass	73
Dispositions, Servia Pass, 15th April	75
The Allied line in Greece and Albania, and General Papagos' proposed shorter line	78
The Olympus-Aliakmon and Thermopylae lines	82
Dispositions in the Olympus passes, 15th April	84
The German advance to 14th April	93
The withdrawal of the 21st New Zealand Battalion from Platamon	96
Sketch made by Brigadier S. F. Rowell before writing orders for withdrawal to Thermopylae	98
Dispositions, dusk 16th April	101
Dispositions, late afternoon 18th April	124
The withdrawal from Pinios	127
Dispositions, night 20th-21st April	136
The embarkation beaches	145
Dispositions at Thermopylae, 24th April	147
Brallos Pass, 24th April	156
Withdrawal from Thermopylae, dusk 24th April	159
Athens area	175
German dispositions in southern Greece	184

	Page
The Aegean Sea	187
The Iraqi frontiers	198
Baghdad-Habbaniya area	199
Crete	203
The German plan	229
Dispositions, Galatas area, morning 25th May	245
Dispositions at 42nd Street	252
The 2/1st Battalion counter-attack at Retimo, 21st May	262
The 2/11th Battalion attack at Perivolia, 28th May	270
Heraklion area	288
Suda Bay-Sfakia area	296
Eastern Mediterranean area	298
The rearguard at Sfakia	303
Palestine-Syria	334
The Palestine-Syria frontier	343
The 21st Brigade's advance, 8th June	348
The 25th Brigade's advance, 8th June	353
The 5th Indian Brigade's advance, 8th-9th June	357
Allied dispositions, dusk 8th June	358
The crossing of the Litani River	361
Litani River-Sidon area	367
The Free French advance to Kiswe, 9th-11th June	374
The 2/27th Battalion at Adloun, 11th June	376
Adloun-Wadi Zaharani area	377
The 2/16th Battalion's attack on Sidon, 13th June	381
Sidon-Damour area	385
Damascus area	393
Dispositions, inland sectors, 15th June	395
Dispositions, Merdjayoun area, dawn 16th June	396
Allied dispositions, Syria, 18th June	413
The attack on Damascus, 20th June	416
Mezze area	421
The advance of Habforce at Palmyra	440
The 2/25th Battalion's advance towards Hasrout, 26th-27th June	462
Palmyra area	466
The advance towards Rharife, 3rd-4th July	475
The 10th Indian Division's advance from Iraq	478
The El Atiqa defences	485
Damour, nightfall 8th July	500
Forward Australian battalions, 11th July	504
Mazraat ech Chouf-Badarane area	506
The attack on Jebel Mazar, 10th-11th July	509
Allied dispositions, Syria, 31st July	516
The Northern flank	533
Tripoli fortress area	535
Location of A.I.F., December 1941	545

PREFACE

THE historian of a force which forms only a part of a larger Allied army is constantly faced by the question on what scale he should attempt to write of the operations of the other contingents in that army. His resources do not enable him to write comprehensively of the experiences of other forces and, in any event, it is not his task. On the other hand he has a responsibility for ensuring that the operations of his own force are seen in proportion, and not larger than life. In this volume this problem presented itself in an interesting variety of forms. In the first engagement which is described, an Australian general commands a force including British and Australian units and some New Zealanders. Afterwards, in Greece, the I Australian Corps, temporarily renamed the Anzac Corps, includes a New Zealand as well as an Australian division, and a British brigade. From time to time New Zealand units are included in Australian brigade groups and vice versa. In Crete an Australian battalion becomes part of a British brigade; in Syria one Australian battalion joins an Indian brigade and then a British one, another serves in a Free French force; a British battalion joins an Australian brigade group; Australian cavalry and artillery serve in a British division; an Australian corps commander controls British, Indian and Free French formations.

As a general rule I have attempted to narrate in some detail the experiences of individual Allied units which were incorporated within Australian brigades. On the other hand, the operations of Allied formations included in the Australian Corps—the New Zealand Division in Greece, for example, or the 6th British Division in Syria—are described in more general terms; the operations of Allied formations in an area remote from the Australian one—for example, the 21st Indian Brigade in Syria—are told in little more detail than usually appears in a Commander-in-Chief's dispatch. Nevertheless the aim has been to enable the reader to see each phase of the operations in true perspective.

In these campaigns the cooperation of navy, army and air force was often of crucial importance. I have briefly recorded those naval and air operations which directly affected the troops on the ground, but the story of the naval and air forces in the Middle East in 1941 will be narrated in detail (from an Australian point of view) in the first volume of the naval series and the third volume of the air series of this history. The medical story is told in the first and second volumes of Dr Allan S. Walker's history.

Books and periodicals quoted are mentioned in footnotes. It is significant of the eventfulness of this brief period that the books thus referred to number more than forty; they include memoirs by or biographies of a number of the senior leaders, political and military, including Mr Winston Churchill, Admiral of the Fleet Viscount Cunningham, Field Marshal Earl Wavell, Field Marshal Lord Wilson, Field Marshal Papagos, General

Catroux, and Marshal of the R.A.F. Lord Tedder. Unfortunately no senior Australian soldier of this period has produced a memoir.

At the tactical level these chapters are based largely on formation reports and formation and unit war diaries with their appended documents and maps; but such records, particularly of operations in Greece and Crete, were sometimes so scanty that this volume depends more than any other in the series on interviews and correspondence with participants. Many of these took great trouble to establish the facts. It may reassure those who are inclined to mistrust such evidence to know that much of it has been perused and checked by other participants, and to reflect that those who provided these post-mortem accounts knew that what they were saying or writing would be open sooner or later to critical examination by others who also were on the spot. Also, as a general rule, the relevant parts of this volume were read in draft form and commented on by the commander or some other knowledgeable member or members of every formation or infantry unit concerned. It is inevitable, however, that some of the emphasis, some of the conclusions and some of the facts and figures will not be completely acceptable to all of these helpers. Among those who have given generous assistance either during the war or since, are:

Lieut-Generals F. H. Berryman, Lord Freyberg, Sir John Lavarack, Sir Iven Mackay, S. F. Rowell, Sir Stanley Savige; Major-Generals A. S. Allen, I. N. Dougherty, S. H. W. C. Porter, C. S. Steele, J. E. S. Stevens; Brigadiers A. W. Buttrose, I. R. Campbell, F. O. Chilton, W. E. Cremor, C. R. V. Edgar, D. Macarthur-Onslow, M. J. Moten, A. W. Potts, W. L. Rau, R. L. Sandover, J. R. Stevenson, H. W. Strutt; Lieut-Colonels A. P. Bennett, A. E. Caro, T. Cotton, A. G. Fenton, A. P. Fleming, R. R. Gordon, R. Honner, J. T. Lang, J. McCarty, R. H. Marson, A. C. Murchison, T. Mills, P. K. Parbury, W. T. Robertson, E. M. Robson, F. A. Stanton, P. D. Starr, F. H. Sublet, R. R. Vial; Majors J. R. Anderson, G. W. Austin, H. McP. Austin, S. B. Cann, H. S. Conkey, C. I. A. Coombes, E. A. Daly, H. M. Hamilton, J. S. Jones, R. R. Macartney, C. W. Macfarlane, G. O'Day, A. C. Robertson, W. B. Russell, C. A. W. Sims, D. E. Williams; Captains C. B. Britten, L. M. Long, D. H. Millar; Lieutenants J. Copeman, A. R. Cutler, VC, B. H. MacDougal, W. N. Macpherson, B. W. Moloney, R. Sheppard.

Other valuable sources were the several regimental histories which are acknowledged in the following pages. While this volume was being revised the trustees of the late Field Marshal Sir Thomas Blamey lent his wartime papers to me and my colleagues; these enabled me to strengthen the concluding chapters of this volume.

I am greatly indebted also to Major-General Sir Howard Kippenberger, Editor-in-Chief of the New Zealand Official War History, and his staff, particularly Messrs W. E. Murphy and I. McL. Wards. They provided much of the documentary material on which the first half of this volume is based, and read and re-read the typescript; correcting many defects and making many valuable suggestions. Brigadier H. B. Latham of the Historical Section of the United Kingdom Cabinet Office, and his colleagues, particularly Major-General I. S. O. Playfair, also gave invaluable support, pointing out errors of fact and emphasis, and making documents available which greatly helped me to write accounts of the higher planning, of the operations of British formations, and of the enemy's story. Much help was obtained from narratives of the campaigns in Greece and Crete written within the British Historical Section by Mr E. E. Rich.

My colleagues Mr G. Hermon Gill, who is writing the naval volumes of this history, Squadron Leader John Herington, who is writing the volumes dealing with the Australian part in air operations in Europe and the Middle East, and Mr Chester Wilmot, who is writing the volume which follows this one in the army series, contributed much valuable correction and criticism. I am indebted to my wife, to whom this volume was read in order that verbal infelicities and obscure terminology might be detected. My principal assistant was again Mr A. J. Sweeting, who assembled the material, did much checking, compiled the biographical footnotes and index and, with the help of my secretary, Miss Mary Gilchrist, prepared the manuscript for the printer. Mr. Hugh Groser drew all the maps.

Some of the description in this volume is based on personal observations. I was with the British force in Greece as a correspondent of Australian morning newspapers, and spent a few days in Crete. I was recalled to Australia, however, before the operations in Syria began.

G. L.

Canberra,
1st March, 1953.

LIST OF EVENTS
FROM 22 FEBRUARY TO 8 DECEMBER 1941
Events described in this volume are printed in italics

1941	22-23 Feb	*Athens conference on British aid to Greece*
	11 Mar	President Roosevelt signs Lend-Lease Bill
	26-27 Mar	*Revolution in Yugoslavia*
	28 Mar	*Battle of Cape Matapan*
	31 Mar	Enemy counter-attack in North Africa
	6 Apr	*German army invades Greece and Yugoslavia*
	11 Apr	Siege of Tobruk begins
	22 Apr	*Embarkation of troops from Greece begins*
	2 May	*Iraqi forces attack Habbaniya*
	20 May	*German troops descend on Crete*
	27 May	*Bismarck sunk 400 miles west of Brest*
	31 May	*Iraqi revolt collapses.*
	1 June	*Embarkation from Crete completed*
	8 June	*Allied invasion of Syria opens*
	15 June	British offensive opens in Western Desert
	21 June	*Allied troops enter Damascus*
	22 June	Germany invades Russia
	3 July	*Palmyra surrendered to British forces*
	9 July	*Damour falls*
	12 July	*Armistice in Syria*
	25 Aug	*British and Russian troops enter Iran*
	29 Aug	Mr Fadden becomes Prime Minister of Australia
	19 Sept	Germans occupy Kiev
	7 Oct	Mr Curtin becomes Prime Minister of Australia
	18 Oct	General Tojo becomes Prime Minister of Japan
	18 Nov	British offensive in Western Desert opens
	28 Nov	Russians retake Rostov
	7-8 Dec	Japanese attack Malaya and Pearl Harbour

CHAPTER 1

BRITAIN AND GREECE

THIS volume is chiefly concerned with three short campaigns fought in the Middle East in the spring and early summer of 1941. In each of them a relatively large Australian contingent took part and in two of them an Australian commanded the main force in the field during a crucial phase. Never before had Australian political leaders been so closely involved in decisions affecting the conduct of military operations, nor had Australian military leaders borne such heavy independent responsibility in the field. At every level, problems of enduring interest to smaller partners in an alliance were encountered. To the Australian infantry these campaigns brought their first experience of large-scale mountain warfare and of large-scale operations in which the enemy dominated the air.

In March 1941 when this phase opened, the British armies in Africa and the Greek army in Albania had inflicted a series of defeats on the Italian army, but, except for some recent skirmishes with a few German units newly arrived in Africa, and some commando raids in western Europe, there had been no contact between the British and German armies since June 1940. It was evident, however, that the German army would soon intervene both in North Africa and the Balkans, either in pursuance of Hitler's own long-range plans or in support of Italy.

When Italy had invaded Greece on 28th October 1940 she intended a lightning campaign which would soon leave her master of the southern Balkans and the Aegean. Instead, to the annoyance of her senior ally, she started a chain of events which was to make Greece briefly a battleground for the two main antagonists—Britain and Germany. An immediate Greek reaction to the Italian invasion had been to invoke a long-standing guarantee that Britain would support Greece if she were attacked without provocation. Promptly a British air force contingent was flown to Athens, and soon four squadrons and part of another were operating from Greek airfields against the Italians in Albania. In November a weak British infantry brigade group was landed in Crete, and about 4,200 anti-aircraft gunners, air force ground staff and depot troops were sent to Athens.

At that time the British Commonwealth stood alone against Germany and her European satellites. Italy's attack on Greece made Greece an ally of Britain against Italy but not against Germany. In the last quarter of 1940 Britain had two main military pre-occupations—the defence of the British Isles against invasion by an otherwise unemployed German army, and the defence of the Middle East against the Italians. The Greeks then neither sought nor needed military reinforcements on a large scale. They promptly defeated the Italian thrust into Greek territory from Albania and themselves took the offensive, with immediate success. When January opened fourteen Greek divisions faced nineteen Italian divisions on a front about 100 miles in length and from 20 to 30 miles within the Albanian border.

The Greeks had thus demonstrated that they could defend their territory against the Italians; but Germany was master of Hungary and Rumania, and should she march southward into Greece through Bulgaria Greece would undoubtedly be overpowered. In January the Germans were known to have twelve divisions and a powerful air force in Rumania. Greece on the other hand had only four divisions left on the Bulgarian frontier, and one of these was due soon to move to Albania. This was the situation when on 6th January the British Foreign Minister, Mr Eden, informed the Prime Minister, Mr Churchill, that

a mass of information has come to us over the last few days from divers sources, all of which tends to show that Germany is pressing forward her preparations in the Balkans with a view to an ultimate descent upon Greece. The date usually mentioned for such a descent is the beginning of March, but I feel confident that the Germans must be making every effort to antedate their move. Whether or not military operations are possible through Bulgaria against Salonika at this time of the year I am not qualified to say, but we may feel certain that Germany will seek to intervene by force to prevent complete Italian defeat in Albania.[1]

A month earlier the British forces in North Africa had opened an offensive, driven the Italians out of Egypt, and on 3rd and 4th January had overcome the Italians' fortress of Bardia in eastern Cyrenaica. On the 8th the Chiefs of Staff in London decided that no effective resistance could be offered to a German invasion of Greece but, nevertheless, on the 10th, after considering Eden's submission, Churchill and the Chiefs of Staff decided that once their army in Cyrenaica had taken the fortress of Tobruk, which was then invested, all other operations in the Middle East must have second place to sending the greatest possible help to the Greeks. Consequently General Wavell, Commander-in-Chief of the British army in the Middle East, and Air Chief Marshal Longmore, Commander-in-Chief of the British air forces there, went to Athens to

---

[1] Quoted in Churchill, *The Second World War*, Vol III (1950), p. 13.

offer to the Greek dictator, General Metaxas, a small immediate reinforcement—a squadron of infantry tanks, a regiment of cruiser tanks and some regiments of artillery.[2] In informal discussion Wavell told the Greek leaders that, in addition to these units, two or three divisions could be dispatched within two months.[3]

Metaxas declined these offers on the grounds that the contingent of artillery and armour would not effectively reinforce the Greek Army and might provide the Germans with a pretext for attacking Greece; he considered that even two or three divisions would be quite inadequate to the task presented by a German invasion. General Papagos, the Greek Commander-in-Chief, said that to establish "a good defensive position and a reasonably strong front" on the Bulgarian frontier reinforcement by nine British divisions with suitable air support would be needed. He wrote later that he advised Metaxas in private that the limited aid which Britain was proposing to give to Greece

would not only fail to produce substantial military and political results in the Balkans, but would also, from the more general allied point of view, be contrary to the sound principles of strategy . . . . In fact, the two or three divisions which it was proposed to withdraw from the Army in Egypt to send to Greece would come in more useful in Africa.[4]

After the Athens conference Wavell told the Chiefs of Staff in London that he himself regarded the proposal to send a few units as "a dangerous half-measure".

In a formal note sent to the British Government on 18th January Metaxas said that he would agree to the disembarkation of a British force in Greece as soon as German troops entered Bulgaria. He informed the Yugoslav Government of his replies to Britain, and later told Papagos that he knew that the Yugoslav Government had passed the information on to Germany.

Because of their uncertainty about the policy which Yugoslavia would follow if the German Army invaded Greece, Metaxas and Papagos faced a most difficult politico-military problem. If Yugoslavia joined Britain and Greece against German attack, the port of Salonika should be held because this was the only effective means of supplying the Yugoslavs; in that case the Anglo-Greek force should hold the well-designed frontier fortifications, named the Metaxas Line, with an eastern flank preferably on the Nestos River. If Yugoslavia remained truly neutral, a withdrawal from this line protecting Salonika to a shorter and stronger line on the Vermion Range, through Edessa to Mount Olympus would be desirable. If Yugoslavia allowed German troops to pass through her territory, however, they could outflank the Vermion passes by way of the Monastir Gap, and Papagos considered that, in that event, the best defensive line would be one through the Olympus passes, along the Aliakmon River

---

[2] The units offered would have been equipped with 65 tanks, 12 heavy guns, 24 field guns, 40 anti-aircraft guns, and 24 anti-tank guns.

[3] A. Papagos, *The Battle of Greece 1940-41* (published in Greek in 1945 and in English translation in 1949), p. 313.

[4] Papagos, p. 315.

and the Venetikos River and thence to a shortened front against the Italians in Albania.[5] These three lines—the Doiran-Nestos position, embracing the Metaxas Line; the Vermion-Olympus line; and a line along the Aliakmon—were to be frequently under discussion in the following weeks.

Three days after receiving Metaxas' note declining help the British Chiefs of Staff instructed Wavell and his fellow Commanders-in-Chief to continue the advance in Cyrenaica as far as Benghazi. At the same time they ordered him to seize Rhodes and other places in the Italian Dodecanese so as to forestall the possible arrival of a German air force in those islands, which lay close to the line of communications with Greece

---

[5] Papagos' comment is: "It shows once again how, in wars involving coalitions, political considerations are frequently opposed to the purely military and sometimes override them."

and Turkey. They also instructed him to form a reserve of four divisions for possible service in the Balkans.

Meanwhile, late in January, the Italians, who now had twenty-one divisions in Albania, opened a counter-offensive. It failed utterly after a few days. Thereupon Papagos decided that the Greek armies—which had been strengthened by the capture by their own troops of much Italian equipment and also by considerable instalments of British and captured Italians arms and vehicles from Egypt—should attack the shaken Italian force in the hope of taking Valona. Loss of that port would greatly slow down the maintenance of the Italian force in Albania, and a further Greek offensive might then drive them out of the country. At the least the capture of Valona would shorten the Albanian front before the Germans attacked in the spring; and the Greek leaders were now convinced that the Germans would do so as soon as the winter ended and the drying of the Balkan roads made large-scale military movement possible. At the request of the Greek King and Papagos, Air Vice-Marshal D'Albiac, who commanded the British air force in Greece, agreed to allow his squadrons to be used in close support of the troops in this offensive, to encourage them to endure the bombing by Italian aircraft and the rigours of a winter campaign in bitterly cold and inhospitable mountains. The offensive was opened with great dash early in February but Italian reinforcements had been hurried to Albania where twenty-six Italian divisions had now been identified, and the efforts of these, combined with exceptionally heavy snow and rain, halted the attack.[6]

Greece had thrown nearly all her resources into this offensive. Her army now contained twenty-one divisions and had the support of a small but efficient British air force. All but six of the Greek divisions were now engaged in the Albanian campaign, and those six, held in reserve or on the Bulgarian frontier, were far below strength.[7]

Meanwhile, on 29th January, General Metaxas had died. The King appointed M. Alexander Koryzis to succeed him as Prime Minister. On 8th February (two days after Australian troops had taken the surrender of Benghazi) Koryzis sent a note to the British Government reaffirming Greece's determination to resist a German attack, repeating that a British force should not be sent to Macedonia unless the German Army entered Bulgaria, but suggesting that the size and composition of the proposed force should be determined

> so that the British Government may be in a position to judge whether, despite the sacrifices which Greece is prepared to make in resisting the aggressor with the

---

[6] During the month the British air force was strengthened by the arrival of six Hurricanes with which the expert pilots of the fighter squadrons achieved some spectacular successes, the greatest being a remarkable fight on 28th February in which, in full view of both Greek and Italian armies, Hurricanes in company with Gladiators were estimated to have destroyed 27 Italian aircraft without loss to themselves. In the first three months of the year the R.A.F. claimed 93 Italian aircraft and probably 26 others for a loss of 8 fighters. The Italian losses were probably over-estimated.

[7] They were the 7th, 12th, 14th (6 battalions), 18th (5 battalions), 19th (3 battalions), 20th (6 battalions with little training). It would be impossible for Greece with a population of only 7,000,000 to maintain these 21 divisions in a prolonged war, particularly in view of the nation's poverty of mechanical equipment.

weak forces which she has available on the Macedonian front, the British force to be dispatched will be adequate together with the Greek forces to frustrate the German aggression and at the same time to encourage Yugoslavia and Turkey to take part in the struggle.[8]

Three days later Churchill and his Chiefs of Staff, adhering to their policy of concentrating on help to Greece and Turkey, decided that the British advance in Cyrenaica must be halted. On the 12th Mr Churchill conveyed this decision to General Wavell, who was informed that Mr Eden and the Chief of the General Staff, General Dill, were due in Cairo on the 14th or 15th February.

> Having surveyed the whole position in Cairo and got all preparatory measures on the move (wrote Churchill to Wavell) you will no doubt go to Athens with them, and, thereafter, if convenient, to Angora. It is hoped that at least four divisions, including one armoured division, and whatever additional air forces the Greek airfields are ready for, together with all available munitions, may be offered in the best possible way and in the shortest time . . . . In the event of its proving impossible to reach any good agreement with the Greeks and work out a practical military plan, then we must try to save as much from the wreck as possible. We must at all costs keep Crete and take any Greek islands which are of use as air bases. We could also reconsider the advance on Tripoli.[9]

Churchill told Wavell that he should not, however, delay the capture of Rhodes "which we regard as most urgent". The occupation of Rhodes was to be the first step in the achievement of the British Government's intentions, which were to help Greece, draw both Turkey and Yugoslavia into the Allied camp, and thus build up a battle front in the Balkans.

We know now that on 12th November 1940 Hitler had ordered his staff to plan the occupation of northern Greece, and had allotted an army of about ten divisions to this task. Later in November the German objective was enlarged to include the whole of Greece, and on 13th December Hitler decided that the invasion would probably take place in March. At this stage, partly as a result of the impression made on Hitler and his staff by the British successes in North Africa and the Greek successes in Albania, a larger German army was allotted to the coming invasion of Greece. The purpose to be attained was to secure Germany's southern flank in preparation for the invasion of Russia, timed to begin some time after 15th May, and in particular to preclude attack on the Rumanian oilfields by British bombers based in Greece.

The size of the army which Hitler could afford to employ against Greece was limited only by the capacity of the Balkan roads. No German formations had been engaged since June 1940, and since then the size of the German Army had been increased and its equipment and training improved. On the other hand Wavell had only two armoured divisions (one now lacking equipment) and eight infantry divisions (not including two small and lightly-armed African formations). Three of the infantry

---

[8] Quoted in Papagos, p. 401. The original French text appears in the Greek edition of Papagos' book, p. 433.
[9] Quoted in Churchill, Vol III, p. 59.

divisions were engaged against the Italians in Abyssinia, and a fourth—the 6th British—had been allotted to the attack on Rhodes. The 7th Armoured Division would not be available until its tanks, worn out after eight months of fighting in North Africa, had been overhauled or replaced. Consequently the divisions available for the garrisoning of Cyrenaica and the proposed expedition to Greece were the 2nd Armoured, 6th, 7th and 9th Australian and the New Zealand. Thus if one armoured and three infantry divisions were to be offered to Greece, as Churchill wished, the greater part of that force would of necessity consist of Australians and New Zealanders.

The cruiser tanks of the 2nd Armoured Division, which had arrived in Egypt in January, were worn, and no tracks were available to repair them except some which had been made in Australia and which "on trial proved to be practically useless".[1] Wavell decided to separate this division into two parts, send the headquarters and one brigade to eastern Cyrenaica and retain the second brigade for possible use in Greece. He planned to leave the seasoned 6th Australian Division in Cyrenaica and prepare to send to Greece first the New Zealand Division and then the 7th Australian Division and a Polish Brigade (formed from Poles who had escaped to the Middle East after the German invasion of their country). Finally he proposed to replace the 6th Australian Division in Cyrenaica with the relatively raw and ill-equipped 9th Australian and send the 6th to Greece.

This would mean that at least one fully equipped and seasoned division would be available for the defence of Cyrenaica for the first month or so, since it was calculated that the dispatch of the total force to Greece would take 10 weeks to complete. General Blamey . . . insisted, however, and as it proved rightly so, that the 7th Division was not sufficiently trained or equipped and that the 6th Division must be the first to proceed. This involved relieving the 6th Australian Division at once by the 9th Australian Division, which was only partly trained and equipped.[2]

The 18th and 25th Australian Brigades having now arrived in the Middle East from England, whither the 18th Brigade had been diverted in June 1940 and where the 25th had been formed, the 7th and 9th Divisions had been reorganised. The 18th Brigade, formed in 1939, and the 25th, formed in June 1940, and both relatively well-equipped, were transferred from the 9th to the 7th Division, which seemed likely to be in action before the 9th. The 21st Brigade remained in the 7th Division. The 9th Division was allotted the 20th, formed in April 1940, and the 24th and 26th, formed in July. The 8th Division, divided between Malaya and Australia, included the 22nd, 23rd and 27th Brigades.

The Australian Prime Minister, Mr Menzies, had arrived in Egypt on 5th February on his way to London for conferences with the British Cabinet. He was in North Africa until the 13th and had discussions with

---

[1] Wavell, *Despatch on Operations in the Middle East from 7 February 1941 to 15 July 1941*. The manufacture of these tracks is discussed in D. P. Mellor, *The Role of Science and Technology*, in the civil series of this history.
[2] Wavell despatch.

General Wavell about the general proposal to offer a force to Greece. After these discussions General Wavell had sent a telegram to Mr Churchill on the 12th February in which he said: "We have naturally been considering problem of assistance to Greece and Turkey for some time. My [telegram] of 11 February to Chief of the Imperial General Staff gave estimate of available resources but hope may be able to improve on this especially if Australian Government will give me certain latitude as regards use of their troops. I have already spoken to Menzies about this and he was very ready to agree to what I suggest. I will approach him again before he leaves." Menzies had also met General Blamey, the commander of the A.I.F. in the Middle East, but Churchill's directive to Wavell was received only the day before Menzies' departure, and Blamey, who was with his I Australian Corps headquarters in western Cyrenaica, had not yet learnt of the proposal to send his corps to Greece; it was not discussed between him and Menzies.

Wavell was not entirely happy about the plan. On 17th February he issued some notes in which his perplexity is evident:

> Owing to the political hesitations of our Greek and Turkish allies, to say nothing of the Yugoslavs, we have been placed in a most difficult situation. Our military objective in the Balkans is purely defensive, for the present at any rate. Personally I can never see much prospect of the Balkans becoming an offensive military front from our point of view. Therefore we want to employ the minimum force to secure our object . . . . On the other hand the Balkans may well become an offensive theatre from the air point of view, since there is a vital objective to the enemy in the Rumanian oilfields . . . . If we can put a sufficient force into Macedonia to ensure the safety of the port of Salonika and to hold its principal passes from Bulgaria, we shall have fulfilled our object . . . . Unfortunately our forces available are very limited and it is doubtful whether they can arrive in time.

He added that another course would be to help the Greeks to hold a line on the Aliakmon River. There was also a fear at Wavell's headquarters (as Menzies was informed when he was in Cairo) that the Greeks would not resist when the time came, a fear which the assurances of Koryzis had not wholly dispelled.[3] Meanwhile, the strength of the air forces in the Middle East was actually waning. Longmore pointed out afterwards that aircraft were arriving from Britain and America in insufficient numbers to replace losses; in the three months to 31st March, for example, losses were 184, arrivals 166. The army in the Middle East would not be substantially increased in the near future. Although convoys were arriving from England at regular intervals they were loaded principally with depot units, equipment and reinforcements. Except for the ill-equipped 2nd Armoured Division, no effective fighting formation had reached the Middle East from England since the fall of France, though plans were then afoot for sending the 50th British Division round the Cape.

---

[3] In December Harry L. Hopkins, President Roosevelt's envoy, had written, after meeting Churchill: "The P.M. impatient—prodding Wavell—but ever giving him his confident support—but Greece must be supported for political reasons and Wavell grudgingly agrees, for these are explicit orders from the Minister for Defence."—R. E. Sherwood, *The White House Papers of Harry L. Hopkins* (1948), Vol I, p. 256.

Eden and Dill arrived in Cairo on the 19th, having been delayed by bad weather. At a meeting there on the 20th Wavell described the force he could make available and (in spite of his doubt that an adequate force could be got there in time) advised proposing to the Greeks that an attempt be made to defend Salonika. Both Admiral Cunningham, commanding the Mediterranean Fleet, and Air Chief Marshal Longmore were doubtful about this feature of the plan. Later Cunningham wrote about the expedition as a whole:

> I gave it as my opinion that though politically we were correct, I had grave uncertainty of its military expedience. Dill himself had doubts, and said to me after the meeting: "Well, we've taken the decision. I'm not at all sure it's the right one."[4]

After this meeting Eden cabled to Churchill that his present intention was to tell the Greeks of the help they were prepared to give them and urge them to accept it as fast as it could be shipped. "There is a fair chance that we can hold a line in Greece," he said. What line should it be? Eden reported that "present limited air forces available make it doubtful whether we can hold a line covering Salonika, which General Wavell is prepared to contemplate. C. in C. Mediterranean considers that he could supply the necessary protection at sea to enable Salonika to be used as base, but emphasises that to do this he will need air protection, which we fear would prove an insuperable difficulty."

In a second cable sent the following day he added that it was a gamble to send forces to the mainland of Europe to fight Germans at that time, but that it was better to suffer with the Greeks than make no attempt to help them, though none could guarantee that they might not have "to play the card of our evacuation strong suit".

At these meetings it was decided to offer command of the proposed force to General Maitland Wilson, who had commanded the British army in North Africa in the opening stages of the offensive there, and was now Military Governor in Cyrenaica. Wavell sent a telegram to Wilson asking him to meet him at El Adem airfield near Tobruk next morning. Wilson was there when two aircraft arrived carrying Eden, Dill, Wavell, Longmore and their staffs to Athens. While the aircraft refuelled Wavell took Wilson aside and told him of his proposed appointment.

Later on the 22nd the delegates reached Athens. Before the military talks opened Koryzis assured the British envoys that in any circumstances Greece would resist German aggression. At a meeting attended by the British and Greek political and military leaders Eden said that Britain could offer three infantry divisions, the Polish Brigade, one armoured brigade and perhaps a second armoured brigade—a total of 100,000 men with 240 field guns, 202 anti-tank guns, 32 medium guns, 192 anti-aircraft guns and 142 tanks. The British force would arrive in three instalments: first, one division and one armoured brigade; second, a division and the Polish Brigade; third, a division, and a second armoured brigade if required. Perhaps five additional air squadrons would be added

---

[4] Viscount Cunningham, *A Sailor's Odyssey* (1951), p. 315.

by the end of March and two of those already in Greece would be re-equipped with Hurricanes. (Actually one of the two single-engined fighter squadrons in Greece was already being equipped with Hurricanes.[5])

General Papagos explained that the Greek army east of the Axios River, that is, in the area south of the Bulgarian frontier, included four divisions—the 12th in Thrace east of the Nestos River, the 18th between the Nestos and the Struma, the 7th and 14th west of the Struma. Together they comprised the Eastern Macedonian Army. Papagos added that if the Yugoslavs were willing to fight it would be fatal to them for the

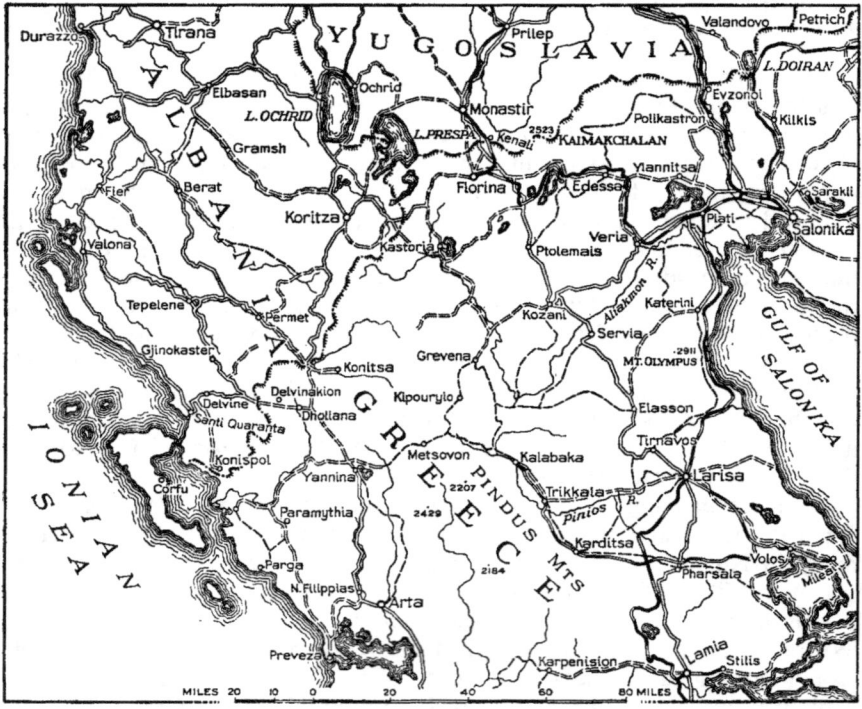

Greeks to abandon Salonika because only through that port could the Yugoslav Army be supplied. However, if Yugoslavia was neutral or allowed the German Army to march through her territory, only fortress troops should be left in eastern Macedonia and a line through the passes of Olympus, Veria and Edessa should be manned. To withdraw the Greek

---

[5] Lt-Col de Guingand, who accompanied Wavell, in *Operation Victory* (1946), p. 57, noted the zeal of his diplomatic colleagues at this conference. "I think it was Eden who stressed and enumerated the 'formidable' resources which we were prepared to send over," he wrote. "It sounded pretty good, but if a real expert had carried out a more detailed investigation, I doubt whether those present would have been so satisfied. Totals of men and guns are generally impressive. In the aircraft flying over I had been asked to produce a list showing totals of items we were proposing to send. My first manpower figures excluded such categories as pioneers, and in the gun totals I only produced artillery pieces. This was nothing like good enough for one of Mr Eden's party who was preparing the brief. He asked that the figures should be swelled with what to my mind were doubtful values. I felt that this was hardly a fair do, and bordering upon dishonesty. I don't know, however, whether figures meant very much to the Greeks by the time they were produced."

troops to this line would require at least twenty days. After such a withdrawal there would be thirty-five Greek battalions in the Vermion-Olympus line, and a motor division in reserve at Larisa. He considered that eight divisions with a ninth in reserve would be needed to hold the proposed line.

Dill and Wavell considered that this Greek force—comprising, after certain new formations had been raised, five or six divisions, together with the four (or their equivalent) from Egypt—"appeared to offer a reasonable prospect of establishing an effective defence against German aggression in the north-east of Greece". It was decided that Eden should send a telegram to Prince Paul of Yugoslavia seeking his views on the threat to Salonika, and it was agreed that "preparations should at once be made and put into execution to withdraw the Greek advanced troops in Thrace and Macedonia" to the Vermion-Olympus line.

At the conference, which continued until 3 o'clock in the morning, the Greek leaders finally agreed to accept the British offer.[6] The Greeks welcomed the appointment of General Wilson to command the British force.

From Athens the delegation travelled to Cairo and thence to Ankara, where they arrived on 26th February. There Eden told the Turkish leaders that Britain was sending about four divisions to Greece and consequently had none to offer Turkey. The Turks said that they lacked adequate military equipment and were unwilling to forgo their neutrality and join in forming a Balkan front until they were better equipped. In any event they regarded the Yugoslav Government as unreliable.

The Turkish leaders feared both Russia and Germany, and Russia more than Germany, and, after the fall of France, seem to have been resolved to keep out of the conflict if they could. Even if they had ardently wished to enter the struggle, the soldiers who ruled Turkey were unlikely to imagine that war could be waged successfully without efficient equipment. In addition, the British defeats of 1940 made a particularly deep impression on the Turks because they themselves had been defeated by British armies in 1918. How powerful must be the German Army! Nevertheless, both Government and people were very friendly towards Britain (as many Australians were later to discover).[7]

---

[6] In *Operation Victory* de Guingand describes how, after the conference, "Eden came in looking buoyant. He strode over to the fire and warmed his hands, and then stood with his back to the fire dictating signals to his staff. They in turn looked nearly as triumphant as he did, and were positively oozing congratulations. Presumably he had done his job and accomplished what he had set out to achieve. He was, therefore, no doubt entitled to be pleased with himself. But whether it was a job worth doing and in our best interests seemed to me very doubtful." In Australia in November 1941 Mr Menzies expressed the opinion that Mr Eden and General Dill had been sent to the Middle East to arrange for the campaign to be undertaken and not to obtain an independent judgment on it.

[7] In *Special Duties* (1946) Air Vice-Marshal A. S. G. Lee, who was on loan to the Turkish Staff College in 1938-1941, wrote: "Although their military and air leaders always showed a sublime outward confidence they knew that their air force, essential shield for the army in Thrace, would disappear in a few days of intensive fighting before a sizeable German air formation. And there were several sub-formations, together with large armoured and other forces, waiting impatiently in Bulgaria and Rumania. The Turks feared that these forces were intended for something bigger than an attack on Greece, and were sure that either Turkey or Russia was to be the victim. They were thus in no mood to listen to the arguments of successive visitors—that they should enter the war." When Germany attacked Russia, this writer added: "Turkey heaved a sigh of relief and wished good luck to them both!" Count Ciano, the Italian Foreign Minister,

On 1st March, while the conversations at Ankara were in progress, a report arrived that the German Army had begun to enter Bulgaria.[8] The British envoys returned to Athens next day. There Mr Ronald Campbell,[9] the British Minister at Belgrade, informed Mr Eden that the Yugoslav Government was frightened of Germany, but there was a chance that "if they knew our plans for aiding Greece they might be ready to help".[1] Major-General Heywood, head of the British Military Mission in Greece, told the British delegates that General Papagos was unwilling to order the withdrawal of his troops from eastern Macedonia to the Vermion-Olympus line until the Yugoslavs had defined their attitude, and that Papagos now said that it was too late to do so, the Germans having entered Bulgaria.

This news greatly disturbed the British leaders, because they had imagined that this withdrawal had already begun. At a meeting with Koryzis and Papagos, Dill said that he thought that it was understood at the previous conference that the movement was to begin at once. Papagos said that his understanding was that the movement was to await a reply from Yugoslavia; he had asked General Heywood each day whether a reply had been received from Belgrade and the answer was always no. Eden and Dill then urged Papagos to withdraw his divisions to the new line forthwith. Papagos replied that he could not now do so, because it would take fifteen days to carry out the move and, as the Germans had now entered Bulgaria, they might attack while the Greek troops were retiring. He added that transfer of troops from Albania was impossible, and proposed that the British force be disembarked at Salonika and sent forward to help his four divisions to hold the passes in Macedonia and defend Salonika. The British staff thus found themselves faced with a plan which they considered unsound and likely to result in the available forces being defeated in detail. At these meetings Eden and Dill found Papagos "unaccommodating and defeatist".[2] At the request of Eden and Dill, Wavell hastened to Athens, arriving on 3rd March.

---

recorded in his diary in April 1942 that the Italian Ambassador at Ankara said to him: "The Turkish ideal is that the last German soldier should fall upon the last Russian corpse."
In May 1940, when France was still fighting, the British and French commanders-in-chief had met the Turkish Marshal Chakmak and discussed the situation created by the successful German attack on France and Italy's imminent entry into the war. Chakmak was sceptical concerning the ability of the Allies to take effective action to support Turkey.
In *From Sea to Sky* (1946) Air Marshal Sir Arthur Longmore, the British Air Commander-in-Chief, wrote of this conference: "The Turk is a realist, there was nothing very much in the way of air support that either the French or ourselves could immediately give him beyond the Hurricanes we had originally supplied at the expense of the Middle East. As a result of the conference I formed the opinion that any further discussions with the Turks as to active participation in any eventuality in which they, themselves, were not attacked would be purely academic."

[8] In fact, the German entry into Bulgaria, which was to have begun on 2 March, was delayed for several days by unfavourable weather.

[9] Sir Ronald Campbell, GCMG, CB. Minister at Belgrade 1939-41, in Washington 1941-45. B. 7 Jun 1890.

[1] Churchill, Vol III, p. 87.

[2] The text of Eden's telegram of 4 March to Churchill describing these discussions is published in *Documents Relating to New Zealand's Participation in the Second World War*, Vol I (1950), pp. 247-9. New Zealand documents quoted in this volume have been drawn from Vol I and Vol II of this work.

The British delegates decided "to enlist the aid of the King in this crisis" and on 4th March, at a meeting which the King attended, Papagos proposed as a compromise that the forces in eastern Macedonia (including the 7th, 14th and 18th Divisions) should remain in the Metaxas Line along the Bulgarian frontier, but that forces in western Thrace be withdrawn except for the garrisons of two forts and a few outposts; and that the 12th Division from western Thrace and the 20th and 19th, his only general reserve, should join the British force on the Vermion-Olympus position. In this way, if Yugoslavia fought, the troops in that position could move forward into the Metaxas Line. If Yugoslavia was neutral the three weak divisions and other smaller groups in eastern Macedonia (they possessed only twenty-one battalions between them) would hold the Metaxas Line as long as they could and then attempt to withdraw to the rear line. The British delegates considered that they now were faced with the choice of accepting Papagos' plan "of attempting to dribble our forces piecemeal up to the Macedonian frontier", or accepting his compromise, or withdrawing the offer of military support altogether. They decided that the first course would be disastrous for military reasons and the third disastrous for political reasons and agreed to the second, with some misgivings. (To adopt the third course would have entailed turning back the first large convoy of British troops, which was due at Piraeus, the port of Athens, on the 7th.) A condition of acceptance of Papagos' compromise plan was that General Wilson should command the whole force on the Vermion-Olympus line. To prevent further misunderstanding the agreement was put in writing.

Thus the British delegates considered the "new and disturbing situation" which faced them on 2nd March so different from that which had been envisaged a week earlier that they contemplated abandoning the whole enterprise. In the telegrams sent to London at the time and in later writings by the participants too much seems to have been made of the facts that during these seven days no Greek soldiers were moved from the thinly-manned line on the Bulgarian border, and that once the Germans entered Bulgaria Papagos was unwilling to move his frontier force back. At least partial acceptance of Papagos' contention that the forces should not be withdrawn from the line forward of Salonika until Yugoslavia's policy had been clarified was implied by Eden on the 5th when he sent the Yugoslav Regent a letter urging him to join the Allies, and instructed the British Minister in Belgrade to inform the Regent that the defence of Salonika would depend on Yugoslavia's attitude.[3]

On the same day Eden cabled to Churchill:

> While recognising the dangers and difficulties of this solution, the military advisers did not consider it by any means a hopeless proposition to check and hold the German advance on this [the Vermion-Olympus] line, which is naturally strong

---

[3] Churchill, Vol. III, p. 87.

and with few approaches. A fighting withdrawal from this line through country eminently suitable for rearguard action should always be possible at the worst.[4]

On the British side the decision had been made and there could be no turning back; and in the minds of the Greeks the impending invasion was stirring ancient memories, and producing a mood, half mystical, half fatalistic and wholly heroic. In the right-wing newspaper *Katherimne*, for example, on 8th March, the day after cruisers had disembarked a few thousand men in British khaki at Piraeus, George Vlachos, an Ajax defying the lightning, wrote an open letter to Hitler in the course of which he said:

It appears—so the world is told by wireless propaganda—that the Germans want to invade Greece. We ask you why. If the operation against Greece was essential to Axis interests from the start . . . Germans and Italians would have attacked us side by side. It is clear therefore that the attack on Greece was not a necessity for the Axis. Why is it so now? To prevent the creation of a front in the Balkans against Germany? But neither Serbia nor Turkey has any reason to let the war spread.

It is perhaps to save the Italians in Albania. But would not the Italians be finally and irrevocably defeated the moment even one German soldier sets foot in Greece? Would not all the world assert aloud that 45,000,000, after attacking our 8,000,000 were now begging for the help of another 85,000,000 to save them? Perhaps you will say 'What about the British?' We reply that we did not bring them here. It is the Italians who brought them to Greece. Do you wish us to bid them begone? Even so, let us tell them to go. But to whom should we tell this? To the living? For we hardly can tell the dead, those who fell in our mountains, who landed wounded in Attica while their country was burning at home, came here and fell here, and found tombs here . . . .

What will your army do, your excellency, if, instead of divisions of infantry and artillery, Greece sends to garrison the frontiers a force of 20,000 wounded, legless, armless, bloody and bandaged to welcome it? Will your army strike at such a garrison? Small or great, the free army of Greeks will stand in Thrace as it stood in Epirus. It will fight. It will die there too. In Thrace it will await the return of that runner from Berlin who came five years ago and received the light of Olympia, and changed it into a bonfire, to bring death and destruction to a country small in size, but now made great, and which, after teaching the world how to live, must now teach it how to die.

What steps had been taken to inform and consult the Governments of Australia and New Zealand about the expedition? As mentioned above Mr Menzies and General Wavell had discussed the plan in general terms in Egypt about 12th February. Mr Menzies had been in London while the Athens conferences were held. He attended a Cabinet meeting on the 24th February—the day after that on which the Greek leaders accepted

---

[4] General Dill apparently continued to have misgivings. On 17th March, when visiting General Neame's headquarters in Cyrenaica, he said: "You are going to get a bloody nose here, Philip, and it is not the only place where we shall get bloody noses." (*Playing With Strife*, by Lt-Gen Sir Philip Neame, 1947, p. 268.) In *Our Armoured Forces* (1945), Lt-Gen Sir Giffard Martel, then commander of the Royal Armoured Corps, wrote (p. 93): "The Prime Minister was in favour of sending them [the Greeks] military forces and he told me so one day in February . . . . I pressed the General Staff view and said that I thought we would rue the day that we sent forces to fight those great German armies in Greece. The whole matter was, of course, inevitably bound up with political considerations that may have outweighed the purely military aspect. As we had taken no clear line, we eventually drifted into a position where we were bound to come to their help, and at that stage the C.I.G.S. [General Dill] agreed with the decision to do so."

the British offer. After the Cabinet meeting (at which Menzies noted an inclination on the part of the subordinate ministers to accept any proposal of Churchill's without question) he sent a cable to the acting Prime Minister, Mr Fadden,[5] outlining the plan and saying that the feeling in London was unanimously in favour of the expedition although it was realised that it would be risky and an evacuation might have to occur; in that event, Churchill considered, "the loss would be primarily one of material and that the bulk of the men could be got back to Egypt". Menzies added that he would not favour the proposal if it was only "a forlorn hope"; but it was being undertaken on the advice of Wavell and Dill who were "able and cautious". Churchill had said that, if Japan attacked, "adequate naval reinforcements would at once be dispatched to Australian waters"—an opinion which, Menzies considered, "must be a little discounted".

> Allowing for all these things (he concluded) though with some anxiety my own recommendation to my colleagues is that we should concur.

On the same day a cable which reached Fadden from the Dominions Office gave further details of the plan and added:

> It was felt that we must take this only remaining chance of forming Balkan front and persuading Turkey and possibly Yugoslavia to enter the war on our side. From the strategical point of view the formation of Balkan front would have advantages of making Germany fight at the end of long lines of communication and expending her resources uneconomically, of interfering with Germany's trade in the Balkans and particularly oil traffic from Rumania and of enabling us to establish platform for bombing of Italy and Rumanian oilfields . . . . Finally from the political point of view, failure to help this small nation putting up a gallant fight against one aggressor and willing to defy another would have grave effect on public opinion throughout the world and particularly in the United States.

On the 26th the New Zealand Government (which had not yet received a copy of Eden's cable about the Athens Conference of the 22nd) concurred in the expedition on the understanding that its division was fully equipped and accompanied by an armoured brigade. It added that it was a matter of great satisfaction that the 2nd N.Z.E.F. was ready to play the role for which it was formed, and that Australian and New Zealand forces were chosen to stand together.

Fadden cabled to Menzies on the 28th that the Australian War Cabinet concurred in the employment of two Australian divisions in Greece but added that consent "must be regarded as conditional on plans having been completed beforehand to ensure that evacuation, if necessitated, will be successfully undertaken and that shipping and other essential services will be available for this purpose if required". This cable was repeated to the New Zealand Government.

In the following week, however, the news from the Middle East—the misunderstanding with Papagos, the closing of the Suez Canal as a result

---

[5] Rt Hon Sir Arthur Fadden, KCMG. Treasurer and Member of Aust War Cabinet 1940-41; Prime Minister Aug-Oct 1941; Treasurer since Dec 1949. Chartered accountant; of Townsville and Brisbane; b. Ingham, Qld, 13 Apr 1895.

of dropping of mines by enemy aircraft, the failure of a British attack on the island of Castellorizo in the Dodecanese,[6] the identification of German aircraft over western Cyrenaica, and a rumoured landing of German armour at Tripoli—was causing alarm in London. On 4th March, Menzies asked that the Greek plan be re-examined. (Advanced elements of the Australian part of the force were due to sail on the 6th.)

On the 6th Churchill sent a gloomy cable to Eden. It contained the following passages:

> Situation has indeed changed for worse. Failure of Papagos to act as agreed with you on February 22, obvious difficulty of his extricating his army from contact in Albania, and time-table of our possible movements furnished by Wavell, together with other adverse factors recited by Chiefs of Staff—e.g., postponement of Rhodes and closing of Canal—make it difficult for Cabinet to believe that we now have any power to avert fate of Greece unless Turkey and/or Yugoslavia come in, which seems most improbable. We have done our best to promote Balkan combination against Germany. We must be careful not to urge Greece against her better judgment into a hopeless resistance alone when we have only handfuls of troops which can reach scene in time. Grave Imperial issues are raised by committing New Zealand and Australian troops to an enterprise which, as you say, has become even more hazardous. We are bound to lay before the Dominions Governments your and Chiefs of Staff appreciation. Cannot forecast their assent to operation. We do not see any reasons for expecting success, except that of course we attach great weight to opinions of Dill and Wavell.[7]

Churchill added that he was reconsidering re-planning to the extent of concentrating on an advance on Tripoli.

Eden replied that "in the existing situation we are all agreed that the course advocated should be followed and help given to Greece. We devoutly trust therefore that no difficulties will arise with regard to the dispatch of Dominions forces as arranged." At this stage, as Wavell wrote later, "there were practical difficulties in any reversal of plan; the troops were on the move and a change would have caused confusion".[8]

The Chiefs of Staff informed Wavell on the 7th that "Cabinet decided to authorise you to proceed with operations and by doing so Cabinet accepts for it full responsibility. We will communicate with Australian and New Zealand Governments accordingly."

Menzies then cabled to Fadden about the "changed and disturbing situation" in Greece on the return of Eden and Dill from Turkey and the written agreement with Papagos which had followed. He said that the Cabinet's military advisers discounted the possibility of a successful thrust by a German armoured force in North Africa and believed that Benghazi could be held. He then underlined two considerations: first, that Eden and Dill had made a written agreement, and second, that Eden, Dill and Wavell considered that the "adventure" had "reasonable prospect of success".

---

[6] A British commando force occupied Castellorizo, but later was counter-attacked and withdrawn.
[7] Churchill, Vol III, p. 90.
[8] "The British Expedition to Greece 1941" by Field Marshal Wavell (*Army Quarterly*, Jan 1950).

I pointed out to Cabinet (he continued) that while Australia was not likely to refuse to take a great risk in a good cause, we must inevitably feel some resentment at the notion that a Minister, not authorised by us, should make an agreement binding upon us which substantially modifies a proposal already accepted by us.

Menzies added that, as an outcome of this protest, Churchill had cabled to Eden that he must be able to tell Australia and New Zealand that the campaign was being undertaken not because of commitments made by a British Cabinet Minister in Athens but because Dill and the local commanders-in-chief were convinced that there was a "reasonable fighting chance". Menzies reported that the Commanders-in-Chief in the Middle East reaffirmed their belief in the proposal and that Generals Blamey and Freyberg (the commander of the New Zealand Division) were "agreeable"; and he added that it was important in relation to the world at large and particularly America not to abandon the Greeks "who have of all our Allies fought the most gallantly". However, as will be seen later, neither Blamey nor Freyberg had been asked specifically whether they agreed or not.

Thus it was puzzling for the Australian Ministers when, on 9th March, a cable from General Blamey reached Mr Spender,[1] the Minister for the Army, in which Blamey asked permission to submit his views before the A.I.F. was committed; the Ministers knew that the A.I.F. was already committed, and had been informed that Blamey was "agreeable". Spender instructed Blamey to express his opinion, whereupon the leader of the A.I.F. sent the following cable from Alexandria on the 10th:

> British Forces immediately available consist of the 6th Australian Division, 7th Australian Division, New Zealand Division, one Armoured Brigade and ancillary troops. 7th Australian Division and the New Zealand Division have not been trained as complete divisions. Available later at unknown date one armoured division. Practically no other troops in the Middle East not fully engaged. Arrival of other formations from overseas indefinite owing to shipping difficulties. Movement now under orders will be completed probably in two months.
>
> The Germans have as many divisions available as roads can carry and capacity can be greatly increased in two months. It is certain that within three or four months we must be prepared to meet overwhelming forces completely equipped and trained. Greek forces inadequate in numbers and equipment to deal with the first irruptions of the strong German Army. Air forces available 23 squadrons.[2] German Air Force within close striking range of the proposed theatre of operations and large air force can be brought to bear early in the summer. In view of the Germans' much proclaimed intention to drive us off the continent wherever we appear, landing of this small British force would be most welcome to them as it gives good reason to attack. The factors to be weighed are *for*:
>
> (a) The effect of failure to reinforce Greece on opinion in Turkey, Yugoslavia and Greece; and *against*
>
> (b) The effect of defeat and second evacuation if such be possible on opinion of the same countries and Japan.
>
> Military operation extremely hazardous in view of the disparity between opposing forces in numbers and training.

---

[1] Hon Sir Percy Spender, KBE. Minister for the Army 1940-41, for External Affairs 1949-51. Australian Ambassador to Washington since 1951. B. Sydney, 1 Oct 1897.

[2] This was the total force in the eastern Mediterranean, but, by some misunderstanding, Blamey believed that a force of 23 squadrons was to be sent to Greece.

Wavell had outlined the plan to Blamey on 18th February.³ When Blamey had said that it must be referred to Australia, Wavell replied that he had already discussed the proposed expedition to Greece with Mr Menzies. He did not ask for Blamey's opinion.

In a discussion with Dill and Wavell in Cairo on the 6th March Eden, who had just received Churchill's cable mentioned above, said that a "really disturbing question was the possible reluctance of the Dominions to engage in the venture". Wavell said that he had informed Freyberg of the latest developments and Freyberg was prepared to go ahead, but Blamey had not yet been consulted. Consequently, later that day, Blamey was summoned to meet Dill and Wavell. In a letter to Spender written on 12th March, Blamey said that at this interview his views on the Greek expedition were again not sought. "I felt that I was receiving instructions," he wrote. When Blamey asked what additional formations would be available he was told that perhaps one more armoured division would be added at an unknown date. Blamey reported that he had said to Wavell that he considered the enterprise most hazardous. In his letter he added that he considered that Dill and Wavell did not give enough weight either to the German capacity rapidly to improve communications in Greece or to German strength in the air. "As it would appear that it will be held that the operation must take place," he concluded, "I beg to urge most strongly that vigorous action be taken to ensure that adequate forces for the task are provided at the most rapid rate possible."⁴

It has been seen above that Blamey understood at this time that twenty-three air squadrons were to support the force. Menzies, however, had been told in London that there was accommodation in Greece for only thirteen though this might be increased by seven in two or three months. This was an optimistic estimate. Seven squadrons were then actually in Greece.⁵

After the interview with Blamey, Dill cabled to the Secretary for the Dominions that Wavell had explained to Blamey (and Freyberg) the additional risks involved in the venture in Greece and both had expressed their willingness to undertake the operations under the new conditions. Both Blamey and Freyberg, however, did not consider that Wavell had *consulted* them about the expedition. Freyberg said afterwards that he was only "given instructions to get ready to go". In one capacity Blamey, like Freyberg, was a formation commander who had been and would be subordinate to one or other of Wavell's army commanders in the field. But in another capacity each was the leader of a national force and a principal military adviser of a government. It was in this capacity that

---

³ On the 17th Wavell had ordered Freyberg to make ready to take his division to Greece. Freyberg was not asked his opinion of the project but understood that Wavell had been in touch with the New Zealand Government.

⁴ It was at this conference that Wavell, as mentioned earlier, had informed Blamey that he proposed to send the 7th Division to Greece before the 6th and Blamey insisted that the 6th was better trained and equipped and should go first.

⁵ A statement was given to Menzies showing that some 480 German aircraft were in Rumania and Bulgaria and 200 could be added in ten days; 402 British aircraft were in the Middle East and 380 on the way thither. From the British pool, however, only a fraction could be sent to Greece.

The Anglo-Greek War Council. Major-General Gambier-Parry, General Metaxas, King George, Air Vice-Marshal D'Albiac, General Papagos.

Group Captain ———, Air Vice-Marshal R. M. Drummond, Rt Hon Anthony Eden, General Sir Archibald Wavell, Lieut-General Sir H. Maitland Wilson, Squadron Leader I. D. McLachlan.

(*Australian War Memorial*)

A naval vessel carrying troops to Greece.

Blamey and Freyberg were expected to advise their Governments on forthcoming operations—and, as will be seen below, were incurring the disapproval of those Governments for not being sufficiently swift and outspoken in their comments on the plans of their superior officers.

Blamey's opinions greatly disturbed the Australian Cabinet. On the 18th March Fadden submitted the Greek problem to the Advisory War Council, but the Opposition members of that body declined to offer any opinion. The Opposition Leader (Mr Curtin) said that the decision had been made by the Government; if the Labour policy had been followed there would be no Australian troops in the Middle East.[6] However, he added, failure to support Greece would have had a bad effect on Spain and on public opinion in the United States.

On 27th March Fadden cabled to Menzies:

> My colleagues and I feel resentment that while some discussions appear to have taken place with the High Command, Blamey's views as G.O.C. of the force which apparently is to take the major part in the operations should not have been sought and that he was not asked to express any opinion. This not only deeply affects the question of Empire relationship but also places us in an embarrassing situation with the Advisory War Council and with Cabinet, particularly as I have there stressed . . . that General Blamey had agreed to the operation.

When Menzies sought a further assurance in London that there was a reasonable chance of success, Churchill informed him that the "real foundation" for the expedition was the estimate made on the spot of the "overwhelming moral and political repercussions of abandoning Greece"—a statement differing from that received earlier from the Dominions Office, which had suggested that the first consideration was a desire to establish a front in the Balkans. At the same time (on 29th March) Menzies cabled to his colleagues in Australia that Blamey knew his powers as G.O.C., A.I.F. and should not have hesitated to offer his views. On the other hand Wavell had informed Blamey at the outset that he had discussed the plan with Menzies (before Blamey had heard of it) and that Menzies had already agreed. In a letter written to Menzies on 5th March Blamey had given his Prime Minister more than a hint of his dilemma—the choice between criticising his superiors' policy and remaining silent despite his fears. He had written:

> The plan is, of course, what I feared: piecemeal dispatch to Europe. I am not criticising the higher policy that has required it, but regret that it must take this dangerous form. However, we will give a very good account of ourselves.

So far as Blamey's actions were concerned, Menzies' attitude was modified when he knew more of the facts. At a meeting of the Advisory War Council in November 1941 he said that "quite frankly" he felt that some pains had been taken to suppress the critical views of Blamey about the proposed operation in Greece. It now appears, however, that Blamey

---

[6] Curtin had been informed of the plan in confidence a few days earlier, but after the Cabinet decisions had been made.

had not expressed to Wavell on 6th March such strongly-critical views as he expressed to Spender on the 12th.[7]

Freyberg also received a rebuke for not having spoken to his government sooner and more frankly. In June the New Zealand Prime Minister, Mr Fraser,[8] cabled from Cairo to his acting Prime Minister:

> I . . . am surprised to learn now from Freyberg that he never considered the operation a feasible one, though, as I pointed out to him, his telegrams to us conveyed a contrary impression. In this connection he has drawn my attention to the difficulty of a subordinate commander criticising the plans of superior officers, but I have made it plain to him that in any future case where he doubts the propriety of a proposal he is to give the War Cabinet in Wellington full opportunity of considering the proposal, with his views on it, and that we understood that he would have done so in any case.

Both Dominion Governments reaffirmed their concurrence in the expedition to Greece, in spite of the disturbing news and opinions they now received. When the cables describing the situation which faced the British envoys on their return to Athens on 2nd March were repeated to the New Zealand Government it replied (on the 9th) that to abandon the Greeks to their fate "would be to destroy the moral basis of our cause and invite results greater in their potential damage to us than any failure of the contemplated operation". It urged, however, the provision of the strongest possible sea and air escort for transports, and a "full and immediate consideration of the means of withdrawal both on land and at sea should this course unfortunately prove to be necessary". Finally the New Zealand Government said that it assumed that the operations would not be undertaken unless the full British forces contemplated could "clearly be made available at the appropriate time".

As a result of these representations about planning a withdrawal, which echoed those in the Australian cable of 28th February, the First Sea Lord, Admiral Pound,[9] cabled to Admiral Cunningham on 24th March that:

> Both the Australian and New Zealand Governments when agreeing to the use of their forces in Greece asked that adequate arrangements might be prepared in advance to withdraw their forces should this be necessary owing to the Greeks who are in line with our forces failing to hold up a German advance. The Chiefs of Staff are very reluctant to send a telegram on this subject, which might have a wide distribution, whilst forces are being put into Greece. It was decided therefore that I should send you, who are chiefly concerned, a personal telegram asking you to confirm that you have this possibility in mind in order that we may be able to reassure the Australian and New Zealand Governments.

Cunningham replied:

> This problem has never been far from my thoughts since decision was reached to move into Greece. The question of evacuation must evidently depend upon the

---

[7] Blamey's experience on this occasion influenced his later policy. At the same meeting of the Advisory War Council, he said that it was now his practice to send advice immediately to the Commonwealth Government on any matter affecting the Australian forces, but that "this had not been the case earlier".

[8] Rt Hon P. Fraser, CH. Prime Minister of NZ, 1940-49. B. Fearn, Ross-shire, Scot., 28 Aug 1884. Died 12 Dec 1950.

[9] Admiral of the Fleet Sir Dudley Pound, GCB, OM, GCVO. First Sea Lord and Chief of Naval Staff 1939-43. B. 29 Aug 1877. Died 21 Oct 1943.

military situation at the time which will obviously dictate what troops can be evacuated and part from which the evacuation can take place as well as type of ship that can be used. The simplest way to ensure an [amphibious] operation is to detain a large number of personnel ships in Mediterranean so as to have them immediately available. Such action appears to me to be a short-sighted policy, however, in view of shipping situation. I can only guarantee that everything possible will be done to withdraw the Dominion troops with British.[1]

Meanwhile Menzies in London and Blamey in Egypt had, each independently, raised another question: whether leadership of the force to be sent to Greece should not be given to the Australian commander. In the last week of February Blamey had suggested to Wavell that he, Blamey, should command the force because a majority of the troops were from the Dominions. On the 26th he reported this in a cable to Menzies. The Secretary of the Australian Department of Defence, Mr Shedden, who was accompanying Menzies, had already suggested to his leader that since most of the fighting strength of the force would be Australian, or certainly Dominion, Blamey should command. Consequently, on 1st March, Menzies made the proposal at a meeting of the British War Cabinet, but was informed that the bulk of the force would be United Kingdom troops. On the 5th March Blamey wrote to Menzies confirming his earlier cable and adding that he had raised the question of command "as a matter of principle and not as a personal matter". He added that despite an estimate by Wavell that Australia would contribute only one-third of a force of 126,000, the Australian contribution was actual, the British largely a forecast, and some of the British units included were not even in existence. "Past experience," he added, "has taught me to look with misgiving on a situation where British leaders have control of considerable bodies of first-class Dominion troops while Dominion commanders are excluded from all responsibility in control, planning and policy."

As a senior staff officer in the old A.I.F. Blamey had seen the gradual "Australianisation" of that force, in which, as late as December 1917, the corps commander, most of his staff, and the commanders of three of the five infantry divisions had been British officers; he knew that the replacement of these and other British senior officers had been achieved only as a result of political pressure. Blamey now controlled a corps of three divisions—the strongest single fighting formation under Wavell's command; he, like Freyberg, was a very senior and experienced soldier; yet every front was commanded by a British general with a British staff: in the Western Desert first Wilson, then O'Connor, and later Neame; in the Sudan, Platt; in East Africa, Cunningham; and soon Wilson in Greece. No immediate change was made in the allotment of commands as a result of Blamey's suggestion—Wilson had been in Athens preparing to take command since 4th March—but Menzies persisted with his proposal that

---

[1] Neither the suggestion that the Dominion Governments were each anxious only about their own contingents, nor that they lacked confidence in the Greeks can fairly be read into the cables sent by those governments, and quoted above.

Blamey be promoted to a larger command, with results which will be recorded later.

There was another factor favouring the appointment of Blamey. Blamey's staff had been carefully selected from a large field of highly-trained officers and was a team, having been in existence for nearly a year; Wilson's had been hurriedly improvised in a theatre where the shortage of competent staff officers was acute, and in his own words was not "a going concern". It had been collected after the Greeks had accepted the offer of British reinforcements in the last week of February. As his senior general staff officer Wilson obtained Brigadier Galloway, who had served him in a similar capacity when Wilson had commanded the army in Egypt. Galloway was then commanding the British brigade in Crete. As his senior administrative officer, he had Brigadier Brunskill,[2] then serving in Palestine.

The imminent transfer of I Australian Corps to Greece faced Blamey with the immediate necessity of reorganising the administration of the A.I.F. In his dual capacity as commander of the A.I.F. as a whole and of the Australian Corps which was part of the A.I.F. he had two separate tasks and two separate staffs to help him perform them. Some of his subordinates considered that steps to depute to a senior officer control of the Australian base organisations were overdue. In Greece he would be far separated from those organisations and unable to deal personally with day-by-day problems of administration affecting those parts of the A.I.F. which were not in his corps. He chose Brigadier Plant,[3] a regular officer hitherto leading the 24th Brigade, as commander of the "Rear Echelon, Headquarters of the A.I.F. in the Middle East", with the temporary rank of major-general. This appointment took effect from 5th March.

Meanwhile the trickling of the expeditionary force into Greece had continued. The air force, which by the end of February consisted of seven squadrons, was increased during March by one more squadron of Blenheim bombers, and early in April by one army cooperation squadron. It was now divided into three groups: one wing, eventually to include four squadrons, was in support of the forces that were preparing to resist the German invasion, another wing of two squadrons was in support of the Greeks on the Albanian front, and a third force of three squadrons and parts of two others was based in the Athens area under Air Vice-Marshal D'Albiac's direct command.[4] In addition a handful of Swordfish aircraft

---

[2] Brig G. S. Brunskill, CBE, MC. Brig i/c Admin Palestine and Transjordan 1937-41; DA & QMG Brit Tps Greece and Crete 1941. Regular soldier; b. Kingsbridge, Sth Devon, Eng, 26 Aug 1891.

[3] Maj-Gen E. C. P. Plant, CB, DSO, OBE, QX6392. (1st AIF: 9 Bn and BM 6 Bde.) Comd 24 Bde 1940-41, Rear Echelon HQ AIF ME Mar-Jun 1941, 25 Bde 1941, NSW L of C Area 1943-46. Regular soldier; of Brisbane; b. Charters Towers, Qld, 23 Apr 1890. Died 17 May 1950.

[4] Finally the squadrons were distributed thus:

Eastern Wing	Western Wing	Athens Area
No. 11(B) Blenheims	No. 112(F) Gladiators	No. 30(F/B) Blenheims
113(B) Blenheims	211(B) Blenheims	80(F) Hurricanes and Gladiators
33(F) Hurricanes		84(B) Blenheims
208(AC) Hurricanes and Lysanders		Dets No. 37(B)
		38(B) Wellingtons

of the Fleet Air Arm arrived in Greece in March and were stationed at Paramythia whence they carried out raids on Durazzo and Valona, the Italians' main supply ports in Albania.

On 5th March, in accordance with the pre-arranged plan, part of the 1st Armoured Brigade and advanced parties of I Australian Corps, and of the New Zealand and 6th Australian Divisions embarked for Greece in the cruisers *Gloucester*, *York* and *Bonaventure*. By 27th March the 1st Armoured Brigade, all but a few units of the New Zealand Division, and one brigade of Australians had landed in Greece. So far no weighty effort had been made by the Germans and Italians to interfere with the movement; only two small cargo ships had been sunk by German aircraft. Admiral Cunningham considered it likely, however, that the Italian fleet would eventually attack the convoy route, and on the 27th a report from the crew of a flying-boat that three Italian cruisers and a destroyer were 80 miles east of Sicily and steaming towards Crete suggested to him that some of the Italian heavy ships were at sea. He immediately took up the challenge. A convoy which was on its way to Piraeus was ordered to steam on until dusk and then reverse its course, and the Mediterranean Fleet sailed from Alexandria as soon as darkness fell. At dawn on the 28th an aircraft from the carrier *Formidable* reported four Italian cruisers and six destroyers; and a few hours later Vice-Admiral Pridham-Wippell's[5] Cruiser Squadron (the British cruisers *Orion*, *Ajax* and *Gloucester* and the Australian *Perth*) which was ahead of the main fleet sighted them. The Italian cruisers withdrew with Pridham-Wippell in pursuit and Cunningham and the battleships hastening after him. At 11 a.m. the cruisers sighted an Italian battleship, which was attacked by aircraft from the *Formidable*. It made off to the north-west. Meanwhile five cruisers and five destroyers were sighted 100 miles to the north. After further air attacks on the Italian battleship—now identified as the *Vittorio Veneto*—its speed was greatly reduced. An Italian cruiser, the *Pola*, was also hit by bombs. Darkness fell before Cunningham's slow battleships could reach the Italian ships. At 10.25 p.m., however, the battleships suddenly came upon the Italian cruisers *Fiume* and *Zara* and promptly sank the *Fiume* and damaged the *Zara*. In the confused night fighting which followed, the destroyers, commanded by Captain Waller,[6] R.A.N., in *Stuart*, finished off *Zara* and *Pola* and sank two destroyers; but the damaged *Vittorio Veneto* managed to increase her speed and escaped. The battle of Matapan, as it was later named, was a notable success. It was unlikely that the Italian fleet would venture out again for some time, and control of the eastern Mediterranean was to be of crucial importance to British fortunes in the next two months.

---

[5] Admiral Sir Henry Pridham-Wippell, KCB, CVO; RN. Second-in-Comd Medit Fleet 1940; Flag Offr Comdg Dover 1942-45; Comdr-in-Chief Plymouth 1945-47. B. 12 Aug 1885. Died 2 Apr 1952.

[6] Capt H. M. L. Waller, DSO; RAN. HMS *Agincourt* 1918. HMAS *Stuart* 1939-41 (Cdr 10th Destroyer Flotilla 1940-41); Comd HMAS *Perth* 1941-42. B. Benalla, Vic, 4 Apr 1900. Lost in *Perth*, Battle of Java Sea, 1 Mar 1942.

On the 8th March, the day after the first contingent of "Lustre Force", as the force for Greece was named, reached Athens, a "Mr Hope" arrived there to see a "Mr Watt". "Mr Hope" was Colonel Peresitch, an officer of the Yugoslav General Staff; "Mr Watt" was General Wilson, who, at the request of the Greek Government, was wearing plain clothes and using an assumed name lest the presence of a British commander in Greece should anger the Germans.[7] The arrival of the Yugoslav officer was in belated response to repeated British requests for talks which would lead to a coordinated plan of action by the three Balkan states which the Germans had not yet overrun—Greece, Turkey and Yugoslavia; hitherto the Yugoslav Government had not dared to arrange even Staff talks.

At that time what likelihood remained of realising the expectation that Yugoslavia might enter the alliance? Prince Paul, due to be Regent until the young King became 18 in September 1941, had succeeded in creating only a precarious balance between the powerful and antagonistic groups within the kingdom. Paul, a well-meaning but ineffective dictator, was acutely aware of the military weakness which the incompetent and corrupt administration had created and of its shortage of arms, particularly since Germany had acquired the Skoda munition factories in Czechoslovakia on which Yugoslavia had formerly relied. Above all he feared a crisis which would provide the radicals, and particularly the Communists (who had been ruthlessly suppressed since 1921) with an opportunity to unseat him. He decided to try temporising with Hitler. As soon as the Bulgarian Premier, on 1st March, signed the agreement with Germany which made Bulgaria a German dependency, Prince Paul paid a secret visit to Berchtesgaden. It was after his return that Colonel Peresitch visited Athens. It now seems evident that Peresitch's task was to collect information which would help Paul to decide whether it would be safer to throw in his lot with the Germans or the Allies.

From the Allied point of view Peresitch's mission was unproductive. He emphasised the importance of maintaining communications with Yugoslavia through Salonika should Yugoslavia join the Allies—"proof," wrote Papagos later "that the evacuation of Eastern Macedonia and the abandonment of Salonika were inadvisable as long as the hope of Yugoslavia coming in had not entirely disappeared."[8] But Peresitch was not communicative and he had no power to commit the Yugoslav General Staff to a plan.

At this stage Wilson was disturbed by the possibility of the German attack descending before his force had been concentrated. Major-General Arthur Smith, who was General Wavell's Chief of Staff, had come to Athens for the talks with Peresitch, and Wilson discussed this possibility with him and

asked for a team of officers whose job would be to reconnoitre positions on to

---

[7] It is certain that these disguises did not deceive the staff of the German Ambassador in Athens for long. German observers in Athens were taking notes of arrivals and departures at the Piraeus, and at the Acropole Palace Hotel where Wilson had his headquarters. It will be seen later, however, that German Intelligence about the size of the British force was wide of the mark.

[8] Papagos, p. 327.

which we could fall back, if necessary, having none to spare from our own troops on whom innumerable calls were being made.[9]

While these talks were in progress in Athens the Italian army in Albania, on 9th March, opened a large-scale offensive in the central sector of the front. In the next sixteen days the Italians employed twelve divisions in a series of attacks against six Greek divisions without gaining any ground. At this stage about one-third of the fighting formations of the whole Italian Army had been committed in Albania against a Greek army inferior in numbers and vastly inferior in equipment.

The deliberations in Belgrade which followed Prince Paul's visit to Germany and Peresitch's to Athens lasted until 24th March. At length the Yugoslav leaders decided to throw in their lot with Germany. On the 24th the Premier, M. Cvetkovic, and the Foreign Minister, M. Cincar-Markovic, left for Vienna where they signed an agreement to adhere to the Tripartite Pact between Germany, Italy and Japan. This news became known in Belgrade two days later. That night a group representing elements which detested Germany, Italy, and Prince Paul and his clique, took swift action. They arrested Cvetkovic, Cincar-Markovic and other senior members of the Government, proclaimed King Peter's accession, and eventually sent Paul and his family into exile.[1] The party which had achieved this *coup d'état* was led by younger officers of the air force and army, and was supported by students and many of the staff of the university, the Orthodox clergy, and the Serbian parties generally. The new Cabinet, headed by the Serb General Simovic, who commanded the air force, was widely representative.

When the news arrived in Athens that Yugoslavia had joined the Axis, plans were discussed between Papagos and Wilson for hurriedly bringing the Greek divisions on the Bulgarian frontier and the Nestos River—the Doiran-Nestos line—back to the Vermion-Olympus line. Soon, however, news arrived of the possibility of a coup in Yugoslavia, and thereupon Papagos urged that the whole Allied force should be advanced to the Doiran-Nestos line. Wilson replied that this was not possible. He explained to the Greeks that "to advance all the troops . . . into Eastern Macedonia (a distance averaging 125-150 miles) with the British element only partly concentrated in face of the hourly expected German attack was to court disaster". When news arrived of the actual coup in Belgrade, Wilson was making a reconnaissance in northern Greece.

The coup in Yugoslavia vastly increased Churchill's optimism; so much so that, on 30th March, he cabled to Fadden in Australia that renewed hope could be cherished of forming a Balkan front with Turkey, and "comprising about seventy Allied divisions from the four Powers concerned". (This was in spite of the fact that the Turks had made it clear that they would remain neutral unless attacked.)

---

[9] Lord Wilson, *Eight Years Overseas* (1950), p. 75.
[1] The British Government gave him refuge in Kenya.

The maintenance of such a front demanded the holding of Salonika and the roads and railways leading from Greece into Yugoslavia. As a result of Papagos' tenacity there was still a substantial Greek force on the Bulgarian frontier, and, although the British troops were being deployed on a line west of Salonika and of the railways leading into Yugoslavia, Greek troops were still forward of them, so that in renewed discussions with the Yugoslavs their supply through Salonika could be discussed as a practical proposal.

With the object of renewing efforts to obtain Yugoslav cooperation, Eden and Dill, who had been delayed at Malta on the way home, flew to Athens, where they conferred with Wilson on 28th and 30th March and agreed that if the Yugoslavs would join the Allies it would probably be essential to hold at least the line covering the Struma River and the Doiran Gap, through which the road and railway from Salonika entered Yugoslavia. At a meeting with the Greek leaders it was agreed to tell the Yugoslavs that if they would attack into Bulgaria and Albania when the Germans advanced into Greece, the Allies would reinforce the line of the Bulgarian frontier and the Nestos River. Papagos informed the British leaders that the Yugoslavs had 24 divisions of infantry and three of cavalry. It was this potentially powerful army that he had always wanted to have on his northern flank. With its help he could swiftly dispose of the Italians in Albania and then might reasonably hope to bog down the Germans on the eastern flank.

On 31st March General Dill flew to Belgrade where he met the Yugoslav leaders. He informed them that the British force in Greece would ultimately reach 150,000 and was then "somewhere near the half-way mark".[2] When the Yugoslavs asked whether the British force would concentrate in the Doiran Gap Dill replied that the Allies had contemplated holding the line of the Bulgarian frontier and the Nestos but meanwhile were established on the Vermion-Olympus line. They could not advance to the forward line without assurances of Yugoslav cooperation. The Yugoslav leaders said that they could not sign any undertaking to help Greece without first consulting the Government as a whole. General Dill said that Britain would give Yugoslavia what help she could. It was arranged that a staff talk between Papagos, Wilson, D'Albiac and General Jankovic, the Yugoslav director of military operations, should be held near Florina in Greece on the 3rd.

This military staff meeting, begun on the night of the 3rd and finished some time before dawn next day, was held at the Kenali railway station just north of the Greek frontier. Jankovic said that possession of Salonika was vital to Yugoslavia. He proposed that the Greek forces east of the Struma and in the Metaxas Line should remain on the defensive, gaining time for the Yugloslavs (who had only four divisions in the south) and the British force to strike the right flank of the German advance in the Struma Valley; the British force would thus form a link between Greek

---

[2] This was an over-statement. About 31,000 men had then landed; others were on the water.

and Yugoslav armies in the area of Lake Doiran-Struma. Jankovic and Papagos also discussed and were in agreement on a plan whereby Yugoslav forces should cooperate with the Greeks in a converging attack on Tirana and Valona in Albania, which, if successful, would expel the Italian army from that country. When Wilson explained that although the British force would finally include three divisions and an armoured brigade, at the moment it comprised only one division, part of a second and an armoured brigade, Jankovic said that General Dill had mentioned four divisions and an armoured brigade. Jankovic's disappointment was evident. Wilson said that he could not reinforce the Doiran area without reconnaissance. He urged that the Yugoslavs, who had few anti-tank and anti-aircraft weapons, should fight the Germans in the mountains. He wrote afterwards that Jankovic

gave one the idea that the Yugoslav Army was already in a defeatist mood at the idea of a blitz attack by the Germans and it was evident that its organisation was pretty confused.[3]

Discussing this meeting in the train as it was travelling back to Athens Papagos and Wilson agreed that the situation remained as before and that they should make sure of the Vermion-Olympus line. When enough Australian troops had arrived to relieve the 12th Greek Division in that line, that division should be moved forward to the left of the Doiran-Nestos line, but this could not be done for eight days.

The discussion with Jankovic made Wilson very doubtful of the value of the Yugoslav Army and he "began to think more and more about the Monastir Gap" through which the Germans could advance into Greece across the rear of the Vermion-Olympus line if the Yugoslavs collapsed.

On 31st March Blamey, now in Greece, where he had reconnoitred the Vermion-Olympus line, sent a cable to the Australian Government which was more in tune with Wilson's worried reflections than with Churchill's hopeful cable of the previous day picturing a Balkan front of 70 divisions. Blamey said that the weakness of the position was in the north where an advance through Yugoslavia or the Edessa Pass would entail the loss of Florina and give the Germans access to the area south from Florina to Servia, which was suitable for armoured units. "The only line of communication available is the railway Athens-Larisa and thence forward by road. In both cases these are defiles which can be subjected to intense air attack at vital points. Air and ground anti-aircraft defences hopelessly inadequate and serious dislocation of lines of communication likely. Can only be met by building up reserves in forward area." He pointed out that the Germans had from twenty-three to twenty-five divisions in Bulgaria, could concentrate from eleven to thirteen of these against the four Greek divisions on the frontier, then turn with from six to seven against the Vermion-Olympus line, which was held by one armoured brigade, the New Zealand Division and two Greek divisions.

---
[3] Wilson, p. 83.

Thus by 4th April hope of enlisting Yugoslavia in a coordinated plan seemed slender. About half of the small part of the Greek Army which was available for defence against a German invasion was on the frontier; the other half was going into position on a line some 120 miles to the rear. Of the three British Dominion divisions which were to help man this rearward line only one and a half had yet arrived in Greece. Papagos who would command the whole Allied force had contended that a total of nine British and Greek divisions with full air support would be needed to establish a "reasonably strong front"; he had eight divisions, of which six were far below strength, and weak air support. Wilson, who commanded the British and Greek force in the rearward position, had asked for a staff to reconnoitre lines of withdrawal, and plans were already being made to embark the British force if necessary. Blamey, commanding the main part of the British expedition, considered it would meet "overwhelming" German forces.

CHAPTER 2

THE GERMAN ATTACK OPENS

THE commander of the British expedition was directly concerned only with that part of northern Greece which lies east of the towering Pindus mountains and west of Salonika. This area was linked with Athens by one main railway. North of Larisa in the wide plain of Thessaly, this travelled through a narrow pass between Mount Olympus and the sea, and thence across the Aliakmon River. Beyond the river it branched, one line going to Salonika, the second city of Greece, and another climbing through the Edessa Pass to the upland valley of Florina and thence into Yugoslavia. From Salonika a second line entered Yugoslavia through the Doiran Gap. The one main road linking Athens with Macedonia travelled into the Florina Valley west of Olympus—not east of it as the railway did—and thence on to Yugoslavia through the Monastir Gap.

Although it was the principal highway of Greece, the Athens-Florina road was second-class by Western European standards. The surface was generally bitumen interspersed with stretches of macadam, often so narrow that two vehicles could not pass, particularly on hills and side cuttings. The Athens-Salonika railway had a single track and was of standard gauge. A branch line linking this to Volos, the one considerable port between those cities, was only one metre wide. There were but 1,653 miles of railway in Greece, and the rolling stock was correspondingly limited. When war broke out there were only some 350 passenger coaches and about 5,000 goods waggons on the Hellenic State Railways, the standard-gauge system,[1] and both rolling stock and fuel were imported.

Piraeus, the port of Athens, was equipped to unload 3,000 tons of cargo a day—enough to maintain a British force of the size contemplated. There now seemed no likelihood of holding Salonika; and Volos, the only other port that could be used effectively to supply the British force, could not accommodate ships of more than 6,000 tons. The small port of Stilis, connected with Lamia by standard-gauge railway, would have been useful, but the Greeks were not willing to make it available because they wanted that dead-end line for storing the railway waggons to be withdrawn from Macedonia when the Germans advanced.

Thus, when Brigadier Brunskill, General Wilson's senior administrative officer, arrived in Athens on 23rd February to prepare for the arrival of the new British force, he could count on only one considerable port and very limited roads and railways. The railways were already maintaining about 100,000 Greek troops in eastern Albania, supplied through Florina,

---

[1] Australians may gain a clearer conception of the capacity of the Greek railway system from the following comparison (figures for 1938 or 1939):

	Greece	Victoria
Area (square miles)	50,000	87,000
Population	7,108,000	1,873,000
Railway mileage	1,653	4,745
Goods waggons and vans	6,456	21,000
Freight carried (000 tons)	2,510	7,258

where so far the Greeks had been unable to build up even thirty days' reserve supplies. Fewer than 400 railway trucks would be available to the British force. Brunskill wrote later:

> The Greek Army was therefore already using its railways almost to maximum capacity, the country had been denuded of every animal, cart and motor vehicle which was fit for use, the army had taken control of all small ships and practically all caiques; the available civilian labour (men, women and children) was all employed, largely on road maintenance. The civil population, moreover, was already badly off for food; there was no meat, and flour was short and they even had to feed wheat to their pack transport owing to the shortage of barley. The British Military Mission in Athens had placed large orders for equipment, stores, food, coal, etc. at home and occasional ships were arriving from Britain, but the program of fulfilment of the orders could not be predicted at all. From a Greek point of view, therefore, the cupboard was nearly bare of local resources; from a British Army point of view nothing was available locally.[2]

One of Brunskill's first steps was to ferry forward to Larisa as soon as possible the stocks of food and ammunition already at the base in Athens; and it was decided that troops arriving at Piraeus from Egypt would also be moved forward piece-meal to Larisa. The object was to place sixty days' supplies for forward troops at this advanced base and to establish forward depots or dumps at Levadhion, Servia, Kozani, Katerini, Veria, Edessa and Amindaion, the intention being to prepare for probable interruption of railway traffic by German air bombardment. By the end of the first week in April 58 days' supplies, 38 days' petrol and lubricants, 70 days' ordnance stores and 14,000 tons of engineer stores had been landed in Greece, and the forward dumps had been established. The engineer stores included 300 tons of explosives which were later to prove of immense value, particularly as the Australian Corps could obtain only three tons for its ordnance echelon instead of its normal entitlement of 30.[3]

By 18th March the 1st Armoured Brigade[4] and about half the New Zealand Division were in Greece. The 16th Australian Brigade disembarked between the 19th and the 22nd. For the men of the Australian division it was a swift transition. On 8th March when the first "flight" or contingent of Lustre Force was landing at Piraeus, the 16th Australian Brigade was at Tobruk, the 19th near Tocra in western Cyrenaica, the 17th in position on the Tripolitanian frontier beyond Agedabia. That day the 16th Brigade travelled back to Mersa Matruh. There the battalions received some equipment, including a new weapon—the Thompson submachine-gun. From Matruh the brigade moved to its old camp at Amiriya, where the men were given leave in Alexandria and renewed acquaintance with the pleasures of the town for the first time since December. Hun-

---
[2] G. S. Brunskill, "The Administrative Aspect of the Campaign in Greece in 1941" (*Army Quarterly*, Apr 1947).

[3] The large supply of explosives was obtained through the foresight of Brig H. P. W. Hutson, Chief Engineer of the force.

[4] This brigade included the 3rd Royal Tanks (cruiser tanks), 4th Hussars (light tanks), 1/Rangers (infantry), 2nd Royal Horse Artillery, and 102nd Anti-Tank Regt. The 3rd had fifty-two cruisers, the Hussars fifty-two light tanks, the vehicles being in good condition except that, as mentioned, their tracks were somewhat worn.

dreds were still on leave in Alexandria on the night of the 17th when an order arrived that the brigade would embark early next day. Military police, who were hurried into the city to summon the holiday-makers to their units, entered cafés and, disregarding secrecy, shouted that all men of the 16th Brigade must return to camp because they were to move next morning. Posters were placed in the streets announcing the news. All night men streamed back to Amiriya, in taxi-cabs, gharries and on foot; by dawn few were missing. For example, when the 2/2nd Battalion embarked only two were absent without leave.

The 2/3rd Battalion embarked next day on the cruiser *Gloucester*, and Brigadier Allen's headquarters and the 2/1st and 2/2nd Battalions and attached troops in merchantmen. The *Gloucester* arrived at Piraeus on the 19th, having left the merchant ships and their escort far behind. One of the more obvious dangers of the expedition to Greece lay in the presence of a considerable Italian air force in the Dodecanese Islands on the eastern flank of the sea route to Athens, and on the 21st the slow ships were attacked by a squadron of Italian dive bombers from that quarter. The Australians fired back with the Brens and with captured Italian Bredas which they had mounted on the decks. Only a tanker was hit, and she did not sink.

As their ships steamed into the gulf towards Piraeus the shores seemed to the New South Welshmen strangely like home—the hard light, the grey-green trees clothing steep hills, and the clear water evoked memories of Australian ports. It was stranger still to find themselves among a friendly people, who cheered them and threw flowers as their trucks drove along the streets to the staging camp at Daphni. For the first time since they had reached the Middle East these men were on the soil of a people who genuinely welcomed them, and in a land as green and pleasant as their own.

> What a contrast! Instead of awaking with eyes, ears and noses full of sand we breathed pure crisp air with the scent of flowers. Flowers!—we hadn't seen them since leaving Australia. After months of desert glare the landscape at Daphni was a dream come true. The troops stood and gazed at the natural gardens full of shrubs and flowers which scented the breeze; at the grasses that made a swishing noise as you walked through . . . . We saw civilians dressed as we used to dress before the war—civilians whom you could trust . . . . From the hillside one could look back into the valley below and see Athens.[5]

The troops who were given leave in Athens acquired an increasing respect and sympathy for the Greeks. "Greeks gloriously happy to see us . . . worth fighting for and with," wrote one young officer in his diary. They found them resolved not to allow pleasure to interfere with the business of war. Greek soldiers were not seen in the city's few cabarets, and bars were closed at midnight. A cup of coffee at a café table appeared to be the only relaxation the drably-uniformed officers and men of the Greek headquarters and depots in Athens allowed themselves—a sharp

---

[5] Lt-Col C. H. Green (then a captain in 2/2 Bn) in *Nulli Secundus Log* (1946). Green was killed commanding the 3/Royal Australian Regiment in Korea in 1950.

contrast to the gaiety and lavish eating and drinking surrounding headquarters in Cairo. The civilians possessed a dignity that the inhabitants of Egypt and Palestine lacked, and there were no beggars or touts.

Most of the men travelled north in crowded railway waggons, but those who went by road in long processions of trucks were hailed by the country folk even more cordially than in Athens. Groups of peasants shouted joyfully, waved and gave the thumbs-up sign, which was gaining as wide a currency among the democracies as the Fascist salutes in Germany and Italy; little girls threw bunches of lilac and buttercups into the moving trucks and boys calling "Englees" and "Zeeto ee Australia"—"long live Australia"—held out handfuls of leaves for the drivers to snatch. It was early spring and the countryside so full of beauty that it would have enchanted the Australians even if their senses had not been starved in the deserts of Egypt and Libya. In Attica the steep hills were clothed with pines. Farther north, in Thessaly, fruit trees in blossom stood in fields in which the young crops were a few inches high, and above the farmlands towered snow-capped Parnassus and Olympus. Some of the fields were still unsown, and old men walked behind the ploughs while women followed scattering the seed—evidently the young men were all at war. Old women were hoeing the fields; little girls drove donkeys laden with brushwood for the fires; small boys with cloaks slung over their shoulders stood herding the sheep and goats which grazed on the foothills, the copper bells at their necks tinkling pleasantly.

> Once away from Athens with its trams and taxis (wrote one observer) the past seemed very close. The peasants lived and worked much as they must have done a thousand or two thousand years ago, when other armies followed much the same roads as ours and gave immortality to these towns and passes. At the end of the second day on the road the convoy with which I went north halted by a wide shallow stream between steep hills. As the sun set the men stripped on the shingle and, standing ankle-deep in clear water, had their first good wash for weeks. Some old shepherds stood and watched, leaning on their crooks. The sun, sinking between two hills, gilded the river where the naked men bathed and shouted. They might have been soldiers of any one of the other armies that have marched past Greek shepherds and their flocks and seen the snows of Olympus against the sky.

On 27th March the 16th Brigade Group bivouacked on grassy slopes in the Servia Pass with Olympus rising above them to the east and the Aliakmon River below them to the north. Every few days another convoy arrived at Piraeus and columns of vehicles rolled northwards through Greece, past the excited villagers and the stolid peasant people—probably giving them the impression that a powerful army was moving forward; their own far larger army had fewer vehicles and thus made less show.

By 1st April the New Zealand Division, concentrating east and north of Olympus, was practically complete. On 3rd April three Australian artillery regiments and two more infantry battalions arrived. On the 4th and 5th the fighting troops in Greece comprised the 1st Armoured

Brigade, the New Zealand Division, and the 6th Australian Division less four infantry battalions and one field artillery regiment.[6]

General Wilson's headquarters had opened at the Acropole Hotel on 7th March.[7] On the 6th General Papagos had informed him that the Greek divisions on the Aliakmon line would be the 19th (Motorised) in the coastal sector, the 12th in the Veria Pass, and the 20th in the Edessa Pass; these would guard the three main passes until the British troops arrived. As the British force went into the line the 12th and 20th Greek Divisions were to side-step to the left. At length the New Zealand Division with the 19th Greek on its right would be in the coastal sector, the 6th Australian would guard the Veria Pass, and the 12th and 20th Greek Divisions would occupy the Vermion Range north of Veria including the wide Edessa Pass.

The next of the senior British commanders to arrive was General Freyberg, who reached Greece on 7th March and promptly went forward to the Vermion-Olympus line. A visit to the 19th and 12th Greek Divisions filled him "with mixed feelings". The 19th was a division only in name. Brigadier Charrington[8] of the 1st Armoured Brigade described it as containing "just over 2,000" men and those "quite untrained"; in his opinion it had "no possible prospect of fighting usefully as a mobile force with its few Bren carriers, motor-cycles, and small cars". The carriers had only recently been delivered to the Greeks. The 12th Division consisted of six battalions of recently-assembled troops and three batteries. It possessed only six motor vehicles—five trucks, and a car for the commander—and otherwise relied on carts and pack animals. The 20th was similarly composed to the 12th but had a few more field guns. Freyberg discovered that the role of the 19th Greek was to occupy 12,000 yards of open country north of Katerini, while his division held 15,000 yards of

---

[6] Nearly 350 units, sub-units and detachments were included in the force that arrived in Greece. A complete list would include a multitude of small but necessary depot units such as mobile laundries, port detachments, field bakeries, bath units, a bomb disposal section, and so on. There were 38 units of armour, cavalry, corps and divisional artillery and infantry—16 New Zealand, 14 Australian, and 8 United Kingdom. The following table shows the dates (sometimes approximate) of their arrival in Greece up to the day of the German invasion. In some instances parts of the units listed did not arrive until later than the date given.

7-9 March (1st Flight)	20 March	21 NZ Bn
102 A-Tk Regt (2 Btys only)	4 NZ Fd Regt	22 NZ Bn
18 NZ Bn	*21 March*	*3 April*
2 Hy AA Regiment RA	NZ Div Cav Regt	2/2 Aust Fd Regt
10-12 March (2nd Flight)	64 Med Regt	2/3 Aust Fd Regt
4 Hussars	26 NZ Bn	2/1 Aust A-Tk Regt
3 Royal Tank Regt	27 NZ (MG) Bn	2/4 Aust Bn
15-17 March	*22 March*	2/8 Aust Bn
2 Royal Horse Arty	2/1 Aust Bn	*In Transit 6 April*
1/Rangers	2/2 Aust Bn	7 Medium Regt
19 NZ Bn	*27 March*	2/1 Aust MG Bn
20 NZ Bn	5 NZ Fd Regt	*Not sailed 6 April*
18 March	6 NZ Fd Regt	2/1 Aust Fd Regt
24 NZ Bn	23 NZ Bn	2/5 Aust Bn
25 NZ Bn	28 Maori Bn	2/6 Aust Bn
19 March	*29 March*	2/7 Aust Bn
2/3 Aust Bn	7 NZ A-Tk Regt	2/11 Aust Bn

[7] Brig Brunskill had failed to persuade Air Vice-Marshal D'Albiac to establish his headquarters in the same building as Wilson's. D'Albiac was still under General Papagos, not General Wilson, and in addition he was opposed to placing both headquarters in a single building where one air raid might disorganise them.

[8] Brig H. V. S. Charrington, DSO, MC. Comd 1 Armd Bde. Brewery director; of Basingstoke, Hants, Eng., b. London, 19 Oct 1886.

more rugged country on the left. He gave orders that his 6th Brigade should occupy the right and the 4th the left of this position.

At this time, when negotiations with the Yugoslavs were still in progress, Papagos wished to stand on the Doiran-Rupel-Nestos line defending Salonika. As mentioned above, Wilson was not willing to do this; nevertheless he agreed to send his armoured brigade forward between the Axios and the Aliakmon as a delaying force, and to instruct the New Zealand Division to take over the coastal sector of the Aliakmon line while the 19th Greek Division moved forward into the Axios Valley and the Doiran Gap to deal with any paratroops who might be landed there. Weak though it was, the 19th Greek Division's departure entailed an appreciable loss to the force on the Aliakmon line, where the New Zealanders now became responsible for a front of some 25,000 yards.[9]

General Blamey did not arrive in Greece until 19th March, but an advanced party of his staff, including Lieut-Colonel Wells,[1] his senior liaison officer, had been there since the 7th.[2] Wells toured the line and was greatly impressed by the unwisdom of trying to hold the open country north of Katerini, rather than the narrow passes to the south. He reported this to Blamey in Athens. Blamey and his chief staff officer, Brigadier Rowell, drove north on 22nd March to reconnoitre. They visited the Greek corps commander at Kozani, and also the 12th and 20th Greek Divisions and the New Zealand Division. Blamey was impressed by the danger of a possible German move through Yugoslavia and the Monastir-Florina Gap and thus across the rear of the defenders' position. He and Rowell considered that the Greek senior officers whom they met were lacking in confidence and not well-informed. They decided that the men would be stubborn fighters and would give a good account of themselves in prepared defences in the mountains, but that it was evident that they could not fight a well-equipped enemy in a war of movement—their transport consisted of pack horses, horse-drawn carts and bullock waggons capable of moving at about one mile an hour. In any circumstances the Greeks would have to be supported by British artillery since their divisions each possessed so few field or medium guns and their only anti-tank guns were some captured from the Italians.

On the 23rd Blamey visited Freyberg who told him that his division was

holding a front of 25,000 yards with two infantry brigades, one field artillery regiment, and no anti-tank guns and that this position would not alter until 4th April [and] even after the arrival of the 5th Brigade and the anti-tank artillery, we should be far too thin on the ground, especially as at that stage the 5th Brigade were due to go into Corps reserve in a position behind the Veria Pass.

---

[9] The Greek troops finally placed under General Wilson's command comprised: 12th Division (6 battalions, three mountain batteries); 20th Division (9 battalions).

[1] Lt-Gen H. Wells, CBE, DSO, VX15120. Snr LO I Corps 1940-41, GSO1 9 Div 1941-43; BGS II Corps 1943-44, I Corps 1944-45. Regular soldier; b. Kyneton, Vic, 22 Mar 1898.

[2] Principal appointments on the staff of I Aust Corps on 6 Apr included: *BGS* Brig S. F. Rowell; *GSO2 (Ops)* Lt-Cols C. M. L. Elliott and A. R. Garrett; *GSO2 (Int)* Lt-Col J. D. Rogers; *Senior Liaison Officer* Lt-Col H. Wells; *DA&QMG* Brig W. Bridgeford; *AQMG* Lt-Col E. W. Woodward; *DDMS* Col W. W. S. Johnston; *ADOS* Col J. T. Simpson; *APM* Maj C. J. Farnington; *CCRA* Brig C. A. Clowes; *CCMA* Brig E. A. Lee; *CE* Brig C. S. Steele; *CSO* Col C. H. Simpson; *DDS&T* Brig D. D. Paine.

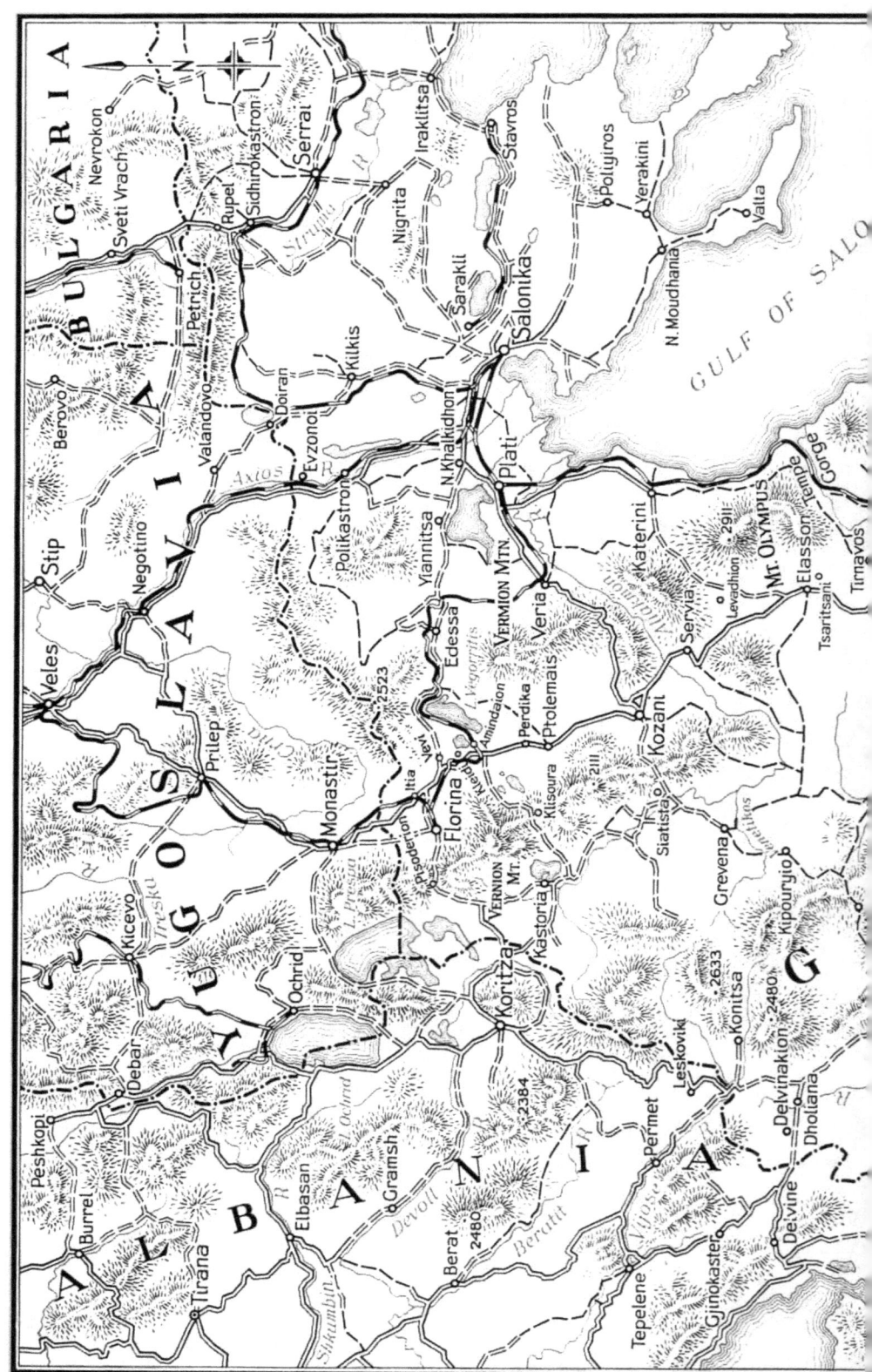

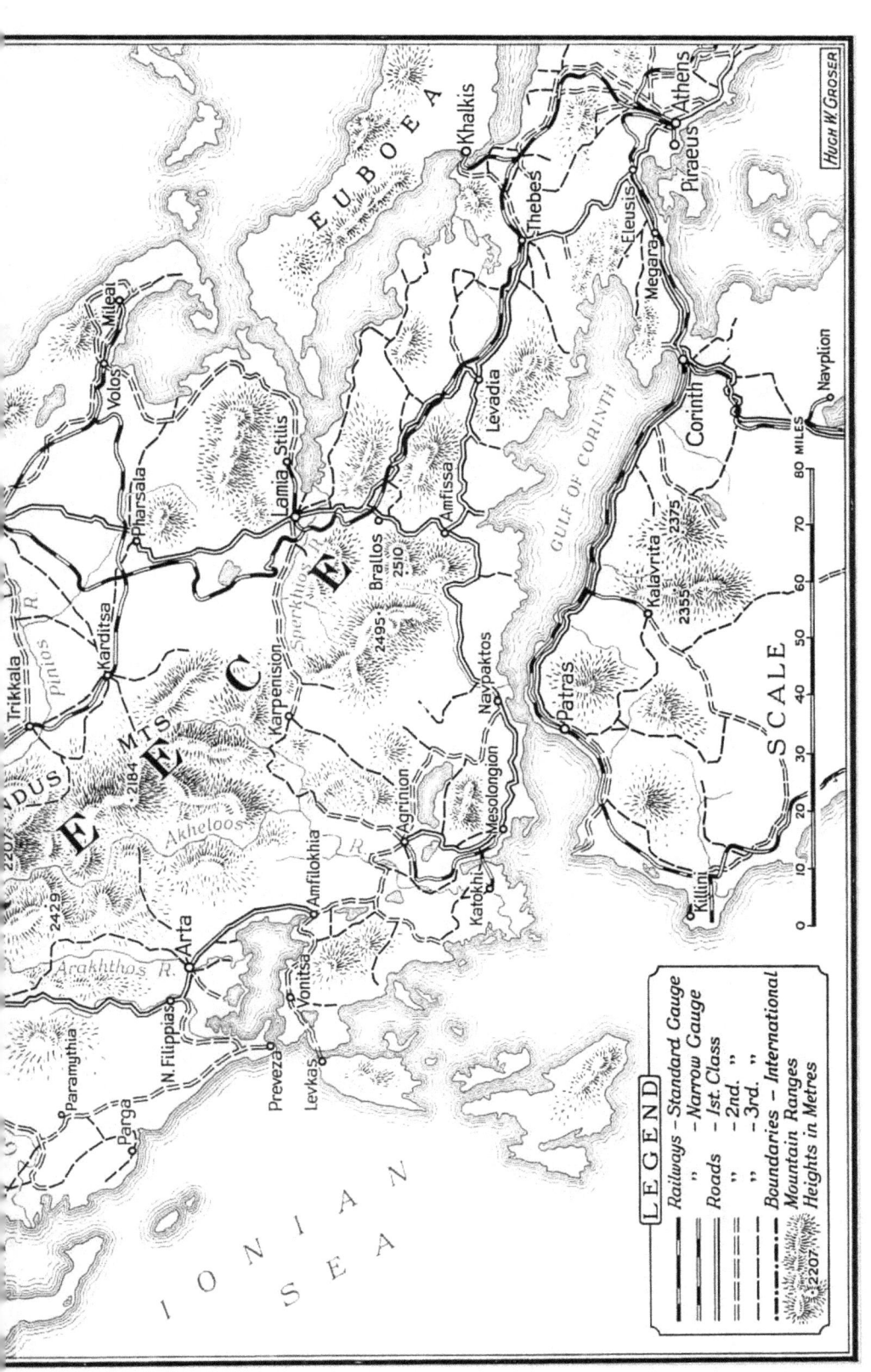

Freyberg contended and Blamey agreed that the line could not be held against a determined attack supported by tanks, and that the wise course would be to pull back to the mouths of the Olympus passes. When he returned to Athens on the 24th, Blamey met Wilson at the British Embassy and obtained his agreement to a plan whereby the New Zealand Division should concentrate on digging and wiring defences in the passes, leaving only the divisional cavalry regiment forward of Katerini. It was agreed that Blamey should establish his headquarters in the Gerania area as soon as possible and take command of the New Zealanders and the troops in the Veria Pass.

After this conference Brigadier Galloway, General Wilson's chief of staff, informed General Freyberg that he should "make certain of the passes round either side of Mount Olympus", but that General Wilson considered that the New Zealand front was less likely to be seriously involved than the northern one. No order was given to Freyberg to withdraw his forward infantry to the passes. In delaying such an order Wilson no doubt took into account that he had undertaken to hold a line forward of Katerini and to withdraw to the passes would entail amending his agreement with Papagos; and possibly took into account the possibility of having to move forward to support the Yugoslavs. He was influenced by the fact that, between Katerini and Edessa, the Florina railway along which travelled most of the supplies for the Greek army in eastern Albania lay east of the Vermion Range and thus forward of the line his force was to occupy.

Meanwhile some preparations were being made to cope with the danger that the Germans might push through southern Yugoslavia, swing south through the Monastir Gap and take the Allied positions in the rear. A suitable area in which to hold such a thrust was where the Florina Valley was narrowed by two large lakes, Vegorritis and Petron. Brigadier Charrington had been instructed, on 17th March, to prepare a route for withdrawal through the Edessa Pass into the Florina Valley, where he could help to meet an advance from Monastir, and his 3rd Royal Tanks (the cruiser tank regiment) did not move forward to the Axios with the remainder of the brigade but remained at Amindaion in the lake area. By the end of March there were in that neighbourhood also the 27th New Zealand Machine Gun Battalion (lacking two companies) and part of the 64th Medium Regiment. However, Charrington's headquarters and the remainder of his brigade were about Edessa, so remote from Amindaion that the detachment there was placed under the command of Brigadier Lee,[3] a British officer recently appointed to Blamey's staff to command the medium artillery, all of which was British. Later the 2/1st Australian Anti-Tank Regiment (less one battery) was added to Lee's command.

On 5th April General Wilson formally took command of the Allied forces in Central Macedonia, with an advanced headquarters at Tsaritsani, a village near Elasson on the main Larisa-Florina road, and a rear head-

---
[3] Brig E. A. Lee, DSO; RA. Regular soldier; b. London, 13 Jun 1893. Died 1942.

quarters at Athens. On the same day General Blamey opened his headquarters at Gerania, a poky village just off the main road on high ground south of the Servia Pass, and took command of the British troops from the sea to the Veria Pass. On his left General Kotulas commanded the Central Macedonian Army, which was the title given to the two Greek divisions in the Vermion mountains north of Veria.

At this stage General Wilson intended that "W" Group, as his force was named, should be deployed as follows: the New Zealand Division on the right from the coast to the Pieria mountains, north-east of Servia, a regiment of the 12th Greek Division in those mountains, one Australian brigade in the Veria Pass, one at Kozani and one at Servia, and the 20th Greek Division and the remainder of the 12th in the Vermion mountains north of Veria. Of the Australian brigades only the 16th, at Servia, was in its intended area. All three New Zealand brigades, however, were in the forward zone. On the 28th March the 6th had taken over the coastal sector formerly held by the little 19th Greek Division; the 4th went into position on its left; and the 5th into reserve in the Olympus Pass, through which the road climbed from Katerini over the mountain and joined the main Larisa-Florina road near Elasson. The New Zealand Divisional Cavalry Regiment was forward of the infantry on the line of the Aliakmon River in a delaying role.

On 5th April—the day on which he took command in the field—General Wilson conferred with General Kotulas at Kozani. Kotulas urged that the Australians should at once begin taking over from the 12th Division, still in the Veria Pass, so that he could use the 12th to strengthen the position held by the 20th in the Edessa area. Wilson said that he hoped that the Australians would have completely taken over in eight days; and later that day he ordered General Mackay, commanding the 6th Australian Division, to occupy part of the Veria position, relieving all but two battalions of the Greek 12th Division; these were to remain on the Australian left in country so rugged that troops could not be maintained there without pack transport.

Mackay had arrived at Gerania on the 5th, having reached Athens on the 3rd. Three of his staff were with him.[4] The German invasion was believed to be imminent, but, of Mackay's brigades, only the 16th was in the forward area. Two battalions of the 19th were moving up, and the 17th had not yet sailed from Alexandria.[5] Indeed so little shipping was available that it had been possible to move the force to Greece at the rate of only about a brigade and a half a week, and that only by transporting some units in cruisers. The third convoy had been delayed by storms and the fourth by the battle of Cape Matapan.

The individual units of Lustre Force were fully equipped but, as had been foreseen, the force as a whole was grievously short of air support

---
[4] Brig E. F. Herring commanding the artillery, Lt-Col R. B. Sutherland, his GSO1, and Mackay's ADC, Lt B. H. Travers. The staff of the 6th Division in Greece also included: *GSO2* Maj A. D. Molloy; *AA & QMG* Col C. E. Prior; *DAAG* Maj. B. J. O'Loughlin; *DAQMG* Maj C. Bowser; *ADMS* Col H. C. Disher; *DADOS* Maj B. W. Pulver; *CRE* Lt-Col L. C. Lucas; *CSO* Lt-Col L. J. Wellman; *CASC* Lt-Col N. B. Loveridge.

[5] Its headquarters sailed on the 6th, the battalions on the 10th.

and armour. For example, Air Vice-Marshal D'Albiac's small air force had only eighty serviceable aircraft to meet a German force estimated at 800, not counting an Italian air force in Albania, or operating over Albania from Italy, of approximately 300. He had only one army cooperation squadron, and it had arrived just as the German attack opened. "Unfortunately this squadron rarely had more than one Hurricane aircraft serviceable at a time and, since the remainder of its aircraft were Lysanders, which it was quite impossible to use in the face of enemy air opposition, the squadron did very little useful work."[6]

So far only one medium artillery regiment had arrived to support a defensive line which, whatever tactics the Germans employed, could hardly be less than 100 miles in length. The Australian division lacked its cavalry regiment, and a number of necessary technical units had not yet arrived. The inevitable splitting of Wilson's headquarters between Athens and a village in northern Thessaly put a strain on his signals. He had, however, an independent signal squadron equipped with the best available wireless sets. He allotted one of its stations to the Greek command at Salonika, and another to Kotulas' headquarters, and held a third ready to join the Yugoslav Army.

On 5th April the only British infantry deployed in forward positions on the Vermion-Olympus line were the 6th and 4th New Zealand Brigades which occupied the line covering Katerini from the sea to the northern foothills of Olympus. The 5th Brigade[7] was in position astride the Olympus Pass, on a front of 15,000 yards and 3,000 feet above sea level. To the left of the New Zealanders was to be the 16th Australian Brigade which, having spent eleven days bivouacked in the Servia Pass, was to begin moving forward on 6th April to the Veria Pass—which Mackay reconnoitred that day. The Allied staff estimated that the Germans had twenty-three to twenty-five divisions in Bulgaria of which six or seven could be concentrated against the Vermion-Olympus line at short notice.

Moreover, while "W" Group was being concentrated, events in Cyrenaica had removed any prospect of the 7th Australian Division and the Polish Brigade joining the force in Greece. Late in February it had become apparent that a German force was being assembled in Libya. On 24th March the Germans occupied El Agheila and on 2nd April entered Agedabia. Two days later both the depleted 2nd Armoured Division and the incomplete 9th Australian Division were withdrawing eastwards with the enemy pressing hard upon them. Thereupon General Wavell ordered one brigade of the 7th Division—the 18th—to Tobruk to help hold that fortress, and decided that the remainder of the division might also have to go to Cyrenaica. When he learnt of this decision, Blamey cabled Wavell that the retention of Libya was not vital whereas the force in Greece would be in grave peril if not built up to adequate

---

[6] J. H. D'Albiac: *Report on Air Operations in Greece, 1940-1941.*

[7] The 21 Bn of this brigade was retained in Athens to perform local security duties, but its place in the brigade was taken by the 28 (Maori) Bn, a tenth infantry battalion of the NZ Division.

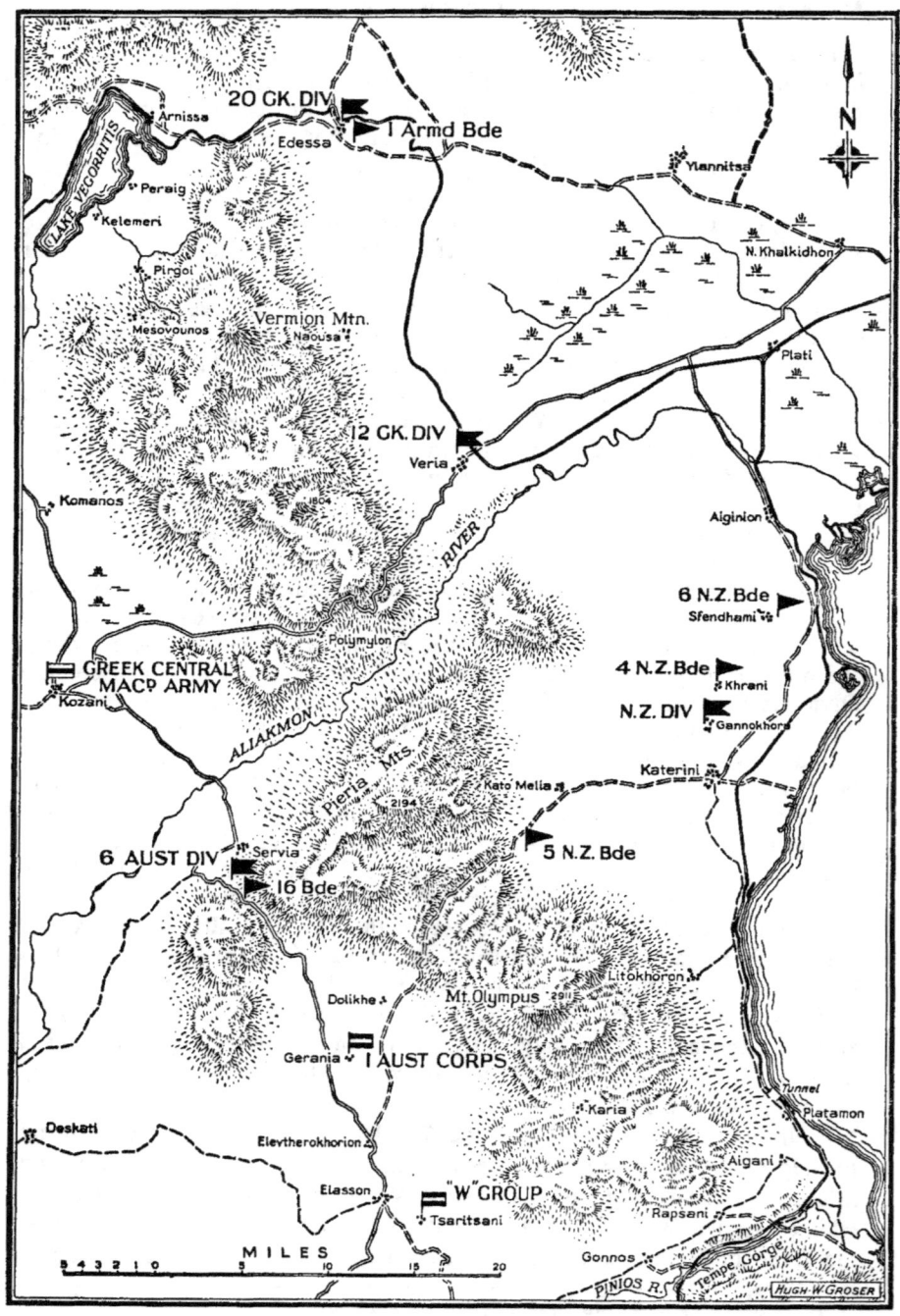

Allied dispositions, 6th April.

strength; but Wavell was convinced that the 7th Division could not be spared from Africa.

Blamey learnt of the decision to retain the 7th Division on the 6th April; that morning, at 5.15, the long-expected news had arrived that the German *Twelfth Army* had begun to advance into Greece and Yugoslavia.

Dawn, 6th April.

The first shock of the German offensive would be taken by the ill-prepared Yugoslav Army and the thin line of Greeks on the Bulgarian frontier. In that area Papagos had withdrawn all except a few units from Thrace, the narrow territory lying between the Bulgarian frontier on the north, the Aegean Sea on the south, and the Nestos River on the west. Apparently for political reasons, however, the garrisons of two frontier fortresses remained in Thrace with three battalions (the Evros Brigade) in support. To the west, on the Doiran-Nestos line the Eastern Macedonian Army was deployed. On its right the Nestos Brigade (three battalions) was to defend the line of the Nestos to a point some 30 miles from its mouth. On its left the 7th Division (five battalions) held a sector which continued the line of the Nestos and, turning west, ended south of Kato Nevrokop. Thence the 14th Division (six battalions) held a sector extending to the Struma River. The 18th Division (five battalions) was deployed from the Struma to the Yugoslav frontier.

Throughout 6th April the German attack in Thrace and eastern Macedonia, though supported by heavy artillery and air bombardment, made little impression on the Greek frontier forts, and on the 7th even the remote forts at Nimphaea and Ekhinos in Thrace were still holding out. Nimphaea was overcome at 11.30 p.m. on the 7th after a prolonged attack by German infantry equipped with flame throwers; but Ekhinos held. The Nestos Brigade was covered by these forts and was not yet in contact with the enemy. The 7th Division, next to the left, was fiercely attacked but gave little ground on the 6th. On the 14th Division's front none of the frontier forts were taken by the Germans that day. In the Struma valley all but one of the forts held out. Farther west, however, German mountain troops advanced between Lakes Kerkinitis and Doiran, due north of Salonika. To meet this threat the Greek Army commander ordered the 19th Division forward to this area, but at the end of the day a gap remained between this division and the 18th.

It was part of the agreement made between the Greeks and Yugoslavs on 4th April that, when the invasion began, they should both attack the Italians in Albania with Tirana and Valona as the objectives. By swift success in Albania they might free their forces there to help meet the Germans on their eastern fronts. Consequently, on the 6th, Papagos ordered his Western Macedonian Army to open an offensive against the Italians next day. However, his Epirus Army was not ready to attack so soon.

A few hours after hearing of the German attack Blamey sent Rowell to Wilson's headquarters to press for an immediate withdrawal of the New Zealand Division to the passes in accordance with the agreement reached by Wilson and himself in Athens twelve days before. At Elasson Rowell's request was answered with the argument that it was still desirable to protect the railhead at Katerini. However, Wilson ordered Freyberg to draft more labour into the Olympus Pass—yet to continue to hold the positions forward of Katerini.

At the same time Wilson's staff began to consider a secondary line— one covering the Olympus passes, pivoting on the Pieria mountains, and then running along the south bank of the Aliakmon. So far as it went this proposed Aliakmon line was identical with the rearmost of the three lines which had entered into Papagos' planning from the outset. To retire to it, however, would have drastic consequences from the Greek point of view; it would entail supplying the Greek army in eastern Albania along the third-grade mountain road from Larisa through Trikkala and Kastoria.

The German Air Force delivered a very serious blow to the British expedition on the night of the 6th-7th. German bombers attacked Piraeus; the steamer *Clan Fraser* loaded with T.N.T. caught fire and exploded; largely as a result of this huge secondary explosion, which was heard and felt throughout the city of Athens, seven merchant ships, sixty lighters, and twenty-five caiques were destroyed, an ammunition train and an ammunition barge were blown up, and quays, offices and shops wrecked. The port was closed completely for two days, and its ability to handle the ships that would reinforce and maintain the British expedition greatly reduced. Afterwards only five of the twelve berths could be used; so many tugs and small craft were destroyed that coal and water could not be obtained by ships lying in the roads; the telephone system was out of action; many skilled workers were killed or injured and others abandoned their jobs.

On the afternoon of the 7th of April the disturbing information arrived at the Greek army headquarters at Salonika that German armoured forces from Strumica in Yugoslavia were moving south towards the practically unguarded Doiran Gap, thus threatening to sweep round the Greek flank and down the Axios Valley to Salonika. The 19th Division which on the 6th had been hurriedly sent to counter the threat of a German advance east of Doiran was now reinforced with some anti-paratroop companies from Salonika and ordered to extend its flank to the Axios, about 40 miles to the west. The German advance-guards entered Doiran on the evening of the 7th. That day the Greek offensive in Albania was opened but made small gains. A Yugoslav division which was to have cooperated failed to do so, but its commander said that he would be ready next day.

In Wilson's area the 19th Australian Brigade, less one battalion, was now coming forward. It had a battalion at Larisa and one near Tirnavos. Its proposed role had been to go in on the left of the 16th Brigade at Veria, but Wilson now ordered it to concentrate near Kozani where it would be available to reinforce either Veria or the Florina Valley.

That day the 16th Brigade began to take up its positions in the Veria Pass. For these Australians a more complete change from conditions in Cyrenaica could hardly be imagined, and to describe their experiences is to describe those of other battalions then digging in above the snow-line. The brigade was perched astride a mountain road some 3,000 feet above the sea, with higher peaks towering above them. Troops in positions on the heights above the pass had to carry all their gear, ammunition and rations, either by hand or on the backs of a few donkeys borrowed from the Greeks. As an example of the difficulties, it took three hours to climb from one end of the 2/2nd Battalion's position to the other; the battalion's headquarters were at 4,200 feet along a foot track which took two hours to climb, and its left company was 2 miles farther on. The normal telephone equipment of a battalion—eight telephones with 8 miles of cable—was quite inadequate for such conditions; one battalion fortunately had increased its equipment to twenty-three telephones and 25 miles of cable by collecting Italian gear captured in Libya, and needed all of it.

From the 8th onwards snow fell intermittently on the mountains and rain in the valleys, and sometimes a fog enveloped the mountains until about 10 a.m.; when the air was clear the Australians could see Salonika, and the mountains of Yugoslavia where the distant battles were being fought. For shelter each platoon had only a tent-fly which sagged under the weight of the snow. Lack of interpreters caused much delay.[8] One advanced party had to speak in signs; for example, they suggested a tank

---

[8] The 2/2nd was fortunate to possess a man who could speak Greek—Cpl G. J. Caling (of Armidale, NSW).

by crawling with one hand forward and saying "Bang, Bang!" The Australians were surprised not only by the primitive equipment of the Greeks but by their lack of tactical knowledge. There is a record of one Greek company which possessed only one automatic weapon (faultily mounted in a conspicuous position) but had piles of stones ready to push down on the advancing Germans. Lieut-Colonel Chilton of the 2/2nd decided not to relieve the Greeks in the defences they had prepared, because he considered these not tactically sound for troops equipped as his were; his company commanders chose new positions. However, the Greeks handed over to the Australian engineers an effective flame-throwing device which won their admiration. It was a fougasse consisting of drums of petrol and crude oil to be projected along the road by a charge of ammonal with "Elektron"[9] turnings for igniting the oil. It produced a flame up to 50 yards long and 5 feet wide.

On 8th April, owing to rain and snow, there was little effective air reconnaissance, but throughout the day enough news of the German advance into Yugoslavia reached Greek and British headquarters to give a fairly clear picture. A British patrol which thrust to the north of Monastir reported that the southern Yugoslav army had collapsed, Veles and Skoplje had fallen, three divisions had surrendered, and fugitive Yugoslav staff officers were collecting at Florina. The patrol led back three Yugoslav tanks and four anti-aircraft guns. Early in the day the German armour advancing through the Doiran Gap thrust back units of the 19th Division and was approaching Kilkis. Papagos requested that the 1st Armoured Brigade take immediate action to strengthen the few Greek troops in the Doiran Gap. It was too late for such measures. Soon after midday the 4th Hussars, who formed a screen on the Axios plain, saw German tanks approaching, whereupon they damaged the railway bridge and blew up a road bridge across the river and, in the evening and during the night, in accordance with orders from Wilson, withdrew to Kozani, part through the Edessa Pass and part through the Veria. A commando party of the Canadian Kent Corps Troops destroyed the oil stocks at Salonika, in accordance with a plan secretly prepared. In conformity with the withdrawal of the Hussars, the New Zealand divisional cavalry regiment blew the bridges over the Aliakmon and the 6th New Zealand Brigade blew up those on its front.

From the Struma eastward the Eastern Macedonian Army was still holding firm, but the German column moving down the Axios Valley reached Kilkis late on the night of the 8th. The 19th Greek Division (scarcely a brigade strong) was swept aside, and nothing then lay between the invading army and Salonika. That night the commander of the Eastern Macedonian Army sent an envoy to the German armoured division in the Axios Valley to propose an armistice, and informed his subordinates that he had done so, but ordered them to fight on until a decision had been reached.

---

[9] An alloy of magnesium and aluminium, used also in incendiary bombs, which ignites easily and burns with an intense heat.

In Albania the Western Macedonian Army had resumed its attack on the morning of the 8th, and the Yugoslavs attacked too, but their gains were small and Papagos ordered that the offensive cease because of the uncertainty of the situation in southern Yugoslavia generally.

Fearing that a German advance through the Monastir Gap would threaten the rear of his Western Macedonian Army in Albania and of "W" Group, Papagos decided to withdraw the troops who were in the mountains north of the Edessa Pass to Lake Vegorritis, where they would link with Wilson's proposed defensive line across the Florina Valley at Vevi. He instructed "W" Group and the Western Macedonian Army that their line would henceforward run from Olympus on the right, through the Vermion range to Lake Vegorritis, and across the valley to Nimfaion at the entrance to the Klisoura Pass, the central of three passes leading through the range flanking the Florina Valley to the west. There the British left would link with the right of the Western Macedonian Army. The linking formation would be the Greek Cavalry Division which, on the 7th, had been moved from Koritza to the Florina area to protect the Pisoderion Pass, the northernmost pass leading west from Florina.[1] He instructed Wilson to send his armoured force towards the Monastir Gap to gain touch with and delay the German advance. As the British force would be too weak to extend its left flank to Nimfaion, the Greek 21st Brigade was to be interposed between the British area and the Cavalry Division. Before these instructions reached Wilson, however, he had made his own plans and issued his orders.

At 11 a.m. on the 8th, at a meeting at Blamey's headquarters, Wilson had already decided that a force should be formed, including Lee's Amindaion detachment and such troops of the 6th Division as became available (except the 16th Brigade), "to stop a blitzkrieg down Florina gap".[2] General Mackay would command it from headquarters near Perdika close to those of General Kotulas, and would be directly under Wilson's command. At the outset his force would include the 19th Brigade (only two battalions), 2/3rd Field Regiment, and Lee's detachment (3rd Royal Tanks, 27th New Zealand Machine Gun Battalion, less two companies, 2nd Royal Horse Artillery, 64th Medium Regiment, 2/1st Australian Anti-Tank Regiment). It was a minute and ill-balanced force with which to meet what might be the main German thrust into Greece.

At the same conference it was decided that the 6th Australian Division should not continue the relief of the 12th Greek at Veria; the Olympus-Vermion-Amindaion line was now to be regarded merely as a rearguard position which would give the division time to form up later on the Aliakmon line which Wilson had considered as a possibility on the 6th. Blamey was ordered to prepare for the occupation of the Aliakmon line, his command including the New Zealand Division, 16th Australian Brigade, and 12th Greek Division. It was decided to transfer the 4th

---

[1] Farther left the 13th Greek Division was placed in the gap between Lake Prespa and Lake Ochrid.
[2] On the 5th Brigadier Clowes of Blamey's staff had been ordered to reconnoitre the Monastir position with a view to siting a delaying position.

New Zealand Brigade to the Servia Pass "to form a pivot on which later withdrawal from the north could be based"; and to leave only mobile forces forward of Katerini in the New Zealand sector. The 6th New Zealand Brigade was ordered to withdraw through the 5th, in the Olympus Pass.

The distribution of command was proving extremely complex. Blamey from his corps headquarters at Gerania now commanded the New Zealand and part of the Australian and the 12th Greek Divisions; there was a Greek commander of the Central Macedonian Army, which now included little more than the 20th Division; Mackay's force was directly under Wilson. Wilson's staff was divided, his advanced headquarters being at Elasson not far from Blamey's, his rear headquarters in Athens, more than 200 miles away. In Athens there were also a British air commander who was independent of Wilson, an independent naval staff, and a British Military Mission. General Papagos' headquarters were also there. Discussing the difficulty of coordinating these diverse commands, Brigadier Brunskill later wrote:

> As regards command, it seemed obvious to army officers that the army commander should have become supreme commander of all British forces in Greece, with the air officer commanding as his deputy. He should have then remained in Athens with the higher staffs of all three British fighting Services and the Ambassador, as closely knit into a team under him as possible. The British Military Mission should have been abolished and the Military Attaché absorbed into the staff. The Australian corps headquarters should have been expanded to command all the British and Greek troops on the Aliakmon position. Dealings with the Greeks should have been direct at all levels. Our habitual excruciating public-school French, with an interpreter to supply missing words, was adequate as a medium for military conversations.[3]

When General Mackay arrived at Lee's headquarters at Sotir a few minutes before midnight on the 8th to take command in the Vevi Gap there was no infantry unit in the area. Brigadier Vasey of the 19th Brigade was present but his 2/4th Battalion was still moving forward, his 2/8th (in obedience to earlier orders) was in the Veria area, and his 2/11th had not yet landed in Greece. The only units Lee commanded were the 64th Medium Regiment, 2/1st Australian Anti-Tank Regiment, and the New Zealand machine-gun battalion. However, the 1st Armoured Brigade had been ordered to concentrate at Amindaion before dawn and therefore Mackay might anticipate that it, like the 19th Brigade, would be included in his force. He decided to place Vasey in charge of the defence of the gap, to add the 1/Rangers, 2/1st Australian Anti-Tank Regiment and the New Zealand machine-gun battalion to his command, and to place the remainder of the armoured brigade in reserve. He put his artillery commander, Brigadier Herring, in control of the three regiments of field and medium artillery. Although it possessed not even a complete brigade of infantry,[4] the force was relatively strong in artillery—an arm in which the Germans, pushing along boggy roads and past demoli-

---

[3] Brunskill, *Army Quarterly*, Apr 1947.
[4] The 2/4 Bn lacked one company which was on duty at Volos.

tions, were likely to be weak, at least at the outset. Mackay and his staff were handicapped by the lack of an interpreter. On the 7th he had managed to exchange some information with the commander of the 12th Greek Division in French, but it had been a slow and irritating process.

At 1 p.m. on 9th April the Greek Commander in eastern Macedonia capitulated. Although, from the Struma eastward, his troops had yielded little territory, despite three days of vigorous attack by far stronger German forces, his army was now isolated. The Greek commander has recorded with pride that on the 10th, when the garrisons of Rupel and other forts formally surrendered, the Germans congratulated them warmly, that the commander of the German *72nd Division* declared that he had

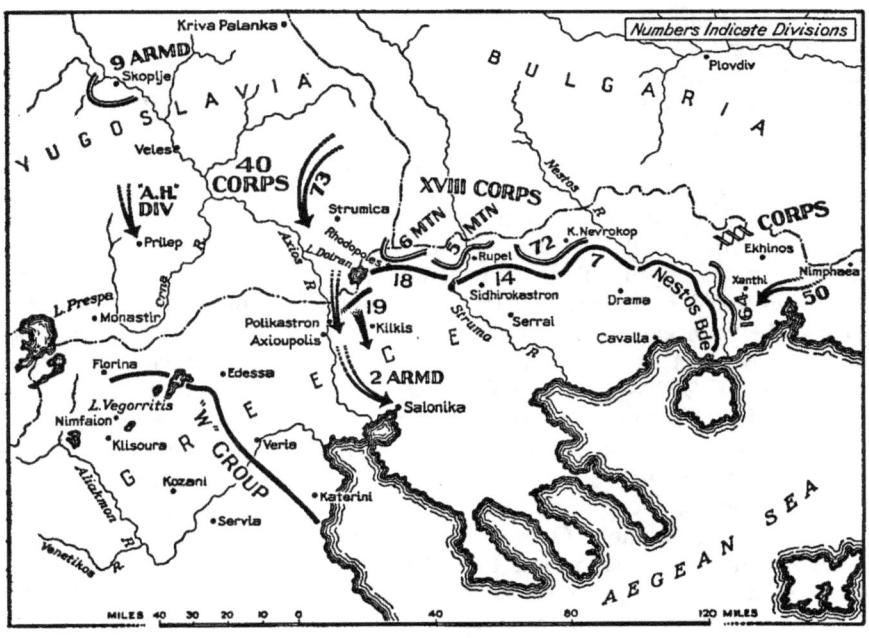

Morning, 9th April.

not met such effective resistance in Poland or France, and that the Greek army was the first in which dive bombers did not inspire panic. He adds that senior German officers said that the Greek forts represented a golden mean between the French, on which too much effort had been spent providing comfortable living conditions and too little on armament, and the forts of "other Powers" in which there was insufficient care for the men and an excess of armament. They praised the skill with which the Greek engineers had provided exit trenches for surprise counter-attacks by the garrisons.

The four-day campaign in eastern Macedonia had followed a course not unlike the invasion of France eleven months before. The German success had been achieved by advancing through the territory of a third party and round the flank of a strong fortified line. The Greek commander had too small a reserve to block or to counter-attack the armoured forces outflanking him. Papagos' understandable determination to hold Salonika—the price of effective cooperation with the Yugoslavs—had resulted in the loss of four of the six Greek divisions available to meet the German invasion.[5]

On the morning of the 9th Wilson issued orders for withdrawal to the Aliakmon line. On the 10th he conferred with Mackay and General Karassos, who had replaced Kotulas in command of the Central Macedonian Army. When he returned to his headquarters he learnt from Brigadier Galloway that General Papagos had been informed of the proposal to withdraw and had approved it. Papagos had asked that Wilson should meet him at Pharsala on the 11th.

As a result of these decisions Papagos ordered preparations for a withdrawal by stages from both Albania and central Macedonia to his third line of defence mentioned above. This line would, on the right, include the Olympus-Aliakmon position, but it would omit the passes west of the Florina Valley. From the British left westward it would follow the Venetikos River, and thence run more or less due west to the sea. This withdrawal would entail the loss not only of nearly all the territory gained in Albania but of practically all Macedonia.[6] The removal of supplies from the base at Koritza was begun. Papagos ordered that the retirement of the Greek forces in the Vermion area across the valley into the mountains to its west was to be "concealed until its completion by means of a vigorous defence by the (British) forces in the Kleidi position". These Greek divisions—the 12th and 20th—were to hold the Siatista and Klisoura Passes, while the Cavalry Division held the Pisoderion.

In his detailed instruction of the 9th April Wilson had defined his "rear defensive line", as it was now called: from the Olympus defiles, via Servia to the escarpment to the west of it, and thence along the south bank of the Aliakmon. On this line a "protracted defence" was to be offered. The Vevi position was to be held as long as possible to gain time for the Greeks to adjust their forces both in Macedonia and Albania, and for the Aliakmon line to be prepared. The Aliakmon front was to be divided into three main sectors. On the right Blamey's command would include the New Zealand Division, the 16th Australian Brigade and the 12th Greek Division except for two battalions on the left; on the left Karassos would command the 20th Greek Division and the remainder of the 12th; to the north was Mackay's force, in which the whole of the 1st Armoured Brigade would now be included. Blamey's forces in the Veria area had the responsibility of holding until the 20th Greek Division and Mackay's force had fallen back. Wilson ordered that the vehicles of the Greek divisions be withdrawn, the 12th's south of the Aliakmon to

---

[5] These four divisions plus the Nestos Brigade were barely equal to two German divisions, even in infantry.

[6] Papagos had warned his subordinates on the 7th April to begin planning such a withdrawal.

Deskati, the 20th's to Grevena, leaving them only with pack animals. The Greeks were to be helped with supplies from British dumps.

During the 9th the New Zealand Division began to adjust its positions. On the right the newly-arrived 21st Battalion was now at the Platamon tunnel in the narrow pass between Olympus and the sea. Warning orders to withdraw into reserve were given to the forward battalions of the 6th Brigade. Divisional headquarters began to move back to Dolikhe. By the evening of the 9th the 4th Brigade had arrived in the Servia area.

Meanwhile, on the 9th, British armoured cars drove forward to a point 5 miles north of Monastir and saw a column of German vehicles accumulating on the north side of the River Crna where the bridge had been demolished. By 4.50 p.m. the German advance-guard had still not entered Monastir and it was evident that they could not reach the positions occupied by Mackay's force that day.

At 6 a.m. on the 9th Mackay and his senior staff officer, Colonel Sutherland,[7] had met General Karassos at Kozani. A difficult three-hour conference followed, during which the commanders exchanged views through interpreters and liaison officers and, in Mackay's opinion, little was gained. Mackay told Karassos that his headquarters would be at Perdika, close to the Greek headquarters; and the British anti-tank guns supporting the left of the Greek 20th Division were increased from a troop to a battery.

During that day the 1st Armoured Brigade and the two battalions of the 19th Australian arrived and began to deploy. On their right was the Dodecanese Regiment in the area of Lakes Vegorritis and Petron. The 2/8th Battalion was next to the left, then the 1/Rangers, astride the road, and the 2/4th on a four-mile front along the hills to the west. The three battalions had travelled in trucks along the greasy roads all night; and the 2/8th had spent the previous night on the road, and the night before that in crowded railway waggons in which sleep was almost impossible. After leaving their vehicles the weary men, fully laden, made long marches to positions allotted to companies and platoons above Xinon Neron where they spent the night of the 9th in the snow without shelter; next morning (the 10th) they began to move forward to new positions on the right at Vevi.

At Vevi the Monastir Valley narrows. To the west steep hills rise to more than 3,000 feet; east of the pass, the lakes Vegorritis and Petron lie across the path of an advance over the foothills. The pass itself varied in width from 100 to 500 yards and followed a winding course through a defile flanked by steep rock-strewn hills with few trees. It was a strong natural position, but on each flank the front was so extended that it was necessary to separate platoons widely, and some could keep in touch only by patrolling the considerable gaps between. On the right and left the steep hillsides and the lack of tracks made it necessary to man-handle

---

[7] Brig R. B. Sutherland, WX1570. (1st AIF: Lt 4 Div Engrs.) CRE I Aust Corps 1940-41; GSO1 6 Div 1941-42; BGS HQ NT Force 1942. Regular soldier; of Kew, Vic; b. Murrumbeena, Vic, 24 Oct 1897. Killed in aircraft accident, 28 Sep 1943.

all weapons and supplies to the forward positions, and rapid movement of troops from one part of the front to another was not possible. In the centre the strong contingents of medium, field and anti-tank artillery and machine-gunners helped to offset the thinness of the infantry line. One platoon of New Zealand machine-gunners was with the left company of the 2/8th, two companies left of the road supporting the Rangers and the 2/4th Battalion. Forward of the Rangers the 2/1st Australian Field Company was completing a mine-field. The 2/4th made contact with the 21st Greek Brigade (part of the Cavalry Division), Lieut-Colonel Dougherty's left company establishing a jointly-held post about five miles west of the road on the western slopes of Hill 1001. Strung out along a front of about ten miles the three battalions waited for the German attack.

In the first quarter of 1941 the German High Command had assembled an army of twenty divisions for the conquest of Greece—Operation MARITA. As mentioned above Hitler issued his directive for the invasion of Greece on the 13th December 1940.[8] In it he stated:

1. The result of the battles in Albania is not yet decisive. Because of a dangerous situation in Albania, it is doubly necessary that the British endeavour be foiled to create air bases under the protection of a Balkan front, which would be dangerous to Italy and to the Rumanian oilfields.
2. My plan therefore is (*a*) to form a gradually increasing force in southern Rumania within the next month, (*b*) after the setting-in of favourable weather, probably in March, to send this force to occupy the Aegean north coast by way of Bulgaria and if necessary to occupy the entire Greek mainland.

On 17th February he ordered that his troops should cross the Danube on 2nd March. The coup in Yugoslavia seriously upset his intention to win Yugoslavia by other than military means, and greatly increased his commitments in the Balkans and contributed to a postponement of the attack on Russia. He declared at a conference on 27th March, the day of the coup, that Yugoslavia must be occupied, and added:

Politically it is especially important that the blow against Yugoslavia is carried out with unmerciful harshness and that the military destruction is done in a lightning-like undertaking. In this way Turkey would become sufficiently frightened and the campaign against Greece later on would be influenced in a favourable way. It can be assumed that the Croats will come to our side when we attack. A corresponding political treatment (autonomy later on) will be assured to them. The war against Yugoslavia should be very popular in Italy, Hungary and Bulgaria, as territorial acquisitions are to be promised to these states; the Adriatic coast for Italy, the Banat for Hungary and Macedonia for Bulgaria.

Hitler ordered that the air force should "destroy the capital Belgrade in attacks by waves". On 4th April M. Molotov informed the German Ambassador in Moscow that the Soviet Government had concluded a treaty of friendship with Yugoslavia; but already the German Army was on the move against Russia's fellow Slavs.

The achievement of Hitler's plan to occupy Greece was allotted to the *Twelfth German Army*, commanded by Field Marshal List. It had fought

---

[8] An earlier directive of 12 November ordered that the army make preparations to occupy northern Greece if necessary.

in France, and had begun to assemble in western Rumania at the end of 1940.⁹ A major problem facing the German commander was to construct sufficient crossings of the Danube to enable him to move his army swiftly through Bulgaria. The only first-class bridge was that at Czernawoda, carrying the railway to Constanta, and, in the spring, the lower Danube is swollen by the thaw and carries down much floating ice. Late in February the river was in fact blocked by ice as far upstream as Giurgiu; and such an interval elapsed before the ice loosened and began to move downstream that the German engineers had time to make only three additional bridges before the *Twelfth Army* began to advance into Bulgaria. One, at Bechet, was broken by a storm while troops were crossing; another was at Turnu Magurele; the third and most important was a 1,200-metre bridge at Giurgiu. The entry into Bulgaria was delayed for several days after 2nd March.

Hitler wished the invasion of Greece to begin on 1st April, but left it to List to fix the precise date, after taking the weather into account. Hitler's order that Yugoslavia must be occupied necessitated the hurried reinforcement of his army in the Balkans. The *Twelfth Army* then included twenty divisions. The attack on central and northern Yugoslavia was allotted to the *Second Army* (Field Marshal von Weichs), which was in the area of Graz in southern Austria. It was to be reinforced by divisions from Germany and France, but chiefly from the *Twelfth Army*, until eventually it would include the following formations:

49th (Alpine) Corps (General Kuebler)
  1st Mountain Division
  79th Division

51st Corps (General Reinhard)
  132nd Division
  101st Division
  183rd Division

46th (Armoured) Corps (General von Vietinghoff)
  8th Armoured Division
  14th Armoured Division
  16th (Motorised) Division

*First Armoured Group*¹ (General von Kleist)
  5th Armoured Division
  11th Armoured Division
  60th (Motorised) Division
  4th Mountain Division
  294th Division
  198th Division

41st (Motorised) Corps (General Reinhardt)
  S.S. "Reich" (Motorised) Division
  "Graf S'rachwitz" (Bulgarian) Division
  "Grossdeutschland" Regiment
  "Hermann Goering" Regiment

---

⁹ In this and later chapters the account of German operations at the army and corps level is based largely on a paper written after the war by General von Greiffenberg, Field Marshal List's chief of staff. Where his account disagreed with that presented by a series of contemporary German battle maps, the evidence of the maps has been preferred.

¹ This Group included two corps headquarters—the *XI* and *XIV (Armoured)*.

The *49th* and *51st Corps* were assembled in the Steiermark province of Austria, the *46th* in western Hungary. The *First Armoured Group* and *41st Corps* were concentrated in Bulgaria and were to remain under the command of the *Second Army* until several days after the invasion began. Of the formations in Austria and Hungary only the *46th Armoured Corps* was ready for action on 6th April.

After the transfer of *41st Corps* and Kleist's group to *Second Army*, List's *Twelfth Army* in Bulgaria would be reduced to:

40th (Motorised) Corps (General Stumme)
  9th Armoured Division
  73rd Division
  S.S. Leibstandarte "Adolf Hitler"
XVIII (Mountain) Corps (General Boehme)
  2nd Armoured Division
  5th Mountain Division
  6th Mountain Division
  72nd Division
  125th Infantry Regiment
XXX Corps (General Hartmann, later General Ott)
  50th Division
  164th Division

In reserve were two divisions, the *46th* and *76th*. The *16th Armoured Division* was deployed on the Turkish frontier throughout this period; no account is taken of this division in this or later statements of the forces available to List.

At the beginning of April the German Army as a whole contained 153 divisions. They included 14 armoured, 8 motorised infantry (3 of these being S.S. divisions and one a light division serving in North Africa), 124 infantry, 6 mountain, and one cavalry. By the beginning of June, 2 armoured and 18 infantry were to be added; and 24 garrison divisions for service in occupied territories. Thus 6 out of the 14 available armoured divisions were allotted roles in the Balkan campaign, and 4 out of the 6 available mountain divisions, but only a small proportion of the available infantry divisions—16 out of 124.

The command of the Balkan operations was allotted to the Commander-in-Chief of the Army, Field Marshal von Brauchitsch, who moved his headquarters from Berlin to Wiener Neustadt, south of Vienna; it was decided to do without an army group commander. The German plan, rapidly revised after the decision to attack Yugoslavia, provided that one armoured division should move across the Drave River on Zagreb while the remainder of Vietinghoff's corps, advancing between the Drave and the Save rivers, attacked Belgrade. Reinhard's infantry corps was to advance towards Zagreb and then wheel towards Belgrade. Kuebler's *Alpine Corps* was to cover the mountainous western flank. This plan—to strike at the heart of Yugoslav resistance—displeased the Italian leaders. General Roatta, the Italian Chief of the General Staff, wished the Germans to attack south-west and deal with the Yugoslav formations opposite Albania; and the Italian Commander-in-Chief, General Ambrosio,

Australian troops on leave in Athens.

(*Australian War Memorial*)

(Australian War Memorial)
Site of headquarters of the 6th Division, south of Olympus.

(Capt B. Brock)
Drawing water from a mountain stream east of Servia.

Piraeus after the raid by German aircraft on the night 6th-7th April. The steamer *Clan Fraser*, loaded with explosives, lies burning on the right.

(*Australian War Memorial*)

Piraeus after the bombing, morning 7th April.

(Maj-Gen I. N. Dougherty)

Lt-Col I. N. Dougherty (on the right) with the C.O. of the flanking Greek battalion at Vevi, Good Friday, April 1941.

(Australian War Memorial)

Greek troops moving along a mountain road, April 1941.

at first declined to follow a German suggestion that the Italian army in Albania should attack the Yugoslavs, but finally agreed to feign an offensive.

List's army was hurriedly regrouped after the Yugoslav *coup d'état*. Kleist's *Armoured Group*, at first including one armoured, one mountain, one motorised and two infantry divisions, was to attack from Sofia northwest towards Belgrade, in cooperation with *Second Army* under whose command it was later to come. Stumme's corps was to advance into southern Yugoslavia, break up the Yugoslav army in the Skoplje area and link with the Italians at Lake Ochrid. Boehme's corps was to thrust through the Metaxas Line. On the left flank Hartmann's small corps was to advance on Cavalla in western Thrace. When this plan was made the German commander believed that the Yugoslavs had sixteen divisions, concentrated mainly round Nish, Skoplje and Veles.

One main problem of the German commanders was to move forward their columns along mountain roads so narrow and winding that there were points where engineers had sometimes to widen them by blasting to make it possible for guns to be hauled round the bends. As a rule more than one division had to share a single road. In Yugoslavia the Drave and Save rivers, which Weichs' army had to cross, were swollen by the thaw.

On the German right, units of Vietinghoff's corps crossed the Mur and Drave rivers against weak resistance, capturing several bridges intact. Many prisoners were taken in the field; deserters from the air force flew to Graz in Austria and surrendered themselves and their aircraft. So few German troops were yet available—only three divisions were on the frontier—that, despite these easy successes, Brauchitsch decided to keep to the original plan—to wait until 10th April before launching the main advance on Belgrade. It was evident that the knowledge of the treachery of the Regent, Prince Paul, his Ministers and a proportion of the military leaders had so shaken the faith of the people that little resistance was likely except by small, stubborn groups which had not succumbed to the general despair.

Farther south, Stumme's corps crossed the frontier in two columns, the *9th Armoured* and the *"Adolf Hitler" Divisions* by way of Kriva Palanka and Kumanovo towards Skoplje, the *73rd Division* towards Veles. Both columns reached the Vardar (Axios) on the 6th; Skoplje was occupied on the 7th; and the *2nd Armoured* was approaching Strumica. Yugoslav resistance was negligible. By the 8th resistance in southern Yugoslavia had been broken and only fragments of the defending divisions remained. The *"Adolf Hitler"* wheeled left and advanced through Prilep into the Monastir Valley; the *2nd Armoured* was approaching Salonika along the Axios Valley.

From the Greeks on the Metaxas Line Boehme's corps met resistance of an entirely different kind. This line resembled the Maginot Line in France and consisted of forts cleverly camouflaged and commanding the main points of entry. Boehme's first task was to break through on both sides of the Rupel Pass with two mountain divisions (*5th* and *6th*) and heavy artillery detachments. The *72nd Division* was to advance from Nevrokop via Serrai and Drama taking the Rupel Pass position in the rear and clearing the way for the *2nd Armoured Division* to sweep down the Axios Valley towards Salonika.

But the forts were doggedly held. The "Hellas" fort fell only after the entire artillery of the *XXX Corps* had been in action against it for thirty-six hours; the Ekhinos fort held out for days in the German rear after the mountain troops had broken through. However, by the afternoon of the 6th the *6th Mountain Division* was at Rhodopoles on the Salonika-Serrai railway. Next evening (7th April) the *5th Mountain Division* broke through west of the Rupel Pass though "some heroic garrisons of a few as yet unconquered forts"[2] were still holding out in the rear, and the *125th Regiment* was held by the Greeks in the defile itself. On 7th April the *72nd Division* had broken the line south of Nevrokop and was moving through Serrai. The *2nd Armoured Division*, swinging round the western flank, occupied Salonika on the 9th.

On the left Hartmann's corps, with its *164th Division* on the right and the *50th* on the left, overcame bitter resistance at the frontier forts and advanced to the sea. Thence the *50th Division* swung west towards Salonika, and the *164th*, using a German steamer, Greek fishing craft, and two Italian destroyers, occupied the islands of Samothrace, Thasos, Lemnos, Mytilene and Chios.

---

[2] Ernst Wisshaupt, "The Balkan Campaign of the Twelfth Army" (in typescript in the library of the Australian War Memorial).

CHAPTER 3

THE REARGUARD ACTIONS IN THE FLORINA VALLEY

SNOW fell on the hills flanking the Vevi Pass during the night of the 9th April, and when the men at infantry posts awoke next morning they found three or four inches of it lying on the greatcoats and blankets that covered them. In the pass below, a stream of Greek and Yugoslav refugees was moving through the British line, as they had been for several days, some on foot carrying a few possessions, some with donkeys or little brightly-coloured farm carts. In this slow procession were groups of Yugoslav soldiers, and parties of Greek police whose well-cut uniforms, neat haversacks and long grey coats were in contrast to the shabby dress of the Greek fighting men.

Two patrols of New Zealand armoured cars (attached to the 1st Armoured Brigade) drove forward, saw the head of one German column six miles north of the Vevi line and another at Sitaria, and returned intact after exchanging fire with the enemy. The air force reported that a large collection of vehicles was still waiting on the north bank of the Crna River in Yugoslavia for the bridge to be repaired. About 10 a.m. on the 10th, after German trucks had been seen near Vevi and farther north near Itia, it was decided that the last of the Greek artillery had passed through the Vevi position, and the Rangers blew up the road ahead of their minefield. From about 1 p.m. onwards the British and Australian guns fired at long range on German vehicles, a shell of the first salvo fired by the 64th Medium Regiment with astonishing luck scoring a hit on a German truck. From their posts overlooking the plain across which the enemy was advancing the artillery and infantry observers watched the column of German vehicles moving south "like a dark grey caterpillar on a great green lawn",[1] and in mid-afternoon saw infantry and tanks deploying behind the Sitaria-Lofoi ridge three miles to the north. The defending artillery continued to fire intermittently at German vehicles and infantry but there was no German fire, their infantry and tanks having evidently outrun the guns. It appeared that there would be no coordinated attack that day. This was fortunate because there were only three battalions of infantry to hold the pass, and although the Rangers and the 2/4th had arrived on the 9th in time to occupy their positions that day, the 2/8th was still scrambling wearily up the hills to fill the gap on the right of the line. When the artillery fire opened on the morning of the 10th the company commanders were on the ridge to the east of the road reconnoitring their positions in an otherwise vacant battalion area. To the north they could see the Germans approaching; to the south their own men finishing an eleven-mile march with a steep climb to the positions on which they had yet to dig in.

---

[1] Capt A. D. Crawford, 2/1 A-Tk Regt, in *Detour—The Story of Oflag IVC* (1946).

This day a German force advancing from Florina into the Pisoderion Pass had been held by the Greek Cavalry Division there. Farther left the German and Italian armies linked with each other in the vicinity of Lake Ochrid. To guard the communications of the Epirus Army against attack from the east Papagos ordered his 11th Division from Leskoviki in southern Albania to the Metsovon area.

When General Wilson met General Karassos and General Mackay at Perdika at 2 p.m. on the 10th April to plan the withdrawal from the Vermion-Veria position, they had decided that three nights would be devoted to this delicate operation, largely because the Greeks lacked motor vehicles. The Greeks would withdraw across the valley and occupy the passes to the west of it. Mackay's force would withdraw to the south. This would concentrate the Greek formations on the left so that there would be one and not three points of contact, as there had been before, and a consequent simplification of command and supply problems. Three Greek battalions would withdraw that night, three on the 11th-12th, and the rearguards and the Dodecanese Regiment, which was on Mackay's immediate right, on the 12th-13th, after which Mackay's force would withdraw. These orders imposed on the raw Greek divisions a wearying march from one mountain range to another, and on Mackay's thin line of infantry the duty of holding an increasing German force for three nights and two days.

A few hours earlier General Blamey, from his headquarters south of the Aliakmon, had given instructions defining the Olympus-Aliakmon position his corps was to hold and, in anticipation of orders to withdraw from Veria, warning the 16th Brigade and 12th Greek Division along what route they would withdraw and where their place in the new line would be. These instructions, issued at 12.10 a.m. on the 10th, proposed that the 12th Greek Division, when withdrawal from Veria was ordered, should cross the Aliakmon on a foot-bridge to be built about eight miles west of Servia and take up a position overlooking the river on the left of the 4th New Zealand Brigade. General Blamey ordered that vehicles not immediately needed should that night be withdrawn south of the "position for protracted defence", and sent Colonel Wells to the 12th Division to coordinate its movement.

So far as they affected the 12th Greek these warning instructions were countermanded within a few hours by Wilson's order outlined above that it should withdraw west to the Siatista Pass and not south across the river—an occurrence which again underlined the weakness of the complicated system of command and the desirability of placing the whole of "W" Group under a single field commander, who would necessarily be Blamey. Early on the afternoon of the 10th Wilson sent a "warning order" to Blamey defining the new line and informing him that his junction with the 12th Greek Division would be in the Kerasia area on the high ground north of the Aliakmon, not south of it as Blamey had anticipated. Wilson's decision was tactically orthodox in that it avoided allowing a river to form the boundary between one formation and another, but Blamey's staff protested, though in vain, that it would be extremely difficult for them to maintain part of their force on the north side of the river that could be reached only along rough tracks and crossed by an improvised bridge. In fact, Blamey's staff had little confidence in the ability of the Greek divisions to reach their new area in good fighting shape and were unwilling therefore to place a flanking force on the far side of the river to link with them.

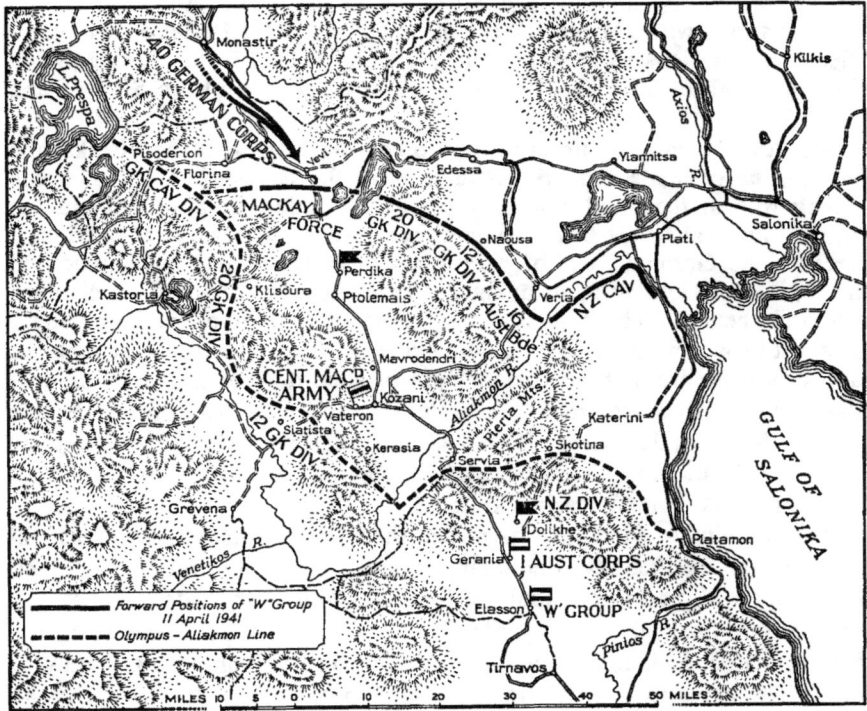

The warning order to the 16th Brigade provided that, having sent the vehicles across the Aliakmon that night, the men must march across the mountains to their new sector on the right of the New Zealanders in the Servia Pass. If the men had been carried on their vehicles through Kozani and across the river to Servia they would have had an easy march of five miles or so to their new position. But, climbing through the mountains, they would have to cover 30 miles on the map and considerably more in fact—up one side of a 3,000-foot range and down the other side to the Aliakmon, and thence another ascent to heights above 3,000 feet. Brigadier Allen reflected that there seemed no point in marching the men so far, but surmised that apparently the aim was to prevent traffic congestion by sending the vehicles off without delay. The real reason for the decision was that Blamey was uncertain whether Mackay's force at Vevi could withstand a powerful blow, and feared lest a break-through at Vevi should catch the 16th Brigade withdrawing along the main road. To march over the hills was safe, though exhausting; when the order was given the plan was to offer a prolonged defence on the Olympus-Aliakmon line and consequently it was believed that the infantrymen would have time to rest before they were engaged in battle.

During the day the New Zealand Division completed its withdrawal to the Olympus passes, taking all its supplies and leaving only the cavalry screen on the Aliakmon. The 5th Brigade was now astride the main Olympus pass with the 6th in rear of it; and the 21st Battalion had completed preparations to demolish the Platamon tunnel in the pass between Olympus and the sea. The 4th Brigade was digging in at the Servia Pass.

At Vevi, in spite of efforts to ensure coordination with the Greeks, the blowing up of roads and bridges in front of the British line cut off some Greek troops; they and civilian refugees continued to pass through the British lines all day. The refugees were watched somewhat anxiously because the Germans' use of paratroops in Holland and their rumoured use of "Fifth Columns", meaning agents or troops disguised as civilians operating behind their enemies' lines, had made their opponents apprehensive lest these devices should be adopted in Greece. One of the advantages an army gains from the occasional use of such devices is that it induces the enemy to disperse troops on protective duties in rear areas. (It was to guard the headquarters of "W" Group, for example, that a company of the 2/4th Battalion had been detached leaving that battalion now with only three rifle companies in the line.)

The morning of the 11th was fine in the Florina Valley, but it was still snowing on the heights; the weary infantrymen were wet through and miserably cold, and throughout the day snow and mist made it impossible to see more than 50 to 100 yards. The men of the 2/8th were worn out, having marched all the previous day and reached their positions only at dusk. The necessity for linking with the Rangers compelled them to take up exposed positions on the forward slopes. When they began to dig in they found the ground so rocky that only shallow trenches could be made. They had been in position a few hours when they heard voices in the darkness calling in English "Stand up, Steve", "Friendly patrol here" and the like. Before it was discovered that these calls came from German patrols probing among their widely-spaced platoon positions, five Australians, a section of New Zealand machine-gunners, and six of the Rangers on their left had been taken prisoner. Brushes with these patrols continued all night, and again the men in the forward companies had little sleep. When daylight came none of the enemy infantry was in sight. At 3 a.m. a company of the Rangers was drawn back on that battalion's right.

Later in the morning a few German tanks appeared; one and then another were disabled by mines in the field forward of the Rangers.[2] The field artillery fired intermittently on German vehicles unloading infantry round Vevi, and on German infantry seen digging in along the road to Kelli. In the late morning and early afternoon German artillery arrived and opened fire. As the day went on fire from heavy mortars and machine-guns sited behind the Lofoi ridge became heavier, causing casualties particularly among the Australian anti-tank gunners on the forward slope. Before any concerted attack had been made on Brigadier Vasey's infantry, however, news arrived of a threatened flanking move by German tanks against a position held by the 20th Greek Division between Lake Petron and Lake Vegorritis. If German tanks broke through here they would threaten the main road at Sotir, six miles south of Vasey's force. To meet the danger a squadron of the 3rd Royal Tanks and a troop of the 102nd Anti-Tank were sent out from Amindaion to the neck of land at Pandeleimon. Moving in snow and sleet over eight miles of ploughed vineyards six tanks broke their tracks, but the Germans did not continue their attempt to advance in this direction and at length the tanks and guns withdrew.

A little before 5 p.m. German infantry, seemingly two battalions, attacked astride the road, but their advance was stopped by artillery fire when they were half a mile from the forward posts. There was yet no artillery observer forward in the 2/4th's area on the left and the fire of the guns was directed by Captain Conkey of the 2/4th by telephone through battalion headquarters. During the next four hours the Germans continued to press forward cautiously feeling for the Australian line and, in the dark, still under well-aimed fire from the Royal Horse Artillery, dug in in dead ground on the lower slopes a few hundred yards forward of the defenders.

The snow was now from six inches to a foot deep over the whole of Hill 1001—the 3,000-foot ridge on which the 2/4th were deployed—and there was snow on the hills on the right flank, where from 10 p.m. the Germans made sharp attacks on the 2/8th, but now it was the Australians who took prisoners.[3] In one night affray two wounded Germans were taken and found to belong to the "*Adolf Hitler*" motorised division of the S.S.[4] The night fighting and the intense cold further wearied the 2/8th, whose men were near the limit of their endurance. Few had

---

[2] On the 10th while this minefield was being laid a pack donkey trod on a mine whose explosion detonated all mines within 100 yards. The mines had been placed three yards apart; thereafter it was considered that five yards would be safer.

[3] This thrust was made by one German company which afterwards reported having lost two killed and three seriously wounded.

[4] The S.S. formations were recruited and administered by Himmler's *Schutzstaffel* organisation and, in his words, were to be a "Nationalist Socialist Soldier Order of Nordic Men". Originally it formed Hitler's bodyguard, and its existence was indicative of his lack of confidence in the support of the army proper. At length part of the S.S. became responsible for guarding the concentration camps, and part—the Waffen S.S. (armed S.S.), a purely military organisation—was placed under the tactical control of the German Army High Command. In 1939 the Waffen S.S. consisted of a number of regiments, including the *Leibstandarte S.S.* "*Adolf Hitler*", 8,000 to 9,000 strong, and totalled about 28,000. These were each expanded into divisions and, as the war developed, more divisions were organised. At the end of 1942, there were eight such divisions and two brigades; finally there were 35 divisions. The "*Adolf Hitler*" had played a leading part in the occupation of Austria and the Sudetenland, and the operations in Poland and France.

blankets because men could not be spared to carry them forward—the arduous scramble into the hills from battalion headquarters to one of the companies took from an hour to an hour and a half. The men could not heat their food. The battalion was now spread across a front of two miles and a half, having taken over part of the Greek front on its right and filled a gap between its left and the Rangers.

To the north-west, in the Pisoderion Pass, the Germans again probed forward against the Greek Cavalry Division on the 11th and were again repulsed. Italian attacks on the Albanian front were also held by the Greeks.

Early on the 11th April General Papagos had discussed the reinforcement of the Allied left flank by transferring troops from Albania, and later in the day informed Wilson's rear headquarters at Athens that he would withdraw his right corps (the III) in Albania, provided the 1st Armoured Brigade operated in the Florina area to protect its withdrawal. British rear headquarters gave an assurance to this effect, evidently ignorant of the situation at the front. Wilson was already contemplating withdrawal. At 3.45 next morning (the 12th) he issued a comprehensive instruction to the formations under his command for retirement to the Olympus-Aliakmon line "as soon as possible". This instruction elaborated the decisions made at his conference with Mackay and Karassos on the 10th. Except for small mule parties the 20th Greek Division, which had been marching across the valley during the 11th, was to be west of the main road by 2 p.m. on the 12th; the Dodecanese Regiment was to come under Mackay's command during its withdrawal. As mentioned above, the 19th Brigade was to withdraw to the Kerasia area, north of the Aliakmon, and link with the Greeks there; but the artillery was to retire across the river; and the armoured brigade, after protecting the withdrawal of the remainder of the force, to Grevena. It was to be south of the new line by 8 p.m. on the 13th. Already the New Zealand brigades had gone back to the Olympus passes; and on the afternoon of the 11th Blamey had ordered that one battalion of the 16th Brigade at Veria should begin to withdraw forthwith.

On the morning of the 12th two of the three nights during which Mackay had been ordered to hold at Vevi had passed without the line being seriously threatened. Yet it was now becoming apparent not only that a concerted German attack would soon be made, but that fatigue and cold would begin to cause serious casualties; already infantrymen were being taken out of the line suffering from exhaustion and frost-bite.

Late on the 11th Mackay had learnt that the commander and staff of the Central Macedonian Army had departed from Perdika to Vateron, without warning him. When he visited the Greek headquarters next morning he found there only a "sickly" colonel named Pappas. Mackay was anxious to begin moving the last Greek regiment—the Dodecanese— across from his right to his left as soon as possible, and he was concerned to learn from Pappas that the regiment was 4,500 strong, not 3,000 as he had been informed the previous day. He wrote an order to the Greeks that they were to begin withdrawing at 3 p.m. and allotted them thirty 3-ton lorries to carry their sick and wounded, estimated at 1,200.

In his detailed orders to the 19th Brigade Mackay said that the 2/4th and 2/8th Battalions were to embus behind the Vevi position; they were to begin thinning out at 7.30 p.m. on the 12th and to begin embussing at 8; and the Rangers (being astride the road) were to cover the withdrawal. All were to be in their vehicles by 4 a.m. on the 13th.[5] Part of the armoured brigade, including one company of the Rangers, withdrawn earlier, was to occupy a position at Rodona and Sotir astride the road six miles to the south to cover the main withdrawal. The rest of the brigade was to occupy a final rearguard position three miles south of Ptolemais, through which the Sotir force would withdraw. After the withdrawal of the 19th Brigade, the whole of the 1/Rangers, the 2nd Royal Horse Artillery, and the New Zealand machine-gunners were to revert to command of Brigadier Charrington of the armoured brigade.

Before Mackay had begun his conference with the sole remaining Greek staff officer the expected German attack developed. At 8.30 a.m. on the 12th, supported by intense mortar and machine-gun fire, the Germans advanced with determination on a wide front east of the road against the left companies of the 2/8th and at the junction of the 2/8th and the Rangers. Their grey-clad infantry moved in close formation—surprising tactics to the Australians who had been schooled in the necessity for dispersion in the attack—and, near the left flank of the 2/8th, succeeded in overrunning the foremost platoon (Lieutenant Oldfield's[6]) all but six of which were killed or captured. The remainder of this company (Captain Robertson's), supported by enfilade fire from the company on its right, held and inflicted casualties on the attackers, Lieutenant Gately displaying notable coolness and determination in a dangerous crisis. About 11 a.m., however, Captain Coombes' company on the Australian left saw the Rangers in the valley below (possibly believing that the 2/8th's positions had been overrun) begin to withdraw. Robertson's remaining platoons fell

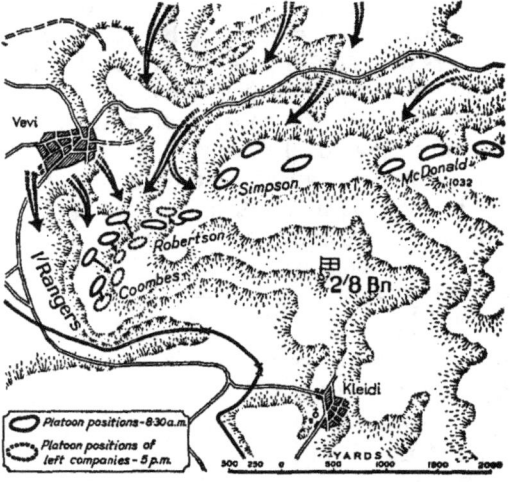

---

[5] An order by the 1st Armoured Brigade said that the forward companies of the Rangers were not to leave the embussing point before 5 a.m. on the 13th.

[6] Lt T. C. Oldfield, VX7066; 2/8 Bn. Clerk; of Albury, NSW; b. Blayney, NSW, 14 Jan 1921. Killed in action 12 Apr 1941. Oldfield had added three years to his age on enlistment in Oct 1939, and thus had enlisted at 18, been commissioned at 19, and killed at 20.

back to positions farther up the slopes and Coombes' men also were moved about 150 yards back. The low ground forward of the 2/8th was now alive with tanks and troop-carrying trucks and guns, but for several hours the Germans made no concerted attack. The right-hand companies of the 2/8th, Simpson's[7] and McDonald's, which were not being attacked, were still able to enfilade German infantry swarming up the hill against the companies on the left and coolly to observe the enemy's tactics. The German infantry jumped from their trucks close to a start-line, formed up and advanced close behind the tanks (as the Australians had done in Libya), one platoon accompanying each of the tanks, which fired briskly using high explosive shell. At intervals the leading infantry sent white Very lights into the sky to indicate their positions to their artillery.

At 2 p.m. Lieut-Colonel Mitchell of the 2/8th, who had reinforced his left with a platoon (from McDonald's company) led with great dash by Sergeant Duncan,[8] ordered a counter-attack which regained some vital ground on top of the ridge at the junction of Coombes' and Robertson's companies. After six hours of intermittent fighting in the pass and on the slopes to the east, the 2/8th still held the heights though their left had been mauled; the Rangers, however, were rallying astride the road about two miles to the rear, but five of the six supporting guns of the 2/1st Anti-Tank Regiment had been left without protection and abandoned. Thus the ridge held by the 2/8th formed a deep salient.

The withdrawal of the Rangers left no infantry forward of the supporting artillery of the 2nd Royal Horse Artillery except a platoon of New Zealand machine-gunners. This was reported to Vasey's headquarters by Captain Grant[9] of the New Zealand machine-gunners and Lieut-Colonel Aikenhead[1] of the R.H.A. but brigade headquarters insisted that the Rangers were still in position. About 3 p.m. Vasey ordered the Rangers to hold until dark, keeping in touch with the 2/8th on their right; but in fact the Rangers were far to the rear of the 2/8th.

Soon afterwards the Rangers made a second withdrawal, this time to the pre-arranged rearguard position at Rodona. On the right about this time a concerted German attack was made. By 4 p.m. the last of the Dodecanese had withdrawn and not only was Mitchell's left being hard pressed but his battalion was under machine-gun fire from heights on his right.[2]

---

[7] Lt-Col C. L. Simpson, VX66. 2/8 Bn and Aust Prov Corps. Police constable; of Box Hill, Vic; b. Leeds, Eng, 21 Apr 1909.

[8] He had been commissioned in February, but his unit was unaware of it.

[9] Lt-Col J. L. Grant, 27 NZ MG Bn. Master butcher; of Christchurch, NZ; b. Timaru, NZ, 19 Mar 1908.

[1] Brig D. F. Aikenhead, DSO, MC. CO 2 RHA 1940-41 and in 1942; CCRA XXX Corps 1941-42; CRA 48 Div 1942-44; CCRA III Corps 1944-45. Regular soldier; of Frome, Somerset, Eng; b. Liverpool, Eng, 29 Jun 1895.

[2] Mackay said afterwards: "the 2/8th thought the Dodecanese had broken. No; but they didn't march in our style, but straggled out, stolid and quiet. They kept off the road, and went their way while we went ours." He was in error in believing that the 2/8th considered that the Greeks had given way. It is important, however, to note that he (and Vasey) were uncritical of the manner in which the Greeks carried out their instructions to withdraw.
German records reveal that some Greeks were still fighting west of Lake Petron at 8 p.m., but it seems certain that the Greeks on the immediate Australian right had withdrawn, according to plan, by 4 p.m.

On the left his headquarters, ammunition dump and regimental aid post[3] were under the fire of German machine-guns sited to his left rear. His telephone wire, which had run through the Rangers' to Vasey's headquarters, went out of action about 4.30 because of the Rangers' retirement, and his line of retreat along the main road was cut. Some time before the renewed German attack opened, Mitchell had summoned the company commanders to issue orders for the withdrawal that evening: to the south-east since it was impossible to withdraw along the road on which German tanks were then moving. Because signal communication at least to some of the companies had been broken Mitchell could not now have countermanded the order to attend a conference even if he had wished. About 5.30, as the company commanders were returning to their men, German tanks and about 500 infantry reached the Australian positions along nearly the whole front, and particularly on Coombes' company on the left. Efforts were made to organise a withdrawal but the tanks, impervious to the fire of anti-tank rifles, were now deep into the Australian position and, in the search for cover, sections were separated from platoons and platoons from companies. When the men reached the floor of the valley behind them, they came under the heavy machine-gun fire that had long been enfilading the headquarters area; dispersed they made their way over the next ridge. Some officers and men decided that if, in their weary condition, the men tried to carry out their weapons and equipment they would be cut off and captured, and that their only chance of escape was to move fast and use what cover the hills offered. In McDonald's company on the right "the men were simply too tired to withdraw carrying weapons, and perhaps 20 per cent threw away Brens and even rifles". A platoon commander in another company ordered his men to drop their equipment. Weapons were lost not because of disorganisation—though the withdrawal became confused as darkness fell—but because of sheer weariness.

On the left Lieutenant Fleming,[4] Mitchell's Intelligence officer, remained to collect stragglers after the battalion headquarters had gone. Tanks were firing and German infantry were moving across the battalion's line of withdrawal and towards Kleidi. When he, with McDonald, Lieutenants Austin,[5] Diffey and others, under fire from a group of tanks 500 yards away, reached the top of the ridge they saw the main body of the battalion plodding wearily south in open order. When darkness fell the men marched on through heavy mud. The leading companies reached the reserve position at Sotir, ten miles from where they had set out, about 9 p.m., and two hours later were at the forked roads at Rodona where their

---

[3] The regimental medical officer, Capt R. R. Anderson (of Perth, WA), and his men carried on coolly under fire throughout the afternoon. Anderson was considered "directly responsible for preventing at least six wounded men falling into the enemy's hands".

[4] Lt-Col A. P. Fleming, OBE, VX3359. 2/8 Bn 1939-41, and air liaison offr on various staffs 1941-45. Journalist; of Melbourne; b. Melbourne, 5 Mar 1912.

[5] Maj H. McP. Austin, VX244. 2/8 Bn, and Aust Prov Corps. Grazier; of Seymour, Vic; b. Skipton, Vic, 8 Mar 1903.

vehicles awaited them. Small parties of weary men arrived to rejoin the battalion at intervals during the night, until about 250 had assembled; about half of the officers and two-thirds of the men were then still unaccounted for.

Meanwhile in the central sector astride the road the guns of the 2nd Royal Horse Artillery with two Australian anti-tank guns filled the gap during the late afternoon and held the German infantry and tanks there. They engaged the advancing enemy over open sights until they were under small arms fire from less than 400 yards, and then were coolly withdrawn. They saved the day.[6]

After having telephoned Mackay and told him that the situation was becoming "serious" Vasey, about 5 p.m., had warned Dougherty on the left, who had not been attacked, that the front had lost all cohesion and ordered him to withdraw to his embussing point south of Rodona. Dougherty ordered his carrier platoon and Lieutenant Wren's[7] rifle platoon to take up a position on his right to cover the withdrawal of his forward companies, the carriers to hold until 8.30 and then to go back along a route well to the west of the main road in case the Germans should be in possession of it; and he sent messages to the companies instructing them to withdraw. In anticipation of such a move Dougherty had already instructed his centre company, Captain McCarty's, to thin out leaving only one platoon on Hill 1001; and Conkey's company on the right had already withdrawn on to battalion headquarters as a result of earlier orders and in consequence of the withdrawal of the Rangers on their right. Dougherty could now communicate with the remainder of McCarty's company and Major Barham's[8] on the left only by runner because the battalion had never enough telephone wire to reach Barham's positions, five miles from the main road and about 1,500 feet above it, and the wire to McCarty's company was broken. Before the runners had climbed the steep snow-covered slopes to McCarty, who had withdrawn one of his two platoons to the rear slopes of the ridge, Captain Luxton,[1] a liaison officer on Vasey's staff, arrived and told him he was to withdraw immediately. McCarty sent two of his men, Corporal West[2] and Private Murphy,[3] to pass the order to Lieutenant Copland, who commanded the platoon still on Hill 1001, and led out the remainder, taking the precaution to keep well to the west of the road, along which the enemy was advancing.

---

[6] "The gun drill, fire discipline and accuracy of shooting of these R.H.A. gunners was truly magnificent," wrote an Australian anti-tank officer, Maj J. P. Love.

[7] Capt E. D. Wren, NX64. 2/4 Bn, and Brit Borneo Civil Affairs Unit 1945. Law clerk; of Strathfield, NSW; b. Sydney, 29 Aug 1919.

[8] Maj K. H. Barham, NX66; 2/4 Bn. Solicitor; of Parramatta, NSW; b. Parramatta, 23 Feb 1911. Killed in action 12 Apr 1941.

[1] Lt-Col T. Luxton, DSO, MBE, VX335. HQ 19 Bde 1940-41; DAQMG 9 Div 1942-43; AA&QMG 6 Div 1943. Merchant; of Melbourne; b. Malvern, Vic, 24 Jan 1912.

[2] Cpl H. West, NX5887; 2/4 Bn. Grazier; of Crowther, NSW; b. Young, NSW, 25 Oct 1916.

[3] Pte A. D. Murphy, NX5882; 2/4 Bn. Farm worker; of Cootamundra, NSW; b. Bodangora, NSW, 20 Feb 1906.

Copland had already intercepted and read a written order to withdraw which Private Coles,[4] a runner from Dougherty's headquarters, brought to the forward slopes of Hill 1001 at 7.30, believing all McCarty's company was still there. Copland directed Coles to McCarty's new position, as he believed, and added to the message a request that a Very light signal should be made if he also was to retire immediately. No signal appeared but an hour later, at 8.30, the two runners whom McCarty had sent forward appeared in the distance and signalled to Copland to move out. At this time German infantry were climbing the forward slopes of Hill 1001. Copland deployed his platoon in readiness to meet attacks from flank or rear and marched his men down the hill to Xinon Neron, four miles away. It was now dark—about 9.30 p.m.—and, after having failed to find a road leading south from the village, though the map showed three, he decided to march east to the main road and then south. Dougherty, believing that Barham and Copland had received instructions to keep well west of the main road, had left Xinon Neron in his carrier at 9 p.m.

When he received the order to withdraw Major Barham delayed the retirement of two of his rifle platoons until two sections of New Zealand machine-gunners who were in support had moved out. These machine-gunners withdrew in their vehicles after having carried all their equipment to the foot of the hill. A troop of Australian anti-tank gunners, under Lieutenant Smith,[5] destroyed their guns and withdrew on foot with the infantrymen. Thus Barham at length arrived at Xinon Neron with two platoons[6] under Lieutenants Irwin[7] and de Meyrick,[8] and with Smith's troop of the 2/1st Anti-Tank. Barham said that he knew well the way to the new embussing point and moved the little force on to and along the main road, in column, with himself, Copland and two others bringing up the rear. Apparently he had not received Dougherty's message telling him to keep well west of the road. Just past the road junction a small group of German motor-cyclists appeared. After an exchange of fire, in which Barham shot a German soldier and then was killed himself, the Germans rode off. The column moved on but only to walk, section by section, into a strong enemy position astride the road. There, covered by Germans in weapon pits, they were disarmed and shepherded into a near-by field. There were about seventy Australians in the group.

The outcome of the engagement was that although the Vevi position had not been held until 8 p.m., as had been planned, except on the 2/4th's sector where Barham's depleted company and Copland's and Wren's

---

[4] Pte G. T. Coles, NX2083; 2/4 Bn. Tin miner; of Newcastle, NSW; b. Tingha, NSW, 19 Nov 1913.

[5] Lt S. Smith, NX70171; 2/1 A-Tk Regt. Insurance clerk; of Chatswood, NSW; b. Petersham, NSW, 19 Sep 1914.

[6] The third platoon, Wren's, mentioned above, had been withdrawn during the afternoon to a position forward of Dougherty's headquarters.

[7] Lt. W. Irwin, NX3593; 2/4 Bn. Insurance inspector; of Sydney; b. Omagh, County Tyrone, N. Ireland, 27 Sep 1908. Killed in action 12 Apr 1941.

[8] Lt J. J. de Meyrick, NX4006; 2/4 Bn. Student; of Casula, NSW; b. Toronto, NSW, 16 Jun 1919. Killed in action 13 Apr 1941.

platoons had been in position until after that hour, it had been held long enough to enable both flanking battalions to complete their withdrawal under cover of darkness. Vasey's handling of his thin line during the critical afternoon had been cool and resolute—one observer recorded the opinion that the atmosphere at his headquarters was "almost too cool and calm"— at one stage this atmosphere may have been due to the failure of headquarters to realise how badly the fight was going.[9] Some casualties had been inflicted on the Germans, but the price the defenders had paid had been far higher in relation to the size of the small force to which they belonged. During that night only 250 of the 2/8th were assembled at Rodona, and many had no weapons. The Rangers also had lost heavily. The 2/4th had only three rifle companies at the outset and the equivalent of one of those companies had now been captured. The artillery had remained in action until the enemy was only a few hundred yards away. The 2/3rd Field Regiment (Lieut-Colonel Strutt[1]) had lost two guns which had become bogged[2] and the 64th Medium one. The Australian anti-tank gunners who, in Mackay's opinion, had been sited too far forward—and they had certainly been a target for German artillery and machine-gun fire all day—had suffered heavy casualties and lost sixteen guns, ten of them in Captain Crawford's[3] 2nd Battery which had been cut off by a demolition in the road and some eighty officers and men captured.

The width of the front Vasey had to hold had made it impossible for him to form a reserve which might have been used to restore the sector lost by the Rangers, and impossible to link the outlying companies on the left by telephone; afterwards Vasey decided that his headquarters were too far back, in the circumstances. If Barham and Copland had received the order to withdraw sooner and had received the order to move well to the west of the road, it is probable that they would have reached the embussing position safely. There were not men enough to organise defence in depth, but only to attempt to hold the crest of the heights, which resulted, in Mackay's words, in "a type of guerilla warfare". The sheer fatigue of the troops, who had been hurried into position after several sleepless nights, and the intense cold, had contributed to the confusion of the 2/8th's withdrawal. "The 2/8th Battalion," wrote Vasey, "was completely disorganised. A large percentage of the men had thrown away their weapons. Subsequently only 50 armed men could be raised from

---

[9] "This action (wrote Mackay afterwards) was characterised by the bold command of Brig Vasey when a less resolute commander might easily have lost control on the evening of 12 April, at which stage the situation was indeed critical. 1/Rangers had been heavily engaged all day and were in a poor state to fight. 2/8 Bn had withdrawn to the east and south-east and were temporarily lost in the command as a fighting unit. Brig Vasey handled the situation with coolness and courage. The support given by 2 RHA, 2/3 Fd Regt and 64 Med Regt during the whole engagement and by the horse and field artillery during the later stages of the withdrawal was of a high order and contributed to the success achieved."

[1] Brig H. W. Strutt, DSO, TX2001. CO 2/3 Fd Regt 1941; A/CRA NZ Div in Crete 1941; CRA 6 Aust Div 1941-42; BRA NT Force 1942-44. Merchant; of Hobart; b. Hobart, 19 Dec 1903.

[2] The withdrawal of the guns of the 2/3rd was covered by a gun commanded by Sgt D. H. Russell (of Darwin), whose coolness "was largely responsible for the other nine guns being got away".

[3] Capt A. D. Crawford, QX6014; 2/1 A-Tk Regt. Manufacturer's agent and farmer; of Brisbane; b. Brisbane, 6 Jun 1914.

the battalion. The C.O. was completely exhausted." This bleak statement was not the whole truth. A battalion hurried from the Western Desert with no time for re-training or even the elementary training of its raw reinforcements, with little proper rest or food since it left Athens seven days before, had been hurried into a position two miles and a half in width and above the snow-line. There they had beaten off confident German patrolling and attacks for two days, withdrawing only when both flanks were in the air, when the battalion was under enfilading machine-gun fire, and tanks were milling round the company areas.[4]

A main task of Mackay's force had been to cover the withdrawal of the 20th and 12th Greek Divisions and Mackay had been constantly anxious to ensure that this was done. After the war Papagos strongly criticised "W" Group for having failed to protect the Greek withdrawal.

> At 6 p.m. on April 12th, though the damage and the losses sustained by the forces defending the Kleidi position in no way justified such a hasty move, Group W ordered its forces who were fighting in this area to withdraw (Papagos wrote) .... The order of withdrawal ... was given by Group W without taking into consideration that immediately west of Lake Vegorritis there were still forces of the 20th Infantry Division, that the 12th Infantry Division was still east of the highway Servia-Kozani-Ptolemais and that Group W had been instructed to hold the Kleidi position until the forces of the 12th and 20th Greek Divisions, which came under its orders, had completed their movements to the west. Moreover, this decision was taken without any warning to the Cavalry Division, whose right wing (21st Infantry Brigade) was in contact with the left flank of the forces defending the Kleidi position. The movement of the 12th Division to the west having been resumed since 9 p.m. on 12th April, following the second order of Group W, was carried out under such great difficulties, owing to bad roads and unfavourable conditions, that only a small section of the forces of the division managed to reach the pass east of Siatista in the night of the 12th to 13th April. The forces of the 20th Division, who also had to change positions in a hurry, came up against such difficulties ... that great disorder ensued; one section was dispersed, their fighting ability was reduced, and only part of them managed to reach the Vlasti-Klisoura area in the night of the 12th to 13th April.[5]

Papagos' criticism is based on the fact that his orders were simply that Mackay's force was to protect the withdrawal of the 12th and 20th Divisions and the whole of "W" Group to be on the Aliakmon line "by April 14th at the latest". In keeping with these orders Wilson, Mackay and the staff of the Central Macedonian Army had agreed on a plan whereby that army would withdraw bit by bit on the nights of the 10th-11th, 11th-12th and 12th-13th. In fact Mackay's force had held the Vevi Pass until after dark on the 12th and was to hold the rearguard position at Sotir six miles to the south during the following night. It is true that after the early hours of the morning of the 12th it was probably impossible for troops of the Greek 20th Division to move along the road leading

---

[4] When he made these generalisations Vasey probably knew little of what was happening to the 2/8th in the late afternoon after its communications (which went through the Rangers' position) had been overrun. Later, in Crete, he talked about the engagement to Major A. S. Key, the second-in-command of the battalion at Vevi and its commander in Crete, and with two company commanders, and left them with the impression that for the first time he had the battalion's story correctly. Both Vasey and Key were later killed in the Pacific war.

[5] Papagos, p. 372.

into the Klisoura Pass, which ran just north of the British rearguard, but the Australians knew that the 20th Division had been ordered to be west of the main road by 2 p.m. and believed they had done so. Mackay's anxiety at this stage was for the Dodecanese Regiment to which he had allotted thirty trucks to accelerate their withdrawal. The retirement of the 12th Greek Division was protected during the whole of the 13th.[6] The truth appears to be that the Greek troops were set too hard a task and were ordered to begin to thin out too late, and that liaison with their staffs was lamentably weak and left much room for misunderstanding. The British and Greek forces spoke different languages not only in the literal sense but in the sense that one was a highly-mobile, expertly-staffed army and the other an army of foot-soldiers served by pack animals which moved so slowly that probably many Greeks who withdrew from the Vermion mountains to the east of the valley on the first night had not yet arrived at the Klisoura and Siatista Passes to the west of it on the third night. Australian accounts of the withdrawal of the Greeks, and German accounts of the dogged fight the 20th and 12th put up in their new positions strongly suggest that Papagos was wrongly informed concerning the proportion of Greeks who did carry out the withdrawal successfully. The 21st Greek Brigade on the left of Mackay's force fought hard after the 2/4th Battalion's withdrawal and later joined the 12th and 20th Divisions. The Greek troops generally seemed dogged and capable of great endurance, and likely to arrive at their destination and make a good stand there.

Meanwhile, on Papagos' orders a large-scale withdrawal of the Greek western armies had begun—a pressing necessity since they occupied a deep salient on the left of the Allied line. During the 12th April the Western Macedonian and Epirus Armies withdrew to positions covering passes on each side of the Albanian frontier. As part of this movement the Cavalry Division was ordered to hold the Pisoderion Pass until the withdrawal was completed, because a German advance through it would cut the road from Koritza along the upper Aliakmon Valley, now the main line of supply of the Western Macedonian Army.

Thus, on the morning of the 13th, the British rearguard was astride the road at Sotir; and Greek rearguards in the three passes through the mountains to the west, one of which—Siatista—was still covered by Brigadier Charrington's force. The rearguard position at Sotir lay across a neck of land about five miles in width between Lake Vegorritis on the right and a marshy area on the left. The rearguard occupied a ridge rising to a height of 600 feet which lies across this gap. The Amindaion creek on the right and the marsh on the left, which came up to the main road, were impassable to tanks. Charrington had obtained Mackay's leave to add the 2/4th Australian Battalion to his force to strengthen his infantry,

[6] Mackay was convinced that he had successfully covered the Greek withdrawal. His ADC, Lt B. H. Travers, wrote in his diary next day: "It was a triumph that two Greek divisions got out without a casualty." Some infantry of the 20th Greek Division marched across the Aliakmon into the area of the 4th NZ Bde and thence on towards Larisa.

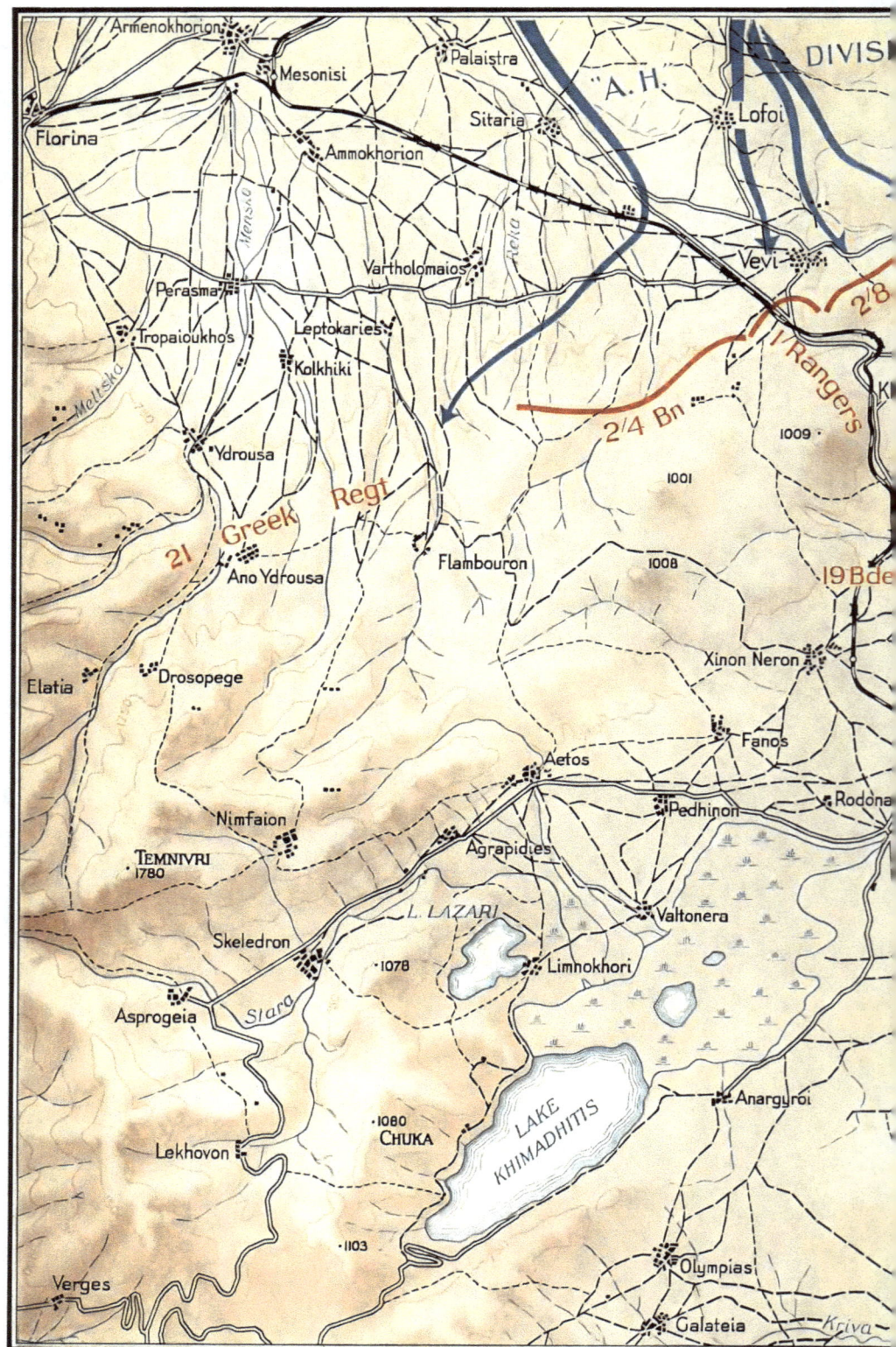

Disposition

of which he still had only a company of the Rangers. The 2/4th, now reduced to two rifle companies, had therefore been halted and deployed during the night on a line some three miles long, on the right of the ridge, with the Rangers on their left, "There was not a murmur from any of the men of my tired battalion," wrote Dougherty two days later, "when told they had to fight this rearguard action." In support were the 3rd Royal Tanks less one squadron, a squadron of the Hussars, the 2nd Royal Horse Artillery, a platoon of New Zealand machine-gunners, and an anti-tank battery of the 102nd Regiment.

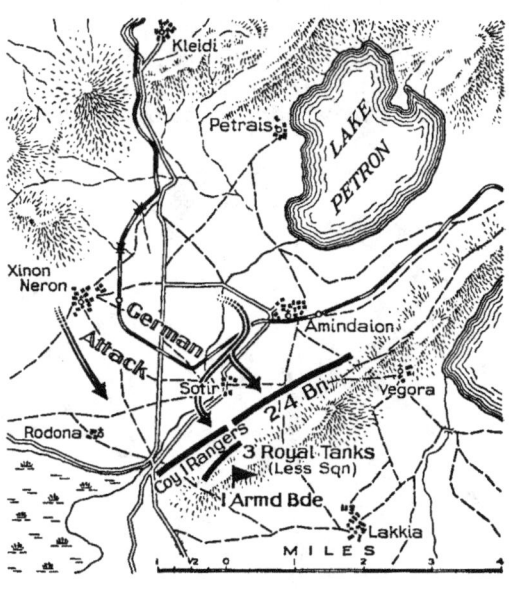

Before dawn Vasey and Dougherty went forward to the companies. As light came they saw the enemy in weapon pits on the flat about 1,000 yards away, and a machine-gun opened up on them as they stood exposed. The British line opened fire not knowing that in between on the ploughed land near Sotir lay the Australian, New Zealand, British and Greek prisoners taken the previous night. Lieutenant de Meyrick and some other prisoners were killed by this fire; the tireless Copland was shot and wounded by a German when trying to signal to the party of prisoners to move west in the hope of avoiding the fire and returning to their own lines. Some of the prisoners managed to reach protection or to hide in the young crops. When the Germans assembled the Australian prisoners after the fight more than 30 out of 123 had been wounded.[7]

---

[7] Later the Germans forced the unwounded men to mend the cratered road. The prisoners watched two attacks on the pass by British aircraft that morning, "both . . . unsuccessful", but a third attack in the evening hit three trucks and killed "quite a number of Germans". At Vevi the men of the *"Adolf Hitler" Division* fed the prisoners and treated them well. Near Florina three dogged and enterprising infantrymen, Cpl P. A. Lane (Wallerawang, NSW), Ptes C. C. Campbell (Wauchope, NSW) and E. Steel (Grenfell, NSW), hid in a drain during a halt and, escaping into the hills, set off on an adventurous expedition which was typical of many other such exploits in the following weeks. They received help from friendly Greeks and reached a point 10 miles from Salonika and thence walked south along the railway line to Leptokaria and through the hills to Elasson. Early in May they changed into Greek tunics and walked as far south as Pharsala meaning to go to Athens, but they were persuaded to go north again by a Greek who said that food was very short in Athens. After further wanderings they arrived at a village in the Volos peninsula where they met Sgt C. J. Skerrett of the 2/2nd Battalion and four others who had fought in a later battle at Pinios. On 22 May these were ferried to the island of Skiathos where they were joined by four other Australian privates. Together they were sailed by Greeks to Skyros, Antipsara and thence to Smyrna, in Turkey, whence they arrived at Haifa in the Polish ship *Warsaw* on 29 June.

Soon after dawn the German infantry advanced in open order supported by machine-gun fire. They were effectively shelled by the R.H.A., but by 7.30 had penetrated the Rangers' position. A squadron of the Royal Tanks then moved forward and stemmed the advance. During the next two hours the rearguard withdrew, unit by unit, while the tanks held the enemy down and finally themselves retired to a position already organised a few miles south of Ptolemais. The 2/4th, which at Vasey's suggestion was withdrawn first, now left the armoured brigade and travelled in its trucks to Kozani and thence south to take up its pre-arranged position with the remainder of the brigade on the left of the Aliakmon-Olympus line.[8] It will be recalled that the plan of withdrawal provided that the armoured brigade should be south of the Aliakmon by 8 p.m. on the 13th, but, with the object of giving the Greek 12th Division more time to complete its withdrawal across the line of retreat, Wilson had ordered

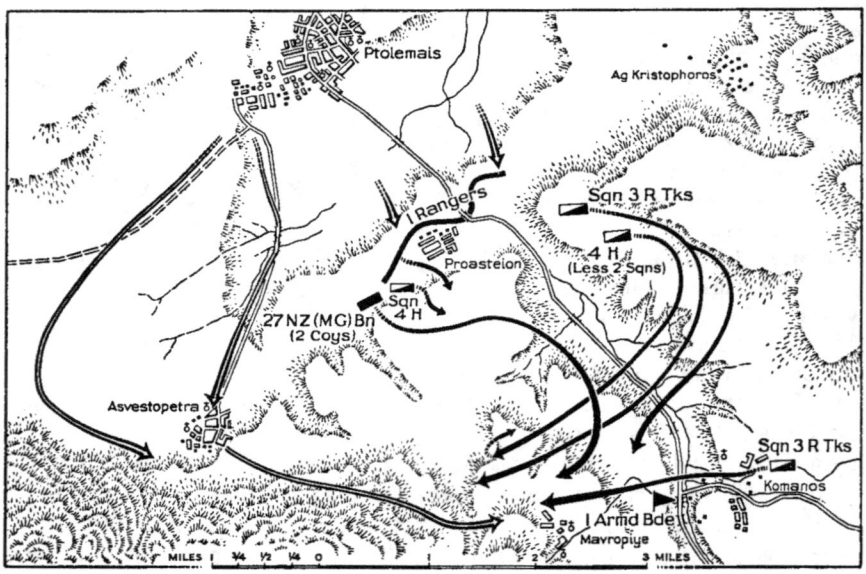

Charrington to hold the German advance as long as he could. Consequently Charrington prepared to maintain a prolonged defence in the second rearguard position. Here Colonel Lillingston[9] with his Hussars, a squadron of the Royal Tanks, part of the Rangers, a battery of anti-tank guns, and two platoons of New Zealand machine-gunners had prepared a position. The road ran through a gorge with hills rising to 1,200 feet above it on either side. The rearguard had a clear view of the German

---

[8] What was believed to be the last party of the 2/4th departed at 8.55 but a section of the 2/4th under a dogged private, L. N. Gardiner (of Adjungbilly, NSW), did not receive the order and held its position until 11.40 a.m. when Gardiner extricated his men, who were almost surrounded. One man was killed and Gardiner himself wounded.

[9] Lt-Col E. G. G. Lillingston, DSO; 4 Hussars. Regular soldier; b. Chaibassa, India, 4 Jul 1892.

tanks and troop-carriers steadily advancing, and of their men repairing the cratered road as they moved forward. By 2.30 the Germans were exchanging fire with the British forward patrols and half an hour later their guns began accurately shelling the Rangers' posts.

The frontal advance was held by the Rangers and the anti-tank gunners astride the road, but about thirty tanks swung over the foothills, round the British left flank and by 7 o'clock were moving towards the road near Mavropiye where Charrington had his headquarters, three miles behind the main British position. Here a fierce fight ensued, German aircraft strafing and dive-bombing the defenders for the first time in the campaign. In the failing light Lieutenant Trippier's[1] gunners of the 102nd Anti-Tank believed that they knocked out eight tanks, and two troops of medium tanks which were hurried into action were considered to have destroyed five more. The men of brigade headquarters went into action with rifles and Brens, and the New Zealand machine-gunners who were then moving back halted and deployed. "It was a most pretty sight," wrote Colonel Waller[2] of the anti-tank regiment. "Blazing tanks and trucks, 2-pounder and 50-mm tracer, flashes from guns and rifles, and bursting shells, with the last afterglow of the setting sun and the dark mass of the mountains as a background."[3] The German attack was held for the time, but Charrington decided to withdraw his force without delay. The withdrawal was covered by the tanks and armoured cars which, when the infantry and artillery had got clear, themselves retired under cover of a smoke-screen unmolested by the battered German tank force. The depleted brigade retired to Kozani and thence along the mountain road to Grevena. A small rearguard stood astride the road at Mavrodendri until 1.30 a.m. on the 14th, but was not attacked by the Germans, who had evidently suffered severely. It then rejoined the brigade at Grevena.

Charrington's brigade had been reduced almost to impotence. Its armoured regiment had been depleted, chiefly by mechanical breakdowns, to one weak squadron. Its infantry battalion had lost half its men; its anti-tank regiment had lost six guns. There was no possibility of replacing the tanks. In two sharp actions they had delayed the Germans' approach to the main British defence line and had knocked out a number of tanks, but the cost was the virtual disappearance of the one small armoured force the Allied army in Greece possessed.

Twenty-six years before, in April 1915, an Australian and New Zealand Army Corps had landed on Gallipoli, where, in eight months of bitter and costly fighting, Australian and New Zealand soldiers had established an enduring military tradition. Several of the senior leaders of the force now in Greece, including Blamey, Mackay and Freyberg, had served at the

---

[1] Maj A. W. Trippier, MC; 102 A-Tk Regt. Stockbroker; b. Ramsbottom, Eng, 30 Aug 1909.
[2] Brig R. P. Waller, DSO, MC. 102 A-Tk Regt; CRA 10 Ind Div 1941-42; CCRA III Corps 1943-44. Regular soldier; b. Westbury, Glos, Eng, 9 Oct 1895.
[3] "With the 1st Armoured Brigade in Greece", by Lt-Col R. P. Waller, *Journal of the Royal Artillery*, Jul 1945.

landing.⁴ In this April, twenty-six years later, Australian and New Zealand brigades were again fighting side by side on a battlefield in the Levant, and old memories were stirred. In the early morning of the 12th Blamey sent the following message to his divisional commanders:

> As from 1800 hrs 12 Apr I Aust Corps will be designated ANZAC CORPS. In making this announcement the GOC ANZAC CORPS desires to say that the reunion of the Australian and New Zealand Divisions gives all ranks the greatest uplift. The task ahead though difficult is not nearly so desperate as that which our fathers faced in April twenty-six years ago. We go to it together with stout hearts and certainty of success.⁵

We now know that soon after Stumme's *40 Corps* had reached the Axios and also had gained contact with the Italians in Albania, Field Marshal List ordered it to wheel south by way of Monastir and Florina to Kozani and thus take in the rear the Greek and British force which was establishing itself on the line Katerini-Edessa-Florina, leaving the mopping-up of the scattered fragments of the southern Yugoslav army to Kleist's *Armoured Group*. For this operation the *5th Armoured Division* was detached from Kleist's Group which was meeting little resistance in Yugoslavia, and added to Stumme's corps, which thenceforward comprised the *5th* and *9th Armoured Divisions, the 73rd Infantry Division*, and the *S.S. "Adolf Hitler" Division*. On the 9th *40 Corps* reached Monastir and on the 10th the *"Adolf Hitler"* crossed the frontier and occupied Florina. That day the German corps, advancing down the Florina Valley, made little progress along the muddy, cratered roads and it was repeatedly attacked by British bomber and fighter aircraft; farther east the *6th Mountain Division* and a detachment of the *2nd Armoured* crossed the Axios and advanced towards Edessa. At the outset the German Intelligence staff's estimate of the British force awaiting them about Kozani and Katerini had included three or four divisions including the 6th and 7th Australian and the New Zealand, with part of the 2nd Armoured—in fact, the force that had been intended for Greece. It seems that their agents

---

⁴ On 25 Apr 1915 Blamey had been a major on the staff of 1 Aust Div, Mackay a captain in the 4 Aust Bn, Freyberg a lieut-commander in the *Hood* Bn of the Royal Naval Division. Rowell had landed on Gallipoli in May as a lieutenant in the 3 Aust Light Horse.

⁵ On 4 March 1940 the Australian Prime Minister, Mr Menzies, had cabled to the New Zealand Prime Minister, Mr Savage, to suggest that the New Zealand Division might be incorporated with the 6th and 7th Australian Divisions in an Australian and New Zealand Army Corps. The New Zealand Government consulted the War Office and General Freyberg. The War Office pointed out that it was not possible at that stage to be certain that a three-division Australian-New Zealand corps would be required to take the field as a complete corps, and suggested that the two Dominion Governments should be prepared in advance to agree to the possible detachment of the New Zealand Division. Freyberg foresaw difficulties. He said that "practical advantages would be gained by fighting in a Corps with Australian divisions, as their great value on the flank and General Blamey's experience give confidence"; on the other hand New Zealand administration would need to be safeguarded; and the Australian approach to defence problems was not entirely similar to the New Zealand Government's. "New Zealand," he said, "desires to assist in the manner best conforming to the British war effort and may not wish to be associated automatically with a possible aggressive Australian attitude regarding strategy." He summed up by saying that they should link up for operational control only, but that the time to link had not yet arrived. On 17 May the New Zealand Cabinet Defence Committee decided that the matter should be discussed with the Australian authorities by Mr Nash, the Minister for Finance, who was to visit Australia. The visit did not take place, and the Australian proposal lapsed—until April 1941. On 6 April 1941, six days before Blamey's announcement, Freyberg had written to his Prime Minister: "We are now linked with the 6th Australian Division; thus the Anzac Corps is again in being." (*Documents Relating to New Zealand's Participation in the Second World War*, Vol II (1951).

in Egypt had served them well by informing them of the composition of the force allotted to Greece, but that their officials in Athens had failed to discover what formations had actually arrived.

The German commander believed that the Australian and New Zealand divisions were on a line approximately east-west from Katerini to Kozani, where, he believed, Corps headquarters were situated. The attack at Vevi was made chiefly by units of the *"Adolf Hitler"* (as Vasey learnt after two prisoners had been taken); there were also tanks of the *9th Armoured Division*. A battalion group attacked at Vevi after dark on the 11th with only one company forward, but the attack was eventually stopped because it was decided that the artillery support was inadequate. The Germans deployed three "battle groups" for the attack on the 12th. On their left one group, including five companies with artillery, was to thrust to Kelli (on the front of the Dodecanese) and thence along the ridge to Petrais; the other group was to advance through Vevi and Kleidi and on to Kozani. A third group was later to advance to Xinon Neron round the British left rear. The group on the German left attacked at 4.20 p.m., reached Kelli at 6.15 and Petrais, where "60 Australians and Greeks were captured", at 8.15. The group in the centre opened a preliminary attack on the dominating feature on the left of the 2/8th Australian Battalion at 10 a.m. (8.30 according to Australian records) and its main attack at 3 p.m., when the whole group advanced astride the road. According to List's chief of staff, Major-General Greiffenberg, the German losses were "relatively high"—about forty men killed. The Germans claimed 480 "English" and 40 Greek prisoners. After this fight the *"Adolf Hitler"* wheeled west towards the Klisoura Pass and the *9th Armoured Division* continued southward. A "fierce tank battle" at Ptolemais followed, in which the *33rd Armoured Regiment* lost four tanks. After this the British force was believed by the Germans to have withdrawn that night behind the Aliakmon. At this stage the Germans were not seriously attacking in the Pisoderion Pass, where they had deployed only a battalion less two companies.

Meanwhile, Vietinghoff's corps of the *Second German Army* had begun its advance on Belgrade through the bridgeheads held since the 6th by the *14th Armoured Division*. On the 9th it crossed the Yugoslav-Austrian border on a front of about 100 miles; on the 10th the *14th Armoured* attacked Zagreb. General Kuhn entered the town that evening with one battalion and was cheered by the people. The *14th Armoured Division* was followed by the *8th*, and both then advanced through Barcs along the road south of the Drave to Vukovar and Mitrovica and on towards Belgrade; the *16th Division* advanced via Nasice to Mitrovica. On the 12th, after a march that had been impeded less by Yugoslav fighting troops than by boggy roads and some demolished bridges, Belgrade was entered by troops of Vietinghoff's corps from the west, of Reinhard's from the north-east, and of Kleist's group from the south. The degree of Yugoslav resistance can be gauged by the fact that in Reinhard's corps only one officer was killed, and he by a civilian.

CHAPTER 4

THE OLYMPUS-ALIAKMON LINE

WHILE General Mackay's force and the Central Macedonian Army were fighting rearguard actions and falling back in the Florina-Kozani Valley, the New Zealand and Australian formations on their right had also been withdrawing to the Aliakmon line, although under less heavy pressure. On the 10th the New Zealand Division had withdrawn to its positions on Mount Olympus leaving the divisional cavalry regiment (with armoured cars and Bren carriers) and a troop of field guns to fight a delaying action from the river back to the Olympus positions. On the afternoon of the 12th the flashing windscreens of a long convoy of German vehicles were seen some 10 miles beyond the river. Motor-cyclists approached the road bridge, which the New Zealanders had demolished, but were dispersed by Bren gun fire. Just before dusk thirty lorries appeared, but quickly withdrew when shells from the New Zealand field guns fell among them. At 9 a.m. on the 13th the enemy tried to cross the river near the road bridge, but from well-concealed positions the defending carriers and armoured cars fired on the German infantry to good effect, and the guns accurately shelled German mortars and vehicles beyond the river and infantry trying to cross the river in rubber boats. It was a fine artillery feat: the foremost New Zealanders were at the southern bank of the river, the Germans were only 100 yards away on the northern bank and the guns were firing from 10,000 yards to the rear.

Enemy tanks advanced and the forward cavalry squadron was heavily shelled by German guns. At 1.30 p.m. the whole delaying force was ordered to withdraw. (This was about two hours before the 1st Armoured Brigade began fighting its final rearguard action at Ptolemais.) The New Zealand cavalry spent the night behind a tank ditch some 10 miles south. At 6 a.m. on the 14th German infantry began to filter across this tank trap and there was a sharp exchange of fire. Then their tanks advanced to the ditch with a strong force of infantry. At 10 a.m. the rearguard was ordered to withdraw to Katerini, and by 4 p.m. it was inside the Olympus defences.

In the meantime the withdrawal of the 16th Brigade to the Servia position had been proceeding. Some donkeys had been collected from the Greek villagers to act as pack animals in the long march over the mountains.[1] On the 9th engineers had cratered the pass. When the brigade received orders to march back to Mount Olympus the infantry destroyed much gear which had been brought forward by the trucks and was too

---

[1] Having failed to obtain mules in Greece where the Greek Army had already commandeered the best, Wilson's staff asked GHQ at Cairo to send mules from Egypt. One shipload of mules was sunk but one was landed and the animals were used later in the Brallos Pass.

heavy for the donkeys to carry away.[2] Tents were burned, reserve ammunition buried, some tools and spare Bren barrels were smashed and, in some companies, all greatcoats and all blankets but one a man were burnt. It snowed at Veria for twenty-four hours before the withdrawal began.

In accordance with Blamey's order that one battalion be withdrawn without delay the 2/3rd had been moved back to the foot of the pass on the 11th and there took up a covering position near the junction of the main road and the track over which the brigade was to march south over the hills and across the Aliakmon River. Two companies of the 2/2nd and two of the 2/1st left their positions in the pass on the 11th, the remainder of the 2/1st and 2/2nd (which supplied the rear party) on the night of the 12th. The long march was to continue all that night and most of the following day—for the rearmost parties even longer. Carrying 100 rounds of ammunition and five days' rations, greatcoats, blanket, groundsheet and haversack, and with donkeys carrying the heavy weapons, the main body of the 2/1st reached Leventes at 3 a.m. on the 13th and thence marched south along the track to the village of Avlianna where the leaders woke a villager to show the way to the pass leading over the mountains to the

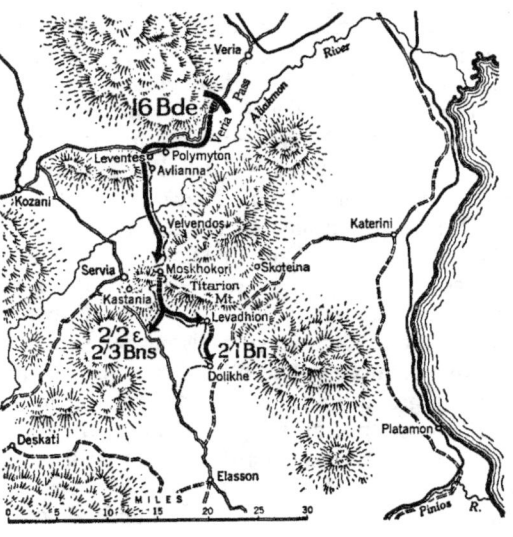

river. They reached the pass after trudging four miles in ankle-deep mud. Now nearly exhausted, they rested in the snow for five minutes in every fifteen, and when a man seemed likely to collapse his mates would distribute his gear among them and help him along. At 6 a.m. they were at the top of the pass and could see the Aliakmon 3,000 feet below and only four miles distant. At the river they were met by a party of seven sappers of the 2/1st Field Company under Lieutenant Cann and Corporal Smeal[3] who ferried them across from 8 a.m. onwards in a punt guided by a wire rope and propelled by the force of the river. When they had climbed to the village of Velvendos, overlooking the river from the south, it was estimated that

---

[2] The Greek peasants' donkey is a small animal able to carry a load of only fifty pounds or so on mountain tracks. One 2/2 Bn man records that at Veria Pass a section leader, Cpl Dick Powell (New Lambton, NSW), finding that he and his men, having only one blanket each, could not sleep in the snow, walked two miles to his coy HQ and alone carried back a tent, "a thing no mule could manage".

[3] Cpl D. G. Smeal, NX1106; 2/1 Fd Coy. Carpenter and rigger; of North Sydney; b. North Sydney, 13 Apr 1910.

they had marched 34 miles from their positions in the Veria Pass. The 2/2nd passed through the rearguard position at Leventes at 6 a.m. and had crossed the river by midday; at that time the 2/3rd began to move south. The tail of the column left Avlianna late in the afternoon and from the heights overlooking the Aliakmon Valley watched, as from a grandstand, German aircraft dive-bombing the Servia Pass. It was 10 p.m. on the 13th before the last platoon of the 2/3rd crossed the river and Corporal Smeal sank the punt and led the last men up to Velvendos. Two companies of the 2/1st Battalion covered the river as the 2/3rd crossed.

It had been a gruelling march even for men hardened by months of severe campaigning and they themselves were surprised that they had been able to endure it. In spite of fatigue, heavy going in mud and snow, and ice-covered slopes so steep that men and donkeys slipped and fell, no equipment had been lost and there were few stragglers—only sixteen were counted at Leventes after the first two battalions had passed. "An epic of endurance, physical and moral," wrote one diarist with pardonable pride.

After General Mackay had left Brigadier Charrington and the 1st Armoured Brigade at the Sotir rearguard position on the morning of the 13th, he had driven south to take command of that sector of the new line occupied by the 16th, 4th and 19th Brigades.[4] At 10 o'clock (the withdrawal from Sotir was then taking place) Mackay met Brigadier Rowell at the bridge on which the main road crossed the Aliakmon, told him that the 19th Brigade was worn out, and learnt from him that Blamey had already ordered a New Zealand battalion—the 26th—to cross the river to reinforce them. Mackay remained at the Aliakmon bridge until 3.20 p.m. (the attack on the rearguard at Ptolemais was then in progress), when he ordered Captain Heugh[5] of the Australian engineers to blow the bridge, which was of three steel-trussed spans, and carried a concrete roadway across a gap of 450 feet. Lance-Corporal Buckingham[6] of the 2/1st Field Company, assisted by sappers of the 580th British Army Troops Company, had placed charges for its demolition. Buckingham fired the charges and all three spans dropped into the river, which was wide and shallow at this crossing. Although the demolished bridge could not be used by vehicles, infantry could still clamber across. Soon after the explosion six British 3-ton trucks arrived on the north bank. Fortunately a pontoon bridge a few hundred yards downstream was still intact, and the trucks crossed it before the engineers sank the pontoons and set the superstructure drifting down the river.

In the Servia Pass, overlooking the bridge and the river, the 4th Brigade had been digging in for three days. On the heights three field

---

[4] Henceforward the Anzac infantry brigades will sometimes be denoted by their numbers only, and the adjectives "Australian" or "New Zealand" omitted. The New Zealand brigades' were the 4th, 5th and 6th, the Australian the 16th, 17th and 19th.

[5] Maj H. Heugh, MBE, QX3708; RAE I Aust Corps. Insurance inspector; of Innisfail, Qld; b. Richmond River, NSW, 18 Feb 1907. Died 10 Aug 1951.

[6] L-Cpl J. R. Buckingham, WX1728; 2/3 and 2/1 Fd Coys. Miner; of Kalgoorlie, WA; b. Sandstone, WA, 15 Jan 1909.

regiments were in position—the 6th New Zealand, 2/2nd and 2/3rd Australian—though the task of the two Australian regiments was to support the Australian brigade on the opposite side of the river. In the course of the day the 26th Battalion had moved to Rymnion, south of the Aliakmon on the left of the 4th Brigade. When it arrived there it had no indication of its role but at length Lieut-Colonel Page[7] managed to contact Brigadier Vasey by an artillery telephone, and learnt that he must join the Australians north of the river.

The two weary and depleted battalions of the 19th Brigade had arrived in their new sector during the 13th. Trucks had carried them to the mountain village of Kerasia whence they marched into the hills while the vehicles returned to Kozani and across the river to Mikrovalton. The

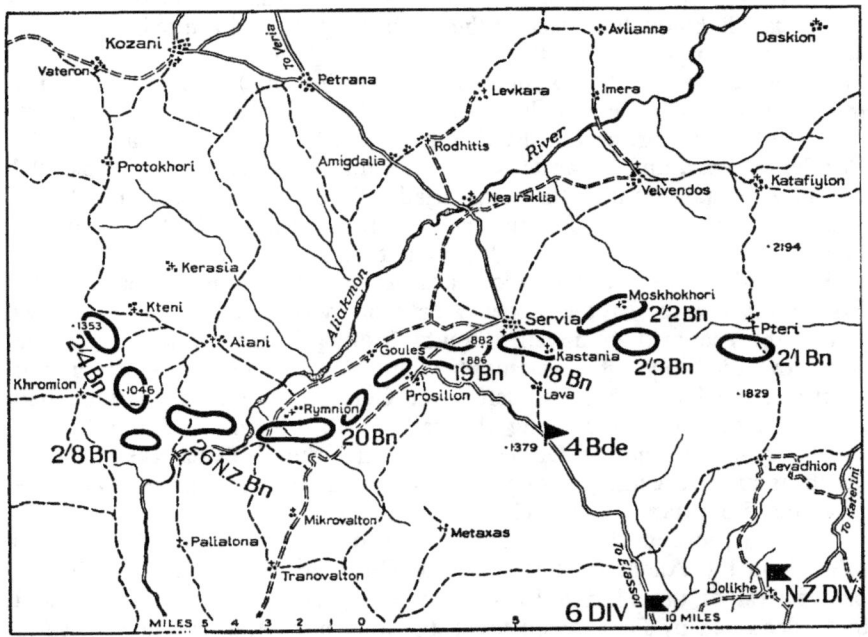

Dispositions, 15th April.

arrival of batches of stragglers had now increased the strength of the 2/8th to 308, not including about fifty men whose vehicles took the wrong turning at Kozani and who were now south of the river.

On the night of the 14th the 26th Battalion crossed the river by a ferry—a folding boat and a rope—and went into position on the Australian right facing north on a front of more than two miles. The boat could hold only three fully-equipped men, and one company was still on the south bank at daybreak and stayed there. The 2/4th Battalion was on the left facing east with one company on a 3,000-foot ridge on the

---

[7] Col J. R. Page, DSO; CO 26 NZ Bn 1940-41. Regular soldier; of Auckland, NZ; b. Dunedin, NZ, 10 May 1908.

right and another on a 4,000-foot mountain on the left overlooking Kteni at the boundary between the British and Greek forces, though no Greek troops were seen in that village by the Australians.[8] The depleted 2/8th was in reserve.

No bridge crossed the Aliakmon west of the main road, though the New Zealand ferry was kept in operation; but engineers had been ordered on the 13th to bridge the river on the 19th Brigade's flank. In the meantime even to send orders to the 19th Brigade was difficult because Vasey's wireless sets were not always effective; Captain Vial,[9] one of Mackay's Intelligence officers, delivered a signal to him by riding his motor-cycle to the river, swimming the stream, and finding a Greek to guide him through the hills to the Australian headquarters.

Thus by the 15th April, all Blamey's corps was in position on the Olympus-Aliakmon line except the 16th Brigade, still moving into its sector on the right of the 4th.

The withdrawal to the Olympus-Aliakmon line placed the Greek Army temporarily in a salient with its eastern side lying along the mountain range to the west of the Florina-Kozani valley, its point in the area of the Pisoderion Pass, and its western side stretching thence, south and parallel to the Albanian frontier, to the Adriatic. Each side of this salient was about 75 miles in length. The eastern, soon to be attacked by the advancing German force, followed a tangled mountain range rising to 6,000 feet and pierced by the second-grade roads through the Siatista, Klisoura and Pisoderion Passes. In the upper Aliakmon Valley these lateral routes joined the road which travelled south through Kalabaka to Larisa and was now the only effective supply route for the Greek Western and Central Macedonian Armies. Before the German attack these armies had been maintained chiefly along the railway to Florina and the Larisa-Florina road, both now in German hands. Thus the Trikkala-Kastoria road (with its branch leading through the Metsovon Pass to Epirus) was now of capital importance to the Greek Army.

Thus far, orders had implied that a prolonged defence would be offered on the Aliakmon line with the Greek armies on the left in the passes west of the Florina Valley and along the Albanian frontier, and the order given by Papagos on the 12th, confirming the new line Wilson's force was to hold, made the British forces responsible for aiding the Greeks with anti-tank weapons (which the Greeks lacked) in the Klisoura and Siatista Passes and the minor pass of Vlasti midway between them. The 6th Australian Division had to be relieved of this task, however, because of its heavy loss of anti-tank guns in the first engagement. Nevertheless, Wilson ordered Mackay to take responsibility for demolitions on the Klisoura road, and the Argos Orestikon-Grevena road[1]; and a troop of

---

[8] Vasey's force included also a company of the 2/1 MG and a battery of the 2/1 A-Tk.

[9] Lt-Col R. R. Vial, DSO, VX3557. HQ 6 Div 1940-41; GSO1 (Ops) HQ NG Force 1942, 1943-44; II Corps 1944, 1945; and other staff appts. Bank officer; of Camberwell, Vic; b. Camberwell, 6 Jul 1915.

[1] On the 12th a section of the 2/1 Fd Coy prepared the road Argos Orestikon-Siatista-Kozani for demolition and handed over to the Greeks. Colonel Lucas, Mackay's chief engineer, wrote later: "The service rendered was not enthusiastically welcomed by the Greek commander, who emphatically vetoed the destruction of the new concrete bridge near Neapolis."

the 102nd Anti-Tank Regiment was placed under the command of the 20th Greek Division at Klisoura.

Cooperation between allies presents a multitude of problems. Differences in equipment complicate supply. Each is likely to possess his own tactical doctrines. Dissimilarity of national temperament can produce major misunderstandings. It was to simplify such problems that the Allied leaders had agreed to impose on the ill-equipped 12th and 20th Greek Divisions the exhausting and hazardous march from the Vermion passes across the Florina-Kozani Valley to the western passes; by that means the Anzac Corps would have the best roads at its service as its more cumbersome—and more powerful—equipment demanded; and the Greeks with their pack animals and lighter weapons would be in the tangle of mountains on the left, supplied along a road incapable of carrying the trucks the Anzac troops possessed.

But of all obstacles that stand in the way of smooth cooperation between allies, the difficulty of achieving mutual understanding is perhaps the greatest, and the allocation of separate sectors, though it reduces the number of points at which this problem occurs, does not solve it. In the campaign in Greece full understanding was made specially difficult by the fact that few Greeks speak English and fewer Englishmen speak Greek. The unwieldy organisation of the British Command added another complication. In direct touch with the Greek leaders were five independent British commands or missions.

On the morning of the 13th Papagos informed the commanders of the armies of Western Macedonia and Epirus that they were finally to withdraw to the line along the Venetikos River (south of Grevena) and running thence through the Pindus and along the western part of the Albanian frontier to the coast at Lake Vutrinto. This would entail withdrawal from the deep salient in which they now lay to a line continuing the British line in an east-west direction. The British line, although perilously long for two divisions, was, in Blamey's words, "an immensely strong natural position"; the new Greek line would be in extremely rugged country. Papagos' orders stated that when the Western Macedonian Army had withdrawn into the upper Aliakmon Valley it would absorb the Central Macedonian and the combined force would continue the retirement along the axis of the Kastoria-Grevena road. The boundary between "W" Group and the Greek Army was to be a line more or less north-south through Deskati. Thus the 1st Armoured Brigade would have to side-step to the east to come into the British area. To reach the new line some Greek formations would have to march about 100 miles. It would be necessary for the Klisoura and Siatista Passes to be held for several days, and the Grevena road for several days more, if the retirement was to be carried out successfully.

In the course of the 13th, however, reports reached Wilson's headquarters which he and his staff considered extremely disturbing. The road through Grevena, along which the 1st Armoured Brigade was withdrawing, was jammed with Greek troops plodding south. The 12th and

20th Greek Divisions were reported to have "disintegrated" on their way to the Siatista and Klisoura Passes, though the Cavalry Division was still well-established in the Pisoderion Pass farther north.

In his dispatch Wilson later wrote that "from the outset, in spite of every possible effort being made to avoid misunderstanding, the Greek Central Macedonian Army failed in every way to carry out its role in the withdrawal. . . . It may be said, in fact, that the Greek 12th and 20th Divisions never regained control after their withdrawal from the Vermion positions, but continued to disintegrate into a disorganised rabble whose main object was to reach Athens."

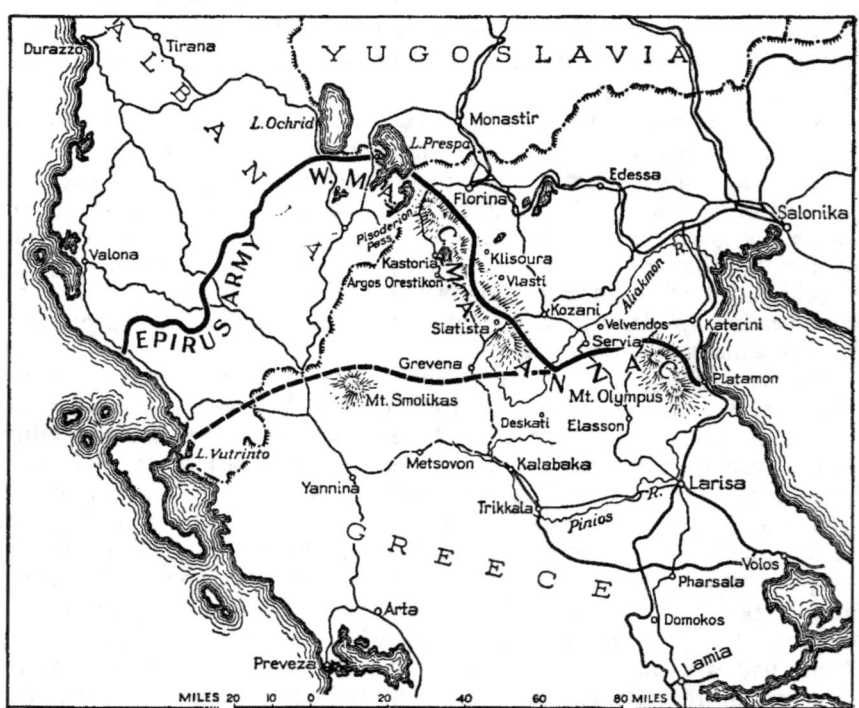

The front line on 15th April and the shorter line proposed by General Papagos.

It seems likely that the conviction of the British leader and his staff that the Greek army east of the Pindus was broken derived partly from early impressions of the poor equipment of the Greek Army and largely from its appearance on the roads. The Greeks tramped along the sides of the roads in small groups, wearing dingy uniforms, and using an odd variety of means of transport such as donkeys, farm carts, and a few old motor vehicles. Particularly might reports of confusion and retreat have reached Wilson from observers at various headquarters, who, in a withdrawal (whether Greek or British) inevitably saw more of the service troops moving back than of the fighting men still at their forward posts.

Nevertheless, on the evidence arriving at his headquarters, Wilson saw a serious threat to his inland flank. If the Germans sped south along the Grevena road they might reach the Larisa bottleneck from that direction and cut his road to Athens. He decided to use his only reserve—the 17th Brigade, whose units were then disembarking at Piraeus—to guard this flank.

On the 13th, Brigadier Savige, commander of the 17th, arrived at Blamey's headquarters for orders. He and his headquarters had reached Larisa on the 11th,[2] but his three battalions and the 2/11th, the missing battalion of Vasey's brigade, had disembarked at Piraeus only on the afternoon of the 12th and were still in Athens. When he arrived at Blamey's headquarters Wilson was there. Savige was instructed to reconnoitre (a) the road leading from Larisa through Kalabaka as far west as the summit of the Pindus mountains about Metsovon—the road leading to the rear of the Epirus Army, and (b) the Kalabaka-Grevena road— along which the 1st Armoured Brigade and the Western Macedonian Army were then withdrawing. Savige immediately set off and, with his liaison officer, Lieutenant Lowen,[3] drove from Larisa, through Kalabaka, without seeing any Greek troops. Thence they drove into the Pindus to a point above the snow-line whence they could see the Adriatic. When they returned to Kalabaka the town was crowded with Greek troops. Early on the 14th Savige was recalled to Blamey's headquarters where a discussion took place in which Brigadier Galloway pressed Wilson's request that the 17th Brigade should be sent promptly to Kalabaka. While these three were talking Rowell entered and said that information had arrived that the Germans had broken through the Greeks on the left. Thereupon Blamey ordered Savige to occupy a line covering Kalabaka. Savige recommended holding an area covering both the road to Grevena and the road through the Pindus and this was agreed to. His force was to include the 2/5th, 2/6th, 2/7th and 2/11th Battalions with artillery and other supporting arms. The 2/5th and 2/11th were expected to arrive at Larisa by rail at 9 a.m. that day.

A written order, not signed until that evening, gave Savige the task of holding the junction of the Pindus and Grevena roads and preparing to move north to support the armoured brigade, probably on the Venetikos River. His force was to consist initially of the four battalions mentioned above, seven cruiser tanks of the 3rd Royal Tank Regiment, two troops of the 64th Medium Regiment, a battery of New Zealand field artillery, a battery of Australian anti-tank artillery, a company of the 2/1st Machine Gun Battalion, the 2/2nd Field Company, and 2/2nd Field Ambulance. The dispatch rider who was to deliver Savige's copy of this order was delayed and Savige did not see it until the morning of the 15th when Lieut-Colonel Garrett, allotted to him from Blamey's staff as "Operations Staff Officer", arrived at his headquarters.

---

[2] On the 12th he had met Blamey on the road and called at Corps headquarters where Rowell had described the situation to him.
[3] Lt-Col I. H. Lowen, VX53. HQ 17 Bde 1940-41; HQ 9 Div 1942-43, 7 Div 1943-44; BM 18 Bde 1944-45. Sales manager; of Kew, Vic; b. Sydney, 8 Jan 1917.

Somewhat more encouraging reports had arrived at "W" Group headquarters early on the 14th. The Greek 12th, 20th and Cavalry Divisions were now reported to be in position on the left, and the Cavalry Division was not yet being heavily pressed. About noon, however, news came that German forces had captured the Klisoura Pass. This threatened the withdrawal of three divisions—the 9th, 10th and 13th—of the Western Macedonian Army.

The loss by the Greeks of the Klisoura Pass underlined the conviction already reached by Wilson and Blamey that the Greeks to the north were disintegrating; in addition German air attacks were now becoming more severe. Since the German attack opened the three squadrons of the Eastern Wing of the British air force had not only hampered the German advance but had been the most reliable source of information about the enemy's movements. On the 6th the Hurricane squadron had attacked twenty Me-109's over the Rupel Pass and claimed to have shot down five without loss to themselves; on the 7th congested columns of vehicles were bombed in Yugoslavia. Bad weather hampered flying from the 8th to the 12th, but on the 13th it was clearer, and German aircraft, now operating from strips hurriedly prepared at Prilep and Monastir, began dive-bombing the forward Greek and British troops. That day twenty-one dive bombers attacked the positions in the Servia Pass, and on the 14th groups of up to fourteen aircraft bombed and machine-gunned the forward positions and the roads leading to them.[4]

On the 13th Wilson had decided that the Greek Army could no longer be relied on, and, after conferring with Blamey that day, a decision to withdraw to the Thermopylae line was made.

> German air activity [he wrote later] was now on the increase and becoming continuous and widespread; the bombing of a town put an end to all civil control and the functioning of police and telegraphs. The railways also were beginning to show the same symptoms. Our air force, which faced superior numbers valiantly, now began to feel the attrition of combat as well as losses on airfields, with the result that its effectiveness began to wane . . . . Farther to the left reports of further disintegration of the Greek forces made me anxious about that flank, fearing that the Germans might thrust down each side of the Pindus on Grevena and Yannina without opposition. There were also reports that Greek troops from the Albanian front were unwilling to take up positions in the line we were now holding and were making for Athens . . . . The increasing gravity of these reports caused me to consider a further withdrawal to a position which the British Imperial troops could hold without reliance on Allied support; this position was at Thermopylae, about 100 miles to the south.[5]

The new line would be astride the Thermopylae, Brallos and Delphi Passes and retirement to it would entail the loss of all Greece north of the Peloponnese except the peninsula, some 35 miles wide, between Lamia and Athens. It would also entail abandoning all prospect of further cooperation with the main body of the Greek Army, and would make it

---

[4] It was the attack on the 13th which the men of the 16 Bde had looked down upon from the heights.
[5] Wilson, *Eight Years Overseas*, p. 89.

possible for the enemy to base his fighter aircraft within range of Athens. It was decided to carry out the withdrawal as swiftly as possible. The British force, well-equipped with vehicles, could complete the manoeuvre in a few days, but it would take weeks for the Greek forces to march back so far. Indeed, Wilson's written order in which the new decision was expressed said that "within the limits of responsibility, Anzac Corps will make every possible effort to ensure that Greek forces do not withdraw on routes available to Imperial forces, and that they do not in any way whatsoever hinder the withdrawal".

It was a drastic decision. When it was made the Anzac Corps was not in serious contact with the enemy at any point, although considerable German forces could be seen massing on the lower ground forward of the three main passes held by the corps. In the mountains west of the Florina-Kozani valley the Greeks held two and had lost one of the three passes leading to the Grevena road along which their Central Macedonian Army was retiring. The withdrawal of that army and the Epirus Army had so far not been seriously molested by the Germans or Italians except that German aircraft were now constantly attacking the Greek and British troops on the muddy, winding Grevena road, and traffic congestion was becoming acute.

More powerful factors were present, however, than those revealed by examination of marks made with coloured pencils on the maps at British or Greek headquarters. Before the campaign began some of the British leaders had little confidence in its success and had begun to plan both withdrawal southward through Greece and an embarkation. Barely half the intended British force had arrived in Greece when the Germans attacked. The British and Anzac commanders lacked confidence in their opposite numbers in the Greek Army and had been appalled at the primitiveness of that army's equipment. The German Army could afford to deploy ground and air forces of overwhelming strength in Greece. How long the Allied force could have stood on the Aliakmon and Venetikos might have remained forever a matter of speculation, had the line held until the withdrawal had been completed. In fact the line was broken—and not only on the Greek front. If the British withdrawal had begun a day later it would have been disastrous for the British force.

Wilson's order for the retirement to Thermopylae was issued at 9.5 a.m. on the 15th. It handed the conduct of the withdrawal to the commander of the Anzac Corps; the advanced headquarters of "W" Group would be withdrawn south of Larisa. "Maximum demolitions in depth on roads and defiles . . . within the time available in order to impose all possible delay on the enemy" were ordered. Four forces had been or were being placed in position to cover the withdrawal. These were the 1st Armoured Brigade (henceforth under Blamey's command) round Grevena and Kalabaka, Savige Force round Kalabaka, one New Zealand brigade (it would be the 6th) round Tirnavos, and one brigade (the 19th) about Pharsala.

At 6 p.m. on the 15th, in obedience to General Wilson's order given to him that morning, General Blamey had issued more detailed and comprehensive orders for the withdrawal he was to conduct. There were to be two phases. The first would begin on the 15th (only six hours of the 15th then remained). During the night the 6th New Zealand Brigade—the first rearguard — would move from its position in reserve in the Olympus Pass to a line covering the two roads between Tirnavos and Elasson, where it would be reinforced by the 2/3rd Australian Field Regiment. The 19th Australian Brigade, after withdrawal from north of the Aliakmon, would move in vehicles to Domokos, south of Pharsala, where it would join a force commanded by Brigadier Lee and including the 2/6th and 2/7th Battalions, a company of the 2/5th, the 2/1st Field Regiment (less a battery), which would form a second rearguard to cover the final withdrawal to the new line. This entailed removing the 2/6th, 2/7th and a company of the 2/5th from the force hitherto allotted to Savige. The 16th Brigade—the left flank guard—would begin to move on 15th April on foot to the main road and thence in vehicles to a position astride the Trikkala-Larisa road at Zarkos with a field regiment in support.

These first moves were designed to bring all troops of the 6th Australian Division behind the passes by 8 a.m. on the 16th, when the second phase would begin. In it Freyberg would become responsible for the front and for the withdrawal through the first rearguard of his 5th Brigade Group from the Olympus Pass and his 4th Brigade Group from Servia on the night of the 17th-18th, "subject to ability to disengage"; on the same night Savige Force was to withdraw through the left flank guard. "The rearguard of 6th New Zealand Brigade Group, the left flank guard of 16th Australian Brigade Group, and the troops holding the coast at pass east of Mount Olympus were to withdraw during the night 18th-19th April, 1st Armoured Brigade covering the final withdrawal across the flat, featureless plain of Thessaly on 19th April. From Larisa to the south, New Zealand Division was allotted the coast road via Volos to Lamia and 6th Australian Division and 1st Armoured Brigade the main road via Pharsala.

(Australian War Memorial)

The Aliakmon bridge, 12th April 1941.

(Maj-Gen C. S. Steele)

After the demolition, 13th April 1941.

(Maj S. B. Cann, 2/1 Fd Coy)
The ferry which carried the 16th Brigade across the Aliakmon River.

This was designed to bring New Zealand Division on the right of the Thermopylae position and 6th Australian Division on the left, in the Brallos Pass. All marching personnel were to be carried in motor transport."[6]

In Athens planning had leapt even farther ahead, for Admiral Cunningham had been informed on 13th April by the naval attaché at Athens that the evacuation of Greece was imminent, and on the 15th that it would probably begin before many days. In Cairo on the 14th General Wavell's joint planning staff completed an outline plan for the embarkation of the whole British force.

A few hours before Wilson's order was signed the Germans gained virtually undisputed control of the air in the forward zone. On the 15th German squadrons made a dawn attack on the airfields in the Larisa area destroying ten Blenheims on the ground. Air Vice-Marshal D'Albiac, who was present when this major calamity occurred, ordered that what remained of the squadrons should withdraw to Athens forthwith. German aircraft then bombed Larisa intermittently throughout the day and heavily bombed Elasson, where Blamey's headquarters were established. The severe loss of aircraft at Larisa and the withdrawal of what was left of the squadrons to Athens placed them too far away to be used in close support of the troops. The men on the ground had seen little of their own aircraft and knew nothing of the skill and daring with which they were being flown against a vastly superior enemy; henceforward few of them were to see a British machine, and German attacks were to become daily more intense.

What had been the condition of the main Greek armies during the 13th and 14th when this decision was made by the British commander? We have seen that on the 13th the Greeks were holding the Germans in the Pisoderion and Klisoura Passes. The withdrawal of the Western Macedonian Army to the Venetikos position proceeded without interference on the 13th and that of the Epirus Army began that night. About noon on the 14th, as mentioned above, the 20th Greek Division was driven from the Klisoura Pass. What remained of this division was ordered to block the Grevena road farther south. During that day and the following night the withdrawal of the 9th, 10th and 13th Greek Divisions of the Western Macedonian Army was not hindered. That day the 11th Division which had been ordered to the Metsovon Pass on the 10th occupied its positions there.

On the 14th the Germans began probing the positions held by the Anzac Corps in the Aliakmon line. It will be recalled that the New Zealand Division was now holding two passes on either side of Olympus—one the narrow coastal ledge along which a road and the railway travelled, at Platamon; and the other the wider Olympus Pass. A detachment of New Zealand engineers of the 19th Army Troops Company, equipped with some ammonal and gelignite, one naval depth-charge, some anti-tank

---

[6] Report on Operations Anzac Corps during the Campaign in Greece, 1941.

mines and a small quantity of other explosives, had the task of demolishing both tunnel and road at Platamon. Only two New Zealand field companies had arrived in Greece, and consequently the army troops company, equipped for work along the line of communication and not for the kind of demolitions that a field company is expected to carry out, had to take the place of the missing field company. Both demolitions were blown on the 14th and both proved unsatisfactory. The bricks lining the tunnel were blown out, but little damage was done to the rock above. The engineers, lacking the pneumatic drills that a field company would have possessed, tried with pickaxes to chip holes for a further charge, but the rock was hard and the second demolition, although more successful, was considered likely to impose a delay of only from four to six hours, if the enemy was left to work without interference.[7] An anti-tank minefield was put down covering the road over the saddle.

Farther left the 5th New Zealand Brigade was deployed in the Olympus Pass (through which travelled the Katerini-Elasson road), with the 23rd Battalion on the right, the 22nd in the centre, and the 28th (Maori) on the left with its left at Skoteina. The 5th Field Regiment and an anti-tank battery were in support. On the 14th, companies of the 24th Battalion were moving into the hills on the left of the Maoris as a first stage of the intended move of the 6th Brigade to a position on the left of the 5th. Some German vehicles were seen in front of the 22nd Battalion about 5 p.m. on the 14th, but by the time the guns obtained leave to fire they had gone. Throughout the night the New Zealanders saw and heard enemy vehicles with their headlights blazing, bringing troops forward. About 11 p.m. a party of motorcyclists rode boldly up the pass, but when machine-gun fire was directed at them some made off; next morning five motor-cycles were lying by the roadway. During the 15th German tanks and vehicles cautiously advanced, evidently trying to find covered ways of approach and to move round the demolitions. They were fired on by the defending artillery, and about 4.30 p.m. German guns began to reply. No real attack developed during the day.

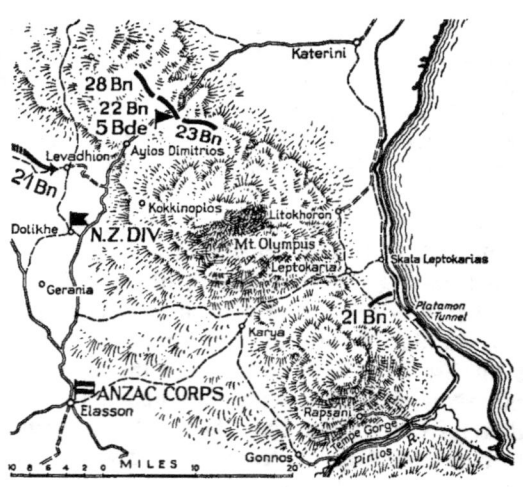

Dawn, 15th April.

---

[7] However, the success of the demolition exceeded expectations. Four days after it fell into German hands the tunnel was still collapsing.

This narrative left the 16th Australian Brigade (which was to fill the gap between the 6th and 4th New Zealand) when, late at night on the 13th, the tail of the brigade crossed the Aliakmon. During the night the leading half of the 2/2nd moved on to Moskhokori; next day the remainder joined it and by midnight the battalion had taken up its position beyond that village. In the morning of the 14th the 2/1st moved through Velvendos to the foot of the mountains and rested there. The 2/3rd remained in the Velvendos area.

That night, when the moon rose at 10.15, the 2/1st climbed to Moskhokori followed by the 2/3rd. There at dawn on the 15th the 2/1st was met by officers from Allen's headquarters with the orders that it should climb five or six miles to its position on the right of the brigade's front. At 6 that morning Corporal Smeal and another sapper who had spent the night at Velvendos with an exhausted infantryman were told by Greek villagers that the Germans had forded the river behind them; the Australians—the last men in the long column—set off with two donkeys, one carrying the sick man and the other their gear. The 2/3rd reached Moskhokori that morning. The weary men were now short of food having lived since the 12th on what they had been able to carry away from Veria Pass. "We stood down at 7 (on the morning of the 15th) and looked hungrily at our rations, debating within ourselves what we could afford to have for breakfast," wrote a sergeant of the 2/2nd in his diary. "I eventually decided on 'mush' and with snow boiled my last packet of biscuits. It was unpleasant—mush without milk or sugar—and one felt as though he was doing a dog out of a good meal."[8]

About 9 a.m. on the 15th the 2/1st reached their new position. It was about 5,500 feet above sea level and seamed with precipitous ravines. The slopes here were two feet deep in snow; they prepared to meet German mountain troops, for only mountain troops were likely to use the mule paths that led into that remote area. They found no sign of New Zealanders on their right (the New Zealanders were six miles to the north-east through rugged mountains). The Australians had been climbing with little rest since the night of the 12th, and had only a greatcoat and one blanket each in which to sleep. The 2/2nd completed its occupation of Hill 1628 south-east of Moskhokori on the 15th; the 2/3rd was in reserve south of the village.

It was difficult to convey the new orders for the withdrawal to Thermopylae to the battalions of the 16th Brigade. There was not enough telephone wire to link them with Allen's headquarters and they could be reached only along bridle paths winding across the slopes of Olympus. Lieutenant Swinton[9] of Allen's staff rode a pony to the 2/2nd, which was to come out first, bearing an order to hand over to the 2/3rd and march out to the southern end of the pass. He reached Chilton at 8 p.m. on the 15th. It was a long and difficult job concentrating companies widely-

---

[8] Sgt (later Lt) D. C. Peirce, NX1603. 2/2 and 2/1 Bns. Bank clerk; of Coffs Harbour, NSW; b. Wollongong, NSW, 26 Feb 1918.

[9] Capt C. N. Swinton, NX1837; 2/2 Bn. Bank officer; of Uralla, NSW; b. Casino, NSW, 24 Aug 1918.

dispersed in rugged country on a dark night, but by 2 a.m. on the 16th the battalion had concentrated and was marching out. The 2/1st Battalion was in country so difficult and snow-bound that the brigade liaison officer could not even find it. On the morning of the 16th, however, the commanding officer, Lieut-Colonel Campbell and his pioneer lieutenant, Fairbairn,[1] found a track back over the mountains and so learnt that the battalion should have withdrawn the previous night.

Meanwhile, farther left, an attack on the troops defending the Servia Pass had begun. From Kastania to Prosilion the position allotted to Puttick's 4th Brigade lay along steep slopes behind a still steeper escarpment below which the ground sloped more gradually to the river from two to four miles away and about 2,000 feet below. At Prosilion in the centre of the position the main road climbed through a gap in the escarpment about 500 yards wide. On the south of the gap—the New Zealanders' side—the main road climbed south-east through a winding valley, and a tributary road travelled south-west and parallel to the river and the escarpment. The battalions had been digging in since dawn on the 11th. The 18th New Zealand Battalion (Lieut-Colonel Gray[2]) was in position north of Lava from a steep ridge north of Kastania on the right to Hill 882 at the top of the escarpment south-west of Servia; the 19th was on a four-mile front astride the pass. The 19th and 20th Battalions each had two platoons of the 2/1st Machine Gun Battalion under command, one of those with the 19th being forward with the infantry posts in the pass itself. By 15th April the 6th New Zealand Field Regiment, one battery of the 7th (British) Medium Regiment and one troop of the 64th (British) Medium Regiment were in support of the New Zealand brigade.

During the afternoon of the 14th artillery observers on these slopes above the Aliakmon, looking down from about 2,000 feet to the river and the country beyond it, watched columns of German vehicles moving south. On the 13th and 14th when squadrons of German fighters and dive bombers, flying low, had attacked the positions in the pass, the only anti-aircraft guns there were four new Skoda weapons of a Yugoslav battery and four Greek guns which had arrived from the north unannounced and taken up positions near the main road. It was still a new and disturbing experience for New Zealand troops to watch the dive bombers approaching in formation, peeling off one by one, diving to about 1,000 feet to release their bombs and steeply climbing again. The Stukas sought out and attacked the gun positions, and dropped bombs along the road in an effort to crater it. Many of them had a screaming device fitted to them to make them more noisy and unpleasant for the troops below. Clearly this onslaught from the air was a prelude to a concerted attack by the German force then moving steadily forward from Kozani. At 2 o'clock on the 14th the head of the German column was seen at Petrana,

---

[1] Lt T. C. Fairbairn, NX9822; 2/1 Bn. Regular soldier; of Campbelltown, NSW; b. Stevenstown, Ireland, 26 Apr 1918.

[2] Brig J. R. Gray. CO 18 NZ Bn; Comd 4 NZ Bde Jun-Jul 1942. Barrister and solicitor; b. Wellington, NZ, 5 Jul 1900. Killed in action 5 Jul 1942.

six miles north of the river. At dusk German guns sent ranging shots across the river, and just before midnight began steadily shelling the Anzac positions; but from 8 o'clock onwards the lights of columns of German vehicles were seen moving from Kozani not south but west into the hills towards Grevena whither the armoured brigade had withdrawn.

On the night of the 14th Brigadier Puttick moved the 20th Battalion to the left flank above Rymnion to link with the 19th Australian Brigade north of the Aliakmon. Thus the front held by his three battalions was increased to 15,700 yards, though of that distance 9,500 were along an escarpment so steep as to be almost unscaleable and watched only by patrols.

Before dawn on the 15th—the day after General Wilson had ordered the retirement from the Aliakmon line—the men in the forward posts of the 19th New Zealand Battalion saw a party of Germans straggling along the road like Greeks, for whom they were at first mistaken. Some of them had passed the sections guarding the road before they were recognised and dispersed by fire from infantry and Lieutenant Sampson's[3] platoon of the 2/1st Machine Gun Battalion forward in the pass. An attack at midday and another at 5.45 p.m. were easily repulsed. Germans ran for cover in the small bushes growing on the hillside but after machine-gunners and riflemen had lashed the area with fire they began to emerge waving white handkerchiefs. The New Zealanders sent forward patrols which rounded up 147 unwounded officers and men and from 30 to 40 wounded Austrian infantrymen of the *9th Armoured Division*. The enemy's total losses were estimated at about 400, though the New Zealanders suffered only eight casualties.[4] Such losses were not surprising in a frontal attack launched without the help of air or artillery bombardment against posts well-sited and securely dug in and commanding a clear view of the slopes up which the attackers must advance.

In spite of their set-backs the Germans continued to press the attack. Parties of enemy infantry assembled in strength in Servia, where the buildings gave cover; the village was kept under constant artillery, mortar and small arms fire. In the course of the night Sampson reported that his position forward in the pass was practically surrounded and enemy infantry was under the scarp where his guns could not reach them. Under cover of darkness he withdrew to a new position higher up the slope. Two platoons of the 19th Battalion made a counter-attack here and drove out a patrol of about forty Germans who had established themselves on the slopes below Prosilion village.

Early in the afternoon of the 15th and before his comprehensive order for the withdrawal was completed Blamey had instructed Mackay that, as a first step, he must move the 19th Brigade back across the Aliakmon

---

[3] Maj R. G. Sampson, MC, QX6063. 2/1 MG Bn 1939-42; 2/3 MG Bn 1942-45; 31/51 Bn 1945. Bank officer; of Launceston, Tas; b. Launceston, 12 May 1914.
[4] A prisoner said that the attack had been made by two rifle companies and one support company. When Brigadier Puttick asked a prisoner why the attack had been made in so absurd a fashion, the Austrian replied that he was afraid "some of our officers are not good at tactics".

that day. Only a few hours of daylight remained, the river was not yet bridged and wireless communication with Vasey was unreliable. The 26th New Zealand Battalion had crossed the Aliakmon by means of a ferry contrived with folding boats travelling along a rope, but the building of a bridge presented greater difficulties. When, at the order of Colonel Lucas,[5] Captain Reddy[6] had reconnoitred the site on the 13th, he had had to walk six miles to reach the New Zealand ferry, and there found a swollen torrent 140 feet wide, flowing at eight to ten knots and about 10 feet deep in midstream. The shortest way out was straight up the side of the hill which rose 1,200 feet in two miles and a quarter. Next day Lieutenant Chester[7] and a section of the 2/1st Field Company were sent forward to build a timber trestle bridge. The men carried picks, shovels, and other hand tools, spikes and rope; a second section (under Sergeant West[8]) was ordered to make a road to the bridge. These teams reached the river after dark on the 14th and began work at dawn next day. They laboured all day, helped in the afternoon by New Zealanders of the 26th Battalion and two sections of a company of British engineers, but were still cutting timber for the bridge when at 2 p.m. an order arrived that it must be ready for the 19th Brigade to cross at 9 p.m. At 10 p.m. the bridge was finished and decked with slats six inches apart—a notable achievement by a small body of sappers equipped only with such tools as they could carry to the river along rough tracks. By the time the final gap of 45 feet was being spanned the leading companies of the 19th Brigade were assembling in the darkness on the opposite bank.

The order to withdraw had not reached Vasey until 5 p.m., although he had received a warning at 1 o'clock. Again, as at Vevi, the 2/4th Battalion was so widely spread that it had not enough telephone wire to reach its outlying company (Captain McCarty). When the order to withdraw arrived Lieut-Colonel Dougherty and his Intelligence sergeant, Falla,[9] had just returned from a visit to that company. Falla immediately returned to the company with the new orders and came out with it—a fine feat of endurance. The fifteen Bren carriers of the two battalions and the ten trucks[1] and guns of the anti-tank battery were driven down to the river blazing a trail for the infantry with their commander, Lieutenant Maddern,[2] leading the way with a hand torch; but when they arrived they found that the bridge could not carry vehicles. An attempt was made to raft a carrier across but the raft was overturned and swept away by the

---

[5] Brig L. C. Lucas, DSO, MC, DX200. (1st AIF: Lt 18 Bn, Capt 2 Div Sig Coy.) CRE 6 Div 1940-42; Deputy Engr in Chief Adv LHQ 1942-45. Architect; of Sydney; b. Townsville, Qld, 6 Nov 1894.

[6] Maj L. G. Reddy, VX184; 2/1 Fd Coy. Civil engineer; of Petersham, NSW; b. Harden, NSW, 22 Nov 1910.

[7] Maj R. R. Chester, NX3523. 2/1 Fd Coy 1940-42; RAE (Water Tptn) 1943-45. Civil engineer; of Sydney; b. Christchurch, NZ, 22 Apr 1906.

[8] Maj N. P. West, MC, NX3592. 2/1 Fd Coy 1940-41; OC 2/22 Fd Park Coy 1942-45. Electrical engineer; of Epping, NSW; b. Broken Hill, NSW, 19 Dec 1903.

[9] Capt J. St H. Falla, MBE, DCM, NX5960. 2/4 Bn; HQ 19 Bde. Insurance agent; of Leeton, NSW; b. London, 4 Nov 1911.

[1] The remaining vehicles were already south of the river.

[2] Maj R. Maddern, TX2025; 2/4 Bn. Schoolmaster; of Launceston, Tas; b. Malvern, Vic, 24 Aug 1912.

current. Consequently the crews smashed the engines of their vehicles with hammers and grenades, the gunners threw breech-blocks into the river, and guns and vehicles were abandoned. However, the company of the 2/1st Machine Gun Battalion carried all twelve of their guns back across the river. The 2/8th and the 2/4th (without McCarty's company) had crossed the bridge by 1 a.m. and, carrying some wounded men on improvised stretchers, began climbing a goat track leading up the steep escarpment to the Mikrovalton road. The 26th New Zealand Battalion formed the rearguard, and remained in position until the 2/4th and 2/8th had crossed. Chester and the New Zealand sergeant in charge of the ferry remained at the bridge and ferry until daylight, awaiting McCarty's missing company, but it did not arrive.

A guide posted at the junction of the track leading to the river seems to have left his post and McCarty's company missed the track. After an arduous night march it reached the river at daylight at a point some miles east of the bridge where the river was 300 yards wide. Some men tried to wade across but after 200 yards the water was too deep. Finally Lieutenant Hyles[3] found in the stream a little boat which would carry seven men at a time, swam out and fetched it, and the company, reduced by its losses at Vevi to sixty men, was ferried laboriously over, Hyles and Lieutenant Millar[4] rowing. By the time each return journey was over the boat had drifted 150 yards downstream and had to be hauled upstream again. When the men began scaling the escarpment they were so weary that they climbed for five minutes and then rested for ten, during which nearly all of them fell asleep. Eventually they reached the 2/3rd Field Regiment, learnt that their vehicles were gone, and remained with the gunners, who were under orders to withdraw and could find room for these weary infantrymen on their trucks.

The Germans were then pressing hard against the Greeks in the passes north of the Aliakmon. On the evening of the 14th when the British anti-tank battery supporting the Greeks at the Siatista Pass withdrew on Brigadier Charrington's orders, the Germans were within 200 yards of the guns, and the Greek infantry were dribbling back. The armoured brigade in the Grevena Pass now lay astride the route of the German flanking move. That night Brigadier Charrington began to move back from the Aliakmon to the Venetikos; so congested was the traffic, which included Yugoslav and Greek trucks, and so rough and narrow the road that it was evening on the 15th before the move was completed. Colonel Waller of the 102nd Anti-Tank Regiment, described the road as being

packed with Greeks, Yugoslavs and British, military and civilians, motor, horse and ox transport, all intermingled, head to tail, and two lines deep wherever the road permitted it. An awful sight, made more dreadful by certainty that the

---

[3] Capt J. H. Hyles, NX34899; 2/4 Bn. Grazier; of Boorowa, NSW; b. Goulburn, NSW, 9 Nov 1914.

[4] Capt D. H. Millar, NX98; 2/4 Bn. Bank officer; of Lismore, NSW; b. Crow's Nest, Qld, 14 Mar 1918.

arrival of the *Luftwaffe* would not be long delayed . . . . It was a clear, bright, sunny day and from about 0700 dive-bombing and machine-gunning attacks were continuous along the whole length of the road. It seemed that aircraft succeeded aircraft almost without a pause—yet we struggled forward and our loss was surprisingly slight . . . . By tremendous efforts we at last reached the river about 1700 hours—12 miles in 16 hours!⁵

On the 14th and 15th the 3rd Royal Tanks had to abandon seven tanks which broke down beyond repair and thus the regiment was reduced to only six out of their original fifty-two, but the brigade was still strong in artillery, the fine 2nd Royal Horse Artillery being "as good as ever" and the 102nd Anti-Tank having lost only six guns. Charrington, however, was perturbed by a report that the Central Macedonian Army was incapable of further effective resistance. He felt that his brigade was no longer able to act as an aggressive fighting formation, that further withdrawal would prove difficult because of the condition of the roads, the congestion and dive-bombing, and that both the brigade's flanks were in the air. Not all of these fears were justified. A patrol of the 4th Hussars, who formed the rearguard, went forward in the evening and discovered that the Germans had not yet crossed the Aliakmon nor were they in Grevena. On 14th April General Wilson visited the 1st Armoured Brigade and ordered it back to Kalabaka.

Meanwhile Savige Force was assembling, though in less strength than had originally been intended. By the night of the 14th seven cruiser tanks of the headquarters squadron of the 1st Armoured Brigade (under Captain Dale⁶), the 2/5th Battalion (less a company) and 2/11th Battalion,⁷ a battery of the 2/1st Australian Anti-Tank Regiment and a company of the 2/1st Machine Gun Battalion had reached Savige at Kalabaka. Next day artillery and other detachments moved in, but at 4 p.m. General Wilson arrived and informed Brigadier Savige that the 2/6th and 2/7th Battalions and the missing company of the 2/5th would not join him but would be needed to augment a new rearguard at Domokos.⁸ This was a consequence of the decision to withdraw to Thermopylae, but Savige had not yet received his copy of the Corps order of 6 p.m. on the 15th placing these battalions under Brigadier Lee's command at Domokos.

The main point of contact between the British and Greek forces was now in the Grevena-Kalabaka area. When Wilson saw Savige on the afternoon of the 15th he told him that about 3,000 Greek soldiers conveyed in trucks provided by "W" Group would be deposited in his area that night and on the following two or three nights. The first 3,000 arrived that evening and, Savige wrote later, "cluttered my forward area

---

⁵ "With the 1st Armoured Brigade in Greece", *Journal of the Royal Artillery*, Jul 1945.

⁶ Maj R. Dale, MC; 4 Hussars. Regular soldier; of Chester, Cheshire, Eng; b. Preston, Birkenhead, Eng, 18 Jun 1912.

⁷ These infantry battalions had reached Larisa by rail at 5 p.m. on the 14th, eight hours later than originally expected.

⁸ The main object of General Wilson's journey was to confer with General Tsolakoglou, commanding the Western Macedonian Army. The meeting had been arranged through Athens but Wilson could find no sign of Tsolakoglou and set off to reach his own new headquarters at Soumpasi, south of Larisa, before dark. (*Eight Years Overseas*, p. 90.)

and added weight to the stream of refugee troops, mule trains and mule carts passing through from Grevena to Trikkala". So far as Savige's staff could discover the Greek troops had been ordered to vacate their positions, leave their weapons and make for Trikkala where they believed they would be refitted and rearmed. At Trikkala, however, no arms or clothing to re-equip these men could be found, but only dumps containing chiefly petrol, ammunition, and British rations.

In the evening Savige met Lieut-Colonel Barter,[9] leader of a British liaison team attached to the staff of General Tsolakoglou, commanding the Western Macedonian Army, and told him that he was anxious to clear his forward defended localities of Greek troops. "I was informed by Barter," wrote Savige afterwards, "that Tsolakoglou was a member of a rich and influential Greek family, who, when a captain, had deserted his company in action during the Balkan War in 1912, but this particular act had no adverse effects upon his subsequent career because of his powerful family connections. Barter . . . held out little hope that Tsolakoglou would cooperate with me in clearing his troops from my F.D.L's,[10] and did not provide any hope that he would fight if the Germans advanced upon us." However, Barter, who spoke Greek fluently, arranged an interview between the two commanders for 9 a.m. next day—the 16th.

The events of the morning of the 16th impressed themselves on Savige's memory and later he wrote an account of them.[1]

General Tsolakoglou was quartered in a two storey stone house in the village some mile and a half north of Kalabaka. The house faced the village square in which there were numerous splendidly-uniformed Greek officers, mainly in small groups, without apparently anything to do. Barter led the way and Garrett accompanied me. We climbed a rickety staircase to the first floor and into a room where Barter introduced Garrett and me to the general. He was a man in his middle fifties, some six foot two inches tall, of splendid physique, and handsome. From memory, he wore a dark uniform and either top boots or leggings, which added to his vigorous personality. A strong odour of perfume filled the room.

On us entering the room the general was partly sitting on a bare table with one foot on the floor. He was holding an egg cup in his hand from which he was scooping out the contents of an egg with a spoon. He rose as he received us, and immediately resumed his position and occupation of devouring eggs.

With Barter interpreting, I expressed my concern at the large number of his unarmed troops cluttering my F.D.L's, crowding Kalabaka, and choking the roads. With a wave of his spoon he said "Machine-gun them. They are all deserters." With a smile, I informed him I was a British officer and we did not act as he advised. I pressed my point and requested his assistance by dispatching a number of his officers to organise his troops and march them to some area outside the area in question, where I expected to fight the Germans in the very near future. I further requested that his officers meet incoming convoys, provided by the British Command, to debus his troops and march them to pre-selected areas outside those areas held by my troops. He airily agreed to do so.

We then listened to Barter's interpretation of the general's repeated evaluation of himself. He by words and stance, drove home the fact that he commanded the

---

[9] Brig A. R. Barter. Asst Mil Attaché, Rome 1939-40; Brit Mil Mission, Egypt 1940-41; Spears Mission 1941; Mil Attaché, Lisbon 1942-45. B. Birmingham, Eng, 6 Nov 1900.

[10] Actually the line of posts held by the forward infantry.

[1] General Savige wrote this narrative in Feb 1951. Some details have been omitted.

"Armies of Macedonia". We listened with attention, and with appropriate dignified fervour, praised him, his troops and the Greek nation. I gathered he was assembling his "Armies of Macedonia" in positions in the Pindus Mountains. I informed him I had made a recce to the summit and that I then had a section of engineers, protected by some infantry, engaged in assisting Greek engineers to place demolitions in the road tunnel. He at once demanded their withdrawal on the grounds that this area was within his command. I pleaded that operational necessity prevented this until his troops were in occupation of the area. His vigorous insistence on the withdrawing of my parties, in addition to his generally unhelpful attitude, raised a feeling in my mind that he did not intend to fight. I expressed this to Barter and Garrett who, while not disagreeing with my view, expressed the opinion that I could not press the question further. I knew I couldn't, so I reluctantly agreed to withdraw them. I felt that the general was double-crossing.

Finally, I reverted to the question of his removal of his troops from my defended localities because of an expected imminent attack on me by the Germans. He asked when I expected the attack. With my tongue in my cheek, and in order to get immediate action, I said "Late this afternoon or early tomorrow morning." He looked at me and said "So soon." I said "Yes." He then promised to issue orders to clear his troops immediately and we agreed to meet again at 2 p.m., at his H.Q., for further discussion about cooperation.

On reaching the main Kalabaka-Pindus Road, I drove to the bridge, which was covered by 2/5 Bn, to meet Lieut-Colonel R. King, from whom I had received a report (as I left to keep the appointment with Tsolakoglou) that trouble was developing with Greek troops in that area. I found King grappling with the problem of moving Greek troops, coming along the road from Grevena, westwards across the bridge; and preventing Greek troops, moving down from the Pindus Mountains, crossing the bridge eastwards towards Kalabaka. Our troops, with fixed bayonets, were holding angry Greek soldiers at each end of the bridge, and literally forcing them to move into, or back into the mountains.

King and I then moved to the bank of a low cutting near the road junction, a short distance east of the bridge. We were there only a few minutes, and it was within half an hour of my departure from Tsolakoglou's H.Q., when a convoy of magnificent cars and charabancs, filled with Greek officers, drove past to cross the bridge. In the second or third car was General Tsolakoglou, who leant out the window and waved farewell to me with a broad smile on his face.

On the 15th about 6 p.m. the head of the German column advancing through Klisoura had reached the Kastoria-Grevena road at Argos Orestikon cutting off the Greek Cavalry Division and the 9th, 10th and 13th Divisions—the main body of Tsolakoglou's army, which began to withdraw westwards along the tracks leading into the Pindus mountains. What remained of the 12th and 20th Greek Divisions this day withdrew west across the Aliakmon to Neapolis and Grevena.

Thus when Savige saw Tsolakoglou next morning Tsolakoglou's army had been reduced to the remnants of two weak divisions round Grevena and a stream of apparently leaderless men trudging south through Savige Force towards Kalabaka and Larisa. The devious Tsolakoglou himself (whose army had now been re-named the III Corps and placed under the command of General Pitsikas, leader of the Epirus Army) had driven west evidently towards Pitsikas' headquarters.

When General Wilson reached his headquarters at Soumpasi after dark on the 15th he found a message from General Papagos asking him to meet him at Lamia at 6 o'clock next morning. Although he left Soumpasi at

1 a.m. to keep this appointment only 50 miles away, the roads were so congested and an air raid caused so prolonged a traffic jam in the streets of Pharsala, that it was 10 a.m. before he reached Lamia. There Papagos described the situation of the Greek Army—the Klisoura Pass had been lost and the Western Macedonian divisions "had taken to the mountains and were likely to turn up at Metsovon or Kalabaka but not for several days".[2] Wilson informed Papagos of the decision to withdraw to Thermopylae and Papagos expressed approval. Papagos appears not to have been aware that the withdrawal was then in progress.[3]

Although on 13th April the greater part of the *"Adolf Hitler" Division* was sent west into the Klisoura Pass, Stumme's main effort was first towards the Servia Pass. It was intended in due course to make a flanking movement through Grevena and turn the Aliakmon sector from the west. The *9th Armoured Division* advanced through Kozani and patrols crossed the Aliakmon on the 14th. The German staff then believed that on the 14th the 6th and 7th Australian and New Zealand Divisions and part of the 2nd British Armoured Division had begun a "full retreat"

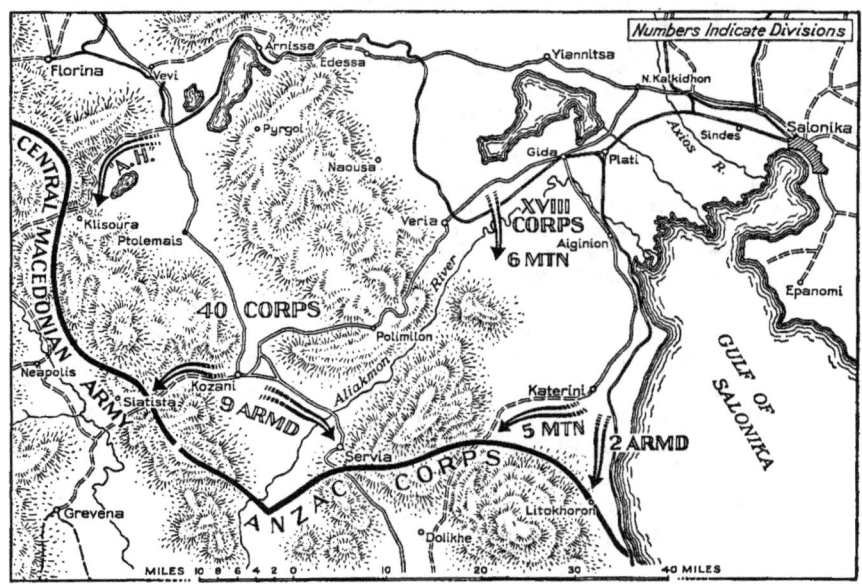

Dispositions, 14th April.

from the Olympus-Aliakmon position, and that there were "withdrawal moves" on the eastern flank of the Greek front. The attack at Servia was made chiefly by the *11th Infantry Regiment* and the German losses were 36 killed, 72 wounded and 190 missing.

It was the *"Adolf Hitler"* which reached the Kastoria-Grevena road on the 15th, thus cutting the communications of the Greek army retreating from eastern Albania.

---

[2] Wilson, p. 91.

[3] Papagos in *The Battle of Greece 1940-41* describing the Lamia conference writes (pp. 379-80): "On the morning of April 16th I met Gen Wilson outside Lamia and after a review of the situation it was decided to order the withdrawal of the British forces to the Thermopylae position. This withdrawal was ordered to begin in the night of April 16th to 17th . . . the written order of withdrawal confirming the oral one given on April 16th, was issued on April 17th on my return to Athens."

The German leaders then moved up the *73rd Division* "to protect the flank of *40 Corps* facing the Greek front". They did not consider that front to have "disintegrated". Indeed on the 15th the evening report of the *Twelfth Army* said: "The Greeks are offering stubborn resistance west of Florina and at Kastoria." (But, at that time, their commander, Tsolakoglou, and his staff, had abandoned them.)

Boehme's mountain corps (the one which had occupied Salonika on the 9th) had at first been ordered to attack the Edessa Pass with one mountain division (the *6th*) and the Veria with the *5th Mountain Division* and *2nd Armoured Division*. However, Stumme's advance to Kozani and the British-Greek withdrawal from Edessa and Veria made that operation unnecessary, and Boehme was ordered to pursue the enemy southwards. The *6th Mountain Division* advanced across the Aliakmon from Veria and began climbing the northern slopes of Olympus on the 14th close on the heels of the 16th Australian Brigade, while the *2nd Armoured Division* advanced towards Larisa both through the Olympus Pass and on the route between Olympus and the sea—that is to say against the weak eastern flank of the New Zealand line where only the 21st Battalion was in position.

Meanwhile in Yugoslavia—and here our account of the operations in Yugoslavia so far as they concern the campaign in Greece can be completed—the German Army was in effective possession of the country lying north and west of a line through Zagreb, Belgrade, Nish and Skoplje by the 13th April. The Italians had advanced to Ljubljana. The Croats, who had welcomed the Germans in Zagreb, declared that there would be no real resistance in Croatia, Dalmatia or Bosnia. What effective Yugoslav forces remained had withdrawn into the vast tangle of mountains to the west. In fact, three German columns aggregating three armoured, two mountain and six infantry divisions had occupied the northern plain of Yugoslavia without a fight; the more difficult task remained of mopping up the forces in the western mountains, and in fact, it was never done; but the fighting in Yugoslavia could now have no influence on operations in Greece. Troops of Reinhard's corps occupied Sarajevo, having travelled part of the way by rail. On the 15th the Yugoslav commander asked for an armistice. The Germans demanded an unconditional surrender, and obtained signatures on the 17th to a capitulation under which the Yugoslav leaders agreed to surrender all war material.

The German superiority in men and tanks was now immense. Field Marshal List had three corps, including three armoured divisions (*2nd, 5th* and *9th*), two mountain divisions, and five of infantry. In reserve he had two infantry divisions. To the north, Field Marshal von Weichs' army, now fourteen divisions, including three armoured (*8th, 11th* and *14th*), had completed its main task and, if necessary, could spare most of its formations to reinforce List. East of the Pindus watershed List's army faced six shattered Greek divisions, and the two divisions of the Anzac Corps.

CHAPTER 5

THE CRITICAL DAYS

EARLY on 16th April the situation of the Anzac Corps was transformed by a realisation that the main threat was to its own eastern flank and not the western flank where the Greeks stood. Hitherto it had appeared that the Olympus passes could be held without great difficulty long enough to enable the Anzac force to disengage in good order, but there had been keen anxiety lest the Germans should advance rapidly through the mountains, along the Grevena road and descend on the plain of Thessaly before the corps had withdrawn through Larisa. From the 14th onwards, however, a series of disturbing reports reached Anzac Corps headquarters from the 21st New Zealand Battalion (Lieut-Colonel Macky[1]) at the Platamon tunnel on the coastal pass east of Olympus, particularly a message that 150 tanks could be seen and the German attack was being pushed hard.

The battalion was attacked by motor-cycle troops during the 15th but repulsed the enemy with heavy loss. A German armoured regiment arrived on the evening of that day. The coastal and the inland flank of the battalion was attacked but held its ground. The Germans were reinforced during the night of the 15th-16th until (as we now know) they had assembled a tank battalion, an infantry battalion and a battalion of motor-cycle troops. Infantry attacked the left New Zealand company at dawn and the tanks attacked along the coast at 9 a.m. When his left company had been out of touch for some time, and two companies farther down the hill were being fired on from the flank and rear, Colonel Macky gave the order to retire. The withdrawal was covered by the reserve company, which was on a ridge south of that pierced by the tunnel. Soon after 10 a.m. Macky reported by wireless to corps headquarters (he had been placed directly under General Blamey's command so that General Freyberg would be freer to organise the withdrawal of the remainder of his division) that he could no longer hold; the battalion's wireless set was then destroyed and most of the telephone cable abandoned.

Already, at 1 a.m., Blamey had ordered his artillery commander, Brigadier Clowes, a cool and experienced regular soldier, to visit the 21st and take any action he considered necessary. Clowes drove during the night to Freyberg's headquarters and thence to Larisa, but there were delays on the road and it was after 8 a.m. before he set out from Larisa towards Platamon. About 11 a.m. he reached a ferry at the eastern end of the Pinios gorge,[2] found the New Zealand battalion there and learnt

---

[1] Lt-Col N. L. Macky, MC; CO 21 NZ Bn 1940-41. Barrister and solicitor; of Auckland, NZ; b. Auckland, 20 Feb 1891.

[2] Herodotus described the gorge when writing of the invasion of Greece by the army of Xerxes: "Now there is a tradition that Thessaly was in ancient times a lake, shut in on every side by huge hills. Ossa and Pelion—ranges which join at the foot—do in fact inclose it upon the east, while Olympus forms a barrier upon the north, Pindus upon the west, and Othrys towards the south. The tract contained within these mountains, which is a deep basin, is called Thessaly. Many rivers pour their waters into it; but five of them are of more note than the rest, namely,

from Macky that one company and part of another were missing. Macky had intended to hold a new position about one mile south of Platamon, but this was found to be impracticable, and the retirement had continued to the mouth of the gorge. At that point the only way across was by a flat-bottomed barge pulled by hand between banks from 20 to 30 feet high. Clowes instructed Macky that it was "essential to deny the gorge to the enemy till 19th April even if it meant extinction", and that support would arrive within twenty-four hours. He ordered him to sink the ferry-boat when all his men had crossed, and hold the western end of the gorge to the last, paying special attention to the high ground north of the river. He predicted that sooner or later the enemy would move along these slopes and outflank any troops in the gorge. He advised Macky, if the enemy broke through the gorge, to fall back to a position astride the point where the road and railway crossed seven miles south of the western exit.

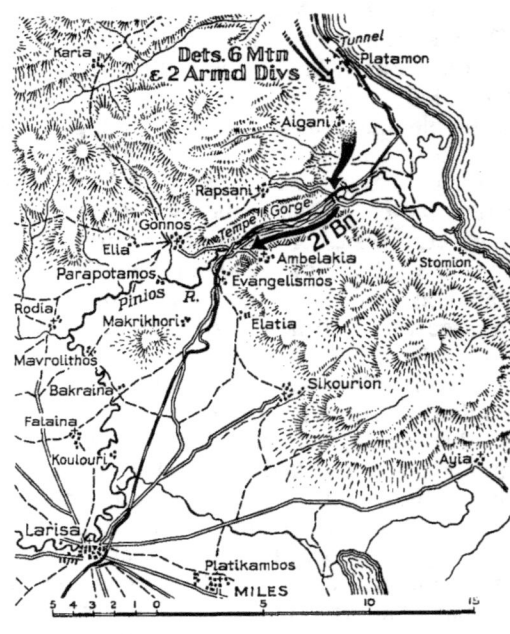

It was late in the afternoon before Macky's men had been ferried across. The four guns with their tractors and limbers were too heavy for the barge, but the heavy vehicles were driven over the railway bridge. The guns swayed too much to be towed across and were man-handled down the bank to the ferry and hauled up the opposite bank. The ferry was then sunk, "but not before a large flock of sheep and goats and their two shepherdesses had been ferried across".

After Clowes had been sent off to take charge of the threatened flank the next problem of Blamey and his staff was to find reinforcements to stop the gap there. The last reserve, Savige's brigade, had been used

---

the Peneus, the Apidanus, the Onochônus, the Enipeus, and the Pamisus. These streams flow down from the mountains which surround Thessaly, and, meeting in the plain, mingle their waters together, and discharge themselves into the sea by a single outlet, which is a gorge of extreme narrowness. After the junction all the other names disappear, and the river is known as the Peneus. It is said that of old the gorge which allows the waters an outlet did not exist; accordingly the rivers, which were then, as well as the Lake Boebeïs, without names, but flowed with as much water as at present, made Thessaly a sea. The Thessalians tell us that the gorge through which the water escapes was caused by Neptune; and this is likely enough; at least any man who believes that Neptune causes earthquakes, and that chasms so produced are his handiwork, would say, upon seeing this rent, that Neptune did it. For it plainly appeared to me that the hill had been torn asunder by an earthquake." (Book VII, Ch 129, Rawlinson's translation.)

partly to form the flank guard at Kalabaka and partly to supplement Lee's force astride the road at Domokos. When, still in the early hours, other disturbing signals had arrived from the right flank, Brigadier Rowell ordered, from Blamey's headquarters, that the first available battalion of the 16th Brigade be stopped on the road so that it could be sent to the Pinios Gorge. Consequently, when the weary men of the 2/2nd Battalion arrived at the main road at 10 o'clock that morning, after marching since 2 a.m., many on blistered feet and most with worn-out boots and torn clothing, Lieut-Colonel Chilton was met by a liaison officer with orders to report to corps. There Rowell told him that the 21st Battalion's final signals had been disquieting and he did not know whether any of the battalion would be left. Brigadier Clowes, he said, had gone out to discover what had happened and had not yet returned.[3] A battery of field artillery, a troop of three anti-tank guns and the carriers of two battalions (the 2/5th and 2/11th) would be placed under Chilton's command, and he would go to the Elatia area south-west of the gorge and take steps to hold the western exit possibly for three or four days. Chilton was greatly impressed and encouraged by the air of calm and cheerful efficiency at corps headquarters.

Chilton set off in a car. Near Larisa he met Clowes returning and learnt that the 21st Battalion was withdrawing into the gorge. After having left his adjutant, Captain Goslett,[4] to collect his battalion's vehicles and arrange for guides through the town—for the roads were crowded with trucks and some of the streets in Larisa were blocked by craters and rubble—Chilton went on to Tempe with his carrier platoon. At dusk he met Colonel Macky, who told him that his men, who were very fatigued, were bivouacked in the village with one platoon covering the road three miles forward in the gorge. His battalion, he said, had suffered only thirty-five casualties at Platamon but had lost much equipment there, including all the signal gear. During the night the remainder of Chilton's weary battalion and the artillery arrived in their vehicles.

Meanwhile Blamey had decided to send Brigadier Allen to take command of a brigade group, consisting of two of his own battalions (including the 2/2nd), the 21st New Zealand, and artillery and other detachments, in the Pinios Gorge. On the 16th Allen was in the foothills of Olympus gaining touch with his 2/1st Battalion, and it was 2 a.m. on the 17th before he arrived at corps headquarters for orders. There Rowell "who was endeavouring to get some sleep under a tree, with the aid of a torch and map, gave Brig. instructions to move on to Pinios Gorge".[5] Allen would take command of all troops there. Eventually these were to include the 2/2nd, 2/3rd and 21st Battalions, 4th Field Regiment (less a battery), a troop of New Zealand 2-pounders, seven carriers of the 2/5th Battalion and four of the 2/11th. His task was to prevent the enemy taking Larisa

---

[3] Later in the morning, however, Col K. L. Stewart, Freyberg's chief staff officer, telephoned Rowell to tell him that he had received a message from Macky that he was withdrawing.

[4] Lt-Col D. L. B. Goslett, MC, NX118. 2/2 Bn; and GSO1 (Ops) II Corps 1945. Insurance officer; of West Kempsey, NSW; b. Melbourne, 4 Jan 1911.

[5] Report on Operations in Greece, 16 Aust Inf Bde.

from the east. At this stage Allen's 2/3rd Battalion was still marching out of the mountains but due to reach the main road that night; its orders were to rendezvous at a point west of Larisa, so, after leaving Rowell, Allen had to go to this point to pass on the new orders. The 2/1st was still at Levadhion high on Olympus, with its vehicles on the Katerini-Olympus pass road nine arduous miles away; on arrival there it came directly under the divisional commander.

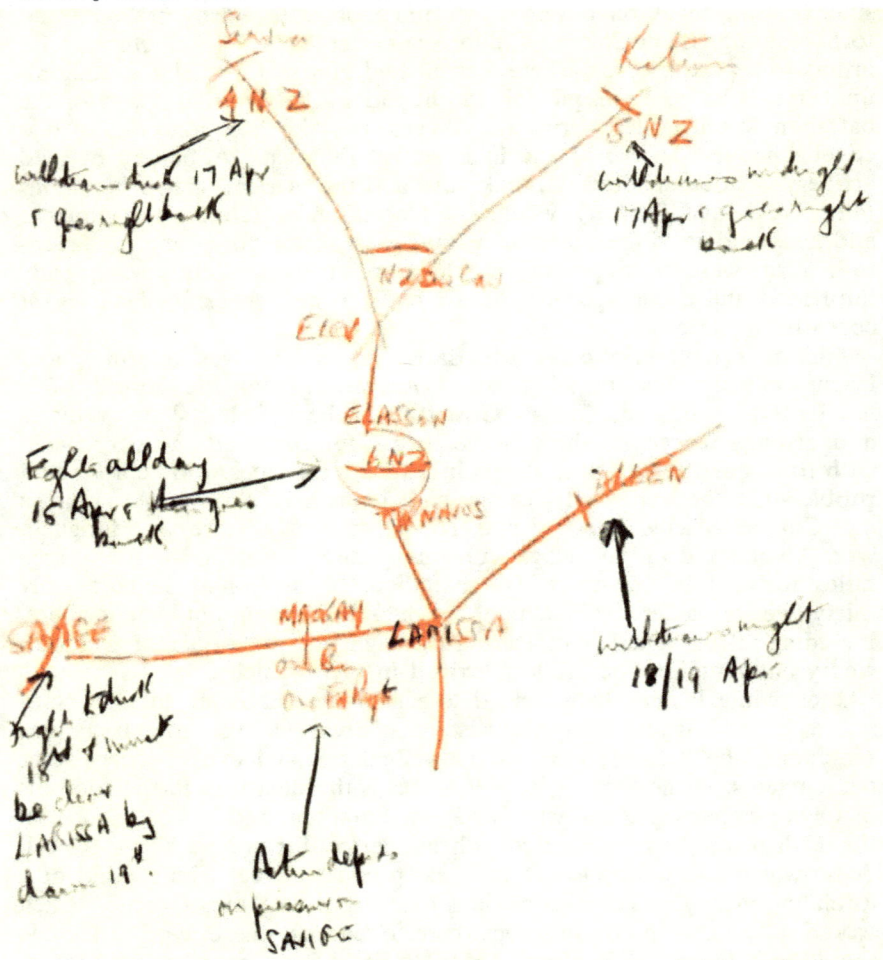

Sketch made by Brigadier Rowell on 16th April before writing the orders for the withdrawal to Thermopylae.

Meanwhile the plans for the withdrawal of the corps were elaborated. In an order late on the night of the 16th Blamey defined the division of responsibility between Generals Mackay and Freyberg during the leap-frogging move back to Thermopylae. Mackay would protect the flanks of the New Zealand Division as far south as an east-west line through Larisa and would control the withdrawal through Domokos to Thermopylae of Savige Force and the Zarkos Force, and finally of Lee Force; the 1st Armoured Brigade would cover the withdrawal of Savige Force to Larisa and thereafter the withdrawal of the 6th Division under whose command it would come; Freyberg would control the withdrawal of Allen Force which was to move along the same route as the New Zealand Division. Blamey further decided to place all engineers under corps control and a conference was held at the junction of the Katerini and Servia roads between Brigadier Steele and Colonel Lucas (Australian) and Colonel Clifton[6] (New Zealand). Blamey hoped that the enemy could be delayed sufficiently to enable the force to conform to the following time-table: 4th New Zealand Brigade to vacate Servia Pass and 5th New Zealand Brigade to vacate Olympus Pass on the night of the 17th-18th, 6th New Zealand to vacate the Elasson position on the night of 18th-19th;[7] Savige Force to withdraw the main bodies to Zarkos on the 17th-18th leaving delaying parties at Kalabaka during the 18th. The final withdrawal of Savige and Allen Forces was to be arranged between Freyberg and Mackay.[8]

Between the force which Allen was to assemble on the south bank of the Pinios, and the right flank of Brigadier Hargest's[9] 5th Brigade, 20 miles away in the Olympus Pass, rose the snow-capped heights of Mount Olympus. Hargest was on its northern slopes; the force at Tempe was in the gorge which bounds the mountain on the south. On a large-scale map Olympus seemed an impassable barrier, but in fact several tracks wound over its slopes and one of these—the track from Skala Leptokarias on the coast, by way of Karya and Gonnos to the Larisa road[1]—offered a

---

[6] Brig G. H. Clifton, DSO, MC. CRE NZ Div 1940-41; CB XXX Corps 1941; Comd 6 NZ Bde 1942. Regular soldier; b. Greenmeadows, NZ, 18 Sep 1898.

[7] On the 15th the 6 NZ Bde had taken up its position in the northernmost rearguard position, the 24 Bn south of Elasson on the east road, the 25th on the west. The third battalion of the brigade, the 26th, having covered the withdrawal of the 19 Aust Bde, to which it was attached, as far as Deskati, was moved into reserve at Domenikon on the 17th and 18th.

[8] Freyberg moved his battle headquarters on the 15th from Dolikhe to just south of the junction of the Servia and Katerini roads; Wilson's were still at Soumpasi, south of Larisa, Blamey's still at Elasson, and Mackay's by the road at the top of the Servia Pass. On the 16th Wilson's headquarters withdrew to Thebes, Blamey's to Soumpasi; and, in the evening, Mackay's to Nikaia, seven miles south of Larisa.

[9] Brig J. Hargest, CBE, DSO, MC; Comd 5 NZ Bde 1940-41. Sheep farmer; b. Gore, NZ, 4 Sep 1891. Killed in action 12 Aug 1944.

[1] Herodotus said that the army of Xerxes moved by way of Gonnos. "Hereupon the Greeks determined to send a body of foot to Thessaly by sea, which should defend the pass of Olympus. Accordingly a force was collected, which passed up the Euripus, and disembarking at Alus, on the coast of Achaea, left the ships there, and marched by land from Lower Macedonia into Thessaly along the course of the Peneus, having the range of Olympus on the one hand and Ossa upon the other. In this place the Greek force that had been collected, amounting to about 10,000 heavy-armed men, pitched their camp . . . . They did not however maintain their station for more than a few days; since envoys came from Alexander, the son of Amyntas, the Macedonian, and counselled them to decamp from Tempe, telling them that if they remained in the pass they would be trodden under foot by the invading army, whose numbers they recounted, and likewise the multitude of their ships. So when the envoys thus counselled them, and the counsel seemed to be good, and the Macedonian who sent it friendly, they did even as he advised. In my opinion what chiefly wrought on them was the fear that the Persians might enter by another pass, whereof they now heard, which led from Upper Macedonia into Thessaly through the territory of the Perrhaebi, and by the town of Gonnus—the pass by which soon afterwards the army of Xerxes actually made its entrance . . . . The Greeks, on their return to the Isthmus, took counsel together concerning the words of Alexander,

promising line of advance for German mountain troops. Similarly on the left of the New Zealanders in the Olympus Pass another main track led over the northern buttress of the mountain through Skoteina and Levadhion. (It was along this track that the 2/1st Battalion had withdrawn.) Thus the German mountain troops might decide to advance not only through the main passes, but also along these lesser tracks, one south one north of Hargest's brigade.

On the night of the 15th-16th (while the 21st Battalion was being heavily attacked at Platamon) men in the forward posts of the 22nd Battalion, the centre battalion of Hargest's brigade, astride the road through the Olympus Pass, heard Germans calling out in English. Thinking it was a ruse to draw fire they remained silent but in the morning found that these Germans had been cutting their wire and lifting mines. Soon after dawn the 22nd was lightly attacked; but the German infantry withdrew when artillery and mortars fired on them. Behind them were many waggons and tanks. Under cover of this attack the Germans had brought up mortars and infantry guns, which were very troublesome. The commanding officer of the supporting field regiment, Lieut-Colonel Fraser,[2] came forward and directed fire which silenced a particularly well-sited mortar.

The Maoris on the left could now see vehicles crowding the road for 14 miles back, as far as Katerini, the first three miles of the column consisting mainly of tanks, troop carriers and motor-cycles. About 8.30 a.m. the leading vehicles swiftly moved forward. The New Zealand artillery observer boldly dropped his range by 800 yards and broke the attack. Soon fourteen vehicles, including two tanks, had been destroyed. From 11 a.m. until 3 p.m. rain and mist made it impossible to see more than a few hundred yards. When the weather cleared the Maoris saw Germans streaming into the deep ravine of the Mavroneri towards the left flank, and beyond effective range.

On the right the 23rd Battalion was in heavy mist. Enemy parties tried to move round the right flank but were thwarted by the defending infantry and gunners until late in the afternoon, when their advance in this direction threatened to hamper the withdrawal. However, reinforcements arrived and drove the enemy back. On the Maoris' sector the enemy had now moved across to the front of the left company and, in the twilight, were forming up in strength on the far side of a ravine through which ran the road to Skoteina. The slopes on both sides were covered with scrub and stunted trees and immediate fields of fire were not more than twenty yards, though the opposite bank could be covered. Suddenly enemy troops began to swarm on to the road and dash along it. They were fired on and fell back, but in a few moments the forward Maori section was

---

and considered where they should fix the war, and what places they should occupy. The opinion which prevailed was, that they should guard the pass of Thermopylae; since it was narrower than the Thessalian defile, and at the same time nearer to them." (Book VII, Chapters 173-5, Rawlinson's translation.)

[2] Lt-Col K. W. Fraser, OBE. CO 5 NZ Fd Regt 1940-41. Asst advertising manager; of Eastbourne, Wellington, NZ; b. Edinburgh, 1 Nov 1905.

sharply bombarded with mortar bombs, grenades and bullets, and the German mountain troops clambered up the hill and, at heavy cost, overran the foremost Maori posts. However, the enemy—probably two companies —had lost heavily and the survivors were gradually pushed back into the ravine. This flank was reinforced and the situation became stable, but the battalion was an hour and a half late in beginning to withdraw along greasy tracks in pitch darkness.

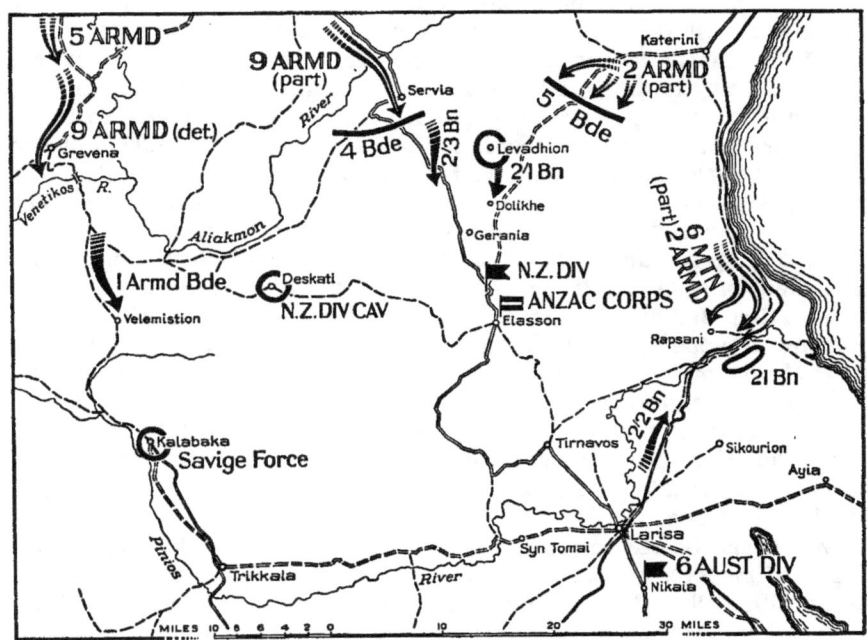

Dusk, 16th April.

The other battalions withdrew more or less according to plan. The route of the 23rd climbed to 2,000 feet above the pass over a shoulder of Mount Olympus and the track was deep in mud. The nine 2-pounders supporting them had been doomed when the action began and after an effort to man-handle them out, were reluctantly tipped over cliffs. Ten carriers and twenty trucks were also abandoned. Craters were blown in the road and the new position was occupied astride the top of the pass seven miles to the south-west (through Ayios Dimitrios and Kokkinoplos) where the brigade was to hold until its withdrawal to the Thermopylae position the following night. As an additional precaution during this withdrawal Freyberg had on the 16th established a force of anti-tank guns, machine-guns, and three platoons of carriers under Lieut-Colonel Duff[3] to cover the withdrawal from the Servia and Olympus Passes.

---

[3] Brig C. S. J. Duff, DSO. CO 7 NZ A-Tk Regt 1940-41, 4 Fd Regt 1941-42; CRA 3 NZ Div (Pacific) 1942-44. Regular soldier; of Wellington, NZ; b. Wellington, 19 Nov 1898.

It took up positions north of Elasson near the village of Elevtherokhorion where the road from Servia joins that from Katerini. Next day two squadrons of the divisional cavalry regiment, which, since the 15th, had been about Deskati guarding a side road which entered the Anzac area from Grevena, took over the role of Duff Force. The carriers of the third squadron remained about Deskati and the armoured cars of the squadron were ordered south to join Allen.

In the Servia Pass the enemy, after the failure of his ill-managed attempts to rush the pass on the 15th, made no further infantry attacks on the 16th, though the artillery duel and the aerial bombing continued. In the morning of the 16th the 2/2nd Field Regiment pulled out its guns and withdrew to join the flank guard at Zarkos. Its orders were to travel by the Servia Pass but, in response to a warning by a New Zealand officer that any vehicles moving along the exposed stretch of road near Prosilion immediately came under accurate fire from the German guns, this regiment (and also some detachments of Vasey's brigade) made a long detour through Karperon and Deskati—an action of which Mackay strongly disapproved. In spite of this the 2/2nd arrived at Zarkos early in the afternoon. After dark on the 16th the 2/3rd Field Regiment withdrew to Elasson to support the 6th New Zealand Brigade in its rearguard position there. In the night drive up the zigzag road one gun fell over the cliff and had to be abandoned—the third gun the regiment had lost since the fighting began. Puttick's left battalion—the 20th—was withdrawn on the night 16th-17th to a position astride the road at Lava to cover the retirement of the brigade the following night, and the 19th swung its left flank south of Prosilion.

Meanwhile Savige, perched in the mountains on the left flank, had deployed his force at Kalabaka. On the 15th he had examined the defensive position allotted to him near the snow line west of the junction of the Grevena and Metsovon roads and rejected it on the grounds that it was in country which offered cover and easy movement to enemy tanks and infantry and could be outflanked. He decided instead to hold a line two miles and a half west of Kalabaka where his left would be on a wide stream—the upper Pinios River—his front covered by a narrower stream and his right, though "tender", could be defended in depth.

In the course of his visit to Savige on the afternoon of the 15th General Wilson had told him that his force might have to get away from Kalabaka in a hurry and that he would need enough vehicles to lift all his men at once. He advised him to keep in touch with the British convoy of motor trucks which was bringing Greek troops into his area from the west. Savige did so and arranged that he should receive eighty vehicles from this source. On the 16th, however, at the urgent request of liaison officers from corps headquarters he handed thirty of these to corps. It was from these officers that he first learnt of the general withdrawal.

The town of Kalabaka was now in turmoil. It nestles between a big cliff "remarkably like Gibraltar in appearance" and the Pinios River. The British medium artillerymen were established at the eastern end of the town and at the foot of the cliff. At night clusters of dwellings on the cliff face were lit up and the lights flickered on and off as doors or curtains were opened or shut. The gunners began to interpret these lights as signals by a Fifth Column, and constant challenges were given and occasional bursts of Bren gun fire directed at the cliff dwellers.

Savige did not have enough troops to police the town and

> the straggling Greek troops, without food, took what they could from the shops and houses (he wrote afterwards). The locals no doubt fired some shots, and possibly some of the few Greek troops with rifles joined in the fun. I believe that, while Greek troops were intent on robbing civilians, the civilians raided the depots to collect rifles and ammunition to protect themselves. Kerosene was particularly short and civilians took their current and reserve needs from the now-unprotected dumps, from which Greek troops had fled to join the procession eastwards.

So far Savige had had no direct contact with the 1st Armoured Brigade, farther north. On the 16th a liaison officer from Wilson's headquarters, returning from a visit to that brigade informed him that the head of its column would pass through Kalabaka that day on the way to Larisa. During the afternoon its leading vehicles began to move through the town. Savige had some anxiety whether the bridge over the Venetikos River, just south of Grevena, would be blown—a responsibility of the armoured brigade. He picked a resolute-looking subaltern named Hughes of the 292nd Field Company, a British unit in his area, and asked him to collect some volunteers to go forward and ensure that the bridge had been blown. Hughes found the bridge intact but the charges ready for firing. He fired them and destroyed the bridge, returning next day.[4]

At 9 p.m. Colonel Wells[5] arrived at Kalabaka from Blamey's headquarters with instructions that Savige Force would hold its positions until midnight on the 18th-19th, and that the 1st Armoured Brigade would cover its withdrawal, the senior of the two brigadiers to command the combined force.

At 1.30 a.m. on the 16th, however, Brigadier Charrington's brigade major had left General Wilson's headquarters with entirely different orders for that brigade: that it should withdraw into reserve behind the Thermopylae line at Atalandi.

The main body of the 1st Armoured Brigade had reached Velemistion that evening having travelled some 20 miles in nine hours along a narrow, cratered road deep in mud, crowded with refugees, and strewn with abandoned vehicles and weapons. Rain and mist had concealed the column from German aircraft, but progress was slow because of the congestion and because detours had to be dug round stretches of road that were otherwise impassable. On the morning of the 17th the brigade continued to move through Kalabaka.

---

[4] Later Savige's staff was worried to learn that there were still Greek troops north of the Venetikos. However, the head of the German column passed through Grevena on the 16th and therefore the bridge was demolished none too soon.

[5] "Tireless in his long journeys, helpful in every possible way, and courageous in all circumstances," wrote Savige afterwards.

At this stage a misunderstanding developed as to the role of the armoured brigade. Brigadier Charrington's brigade major, when he arrived at Kalabaka, received a message telling him to remain there until the brigade arrived. He spent the 16th there and in the afternoon was asked whether he could arrange with Brigadier Charrington that the armoured brigade should cover the withdrawal of Savige Force. In his opinion it was impossible in view of the orders he had received from General Wilson for the whole brigade to cooperate, but he finally agreed that it should detach a small party to guard the bridge and cover the withdrawal.

About 10 a.m. on the 17th Brigadier Charrington arrived, and, after some discussion, this arrangement was confirmed. The result was that the detachment—a carrier platoon (Rangers), a troop of anti-tank guns, a platoon of New Zealand machine-gunners and two troops of the New Zealand Cavalry—remained at the Velemistion bridge forward of Savige's position, and the armoured brigade as a whole continued to withdraw. At this stage (10 a.m. on the 17th) neither Charrington nor Savige had received Blamey's written order of 6 p.m. on the 16th, but, as mentioned above, Savige had been told by the liaison officer the previous afternoon that the armoured brigade was to cover his withdrawal, both brigades coming under the command of the senior brigadier.[6] The written order reached him at 12.30 p.m. on the 17th; that afternoon he informed corps headquarters that the armoured brigade was already withdrawing.

The armoured regiment of Charrington's brigade had been sorely tried by the mechanical faults that developed in their worn tanks and by defective tracks with which these were fitted. The break-down of most of the tanks that survived the rearguard actions in the Florina Valley was largely due to "W" Group's faulty decision to withdraw the brigade over a rough mountain road which had not been reconnoitred, instead of down the main road. This laborious journey had wearied the men, and the fact that for days the brigade had struggled along a road crowded with retreating Greeks and Yugoslavs had depressed their spirits.

It was on the 16th that General Wilson met General Papagos at Lamia and informed him of his decision to withdraw to Thermopylae. In Athens that day the Metropolitan Bishop of Yannina, a power in the land, urged the Prime Minister, M. Koryzis, to give up the struggle. Since the 14th senior commanders in Epirus had been making the same proposal.[7] On the 15th indefinite leave had been given to Greek troops in rear areas and many of these were now wandering round the streets of Athens. That morning General Wavell had sent a message to Wilson that "we must of course continue to fight in close cooperation with Greeks but from news

---

[6] General Wilson had placed the 1st Armoured Brigade under General Blamey's command from the time of its receipt of an operation order issued at 9.5 a.m. on the 15th but on the 17th Brigadier Charrington did not know of this. On the 16th, at 11.55 p.m. Blamey had issued instructions that the brigade was to cover the withdrawal of Savige Force to Larisa and thereafter the withdrawal of 6 Div, under the direction of General Mackay.
The war diary of the armoured brigade records that on the morning of the 17th the brigade major arrived with orders that the brigade should withdraw to Atalandi about 180 miles away and behind the Thermopylae line.

[7] Papagos, p. 382.

here it looks as if early further withdrawal necessary". Further withdrawal could only mean embarkation from Greece.

In most of Thessaly the 17th of April, like the 16th, began with drizzling rain and mist, so that again the crowded traffic on the main road was often concealed from German aircraft, and the clouds lying low on the hills made flying dangerous; in the afternoon, however, the sky cleared in some areas and German aircraft attacked the columns of trucks. The road was packed with vehicles—fighting troops moving back to the Domokos position (the weary men lying sleeping, packed on the floor of each vehicle), depot units withdrawing to Thermopylae and a few, very few, Greek trucks, cars and aged omnibuses crowded with troops. Against this stream were moving the vehicles which were carrying supplies forward. Frequently the two processions became locked and movement ceased until the tangle had been straightened out. Where the narrow road zigzagged over the pass—between Elasson and Tirnavos, or at Pharsala or Domokos—trucks were packed head to tail for hours on end, the procession moving for a mile or two, then stopping, then moving on, then stopping again. The machine-gunning of vehicles on the 14th and 15th had made many of the drivers nervous, and the appearance of an aircraft in the distance—sometimes a Greek or a British machine—would cause a convoy to halt while drivers and passengers jumped from the trucks and ran off the road to temporary cover in the fields. Beside the road plodded an ever-increasing number of Greek soldiers, shabby and weary, and heavily laden with kit. Some wore cloth caps, some Italian helmets, some British helmets. There were Greeks riding donkeys and Greek cavalrymen with their cloaks shining in the rain riding tired horses whose heads drooped. Occasionally would be seen a civilian car loaded with refugees, a pair of carts being dragged by a farm tractor, a farm cart carrying a whole family and perhaps the bodies of a few fowls dangling at the back. Here and there were well-cared-for and neatly-uniformed Greek police with motor-cycles and side-cars.

Larisa, the largest town on the road, through which all must pass, was now in ruins, the damage having been caused partly by earthquake and partly by air attack. Notice boards marked spots where unexploded bombs had buried themselves. The bridge across the Pinios at the northern entrance to Larisa was witness to the improbability of a bomber hitting a smallish target. Within a hundred yards a dozen bomb craters gaped, yet it was still intact.

Larisa was the site of a well-stocked British canteen whose staff had abandoned it. This might have had serious consequences. On the night of the 16th and during the 17th many truck-loads of Anzac and British troops each loaded on a case of beer. Some drivers drank a bottle or two and, being extremely weary and hungry, went to sleep farther along the road and could not be wakened.

Not only were the roads becoming dangerously congested but the railways were disorganised. The confusion can be illustrated by the experiences of the two battalions of the 17th Australian Brigade on their move from Athens to Thessaly. The train carrying the 2/6th stopped south of Pharsala for nine hours on the night of the 14th-15th because the crew feared that it might be attacked from the air. The train bearing the 2/7th was under a prolonged attack from the air near Larisa on the following night, and the crew disappeared. However, in the early hours of the morning some Victorian railwaymen led by Corporal "Jock" Taylor, who had shown himself in the fighting in Cyrenaica to be an outstandingly cool and intrepid leader, Corporal Melville,[8] and Private Naismith,[9] fired one engine and left it with the fire-box door open as a decoy to delude the German aircraft and, while bombers were attacking it, manned another engine 500 yards away and made up a train into which the battalion was loaded and taken to Domokos.

In the front line, however, the 17th passed relatively quietly. This comparative calm demonstrated how effectively a retiring force moving back by carefully-planned stages into well-picked positions, and demolishing roads and bridges behind it, could delay an advancing army. Before the enemy could locate and counter the defending artillery in the Servia and Katerini Passes, the defenders had moved from the foot to the top of each pass, cratering the road. The Germans had then to probe forward and find the new positions, to repair the road and bring up their guns—because, where they could not deploy their tanks, they could do nothing without their guns.

In the Pinios Gorge during the 17th Colonels Chilton, Macky and Parkinson[1] were able to prepare their defences with relatively little interruption, although there was no time for elaborate reconnaissance or planning, nor time to move farther forward astride the defile if that had been considered desirable. Before Allen arrived the young veteran Chilton had deployed the force, Macky agreeing to his proposals for siting the New Zealand battalion. The narrow, steep-sided gorge was about five miles long. The river running through it was from 30 to 50 yards wide and fast-flowing. The railway travelled along the north side of the river, the road along the south. At the western end of the gorge the railway crossed the river and turned south towards Larisa. The Australian decided that the first necessity was to prevent enemy tanks from emerging from the defile. He arranged for a new crater to be blown in the road and for the New Zealand battalion to be disposed east of Tempe at the exit from the defile to cover it. He deployed his own battalion to protect the left flank against attack by infantry across the river from Gonnos and to give depth to the defence of the defile—although, if the New Zealanders were

---

[8] Cpl A. H. Melville, VX4699; 2/7 Bn. Green keeper; of Merbein, Vic; b. Greenock, Scotland, 12 Mar 1905.

[9] Sgt A. K. Naismith, DCM, VX4838; 2/7 Bn. Tobacco grower; of Gunbower, Vic; b. Bendigo, Vic, 10 Mar 1915.

[1] Maj-Gen G. B. Parkinson, CBE, DSO. CO 4 NZ Fd Regt 1940-41; Comd 6 NZ Bde 1943-45 (GOC 2 NZ Div Mar 1944). Regular soldier; of Christchurch, NZ; b. Wellington, NZ, 5 Nov 1896. (Parkinson had been sent to Pinios by the CRA of the NZ Div, Brig R. Miles. One battery of Parkinson's regiment was now detached to Savige Force, one (the 26th) to Allen Force; his headquarters was at Tirnavos and he with a handful of men from his headquarters was with Chilton.)

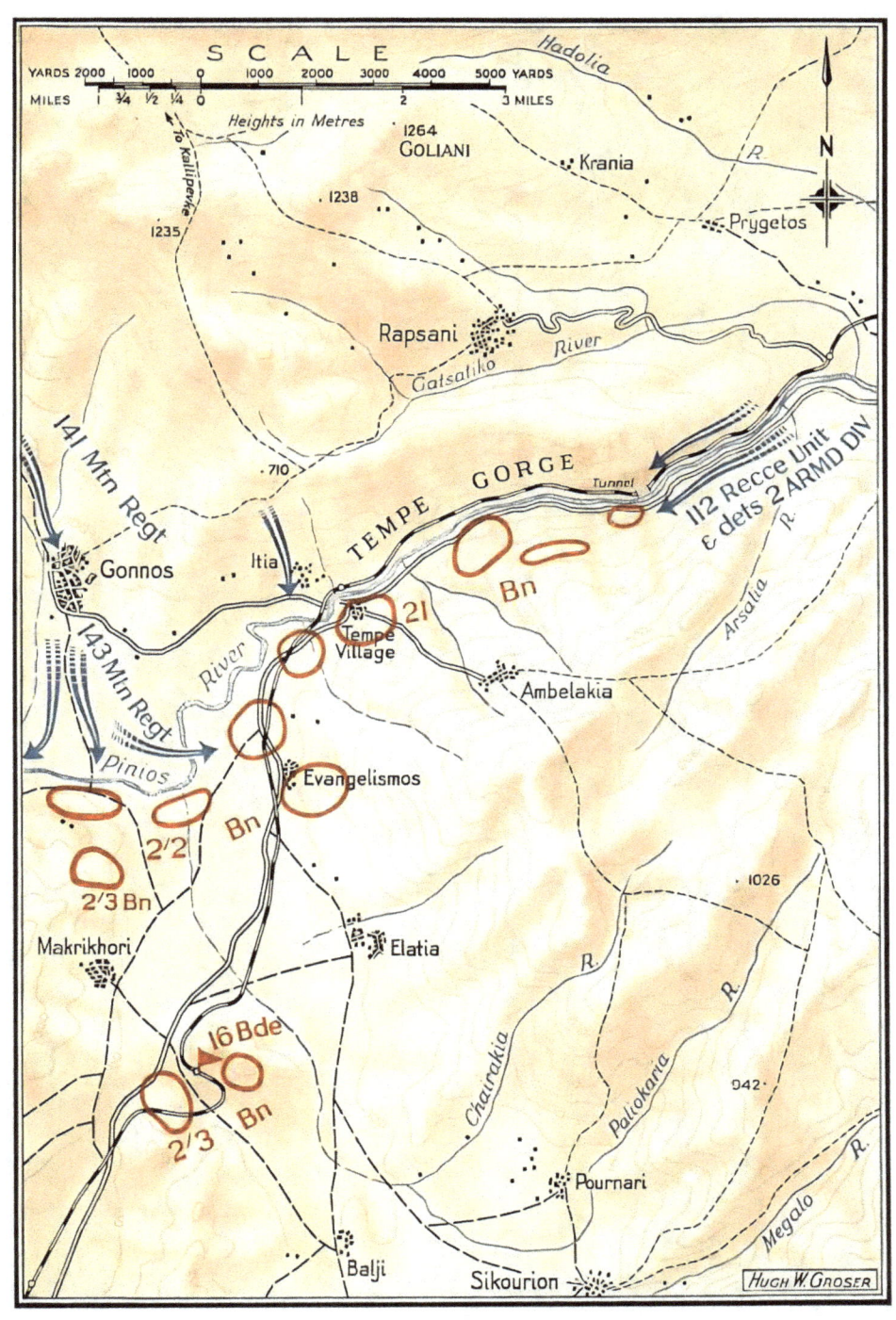

Dispositions 17th April

thrust aside and the enemy tanks able to fan out on the flats the position of the 2/2nd would be precarious. Thus the 21st New Zealand was disposed with one platoon at the road-block, and the remainder of the forward company, with one anti-tank gun, astride the road a mile to the west; one company on the slopes overlooking it; and two companies with two anti-tank guns in echelon across the road at Tempe, with a flank on to the slopes above. Chilton's companies were placed along and astride the western exit, at intervals of about 1,000 yards, covering road, railway and river flats. The right company, with one anti-tank gun, was placed astride the road, and on the river flats where the stream bends deeply to the west; another company astride the road and railway forward of the village of Evangelismos, and a third round the southern edge of this village. A platoon from one of these companies was placed on a 1,005-metre hill above Ambelakia, the summit of the ridge overlooking the Pinios. At the suggestion of Brigadier Allen, who arrived at 1 p.m., Chilton extended his flank by placing his fourth rifle company on the high ground overlooking the river a mile west of the road.[2] The gap of some 3,000 yards between this company and the next was covered by the carriers assisted later by a platoon of the 2/3rd.

The 2/2nd's tools arrived during the morning and weapon pits were dug. In some places were low stone walls which could be incorporated into the hastily-prepared defences. A treasured hoard of Italian signal wire captured in Libya made it possible to link the dispersed companies. There was no barbed wire nor any anti-tank mines, though mines would have transformed the situation. In the afternoon sappers of the 2/1st Field Company placed some naval depth charges in the culverts on the pass, to be blown after the last troops had gone.

The 2/3rd—Allen's third battalion—had reached the main road south of the Servia Pass at midnight on the 16th-17th, marched for two hours to reach their vehicles, and driven through Larisa to the Pinios area. When the battalion reached its destination one company was employed patrolling the roads to Sikourion and Ayia along which the enemy might make a flanking move against Larisa from north-east and east. The three remaining rifle companies were below strength because, on the way through Larisa, the drivers of several trucks mistakenly followed the main stream of traffic towards Lamia and lost touch with the battalion.

Allen, anxious about the left flank, ordered Lieut-Colonel Lamb[3] of the 2/3rd to extend it still farther by placing one company (Captain Murchison) on high ground north of Makrikhori looking across the river towards similar high ground at Gonnos and left of and higher than the company which Allen had already ordered Chilton to place on the heights west of the road. The remaining two companies of the 2/3rd were in reserve astride the road some four miles south of the 2/2nd Battalion's

---

[2] Allen Force finally included 2/2, 2/3 (Aust) and 21 (NZ) Bns, a tp of 33 NZ A-Tk Bty, 26 Bty of 4 Fd Regt and a tp of the 27 Bty which had been with the 21 Bn throughout, and 3 guns of the 2/1 Aust A-Tk Regt. Three a-tk guns were with the 21 Bn, four with the 2/2.

[3] Lt-Col D. J. Lamb, OBE, NX45. CO 2/3 Bn 1941, 2/2 Gd Bn 1942-45. Sales manager; of Cronulla, NSW: b. Sydney, 21 Aug 1903.

position. Because it had been forced to jettison much of its equipment at the Veria Pass before marching out across the hills, the 2/3rd had few tools, no barbed wire, no anti-tank mines, and so little signal wire that Lamb had to keep in touch with his companies by runner. The men of both battalions were extremely weary; beginning on the night of the 12th they had spent every night but two in long marches and on those two they had been sleeping with only blanket and greatcoat to protect them against intense cold.

Before the companies settled in their new positions, the leading German patrols appeared. In the afternoon of the 17th small bodies of men with pack animals were seen on the ridge above Gonnos and Very lights were fired from these heights when German aircraft flew overhead. The New Zealanders reported that they were being fired on from high ground to the east. During the evening a line of men with mules was seen entering Gonnos. After dark Captain Hendry, commanding the left company of the 2/2nd, sent a platoon under Lieutenant Colquhoun[4] across the river in a punt to explore Gonnos and eastwards to the river at Tempe. This patrol reported that there were Germans in Gonnos, and small bodies of men with pack animals were moving west towards Elia. At 11 p.m. a party of Germans attacked three of Colquhoun's men left guarding the ferry and in the affray, and before the Germans made off, a German was killed and an Australian wounded.

Meanwhile, on the Australian right, Lieutenant Arnold[5] and Sergeant Tanner[6] in the afternoon had led a platoon of the 2/2nd along the earth road through the gorge. They passed through the New Zealand posts and continued, believing the German advance-guard still to be far away. As they drew level with a railway tunnel (on the other side of the river just ahead of the forward posts) there was a burst of fire from about 150 yards away on the other side of the stream. Two men, including Corporal Lyon,[7] a section leader, fell seriously wounded and two others were hit. The leading Australians took cover and they and a New Zealand platoon returned the fire of a party of German infantry and a tank which had run along the railway as far as the tunnel (which had been blocked). The duel lasted for two hours, until dusk, when Arnold and Tanner led their men out. Men of the 21st New Zealand later brought in two wounded Australians.

It will be recalled that Blamey's orders required the New Zealand Division to withdraw along the Larisa-Volos road, leaving the section of the main road between Larisa and Lamia to Mackay. The road to

---

[4] Capt C. T. Colquhoun, MC, NX1400. 2/2 Bn; RAE (Water Tpt) 1945. Baths manager; of Muswellbrook, NSW; b. Cessnock, NSW, 12 Nov 1914.

[5] Maj M. G. de L. Arnold, NX12405; 2/2 Bn and Trg Appts. University student; of Rose Bay, NSW; b. Strathfield, NSW, 6 Oct 1916.

[6] Lt R. R. Tanner, NX1746; 2/2 Bn. Butcher; of Wallabadah, NSW; b. Wallabadah, 13 Nov 1917. Killed in action 20 Oct 1942.

[7] Cpl F. G. Lyon, NX1914; 2/2 Bn. Farmer; of Coonabarabran, NSW; b. Junee, NSW, 12 Jun 1918. Died of wounds 19 Apr 1941.

Volos, however, was little better than an earth track, classed as a third-grade road even on Greek maps. It travelled over flat country and the rain had made it very boggy. Freyberg wrote to Blamey on the 17th to inform him that he had arranged with Mackay that morning to use "his road".[8] Having made this arrangement Freyberg ordered his 5th Brigade to begin embussing in the afternoon. Two battalions were now astride the top of the pass three miles south of Ayios Dimitrios, while the third, the 23rd, rested at Kokkinoplos with one company forward covering the muddy track leading through the village. The craters blown in the road delayed the Germans so effectively that none were seen on the front until 6 p.m. when a small body of infantry appeared at Ayios Dimitrios. The withdrawal was then well under way, and the Germans were dispersed by the fire of a troop of guns which, with two companies of infantry, formed the rearguard. The trucks carrying this brigade followed the crowded main road—the Australian division's road—only to Pharsala and thence joined the eastern road at Almiros.

Similarly in the Servia Pass there was no infantry fighting during the 17th, though the artillery fired intermittently during the day. The New Zealand guns were withdrawn late in the afternoon; the infantry were not to begin embussing before 8 p.m. The rearguard under Lieut-Colonel Kippenberger[9] of the 20th, who was to control the demolitions, was to be out of the pass by 3 a.m. on the 18th. The 19th Battalion was out before midnight, and on the road moving south, its vehicles well-spaced and travelling at good speed. The 18th had a difficult and arduous withdrawal and at 3 a.m. two of its companies had not arrived at the point where Kippenberger was waiting to order the first demolition. One company arrived at nearly 4 o'clock, the other soon afterwards, and Kippenberger ordered Captain Kelsall,[1] the engineer officer with him, to demolish the road. Immediately after the explosion there were cries from a few New Zealanders still on the other side. They and still later stragglers were awaited. It was 6 a.m. before Kippenberger ordered the final demolition. Except for this rearguard (whose later experiences are described below) the hazardous withdrawal from the Servia Pass was complete. The road was now covered by Brigadier Barrowclough's[2] augmented 6th Brigade Group back at Elasson.

Next to the left—but 35 miles away as the crow flies and 80 miles by road—lay Savige Force round Kalabaka. Between the late afternoon of the 16th and early afternoon of the 17th he had received four visits from liaison officers. The first discussed administrative arrangements, the

---

[8] The letter did not reach Blamey until 10 p.m. by which time the 5 NZ Bde's trucks were passing his headquarters at Soumpasi, 15 miles south of Larisa.

[9] Maj-Gen Sir Howard Kippenberger, KBE, CB, DSO. (1914-18: Pte Canterbury Regt.) CO 20 NZ Bn 1939-41; Comd 10 Inf Bde Crete May 1941, 5 Bde 1942-43; GOC 2 NZ Div 1943 and 1944. Editor-in-Chief NZ War Histories since 1946. Barrister and solicitor; b. Ladbrooks, Canterbury, NZ, 28 Jan 1897.

[1] Capt D. V. C. Kelsall, NZ Engrs. Civil engineering student; b. Taihape, NZ, 13 Dec 1913.

[2] Maj-Gen H. E. Barrowclough, DSO, MC. (1914-18: CO 4 Bn, NZ Rifle Bde.) Comd 6 NZ Bde 1940-42; GOC 1 NZ Div 1942, 2 NZEF in Pacific and 3 NZ Div. Barrister; of Auckland, NZ; b. Masterton, NZ, 23 Jun 1894.

second (mentioned above) conveyed the order from Anzac Corps that Savige Force was to hold its positions until midnight on the 18th, when its withdrawal would be covered by the 1st Armoured Brigade. The third arrived at 12.30 p.m. on the 17th with the written Corps instruction, which provided that Savige should withdraw his main bodies to Zarkos during the night 17th-18th but leave a rearguard at Kalabaka during the 18th. An hour and a quarter later a liaison officer (Captain Grieve) arrived from the 6th Division with instructions to withdraw that night covered by the 1st Armoured Brigade. Grieve also brought the disturbing information that the road between Trikkala and Larisa was jammed with vehicles of the armoured brigade and vehicles, mules and men of the Greek Army, and that the bridge over the Pinios east of Zarkos had been demolished and a by-pass road, through Tirnavos, was very boggy.

The mishap to this bridge occurred when some engineers exploded a test charge. They were doubtful whether the commercial gelignite (or dynamite) which was the only explosive they had, would be satisfactory for cutting the steel trusses. To test it they exploded a small charge on a bridge member considered to be redundant, but the impact unsettled one whole truss, of some 90-feet span, and dropped one end of it into the river. Soon afterwards Lieutenants Gilmour and Nolan[3] of the 6th Division's engineers found that Larisa could be reached by two alternative routes: the first a short detour over another bridge a few miles north of the bridge which had been accidentally destroyed, and the second a much longer detour by a side road to Tirnavos and thence south to Larisa.

The problem which faced Savige on the afternoon of the 17th was a ticklish one. The road behind him was packed with vehicles, a bridge on the only reasonably good road back had been broken, and he still needed time to complete demolitions aimed at delaying a German advance from Grevena. The armoured brigade had departed and could not cover his withdrawal. The task of covering the western flank of the whole force until next day appeared to him still to be important. He decided that the right course was to remain where he was until the road was clear behind him, even though that entailed disregarding the latest order. He sought the views of his unit commanders and they agreed with him. Thereupon he gave Grieve a written statement for General Mackay setting out the reasons for his decision and saying that he would thin out on the 18th, if he could, and that he anticipated being able to remain where he was until the night of the 18th-19th. That evening a plan of withdrawal was worked out.[4]

---

[3] Maj R. K. J. Nolan, NX37. 6 Div Engrs; 52 Fd Pk Coy 1942-44; 2/14 Fd Pk Coy 1944-45. Engineer; of Lockhart, NSW; b. Lockhart, 11 Dec 1914.

[4] Savige wrote afterwards: "From 14 to 17 April I was under direct orders of Anzac Corps. Late on 17 April I was reverted to the command of my own division . . . . As commander on the spot I was placed in the invidious position of deciding what my new commander would have me do were he aware of previous orders (delivered chiefly by L.O's), general requirements, and the present position on my front . . . . In the final divisional instructions, received in a letter, I was ordered to keep Commander 1 Armoured Brigade informed of the progress of my withdrawal. When that instruction was written Commander 1 Armoured Brigade was beyond Larisa . . . . Commanders switched from one command to another must experience the feeling of being between the hammer and the anvil."

At 1.30 a.m. on the 18th Grieve returned to Kalabaka with orders from Mackay that Savige should begin withdrawal during the night, reconnoitre the Zarkos position, concentrate round Syn Tomai (just beyond the demolished bridge), inform the division of his expected disposition at 5 p.m. on the 18th, and keep the 1st Armoured Brigade informed of his withdrawal. It was evident that, when these orders were given, Mackay's staff still did not know that the armoured brigade had already withdrawn—the head of its column was then at Pharsala. Savige informed Grieve that his withdrawal would begin immediately—he had already sent out his British medium artillery and his New Zealand battery less one troop—and that he expected to be in the Larisa area not later than 5 p.m., possibly earlier if the state of the roads allowed.

During the 17th Brigadier Lee's rearguard force at Domokos was assembled. From the north arrived the 2/4th and 2/8th Battalions, the 2/8th now 533 strong but short of weapons. The men of the newly-arrived 2/1st Field Regiment, who had been carried forward by train to Larisa, though their guns were halted at Domokos, arrived late that night. The 2/6th Battalion had arrived at Domokos by train on the 16th; the 2/7th, in the train its own men had made up and driven, arrived from Larisa whither they had been carried on, on the morning of the 17th. By nightfall on the 17th the 2/6th Battalion (plus a company of the 2/5th which had travelled from Athens with it) was in position on the right of the road on the foothills north of Domokos, the 2/7th on the left. The depleted 2/4th and 2/8th were in reserve.[5]

Thus by midnight on the 17th four of the seven brigades in the British force, hidden from enemy aircraft by the providential rain and mist, had passed safely through the Larisa bottleneck and were in either the Domokos or the Thermopylae positions or strung out along the road to Lamia. One of the two critical days was over, but the more hazardous task still lay ahead: to extricate the three remaining brigades (two of which were certain to be hard pressed throughout the day) along three roads converging at Larisa, and thence along a single crowded road across the plain of Thessaly, over one pass at Pharsala, over another at Domokos, and to the escarpment overlooking Lamia.

By 18th April there were signs that organised Greek resistance would not last much longer. Greece was a police state, as was Germany, and the political ideals of some of the Greek political and military leaders were closer to those of Germany than of Britain, and, in the eyes of these men, Germany carried immense prestige. It would not be difficult for the Germans to find a distinguished quisling if she needed one.

The Macedonian armies of Tsolakoglou had virtually disappeared. The retreating Epirus Army was under constant air attack and a great part

---

[5] Forward of Lee's Force, protecting the aerodrome just south of Larisa, were the 2/1 Bn, 2/2 Fd Regt and part of the 2/1 Anti-Tank—the balance of the intended Zarkos rearguard, the remainder of which had been diverted to the Pinios Gorge. The 2/1 Bn had reached the Syn Tomai area at noon on the 17th. It was then ordered to defend Larisa airfield against possible parachute attack.

of the force had to withdraw across a single bridge which had now been twice destroyed and twice repaired. Its supply difficulties, in Papagos' words, "were practically insuperable".

On the 16th, after Wilson's conference with Papagos at Lamia that day, Wavell had sent a telegram to Mr Churchill informing him what had been said, including Papagos' proposal that the British force should leave Greece. Churchill replied on the 17th:

> We cannot remain in Greece against wish of Greek Commander-in-Chief, and thus expose country to devastation. Wilson or Palairet[6] should obtain endorsement by Greek Government of Papagos' request. Consequent upon this assent, evacuation should proceed, without however prejudicing any withdrawal to Thermopylae position in cooperation with the Greek Army. You will naturally try to save as much material as possible.[7]

That day General Wilson hastened to Athens where he attended a conference with the King, General Papagos, the British Minister (Sir Michael Palairet), Air Vice-Marshal D'Albiac and Rear-Admiral Turle.

> The discussion which ensued (wrote Wilson later) revolved round the following: whether it was possible to carry on the war; whether it would be advisable for the British-Imperial Forces to hold on or evacuate, and the possible effect of the latter on the civil population; the danger of disintegration of the Greek Army in Albania; the prospect of the British sending more reinforcements, army and air; the collapse of Yugoslavia, who the day previously had passed under German domination, all organised resistance having ceased after eleven days of war resulting in the possibility of further German forces being directed against Greece.
> The military situation was gloomy enough, but I was shocked at what came to light concerning the political position that the Greek Government had drifted into. The bad feeling in Athens had alarmed the Government, who were now thinking of leaving that city for the Peloponnesus but feared, if it did so, resistance would cease and that the troops would realise the critical situation; already at Yannina there had been an indiscretion and men had been sent on leave under the impression that the war was over; the propaganda of the Greek Government was having no effect in countering that of the Germans with the result that defeatism was now getting widespread. I informed the conference that I would bring all that had been discussed to the notice of Wavell, who was arriving in Athens next day.[8]

That evening the Prime Minister, M. Koryzis, "after telling the King that he felt he had failed him in the task entrusted to him" committed suicide.[9]

In London an evacuation was now considered inevitable and imminent. On the 18th Churchill issued a directive to the Chiefs of Staff and Commanders-in-Chief instructing them that they "must divide between protecting evacuation and sustaining battle in Libya. But if these clash, which may be avoidable, emphasis must be given to victory in Libya."

---

[6] Sir Michael Palairet, KCMG. Minister to Greece 1939-42, Ambassador 1942-43; Under-Secretary of State in Foreign Office 1943-45. B. 29 Sep 1882.

[7] Quoted in Churchill, Vol III, p. 200.

[8] Wilson, p. 93.

[9] Quotation from cable of 19 April, Dominions Office to Prime Ministers of Australia and New Zealand.

Crete will at first only be a receptacle of whatever can get there from Greece (he added). Its fuller defence must be organised later. In the meanwhile all forces there must protect themselves from air bombing by dispersion and use their bayonets against parachutists or airborne intruders if any.[1]

Although an eventual embarkation was now a foregone conclusion, Wavell, on this day, instructed Wilson not to hurry it. In a message to him he said:

If you can establish yourself securely on Thermopylae line see no reason to hurry evacuation. You should engage enemy and force him to fight. Unless political situation makes early withdrawal imperative you should prepare to hold Thermopylae line for some time. This will give more time for defence of Crete and defence of Egypt to be strengthened as well as arrangements for evacuation to be made without too much haste.

None of this was known to the Anzac divisions in the field, now approaching what seemed likely to be the critical hours of the campaign. The 18th April was clear and fine. In the Pinios Gorge—still the danger spot—about 7 a.m. German troops were seen moving down the slopes from Gonnos south-east towards the river. They increased in numbers until it appeared that a battalion was deployed there, and another battalion (or so it seemed) was moving west from Gonnos along the tracks leading towards the main road between Elasson and Tirnavos. Captain Hendry, commanding the left company of the 2/2nd Battalion, reported that the enemy battalion moving west presented a good artillery target. No artillery observer had yet been established on this hill, but until one arrived Hendry, by telephone, directed fire on the enemy across the river. It was still early in the morning when, from the high ground, a trickle of men were seen moving south along a track from Parapotamos. The watchers thought at first that these dun-clad figures were Greek refugees— they had seen many such during their long marches north of Olympus. However, about 9 o'clock Hendry sent Lieutenant Watson's[2] platoon down the hill to see what was happening in the village and to destroy a boat that had been used to ferry small parties of men across. As the patrol approached Parapotamos it came under sharp fire, and a long fight began in which a corporal, Baker,[3] was mortally wounded and two others wounded.

Meanwhile, in response to Hendry's report that enemy troops were moving round his left and out of range, Chilton sent out his carrier platoon to intercept them. Lieutenant Love[4] led six of his carriers forward towards the river, and when they reached the exposed side of the hill concealed them beside the track and sent a section forward on foot to a point whence they could see the boat and, within light machine-gun

---

[1] Quoted in Churchill, Vol III, p. 201.
[2] Maj G. C. Watson, NX12171; 2/2 Bn. Public servant; of Canberra; b. Broughshane, County Antrim, N. Ireland, 25 May 1918.
[3] Cpl A. A. Baker, NX1395; 2/2 Bn. Carrier; of Toronto, NSW; b. Mosman, NSW, 21 Nov 1917. Died of wounds 18 Apr 1941.
[4] Lt J. T. Love, NX70225; 2/2 Bn. Orchardist; of Kingsford, NSW; b. Walcha, NSW, 6 Nov 1911. Died of wounds 24 Apr 1941.

range, German mortars firing. Love then brought the carriers forward but they immediately came under hot fire from the mortars which killed one man, mortally wounded Love and wounded four others of his platoon, and also Watson who had withdrawn his men in this direction. Sergeant Stovin[5] and Private MacQueen[6] silenced a German mortar with Bren gun fire while Corporal Lacey,[7] deliberately exposing himself to create a diversion, organised the rescue of the wounded and withdrew the carriers to sheltered ground. Stovin then established his platoon, dismounted, on this flank.

Hendry was now, about 11 a.m., for the first time in touch with Murchison's company of the 2/3rd on his left rear. Because some of its trucks had missed the road at Larisa this company had a strength of one officer and about fifty men but increased bit by bit during the day. It had no tools with which to dig in, but took up its position as best it could.

Meanwhile, early in the morning while it was still misty, about forty Germans appeared on the bank of the river opposite Buckley's company—the right flank of the 2/2nd. The Germans were bunched in a way that puzzled the Australians, who fired on them and "wiped them out".

Throughout the morning German activity on the front of the 21st Battalion increased and by midday a heavy attack was in progress. The Germans cleared away the road-block and their tanks came through. The first tank knocked out the nearest 2-pounder gun and the second tank advanced past it. These and other tanks farther back and German infantry across the narrow gorge fired on the exposed positions of the 21st on the bare forward slopes of Mount Ossa.

> The foremost platoons were pushed back and the anti-tank crews out in front of them waited and watched. Three tanks moved slowly along the road below. When the nearest was almost under the noses of the nearest gunners they fired. Two tanks were knocked out and the third hit several times; the gun fired 28 rounds all told. But by now enemy infantry had crossed the river behind the gunners and called on them to surrender. One gun crew escaped and squads of infantry with machine pistols crept close to another gun while mortars across the river concentrated on it; the crew was driven off or captured. The tanks were then engaged by indirect fire from the field guns and they stopped for some hours. With tanks a stone's throw below, scorching the hillsides with machine-gun fire, and large bodies of infantry just across the gorge, the remaining 21st Battalion positions on the bare slopes south of the river became less and less tenable. Platoon by platoon the unit fell back. Over the crest of the main ridge (on which stands the village of Ambelakia) were innumerable gullies in which it was impossible to collect the scattered fragments of the battalion. Elements continued to hold out higher up the ridge but the battalion was losing its cohesion.[8]

---

[5] WO1 R. C. Stovin, NX2396; 2/2 Bn. Salesman; of Sth Murwillumbah, NSW; b. Bath, Somerset, Eng, 1 May 1908.

[6] Cpl A. A. MacQueen, MM, NX2383; 2/2 Bn. Farmer; of Casino, NSW; b. Woolner's Arm, NSW, 18 Oct 1910.

[7] Lt A. R. Lacey, MM, NX2389; 2/2 Bn. Clerk; of Ballina, NSW; b. Sydney, 1 Jan 1912.

[8] For this account the author is indebted to the New Zealand War History Section. Other descriptions of New Zealand actions in this volume are chiefly based on material generously supplied by that section.

(Maj S. B. Cann, 2/1 Fd Coy)

A soldier and his donkey arrive at the Aliakmon River crossing.

(Unknown New Zealand sapper)

The bridge built by the 2/1st Field Company to carry the 19th Brigade across the Aliakmon.

(New Zealand War History Branch)
Lieut-General Sir Thomas Blamey, Lieut-General Sir H. Maitland Wilson,
and Major-General B. C. Freyberg.

(New Zealand War History Branch)
An observation post of the 6th N.Z. Field Regiment in the Servia Pass,
overlooking the Aliakmon River.

At 11 o'clock small parties of New Zealanders had begun to withdraw through Buckley's position declaring that German tanks were advancing along the road behind them and, at 11.30, the crew of the anti-tank gun in his area was missing. During the morning Chilton had several telephone conversations with Macky, who told him that Tempe village was under heavy mortar fire and his men were engaging enemy troops across the river. Then, about midday, the telephone to Macky became silent. Soon afterwards more small parties of New Zealanders began to move through the Australian positions, most leaderless, though one complete platoon under Lieutenant Southworth[9] reported to Chilton and was put into position near Evangelismos. The greater part of the New Zealand battalion had moved south and south-east up the slopes of Ossa. Just before Macky's telephone was cut off, however, his Intelligence officer had spoken to Allen's headquarters saying that German tanks were in Tempe and the battalion was withdrawing to the hills.

Soon after losing communication with the 21st, Chilton was telephoned by Buckley and told that New Zealand troops retiring along the road were saying that the German tanks had reached Tempe. Chilton told Buckley to warn the anti-tank gun in his locality to cover the exit from the village, but Buckley reported that the crew of this gun had gone, taking the breech-block with them.

After the withdrawal of these New Zealanders the Australian battalion was not heavily pressed for more than two hours, though the whole area was under intermittent mortar and machine-gun fire. As we have seen the German tanks were halted round Tempe, under artillery fire. So far the Australians had lost about forty killed and wounded. Then at 3 p.m. a concerted attack began. First thirty-five aircraft appeared and for half an hour circled Makrikhori railway station near which Allen's headquarters were established, dropping bombs, one of which smashed the little railway station.

The foremost platoon of the 2/2nd was Lieutenant Lovett's, about 400 yards forward of Buckley's headquarters. A tank drove through its position and, with the tank between them and company headquarters, most of the platoon fell back across the road to the slopes on the south side, Lovett himself being wounded and later made a prisoner. At this stage an Australian anti-tank gun in Buckley's area was disabled and the crew put their hands up, but were shot at by the advancing tanks of which there were now three on the road.

Meanwhile a heavy infantry attack had been made on Captain Caldwell's company next to the left.[1] What appeared to be a German battalion began to wade the river on his left, supported by machine-gun fire from the slopes above. As they moved across the river and on to the flats they were met by intense and accurate fire from the Bren gunners not only of this company but of the next to the left and from battalion head-

---

[9] Lt W. G. Southworth; 21 NZ Bn. School teacher; of Auckland, NZ; b. Christchurch, NZ, 30 May 1918. Killed in action 22 May 1941.

[1] It was a platoon short, one having been sent off to patrol with a platoon of "B" Coy the 1,005-metre hill to the east.

quarters, and were showered with bombs by Sergeant Coyle's[2] two 3-inch mortars. In an hour and a half, firing until the barrels were "almost red hot", the youthful Coyle, Corporal Evans[3] and their team lobbed 350 bombs with deadly effect among the advancing Germans as they reached the rushes on the south bank of the river, and on the rafts on which they were crossing. The infantrymen saw broken rafts and many dead bodies floating down the stream. This fire and the fire of the Bren guns broke the attack across the river, but the tanks continued to press forward along the road.[4]

At 5 p.m. the telephone line to both Buckley's and Caldwell's companies was broken. Private Thom[5] rode forward under fire on a motorcycle, found the break and brought back a message from Caldwell; whereupon Lance-Corporal Steadman[6] and two others laid a new line to Caldwell's company under brisk fire, and arrived at their destination only in time to find the company withdrawing and their retreat cut off.

On the left Hendry had reported to Chilton by telephone at 4 p.m. that the enemy was steadily moving round his left flank and digging in south of Parapotamos. Chilton ordered him to withdraw his platoon from the river bank and with Sergeant Stovin's carriers make a counter-attack against the Germans on the flats to the west. After this the line to Hendry's company was broken. Hendry was organising the counter-attack when Murchison arrived with an order, timed 3.45 p.m. and signed by Captain Walker,[7] adjutant of the 2/3rd, stating that "B" Company of the 2/3rd was "now withdrawing" and Murchison would coordinate his withdrawal with that of the company of the 2/2nd nearest to him. It was then 4.30. Hendry, a schoolmaster by profession, was somewhat puzzled by this order, and advised the younger man, Murchison, to make sure that he did not lose it because, he said, sometimes questions were asked afterwards about withdrawals. Thus at 4.45 the two companies began to withdraw platoon by platoon, the last platoon of Hendry's company being covered by Stovin's carriers which took the last infantrymen out. Mortar bombs were bursting on the hill but the German infantry were not pressing hard. The Australians marched to Makrikhori where they boarded their trucks and drove south to brigade headquarters and the reserve companies of the 2/3rd. Chilton knew nothing of this withdrawal or the order which pro-

---

[2] Capt G. Coyle, NX1250; 2/2 Bn. Labourer; of Newcastle, NSW; b. Toowoomba, Qld, 3 Oct 1922. (Earlier in the day Coyle, using extra charges, had succeeded in knocking out German mortars well beyond the normal range of the British mortars.)

[3] WO2 F. P. Evans, MM, NX1294; 2/2 and 2/1 Bns. Telegraph linesman; of Newcastle, NSW; b. Sydney, 14 Nov 1914.

[4] When the German tanks appeared Coyle, having fired all but six rounds of his ammunition, sent his weapons to the rear in a truck while he and his detachment remained and fired on with their rifles. However, a shell from a German tank hit and disabled the truck before it had gone far.

[5] Cpl J. G. Thom, NX1318; 2/2 Bn. 3 Bn Royal Australian Regiment, Korea. Labourer; of Lambton, NSW; b. Sydney, 14 Jun 1918.

[6] L-Cpl J. P. Steadman, NX1569; 2/2 Bn. Timber worker; of Taree, NSW; b. Taree, NSW, 23 Aug 1910.

[7] Maj E. S. Walker, NX261; 2/3 Bn 1939-42, and staff appointments. Bank officer; of Turramurra, NSW; b. Chatswood, NSW, 9 Oct 1917.

duced it, but when, between 4.30 and 5, firing ceased on the Makrikhori slopes he concluded that the companies there had been overrun.[8]

Buckley's company, on the slopes above the road, was now firing down from 100 yards' range at a group of German tanks. Each tank was dragging a trailer carrying seven or eight infantrymen while other infantry followed, the men on the tanks waving them on. As they neared Caldwell's company one tank was hit and stopped by a shell from one of the two forward 25-pounders, then three more were hit; none of the crews emerged and the tanks were assumed to have been destroyed. Other tanks followed up. For about forty minutes these "milled round firing madly and moved on the flats north of the road". Ten tanks, closely followed by infantry, broke into Caldwell's position. It was then 6.5 p.m.

Caldwell withdrew his headquarters, first 150 and then 400 yards from the road, whence, like Buckley's company on his right, his men watched about eighteen tanks move forward; as they emerged from the defile the tanks deployed and moved south astride the road. Infantry and, at a short distance, another six or eight tanks, followed.

> Supporting infantry were not energetic in mopping up (wrote Caldwell later), and no patrols or flank guards moved in the hills to the east of the road which entered Evangelismos from the north-east.

Shortly after 4 p.m. General Freyberg had spoken to Chilton on the telephone seeking news of his 21st Battalion, and asking Chilton whether he could get a message to them. Chilton said that would be impossible. Freyberg asked whether Chilton thought that he (Freyberg) could reach Chilton's headquarters. Chilton replied that the way was still open but it seemed likely that tanks would soon block it. Chilton described the situation; Freyberg asked him to do what he could to collect any stragglers. "You've a fine man up there," said Freyberg to Allen, "he's as cool as a cucumber." He said good-bye to Allen and wished him luck. Allen assured him that all would be well. Soon afterward's Chilton's line to Allen's headquarters died. Allen and his brigade major, Hammer,[9] then wrote a detailed order for the withdrawal of the force (Hammer had outlined this order to Chilton while the telephone was still in action), and at 5.30 handed it to Lieutenant Swinton, one of the liaison officers, to deliver to Chilton and Parkinson. Swinton set out in a carrier along a road congested with men and vehicles. When he reached the forward artillery positions he was informed, wrongly, that Chilton's headquarters had been overrun by tanks; he could see men in the hills to the east. He handed Parkinson's order to the officer commanding the guns and drove up the slope, hoping to find Chilton among the troops on the slopes, but the carrier could not climb through the gullies and he returned to brigade headquarters.

---

[8] Both company commanders misunderstood the intention of the order, which was that Murchison's company should withdraw at the same time as the company of the 2/2nd Battalion next to it; that is, that the 2/3rd company should move with the 2/2nd, not the 2/2nd company with the 2/3rd.

[9] Brig H. H. Hammer, CBE, DSO, VX24525. BM 16 Bde 1941; CO 2/48 Bn 1942-43; Comd 15 Inf Bde 1943-45. Manufacturers' agent; of Ballarat, Vic; b. Southern Cross, WA, 15 Feb 1905.

What had happened was that when the tanks fanned out in the Evangelismos area Lieutenant Moore,[1] commanding eleven carriers (some from the 2/5th and 2/11th Battalions), formed the vehicles up, hull down, astride the road and railway to cover the withdrawal of the infantry. Here a point-blank duel took place between the tanks and a New Zealand 25-pounder sited about 100 yards west of Chilton's headquarters. Two tanks were hit and set on fire, and the gun crew and a leading tank then exchanged shots until a shell from the tank destroyed the ammunition limber; thereupon the crew coolly withdrew, carrying the breech-block with them. In accordance with Parkinson's order the other guns were hauled out, one troop covering the withdrawal of the two others as they leap-frogged back at 1,000-yard intervals. This left only one 2-pounder in a defiladed position near Chilton's headquarters; about 6.30 this gun and its crew were withdrawn without orders from Chilton. A dense cloud of smoke was rising from the burning tanks and drifting south-west, making a smoke screen under cover of which more tanks and infantry moved on the flat west of the road. At this time runners at length arrived from both Buckley's and Caldwell's companies announcing that those companies had retreated up the slopes of the hill—the first news of these companies for more than an hour, the time taken by the runners to climb round the hills to the headquarters of the battalion.

The German tanks, their crews made cautious by their losses on the road, and evidently not knowing that no guns remained, took up hull-down positions and fired briskly. Their fire forced out the carrier platoons, Lieutenant Gibbins' platoon of the 2/3rd, and Lieutenant Southworth's of the 21st New Zealand, which were in the neighbourhood of battalion headquarters.[2]

The signal truck had been under fire and Chilton ordered Lieutenant Dunlop,[3] his signals officer, to withdraw to cover. While he was doing so the truck was disabled by a tank shell. Corporal Hiddins,[4] however, returned, jumped on the truck and began to drive it to cover. He was about to start the vehicle when a tank appeared in the lane ahead, whereupon he backed the truck and turned into a ploughed field and was half way across when it was hit by a shell and burst into flames. The brave Hiddins was not injured and escaped to shelter.

Tanks and infantry were now moving from the north, north-west and south-west on to the area south of Evangelismos where battalion headquarters and Captain King's[5] company were in position. At 6.45 Chilton decided that King's company would soon be surrounded and could not delay the advance of the tanks or infantry along the flat country west

---

[1] Capt R. McC. Moore, NX1916; 2/2 Bn. Grazier; of Boggabri, NSW; b. Sydney, 14 Apr 1907.
[2] Lt K. J. McPherson, of brigade headquarters, who had volunteered to take charge of the NZ carriers also in the area, was mortally wounded here.
[3] Maj J. W. Dunlop, NX3206; 2/2 Bn. Paper merchant; of Sydney; b. Sydney, 20 May 1910.
[4] Cpl A. J. Hiddins, MM, NX1830; 2/2 Bn. Plumber; of Armidale, NSW; b. Armidale, 20 Sep 1918.
[5] Capt E. H. King, NX319; 2/2 Bn. Painter; of Sydney; b. Hobart, 12 July 1914.

of the road. He ordered it to withdraw. It moved out in good order and Chilton followed.

A section commanded by Corporal Kentwell[6] covered the withdrawal of Chilton's little headquarters, firing with anti-tank rifle and Bren until tanks were 50 yards away and then dribbling back to take up another position farther up the hill. Thenceforward until dark the parties of 2/2nd Battalion men climbed up into the hills taking what cover the land offered from the brisk fire of German tanks and infantry below.

At 5.45 Hendry's and Murchison's companies began to arrive at Allen's headquarters, and the New Zealand guns which had been in support of the 2/2nd were moving through the area. It was evident that the 21st and 2/2nd (except one company) were cut off. Allen's orders from Freyberg were to deny the enemy a line through the Tempe-Sikourion road junction until 3 a.m. He told Lieut-Colonel Lamb of the 2/3rd to stop the gunners and place them in a covering position where road and railway crossed.

Allen moved his own headquarters back to this position. He was confident that he could hold the enemy on this line until after dark, when the task would become much simpler. There were several places between that point and Larisa where successive rearguard positions could be held in the darkness with few troops. In the new position one company of the 2/3rd was on a hill on the right of the road, Murchison's company of the 2/3rd and Hendry's of the 2/2nd on low ground on the left with carriers extending the flank and more carriers and a third company of the 2/3rd, only some thirty strong, in reserve.

Allen now had a considerable collection of carriers. There were the carrier platoons of three Australian battalions, the 2/2nd, 2/5th and 2/11th (each of the 2/5th and 2/11th about half strength), and some carriers of the 21st New Zealand; and, in the course of the afternoon, two armoured car troops and a carrier troop of the New Zealand divisional cavalry arrived. His infantry strength, however, had been reduced to one company of the 2/2nd and two of the 2/3rd, both reduced in numbers by the fact that some of the trucks that had lost their way on the night of the 16th-17th had not yet rejoined.[7] The whole area had been bombed and strafed intermittently during the day by aircraft attracted by the collection of vehicles and men, and some trucks hit earlier in the afternoon were still burning. About 7.30 p.m. five German tanks appeared, moving astride the road, and were met by a hail of harmless fire from rifles and Brens. Two of the New Zealand 25-pounders were moved up into the line and swung into action in the open, firing at the tanks at close range. Later one of the infantrymen described the scene:

---

[6] Cpl R. N. Kentwell, NX2255; 2/2 Bn. Butter grader and tester; of Byron Bay, NSW; b. Thornleigh, NSW, 25 Dec 1912. Killed in action 18 Apr 1941.

[7] As mentioned above, a third company of the 2/3rd, under Capt P. K. Parbury, was on the right in the area of Sikourion; the fourth, only 65 strong at the beginning of the day, had lost an officer and 6 men killed or wounded in an air attack early in the afternoon, and a truckload of some 20 officers and men who, through some misunderstanding of orders and in the confusion that developed to the rear of brigade headquarters, departed for Larisa.

The officer stood out in the open directing the fire, the crews crouched behind the shields and fed and fired the guns while everything the enemy had was being pelted at them . . . . They looked like a drawing by someone who had never been to a war, but the whole thing was unreal. They got two tanks, lost one gun and pulled the other gun and their wounded out, having done what they could. There was nothing to stop the tanks then, and they formed up and came on.

A squadron of aircraft then appeared from the direction of Larisa and made strafing runs across the area at the infantry and carriers who fired back with rifles, Brens and even anti-tank rifles. On the left the tanks pressed forward in the dusk firing until they were in the midst of Hendry's men.

At one stage (wrote Hendry) a group of fifteen to twenty men were round a tank firing rifles and L.M.G.s to no apparent effect. This tank crushed two men,[8] Privates Cameron[9] and Dunn.[1] The feeling of helplessness against the tanks overcame the troops and they began to move back in small parties to the trucks.

This movement rapidly spread along the line. "By this time," wrote a sergeant commanding a platoon in Murchison's company, "Arthur Carson,[2] a D.C.M. from the last war, was beside our platoon with his pioneers and I asked him if any orders had come through. 'Some are going back,' said Arthur, 'but we have no orders to withdraw.' Arthur spoke in his usual quiet manner, as though he was back in camp and a fatigue party hadn't arrived to dig a drain for him. I sent a man back to find out what was doing, and it appeared that we were left like a shag on a rock and the rest were on the trucks withdrawing."

Murchison signalled his platoons to withdraw to the road and board the trucks. Lamb had already ordered Major McGregor's company on the right of the road to withdraw. There was then little daylight left and when Lamb halted the vehicles and began forming the infantrymen and carriers across the road 1,000 yards farther south it was dark. The new line was in the shape of a tilted "L" with its shaft across the road and its base beside the railway line on the left, and the men lying close enough together in the darkness to be able to touch one another.

This time we really did think it was the end (wrote the platoon commander quoted earlier). I started to get the platoon together more for sentiment's sake than for usefulness, for the colonel was telling them to go down wherever they were, but Arthur, who turned up again beside me, said: "We're not platoons here. We are the A.I.F."

In a few minutes the leading tank appeared. A man who was standing waist high in the turret of one of them peering out was riddled with

---

[8] The softness of the ploughed ground saved them from fatal injuries.
[9] Pte K. D. Cameron, NX15476; 2/2 Bn. Railway officer; of Condobolin, NSW; b. Condobolin, 5 Feb 1907. At this stage Cameron was acting as a platoon commander.
[1] Pte R. K. Dunn, NX2397; 2/2 Bn. Monumental mason; of Murwillumbah, NSW; b. Broken Hill, NSW, 17 Nov 1918. Died 3 Jun 1941.
[2] Sgt A. L. Carson, DCM, MM, NX5027; 2/3 Bn. (1st AIF: Cpl 2 Bn.) Rigger; of Rozelle, NSW; b. Balmain, NSW, 2 May 1893. (Served in 1st AIF as Carlson. In May 1917 he had been recommended for the award of a Victoria Cross.)

bullets and slumped forward. Lamb shouted to the men to make every shot tell and that the tanks could not fight in the dark. The tank stopped and fired shells and tracer bullets at random and fire appeared to be coming from other tanks behind it; an ineffective hail of rifle and machine-gun fire answered this. The tank withdrew. Allen then ordered Lamb to take the force back to a point where the road crossed a swampy area north of Larisa. Allen and his staff remained to see the position cleared; New Zealand armoured cars covered the withdrawal.

It was a fantastic battle (wrote Allen afterwards). Everybody was on top (no time to dig in), and all in the front line, including artillery, Bren carriers, infantry and various unit headquarters, with unit transport only a few hundred yards in rear. Some confusion could be expected with every weapon firing and aircraft strafing from above. If you saw it at the cinema you would say the author had never seen a battle. We had to hold this position until after dark and thanks to the morale of the force it was done. As expected the pressure eased after dark—but I have often wondered why the enemy did not follow up his success if only with infantry patrols.

The Larisa road, which was narrow, with ditches each side, was now crowded with moving vehicles. When, about 10 p.m., the leading lorry reached the level crossing two miles from Larisa it was halted at a railway truck that had been pushed across the road. There was a burst of fire which killed or wounded nearly every man in the vehicle, including Captain Flashman,[3] medical officer of the 2/3rd. Sergeant-Major Hoddinott, with some others, jumped from the lorry and, lying by the road, he saw a party of (it seemed) about fifty Germans firing, throwing grenades and calling for surrender. Four New Zealand carriers appeared. Their commander decided that they should force their way through the Germans, the trucks following them. Lieutenant Johnson,[4] who had commanded the Australian anti-tank guns at Tempe, and who was with the carriers, wrote afterwards:

Upon proceeding 100 yards the leading carrier ran into what I presume was a land mine, slewed across the road and blocked any further movement forward. The efforts of approximately six men failed to roll the carrier off the road, it still being under continual machine-gun fire and sniping, and the troops were told to take cover off the road. [I and Gunner Aldridge[5]] contacted a second lieutenant of the N.Z.E.F. who had with him several of his own men. He expressed his determination to attack the machine-gun nest on the left of the road and wanted personnel to accompany him. Bombs were obtained from one of the carriers and we attempted to encircle the nest. During this time fire from the enemy was still kept up. As far as I can ascertain it took us nearly an hour to overrun this position. It was situated between the rails and sangared in with stones. Four men were in the post .... All four men were killed. After destroying the gun we withdrew back on to the flat ground. During the operation several New Zealanders received wounds. Owing to the casualties it was decided not to attack the other machine-gun post but to make our way round Larisa.

---

[3] Capt J. A. F. Flashman, NX150; RMO 2/3 Bn. Medical practitioner; of Potts Point, NSW; b. Sydney, 17 Nov 1908. Killed in action 18 Apr 1941.

[4] Capt C. M. Johnson, MC, DX176. 2/3 Fd Regt; 2/1st A-Tk Regt 1941-45. Regular soldier; of Drummoyne, NSW; b. Ariah Park, NSW, 9 July 1919.

[5] Gnr J. Aldridge, DX183; 2/1 A-Tk Regt. Labourer; of Carlton, NSW; b. Carlton, 10 Sep 1911.

Johnson and Aldridge went back among the vehicles to find others of their men, but, failing to do so, they and some of those round about split into small parties and skirting the remaining German post, made towards Larisa.[6]

Meanwhile the column behind had halted well short of the ambush, where tracer fire and flares could be seen, and a rumour had run back along the line that the Germans were in Larisa. Lamb decided to divert the column to the left to the Volos road (as he thought) and, one after another, the crowded trucks and carriers turned left off the main road on to the boggy tracks or into the fields and set off south-eastwards. In fact the first road they would meet did not lead to Volos but was a dead-end road to a village on the coast south of Mount Ossa.

Thus, at dawn, most of what remained of Allen's force was dispersed in small groups of vehicles ploughing along boggy farm tracks east of Larisa; part of it was finding its way through Volos to Lamia. The 21st New Zealand Battalion had been pushed into the hills above Tempe; most of the 2/2nd into the hills above Evangelismos.[7] The force had carried out its orders to deny the Tempe-Sikourion road junction until 3 a.m., but a party of German troops—its strength unknown to Allen or Lamb—had moved round its left flank and cut the road to Larisa.

It will be recalled that, on this critical day, three rearguard forces were to withdraw through the Larisa bottleneck—Allen's from the Pinios, Barrowclough's from Elasson and Savige's from Kalabaka. Each held a position astride one of the three main roads leading south, but between those roads were a number of tracks through the hills. For instance, from Gonnos, on the heights which Allen's force overlooked, fanned three tracks, one to Elasson, one to the Tirnavos area, and a third to a point on the main road between the two, and all day Allen's men had watched German troops moving west and south-west along them towards the New Zealand rear. Early in the afternoon Allen's left company had been briskly engaged with Germans established on the southernmost of these tracks where they were well situated to move either to Tirnavos or Larisa without interference.

At dawn on the 18th the New Zealand Cavalry Regiment with two of its squadrons and two anti-tank troops under command was guarding the junction of the roads from Servia and Katerini. The rearguard for the 4th Brigade had been thinned out until it consisted only of Colonel Kippenberger, his driver and batman, some sixty sappers and three Bren carriers. As mentioned above, this rearguard had delayed several hours to collect stragglers.

---

[6] Johnson was captured by a German patrol near Lamia and put into a prison camp in that town containing 180 New Zealanders. He escaped with CSM Hill of the 21 NZ Bn, and, after spending several weeks in Greece, was taken, with others, in small boats to Turkey.

[7] The 2/2 Bn lost 3 officers and 41 others killed or wounded, and 6 officers and 55 others (some of whom were wounded) taken prisoner. The 2/3 lost about 40 killed and wounded and about 60 taken prisoner.

The foremost cavalry squadron had one detachment with one 2-pounder portee (gun mounted on a vehicle) astride the road to Servia and another with three portees on the Katerini road. The second squadron was just south of the junction with four anti-tank guns dug in. While the men on the Katerini road were getting breakfast they were surprised to see four tanks and some motor-cycles coming down the road from Katerini. They had expected the demolitions to delay the enemy's vehicles for some days. They went into action, knocked out two tanks and drove the motor-cyclists back. The detachments then withdrew behind the rear squadron. Kippenberger's rearguard from Servia arrived in the midst of this engagement and before they quite knew what was happening the engineers and carrier crews were being fired on at short range by German tanks. The men either took to the hills or were killed or captured. Kippenberger led one party out on foot over the hills to the south and after some hours reached the 25th Battalion.

Meanwhile the German tanks attacked again, this time along both roads, but the anti-tank gunners quickly knocked out at least four tanks, two armoured cars, and a lorry. When word arrived that all other troops were behind the defences of the 6th Brigade this rearguard withdrew.

The 6th Brigade was deployed south of Elasson where two roads lead to Larisa, one over the steep Menexes Pass to the south-east and the other south-west by an easier but longer route. The 24th Battalion guarded the eastern route, the 25th the western; the 26th was in reserve round Domenikon. The infantry was supported by the 2/3rd Field Regiment (with twenty 25-pounders), and with a troop of the 64th Medium Regiment under command; two groups (eight 25-pounders) of the 5th New Zealand Regiment in an anti-tank role behind the 25th Battalion; a battery (twelve 25-pounders) of the 5th Regiment in reserve at Domenikon; and seven 2-pounders dug in and four mobile in the 25th Battalion area. Thus there were no guns near the 24th Battalion but the steepness of the pass, demolitions and mines were thought to provide an adequate protection against tank attack in its area, and the country in front of the infantry could be brought under fire from the field guns to the east.

German tanks closely followed the withdrawal of the New Zealand cavalry, and by about 10.30 the medium guns were firing on enemy vehicles bunched in the hills north of Elasson. The field guns of the 2/3rd caught groups of enemy tanks at ranges up to 10,000 yards and hit numbers of them. This accurate fire and the difficulty of putting vehicles across the river prevented the Germans concentrating for a serious attack until late in the day. Dive-bombers passed overhead in groups of from forty to sixty at regular intervals to harass the columns farther south, but only one bomber attacked the 6th Brigade. The medium guns ran out of ammunition early in the afternoon and withdrew, but by a fortunate accident the Australian gunners were lavishly supplied with ammunition. Before the withdrawal from the Katerini Pass the 5th New Zealand Regiment had been ordered to carry one load of ammunition from the 4th's positions at Ayios Dimitrios to the position south of Elasson. The order was misunderstood; the drivers worked all night on wet and crowded roads and moved back all the considerable dump of ammunition that had been stored at Ayios Dimitrios in readiness for a prolonged stand in the pass. After the medium guns were withdrawn most of the firing was done by the 2/3rd. The artillery observers gave the batteries such

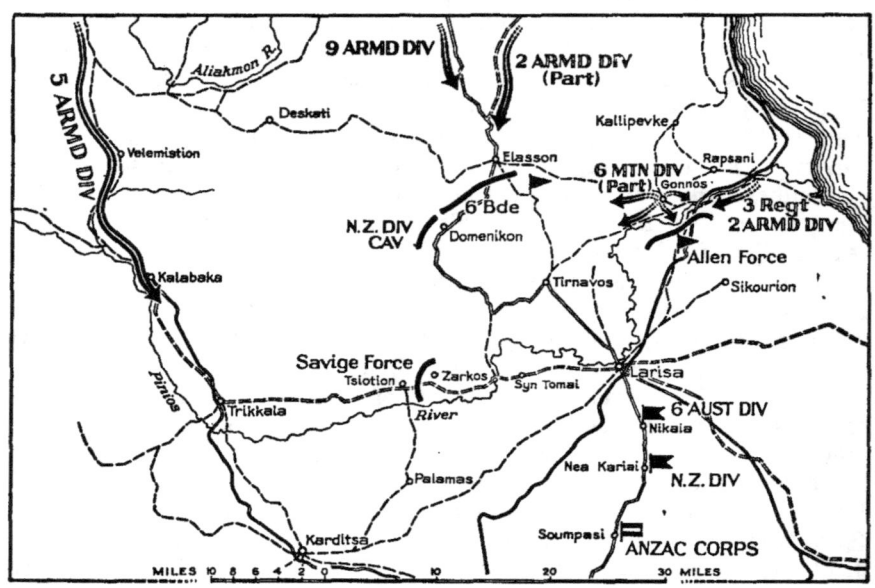

Late afternoon, 18th April.

targets as "15 cruiser tanks", "30 tanks", "12 vehicles", "5 tanks", "6 tanks". "Exciting day," wrote the diarist of the 2/3rd Australian, "in which 6,500 rounds were fired by the regiment. Tanks appeared in the early morning and troops formed up but the consistent shooting of the regiment stopped the enemy and the infantry made no contact." Indeed, all day the advance of what was evidently a powerful enemy force, with a battalion or more of tanks advancing over open, rolling country, was held chiefly by demolitions and the fire of twenty-four field and medium guns.

Just before dusk, however, when the rearguard was beginning to thin out, the enemy attacked. Shells fell in the 24th Battalion's position and a column of lorries, led by tanks, advanced up the road to the Menexes Pass. Leading tanks struck mines and soon the 2/3rd Field Regiment was pumping shells among the tanks. German infantry dismounted and advanced against the forward positions of the 24th as it was withdrawing in accordance with the plan, but the attackers succeeded only in delaying the withdrawal for a time. On the eastern flank the Australian guns were pulled out troop by troop and the infantry thinned out until only a troop of New Zealand field guns, four anti-tank guns and small parties of infantry were left. The field guns fired heavily until 11:30 p.m. when the force moved back swiftly, blowing culverts on the way. It reached Larisa about 3 a.m. The 24th and 25th Battalions took the road to Volos; the 26th Battalion travelled from Larisa by train.[8]

It remains to record the experiences of Brigadier Savige's force on this day. Savige had placed Lieut-Colonel King of the 2/5th in command of a rearguard consisting of one company of infantry and detachments of tanks, artillery and machine-guns, which took up a position about five miles east of Kalabaka, with orders to retire one hour after the main body had passed him. The 2/11th were on the road to Zarkos before dawn and had occupied a position there by 10 a.m. At 11 a.m. the 2/2nd Field Company[9] began blowing up sections of the road, having prepared demolitions at eight points extending from a tunnel three miles beyond Kalabaka on the west to road bridges in Trikkala to the east. Part of Savige Force crossed the Pinios over the undamaged bridge on a by-pass road a few miles north of Syn Tomai, but about 11.30 a.m. three enemy aircraft bombed this bridge which had been prepared for demolition. One bomb dropped near the bridge, the explosive charges were set off either by bomb splinters or sympathetic detonation, and the bridge was destroyed. The only route for vehicles was now a long detour through Tirnavos. The engineers improvised a ferry over the river near the demolished bridge on the main road and the men who remained on the western side crossed this way. The empty vehicles were sent through Tirnavos whence they circled round through much-bombed Larisa to the east bank of the river and picked up the men waiting there.

Meanwhile in an order timed 1 p.m. Mackay had instructed Savige to move the 2/11th Battalion from Zarkos to a position on the west bank of the river to defend the left flank until 3 a.m. on the 19th—the same time as that at which Allen had been ordered to defend the right flank. This order caused Savige some concern as it would entail moving the 2/11th across the river in the early hours of the next morning in darkness. He decided that his role could be carried out equally well on the east bank and moved the 2/11th across the river in the ferry in the late afternoon and early part of the night. His force as a whole was to begin moving south at 9 p.m., the rearguard at 3 a.m.

In the late afternoon the engineers responsible for demolitions along this section of the Pinios and for the two mishaps, reported to Major Wilson,[1] commanding the 2/2nd Field Company, that a bridge between Tsiotion and Palamas had not been blown or even prepared for demolition. Wilson found it impossible to reach this bridge from the south bank

---

[8] It travelled 130 miles to Kifisokhori. It was an eventful journey. No signals worked, and abandoned trucks had to be pushed in front of the engine until a siding was found. The engine failed on a steep grade north of Lamia and five trucks were uncoupled and the troops packed into the remaining nine. South of Lamia the train was under frequent air attack.

[9] This company had landed in Athens from Egypt on the 13th, reached Kalabaka on the night of the 15th, prepared its demolitions on the 16th, and blew them on the 18th.

[1] Col J. G. Wilson, OBE, VX164. OC 2/2 Fd Coy, and Asst Engr-in-Chief LHQ 1943-45. Member Melbourne Stock Exchange; of Toorak, Vic; b. Brighton, Vic, 13 Jul 1913.

of the Pinios, but feared that it might give the Germans a route to Pharsala through Karditsa. He therefore assembled a small demolition party under Warrant-Officer Crawford. This party, with a utility, was ferried back across the Pinios and put on to the Trikkala road at dusk. There were then no British troops on the Trikkala side of the Pinios. Crawford led the party back to the bridge and destroyed it. About midnight they rejoined the rearguard on the eastern bank.

The 2/11th Battalion was deployed on the east side of the Pinios by 8 p.m. A quarter of an hour later the 2/5th set off towards Larisa in its vehicles. The 2/11th followed at 3 a.m. and the tail of its column cleared Larisa about 4 a.m.

It will be recalled that after the failure of the German attack at Servia the greater part of Stumme's Corps (*5th* and *9th Armoured*, "*Adolf Hitler*" and *73rd*) swung west towards Grevena, and Boehme's moved south round the eastern side of Olympus leaving a relatively weak force facing Servia. On the 15th the *5th* and *6th Mountain* and *2nd Armoured Divisions* and a detachment of the *72nd* were advancing against the eastern Olympus passes.

The *2nd Armoured Division* was divided into two groups. One, including five infantry battalions, one armoured unit (the *II/3rd*), and the equivalent of two artillery regiments, advanced up the Olympus Pass. The other, including the remaining two battalions of the *3rd Armoured Regiment*, one infantry battalion, the equivalent of two more battalions (cyclists and engineers used as infantry), and two artillery regiments, were concentrated against the 21st New Zealand Battalion at Platamon. German accounts speak of "fierce battles" between Olympus and the sea.

After Platamon the German force advancing into the Pinios Gorge was augmented from the *6th Mountain Division* until it included three armoured units (two battalions of the *3rd Armoured Regiment* and the *112th Reconnaissance Unit*, all totalling some 150 tanks), five infantry battalions, and the equivalent of two more, three and a half artillery regiments.

On the 16th the *6th Mountain Division* began a wide outflanking move across the southern slopes of Olympus on the track through Leptokaria and Kallipevke to Gonnos, and early on the 17th the leading battalion (*III/143rd*) began arriving at Gonnos. The divisional commander reached Gonnos at 4 p.m. and at 11.30 that night he issued orders for an attack by the *III* and *II Battalions* of the *143rd* next morning.[2] Its object was to cross the river and cut the road behind the British force. Meanwhile the leading troops of the *2nd Armoured*—the *I/3rd Armoured Battalion*—with the *112th Reconnaissance Unit* (of the *6th Mountain*) had reached the entrance to the Pinios Gorge early on the afternoon of the 17th. They found a ford, and some infantry and five tanks crossed the river. The water was so deep that the tanks were almost covered and two were bogged. A cycle squadron pushed forward that evening and came under heavy fire but "pushed the enemy back 800 yards" (this was Lieutenant Arnold's patrol). That night the Germans south of the river were accurately shelled.

When the Germans in the gorge resumed their attack next morning they made little progress because of the severe artillery fire. About 1.30 p.m. a coordinated attack was made along both sides of the gorge. Two tanks were hit and set on fire and for a time only three remained in action. Meanwhile at 9.30 the *III/143rd Battalion* had sent patrols across the river where, they reported, they took "the

---

[2] In this and other reports of German operations an hour has been added to all times given in German reports. Part of the Balkans were one hour fast on GMT, part two hours. It is evident that German watches were one hour faster than GMT, British two. For instance a "very successful" Stuka attack on Allen's headquarters was recorded at the receiving end as having taken place at exactly 3 p.m., but in the German reports at exactly 2 p.m.

English" in Parapotamos (Lieutenant Watson's patrol) by surprise and forced them to fight a delaying action. The remainder of the battalion trickled across the river during the morning. The *1/143rd Battalion* was to make a feint attack while the *III/143rd* was crossing, and then follow it over. It made a serious attack at 3 p.m., its immediate objective being Evangelismos. It got across the river by 4.30 p.m. but "the enemy offered stubborn opposition and some of our heavy weapons were casualties, so the attack made very slow progress. Not until 1730 (1830) hours did we break into the enemy's position after hand to hand fighting." This battalion lost 12 killed, one missing and 69 wounded during the day (most of them probably caused by Caldwell's company). The *112th Reconnaissance Unit*, leading the advance along the gorge reported that it reached the outskirts of Tempe at 4.30 p.m. and the village was taken at 5.45. By 6.30 the *I and II Battalions* of the *143rd Regiment* were pressing on towards Makrikhori railway station and two battalions of the newly-arrived *131st Regiment* were also crossing the river. By 7 p.m. the German tanks had passed through Evangelismos and advanced beyond Makrikhori station where, they reported, they were counter-attacked by "English tanks" (evidently the Bren carriers) and "salvo after salvo of heavy enemy shells from the Larisa direction prevented the thrust from making any more headway before dark".

It was the *2nd Company* of the *143rd Mountain Regiment* that cut the road between Allen Force and Larisa. It was given the task of crossing the river on the division's extreme right flank, climbing the 1,500-foot hill west of Makrikhori and blocking the Tempe - Larisa road and railway, and finally advancing to the northern edge of the town. Some of the Germans forded and swam the river at 10.30 a.m. on the 18th, the others were ferried over. The commander, Lieutenant Jacob, seeing the enemy (Murchison's company of the 2/3rd) on the hill one mile north-west of Makrikhori, decided to swing wider to the west, and the company went through the villages of Mavrolithos, Bakraina and Koulouri and aimed at the level crossing about two miles and a half from Larisa. They reached the crossing about 8 p.m., cut the telephone lines and pushed railway trucks across the road. There they first captured a convoy of nine or ten trucks. At 10.30 p.m. a long convoy approached. A "light tank" (probably the carrier mentioned by Lieutenant Johnson above) which was leading was knocked out with an anti-tank rifle. At 11.30 p.m., according to the German account, two armoured cars advanced firing but the Germans replied with "terrific effect". "The Australians made a determined effort to overrun the German positions on the railway embankment, coming into very close range but our accurate fire inflicted heavy casualties." About 1 a.m. what Jacob thought was a heavy tank was knocked out. Finally some 30 Australians surrendered, 8 to 10 dead and about 20 wounded were left behind, and others were trying to escape south-east. At dawn the German company moved towards Larisa. Near the town it was overtaken by detachments of the *2nd Armoured Division* and the two entered the town together soon after 7 a.m. on the 19th.

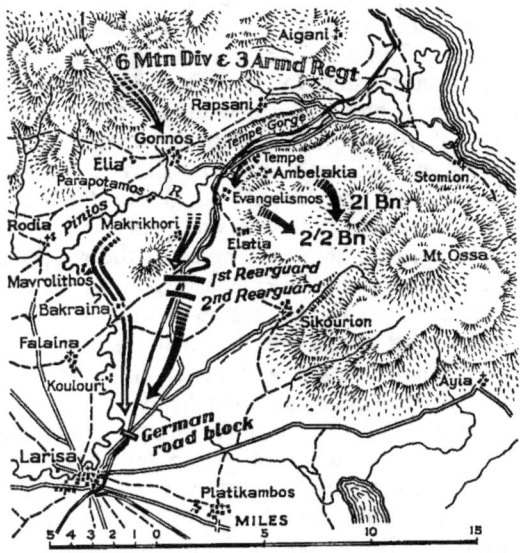

While the fight at Pinios was in progress three other armoured columns were converging on Larisa. That part of the *2nd Armoured* which advanced through the Olympus Pass had reached the main road on the 18th, and linked with the *9th Armoured* advancing south from Servia, whose advance had been so effectively checked by the New Zealand rearguard at Elasson. On the evening of the 16th detached units of the *9th Armoured Division* reached Grevena and some turned east towards Deskati while others were engaged by "strong enemy rearguards"—apparently Greeks—at the Venetikos bridge. The *5th Armoured Division* now took over the advance towards Kalabaka. It spent the 17th bridging the Venetikos and at 7 p.m. on the 18th was nearing Kalabaka. That day List ordered Stumme, in addition to pushing on to Lamia, to send a force over the Metsovon Pass in the Pindus range against Yannina.

The 18th had been a day of keen anxiety for the commanders not only because of their fears that one or other of the two eastern rearguard forces might be thrust back to Larisa before the others were through the bottleneck, but because of the possibility that the German bombers might block the road south of Larisa along which the retiring columns were pouring. Thus not only were messages from the rearguards anxiously read, but the long road from Larisa to Lamia was scanned with anxious eyes. Soon after dawn it was evident that the sky would be clear enough to give the German aircraft a field day. There would be no opposition from anti-aircraft guns, for now there were none so far north, nor was it likely that any fighter aircraft would be available to protect the convoys.

At daylight on the 18th the endless procession of trucks was moving fast along the road south of Larisa. To watchers at corps headquarters at Soumpasi and Mackay's headquarters at Nikaia it was evident that for the time the withdrawal was proceeding smoothly. But, at 9.30, a loud explosion was heard six miles to the south. German aircraft had attacked the bridge over the Enipeus River north of Pharsala, had missed it, but hit a truck-load of explosives, which were detonated and blew a huge hole in the road on an embankment leading to the bridge. The traffic slowed down, then stopped and began to bank up until there was a column of stationary vehicles jammed head to tail for 10 miles. Above the line of vehicles groups of German aircraft roared at intervals of a few minutes. Some vehicles were hit and a few began to burn. Brigadier Steele, the forceful Chief Engineer of Anzac Corps, arrived quickly at the break in the road and directed repairs. The crater was 25 feet in diameter and about 16 feet deep, and on the embankment at the north end of the crater lay a bulldozer disabled by the explosion. It was too heavy for a truck to haul away and added a second obstacle. Steele sent an officer back along the line of vehicles to order every driver to bring his pick and shovel to the spot, and teams from several units, including a Cypriot pioneer company, were soon at work filling the crater and cutting a detour. Lieutenant Cann with a party of sappers blew up uprooted concrete beams projecting into the new by-pass, and for some four hours controlled traffic at the spot. Several miles farther south Lieutenant Ballantine[3]

---

[3] Maj R. L. Ballantine, NX35059. 2/2 (2/22) Fd Pk Coy 1940-44; OC 13 Fd Coy 1944-45. Engineer; of Waroona, WA; b. Perth, WA, 12 Mar 1915.

strengthened a track in marshy ground round the edge of another crater by using folding boats as corduroy.[4] At length a gradual track was cut down the embankment past the main crater and up again to the bridge.[5] Perhaps twelve other bombs directly hit the road between Larisa and Brallos, although with less serious effects.

However, the position was so disturbing that at 2 p.m. Brigadier Rowell obtained Blamey's permission to go forward to Mackay and Freyberg to ascertain whether the withdrawal could be postponed for twenty-four hours. When he reached Mackay's headquarters at Nikaia at 4 o'clock there were reports that the enemy was across the Pinios; it was evident that there could be no postponement. Indeed, there seemed a danger that the enemy might be in Larisa in time to cut off half the fighting part of the force and to pursue the congested column down the road to Lamia. Actually, by that time the crisis had passed. At 1.30 p.m. the detour at Pharsala was in action and the long column was moving forward again.

The air attacks did not cease, but as the day went on it became increasingly apparent that the enemy aircraft, though noisy and nerve-wracking, were doing remarkably little damage to men and vehicles. In spite of the fact that the Germans could put into the air enough aircraft to enable them always to be attacking in strength somewhere between Larisa (which was bombed half a dozen times during the day) and Lamia, and that the column, 70 miles long, lay defenceless on the road below them, relatively few men were hit and vehicles disabled, though there was much noise and smoke. Freyberg and Mackay particularly were taking pains to encourage by their example a disregard of the nuisance in the air. On this and the succeeding days each of these commanders was seen at his full stature. The qualities that had made them outstanding young fighting leaders in the previous war were evident and their influence seeped down through the force. Some saw Freyberg standing nonchalantly and alone while an aircraft machine-gunned him, and missed; or saw him coolly clearing a traffic jam among the trucks of a withdrawing infantry rearguard.[6] Others heard of Mackay sitting in the open, apparently unconcerned, during an air attack; or of Mackay waiting at the rearguard position at Domokos on the 19th during an air attack that lasted two-and-a-half hours, when his car was hit and his driver wounded. Each was frequently forward with a rearguard brigade at critical periods. From a psychological point of view as well as tactically the 18th was the critical day, and after it had passed, and partly because of the example of the

---

[4] "These expensive boats were smashed to matchwood," wrote Steele later, and "without prior approval of the Business Board." Steele was an implacable enemy of business boards and such-like, which, he believed, only achieved delay and circumlocution.

[5] At 11.15 a.m. Blamey's headquarters sent the following signal to Wilson's headquarters now at Thebes: "Owing condition Volos road we can use only main road. General Blamey says you must repeat must provide fighter protection for road Larisa-Lamia throughout day. Road badly holed at Pharsala and long column halted northwards." At 2.35 p.m. this was followed by another appeal: "Fifty enemy aircraft bombed and machine-gunned our columns Larisa-Lamia road at 0930 hrs. Then followed intermittent attacks throughout morning and now at 1430 hrs continuous attack is being made. This road is our life-line for next few days and we must have air protection if humanly possible."

[6] At Volos about dawn on the 19th.

leaders, partly because of the coolness and dogged stamina of the fighting men, there was no danger of depression or panic seizing the force. Thereafter discipline became more rigidly observed, not less, and spirits rose, though in defeat.

The German Air Force signally failed to exploit its superiority on this critical day. If, having broken the road as it did near Pharsala, it had concentrated on that point and kept aircraft over it continually it would probably have halted the column all day, and on the following days might have caught and defeated the greater part of the corps before it had reached the relative security of the Thermopylae position. As it was, the German bombers dispersed their effort, attacking singly or in small groups at intervals along the road, and interrupting the progress of the column for only short periods. Later in the war more effective tactics would have been used.

CHAPTER 6

THE THERMOPYLAE LINE

GENERAL Wavell arrived in Athens on the 19th April and immediately held a conference at General Wilson's quarters. Although an effective decision to embark the British force from Greece had been made on a higher level in London, the commanders on the spot now once again deeply considered the pros and cons. The Greek Government was unstable and had suggested that the British force should depart in order to avoid further devastation of the country. It was unlikely that the Greek Army of Epirus could be extricated and some of its senior officers were urging surrender. General Wilson considered that his force could hold the Thermopylae line indefinitely once the troops were in position.[1] "The arguments in favour of fighting it out, which [it] is always better to do if possible," wrote Wilson later,[2] "were: the tying up of enemy forces, army and air, which would result therefrom; the strain the evacuation would place on the Navy and Merchant Marine; the effect on the morale of the troops and the loss of equipment which would be incurred. In favour of withdrawal the arguments were: the question as to whether our forces in Greece could be reinforced as this was essential; the question of the maintenance of our forces, plus the feeding of the civil population; the weakness of our air forces with few airfields and little prospect of receiving reinforcements; the little hope of the Greek Army being able to recover its morale. The decision was made to withdraw from Greece." The British leaders considered that it was unlikely that they would be able to take out any equipment except that which the troops carried, and that they would be lucky "to get away with 30 per cent of the force".

This British discussion was followed by a conference at the Greek King's palace, attended, as on the previous day, by the King himself, Sir Michael Palairet, General Papagos, General Wilson, Air Vice-Marshal D'Albiac and Rear-Admiral Turle; but, on this occasion, also by General Wavell and by General Mazarakis, a leader of the Venizelist Republican party to whom the King had suddenly offered the Prime Ministership.

Wavell, who spoke first, said that the British Army would fight as long as the Greek Army fought. On the other hand it would embark if the Greek Government wished. Papagos then said that the morale of the Greek Army had been shaken. The Epirus Army had now to be supplied along a single road (through Yannina) and the vehicles available were too few to maintain that army in the field. Some of the senior officers wished to cease fighting. The King, the Government and the high command had had to order them to fight on. Greece would be devastated if the armies continued fighting for another month or two. Palairet then read a telegram from Mr Churchill to the effect that if the British force left Greece it must

---

[1] Baillie-Grohman, Report.
[2] Wilson, pp. 93-4.

be with the full consent of the Greek King and Government. Mazarakis said that "he had been called in too late to retrieve the situation and that evacuation was the best solution".[3] It was decided that the British force should be embarked and that

> the Greek forces in Epirus should continue fighting as long as possible, or at any rate as long as [required for] the withdrawal of the British forces . . . . The war was of course to continue in the islands with all the means and the naval forces available, since Greece was indissolubly bound up with Britain and her resolve was to fight to the end by the side of the British Empire.[4]

The belated effort to bring the Venizelists into the Government failed. They had been obliterated from Greek public life after 1935, when Metaxas established his dictatorship. In 1935, and later, large numbers of republican army officers had been dismissed. When the Italians invaded Greece some relatively junior officers of republican leanings were allowed to rejoin the army but none of the rank of colonel or above was recalled.[5]

These republican officers considered the monarchists generally to be half-hearted about the war and inefficient. They thought that, as soon as Italy attacked, a coalition government should have been formed and the compulsorily-retired republican officers recalled. Now, at the eleventh hour, the King proposed to form a coalition government. Mazarakis agreed to lead a coalition on condition that M. Maniadakis, the Minister for Internal Security, who controlled the police force, was excluded.

> As this matter affected security (wrote Wilson afterwards) it was referred to my headquarters for decision as to the advisability of a change at this juncture; in view of the impending evacuation we were unable to agree to any step which would tend to loosen the control exercised by the police in Athens. (Two years were to elapse before a Venizelist entered the Greek Government.)[6]

It was ironical that, as a result of a British decision, the followers of the great Greek liberal who had been a devoted ally of Britain and France in the first world war should thus have been excluded from the Greek Government in this crisis.

Although, on the 18th, Mr Churchill had issued a directive about the principles that should govern the evacuation, on the 20th, evidently encouraged by news that the British force was successfully falling back to the Thermopylae line, he wrote to Mr Eden in an optimistic vein.

> I am increasingly of the opinion that if the generals on the spot think they can hold on in the Thermopylae position for a fortnight or three weeks, and can keep the Greek Army fighting, or enough of it, we should certainly support them, if the Dominions will agree . . . every day the German Air Force is detained in Greece enables the Libyan situation to be stabilised, and may enable us to bring in the extra tanks [to Tobruk]. If this is accomplished safely and the Tobruk position holds, we

---

[3] Wilson, p. 95.
[4] Papagos, p. 382.
[5] In *Greek Resistance Army* (Eng edition, 1951) General Sarafis, one of the republicans, says that General Heywood (the leader of the British Military Mission to Greece) presented a list of 600 such officers to the Government and asked that they be employed, but the Government refused.
[6] Wilson, p. 95.

might even feel strong enough to reinforce from Egypt. I am most reluctant to see us quit, and if the troops were British only and the matter could be decided on military grounds alone I would urge Wilson to fight if he thought it possible. Anyhow, before we commit ourselves to evacuation the case must be put squarely to the Dominions after to-morrow's Cabinet. Of course, I do not know the conditions in which our retreating forces will reach the new key position.[7]

It was too late, however, for such a change of heart and change of plan. That day there was a meeting of Greek generals in Epirus. With the support of the Bishop of Yannina, General Tsolakoglou (whom we last saw driving westward from Kalabaka leaving his troops behind him) and his two fellow corps commanders, removed General Pitsikas, the leader of the Epirus Army, from his post, and opened negotiations for surrender with the commander of the *"Adolf Hitler"* Division, then nearing Yannina. Next day at Larisa, Tsolakoglou signed an agreement to surrender. When Papagos learned of Tsolakoglou's preliminary negotiations he sent a signal to Pitsikas ordering him to dismiss Tsolakoglou immediately, but Pitsikas had already been deposed.[8]

That day the gallant little British air force struck its last blow. About 100 German dive bombers and fighters attacked the Athens area. The fifteen Hurricanes which were still serviceable went up to intercept them and reported having brought down twenty-two German aircraft for certain, and possibly eight others, for a loss of five Hurricanes.

Meanwhile, at 2 o'clock on the morning of the 21st, Wavell arrived at Blamey's headquarters and informed him that the force was to be evacuated as soon as possible. At that stage it was considered that embarkation would not begin before 27th April; but, at a conference between Wilson, Blamey, and Rear-Admiral Baillie-Grohman[9] (in charge of the naval arrangements ashore) on the roadside near Thebes the following night, Wilson informed Blamey that as a result of the surrender in Epirus he had decided to accelerate the program. It would be Blamey's task to deliver the first troops to the beaches by dawn on the 24th, for embarkation on the night of the 24th-25th.

In the meantime the Anzac Corps had gone into position on the Thermopylae line. By sunrise on the 19th it had succeeded in placing some 40 to 50 miles of cratered roads and demolished bridges between itself and the German advance-guard. The Germans were not then in Larisa, where police of the 7th Australian Division's provost company were still coolly directing the few vehicles straggling behind the main columns. The 6th New Zealand Brigade group was in Volos; the divisional cavalry and a company of the 25th Battalion occupied a rearguard position across the

---

[7] Quoted in Churchill, Vol III, p. 202.

[8] It seems likely that the Greek corps commanders were anxious to surrender to Germans rather than Italians, whom they had defeated and whom they despised. The Italian leaders protested against the action of the German Army in accepting the Greek surrender without consulting them, and as a result a second surrender agreement, whereby the Greeks capitulated also to the Italians, was signed at Salonika on the 23rd.

[9] Rear-Adm H. T. Baillie-Grohman, CB, DSO, OBE; RN. Comd HMS *Ramillies*, 1st Battle Sqn, Medit 1939-40. Flag Officer attached GHQ ME 1941; Rear-Adm Comb Ops 1942. B. Victoria, Brit Columbia, 15 Jan 1888.

roads leading into that town. Stragglers of the 21st Battalion and the 2/2nd from Tempe arrived at Volos during the morning; other parties from those battalions and the 2/3rd were dispersed in the hills to the north and west.

At dawn the retreating Anzac column on the main road from Larisa to Lamia was still more than 10 miles in length, the vehicles closely spaced and an easy target for air attack. The day again was fine but, luckily for the long convoy, German aircraft did not appear in force until some hours after daylight, and by then the vehicles were moving steadily south. There were heavy attacks by groups of up to twenty-seven aircraft from 7 a.m. to 8.30, then a lull, a second attack by twenty-one at midday, and another lull until about 2 o'clock. In the early afternoon the Domokos rearguard and the road south of it were attacked continuously for two hours and a half. The tail of Savige Force was then some miles past Domokos.[1]

The column was making painfully slow progress and most of the troops spent the whole day packed in their vehicles under fire from an enemy against whom they could not hit back. A typical experience was that of the 2/1st Battalion. At dawn it was 10 miles north of Lamia in the middle of a congested column. It did not pass through Lamia until 10 a.m.; then the column was halted under air attack on the straight road, the trucks almost head to tail and, in places, two abreast. At length the column began to move again, but it was 5 o'clock before this battalion reached its positions in the Brallos Pass.

Many vehicles were hit but few disabled. One officer who was towards the rear of the column remembers having seen only six abandoned vehicles between Larisa and Lamia. It seems certain that more vehicles were lost as a result of being bogged, breaking down, or running over the edges of the narrow roads than as a result of direct damage by air attack. In men, to take two instances, the 2/5th Battalion lost thirteen killed and twenty-four wounded during the day, and the 2/11th Battalion four killed and eleven wounded; these appear to have been the heaviest casualties inflicted on Australian battalions by air attack in any day in this campaign.[2] Attacks with light bombs and machine-guns against troops dispersed in defensive positions were ineffective, and everywhere the softness of the ground limited the effect of the bombs. For example, the 2/6th, deployed beside the road at Domokos, reported that its area had been attacked by twenty to thirty aircraft at 7.30 and again at 12.15, and, later in the afternoon, by relays of aircraft for two hours and a half; yet its only losses were one officer (Lieutenant Williams[3]) killed, and two men wounded. Mackay's driver was wounded here. Farther north the driver of Lieut-Colonel Louch of the 2/11th was killed and their car run off the road, Louch being badly shaken. Brigadier Savige's driver had his foot broken by a great clod of earth thrown up by a bomb. Dive bombers made an effective attack on Brigadier Steele's engineer headquarters group at the foot of Brallos Pass.

---

[1] The last vehicle was a truck containing Captain Honner and a few men of the 2/11th Bn, who had been the last to leave Savige Force's rearguard position at Syn Tomai.

[2] Three men of the 2/11th were killed and six wounded by a single bomb.

[3] Lt T. H. Williams, VX4554; 2/6 Bn. Agricultural student; of South Yarra, Vic; b. Corowa, NSW, 14 Sep 1905. Killed in action 19 Apr 1941.

His medical officer, Captain Weir,[4] and a sapper were killed, and his adjutant, Captain Reddy, and two others wounded.

It was impossible for commanders to control the slowly-moving column in which their cars were merely links in the long chain. By the roadside, during a halt, Steele and Savige met and agreed with each other that it was inadvisable for staff cars to weave their way forward when the column was halted, to discover what was causing the delay, because of the risk that the troops might interpret this as signifying that officers in staff cars were "beating it". These leaders, like Mackay, Freyberg and other senior officers, made themselves conspicuous at the roadside, or went calmly about their duties at their headquarters, setting an example of cool behaviour under fire.[5]

Mackay spent the 19th, from 7.30 until about 4 p.m., at the Domokos rearguard position, so that he could see for himself the problem facing Brigadier Lee there. Lee's force had originally included four battalions— 2/4th, 2/8th, 2/6th and 2/7th—a company of the 2/5th, and artillery and engineers. On the 18th Lee had decided that it was unlikely that he would be hard pressed by the enemy before the remainder of the New Zealand and Australian divisions had passed through Lamia. He therefore ordered the 19th Brigade (2/4th and 2/8th Battalions) to withdraw to the Thermopylae position, but retained one company of the 2/4th.[6] Mackay approved this decision when he arrived at Lee's headquarters on the morning of the 19th.

That morning it was discovered that a train-load of petrol, ammunition, gun-cotton and ammonal was standing at a railway siding two miles north of Domokos. Lieut-Colonel Walker of the 2/7th decided that so valuable a cargo should be driven back to Athens, and the ubiquitous Corporal Taylor, the same who had made up a train at Larisa and carried the battalion back to Domokos, went forward early in the afternoon with Corporal Edwards[7] and six other volunteers, all Victorian railwaymen, to drive the train to safety. A squadron of German aircraft saw the steam rising and circled overhead bombing and machine-gunning the station and train. Taylor was in the engine alone, with his team lying under cover awaiting his signal to jump aboard, when the trucks exploded with a shattering roar and a huge mushroom of smoke rose into the air. The blast was so powerful that men in the infantry positions two miles away

---

[4] Capt S. I. Weir, VX215; AAMC. Medical practitioner; of Geelong, Vic; b. Deniliquin, NSW, 11 Jun 1906. Killed in action 19 Apr 1941.

[5] A senior officer described a scene at Mackay's headquarters south of Brallos next day, during a "particularly hectic" air attack. "I noticed Mackay moving in front of his tent quite unconcerned about the movement of enemy planes. He neither looked at the planes nor at the men dashing about, but they saw him, and those moving towards shelter stopped, and many of those who had gained shelter returned to their duties. Personal example is the only paying proposition in such circumstances."

[6] Lee then had two battalions, 2/6 and 2/7 (plus a company of the 2/4), the 2/1 Fd Regt less a battery, a company of the 2/1 MG, and five cruisers of the 3 Royal Tanks, and the British anti-tank battery which had been with Savige Force and had dropped out of that column on reaching Domokos. As already mentioned the 2/6 Bn, plus a company of the 2/5, was in position to the east of the road, the 2/7 and Capt Rolfe's company of the 2/4 on the west.

[7] Lt A. D. Edwards, MBE, VX5552; 2/7 Bn. Builder; of Warrandyte, Vic; b. Warrandyte, 4 Oct 1913.

felt the force of it. It thrust the engine violently along the rails, and thus its power was cushioned. Taylor survived, and, to the astonishment of those in the pass who had given the railwaymen up for dead, he arrived back at the battalion, leading his men, his hair singed but otherwise unharmed.[8]

Late in the afternoon Mackay decided that Lee's force would soon have done its job—to ensure that the New Zealand and Australian brigades withdrew through Lamia without interference by German troops. He therefore ordered Lee to pull out the main part of his force at dusk, and himself moved south to his new headquarters beyond Brallos. Lee, who had understood that he would have to hold the Domokos Pass until the night of the 21st-22nd, had already sent Captain Luxton out to ascertain when the New Zealand troops moving along the Volos road would have passed through Lamia. At dusk Luxton returned with information that the New Zealanders were clear of Lamia, but that Brigadier Allen did not know the whereabouts of his brigade. Thereupon, at 9 p.m., Lee ordered the main portion of his force to withdraw forthwith, but organised a small rearguard to hold astride the road 10 miles farther south. This was at the southern exit from the range separating Lamia from the plain of Thessaly, whereas Domokos was at the northern exit.

Night, 20-21 April.

Meanwhile at 7 p.m. the road had been blown in several places. In error some demolitions were made behind positions held by the 2/6th and as a result two anti-tank guns had to be destroyed and abandoned. Worse still, at 8 p.m. several vehicles appeared on the road forward of the Domokos force and men climbed from them

---

[8] Next day at Levadia above the Brallos Pass three trains loaded with petrol, gun ammunition and anti-tank mines were set alight as a result of a heavy German air attack, and the ammunition began to explode. Sgt H. Killalea of the Corps Signals, with Dvr McDonald of the New Zealand Divisional Supply Column, boarded a locomotive, discovered how to drive it, and saved 28 trucks of petrol and ammunition by shunting them a safe distance. They then loaded on to waggons a considerable quantity of petrol and ammunition, working not far from railway trucks in which 25-pdr and 60-pdr shells were exploding at intervals. Sig W. J. Truskett (of Caulfield, Vic) coolly salvaged other equipment from the burning trains. (Killalea, of St Kilda, Vic, had served in the previous war in which he had won an MM.)

and began to repair the demolitions. On Lee's orders the gunners fired at them until it was discovered that these were trucks loaded with British engineer and ordnance men and Cypriot pioneers, who had been left behind. A patrol was sent out to bring them in and to destroy their trucks. The withdrawal from the Domokos position was completed by 10.30.

Lee appointed Major Guinn[9] to command the new rearguard position and instructed him to delay the enemy until the last Australian and New Zealand forces had passed through Lamia. Guinn was not informed of his role until early in the morning on the 20th, and when he arrived at the Lamia Pass his little force—a company of the 2/6th, a company of the 2/7th, a company of the 2/1st Machine Gun Battalion, a detachment of anti-tank guns, and five tanks—had already been placed in position in the dark by Lieut-Colonel Wells of the corps staff.[1] When daylight came Guinn decided that some of the infantry were too exposed to observation from the air, and that if he was to avoid air attack and to surprise the enemy's troops when they appeared, he must conceal his positions. This was done and troops and guns were well concealed before any scouting aircraft arrived.

The company of the 2/7th was deployed astride the road and to the right of it; the company of the 2/6th on the left and the tanks in a small copse about a mile forward and a mile to the right of the road. About 11 a.m. a German troop-carrying aircraft landed near the village of Xinia on flat land about three miles from the Australian positions, and at the same time vehicles began to move down the slopes from Domokos. Lieutenant Morris[2] commanding one of the platoons of the 2/7th collected three N.C.O's and led them downhill to capture the aircraft. The company commander, Lieutenant Macfarlane, called to them to come back and the N.C.O's heard and returned, but Morris went on and eventually himself was taken prisoner.

About 2.15 p.m. a group of four German motor-cycles with side-cars appeared, followed at 500 yards by a fifth cycle. The rearguard had been so well concealed on the scrubby slopes that several reconnaissance aircraft which flew low over the pass during the morning and fired into patches of undergrowth evidently failed to detect any of the positions; and the four leading motor-cyclists rode right into the Australian area, where all were killed or wounded by a sudden burst of fire. A little later the fifth motor-cyclist advanced along the road at high speed, saw the wrecked cycles on the road, made a sharp skid turn and got away. At this stage the officer commanding the tanks withdrew his tanks from the wood, where they had been lying concealed and ready to counter-attack.

Later one tank was moved forward to each of the northernmost knolls to engage such German tanks as should appear. An armoured car coming into view was hit by a shell from one of them. A German tank next

---

[9] Lt-Col H. G. Guinn, DSO, VX33; CO 2/7 Bn 1941-44. Commercial traveller; of East Malvern, Vic; b. Carrum, Vic, 21 Mar 1900.
[1] The tanks and anti-tank guns had been detached from Savige Force as it passed through Domokos.
[2] Lt J. I. Morris, VX9889; 2/7 Bn. Accountant; of Sydney; b. San Francisco, USA, 11 Jan 1915.

appeared, was fired on, and made off in reverse. A rain-storm lasting about half an hour then enabled the Germans to bring forward several mortars which fired until silenced by the Australian machine-guns. Thus far all had gone well. The rearguard was concealed and the enemy came under accurate fire as soon as he appeared across the flat ground at the foot of the pass. At 4.30 p.m. a message arrived from Lee stating that all New Zealand and Australian convoys had passed through Lamia; Guinn was to decide when he would withdraw.

At 5 o'clock the enemy opened fire with four light guns. Guinn had given orders that when the enemy opened fire with artillery the rearguard should withdraw. The tanks began to move out, but one was hit and abandoned in the fields east of the road. The officer commanding the company of the 2/6th on the west of the road then ordered his platoons to withdraw, but told Lieutenant Hayes[3] to remain in position near the road until Lieutenant McCaffrey's[4] platoon on the knoll to the left had come in. The company commander had ordered the infantrymen to hurry; and as the men began to move in some haste and confusion up the slopes to the road, the German mortar crews, hitherto unable to find any definite target, saw them and bombs began to drop among the hurrying clusters and amid the machine-guns, which were hot and easily distinguished by the steam rising from their water jackets. Two cruiser tanks held the road while the infantrymen withdrew. After some of the infantry had already embussed Lieutenant Austin's[5] machine-gunners came out, leaving one gun to cover the engineer party which was to set off the charges in the road. Macfarlane's company of the 2/7th on the right had withdrawn in good order, and when Guinn was told by his officers that all their men had come in he reported to Lee, who had now arrived. Lee told him to go back to Vasey's brigade. The last of the trucks then withdrew.[6]

From Allen's force during the 19th and 20th small parties of the 2/2nd and 2/3rd Battalions arrived in the Brallos area. Colonel Lamb (2/3rd) reached divisional headquarters near Gravia at 3 p.m. on the 19th and reported that he had not seen Allen since early that morning and did not know where the bulk of his battalion was. On orders from Colonel Sutherland, Mackay's G.S.O.1, he established at Amfiklia a collecting post for any more of his men who might come in. Major Edgar,[7] second-in-

[3] Maj P. B. Hayes, VX5101; 2/6 Bn. Grazier; of Birregurra, Vic; b. Colac, Vic, 10 Sep 1911.

[4] Lt J. McCaffrey, VX7622; 2/6 Bn. Coffee lounge proprietor; of St. Kilda, Vic; b. 7 May 1913.

[5] Maj G. W. Austin, NX155; 2/1 MG Bn. Farmer; of Yanco, NSW; b. Narrandera, NSW, 24 Sep 1905.

[6] In the withdrawal some parties were missed. Lieutenant Hayes had remained in position until he had seen the orderly withdrawal of McCaffrey's platoon along a route protected from mortar fire. He sent out his platoon, and then himself came out with three others—a weary Bren gunner, Pte P. C. Purves (of Northcote, Vic), Sgt C. H. Jenkins (Thornbury, Vic) and another man who had been in a lookout high on the ridge and had not been warned of the withdrawal. They were marching along the road when an engineer ahead of them shouted a warning. The infantrymen flung themselves to the ground just as a demolition charge exploded in the road 20 yards beyond. Two more explosions followed, so close that Hayes' men were among the falling debris. With his party now increased to six by the addition of three men of the army service corps who had missed their company in the withdrawal from Domokos, Hayes thereupon set out to walk to the Brallos Pass 15 miles away. The demolitions delayed the enemy so successfully that the Australians were able to reach Lamia without mishap at 2.30 a.m. on the 21st and at 9.30 walked into the 25th New Zealand Battalion's lines whence they returned to their own unit.

[7] Brig C. R. V. Edgar, CBE, DSO, NX140. CO 2/2 Bn 1941-43; Comd 4 Inf Bde 1943-45. Bank officer; of Manly, NSW; b. Wedderburn, Vic, 9 Jul 1901.

command of the 2/2nd, had already established a "straggler post" between Amfiklia and Levadia (whither Blamey's headquarters had moved on the 18th) and during the day 7 officers and 297 men of that unit had collected, including Hendry's company and sundry officers and men of the headquarters company. Most of the 2/3rd Battalion's vehicles after ploughing along the tracks east of Larisa during the night made their way to Lamia either through Volos or by rejoining the main road south of Larisa. By the 20th the 2/3rd had reached a strength of about 500.

Several parties of New Zealanders and men of the 2/2nd and 2/3rd whose vehicles had bogged in the country east of Larisa on the night of the 18th managed by hard marching over the foothills of Mount Othrys to reach the New Zealand Division before it finally withdrew from the Thermopylae position. One party of nine, under Sergeant-Major Le Nevez, reached Volos and there bailed up a car and drove to Lamia. Along the roads followed by these men and by others who escaped to Crete or Turkey, the village women, sometimes in tears, gave them food and the men acted as guides and kept them informed, not always accurately, of the Germans' progress. Brigadier Allen himself had driven eastward, making for the Volos road, but went along the dead-end road. There he found fifty or sixty men. Leaving one of his officers, Lieutenant Hill-Griffiths,[8] with this party with instructions to keep moving south, he himself drove back to the main road, skirting Larisa in daylight. Another small party marched and hitch-hiked for four days and reached Akladi on the north shore of the Gulf of Lamia. There they seized a boat and, with Germans visible in the village and the New Zealand artillery firing registering shots overhead, they rowed across the gulf and on the 23rd joined the New Zealand Division.

Meanwhile, in the Thermopylae line, the British force awaited the German columns. In a message written at Corps headquarters late on the 19th and received by Mackay at 10.15 a.m. on the 20th—the twelve hours delay indicating the congestion on the roads and the difficulty of night driving—the new tasks were defined. General Wilson's headquarters were at Thebes, Corps headquarters at Levadia, Freyberg's near Longos. Mackay was ordered to move his headquarters back from near Gravia to near Ayia Marina—a decision of which Mackay disapproved on the ground that it removed his staff 20 miles from the forward troops at Brallos.[1] Freyberg was given the task of defending the coastal pass, Mackay the Brallos.

The Thermopylae position was at the neck of the long peninsula embracing ancient Locris, Phocis, Boeotia, and Attica. A watcher standing at the top of the Brallos escarpment and facing north looks down on the large town of Lamia in the plain 4,000 feet below through which the

---

[8] Capt K. Hill-Griffiths, NX74; 2/1 Bn. Bank officer; of Sydney; b. Sydney, 1 Oct 1910.

[1] Mackay also considered that the danger of airborne or parachute troops landing in the valley behind his brigades provided another reason why his headquarters should have been farther forward. He decided that, in such circumstances, divisional headquarters "must get forward and possibly forward of the reserve brigade".

Sperkhios River runs into the sea. From Lamia the straight main road travels due south across the flats and then zigzags up the face of the escarpment to Brallos and the rolling uplands beyond; a second road branches at Lamia across the Sperkhios and travels eastwards between the foot of the escarpment and the sea.

It was along this coastal route that the army of Xerxes the Persian advanced on Athens, and on a coastal road south-east of Lamia that Leonidas and a gallant company of Spartans were outflanked and overwhelmed by a Persian force which followed a goat track over the foothills and descended in their rear. The silting of the Sperkhios delta in the succeeding centuries had thrust the coastline some five miles to the east, but for "Thermopylae" write "Molos", and a modern defender of the pass is in a position like that on which Leonidas stood.

The area between Molos and the Brallos Pass covered only one-third of the neck of the peninsula; to the south-west between Brallos and the Gulf of Corinth lay a tangle of mountains rising to 6,000 feet, entered from the west by secondary roads at Gravia and Amfissa. Even if the two passes were held, there would be danger of the defenders being outflanked on both the east and the west—on the New Zealand side by an advance along the island of Euboea, on the Australian either by local flanking movements up the mountain tracks west of Brallos, or by a wider move down the road leading from Epirus, and thence along the north coast of the Gulf of Corinth to Amfissa. Indeed the front was too long to be defended by two divisions—as was pointed out to General Wilson by General Blamey in a message sent on the afternoon of the 20th; Blamey did not then know that a decision to embark had been reached the day before.

On the New Zealand sector the 5th Brigade was deployed along the coast road, the foothills south of Lamia, and the Sperkhios River. The 4th Brigade was on the right where it had established coast-watching patrols, the 6th was in reserve. In the forward brigade the 22nd Battalion, on the right, was on a ridge west of Molos with three companies forward. The 23rd, on the left, had one company on high ground overlooking the coast road, one forward at the bridge over the Sperkhios, another at the bridge over a tributary stream half a mile to the south, and a fourth on the high ground to the south-west linking with the Australian position.

The first Australian infantry to arrive in the Brallos area had been Vasey's incomplete 19th Brigade—the 2/4th and 2/8th Battalions, the latter far below strength. In the course of 19th April the 2/1st and 2/5th were placed under Vasey's command, and that day and during the early hours of the 20th the 2/11th rejoined the brigade for the first time since its arrival in Greece.

Early in the afternoon Mackay issued orders for the defence of the new line. He instructed Vasey, with his five battalions, to hold an area from the 1399-metre hill east of the road to the railway tunnel west of Brallos (five miles). Vasey had already placed the 2/5th on the extreme right, to link with the left of the New Zealand Division, the 2/1st astride the loop in the main road and the 2/4th on the left over the railway tunnel; thus his forward positions were well in advance of the area he was now ordered to hold. In immediate reserve at the top of the pass he placed the depleted 2/8th, and astride the road north of Brallos his main reserve —the 2/11th, a company of the 2/1st Machine Gun, and carrier platoons of the 2/1st and 2/5th Battalions.

The 1st Armoured Brigade which had been resting at Atalandi was now ordered to Thebes. Its 102nd Anti-Tank Regiment, however, was sent forward to Freyberg, who placed it with his machine-gun battalion at Longos, facing the western end of Euboea. The tank regiments had now worn out more of their few remaining tanks—the 4th Hussars had been forced to abandon seventeen on the Lamia Pass. General Wilson ordered the 3rd Royal Tanks to Athens for local defence, and sent the 2nd Royal Horse Artillery to join the New Zealand Division, thus reducing Brigadier Charrington's brigade at Thebes to one infantry battalion (the 1/Rangers), the Hussars, and the ancillary troops. On the 21st the brigade was further dispersed. The Hussars were sent south to Glyphada, near Athens, under the command of Force headquarters. Because of reports that the enemy had landed on Euboea, whence he might move on to the mainland by way of Khalkis and cut the communications of the British force at Thebes, the Rangers were sent to Khalkis.

That day the New Zealand Division's front was adjusted. The 6th Brigade moved forward to just east of Molos and took over the 28th Battalion's sector, the 24th taking position north of Molos with its right on Ayia Trias to protect the anti-tank guns on the coast road, the 25th covering the road from Alamanas bridge to Molos, and the 26th remaining in reserve. The 5th Brigade moved the 22nd Battalion to the left of the 25th and the 23rd brought in the company on the heights towards the Brallos road when these were taken over by the 2/5th. Three troops of the 64th Medium Regiment, the three field regiments of the division, one battery of the 2nd Royal Horse Artillery, the New Zealand anti-tank regiment and the 102nd were in support of the two brigades, and seventeen guns of the 5th Regiment were forward with the infantry to deal with tanks.

During the 21st, on the Australian front, the 2/11th relieved the 2/5th in the rugged, scrub-covered country on the 19th Brigade's right. At midday on the 20th Savige, whose brigade then included only the 2/6th and 2/7th Battalions, the 2/5th being in Vasey's, had received orders from Sutherland to guard four road and track exits from the mountains to the west of the Brallos position and cover the Lamia-Brallos road in depth from a point one mile north-west of Brallos. The effect of this would be to echelon the 17th Brigade behind the 19th and protect the left flank. At dusk, however, Savige received new orders, issued to him by Rowell in Mackay's presence. These were to take over part of Vasey's left flank and occupy a line covering the gorge through which the railway ran and extending along high ground about one mile to the west of Oiti (Gardikaki). In addition his left flank was to be refused for a further distance of about a mile and a half. His total front would be about six miles measured on the map. The road and track exits on the west were now made the responsibility of the 16th Brigade (two weak battalions). In conference on the 21st Savige and Vasey agreed that Savige should take over all the ground which Vasey then held west of the Lamia-Brallos road.

The country on this flank was extremely rugged. A road marked on the map as leading into the area was found to peter out, but another practicable road was found which was not on the map. By dusk on the 21st the 2/7th Battalion was in position from the main road about four miles forward of Brallos to the railway and just beyond, with the 2/6th extending the line for about four miles to the west. That day the 2/5th Battalion returned to Savige's command and went into reserve just west of Brallos.

Thus, as deployment continued, the disadvantages of the new position became increasingly apparent. Each of the two main roads needed at least a division to defend it, and although the New Zealand Division was still "reasonably complete", three battalions of the Australian had been greatly reduced in strength.[2] It seemed probable that the enemy would make a flanking move along the island of Euboea. The New Zealand Division's positions could be shelled by guns concealed in the rolling country across the strait, whereas its own guns were in exposed positions on the face of an escarpment or at its foot. The plain of Thebes offered the enemy an excellent field in which to land paratroops in the rear of the defending force, which could spare only a few carriers and other troops to protect that area. The left flank was open to attack by an enemy force moving from Epirus towards Amfissa and the Delphi Pass. This danger was underlined by the news that the *"Adolf Hitler" Division* had reached Yannina, the Greek Army of Epirus had surrendered, and the way to the Gulf of Corinth lay open.

The last account of the German operations left the head of the *40 Corps* at Kalabaka. Thence, in obedience to List's order, General Stumme ordered the *"Adolf Hitler" Division* to swing west through the Metsovon Pass towards Yannina against General Pitsikas' Greek Army of Epirus. It was approaching Yannina on 20th April when Tsolakoglou, to the surprise of both German and Italian leaders, sent his written offer to capitulate to the commander of the advancing German division. Tsolakoglou was flown to Larisa next day and there he surrendered to List's chief of staff, Greiffenberg. "In recognition of their brave bearing," wrote Greiffenberg in 1947, "all Greek officers retained their side-arms, and the men were not looked upon as prisoners of war but were to be demobilised at once by the Greek Command and repatriated."[3]

On 19th April, after the capture of Larisa, the *5th* and *2nd Armoured* and *5th* and *6th Mountain Divisions* followed the retiring British force along the main road to Lamia, German aircraft "repeatedly and successfully" attacking the retreating columns in the Thessalian plain; Volos was entered on the 21st. Cratered roads delayed the German advance.

It is evident that at this stage the German commanders had more troops than they could move with reasonable speed. Their maps show that, at dusk on the

---

[2] The 2/8th, 2/2nd and 2/3rd.
[3] Tsolakoglou himself became head of the Greek Government under the Germans from May 1941 to November 1942. In May 1945 he was sentenced to death and military degradation by a tribunal established by the restored Greek Government, but with a recommendation to mercy. His sentence was mitigated because of ill-health, and he died in a military hospital on 22 May 1948.

21st, from south to north along the Lamia-Larisa road, were strung out the *5th Armoured, 6th Mountain, 2nd Armoured* and *5th Mountain Divisions*, the *9th Armoured* remaining in the Elasson area.

By nightfall on the 20th April no hint that the British forces would be embarked had reached the corps in the field. Mackay and Freyberg had been impressing on their subordinates that there would be no more withdrawals. "I did not dream of evacuation," said Mackay afterwards. "I thought that we'd hang on for about a fortnight and be beaten by weight of numbers." Brigadier Vasey commanding the force astride the Brallos Pass had given an order: "Here we bloody well are and here we bloody well stay," which Bell,[4] his brigade major, translated: "The 19th Brigade will hold its present defensive positions come what may."

As mentioned above, Wavell arrived at Blamey's headquarters about 2 a.m. on the 21st and informed him that Tsolakoglou had surrendered, and that the British force was to be embarked. Later in the day Wavell gave Wilson a written order to embark the force on the basis of the plan prepared by the joint planning staff, and in cooperation with Rear-Admiral Baillie-Grohman. Wilson was given liberty to fix the starting day. Subject to the prior needs of the troops under his command he would, as far as possible, embark "any Greek personnel, etc., desired by the Greek Government". Every soldier must bring out as much equipment as he could carry. The order continued:

> Should part of the original scheme fail or should portions of the force become cut off, they must not surrender but should endeavour to make their way into the Peloponnese or into any of the adjacent islands. It may well be possible to rescue parties from the Peloponnese at some considerably later date. You should bear in mind the possibility of later being able to evacuate transport, guns, etc., from the Southern Peloponnesian ports or beaches.

After the conference between Wilson, Blamey and Baillie-Grohman at the roadside near Thebes on the night of the 21st, Blamey returned to Levadia arriving there before dawn on the 22nd. About 8 a.m. Mackay with Sutherland and Colonel Prior, his senior administrative officer, arrived for orders, and were given an outline of the plan. Freyberg's headquarters were so distant that a liaison officer (Wells) carried the news to him.

Wilson's detailed order confirming his plan for withdrawal from Greece was not issued until the morning of the 23rd, after Blamey and Freyberg had issued orders based on his verbal instructions. Wilson's order stated that the force was now organised into Anzac Corps, 80 Base Sub-area, 82 Base Sub-area (formed from the 1st Armoured Brigade), and the following group of units directly under Wilson's command: 4th Hussars, 3rd Royal Tanks, New Zealand Reinforcement Battalion, Australian Reinforcement Battalion. Those units were in the Athens area; thus not only was it convenient for Force headquarters to control them, but they provided some fighting troops whom it could employ in an emergency.

---

[4] Lt-Col A. T. J. Bell, OBE, VX41. RAE 6 Div 1939-41; BM 19 Bde 1941, and various staff appts in RAE. Regular soldier; of Melbourne; b. Melbourne, 10 Oct 1913.

Wilson's order added that one New Zealand brigade would occupy a covering position on the ridge south of Kriekouki (Erithrai),[5] south of Thebes on the Athens road, and named four beaches or pairs of beaches from which embarkation would take place. It also specified the staffs which would be in charge of these, the groups to be embarked, and the nights of their embarkation. The first were to leave on the 24th-25th, the last on the 26th-27th. The embarkation areas were Rafina ("C" Beach), Porto Rafti ("D" Beach), Megara ("P" Beach), Theodora ("J" Beach), Navplion ("S" and "T" Beaches).[6] The order added that as many guns as possible were to be brought out; those remaining were to be made useless by removing the breech-blocks, and all gun sights and such technical equipment as could be carried were to be brought away. No fires were to be lit. Certain stores and workshop equipment were to be handed over to the Greeks. Officers and men must wear full equipment but not packs; they might carry hard rations in greatcoat pockets, but no other articles would be allowed aboard the lighters.

Blamey's order to the corps, issued at 4 p.m. on the 22nd, stated that the covering force at Erithrai would include the 4th New Zealand Brigade, 2/3rd Field Regiment, one Australian anti-tank battery, 2/8th Australian Field Company, and one company of the 2/1st Machine Gun Battalion. "Except in the case of the move of the covering force to its covering position, only optical and technical instruments, personal arms and equipment that can be carried on the man, automatic weapons and machine-guns, together with what ammunition can be carried on the man will be moved," it added. "Otherwise technical vehicles not being used for troop-carrying and guns will be destroyed." This entailed the destruction of all guns except those of the regiment and battery mentioned above—a precipitate step in view of the complications that might ensue. It will be seen that this part of the order was later countermanded.

In daylight on the 22nd reconnaissance parties and certain unessential units were to move south in small columns. That night (22nd-23rd) the covering force should take up its position astride the Athens road, which it must deny to the enemy until early on 26th April. On the 23rd-24th one brigade group from each division, having thinned out during the day, was to move to its concealment area near its place of embarkation, the Australian brigade group to Megara, the New Zealand to Marathon. On the night of the 24th-25th these two groups would embark and the remaining brigade group of each division (the depleted 6th Division having been divided into only two groups) would each move to their allotted conceal-

---

[5] The order gave this task to "one NZ div"; evidently "one NZ bde" was intended.
[6] Before the German attack opened Gen Wilson's administrative staff had reconnoitred beaches likely to be useful for landing supplies should Piraeus and Volos be put out of action but "a secret underlying motive," wrote Brig Brunskill later, "also was the possible use for evacuation". The requirements of a beach suitable for embarkation were a motor road to within a mile or so of the beach, an assembly area near by where trees would conceal vehicles and men from aircraft, a supply of water, and a steeply shelving beach to enable small craft to run ashore without stranding. The general plan was that troops should drive from the forward areas to the assembly place in one bound by night, should lie concealed the following day, destroy their vehicles and guns at dusk, and embark between 11 p.m. and 3 a.m. thus allowing the ships to approach the beach by night and be well away at daylight.

ment area. On the 25th-26th these groups would embark. The covering force would embark on the 26th-27th. At 8 p.m. on the 23rd Blamey's headquarters was to close and make its way to its point of embarkation; Wilson's headquarters would thenceforward directly control all operations.

The embarkation beaches.

On 22nd April General Freyberg chose his 5th Brigade to move first to the point of embarkation; it was to go along the coast to Ayia Konstantinos on the night of the 22nd-23rd, and to the Marathon beaches the following night. On the night of the 24th-25th the 6th New Zealand Brigade was to withdraw. Whereas the corps order had implied that only the covering force would retain heavy weapons—and only as far as the covering position—Freyberg ordered units to "retain all their fighting equipment until embarkation".

Mackay decided that his first brigade group, to withdraw on the 23rd-24th, should consist of Allen's depleted brigade (less the 2/1st Battalion), Savige's brigade, and part of the 2/8th Battalion; it would be named "Allen Group", Allen, as senior brigadier, being in command. On the 24th-25th Vasey's brigade—including the 2/1st, 2/4th, 2/11th Battalions, two companies of the 2/8th, the 2/2nd Field Regiment, a battery of the 2/1st, and the 2/1st Field Company—would follow.

While these orders were being issued the artillery duel was becoming hotter along the whole front. The weather was still clear, and German vehicles were seen moving along the road north of Lamia and small groups of tanks and infantry moved south of that town. As the day went on, however, it became apparent that although three days had elapsed since the enemy had entered Larisa he was not yet ready to attack, presumably because the cratered roads were delaying guns and vehicles.

When the 2/2nd Field Regiment was climbing the Brallos Pass, Brigadier Herring, commanding the 6th Divisional Artillery, had ordered that two guns be pulled out and sited on the forward slope of the escarpment about two-thirds of the distance up the slope to cover the demolished bridge over the Sperkhios River. They were placed 15 feet apart on a mere ledge at the side of the road in the area held by the 2/4th Battalion and with them was an Italian Breda anti-aircraft machine-gun manned by a British crew. About 6 p.m. on the 21st the first German vehicles emerged from Lamia and began moving south along the straight road on which the guns had been carefully ranged. The gunners opened fire at 10,900 yards and, in three rounds, hit and stopped the leading truck, whereupon the remainder hastily retired to Lamia.

Throughout the night these gunners, and observers perched 400 yards farther up the slope, saw the lights of seemingly hundreds of vehicles moving down the pass into Lamia. On the morning of the 22nd four enemy guns—evidently mediums—opened fire from a wood south-east of Lamia well beyond the range of the Australians' 25-pounders, and a column of vehicles again began moving south towards the Sperkhios. Each time these vehicles came within range the Australian guns opened fire and as regularly the German medium guns replied, their shells bursting closer and closer until they were landing within 15 feet of the gun pits. One German shell hit a truck carrying smoke shells which exploded and covered the area round the Australian guns with smoke for half an hour. A trailer carrying high-explosive shells was set on fire and the shells began to explode. A dump of charges was hit and exploded, setting the scrub ablaze. Some enemy field guns which had been brought forward to the Sperkhios now began to fire, and the Australian guns replied.

By 1 o'clock in the afternoon one Australian gun was out of action through oil leaking from the recuperator. At this stage Lieutenant Anderson,[7] the young officer in command, saw that about twenty trucks had come forward to the foot of the escarpment on the left and were unloading infantrymen there. He and his men lifted the trail of the gun on to the edge of the pit so as to depress it enough to fire down the face of the hill and, using a weak charge lest the recoil should cause the gun to somersault, fired more than fifty rounds into the enemy infantry. This drew heavier shelling from the German medium guns. The Australian crews took shelter, and when they returned found that the carriage of the remaining gun had been hit and would not operate. It was then 4 p.m. The duel had lasted eight hours, and although more than 160 shells had burst round

---

[7] Capt J. R. Anderson, MC, VX587; 2/2 Fd Regt. Accountant; of Brighton Beach, Vic; b. Melbourne, 21 Jul 1914.

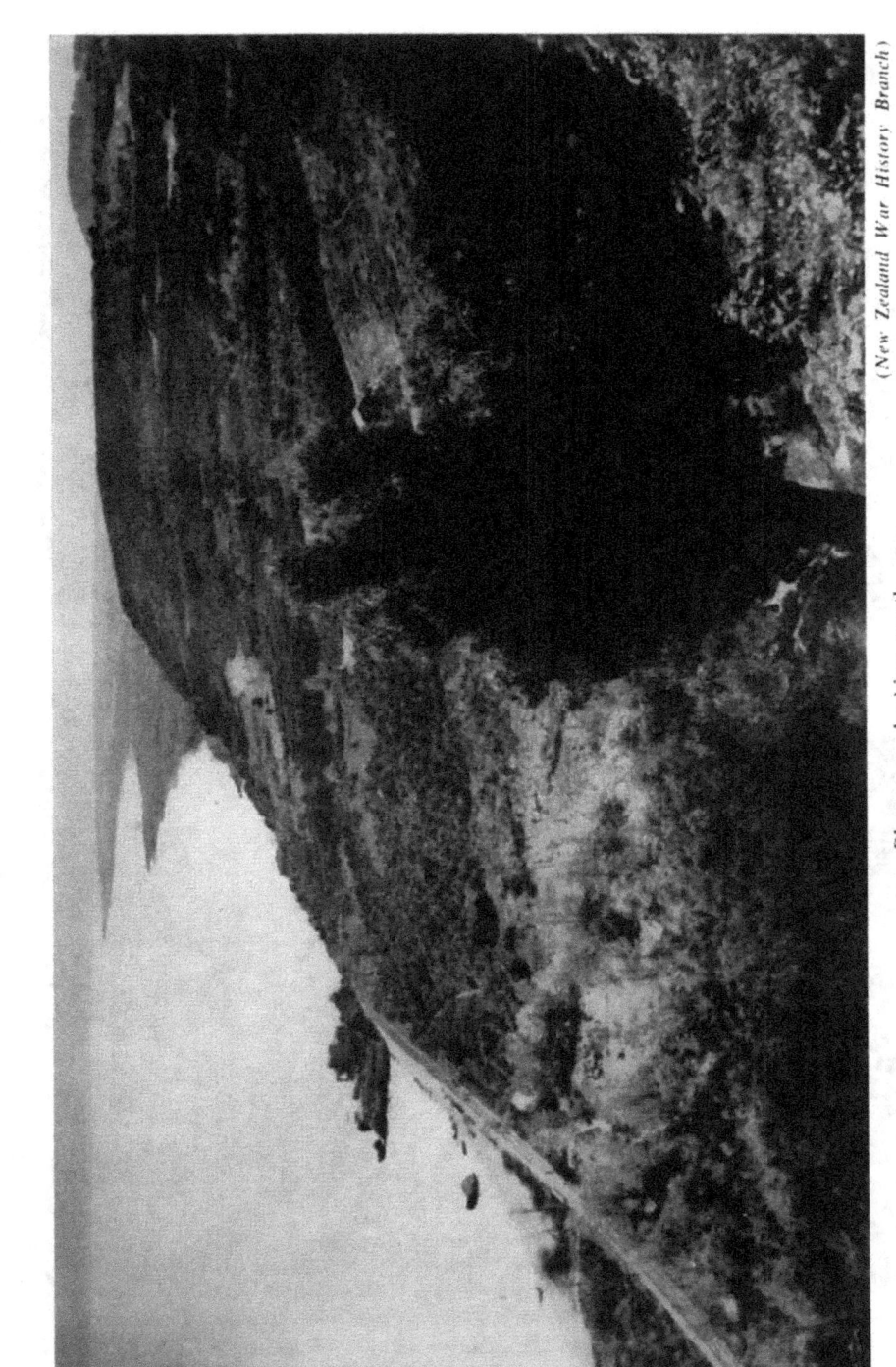

Platamon, looking south.

(New Zealand War History Branch)

Larisa during an air raid.

(New Zealand War History Branch)

An enforced stop on a train journey from Larisa during the withdrawal to the Thermopylae line.

the two exposed guns and dozens of rounds of their own ammunition had been set on fire or exploded and trucks smashed, not a man on the scarred and smoking ledge had been hit. Anderson sent half his men back up the hill with the sights and breech-block of the damaged gun and with his two sergeants, Ingram[8] and Lees,[9] and the remaining crew tried to put the other gun into action. The German guns now opened fire with deadly

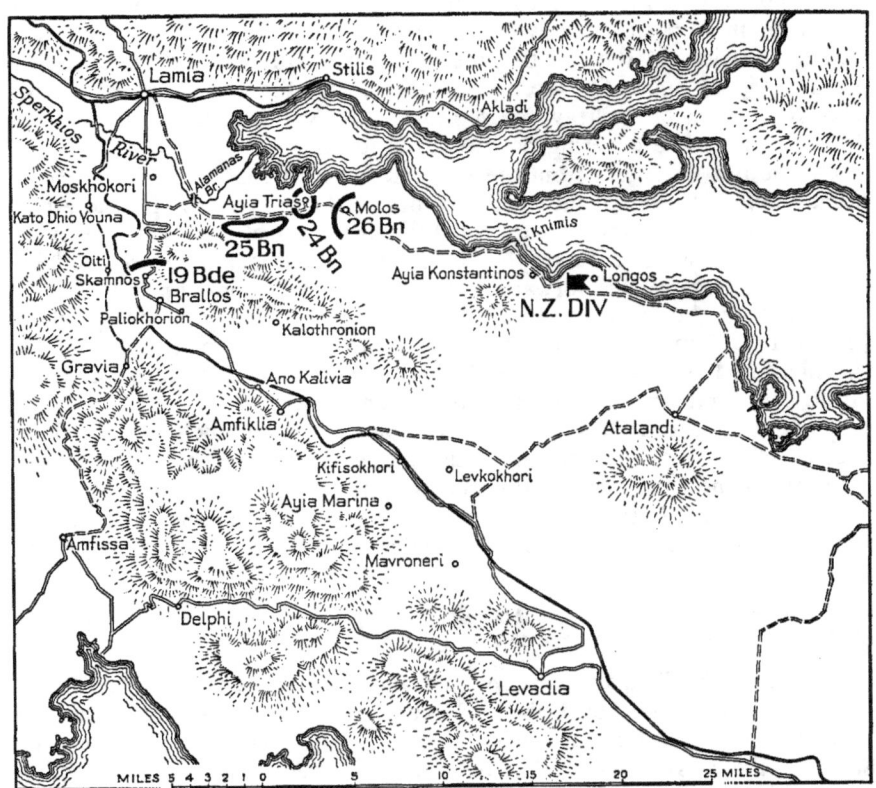

Morning, 24th April.

accuracy. One man was killed and another wounded on the hillside some distance above the guns; then, at the guns, five men were killed and three wounded, one fatally, leaving only eight unwounded, including Anderson. At dusk, after the wounded men had been carried out, Anderson and Gunner Brown[1] returned to the guns and brought away the sights and striker mechanism, and the discs and paybooks of the dead.

---

[8] Sgt L. S. Ingram, VX562; 2/2 Fd Regt. Physical culture instructor; of Albert Park, Vic; b. Albert Park, 10 Oct 1915. Killed in action 22 Apr 1941.

[9] Sgt J. H. Lees, VX809; 2/2 Fd Regt. Butcher; of Prahran, Vic; b. Abbotsford, Vic, 5 Sep 1913.

[1] Gnr E. S. Brown, MM, VX932; 2/2 Fd Regt. Tram conductor; of Kew, Vic; b. Coburg, Vic, 13 May 1908.

It will be recalled that, in consequence of the decision to embark, the defence of the Thermopylae Pass was left to Barrowclough's 6th Brigade. The four companies of the 25th Battalion were in position overlooking the road and the river, the 24th astride the road at Ayia Trias, and the 26th in rear of it astride the road at Molos. Seven artillery regiments (four field, one medium, and two anti-tank) were in support—a formidable array. Forward were sixty men of the 22nd in "skeleton positions" on the left of the main position, sixty of the 23rd at the bridge over the Sperkhios and the carriers of the 5th Brigade which were to patrol the flats north of the road at night. On the night of the 22nd the 5th Brigade, having destroyed much of its heavy gear, moved to Ayia Konstantinos, and the 4th Brigade to the covering position at Erithrai.

On the 6th Division's front the rearward guns of the 2/2nd Field Regiment continued firing at the Sperkhios bridge. In the course of 22nd April German patrols had moved on to high ground west of the road and overlooking the position occupied by the 2/1st Battalion and overlooked by the 2/4th. Because his forward posts were so far from the road Vasey decided to withdraw them about two miles to a more compact position just north of Brallos. The vehicles did not arrive at the right time and on the night of the 23rd-24th the 2/11th Battalion had to make an arduous climb back to the position it had left not long before.

On the 21st and 22nd the troops deployed in and behind the Thermopylae line were attacked from the air as heavily as before.[2] On the morning of the 21st a reconnaissance aircraft was flying low over the area occupied by the 2/1st Field Company when Sapper Atkinson[3]—a noted marksman—put a Bren gun to his shoulder and fired a burst into the plane which

seemed to stop in mid-air (wrote the unit's diarist), nosed over, hit the ground and exploded in a burst of flame and thick oily smoke.

The 23rd April again was fine. During the day it was reported that the enemy had landed on Euboea. Reconnaissance aircraft saw no movement on the island but nevertheless Wilson's staff were anxious about the safety of the crossing at Khalkis. Freyberg was ordered to take what action he could to reinforce the 1/Rangers there, and Charrington to hold the crossing until 9 p.m. on the 25th when the 6th Brigade would be well south of it. He was told that the 6th would leave a rearguard on the high ground north of Tatoi until the Rangers had passed through. Thereupon the Rangers withdrew a company that had been placed on the Euboea side of the crossing and blew charges on the bridge.

In the Thermopylae sector during the 23rd the British medium guns, under intermittent attack by dive bombers, engaged German artillery east

---

[2] Savige wrote afterwards that, on the 22nd, when three enemy planes reached a spot south of his headquarters "one pulled off and flew at right angles and made a straight line of smoke; the next went a little further and made a perfect smoke circle; the third further still, made another straight line of smoke parallel with the first. This was no sooner finished when bombers appeared and bombed all vehicles and tented areas except those within the area marked by the smoke circle. Therein, and on the ground, was our field ambulance."

[3] Spr J. Atkinson, NX8453; 2/1 Fd Coy. Butcher, of Gulgong, NSW; b. Mudgee, NSW, 18 Oct 1905.

of Lamia. In the evening a German advance towards the Sperkhios bridge was stopped by the detachments of the 22nd and 23rd Battalions (which withdrew during the night, the infantry to Molos and the carriers to a rearguard force under Colonel Clifton at Cape Knimis). Thinning out had continued during the day. The 4th Field Regiment, less a battery, withdrew and joined the 5th Brigade, which moved during the night to its concealment area near the embarkation beach at Marathon.[4]

On the 23rd the 19th Brigade withdrew to its new position at Brallos. A rearguard was formed by two companies of the 2/1st Battalion on top of the pass overlooking the Lamia plain. After having put these companies in position Colonel Campbell reconnoitred a circuitous mountain road along which they could withdraw next day.

Meanwhile the possibility of the enemy cutting across the line of retreat by way of the Delphi Pass was causing uneasiness at Wilson's headquarters. Greek headquarters ordered a detachment of infantry and anti-tank guns to Navpaktos and a battalion (the Reserve Officers' College Battalion— perhaps the only competent unit left to them) to Patras with some field guns, the task of the two forces being to prevent an enemy advance along either the north or south shore of the Gulf of Corinth. General Wilson sent also to Patras the 4th Hussars, its fighting vehicles now reduced to twelve light tanks, six carriers and an armoured car, and most of its men organised in rifle troops. In the morning the air force reported that there was no significant movement along the road leading from Yannina, but early in the afternoon a report reached Blamey's headquarters that hundreds of vehicles were streaming south from that town. Rowell calculated that they might reach Delphi next day, and informed Blamey, who decided to demolish the road at Delphi and establish a force covering it.

He ordered Brigadier Steele to damage the road so thoroughly that the enemy would be delayed for twenty-four hours even if the demolitions were not defended. Steele collected a party of sappers and took them some 30 miles towards Amfissa. As they returned they destroyed bridges and culverts and cratered defiles. Finally Steele reconnoitred a site covering the last demolished bridge about three miles east of Levadia. The force to occupy this position was detailed by General Mackay and consisted of the 2/5th Battalion (Lieut-Colonel King) with a troop of field guns and a company of machine-gunners. King's column drove throughout the night with lights on[5] (German aircraft had rarely attacked at night) and by dawn was in position three miles west of Levadia covering demolitions in the road.

On the 22nd the German Air Force again attacked the Athens aerodromes in force and Air Vice-Marshal D'Albiac had sent the remaining Hurricanes to Argos, where on the 23rd the Germans struck again and

---

[4] The 21 Bn, only 132 strong, moved on to Rafina. The 28th (Maori) had taken the place of this bn in the bde.

[5] On the 21st Mackay had ordered that, except on moonlit nights, vehicles would use dimmed headlights provided that they were not visible to the enemy on the ground. Lights, he ordered, were to be switched off only when vehicles were halted.

destroyed thirteen of them on the ground. D'Albiac ordered the remainder to Crete.

At Athens the King of Greece announced that he would transfer his government to Crete and continue the fight there. The officers of the British Base Sub-area in Athens paid all outstanding accounts, the supply depot was handed over to the Greeks,[6] the canteen stores to the American Red Cross, and the Pioneer Corps companies (mostly Palestinians, Arabs and Cypriots under middle-aged British officers) were taken by train to Argos and Navplion. A party of New Zealand nurses and 400 walking wounded were sent to Argos, and other wounded to Megara.

At 3 a.m. on the 23rd Colonel Rogers, Blamey's senior Intelligence officer, and six other officers[7] appointed by Blamey to report at Wilson's headquarters for embarkation duties, had arrived at Athens. Searching for an officer of Wilson's headquarters who could give him instructions, Rogers at length found Major Packard[8] of Wilson's staff who appeared to be coordinating all arrangements with the navy. Packard said that the Australians' role would be to provide beach parties for Rafina, Porto Rafti and Tolos. Rogers appointed these parties, and detailed officers to establish liaison with the New Zealand and the Australian divisions and to ensure that the groups knew the routes they should follow.[9]

On the night of the 23rd-24th the withdrawal of the 17th Brigade from its position on the left of the line and the movement of the combined 16th and 17th Brigades to Megara to await embarkation were achieved remarkably smoothly. Savige's orders provided that the 2/6th Battalion on the left would begin thinning out at 7 p.m. and hold its forward posts until 9, the 2/7th would begin thinning out at 8.30 and hold its forward posts until 9.30. Despite the fact that the forward battalions were deployed over a six-mile front and had to scramble out of extremely rough country, the time-table was adhered to. At daybreak Colonel Prior of Mackay's staff halted the column at Eleusis, where there was good cover and, all that day (the 24th), the men of "Allen Group" lay concealed and resting in olive groves on each side of the Athens road. The diarist of the provost company of the 6th Division underlined the wisdom of Mackay's order that lights (dimmed) should be used in the withdrawal.

---

[6] Next day Gen Freyberg saw Greeks looting some of the dumps in the Athens area.

[7] They were: Majs G. E. W. Hurley (of Melbourne), K. A. Wills, C. C. F. Spry (Brisbane), E. Mander-Jones (Wahroonga, NSW), and Capts A. W. Aubrey (Sydney) and L. Luxton (Adelaide). Additional officers and other ranks were to join them from Australian headquarters and 6th and NZ Divisions.

[8] Maj-Gen C. D. Packard, CB, CBE, DSO. GHQ ME (Plans) 1941; GSO1 Eighth Army 1941-42; CO 1 RHA 1942-43; Dep Ch of Staff 15 Army Gp 1944-45. Regular soldier, of Copdock, nr Ipswich, Eng; b. Bramford, Suffolk, Eng, 17 May 1903.

[9] Col Rogers afterwards wrote that he explained to his officers that "there seemed to be some uncertainty at Force HQ in respect to responsibility for ensuring that all the necessary and complex details of embarkation were completely understood and acted upon, and we proposed therefore to accept the responsibility ourselves, not only for embarkation at those beaches for which we were required to provide parties, but also to see that all Australian and New Zealand units knew the precise routes by which they would proceed to beaches, the bases at which they would assemble and the beaches from which they would embark". Rogers made the following principal appointments: Staff officer, Maj Hurley; Liaison officer to NZ Div, Maj Wills; LO to 6 Div, Maj Spry; OC roads and traffic, Maj E. Mander-Jones; OC "D" Beach collecting area, Maj A. W. Sheppard; "T" Beach collecting area, Maj B. J. O'Loughlin; "T" Beach party, Maj F. W. MacLean; "C" Beach collecting area, Maj S. J. Kelly; "C" Beach party, Maj T. H. E. Oakes; "D" Beach party, Maj G. F. Bertrand.

Orders were that Div troops would pass starting point at the junction of the Atalandi-Athens roads 15 minutes after N.Z. troops had passed through about 0000 hrs, and 16 Bde about 0300 hours. The N.Z. troops and vehicles coming through had no lights and march discipline was poor, consequently there was considerable delay . . . and the end of the column did not pass until 0130 hrs . . . much congestion at Levadia due to Greek troops trying to cut in. From then on only trouble occasioned by odd groups of vehicles. Traffic control excellent and an average speed of 20 M.I.H. (miles in the hour) was maintained until camping area was reached near Eleusis. Distance covered [by 6 Div troops] was 72 miles and all troops reached their destination by 0700 hours . . . . A very remarkable performance considering the heavy traffic on the road, entirely due to good traffic control.

The operation order for the embarkation was the last which Anzac Corps issued. At 8 p.m. on the 23rd, Corps headquarters closed at Levadia and opened at Mandra. It ceased to function at midnight on the 23rd-24th. At that time General Blamey reported to General Wilson in Athens and was ordered to embark next morning in a flying-boat for Alexandria, where he was to see Admiral Cunningham "and press on him the urgency of their position". Blamey then returned to Mandra and informed Rowell of this order. He told him also that Wilson had said that it would now be impossible for troops to embark from the Athens beaches as arranged and that the plan would have to be revised to provide for embarkation of larger numbers from beaches in the Peloponnese. Rowell protested that, in view of this changed situation, Anzac Corps headquarters should remain, but Blamey replied that he had been ordered to go.

Blamey arrived at Alexandria at midday on the 24th and immediately saw Cunningham who (in Blamey's words) "had not till then been fully impressed with the full seriousness of the position, and immediately sent out all available vessels to assist". On the other hand Cunningham had been informed on the 22nd that the first day of the embarkation had been advanced to the 24th, and enough ships to carry out the first embarkation had been sent out.

When he reached Egypt Blamey was appointed Deputy Commander-in-Chief of the British forces in the Middle East. On 26th February he had informed Mr Menzies that he had suggested to General Wavell that, since Australians were to form the largest contingent in Greece, he (Blamey) should command the whole force. This suggestion, which was later raised by Mr Menzies at a meeting of the British War Cabinet, was not accepted. In April, however, the Secretary of the Australian Defence Department, Mr Shedden, who was with Menzies in London, suggested that Blamey be considered for the Western Desert Command. On 19th April Menzies discussed Blamey's future with Dill, who consulted Wavell. Wavell recommended that Blamey be appointed his deputy, the Australian Government concurred, and Blamey took up the new appointment as from 23rd April —thus, incidentally, becoming senior to the commander under whom he had just been serving in Greece.

When Anzac Corps headquarters closed direct control of the embarkation passed to Wilson's headquarters. On the afternoon of the 24th both

Mackay and Freyberg received an order from that headquarters that they and their staffs were to embark that night. In consequence of this order the officers and men of Mackay's headquarters set off for the Argos area, their appointed place of embarkation, late that afternoon. Mackay and his aide-de-camp embarked in a flying-boat and were flown to Crete early next morning. The remainder had sailed in a cruiser during the night.

Freyberg, however, disregarded the order to embark. When it arrived his forward troops were in the midst of a hard fight against German tanks at the Thermopylae Pass. Freyberg wrote later:

> I cabled back to G.H.Q., Athens, and told them I was being attacked by tanks, fighting a battle on a two-brigade front, and asked who was to command the New Zealand troops if I left. I was given the answer of "Movement Control". I naturally went on with the battle. After that I never received an order as to my disposal.

At this stage three Australian brigades, three New Zealand brigades, one British brigade, and the throng of base units, labour battalions and Yugoslavs were still in Greece. If Freyberg had obeyed the order to embark only Wilson's staff would have remained to control seven fighting formations, several detached units, and a multitude of base troops.

On the 24th (as Wilson had forecast to Blamey) the plan of embarkation was revised with the object of moving farther south, reducing the numbers to be lifted from Theodora, Argos and Navplion, and making more use of destroyers and of the comparatively distant beach at Kalamata. Finally Theodora was abandoned and Brigadier Parrington[1] was sent to take command at Kalamata. Arrangements were made also to take aboard there about 2,000 Yugoslav soldiers and refugees who had retreated down the Greek peninsula. Under the revised plan one of the largest groups, Allen's combined 16th and 17th Brigades, would not embark from Megara on the 24th-25th but would move to the Argos area and possibly make a further move to Kalamata and not embark until the 26th-27th. The embarkation would now probably be made as follows:

April	Athens Beaches	Megara	Navplion	Tolos	Kalamata
24th-25th	5 Bde	—	Corps R.A.F. etc.	—	—
25th-26th	19 Bde part 1 Armd Bde	—	—	—	—
26th-27th	6 Bde part 1 Armd Bde	4 Bde	Base details 3 R Tanks 4 Hussars	Base details	16 Bde 17 Bde 4,000 base

The error of ordering the corps and divisional commanders from Greece was now clearly revealed. Under the new plan Allen Group would embark

---
[1] Brig L. Parrington, MC; RA. Regular soldier; b. Holborough, Kent, Eng, 24 Feb 1890.

not that night from Megara, at the same time as its divisional staff embarked from Navplion, but two nights later, and probably from a beach more than 100 miles away. Allen's staff consisted only of his brigade major (Hammer); his Intelligence officer, Captain Lovell;[2] and two young junior officers from the divisional staff (Captain Vial and Lieutenant Knox[3]); yet the strength of his group approached that of a division—it included seven battalions and two artillery regiments.[4] He organised it into four sections: the 16th Brigade and attached troops under Colonel Lamb; 17th Brigade and attached troops under Brigadier Savige; a section including the machine-gun and anti-tank unit under Lieut-Colonel Gooch;[5] and a section including the corps engineers and signallers and others under Lieut-Colonel Kendall.[6]

The revision of the plan of embarkation made it necessary to take new defensive measures especially against possible German paratroop attack at Corinth and in the Peloponnese. A small force of New Zealand engineers and infantry and British anti-aircraft artillery ("Isthmus Force") was sent to Corinth to prepare demolitions and keep the roads open. In addition Brigadier Lee was appointed area commander in the Peloponnese with the special task of guarding the now-abandoned airfields.

On 24th April the capitulation of the Greek Army had been confirmed. General Papagos resigned. One of the last orders to the Greek troops had been to keep off the roads of southern Greece to facilitate the movement of the British force. That day King George and some of his Ministers left Athens in a flying-boat for Crete to re-establish the government there.

It will be recalled that in the Molos bottleneck the 24th Battalion was on the right, the 25th on the left and the 26th in reserve. The junction of the forward battalions was the main road, whence the front of the 24th ran north-east to the sea, and of the 25th westward along the road to within three miles of the Alamanas bridge. The gap between the 25th's left and the right of the Australians in the Brallos Pass could not be effectively covered by fire. The dried marshes to the north were passable by tanks and it seemed clear that an effective tank attack on the Molos position could come only from that direction and that a tank attack along the road could easily be dealt with. Consequently the field guns were sited where they could fire most effectively on the marshes. The two battalions were supported by a medium regiment, four field regiments (three New Zealand, one Royal Horse Artillery), two anti-tank regiments and a light anti-aircraft battery.

---

[2] Lt-Col D. J. H. Lovell, NX53. 16 Bde; CO 55/53 Bn 1942-45. Bank officer; of Haberfield and Bellevue Hill, NSW; b. Stanmore, NSW, 17 Dec 1911.

[3] Maj D. W. R. Knox, VX174; 6 Cav Regt. Merchant and Agent; of Toorak, Vic; b. Melbourne, 4 Dec 1916.

[4] 2/2, 2/3, 2/5, 2/6, 2/7, 2/8 Inf and 2/1 MG Bns; 2/1 Fd Regt, 2/1 A-Tk Regt.

[5] Brig T. N. Gooch, CBE, WX1571. BM 21 Bde 1940; CO 2/1 MG Bn 1941 and various staff and trg appts. Regular soldier; of Sydney; b. Mount Morgan, Qld, 10 Jan 1899.

[6] Maj-Gen R. Kendall, CBE, VX12703. CO Sigs I Corps 1940-41 and 1942-43; Aust Mil Mission Washington 1943-45. Regular soldier; of Melbourne; b. Sydney, 1 Nov 1897.

The fight began in earnest about 2 p.m. on the 24th, when two German tanks moving across the swamp land in front of the 25th were knocked out at long range by field guns. No other tanks attempted to cross the marshes. Motor-cyclists and cyclists, followed by four tanks, then drove along the road. The infantry moved into the hills south of the road when the 25th Battalion fired on them; soon the left of that battalion was under heavy fire from the hills west and south-west and was gradually pushed back. About 3 p.m. the main German attack opened. A group of tanks pushed along the road followed by lorry-loads of infantry and more tanks. Heavy and accurate artillery fire was brought down, but within an hour tanks were getting close to the 25th. One thrust at 4 p.m. was pushed back, but another heavier one followed and tanks advanced into the infantry positions. Numbers of these were hit by field gunners of the 5th Field Regiment, the foremost troop of which was largely in front of the infantry. One gun under Lieutenant Parkes[7] hit tank after tank at ranges from 400 to 600 yards. With burning hulls in front of them and behind them, some of the surviving tanks tried to get away but mostly failed to manoeuvre past the derelicts blocking the road. They were shielded, however, by tanks knocked out in front and screened by smoke and turned their fire on to the 25th Battalion, which suffered heavily.

By 5.15 p.m. fourteen tanks had advanced almost to the extreme right of the 25th. Two more then advanced but the leader was quickly destroyed by the guns when it reached a little bridge on the right boundary of the 25th. For six miles westward from the bridge wrecked tanks were smoking. At least fifteen were knocked out during the day and many others damaged. One gun, whose layer was Bombardier Santi,[8] had set nine tanks on fire; this gun and another destroyed a total of eleven between them.

At this stage Brigadier Miles,[9] commanding the artillery, ordered defensive fire by three regiments on the road by Thermopylae and this defeated all further attempts to bring tanks forward. Towards the end of the day, however, penetration to the rear of the 25th became threatening. It was countered by sending two carrier platoons into the hills and two companies, one from the 26th and the other from the 24th, to extend the 25th's flank. After dark, drivers drove boldly along the road past the destroyed German tanks and picked up the gallant crews of those guns that were now in front of the infantry. During the day enemy air attack had little effect on the fighting, though it made movement difficult behind the front.

In the afternoon Freyberg had received the disturbing news that the trucks of the ammunition column which were to carry out some of the infantry could not be found. He immediately told Miles that as many of the infantry as possible were to be carried on the artillery vehicles, and the remainder would march. After dark the enemy infantry pressed forward

---

[7] Capt H. K. Parkes; 5 NZ Fd Regt. Accountant; b. Dunedin, NZ, 5 May 1918. Killed in action 24 Oct 1942.
[8] Bdr E. W. Santi, DCM; 5 NZ Fd Regt. Tinsmith; of Wellington, NZ; b. 27 Dec 1917. Killed in action 29 May 1941.
[9] Brig R. Miles, CBE, DSO, MC. (1914-18: CO 15 NZ Fd Bty; BM NZ Div Arty.) CRA NZ Div 1940–41. Regular soldier; b. Springston, Canterbury, NZ, 10 Dec 1892. Died 26 Oct 1943.

with determination and the artillery duel continued. At 9.15 p.m. the good news arrived that the ammunition vehicles were on the way, and soon afterwards the troops began to thin out and board them. The medium and field guns were destroyed, the last of them—guns of the 2nd Royal Horse Artillery—at 11.50. By midnight the last vehicles were clear of Molos and the long column was moving south through the rearguard at Cape Knimis and thence to Atlandi. Thenceforward they drove with full lights on, down the main road and through the main rearguard at Erithrai.

By midday the column had travelled 100 miles and was passing through Athens. Miles had been sent forward to Athens to arrange for Force headquarters to picquet the street corners and guide the column through, but he arrived at the Acropole Hotel only in time to meet the last two officers of Wilson's staff leaving it. Consequently he had to determine a route, return to the head of the column, meet the leading trucks, and post at street corners utterly weary men who had fought the previous day and travelled that night and half the next day.

In Athens the long column of battered, muddy trucks, many bearing the scars of battle, had "a most pathetic, touching reception".

> No one who passed through the city with Barrowclough's brigade will ever forget it. Nor will we ever think of the Greek people without the war recollection of that morning—25th April, 1941. Trucks, portees and men showed plainly the marks of twelve hours battle and the 160 miles march through the night. We were nearly the last British troops they would see and the Germans might be on our heels; yet cheering, clapping crowds lined the streets and pressed about our cars, so as almost to hold us up. Girls and men leapt on the running boards to kiss or shake hands with the grimy, weary gunners. They threw flowers to us and ran beside us crying: "Come back—you must come back again—Good-bye—Good luck."[1]

"They appeared heart-broken," wrote Freyberg, "that our efforts to help them had brought disaster upon our force."

Meanwhile on the left flank, high in the hills, the 19th Brigade had also felt the weight of the German attack. Astride the main road, the 2/11th Battalion now commanded by Major Sandover,[2] Colonel Louch having been invalided out, was deployed with one company (Lieutenant McRobbie) to the east of the road, two (Captain Jackson[3] and Captain Wood[4]) west of it and one company in support. The battalion did not finish arriving in its new position until 5 a.m., after a long night march from its former position in the hills on the right. To the right of the 2/11th and under its command was a group of one officer and 48 men of the 2/8th. The 2/1st Battalion (less two companies) was covering the tracks leading through Kalothronion to the right rear of the 2/11th's position.

---

[1] Lt-Col R. P. Waller "With the 1st Armoured Brigade in Greece," *Journal of the Royal Artillery*, Jul 1945.

[2] Brig R. L. Sandover, DSO, WX5. CO 2/11 Bn 1941-43; Comd 6 Inf Bde 1943-45. Accountant and coy director; of London, and Perth, WA; b. Richmond, Surrey, Eng, 28 Mar 1910.

[3] Lt-Col D. A. C. Jackson, OBE, MC, WX32. 2/11 Bn; CO 2/6 Bn 1945. School teacher; of South Perth, WA; b. Guildford, WA, 12 Jul 1916.

[4] Capt S. F. Wood, WX1527; 2/11 Bn. School teacher; of South Perth, WA; b. London, 28 May 1904. Killed in action 28 May 1941.

One company of the 2/1st, under Captain Embrey, was detached to cover demolitions in the defile at Gravia through which ran a road from Amfissa, toward which, as mentioned above, German troops from Epirus were reported to be advancing. The 2/4th Battalion was in position astride the road five miles south of Brallos. Vasey ordered that the 2/1st was to retire on to the main road during the 24th, arriving there about 6 p.m.

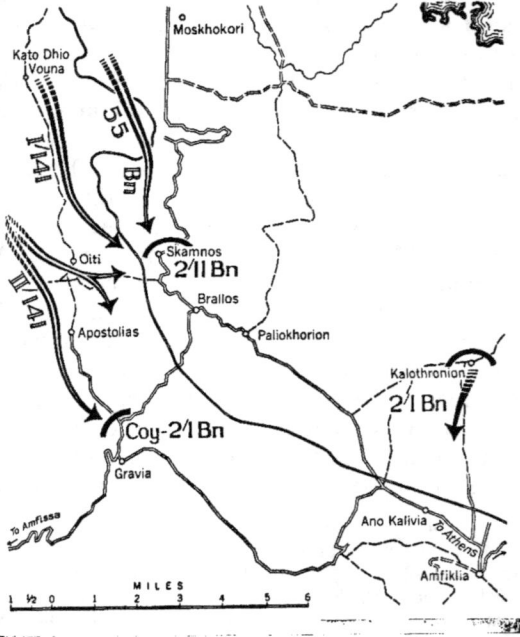

The gun positions of the 2/2nd Regiment had been severely attacked by aircraft on the 23rd; foreseeing other raids, the commanding officer, Colonel Cremor, ordered that the guns be moved at night to new positions 1,000 to 1,500 yards to the rear, but that camouflage nets be left over the old pits. These pits were in the area now occupied by the 2/11th Battalion, which adjusted its positions to keep well clear of them. In the morning 65 dive bombers came over and in two hours made 125 bombing attacks on the abandoned positions then occupied by Captain McPherson,[5] observing for the regiment, and four men.

Early in the morning of the 24th German trucks were seen in the distance crossing the repaired bridge over the Sperkhios and tanks moving south along the road and then wheeling eastwards against the New Zealanders. At 11.30 machine-gunners (of the 2/1st Machine Gun Battalion) attached to the 2/11th began firing on advanced enemy infantry on the near side of the railway line; there was intermittent fire throughout the day until at 4.50 the enemy began showering mortar bombs on the left company of the battalion, killing or wounding the commander (Wood), all the section leaders and eight others in one platoon, and disabling one of the supporting Vickers guns. This bombardment was the prelude to a determined attack. At 5.40 after exchanges of fire in which Germans were shot on the edge of the scrub at 30 yards' range, the forward companies were withdrawn. Sandover brought his reserve company (Captain

---

[5] Maj R. E. McPherson, MC, VX351. 2/2 Fd Regt 1939-43; CBO I Corps 1944-45. Mechanical engineer; of Ascot Vale, Vic; b. Brunswick, Vic, 16 Dec 1913.

McCaskill[6]) forward to a hill to the south of the vacated ground which it and the attached machine-gunners covered with fire.

By this time the 2/1st had withdrawn to the main road, as planned, and was facing the mountain road along which it had come. On the western flank, however, German infantry had appeared to the west of Gravia about 6 p.m., and there Captain Embrey's detached company of the 2/1st exchanged fire with them until dusk. Also about 6 o'clock Vasey, fearing a break-through on the 2/11th's front, decided to accelerate the withdrawal by ordering the 2/1st, 2/4th and the attached troops to embus at 8 p.m., not 8.30 as planned; and told Sandover that he need hold his positions till 9 p.m. only, not 9.30 p.m.

After Vasey had withdrawn the 2/1st, except for Embrey's company, the German infantry were firing on the right company of the 2/11th and on the detachment of the 2/8th Battalion on high ground on the right flank. Sandover withdrew the latter to Brallos village and reinforced his left company with two carriers. Meanwhile Captain Honner, his second-in-command, had organised a new position placing survivors of Wood's company on a line to the left of the road to the rear of the forward companies. Jackson's company was now withdrawn to the new position. The battalion was firmly in position but in danger of attack on either flank. However, the German infantry seemed to tire, and whereas at 8 o'clock they were still thrusting hard, half an hour later there was no real pressure on the West Australian posts. Sandover ordered the two forward companies to begin withdrawing at 8.50 and abandon their positions at 9, falling back through the companies deployed astride the road to the rear.

Originally the 2/2nd Field Regiment had been ordered to destroy its guns at Brallos, but later in the afternoon Cremor was ordered to preserve them and move them south, each with thirty rounds of ammunition. At that stage there were not thirty rounds a gun remaining, and they were still in action. So that some shells would be left, firing was reduced to one round from each gun every five minutes—enough merely to remind the enemy that they were still there. At 8.30 p.m. the guns were withdrawn. The only road that would carry heavy and concentrated traffic was the main road through Brallos. On Vasey's orders the 2/1st Field Company, equipped only with hand tools, air compressors and a limited quantity of explosive, had made a track some three miles long from Brallos north-east over very rough country to the gun positions. This was used to withdraw the 2/2nd Field Regiment, and then was demolished by the engineers who had so recently made it.

At 9 p.m. McCaskill's company of the 2/11th withdrew along the main road and McRobbie's round the right flank. Just as McRobbie's last platoon was leaving its position Corporal Brand[7] was badly wounded and the

---

[6] Capt D. M. McCaskill, WX37; 2/11 Bn. Mechanical draughtsman; of Mount Lawley, WA; b. Shepparton, Vic, 20 Feb 1916.

[7] WO2 D. Brand, WX1030. 2/11 Bn 1939-42; VDC 1942-44. Miner; of Mullewa, WA; b. Dongarra, WA, 1 Aug 1912. MLA since 1945; Minister for Housing 1949, for Works and Water Supply since 1950.

platoon returned to its posts for ten minutes to ensure that he was carried safely to the rear.

Meanwhile the 2/8th detachment had been sent back to Brallos to embus and Embrey's company of the 2/1st had been called in. There was now no pressure on the main rearguard position. When the road behind the rearguard was clear Honner, whom Sandover had left in command of the forward companies while he supervised the embussing at Brallos, started a leap-frog withdrawal, one company moving back a few hundred yards and the other then moving through it. The embussing was slow because each vehicle had to reverse down a side track to turn. While it was in progress Bell, Vasey's brigade major, appeared and said that Vasey was anxious lest the enemy troops who had been moving round the western flank and appeared to be in Gravia should reach the Ano Kalivia road junction before the brigade had passed it. Bell at once left with three carriers with the intention of blocking the southern road. At 10.15 as the last trucks moved off south-east along the road, the men kneeling in the vehicles with their automatic weapons pointing outwards, German Very lights were rising 500 yards south of Brallos.

There remained one other rearguard to the north of the force at Erithrai —King's 2/5th Battalion group in position just west of Levadia covering the road leading through Delphi. As mentioned earlier it had been placed there on the 23rd because of reports that German vehicles were moving along the road from Epirus in the direction of Delphi and might cut the Athens road. In fact they were probably Greek vehicles. The German advance from Yannina had not yet begun. Untroubled, the 2/5th moved out from its positions at 3 a.m. and drove south to rejoin (it hoped) the 17th Brigade to which it belonged. Thus, by the early morning of the 25th the whole of "W" Group had moved through the rearguard at Erithrai and, again, miles of cratered roads separated it from the advancing German army.

On 20th April the four German divisions which had been in action in the Aliakmon-Olympus area were bunched between Elasson and Larisa, and the pursuit of "W" Group was taken up by the *5th Armoured Division*. This formation had made a remarkably rapid march: from Sofia, which it left on 7th April, it had advanced north-west to Nish in Yugoslavia, helped to disperse the defending forces there, swung south in the wake of the corps which was moving down the Florina Valley, and reached Monastir on the 13th. Three days later it was at Grevena, and, on the 18th, was approaching Kalabaka, whence, travelling through Karditsa not Larisa, it cut in and reached the Larisa-Lamia road ahead of the *2nd Armoured Division*. It advanced to Lamia, where the *6th Mountain Division* joined it on the 23rd. The attacks on the Thermopylae position were made by these divisions and part of the *72nd*. The German plan was to send a mountain regiment through the hills west of the Brallos Pass towards Gravia, while the main force attacked along the coast road towards Molos.

The force which was to encircle the Anzac left flank at Gravia included the *I* and *II Battalions* of the *141st Regiment* and a dismounted motor battalion of the *5th Armoured Division*. It reached Kato Dhio Vouna early on the 22nd and thence found it very heavy going. At 2 p.m. it reported seeing "English outposts" withdrawing south and east. By nightfall the troops of the motor battalion were "completely exhausted", and from 11.30 p.m. onwards they were shelled, and got little rest that night. The next day was spent resting and reorganising. The Commander, Colonel Jais, decided to attack toward Brallos at 6 a.m. on the 24th. On the morning of the 24th the German commanders learnt that the main body of the defending force had withdrawn. In consequence the *II/141st Battalion* was ordered to advance south-east and cut the road about five miles south of Brallos while the remainder of Jais' group attacked towards Brallos. At 7.30 a.m. dive bombers attacked the Australian positions. The main thrust against the 2/11th was made by three companies of the *141st Mountain Regiment* and two of the *55th Motor Battalion*, with a machine-gun platoon and a heavy mortar section attached to each company. The *55th* was effectively shelled and at 11.30 was pinned down by artillery and machine-gun fire. "It seemed almost impossible to get out of the zone of fire and advance," the battalion reported. "Any movement, even by individual men, was seen by the enemy and engaged at once with HMG fire.

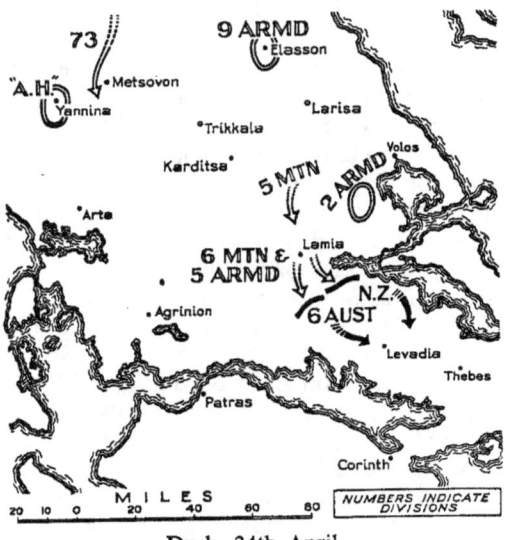

Dusk, 24th April.

We lost one killed and several wounded. It took several hours for the troops to approach the enemy and reach the northern slope of the heights just west of Skamnos."

Later the *I/141st* on the right drew level with the *55th* at midday and the enemy artillery fire was switched on to it. During the afternoon the Germans continued to press forward and about 6 p.m. came under fire from heavy machine-guns which were well camouflaged and had not fired before. At this stage, however, their heavy mortars arrived forward and these silenced one Australian post after another. According to the German account, the attackers then "stormed" Skamnos at 7 p.m. and the positions south-west of it about 8 p.m. (This is an exaggeration; the forward Australian companies were still in position at 9 p.m. and the German pressure slackened about 8.30.) At 8.30 the leading company of the *II Battalion* was a few hundred yards from the Brallos-Gravia road. About midnight the leading Germans reached Paliokhorion.

The attack towards Molos on the New Zealand front was opened by a reconnaissance unit, a cavalry squadron, two cycle squadrons and an infantry battalion. These made insignificant progress and in the afternoon a company of 18 tanks, including four Mark IV's armed with 75-mm guns, advanced. Twelve of these became total losses, and, of the 70 who manned them, 7 were killed and 22 wounded. The other units appear to have suffered about 70 casualties.

This was the second time within a fortnight that German armoured forces, hitherto seemingly invincible, had been halted with heavy loss by resolute infantry and artillery. At Tobruk on 11th April an attempt to break into that fortress had been defeated, the Germans leaving 17 wrecked tanks on the field. About the same number were knocked out at Thermopylae, though the Germans regarded only 12 as total losses. On 1st May a similar attack would be defeated at Tobruk, with even heavier casualties.

CHAPTER 7

THE EMBARKATION FROM GREECE

WHILE the rearguards were travelling south from the Thermopylae line on the night of 24th-25th April the first of the three big embarkations provided for in the plans of "W" Group was carried out.[1] At Porto Rafti the embarkation of the 5th New Zealand Brigade Group and other units totalling about 5,750 was achieved without a hitch, under the direction of a team of Australian officers led by Major Sheppard,[2] the legal officer of the 6th Division. The troops lay under cover until after dark, when they were marched to the beach and ferried to *Glengyle* and the cruiser *Calcutta* in two landing craft. The ships took them aboard at the rate of 1,500 an hour until, about 2 a.m., there were some 5,000 in the transport and 700 in the cruiser and they sailed.

The evacuation from Navplion and Tolos Bay proceeded less smoothly —on this and later nights—partly because there the men were drawn largely from a variety of base units and were less well-organised than those of the fighting formations. Embarkation was controlled by Lieut-Colonel Courage;[3] Major O'Loughlin[4] was in charge of the dispersal area. There was an Australian staff at Tolos and a British at Navplion. At 6.30 a.m. on the 24th O'Loughlin found the little town of Navplion crowded with men and vehicles. Having selected eight dispersal areas and placed officers and N.C.O's in charge of them he sent the officers into the town to find unit commanders and instruct them to lead their units out to one of the dispersal areas. By 10 a.m. the town had thus been emptied of most organised bodies and their vehicles, and contained only small groups, stragglers and abandoned trucks. A section of the 2/2nd Field Workshop Company was given the task of moving abandoned vehicles out of the town, and the stragglers were assembled into a single party and led to one of the dispersal areas, each of which had been chosen with the object of housing about 1,000 men and 150 vehicles.

Between 7,000 and 8,000 men collected in the Navplion area during the 24th, though only 5,000 had been planned for. After dark in bands of fifty they marched through the streets, which had been bombed and machine-gunned during the day and were strewn with glass; and at 10.30 began to embark in barges and ships' boats. All went well until the transport *Ulster Prince* ran aground at the harbour entrance. She was refloated but ran aground again near the wharf. However, by 3 a.m., despite the loss of the *Ulster Prince*, 6,600 men (1,600 more than the pre-arranged

---

[1] Some 1,300 base troops, British civilians, and 150 Germans captured at the Servia Pass had been embarked in small Greek ships at Piraeus on the nights of the 22nd and 23rd.
[2] Col A. W. Sheppard, MC, NX68. 2/4 Bn 1940, DAAG 6 Div 1941-42, AAQMG NT Force 1942, Dir of Org LHQ 1943-45. Journalist-Secretary; of Lindfield, NSW; b. Welbeck, London, 2 Jun 1910.
[3] Lt-Col J. H. Courage; Pioneer Corps. Director; b. Kirkby, Fleetham, Yorks, Eng, 16 Aug 1904.
[4] Lt-Col B. J. O'Loughlin, OBE, VX130. 2/7 Bn 1939-40; DAAG 6 Div 1941, I Corps 1941-42; AAG First Army 1942-44, II Corps 1944-45. Law Clerk; of Richmond, Vic; b. Murray Bridge, SA, 16 Aug 1904.

number) had been embarked in the ship *Glenearn*, the cruiser *Phoebe*, the destroyers *Stuart* and *Voyager*, and the sloop *Hyacinth*.[5] The troops who embarked included Australian Corps headquarters, 6th Australian Divisional headquarters, the 4th Survey Regiment, 16th Heavy Anti-Aircraft Battery, base troops, and about 150 Australian and New Zealand nursing sisters who were carried in *Voyager*. There was no embarkation from Tolos that night.

Meanwhile, an effort to embark troops from Piraeus that day had ended disastrously. On the 24th the large yacht *Hellas* arrived at that devastated port. Her captain said that she could carry 1,000 passengers; she took on board some 500 British civilians, mostly Maltese and Cypriots, and about 400 wounded and sick men from the 2/5th Australian General Hospital, and about as many from the 26th British General Hospital. At 7 p.m. German aircraft attacked, hit her with two bombs and set her on fire. Passengers and wounded men were trapped in burning cabins; the only gangway was destroyed, and eventually the ship rolled over. Estimates of the number who died range from 500 to 742. Among them was the mortally wounded Colonel Kay,[6] commander of the 2/5th Hospital, who was organising the embarkation of patients.

During the night of the 24th-25th Allen Group moved out from Megara under orders to go to the Argos area for embarkation. At 1.30 a.m., as the long column was passing over the Corinth bridge, Brigadier Savige was stopped by a staff officer from Brigadier Lee with a request that he detach a battalion to Lee's force to help guard the area against possible attack by German armour from the north or against paratroops. Savige ordered his staff captain, Major Bishop, to halt the 2/6th Battalion and instruct Lieut-Colonel Wrigley to detach a force for this task, and himself went on to meet Lee who "seemed to have little information about the plan of embarkation". It was finally agreed that three companies of the 2/6th plus two platoons should be deployed on tasks nominated by Lee.

In consequence Captain Dean's[7] company was halted and placed on the north side of the canal in defence of the bridge, under command of Colonel Lillingston of the 4th Hussars; and Captains Jones'[8] and Carroll's[9] companies with two platoons of the remaining rifle company were halted by

---

[5] The Navplion Beach-master's report states that a total of 5,500 were embarked but the Vice-Admiral, Light Forces, reported the following detailed figures:

Phoebe	1,131
Glenearn	5,100
Voyager	340
Stuart	1
Hyacinth	113
	6,685

[6] Col W. E. Kay, DSO, NX441. (1st AIF: 1 Fd Amb, and CO 2 Fd Amb 1917-18.) CO 2/5 AGH 1940-41. Medical practitioner; of Waverley, NSW; b. Glen Innes, NSW, 3 Jan 1888. Died of wounds 26 Apr 1941.

[7] Capt H. A. Dean, MC, VX140; 2/6 Bn. Farmer; of Geelong, Vic; b. Geelong, 11 Sep 1909.

[8] Lt-Col J. S. Jones, VX181. 2/6 Bn 1939-43; CO 4 NG Inf Bn 1945. Textile manufacturer; of Ballarat, Vic; b. Ballarat, 7 Jul 1915.

[9] Maj K. A. Carroll, VX57. 2/6 Bn 1939-43; 24 Bn 1943-45. Bank officer; of Colac, Vic; b. Donald, Vic, 8 May 1912.

Lee near the two adjoining airfields north of Argos. Lee ordered Jones, who was senior to Carroll, to place one of these companies to defend the airfields and send another to join the 4th Hussars at Corinth; it was to travel in one-ton vans so that parties with their own transport could be attached to scattered detachments of the Hussars. Jones took his own company back; having obtained twelve vans from his battalion at Argos, he drove forward, and about 5.30 arrived at the edge of Corinth where he was halted by General Freyberg, bound for a new headquarters near Miloi. Freyberg informed him that Corinth had been bombed and the road was out of action and beyond repair. After hearing of Jones' task, Freyberg said that the object of the force at Corinth was to ensure the withdrawal of 6,000 troops to the Peloponnese, and the Australians could best serve this purpose by clearing a detour through the town, otherwise there would be a traffic jam and the stationary column would be bombed. Jones set his men to work under attack by German aircraft flying low above the roof-tops.

Later Colonel Lillingston allotted Jones the task also of defending a ridge running parallel with the road south of the canal against low-flying aircraft and paratroops. Jones returned to Corinth and found that his men, in spite of fatigue and frequent attacks by aircraft, had almost completed the new route. He left small parties to finish and maintain the work, and took the remainder out of the town, leaving it about 9 p.m. "just as the leading vehicles of the withdrawing column reached the beginning of the detour". The company was in position by midnight and spent the remainder of a second almost sleepless night digging weapon pits.

In order to avoid heavy loss of ships as a result of air attack against vessels operating off the beaches near Athens, the staff of "W" Group radically amended the plan of evacuation with the objects of guarding the beaches of Attica and the Peloponnese against attack from the north and north-west, and embarking more men at beaches farther south. Inevitably this necessitated prolonging the period of embarkation.

As noted above the embarkations on the 25th-26th and 26th-27th were to have been:

25th-26th: 19th Brigade and others, from Athens beaches;
26th-27th: 6th Brigade and armoured brigade from Athens beaches, 4th Brigade from Megara. Various units from the Argos beaches. 16th and 17th Brigades and others from Kalamata.

The new orders by Group headquarters now required the 4th Brigade to hold at Erithrai 24 hours longer and move to the south bank of the Corinth Canal on the 26th-27th; and the 6th Brigade to move from the Athens area to Tripolis in the Peloponnese, there to block the roads leading north-west and south-west. In eastern Attica Brigadier Charrington was ordered to establish a rearguard including the 1/Rangers, part of the New Zealand Cavalry, eight New Zealand 25-pounders, and twelve New Zealand anti-tank guns, to hold the high ground north of Tatoi, thus guarding the Athens beaches from the north, until dusk on the 26th, and

The approach to Pharsala bridge from the north on 18th April 1941, after German aircraft had scored a direct hit on a truck loaded with ammonal.

(*Maj S. B. Cann, 2/1 Fd Coy*)
Burning trucks on the plain south of Lamia.

The road to Brallos Pass, looking north.

(Capt B. Brock, 2/2 Bn)

Brallos Pass, viewed from the arch bridge.

(Maj S. B. Cann, 2/1 Fd Coy)

(Maj S. B. Cann, 2/1 Fd Coy)

A Henschel 126 reconnaissance plane brought down on 21st April by Sapper J. Atkinson, 2/1st Field Company, with a Bren gun fired from the shoulder.

(New Zealand War History Branch)

Air attack on the way to Monemvasia.

(*Australian War Memorial*)

On a ship evacuating troops from Greece to Crete.

then withdraw to Rafina for embarkation on the 26th-27th. That night 8,000 troops of many units were to embark at Kalamata and a similar number at the Argos beaches. The withdrawal of New Zealand troops after the night of the 26th-27th (when the 4th Brigade and Isthmus Force would be on the south bank of the Corinth Canal and the 6th Brigade round Tripolis) was to be "directed with all possible speed on any or all of the following": Monemvasia, Plytra, Githion and Kalamata—all on the south coast of the Peloponnese.

The new plan required that the New Zealand troops and those attached to them should embark at these southern beaches on the 28th-29th and 29th-30th "in approximately equal proportions". Those left over at the Argos beaches on the 26th-27th were to "proceed as quickly as possible" to Monemvasia, Plytra or Kalamata. On the 25th-26th the 19th Brigade Group would be embarked from Megara and not the Athens beaches.

As a result of these orders Vice-Admiral Pridham-Wippell was informed on the 24th that the numbers to be embarked would be:

25th-26th: 5,000 from Megara;
26th-27th: 27,000;
27th-28th: Nil;
28th-29th: 4,000 from Githion and Monemvasia;
29th-30th: 4,000 from Kalamata, Githion and Monemvasia.

Thus a program which was to have been completed with the lifting of five brigades and thousands of unbrigaded troops on 26th-27th was now to be extended for three more nights. It provided that, on the night of the 26th-27th, Freyberg, having withdrawn his 4th Brigade and Isthmus Force to the south bank of the Corinth Canal, would blow demolitions there to impede the pursuit. Freyberg was to take command in the Peloponnese as soon as he passed south over the canal on the 25th. He ordered the remaining squadron of his cavalry regiment with the carriers of the 22nd and 28th Battalions to the Corinth Canal to help hold the bridge.

Meanwhile, at the Argos airfields, Lee had assembled a force consisting of one company and two platoons of the 2/6th Battalion (mentioned above), a squadron of the 3rd Royal Tanks, the men of the 2nd Heavy Anti-Aircraft Regiment (their guns having been destroyed) and two anti-tank guns.[1]

In accordance with this revised plan the only formation to be embarked on the 25th-26th was the 19th Brigade Group from Megara. About midday Wilson's staff had decided that this brigade group plus the 1,100 wounded at Megara could not all be embarked there that night, and Major Spry,[2] an Australian liaison officer, was sent to tell Vasey to retain enough vehicles to carry the surplus men to the Marathon beaches. When Spry

---

[1] The Australian company and two platoons remained in this area performing various tasks until 9 a.m. on the 26th when they were withdrawn, with the anti-aircraft regiment, to Monemvasia. There they came under the command of the 6th New Zealand Brigade and at length embarked with it at 3.30 a.m. on 29 April.

[2] Col C. C. F. Spry, DSO, VX7. GSO3 (Ops) I Corps 1940-41; GSO1 7 Div 1942-43; DDSD LHQ 1943-45. Regular soldier; of Brisbane; b. Yeronga, Qld, 26 Jun 1910.

arrived most of the vehicles had been destroyed (in accordance with earlier orders from Wilson's staff) but enough remained to carry 300. The men of the 19th Brigade Group had slept under the olive trees during the day. That night, carrying rifles, sub-machine-guns, Brens, and anti-tank rifles, they were ferried to the transport *Thurland Castle,* the cruiser *Coventry,* and the destroyers *Havock, Hasty, Decoy, Waterhen* and *Vendetta.* From a beach where there were two jetties all the 19th Brigade Group[3] were taken aboard, but at the neighbouring beach where there were 2,000 sick and wounded men and technical troops, only 1,500 had been embarked by 2.30 a.m. when the last lighter departed. The troops embarked here included the remaining nurses—forty Australian from the 2/5th Australian General Hospital and forty British from the 26th General Hospital—carrying only haversacks and a blanket each.[4] Altogether 5,900 troops were taken off, and some of those who remained were taken in trucks to the Marathon beaches. The *Thurland Castle,* on which were the nurses, most of the 2/11th Battalion, and others, was dive-bombed several times on the way to Crete, but was not hit, though several men were wounded by splinters.

The detachment sent on 23rd April to guard the left flank—2/5th Battalion, one troop 2/1st Field Regiment, and a depleted company of the 2/1st Machine Gun Battalion—had arrived at Megara on the 25th but, finding that no arrangements had been made to embark his force there, Lieut-Colonel King pushed on to join his own brigade, which he did at Miloi that afternoon. One company of the 2/5th had been left to cover a demolition near Delphi and followed the battalion at a distance. A man in this company wrote an account of its withdrawal:

> The movement from then on was blind; we proceeded on, asking M.P's for the embarkation beach; they sent us on. We arrived at Corinth and met members of the 2/6th Battalion, who sent us on. We refuelled there as we were told that we had a further 30 miles to go . . . . We arrived at Argos; again we were sent on. By this time we moved as controlled; we had no idea where we were going or where the battalion was in position. We arrived at Tripolis at approximately 0600 hours and were again told to go on. By this time we were in convoy of mixed troops. We met officers from other units, but they could give us no information. They did not know where they were going. We continued on the road and occasionally met M.P's who sent us on. The Greeks at various villages were wonderfully kind and gave us bread, fruit and water. At approximately 1100 hours, 26th April, we arrived at a village eight miles from Kalamata . . . . We were told that the 2/5th Battalion was at Kalamata.

This isolated company was pursuing Allen Group—the largest single force now moving south—which had arrived at Miloi from Eleusis early on 25th April and again dispersed for the day. In the afternoon Allen

---

[3] The 19 Bde Gp included the 2/1, 2/4 and 2/11 Battalions, two coys of the 2/8, the 2/2 Fd Regt, one bty of the 2/1 Fd Regt, one bty of the 2/1 Aust A-Tk Regt, the 2/7 Fd Amb, and engineers, signallers and other technical troops. The 2/2 Fd Regt disabled the guns and preserved all optical instruments.

[4] General Blamey had left instructions that all Australian nurses must be taken off. However, on the 25th, Brigadier D. T. M. Large, the British Director of Medical Services, was doubtful whether it would be safe to embark them and whether they could be spared. At length, at the urging of Major E. E. Dunlop (the Australian medical liaison officer), Colonel Rogers and Lieut-Commander P. C. Hutton (in charge of the naval party at "P" Beach), Large agreed, and they were hurried to Megara in trucks that night.

received orders, forecast the previous day, to move that night through Tripolis to Kalamata. The column moved off at 8 p.m.[5] For the third consecutive night this column of 600 vehicles containing 6,000 men had a journey of 90 miles by the map—farther in fact—this time along winding mountain roads.

> The march throughout was an exceedingly good one (wrote Allen afterwards[6]) and the M.T. drivers are to be commended for their sterling work. In the darkness, driving from dusk to daylight, using only dim lights, it was no easy task . . . . 6 Aust Div Provost gave valuable assistance.

At Eleusis the group had been ordered to collect an additional seven days' rations and plenty of oil and petrol, and did so. This enabled it to supply many British, Palestinian, Cypriot and Yugoslav troops who joined the column or were encountered at Kalamata, where the group arrived after daylight on the 26th.

On the night of the 25th-26th General Wilson left Athens to set up his headquarters at Miloi. He crossed the Corinth bridge about two hours before dawn. At that stage the outlook seemed encouraging. Two brigade groups—one New Zealand and one Australian—and some 7,000 base troops had been embarked; and the whole force, except the 4th New Zealand Brigade Group, the rearguard drawn from the 1st Armoured Brigade, and some other detachments were south of the Corinth Bridge.

A flat sandy isthmus only three miles wide at its narrowest point links the Peloponnese with the remainder of Greece; through that isthmus had been cut a canal 70 feet in width and 26 or more in depth capable of floating ships up to 5,000 tons. Across the canal ran a bridge carrying the road and railway which passed through Corinth, which is on the coast south-west of the canal. Fear of paratroops, known to be with Field Marshal List's army, had now led to the assembly in the Corinth area of a small patchwork force of all arms. On the north and south banks of the canal were a detachment of the 4th Hussars, a squadron of New Zealand divisional cavalry, the carriers of 22nd and 28th Battalions, Major Gordon's[7] company of the 19th New Zealand Battalion, Captain Dean's company of the 2/6th Battalion, a section of 6th Field Company of the New Zealand Engineers, some British engineers, and a section of Bofors guns of the 122nd Battery. The New Zealand engineers assisted by Lieutenant Tyson[8] of the British engineers had prepared the bridge for demolition and the ferries had been destroyed. At Corinth and on the flat ground south of the canal was the headquarters of the 4th Hussars, but the three squadrons of the regiment were dispersed along the south shore of the

---

[5] In the column were four Yugoslav anti-aircraft guns (new weapons from the Skoda factory) which had joined the force on the Aliakmon.

[6] Report on Operations in Greece, 16 Aust Inf Bde.

[7] Maj R. K. Gordon; 19 NZ Bn. School teacher; of Wanganui, NZ; b. Parewanui Bulls, NZ, 19 Feb 1899.

[8] Maj J. T. Tyson, MC; RE. Scientist; of London; b. London, 16 Feb 1916.

Gulf of Corinth as far as Patras, 70 miles to the west, and only thirty men and four tanks remained with Colonel Lillingston. Jones' company of the 2/6th was deployed on high ground south of the canal, overlooking its eastern end; Dean's company on the north side. In the area were three 3.7-inch anti-aircraft guns, eight 3-inch, and sixteen Bofors, the latter dispersed along the route from the canal to Argos 30 miles south.

The area had been attacked from the air at intervals during the previous four or five days, and on the evening of the 25th aircraft had silenced some anti-aircraft guns. Early the following morning the attack was resumed. About 6.30 a.m. a flight of bombers approached flying low and hit and destroyed a heavy anti-aircraft gun on the slopes south-east of the canal. About 7 a force of some 120 medium and dive bombers and fighters arrived and began a thunderous attack, the dive bombers leisurely circling to find their targets—chiefly guns and groups of vehicles—and then diving on them. Throughout the attack fighters systematically machine-gunned the area. At length the fire of the anti-aircraft guns was subdued. About 7.15 there appeared many large aircraft of a type new to the defenders. They flew in groups of three very slowly at about 300 or 400 feet. From the outer aircraft of each group dropped a descending line of men in parachutes, and from the inner machine canisters of stores. In half an hour a force variously estimated by the defenders from 800 to 1,500 men was dropped astride the canal and near Corinth.

In a few minutes the German paratroops had occupied the bridge and were rounding up prisoners, largely depot troops. Lieutenant Tyson who had helped to prepare the bridge for demolition and Captain Phillips,[9] in charge of traffic movement at Corinth, fired at the charges with rifles. One of their shots is believed to have detonated a charge, and the bridge was completely destroyed.

The defenders opened fire on the paratroops and the strafing aircraft as soon as the drop began.

The German aircraft had heavily machine-gunned the positions held by Dean's company. Two bombs dropped in one platoon area showered sand into the air so that it covered the weapons and the automatics could not be made to fire again. The paratroops who landed round this company vastly outnumbered the Australians. The platoon which had been bombed was soon overcome and it was not long before the remaining platoons (Lieutenants Richards[1] and Mann[2]) were hard pressed. Two gliders each carrying twelve men landed in Richards' area, but he and his men promptly killed or wounded all their occupants. However, this platoon was later overcome and the survivors captured.

An aircraft-load of paratroops floated down into the area held by Mann's platoon. The Australians shot some of them as they came down. "Some of the enemy were firing as they descended but most were too busy swing-

---
[9] Maj J. F. Phillips, MC; Devonshire Regt. DAAG Movt Control ME 1941. B. Plymouth, Eng, 21 Dec 1906.

[1] Lt G. T. E. Richards, VX3948; 2/6 Bn. Watchmaker and jeweller; of Wonthaggi, Vic; b. Cootamundra, NSW, 14 Jan 1914.

[2] Lt W. R. Mann, VX3933; 2/6 Bn. Clerk; of South Yarra, Vic; b. Melbourne, 17 Nov 1915.

ing about," wrote an Australian afterwards. Mann's platoon was soon under fire from paratroops on bare mounds of clay immediately overlooking it. Seeking cover Mann was wounded and several of his men killed.

Company headquarters were closely attacked. Several grenades were thrown into the trench which the headquarters occupied but were thrown out again by Private Coulam,[3] the company clerk, until one exploded in his hand and wounded him seriously in the face. Warrant Officer Stevenson,[4] the company sergeant major, fought on with great determination here, and he and others beat off the enemy for about three hours. At first this handful of men fought on hoping for the arrival of the tanks of the Hussars which Colonel Lillingston had said would cover their withdrawal if it became necessary; but at 11.45, and when no ammunition remained except a few rounds for a pistol, this group capitulated. Not till then did they learn that the bridge had been blown up and, for that reason alone, the tanks could not have come to their assistance. In the course of the action ten men of the 2/6th Battalion were killed and two officers (Lieutenants Mann and Hunter[5]) and eleven men wounded. Some New Zealanders in the neighbourhood fought on for another quarter of an hour and then were overcome.

No Germans landed in the area of Captain Jones' company south of the canal but before long paratroops supported by machine-gun fire were advancing towards its position. Jones decided that there was nothing for it but to withdraw towards Argos while he could. Enemy transport aircraft evidently mistook the Australians for their own men advancing south and dropped weapons and supplies in their path. The Australians, joined by Captain Phillips and Lieutenant Tyson and an officer of the Hussars, fell back into the hills south-east of the isthmus. About 9 p.m. they were overtaken by two companies of the 26th Battalion which had been sent north to help to extricate Isthmus Force. This battalion lent vehicles to the Australians, who remained with this unit until embarkation. Meanwhile an officer of the New Zealand engineers had organised remnants of the Isthmus Force, including the New Zealand cavalry squadron, and they withdrew to Tripolis. Of the troops who had been left at Megara some 500 were intercepted by the German paratroops on their way to Corinth; some made their way back to Athens; some joined the 4th New Zealand Brigade and embarked with them; a few sailed from Megara in a caique.

> The attack on Corinth was made by the regimental headquarters, two battalions, and an attached heavy-weapons company of the *2nd Parachute Rifle Regiment* (Colonel Sturm). The regiment lost 63 killed, 158 wounded and 16 missing, but captured 21 officers and some 900 men of British, New Zealand and Australian units and 1,450 Greeks.

For a time Wilson's and Freyberg's headquarters, both now at Miloi, heard only vague reports of the action at Corinth. The first information

---
[3] Pte C. Coulam, MM, VX3838; 2/6 Bn. Footwear salesman; of Auckland, NZ; b. Auckland, 11 May 1905.
[4] WO2 E. J. Stevenson, MBE, VX3501; 2/6 Bn. Brewery employee; of Preston, Vic; b. Richmond, Vic, 11 Sep 1903.
[5] Lt A. Hunter, MC, VX3439; 2/6 Bn. Tourist; b. Johannesburg, Sth Africa, 23 Feb 1914.

suggested that it was on a minor scale, and Brigadier Barrowclough was ordered merely to send two companies northwards to save the bridge (across which the Erithrai rearguard was to pass that night). Later, when it became apparent that the enemy held the canal strongly, Barrowclough was ordered to defend the pass north of Argos that night to cover the embarkation from the Argos beaches; thereafter he was to defend the road about Tripolis until the 27th-28th and then withdraw to Monemvasia. He placed the 26th Battalion in the pass north of Argos, the 24th Battalion at Tripolis to defend that vital road junction, and the 25th in defence of the western approaches to Miloi. Lee's patchwork force at the Argos airfields was ordered to move south that night and prepare to defend the embarkation area at Monemvasia.

The parachute attack had cut the British force into two main sections: first, the main force from Argos southwards; second, the rearguard forces —the 4th New Zealand Brigade and the 1st Armoured Brigade detachment—astride the roads north-west of Athens, and the artillerymen awaiting embarkation at the Marathon beaches. Having placed infantry across the roads leading from north and west into the southern Peloponnese, Freyberg sent orders by wireless to the 4th Brigade Group that it should embark from the Athens beaches on the 27th-28th.

Wilson informed Freyberg that he (Wilson) would embark that night and Freyberg would then take command of all troops in the Peloponnese and embark himself from Monemvasia on the 28th-29th. Thus for the next two days Freyberg would be the only general officer in Greece. At this stage two brigades were cut off north of Corinth—one in action with the enemy, and one awaiting embarkation; in the Peloponnese were the 6th Brigade at Tripolis, the 16th and 17th at Kalamata. In addition there were some 8,000 ill-organised depot troops and others at Kalamata or on the way there, and 6,000 round Argos.

As the fighting force which would remain under Freyberg's command by dawn on the 27th (if the embarkations were successfully carried out that night) would amount to approximately one division—chiefly the 4th and 6th New Zealand Brigades and what remained of the 1st Armoured Brigade—it was evidently considered appropriate that a divisional commander should take control. On the other hand, when the dispersion of Freyberg's brigades and the presence in Greece of more than 10,000 often ill-organised base troops are taken into account, the decision on the 26th to close Group headquarters seems as precipitate as the decision on the 24th to send out Blamey and Mackay. Afterwards Freyberg considered the situation on the morning of the 27th "chaotic". As described below, about 19,000 men were embarked on the night of the 26th-27th. On the morning of the 27th, however, one of Freyberg's brigades was at the Marathon beaches cut off by the German force at Corinth; another was in the Peloponnese; he had not been informed that there were some 8,000 troops at Kalamata, including about 800 of his own New Zealand reinforcements, or that there were perhaps 2,000 troops round Navplion.

The embarkation of about 39,000 men was a fine achievement—better than Wavell and Wilson had believed possible at the outset—but the 39,000 included only one-third of the New Zealand Division. Failure now would be a national calamity in that distant country—and deeply distressing to Australia, practically all of whose fighting units had been embarked under the protection of the two New Zealand rearguards.

It remains to record the events in the outlying areas during the 26th April. The three squadrons of the 4th Hussars which had been dispersed along the south shore of the Gulf of Corinth assembled at Patras at midday, moved out from Patras at 2 p.m. and travelled south over the mountains by way of Kalavrita.

Of the troops north of Athens and now cut off from their commander in the Peloponnese, the 1st Armoured Brigade detachment and the artillerymen at Rafina were already under orders to embark on the night of the 26th-27th. The armoured brigade detachment had been in position north of Tatoi during the day. Nothing was seen of the enemy, but a rumour—ill-founded—was heard that German troops had entered Athens in the evening, presumably from Corinth. Consequently a company of the Rangers was sent to block the roads from Athens to Kephissia and Porto Rafti. After dark the rest of the battalion and the New Zealand cavalry drove to Rafina where the rearguard company joined them later in the night.

The 4th Brigade at Erithrai lay concealed, and in the early morning was not detected by scouting aircraft. At 11 a.m. a closely-spaced German column of about 100 vehicles led by tanks and motor-cars began to climb up the road from Thebes. When the tail of the column was in range, accurate fire by the Australian guns dispersed them. The German troops were seen to scatter and then board their trucks again and drive back to Thebes leaving eight vehicles on the road. About midday came the expected attack by German aircraft, the rearguard having now revealed its position, and soon after 1 o'clock German artillery began firing. An artillery duel continued all the afternoon, tanks occasionally probing forward. A tank was directly hit late in the afternoon and infantry moving towards the left flank were dispersed by machine-gun fire at 3,000 yards. During the afternoon enemy vehicles were seen streaming east along the road towards Skhimatarion. News of the paratroop landing at Corinth had arrived at 2 p.m. and the orders to embark at Porto Rafti at 7. At 9 o'clock the brigade began to embus and soon was rolling along the road at 30 miles an hour, the engineers blowing a series of craters behind it. Knowing nothing of the rumour that the Germans were in Athens, Puttick (who had sent a platoon to guard the road junction west of Eleusis) took his force through Eleusis and Athens to Porto Rafti.

As noted above three large-scale embarkations were to take place on the night of 26th-27th: from the Athens beaches, the Argos beaches, and Kalamata. The troops at the Athens beaches included Brigadier Miles' big artillery group at Porto Rafti, and the depleted 1st Armoured Brigade at Rafina.

At Porto Rafti the single landing craft, which was the only means of loading, had first to go to Kea Island to bring in 450 men whom it had landed there on the 24th-25th. This delay was likely to prevent the program being carried out. When Brigadier Miles learnt of this, he ordered the 102nd Anti-Tank Regiment and the 2nd Royal Horse Artillery to Rafina. The gunners had brought to the beaches all the equipment that could be carried, even heavy No. 11 wireless sets, and it was a shock to learn that when the 5th Brigade had embarked on the 24th-25th the naval beach-master had ordered that all arms and equipment be discarded. Miles ordered that all the equipment which the men were carrying and also the 2-pounder guns must be taken on board. However, when the time came this was found to be impossible.[6]

At both Rafina and Porto Rafti the embarkation was carried out as coolly and efficiently as on the 24th. The *Glengyle* and *Salween* were loaded and some 2,720 were embarked in the cruiser *Carlisle* and destroyers *Kingston* and *Kandahar*, but when *Glengyle* sailed from Rafina at 2 a.m. 800 of the 1st Armoured Brigade, including Charrington's headquarters, 250 of the 1/Rangers, and 117 of the 102nd were still on the beach. Major Sheppard had intended to embark his staff that night according to his orders, but at 1.30 a.m. on the 27th he learnt that the 4th New Zealand Brigade had now to be embarked from the Marathon beaches the following night. He ordered half his staff to embark, and hurried towards Athens by car to find and guide Puttick's column, meeting Lieut-Colonel Russell[7] and the 2/1st Field Ambulance moving along the Athens-Markopoulon road. By daylight Puttick's force was lying under cover. At 9.25 a.m. on the 27th German troops entered Athens.

It had been intended to send the landing ship *Glenearn* to Navplion on the 26th-27th but she was bombed and disabled that evening,[8] whereupon Vice-Admiral Pridham-Wippell took his flagship (H.M.S. *Orion*) and the Australian cruiser *Perth* to Navplion (where another cruiser, four destroyers and two transports were assembled). He detached H.M.A.S. *Stuart* to Tolos.

Stuart (Captain Waller) began embarking troops at Tolos beach at 11.15 p.m., the men wading to a landing craft which ferried them to the ship. Soon *Stuart* reported that she was full. She transferred her troops to *Orion*, asked for the help of a cruiser, and returned with *Perth* to Tolos. Again and again the landing craft was stranded temporarily on a sand bar about 30 yards from the shore. The naval beach-master had warned Colonel Courage, the area commander, against this bar but had failed to persuade him not to use this beach. At 4 a.m. about 2,000 had been embarked and some 1,300 were still ashore. Four officers of the Australian

---

[6] The 102nd carried breech-blocks and sights on board and threw the barrels into the sea.
[7] Col R. H. Russell, DSO, NX168. CO 2/1 Fd Amb 1941; ADMS 3 Div 1943-44. Medical practitioner; of New Lambton, NSW; b. Sydney, 12 May 1900. Killed in aircraft accident 5 Mar 1945.
[8] The destroyer *Griffin* towed her to Suda Bay, and thence the sloop *Grimsby* towed her to Alexandria.

embarkation staff had been embarked leaving only O'Loughlin, Major MacLean and Captains Bamford and Grieve.

At Navplion the *Ulster Prince,* which had now been bombed and burnt out by German aircraft, obstructed the little harbour and made it impossible for destroyers to come alongside the quay. A choppy sea rendered it dangerous to embark men in small boats and, in the darkness, a number were washed overboard and drowned. Finally, at 4.30 a.m., dangerously late, the ships sailed with about 2,600, having left 1,700 ashore. Having departed so late the *Slamat,* carrying about 500, was still within easy range of German aircraft at dawn. She was discovered and at 7.30 a.m. was sunk. The destroyers *Wryneck* and *Diamond* picked up the few survivors.[9] Later the two destroyers were themselves sunk. Only one naval officer, forty-one ratings and about eight soldiers were rescued. Of those left at Navplion 400 moved down the coast in a tank landing craft, later bombed and sunk; and 700, including the Australian Reinforcement Battalion, were sent to Tolos where they hid for the day. At intervals during the day German aircraft arrived overhead and cruised round dropping small bombs and machine-gunning at so low an altitude that the men lying in the shadow below could see the pilots and gunners clearly and could scarcely believe they themselves were not seen. The air crews were evidently trying to provoke retaliation or movement by the men below but they lay motionless.

At Kalamata from 18,000 to 20,000 troops were now assembled, about one-third being of Allen Group (the 16th and 17th Brigades and corps troops) and most of the remainder a medley of base troops, Yugoslavs and others. The survivors of the 4th Hussars and the New Zealand Reinforcement Battalion were on their way to Kalamata.

Brigadier Allen had urged upon Brigadier Parrington, who was in command of the embarkation area, that fighting men, being the most valuable, should be embarked first. Parrington issued an order late in the afternoon stating that the men were to be divided into four groups. The first included Allen's two brigades; the second, under Colonel Lister,[1] comprised all troops north-east of Kalamata; the third, under a Major Pemberton, those who had arrived by train; and the fourth, under his camp commandant, those not elsewhere included. All these were divided into parties of fifty each and each party was allotted a serial number. Allen's force was given numbers one to 150, Lister's 151 to 300, Pemberton's 301 to 400. The troops were to march to the beach or quay and report to a control post there, where a ship would be allotted to them. It was essential, wrote Parrington, that "the highest standard of discipline be observed in accordance with Imperial traditions". Allen, Savige and their staffs allotted serial numbers within their own force. Medical units came first, then artillery, engineers, infantry and so on. The men were in good

---

[9] The troops embarked at Navplion this night were mostly headquarters and base troops but included also the 3 Royal Tanks less one squadron.
[1] Lt-Col M. D. B. Lister, DSO, MC. 5 and 6 Bns RTR. B. Waterford, Ireland, 6 May 1899.

heart, though weary and disappointed; the Australian leaders resolved to ensure that their units left Greece as a disciplined force, the more so because a majority of the men at Kalamata were now officerless and disorganised and there was evident danger of a panic among them. Allen ordered the commanding officers to take "active measures to prevent troops other than Australian and British troops under the command of Allen Group from filtering on to the ships". He ordered his provosts on the 26th to shoot any man who "fired a shot, lit a fire or panicked". In a written order Lieut-Colonel Walker of the 2/7th said:

> The C.O. directs that every effort be made to present a soldier-like show and he expects every man from private upwards to do his bit towards concluding this effort successfully. On the march, step, dressing and general discipline must be maintained. Stragglers cannot be catered for and can only be left behind.

In the evening the men began to damage or bury their kits. In the course of the 26th it was agreed in conference between Allen and Parrington that the method to be employed to destroy vehicles would be to drain oil and water and run the engines until they seized—as had been done at most beaches. Allen, however, was instructed not to destroy his vehicles until ordered by Parrington's headquarters, in case they were needed to carry his force to yet another place of embarkation. It was decided to hand the vehicles to Parrington for use by the remaining troops; but later that night "at a most inconvenient time", as Allen wrote later, he was ordered to destroy the vehicles, but not to use the method of running the engines without oil and water. Instead tyres were slashed and engines smashed with axes or hammers.

About 10 p.m. the troops saw lights out to sea, coming closer and closer to the shore. Orders were given and the lines of waiting men began to march forward, in threes and in step, carrying weapons and spare boxes of ammunition. As the head of each column neared the shore they could see the dim shapes of destroyers in the bay and an occasional light flashing on the wharf where soon two destroyers were tied up with gangways at bow and stern. The men filed quietly aboard, and, when a destroyer was loaded and cast off, those who remained sat on the wharf in their ranks and waited for the next. There is one recorded incident of leaderless troops attempting to rush a ship. A crowd from the Auxiliary Military Pioneer Corps which was recruited from Cypriots and Palestinians tried to press forward to the destroyer *Hero*, but a platoon of the 2/2nd Battalion thrust them back with rifle butts.

> The behaviour of the troops was outstandingly good and orderly (wrote Savige later). The column had moved, in several heads, to the road which led to the quay. Ranks were maintained and threes were unbroken. Everybody was exhausted but the unit job was always well in hand. Not only were the troops acting splendidly, but there was an atmosphere of complete faith in their officers and N.C.O's. In checking passing units, to ascertain who they were, the reply always quoted their serial number. Their sense of security was so great that, on the approach of a body of troops, I would ask where their officer was. I would make myself known to him, and only thus could I obtain the identity of each unit. When they reached the quay, men stood fast in their tanks. Naval officers, who

were present at Dunkirk, expressed their surprise at all troops carrying their weapons and equipment, and spare boxes of S.A.A.

Savige received the new instruction about destroying vehicles about 9.15 p.m. The vehicles of three of his battalions—2/5th, 2/6th and 2/7th —and of the 2/2nd Field Ambulance were still on the far side of Kalamata. Savige gave Captain Gray[3] the task of organising the destruction of the vehicles and arranging the transport of the drivers to the beach. About 11.30 the drivers had not arrived. Savige pointed out to Gray that he alone knew where their various rendezvous were and the routes along which they would reach them and asked him to go back and try to get them forward in time.

About 2.15 a.m. Savige found that his 2/7th, 2/8th Battalions, his engineers and field ambulance had embarked, and his 2/6th Battalion, 2/1st Field Regiment and brigade headquarters were drawn up beside a destroyer which was then berthing. The 2/5th Battalion was missing. It was found behind the solid mass of troops waiting to embark after Allen's force, and was led forward and embarked.

It was then about 2.45, and Allen had just been informed that no more destroyers would pull in that night but that ships would return the following night. Gray and the drivers had not arrived and therefore Allen decided to leave two of his staff officers, Captains Woodhill[4] and Vial, ashore to collect these men and embark them next night. Believing that all except these drivers had embarked, Allen and Savige boarded the last destroyer, but it had just swung away from the wharf when Captain Tyrrell,[5] in charge of the men of 17th Brigade headquarters, called from the quay; his men were standing there in their ranks.

In fact it turned out that several other groups from Allen's force had been left behind—a detachment of the 2/1st Field Regiment and the commanding officer, Lieut-Colonel Harlock,[6] who was trying to ensure its embarkation; the Yugoslav anti-aircraft gunners; and some others. The total number embarked is uncertain but certainly exceeded 8,000—by far the largest number taken off one beach on a single night.[7]

---

[3] Capt A. W. Gray, MC, VX180; 2/6 Bn. Shop assistant; of Red Cliffs, Vic; b. Melbourne, 9 Nov 1912.

[4] Capt P. J. Woodhill, NX12261; 2/2 Bn. Public servant; of Rabaul; b. Camden, NSW, 10 Oct 1906. Died 26 Nov 1941.

[5] Capt W. A. Tyrrell, MBE, NX188; AASC 6 Div. Importer; of Lindfield, NSW; b. Glen Innes, NSW, 12 Dec 1911.

[6] Brig H. G. F. Harlock, VX20314; CO 2/1 Fd Regt 1941. Regular soldier; of Melbourne; b. Camperdown, Vic, 20 Aug 1900.

[7] The beach staff's report gives the number as 8,000, a suspiciously round figure. The Vice-Admiral's report gives the following totals: *Dilwarra*, 2,400; *City of London*, 3,500; *Costa Rica*, 2,500; *Defender*, 250 (and the Yugoslav Crown Jewels). The troops were ferried to these transports by the destroyers *Defender*, *Hero* and *Hereward*, but it appears that only *Defender* retained troops on board. The cruiser *Phoebe* and sloop *Flamingo* were also in the convoy. The embarked strength of the 17 Bde Gp this night was recorded:

	Offrs	ORs		Offrs	ORs
Bde HQ	4	103	2/6 Bn	17	290
2/1 Fd Regt	23	270	2/7 Bn	32	728
2/2 Fd Coy	5	200	2/8 Bn	23	440
2/5 Bn	29	546			

(The weakness of the 2/6 Bn was due to the absence of three rifle companies and part of another at Corinth or Argos. One battery of the 2/1 Fd Regt had embarked with the 19 Bde Gp.)

One man who waited in vain that night described the scene:

> We just came, in straggling dozens and scores, to a line of figures in the darkness, all facing to the left. We tried to move around them, and saw that they were in a queue. It was quite unreckoned for, and shocking. We got to the end and there, with the light coming off the water, we could see it and it was up to twenty men deep and two hundred yards long, a great packed rectangle of thousands of men. They stood very still, not talking, not smoking; there was an occasional cough, and over the top of the block there played a continual little motion as men raised themselves off their heels to look to the front . . . .[8]

On the 27th Admiral Pridham-Wippell was near the end of his resources. Suda Bay was crowded with ships packed with troops. All available transports were filled and it was likely that any future embarkations must be carried out by naval vessels. He decided to send his laden transports—*Glengyle, Salween, Khedive Ismail, Dilwarra, City of London,* and *Costa Rica*—not to Crete but to Alexandria, escorted by one force of cruisers and destroyers and protected from the north-westward by another. Soon after dawn the air raid alarm sounded in the ships of the Kalamata convoy.

> The men came up on to the deck with a spontaneous rush (said one of them later) and ran to pick gun positions. It was one of the finest things I've seen—the way these worn-out men sprang to the defence of the ship.

On the *City of London,* for example, eighty-four Vickers, Brens and Hotchkiss machine-guns and anti-tank rifles were mounted and fired at the attacking aircraft. A near miss brought an avalanche of water over the forecastle of *Costa Rica,* from whose decks every Vickers gun and Bren on board was in action thickening the fire from the cruiser and destroyers. There were further attacks during the morning but without effect, though seven enemy aircraft were shot down. At 2.40 p.m., however, an enemy aircraft was seen, too late, gliding out of the sun. Its bomb struck the water 7 or 8 feet from the *Costa Rica,* whose engines stopped immediately. At 3 o'clock water was coming in fast through gaps in the plates on the port side. The troops were ordered to fall in. There was room for some of the 2,500 on deck, but most lined the alleyways or stood along the lower deck in darkness, silently on parade. The destroyer *Defender* came alongside. At this stage four men of the ship's crew came on deck, threw a few rafts overboard and shouted "Every man for himself", whereupon about twenty soldiers left the ranks and jumped overboard. This delayed the destroyer *Hero* which was coming along the port side and whose crew had to pull these men from the water. The *Costa Rica* was rising and falling 18 or 20 feet in the water and men had to swing down the side on ropes and jump for the deck of the *Defender*. When she was filled the destroyer *Hereward* came alongside. Among the last to jump on to her were those manning machine-guns, who had been ordered to remain in case the aircraft attacked again. Finally, when *Costa Rica* was listing so steeply that a man could step off the lower bridge on to the deck of a

---

[8] Tom Burns in "Calamity Bay", *Penguin New Writing No. 19.* Burns served with The Friends' Ambulance Unit and was taken prisoner at Kalamata.

destroyer, the *Hero* replaced the *Hereward* and the Dutch ship's officers and about twenty soldiers who remained jumped on to her deck. The trans-shipment took forty-five minutes. The troops aboard included the 2/1st Machine Gun Battalion, the 2/7th Battalion, part of the 2/8th, and a company of the 2/1st.

Thus, on the night of the 26th-27th about 19,000 troops embarked. Of the transports employed two had been sunk by German aircraft before they were out of range—the *Slamat* with a loss of nearly all on board, the *Costa Rica* without the loss of a man. Two destroyers had been sunk. It

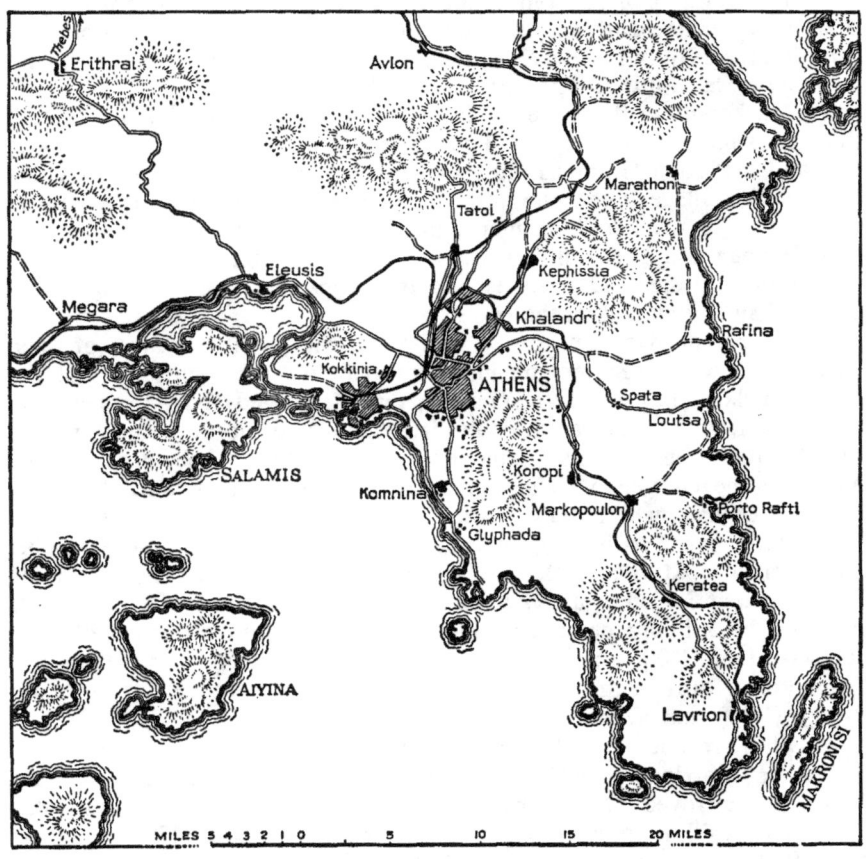

was not a heavy price for such an achievement. There remained in Greece the 4th Brigade Group and part of the armoured brigade near the Athens beaches, about 2,500 men at the Argos beaches, the 6th Brigade Group at Tripolis, several units and detachments at Monemvasia, and more than 8,000 men at Kalamata.

While the 4th New Zealand Brigade was moving to a defensive position about 500 yards east of Markopoulon on the Athens-Porto Rafti road, it was detected about 11 a.m. by some twenty-three German aircraft and severely machine-gunned. This fire exploded a shell in an ammunition waggon of the 2/3rd Field Regiment, which again produced other explosions and soon shells were bursting everywhere, vehicles burning, and the ripe crops in the fields and the trees in the pine woods blazing fiercely. Nine guns of the 2/3rd or the anti-tank battery attached to it were destroyed, and six artillerymen and a larger number of New Zealand infantrymen were killed by the explosions; about 30 were killed or wounded in the 20th Battalion. Into the blazing woods squadrons of German aircraft poured bombs and machine-gun fire at intervals. By 1 p.m., however, the 18th and 20th Battalions were in their intended position forward, the 19th in reserve and the 2/3rd Field Regiment in support, with some guns well forward in an anti-tank role.

In Markopoulon the Greek villagers crowded at their doors to watch the troops move up to the line. Though they knew the campaign had been lost and that soon Germans and not New Zealanders would be marching through the village street, and although some stood glum and silent, others threw roses to the marching men and strewed them on the road at their feet. Women and girls ran forward with cups of water and old men gave the thumbs-up sign. The woods and the crops were still blazing and a cloud of smoke hung over the countryside.

About 3 p.m. a column of 50 to 100 German vehicles, most of them light tanks, were seen moving into Markopoulon. The guns did not fire on the village, but whenever German tanks emerged from it they were met by a heavy concentration of fire from guns and mortars, and throughout the afternoon the tanks remained in the sanctuary the village offered. Many of the German vehicles passed across the front towards the little port of Loutsa, where they perhaps expected to find the main force. The attack, expected hourly, never came, though there was more strafing from the air. At 6 o'clock the brigade began destroying its remaining trucks, and at 8.45 the guns. At 9 o'clock the men in the forward positions marched back into a perimeter which the reserve battalion, the 19th, had formed about 1,000 yards from the beach. The troops were embarked from Porto Rafti in the cruiser *Ajax* (2,500 men), and destroyers *Kimberley* (700) and *Kingston* (640).

It will be recalled that there remained at Rafina, 10 miles to the north, Brigadier Charrington and about 800 of the armoured brigade. All guns had been destroyed. During the 27th this force had taken up a concealed defensive position round the beach, the Rangers, about 250 strong, on the left, the anti-tank gunners and New Zealand cavalry regiment in the centre and on the right. Early in the day German aircraft bombed the wrecked vehicles on the hills north of Rafina and the village itself, and flew low over the hidden troops but without seeing them. In the morning a party of the anti-tank regiment under Lieutenant Pumphrey,[9] who knew

---
[9] Lt J. L. Pumphrey; 102 A-Tk Regt. Student; b. Inverness, Scotland, 22 Jul 1916.

classical Greek, took possession of a caique in the harbour; if no ship arrived at Rafina that night—and none was expected—the caique would be useful.[1] About 250 men were allotted to her and at 6 o'clock Charrington and the remaining 600 began to move towards Porto Rafti, where it was known that an embarkation would take place that night.[2] Later he decided that the enemy between Rafina and Porto Rafti was too strong; and meeting liaison officers from the 4th Brigade who said that a ship would be at Rafina that night, he turned back to rejoin the 250 in the caique. In the meantime the owner of the caique—a pro-German the villagers declared—had disappeared, having first ensured that his ship's auxiliary engine could not be started. Nevertheless the caique was loaded with men and was preparing to set off under sail when at 1.15 a.m. the dim shape of a destroyer appeared off shore. It was the *Havock* whose captain, Lieut-Commander Watkins,[3] had learnt that men were left at Rafina and had steamed from Porto Rafti to pick them up. Brigadier Charrington and the main body of troops had now returned, and by 4 a.m. the 800 were aboard the destroyer and on the way to Crete.

There had been no embarkation from the beaches of the Peloponnese that night (27th-28th April). The transports used on the 26th-27th were then at Alexandria; four cruisers and twelve destroyers had been engaged escorting or protecting them.

Meanwhile at Miloi and Tripolis the 6th Brigade saw no signs of the enemy except in the air. Freyberg ordered Barrowclough to hold till dark and then move back to Monemvasia as fast as he could. Consequently at midday he began thinning out his troops. The 26th Battalion moved south under air attack, which though frequent, caused only three casualties. The remainder of the brigade, with Freyberg's battle headquarters, moved at night, and by daylight on the 28th had travelled 120 miles and was concealed within the defensive line at Monemvasia.

At Monemvasia Lee already had his force in position; and Colonel Clifton and the New Zealand engineers had placed in the road depth-charges from a Greek destroyer which was aground in the harbour. The rear party of Group headquarters, including Rear-Admiral Baillie-Grohman, was established near by, and Colonels Quilliam[4] and Blunt[5] (the military attaché at Athens) had collected the local caiques in case of need. The inhabitants had been induced to go to villages in the hills so that the town would appear to scouting aircraft to be deserted.[6]

---

[1] Another caique which had been reconditioned by the NZ beach party for an emergency, disappeared during the night 26th-27th.

[2] Maj T. H. E. Oakes, second-in-command of the NZ A-Tk Regt, had walked through the German lines to Porto Rafti and back that day—30 odd miles of very rough going—to arrange this.

[3] Lt-Cdr G. R. G. Watkins, DSO, DSC; RN. In HMS *Havock, Kent, Devonshire* and *Norfolk*. B. 2 Sep 1910.

[4] Col C. D. Quilliam, OBE. GSO1 GHQ ME 1939-42; Paiforce 1942-43. Regular soldier; b. Dublin, 11 Jun 1898.

[5] Brig J. S. Blunt; RA. Mil attaché, Athens 1941; Brit Mil Mission to Bulgaria (head of Army Sec) 1944-46. Regular soldier; b. 6 Jul 1898.

[6] During the day Lee's force was joined by about forty of the 4th Hussars who had escaped from Corinth.

At the Argos beaches—Navplion and Tolos—there were now more than 2,000 troops, many without rations, and the number was increasing as parties of stragglers arrived. Enemy aircraft were overhead during the day machine-gunning and bombing. A rearguard force was organised from the Australian Reinforcement Battalion and some 200 men of the 3rd Royal Tanks, the only fighting detachments in the area. Destroyers were expected on the night of the 27th-28th but none arrived, and at 3 a.m. the troops who had assembled ready to embark dispersed to spend another day in hiding. At 4 a.m. Major O'Loughlin gave Major MacLean 150,000 drachmae (about £250) from a fund of 250,000 issued at Servia a fortnight earlier for hire of donkeys, and sent him and a naval officer along the coast to collect small boats to speed the embarkation on the next night, and caiques in case no ships arrived. Sixteen boats were found but when the Greek owners learnt that the Germans were near they were unwilling to provide them at any price.

At Kalamata about 6,000 out of more than 8,000 men were unarmed and largely leaderless base troops, Palestinian and Cypriot labourers of the pioneer corps, Greeks, Yugoslavs, and Lascar seamen from ships sunk off Greece. The only organised fighting troops were the New Zealand Reinforcement Battalion (about 800 men under Major MacDuff[7]), a force of 380 Australians (including about 70 of the 2/1st Field Regiment and the transport detachments of the battalions of the 17th Brigade, all under Lieut-Colonel Harlock[8]), and about 300 men of the squadrons of the 4th Hussars who arrived that day. At dusk on the 27th, as the troops were forming up to march to the beach and the quay again, about twenty-five bombers came over and, making their runs at no more than 500 feet, for an hour dropped sticks of bombs across the already battered town. When they had gone the men patiently formed up again and stood waiting for the ships as they had done the night before. But no ships appeared off Kalamata that night, and at 1 a.m. the troops dispersed to their lying-up places among the trees. The 4th Hussars were given the task of providing an outer defence for Kalamata; the New Zealand battalion was to be in position at 7.30 p.m. to cover the hoped-for embarkation on the night of the 28th.

---

[7] Maj A. P. MacDuff; 20 NZ Bn. Commercial traveller; of Christchurch, NZ; b. 29 Aug 1906.

[8] This patchwork force was organised into the following detachments (some of the figures are approximate):

	Officers	Men
2/1 Fd Regt	7	64
16 Bde	2	3
17 Bde	2	50
2/5 Bn	1	53
2/6 Bn	1	50
2/7 Bn	1	50
Corps petrol company		20
2/1 MG Bn	1	4
Corps signals		20
Det from Daphni Staging Camp	4	40
Corps headquarters		7
	19	361

(Lt-Col T. G. Walker, 2/7 Bn)

The stern of the sinking *Costa Rica* viewed from the *City of London*, the nearest ship in the convoy, with HMS *Defender* on the left. 27th April.

(Capt B. Brock, 2/2 Bn)

A group of officers and men of the 2/2nd Battalion on the eve of their departure from the Aegean island of Euboea, 8th May 1941.

Back row: Pte M. J. Sanders; Cpl J. W. H. Fuller; Cpl H. J. Honeywell; Lt-Col F. O. Chilton; Capt C. H. Green; Capt B. Brock; Lt A. K. Bosgard; Capt A. A. Buckley; Cpl J. Shanahan.

Front row: Pte J. A. E. Whitton; L-Sgt R. C. Smith; Pte H. R. Brown; Pte W. Schofield.

Of the nine officers and N.C.O's in this photograph four were subsequently killed: Honeywell, Shanahan and Bosgard in New Guinea; and Green when leading a battalion in Korea in 1950.

(Maj S. B. Cann, 2/1 Fd Coy)

(Australian War Memorial)

Australian troops resting on the shores of Suda Bay.

Of the groups which remained in Greece on the 28th only one—the New Zealand brigade at Monemvasia—was a substantial, armed and disciplined fighting force (but without artillery weapons). The plan was to embark it in a cruiser and four destroyers that night, to send two cruisers and six destroyers to take off an estimated 7,000 men at Kalamata (actually there were more than that) and to send three sloops to Kithera Island whither some 800 had been transported in caiques and a landing craft.

That night the men on Kithera were ferried to the sloops in the landing craft, and then taken to Suda Bay, the sloop *Hyacinth* towing the landing craft. Embarkation went smoothly at Monemvasia. The destroyers *Isis* and *Griffin* arrived at 10.30 p.m. on the 28th and the cruiser *Ajax* and destroyers *Havock* and *Hotspur* about 1 a.m. The troops, having destroyed their vehicles, were ferried out to them in barges and local fishing boats. By 4 a.m. on the 29th the whole force including General Freyberg and Rear-Admiral Baillie-Grohman were embarked.

Meanwhile the Germans had been thrusting deeper into the Peloponnese. On the morning of the 28th reports had arrived that German parachute troops were near Navplion; whereupon the senior officer, Colonel Courage, announced that officers and men were free to make for the hills, and that he himself was doing so.

The group at the Tolos beach near by included a rearguard of the "Australian Composite Battalion" organised from troops in the Athens area. It had arrived at Argos before dawn on 26th April. It received an order to move to Kalamata prepared to fight a rearguard action. While in the Tripolis Pass it had been attacked by bombers and fighters, the road was made impassable, and one half of the battalion, under Major J. Miller and Captain D. R. Jackson, took up positions near Tripolis. There Jackson received orders from Brigadier Lee to cover the embarkations at Navplion and Tolos—the Argos beaches. The half-battalion, about 130 strong, took up a position covering Tolos beach, Navplion having then been abandoned. On the morning of the 28th, when all officers of the force round Navplion were instructed that those who wished to do so might break away, Miller and Jackson elected to fight on in an attempt to deny the beach to the enemy for another night. Jackson's group was deployed left of the road to Navplion and Miller's right of it. Early in the afternoon they engaged a column of Germans in trucks and captured carriers. After a fight lasting some three hours the little Australian force was overcome.

During the afternoon news was spreading among the troops round the beach that the force had surrendered. Most of the men did surrender, but in the confusion many parties from Tolos escaped, some in boats seized on the spot, some walking south along the coast until they found serviceable caiques.[9]

At Kalamata Parrington had organised his motley assemblage of troops into four groups ready for embarkation that night. First to embark were

---

[9] O'Loughlin and Bamford, for example, walked along the coast, and after many adventures, reached Crete on 9 May with 59 troops whom they had collected.

to be the wounded and their stretcher-bearers; next Pemberton Force, 1,400 men chiefly of the 80th Base Sub-Area; then Harlock Force, now comprising the Australians and New Zealanders; then Lister Force—some 2,400 British troops chiefly from depot units, 100 Indian mule drivers, about 2,000 Palestinian and Cypriot labourers; and lastly perhaps 2,000 other labourers, Yugoslavs and Lascars.

About 4 o'clock in the afternoon the Hussars patrolling north of Kalamata reported that they had been 25 miles from the port and made no contact with the enemy. Two hours later, however, as the troops were moving down to the beach to be ready to embark, German troops, having overrun the Hussars, drove into the town and to the quay, and captured the naval beach-master. Furious firing broke out round the quay. Harlock and other officers hurried parties of troops to the scene. MacDuff's New Zealand battalion fixed bayonets and charged towards the quay.

The fighting that followed was extremely confused. Only 70 of the 400 Australians under the command of Captain Gray could be used in this attack because of shortage of weapons. Gray divided these into two platoons, one of which joined the New Zealanders, while Gray led the other in an attack along the sea front. A concerted attack began about 8.15 p.m. By 9.30 the quay had been recaptured, two field guns which the Germans had established there had been taken, and about 100 of the enemy had been made prisoners.

The attacking German force consisted of two companies with two field guns. It was drawn from the *5th Armoured Division*. The Germans lost 41 killed and "about 60 wounded".

While this fighting was in progress the cruisers *Perth* and *Phoebe* and the destroyers *Nubian, Defender, Hero, Hereward, Decoy* and *Hasty* were approaching Kalamata. *Hero,* which was sent on ahead, arrived off Kalamata at 8.45 p.m., and received a signal, flashed from the harbour, that the Germans were in the town. *Hero* closed the beach and landed her first lieutenant. She then wirelessed *Perth,* whose captain, Bowyer-Smyth,[1] was senior officer of the squadron, that the Germans were in the town but British troops were to the south-east of it. At 9.10 p.m. *Perth* and the rest of the force, then 10 miles from Kalamata, saw tracer fire and a big explosion. At 9.30 *Hero's* first lieutenant reported that the beach was suitable for evacuation, and *Hero* signalled *Perth* accordingly, but because of a wireless defect this message did not reach *Perth* until 10.11 p.m. Meanwhile, acting on the earlier signal, Bowyer-Smyth, at 9.29 p.m., turned his force about and retired at 28 knots, ordering *Hero* to rejoin. By the time he received *Hero's* second signal Bowyer-Smyth was well on his way south and decided to continue retirement. *Hero,* joined later by the destroyers *Kandahar, Kimberley* and *Kingston,* remained until about 3 a.m., when they sailed, having taken on board some of the wounded and about 300 others.

---

[1] Capt Sir Philip Bowyer-Smyth; RN. Comd HMAS *Perth* 1940-41. B. 4 Feb 1894.

As soon as the destroyers had gone Parrington assembled all troops on the beach, summoned the officers and told them that the navy could do no more because of enemy naval action and that he proposed to send a message to the enemy that he would surrender at daybreak. Those who did not wish to surrender should be out of the area by 5 a.m., when it would be becoming light. Some of Parrington's listeners received the impression that commanding officers should consider it their duty to remain. Colonel Harlock, in command of the Australians and New Zealanders, said that he would remain. Parrington then sent an officer with a German prisoner who could speak English to the German headquarters to say that no resistance would be offered after 5.30 a.m.

That night there were probably 8,000 troops at Kalamata (not all British), perhaps 2,000 at Navplion and Tolos. No plan was made to embark the men at Navplion where it might be expected that the German advance-guard would arrive (as it did) that day. At Kalamata, however, the planned embarkation, if it had not been upset by the alarm caused by the arrival of a German detachment which the defending force dealt with, might well have removed most of those who remained.

After the 28th-29th Admiral Cunningham instructed Admiral Pridham-Wippell to attempt to bring off troops who might be straggling along the coast south of Kalamata. The destroyers *Isis*, *Hero* and *Kimberley* picked up 33 that night and 202 the next, when *Hotspur* and *Havock* also embarked 700 who had collected on the island of Milos. Among the Australians picked up south of Kalamata were Captains Woodhill and Vial, mentioned above, and Lieutenant Sweet[2] with a party of five of the 2/5th Battalion.[3]

---

[2] Lt-Col H. G. Sweet, VX7562. 2/5 Bn 1940-43; 58/59 Bn 1944-45. Clerk; of Elwood, Vic; b. St Kilda, Vic, 22 Jun 1918.

[3] Precisely how many were embarked each night can never be known; often the variation between one estimate and another is considerable. For example, the number embarked at Navplion on the 24th-25th was estimated by the beach-master at 5,500, by Admiral Pridham-Wippell at 6,685. The following table is based on figures given in Pridham-Wippell's dispatch. (The night on which the main body of each of the seven brigades embarked is also shown.)

	Night 24-25	Night 25-26	Night 26-27	Night 27-28	Night 28-29
Rafina and Porto Rafti	5,750 (5 NZ)	—	6,300 (1 Armd)	4,640 (4 NZ)	—
Megara	—	5,900 (19 Aust)	—	—	—
Tolos and Navplion	6,685	—	4,520	—	—
Monemvasia	—	—	—	—	4,320 (6 NZ)
Kalamata	—	—	8,650 (16 & 17 Aust)	—	332

Before the night of the 24th-25th about 1,300 were embarked at Piraeus; 820 were embarked from the island of Kithera on the 28th-29th; 250 from Kalamata and 700 from Milos after the 28th-29th. By 14 April 60,394 army and 2,217 air force personnel, a total of 62,611, had been taken to Greece by sea. Admiral Pridham-Wippell's dispatch of 5 May 1941 states that 50,672 (including 500 lost in the sinking of the *Slamat*) were embarked. But the losses in British, Dominion and colonial troops and air force in Greece totalled 14,700, whereas the difference between the total number of men landed in Greece and Admiral Pridham-Wippell's figure of embarkations, excluding those lost in the *Slamat*, is only 12,439. However, this difference of 2,300 is possibly accounted for by the embarkation of Greek troops, British civilians and others, by counting the same men twice during transfer from sinking or damaged craft, and by other similar errors.

I am indebted to Brigadier H. B. Latham, of the Historical Section of the United Kingdom Cabinet Office, for most of the above figures, and for others affecting the force as a whole which follow later.

There remained in Greece one organised Australian unit—a detachment of the 2/5th General Hospital commanded by Major Brooke Moore[4] and including six other officers and 150 other ranks. It was charged with the care of 112 patients, all too ill to be moved, and other casualties who might arrive. On the morning of the 27th the Germans came and placed a guard over the hospital area, which was at Kephissia, near Athens, but the Australians were allowed to continue their work unhindered. On 1st May Germans took the hospital's portable X-ray machine to replace one of their own, which had broken down, and next day took some of the hospital's reserve of rations.

On the 7th, on German orders, the hospital began to move to Kokkinia, a suburb of Athens; on the 10th, the day after the completion of the move, 29 wounded, with 9 New Zealand medical and 4 dental officers arrived from the south. On the 13th 50 patients arrived from the detachment of the 26th British General Hospital which had remained at Kephissia, and in the next few days 140 more, accompanied by rations and equipment. The British hospital was thereupon disbanded by the Germans, most of its medical staff being distributed to prison camps in the Peloponnese; but some medical officers went to the 2/5th Hospital. By the 20th, the strength of the 2/5th had risen to 28 officers and 188 other ranks, and in their care were more than 600 patients.

Late in May casualties began to arrive from Crete, and within a fortnight 1,500 patients had been admitted. Most of them had been severely wounded, many had received no medical attention since their first treatment in the field and were virtually without clothing. By the end of the month the hospital was overflowing and a hospital annexe for walking wounded had been opened. There the accommodation was poor and draughty, the sanitation primitive. Early in June the number of patients had increased to 1,590, and from time to time batches were sent to Salonika on the way to Germany. Gradually the numbers of patients dwindled. The convalescent section was closed in September and the whole hospital in December, when the staff of the unit was moved to Germany. The hospital had treated 3,026 military and 50 civilian patients. The Germans had been generally friendly and helpful, and, when stocks of dressings and drugs had dwindled, had replenished them.[5]

The losses of the German *Twelfth Army* in Greece were 1,160 killed, 3,755 wounded and 345 missing; these figures were announced by Hitler soon after the campaign ended.

The total strengths of the British, Australian and New Zealand contingents in Greece were: British Army 21,880, Palestinians and Cypriots

---

[4] Maj Brooke Moore, NX12361; 2/5 AGH. Medical practitioner; of Bathurst, NSW; b. Bathurst, 29 Aug 1899.

[5] The experiences of the 2/5 and 2/6 AGH's in Greece and of the other Australian medical units there are described in Allan S. Walker, *Middle East and Far East*, in the medical series of this history.

26-27 Apr THE ALLIED LOSSES 183

4,670, R.A.F. 2,217, Australian 17,125, New Zealand 16,720. So far as they can be ascertained, the losses suffered by the contingents were:[6]

	Killed	Wounded	Prisoners
British	146	87	6,480
R.A.F.	110	45	28
Australian	320	494	2,030
New Zealand	291	599	1,614
Palestinian and Cypriot	36	25	3,806

After the Anzac Corps withdrew from the Thermopylae-Brallos position the German columns slowly progressed along the cratered roads to Athens where, as we have seen, the first troops to arrive came from Corinth on the morning of the 27th. The *"Adolf Hitler"* Division at Yannina with an open road before it did not begin to advance south to outflank the Anzac rearguard position until the 26th. (The *73rd Division* remained in Epirus to police the surrender of the Greeks.) The *"Adolf Hitler"* reached Patras on the 27th, and remained in that area until the organised embarkation was over. The fast-moving *5th Armoured Division*, how-

---

[6] The losses sustained by infantry and artillery units of the 6th Australian Division and the New Zealand Division were:

	Killed	Wounded (and not made prisoners)	Prisoners
Australian:			
2/1st Battalion	16	17	51
2/2nd Battalion	14	16	112
2/3rd Battalion	12	31	62
2/5th Battalion	21	26	47
2/6th Battalion	28	43	217
2/7th Battalion	7	13	73
2/4th Battalion	26	38	163
2/8th Battalion	21	33	106
2/11th Battalion	32	32	37
2/1st Machine Gun Battalion	—	5	7
2/1st Field Regiment	6	7	60
2/2nd Field Regiment	11	10	23
2/3rd Field Regiment	7	17	2
2/1st Anti-tank Regiment	18	16	79

	Killed	Wounded	Prisoners
New Zealand:			
Divisional Cavalry Regiment	11	14	43
18th Battalion	26	57	97
19th Battalion	24	37	132
20th Battalion	25	55	69
21st Battalion	15	35	225
22nd Battalion	12	23	18
23rd Battalion	10	12	30
28th (Maori) Battalion	16	17	87
24th Battalion	10	12	130
25th Battalion	20	60	108
26th Battalion	17	40	47
27th (Machine-gun) Battalion	8	17	29
4th Field Regiment	7	21	61
5th Field Regiment	3	11	32
6th Field Regiment	3	16	20
7th Anti-tank Regiment	19	33	61

The British armoured, infantry and mobile artillery units suffered the following losses:

3rd Royal Tanks	289	102nd R.H.A.	277
4th Hussars	465	64th Medium Regiment	53
1/Rangers	198	7th Medium Regiment	181
2nd R.H.A.	113	106th R.H.A.	177

Men who were wounded before being made prisoner or who died of wounds in enemy hands are not included under the heading "prisoners" in the New Zealand table but are so included in the Australian figures.

ever, pushed into the Peloponnese on the 28th, reaching Argos, Navplion and Tripolis that day and Kalamata that night.

On the 28th April ten German divisions were in Greece and they were deployed thus:

Peloponnese,	5th Armoured, "Adolf Hitler"
Athens-Lamia,	2nd Armoured, 5th and 6th Mountain
Thessaly,	9th Armoured
Grevena-Yannina,	73rd
Katerini,	72nd
Salonika,	50th
Eastern Macedonia and the Aegean,	164th

Three infantry divisions (*50th, 72nd* and *164th*), two mountain (*5th* and *6th*) and the *2nd Armoured* had fought the Greeks in eastern Macedonia. Two infantry divisions (*"Adolf Hitler"* and *72nd*), two mountain divisions (*5th* and *6th*) and three armoured divisions (*9th, 2nd* and *5th*) had been engaged against the Anzac Corps. Three divisions of Field Marshal List's *Twelfth Army* (*46th, 76th* and *198th*) were still relatively idle in Bulgaria and southern Yugoslavia when the fighting in Greece ended. Thus, if a prolonged resistance had been offered on the Thermopylae line, List, without calling for help from the three armoured, two mountain and eight infantry divisions of the *Second Army* in central and northern Yugoslavia, could have deployed against the Anzac Corps, three armoured, two mountain, and eight infantry divisions.

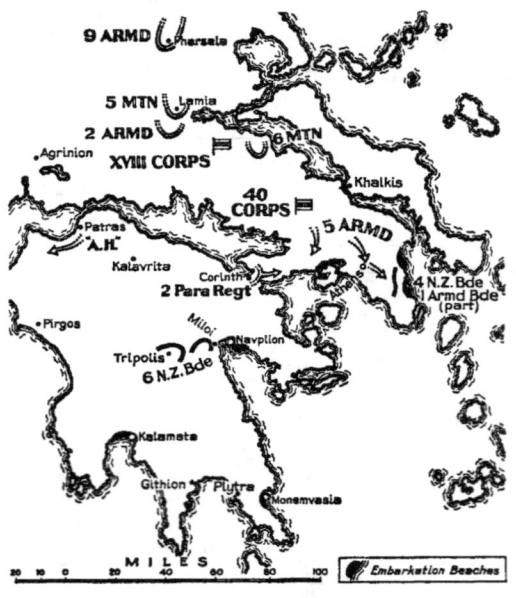

CHAPTER 8

ESCAPES TO CRETE AND TURKEY

AFTER destroyers had embarked the last parties, and the Germans had rounded up their prisoners—chiefly at Kalamata and Navplion—there were many British soldiers at large in Greece, some hundreds of whom contrived to escape to Turkey and elsewhere in the following months and eventually to rejoin their units. It is within the scope of this narrative to record the fate only of the larger Australian parties and of some individuals who were typical of other determined and enterprising escapers.

The largest such groups of Australians belonged to Lieut-Colonel Chilton's 2/2nd Battalion, most of which was cut off in the Pinios Gorge. During the night of the 18th-19th (ten days before the last large embarkation) that battalion was thrust into the hills above Tempe. Next day many of its scattered parties collected in the foothills of Mount Ossa; at the end of that day Major Cullen,[1] of Chilton's headquarters company, had twelve officers and 140 others, including some of the 21st New Zealand Battalion, under his command. Chilton, however, and the headquarters men who had been with him at dusk the previous day were not among them. Cullen marched his force to the coast near Karitsa hoping to find a naval vessel, but, after two days, the group, by mutual agreement, broke into small parties; the villages were small places of only from six to twenty houses and unable to provide food for large bodies of troops. Cullen had distributed some 200,000 drachmae belonging to the regimental funds among the officers in charge of the small parties and they were thus able to buy food, particularly sheep and pigs—though generally the villagers refused to accept payment.

Most of these men went south, and on 25th April the majority, having reassembled, were ferried by Greeks to Skiathos, whence in stages they sailed in luggers to Chios. Here the people were most hospitable; the women provided a free meal in the public school, and a Greek shipowner, Mr D. G. Limos, lent Cullen and Captain Trousdale[2] of the 21st New Zealand Battalion 150,000 drachmae. The Turkish coast was only 10 miles away but, fearing that they would be interned in Turkey, they arranged to join a 150-ton vessel which was leaving for Crete carrying 400 Greek officers and men. On the night of 29th April the ship sailed from Chios amid the cheers of a crowd on the waterfront. It went from island to island, and two days later met a vessel containing another large party including Captain Jackson. Jackson had been captured after the rearguard action at Tolos, mentioned above, but had escaped and reached the coast. There he and others seized a steamer at pistol point, and eventually collected a party of about 280, including about 100 Australians, 100

---

[1] Lt-Col P. A. Cullen, DSO, NX163. 2/2 Bn 1939-42; CO 2/1 Bn 1942-45. Chartered accountant; of Woollahra, NSW; b. Newcastle, NSW, 13 Feb 1909.

[2] Lt-Col A. C. Trousdale, MC. CO 1 Bn Nth Auckland Regt 1942-1943; CO 21 NZ Bn Jun-Jul 1942. Estate agent; of Howick, Auckland, NZ; b. Canada, 20 Oct 1895.

Greeks, and some Communists and Jews. On 4th May both ships sailed for Heraklion in Crete where the passengers landed on 5th May.

Because there was no room for them in the ship, a party of 97, later increased to 133, had been left behind at Chios, under Captain King, of the 2/2nd. The Greek Commandant, the Harbour Master and the Mayor (who had taken over responsibility for the British troops who remained) regretfully told King that there was not enough oil on the island to take a caique to Crete, but they could arrange a caique to Turkey. After making further efforts to obtain a vessel that could make a longer voyage they sailed, with Mr Noel Rees, British Vice-Consul at Chios, to Cesme in Turkey where, after a little hesitation, they were warmly welcomed. With the devoted help of Rees, Colonel Hughes[3]—an Australian—and others, they obtained a Greek yacht, the *Kalamara,* and in it King's party and another ten officers and men from Mytilene led by Lieutenant Harkness[4] sailed through the Italian Dodecanese islands and arrived in Cyprus on the 7th May. Hughes had spent many years in Turkey as an officer of the Imperial War Graves Commission, was *persona grata* with the Turks and well qualified to take part in the delicate task of organising the escape of prisoners through this neutral, though friendly, country.

Meanwhile Colonel Chilton and three men who were with him in the Pinios Gorge at first attempted to reach the 2/3rd Battalion but, having concluded that it had withdrawn, they began marching south-west. They passed through Sikourion and, farther south, came upon abandoned Australian and New Zealand lorries bogged in the plain east of Larisa and took tins of bully beef from them. Chilton's small party was joined by other groups. Tramping chiefly by night, avoiding the roads along which German convoys were streaming, and guided by devoted Greeks, they reached Euboea where they were joined on 7th May by Captains Buckley, Green[5] and Brock,[6] Lieutenant Bosgard[7], and five others who had also tried to walk back to their own force south of Lamia, and eventually, after days of arduous trudging in the hills, had reached this island. On the 8th May, they obtained a boat and sailed to Skyros by way of Skopelos. There they met a party of sixteen men, including Sergeant Peirce of their own battalion, who had news of the escape of Cullen's large party.

Peirce's party, after much wandering, had been landed on Skyros by a Greek sea captain on the 7th May. In his diary Peirce wrote an account, typical of many, of the kind of warm welcome which Greek peasants and fisherfolk gave to the fugitives:

---

[3] Col C. E. Hughes, CBE. (1st AIF: Lt 1 LH Regt.) Dep Dir of Works Imp War Graves Commn, Gallipoli 1919-25; Chief Admin Offr, Imp War Graves Commn Eastern District 1925-36; Aust Govt Commnr in Egypt 1937-40. Att RAF ME 1940. Civil Engineer; of Deloraine, Tas, and Cairo; b. Launceston, Tas, 6 Sep 1890. See C. E. W. Bean, *Gallipoli Mission* (1948) for a sketch of this officer.

[4] Capt J. B. Harkness, NX12284. 2/2 Bn; RAE Water Tptn. Accountant; of Mosman, NSW; b. Mosman, 5 Jan 1908.

[5] Lt-Col C. H. Green, DSO, NX121. 2/2 Bn, and CO 2/11 Bn 1945. CO 3 Bn Royal Aust Regt Korea 1950. Farmer; of Ulmarra, NSW; b. Sth Grafton, NSW, 26 Dec 1919. Killed in action, Korea, 2 Nov 1950.

[6] Capt B. Brock, NX239; 2/2 Bn. School teacher; of Woonona, NSW; b. Darwin, 31 Mar 1907.

[7] Capt A. K. Bosgard, NX34872; 2/2 Bn. Bank clerk; of Mosman, NSW; b. Sydney, 8 Feb 1914. Killed in action, 27 Nov 1942.

Eventually about 5 p.m. (on the 25th April) we arrived at Zagari amidst much weeping by the fairer sex and were taken to a house where we were more or less put on exhibition. Most of the people who visited us left something for us to eat and within a short while we had each partaken of three eggs, half a glass of goat's milk with plenty of bread and cheese . . . . Blankets arrived and soon we adorned the floor in slumber again. At 10 p.m. we were awakened for another feed consisting of three more eggs each, with bread, olives and a sip of milk. We were then told to pack up and we were taken to another house about a mile away where an old codger thought he could speak English and we had some fun with him till another meal arrived. Two low tables were placed together and cloths put on, then dishes of vegetables, mostly potato, two dishes of fried eggs, one of olives and one of small fish like sardines.

On the 10th this party was awakened by a Greek soldier who was with them and told that a boatload of Germans had landed. The "Germans" were Colonel Chilton and his group, now sixteen strong. After some narrow escapes from detection by German aircraft, since the enemy now occupied Chios and Mytilene, the combined party reached the Turkish coast near Smyrna.

> On the way down to Smyrna we met two elderly Turkish colonels (wrote Chilton later). Both had been wounded by Australians during the first war, and they were very proud of it. They said they had squarely beaten us at Gallipoli, even though we made up for it later. They appeared to have the greatest admiration for the Australians of those days—in fact, they echoed sentiments I have heard expressed by our chaps about the Turk. The first man we saw at Smyrna was Colonel Hughes. What a joy he was—and imagine our surprise at being greeted by such a typical Australian. We were quartered in the barracks, but he had laid on everything—hot baths, haircuts, underclothing, food, beer, cigarettes, sweets and goodness knows what else. We also learned for the first time what had been happening in the world. We were delighted to know that Tobruk was holding out.

Sergeant Tanner and another group of eighteen men of the 2/2nd were already in Hughes' care at Smyrna. In civilian clothes, and with instructions to tell anyone who asked questions that they were "English civilian engineers", they all went by train to Alexandretta and thence by Norwegian tanker to Port Said where they arrived on 24th May. On this ship, the *Alcides* (7,634 tons) there were some 250 refugees, including 66 Norwegians who had escaped by way of Russia. It was not until he reached Gaza that Chilton learnt the answer to the question that had worried him from the time that his battalion had been forced back by German tanks: whether his battalion had delayed the enemy long enough to enable the remainder of the force to get through Larisa safely.

Corporal Irvine[8] of the 2/2nd Battalion with two other men of his unit and one of the 21st New Zealand, after having failed to obtain a boat, decided to walk to Turkey by way of Salonika, but, after two days, met a Greek who offered to obtain them a passage to one of the islands. On the 11th May they were taken to Skiathos and thence to Skopelos. There they found it difficult to obtain a boat since "the islands were constantly patrolled by sea and air, oil and benzine were unprocurable, and all serviceable boats were commandeered to take Germans to Crete". Eventually a friendly Greek who had been in touch with the British consuls in Greece helped them to obtain a passage to Cesme in Turkey where they arrived on 2nd August and whence, after ten days in quarantine, they were sent to Syria.

Numbers of men taken prisoner in the Peloponnese escaped from prison camps, from trains or from columns of marching prisoners farther north. Such an escape was made by Warrant-Officer Boulter,[9] captured at Kalamata on 29th April. Next day the prisoners were taken by train to a camp at Corinth where, he was told, about 10,000 British prisoners were assembled, including 350 officers. There were also 4,000 to 5,000 Italians who had been captured by the Greeks, released, and rounded up again

---

[8] Cpl L. J. Irvine, NX1755; 2/2 Bn. Builder's labourer; of Narrabri, NSW; b. Adelaide, 12 May 1914.

[9] Capt T. A. M. Boulter, MM, VX13678; Aust Int Corps. Barrister and solicitor; of Melbourne; b. Frankston, Vic, 31 Mar 1916.

by the Germans. Sanitation was bad and there was much dysentery. While at Corinth the prisoners watched aircraft taking off for Crete and returning bullet-riddled or with broken wings. On 5th June began a move of all prisoners to Germany. Because railway bridges had been destroyed the prisoners were marched to Lamia.

Boulter escaped on 7th June by jumping into some low scrub beside the road and lying there until dark. That evening he obtained clothing from a Greek and for some days worked in the fields in return for food and shelter. Thence he was sent to a remote and self-contained mountain village on Mount Oiti near Lamia where he was joined by two other Australians, a British pilot, and a Pole. They decided to make their way to Euboea and thence from island to island to Turkey. They left the friendly villagers, crossed the railway and main road, climbed the Kallidromon mountains and reached the coast where, on 22nd June, a fisherman ferried them to Euboea. Here, among Greeks they listened to the B.B.C. broadcasting the news that Germany had invaded Russia. The Greeks made the fugitives so comfortable that all but Boulter decided to remain where they were. He walked through the hills to the east coast of Euboea and then along it seeking in vain for a passage. He could now speak "quite a little Greek", and he eventually reached a monastery, where (as always at the monasteries) the priests treated the fugitive with great sympathy, and the bishop arranged with a fisherman to take him to Skyros, first stage in the escape of many Allied soldiers. He walked across the island to Skyros town, and there met a Greek who had already been paid by the Consul at Smyrna for ferrying escapers thither. They reached Smyrna on 25th July after three days at sea, and sailed to Haifa on a Greek tramp about ten days later.

Gunner Barnes,[1] 2/1st Field Regiment, was taken prisoner at Kalamata on 30th April, jumped from a train 80 miles north of Salonika, and wandered through northern Greece. He was helped by Greeks for about six weeks, when he sailed with Greeks from the Mount Athos peninsula to Turkey, and thence rejoined his unit.

Fugitives were still at large in 1942 when the resistance movement in Greece had developed in strength. Lieutenant Derbyshire[2] of the 2/2nd Battalion escaped from a prison camp near Athens with three other officers. At length they separated, Derbyshire establishing himself in Athens where he met Greeks who were active in the resistance movement, and he took part in sabotage exploits. Like other fugitives at large in Athens, he saw and suffered the famine that followed the German-Italian occupation. Long afterwards when commanding a forward company at Dagua in New Guinea he said:

> The peasants did not feel the pinch as much as the people in the cities where the poorer classes lived in dreadful poverty. Few had work and, because of inflation, those who did received about enough in a month to get enough food for a day. Men,

---

[1] Gnr C. E. Barnes, NX3317; 2/1 Fd Regt. Labourer; of Woollahra, NSW; b. Harbord, NSW, 13 Nov 1921.

[2] Capt M. Derbyshire, MC, NX12177; 2/2 Bn. Motor trimmer; of Wagga, NSW; b. Launceston, Tas, 27 Jun 1915.

women and little children starved to death and died in the streets. Little kids of three or four, with old faces, fought in the gutters with the few stray dogs left for small scraps of food or bone. For meat we used horses, donkeys, dogs and cats and all kinds of shell-fish.

In the winter of 1942 Derbyshire joined a party of ten Britons and Greeks who had arranged to embark in a caique on the east coast of Euboea. After five days of walking and climbing they joined the caique and crossed to Turkey, and thence, with the help of the Consulate-General, travelled by railway to Syria.

The experiences of only some Australians who escaped have been described. Other Australian, New Zealand and British soldiers had equally exacting journeys and exhibited similar fortitude. A number of Australian officers and men who escaped survived to hold important posts or give long regimental service. For example, in 1945, Chilton was commanding the 18th Brigade in Borneo, Cullen the 2/1st Battalion in New Guinea, Green the 2/11th, Buckley the 2/1st Pioneer, Jackson the 2/28th; Miller died of scrub typhus in New Guinea in 1942 after leading the 2/31st Battalion through the Owen Stanleys campaign.

CHAPTER 9

RETROSPECT

THE British expedition to Greece was undertaken partly with the object of establishing a front in the Balkans in cooperation with Greece and, it was hoped, Turkey and Yugoslavia, and partly because the British nations had a moral obligation to give substantial help to the hard-pressed Greeks, whom they had guaranteed to assist against any aggressor. The moral obligation was felt the more deeply because Greece was the only surviving ally of the British Commonwealth, and, although a small nation, had fought resolutely—and with success—against the Italians, and was willing to defend herself against Germany. Leaders in Britain and the Dominions were anxious about the unhappy results that might follow, particularly in the United States, if Britain failed to support her ally with all her strength. In their view, the expedition had to be undertaken to maintain the prestige of the British Commonwealth, if for no other reason.

In January the Greek leaders had declined a British offer of help on the grounds that it was so small that not only would it be ineffective but likely to provoke German retaliation. The offer to send a force to Greece was finally accepted, but a condition imposed by the Greeks was that the British force should not arrive until the German Army had entered Bulgaria —when an invasion of Greece was virtually inevitable, and when there would be little time left to transport an effective force from Egypt and build up an enduring front in the Balkans.

The Greek leaders were grateful. Later Papagos wrote that he considered that it was not for military but political reasons that Britain offered aid.

> For Greece to be crushed without a single British soldier striking a blow in her defence would have meant a flagrant breach of the promises so repeatedly given (he said). Such a defection might well have provoked an outcry against the British Government on the part of the British people and Press. Also it would certainly have had an unfavourable effect on American public opinion.... In any case, we Greeks, regardless of the effectiveness of the British aid, owe a debt of gratitude to the British Empire, whose sons came to Greece to fight and get killed by our side.[1]

A Greek republican leader, General Sarafis, afterwards outstanding in the Resistance Army during the German-Italian occupation, went farther and declared that it was Greece who had failed to fulfil her obligations to Britain. In common with other republicans and liberals in Greece, he regarded the monarchists as only half-hearted enemies of Nazism.

> Our British allies were left to continue the fight alone and exposed (he wrote); and thus, at Thermopylae where Leonidas and his 300 Spartans fell, a singular thing came to pass—the Greeks were absent while the British fought. We ought to have put up a defence to the last moment, to have constituted ourselves the rearguard and facilitated the retreat of the British and of as many Greek troops as possible for use on another front.

---

[1] Papagos, p. 316.

The responsibility for this does not lie with our people, who did their duty to the fullest extent. Nor are the generals who capitulated alone responsible but, rather, all our rulers who not only did not take proper measures to prevent surrender, but by their general attitude suggested that very thing.[2]

Opinions will differ on the question whether the expedition was necessary to maintain the prestige of the Allied cause, particularly in the United States. On the one hand is the down-to-earth military opinion forcibly expressed by General Blamey, that another defeat would do more harm than good to the reputation of the British Commonwealth. On the other is the point of view of Britons, in England and the Dominions, who were sensitive to any possible slur on British honour, particularly since the surrender at Munich, and who were convinced that the spectacle of one great Power standing by its promise or duty to a little one was of immense value to the cause, whether in the United States or in the world at large.

The principal aim of the British intervention, however, was to establish a Balkan front; yet at no time does there seem to have been sufficient good evidence to justify the hope entertained by Mr Churchill and his colleagues that Turkey or Yugoslavia would take effective steps towards combined action against attack by Germany. The hopes of the Ministers in London seem to have been based either on inaccurate information or excessive optimism. Thus, very soon after Britain decided to send a large expedition to Greece, the then leaders of Yugoslavia virtually surrendered to Hitler, and the Turks made it clear, as they had done before, that they considered that Britain lacked sufficient military strength to intervene effectively in the Balkans. The Greek leaders agreed with them on this point.

All but four weak divisions of the Greek Army (later two more weak divisions were hurriedly formed) were engaged against a stronger Italian army in Albania. The most that Britain could offer was approximately four divisions, including only a brigade of armour. On the other hand the only limit on the force that the German Army could employ was the capacity of the roads to carry them. (This, as the operations showed, was a genuine limit, because when the British embarkation from the Peloponnese ended fewer than one-third of the divisions of the German *Twelfth Army* had managed to reach southern Greece.) In the event the German staff greatly over-estimated both the force opposed to them and the ability of the Balkan roads to carry their own army, and made available against Greece and Yugoslavia an extravagantly large army group of twenty-seven divisions, including seven armoured (one of which spent April on the Bulgarian-Turkish frontier). The actual conquest of Yugoslavia and Greece was achieved by a fraction of the troops the Germans laboriously deployed. In the face of such reserve power, detailed examination of Allied supply problems, the state of the Greek Army, and the degree of Allied inferiority in the air, would be prolix.

When the invasion of Greece began the exact date of the invasion of Russia had not been fixed by the German High Command. In December

---

[2] S. Sarafis, *Greek Resistance Army* (Eng. trans. 1951), p. xxvi.

it had directed that preparations must be complete by 15th May; on 24th January the 1st June was mentioned as the estimated date. Immediately after the coup in Yugoslavia, however, the invasion of Russia was postponed for about four weeks—an inexact decision since the date of the proposed operation had never been fixed. On 6th April plans for the occupation of Yugoslavia were complete and it was decided that the invasion of Russia could begin on the 22nd June. This date was confirmed on 30th April. Thus the date was tentatively fixed on the day on which the attack on Greece and Yugoslavia opened and confirmed as soon as the Greek campaign ended.[3]

The Germans rapidly re-deployed their Balkan armies for the attack on Russia. By 14th May only three armoured and fifteen unarmoured divisions remained in the Balkans; by 21st June no armoured divisions and seven unarmoured divisions. On 21st June seventeen armoured and 106 unarmoured divisions of the German Army, and other formations provided by the satellite nations, were deployed on the Russian front.

General Papagos later expressed a conviction that the wise course for Britain would have been to concentrate on the conquest of Libya rather than the defence of Greece. General O'Connor, the commander in the field in Cyrenaica, believed that, given full naval and air support, he could have taken Tripoli, had it not been that his advance was halted to enable the force to be sent to Greece—and a fortnight was to pass between the end of the fighting in Cyrenaica and the day on which the Greek leaders accepted the British offer of military help. Before the British and German Armies met in Greece, the reduced garrison of Cyrenaica was in retreat.

> The outstanding lesson of the Greek campaign (wrote General Blamey in his dispatch) is that no reasons whatever should outweigh military considerations when it is proposed to embark on a campaign, otherwise failure and defeat are courted. The main principles that must be satisfied are that the objects to be secured should be fully understood, the means to achieve the objects should be adequate and the plan should be such as will ensure success. All three essentials were lacking in the campaign in Greece, with the resultant inevitable failure. As far as my limited knowledge goes, the main reason for the dispatch of the force appears to have been a political one, viz., to support the Greeks to vindicate our agreed obligations.

It has been seen that Dill, Wavell and Cunningham undertook the expedition with some misgivings though they did not doubt its correctness; but it would have been difficult for them to oppose it. The British Cabinet made it clear at an early stage that it was determined to establish a force in the Balkans if it could, and the personality of the British Prime Minister must be taken into account in any assessment of the decisions of his immediate subordinates. In experience of the conduct of policy in war he towered above his contemporaries, whether in Europe or America. He was autocratic, had a considerable knowledge of military and naval affairs, and an uncommon grasp of their details; he was supported by immense

---

[3] This summary has been derived from a detailed monograph prepared in March 1952 by the Enemy Documents Section of the Historical Branch of the UK Cabinet Office.

prestige, and it required men of phenomenal strength and forthrightness to tell him that he was wrong. The Australian Prime Minister, Mr Menzies, was astonished at the manner in which he dominated his Cabinet.

In other circumstances the Dominion Governments concerned might have vetoed the adventure. Throughout 1940 and 1941, however, the Dominion Governments were not informed on questions of military policy fully and promptly enough to enable them to make important strategical decisions, and, in addition, were clearly impressed by the necessity of presenting a united front. The habit of accepting the solution offered by senior British leaders was deeply engrained.

When facing a crucial problem Menzies might have been expected to consult Blamey, and Blamey to have expressed his opinion to his minister, as he had the right to do. But, as a result of misunderstandings, Menzies had been told in London that Blamey agreed, Blamey in Egypt that Menzies agreed. In any event (and it is in this respect that, in this episode, the method of cooperation with the Dominions chiefly failed), when the Dominion leaders were consulted it was too late. The British envoys had offered to Greece an army consisting chiefly of three divisions—two Australian and one New Zealand—and it had been accepted by the Greeks. The Dominion Governments were left a choice between concurrence on the one hand and, on the other, a veto which would have required the British Commonwealth to break an undertaking with its ally. They concurred. For any disregard of their rights and responsibilities the Dominion Ministers themselves were largely responsible. It was their duty to ensure that they were adequately informed on military matters, and to assert their right to swift and adequate information from London and effective consultation.

The record of the consultations between British and Greek commanders is a sorry tale of misunderstanding, and the campaign opened in an atmosphere of mistrust. One principal object of the British political leaders was to establish cooperation with Yugoslavia, and the Greeks were particularly anxious that this should be done. With sound logic Papagos was resolved to attempt to hold Salonika, the only port through which Yugoslav resistance could be maintained, until the attitude of Yugoslavia had been defined. The British commanders saw the advantage of holding Salonika but, after learning of the dispositions of the Greek Army, decided that it would be advisable to deploy on the Olympus-Vermion line in country difficult to an attacker. The coup in Yugoslavia revived the possibility of holding a line forward of Salonika, but efforts to establish an effective liaison with the Yugoslav Army proved unsuccessful.

Lack of confidence in the Greeks, established in the minds of the British and Dominion commanders before the fighting opened, strongly influenced the conduct of the campaign. General Wilson decided to withdraw from the Aliakmon position because, he believed, the Greeks had disintegrated on his left. It has been seen, however, that the more dangerous breach of the Allied line occurred not in the Greek sector on the left, but on the right of the Anzac Corps. That Corps was not strong enough to hold the Olympus-Aliakmon line against the forces which the Germans could bring against them. Later, when the British force retired and occupied the Thermopylae position, and the Greek army in Epirus surrendered, the capitulation of that army was given as a reason why the Thermopylae position would be untenable. Actually no threat to the Anzac force developed from that flank; and, whatever happened in Epirus, the Thermopylae position could not have been held against List's army by the depleted Anzac Corps. It was regrettable that efforts were made to place responsibility for failure on the Greeks who had fought well against both Italians and Germans. Finally, the military planning of the embarkation was left until too late, and two commanders and staffs well qualified to take part in controlling an orderly and complete withdrawal and embarkation were sent out of Greece too early. In retrospect it is evident that a more deliberate withdrawal could have been carried out and thousands of base troops who were left behind could have been saved.

Pride is a military virtue. The soldier is "jealous in honour, sudden and quick in quarrel, seeking the bubble reputation even in the cannon's mouth". The reputation of a senior commander seldom survives a failure. A humiliating feature of a set-back in which the foot-soldier has stood his ground but the general management has been faulty is the recrimination that follows and may infect the troops as well as their leaders. An Air Force officer from Greece wrote of the scene in Cairo immediately after the evacuation:

> At both Army and Air Headquarters during the next few days there was a hum of splenetic activity, reminiscent of an overturned beehive. Everybody was writing out reports, the Army blaming the Air Force . . . the Air Force blaming the Army . . . . The atmosphere was full of acrimonious tension, which was felt even by other ranks, for there were incidents at Alexandria between soldiers just in from Greece and men of the R.A.F., some of whom had never even been there.[4]

Before the war it had been generally realised that air attack would be more accurate and persistent than in the war of 1914-18; actual experience of air assault on rear positions and convoys vividly impressed some senior commanders and staffs in 1940 and 1941, and gave them temporarily an exaggerated conception of the power of aircraft (in the numbers available in those years) decisively to influence fighting on the ground. Some of them asserted that British air inferiority had been a decisive factor in Greece. If so much as a platoon had altered its position because it had been attacked from the air, or if substantial casualties had been inflicted on the rearguards by aircraft, or the transport and supply of the force seriously impeded because they had destroyed its trucks, there would be support for such a contention. The fact was that the German Air Force failed to achieve any of these results in Greece; its greatest success was the destruction wrought in the port of Athens. The time was then distant when

---

[4] A. S. G. Lee, *Special Duties* (1946), p. 111.

air power, vastly stronger than that employed by the Germans in Greece, considerably more accurate in its fire and more closely coordinated, would be able to play a part comparable with, say, the artillery in an action on the ground.

After the campaign there was also much discussion of equipment—whether the force as a whole was adequately armed, whether the unit and the man were as well provided as their enemy. In fact the British formations in Greece were probably no better or worse armed than their German adversaries, who were happy to refit vehicles and weapons captured in this as in earlier campaigns. The infantry were flung into a mountain campaign against expert mountain troops who were better equipped and trained than they were for such operations. Nevertheless, at short notice they converted themselves into mountain troops to the extent that they covered the ground and solved the new tactical problems. Inevitably useful lessons were learnt as a result of first meeting with another first-class army—for the Anzac Corps was a well-trained force and in fine fettle—but the defeat suffered by the Corps was not the result of lack of equipment within the formations but of the deployment of an enemy force stronger both in armour and infantry.

The Anzac Corps carried out a series of successful rearguard actions—in each of its positions the clash did not come until after plans for the next withdrawal had been made; each was a rearguard action in the strictest sense of the word. Perhaps the most important military lesson of the campaign was its demonstration of the extent to which, in such rugged country, artillery, with reliable infantry ahead, could halt and confuse a pursuer, and, after each retirement, engineers, cratering the roads at well-selected places, could delay for days the advance of a force tied to a multitude of laden vehicles—as was the German. In retrospect, the fighting withdrawal of more than 300 miles, generally along a single road, with the loss of but one fighting unit, seems an outstanding military achievement.

CHAPTER 10

THE PROBLEM OF CRETE

THERE were good reasons why the Germans should attempt to advance southward through the eastern Mediterranean and occupy Crete. It was desirable for them to rob their enemy of potential air bases only 700 miles from the Rumanian oilfields, and by so doing gain for themselves bases which lay only 250 miles from North Africa, and from which, as from Rhodes and the Dodecanese, they could harass British shipping. To attempt a purely seaborne invasion of Crete would be hazardous in view of the unreliability of the Italian Navy; however, the German Army possessed a large force of paratroops and had already used them with success in Holland and at Corinth. If these could seize one or more of the Cretan airfields, other troops might be landed from the air, and perhaps still more troops, with heavier equipment, be ferried in small ships from southern Greece.

In March the defence of Crete against heavy airborne attack had been exercising the minds of leaders and staffs in Cairo—as in London. During April, however, other demands had been pressing upon the British Commanders-in-Chief in the Middle East, and it is impossible to appreciate their problems without knowledge of the calamitous events which had been occurring in other areas.

During the campaign in Greece an Axis army had been rapidly advancing through Cyrenaica. It was the threat offered on this western flank that led to the decision not to send the 7th Australian Division and the Polish Brigade to Greece but to retain them to reinforce the army in North Africa. There, in the early days of April, the 2nd Armoured Division and the 9th Australian Division had been thrust back.[1] Three British generals, including O'Connor, had been captured. By 11th April the 9th Australian Division, a brigade of the 7th, and the 3rd Armoured Brigade had been isolated in Tobruk. On the 13th, German and Italian forces attacked Tobruk but were repulsed; farther east, they took Salum and Halfaya Pass. At these points the advance was halted, but the British forces which were holding at Tobruk and east of the Egyptian frontier were perilously weak.

It was fortunate that, early in April, the Italian army in Abyssinia was decisively beaten, and, as a result, General Wavell would soon be able to bring reinforcements northward from that theatre. On the other hand disturbing events were occurring in Iraq on his remote eastern flank—events which in their ultimate effect were to govern the future operations of a large part of the Australian force.

From the beginning of the war the British leaders had to take into account the possibility that the nationalist leaders in Iraq would seize the

---

[1] These operations will be described in detail in the next volume in this series—C. Wilmot, *Tobruk and El Alamein*.

chance to expel the British garrison, which had been reduced to a shadow
—an air force school and depot equipped with training aircraft and a few
troops to guard them. Nevertheless, it was vital to Britain that Iraq should
remain under the control either of rulers well-disposed to Britain, or failing
that, of a British army. The oil from Persia was piped to Basra in Iraq,
the oil from Iraq to Haifa. It would have been calamitous if these supplies
had been cut off; and, if Iraq was in the hands of a pro-German clique,
the Germans might be tempted to march through Turkey to Iraq and
establish themselves and their submarines and aircraft on the shores of the
Indian Ocean.

The anti-British movement in Iraq was headed by Rashid Ali, who had
been Prime Minister from April 1940 until January 1941. He was strongly
supported by the Grand Mufti of Jerusalem, a vigorous leader of the Arab
Nationalist movement and an enemy of Britain. The Grand Mufti in
September had approached the German Government with a plan for
stirring up anti-British movements in Iraq, Syria and Transjordan, but
the German Government had then been unenthusiastic.

Because Iraq had virtual independence and possessed an army of more
than 50,000 men—trained and equipped by Britain and commanded by
Iraqi officers who had passed through the British staff college—Arab
nationalists throughout the Middle East looked to Baghdad to raise their
banner at an opportune moment.[2] In January the Germans began to

---

[2] This army was organised in four divisions with a total of 18 four-gun batteries of artillery.

reconsider the Grand Mufti's proposal and to seek means of trickling arms into Iraq. Early in April Rashid Ali became Prime Minister, and the Amir Abdul Illah, uncle of the infant King and a supporter of British influence, who was acting as Regent, having learnt that the new Prime Minister intended to arrest him, fled to Basra and thence to Transjordan.

Thereupon, the British Government decided to land a force at Basra, calling upon its treaty right to pass limited numbers of troops through Iraq. A brigade group of the 10th Indian Division which was then embarking at Karachi for Malaya was diverted to Basra where it landed without incident on 18th April. Responsibility for control of the force in Iraq was then transferred to the Commander-in-Chief in India, who, since January 1941, had been General Sir Claude Auchinleck.[3]

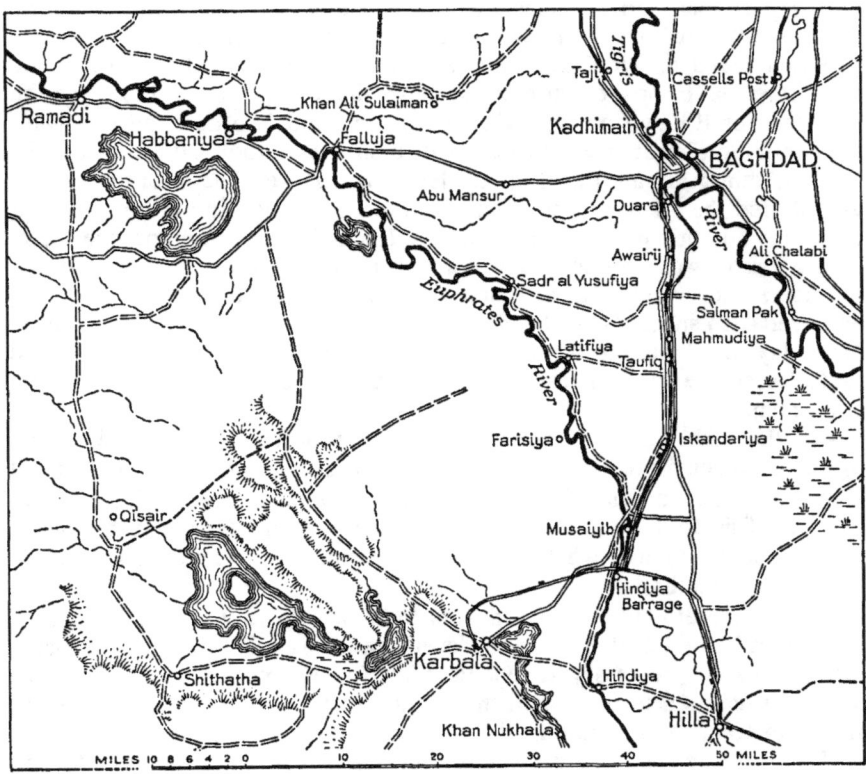

The new Iraq Government declared that no more British troops must enter Iraq until the brigade at Basra had moved on. On 28th April, however, the British force at Basra was slightly reinforced. The following day two infantry brigades of the Iraqi army supported by armoured cars and

---

[a] Field Marshal Sir Claude Auchinleck, GCB, GCIE, CSI, DSO, OBE. C-in-C India 1941 and 1943-1946; GOC-in-C ME 1941-42. Regular soldier; b. 21 Jun 1884.

artillery—twelve 18-pounder guns and some howitzers—surrounded the British cantonment at Habbaniya and trained their guns on it.

Habbaniya, on the south bank of the Euphrates 50 miles west of Baghdad, contained the headquarters of Air Vice-Marshal H. G. Smart's Iraq Command of the Royal Air Force, No. 4 Flying Training School (about 1,000 men of the R.A.F. in all), a company of eighteen armoured cars of the R.A.F., and five companies, totalling 1,000 men, of Assyrian (Christian) and Kurdish troops led by twenty British officers. The area was surrounded by a fence along which, at intervals of 500 yards, were fourteen blockhouses, but was overlooked by a plateau.

The eighty training aircraft in the flying school were hastily formed into four squadrons manned by instructors and students. Smart could also call on some Wellingtons that had been flown to Shaiba, where there was also an army cooperation squadron, No. 244, supporting the force at Basra. On the 30th 350 men of a British battalion were flown in from Basra.

When asked to withdraw, the Iraqi commander replied that he would open fire on troops or aircraft leaving the camp. Thus the situation remained until dawn on 2nd May when, on Smart's orders, all the available training aircraft were loaded with bombs and took off from the airfield. Within a minute the Iraqi artillery opened fire. The aircraft bombed and strafed the Iraqi gun positions, in three days silencing more than half of them; but this did not dissuade the Iraqis from continuing the siege. The garrison was outnumbered and had no artillery except two old 18-pounders. Nevertheless it patrolled vigorously by night and, on 5th May, achieved such success that the Iraqis began to withdraw to a safer distance. Next day the British troops and Iraqi levies defeated an enemy rearguard and cleared the plateau, capturing more than 400 men and much useful equipment.

On the fifth day the Iraqis were on the defensive. Four Blenheim fighters had reinforced the squadrons at Habbaniya, and Air Vice-Marshal D'Albiac, now commanding the air force in Palestine and Transjordan, had established a base at the "H.4" Pumping Station near the Iraq frontier to prevent the enemy, whether Iraqi or German, from landing aircraft at "H.3" or at Rutba.[4]

Lieut-General Quinan[5] arrived from India on 7th May to take command. He was informed that he was to develop and organise the port of Basra "to any extent necessary to enable such forces, our own or Allied, as might be required to operate in the Middle East, including Egypt, Turkey, Iraq and Iran, to be maintained", to secure control of all communications in Iraq, and be ready to protect the Kirkuk oilfield and the pipe-line to Haifa, the Anglo-Iranian Oil Company's installations, and the R.A.F. depots at Habbaniya and Shaiba. He was informed that his force would be increased to three infantry divisions and possibly one armoured division.

---

[4] Stations on the pipe-line from Iraq to Haifa were named with an "H", and a serial number, those on the line to Tripoli with a "T" and a serial number.

[5] Gen Sir Edward Quinan, KCB, KCIE, DSO, OBE. GOC Iran and Iraq 1941, Tenth Army 1942-43, NW Army in India 1943. Regular soldier; b. 9 Jan 1885.

At this stage control of operations in Iraq were transferred from Auchinleck to Wavell, who could not, however, send help on the scale envisaged. It was important to crush the Iraqis quickly before the threatened attack on Crete opened. A flying column which eventually included an incomplete mechanised cavalry brigade (the 4th), an incomplete artillery regiment, 250 men of the Transjordan Frontier Force, part of the 1/Essex Regiment and a company of armoured cars of the R.A.F., was assembled at H.4 and sent across the desert. Having recaptured Rutba on 10th May, it arrived at Habbaniya on the 18th. On the 19th the Habbaniya garrison made a cleverly-organised attack on Falluja, across the Euphrates, now the main Iraq position in the area, and captured it. Thence the column from Palestine assisted in defeating a determined counter-attack and drove the Iraqis back to Baghdad where an armistice was signed by the Mayor on 31st May and a friendly government was established.[6] Rashid Ali, the Italian Consular staffs and the Mufti of Jerusalem had fled to Persia. By this time the two other brigades (the 21st and 25th) of the 10th Indian Division had arrived at Basra.

At the time, the revolt appeared to British leaders to be part of a coordinated German offensive against Crete and Iraq. But we know now that during May the German air force in the eastern Mediterranean was concentrated against Crete, and the flimsy help that Hitler was willing to spend in Iraq was confined to the supply of French weapons from Syria and a "limited" air force, which was to be "an agent for promoting greater self-confidence and will to resist among the Iraq armed forces and civilians".[7]

Such efforts as the Germans and Italians made to help the Iraqis were belated and parsimonious. After discussions lasting for the five weeks which followed Rashid Ali's coup, Rudolph Rahn, a vigorous member of the foreign propaganda department of the German Foreign Office, was sent to Syria (in the second week of May) to organise the sending of supplies to the Iraqis; and a Major von Blomberg flew to Damascus to reconnoitre airfields in Syria and Iraq with the object of flying two squadrons in. Iraqi anti-aircraft gunners mistakenly shot down Blomberg's aircraft when it appeared over Baghdad, and he was killed.

Nevertheless, from 13th May onwards German aircraft based at Mosul and Erbil were in action in Iraq, and later in the month Italian aircraft took part. On 16th May three Heinkels attacked Habbaniya and did severe damage—more than the Iraqi artillery and aircraft had done in five days. By the 28th, however, only one German fighter and one bomber were still serviceable.

Rashid Ali and his followers were bitter about the failure of Germany and Italy to give substantial help. Rahn had sent from Syria some captured French arms but they proved useless; the Germans had delivered no gold—an essential ingredient of an Arab revolt. The Chief of the

---

[6] On 16 May the Russian Government had established diplomatic relations with the Iraqi Government of Rashid Ali.

[7] *Fuhrer Conferences on Naval Affairs, 1941* (published by the Admiralty, 1947).

German General Staff, General Halder, wrote in his diary on 30th May that "owing to deficient preparation and the impossibility of sending effective support, the Iraq show, which is more in the nature of a political rising than a conscious fight for liberation, must eventually peter out. Whatever the outcome, however, it did force the British to spread themselves critically thin, both during the Crete operations and at a time when our situation in North Africa was rather precarious".

Even this was an over-estimate of the effect of "the Iraq show". It was a source of great satisfaction to the British Commanders-in-Chief that before the attack on Crete opened the Iraq army had been defeated. By bold action and at remarkably little cost, the British forces had asserted their control of Iraq and its oilfields, the pipe-line to Haifa, and the outlet of the Persian oil. The effort had involved merely a brigade from Palestine and two brigades of Indian troops destined for Malaya. The success of British arms and the weakness of Axis support for Iraq restored British prestige in the Arab world, affecting the attitude of nationalists not only in Iraq but in Syria, Lebanon and Palestine.

Meanwhile in an effort to halt the German-Italian offensive in Africa, Mr Churchill on 14th April had ordered that the Mediterranean Fleet must make the port of Tripoli unusable. Admiral Cunningham objected to a proposal that the battleship *Barham* be sunk at the entrance to the harbour, but at length, on 21st April, he bombarded the port and emerged with his fleet unscathed. Later in April, on Churchill's orders, a convoy of five ships carrying 240 tanks, including 180 infantry tanks, was sent through the Mediterranean to help re-equip Wavell's armoured regiments. On the night of the 8th-9th May one ship of the convoy struck a mine when nearing the narrow passage between Sicily and Tunisia and sank, but the others continued. Encouraged by this success Churchill suggested that one ship should unload a few tanks in Crete on the way eastwards but the Chiefs of Staff "deemed it inadvisable to endanger the rest of the ship's valuable cargo by such a diversion".[8] Churchill then suggested that twelve tanks should be shipped to Suda Bay as soon as the main cargoes had been discharged at Alexandria, and this was ordered. Wavell replied, however, on 10th May that he had already arranged to send six infantry and fifteen light tanks to Crete.

The steep and narrow mountain range which forms the backbone of Crete falls sharply into the sea along most of the south coast, but in the north are three largish areas of flatter land where cereals, vines and olives were cultivated on terraced slopes or on small pockets of level ground. Of these the westernmost was round Suda Bay and Canea, the capital, which had a population of 36,000; the next had its centre at Retimo about 30 miles east of Canea. The easternmost was at Heraklion, the largest town and port, and with a population of 43,000.

---

[8] Churchill, Vol III, p. 223.

Near each of these towns an airfield had been made, and there were no other airfields on the island. Only one road that could be used by motor vehicles travelled the island from east to west and for most of its length it ran close to the northern shore. Five secondary roads crossed the island from north to south: one joined Maleme, the airfield near Canea, to the south coast; another climbed over the range from Suda Bay towards Sfakia but degenerated into a goat track five miles from that village; a third and fourth linked Retimo and Heraklion with Timbakion; and at the extreme eastern end of the island a fifth travelled over the narrow isthmus of Ierapetra. Suda Bay was the only port that could accommodate large freighters and it had only one jetty and no crane. From the defenders' point of view Crete "faced the wrong way with its three aerodromes, two harbours and roads all situated on the north coast".[9]

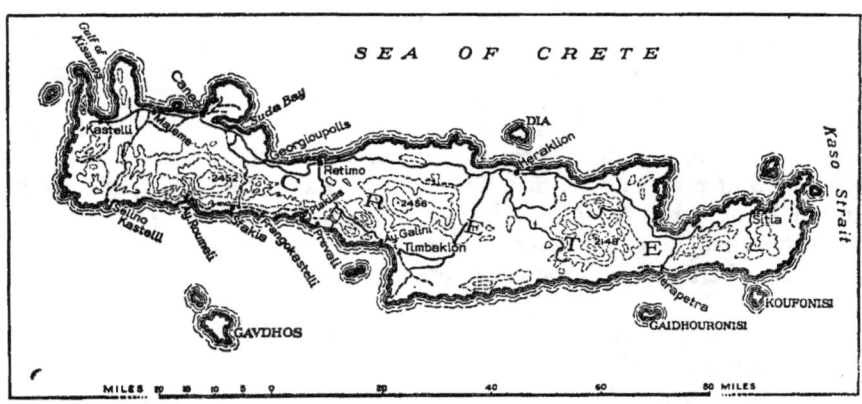

After a British garrison, including two infantry battalions of the 14th Brigade and a substantial contingent of anti-aircraft artillery, had been landed in Crete in November 1940, the Greeks had sent their 5th (Cretan) Division to fight in Albania, leaving only training units on the island. When late in November a proposal to add an Australian brigade to the garrison was abandoned, a commando unit, 385 strong, was temporarily stationed in Crete; the British force on the island then totalled 3,380; the Greek 3,733 with only 659 rifles.[1] In this period the policy was to maintain a garrison of one British and one Greek brigade, but to build up a base able, if necessary, to accommodate a full division and some ancillary units. In December Mr Churchill urged that "many hundreds of Cretans" be employed enlarging and improving the aerodromes. In February 1941, the 14th Brigade was brought to strength by the addition of a third battalion, but in the meantime the Greek troops had been reduced to fewer than 1,000.

---

[9] B. C. Freyberg, Report on the Battle for Crete, August, 1941.

[1] In *Greek Resistance Army* General Sarafis writes that the Metaxas Government had taken care to disarm the islanders because of the island's republican tradition and sympathies.

Indeed, in December and during the first three months of 1941 few preparations were made to meet a possible invasion. The garrison was placed where administration was easy, water plentiful, and malaria absent. Six officers in rapid succession held command. Brigadier Tidbury[2] was replaced by General Gambier-Parry on the 8th January; General Gambier-Parry went away to take command of the 2nd Armoured Division and Lieut-Colonel C. H. Mather (52nd L.A.A. Regiment)—the senior officer then remaining—commanded from 2nd to 19th February. Thereafter Brigadier Galloway commanded until the 7th March, when he was appointed to General Wilson's staff in Greece, and Mather again took over temporarily. Brigadier Chappel[3] (newly appointed to the 14th Brigade) next commanded, from 21st March to 26th April. Then Major-General Weston[4] of the Royal Marines, who had recently arrived from England, took over. He had already visited Crete and made a reconnaissance.

The arrival of Weston was partly the result of a decision made on 1st April by the Commanders-in-Chief to make Suda a fleet base and not merely a fuelling station. This decision was in tune with the action of the Chiefs of Staff in London in ordering to Crete, in January, the "Mobile Naval Base Defence Organisation", which Weston commanded. The M.N.B.D.O. had been initiated a few years after the previous war with the object of providing the fleet with a base which could be rapidly established in any part of the world; doubtless it was considered most improbable that the commander of this organisation would be placed in a situation where he would be called upon to conduct operations against an invader.

The M.N.B.D.O. included a landing and maintenance group whose task was primarily to build a naval base, including buildings, jetties and roads; a defence group, including coast, anti-aircraft, anti-tank and searchlight batteries; and a land defence force including rifle companies, light artillery batteries and machine-gunners. Its total strength was 8,000, but only the landing and maintenance group, a searchlight regiment, one anti-aircraft regiment and some other specialists—about 2,000 men in all—would arrive in Crete before the invasion began. At the time of the evacuation from Greece the anti-aircraft batteries on Crete were: 151st and 234th Heavy; 159th, 156th, and 7th (Australian) Light Batteries; and 304th Searchlight Battery. As a result of the arrival of M.N.B.D.O. units, and of other additions from Egypt, the anti-aircraft defences on Crete late in May included sixteen 3.7-inch, sixteen 3-inch, thirty-six 40-mm guns, and twenty-four searchlights. (The Chiefs of Staff had in November accepted in principle that at least fifty-six heavy and forty-eight light guns and seventy-two searchlights were needed.)

---

[2] Brig O. H. Tidbury, MC. Comd 18 Inf Bde 1939-40, Crete Force Nov 1940-Jan 1941; Sub-Area Comd UK 1941. Regular soldier; b. Trowbridge, Wilts, Eng, 10 Dec 1888.

[3] Maj-Gen B. H. Chappel, DSO. Comd 14 Inf Bde 1941; GOC 6 and 23 Ind Inf Divs. Regular soldier; of Bedford, Eng; b. Belgaum, India, 25 Nov 1895.

[4] Lt-Gen E. C. Weston, CB. Comd MNBDO 1940-43; Ordnance Board 1943-45. Royal Marine officer; of Liss, Hants, Eng; b. Kentish Town, London, 5 Jun 1888. Died 1950.

As a result of the failure in Greece, Crete ceased to be the site of a relatively sheltered naval station and became the foremost Allied position facing the German advance through the Balkans. Indeed, a week before Weston took command, the intention to hold an Allied front in Greece had been abandoned; and, two days before, the first large-scale embarkation from Greece took place and troops from Greece were being hastily landed in Crete in their thousands so that the ships could hurry back for more.

Eleven days before he actually assumed command General Weston had made a report on the defence of Crete. He said that he considered that if Greece was overrun a major invasion by sea would become possible. He decided that one brigade group was needed at Suda-Maleme, and another at Heraklion with a detachment at Retimo. Three days later General Wavell warned Weston of the possibility of attack by airborne troops. On the 24th April, Wavell's joint planning staff reached the conclusion that airborne attack would probably be delayed until it could be sustained by sea—perhaps three or four weeks after the mainland had been overrun—and that, ultimately, a garrison of three brigades would be required. In the meantime the existing garrison should be increased to two brigades, all fresh troops; any troops arriving from Greece should be taken to Egypt; three fighter squadrons should be based on Crete. After having considered these reports, and apparently expecting that he would have about a month for preparation, Wavell decided not to send additional troops (except one mountain battery when available) until the embarkation from Greece was finished. Two months' supplies for two brigades were to be landed as soon as possible.

Thus, although the possibility of an evacuation from Greece had been in mind since early in March, plans and preparations to defend Crete against a major attack were not initiated until the middle of April. Much that could have been done in the meantime—reconnaissance, shipping of vehicles, improvement of roads and harbours, the equipment and training of Greek forces, and the establishment of effective liaison with them—remained undone. The responsibility rests not with the succession of local commanders, whose role was to administer a small garrison, but higher up, whence came no directions to begin effective preparation to defeat invasion.

When Weston took command one of his most pressing responsibilities was to accommodate and feed perhaps 50,000 men rescued from Greece. Already on the 17th April (four days before the embarkation from Greece was ordered) tents, clothing and blankets for 30,000 men had been asked for from Egypt. A trickle of troops and civilian refugees began to arrive from Greece on the 23rd April. On the 25th, in the first large-scale shipment from Greece, some 5,000 troops were put ashore at Suda Bay; and, in the succeeding days, transports and warships disembarked 20,000 more. There were no tents to shelter the new arrivals. They were guided to bivouac areas among the olive trees, where, lacking even blankets and greatcoats, they had to sleep on the ground with no covering but their clothes. Some had no mess gear. In the first few days there was little for many to do except rest under the olive trees, forage for food and equipment, eat—and perhaps get into trouble. The men, used to drinking beer, found the heavy Greek wines treacherous. Even fighting units which had landed organised and more or less complete in numbers lacked tools with which to dig field works. "Officers and men on arrival from Greece were sent, as far as possible, to any of their unit who had arrived previously and had been organised under an officer . . . . The only cooking utensils were petrol tins; a very large number of men fed out of tin cans as there were no mess tins, knives, forks or spoons available in ordnance in large quantities." Meat-and-vegetable tins were used as pannikins, herring tins as dixies, and spoons and forks were whittled out of wood.

> It was hard to get clean clothes and lice appeared (wrote an Australian). We had a long fight with them—the boys would do a day in underpants while the women washed their clothes, and they are great washerwomen; but until the great day when we were given a shirt and shorts each, the lice were always with us. I had a blanket and greatcoat, but for a week or more shared the blanket with three others. We would sleep in a row with greatcoats on and the blanket over our feet . . . . I slipped into Canea and bought a brush and razor. Except for a table knife that was all my equipment.

"Conditions very peaceful in the pleasant waiting existence," wrote the diarist of a New Zealand unit concerning these first days, "parties bathe in the Mediterranean and bask in the sunshine: the area is fertile with vineyards, cornfields and vegetable patches, and orange vendors ply a steady trade."

The arrival in Crete of officers from Greece who were senior to Weston accelerated the rate at which the command of the garrison changed hands. When General Wilson arrived, it was to him, as senior officer, that General Wavell sent a signal that Crete must be denied to the enemy, that until they could be moved to Egypt all troops from Greece were available to defend the island, and that the air force could not send more aircraft "for some time to come". "In view of our present shortage troops, British element garrison should be kept to essential minimum and fullest use should be made of reliable Greek troops," he added. It seems that Wavell and his staff then had little conception of the condition of the units arriving from Greece or the general disorganisation on the island as a result of the rapid unloading of tens of thousands of ill-equipped troops. General Wavell asked General Wilson, in conjunction with General Weston and General Mackay, to examine the problem of what should be the essential permanent garrison in Crete. (Mackay had departed for Egypt, however, on the 29th April, believing that the greater part of his division was there.)

At that time one battalion of the garrison (2/Black Watch) was at Heraklion and the remainder of the 14th Brigade in the Suda Bay area. The air force under Group Captain Beamish[5] included four depleted squadrons from Greece—No. 30 with from six to eight serviceable Blen-

---

[5] Air Vice-Marshal G. R. Beamish, CB, CBE. Comd RAF Crete 1941; Air HQ Libya 1941-42; AOC 44 Gp 1943-45. Regular airman; of Coleraine, Co Derry, N. Ireland; b. Dunmanway, Co Cork, Ireland, 29 Apr 1905.

heims, Nos. 33 and 80 with six Hurricanes between them, No. 112 with six serviceable Gladiators—and one squadron from Egypt (No. 203) with nine Blenheims. At Maleme was also No. 805 Squadron of the Fleet Air Arm.

Wilson reported that the enemy would not improbably attempt a combined seaborne and airborne attack in the near future. His estimate of the necessary garrison somewhat exceeded those of Weston and the joint planners: three brigade groups each of four battalions and one motor battalion distributed between the Suda Bay area and Heraklion. He concluded: "I consider that unless all three Services are prepared to face the strain of maintaining adequate forces up to strength, the holding of the island is a dangerous commitment, and a decision on the matter must be taken at once." Here he indicated a basic problem: how was a defending force to be maintained? There was a limited store of supplies and limited equipment for a garrison of one brigade totalling some 5,000 men; this store was in process of being increased to 90 days' supplies for 30,000 men. From Greece, however, had come perhaps 25,000 men, who, besides being fed, needed to be largely rearmed and reclothed, and who possessed no vehicles or heavy weapons and little ammunition. Ships carrying supplies from Egypt had to make a hazardous voyage to ports on the north coast and use ill-equipped harbours where unloading was slow. The problem of supply was complicated by the presence on the island of a population exceeding 400,000, partly dependent on imported grain, and of 14,000 Italian prisoners of war captured by the Greeks.

On 28th April M. Tsouderos, the Greek Prime Minister, whose Government was now established at Canea, presided at a meeting which Generals Wilson and Weston, Air Vice-Marshal D'Albiac, Rear-Admiral Turle, and Group Captain Beamish attended. The Greek representatives explained that the Greek forces under General Skoulas consisted of 2,500 gendarmes, 7,500 soldiers, and 1,000 reservists, organised into eleven battalions none of which was well equipped. They asked that a British general be appointed to command the Allied forces on the island, and that the Greek troops be armed with British weapons.

In London that day the Joint Intelligence Committee had estimated that the Germans had aircraft enough round the eastern Mediterranean to enable them to land from 3,000 to 4,000 paratroops or airborne troops on Crete in a first sortie, and might make from two to three sorties in a day from Greece and three or four from Rhodes. This estimate was immediately passed on to Cairo; and, the same day, Churchill sent Wavell the following message:

> It seems clear from our information that a heavy airborne attack by German troops and bombers will soon be made on Crete. Let me know what forces you have in the island and what your plans are. It ought to be a fine opportunity for killing the parachute troops. The island must be stubbornly defended.[6]

Wavell replied that in addition to the original garrison of three battalions and the anti-aircraft and coastal batteries, Crete now contained

---
[6] Quoted in Churchill, Vol III, p. 241.

some 30,000 men evacuated from Greece. "It is just possible," he added, "that plan for attack on Crete may be cover for attack on Syria or Cyprus, and that real plan will only be disclosed even to [their] own troops at last moment."

Churchill proposed that General Freyberg, for whose courage he had great admiration, should be placed in command in Crete, and General Wavell agreed.

On the 29th April the convoy carrying Freyberg and his staff and the 6th New Zealand Brigade reached Suda Bay. Freyberg went ashore with his chief of staff, Colonel Stewart, and senior administrative officer, Lieut-Colonel Gentry,[7] thinking to obtain a passage by air to Egypt, where he understood his division would be assembled and reorganised, and to visit his 5th Brigade which he knew was staging in Crete (he did not know that other New Zealand troops were on the island). It was arranged that he should set off for Egypt early next morning in a flying-boat, but, when morning came, he was instructed to remain and attend a conference at Canea a few hours later. In his report Freyberg described the meeting:

> We met in a small village between Maleme and Canea and set to work at 11.30. General Wavell had arrived by air and he looked drawn and tired and more weary than any of us. Just prior to sitting down General Wavell and General Wilson had a heart-to-heart talk in one corner and then the C-in-C called me over. He took me by the arm and said "I want to tell you how well I think the New Zealand Division has done in Greece. I do not believe any other Division would have carried out those withdrawals as well." His next words came as a complete surprise. He said he wanted me to take command of the forces in Crete and went on to say that he considered Crete would be attacked in the next few days. I told him that I wanted to get back to Egypt to concentrate the division and train and re-equip it and I added that my Government would never agree to the division being split permanently. He then said that he considered it my duty to remain and take on the job. I could do nothing but accept.

It was in the course of their "heart-to-heart talk" that Wavell had told Wilson that he wished him "to go to Jerusalem and relieve Baghdad". To Wilson this

> came as a surprise as I had no idea what had been happening outside Greece for the last three weeks.[8]

At the conference it was decided that the likely scale of attack was by 5,000 to 6,000 airborne troops and possibly seaborne troops also, launched against Maleme and Heraklion airfields; no additional air support could be provided. Freyberg took Wavell aside and told him that there were not enough men on Crete to hold it, and that they were inadequately armed; and he asked that the decision to defend the island be reconsidered if aircraft were not to be available. Wavell, however, said that the scale of the probable attack had possibly been exaggerated, that he was confident

---

[7] Maj-Gen W. G. Gentry, CBE, DSO. AA & QMG NZ Div 1940-41; Comd 6 NZ Bde 1942-43; Dep CGS (NZ) 1943-44; Comd 9 NZ Bde 1945. CGS (NZ) since Apr 1952. Regular soldier; of Lower Hutt, NZ; b. London, 20 Feb 1899.

[8] Wilson, *Eight Years Overseas*, p. 102.

that the troops would be equal to their task; efforts would be made to obtain fighter aircraft from England. He told Freyberg that in any event Crete could not be evacuated because there were not enough ships to take the troops away.

> The main defence problems which faced me in Crete were not clear to me at this stage (wrote Freyberg afterwards). I did not know anything about the geography or physical characteristics of the island. I knew less about the condition of the force I was to command. Neither was I aware of the serious situation with regard to maintenance and, finally, I had not learnt the real scale of attack which we were to be prepared to repel.

Freyberg received the estimate noted above of the possible scale of a German attack on 1st May. He decided that the sooner he "introduced a little reality into the calculations for the defence of Crete the better", and immediately sent a telegram to Wavell stating that his forces were "totally inadequate to meet attack envisaged", and that unless the fighter aircraft were increased and naval forces made available he could not hope to hold out with a force devoid of artillery, with insufficient tools for digging, inadequate transport, and inadequate reserves of equipment and ammunition.[1] He urged that if naval and air support were not available, the holding of Crete should be reconsidered, and announced that it was his duty to inform the New Zealand Government "of situation in which greater part of my division is now placed". Thereupon he cabled to his Prime Minister describing the position and adding:

> Recommended you bring pressure to bear on highest plane in London either to supply us with sufficient means to defend island or to review decision Crete must be held.

Two days later Wavell sent a message to Freyberg stating, reassuringly, that he considered the War Office estimate of the scale of attack exaggerated, and informing him that naval support would be given, efforts were being made to provide air support, and artillery and tools would be sent. "I am trying," he added, "to make arrangements . . . to relieve New Zealand troops from Crete and am most anxious to re-form your division at earliest opportunity. But at moment my resources are stretched to limit."

Wavell had sent a cable to Dill on the 2nd in which he said that "at least three brigade groups" and a "considerable number of anti-aircraft units" were required to garrison the island effectively. He described the existing garrison as comprising three British regular battalions, six New Zealand battalions, one Australian battalion, and two composite battalions of details evacuated from Greece. He added that the troops from Greece were weak in numbers and equipment and there was no artillery; and the scale of anti-aircraft defence was inadequate. "Air defence," he added, "will always be a difficult problem." This estimate implied, however, that if arms and equipment were sent to Crete the garrison on the ground would be adequate. Moreover, it was evidently so difficult to ascertain what forces were on Crete that Wavell's list of the units there had considerably under-

---
[1] Freyberg, Report.

stated them. There were seven, not six, New Zealand battalions (not including part of a machine-gun battalion); four Australian battalions, not one (not including a full machine-gun battalion and half of a fifth infantry battalion).[2]

General Blamey, now in Cairo as Deputy Commander-in-Chief, agreed with the current estimates of the force needed to hold Crete. In response to a request from the anxious Australian Cabinet, Blamey cabled, on 6th May, that he considered that Crete should not be abandoned without the sternest struggle. A possible scale of attack would be by one airborne and one seaborne division, the first sortie being made by one-third of an airborne division. (It will later be seen that the British Intelligence estimates were remarkably accurate.) The troops required to defend the island were three infantry brigade groups with coastal and harbour defences and a "reasonable air force": the forces available were the 14th British Brigade and troops from Greece who were adequate in numbers but had no artillery. He considered that the 16th British Brigade, more artillery and fighter squadrons should be sent. "Situation far from satisfactory," he added, "but everything possible being done to improve it." He expected that most of the A.I.F. would be withdrawn as soon as the 16th British Brigade could be sent in.

Meanwhile, on the 3rd May, Churchill had followed Freyberg's message to the New Zealand Government with one of his own to the New Zealand Prime Minister, Mr Fraser, then in Cairo, in which he said that every effort would be made to re-equip the New Zealand Division, particularly with artillery "in which General Wavell is already strong".[3] From New Zealand, the acting Prime Minister cabled to Freyberg on the 4th that his government had made urgent representations to the United Kingdom Government on the lines he had indicated. Next day Freyberg sent a cable to Churchill in the course of which he said that he was "not in the least anxious about an airborne attack" and added:

> I have made my dispositions and feel that with the troops now at my disposal I can cope adequately. However, a combination of seaborne and airborne attack is different. If that comes before I can get the guns and transport here the situation will be difficult. Even so, provided the Navy can help, I trust that all will be well.

Freyberg sent a message to Wavell that day urging that about 10,000 men who were without arms "and with little or no employment other than getting into trouble with the civil population" should be evacuated.

Freyberg had established his headquarters in dug-outs in the foothills east of Canea and was at work reorganising and redeploying his force. As chief staff officer he retained Colonel Stewart; his senior administrative officer was Brigadier Brunskill, the British officer who had occupied a similar post on Wilson's staff in Greece; his artillery commander was Colonel Frowen of the 7th Medium Regiment, the same who had played

---

[2] As a result of this cable (quoted in Churchill, Vol III, p. 244) the impression seems to have persisted in London during the following weeks that the Australian contingent on Crete comprised a very small part of the whole force.

[3] Quoted in Churchill, Vol III, p. 246.

(Mrs. G. A. Vasey)

Brigadier G. A. Vasey, who commanded the Australians on Crete.

(2/4 Bn War Diary)

Near Heraklion.

(Maj S. B. Cann, 2/1 Fd Coy)
Suda Bay during a bombing attack. The smoke in the lower picture is rising from two tankers set alight by attacking aircraft. t.

a leading part in making the artillery plan at Bardia. The filling of staff posts was a difficult problem because Freyberg had brought only two of his divisional staff ashore, yet had to create, in effect, a corps staff, and also a new staff for the New Zealand Division now commanded by Brigadier Puttick.

The garrison of Crete—about which, in the confusion, the leaders in Cairo and London were somewhat ill-informed—now included five main contingents: the 14th British Brigade and other troops of the original garrison; the incomplete New Zealand Division; a number of Australian units and detachments from Greece; part of the 1st Armoured Brigade and some personnel of other British units from Greece; some 10,000 Cretan recruits, very raw.

The New Zealand Division on Crete included the 4th and 5th Brigades, with seven infantry battalions—18th, 19th, 20th, 21st, 22nd, 23rd and 28th (Maori)—and a majority of the divisional troops.[4] The 6th Brigade Group, which had sustained small losses on Greece, had called at Suda Bay, but, on naval orders, had been sent on to Alexandria. The Australian contingent consisted principally of three groups fortuitously landed on Crete. First there was the 19th Brigade Group (at that time including the 2/1st, 2/4th and 2/11th Battalions, half the 2/8th Battalion and the 2/2nd Field Regiment), which had been embarked from Megara on the 25th-26th; then those Australians who had been taken off the sinking *Costa Rica* and carried to Suda Bay in destroyers (among these were the 2/7th Battalion, the 2/1st Machine Gun Battalion, and about half of the 2/8th); finally there were the 2/3rd Field Regiment (which had embarked with the 4th New Zealand Brigade) and other units and detachments.

After the departure of General Mackay and his staff, Brigadier Vasey, as senior Australian officer in Crete, found himself not only in command of an Australian brigade group but bearing a responsibility for a total of some 8,500 troops, including almost-unarmed units equivalent to a second brigade, besides parties of varying size belonging to about thirty other separate units. There was no other Australian brigadier on the island. Vasey, like Freyberg, was anxious to send his unarmed men to Egypt, and on the 5th May he dispatched a message through Freyberg's headquarters to A.I.F. headquarters recommending the removal of some 5,000 such troops and stating that he had organised four battalions (2/4th, 2/7th, 2/8th and 2/11th[5]) with the 2/8th Field Company, a company of the 2/1st Machine Gun Battalion, and the 2/7th Field Ambulance for garrison duties. The implication was that other units and detachments should be removed.

Having received no reply to this signal Vasey, on the 12th, sent a letter to Brigadier Rowell, now senior at Australian Corps headquarters, by an officer who was returning to Egypt. In it he explained that the 2/4th Battalion was then at Heraklion, that he commanded four battalions and

---

[4] Before Freyberg's arrival Weston had allotted the New Zealand force, then consisting only of the 5th Bde, to the defence of the Suda-Maleme area.

[5] The 2/1 Bn was inadvertently omitted from this signal.

an artillery regiment in the Retimo sector, and that there was an Australian composite battalion in the Suda Bay area. His first problem, he said, was the dispatch of troops from Crete. General Freyberg had ordered that no troops with an operational role should depart until replaced. He had heard that it was intended to re-form the 17th Brigade as soon as possible, but he was sure that Freyberg would resist sending any armed infantry from Crete. Vasey pointed out also that no letters had arrived in Crete (he himself had received none since he left Egypt for Greece in March). "Every time I go round and see any of the troops," he added, "the first question is 'When is the mail coming?'" He asked also for a pay staff and a canteen and pointed out his shortage of medical supplies, and hats. Every man then had a blanket and he hoped each would soon have a groundsheet and greatcoat.

> On the whole (he wrote) the discipline of the unarmed and more or less unemployed personnel is fair. There have been a few major incidents including an alleged murder, but so far we have always been able to apprehend the culprits. I have taken to myself the power to convene FGCMs (field general courts martial) and cases are proceeding apace.... I hope the Legal Staff Officer will review the proceedings of the courts martial with a kindly eye.

The British contingent included, in addition to the fresh 14th Brigade (in Freyberg's words) "four weak and improvised battalions from Rangers, Northumberland Hussars, 7th Medium Regiment, 106th Royal Horse Artillery", the units of the mobile naval base, all the coast artillery, nearly all the anti-aircraft artillery, and a number of base units.

The 10,000 Greek troops were organised in three garrison battalions —one each at Canea, Retimo and Heraklion—and eight recruit battalions. As noted above the 5th (Cretan) Division had long since been sent to Albania, and now had been captured there. The recruits on Crete had been given only a few weeks' training; although five types of rifle were in use some men had none; there were only about 30 rounds a rifle; few men had fired a shot. Freyberg was anxious to reorganise and rearm the Greeks. On the 5th he informed Wavell that the King of Greece had placed what remained of the Greek Army under his command, and that he intended to lend to the Greeks Brigadier Salisbury-Jones[6], and a number of other British officers to help with their training. Four days later he wrote to Wavell's chief of staff, Major-General Arthur Smith, that the Greeks were pressing him to raise a Cretan militia, but that that was dependent on receiving arms and settlement of a policy for the future of the Greek Army. "I am impressed with the Greek rank and file," he wrote, "but a great deal of dead wood must go, especially officers.... I am certain that one division could be raised at once, and two divisions eventually, if the problem is tackled at once before they become despondent from lack of equipment and employment." On the 11th Freyberg informed Smith that the Greek leaders had agreed that the Greek troops should be

---

[6] Maj-Gen A. G. Salisbury-Jones, CBE, MC. (1914-18: Coldstream Guards.) Liaison officer, Syria, 1924-1926; CO 3/Coldstream in operations in Palestine 1938-39; head of mission to General Weygand in Syria 1939-40, to South Africa 1941-44. B. 4 Jul 1896.

organised on British war establishments and brigaded with British troops. The immediate aim would be to raise and arm twelve battalions and three field batteries.

It is evident, however, that the political disunity of Greece and the weakness of the leadership placed immense difficulties in the way of rapid and effective organisation of a Cretan army on the lines pictured by Freyberg.

On the 3rd May, Freyberg issued an instruction defining the organisation and role of "Creforce", as it had been entitled since November. The infantry allotted to the Heraklion sector (Brigadier Chappel) comprised the 14th British Brigade (two battalions), the 2/4th Battalion,[7] the 7th Medium Regiment armed with rifles, and two Greek battalions; to the Retimo sector (Brigadier Vasey) four Australian battalions (2/1st, 2/7th, 2/11th and 2/1st Machine Gun[8]) and two Greek; to the Suda Bay sector (Major-General Weston) the M.N.B.D.O., the 1/Welch, the 2/8th, and one Greek battalion; to the Maleme sector the New Zealand Division comprising the 4th Brigade (now commanded by Colonel Kippenberger), the 5th (Brigadier Hargest) and three Greek battalions.[9] The 1/Welch and 4th Brigade (less one battalion) were in Force reserve, but administered by their sector commanders. Those commanders were instructed to dispose one-third of their troops on or round the landing grounds and two-thirds "outside the area which will be attacked in the first instance". The attack would probably take the form of intensive bombing and machine-gunning of the airfields and their vicinity, a landing by paratroops to seize and clear the airfields, and finally the landing of troop-carrying aircraft. In addition seaborne attack, probably on beaches close to the aerodromes and Suda Bay, must be expected.

On 8th May it was estimated that the original garrison of Crete numbered 5,300, and the troops from Greece 25,300. It was hoped that by 15th May the original garrison would have been increased to 5,800 and other contingents reduced to: New Zealand 4,500; Australian 3,500; other British 2,000. A policy was adopted of using ships returning empty after landing supplies, to take away men, chiefly of service and base units, for whom there was no role in Crete, but the ships could take only limited numbers. The navy had lost ships in the embarkation from Greece and was fully occupied. As the weeks passed and air attacks on Suda Bay and shipping increased, it became evident that it would not be possible to remove all the unwanted troops who had arrived from Greece. Of these some 3,200 British (including Palestinians and Cypriots), 2,500 Australians and 1,300 New Zealanders were sent on to Egypt; by 17th May

---

[7] Henceforward, except where ambiguity is possible, the prefix "British", "Australian" or "New Zealand" will be dropped from the titles of most units. Australian units are adequately distinguished by the prefix of 2/ (as in 2/4th Battalion). As mentioned above the New Zealand battalions on Crete were the 18th, 19th, 20th, 21st, 22nd, 23rd, 28th (Maori) and part of the 27th (Machine Gun).

[8] Later the main body of the machine-gun battalion was embarked for Egypt and the 2/8th allotted to this sector.

[9] Of the 7 LAA Battery, the only Australian anti-aircraft artillery on the island, two troops were allotted to Heraklion, one troop to Maleme, and the remainder of the battery to Suda Bay.

the garrison included about 15,000 British, 7,750 New Zealanders, 6,500 Australians, and 10,200 Greeks.[1]

Unneeded men of the R.A.F. were also moved to Egypt, many being ferried by No. 230 Squadron, which itself returned to Egypt on 30th April. There were then the following squadrons on the island:

	Station	Aircraft
30 Squadron	Maleme	12 Blenheims
33/80 Squadron	Maleme	6 Hurricanes
112 Squadron	Heraklion	12 Gladiators
805 Fleet Air Arm Squadron	Maleme	6 Gladiators and Fulmars

General Freyberg was anxious to arrange the departure of the King of Greece and his Ministers, who were at Canea. Almost every day the Canea area was being bombed. "It seemed to me," wrote Freyberg afterwards, "that in the circumstances the front line—and Canea during the middle of May was certainly very much in the front line—was not the right place for the King and the National Government.... I did not see any reason to expose those important and gallant people to the risk of being killed or wounded or, far worse, captured." Freyberg received a cable from the Foreign Office stating that the Greek political leaders were not to be exposed to undue risk and that he was to be the judge of what undue risk was, but emphasising that their presence in Crete was having an important effect at home and in neutral countries and that the King should remain until the last possible moment. Consequently, on the 9th May, Freyberg reached an agreement with the King that he and the Government should depart on the 14th and the decision be explained to the people of Greece. However, soon afterwards, he received a cable that the British War Cabinet felt very strongly that the King and Government should stay, even if the island was attacked. Thereupon Freyberg informed the King and M. Tsouderos that for the moment, there was no reason for them to go. Freyberg invited them to go into quarters within the defended area, but it was finally agreed that they should live in houses in the foothills well south of the perimeter ready to move farther south into the mountains if need be. Freyberg provided a platoon of the 18th Battalion under Lieutenant Ryan[2] as a guard and asked Cairo to provide a warship or flying-

---

[1] On the 5th the hospital ship *Aba* sailed with 602 patients aboard. The *Aba* returned on the 16th and embarked 561 patients. On the 9th 763 Australians were embarked. A total of 2,041 were in the convoy of 5 merchant ships, 2 destroyers and 2 sloops. On the 14th another 1,721 embarked, including 1,200 New Zealanders. Except for 18 officers and 414 men of the 2/1 MG Bn these nearly all belonged to medical and other service units. After that the strengths of Australian infantry and field artillery units in Crete were approximately:

2/1 Bn	.	.	.	32 Offrs and 550 men
2/4 Bn	.	.	.	33 ,, ,, 520 ,,
2/7 Bn	.	.	.	31 ,, ,, 550 ,,
2/8 Bn	.	.	.	14 ,, ,, 370 ,,
2/11 Bn	.	.	.	35 ,, ,, 610 ,,
2/1 MG Bn	.	.	.	6 ,, ,, 164 ,,
2/2 Fd Regt	.	.	.	34 ,, ,, 520 ,,
2/3 Fd Regt	.	.	.	26 ,, ,, 476 ,,

The 16 Bde Composite Bn (2/2 and 2/3 Bns) had 16 officers and 427 men, the 17 Bde Composite Bn (2/5 and 2/6 Bns) 20 officers and 367 men. The 2/8 Fd Coy was 150 strong.

[2] Maj W. H. Ryan, OBE. 18 NZ Bn, and 18 NZ Armd Regt 1942-45. Civil engineer; of Mangaia, Cook Is; b. Auckland, NZ, 1 Jun 1911.

boat to take the King and his party away if necessary. Colonel Blunt, the British military attaché, was put in charge of the whole group.

Another embarrassment was the presence on Crete of the 14,000 Italian prisoners of war. After prolonged negotiations with the Greeks, who feared that to hand over these prisoners might be contrary to international law, it was agreed that they should be taken to Egypt and thence India, but they were still on the island on the 20th May.

Meanwhile a trickle of equipped troops and of arms and supplies for the men from Greece was reaching Crete. During May part of the M.N.B.D.O. —some 2,200 marines equipped principally with coast and anti-aircraft guns and searchlights—a troop of mountain artillery armed with 3.7-inch howitzers, a troop of sixteen light tanks, six infantry tanks, and two infantry battalions (2/Leicesters and 1/Argyll and Sutherland Highlanders) arrived from Egypt. The 2/Leicesters were landed at Heraklion on 16th May from the cruisers *Gloucester* and *Fiji*; the 1/Argyll and Sutherland Highlanders and two infantry tanks were landed by the *Glengyle* at Timbakion on the south coast on the 19th.[3] It was Wavell's intention that this battalion group should form a reserve to the Retimo and Heraklion forces.

It has been mentioned that on 2nd May Wavell reported that there was no field artillery on Crete; on the 6th Blamey in a cable to the Australian Government emphasised that the troops landed on Crete from Greece had no artillery, and on the 3rd Churchill had cabled to Fraser, the New Zealand Prime Minister, then in Cairo, that every effort would be made to re-equip the New Zealanders particularly with artillery, in which Wavell was "already strong". On the 7th Wavell had sent a cable to Freyberg in the course of which he said that he was trying to arrange the dispatch of about half a dozen infantry tanks and some light tanks and that he could make the 16th (British) Infantry Brigade available if ships could be found but "probably better to complete equipment of fighting units now without arms". He asked Freyberg to cable his principal requirements. Freyberg replied:

> First. Agree not desirable at this juncture to attempt to land 16th Inf Bde and broadly speaking do not require additional personnel of any arm as a first priority. Prefer concentrate on landing essential equipment and stores. Second. Agree infantry tanks with crews and light tanks valuable also carriers. Third. Ample artillery personnel available also sights and directors without stands. 25pr ammunition could be unloaded off Runo if guns available. Otherwise hasten despatch of 75 mm guns. Tractors and artillery signal equipment will also be needed. Fourth. Other weapons required. Vickers guns and belts complete at least 24. Tripods for existing guns 30. Bren guns with magazines all possible to meet existing shortage of 300 and magazines for existing 300 guns. Rifles and bayonets 5000 for British plus 500 for Greeks. Mortars 2-inch and 3-inch as many as possible. Fifth. Hasten despatch of 20 cars and of motor-cycles already asked for but increase from 30 to 100. Also expedite 70 15-cwt trucks and balance of one reserve MT Coy predicted in fourth of your [signal] of 3rd May as part of next convoy. Sixth. Ammunition. .303 inch bandoliers

---

[3] These battalions were drawn from the 16th British Bde (mentioned above by Blamey), whose headquarters and third battalion—2/Queen's—remained in Egypt.

5 million carton 2 million stripless belts half million. ATK rifle 10000. Mortar ample supply with weapons you send. Thompson sub-machine gun 100000. Grenades H.E. 3000. Seventh. Signal equipment repeat demand of 4th May plus major items of . . . equipment [on the establishment of] three infantry brigade signal sections. Eighth. Workshops and personnel and spares and ammunition and POL for any tanks sent. Ninth. Diesel oil 6000 gallons. Tenth. No shore installations here capable of lifting heavy tanks.

The 6th Australian and the New Zealand Divisions had lost their guns in Greece, and so had the three British field or medium regiments there. The British formations in the Middle East generally had always been short of field artillery, and that was a factor which operated against organising into divisions the considerable number of well-trained regular infantry battalions in Egypt and Palestine. The Australian force, however, possessed a considerable pool of trained field artillery regiments. Of the 9th Division's three such regiments only one—the 2/12th—was in Tobruk; two others— the 2/7th and 2/8th—were in reserve in Egypt. There were also the three regiments of the 7th Division—2/4th, 2/5th and 2/6th. Two regiments of "corps artillery", not attached to any particular division, arrived from Australia in May, but had no guns.

On the 20th May five Australian field artillery regiments in Egypt— 2/4th, 2/5th, 2/6th, 2/7th and 2/8th—were equipped with guns. The guns of these five regiments included 36 modern 25-pounders, 59 old 18-pounders (some in poor condition), and 24 4.5-inch howitzers. In the last week of May the 2/4th and 2/6th between them drew 24 additional 25-pounders from the depot at Tel el Kebir. Thus, by the end of the month the Australian regiments in reserve at Mersa Matruh and Ikingi Maryut held 60 25-pounders. To have withdrawn these guns from the idle Australian regiments and sent them to Crete would have enabled each of three regiments there to be armed with 20 guns—almost their full establishment. The presence on Crete of 60 25-pounders would have transformed the situation. In the event no 25-pounders were sent to Crete. Among the shipments of arms which did arrive from Egypt were forty-nine Italian and French field guns.[4] These enabled some artillery units to be partly rearmed but there were not enough, even of guns such as these, to equip all the artillery regiments, and several (including 102nd Anti-Tank, part of the 106th Royal Horse Artillery, the 7th Medium, and 2/2nd Australian) were armed as infantry.

In his report Freyberg wrote that evidently 100 guns were dispatched. "Sufficient to say that many did not arrive, others came without their instruments, some without their sights, some without ammunition, and some of the ammunition without fuses . . . . The gunners . . . were either British Regular Army, Australians or New Zealanders; men of infinite resource and energy; they set to work and one lot made a sighting appliance out of wood and chewing gum. Another lot of gunners made out charts which enabled them to shoot without sights or instruments. Nobody groused . . . and everybody got on with the job." Some of the Italian guns were 75-mm

---

[4] There were also the mountain guns—eight of them—referred to above.

and some 100-mm. The rifles and machine-guns which were landed included American and Italian as well as British weapons.

While these plans were being made the defenders were under constant air attack. Shipping in Suda Bay had been regularly attacked from the air even before the embarkation from Greece began. There were particularly heavy air raids during 3rd May, and on the 4th the labour troops who had been unloading the ships were replaced by volunteers, chiefly from Australian engineer units and the 2/2nd Field Regiment, and commanded by Major Torr[5] of the Australian engineers. These carried on unloading except when aircraft were directly attacking the ship they were working on. One of their best achievements was to retrieve a number of Bren carriers from a sunken ship with its upper deck several feet under water.[6]

At length the air attacks were causing such heavy loss that it was decided to use only ships fast enough to enter the danger area after dark, unload and be out of the danger area next morning. This could be done only by vessels of about 30 knots speed, and necessitated arriving at the pier about 11.30 p.m. and departing at 3 a.m. From 29th April to 20th May, 15,000 tons of army stores were unloaded from fifteen ships, eight of which were sunk or damaged. This rate of supply was less than half that considered necessary to maintain such a force—quite apart from the needs of the 400,000 Cretans. The reduction in the number of supply ships arriving in Crete made it apparent that the island could not be held indefinitely if air attack continued to be as heavy as it was during the first three weeks of May. By 19th May thirteen damaged ships lay in Suda Bay. The use of a port on the south coast would have greatly simplified the problem, but there was no unloading equipment there and much improvement of the roads would have been needed to bring equipment landed in the south to the garrisons in the north.

On the 14th May the organisation of the New Zealand Division was expanded by the formation of the 10th Brigade,[7] consisting of the 20th Battalion, a composite battalion of artillery and army service corps men, and the 6th Greek Battalion. Colonel Kippenberger was given command of this new formation, Colonel Falconer[8] taking the 4th Brigade until the 17th, when he was replaced by Brigadier Inglis[9] who had been commanding the 9th Brigade in Egypt.

What steps had been taken to deploy the increased force then in Crete? West of Canea, in the Maleme sector, the problem was to defend the air-

---

[5] Brig A. G. Torr, CBE, DSO, NX171. OC 2/1 Fd Coy 1939-41; GSO1 (Engrs) HQ AIF ME 1941-42; CE HQ NG Force 1943, I Corps 1943-44, First Army 1944-45. Chartered engineer; of Vaucluse, NSW; b. Sydney, 8 Apr 1907. Died 9 Aug 1952.
[6] From 17 May the Suda Docks group was commanded by Lt-Col G. C. McNaught of the NZEF.
[7] The New Zealand troops in Egypt, exclusive of the 6th Brigade, were organised into a 9th Brigade.
[8] Brig A. S. Falconer, CBE, DSO, MC. CO 23 NZ Bn 1940 and Mar to May 1941; Comd 5 Div (in NZ) 1942-43. Tobacconist and secretary; of Dunedin, NZ; b. Mosgiel, NZ, 4 Nov 1892.
[9] Maj-Gen L. M. Inglis, CB, CBE, DSO, MC. CO 27 NZ (MG) Bn 1940; Comd 4 NZ Bde 1941-42, 4 Armd Bde 1942-44; GOC 2 NZ Div Jun-Aug 1942 and Jun-Jul 1943. Barrister and solicitor; of Timaru, NZ; b. Mosgiel, NZ, 16 May 1894.

field and a long beach. Brigadier Puttick placed his 5th Brigade to cover Maleme and the near-by beaches; the 10th occupied a position facing west astride the coastal plain and west of Galatas; the 4th Brigade was in the area east of Galatas under orders to be prepared "to move at short notice in any direction in a counter-attack role", perhaps with the 1/Welch under its command.

Farther west at the little port of Kastelli was the 1st Greek Regiment of 1,030 men nearly all recruits aged 20 and 21, ill-clad, poorly officered and possessing only 600 rifles. Major Bedding[1] (19th Battalion) and thirteen other New Zealand officers and N.C.O's were attached to them. There were also forty-five gendarmes and a well-organised and high-spirited home guard of about 200 with a variety of arms, including shotguns.

General Weston, who commanded the force in the Suda Bay-Canea sector, had to protect the harbour and the base. Improvised Australian battalions were deployed east of Suda Point, other improvised units were on a line south of Canea to prevent enemy paratroops who might land in the olive groves from advancing into the town, and a detachment was placed on the Akrotiri Peninsula. The improvised Australian battalions in the Suda Bay force were grouped under Lieut-Colonel Cremor, and included his 2/2nd Field Regiment (employed as infantry), two weak battalions—the 16th Brigade Composite Battalion and the 17th Brigade Composite Battalion—and a detachment of engineers and another of artillerymen.[2] Gradually these units were armed, the 16th, for example, at length receiving American rifles for all its men, six Brens, but each with only one magazine, one Vickers gun without a tripod, two Hotchkiss guns with improvised mountings and three mortars without base plates.

Next to the east, in the Retimo sector, Brigadier Vasey had two main tasks: to defend the harbour and airfield of Retimo and the adjacent beaches, and to prevent a seaborne landing in Georgioupolis Bay whose eastern end was some seven miles to the west. He allotted two Australian battalions (2/1st and 2/11th) to Retimo, two (2/7th and the weak 2/8th) to Georgioupolis. At Heraklion were four British, one Australian and three Greek battalions. The principal formations and units in each sector were:

Maleme Sector:
  New Zealand Division (Brigadier Puttick)
    5th Brigade (21st, 22nd, 23rd and 28th (Maori) Battalions and N.Z.E. composite infantry unit, 327 strong). Total strength, 3,156.
    10th Brigade (20th Battalion, Composite Battalion, detachment of New Zealand Cavalry, 6th Greek Regiment, 8th Greek Regiment). Total strength, 1,989 New Zealand troops, and 2,498 Greeks with 36 New Zealanders attached. The 20th Battalion was nominally in the 10th Brigade, but was not to be employed without the approval of the New Zealand Division. The field artillery included ten 75-mm guns and six 3.7-inch howitzers; there were two infantry and 10 light tanks.

---

[1] Maj T. G. Bedding; 19 NZ Bn, and CO 1 Greek Regt May 1941. Physical instructor; of Pahautanui, NZ; b. Eketahuna, NZ, 18 Nov 1909.

[2] Major L. G. H. Dyke (of Melbourne) took temporary command of the 2/2 Fd Regt until he was appointed Australian liaison officer at Creforce headquarters and Major R. F. Jaboor (of Hawthorn, Vic) took over.

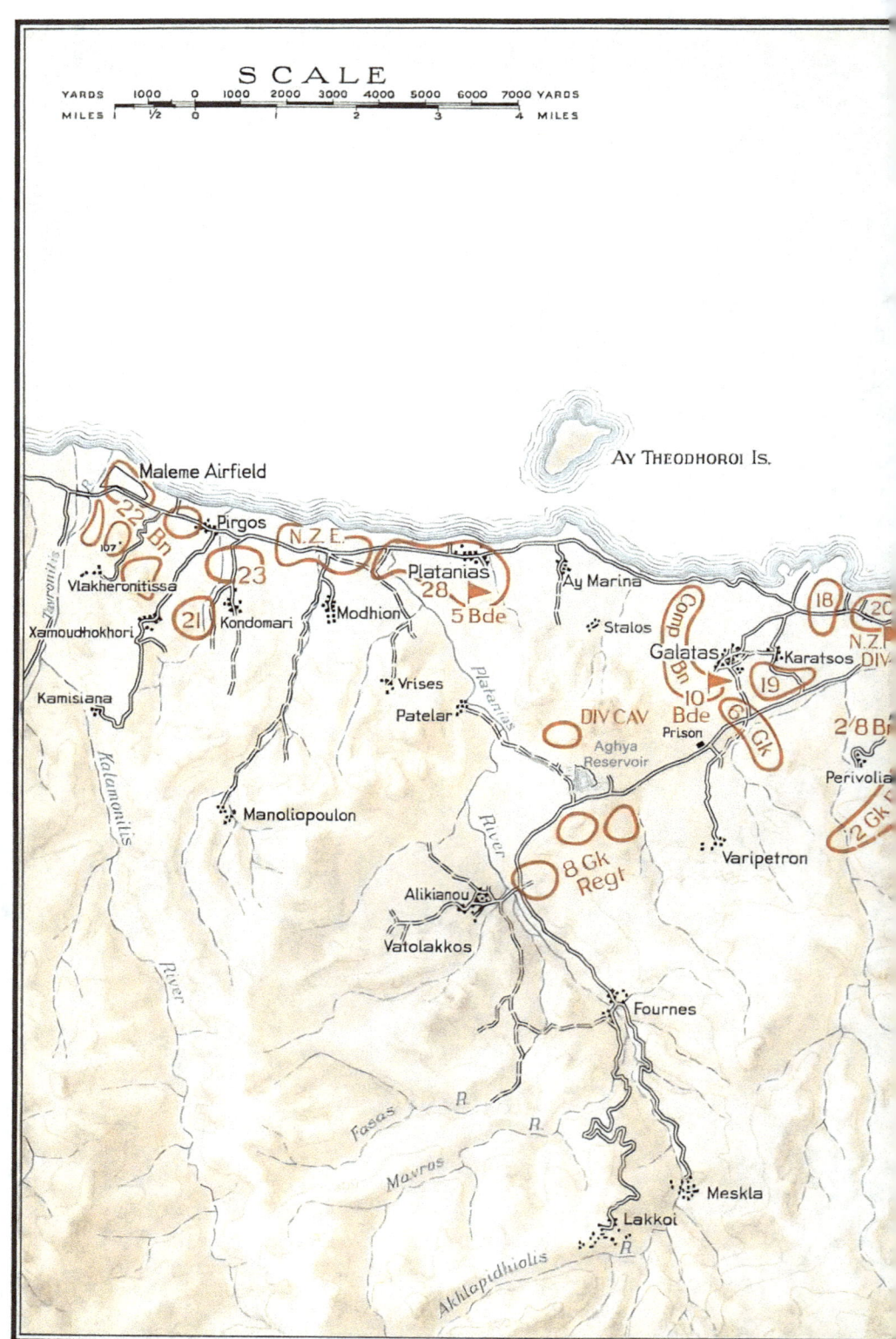

Dispositions, Suda-Maleme

a. 19th May

Force Reserve:
  4th New Zealand Brigade (18th, 19th Battalions). Total strength, 1,563.
  1/Welch, 854 strong

Kastelli Sector:
  1st Greek Regiment (1,030 strong)

Suda Sector: (Major-General Weston)
  M.N.B.D.O.
  1/Rangers
  102nd Anti-Tank (as infantry)
  106th R.H.A. (as infantry)

Cremor Force
  2/2nd Field Regiment (as infantry)
  16th Australian Composite Battalion
  17th Australian Composite Battalion
  Group "A" (600 men of R.A.A.)
  Group "B" (600 men of R.A.E.)
  2nd Greek Regiment
  The Australians in this group totalled 2,280 officers and men. The several anti-aircraft units and detachments in the Suda sector possessed sixteen 3.7-inch, ten 3-inch, and sixteen Bofors guns. There were eight coast defence guns of various calibres.

Retimo Sector: (Brigadier Vasey)
  19th Australian Brigade (2/1st, 2/11th, 2/7th, 2/8th Battalions).
  Three Greek regiments (each of battalion strength).
  One battery of the 2/3rd Field Regiment with fourteen guns of various models was in this sector. There were two infantry tanks at Retimo.

Heraklion Sector: (Brigadier Chappel)
  14th Brigade (2/Black Watch, 2/York and Lancaster, 2/Leicester, 2/4th Battalion, 7th Medium Regiment—with rifles).
  Three Greek regiments (each of battalion strength). There were thirteen field guns in support, ten light and four heavy anti-aircraft guns, four infantry tanks (including two landed at Timbakion on the 21st) and six light tanks. On the 19th the 1/Argyll and Sutherland Highlanders were also at Timbakion waiting to move to Heraklion.

On 13th May systematic large-scale bombing of the defended areas had begun.[3] The British fighter aircraft were flown nightly to Retimo airfield to avoid the bombing at Maleme and Heraklion. On the 16th Intelligence reports predicted that Crete would be attacked on the 17th, 18th or 19th by the *XI German Corps* including the *22nd Airborne Division,* 25,000 to 35,000 men coming by air and 10,000 by sea. The objectives would be Maleme, Canea and the valley south-west of it, and Retimo. There would be a sharp attack by some 100 bombers and fighters and then 600 troop-carrying aircraft would drop waves of paratroops.

While Creforce as a whole was preparing for this coming invasion, the anti-aircraft gunners were in action every day and often many times a day against German aircraft. The ships in Suda Bay were the principal target. On the 19th a new fire system was put into effect whereby an "umbrella" of bursting shells was put up over the pier when ships discharging cargo

---

[3] On 18 May eight bombs were dropped in the hospital area killing four and wounding four. When General Student was tried at Luneberg, Germany, in May 1946, Brig Inglis gave evidence that he thought that the bombs were intended for troops bathing in the sea.

were attacked. Thereafter no bomb hit either a discharging ship or the jetty. Nevertheless the batteries round Suda, armed with a total of 16 modern 3.7-inch guns, and 10 older 3-inch guns, with 16 light Bofors guns, were not strong enough to give adequate protection against heavy air attack. At Retimo there were no anti-aircraft guns; at Heraklion four 3-inch and, initially, 10 Bofors. In the period up to 20th May, however, no anti-aircraft gun was irreparably damaged and the total casualties to the gunners were 6 killed and 11 wounded.

Although the equipment received was far less than was needed to refit them, the units deployed it with skill and enterprise. As the preparations continued, Freyberg's confidence increased, and late on 16th May he sent the following cable to Wavell:

> I have completed plans for the defence of Crete and have just returned from a final tour of defences. I feel greatly encouraged by my visits. Everywhere all ranks are fit and morale is now high. All defences have been strengthened and positions wired as much as possible. We have 45 field guns in action with adequate ammunition dumped. Two infantry tanks are at each aerodrome. Carriers and transport still being unloaded and delivered. 2nd Battalion Leicesters have arrived and will make Heraklion stronger. I do not wish to seem over-confident but I feel that at least we will give an excellent account of ourselves. With help of Royal Navy I trust Crete will be held.

On the 18th the following message reached Freyberg:

> All our thoughts are with you in these fateful days. We are glad to hear of reinforcements which have reached you and strong dispositions you have made. We are sure that you and your brave troops will perform in deed of lasting fame. Victory where you are would powerfully affect world situation. Navy will do its utmost. Winston Churchill.

It was evident that there would be little air support in the coming battle. On 24th April Air Chief Marshal Longmore, after a visit to Crete, reported to the Chief of the Air Staff in London that a squadron of Hurricanes, with 100 per cent reserve of pilots and a generous rate of replacement, should be able to defend the Suda Bay naval base, but he doubted whether such a squadron could be kept up to strength because of the demands of North Africa and the probable heavy losses in Crete. In fact, on 19th May only four serviceable Hurricanes, three Gladiators and two Fulmars remained in Crete. That day one Hurricane was shot down over Maleme and the last Fulmars destroyed on the ground. Up to that time it was believed that the handful of defending fighters had shot down 23 enemy aircraft and possibly 9 others. Freyberg told Beamish that "it would be painful to see these machines and their gallant young pilots shot down on the first morning", and with the agreement of Mr Churchill the few machines that remained were sent to Egypt. General Freyberg wished to mine all airfields, but was not allowed to because it was intended that fighters should return as soon as possible. All three fields had to be preserved.

CHAPTER 11

THE LOSS OF MALEME AIRFIELD

THE 20th May was clear and still. About 6.45 in the morning, a far larger force of enemy bombers and fighters than usual appeared over the Suda-Maleme area and attacked the airfield and the area round it, Canea, the anti-aircraft batteries, and all roads. Great clouds of dust raised by bursting bombs obscured the view of the anti-aircraft gunners, who were already jaded by the daily attacks of which they had been a principal target. Each gun now received the attention of two or three dive bombers, and many were knocked out. Soon it was evident that this bombardment was not the "daily strafe" but the prelude to the long-expected invasion.

To all who saw it the scene which followed was perhaps the most majestic in their experience. Afterwards General Freyberg described it thus:

> I stood out on the hill with other members of my staff enthralled by the magnitude of the operation. While we were still watching the bombers, we suddenly became aware of a greater throbbing in the moments of comparative quiet, and, looking out to sea with the glasses, I picked out hundreds of planes tier upon tier coming towards us—here were the huge, slow-moving troop carriers with the loads we were expecting. First we watched them circle counter-clockwise over Maleme aerodrome and then, when they were only a few hundred feet above the ground, as if by magic white specks mixed with other colours suddenly appeared beneath them as clouds of parachutists floated slowly to earth.

Those nearer Maleme knew that before the dust of the bombs had cleared some seventy-five gliders had silently landed; perhaps forty-five of them west of the airfield, but small groups of three or four at various points between Maleme and Suda. The parachute troops appeared to drop west, south, and east of the airfield, east of Galatas, near the 7th General Hospital, on the road leading down from the hills (past a reservoir and a prison) to Galatas, and round Alikianou, farther south along that road.

The bombardment broke all signal lines leading from Puttick's headquarters about a mile south-west of Canea, and for several hours he had only meagre information from his units. His lines to Freyberg's headquarters were not repaired until 11 a.m. For some hours, in some instances for the whole day, there was little more communication between the battalions deployed between Canea and Maleme than between the groups of Germans broadcast among them.

Maleme airfield—the vital ground—was in the area of the westernmost New Zealand battalion, the 22nd. If the men dropped from the sky could seize and hold that airfield they might be reinforced by large bodies of infantry landed in transport planes and generously supplied with heavy weapons. "A blanket of dust and smoke" had concealed the landing of the gliders, most in the bed of the Tavronitis. Then parachute troops—there seemed to be from 400 to 600—descended round the battalion area which was about a mile and a half wide from north to south. A few gliders and a few paratroops landed in the 22nd Battalion's area, some of the gliders coming to earth within the lines of the westernmost company—Captain Campbell's.[1] Some paratroops landed just south-west of Pirgos, overran one New Zealand platoon of the headquarters company but were unable to dislodge the rest of it. Others, landed in the battalion area, were few but managed to interrupt communication by runners. Lieut-Colonel Andrew[2] thought the whole of the headquarters company lost, but the real threats to the defence came only from troops landed outside the battalion area.

Near Campbell's company the centre of the landing was the western bank of the river. Perhaps half a dozen gliders, from which few survived, and some twenty paratroops landed within his area. Germans who came down on the western bank crossed the river, dodging from pylon to pylon of the bridge, entered the R.A.F. offices and camp just south-east of it, and drove the non-combatants therein up the hill towards the headquarters of the 22nd. Campbell's right platoon, outnumbered and enfiladed, had to fall back, leaving a gap between his company and Captain Johnson's[3] to the north. After this Campbell's company held firmly. He heard, after dark, that battalion headquarters had withdrawn, but did not believe it. However, when he led a party in that direction after dark to obtain water and ammunition he found that it was so, and decided that he too must withdraw.

At 3 o'clock next morning the withdrawal began, each platoon following a different route. One moved south and then east into the hills, eventually crossing the island; another making south beside the river was captured; the third went eastward and eventually reached the rear battalions of the brigade.

Part of one of the other four rifle companies of the 22nd was deployed on the airfield; the westernmost platoon (Lieutenant Sinclair[4]) was holding a front of 1,400 yards on that edge. Fourteen gliders landed along its front in the Tavronitis and many paratroops arrived at the same time. The crews of the anti-aircraft guns were overpowered and one by one Sinclair's men were hit. The sections held out until the middle of the afternoon, though under fire from all directions except due east. At dusk Sinclair himself, who had been wounded, and his last remaining man, also wounded, were taken prisoner. Eight in his platoon were killed, fifteen wounded and only two not hit.

Elsewhere the 22nd generally held its ground—the eastern side of the airfield and the slopes south of the main road, which bounded the airfield on the south—although small enemy groups were wedged between two of its companies, and between it and the 21st Battalion. In Pirgos paratroops had landed in the streets and on the flat roofs. Most of the first group

---

[1] Col T. C. Campbell, DSO, MC. CO 22 NZ Bn 1942-44; Comd 4 NZ Armd Bde 1945. Farm appraiser; of London; b. Colombo, 20 Dec 1911.

[2] Brig L. W. Andrew, VC, DSO. (1914-18: Lt 2nd Bn Wellington Regt.) CO 22 NZ Bn 1940-42 (Comd 5 NZ Bde Nov-Dec 1941); Area Comd, Wellington 1943-46. Regular soldier; of Khandallah, Wellington, NZ; b. Ashhurst, NZ, 23 Mar 1897.

[3] Capt S. H. Johnson; 22 NZ Bn. School teacher; of Auckland; b. 5 Oct 1910.

[4] Capt R. B. Sinclair; 22 NZ Bn. Clerk; of Gisborne, NZ; b. Gisborne, 3 Jan 1918.

were shot as they fell; a second group arriving about 10.30 was also overcome, and by midday only small parties were in the area, moving along drains and through the vineyards trying to find one another and organise.

At 5.15 p.m. Colonel Andrew, a regular soldier who had won the Victoria Cross as a lance-corporal in 1917, had decided to use two infantry tanks that were under his command, with a platoon reinforced by a few British Bofors gunners, to thrust west along the road, but the crew of one tank found their gun to be unusable and withdrew; the other tank reached the river flat and was there abandoned.

By 9 p.m. the enemy had a weak grip on the western edge of the airfield and the area between Vlakheronitissa and Xamoudhokhori, and was increasing his hold on Hill 107, which dominated the airfield. Andrew decided to withdraw and consolidate the battalion on his rear rifle company on the eastern of the two ridges the battalion held, thus abandoning a belt of country about 1,000 yards wide east of the Tavronitis. At dawn next morning the survivors of the battalion, with parties of gunners and air force men from the airfield, were moving east in groups towards the Pirgos-Xamoudhokhori track.

East of the 22nd, the 23rd Battalion (Major Leckie[5]) overlooked the main road and was itself overlooked by the 21st Battalion on the higher slopes to the south. Gliders and paratroops who landed in and round the 23rd's area were soon killed or dispersed; it was estimated that about 400 were killed in the air, in trees, or on the ground. By midday the area was fully under the defenders' control, and their machine-guns and mortars were raking the beaches and the eastern edges of the airfield. However, efforts to get into touch with the 22nd Battalion failed. Late in the afternoon one company of the 23rd and one of the 28th (Maori) were sent west to reinforce the 22nd. The Maori company had a sharp skirmish with Germans and killed perhaps thirty. The company of the 23rd formed a rearguard while the 22nd withdrew; the Maori company found the headquarters of the 22nd deserted, and, retiring, met part of one of the companies of the 22nd and Andrew with it. It was then about 2 a.m.

Some 100 parachutists who landed on the slopes held by the 21st Battalion (Lieut-Colonel Allen[6]) were killed or captured. Allen's orders left him the choice of replacing the 23rd if that battalion counter-attacked, supporting the 22nd, or holding his positions on the vine-covered ridges. Because paratroops had landed in his area and more might come, Allen decided to remain where he was, but sent one platoon to clear the enemy from Xamoudhokhori and Vlakheronitissa. It cleared Xamoudhokhori but found Vlakheronitissa too strongly held.

East of the 23rd Battalion was the N.Z.E. detachment (an infantry unit improvised from engineer companies), and partly in its area and partly in the 23rd's and 21st's was the 27th Battery, armed with two English 3.7-inch howitzers (mountain weapons), three Italian 75-mm guns, and

---

[5] Col D. F. Leckie, OBE. CO 23 NZ Bn 1940-42. School teacher; of Invercargill, NZ; b. Dunedin, NZ, 9 Jun 1897.
[6] Lt-Col J. M. Allen; CO 21 Bn 1941. Farmer; b. Cheadle, Eng, 3 Aug 1901. Killed in action 28 Nov 1941.

four French 75's. Parachutists who were landed round the guns were overcome, as were some who descended round the N.Z.E. detachment and the 28th (Maori) Battalion (Lieut-Colonel Dittmer[7]), from which two platoons sallied forth in the afternoon and mopped up a party of Germans assembled at a mill 600 yards forward of the N.Z.E. positions.

Thus at dawn on the second day all four battalions of Hargest's 5th Brigade had overcome the Germans landed in their areas except the 22nd —the battalion that had occupied the most important ground. It had been seriously mauled and had withdrawn, leaving only isolated parties within half a mile of the airfield. No counter-attack had been made by the brigade as a whole. In view of the number of German fighters and bombers continually overhead, and the uncertainty of communications, it would have been impossible to organise an effective counter-attack.

Farther east Colonel Kippenberger's 10th Brigade held a wide front extending to the foothills just west of Canea. On the coastal flank was the Composite Battalion holding a front of 3,200 yards from the coast south to the foothills. Farther south were the 6th and 8th Greek Regiments[8] and the Divisional Cavalry (190 men fighting as infantry), these last two being far into the foothills to the south-west. The Composite Battalion consisted of about 1,000 gunners and drivers relatively untrained as infantry; the 2,400 Greeks were ill-armed recruits with a few weeks' service.

As soon as the preliminary bombing had ceased, on the 20th, a strong force of paratroops and gliders landed in and round the 10th Brigade area, and particularly round Galatas, the Aghya prison, where probably 1,500 landed, and thence to Alikianou. When Colonel Kippenberger arrived panting and alone at the small house that he had arranged to use as his battle headquarters he found a German sniper in occupation; he stalked the German and shot him.

Within half an hour the 6th Greek Regiment had exhausted its ammunition and was broken; some 400 who fell back towards Galatas were rallied by Captain Forrester[9] of the Queen's, a liaison officer with the Greeks, who formed a line linking with the 19th Battalion which was round Karatsos, and the Composite Battalion.[1] The Germans were now attacking along the Prison-Galatas road, and the cavalry and the 8th Greek were out of touch. This attack drove in the left of the Composite Battalion (held by the Petrol Company) and Colonel Kippenberger's brigade headquarters. By midday, however, parties of Germans landed in Galatas had been rounded up.

The Germans renewed their attack up the Prison-Galatas road at 4 p.m., but were repulsed. About this time the cavalry arrived in the Galatas area,

---

[7] Brig G. Dittmer, CBE, DSO, MC. CO 28 (Maori) Bn 1940-42; Comd Fiji Mil Forces and Fiji Inf Bde Gp 1943-45. Regular soldier; of Auckland, NZ; b. Maharahara, NZ, 4 Jun 1893.

[8] The Greek infantry in this sector was organised into regiments each including two battalions intended to be about 600 strong. They are therefore referred to as regiments although in fact each had the numerical strength of little more than a battalion, and far fewer weapons than a battalion needed.

[9] Lt-Col M. Forrester, DSO, MC. CO 1/6 Queen's 1943. B. Portsmouth, Eng, 31 Aug 1917.

[1] 1 Lt Tp RA, with four 3.7-in howitzers emplaced just south of 19 Bn was overrun after three of the guns had been disabled by the gunners.

having withdrawn from their isolated position north of the reservoir; they were placed in the sector weakly held by the Greeks east of Galatas and formed a link between the Petrol Company and the 19th Battalion. The 8th Greek was still out in the foothills, isolated but fighting strongly; reports arrived that in the Prison area, now firmly in German hands, the enemy seemed to be clearing a landing ground.

In the area held by the 4th Brigade (Brigadier Inglis) which was just east of the 10th and included Brigadier Puttick's divisional headquarters, parachute troops landed round Karatsos village, and, later, in vineyards north of the coast road and south of the 7th General Hospital, which was on the small peninsula in this area. When he learnt that the hospital had been captured Inglis ordered a company of the 18th to retake it. They achieved this with little opposition early in the afternoon.[2] Other paratroops captured the 6th Field Ambulance, in this area, and shot the commanding officer, Lieut-Colonel Plimmer.[3]

Because of broken telephone lines and wireless failures Freyberg had received scanty reports during the first few hours, but by 11 a.m. he decided that Maleme was the danger point and ordered that the 4th Brigade less the 1/Welch be returned to Puttick's command, thus allotting him the whole of his reserve except one battalion. Brigadier Puttick, whose reports from the 5th Brigade had so far been cheerful and confident, at first decided that to use these reserves for a counter-attack would leave the coast open to attack by a force then known to be at sea; such an attack might cut off his whole division. In the late afternoon, however, reports that the enemy appeared to be clearing a landing ground near the prison made the 4th Brigade area seem no less dangerous than Maleme. At length, at Kippenberger's suggestion, Puttick agreed to an attack on the prison, and this was launched at 7.15 p.m. by Lieut-Colonel Blackburn's[4] 19th Battalion supported by a troop of three light tanks of the 3rd Hussars, this battalion of the reserve brigade thus advancing into the area of the adjoining brigade (Kippenberger's). Two companies of the 19th advanced west from Galatas, then south. By 8.30, having overcome sturdy resistance, they were 1,400 yards north of the prison; light was fading and the tank commander considered that he could do no more that night, and at 10 p.m. the two companies formed a leaguer round the tanks. In the meantime Kippenberger had been given to understand that the 19th was now under his command. He decided that the attack had been made too late and with too-weak forces and should be cancelled. Next morning patrols reached the attacking companies with orders to withdraw, and they rejoined their battalion.

---

[2] A large party of patients who were able to walk were being shepherded westward by a German guard when New Zealanders dispersed the guard and freed them. For a time the patients were in the midst of the fire fight. This incident bred a rumour that during attacks the Germans had deliberately driven prisoners in front of them.

[3] Lt-Col J. R. L. Plimmer; CO 6 NZ Fd Amb 1941. Medical practitioner; of Wellington, NZ; b. Wellington, 28 Feb 1901. Killed in action 20 May 1941.

[4] Lt-Col C. A. D'A. Blackburn. CO 19 NZ Bn in 1941; 1 NZ Army Tk Bde 1942-43; CO 1 Army Tk Bn 1943. Public accountant; of Gisborne, NZ; b. Hamilton, NZ, 8 May 1899.

It was unfortunate (reported Kippenberger later) that 19th Battalion was not placed under command earlier, as in consequence the forward commander, in touch with the situation, was unable to assist or direct the attack in any way, and it was consequently abortive. Considerable help could have been given by the Divisional Cavalry detachment, by the Greeks, who always advanced cheerfully, by parties from the Composite Battalion and by the guns and machine-guns, none of which in fact knew anything about the operation until too late.

Thus, by the night of the 20th, the Germans had a foothold on Maleme airfield, but it was still commanded by the defenders' guns; a belt of tactically important ground east of the Tavronitis had been lost; and a German force was strongly established on the slopes round the prison and the reservoir whence they threatened to cut through the centre of the elongated position occupied by the New Zealand Division on the coastal shelf and the foothills overlooking it.

Meanwhile, in General Weston's Suda-Canea area east of the New Zealand Division, paratroops and gliders had landed south of Canea and on the Akrotiri Peninsula bounding Suda Bay to the north.[5] Some 700 men of the Composite Battalion near Perivolia dealt with paratroops landed in the woods near by. The King of Greece had been staying in a house close to the camp, and after their morning's good work General Weston named this force the Royal Perivolians. It will be recalled that the protection of the King and his party had been entrusted to a New Zealand platoon under Lieutenant Ryan. Parachutists landed in the garden of the King's house. Protected by the New Zealanders and some armed Cretans the King and his Ministers made their way into the hills.[6]

Fifteen gliders were released over the sea near the Akrotiri Peninsula but only eleven reached the land and some of those were shot down; the Northumberland Hussars soon killed or captured most of the survivors. Other gliders landed south of Canea round a group of anti-aircraft guns. The gunners had few rifles and Germans overcame them, but were contained by the 1/Rangers and a section of carriers from the 1/Welch (in reserve on the outskirts of the town). These were reinforced in the afternoon by two platoons of Royal Marines and some Greeks of the 2nd Regiment, and the gun sites were recaptured. By nightfall only isolated groups of Germans remained in the Suda-Canea area, into which, late in the afternoon, was brought the 2/8th Battalion from Georgioupolis; it went into position on a 2,000-yard front west of Mournies with the Perivolians on the right, the 2/2nd Field Regiment on the left, and the 2nd Greek Regiment extending the line.

---

[5] Weston had the Northumberland Hussars (as infantry) on the Akrotiri Peninsula; south of the road junction, west of Canea, he had placed a composite battalion of 700 rifles; on a line running south from that point to Mournies the 2nd Greek Regiment, and on a reserve line from the Composite Battalion to the monastery south of Canea the 2/2nd Field Regiment and part of the 1 Rangers. On his eastern flank along the southern shore of the bay were, at Meg Khorafia part of the 2/3rd Field Regiment, at Suda Point the 17th Australian Composite Battalion (270 rifles), and at Kalives the 16th Australian Composite (350 rifles). Between these flanking forces was a variety of detachments of coast and anti-aircraft artillery, base troops and unarmed men.

[6] The party, consisting of the King of Greece, a few of his staff, the British Minister, the naval attaché and about 40 others, crossed the island to Ayia Roumeli, where it embarked in H.M.S. *Decoy* and *Hero* on the night of the 22nd.

(2/4 Bn War Diary)

The bombing of Heraklion.

(New Zealand War History Branch)
German transport planes and supplies on a Greek airfield, May 1941.

(Captured photograph)
Troops of the 5th German Mountain Division boarding a transport aircraft in Greece.

The invasion. Parachutes over Suda Bay.

German parachute troops over Suda Bay, 20th May 1941.

The south coast of Crete viewed from above Sfakia, May 1941.

(Maj S. B. Cann, 2/1 Fd Coy)

As mentioned above, a Greek force was protecting the harbour of Kastelli near the western end of the island. Germans landed east of the town and north and south of the main road near by. The Greeks sallied out and attacked them so effectively that by 11 a.m., after a grim fight, only one small enemy group was still resisting. A platoon led by Major Bedding captured this post. The Germans lost some 50 killed and 28 prisoners; 57 Greeks were killed and 62 Greeks and one New Zealander wounded.

The present chapter will tell no more about the fighting in the other sectors—Retimo and Heraklion—than was known to General Freyberg at the time. These places were not attacked until late in the afternoon of the 20th. That night at Retimo most of the paratroops were overcome, but one group held strongly on a ridge overlooking the airfield from the south-east. At Heraklion all who dropped within the defended area were disposed of except for parties of snipers, but fighting was in progress in the town. Signal communications were so poor that Freyberg's report to Wavell that night said: "So far I think we hold Maleme, Heraklion and Retimo aerodromes and the two harbours. Margin by which we hold them is bare one .... Everybody here realises vital issue and we will fight it out."

Admiral Cunningham had kept naval forces ready to defeat a seaborne attack on Crete since 14th May. He considered that the three most likely landing places were Canea, Retimo and Heraklion, but that Kisamos Bay and Sitia were also possibilities. Consequently he established three "light" forces (of cruisers and destroyers), one to protect Heraklion and Sitia, another Retimo, and a third north-west Crete. Two battleships and five destroyers were to take up a position by night westward of Crete to cover the lighter ships. In reserve at Alexandria were two battleships and his only aircraft carrier, *Formidable* (which now possessed only four serviceable aircraft). On the night of the 20th-21st six Italian motor-boats were seen in Kaso Strait; when fired on by a force consisting of the cruisers *Naiad* and *Perth* and four destroyers, they retired after four boats had been damaged. No other enemy ships were seen.

It is now known that the proposal that Crete should be captured by parachute and airborne troops was made to Field Marshal Goering on 15th April by General Lohr, commander of the *Fourth Air Fleet*.[7] Hitler was persuaded that airborne attack on Crete was practicable, and command of the whole operation was given to General Lohr who had controlled the air operations in Greece. His force included General Student's *XI Air Corps*[8] (glider and parachute troops) and General von Richthofen's *VIII*

---
[7] The account of German operations against Crete is based chiefly on a detailed report by *XI Air Corps* and on a variety of captured German documents held by the United States War Department and translated by Mr W. D. Dawson of the New Zealand War History Branch.

[8] It had been intended to include the *22nd Infantry Division* which had been landed from the air in Holland but, according to the German official account, it could not be transported from Rumania where it was guarding the oilfields. According to Student, in conversation with Capt Liddell Hart after the war, Hitler was so concerned about possible sabotage of the oilfields that he refused to release it.

Air Corps (a purely air formation). The concentration of the attacking troops round the airfields at Corinth, Megara, Tanagra, Topolia, Dadion, Eleusis and Phaleron in southern Greece was completed by 14th May. The force defending Crete was estimated at one division plus troops that had escaped from Greece.

Student had hoped to launch simultaneous attacks on Maleme, Canea-Suda Bay, Retimo, and Heraklion, but Richthofen would not guarantee complete air protection for four simultaneous attacks, and consequently plans were made to attack Maleme and Canea with airborne troops at 8.15 in the morning and Retimo and Heraklion at 4.15 in the afternoon.[9] In addition four groups comprising sixty-three small commandeered vessels and seven merchantmen were organised under Admiral Schuster, to transport one infantry battalion, some other men, heavy weapons, pack animals and supplies to Crete. The first was to reach the beaches west of Maleme on the first day, and the second the coast east of Heraklion on the second day, but at the last moment it was decided that the British fleet was too active to permit a landing on the first day and that both groups should land on the second.

General Student's *XI Air Corps* included General Sussmann's *7th Air Division* (paratroops), General Meindl's *1st Assault Regiment* (glider-borne), and the aircraft group (General Conrad) whose chief task was to transport the fighting part of the corps. *The Assault Regiment* included four battalions each of four companies. The *Air Division* included three regiments, each of three battalions. Each battalion had three rifle companies; the regiment included also a *13th* (artillery) and *14th* (anti-tank) *Company*. The division possessed in addition a battery of artillery, an anti-tank, a machine-gun and a pioneer battalion. To the corps was added also the *5th Mountain Division* with three rifle regiments (one from the *6th Mountain Division*) and a battalion of tanks.

The plan provided that, after the *7th Air Division* and the *Assault Regiment* had been dropped, part of the *5th Mountain Division* would be landed on the captured airfields and part taken to Crete by sea. Thus, in the initial stages, 750 men would descend in gliders and 10,000 in parachutes, while 5,000 would be landed in aircraft and 7,000 from ships. The aircraft available for transport were from 70 to 80 towed gliders, and from 600 to 750 Junkers transports (Ju-52's), able to carry 5,000-6,000 men and their equipment in one lift. The supporting air bombardment was to be given by *VIII Air Corps* which possessed 430 dive bombers, 180 fighters and 40 reconnaissance aircraft. The information which General Wavell thought exaggerated had thus proved remarkably correct.

The attacking troops were divided into three groups—West, Centre and East. The West Group under General Meindl consisted of the *Assault Regiment* (less half of the *I Battalion*) a combined anti-aircraft and machine-gun battalion and a medical platoon. Its task was to capture

---

[9] German time was an hour earlier than British in this area at this time. In this account of German operations an hour has been added to the times recorded in German reports.

Maleme airfield and keep it open for aircraft, to reconnoitre westward to Kastelli and the Gulf of Kisamos, and to advance southward and eastward to meet the Centre Group. That group (with General Sussmann, commander of the *7th Air Division*) consisted of two forces. The first comprised the *3rd Parachute Regiment,* the remaining half-battalion of the *Assault Regiment* and the division's pioneer battalion, and its task was to capture Canea and Suda. Its second force comprised the *2nd Parachute Regiment* (less one battalion); its task was to take Retimo, whence it was to send troops westward to attack Suda Bay from the east. Little resistance was expected at Retimo. The East Group of four battalions was to capture Heraklion and its airfield and prepare the way for the landing of troops by sea.

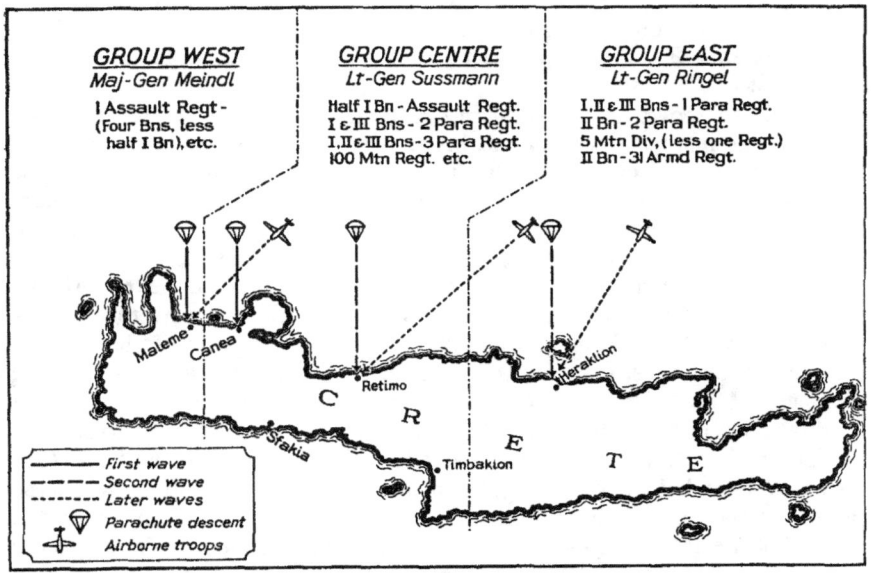

The German plan

The gliders of the West Group landed where intended and their occupants achieved their initial tasks, namely to capture a tented camp near the airfield (probably the air force camp), overcome the anti-aircraft guns at the mouth of the Tavronitis, and capture the bridge over the river intact. The *III Battalion* (Major Scherber) was to land along the Maleme-Platanias road and capture the airfield from the east. It was wrongly landed in the hills south of the road, because aircraft commanders were overanxious lest they land their men in the sea. Instead of descending along the road between Pirgos and a point two miles east, they landed along a line parallel to the road but about half a mile south of it. Many were shot while falling or when caught in trees and others were killed on the ground; finally all the officers were killed or wounded and only 200 remained alive of a battalion of 600.

The *IV Battalion,* with General Meindl, was to land west of the Tavronitis bridge. The task of its *16th Company* was to cross the island to Selino Kastelli. This company fought its way southward against Greek guerillas; the remainder (with the *8th Company* of the *II Battalion*) was committed to an attack eastward to help the glider troops.

When Meindl himself landed about 8.30 a.m. the glider troops were heavily engaged, but he had the greater part of two battalions organised and ready to carry out his orders. There appeared to be a strong defence line round the airfield. He ordered a frontal attack astride the bridge by four companies (*8th, 13th, 14th, 15th*) while two companies (*5th* and *7th*) made a flanking movement to the south. Meindl was soon seriously wounded and Major Stenzler took command of the forward troops. By evening the main body of the regiment had gained the western edge of the airfield and the northern slope of Hill 107 (the centre of the 22nd New Zealand Battalion's position) and the detached companies were south-east of that hill.

As related above, the force to land in the Canea-Suda Bay area included General Sussmann. Sussmann and his staff set off in five gliders. One containing the general crashed on the island of Aegina near Athens and the occupants were killed. Thereafter Colonel Heidrich of the *3rd Regiment* commanded the division. The *I/3rd Battalion* landed near the prison and re-formed, captured the heights there, and advanced as far east as Perivolia. There they met a company of the *III/3rd,* landed near Perivolia instead of round Galatas, and advanced on Mournies, but were thrust back (by the Royal Perivolians and Greeks). Another company of the *III/3rd* was practically destroyed near Galatas; a third succeeded in taking Cemetery Hill south-east of Galatas; a fourth, instead of landing at Karatsos descended with the *I/3rd Battalion* and attached itself to it.

The *II/3rd Battalion* (which lacked its *8th Company* but had the *13th* and *14th*) landed between the prison and the reservoir and between the prison and Galatas and became involved in the heavy fighting with the 10th New Zealand Brigade. The pioneer battalion landed on high ground north of Alikianou, captured a power station in the area and became involved in a hard struggle with the Greeks of the 8th Regiment.

When, at 9 a.m., Heidrich landed near the prison he had approximately three full battalions in the Alikianou-Prison-Perivolia area. He was disturbed to find that the landing area was commanded by the opposing troops on the heights round Galatas, and organised an attack by one company towards those heights. In the afternoon, after another company had been thrown in, the Galatas height (Pink Hill) was taken. In the evening, "because of a misunderstanding", it was abandoned, and the attacking companies and also *I/3rd Battalion* from Perivolia were withdrawn and a defensive front facing Galatas was formed. During the night, on Heidrich's orders, the pioneers fought their way to the prison area. Thus what was left of his regiment was deployed defensively from the heights west of Perivolia on the right to the Alikianou area on the left. Heidrich considered that his four battalions, two of which had lost heavily, were just strong enough to withstand the counter-attack he expected on the 21st.

It was not until the morning of the 21st that Freyberg learnt of the extent to which the 22nd Battalion had been thrust off its ground. It was reported to him, however, that the airfield was still covered by his artillery and machine-guns, and could not be used by the enemy. A severe dive-bombing of the defenders began before 9 a.m. Then arrived more disturbing news: that not only were more paratroops descending but transport aircraft were landing in the bed of the river west of Maleme and on the undefended beaches farther west.

Puttick's Intelligence staff correctly estimated that two German regiments had landed, one about Maleme and one south of Galatas, and that they were intent on advancing east. Puttick considered that the most important task was the recapture of Maleme airfield, but measures to carry out that task proceeded at a snail's pace. At a conference at the 23rd Battalion headquarters about 2 a.m. on the 21st it was decided that the 23rd should hold its position next day and that the battered 22nd, now only about two companies strong, should be withdrawn to the lines of the 23rd and 21st for reorganisation. Thus, at dawn, the 22nd Battalion was fitted into the lines of the 23rd and 21st, whence a certain amount of fire covered the airfield. Scores of weary, unarmed men of the Royal Air Force and the disabled anti-aircraft batteries, and the Royal Marine Artillery were now drifting east through the New Zealand lines.

Throughout the 21st, the 5th Brigade, still almost isolated, was bombed and machine-gunned from the air, and pressed by the enemy on the ground. It held its positions, except that the machine-gun platoon with the 23rd Battalion was withdrawn from one useful height. The Vickers guns and mortars fired on aircraft landing on the airfield until, by late afternoon, their ammunition was exhausted. At a conference of commanding officers at the headquarters of the 23rd Battalion it was decided that next day the 23rd should counter-attack and reoccupy the ground it had lost.

Meanwhile the German transport aircraft were pressing their advantage boldly. At 8.10 a.m. in spite of the fire of nine guns[1] of the 27th Battery and a platoon of machine-guns, an aircraft landed on Maleme airfield, unloaded and took off again—a significant event. Later several troop carriers landed and took off at the west end of the field. About 4 p.m. a steady stream of aircraft began landing. Thus the Germans had achieved their first main objective—to gain the use of an airfield—although their hold on it was still insecure.

Farther east the situation within each New Zealand sector was even more reassuring than on the previous day. Large numbers of paratroops dropped on and round the Maori battalion's area about 3.40 p.m. The Maoris attacked the newcomers with vigour and by nightfall had cleared

---

[1] There were four French 75's, three Italian 75's and two British 3.7 mountain howitzers.

their own area and most of the country between them and the New Zealand Engineers, where, however, one group of Germans established itself. Within the 4th Brigade's area only isolated parties of Germans were at large on the 21st. Early in the afternoon a company of the 19th Battalion supported by fire from a squadron of the New Zealand Cavalry attacked Cemetery Hill but German mortar and machine-gun fire was too heavy. This bald hill was too exposed and neither side could hold it.

Although the recapture of Maleme airfield was now the main necessity, a task of almost equal importance was to prevent the German force in the Aghya area from advancing north to the coast and thus cutting the New Zealand Division in two. Thus when it was reported that morning that some eighty paratroops had descended on the slopes well south of the Maori battalion and troop carriers were seen flying towards the Aghya reservoir, a Maori patrol was sent out to see what was happening over the hills to their south. It found that Germans who had apparently filtered down from the reservoir area had established posts between the Maori and N.Z.E. detachment.

What plans were being made to counter the two threats? At 11.15 a.m. Hargest had proposed to Puttick that an attack should be made towards Maleme by the Maori and another battalion; it should be made at night because machine-gun fire from the air did not permit large-scale movement by day. Late in the afternoon Freyberg held a conference (which Brigadier Vasey attended) at which he decided that he would bring an Australian battalion from Georgioupolis in trucks to replace the 20th New Zealand, which would then move west in the vehicles the Australians had used, reinforce the 5th Brigade, and be available for a counter-attack. Later in the evening Freyberg ordered his troop of the 2/3rd Field Regiment and a section of the 106th Royal Horse Artillery (an anti-tank unit) to join the New Zealand Division for shelling the airfield. The former commander of the 2/3rd, Lieut-Colonel Strutt,[2] had that day been appointed to command the artillery of the New Zealand Division.

The detailed plan was that the 20th Battalion would advance between the road and the beach, three light tanks along the road, and the Maoris on the left of it. The attacking troops would form up about 400 yards west of the Platanias River. The first objective was Pirgos, where the troops would rest for thirty minutes; the second objective was the airfield on the right and the river on the left. If successful the attack would carry the advancing troops right through the 5th Brigade. Aircraft from Egypt would bomb the areas west of the advancing troops from midnight until 2.30 a.m.

Freyberg learnt that the 21st May had been a fairly successful day at Retimo, where the 2/1st Battalion had recaptured the heights south-east of the airfield, although an enemy group remained astride the road leading west to Canea and the road leading east to Heraklion. At Heraklion

---

[2] The coolness and efficiency of Colonel Strutt and his regiment had greatly impressed the New Zealanders whom they had supported at Elasson in Greece on the 18th April, at Erithrai on the 26th, and at Porto Rafti on the 27th.

the enemy had captured the harbour but was later driven out. In both areas the enemy had failed to take the airfield and was on the defensive.

During the 21st British naval forces were waiting south of Crete ready to resume their sweeps north of the island during the second night. One force was bombed continuously from 9.50 a.m. to 1.50 p.m., and the destroyer *Juno* was sunk. In another force the cruiser *Ajax* was damaged by near misses. At this juncture, however, aircraft reported enemy small ships steering towards Crete from Milos, and that night the three light forces made a sweep along the north coast. At 11.30 p.m. *Dido, Orion,* the damaged *Ajax* and four destroyers met a convoy, chiefly of caiques crowded with German soldiers, 18 miles north of Canea. The British ships fired on them for two hours and a half, sinking or setting fire to one or two steamers, at least a dozen caiques, a small pleasure steamer and a steam yacht. One of the escorting destroyers, the *Lupo,* was hit but did not sink.

The German commander had decided on the 21st that success depended on the prompt capture of an airfield and that it could only be Maleme since Retimo and Heraklion were firmly in enemy hands; all measures were to be concentrated on achieving this. General Student decided to land his two remaining parachute companies (of the *2nd Regiment*) in his enemy's rear east of Pirgos while the *Assault Regiment* attacked from the west; *VIII Air Corps* was asked to silence the enemy battery that was firing on the field. The *II Battalion* of the *100th Mountain Regiment* was to be embarked in transport aircraft in Greece and be ready to land at Maleme from 4 p.m. onwards—these were the troops seen arriving at Maleme that afternoon. Twenty of their aircraft were destroyed in the process.

At dawn the Germans round Maleme had advanced from the positions reached the night before, occupied Hill 107, moved across the airfield, and formed a line on its eastern edge. They then organised an attack on Maleme and Pirgos, abandoned by the New Zealanders the night before, and occupied them.

In the Prison Valley the German position remained practically unchanged throughout the 21st. The German commander, Colonel Heidrich, expected a British counterattack, but none came. When the two parachute companies jumped into the Platanias area they fell among troops who were ready for them, and lost heavily; but one group of eighty men succeeded in establishing itself in a farm on the outskirts of Pirgos near the beach.

As for the invasion by sea, it is now known that the delayed convoy of small ships that was to transport to Maleme a mountain battalion—*III Battalion* of *100th Mountain Regiment*—part of an anti-aircraft regiment and some heavy weapons groups, 2,330 men in all, sailed early in the morning but returned because of the presence of British naval ships. It sailed again about midday and was off the coast of Crete when it was discovered by the British squadron and "dispersed with heavy losses"—about 320 men. "Due to the courageous action of the *Lupo* (an Italian destroyer) . . . and to the scattered formation of our ships, only a small portion of the flotilla was caught and destroyed." Many were rescued later by Italian speedboats and destroyers.

The German plan for the 22nd was that the *Assault Regiment* should hold its gains and reorganise, and the mountain troops should assist in holding the airfield. During the day more mountain troops were to arrive and were to make an enveloping attack through the hills. Student informed Major-General Ringel, commanding the *5th Mountain Division,* that he would be placed in command of all troops on Crete, and his task would be to clear the island from west to east.

"On the evening of the second day of the invasion," said the diarist of Ringel's division, "the situation seemed to be balanced on a knife-edge. If *II/100th Mountain*

Battalion had landed with light casualties, the defences of Maleme airfield would be considerably strengthened, but a heavy, concentrated British counter-attack would force the defenders to fight for their lives."

The "heavy, concentrated counter-attack" was, in fact, to take place that night. Although no Australian unit would take part, its commencement, as noted above, was to await the arrival in the New Zealand Division's area of one of Vasey's battalions from Georgioupolis, 18 miles away. During the first two days of the battle Vasey's force at Georgioupolis had not been engaged. It will be recalled that it included the 2/7th Battalion, about 580 strong. The 2/7th was a tried unit which had seen hard fighting at Bardia in January, and in February and March had been in the forward position round Marsa Brega in western Cyrenaica under daily attack from the air. Service in Greece followed. It probably had more experience of German air attack than any other unit in Crete. Its losses in Greece had not been great.

On the morning of the 21st Brigadier Vasey had told Lieut-Colonel Walker of the 2/7th that he wished to use that battalion to clear the road to Retimo and re-establish communications with the other half of his brigade, after which his battalions should be used to reinforce the New Zealanders round Maleme. At the conference at Freyberg's headquarters on the afternoon of the 21st, however, Vasey had learnt that the 2/7th was to relieve the 20th New Zealand that night to enable it to counter-attack towards Maleme. This decision left Vasey with no troops under his command except the 2/7th Field Ambulance and a detachment of engineers. His 2/1st and 2/11th Battalions were cut off at Retimo where Colonel Campbell of the 2/1st was now in command; his 2/8th was under Weston's command round Perivolia, south-west of Canea. Vasey asked to be allotted an area where he could command the 2/7th and 2/8th—a request that was to be granted late next day.

On the morning of the 21st Vasey had informed Walker of the 2/7th that his plan to clear the road to Maleme would not be realised, but that he thought that the 2/7th was to be used to counter-attack towards Maleme. Walker and his Intelligence officer, Lieutenant Lunn,[3] had then accompanied Vasey to the New Zealand conference, Walker having first warned his second-in-command, Major Marshall, to have the battalion ready to move at 8 p.m.—just before dusk. It was not until the conference ended, late in the afternoon, that Walker learnt of the actual plan. He sent Lunn hurrying eastward to pass on the orders to his second-in-command, while he himself went forward with Brigadier Inglis to reconnoitre the new area. Their journey was slow because of frequent stops during attacks from the air. On the way Walker told Inglis that he did not like the plan: to attempt to bring forward by night a battalion that lacked its own transport, was 18 miles away, and not connected to headquarters by telephone, in time for it to relieve another battalion that was to make an attack

---

[3] Maj H. T. Lunn, VX4635; 2/7 Bn and trg appts. Auctioneer; of Mildura, Vic; b. Havelock, Vic, 22 Dec 1905.

the same night. Inglis said that a well-trained battalion could carry out such a relief in an hour.

Before Lunn arrived, Marshall, about 4 p.m., had received orders from Beresford,[4] Vasey's staff captain, to move off "as near to 5 p.m. as possible".

> During the afternoon (wrote Marshall in his diary later that year) the transport arrived in dribs and drabs from all sorts of sources . . . . The drivers were all unnerved by bombing and the threat or sound of planes and were sheltering away from their trucks as they considered their vehicles the targets . . . . I hoped to get away at 5 p.m. and speeded things up. Odd planes had been over our area all day and nothing had happened. Just as we had completed the embussing of the battalion in their areas with the exception of "D" Company, whose drivers were still coming in, some enemy planes . . . discovered us . . . . The planes were concentrating as well on a supply dump about a mile further on nearer to Neo Khorion. Everyone else was ready except "D" Company so I left Halliday to hurry them on and I started off with the planes still around. It followed on our idea from Greece that the best way is to just go on in the face of an attack . . . . We whizzed down the road and passed the food dump and breathed again. Then we turned a corner and found half a dozen planes above with the obvious intention of attacking us somewhere. I stopped the column until I was sure Savige with "A" Company had caught up and then we sailed on. It was rather exhilarating. The planes had now obviously got on to us, but the road was winding along a valley and there were few straight stretches. The planes cruised about those straight stretches waiting for us . . . . Twice I watched a plane single us out, bank and turn to machine-gun us along the straight and I told the driver to crack it up. It then became a race to the curve . . . . We streaked along and I hoped the battalion was following.

At Suda Marshall met Lunn, left him to bring on the three rear companies which had not yet arrived there, and himself continued forward with the two leading companies. It seems probable that the head of the column departed from Georgioupolis between 5 and 6 p.m., the tail of the column ("E" Company—Headquarters company acting as a rifle company) about 8 p.m., when the leaders were just arriving in the 20th Battalion's area. The relief of the 20th Battalion seems to have been completed about 11.30 p.m.[5]

Brigadier Hargest went forward to Platanias village a little before midnight on the 21st to await the arrival of the attacking battalions. The Maoris had assembled at the start-line about 11.30 p.m. but there was yet no sign of the 20th. At length about 2.45 a.m. its two leading companies arrived. About 3.30 a.m. the attacking force moved off—two companies of the 20th leading on the right; on the left the Maoris who had then been waiting on the start-line for nearly four hours.

Soon the 20th, advancing through country scattered with vines and shrubs and cut by ditches, was fighting along its whole front. German resistance increased as the line neared the airfield. The Maoris made good progress while it was still dark, the tanks on the road following the leading

---

[4] Capt B. D. Beresford, WX1551. HQ 19 Bde, and BM 30 Bde 1942. Solicitor; of Portland, Vic; b. Kalgoorlie, WA, 28 Sep 1910. Killed in action 7 Dec 1942.

[5] After the war Major Miller, commanding the last company but one, recollected that he completed relief of the corresponding New Zealand company between 9.30 and 10 p.m.; Captain G. H. Halliday, commanding the last company, that the New Zealand company commander left him after handing over about 11.30 p.m.

infantry, and when light dawned the Maoris were ahead of the 20th, which had met stiffer opposition. The leading tank was hit and disarmed, and all three moved back behind a bend in the road. On the right the 20th fought its way through the northern part of Pirgos and reached the cleared land near the airfield, but heavy fire drove the right company into the cover of bamboo thickets about 100 yards from its edge. Now that it was light the attackers were under intense fire both from ground and air. Lieut-Colonel Burrows[6] of the 20th decided to withdraw his battalion behind the Maori so that if the Maori seized the field the 20th could occupy the high ground south of it.

On the left, as part of the main attack, the 21st Battalion had advanced to occupy Hill 107 and the wireless station. The attack began at 7 a.m. At 8.30 the wireless station was captured and soon afterwards Xamoudhokhori, but thereafter strong opposition was encountered.[7] During the afternoon, in view of the failure of the main attack along the coast, the companies fell back some distance under heavy enemy pressure. The withdrawal of the exposed right flank was organised by 2nd-Lieutenant Upham,[8] who had been an outstanding leader throughout the attack, and Sergeant Kirk.[9] As the 20th Battalion withdrew German aircraft were landing and their occupants jumping out and going straight into the fight. Eventually the 20th crossed the road and came in behind the Maoris.

The Maoris were now holding a continuous line with two faces—one looking west with its left flank bent back towards the 21st Battalion and the other looking north with its right linking with the 23rd.

A platoon of the 2/1st Australian Machine Gun Battalion hitherto with the 4th Brigade was sent forward to the 5th on the evening of the 22nd. According to Hargest it "ran clean into a Hun attack and in five minutes lost everything they had—vehicles, guns, ammunition".

Throughout 22nd May the 28th continued to probe west and north testing the enemy's strength. In the afternoon Dittmer consulted the commanding officers of the 23rd (Leckie) and 22nd (Andrew) and a message was written to Hargest describing how things stood.

Thus the counter-attacks towards Maleme had gained no vital ground. If the main advance—that of the Maori and the 20th—had begun earlier it might have made further progress, but it is questionable whether even if a line had been established west of the airfield, it could have been maintained. Vasey and Walker considered that it would have been a better plan to attack with the 2/7th Battalion, thus avoiding the delay caused by the relief, and thus putting a fresher and more-experienced battalion into the fight, but it now seems unlikely that such a plan would have

---

[6] Brig J. T. Burrows, DSO. CO 20 NZ Bn 1941-43; Comd 4, 5 and 6 NZ Bdes at times during 1942-44. School teacher; b. Christchurch, NZ, 14 Jul 1904.

[7] Lt W. G. Southworth who had fought with distinction with the 2/2 Bn at Tempe in Greece was killed here.

[8] Capt C. H. Upham, VC and bar; 20 NZ Bn. Govt land valuer; of Conway Flat, Hundalee, N. Canterbury, NZ; b. Christchurch, NZ, 21 Sep 1908. In the advance Upham had thrice led attacks on enemy machine-gun posts. He was awarded the Victoria Cross for his courageous conduct this night, and later.

[9] Capt V. D. Kirk, DCM. 20 and 23 NZ Bns. Winchman; of Blackball, NZ; b. Blackball, 17 Sep 1915.

achieved decisive results. The Germans had then landed two brigades and part of a third in the Maleme-Suda area. They had lost heavily, but so had the defenders. If the airfield had been denied to the enemy and the navy could have prevented reinforcement by sea, a long struggle would have begun between forces approximately equal in trained infantry and both poorly equipped with artillery. The outcome would probably have depended on which side first ran short of food and ammunition. As it was, lack of supplies was already causing Freyberg keen anxiety, but the Germans had enough aircraft to maintain continuous supply though perhaps on a modest scale. German aircraft were still landing on Maleme, each machine increasing by a little the German strength.

About 11 a.m. on the 22nd, a will-o'-the-wisp impression had developed at Hargest's headquarters that the Germans might be abandoning Crete, because men were seen running towards the steady stream of aircraft that had been landing on the airfield, and eleven fires were counted. To test this theory Puttick ordered Kippenberger to send out strong fighting patrols all along his front. The strong resistance encountered by these dispelled the illusion. But in response to information that the enemy might be preparing to abandon Crete, Kippenberger had also ordered the 19th Battalion to advance south astride the Suda Bay-Prison road on a front of 800 yards to a Turkish fort on one of three pyramid-like hills south-east of the prison. The attack opened at 3 p.m. The German positions were strongly held, however, and the two attacking companies withdrew in the early evening, having lost twelve men. About 7 p.m. the Germans themselves attacked, on a front of about 700 yards west of the Galatas-Prison road towards Galatas and the position held by the Petrol Company. Kippenberger ordered an immediate counter-attack by such forces as were available. He himself was on the left flank with a small force preparing to take part in the counter-attack when a detachment of Greeks from in and round Galatas joined by some civilians and led by Captain Forrester of the Queen's dashed at the advancing Germans. "A most infernal uproar broke out across the valley," wrote Kippenberger later. "Over an open space in the trees near Galatas came running, bounding and yelling like Red Indians, about a hundred Greeks and villagers, led by Michael Forrester. It was too much for the Germans. They turned and ran without hesitation."[1]

In the afternoon Freyberg had ordered a further attack on the airfield but before this could be organised the German advance against the 10th Brigade front developed, and Puttick learnt that the coast road between the 4th and 5th Brigades was commanded by a German detachment. Puttick decided that to proceed with the proposed attack by the 5th Brigade would be to risk it being cut off. That night at a conference between Puttick and Stewart (whom Freyberg had sent forward) it was decided that the 5th Brigade should withdraw to the line of the "Wadi" Platanias, that is to say, to abandon all the ground then held to about two miles and a half to the westward. In effect this decision, made about

---

[1] H. K. Kippenberger, *Infantry Brigadier* (1949), p. 59.

10 p.m. on the 22nd, was an acceptance that Crete had been lost. Thenceforward the enemy could use the airfield without hindrance.

It was just before dawn on the 23rd when Hargest's brigade major arrived with these orders at the headquarters of the 23rd Battalion. During the early part of the morning the withdrawal was carried out. The 28th formed the rearguard, and its last parties came out about 6.30 a.m.

The Canea-Suda sector was now free of Germans except for small isolated parties on the Akrotiri Peninsula, some of which were rounded up by the 1/Welch that day. The 2nd Greek Regiment and the 2/8th Battalion, now commanded by Vasey, moved forward and occupied a line along a wadi about 1,000 yards west of Mournies. In this position Vasey was placed under Puttick's command and the defence of the flat area south of Canea fell to the 2/2nd Field Regiment, a company of the 1/Rangers and a marine battalion of some 700 men improvised by Major Garrett,[2] of the marines, from anti-aircraft and searchlight units. Canea had been bombed intermittently, and Weston feared lest heavier attacks might cause a panic among the civilians there. Consequently on the night of the 22nd most of the civilians were persuaded to leave the town and take shelter in the villages in the hills.

At Retimo during the 22nd Colonel Campbell's force attacked the enemy groups astride the road both east and west of this position, but without complete success. From Heraklion came the disturbing news that the Germans were established across the road leading to Timbakion on the south coast, the most suitable place at which to land reinforcements. That night at 9.30 the headquarters of the 16th British Brigade and the 2/Queen's (its remaining battalion) with eighteen vehicles sailed from Alexandria in the landing ship *Glenroy* with the intention of landing at Timbakion and reopening the road to Heraklion.

On the morning of the 22nd a naval force, including *Naiad, Perth, Carlisle* and destroyers, engaged enemy ships between Heraklion and the island of Milos. *Perth* sank a caique loaded with troops, then saw a destroyer and many caiques. These were engaged but the squadron was under heavy air attack and anti-aircraft ammunition was running low; Rear-Admiral King[3] withdrew.[4] The enemy made intense air attacks on other naval forces and the cruisers *Fiji* and *Gloucester* were sunk. At 10.30

---

[2] Lt-Col R. Garrett, DSO, OBE. CO 1 Hvy AA Regt, RM, 1942-45. Royal Marine officer; of Southsea, Eng; b. Kalmunai, Ceylon, 11 Nov 1903. Died by drowning 1952.

[3] Admiral E. L. S. King, CB, MVO; RN. Ch of Staff to C-in-C Home Fleet 1938-40; Comd Cruiser Sqn 1940-41; Asst Ch of Naval Staff 1941-42; Principal naval liaison offr to Allied Navies 1943-46. Of Ruan Minor, Helston, Cornwall; b. Windom, USA, 22 Feb 1889.

[4] In his dispatch of 4 Aug 1941 Admiral Cunningham wrote: "The situation was undoubtedly a difficult one for him, as this attack was certainly on a majestic scale, but it appears that no diminution of risk could have been achieved by retirement and that, in fact, the safest place for the squadron would have been among the enemy ships. The brief action did, however, have the effect of turning back the convoy, and the troops, if they ever did reach Crete, were not in time to influence the battle.

p.m. on the 22nd a signal from Rear-Admiral Rawlings[5] of the 7th Cruiser Squadron reached Admiral Cunningham reporting this loss, and through an error of handwriting it was also made to appear that the battleships had no pom-pom ammunition left. Cunningham thereupon ordered all naval forces to withdraw to Alexandria except the transport *Glenroy* and her escort.

In accordance with these orders, at daylight on the 23rd Captain Lord Louis Mountbatten[6] with the destroyers *Kelly, Kashmir* and *Kipling* were withdrawing from Canea to Alexandria when they were attacked by dive bombers. At length *Kashmir* and then *Kelly* were hit and sunk. Still under air attack *Kipling* picked up the survivors, leaving the scene at 11 a.m. At 11.27 a.m. Cunningham decided to order *Glenroy* and her escort to return to Alexandria. However, the effort to carry supplies through to the defending force did not cease; that night two destroyers unloaded ammunition at Suda Bay and the fast mine-layer *Abdiel* left Alexandria carrying ammunition and stores.

Thus the protection of Crete from seaborne attack was proving costly. By the morning of the 23rd, in addition to the ships mentioned, the destroyers *Juno* and *Greyhound* had been sunk, and the battleships *Warspite* and *Valiant* and cruisers *Ajax, Naiad* and *Carlisle* damaged. As well the ships in Suda Bay had been persistently bombed and now only wrecks remained, including the half-submerged cruiser *York* which had been torpedoed in harbour by an Italian motor-boat on 26th March.

"Suda Bay was a melancholy sight," wrote an observer.[7] "Besides H.M.S. *York*, there were also two destroyers, half a dozen merchantmen, and ten or twelve other craft, big or small, in a more or less disabled condition. Some of them were burning furiously and sending tall columns of black and white smoke up into the sky . . . . The hulls . . . were outlined by a dull red rim of flame, which every now and then would flicker dimmer or brighter. Occasionally, when something more inflammable ignited in the holds, a yellow-white flare burst suddenly upwards in a shower of sparks and illuminated the surrounding shore."

In the course of the 22nd May two more German mountain battalions—the *I/100th* and *I/85th*—were landed on Maleme field. The landing ground was now littered with burning and wrecked aircraft but again and again was cleared with the help of captured tanks employed as tractors. General Ringel, now in command of all troops on the island, was ordered to secure Maleme, clear Suda Bay, relieve Retimo, advance to Heraklion, and, at length, secure the whole of Crete. His troops had the immediate task of attacking towards Canea, but this plan was upset by the New Zealand counter-attack. "The enemy attacked unexpectedly from Pirgos towards Maleme with the support of tanks," said the report of *XI Air Corps*. "In a deter-

---

[5] Admiral Sir Bernard Rawlings, GBE, KCB; RN. Comd 1 Battle Sqn 1940, 7 Cruiser Sqn 1941; Asst Ch of Naval Staff, Foreign, 1942-43; Flag Offr, Eastern Medit, 1943-44; Second-in-Comd Brit Pacific Fleet and Cdg Brit Task Forces 1944-45. B. 21 May 1889.

[6] Admiral Rt Hon Earl Mountbatten, KG, GMSI, GMIE, GCVO, KCB, DSO; RN. In Comd HMS *Kelly* and 5th Destroyer Flotilla 1939-41, HMS *Illustrious* 1941; Chief of Combined Ops 1942-43; Supreme Allied Comdr, South-East Asia 1943-46; Viceroy of India 1947, Governor-General 1947-48. B. Frogmore House, Windsor, Eng, 25 Jun 1900.

[7] T. Stephanides, *Climax in Crete* (1946), pp. 73-4.

mined counter-attack Captain Gericke drove the enemy back into Pirgos. The heights south of Pirgos remained in the enemy's possession."

In the evening Ringel organised the force into three groups. One (Major Schaette with an engineer battalion), to protect Maleme from west and south. Another, including most of the parachute troops, under Colonel Ramcke was to attack Canea in cooperation with a third group—*100th Mountain Regiment*—under Colonel Utz, which was to envelop the defenders east of Maleme by advancing through the hills to the south.[8]

Pending this action a group of 150, organised by Colonel Heidrich from parts of the *III/3rd Parachute Battalion* and the *Pioneer*, advanced north towards Stalos to command the coast road. It reached Stalos at 6 a.m. on the 23rd without meeting opposition.

On the 23rd Schaette's group probing westward, encountered "snipers" (Greeks of the 1st Regiment) round Kastelli, and "atrocities were reported". "The division decided to advance in all possible strength against these bestial hordes," wrote the diarist of the *5th Mountain Division*. "It was hoped to put a stop to this state of affairs by taking hostages and initiating reprisals." As noted above the detachment of parachute troops dropped at Kastelli on the 20th had all been killed or had surrendered. German reports, however, state that, of 57 parachute troops dropped at Kastelli, 40 had been "mutilated" and 17 "took refuge" in a gaol. The German report adds that Kastelli was dive-bombed early on the 24th and later in the day attacked by a German battalion—Schaette's *95th Engineers*—which took it that afternoon after a fight in which 200 Greeks were killed or wounded and 15 prisoners taken, including two New Zealand officers.

In a report by a senior German medical officer it is stated the 200 men of Kastelli were shot as a reprisal for atrocities.

On the other hand Major Bedding, the senior New Zealand officer attached to the Greek battalion, at Kastelli reported that he took over and gaoled the German prisoners taken there at the request of the Greek colonel who was afraid his own men might kill them, that he included some New Zealanders in the guard "for safety's sake", and that he saw no prisoner badly treated by the Greeks.

This episode marks the beginning of the numerous German "reprisals" against the Cretans. Parachute troops (57 according to Bedding) were landed among the 1st Greek Regiment (about 1,000 strong with 600 rifles). In the ensuing fight from 40 to 50 Germans were killed and from 17 to 28 imprisoned. A larger number of Greeks were killed. Since nearly half the Greek troops lacked rifles it would not be surprising if Germans had been killed with knives and clubs. According to a German report the dead had been slashed in the neck or body, had their private parts cut or eyes gouged out; as a reprisal 200 men of the town were shot.

Later the Germans made a judicial investigation of this incident and of many other rumours of mutilation. A report is available from the Chief Medical Inspector of the *Luftwaffe* and it says, in part: "Judge Rudel, a member of the enquiry commission in Canea said . . . that all interrogations had revealed a total of 6 or 8 cases of mutilation in Kastelli, about 15 more scattered elsewhere, and only 2 or 3 at Retimo. From all investigations it appeared that no enemy soldiers had been guilty of mutilation. The crimes were all attributed to fanatical civilians. Judge Rudel emphasises the fair way in which the British and New Zealanders had fought. They had protected German prisoners whenever possible and had saved them from the wrath of the civilians, even going so far as to fire on the mobs."

This episode has been narrated in some detail because it seems to be a rare one of its kind in which the chain of events can be fairly well established—the exaggerated accusation, the savage retaliation, and the belated discovery of the truth, or a reasonable approximation to it. It also may help the reader to assess charges made against the Australians and New Zealanders after an action described later in this chapter.

---

[8] At this stage Utz's regiment included *I/100th, II/100th* and *I/85th Battalions*.

On the night of the 22nd General Wavell sent a signal to General Freyberg informing him that it was impossible to land reinforcements at Suda and the "gallant troops must stick it". He had great hopes that the enemy could not "stay the pace much longer". He was arranging for a commando unit to land on the south coast and cross the island. He added: "If you report that situation at Maleme is really serious hope to arrange for R.A.F. to send fighters to strafe enemy tomorrow till ammunition and petrol exhausted and then land within your protection." In another message that night Wavell suggested that Freyberg consider the possibility of moving units from Retimo to Canea and from Heraklion to Retimo, replacing those from Heraklion with new troops landed at Timbakion. This impractical suggestion underlined the scanty nature of the information that had reached Wavell's headquarters, but although Freyberg's messages had been unprecise, the facts known at Cairo should have shown the impossibility of the proposed manoeuvre, which would have to be made chiefly on foot since there were not enough vehicles on Crete to carry large bodies of men. Was it intended that they should be undertaken simultaneously, or was Heraklion to wait until the reinforcements from Timbakion had marched across the island, Retimo to wait until units reached them from Heraklion, and Maleme-Suda Bay—the crucial sector —to pin its hopes on the arrival of reinforcements from Retimo?[9]

Freyberg's reply to Wavell next morning gave a clearer picture than his messages of the previous three days. The road from Suda to Retimo was held by the enemy and also (he believed) the road from Retimo to Heraklion. There were no vehicles at Retimo. "Heraklion now in touch with Argyll and Sutherlands and I have ordered them to concentrate battalion and tanks at Heraklion preparatory to reinforcing Suda garrison if possible by road." Freyberg added that his troops at Maleme were cut off and that he had decided "to readjust present insecure position and make ready for secure defence". He added:

I have decided (1) that I cannot continue to chance all rear areas and coast line and (2) that troops cannot fight on without a rest. Am therefore taking up line which will lessen my responsibilities. Enemy is now approaching equality in numbers[1] .... We can fight on as long as maintenance does not break down.

Later in the day Freyberg received a cable from Churchill: "The whole world watches your splendid battle on which great things turn." "However splendid the battle might appear in the eyes of the world," Freyberg wrote later, "the situation was rapidly deteriorating in the Maleme sector."

---

[9] Next day (23rd) Freyberg informed Wavell that he had only 150 15-cwt trucks and 117 other load-carrying vehicles, that the only road to the south coast which could be negotiated by trucks was that to Timbakion, and that it served Heraklion only.

[1] We know now that this was an underestimate of the German strength. The strength of Freyberg's infantry battalions on the 24th was: 18th, 500; 19th, 450; 20th, 382; 21st, 194; 22nd, 233; 23rd, 265; 28th, 459; 2/7th, 580; 2/8th, 380. The Composite Battalion had 650 men, the NZE 340. The total strength of the New Zealand and Australian troops in the division was 5,573, of the Greeks attached to it about 900. In fact, the division had little more than the strength of a brigade group in men and was weaker than such a group in heavy weapons. The Germans had by then landed approximately four regiments.

On the Platanias line the Maori battalion occupied its former position; the 23rd faced north on the high ground between the Maori and Ayia Marina; the depleted 21st and 22nd and the New Zealand Engineers faced north linking the 23rd Battalion and the 4th Brigade. All units were in position by 10. Air attacks on the withdrawing troops were relatively light. All day the German aircraft concentrated on the roads from Canea to Suda and Canea itself. Freyberg had "never seen such vicious bombing". In the withdrawal the 27th Battery—the main support of the brigade during the long battle—was able to extricate only two guns (French 75's). In the new position Colonel Strutt had eight 75's (of 27th Battery and 2/3rd Australian Field Regiment), two Bofors and two 2-pounders.

The Germans closely followed the withdrawal, and throughout the day there was sharp fighting on the road where the bridge crossed the Platanias River. The artillery shelled the attackers accurately and put their light guns out of action. While this was happening the men on the ridges above the road saw an encouraging and gallant attack by twelve British bombers on Maleme airfield where 130 transport planes were standing. Six could be seen burning. The strongest pressure against the elongated position of the 5th Brigade came not from the west but from the south as the Germans advanced from the Prison area. At Stalos on the heights south of the 5th Brigade's new position a group of about 150 men under Major Heilmann had been established since 6 a.m. It was engaged by a strong patrol of the New Zealand Army Service Corps which killed some fifteen Germans. Then it was attacked from the north-east by a platoon of the 18th Battalion and all but one of its posts had been taken when the platoon was recalled by the company commander, who was under the impression that the heights were more strongly held than they were.

All hope of denying Maleme to the enemy having been abandoned and the New Zealand Division having withdrawn into a defensive position, there were good reasons to fall back still farther in order to reduce the area over which the force was strung out. Puttick had met Freyberg about 11 a.m. and they agreed that the battered and weary 5th Brigade should move into reserve that night; Inglis of the 4th Brigade would take over the units of 10th Brigade and command the right of the new front line. The left would be formed by Vasey's 19th Brigade which would be west of Perivolia. In the afternoon of the 23rd, to enable the 19th Brigade to fulfil its new role, the 2/8th was advanced to a position on the creek west of Perivolia on the left of the 2/7th, which had been moved into the area that morning. The 2nd Greek, extended south-west from Perivolia, formed the left flank.

That night all the troops in the Platanias area withdrew on foot behind the lines of the 4th Brigade. There were vehicles enough to carry only the wounded and the heavy weapons.[2]

Freyberg was handicapped in his control of the isolated sector at Retimo because there were no ciphers there and messages had to go in clear. At

---

[2] The battery of 6-in. coast guns at St John's Hill helped to cover this withdrawal by firing into the German positions, but after eighteen rounds German aircraft dropped flares and to avoid observation the guns ceased to fire.

Heraklion the ciphers had been destroyed on the 20th during the parachute landing, but messages could be sent there secretly by submarine cable. On the 23rd Freyberg ordered a company of the 1/Rangers with two anti-tank guns to advance east from Suda and open the road to Retimo airfield. They reached Retimo town that day, and about 8 p.m. were met by Captain Lergessner,[3] whom Colonel Campbell had ordered to make his way through the foothills to the town and travel thence to Suda to give information to Freyberg's headquarters and seek instructions. Lergessner had set out before Campbell learnt by wireless that the Rangers were coming. Knowing the strength of the German position astride the road Lergessner tried without success to dissuade the company of the Rangers from attacking. He stayed with them that night, witnessed an unsuccessful attack next morning, and then pushed on to Suda, followed later in the day by the remnant of the Rangers' company.

The two infantry tanks which had been landed at Timbakion on the night of the 19th-20th reached Heraklion on the 23rd with news that the Argyll and Sutherland Highlanders (also landed at Timbakion that night) were on their way. The infantry tanks, with the one remaining "runner" of those that had been at Heraklion throughout, and two 75-mm guns were sent to Suda in a lighter.

Efforts to reinforce Crete continued. Although *Glenroy* had been turned back, *Abdiel* sailed from Alexandria with Lieut-Colonel F. B. Colvin and 195 of "A" Battalion of a commando (then called "Special Service") force under Colonel Laycock,[4] and to be known as "Layforce". *Abdiel* carried also medical stores, rations and ammunition.

The German staff believed that the British fell back because of "the enveloping advance of the Utz Group". Ramcke's Group followed the retiring troops "engaging enemy rearguards, who fought with great determination". That night General Ringel ordered a strong group from the *85th Mountain Regiment* to move through Alikianou and continue east through the mountains towards Suda Bay, with the object of outflanking the British in the Galatas-Suda area and penetrating to Retimo to support "the hard-pressed *2nd Parachute Rifle Regiment*". It was evidently because the German commanders' eyes were on the next objective—Suda Bay—that their aircraft were ordered to concentrate on targets there, and the withdrawing 5th New Zealand Brigade escaped relatively lightly.

At Stalos that afternoon, Major Heilmann's group was joined by the *II/100th Mountain Battalion,* and at last the force from Maleme was united with that in the Prison area. During the day two mountain artillery units, one mountain armoured unit and most of a motor-cycle battalion landed on Maleme airfield.

On the morning of the 24th the western flank of Creforce was an arc curved round the south-west of Canea with a radius of some three miles.[5]

---

[3] Capt E. T. Lergessner, NX146; 2/1 Bn. Regular soldier; of Sydney; b. Cooran, Qld, 28 Nov 1906.

[4] Maj-Gen R. E. Laycock, CB, DSO. Chief of Combined Ops 1943-47. Regular soldier; b. London, 18 Apr 1907.

[5] Behind the position held by the New Zealand Division was the reserve position held by the foremost troops of Weston's force along the creek through Mournies. It was occupied (from the right) by the Royal Perivolians, an improvised force of marines and the 2/2 Fd Regt armed with rifles. This force was entitled the Suda Brigade and was commanded by Lt-Col A. F. Hely of the 106 RHA, which was in reserve.

Against it were pressing the now-combined German forces from the Maleme and Prison areas, and a strong force of mountain troops was advancing east through the hills to descend on Suda Bay from the south and encircle the defenders. Across the path of these mountain troops lay only the 8th Greek Regiment which had been cut off from the main force since the landing of paratroops in the Prison area.

During the afternoon strong German patrols probed the 4th Brigade's front and there were signs that the enemy was preparing a large-scale attack. About 4 p.m. a heavy thrust was made on the 18th Battalion (Lieut-Colonel Gray). Some forward posts were driven in but later the line was restored by a counter-attack. At dusk some posts were again abandoned and again retaken. During the afternoon the German aircraft concentrated on Canea and bombed it so heavily and systematically that it seemed that they intended to thoroughly wreck the town.

The daily cable received from Cairo on the 24th seemed to Freyberg "to indicate that the Deputy C.-in-C. General Blamey was officiating". It was clear and direct: "Guts and determination of yourself and troops are splendid example to all. We have evidence that Germans have great difficulties. We are doing our best to help you." That day Freyberg learnt of the failure of the detachment of the 1/Rangers to clear the road to Retimo, and that a new body of paratroops had landed west of Heraklion and blocked the advance of the Argylls from Timbakion. But that day also, at 9.30 a.m., three British destroyers sailed from Alexandria carrying the remainder of the two commando battalions that comprised Layforce; Colonel Colvin and the first instalment were put ashore that night at Suda by the *Abdiel*.

By this time two German airborne regiments and one mountain regiment were concentrated against the New Zealand Division, and a second mountain regiment was moving through the hills to the south towards Suda Bay. The Germans on the northern wing were formed into three groups for an attack on the Galatas heights: the *Assault Regiment* to attack the heights north-west of Galatas; the *100th Mountain Regiment* to attack Galatas; and the *3rd Parachute Rifle Regiment,* after Galatas had fallen, to attack astride the Alikianou-Canea road. On the 24th one mountain battalion and a half, as well as a reconnaissance and an anti-aircraft unit were landed at Maleme.

The New Zealanders were convinced that the strong concerted attack begun on the 24th would reach a climax on the 25th. Inglis was given a direct call upon the reserve—the four tired and depleted battalions of the 5th Brigade, less than 1,400 strong. During the morning air attacks and mortar and machine-gun fire on the western front became more and more intense. Enemy parties were seen massing opposite the 18th Battalion on the coastal flank. In the afternoon dive bombers attacked the whole area of the 4th Brigade and, as soon as they ceased, the German infantry advanced behind intense fire from mortars and machine-guns, the strongest pressure being against the 18th which was soon engaged in a fierce fight. The right company was overwhelmed and the centre company was being fired on from all sides. Colonel Gray, carrying a rifle

25 May ROUND GALATAS 245

and bayonet and shouting "No Surrender!" led forward a party of men from his headquarters to restore the line, but the enemy was too strong.[6]

Brigadier Inglis sent forward two companies of the 20th Battalion. Kippenberger, in command of the troops in the forward area, ordered them to the right of the ridge occupied by the Composite Battalion. When they arrived there they found the Composite "nearly all gone"; yet they halted the enemy advancing through the gap on the right of the front, 2nd-Lieutenant Upham again playing a gallant part. But the enemy was now thrusting hard along the Prison-Galatas road.

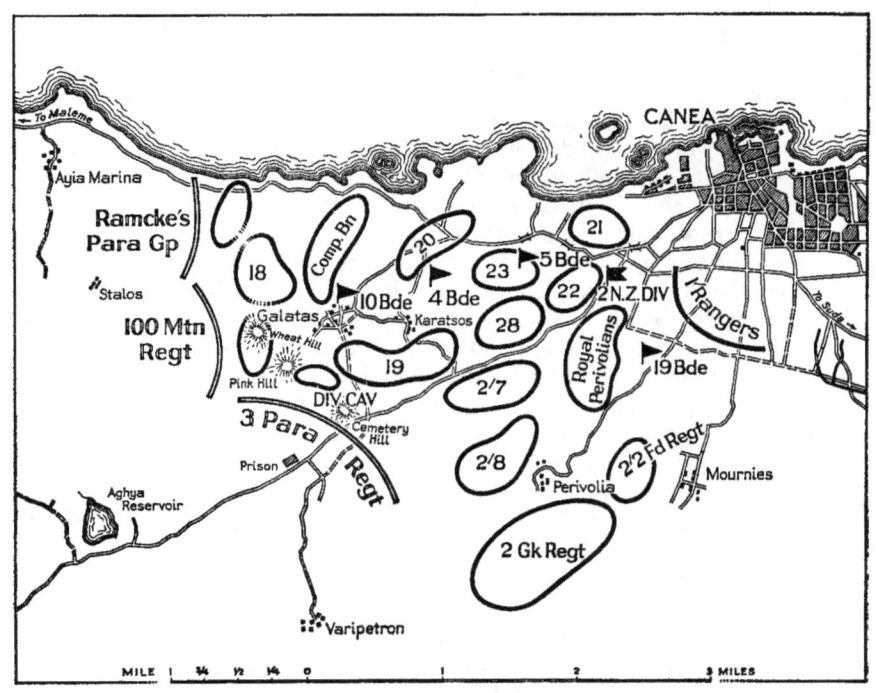

Morning, 25th May

Matters were now looking grave (wrote Kippenberger later), for John Russell[7] reported that he was being hard pressed, and a trickle of stragglers was coming back past me. I sent Brian [Bassett[8] his brigade major] on foot to tell Inglis the position and say that I must have help. There were nearly 200 wounded at the Regimental Aid Post, close to headquarters. Our two trucks worked incessantly, taking them down to the Advanced Dressing Station in loads like butcher's meat. Then the position worsened. Wheat Hill was abandoned without orders. This exposed Lynch's[9]

---

[6] During the day the 18th lost almost 100 killed.

[7] Lt-Col J. T. Russell, DSO. NZ Div Cav 1940-42; CO 22 NZ Bn 1942. Farmer; b. Hastings, NZ, 11 Nov 1904. Killed in action 6 Sep 1942.

[8] Maj B. I. Bassett; 23 NZ Bn and BM 4 NZ Bde. Barrister and solicitor; b. Christchurch, NZ, 12 Sep 1911. Killed in action 5 Jul 1942.

[9] Lt-Col R. J. Lynch, MC; CO 18 NZ Bn 1942. Sales manager; b. Waihi, NZ, 24 Oct 1909. Died of wounds 26 Sep 1942.

company in the centre of the Eighteenth line and it fell back, still fighting savagely. Suddenly the trickle of stragglers turned to a stream, many of them on the verge of panic. I walked in among them shouting 'Stand for New Zealand!' and everything else I could think of.[1]

Kippenberger filled the gaps by sending in reinforcements as they reached him from Inglis: the 4th Brigade Band lined a wall 100 yards in front of his headquarters, the pioneer platoon of the 20th and the Kiwi Concert Party carried the line farther to the right; a company of the 20th extended it farther. Orders were sent to the main body of the 20th to pull back and take up a position on the right of these groups.

The 23rd Battalion was now reaching the threatened area. Kippenberger decided that "it was no use trying to patch the line any more; obviously we must hit or everything would crumble away". Two companies of the 23rd were ordered to advance and retake Galatas, one company advancing on either side of the road, with two light tanks under Captain Farran[2] leading. The tanks rumbled off and the infantry (which now included several detachments from other units) followed cheering and shouting. "From Galatas streamed hundreds of tracer bullets, multi-coloured flares and whistling mortar bombs." The advance reached the narrow, cobbled streets of the town. The leading tank had a track blown off but the other continued. While Germans threw grenades at them from second-storey windows, the troops advanced to the central square. There the leading tank was disabled and Farran wounded. Round the square a fierce hand-to-hand fight followed; rifles and Tommy guns were fired from the hip, bayonets and rifle butts were used; at length the last Germans fled into the olive groves west of the village. The German advance had been decisively halted.

Against the 19th Brigade, next to the left, there were no attacks that day. The 2/8th was ordered to advance 1,000 yards at dusk to relieve the pressure on the New Zealanders, but after the success of the New Zealand counter-attack this order was cancelled. Nevertheless, that night the situation was extremely disturbing. Casualties were mounting, fatigue increasing, and the prolonged air attacks were lowering the defenders' spirits. Units of the 4th and 5th Brigades, both of which had now lost heavily, were intermingled in the front line. Puttick decided to shorten his front by withdrawing from the Galatas area to a line through Karatsos running north and south from the right flank of the 19th Brigade.

Meanwhile the 8th Greek Regiment was standing firm. It was not then realised that, reinforced by villagers, it was strongly resisting the detachment from the German *85th Mountain Regiment* (Colonel Krakau), which was attempting to encircle the whole British force. In the past few days the Greeks had expelled the Utz Group of airborne troops from the Alikianou area, and forced it to establish a protective line south of the

---

[1] Kippenberger, p. 64.
[2] Maj R. A. Farran, DSO, MC, 3 Hussars 1940-42; 2 i/c 2 Special Air Service Regt 1943-45. Regular soldier; of Codsall, Staffs, Eng; b. Purley, Eng, 2 Jan 1921. Author of *Winged Dagger* in which these and other operations are described.

reservoir; now, on the 25th, they were roughly handling Krakau's mountain regiment sweating its way over the hills to the south-west.

General Student himself arrived in Crete on the 25th. It was the *II Battalion* of the *Assault Regiment* followed by the *IV* which, after heavy losses, captured the heights north-west of Galatas, and the *100th Mountain Regiment* that took Galatas itself. That day two more mountain battalions and a motor-cycle company landed at Maleme.[3]

On the 25th Puttick sent Freyberg a message that heavy attacks had "obviously broken" the line at Galatas and that he was trying to form his new line running north and south from the right flank of the 19th Brigade. "Am exceedingly doubtful on present reports," he concluded, "whether I can hold the enemy tomorrow (26th)." Later that night one of the liaison officers with the Greeks called on Freyberg and "made it clear that the Greeks were about to break".

About one o'clock on the morning of the 26th an order was issued confirming Puttick's decision to withdraw: the division would retire to the new line, which was along the creek about a mile and a half west of Canea. On the right would be the 21st Battalion, with a cavalry detachment, an engineer company and a company of the 20th under its command; in the centre the 19th Battalion; on its left the 28th (Maori) which would link with the 19th Brigade (one battalion and a half). The Prison road would form the boundary between brigades. By dawn the 5th Brigade was on the new line. The men were weary, hungry and jaded. "There were many stragglers," said Puttick's report. "Isolated groups of very tired men were hard to find in the thick olive groves and constant air attack on any movements made re-grouping difficult." Apparently the men of some base units at Suda had been ordered to make their way over the hills to Sfakia on the south coast. The news spread and combatant troops who could not find their units moved along the road with them.

That morning at 9.30 after a conference with Captain Morse,[4] the naval officer in charge at Suda, and Group Captain Beamish, Freyberg had sent the following cable to Wavell:

> I regret to have to report that in my opinion the limit of endurance has been reached by the troops under my command here at Suda Bay. No matter what decision is taken by the Commanders-in-Chief from a military point of view our position here is hopeless. A small ill-equipped and immobile force such as ours cannot stand up against the concentrated bombing that we have been faced with during the last seven days. I feel that I should tell you that from an administrative point of view the difficulties of extricating this force in full are now insuperable. Provided a decision is reached at once a certain proportion of the force might be embarked. Once this sector has been reduced the reduction of Retimo and Heraklion by the same methods will only be a matter of time. The troops we have with the exception of the Welch Regiment and the Commando are past any offensive action. If you decide in view of whole Middle East position that hours help we will carry on. I would have to consider how this would be best achieved. Suda Bay may be under fire within twenty-

---

[3] Early in the morning of the 25th Hurricane fighters and Blenheim and Maryland bombers attacked the Maleme airfield. It was estimated that they destroyed about 24 transport aircraft and fighters.

[4] Vice-Adm Sir Anthony Morse, KBE, CB, DSO; RN. Naval Offr i/c at Suda, Crete, 1941; Flag Offr, Malaya 1945-46. B. 16 Oct 1892.

four hours. Further, casualties have been heavy, and we have lost the majority of our immobile guns.

Freyberg then saw Inglis and told him that the line must be stabilised and that Inglis would be placed in command of the Force reserve and go forward to relieve the New Zealand Division. Kippenberger would replace him in command of the 4th Brigade (18th and 20th Battalions).

Meanwhile both the forward brigades had been strongly attacked. The 5th Brigade's line was held by the 21st, 19th, 28th, 22nd and 23rd Battalions, each little stronger than a company. Detachments of the engineers, cavalry and others thickened the line. At 11.15 the engineers in the 21st's sector on the right were thrust back by a German attack but counter-attacked and retook the lost ground. The attacks increased in intensity in the afternoon and the battalion lost eighty men in the day, but the flank held.

The 19th Battalion was under heavy pressure, and at 2 p.m. two platoons were forced out of their posts but a new line was formed 150 yards back; by 5 p.m. the original posts were retaken. Next to the left the 28th (Maori) repulsed German attacks. From about 10.30 a.m. onwards enemy infantry, supported by air and mortar bombardment, attacked the left flank of the Australians and pushed into a gap between it and the 2nd Greeks.

The threat to two Australian platoons on the left was such that they were withdrawn some distance towards Perivolia, and there held on. In the afternoon the attack was intensified and at length the 2/8th was ordered to withdraw to its original positions outside Mournies, and the 2/7th received similar orders. They withdrew about 5 p.m. and fitted in among the Marines round Mournies.

That morning Vasey had been confident that his line could be held that day and the next; at 5 p.m. he was convinced that the situation on his left was critical.

While Puttick's headquarters were being moved back (to a point about a mile south of Canea) a letter reached him from Freyberg informing him that he and Weston were to establish a joint headquarters; later Freyberg informed Inglis that he was to command a new "Composite Brigade" consisting of the 1/Welch, Northumberland Hussars and 1/Rangers—the principal infantry units of Weston's command—and relieve the 5th New Zealand Brigade after dark. Puttick doubted whether the relief could be carried out before the 5th was forced off its line. He considered the men near the end of their endurance: as has been said the battalions were little stronger than companies; air attack was almost unceasing, and any vehicle that moved on the road was strafed; all signal communications had been broken. Puttick walked back to Freyberg's headquarters to place the problem before him. There, at 3.15 p.m., Freyberg told him that it was essential to hold his present line because two destroyers were to arrive at Suda that night and unload commando troops and 80 tons of food and ammunition. He added that since the New Zealand Division was now in the Canea-Suda area it would be under Weston's command.

It took Puttick three hours to visit Force headquarters and return. Meanwhile the German advance round the left flank was continuing. About 5 p.m., before Puttick's return to his own headquarters, Vasey visited Hargest and informed him that the Germans were encircling his exposed flank and some enemy machine-guns were firing from his rear. He asked when Hargest was going to withdraw because he was certain he would have to do the same. When Puttick arrived soon afterwards he decided that the situation had seriously deteriorated. He was now convinced that withdrawal was unavoidable chiefly because of the enemy movement round Vasey's flank; he was equally certain that the proposed relief by Inglis' force was impracticable.

After consulting Vasey and Hargest and obtaining their agreement Puttick decided to propose to Weston, his new commander, that the Welch should take up a covering position from Kristos to Tsikalaria, with the commando extending the line southwards to the road at Ayia Marina. This implied a withdrawal well to the east of Canea, and Puttick was writing a report to that effect about 6 p.m. when Weston arrived at his headquarters. Puttick made his proposal. Weston telephoned Vasey who said that he now considered it impossible to hold his present line until dark next day—which meant that a withdrawal should be made that night. Weston then told Puttick that he could not make such a major decision himself and, about 6.10, left to consult Freyberg.

When Weston returned to Canea he was forced by heavy bombing to leave the town. Puttick heard nothing from him, and between 8 and 10 p.m. sent a series of wireless messages seeking guidance from Freyberg's headquarters; the only reply came at 10.10, informing him that Weston would give him his orders. Thereupon, again after consulting Vasey, he decided on his own authority to order a withdrawal to a defensive position at the head of Suda Bay as proposed to Weston, with 19th Brigade on the right of Kristos and the 5th on the left. The 4th Brigade would withdraw to Stilos on the road to Sfakia. He gave orders to this effect at 10.30, and sent an officer back to inform his seniors. In conformity with this decision, Vasey instructed his battalions to withdraw, and informed the Greeks and the British detachments in his area of his intention.

In the meantime Freyberg and Weston had met twice—about 7.30 p.m. and about 10.15. On the first occasion, when told by Weston that the New Zealanders could not hold another night, Freyberg ordered that they be relieved by the Composite Brigade. The Composite Brigade was warned to be ready to move at 8.30. Weston inaccurately informed Freyberg that at the moment the New Zealanders were holding but the Australians were coming back. Freyberg at once wrote to Vasey that he must continue to hold a line in the wadi 1,000 yards east of his position of that morning until dark on the 27th. This order did not reach Vasey until about 11 p.m. when he had already ordered a withdrawal. He consulted Puttick, and learnt that the New Zealanders had not yet received similar orders to hold on and were withdrawing. He decided that if he stayed where he was "with the Greeks dispersed on my left flank and the New Zealanders withdrawn from my right" his two battalions would be captured; and after consulting Puttick and obtaining his approval continued his withdrawal. "This decision was reinforced when after the first message to 2/7th Battalion I received information that the withdrawal of the battalion had already commenced and that they were being followed up closely by the enemy." The battalions disengaged and began marching to the new line along "42nd Street", a north-south road through an old bivouac area between Suda and Canea.

Freyberg's belated order to the New Zealanders reached Puttick at 1.45 a.m.: he was to hold the old line until relieved by the Composite Brigade. Puttick reached Weston's headquarters at 2.15 a.m. When he asked why no orders had been given to the New Zealand Division the previous evening, General Weston told him that it was no use sending orders since he, Puttick, "had made it very clear that the New Zealand Division was retiring whatever happened". He added (Puttick wrote later) that he had troops on the new line and did not want Hargest's and Vasey's brigades there. Puttick told Weston that his brigades would hold their new line until Weston ordered them to retire. At this stage communications were fatally slow. Under the complex system of control that had then been established, hours not minutes were consumed obtaining a reply from a senior commander. Orders had to go from Freyberg to Weston to Puttick to Vasey. Between 6.10 p.m. when Weston left Puttick's headquarters and 1.45 a.m. when a message from Weston was handed to Puttick, only one order was received from Weston or Freyberg; this was about 11.15 p.m. when Puttick's subordinate, Vasey, received an order direct from Weston and without Puttick being informed. In the intervening seven hours Puttick had ordered a withdrawal on his own authority, and it was being carried out.

Perhaps the New Zealanders were capable of longer resistance than Puttick and Hargest believed. But, as often occurs in an exhausting withdrawal, alarm increased in proportion to the distance from the front line. Commanders are older and less resilient than the men in the battalions; they and their staffs see much of the wounded and non-combatant troops and are apt to judge the condition of the front-line troops, perhaps still holding firmly, by the condition of the shaken men seen in the rear areas.

When the 5th and 19th Brigades withdrew Colonel Hely[5] ordered the withdrawal of his Suda Brigade ("S" Battalion of the Royal Marines, 2/2nd Field Regiment, "Royal Perivolians" and 106th Royal Horse Artillery) from Mournies where it had been in reserve. Meanwhile the Composite Brigade (the 1/Welch, 1/Rangers and Northumberland Hussars) was carrying out its orders to advance and occupy a position about a mile west of Canea. Its acting commander, Lieut-Colonel Duncan[6] of the Welch, did not know that the Suda Brigade had retired and there was no support on his left.

---
[5] Brig A. F. Hely, CB, CBE, DSO. CO 106 RHA 1939-41, 60 Fd Regt 1941-42; CRA 7 Ind Div 1942-45; GOC 7 Ind Div in 1945. Dental surgeon; of Liverpool, Eng; b. Liverpool, 2 Aug 1902.
[6] Lt-Col A. Duncan, MC. CO 1/Welch. Regular soldier; b. 9 Dec 1895. Weston had not yet handed the command to Inglis.

Thus, in the night, the 5th and 19th Brigades fell back past the "smouldering dust heap" of Canea to their position just west of Suda. "A" Battalion of Layforce was near Suda village.[7] On the withdrawal the Australians, to their surprise, saw no sign of the British brigade that was to come up and act as rearguard. Evidently it was moving along the coast road while the Australians withdrew on the inland road. During the night the 4th Brigade withdrew to Stilos. Inglis, unable to locate the units of the Composite Brigade during the day, returned to the command of the 4th Brigade and Kippenberger to command of the 20th Battalion.

About 1 a.m. Weston realising the danger of the Welch's position sent orders to Colonel Duncan to withdraw. The order appears to have reached him too late, if at all. The Welch were forward with the depleted Rangers and Northumberland Hussars supporting the left flank. A German attack opened at dawn. By 9 a.m. one of the two forward companies was surrounded and the other had lost heavily; Duncan decided to withdraw to the Kladhisos Creek, and as the enemy was encircling his flank, he ordered the two rear companies under Major Gibson[8] to move west of Suda to cover the withdrawal of the remainder. As they did so, they could hear heavy firing at 42nd Street five miles to the rear of their original positions. Gibson and his men reached Suda. However, a gallant handful of the Welch held out on the coast until the morning of the 28th, when the Germans discovered that they had been delayed for more than eighteen hours by a small party under a sergeant.

General Weston was not at 42nd Street when the New Zealanders and Australians arrived. At length Puttick and Vasey picked positions for their depleted brigades along the "street"—a straight earth road through the olive groves. The line was held (from the right) by the 2/8th (astride the main road), 2/7th, 21st New Zealand, 28th, 19th, 22nd. They were packed tightly—the 28th, for example, on a front of 250 yards, and the depleted 21st on a far narrower one. During the night Freyberg visited the Australians and noted that they seemed "absolutely confident". Then he watched the eighty tons of supplies being unloaded at Suda pier.

Colonel Dittmer, commanding the Maoris, saw Colonel Walker and Colonel Allen between 9 and 10 a.m. and told them that if the enemy came to close quarters his battalion would open fire and then charge. Walker and Allen agreed that their battalions would cooperate.

About 11 a.m. the Australians saw some 400 Germans advancing astride the Suda Bay road. The 2/7th had two companies forward. Major Miller,[9] commanding the one on the right, sent forward a patrol under Lieutenant McGeoch to keep them under observation while he planned

---

[7] That night the remaining 750 of Layforce were landed at Suda from *Abdiel*, *Hero* and *Nizam*, which took away 930 walking wounded and other unwanted men. On the 26th also the final effort to send substantial reinforcements to Crete was abandoned. The landing ship *Glenroy* which, late on the 25th, again set out from Alexandria carrying the 2/Queen's was attacked by dive bombers and damaged. At 9.15 p.m. on the 26th she was ordered back to Alexandria.

[8] Lt-Col J. T. Gibson, DSO. CO 1/Welch 1942-44, 2/Welch 1944, 1/5 Welch 1944. Regular soldier; b. Deal, Kent, Eng, 18 Sep 1903. Died of wounds 20 Sep 1944.

[9] Maj W. V. Miller, VX192; 2/7 Bn. Salesman; of Murrumbeena, Vic; b. Geelong, Vic, 11 Jul 1907.

a counter-attack and sent this information to Captain Nelson,[1] commanding the company on his left, with a suggestion that he should join the attack. He dispatched a runner to Colonel Walker. Miller was on his way forward to join McGeoch when firing began. He signalled the company forward, and when it arrived placed a platoon on each side of McGeoch's patrol. The Germans, who were raiding an abandoned depot, were taken by surprise, and, after a few minutes firing, broke and ran. Meanwhile Nelson's company had come up on the left flank. Both companies now rose and charged the fleeing Germans. Nelson, a high-spirited youngster, was hit in the shoulder as he ran forward waving to his men to follow. Lieutenant Bernard then took command and, though he too was soon wounded, continued to lead the charge. Sergeant Reiter's[2] platoon drove the Germans from the cover of the abandoned depot, Reiter continuing to lead his men in a bayonet charge though wounded in the head.

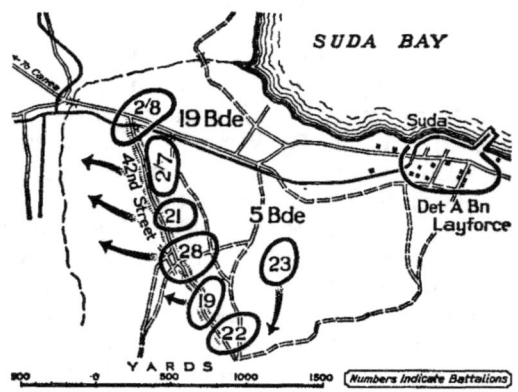

Farther left Private Baxter[3] raced ahead armed with a sub-machine-gun and put to flight a group of Germans firing from the shelter of a wadi. As they ran from Baxter they threw their arms away. The advance continued for more than a mile.

Possibly before the Australian charge began, the Maoris, and also the 21st on their right and the 19th on their left, had begun a similar charge.[4] The New Zealanders charged some 600 yards, until few Germans were visible except some making off at high speed. The Maoris estimated the dead on their front at more than 80. The Australians estimated that about 200 Germans were killed; they took three prisoners. In the charge the 2/7th lost 10 killed and 28 wounded; and 14 of the Maoris were hit.

Miller at length had halted the Australians' advance, there being no further cover from view from the air. Lieutenant Bolton[5] arrived forward

---

[1] Maj St E. D. Nelson, VX237; 2/7 Bn. Law clerk; of Geelong, Vic; b. Caulfield, Vic, 18 Mar 1919.

[2] Lt F. A. Reiter, MC, MM, VX4024; 2/7, 31/51 Bns. Labourer; of Kardella, Vic; b. Meeniyan, Vic, 10 Mar 1918.

[3] Pte B. A. Baxter, MM, VX41609; 2/7 Bn. Labourer; of Malvern, Vic; b. Glenferrie, Vic, 16 Aug 1916.

[4] There is uncertainty about which unit charged first. Colonel Dittmer wrote later: "After heavy enemy mortar fire also MMG fire the enemy was seen in undergrowth just the other side of 42nd Street, the 28th and at least some other units opened fire, then the front companies of 28 Bn under shouted orders of the company commanders leapt up and dashed across the road and commenced to mix things. Very soon afterwards the 2/7 Australian, and about the same time the 21st, moved forward . . . . From where I was with reserve company I could see what happened . . . the 28 Bn thought the 2/7 Aust Bn a really great unit and does not wish to deprive the 2/7 of any credit that is its due." (From notes written in 1950 by Dittmer to General Kippenberger, Editor-in-Chief of the New Zealand War Histories.)

[5] Capt W. B. Bolton, VX110; 2/1 MG Bn. Stock and station agent; of Horsham, Vic; b. Horsham, 22 Mar 1914.

with a Vickers gun and fired on the fleeing enemy with good effect. The advancing Germans had received a severe shock, and made no further attack that day, though in the afternoon there was close contact along the whole front. During the day, however, hundreds of Germans were seen moving round the hills to the south steadily encircling the Australian and New Zealand position.

Weston was in command of the rearguard, but communications had failed and Vasey and Hargest did not see him or hear from him that day. Vasey and Hargest had decided to keep together and try to coordinate the withdrawal. In the course of the 27th they met the commander of a battalion of Laycock's force, who had orders from Weston to occupy a delaying position on the road to Sfakia. Thereupon Vasey and Hargest decided to withdraw that night to Neo Khorion, south of Stilos, in the hope that Layforce would be covering that area. Their plan was that the 5th Brigade would go to Stilos, the 19th Brigade to Neo Khorion with the 2/8th Battalion at the junction of the road from Kalives and the 2/7th linking with the New Zealanders at Stilos. At 9 o'clock, when the rearguard at 42nd Street was due to disengage and begin its long march to Stilos, it was still light and the withdrawal was delayed until after 10. The head of the column reached Stilos, 14 miles away, at 3.30 a.m. on the 28th. Weston had in fact ordered Laycock (who had landed only a few hours earlier) with his "D" Battalion to take up a rearguard position at Babali Inn farther south, and had attached to his battalion two infantry tanks and three carriers.

General Weston appears to have gone southward to survey the line of withdrawal, and, when he turned back, found it almost impossible to move against the tide of vehicles, troops and civilians now streaming along the road winding up into the mountains towards Sfakia.[6] These were largely the gunners and base troops from Suda and the men of the several improvised infantry units that had been in that area. Freyberg wrote later:

> There were units sticking together and marching with their weapons—units of one or other of the composite forces that had come out of the line—but in the main it was a disorganised rabble making its way doggedly and painfully to the south. There were thousands of unarmed troops including the Cypriots and Palestinians. Without leadership, without any sort of discipline, it is impossible to expect anything else of troops who have never been trained as fighting soldiers. Somehow or other the word Sfakia got out and many of these people had taken a flying start in any available transport they could steal and which they later left abandoned . . . . Never shall I forget the disorganisation and almost complete lack of control of the masses on the move as we made our way slowly through that endless stream of trudging men.

Lieutenant Stephanides also described the scene:

> I knew that I was taking part in a retreat; in fact I wondered if it should not be called more correctly a rout as, on all sides, men were hurrying along in disorder. Most of them had thrown away their rifles and a number had even discarded their

---

[6] Weston wrote afterwards: "I was able to have little influence on the rearguard operations until Thursday (29 May), owing to the extreme difficulty of movement on the road . . . . The fact that the rearguard actions were effectively and successfully conducted was due mainly to the excellent cooperation between New Zealand and Australian brigadiers and Colonel Laycock."

tunics, as it was a hot day . . . . Nearly every yard of the road and of the ditches on either side was strewn with abandoned arms and accoutrements, blankets, gas-masks, packs, kit-bags, sun-helmets, cases and containers of all shapes and sizes, tinned provisions and boxes of cartridges and hand grenades; now and then one ran across officers' valises and burst-open suitcases.[7]

A reply was now received from Cairo to Freyberg's outspoken signal of the 26th in which he had declared the situation "hopeless". It said that Major-General Evetts[8] was arriving as liaison officer and suggested that the Suda-Maleme force should retire on Retimo and hold the eastern part of the island. Freyberg "did not derive much comfort from this helpful advice which indicated complete ignorance of the strength of the Retimo road-blocks and of the latest reports of a German sea landing at Georgioupolis". Accordingly, at 1 a.m. on the 27th, he sent Wavell a message stating that Retimo was practically foodless and without ammunition, and all guns in the Maleme-Suda sector had been lost because of lack of tractors; the force could survive only if food was landed at Sfakia at once. The only chance of saving some of the force lay in withdrawal to Sfakia. Freyberg himself received a letter from the Greek commander, General Skoulas, stating that the position of the Greek forces was so difficult that they had begun to disintegrate at many points.

In the afternoon Freyberg received orders to abandon Crete. That morning Wavell had asked London for instructions and, having received no reply by 3.50 p.m., had then sent orders to Freyberg to evacuate Crete. This decision was confirmed from London a few hours later. News of the coming evacuation could not immediately be sent to Colonel Campbell at Retimo because Campbell had no ciphers, but it had been arranged that Lieutenant Haig,[9] Royal Navy, should carry ten tons of rations to Retimo that night, and Freyberg told an officer to tell Haig of the order to embark so that he could pass it to Campbell. However, Haig departed before the officer delivered the message. In the meantime Freyberg's headquarters set out for Sfakia and it was not until next day that he knew that the message had not reached Haig. He asked Cairo to drop it by aircraft.

From the German point of view the 26th and 27th were days of great success. The *Assault Regiment* pushed on to two kilometres west of Canea; farther south the *100th Mountain Regiment* took Karatsos; advancing from the Prison Valley, the *3rd Parachute Regiment* took Perivolia. Still farther south Krakau took Alikianou. During the day one mountain battalion and a half, and additional artillery were landed on Maleme airfield. Nevertheless the German units were depleted and weary; the *3rd Parachute Regiment,* for example, had been reorganised after Galatas to form one weak battalion.

General Ringel planned to continue the encirclement of Canea on the 27th and, having done so, to pursue towards Retimo. Five columns were now advancing east; Krakau's group farthest south was aimed at Ayia Marina (the Ayia Marina south of 42nd Street). Jais' group (the *141st Mountain Regiment*) was next to the north; then Heidrich's *3rd Parachute Regiment*; then Utz's group (*100th Mountain Regiment*), and finally Ramcke's group on the coast.

---

[7] T. Stephanides, *Climax in Crete,* p. 113.
[8] Lt-Gen J. F. Evetts, CB, CBE, MC. GOC 6 Brit Div 1941; Asst Ch Imp Gen Staff 1942-44; Senior Mil Adviser, Min of Supply 1944-46; Chief Executive Offr Joint UK-Australian Long Range Weapons Board of Administration 1946-51. Regular soldier; b. Naini Tal, India, 30 Jun 1891.
[9] Lt-Cdr R. A. Haig, DSC; RN. Landing Ship *Glenroy* 1941. B. 18 Sep 1912.

It was Jais' regiment (the one which had fought the 19th Brigade in the rearguard position at Brallos in Greece) which had the "fierce and costly encounter" at 42nd Street. At 6.45 a.m. it had received orders to push through to the head of Suda Bay and cut off the enemy's retreat. The *I Battalion* led the advance. From about 11 a.m. for more than half an hour no word arrived from the leading battalion. Jais decided that it had been dispersed by a counter-attack and he halted the *III Battalion*, which was following, until the situation was cleared up. About 2.30 p.m. Major Forster, commander of the *I Battalion*, arrived at Jais' headquarters. He reported that his battalion had come unexpectedly on the "English" positions 2.5 kilometres west of Suda village in thick olive country. Part of the leading company had run on to a minefield and the battalion had heavy casualties in a few minutes. The English threatened to surround the battalion completely, and therefore the fighting troops were pulled back, suffering further casualties as they came. Most of the officers and many other ranks had been killed or wounded. The battalion was withdrawn west to high ground where the *III/141st* had taken up defensive positions.

In a report written later Forster said that his unit had "very heavy casualties". He added: "I consider it impossible that all the dead we afterwards found [121 men] were killed during the action." Private Kumnig, who stated that he went to the battlefield several times, reported that he "assumed that the English, before abandoning the battlefield, had either shot or stabbed every wounded German on the field". A number of the German dead had stab wounds or broken skulls. A Sergeant-Major Hoyer reported that "throughout the battlefield there was not a single English corpse with a bayonet or butt wound. I saw about 20 dead . . . New Zealanders and Australians".

In reply to questions about this incident Lieut-Colonel Walker wrote, in 1952: "In building up his forward troops for the counter-attack the enemy had concentrated a large number of automatic weapons forward. These were overrun and captured by us in the first few moments of the attack, and the captured weapons used in the following stages with great effect. In close fighting of this nature, as it was amongst olive trees, a burst of automatic fire is almost certain to prove fatal, as would also bayonet wounds. In point of fact, we captured three wounded men and it would be reasonable to suppose that some wounded men got back to German areas. Outside the heat of the moment in battle, or when wounded men still continued to engage us, no man either wounded and offering to surrender, or unwounded and offering to surrender was shot."

Referring to accusations made by Germans in June 1941 to him personally, Walker added: "The German accusation against me concerned in the main, so far as I can remember, the specific case of a number of men unarmed who were found shot at the foot of a wall. None of us knew anything of this incident, and it is more than probable that they were running away and the delay in scaling the wall caused their death. It is of course quite legitimate to fire on anyone who fails to surrender."

By 10 a.m. on the 27th the *3rd Parachute Regiment* had fought its way to the wireless station; and about 2 p.m. on the 27th it entered Canea together with the *100th Mountain Regiment* and Ramcke's group. Forty guns and about 1,000 prisoners were taken. In the evening Krakau's mountain troops of the *85th Regiment* occupied the heights west of Stilos.· During the 27th the remainder of the *5th Mountain Division* and a battalion of the *6th Mountain Division* were landed at Maleme.

The rearguard—5th and 19th Brigades and Layforce—had, by a very narrow margin, succeeded in reaching the foot of the road leading over the mountains to Sfakia but now was fairly firmly deployed along that road from Stilos to Babali Inn (properly Babali Hani), ready again to protect the main column which packed the road to the south. Before the retreat and embarkation of the Maleme-Suda force is described let us turn to the isolated sectors at Retimo and Heraklion.

CHAPTER 12

DEFENCE OF RETIMO

ROUND Retimo the mountains, sloping steeply down to the sea, were cut at every mile or so by deep gullies which ran out into a coastal shelf varying in width from 100 to 800 yards and terminating in a shingle beach. About five miles east of Retimo, a compact town with a population of about 10,000, lay the airfield, which was about 100 yards from the beach and parallel to it. Immediately overlooking the airfield was a narrow ridge varying in height from 100 to 200 feet.

To understand the problems facing Lieut-Colonel Ian Campbell, who became the commander of the force defending Retimo airfield, it is necessary to see this ridge in some detail. A spur, which the Australians named Hill "A", jutted to within 100 yards of the sea, commanding the eastern end of the airfield; about 1,000 yards east of Hill "A" was the small village of Stavromenos whose main building was an olive oil factory with a 50-foot chimney. The ridge itself, separated from the main mountain system to the south by a narrow valley sheltering the villages of Pigi and Adhele, blended into the mountains about two miles east of the airfield, but, to the west, terminated abruptly just short of the village of Platanes, where the road from Kirianna through Adhele joined the main coast road. From the south the landing ground was dominated by Hill "D", which rose between the Wadi Bardia[1] on the east and the Wadi Pigi on the west. Between the Wadi Pigi and the Wadi Adhele the ridge continued. Beyond the Wadi Adhele lay Hill "B" which broadened out at its western end overlooking Platanes. To the west, overlooking Perivolia, was Hill "C". Olive trees covered the whole area except the coastal plain, the inland valley near Pigi and the seaward slopes of Hills "A" and "B". On these northern slopes were vineyards in full leaf, offering good cover. All the hillsides were terraced in steps up to 20 feet high, and thus men could move round the spurs without being seen by those higher up.

Since 30th April, when Campbell's 2/1st Battalion arrived to take over the defence of the landing ground from Greek troops, the force had been steadily built up, until by 19th May there was the equivalent of a brigade group disposed to defend the air strip.[2] Although the Australian infantry

---

[1] The hills and gullies were named by Lt-Col Campbell. After the Libyan campaign the men of 6 Div long continued to describe creeks and gullies as "wadis". It was natural that Campbell should name one wadi "Bardia", because the 2/1st led the attack in that battle.

[2] The strength and equipment of the units were:

2/1 Bn, 620 officers and men, adequately equipped with rifles, Bren light machine-guns and anti-tank rifles. The headquarters company was organised as a rifle company. There were two 3-inch mortars but without base plates, and two carriers.

2/11 Bn, 650 officers and men, fully equipped with rifles, Brens, anti-tank rifles and sub-machine-guns. There were two 3-inch mortars but without base plates, three (instead of nine) 2-inch mortars, two carriers.

Four improvised battalions of Greeks, 2,300 men in all, equipped with 800 American Springfield rifles, and 1,500 Greek rifles, with about ten rounds of ammunition a rifle and some old French machine-guns.

A force of 800 well-disciplined Cretan police.

6 Bty, 2/3 Fd Regt, about 90 men, equipped with four 100-mm Italian guns, four 75-mm

was adequately equipped with small arms, ammunition for them was limited. There were only five rounds for each anti-tank rifle, eighty bombs for each of the four 3-inch mortars. The medium machine-gunners had but sixteen belts of ammunition to a gun. Uniforms and boots were in need of repair and few men received any replacements in Crete.

Unlike the defenders at the other two landing grounds, where there was both heavy and light anti-aircraft artillery, the force at Retimo had none, nor had they armour-piercing small arms ammunition. Consequently German bombers and fighters would be able with relative safety to fly low over the area and only their thin-skinned troop carriers would be in danger from the defenders' small arms fire. The 2/1st Battalion had no signalling equipment except three telephones and some cable brought by the gunners; these Campbell used to link his headquarters with Hills "A" and "B". Except for a few runners and the men required to maintain these three telephones, all signallers became riflemen. The 2/11th had a telephone for each company but very little cable. Communication between the two battalions was by runner. Enough barbed wire was received to make it possible to fence the whole front and the airfield.

There were rations enough to last ten days, but four days' supply had been moved to the end of the road to Mesi so that the force could fall back there if it was pushed off the ridge above the airfield. The food supply was supplemented by buying pigs, vegetables, eggs, and goats' milk from the farms and villages; the West Australians of the 2/11th Battalion hired milking goats and kept them in their lines.

Because the olive trees masked the southern slopes of the ridges the field guns and all but two of the medium machine-guns were placed well forward on Hills "A" and "B", whence there was a clear field of fire north, east and west. The remaining two machine-guns were sited on the ridge above Hill "B". On Hill "A" Campbell placed one company of the 2/1st, two 100-mm and four 75-mm guns and a platoon of machine-gunners. The remainder of the battalion occupied Hill "D" and the slopes overlooking the landing ground from the south. Here were four companies, the headquarters group having been converted into a rifle company because it lacked its normal equipment—mortars, vehicles, signal and pioneer gear and all except two carriers—and on a forward spur of this hill, whence he could see the whole coastal plain from Hill "A" to Retimo, Campbell placed his headquarters. The 4th Greek Battalion was stationed on the ridge between the Wadi Pigi and the Wadi Adhele with the remaining three Greek battalions in reserve among olive trees south of Pigi village.

The 2/11th Battalion (Major Sandover) occupied the ridge from the Wadi Adhele to its western end at Hill "B" with three companies forward facing north. Initially the role of the 2/11th was to form a reserve to the 2/1st Battalion in defence of the airfield. One company was held in the

---

American guns with no sights (they were sighted through the barrel).
Two platoons, 2/1 MG Bn.
One section, 2/8 Fd Coy, without explosives and with practically no equipment.
One company (augmented), 2/7 Fd Amb.
Detachment, 7 Royal Tank Regiment, with two Matilda tanks.
There were also detachments of AASC, Signals, and a naval and an air force signals detachment.

rear ready to reinforce the 2/1st if required; the battalion's reserve was the transport platoon. On Hill "B" which jutted towards the sea, were also two 100-mm guns and one platoon of the 2/1st Machine Gun Battalion (Lieutenant McKerrow)[3] less one section at the eastern flank of the battalion near the Wadi Adhele. The two tanks were stationed under olive trees in the Wadi Pigi, whence they could issue forth to counter-attack if an enemy force obtained a foothold on the landing ground. The infantrymen were in weapon pits under olive trees or otherwise concealed so that they could be seen from neither the ground nor the air. Proof of the effectiveness of the camouflage—and guidance in improving it—had been obtained on the 16th when a very low-flying German reconnaissance aircraft crashed near the landing ground and in it were found aerial photographs dated the 8th—before the 2/11th arrived—showing that only one of the defenders' positions had been located. It was forthwith altered.

Campbell put the town of Retimo out of bounds because in the early days a few men on leave there drank too freely of the potent local wine, and he was rightly anxious that nothing should upset the cordial relations with the Cretans. Small parties of provosts were placed in Retimo and all the villages.

At 9 a.m. on the 20th the troops at Retimo saw fourteen fat troop-carrying aircraft approach the airfield but wheel right towards Canea. The long-awaited assault had begun. At 12 o'clock twenty troop carriers flew east past Retimo towards Heraklion. At 4 p.m. about twenty fighters and bombers arrived over Retimo and bombed and machine-gunned the area round the airfield. It was evident the camouflage was so thorough that the air crews could see no definite targets, and only two or three men were hit. However, the raw 4th Greek Battalion, although no bombs had fallen in their area, began moving back up the ridge. Australian N.C.O's were sent from the left of the 2/1st and right of the 2/11th, and they steadied the Greeks, led them forward to their original front line and stayed with them there. (One of these N.C.O's, Corporal Smallwood,[4] not only led the Greeks back to their positions but later took forward a large patrol of them to the main road capturing some twenty prisoners.)

After this ineffective strafing had continued for a quarter of an hour, twenty-four troop-carrying aircraft appeared. They came from the north towards Refuge Point, some miles to the east, then turned west, flying parallel to the coast, slowly, at about 400 feet. Other groups of troop carriers followed until 161 had been counted. One force of paratroops jumped when they were east of the airfield and floated down in an area three miles long and half a mile wide from east of the Olive Oil Factory to the eastern end of the airfield. A second force landed in sections along the coastal shelf from the western end of the airfield to the outskirts of Retimo itself. The landing was completed in thirty-five minutes. The slow-

---

[3] Capt I. McKerrow, VX15675; 2/1 MG Bn. Farmer; of Swan Hill, Vic; b. Swan Hill, 16 Jul 1916.
[4] Cpl R. G. Smallwood, MM, NX4088; 2/1 Bn. Drover; of Elizabeth Bay, NSW; b. Norbury, Eng, 8 Nov 1914.

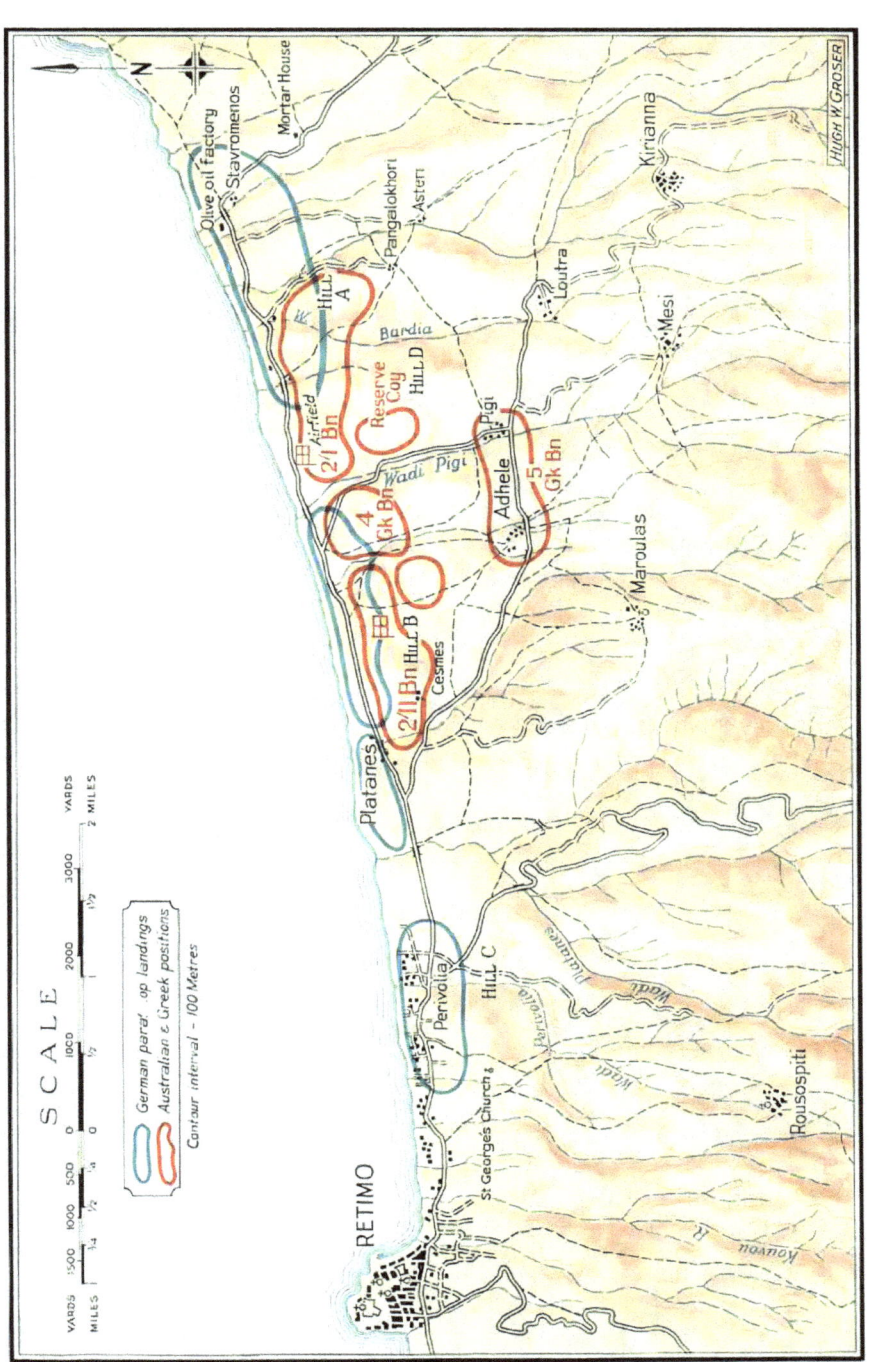

Situation at Retimo, evening, 20th May

flying, flimsy transport aircraft were a relatively easy target, and every weapon on the ground blazed at them as they passed across the front at a range of little more than 100 yards. Seven troop carriers and two other aircraft were shot down, most of them crashing in flames near Perivolia at the western end of their run. Other aircraft were on fire as they flew homewards.

On Hill "A", the vital ground overlooking the eastern end of the airfield, a considerable number of paratroops landed right on the closely-defended area—a hill about 200 yards by 300—held by one company of infantry (Captain Channell's[5]), six guns and four Vickers machine-guns. There followed a bitter series of fights between sections or platoons of Australians on the one hand and, on the other, such groups of paratroops as survived long enough to organise and go into action. On the east of the line paratroops landed on top of one platoon of infantry, the 75-mm guns, and the two Vickers guns, under Lieutenant Cleaver.[6] Crew after crew of the Vickers guns were shot down, and the guns were finally put out of action by a German mortar bomb. The surviving gunners of the 75's, who had no small arms except three pistols, withdrew to the battery headquarters farther up the ridge, carrying their breech-blocks with them. There they fought on, using some captured weapons, and held their positions until a concerted German attack about 9 p.m. Of the crews of the remaining two machine-guns farther west, few survived, but three isolated infantry posts still held out on the northern slopes, and the remainder of Channell's company was across the neck of the hill. Campbell sent two platoons (Lieutenants Craig[7] and Kiely[8]) from his central company, which was not engaged, to prevent the Germans from advancing west from Hill "A", and they moved across the Wadi Bardia under fire. Although the Germans possessed most of the top and eastern side of "A", it was dangerous for them to advance out of the vineyards and down the western slopes because they were under observed fire from Captain Travers' company on the spur west of the Wadi Bardia. Campbell also sent a platoon to reinforce Channell on Hill "A" and to clear the vineyards on the north-west side of the hill. This platoon reached Channell's headquarters about 6.30 but was unable to advance across the north-west slopes, where paratroops were now firing from excellent cover among the vines and terraces. During this fight, because so many of the paratroops had landed in the midst of the defenders, the supporting German aircraft at first were helpless and flew round looking for targets on which they could fire without endangering their own men.

Meanwhile, at 5.15 p.m., Campbell had ordered the two tanks to advance down the Wadi Pigi and swing right across the airfield and then along the road to attack the Germans east of Hill "A". However, one tank stuck

---

[5] Capt D. R. Channell, MC, NX115; 2/1 Bn. Radio announcer; of Padstow Park, NSW; b. London, 7 Dec 1909.
[6] Lt E. H. R. Cleaver, TX2021; 2/1 MG Bn. Tailor; of Manly, NSW; b. Glasgow, Scotland, 5 Jun 1909.
[7] Lt N. W. Craig, NX2632; 2/1 Bn. Traveller; of St Arnaud, Vic; b. St Arnaud, 16 Apr 1917.
[8] Capt V. A. Kiely, MC, NX12173; 2/1 Bn. Bank clerk; of Sydney; b. Sydney, 25 Jul 1918.

in a drain on the north side of the airfield and the other, after passing east of Hill "A" and firing a few shots, fell into a wadi eight feet deep.[9]

Farther to the left the few paratroops who landed in front of the main body of the 2/1st Battalion and the 4th Greek Battalion were soon all killed or captured, as were the few who came to earth within the 2/11th's wired area on Hill "B". Other groups came down among the vineyards north of the 2/11th under a searching fire and were killed or forced to seek cover among the vines and huts before they had time to organise.[1] Many Germans were dead when they landed. In one party of about twelve who descended compactly between two sections on the left of the 2/11th, every man had been riddled with bullets as he floated down. However, strong parties, estimated at 500 by Captain Honner, commanding the left company, were seen moving westward toward Perivolia beyond the range of the West Australians' machine-guns.

Sandover ordered a quick northward advance along his whole line to mop-up the Germans on the low ground before dark. There was considerable opposition in places and by nightfall the main road had not been reached at all points along the front. While daylight lasted the West Australians had the advantage of overlooking the enemy, but after dark the enemy, concealed in the vineyards, could inflict disproportionate casualties on the patrols. Sandover decided to withdraw his companies within the wire for the night, but to send out patrols, particularly on the left, to stop the Germans moving towards Retimo. By 10.30 p.m. the battalion had collected eighty-four prisoners and "a mass of captured arms". The night patrols had difficulty in finding the scattered Germans hiding among the vines and terraces, but only a few were believed to have escaped from the area which was combed. Sandover, who could speak German, questioned the prisoners, most of whom expressed the comforting opinion that no more paratroops would be landed. He also translated a captured code of signals and, as a result, his men next day laid out on the ground the sign calling for mortar bombs, and a German supply aircraft obediently dropped some.

On the first evening Campbell, unaware of what was happening elsewhere on the island and knowing that the Germans controlled most of the vital Hill "A", sent a request to General Freyberg, by wireless, for reinforcements[2] and, at dusk, issued orders for two attacks at dawn next morning, the 2/1st to clear the enemy from Hill "A", and the 2/11th to clear them from the low ground between it and the sea, each Australian battalion being assisted by one Greek battalion which would strike north against the southern flank of the German force opposing each Australian battalion. With the eastern Greek battalion Campbell sent his second-in-

---

[9] Lt Simpson, who commanded these tanks, was killed on getting out of the tank that lodged in the drain.

[1] The ground on the left of the 2/11th offered so much cover that parachutists who had landed only a few yards from the Australian posts were invisible. Pte F. Graffin (of Kalgoorlie, WA) dashed out repeatedly and killed such men with his bayonet until he himself was killed by a German bullet.

[2] At midnight a wireless message arrived from Freyberg regretting his inability to send reinforcements and wishing Campbell luck.

command, Major Hooper,³ while Major Ford⁴ of the Welch Regiment, who was liaison officer with the Greeks in this sector, was to accompany the western force.⁵

However, during the night the Germans on Hill "A" anticipated such an effort so far as it affected their position by pressing forward against the remaining Australian posts on that hill. They overran one section of the isolated platoon, the remainder of which withdrew on to the company headquarters. The Germans advanced on to the airfield and captured the crews of the stranded tanks; most of these Germans withdrew by dawn, but about forty remained behind the bank of the beach. Thus at dawn, when the attack was to begin, only one section of Channell's company (Corporal Johnston⁶), though surrounded and overlooked by Germans, was still holding out, very gamely, on the forward slopes of the hill; the remainder of the company, now reinforced by two additional platoons, was across the neck of Hill "A".

Channell led his men into the attack at dawn, the plan being to move round the sides and over the top of the hill. It appeared to the Australians that the Germans had arranged to attack almost simultaneously and under an intense barrage of mortar bombs. Into this fire Channell's men advanced 60 to 100 yards; Channell and Lieutenant Delves⁷ were wounded, and the company was driven back until it was clinging to a line on the western edge of the neck of the hill.

Captain Moriarty's company and the carrier platoon (though without carriers) arrived about 6 a.m. from Hill "D" to give support if it was needed and found that the attack had failed. Thus at 6.15 there were at the neck of Hill "A", where Moriarty took over command, the survivors of nearly half of Campbell's battalion; and the Germans were pressing hard. Moriarty telephoned to battalion headquarters that the position was "very desperate", whereupon Campbell led one of the companies still in hand along a sheltered route across the Wadi Bardia, and leaving part of it round the wadi, took the remainder on. He reached Moriarty about 7 a.m. and ordered him to manoeuvre the enemy off Hill "A" as soon as possible. About this time the Australians were cheered to see a German bomber drop six bombs on the German front line on the neck of Hill "A".⁸

Moriarty organised his force—now including platoons from four companies—into four groups and, about 8 a.m., attacked northwards. The attack was carried out with dash and succeeded brilliantly. On the right Lieutenant Rogers with four platoons (including the pioneers and the carrier crews) advanced along the eastern slope of the hill, then turned

---

³ Maj G. F. R. Hooper, NX128; 2/1 Bn. Traveller; of Mosman, NSW; b. Elsternwick, Vic, 15 Jan 1904.
⁴ Maj F. J. V. Ford; 1/Welch. Regular soldier; b. 13 Oct 1917.
⁵ Campbell had assumed command of the force in which he, a battalion commander of a few weeks' standing, was the senior officer. Because he did not wish to rob the fighting units of officers, his staff consisted only of his adjutant, Lt Willmott, and quartermaster, Capt Lergessner. His Intelligence officer had been invalided to Egypt and his Intelligence sergeant was sick.
⁶ Cpl H. H. Johnston, DCM, NX2470; 2/1 Bn. Plumber's apprentice; of Eastwood, NSW; b. Northbridge, NSW, 21 Jan 1918.
⁷ Lt W. P. Delves, NX7597; 2/1 Bn. Regular soldier; of Sydney; b. Melbourne, 19 Mar 1909.
⁸ Prisoners said later that these killed sixteen men.

east down the slope, took twenty-five prisoners and moved on to the hill east of "A", while one of his platoons under Lieutenant Savage[9] advanced north to the road. In the centre Lieutenants Whittle[1] and Gilmour-Walsh[2] (each with two platoons) advanced and occupied the eastern and northern face of Hill "A", recapturing the 75's. On the left Lieutenant Mann[3] moved round the terrace on the west of the hill and, having taken thirty-four prisoners, joined Savage on the road. Meanwhile Lieutenant Craig in the Wadi Bardia also moved forward to the main road. The Germans who survived escaped round the spurs south of the road to the shelter of the beach.

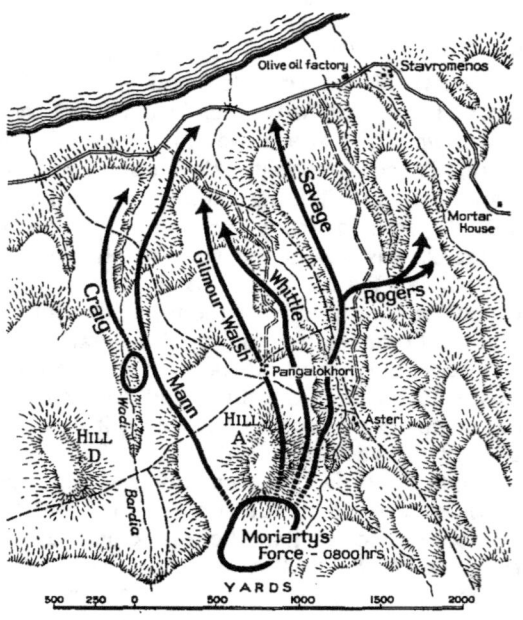

Thus, eighteen hours after the landing, the one German force that had succeeded in occupying a height commanding the airfield had been driven off, and only scattered parties of paratroops survived in the six miles of coastal plain between Perivolia and Hill "A". However, some of these surviving groups, though small, were enterprising and aggressive. Early on the 21st several of them filtered round the rear of the Australian positions and one, twenty strong, entered the dressing station at Adhele, ordered the men there to surrender and then moved on north towards the 2/11th, but were rounded up there by a party of West Australians. Two of these Germans were killed while changing into Greek uniforms. Other Germans, moving east behind the 2/11th, pushed on through Pigi and thence down the road towards the aerodrome. They captured Lieutenant Willmott,[4] whom Campbell had sent to stir the Greeks on the east into action, but the captors were themselves ambushed and captured by the engineers and transport sections, and Willmott was released.

During the day the 2/1st and 2/11th cleared the few remaining Germans from the coastal plain between Hills "A" and "B".[5] These enemy

---

[9] Lt B. M. Savage, NX173; 2/1 Bn. Livestock officer; of Bathurst, NSW; b. Blackwood, SA, 5 May 1912.
[1] Lt J. S. Whittle, NX8691; 2/1 Bn. Clerk; of Ashfield, NSW; b. Marrickville, NSW, 12 Oct 1918.
[2] Lt A. H. Gilmour-Walsh, NX4129; 2/1 Bn. Accountant; of Manly, NSW; b. Sydney, 8 Nov 1913.
[3] Capt G. W. Mann, MC, NX7646; 2/1 Bn. Grazier; of Batlow, NSW; b. Petersham, NSW, 4 Mar 1913.
[4] Lt R. Willmott, NX3871; 2/1 Bn. Advertising agent; of Sydney; b. Sydney, 19 Apr 1911.
[5] Lt C. Stanton was killed during the mopping up immediately north of the airfield.

parties were under fire from the Australians' machine-guns above them and had been pinned down behind such cover as the low ground offered. Among the prisoners taken by the 2/11th was Colonel Sturm, commander of the whole German force. He carried his orders with him, and from these it was learnt that the plan had been to land one battalion of his regiment east and one west of the airfield, about 1,500 men in all. (By error two companies intended for dropping west of Hill "B" had been dropped east of Hill "A".)

Of the Greek battalions sent to each flank, the one accompanied by Major Ford reached the ridge south of Perivolia by nightfall on the 21st, but round Perivolia the Germans had collected in considerable strength, though they were loosely contained by the 2/11th on Hill "B" and by the Greeks in the hills to the south and the sturdy force of 800 Cretan police who had ejected all Germans from Retimo and were astride the road between the town and Perivolia. The 2/11th was not aware that Greeks would be moving west, and there was an exchange of fire between the westernmost Australian platoon and a Greek force. The other Greek battalion, on the right, cleared small parties of Germans from the village south of the Olive Oil Factory, but by night had not reached the crest of the ridge there whence they could have threatened the Germans on the coastal plain below. Campbell relieved Channell's battered company on Hill "A" with Captain Embrey's. His field gunners, now plentifully supplied with German small arms, were back at their guns. He sent a message to Freyberg's headquarters reporting that the situation was well in hand.

However, although the airfield and the positions commanding it were secure, two strongly-established groups of Germans remained, one on the east, in and round the Olive Oil Factory, astride the road to Heraklion; the other at Perivolia across the road to Suda Bay. Campbell ordered that on the 22nd each of these should be driven out. The 2/11th was to thrust west towards Perivolia, and two companies of the 2/1st east towards the factory. Near the factory the advancing Australians were joined by the Greeks from the south and found Germans strongly ensconced in the thick-walled buildings there. Moriarty's company, advancing along the ridges, made good progress and Campbell ordered an attack about 10 a.m. if fifteen minutes' artillery bombardment by Captain Killey's[6] guns on Hill "A" seemed effective. The guns fired what ammunition Killey considered they could afford, but already the gallant Moriarty, while reconnoitring, had been shot dead by a German rifleman, and Lieutenant Savage—the only other officer of his company—had been wounded. The attack did not start.

Campbell then planned a converging attack, to be made at 6 p.m. after artillery and mortar bombardment: 200 Greeks would move secretly down one wadi and forty Australians would crawl down another, and then charge, while the remaining troops of Captain Travers' company fired down into the factory from the heights overlooking it 100 to 200 yards away.

---

[6] Capt G. H. Killey, MC, WX28; 2/3 Fd Regt. Bank officer; of South Perth, WA; b. Narrogin, WA, 6 Jan 1914.

However, the Greek troops did not move at the appointed time, though the forty Australians, gallantly led by Mann, rushed forward with a yell from their wadi. Many fell, and the survivors took shelter behind a bank about 40 yards from the factory. Campbell, who was near by, called to Mann not to move until the Greeks attacked. Corporal Thompson[7] shouted back that Mann had been seriously wounded[8] and that he (Thompson) was now in command of the few men who remained. Campbell then decided that the attack could not be pressed, and ordered the Greeks to keep the factory under fire but not to advance. At dark, when the Australians, pinned down near the factory, were able to withdraw, he sent his two companies back to their original positions overlooking the airfield, leaving the Greeks to contain the Germans in the factory.

On the left the last of the small parties of Germans in the rear of the 2/11th withdrew during the night and in the afternoon the left flanking company (Captain Honner) advanced without opposition through Cesmes to the wadi through Platanes, where they came under fire from houses farther west. On previous days the West Australians had used German signals to mislead the enemy, and now, just east of the Wadi Platanes, Honner laid on the ground a signal calling to German aircraft for bombs on Perivolia, and the German aircraft obeyed.[9] Sandover ordered Honner to advance astride the road to the creek west of the road fork at Perivolia. Honner's men, supported by a captured German mortar and one of their own, attacked and occupied the group of houses on the small ridge about half way to the objective with a loss of one man killed and two wounded. Beyond the houses the land sloped downwards and further advance would be observed by the Germans, strongly established 1,000 yards ahead on the edge of Perivolia in buildings, behind stone walls and in the Church of St. George, whose churchyard was surrounded by a stone wall, and which overlooked the ground across which the 2/11th was to attack. His 100 men were under fire from mortars, machine-guns and light artillery.

It was then late in the afternoon and when a runner arrived to report that Captain Jackson's company was moving forward to support him, Honner (who was the senior company commander of the battalion) decided to make a leap-frogging attack in the darkness with both companies between the road and the coast, where three parallel ditches spaced at intervals of a few hundred yards and about two feet deep offered some cover. As the light faded Jackson advanced to the second of these without difficulty. Honner was following with his own company when Sandover arrived. Sandover understood that the Greeks were about to attack the Church of St. George. This seemed to him to be a vitally-important position,

---

[7] Lt N. O. Thompson, NX2618; 2/1 Bn. Labourer; of Balmain, NSW; b. Cottesloe, WA, 12 Oct 1913.

[8] Mann had previously been wounded at Bardia.

[9] The diarist of the *5th Mountain Division* recorded that, on the 22nd, "reports from various sources that weapons and supplies were being dropped in the wrong places led to the definite conclusion that the Greeks and British were using swastika flags taken from dead or captured paratroops for deception purposes, and thus causing our aircraft to drop supplies in the wrong places or make false reports".

but he was anxious to avoid a further unfortunate clash with the Greeks. The volume of German fire made it appear doubtful whether a frontal attack would succeed across the open ground ahead, and he ordered the two companies to remain where they were and dig in. They heard much noise and shooting around Perivolia. It appears that, in the night, the Greeks advanced, captured some prisoners, and withdrew.[1]

On the 23rd Campbell received an encouraging wireless message from General Freyberg: "You have done magnificently"; and later in the day came word that a company of the 1/Rangers was advancing from Canea to clear a way through Perivolia. It will be recalled that, before this news arrived, Campbell had sent off Captain Lergessner westwards with instructions to carry a message to Suda; he was also to take a mule train to Retimo to collect food. Lergessner could not get the mules over the steep hills but he himself scrambled to Retimo where he met the company of the Rangers, and (as noted above) failed to dissuade them from attacking.

When mopping-up east of the airfield, the Australians had captured the paratroops' medical aid post and, on 23rd May, the medical officer of the 2/1st arranged with the German medical officers, first, that these should remove their wounded from the aid post in no-man's land west of Stavromenos to the Australian dressing station in the valley near Adhele, where henceforward Australian and German medical officers and orderlies worked side by side;[2] and, second, that there be a three hours' truce so that both sides could collect these and other wounded lying between Hill "A" and the factory. About half an hour later Captain Embrey led in a blindfolded German officer from the factory with a message demanding that the Australians surrender, on the grounds that the Germans had succeeded at the two other landing places and the Australians' position was hopeless. Campbell refused and punctuated his decision by spending a few more of his precious shells on the factory when the truce was over.

On the left the Greeks promised Sandover that on the 23rd they would drive the Germans from St. George's Church. Accordingly during the morning the West Australians shelled the church with a captured anti-tank gun until the Germans abandoned it; but the Greeks failed to follow up. That afternoon about fifty German aircraft appeared and, evidently obeying signals from the Germans in Perivolia, attacked the area between that village and Platanes for five hours. Jackson's company, nearest the Ger-

---

[1] That night a British aircraft, evidently mistaking the flat ground east of Perivolia for the airfield, dropped two bags of .303 ammunition, one near the German line and the other in front of Jackson's company, which recovered it.

[2] On the 23rd there were at the dressing station in addition to the Australian officers (Maj J. D. Palandri and Capts F. E. Gallash and M. Mayrhofer—all of Perth, WA) and orderlies, two German medical officers and some orderlies, to whom tents of their own had been allotted, and two or three Greek medical officers and medical students. By the 24th there were 147 Australian patients, 51 Greek and 252 Germans. Day by day as more wounded men arrived, more tents were put up until there were fifteen occupied by Australians, eight by Germans and four by Greeks; and every day Capts A. G. G. Carter (Melbourne) of the 2/1 and J. J. Ryan of the 2/11 sent in captured medical supplies without which the dressing station—now a small hospital—could not have functioned. The number of German patients was reduced by sending walking wounded to the prisoner compound, and on the 29th there were 232 Germans, 181 Australians and 62 Greeks at the dressing station.

mans, escaped with nine casualties,[3] but Honner's and the mortar platoon next to them lost three men killed and twenty-seven wounded. Where the bombardment was hottest Privates "Slim" Johnson[4] and Symmons[5] kept a Bren gun in action though both were wounded, and refused to move to a safer position where they would have a less clear view. For a time the aircraft circled round setting fire to houses and crops. At sunset the Germans on the ground attacked from Perivolia, but were beaten off. "Our forward troops," wrote an Australian, "stood up and shot them down like rabbits." When the attack was over the survivors of Honner's company were replaced on the left by Captain McCaskill's, which made ready to attack with Jackson's as soon as the Rangers appeared, but nothing was seen or heard of them.[6]

The reoccupation of Hill "A" and the coastal plain had placed Campbell again in possession of the two tanks. Carrier crews of the 2/1st found that they were undamaged and discovered how to drive them. At dawn on the 24th one tank thus recovered by the efforts of Lieutenant Mason of the Royal Army Ordnance Corps was used to reconnoitre the Olive Oil Factory, and later in the morning Mason drove it along the road past the factory to a house where Germans had been collecting. The Germans sheltered in the house and remained there.

That night Campbell guided this tank to the road junction west of Hill "B", and just before dawn handed it over to Sandover to support a new attack towards Perivolia. The tank moved forward at first light on the 25th but a Blenheim aircraft flying low overhead alarmed the inexperienced driver and caused him to blunder over a culvert into a creek. It was hastily camouflaged to hide it from patrolling aircraft and rescued towards evening. Next morning (the 26th) it again advanced towards St. George's Church, but when it was nearing the objective a German shell hit the turret, jamming it and stunning the commander (Lieutenant Greenway[7]) and again the attack was abandoned.[8]

---

[3] Including Lt F. L. Clarke (Burekup, WA), fatally wounded. Although many bombs were dropped and dug huge craters in the soft ground practically all, if not all, the casualties were caused by cannon and machine-gun fire.

[4] Pte H. C. Johnson, MM, WX788; 2/11 Bn. Carpenter; of Kalgoorlie, WA; b. Kalgoorlie, 21 Jan 1917.

[5] Pte F. W. Symmons, WX739; 2/11 Bn. Storeman; of Northam, WA; b. Geraldton, WA, 4 Jun 1917. Died of wounds 23 May 1941. (His father and an uncle had both fought with the old 11 Bn in 1914-18.)

[6] The officer commanding this company of the Rangers decided that the Germans were immune to his weapons—Brens and one 2-pdr anti-tank gun—because they were in stone houses and a thick-walled church and, having learnt from Lergessner that the Australian force was in good shape, telephoned Freyberg's headquarters asking whether in the circumstances he should attack. He was ordered to do so. The attack at dawn on the 24th was a costly failure and the surviving Rangers were embussed and returned to Canea.

[7] Capt G. J. Greenway, MC, WX976; 2/11 Bn. Station overseer; of Murchison River, WA; b. Cottesloe, WA, 4 Oct 1903.

[8] The 2/11th lost four killed and twenty-six wounded (including Capt McCaskill) this day, some through air attack. Capt Ryan went forward with stretcher-bearers under the Red Cross flag to collect men lying wounded on the forward slope. The Germans ceased fire while the wounded men were collected.

At this stage a sniping party led by Warrant Officer C. W. Mitchell (of Perth, WA) and using a captured German rifle with telescopic sights had been established in foothills on the left, whence they caused much annoyance to the Germans. Signalman A. R. Mulgrave (of Kalamunda, WA) was estimated to have caused over 20 casualties at ranges of over 900 yards.

Meanwhile the 2/1st, using a captured mortar, had, on the 25th, bombed some thirty Germans out of the house on the extreme right. This greatly heartened the Greeks, who forthwith occupied the house, but the Germans in and round the factory were well armed and aggressive and kept the Australian gunners under heavy and accurate mortar and machine-gun fire. At 9 o'clock on the 26th, hearing that this fire had diminished, Campbell sent a tank and a platoon of Embrey's company to explore. Embrey himself led the infantry which reached the outskirts of Stavromenos, covered by the tank and by fire from the 75-mm guns on Hill "A". Having gone so far without meeting opposition he decided to attack, and the artillery fire was stopped as he and his men jumped the wall and captured the factory, taking forty-two wounded and forty unwounded Germans. From these they learnt that at 3 a.m. the three surviving officers with thirty men had made off eastwards.[9] There were now 500 German prisoners penned in a cage under the southern side of Hill "D".

Since the invasion began Campbell had received from Freyberg's headquarters only such news as could be sent to him by wireless in clear language, and he knew that if any secret plans were proposed—an embarkation, for example—news of them would have to be sent to him by other means. On the 26th Lergessner arrived from Canea, bringing the first news of the failure of the Rangers on the 24th; but he added that there was no talk of evacuation at Force headquarters.

The second tank was now in working order and, during the night of the 26th-27th, Campbell guided it to Sandover to support yet another attack towards Perivolia, this time by two companies. Before daylight Honner's company, only sixty strong until reinforced by some transport drivers, and that of Captain Gook[1] (who had succeeded McCaskill), had moved stealthily forward to the farthermost ditch, only 75 yards from the German positions, and there waited for the tanks to arrive. At dawn the two tanks appeared, each commanded by an Australian infantry officer. Lieutenant Lawry's[2] on the left was near the German line when it was hit by a shell and set on fire. The crew of the other (under Lieutenant Bedells[3]), unaware that the infantry had crawled to the farthermost ditch, opened fire in the dim light causing two casualties. The infantrymen had to wave signals back to the tank and thus betrayed their presence to the Germans. Thirty yards beyond the ditch the tank struck a land mine which knocked off a track. It lurched on for a few yards and was bogged in sand. A mortar bomb blew the top of the turret open and as Bedells was trying to close it a second bomb severed the fingers of one hand and a third disabled his guns, which had been kept in action to the last.[4] Lawry and one of his men, wounded and scorched, crawled back to safety. Bedells and his crew remained in the tank until nightfall.

---

[9] Lt A. A. Herron (Strathfield, NSW) was fatally wounded in this attack.
[1] Capt W. W. Gook, WX16; 2/11 Bn. Printer; of West Perth, WA; b. London, 8 Jul 1916.
[2] Lt P. C. Lawry, MC, NX2638; 2/1 Bn. Jackeroo; of Inverell, NSW; b. Inverell, 2 Jul 1914.
[3] Lt J. G. Bedells, WX13; 2/11 Bn. Clerk; of Cottesloe, WA; b. Cottesloe, 25 May 1918.
[4] The German mortarman afterwards told Bedells that his mortar was 100 metres distant and ranged precisely on the spot where the tank bogged.

Honner had just decided that with both tanks out of action it would be useless for the infantry to attack, when Gook wormed his way into the ditch and announced that his forward platoon (Lieutenant Roberts[5]) could not be found. After further reconnaissance Gook returned to say that the missing platoon must have attacked and broken into the Perivolia position. In an account written after the campaign Honner described what followed:

> That left me only one thing to do—attack to help Roberts out of trouble or to complete the success he had started. I knew I'd have to lose men but I couldn't lose time. A section from 14 Platoon—nine men—was ordered to move to a low stone wall fifty yards ahead round a well about twenty-five yards from the German line, to cover with Bren fire our attack across the open. They raced along the low hedge to the well. The leader, Corporal Tom Willoughby,[6] was nearly there before he fell. The man carrying the Bren went down. Someone following him picked it up and went on until he was killed, and so the gun was relayed until it almost reached the well in the hands of the last man, and he too was killed as he went down with it. Eight brave men died there—Corporal Willoughby, Lance-Corporal Dowsett,[7] Privates Brown,[8] Elvy,[9] Fraser,[1] Green,[2] G. McDermid,[3] and White.[4] The ninth man, Private Proud,[5] was hit on the tin hat as he jumped up, and fell back stunned into the ditch. As the first man fell a stretcher-bearer dashed out, went down beside him, saw he was dead, decided that the others were probably dead also, and lay there until rescued an hour or so later. Then we tried the other side. Lieutenant Bayly[6] headed a party (along a forward leading tributary of the ditch) but he was the only one in the leading group not hit. Private "Blue" Pauley[7] was hit here and so was young Fitzsimons[8] who had been wounded on the 23rd but got away from the dressing station to rejoin his company when he heard it was going into action again. This time he was stopped with hits in the arm, chest and legs. Gook's runner was also hit; and then Gook came along the ditch from the left to say Roberts' platoon was lying doggo along the far end of it. I wrote a hurried report of the situation . . . . Snipers occupied the houses overlooking us and it seemed that it would be difficult to leave the ditch but safe to stay all day (to protect the tank crew). Everyone leaving the ditch since daylight, except the stretcher-bearer, had been hit, but I wanted to get my message back and I wanted to direct the putting down of smoke (we had none) to cover a party to bring in our wounded (we did not know they were dead).

---

[5] Lt F. E. Roberts, WX528; 2/11 Bn. Shipping clerk; of Bunbury, WA; b. Bunbury, 29 Sep 1914.

[6] Cpl T. R. Willoughby, WX786; 2/11 Bn. Baker; of Scarborough Beach, WA; b. Kalgoorlie, WA, 5 Sep 1908. Killed in action 27 May 1941.

[7] L-Cpl A. E. Dowsett, WX1869; 2/11 Bn. Farmer; of Wandering, WA; b. Wandering, 10 Nov 1916. Killed in action 27 May 1941. Dowsett was an outstanding racing cyclist.

[8] Pte C. Brown, WX1013; 2/11 Bn. Builder; of Perth, WA; b. London, 6 May 1905. Killed in action 27 May 1941.

[9] Pte C. J. Elvy, WX842; 2/11 Bn. Farm labourer; of Narlingup, WA; b. Littlehampton, Eng, 22 May 1917. Killed in action 27 May 1941.

[1] Pte J. R. Fraser, WX471; 2/11 Bn. Fibrous plasterer; of Perth, WA; b. Perth, 7 Aug 1919. Killed in action 27 May 1941.

[2] Pte F. W. J. Green, WX6115; 2/11 Bn. Miner; of North Perth, WA; b. Ravensthorpe, Phillips River, WA, 8 Mar 1908. Killed in action 27 May 1941.

[3] Pte G. R. W. McDermid, WX1658; 2/11 Bn. Fireman; of East Fremantle, WA; b. Ayr, Scotland, 6 Dec 1913. Killed in action 27 May 1941.

[4] Pte R. G. White, WX6806; 2/11 Bn. Road grader hand; of Pinjarra, WA; b. Pinjarra, 5 Jun 1911. Killed in action 27 May 1941.

[5] Pte W. F. Proud, WX2314; 2/11 Bn. Miner; of Kalgoorlie, WA; b. Tuckanarra, WA, 18 Sep 1905.

[6] Maj C. W. Bayly, MC, WX334; 2/11 Bn, and OC 2/8 Ind Coy 1942-43. Accountant; of Perth, WA; b. Kew, Vic, 5 Sep 1916.

[7] Cpl W. H. Pauley, WX695; 2/11 Bn. Labourer; of Wickepen, WA; b. Narrogin, WA, 28 Feb 1915.

[8] Pte D. W. Fitzsimons, WX1043; 2/11 Bn. Public servant; of Victoria Park, WA; b. Perth, WA, 23 Apr 1920.

Honner decided to carry the message back himself, reasoning that there was no need for him to remain now that the attack had ceased; and he was anxious to receive fresh orders personally. He tied the message to his wrist and arranged for two men to follow him at intervals of five minutes to ensure that the message went through. Under hot fire from Perivolia Honner "crawled, wriggled, rolled and zigzagged" across the half mile of open country between the ditch and the nearest houses unscathed; the two who followed him—Warrant Officer Anderson[9] and Private Donaldson[1]—were both hit.

> No smoke was nearer than three miles away (wrote Honner) so the R.M.O., Ryan,[2] who was at the houses [after consultation with Sandover] decided to go out again with a Red Cross flag. Out he marched with his stretcher-bearers using the German light-running, wheeled stretchers—and the enemy ceased firing while he made his half-mile march forward, a bit doubtful whether the Germans would allow him as close to their trenches as our casualties were. He found Willoughby's men all dead . . . looked into the German line and saw it bristling with machine-guns as they waved him away; and brought back our wounded.

As the loss of the two tanks and the shortage of artillery ammunition made a successful daylight attack against Perivolia impossible, Campbell ordered Sandover to assault the village that night.

By this time the 2/11th had exhausted its mortar ammunition and many men were using captured small arms. Sandover planned an attack by two companies astride the road leading into Perivolia from the south-east. Captain Jackson's was to capture the crossroads and exploit to the sea; Captain Wood's to seize the houses east of the road junction and, when it could, to exploit boldly. Lieutenant Royce's[3] platoon was to follow Wood and guard his left and Honner and Gook were to carry out offensive patrols on their own front and attack machine-gun posts on the right, but to withdraw from this exposed position at dawn.

Jackson's company set off in the darkness at 3.20 a.m. on the 28th, but had not gone 400 yards when Greeks opened fire on St. George's, despite a request that they should not fire during the advance. Immediately the head of the Australian column came under heavy fire at short range. However, the company pressed on, gained the crossroads and penetrated along the wadi towards the sea. Wood's company advanced and bombed the houses on the main road, but ran into heavy grenade and mortar fire which wounded Wood, and two platoon commanders, Lieutenants Bayliss[4] and Lee.[5] The responsibility had been placed upon Wood of deciding

---

[9] WO2 D. A. Anderson, WX464; 2/11 Bn. Breadcarter; of Claremont, WA; b. Portree, Isle of Skye, Scotland, 16 Apr 1908.

[1] Pte A. T. Donaldson, WX1050; 2/11 Bn. Tramways employee; of Nedlands, WA; b. Aberdeen, Scotland, 19 Oct 1902.

[2] Lt-Col J. J. Ryan, MC, QX6083. RMO 2/11 Bn; CO 11 Fd Amb 1945. Medical practitioner; of Wooloowin, Qld; b. Brisbane, 11 Jan 1910.

[3] Maj G. E. Royce, MC, WX248; 2/11 Bn. Accountant; of Claremont, WA; b. Katanning, WA, 15 Oct 1917.

[4] Lt H. E. Bayliss, WX942; 2/11 Bn. Newspaper editor and printer; of Moora, WA; b. Moora, 7 Aug 1913.

[5] Lt V. Lee, WX425; 2/11 Bn. Greengrocer; of East Perth, WA; b. Llandilo, South Wales, 18 Jun 1913.

whether the attack could continue or not. At 4.33 Lieutenant Scott,[6] the only unwounded officer, on the orders of Wood, who lay mortally wounded, fired two green Very lights—the signal that the company was withdrawing, and repeated the signal a few minutes later.

The depleted companies to the east of Perivolia were now caught by machine-gun fire on fixed lines.[7] They withdrew before dawn, but of Wood's company only forty-three came back.[8]

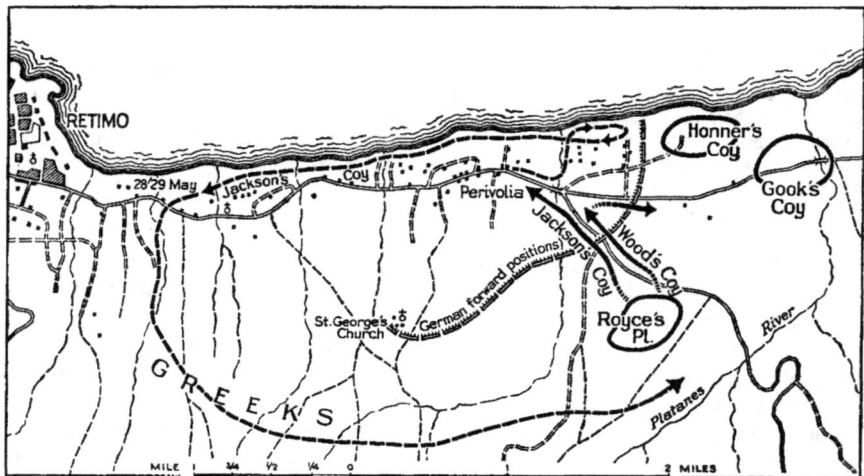

Some of Jackson's men told him that the signal to withdraw had been fired, but neither he nor any of his officers had seen it and he decided not to act on the reports, thinking that perhaps a German signal had been seen. It being then too late to withdraw under cover of the darkness, he decided to occupy houses in Perivolia west of the crossroads and behind the German line, and remain during daylight on the 28th.

There were no Germans in the houses they occupied, although they found signs that some had departed not long before. Soon after dawn a German ran into one house and was captured.[9] An enemy anti-tank gun shelled another, causing the platoon in it to withdraw to a third.

---

[6] Lt H. H. Scott, WX980; 2/11 Bn. Clerk; of Perth, WA; b. Perth, 20 Feb 1917. Killed in action, New Guinea, 3 Jan 1945.

[7] One man was killed and Lt A. C. Stoneham (of North Perth, WA) and four wounded. Of the four, one (Pte C. T. McDonald of Cottesloe, WA), who died later that day, had been previously twice wounded and two (the brothers B. M. and D. R. Rogers) previously once wounded.

[8] Later in the day Capt Ryan, anxious about the wounded men of Wood's company, collected a team of stretcher-bearers and marched again toward the German lines. A German officer levelled a pistol at him and ordered him to stop but he marched on until a German captain arrived who spoke to him in English and took him blindfolded to the German headquarters, where an arrangement was made that trucks (which would have to pass through the German lines) would take a load of equal numbers of seriously wounded Australians and Germans to Suda Bay. The first truck went along the road that evening but was turned back at the German lines.

[9] Sandover interrogated this prisoner, who stated that all the men in his aircraft had come down in the sea and, so far as he knew, he was the only survivor. He and a friend had thrown their weapons away when Bedells' tank got so close on the 27th and were about to surrender when the tank was halted.

Early in the afternoon the enemy severely bombed one house but no attack followed; all the occupied buildings were kept under frequent machine-gun fire from St. George's Church and the seaward flank, but although the walls were perforated and men were half-choked with dust, none was hit by this fire. Jackson decided to withdraw after dark not west or south, as he thought the enemy would expect, but along the wadi to the beach and thence break through the enemy line eastwards along the beach. Jackson had no means of communicating with battalion headquarters, but that headquarters could assess where he was by the firing which had gone on all day. Sandover judged that he would try to break out in the darkness, and, accordingly, the artillery opened fire on the forward German posts as soon as it was dark—and used up most of its remaining ammunition on this task. About 9 p.m. Jackson's company moved off with one wounded man on a stretcher and others walking in the middle of the column. They reached the beach undetected and moved along it crouching until the leaders neared a wrecked aircraft which the enemy used as a strong point. There two machine-guns opened, and the Australians took cover by lying in the water under shelter of a slight bank.

After a quarter of an hour this fire ceased. Jackson decided that he would lose many men if he continued to advance eastward with enemy machine-guns on his flank; he would therefore turn about and withdraw through the rear of the German area. They moved west, coming under fire only once, until they reached the outskirts of Retimo where, now extremely weary, they took shelter in a large villa for the night. Next morning two of the wounded, including Sergeant Hutchinson,[1] who afterwards died, were too ill to move, whereupon Jackson left them at the villa with a medical orderly, Private Whyte,[2] and one other man who was to seek medical aid from Retimo; the others crossed the road, bringing their prisoner with them, moved into the foothills and circled round the south of the German area, reaching their battalion about midday on the 29th. Of some seventy men who had gone into the attack about twelve had been wounded.

After the failure of this attack, Campbell decided that he had not enough men to risk another thrust against enemy troops who were so far from the airfield, the protection of which was his main task. It was on the night of the 2/11th's attack (27th-28th) that the lighter arrived from Suda Bay under Lieutenant Haig, carrying two days' rations for the Retimo force. Haig, who was known to the force at Retimo, having ferried supplies there before the attack, had orders to march across country to Sfakia after delivering the rations; but it will be recalled that he had left Suda before receiving Freyberg's message to Campbell that the whole force was to withdraw. When Freyberg asked Cairo to have a message dropped to the garrison, the following was written:

---

[1] Sgt S. M. Hutchinson, WX1051; 2/11 Bn. Municipal clerk; of Geraldton, WA; b. Geraldton, 21 Jan 1918. Died of wounds 15 Jun 1941.

[2] Pte A. Whyte, MM, WX970; 2/11 Bn. Orchardist; of Perth, WA; b. Edinburgh, Scotland, 10 Sep 1909.

We are to evacuate Crete. Commence withdrawal night 28-29. Leave parties to cover withdrawal and deceive enemy. If liable to observation move only by night and lie up by day. Embark Plaka [Plakias] Bay east end night 31st May-1st June. Essential place of embarkation be concealed from enemy and therefore you should be in embarkation area and concealed by first light 31st May. Make best arrangement you can for wounded. Most regrettable we can do nothing to help you in this respect. Hand prisoners over to Greeks. You and your chaps have done splendidly. Evacuation is due to overwhelming enemy air superiority in this sector. Cheerio and good luck to you.

On the 28th aircraft dropped some cases of food and ammunition at Retimo and may have dropped this message too. If so it was not picked up. On the 29th, presumably in the dark, a slang message understandable by Australians, was dropped to the Retimo force ordering the garrison to fight its way out to the south coast.[3] Later a second message was sent— the Hurricane that carried it did not return. None of these missives reached the force at Retimo, where no friendly aircraft appeared in daylight after 25th May. The No. 9 wireless set at Retimo was working perfectly on the 28th and 29th but the sets at Freyberg's headquarters appeared to have gone off the air.

After dusk on the 29th Major Hooper, who had been with the Greeks on the eastern flank, reported to Campbell that the Greeks declared that a large German force was advancing from the east—the direction of Heraklion. Soon afterwards the Greeks learned that Maleme and Heraklion were in German hands and the four Greek battalions began to withdraw into the mountains. Having received no permission to leave his post, Campbell at once ordered the whole of the 2/11th to occupy the position the 4th Greek was abandoning, but at Sandover's request he agreed that one company (Honner's) be left on the ridge overlooking the Germans in Perivolia, and that the artillery be left on Hill "B". German light artillery began ranging on the Platanes road junction in the late afternoon. At midnight Greeks brought news that Germans were arriving from the west and that 300 motor-cyclists had entered Retimo.

Campbell's only source of news from outside his own area was now the B.B.C., which announced that the situation on Crete was "extremely precarious". There was only enough food to last one more day. In the hope that naval vessels would arrive and remove his force, Campbell had ordered the patrol that policed the beach at night to signal the letter "A" out to sea every twenty minutes, but there had been no reply. Next morning at 6 o'clock Honner's company, again on the left flank watching Perivolia, reported that they could hear what sounded like many motor-cycles, warming up beyond Perivolia, and that the ridge they held was under artillery and mortar fire. About 9.30 three tanks appeared on the left of the 2/11th followed by a procession of about thirty German motor-cyclists, accompanied by some light field guns. A little later Campbell

---

[3] The message was: "Waratahs Bulli Puckapunyals St Kilda Gropers Albany Bogin Hopit." Waratahs would be understood to mean New South Welshmen, Puckapunyals Victorians and Gropers West Australians. Bulli, St Kilda and Albany are all seaside towns south of the capital cities of their States. "Bogin Hopit" may be translated "Fight your way out; get moving".

was informed that German tanks were behind the 2/11th and in the valley behind Hill "D".

Campbell decided that he could now carry out his task—to deny the airfield to the enemy—for only an hour at the most and only at heavy cost. The fact that Lieutenant Haig had been ordered to Sfakia suggested that Sfakia was the embarkation point; it was three days' journey away and his force could not possibly reach it. His men had been on half rations for three days and now had food only for that day, and it seemed to him unfair to make for the mountains and rely on the Cretan villagers to feed so large a force, specially as the Germans had dropped leaflets threatening to shoot any who helped the British. "The only hope," he wrote later, "would be every sub-unit for itself, which would, I knew, result in many being shot down, because, though olive trees are excellent cover from aerial observation, their widely dispersed bare trunks offer little protection against ground observation. I considered that the loss of many brave men to be expected from any attempt to escape now, and the dangers and penalties to which we must expose the Cretan civilians, were not warranted by the remote chance we now had of being evacuated from the south coast."

Campbell told Major Ford and Major Bessell-Browne,[4] his artillery commander, that he proposed to surrender, and they agreed. He then telephoned Sandover, told him that further resistance would result in useless waste of lives and asked his opinion. Sandover, who had not heard that the Germans were advancing from Heraklion, asked whether there was news from there, because, if Retimo surrendered, the Germans advancing from the west might surprise the force at Heraklion. Campbell said that he thought "the show had packed up there". Sandover said that he proposed to tell his men to destroy their arms and make for the hills. During this conversation heavy fire was being exchanged between the German force and Honner's company blocking the road from Perivolia.

With his company only some forty strong Honner had been ordered, on the evening of the 29th, again to take over the position on the western ridge; he was given some men of the anti-aircraft platoon under Lieutenant Dundas[5] to increase his numbers. As Sandover had ordered him to withdraw if attacked by overwhelming forces, Honner left his group in the Platanes wadi, with a Bren gun guarding the bridge, to cover his line of withdrawal. The remainder—his headquarters men, one platoon of twelve men under Corporal Cunnington,[6] and the anti-aircraft men under Lieutenant Dundas—he led forward to the ridge and deployed in the houses and between these and the sea. When the German tanks and infantry attacked after an hour's bombardment, Corporal Young[7] and three

---

[4] Maj I. J. Bessell-Browne, MBE, WX8; 2/3 Fd Regt. Managing agent; of Perth, WA; b. South Perth, 30 Oct 1910. (Son of Brig-Gen A. J. Bessell-Browne, CRA, 5 Div 1st AIF.)

[5] Lt K. I. Dundas, WX781; 2/11 Bn. Bank clerk; of Kalgoorlie, WA; b. Katanning, WA, 7 Mar 1914.

[6] Cpl E. A. Cunnington, WX941; 2/11 Bn. Farmer; of Moora, WA; b. Albany, WA, 3 Feb 1913.

[7] Cpl J. T. Young, WX1860; 2/11 Bn. Truck driver; of Bassendene, WA; b. York, WA, 15 Nov 1914.

men posted on the road on the left flank held their fire until the tanks were close, then blazed at them with their Bren gun so fiercely that the tanks swerved off the road on to the hillside to the south where a line of motor-cycle machine-gunners were now pouring fire into the Australian position. The Germans began to advance south of the road towards the Wadi Platanes. Seeing that he might be cut off Honner ordered a withdrawal, led his headquarters and the anti-aircraft men east along the beach and ordered Cunnington to fight his way back to the remainder of the company; this they did "leap-frogging in perfect tactical style, one group blazing at the Germans (who were held on the hill south of the road) while another streaked past to the next patch of shrubbery". After Cunnington's men reached the Wadi Platanes the whole company withdrew through the dust and smoke of the bombardment by artillery, mortars and machine-guns.

When Honner at length reached battalion headquarters Sandover was conferring with the other company commanders, having just spoken to Campbell on the telephone and told him that he was in favour of making for the hills. The spirited resistance offered by the handful of men in the Platanes-Perivolia road had delayed the enemy advance but two tanks were approaching the front of the battalion; those men who still had ammunition were firing at them. Sandover instructed his officers

that all men should be told there was no known chance of rescue nor source of food, and then be given the choice of surrendering or going. If they wanted to go they'd better go quickly as the back road might be cut.

He added that the sector commander had been informed of this and had wished them good luck. "I am going myself," said Sandover, "we'll think what to do when we get out of this." The battalion area was now under heavy fire from the tanks—although most of it went over the heads of the forward troops. The German gunners were shouting: "The game's up, Aussies!"

Major Heagney,[8] the second-in-command of the battalion, who, though still in poor health, had managed to rejoin the battalion from hospital, and a number of other officers decided to remain. Sandover then left with a party of officers and other ranks. This group halted in a gully behind the Greeks who were concentrating south of the Adhele road. Here others, including Honner, caught up.

My party (Honner wrote) must have been the last organised group to leave the battalion area. It included three men wounded in the morning fight and we were joined by Private Shreeve,[9] wounded in the arm eight days earlier, who left the dressing station with his arm in a sling to be with us. When we caught up the main body I found I was the only man with a map—a Greek map and it was our standby for the next three months.

---

[8] Maj B. S. Heagney, WX22; 2/11 Bn. Accountant; of South Perth, WA; b. Victoria Park, WA, 22 Jun 1906.
[9] Pte R. H. Shreeve, WX6136; 2/11 Bn. Miner; of Kalgoorlie, WA; b. Williams, WA, 29 Apr 1917.

Among those who arrived at this stage was Lieutenant Murray,[1] whose pioneer platoon had been working in Retimo when the attack opened and who had led it back through the hills to the battalion. While in Retimo he had heard a naval officer speak of landing craft at Ayia Galini on the south coast. Sandover distributed regimental funds and a few biscuits and the men then split into two main groups, one led by himself and one by Honner.

Campbell on Hill "D" had ordered Lergessner to make a white flag and display it, and at the same time he sent messages by telephone or by runner to all units and sub-units informing them of the surrender and telling them to display white flags and assemble at the north-west corner of the airfield. A quarter of an hour later, as the German fire continued, he himself tied a towel to a stick and walked down the track towards the airfield. At the time of the capitulation some 500 German prisoners, including their force commander, were held by the Australians, but were then liberated. The Australians had lost about 120 killed;[2] but some 550 Germans had been buried and it was believed that their total loss considerably exceeded that number.

As the defenders had learnt when Colonel Sturm was captured, the German force that attacked Retimo consisted of the *2nd Parachute Rifle Regiment* with two instead of its normal three battalions. Its task was to capture the harbour and landing ground. Sturm, a paratroop leader of 52 years, who had commanded the regiment in the attack at Corinth, divided his force into three groups. Major Kroh with the *I/2nd Battalion* less two companies, but with a machine-gun company and heavy weapon detachments added, was to land east of the airfield and capture it; Sturm and his headquarters would come down with one company and two platoons between the airfield and the Wadi Platanes; Captain Wiedemann with the *III/2nd Battalion,* two troops of artillery and a company of machine-gunners would land between the Wadi Platanes and Perivolia and take Retimo.

Major Kroh's battalion was landed on the coastal plain east of the airfield except for himself and his headquarters and one company who were put down three miles to the east, beyond Refuge Point, on ground so rocky that many men were disabled while landing. Two companies landing close to the airfield immediately came under fire from well-concealed positions on Hill "A". All the officers of one company were killed and both companies lost very severely before the men could reach the weapon

---

[1] Maj J. D. Murray, OBE, WX244. 2/11 Bn; BM 19 Bde 1943-45. Audit clerk; of East Fremantle, WA; b. Fremantle, WA, 15 May 1918.

[2] The battle casualties in the Australian battalions were:

	Killed	Wounded	Unwounded Prisoners
2/1 Bn	43	64	511
2/11 Bn	53	126	423

In Crete, as in Greece, the 2/11th sustained heavier battle casualties than any other Australian battalion.

containers. Kroh hurried west with the company landed near Refuge Point, and collected the remnants of the machine-gun company and two companies (*10th* and *12th*) of the *III/2nd Battalion* which had been dropped wrongly in this area. "These elements (of *III/2nd Battalion*)," states the German account, "found themselves among strongly occupied enemy positions [the company of 2/1st Battalion, platoon of 2/1st Machine Gun Battalion and gunners of 2/3rd Field Regiment on Hill "A"] and, fighting in small groups against superior forces, were mostly destroyed." With this force—what was left of his own battalion and about half of Wiedemann's—he had by about 6.30 p.m. a firm foothold on Hill "A". He planned to attack the airfield next day.[3] (It seems probable that the survivors of the German companies who clung on to Hill "A" were chiefly responsible for the success; and that the arrival of Kroh's group only confirmed it.)

Of Wiedemann's *III/2nd Battalion* only *9th* and *11th Companies,* the artillery troops and the heavy weapons were landed correctly. Wiedemann collected these and advanced west under "constant flanking fire from the heights south of the road". He occupied Perivolia and thrust into the outskirts of Retimo. The German account states that he was strongly counter-attacked from the south-west and was fired on by artillery from that direction (actually there were no guns there). Withdrawing his detachments from Retimo, he organised a "hedgehog" position about Perivolia and beat off the enemy. It therefore appears that it was chiefly the Cretan police who repulsed the western battalion of the German force and confined it in Perivolia.

The escort of Sturm's headquarters—*2nd Company* of Kroh's battalion and heavy weapon detachments—mostly jumped into strongly-held positions (those of the 2/11th), and was "completely destroyed". Sturm himself with a few men landed north of the road and was unable to get into touch with the other groups.

At 5 a.m. on the 21st (according to the German account) Kroh on Hill "A" experienced a strong British attack from the west—the Wadi Bardia—but beat it off. (This was Channell's attack; the starting time was actually 5.25 a.m.) About 9 a.m. he was attacked again (by Moriarty's force), his flank was enveloped and he was forced to retire east to the Olive Oil Factory where he reorganised and beat off repeated attacks. The German account adds: "In a daring storm troop undertaking, 56 parachute riflemen captured by the British were rescued from captivity." (It has been impossible to discover any foundation for this report.) Wiedemann's group, though severely bombed by its own aircraft, extended its defensive position at Perivolia and repulsed "enemy counter-attacks and shock troop operations" (evidently by the 2/11th Battalion).

---

[3] The companies in a German regiment are numbered consecutively throughout the regiment. *Companies 1* and *4* of *I/2 Bn* (the first battalion of the *2 Regt*) were those that landed east of Hill "A" and had now virtually ceased to exist. Kroh, according to the German account, had led the survivors of *3 Company* and the machine-gun company, plus *10* and *12 Companies* (of the *III, 2 Bn*), which were landed in his area in error, in a successful attack on Hill "A".

Thus the remnants of the *III/2nd Battalion* were penned in the solid houses of Perivolia, and those of the *I/2nd* in the equally strong Olive Oil Factory. A supply point for the troops in the factory was established on hilly ground near the coast five miles to the north-east, with a detachment to defend it against "Greek troops and guerillas" who were active there and wherever else the Germans ventured inland. (The German account does not record the expulsion of the Kroh group from the Olive Oil Factory, and the surrender of most of the survivors of that group.)

On the night of the 27th-28th a force consisting of a motor-cycle battalion, several detachments of artillery and one mountain reconnaissance detachment, commanded by Lieut-Colonel Wittman, set off from the Suda area towards Retimo. It broke the resistance of strong rearguards at Meg Khorafia but made slow progress until other mountain troops had taken Vamos. It reached Retimo on the afternoon of the 29th and, driving off strong enemy forces (Cretan police and Greek infantry) east of the town, joined Wiedemann's group at Perivolia. That evening Wittman was reinforced by two tanks (of the *II/31st Armoured Battalion*). On the 30th it attacked "a strong enemy group" (actually a platoon and a few more of the 2/11th) east of Perivolia. "As the result of the artillery bombardment and of the advancing tanks and motor-cycle rifles some 1,200 Australians surrendered"; and Kroh "surrounded by the enemy at the factory" was "liberated". (In fact, as already mentioned, Kroh and some officers and men had slipped away from the factory on the night of the 25th-26th, and the factory and the eighty officerless men remaining had been in Australian hands since the 26th.)

The Germans found the Australians "not in any way dispirited. They are friendly and calm and simply declare: 'We do not want any more,' just as if they had given up a sporting test match." A German account records a conversation between an "excellent colonel" (Campbell) and a German major who "led the conversation into other fields"—the German cause and why kindred nations should fight. Campbell's cool and tactful replies persuaded the ardent German that "it was hopeless; the fight must be carried to a finish; God's iron plough, war, must tear up man's earth before the seed of the future can grow".[4]

At Retimo two highly-trained parachute battalions floated down on ground occupied by two somewhat depleted but high-spirited and expert battalions of Australian infantry, which were supported by about 3,000 Greeks, mostly ill-armed and untrained but including a fine improvised unit of 800 Cretan police. The German landing was muddled, with the result that the attacking force was in confusion early on the second day, its elderly commander and his plans captured, and a large number of his men killed or made prisoner. The surviving Germans were in two groups —one to the east grimly on the defensive, the other penned between the

---

[4] These quotations are from *Gebirgsjager auf Kreta*, translated by Lt B. de B. McGeoch, 2/7 Bn, when a prisoner in Germany.

left Australian battalion and the resolute Cretan police. In retrospect it seems that the afternoon and night of the 21st were critical. If on that day more coordinated use had been made of the valiant but ill-organised Greeks and the attack had been pressed, not frontally along the open road but along the foothills, the small force of Germans in Perivolia would probably have been overcome. Possibly Campbell would have achieved fuller coordination if he had set up a brigade headquarters and not, devotedly, given himself the double task of commanding both the force as a whole and his own battalion. To have overcome the Germans in Perivolia and opened the road to Suda would not have affected the outcome in Crete, but it would have enabled the Retimo force to receive news from Freyberg, and perhaps to have marched to the south coast for embarkation.

The differing responses of the two commanding officers when defeat was certain are specially interesting in view of later experiences of other parts of the A.I.F. Campbell, the regular soldier, kept his unit together and surrendered it as an intact body of troops still under his command. Sandover, the citizen soldier, advised his men to scatter and try to escape, and as a result 13 officers and 39 other ranks of his battalion reached Egypt; it seems that 2 officers and 14 others of the 2/1st Battalion escaped. In other connections the propriety of each course of action has been discussed at length, and in any group of soldiers there will probably always be some who would approve one course and some another.

CHAPTER 13

HERAKLION — DEFENCE AND EMBARKATION

At Heraklion Brigadier Chappel commanded a force which, like the other garrison, was short of artillery but was relatively very strong in both the quality and quantity of its infantry. To three British regular battalions, at full strength or near it, had been added the 2/4th Australian (which had emerged from Greece about 500 strong and had since received a batch of reinforcements), and the 7th Medium Regiment armed as infantry. There were also three raw Greek battalions. Thus there was nearly enough infantry for a division, but Chappel had only thirteen obsolescent field guns, fourteen anti-aircraft guns, and two heavy tanks and six light ones. His task was to hold the port and the airfield.

The port was the outlet for the largest area of continuous settlement in Crete—the wide saddle lying between the 8,000-foot mountain which the ancients called Ida on the west and, some 25 miles to the east, a lower mountain, Dicte, where the ancients believed that Zeus was born. Heraklion itself was a walled town of about 36,000 inhabitants—larger than Canea, the capital; it is indicative of the relative fertility of the wide Heraklion depression that Knossos, the centre of early Minoan civilisation, lay in this upland valley on the slopes three miles south of the modern town. Above the ruins of the palace of Knossos towered the bare, grey peak of Dicte; on the lower ridges and in the valleys the modern villagers grew grain, vines and olives.

The airfield lay on the coastal plain about three miles east of the town, and thus Brigadier Chappel faced a problem that resembled Colonel Campbell's at Retimo—to defend a town and its harbour, an airfield some distance east of it, and the intervening beach on which attackers might be landed from the sea. The defending force was dispersed over an area four miles from east to west and two from north to south. On the right the 2/Black Watch occupied the airfield and the heights to the south-east,[1] next to the left the 2/4th was on and around smooth twin hills which the Australians named the Charlies,[2] so littered with large boulders that the men built sangars to fight from and trenches only for shelter. Next were the 2/Leicesters (in reserve) and the 2/York and Lancasters who linked with the Greek brigade (one trained garrison battalion and two of recruits) which occupied the town itself. On the coastal ledge north of the two last-named British battalions the 7th Medium Regiment, organised as a small infantry battalion with three rifle companies, held the Nea Alikarnassos area round brigade headquarters. Twelve Bofors guns were sited round the airfield and nine 100-mm and four 75-mm guns grouped south-

---

[1] The 2/4th was on the right until 10 May when it changed places with the Black Watch in order to place a better equipped unit on that flank to guard against a possible landing on the beaches to the east.

[2] An Australian slang term meaning breasts.

west of it.³ Chappel instructed the anti-aircraft gunners to fire when they saw fit, but ordered all other troops to remain concealed until the preliminary air bombardment had ended. The gunners were ordered not to fire on the airfield until directed, Chappel's intention being to give this order only if troop carriers landed in strength or the anti-aircraft guns were knocked out. The Leicesters had been given the task of counter-attacking paratroops if they landed on the airfield, or south and west of it between the Charlies and the low ground forward of them and to the north-west. A heavy tank was hidden at each end of the airfield, and the six light tanks were disposed south-east of it. Chappel's orders to the infantry were to attack the enemy the moment he landed.

From the 12th onwards German aircraft bombed the Heraklion area intermittently. On the 13th bombers were overhead at dawn, and again at 6 p.m. when a single Gladiator attacked five German bombers and led them down to within range of the Bofors guns. The gunners failed to score a hit on that occasion, but shot down one bomber in a raid later that day. On the 14th about forty aircraft attacked and were met by two Hurricanes that had arrived at Heraklion the night before. One made a forced landing, the other was not seen again. On the 16th and 18th German aircraft machine-gunned the area; about this time a lone reconnaissance aircraft was shot down by a Bofors gun of the 7th Australian Battery. These attacks caused very few casualties, the defenders being securely dug in and well concealed, and having overhead protection. Indeed, they proved of value to the defenders by testing the effectiveness of their positions and adding to their confidence.

On 19th May a group of German aircraft machine-gunned the Heraklion area early in the morning, and a smaller group in the evening. Next day the attacks began early and were far heavier. By 11 a.m. the defenders knew that paratroops had landed on the main body of Creforce round Suda Bay and, weary but confident, awaited the attack that would certainly soon fall on them. About 4 p.m. forty or fifty bombers, dive bombers and fighters arrived and began a noisy and sustained onslaught, evidently the

---

³ Details of Heraklion force were:
HQ 14 Inf Bde
2/Black Watch (867 offrs and men)
2/York and Lancs (742)
2/Leicester (637)
2/4 Aust Bn (550)
7 Med Regt (450, armed as infantry)
Detachment 3 Hussars (6 light tanks)
Sqn 7 Royal Tank (2 "I" tanks)
234 Med Bty (13 field guns)
Two tps 7 Aust LAA Bty (8 Bofors)
Tp 156 LAA Bty (4 Bofors)
2 Secs "C" HAA Bty, RM (four 3-in AA guns and some pom-poms)
Sec 42 Fd Coy RE
Det 189 Fd Amb
One Greek Garrison Bn
3 Greek Recruit Bn
7 Greek Recruit Bn

There were some RAF men at the airfield. The British battalions were fully armed. The 2/4th had consisted of only three rifle companies until 11 May when 3 officers and 129 men, who had been left at Suda because they lacked weapons, rejoined, enabling the fourth rifle company to be re-formed. Besides its rifles and one Bren or sub-machine-gun to a section, the battalion had three 3-inch mortars minus base plates, six carriers and four Vickers guns.

The Australian light AA battery was commanded by Maj J. A. Hipworth (of Kerang, Vic).

prelude to a landing of paratroops. For more than an hour the area was ceaselessly bombed and machine-gunned by aircraft which came so low that more than one flew below a strand of barbed wire which the troops had strung tautly between the two Charlies.[4] The noise was stunning; the bombs, falling at intervals of a few seconds or less, made the ground quake; but again few men were hit. In the 2/4th Battalion no man was struck by a bomb fragment or a bullet fired from the air during the whole operation at Heraklion.

It was 5 o'clock, after a short lull in the attack, when the first slow troop-carrying aircraft appeared from the north and north-east. As the first lines of parachutes fell and opened the alarm was given, in some areas by the beating of an improvised gong and elsewhere by shouts of "Parachutists!" For two hours, at intervals of about twenty minutes, one group of transports after another arrived and dropped its cargo of men and arms from a sky now clear of fighters and bombers, until more than 240 aircraft (Ju-52's) had been counted—enough to carry more than 2,000 men and their equipment.

I was spellbound by the futuristic nature and the magnificence of the scene before me (wrote one young soldier[5]) . . . . It wasn't long before they were coming in along about five miles of coastline and as far as the eye could see they were still coming. They were about 100 feet above the water and rose to about 250 feet as they came over the coastline, dropped their parachutists, dived again and turned back to sea . . . . I saw many Huns drop like stones when their parachutes failed to open. I saw one carried out to sea trailing behind the plane with his parachute caught in the tail. The men all had black 'chutes; ammunition and guns were dropped in white ones.

The Australians' Bofors, the Marines' 3-inch guns and pom-poms, and the infantrymen's machine-guns, hit and brought down at least fifteen aircraft. The Australians considered their guns to be "sited to perfection". One German aircraft caught fire as the men were jumping, and each dropping parachute vanished in a little puff of smoke, its passenger hurtling to the ground. The troops jumped from another as it was losing height, and all hit the earth before their parachutes opened. Many were shot as they floated down. Probably more than 200 of the attackers were killed in the air or as they struck the ground. Most appeared to land round the airfield or west of the town on Buttercup Field—precisely where landings had been considered most likely; but others, including the earliest waves, tumbled down in East Wadi, on the Charlies, round the Greek Barracks south-west of the Charlies, at Nea Alikarnassos, or to the west of Heraklion. At 7.20, after a renewal of the bombing, men were seen dropping two or three miles east of East Beach far outside the fortress area.

All the battalions promptly attacked the invaders, and most of the paratroops who had landed in the infantry areas were picked off by the defenders before they could rally and collect their gear. The Black Watch (Major Pitcairn[6]) soon cleared the airfield except for a few snipers and

---
[4] None were caught by it and eventually it was broken by a bomb explosion.
[5] Cpl N. M. Johnstone (of Taree, NSW).
[6] Lt-Col A. A. Pitcairn; 2/Black Watch. Regular soldier; of Edinburgh; b. Edinburgh, 9 Mar 1901. Killed in action 20-21 Nov 1941.

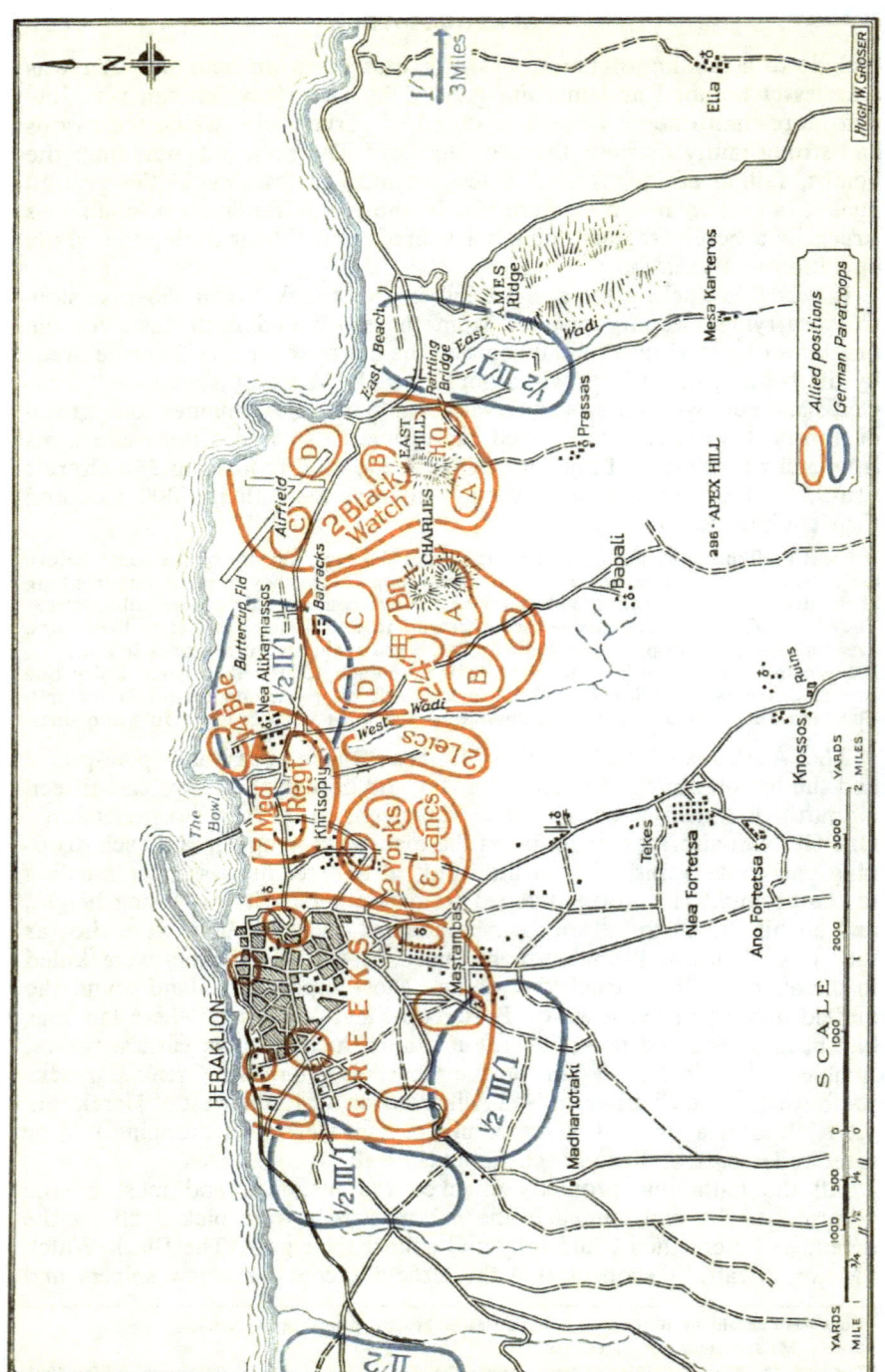

Evening, 20th May

some men who installed themselves at the barracks; the Scots also advanced east of East Hill and cleared East Wadi. All but a few of the group which descended round the barracks were eliminated by Captain Rolfe's company of the 2/4th, which killed about ninety for a loss of three Australians killed and nine wounded. In the 7th Medium Regiment's area a German lobbed a grenade into the headquarters, severely wounding the commanding officer, Major Snook.[7] The gunners of 234th Medium Battery killed 175.[8] Seldom was quarter given on either side.

At 6.15 Chappel ordered a counter-attack towards Buttercup Field by the carrier platoon of his reserve battalion—the Leicesters—and a platoon of the York and Lancasters, and the area was freed of paratroops by 9.30 p.m. All night there was intermittent rifle and machine-gun fire throughout the eastern area and much firing of flares by groups of Germans trying to assemble their scattered men. Still farther east was the 220th "Air Ministry Experimental Station" (a radio-location post) guarded by a platoon of the Black Watch; at dawn the post was abandoned and its men set off to rejoin their battalion. In the early morning the outposts of the Black Watch, mistaking the blue of the approaching air force uniforms for German grey, fired on them; they did not reach safety until the evening.

In the Greek area, however, though the paratroops who landed in the outpost positions had been quickly subdued, some who descended close to the town walls managed to force an entry through the North and West Gates. Throughout the night there was bitter fighting in the streets, the Greeks, soldiers and civilians alike, attacking the invaders with any weapon that came to hand. The Greeks were reinforced by a detachment of the York and Lancasters. By 10.30, however, a party of Germans had reached the quay, and by morning others had dug in at the southern edge of the town.

Nevertheless, in spite of the presence of these parties in the town, and of a larger force east of Chappel's position, it was evident on the morning of the 21st that the attack had failed. A considerable part of the German force had been caught and destroyed before it could organise itself. The British and Greek losses had been light; indeed the defenders were now stronger than before, having added to their equipment useful quantities of German arms and ammunition, wireless sets and rations. Henceforward there was not a platoon that did not possess more than its normal quota of weapons.[9]

At dawn next day German reconnaissance aircraft appeared overhead and at 9 o'clock transports began dropping supplies. On this and later days the defenders captured German Very pistols, orders, and signal strips, and were thus able to send messages to the German air crews to drop supplies to them; the Australian battalion, for example, received machine-guns, wireless sets, mortars, a motor-cycle and side car, chairs

---

[7] Maj R. J. B. Snook, DSO; 7 Medium Regt. Regular soldier; b. 8 Jul 1899.

[8] Not all of these gunners were armed. Lt D. H. Millar of the 2/4th found five in a dugout. A man at the entrance had a rifle while the remainder were behind him each holding a large stone.

[9] Gunner K. McK. Robertson (Edenhope, Vic) of the 7th Aust LAA Bty assembled a German 20-mm gun, which was used with some success.

and tables, a tent, and much food and ammunition. They sent most of the German weapons to the ill-equipped Greek battalions. The German air crews at length realised that they were being misled, but the defenders continued to upset the enemy's signals by firing Very lights whenever the Germans on the ground did so.

Meanwhile, at 9 in the morning, the German force in the east supported by light guns advanced towards the Black Watch on East Hill and began to infiltrate on to the eastern end of the airfield; but both there and in East Wadi they made little progress in the face of the defending artillery and small arms fire. A party in the village of Prassas was rounded up; farther west a patrol of the 2/4th moved out to Babali and drove off a small German force; a German party moving towards Heraklion along the Knossos road was repulsed with severe casualties. However, in and around the town itself the enemy was still established; he now held the harbour and was attempting to push eastwards, and the Greeks were running out of ammunition. During the day, however, the Greeks were able largely to rearm themselves with captured weapons and, in the evening, a concerted attack by them reinforced by a platoon from the Leicesters and one from the York and Lancasters cleared practically all Germans from the town. At 5.5 p.m., the Germans received reinforcements—eleven troop carriers dropped their men east of East Wadi. It was evident, however, that the enemy would need more powerful support if he was now to make any impression on the fortress.

We now know that the task of capturing Heraklion had been entrusted to Colonel Brauer with four battalions—the three battalions of his own *1st Parachute Rifle Regiment* and one of the *2nd Regiment,* together with an anti-aircraft machine-gun company and other detachments. Student, the commander of the *XI Air Corps,* complained when the campaign was over that his Intelligence officers had generally estimated the defenders at about one-third of their actual strength. At Heraklion the error may have been even greater, because there were in fact eight battalions in an area in which the Germans planned to land two. Even after the battle the German staff did not know the strength of the force at Heraklion but estimated it at "three British and two Greek battalions with tank detachment".

The *II/1st Parachute Battalion* was to take the airfield by surprise; the *III/1st* to capture Heraklion from west and south-west; the *I/1st* to take the wireless station at Gurnes, five miles east of the airfield; the *II/2nd* to land west of the *III/1st* and assure protection from the west. All formations were to be parachuted simultaneously at 4.15 p.m., which involved leaving Greece in formation at 2 p.m. However, when the transports returned between 10 and 11 a.m. from delivering the first sortie to the Suda area, it was found that many had been destroyed, and others now broke down and cluttered the runways. So greatly had the force of transports been reduced that 600 men of the Heraklion force were left behind. In addition, refuelling was slow, and a blinding dust rose over the airfields. In the general confusion the departure of some groups was delayed as much as three hours and a half, and both fighter and transport formations were dispatched in wrong order and late, so that they arrived at the objective in relatively small groups at intervals from 4 to 7 p.m. The attack aircraft were able to remain over the target only until 5.15 before returning to refuel, and consequently most of the troops were landed without their protection. It was found that the bomber attacks by *VIII Air Corps* "had not destroyed the enemy". At the time the German leaders believed that bombers could "destroy" infantry even though well dispersed and dug in; actually they had inflicted negligible casualties.

The aircraft carrying the *II/1st Battalion* arrived in dribs and drabs, the last contingent being two and a half hours late. Several machines crashed in flames and many riflemen were killed in the air "because of the configuration of the ground, which necessitated jumping at 200 metres"—a relatively long descent. In the easternmost group of this battalion, landed in East Wadi, all the officers except Captain Burckhardt, the commander, were killed during or soon after the landing. At dark Burckhardt had collected from sixty to seventy survivors at the foot of Hill 182 (A.M.E.S. Ridge). His west group (Captain Dunz) landed at the western edge of the airfield (in and round Buttercup Field and the barracks) and—the Germans believed—"was destroyed within twenty minutes" (actually parties of survivors held out longer). Only five men succeeded, by swimming along the coast, in rejoining Burckhardt, whose battalion was virtually destroyed, losing 12 officers and 300 men killed and 8 and 100 wounded.

Of the *I/1st Battalion*, destined for Gurnes, only one company was landed at the right time; two others landed three hours late and the fourth did not leave Greece that day. The battalion occupied the wireless station, which was undefended. When Colonel Brauer and his regimental headquarters came down there at 7.40 he decided to push on, with part of the *I/1st* under Lieutenant Count Blücher, to the airfield, which he believed to be occupied by the *II/1st*. About 12.40 a.m. he reached the eastern slope of the airfield plateau and, to his surprise, encountered strong enemy fire—from the Black Watch. During the night Blücher and one platoon reached the high ground east of the airfield.

The *III/1st Battalion* was landed west and south of Heraklion "late and far extended". It lost men during the landing but the remainder were organised under Major Schulz and advanced to the town wall where they were held by the Greeks. Schulz withdrew his men to the ridge 500 yards westward. Of the *II/2nd Battalion* two companies had to be left behind for lack of aircraft, and the depleted battalion landed in an undefended zone nearly two miles west of Heraklion.

Brauer decided to attack from the east and west early on the 21st. On the east he had a battalion (less one company and less one platoon, both wiped out by Cretan guerillas near Gurnes); on the west, against the ill-armed Greeks, he had one battalion which had lost fairly heavily and a fresh half battalion. Convinced that an attack across East Wadi could succeed only under cover of the dark and that there was not time to reorganise, Brauer sent in his still-scattered companies and platoons piecemeal. One aim was to establish touch with Count Blücher whose platoon was now isolated on the eastern edge of the field. This attack made no impression on the Black Watch who were supported by artillery and mortars, whereas, Brauer complained later, his men had only the support of five heavy machine-guns. Next morning the detachment on the airfield was overcome by tanks, the resolute Blücher being killed, and at dusk Brauer withdrew his force to a defensive position on the western slope of A.M.E.S. Ridge.

Meanwhile Brauer had sent an order by wireless to Major Schulz to "attack airfield Heraklion with all available forces". Schulz did not receive this message, but intercepted a signal from *VIII Air Corps* that Heraklion was to be attacked from the air from 9 to 10 a.m. and decided to follow up this bombardment by attacking at 10.30. He asked Captain Schirmer of the *II/2nd* for assistance and Schirmer sent him a platoon and a section, but said that he could not spare more men for the task of protecting the force against attack from the west (though he was engaged there only with weak guerilla forces). Schulz formed his force into two groups, one (Lieutenant Becker) to penetrate the town through the North Gate and occupy the harbour, the other (Lieutenant Egger) would enter by the West Gate. Egger's group forced its way into the town but counter-attacks thrust it north on to Becker's force which succeeded in capturing an old Venetian fort in the harbour. "About 1600 [1700] hours," says the report of *XI Air Corps*, "a major of the Greek Army offered the surrender of the town, but the British in the town forced the Greeks to fight on and advanced with strong forces from the east and south against *II Battalion* of the *1st Parachute Rifle Regiment*. Because of lack of ammunition the battalion was forced, under cover of darkness, to fall back to its starting place west of the town leaving patrols in touch with the enemy. The absence of a coordinated control of the elements of *III/1st Battalion* fighting on the western wing and *II/2nd* was an important factor in this failure."

This self-criticism confirms the evidence that, from beginning to end, the German commanders under-estimated the strength of the defenders at Heraklion. Nevertheless, even if the German attacks had been coordinated, it is unlikely that the result would have been different. The Black Watch was unshaken by the ill-organised probing in which Brauer spent his already-weakened force; and, even if a Greek officer had surrendered in Heraklion, it is doubtful whether his men would have ceased fighting; and, if they had, the town and harbour would still have been under fire from the York and Lancasters and the 7th Medium on the slopes to the east. In addition Brigadier Chappel had a reserve—the Leicesters—who far outnumbered the Germans in the town.

As it was, on the morning of the 22nd, patrols from the York and Lancasters mopped up the few snipers who remained in the town; during the morning one of the last two snipers in the Greek barracks near the airfield was killed and the other escaped.[1] The Black Watch sent out many patrols and drove the last Germans from the east end of the airfield,[2] but found the enemy positions at Rattling Bridge, in East Wadi, and on A.M.E.S. Ridge too strongly held to be successfully attacked. This caused Brigadier Chappel some concern because the German guns on East Ridge might enfilade the airfield, and he sent a company of the Leicesters to reinforce the Black Watch, thus using a considerable part of his counter-attack battalion for a defensive role. The battalion commander of the Black Watch sent patrols as far south as Apex Hill, and the 2/4th Australian, next to the left, again patrolled as far as Babali, but these manoeuvres left the German positions on A.M.E.S. Ridge unharmed. When Chappel, at 3.50, ordered the Black Watch to attack A.M.E.S. Ridge the reply was given that the Black Watch had not enough troops; it was a task for the reserve. Still another company of the Leicesters was ordered to support the Scottish battalion, but did not arrive until the following day.

During the day such of the enemy dead as still lay within the defended area were buried—in the British area 950 German corpses had been collected by nightfall on the 22nd, and some 300 were piled in the Greek area, but many others lay where they could not be reached without undue risk of coming under fire. During the day at Heraklion itself no attack was made by either side; the Greeks reported that German troops west of the town had driven Cretan women and children in front of them, but had ceased when the Greek commander sent forward a message threatening to kill all his prisoners if the practice was continued.

Throughout the area Greek civilians were mingled with the troops, and increasing numbers of them were now armed with German rifles which they fired with so little discrimination that in some places they were a

---

[1] According to one account the body of a Scottish soldier was found in the barracks with no uniform, suggesting that the last German had escaped in the Scot's dress.
[2] These were probably the survivors of Count Blücher's platoon.

greater menace than the enemy. During air attacks women and children from the town and villages would crowd into the troops' trenches. In the area of the 2/4th, two families lived near Colonel Dougherty's headquarters, and some 200 civilians were in caves in a single company area.

On the 23rd German aircraft were overhead at intervals throughout the day, bombing, machine-gunning and dropping supplies. Early in the day it became apparent that the Germans were concentrating on the east with the intention of securing the airfield, and a report was received that troop-carrying aircraft were landing east of East Ridge. Two companies of the Leicesters who were sent east to make a raid in this direction returned in the evening with the news that the Germans there were not strong in numbers but had a large proportion of machine-guns. Elsewhere too the garrison widened the area under its control. Colonel Dougherty sent Lieutenant Kesteven[3] and his platoon to occupy Apex Hill, a high knoll overlooking Babali and more than a mile outside the perimeter, and thence to watch the movement of German troops in the hill country through which they might be switched from one flank to another.[4]

On the 23rd two encouraging reinforcements were received. About midday two Matilda tanks arrived from Timbakion on the south coast on their way to Suda, and their leader brought news that the 1/Argyll and Sutherland Highlanders (Lieut-Colonel Anderson[5]) were on the way from Timbakion to Heraklion. (The two tanks, with the only Matilda of the Heraklion force still in running order, and two field guns, were loaded on a lighter and sent to Suda Bay.) Early in the afternoon six Hurricanes arrived overhead from Egypt, but the naval anti-aircraft guns, mistaking them for Germans, fired and shot two down. Three then returned to their base, but the sixth landed. Later, during a particularly heavy raid by about fifty German aircraft, chiefly on the town itself, six more Hurricanes arrived, fought the attacking aircraft and finally landed on the field, four of them with damaged tail wheels. Thus few remained serviceable out of these two flights sent from Egypt to attack transports arriving at Maleme.

After a severe bombing raid on Heraklion the Germans to the west sent forward a message that the town would be destroyed unless the Greeks surrendered. The ultimatum was rejected, though the raid had been both destructive and spectacular. Great clouds of yellow and red smoke poured from the dock area where a store of chemicals was hit; and, because of the mounting casualties and the threat of worse to come, the British commander ordered that all civilians must leave the town, and the York and Lancasters took over its defence with two companies in the town itself and a road-block to the west. The Greeks, now reorganised into two battalions each about 1,000 strong, were concentrated round Arkhania with orders

---

[3] Lt K. L. Kesteven, MC, NX4012; 2/4 Bn. Sales statistician; of Strathfield, NSW; b. Belmore, NSW, 22 Jul 1915.

[4] "Too far out to protect the airfield, too close to be allowed to fall into enemy hands, [Apex Hill] brooded over the whole arena of the battle of which the heart as well as the object was the airfield itself." B. Fergusson, *The Black Watch and the King's Enemies* (1950), p. 77.

[5] Col R. C. B. Anderson, DSO, MC. CO 1/A & SH 1940-42. Regular soldier; b. 3 Nov 1901.

to guard the hospital at Knossos, to keep the road open, and to engage in guerilla warfare.

Next day—the 24th—the Germans began to carry out the threat to destroy Heraklion. Bombing began early in the morning and continued at intervals all day. In the morning about forty transports dropped men and supplies south-west of the town. The paratroops landed in the midst of a fight between the 1/Argyll and Sutherland, on its way from Timbakion, and Germans astride the road in that area. The Argylls were far below

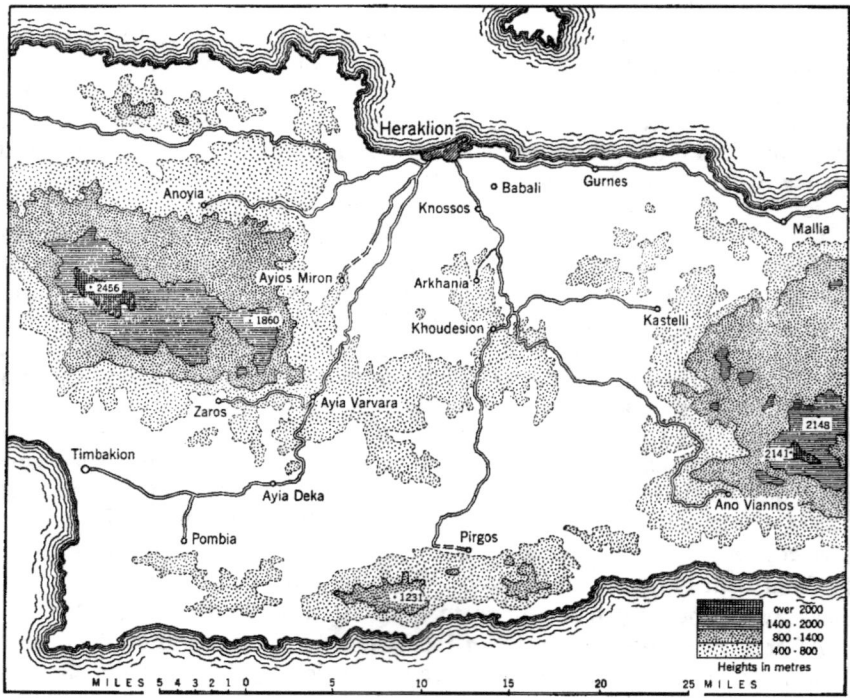

strength, having left detachments at Timbakion and Ayia Deka, and withdrew some distance having lost 2 officers and 20 other ranks. The extremely fluid state of affairs outside the perimeter is illustrated by the fact that, in spite of this repulse, a convoy of lorries carrying chiefly air force men succeeded in travelling along this road to help make a landing ground at Ayia Deka. It was evident that Germans were moving through the hills from west to east, evidently in preparation for an attack from the eastern flank, an impression that was supported by information that aircraft were landing on the beaches at Mallia about 15 miles to the east.

The 25th opened with an attack by the German force west of the town which was repulsed by the two companies of the York and Lancasters and one of the Leicesters. On the 24th an advanced party of the Argyll and Sutherland had entered the fortress area, and on the morning of the

25th the main body (the equivalent of about two companies) arrived, having marched through the hills. They took over the sector which the Leicesters had occupied west of the 2/4th and such of the Leicesters as were not retained in the line became the mobile reserve.

The Argylls soon found themselves in the centre of a confusing action. On the early morning of the 26th, before they had time to find their bearings, a column of about 300 Germans, moving eastward, clashed with them on Cemetery Ridge just east of the town and captured a few of their men. The Leicesters (Lieut-Colonel Cox[6]) counter-attacked along the ridge and restored the situation, although they suffered severely. In the confusion the Argylls, mistaking the Australians to the east of them for the enemy, fired on them until Falla, the cool Intelligence sergeant of the 2/4th, went forward and explained who was who. Soon this strong German column was concentrated between the 2/4th and Kesteven's platoon on Apex Hill.

It will be recalled that Kesteven had been sent to occupy this 1,000-foot hill on the 23rd. On the 24th and 25th the outpost was unmolested, and with a lamp Kesteven signalled information to Dougherty's headquarters. At dawn on the 26th all Kesteven's posts reported the large number of Germans moving eastward through the hills; finally it appeared that some 500 were thrusting towards the wadi west of Apex Hill and 200 approaching the ridge south of it. At 7 a.m. the enemy began advancing against the hill from the north, west and south. Kesteven signalled to his battalion that he was about to fight his way out, as he had been ordered to do in case of heavy attack. He decided to move down the rocky northern face of the hill, form up when he reached the limit of the rocks, and counter-attack the smallest of the groups surrounding him—the German party approaching from the north. After sending ahead most of the platoon under Lieutenant Sargent[7] (who had arrived on the previous day with a ration party) he presently brought up the rearguard of four men and ordered the attack.

As soon as the Australians emerged from the protection of the rocks they met sharp fire from their front and flanks. One man was killed and two, including Kesteven, wounded. Sergeant Swanson[8] took control and, hurling a grenade, led the way straight at some fifty Germans who lay between them and their objective—the lines of the Black Watch. Firing their rifles, the men charged down the hill, overcame the Germans, killing many of them, and reached the shelter of a creek. Only one man was hit despite the fire of fifty more Germans on their left. From the creek they made their way without incident to the Black Watch and thence to the 2/4th.

The German move across the front confirmed their hold on the Knossos road and appeared to be aimed at cutting off the garrison from the south,

---

[6] Brig C. H. V. Cox, DSO, MC. CO 2/Leicester. Regular soldier; b. 22 Apr 1895.
[7] Capt A. H. Sargent, NX70177; 2/4 Bn. Wool classer; of Inverell, NSW; b. Brighton, Eng, 2 Jul 1908.
[8] WO L. R. Swanson, DCM, NX8748; 2/4 Bn. Regular soldier; of Manly, NSW; b. Balmain, NSW, 28 Apr 1918.

whence, the Germans knew, reinforcements had arrived. They were already in control of a British advanced dressing station—which had unwisely been placed outside the perimeter at the Villa Ariadne at Knossos—but did not interfere with the medical work of the station. Indeed, on the evening of the 26th, a German medical officer and stretcher-bearers, carrying a white flag, brought a wounded Highlander and a wounded German into the 2/4th's lines; and Captain Tomlinson,[9] the regimental medical officer, and the German agreed that in future the Germans would carry any severely wounded Australians whom they might find in that area half way across no-man's land and Australian stretcher-bearers would go out and fetch them to their aid post. In this no-man's land, of which Babali village was the centre, there were frequent patrol clashes by day and night and the village itself, a place of twelve or so houses, was often raided by Germans in search of food.

The killing of civilians by Germans in this area, and of Germans by armed civilians and Greek troops fighting guerilla fashion caused anger on both sides. The Australians were convinced that German raiding parties had brutally killed civilians; the Germans, for their part, dropped pamphlets in Greek and English signed "The German High Command" declaring that because of atrocities punishments would be administered "in the manner of his own cruel action, no matter be he or she a man or a woman" and towns and villages would be razed. After this threat Heraklion and Babali were heavily bombed. The pamphlets were as ineffective as paper bombardments invariably are, except when a defending force is already demoralised. Indeed, with a high-spirited force, printed threats or taunts tend to raise its mettle.

Although the British position had not been dented and the enemy gave no indication of being able to mount a concerted attack, Brigadier Chappel had reason to be increasingly anxious about the position in Crete as a whole. On the night of the 26th-27th he sent a message to General Freyberg, by way of Cairo, stating that the enemy was strongly established astride the road leading south, parachute landings were being made outside his reach, all his positions and the aerodromes were commanded by enemy troops on higher ground, and ammunition was running short. He asked for guidance whether he should attack and open the road to the west or south. From Cairo came a request for information whether the Argyll and Sutherland had arrived, whether a break-out to Timbakion could be made, and whether Heraklion harbour could be used. Later on the 27th Chappel was informed that the island was to be abandoned. He did not pass on this information until dawn next day, when he summoned commanding officers to a conference and told them that the whole force was to embark that night. A time-table was distributed and the commanders returned to their units to organise the withdrawal.

That day—the 28th—the enemy was particularly active in the air. About 11.15 a.m. twenty troop carriers and at 11.45 sixty-four dropped

---

[9] Lt-Col P. A. Tomlinson, OBE, NX87. CO 2/11 Fd Amb 1943-44. Medical practitioner; of Epping, NSW; b. Wyong, NSW, 9 Jul 1913.

parachutists east of the perimeter, which was very heavily bombed all day, but no move was made by the men on the ground. Meanwhile the British garrison damaged its vehicles and destroyed its stores; charges timed to explode next morning were placed in the petrol and ordnance dumps; the routes the battalions would follow to the mole were reconnoitred.

In the morning of the 28th, in obedience to the British plan, the cruisers *Orion*, *Ajax* and *Dido* and six destroyers had sailed from Alexandria. From 5 p.m. onward the squadron was heavily attacked and *Ajax* was damaged and ordered to return to port. The remaining ships arrived off Heraklion at 11.30 p.m., the cruisers remaining outside the little harbour, and the destroyers going in four at a time to ferry the troops, the first of whom were waiting at the mole. In the darkness, the force filed through the town to the port, company by company and unit by unit until, about 1 a.m., the last posts were silently abandoned. The town itself, a crowded place of narrow streets and close-set buildings, was in ruins.

Heraklion (wrote Captain Tomlinson) was one large stench of decomposing dead, debris from destroyed dwelling places, roads were wet and running from burst water pipes, hungry dogs were scavenging among the dead. There was a stench of sulphur, smouldering fires and pollution of broken sewers. Conditions were set for a major epidemic.

In this ugly setting the embarkation was carried out with hardly a hitch, though there was much anxiety when, after midnight, the troops still in the forward posts learned that the time-table had been put forward one hour, and they had to hurry along the routes to the town fearful that they would be too late—the Australians knew from their experiences in Greece that the naval ships could not wait. The force sailed at 3 a.m. with all the British troops on board except a detachment guarding the roadblock at Khoudesion, and, of course, the wounded in the German-occupied dressing station at Knossos.[1]

The Greeks were not informed of the embarkation on the ground that the activity of the Germans in their area made it impossible for the orders to be safely conveyed to them and in any event the ships could not carry many more troops. The decision may seem callous when examined from a distance, but it can hardly be disputed that to have attempted to organise the embarkation of the semi-trained Greeks might have endangered the whole delicate operation. It was one task to withdraw to the harbour a force of disciplined troops from defences in which the position of every section of riflemen was known; another to assemble and march back the two Greek battalions which had for some days been operating as a guerilla force.

---

[1] Lt L. F. Howlett (of Scottsdale, Tas), who had been wounded twice but had remained on duty, embarked with the 2/4 Bn. He had been a patrol officer in the New Guinea Administration before the war and later joined the Australian New Guinea Administrative Unit; on 21 Jun 1943 he was killed by the Japanese while leading a two-man patrol in the Markham Valley.

The steering gear of the destroyer *Imperial* failed, a result of bomb damage on the voyage out, and after her crew and her troops had been transferred to the *Hotspur* she was sunk with a torpedo. This was the first of a series of cruel losses. About 6 a.m., as the ships turned into Kaso Strait at the eastern end of the island, about 100 German dive bombers appeared. The weary troops were wakened by the din and concussion of guns. The destroyer *Hereward* was hit and beached and her crew and the troops on board taken prisoner. The cruisers were the chief targets. The *Orion* was hit three times, *Dido* once. In *Orion* about 100 were killed and 200 wounded. In *Dido* 103 out of 240 of the Black Watch on board were killed. The attacks continued at intervals for eight hours and 400 individual dive-bombing attacks were counted.[2]

> These destroyer commanders are out on their own (wrote Corporal Johnstone). As soon as the planes appear overhead you can feel the boat lift out of the water as she puts on speed. Then the deck rolls over at an angle of about 45 degrees. Then back it comes again and down goes the other side as she zigzags, turns and squirms at 40 knots, trying to spoil their aim. Down comes the Stuka and lets his bomb go at about 500 feet. The commander watches the bomb, judges where it is going to fall, turns his boat almost inside out and generally manages to dodge it. Meanwhile every gun is firing all the time and the noise is deafening. The 6-inch and 4-inch guns shake the whole boat and the multiple pom-pom is going like a steam hammer. Four-barrelled multiple machine-guns mounted on each side of the ship add to the general din. Besides all these a lot of our boys had their Brens mounted on deck and were doing their best to add to the row . . . occasionally as the bomb was coming down I glanced at the sailor sighting and firing the pom-pom and I didn't see the slightest sign of emotion on his face, even though the bomb only missed by about three feet and lifted our boat out of the water.

At 2 p.m., as the squadron neared the Egyptian coast, the German attacks ceased, and at 9 p.m. the ships reached the safety of Alexandria.

Although the defenders of Heraklion did not know it, their local success had seriously upset the whole German plan. This provided that part of the *5th Mountain Division* should be landed at Heraklion by sea and air as soon as the paratroops had seized it. The small craft that were to have entered Heraklion harbour were recalled to Piraeus, however, and, from the 22nd May onward, the role allotted to the *1st Parachute Regiment* at Heraklion was not to enable German aircraft to use the Heraklion airfield but to prevent British aircraft from doing so. The Corps commander, General Student, hoped, however, to reinforce Colonel Brauer at a later stage so that at least he might capture the airfield. On the 23rd and 24th the Germans saw seven British fighters and a bomber on the airfield "in spite of intense destructive fire" from their positions on East Hill. On the 24th Brauer was reinforced by a battalion made up of those remnants of the *7th Air Division* that had been left behind on the 20th—two heavy-weapon and two rifle companies, some 400 men in all. The report of *XI Air Corps* states that it was impossible to ascertain whether the paratroop landing ground in the Gurnes area was free of

---

[2] It appears that about 48 Australians of the 2/4 Bn and 2/3 LAA Regt were killed in these air attacks.
  Most of the Australian anti-aircraft gunners were on *Hereward*. One of them wrote afterwards: "Lieutenant Jim Mann of 'B' Troop [Lt J. G. Mann, a Melbourne barrister and Rhodes Scholar] was an inspiration to all on board because of the soldierly way in which he helped organise the 'Abandon Ship', and saw that men had something to keep them afloat. He was one of the last to leave and was drowned. When his turn came all floating material had been used. In the water we were strafed and bombed by a Stuka for a short while. Later an Italian Red Cross plane arrived and kept the Stuka away, by circling round the men in the water. Italian motor torpedo boats took the survivors to Scarpanto and later an Italian destroyer took us to Rhodes."

the enemy, and therefore (to the surprise of the defenders who had guessed that the German plan was to attack from the east) the reinforcements were landed west of Heraklion. "Shortly after landing the battalion engaged in a brief fight with a platoon of British who had advanced towards the landing areas from the south" (the advance-guard of the Argyll and Sutherland Highlanders). "The British were killed or taken prisoner." On the 24th Brauer was ordered by Student to unite the western and eastern group and, with the heavy weapons of the combined force, to prevent the British from using the airfield.

Major Schulz's force moved eastward from Heraklion on the night 25th-26th May over "difficult ground occupied by the enemy". At dawn Schulz "attacked the weakly-held Hill 296 (Apex Hill) . . . from several directions and captured it". From this hill Schulz established contact with Brauer and there his men beat off "counter-attacks by weak enemy forces from the direction of Knossos". (These were Greeks.)

On the 27th yet another improvised battalion formed from the remnants of various units of *XI Air Corps* was landed in the Gurnes area, and Brauer was instructed that, after a preliminary air bombardment, he was to capture the airfield and keep it open for German aircraft. He decided that he had not time to prepare an attack for the 28th but that it should open on the afternoon of the 29th.[3] However, on the night of the 28th, the Germans saw ships off shore; and next morning patrols found the airfield unoccupied and the town empty. The German report adds: "500 prisoners were taken . . . 200 of our own prisoners were set free. Greek forces of approximately 1,000 officers and men still remaining in the eastern part of the island capitulated" (evidently another 1,000 Greek soldiers had either gone into the hills or had prudently become civilians overnight).

From the German point of view the operation against Heraklion had been a series of minor disasters in which one error was piled on another. In the first place the plan was based on faulty intelligence which greatly under-estimated the British garrison. But, even if the defending force had been only one-third as strong, that would not have justified giving Colonel Brauer's force four simultaneous objectives —Gurnes, the airfield, the town, and west flank protection—instead of concentrating it against one at a time. Finally, the tactical error, common to most German paratroop operations on Crete, was made of landing a great part of the attacking force in the midst of a closely-defended area, a practice that proved disastrous where their antagonists were experienced troops, well dug in. And, because no account had been taken of the probability of transports being destroyed and damaged in the first sortie, the second wave was not only seriously under strength but could not maintain its time-table and landed piecemeal.

Having lost nearly half his force in consequence of these errors and omissions on the part of the higher command, Brauer's only opportunity of local success lay in concentrating his force and attacking a single objective—the airfield or the harbour. Instead he kept his forces apart and made ineffective thrusts at both objectives and, having failed, remained inactive until the 24th when he was ordered to concentrate on the eastern flank and keep the airfield under fire. On the 28th, when he was reinforced by two battalions, he was still laboriously concentrating for an attack. It appears that the initial failures and the heavy losses and confusion which they entailed dealt Brauer and his subordinates a shock from which they never fully recovered.

Should the British commander have been more active in the face of an attacker whom he had so thoroughly disorganised? His signal of the 27th to General Freyberg shows that he had considered, among several courses of action, gaining control of the road to the south coast or opening the road to Retimo. Brigadier Chappel's defined task, however, was to hold airfield and harbour. This he did with complete success. After the fight for

---

[3] On the 28th an Italian regiment was landed at the eastern end of Crete from the Dodecanese.

Crete had been lost, a gallant but costly naval enterprise enabled the force to be picked up and taken to Egypt, where, in those days, four good battalions were a reinforcement of greater relative value than a division would have been a year later.

CHAPTER 14

RETREAT AND EMBARKATION

By the morning of 28th May the force at Suda had disengaged and was already distributed along the road which climbed over the island to Sfakia. That road wound up and across Crete's backbone, reaching a height of 3,000 feet. Some seven miles from Sfakia it passed through the upland plain of Askifou, a basin about one mile in width and two in length. Farther on, the road ended a mile and a half from the little beach at Sfakia, and thence only foot tracks led down to the sea. The task of General Freyberg's fighting troops was to hold a series of rearguard positions astride this mountain road, along which a densely-packed column was now retreating, and finally to disengage and embark.

In the morning of the 28th General Freyberg, whose headquarters were now established in the Askifou plain, sent General Weston an order placing all troops in the western sector of Crete under his command. Freyberg informed Weston that 1,000 men were to be embarked that night, 6,000 on the 29th-30th, 3,000 on the 30th-31st, 3,000 on the 31st-1st; the 4th Brigade was to hold a position at the northern entrance to the plain of Askifou until darkness fell on the 29th; an improvised Marine battalion to hold a position south of the plain until darkness on the 31st—the night on which the 5th and 19th Brigades were to embark. Next day the marines and Layforce were to form a final rearguard.

At dawn on the 28th the 5th New Zealand and 19th Australian Brigades, each little stronger than a battalion, were deployed along the Sfakia road from Beritiana, which was only half a mile from Suda Bay, to Babali Inn, about six miles inland. A company of Layforce and two companies of the Maori battalion were astride the road at Beritiana. The 5th Brigade was grouped round Stilos with the 23rd Battalion forward and the 21st, 19th, remainder of the Maori and 22nd echeloned behind. The 19th Brigade was about Neo Khorion, with the 2/8th Battalion astride the road leading up from Kalives and the 2/7th in rear of the New Zealanders on the Stilos road. At Babali Inn, some two miles south of Neo Khorion, was the remainder of Layforce. The two brigades were to withdraw that night.

By 6 a.m. on the 28th the Germans reached the commandos and Maoris at Beritiana and had them under fire; in two hours they surrounded these rearguard companies and were streaming past them towards Stilos. The surviving commandos withdrew through the Maoris' positions at 11 a.m. and at 12.30 Captain Royal[1] began to withdraw his Maoris. They succeeded in fighting their way back to their unit. At 6.30 the German attack reached the 5th Brigade; there it was stopped with severe loss, probably fifty being killed or wounded.

---

[1] Maj R. Royal, MC. 28 (Maori) Bn 1940-41; 2 Maori Bn 1942-43 (CO May-Jun 1943). Civil servant; of Wellington, NZ; b. Levin, NZ, 23 Aug 1897.

About 8 a.m. a large procession of Italian prisoners had moved along the road from the south toward the New Zealand rear carrying white flags. Brigadier Hargest allowed them through his lines in the hope that they would embarrass the enemy. When they reached Stilos they came under German mortar fire and scattered.

About 9 a.m. Hargest and his battalion commanders held a conference (which Brigadier Vasey attended) at which it was decided that their men were not fit to fight all day and march all night, and therefore should begin to move back that day. Vasey agreed, and it was arranged by him and Hargest that, while the 2/7th acted as rearguard, the 5th Brigade headquarters (about 140 men including the band) would march south to Babali Inn and reinforce the line Layforce was holding there. The battalions would then pass through this line to Vrises at the junction of the Georgioupolis and Suda roads, where Hargest hoped to hide his men during the heat of the afternoon. The forward units thinned out and withdrew in good order, the men marching in single file on either side of the road with sections well spread out.

When the 2/8th arrived at Babali about 2 p.m. it took position with Layforce, and Hargest's headquarters moved on to Vrises, followed by the 5th Brigade and the former rearguard, the 2/7th Battalion, which left Babali in the afternoon after having been held in reserve there for some hours. The enemy followed fast and at 1.35 p.m. attacked the Babali rearguard. Until dusk Layforce was under intermittent machine-gun fire, though, throughout the day, for the first time since the 20th, air attack was inconsiderable, probably because the German aircraft were concentrated over Heraklion.

At 9.15 p.m. this rearguard began to withdraw to Vrises. There the 5th Brigade and the remainder of the 19th had assembled early in the afternoon and thence, after a few hours' rest, the New Zealand battalions at 6 p.m. had moved on with the intention of reaching Syn Ammondari, 12 miles away, that night. This necessitated an exacting march up hill to the top of the pass. The men were footsore and very weary. Near Cadiri engineers blew up the road before the rearguard had passed and caused a galling delay to the infantrymen who had to make a difficult detour round the demolition. The 4th Brigade was already deployed at the entrance to the Askifou plain, the 23rd Battalion having established a covering position at Amygdalokorfi.

The 2/7th had marched back to the Askifou plain where it took position just north of Askifou village itself. It was in good heart and in perfect order. As it was marching that night, dispersed in sections on each side of the road, a German aircraft dropped a flare. Walker sent a spoken message along the column that if a flare was dropped again he would blow his whistle and every man would lie face downward off the road. The message was repeated swiftly back along the column and forward again. Another flare was dropped, the whistle blown, and instantly every face was on the ground (where they would not catch the light), every body motionless, and the flare illuminated only an empty road.

The 2/8th was now wearily marching towards the Kerates area, where it arrived about 5 a.m. Layforce followed, withdrawing to Imvros south of the plain.

> According to the German report, in the morning of the 28th May, the *85th Mountain Regiment* after "bloody hand-to-hand fighting" had destroyed two British "medium tanks", captured Stilos, and "made prisoners a British battalion" [evidently a large part of "A" Battalion of the commandos]. It continued the pursuit towards Sfakia, but was held for the remainder of the day. The German commander considered that the defenders would withdraw at dusk, and decided to await this event and continue his advance next morning.
>
> On the 27th and 28th General Ringel, not realising that the main body of the defending force was in retreat southwards towards Sfakia, had ordered the three mountain regiments to thrust eastward towards Retimo. Even on the 29th he detached only the *100th Mountain Regiment* to take up the pursuit towards Sfakia while the *85th* and *141st Regiments* pressed on towards Retimo.

Meanwhile, round Sfakia, General Weston had been preparing for a series of embarkations. Early on the afternoon of the 28th he went to Imvros, where Major Burston[2] commanded a group which included the headquarters of the 2/3rd Field Regiment and other detachments. Weston arranged that Burston should organise about 60 men of the 2/3rd Field Regiment to guide units from the top of the escarpment to the beach. Burston and Captain Forbes[3] reconnoitred the escarpment and disposed their men along a track winding across the Komitadhes ravine and through Komitadhes village, and that night these guides kept the flow of traffic moving steadily to the beach.[4]

At Sfakia that night (the 28th) four destroyers embarked 230 wounded and 800 British troops, including the men of the air force. It was on this

---

[2] Maj V. C. Burston, MBE, VX29; 2/3 Fd Regt. Maltster; of Toorak, Vic; b. Brighton, Vic, 23 Dec 1908.

[3] Maj A. M. Forbes, MC, WX1521; 2/3 Fd Regt. Dry cleaner; of Mount Lawley, WA; b. Northampton, WA, 12 Sep 1914.

[4] Lt-Col Cremor and Capt F. H. Wood of the 2/2 Fd Regiment also commanded control points on this night.

night also that three cruisers and six destroyers took off practically the entire force at Heraklion. The misfortunes of the Heraklion convoy, already related, greatly influenced the decisions that followed these fine achievements. At 9 p.m. on the 28th a force consisting of the cruisers *Phoebe* and *Perth, Calcutta* and *Coventry,* the transport *Glengyle,* and three destroyers left Alexandria to embark troops at Sfakia the following night—the 29th-30th. Major-General Evetts who was to "coordinate the embarkation"— a large task for a newcomer—flew from Alexandria to Cairo on the 29th where he discussed the plans with General Wavell. After consulting also General Blamey and Air Marshal Tedder,[5] Wavell informed Admiral Cunningham that he considered that the Glen ships and cruisers should

not be risked, but that embarkation in destroyers should continue. Thereupon Cunningham consulted the Admiralty, recapitulated his mounting losses, but said that he was ready to continue the evacuation as long as a ship remained. The Admiralty ordered that the *Glengyle* be turned back but the other ships continue. However, this order did not arrive until 8.26 p.m., when the force was approaching Sfakia; Cunningham decided that it was then too late to recall *Glengyle* and informed the Admiralty that instead he was sending three additional destroyers (*Stuart, Jaguar* and *Defender*) to meet her and to rescue troops from any ship damaged by air attack.

Meanwhile plans based on previous arrangements were being made on shore for the first large-scale embarkation from Sfakia. At 2 p.m., at a conference at Vasey's headquarters, Weston ordered that the 4th Brigade, after having held the Askifou rearguard position until nightfall on the 29th, should withdraw to the beaches. By dawn on the 30th, the 19th

---

[5] Marshal of the RAF Lord Tedder, GCB. AOC-in-C RAF ME 1941-43; Air C-in-C Medit Air Comd 1943; Dep Supreme Comd under Gen Eisenhower 1944-45. B. 11 Jul 1890. (Tedder had replaced Longmore early in May.)

Brigade, comprising the 2/7th and 2/8th Battalions, with the marine battalion, and supported by two guns of the 2/3rd Field Regiment, were to occupy a final rearguard position, covered by a rear party comprising the remaining three light tanks of the 3rd Hussars and three carriers of the 2/8th. The rearguard position was near Vitsilokoumos in the hills covering Sfakia. Vasey would probably be responsible for holding this position until the night of the 31st-1st, but there was a possibility that the embarkation would be hastened and the rearguard could embark on the night of the 30th. The 5th Brigade should move to the dispersal area above Sfakia, and Layforce to Komitadhes to cover the exits of a ravine along which the enemy, by-passing the road, might approach the beach from the west.

On the morning of the 29th the 23rd Battalion was holding the entrance to the Askifou plain. At 7.15 a.m. large numbers of Germans were seen advancing towards it. The battalion had been reduced to the strength of only about a company. It had only five officers and, at the end of the day, was commanded by a lieutenant, R. L. Bond.[6] The men were weary, hungry and short of water. Hargest's brigade major, Dawson,[7] solved the water problem by collecting all the glass bottles and other containers he could find in Sin Kares, filling them and sending them forward in a truck.

During the afternoon the enemy edged forward but the battalion withdrew without incident, and from Sin Kares the men were carried back in trucks, of which a few remained. By 9 p.m. they had passed through the 4th Brigade's main rearguard position on the southern edge of the Askifou plain and the 4th had begun to move back. Between 10 and 11 p.m. on the 29th, the 5th, and at daylight on the 30th, the 4th reached the end of the tarred road above Sfakia. In this dispersal area were crowds of men, chiefly base troops, who had lost their units. "The place was literally swarming with men of all sorts," wrote Hargest later, "and nearly all (of) units who had straggled and were now at a loose end, eating up rations and using water that fighting troops needed. Down below on the sea coast it was supposed to be worse." The lack of food and water was now crucial.

During the 29th Burston and Forbes of the 2/3rd Field Regiment had improved their traffic control organisation along the Komitadhes track and had converted it into a "sheeprace", so that "once a man got into the flow of traffic he just could not (and was not allowed to) stop". Later, men who dispersed in the scrub to the west of the ravine during air attack found an old track connecting Sfakia and Askifou and thenceforward a proportion of the men moving down to the beach used this track, but most of them streamed through Komitadhes.

The naval squadron arrived off Sfakia at 11.30 p.m. on the 29th. Men were ferried to the ships in the *Glengyle's* landing craft (three of which she left behind for use in later embarkations) and in two landing craft carried

---

[6] Capt R. L. Bond. 23 NZ Bn 1940-41; enlisted AIF 1942 (Army No. NX149208), served with II Corps as a capt. Brewer; of Adelaide; b. Gympie, Qld, 19 Feb 1908.

[7] Lt-Col R. B. Dawson, DSO. BM 5 NZ Bde 1941 and 1942; 6 NZ Bde 1942-43; Senior Tactics Instr RMC Duntroon 1943-46. Regular soldier; of Lower Hutt, NZ; b. Rotorua, NZ, 21 Jul 1916.

in the cruiser *Perth*. By 3.20 a.m. on the 30th about 6,000 men had been embarked, including 550 wounded, and the squadron sailed. It had been hoped to take more but the small size of the beach, the absence of an extensive dispersal area and faulty control slowed embarkation. On the return voyage the ships were attacked from the air; *Perth* was hit and a boiler room put out of action, but she was not disabled. Puttick and most of his staff were embarked that night. An order from Wavell to Freyberg to embark arrived in time for Freyberg to leave on the 28th, but, as in Greece, he decided that he should not go away until most of the force had been evacuated.

In the rearguard position Vasey had the 2/7th forward astride the road, the weak 2/8th holding a large wadi on the left flank, and the marines in reserve. In support were the two 75-mm guns of the 2/3rd Field Regiment under the resolute Captain Laybourne-Smith[8]—these were the only guns to cross the mountains—and two machine-guns of the 2/1st Machine Gun Battalion under Lieutenant Bolton.[9] The brigade was to hold this position during the 30th and 31st and to embark that night. Forward of the infantry and about a mile north of Imvros the three light tanks of the 3rd Hussars commanded by Major Keith covered a detachment of the 42nd Field Company which was to crater the road in four places when the tanks drew back.

At 5 a.m. the three carriers of the 2/8th Battalion under Sergeant Trethowan[1] joined the tanks. The German advance-guard was attacking as the carriers arrived and one of the tanks had been disabled by a shell. A lively rearguard action followed. Keith told Trethowan that their task was to hold the enemy until 5 p.m. that day. In the pass north of Imvros, Trethowan and three men dismounted and engaged the advancing Germans until Keith ordered him to retire to the village as the enemy's machine-gun fire outranged his. At Imvros a new position was taken up by the tanks and carriers, with two machine-guns under Trethowan forward of them beside the road. After an exchange of fire with a number of German groups, the tanks, carriers and dismounted men moved back beyond a sharp turn and took up a position on the road and on a hill above it and again awaited the Germans.

The enemy came into range with troops in trucks followed by walking personnel (reported Trethowan afterwards). They were an easy target, and the first column when fired upon scampered for cover while their trucks tore down the road and gained cover . . . . The enemy began searching fire with mortars and machine-guns but failed to locate us. A column of marching troops came into range on the road soon after and we dealt with them in a similar manner.

---

[8] Maj G. Laybourne-Smith, MC, SX1456; 2/3 Fd Regt. Architect; of Millswood, SA; b. Adelaide, 21 Feb 1908.

[9] During the next two days Bolton and his men kept his guns in action despite constant mortar and machine-gun fire. Finally one gun was being served by only one man—Pte H. L. Berry (of Echuca, Vic).

[1] Capt J. M. Trethowan, MC, VX6300; 2/8 Bn. Farm hand; of Donnybrook, Vic; b. Preston, Vic, 12 Dec 1912.

German mortar fire at length forced the dismounted Australians off the knoll from which they had been firing, but, accompanied by a tank, they advanced again around a bend in the road and surprised and dispersed a hostile party. Thereafter the enemy ceased to advance along the roads but moved over the hills on the west, whence he fired on the rearguard. At 4 p.m. orders arrived to go back to the beach. In the withdrawal along a road now swept by enemy fire from the left flank two of the little party of Australians—Sergeant Cooper[2] and Private Marshall[3]—were wounded. The carriers were wrecked by their crews on reaching the end of the road, after they had passed through the positions held by the 2/7th.

About 3 p.m., while this action was in progress, men of the 2/8th saw troops advancing dressed in dark jackets and khaki shorts, looking like men of the Greek air force. It was eventually decided that they were Germans and they were fired on and dispersed. A patrol identified the corpses of twenty-five Germans.[4] Further patrols were fired on during the night, and next day more than 100 dead were counted. During the day German patrols, again infiltrating round the western flank, reached to within a few hundred yards of Freyberg's headquarters; against them was sent a platoon of the 20th Battalion under the heroic 2nd-Lieutenant Upham, which silenced a machine-gun and killed 22 Germans.

Although the embarkation on the 29th-30th had taken away some 6,000 men, including many wounded (though hundreds remained), the greater part of the New Zealand Division was still in Crete. Determined to do all he could to save his men, Freyberg, still disobediently on Crete, sent a signal through the British Embassy at Cairo to the Prime Minister of New Zealand, Mr Fraser, who was there: "Can you get more ships to evacuate us tomorrow night. Urgent." He received the following signal from Cairo in reply:

Confirmed destroyers are coming tonight Friday. Everything possible is being done to rescue you and risks more than justifiable are being taken. Fraser and Blamey are being fully consulted and are behind all decisions. Vasey is to embark tonight if possible. Both Sunderlands arrive tonight 30-31 May weather permitting. Sunderlands being sent tonight dusk but may be stopped by weather. Do not therefore lose opportunity of coming in warship tonight.

It was learnt from other signals from Cairo and the navy that only four destroyers would arrive that night, and only 2,000 men could be picked up. Weston selected the 4th and 5th Brigades to go. These together comprised more than 2,000 men, and it was therefore decided that one battalion must stay. Hargest chose the 21st—the strongest—and it was placed under Vasey's command. Later Captain Morse, the naval officer in charge, announced that only 1,000 could be embarked, and at length it was decided to send off 230 men from each battalion of the 4th Brigade and the Maori

---
[2] Capt L. C. Cooper, VX6405; 2/8 Bn. Contractor; of Albury, NSW; b. Bristol, Eng, 6 Sep 1912.
[3] Pte G. Marshall, VX5301; 2/8 Bn; HQ Gd Bn. Labourer; of Eaglehawk, Vic; b. Wyuna, Vic, 17 Feb 1905. (He was believed to have served in the old AIF, and to be much older.)
[4] It appears that German mountain troops were wearing articles of abandoned British tropical clothing, their own being too heavy. They wore their own tunics and headgear, however.

battalion; the 5th Brigade would remain, and at length the 21st Battalion was placed under its command.

The thousands of non-combatant troops awaiting embarkation were now grouped in three main areas: some still on the hillside between what Weston described as the "top storey", where the rearguard was in position, and the "bottom storey"; others collected in the Komitadhes ravine; some grouped round Sfakia itself. In the ravine Major Bull[5] of the New Zealand artillery controlled some 3,000 men including New Zealanders of several units and many stragglers. By arrangement with Burston he organised the stragglers into fifties, and perhaps a dozen such groups were embarked this night.

Four destroyers had duly sailed from Alexandria at 9.15 a.m. on the 30th to continue the embarkation, but at 12.45 one of them, *Kandahar*, developed a mechanical defect and was ordered to return; at 3.30 three aircraft attacked and damaged *Kelvin*, which also was recalled. It was evidently as a result of these losses that Weston was informed that only 1,000, not 2,000 would be embarked; but by 3 a.m. on the 31st the remaining destroyers—the Australian-manned *Napier* and *Nizam*—had embarked some 1,510 troops, including the reduced 18th, 19th, 20th and 28th Battalions. At 11 p.m. Freyberg, Captain Morse, and selected officers of Freyberg's and Weston's headquarters, the British and Greek air forces, the navy and the marines had left for Egypt in two Sunderland flying-boats.

At least a nucleus of one of the two New Zealand brigades on Crete had now been embarked; three battalions remained. Of the five Australian infantry battalions on Crete, however, two had been captured and two more remained on the "top storey" above Sfakia. It was estimated that the total force round Sfakia now included some 1,200 New Zealand, 1,250 Australian and 1,550 British infantry (including some 900 improvised from artillery and marine detachments), and some 5,000 depot troops and scattered detachments.[6] All the rations had now been issued, the men were hungry and thirsty, and for that reason alone it would be impossible for the force to offer a prolonged resistance. No adequate plan had been made to provide reserves of food and ammunition. In addition it required much labour to supply the rearguard on the top storey with water. Twelve men working for eight hours were able to carry to the 2/7th and the Marines only 250 gallons.

Weston had informed Hargest at 7.30 a.m. that probably 2,000 would be embarked that night (31st May-1st June) and they would be allocated thus: 5th Brigade, 950; 2/8th Battalion, 200; British troops, 850. Commanders should, however, be prepared to increase those numbers at short notice. Weston informed Middle East Command that its plan would necessitate leaving 5,400 troops behind. Later he learnt from Wavell that Admiral King had been authorised to increase the number embarking to

---

[5] Maj M. A. Bull; 5 NZ Fd Regt. School teacher; of Timaru, NZ; b. Christchurch, NZ, 14 Oct 1907.

[6] These figures were checked by the number of ration chits issued and were considered to be within 5 per cent of the true total.

3,500.⁷ Weston thereupon increased the allocation of New Zealanders to 1,400, and, climbing the hill, informed Vasey that an additional 500 Australians should be embarked that night. His intention was to allot the places proportionately among British, Australian and New Zealand troops. This made it possible for Vasey to arrange for the embarkation not only of the 2/8th but the 2/7th and his own headquarters. He ordered that his headquarters and the Marines should move to the beach at 9 p.m., the 2/7th at 9.15.

Weston informed Middle East Command that it would still be necessary to leave more than 5,000 troops behind, and that, if they were not supplied with rations, they would have to surrender. He asked for instructions; but before his request could be answered the wireless batteries were exhausted and communication with Cairo ceased.

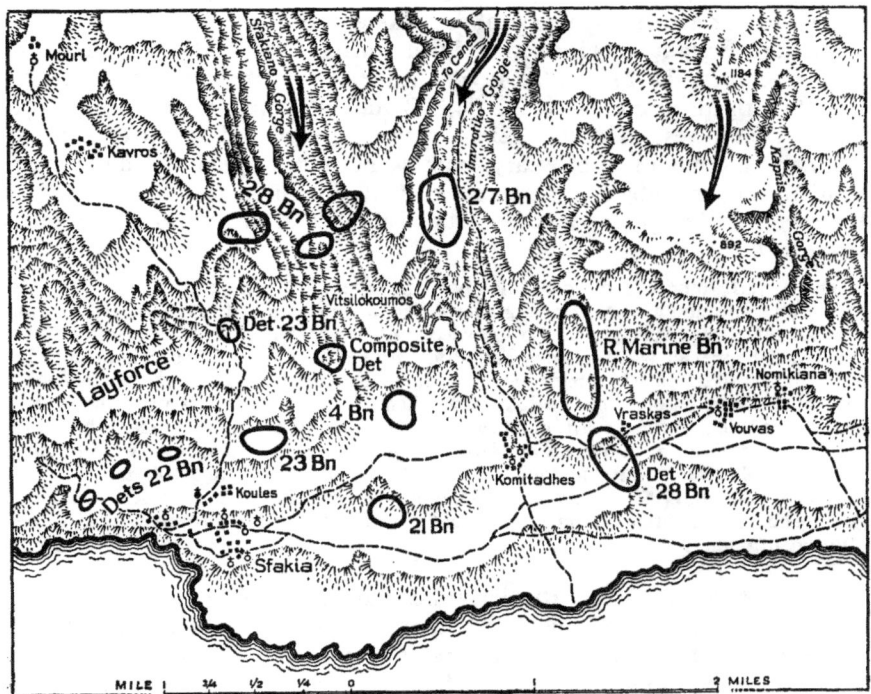

In Cairo General Blamey, perturbed at the small number of Australians who had been embarked, asked that a ship be sent to Plakias, on the south coast between Sfakia and Timbakion, where he believed that a number of Australians were waiting—he knew that two of the Australian battalions could not be at Sfakia. Cunningham said that it was then too late to alter the destination of the ships.

---

⁷ The reason for this change was that the New Zealand Prime Minister, Mr Fraser, had urged Admiral Cunningham to send an additional ship, and the cruiser *Phoebe* had been added.

After the slaughter of their advance-guards on the 30th the Germans made no attack on the 19th Brigade on the 31st, apparently contenting themselves with firing on the positions held by the 2/7th and the Marines. There were no air attacks until evening when three Messerschmitts bombed the troops forming up to embark. Vasey was confident that his men on the heights could hold their rearguard position until the night of the 1st-2nd June if necessary, provided the vulnerable beach area with its thousands of leaderless men was also held. Yet it could be seen that Sfakia was being systematically encircled. The enemy had an observation post on a hill on the right rear of the 2/7th, out of range of Laybourne-Smith's Italian guns. In the course of the day it was learnt that enemy patrols were between Frangokastelli and Sfakia and were moving on Loutro from the west. Layforce, a new unit flung late into the fight, was relieved at Komitadhes by the remaining part of the Maori battalion and moved to the area immediately about Sfakia.

The 5th Brigade now formed an inner perimeter round Sfakia: the 28th at Komitadhes, the 21st in the ravine in the centre, the remaining men of the 4th Brigade (now called the "4th Battalion") west of the ravine, the 23rd farther west, and the 22nd on tracks west and north of Sfakia. Within this double line of weary, hungry, but still dogged and disciplined soldiers was assembled a mere crowd of ill-organised men; the vigorous Hargest, who had placed a cordon round the beach to control this throng, wrote:

> There were hundreds of loose members, members of non-fighting units and all sorts of people about—no formation, no order, no cohesion. It was a ghastly mess. Into all this I was hurtled with no knowledge of it and with my hands already full. What had happened was that men had straggled; small units like searchlight detachments had walked off when their job was done; isolated troops of gunners, engineers, field ambulance, with no one to look after them. But the stragglers were the worst, lawless and fear stricken. At night they rushed for water and ravaged the food dumps and crept back into caves at dawn—a hopeless lot—Greeks, Jews, Palestinians, Cypriots helped to swell the total. My mind was fixed. I had 1,100 troops—950 of the brigade and 150 of the 20th Battalion. We had borne the burden and were going aboard as a brigade and none would stop us. All day I answered pleas to be allowed to come . . . .

Many of the troops—particularly those to whom Hargest here refers—were now starving and plagued by thirst. There was no water supply on the south coast except from one insanitary well, and no adequate plans had been made to provide stores of food or ammunition for the thousands who were assembling round Sfakia. Some stragglers were so hungry that they ate snails. The long march had brought most men close to the limit of endurance.

At 7 p.m. Vasey's brigade major, Bell, informed Walker of the 2/7th that he was to withdraw to the beach that night. Walker fixed the time to begin withdrawal at 9 p.m. and his adjutant, Lieutenant Goodwin,[8] wrote the following order:

---

[8] Capt H. K. H. Goodwin, TX736; 2/7 Bn. Publican; of Woodbridge, Tas; b. Moonee Ponds, Vic, 14 Mar 1904.

1. Cancel all previous orders.
2. MONT [code name for 2/7 Bn] will move tonight.
3. First elements 2100 hrs.
4. Last 2115 hrs.
5. Bn H.Q. closes 2100 hrs.
6. Assembly area at foot of track. Guides will direct from main road. Coys will form up in this area.
7. Silence. Movement must be swift and catlike. It must be impressed on all ranks that accurate timing, pace and SILENCE will make successful move.

Howard K. Goodwin, Adj.

At 9.30 Weston handed to Colonel Colvin of Layforce a written order pointing out that the wireless set would soon give out, no rations were left, and no more embarkations would take place after that night.

> I therefore (he concluded) direct you to collect such senior officers as are available in the early hours of tomorrow and transmit these orders to the senior of them. These orders direct this officer to make contact with the enemy and to capitulate.

Meanwhile at 6 a.m. on the 31st Admiral King with *Phoebe, Abdiel, Hotspur* and *Jackal* sailed from Alexandria for the final embarkation. Small though it was, this squadron comprised a substantial part of the fleet now left to Cunningham, who had warned the Admiralty that, assuming no more ships were damaged, he would be left with only two battleships, three cruisers, the minelayer *Abdiel,* and nine destroyers fit for service in the whole Mediterranean Fleet.

Having been informed by Weston that there would be no further embarkation after the 31st Burston instructed Forbes to have his guides at the embarkation point by 9 p.m. He himself then went across country to the beach to try to preserve control there. He wrote later that

> by nightfall organisation had completely broken down at Sfakia and troops were reaching the beach by the alternative route [to the west of Komitadhes] or just across country in small batches. With the withdrawal of the guides and their organisation from Komitadhes and the track the situation became hopeless, but Captain Forbes managed to get his men to the beach about 0100 hrs . . . as a disciplined unit. All were embarked on the last boat to leave the island.[9]

The ships had arrived off Sfakia at 11.20 p.m. The three landing craft which had been left on the beach were ready loaded and promptly went alongside. The 5th Brigade was in a dense column whose head was on the beach. Through a cordon it had formed passed the 21st, 22nd and 23rd Battalions, the remainder of the 20th and 28th, and the 2/8th (203 men) —but only 100 of the Marines, 27 of Layforce, and 16 of the 2/7th. When the ships sailed at 3 a.m. about 4,050 had embarked.

Thus the 2/7th Battalion and most of the Marines and Layforce had been left behind. The reasons why the 2/7th was not embarked are set out in Vasey's report:

> The route lay along a wadi and a very narrow track which ended up winding through the village of Sfakia. When some little distance from the beach it was found

---

[9] Burston himself declined to embark while others of the 2/3 Regiment were still on the island (including Laybourne-Smith and his gunners) and became a prisoner.

that this road was blocked with men sitting down and many officers challenged anyone approaching wanting to know what they were. Other officers represented themselves as MCO's (Movement Control Officers) and eventually one of these said only single file was allowed through from that point and that 19th Aust Inf Bde would have to wait. With the exception of myself and two staff officers, who went forward to see what the situation was in front, 19th Aust Inf Bde remained in this position for some time. On arrival at the beach I found the embarkation proceeding smoothly and troops filling the boats brought in from the ships reasonably quickly. Not long afterwards, however, it was noticed that troops were not available on the beach when boats came in and there was considerable delay in getting the boats filled and away to the ships. I sent my two staff officers back to investigate the reason for this and to see if brigade HQ and the 7th Battalion had got through and down to the beach. They were absent some considerable time but the rate of movement of troops on to the beach had improved.

19th Aust Inf Bde [headquarters] arrived on the beach at about 0215 hrs and they reported that they had been continually hampered in their movement forward . . . through lack of control in the area behind the beach.

Later Vasey was informed that the commanding officer of the 2/7th had arrived on the beach, and, concluding that all was well, he embarked with his staff. He did not learn the truth until he arrived at Alexandria.

When the 2/7th had begun to withdraw at 9.30 p.m. its leaders knew from their experience in Greece that it was a race against time. Later, in a German prison camp, Major Marshall, the second-in-command, who was with the last company, wrote:

I could have no mercy on them and I had to haze them and threaten them and push them into a faster speed. We crossed the road and stumbled on after Atock[1] (of the Intelligence section) who was guiding us down the centre of this rocky valley. Falls were numerous but I would permit no delay as I knew that time was against us. One of the "A" Company men fell and refused to get up, wanting to be left where he fell and not caring if he were captured or not . . . . I pulled him up and supported him for the next five miles; every time we stopped he sagged and pleaded to be left.

At length this last company caught the remainder of the battalion, but just short of Komitadhes village there was a halt. Marshall went forward and found Lieutenant Lunn with another company; Lunn said that the remainder of the battalion had moved off on a different route to the one he had reconnoitred and he dared not abandon the company that he was guiding. Sergeant Thomas[2] of the Intelligence section thereupon guided the two companies over "nightmare country" in pitch darkness until the weary column reached the beach road, and heard the voices of others of their unit; some were so tired that they fell to the ground and slept.

When its turn came the column moved on slowly down the cliffs above the beach itself. The path was jammed with unarmed men. The head of the 2/7th reached the beach and Colonel Walker immediately sent a few of his men on to a landing craft waiting there. The craft departed and the battalion, drawn up in order on the beach and the road, waited for

---

[1] Pte J. K. Atock, VX5403; 2/7 Bn. Chemist; of East Hawthorn, Vic; b. Sydney, 28 Mar 1919. Shot while a prisoner, 13 Jul 1941.

[2] Maj H. W. Thomas, DCM, VX3961; 2/7 Bn and Intelligence appts. Hosiery mechanic; of Armadale, Vic; b. Prahran, Vic, 12 Nov 1916.

it to return. An officer on the last barge watched the battalion standing there "quiet and orderly in its ranks".

Then came the greatest disappointment of all (wrote Marshall, who was on the beach). The sound of anchor chains through the hawse . . . I found Theo [Walker] and we sat on the edge of the stone sea wall. He told me that things were all up and that the Navy had gone . . . . All our effort and skill wasted.

In the dark early hours Walker and Marshall discussed the possibility of fighting a way along the coast in the hope of being picked up by naval ships. Later some of Walker's men came to him and said that officers and men on the beach were flying white flags. "Shall we shoot them?" they asked. Walker went down and found Colonel Colvin and another, who asked him the date of his promotion, and, learning that he (Walker) was the senior, handed him Weston's order, quoted above. Walker decided that resistance was hopeless. He told his men to destroy their equipment and escape if they could. Hundreds of unarmed men were waving white flags, and soon German aircraft began shooting at them. With Goodwin, his adjutant, Walker climbed to Komitadhes, where he met an Austrian officer and surrendered to him. "What are you doing here, Australia?" asked the Austrian in English. "One might ask what are you doing here, Austria?" replied Walker. "We are all Germans," said the Austrian.[3]

German reports record that by the afternoon of 29th May the *100th Mountain Regiment* was two miles south of Alikambos. Next day, after having thrust back "strong enemy detachments" (the small party of tanks of the 3rd Hussars and carriers of the 2/8th), it met the British rearguard near Imvros. Its position near the end of the made road was so strongly held that the German commander was compelled to make flanking attacks, sending one company east and two west of the road. These companies failed to find the British flank, and, later on the 30th, one company was dispatched on a wider outflanking move through Asfendhon towards the coast some four miles east of Sfakia and another along the heights well to the west of the road. The Germans now occupied Hill 892 east of the road, and thence their observers saw the British troops crowded round Sfakia and Komitadhes. They made no attack that day but waited for the flanking moves to encircle the force (these were observed by the British rearguard). On the morning of the 1st June four dive bombers and four fighters arrived and attacked the Sfakia area, and a light gun that had been hauled on to Hill 892 began shelling the enemy. White flags were raised. Thereupon the *I* and *II Battalions* of the regiment advanced to Komitadhes and Sfakia; they at length took prisoner (according to their reports) some 9,000 British and 900 Greek troops. The German commander seems to have had no inkling that, the night before, a flotilla had arrived off shore and embarked 4,000 men.

On the 1st June thousands of British troops were still at large in Crete, and in the succeeding months perhaps 600 of them made their way back to Egypt in landing barges, fishing boats and submarines.

The three motor landing craft[4] that had been used to ferry men to the warships remained at Sfakia and it was one of these that carried the largest

---

[3] On the 2nd Walker and Goodwin escaped, but they were recaptured two days later. On the 12th a colonel of German paratroops invited him to a meal. "He says," Walker wrote in his diary, "our generals did everything to assist him. Cannot understand why we ever gave ground and did not attack. Neither can we. Said our counter-attack at Suda was only decent fight we gave them . . . . Troops had a concert at night finished up with *Rule Britannia* and *God Save the King*."

[4] These MLC's, forerunners of the LCM's (Landing Craft Mechanised), were designed to carry 100 men or two 15-cwt trucks. They had a speed of seven knots.

party to escape after organised embarkation ceased. On the 1st it set off containing five officers (including Major Garrett of the Royal Marines; Lieutenants K. R. Walker,[5] 2/7th Battalion, and Macartney,[6] 2/2nd Field Regiment) and 135 others, including 56 Marines. That day it reached the island of Gaydhapoula, eighteen miles from the coast, where the engines were overhauled and rations collected; that night it started for Africa. The petrol was exhausted next day, and the craft drifted on the 2nd, 3rd (a despondent Palestinian soldier shot himself that day), and 4th. On the 5th a sail was made by lacing seven blankets with bootlaces and the barge got under way, though when she veered out of the wind the fit men had to go over the side and push her into it again. That day the ration was reduced to half a biscuit covered with bully beef and half a cup of water per man. On the 6th there was no wind. On the 7th a man died of exposure. By the 8th all the men were very weak; Garrett held a church service, "which did a lot to help us along". That evening land was seen; and "with expert handling of sail by Corporal Nugent[7] and Private Legge,[8] and wonderful knowledge of sailing by Major Garrett eventually beached at 0230 hours on 9th June . . . . Position approximately nineteen miles west of Sidi Barrani".

Lieutenant Day[9] of the Welch Regiment took charge of another landing craft at Sfakia on 1st June and put to sea with a company of forty-four including men of his regiment, marines, commandos, five Australians and a Greek. They stopped at a small island to collect food and water, and on the evening of the 1st when they set a course for Derna they had eighty gallons of petrol, one tin of biscuits, nine of beef, four of meat and vegetables, two of bacon, one of fruit and "the unexpended portion" of a sheep given by the Greeks on the island.[1] The petrol was exhausted at midday on the 2nd. A sail was made for the barge with two blankets, and Day with seven men of his regiment and Driver Anstis[2] and Private Green[3] boarded a long boat they had been towing and set off, using an improvised sail and four oars, to obtain help. No more was seen of them by the men in the barge, but they eventually reached Egypt. Private Hansen[4] took control of the landing craft. "He said he was able to navigate as he had knocked about a lot," wrote Horne.[5] "From 2nd to 5th June we had biscuits only to eat but these gave out on the 5th. From then on

---

[5] Maj K. R. Walker, DSO, VX4740; 2/7 Bn. Motor salesman; of Mildura, Vic; b. Essendon, Vic, 25 Aug 1917.

[6] Maj R. R. Macartney; 2/2 Fd Regt and Public Relations. Journalist; of Elsternwick, Vic; b. Elwood, Vic, 14 Aug 1916.

[7] Sgt H. Nugent, NX4358; 2/2 Bn. Farmer; of Grafton, NSW; b. Woolgoolga, NSW, 29 Mar 1914

[8] Pte A. B. Legge, NX2080; 2/2 Bn. Butter factory hand; of Glen Innes, NSW; b. Glen Innes, 6 Oct 1917.

[9] Lt G. M. Day; 1/Welch. Motor engineer; of Swansea, Eng; b. Cardiff, Wales, 9 Dec 1918.

[1] An account of this voyage was written by Pte H. R. Horne of the 2/7 Bn.

[2] Cpl A. F. Anstis, VX4681; 2/7 Bn. Cycle mechanic; of Mildura, Vic; b. Ballarat, Vic, 25 Oct 1916.

[3] Pte J. B. Green, VX4690; 2/7 Bn. Labourer; of Wentworth, NSW; b. Wentworth, 7 Aug 1918.

[4] Pte I. Hansen, VX12399; 2/7 Bn. Truck driver; of Aspendale, Vic; b. Metung Lakes, Vic, 27 Sep 1911.

[5] Pte H. R. Horne, VX11721; 2/7 Bn. Weaver; of Clifton Hill, Vic; b. Clifton Hill, 24 Sep 1919.

we had nothing to eat but were able to keep to our ration of water (four spoonsful night and morning) . . . . About 8th June some of the commandos started to drink sea water. Hansen had a Tommy gun and told them that if they did not stop he would take severe action. This threat effectively stopped them." They reached land near Sidi Barrani on the 10th having had no food for five days.

An enterprising private of the 2/11th Battalion, Harry Richards,[6] "rescued" a third invasion barge, *96 SD 15,* and concealed it in a cave. It had eighty gallons of petrol and Richards decided that he could take off fifty men and sail them to the African coast, calling at Gavdhos Island on the way to replenish food, water and fuel. The barge started at 9.20 p.m. on 1st June. As it moved noisily into open water Germans opened fire with two machine-guns but Richards and his engineer, Taylor,[7] soon had it moving at top speed. Just before dawn next morning it ran aground on Gavdhos. There the passengers filled the water containers. Finding that only fifty-five gallons of petrol remained and food was short, Richards appealed for volunteers to remain on the island and so give the others a reasonable chance of reaching Egypt. Ten men stood aside, and at dusk the barge set sail, now with two officers and fifty men including one Greek. On the afternoon of the 3rd MV *Leaving,* as Richards named his craft, met another barge sailing south; at 5.30 he wrote in his log: "Here is where we want a lot of luck as now our petrol is all used up and still have over 100 miles to go." On the 4th and 5th the barge sometimes drifted, sometimes moved at "a fair speed" with a sail made by Richards from four blankets. On the 5th the food was practically exhausted and for the next three days consisted of only some tins of margarine and cocoa which Richards mixed and issued in small quantities, with hot cocoa made with water. On the morning of the 8th the men were very weak. Richards wrote in his log:

> Sunday 8 Jun 0900 hrs. Flat calm—more cocoa and margarine—all hands very weak and conditions becoming worse hourly. At this stage I have had to address some of the members in words I cannot write—just the same moaning few.
>
> 1000 hours. I have called all members together and we held a service which was conducted by [an English sergeant]. I might mention here that every man on the boat put his heart and soul into this service.
>
> 1030 hrs . . . I have sighted land but am afraid for the time being to announce this as it might be trick of imagination, but no—as I creep nearer I distinguish land clearly.

For fourteen more hours the barge drifted towards land and grounded near Sidi Barrani at 2.30 a.m. next day. Richards' "care for us was beyond description", wrote one escaper. "He exercised his command in a most masterly manner and inspired every one of us to keep his spirits up."

To turn to the experiences of men left elsewhere in Crete: as mentioned above, Major Sandover and Captain Honner, on the 30th, had set out to lead two large parties of the 2/11th Battalion from the Retimo area

---

[6] Pte H. Richards, DCM, WX1944; 2/11 Bn. Farm hand; of Perth, WA; b. Normanville, WA, 24 Dec 1908.

[7] Pte A. H. Taylor, 5431; HQ NZ Div. Farmer; of Waipu, NZ; b. Auckland, NZ, 25 Jul 1905.

to the south coast. By 4 p.m. next day the leading parties were 10 miles north of Ayia Galini. Next day they reached the village and found there about 600 troops, including 300 of the Argyll and Sutherland from Heraklion, some of the Black Watch, and parties of naval and air force men. During the day about 200 Australians, chiefly of the 2/11th, 2/1st Machine Gun and 2/3rd Field Regiment came in. The senior officer there was Major McNab,[8] and the group included Major Ford who had been liason officer with the Greeks at Retimo, and Major Hooper, Campbell's second-in-command, who had also been with the Greeks.

In the cove two landing craft were stranded. The naval officer in charge said that they could not be got into the water but Private McDonald[9] and Corporal Lee[1] of the 2/1st Machine Gun Battalion collected a party which grew to fifty officers and men and after two days of labour succeeded in launching one. Captain Fitzhardinge,[2] a leader in this party, then took three men in a small sailing boat to Timbakion to collect provisions. While they were there German motor-cyclists arrived and opened fire on them. They dashed to the boat and two men lay in the bottom while Captain Fitzhardinge and Private Mortimer[3] swam and towed it from the beach. The boat was repeatedly hit and Lieutenant Bedells[4] was wounded in three places; but they reached Ayia Galini. The landing craft was provisioned and it set out at 8.30 p.m. on 2nd June carrying eleven officers and sixty-six other ranks, with Fitzhardinge in command and Sergeant McWilliam of the South African Air Force as engineer. At 3 a.m. an Italian submarine stopped the craft and took off nine (all except two) of the officers (including three Australians—Fitzhardinge, Lieutenant Morish,[5] and Ryan, the gallant medical officer of the 2/11th). These officers were taken to Italy. On 5th June the landing craft, with Sergeant McWilliam in command, beached at Mersa Matruh, close to the positions of the 2/7th Field Regiment, in which a brother of Fitzhardinge and a brother of Morish were serving.

Meanwhile British aircraft had appeared and given signals at Ayia Galini, and the remaining men were filled with hope that a vessel would be sent to take them off. None came, however, and on 6th June a party of Germans arrived and demanded surrender. "Everyone was very hungry, cold and beginning to despair, some were bootless and nearly all chucked it in," wrote Sandover later. He himself, however, and five of his officers, were bathing in the river some distance away and they made for the hills again.

Meanwhile one of the West Australians had made a single-handed

---

[8] Brig G. A. C. McNab, CB. Mil attaché Bucharest and Prague 1938-41; 1/A & SH 1941; Allied Mission to Hungary 1944-45. B. London, 23 Dec 1899.

[9] Cpl R. McDonald, VX6508; 2/1 MG Bn. Labourer; of Pittsworth, Qld; b. Pittsworth, 7 Nov 1905.

[1] Sgt J. P. Lee, VX5510; 2/1 MG Bn. Grocery manager; of Melbourne; b. Swan Hill, Vic, 30 May 1910.

[2] Capt J. B. Fitzhardinge, MBE, WX9; 2/3 Fd Regt. Architect; of Claremont, WA; b. Manly, NSW, 15 Feb 1911.

[3] Cpl W. A. Mortimer, WX983; 2/11 Bn. Truck driver; of Subiaco, WA; b. Elsternwick, Vic, 18 Aug 1916.

[4] Maj T. C. Bedells, WX14; 2/11 Bn. Insurance clerk; of Cottesloe, WA; b. Cottesloe, 28 Feb 1914.

[5] Lt J. C. Morish, SX1154; 2/3 Fd Regt. Clerk; of Kings Park, SA; b. Adelaide, 11 Aug 1916.

escape. He was Private Carroll[6] who took a sixteen-foot Greek fishing boat which lacked even rowlocks or oars. He used a six-foot piece of driftwood as a mast, a fishing spear as a boom and a piece of bamboo as a peak, and made a sail from a piece of light and ancient canvas found in a flour mill. He set sail on the night of the 11th June. Next morning he was fired on by a German reconnaissance aircraft. He had intended to sail along the coast and find some companions, but after coming under fire at each attempt to return to the coast he set off alone for Egypt. He had six tins of chocolate and two gallons of water; the African coast was 350 miles away and he estimated that in a medium breeze his speed would be three knots. Carroll made slow progress for six days. He wrote afterwards:

At dawn on the seventh morning a strong north-wester blew up and by 1000 hours had developed into a gale. I was obliged to alter my southerly course and run before the wind. Up till then I had used [for a guide] a pen knife mounted on a piece of board. When the blade cast a fine shadow I knew I was heading due south. Sailing by night I used the north star as a guide. For more than twenty-four hours I ran before the wind, surfing the waves which must have been twenty or thirty feet high. My eyes were giving me a lot of trouble, the left being badly affected gave me a blind side making it difficult to judge the waves. A little after sunrise I could see a haze in the sky away to the south. Taking a chance I pushed the boat across the waves, it was quite a battle holding her against them, they were striking me broadside on. The mast being a misfit began to kick from side to side. Twice I took a risk and left the tiller to brace it with floor boards but was nearly swamped. Hoping the planks would hold out long enough, I kept on and sighted land about 0800 hours. I gave her every bit of canvas she had, not caring a hang what happened now. About 1000 hours she began to leak badly, forward on the port side. With still a good distance to go the water commenced to beat me; trying to bail and steer at the same time was impossible, I couldn't keep my feet. Land appeared to be only a few miles off but it must have been nearer ten.

When the boat filled and overturned and the mast smashed a hole in the bottom, my dreams of sailing into Alexandria went with it. Tying my tunic to the rudder clamps I fixed the water tin, almost empty now, across my shoulders and struck out for the shore. It took me seven hours to reach land, swimming, floating and surfing. From the crest of the waves I could see the breakers pounding on the rocks and dashing spray feet into the air. This was about the closest call I'd had up to date and I had a terrific struggle to try and keep from being carried on to the rocks and retain my hold on the tin. If I couldn't find a place to go in, I thought it might serve to take the impact, giving me a chance to scramble clear before the next wave hit me. Fortunately I was able to work my way along to a small patch of sand and came ashore, the breakers spinning me around in all directions. I had to crawl on my hands and knees, feeling too giddy to walk.

I drank most of the water I had left, wrung the water out of my trousers, the only article of clothing I had, and started inland. I knew the road ran somewhere near the coast. The ground was too rough on my bare feet, so I returned to the beach and headed east along the sandhills. After walking for about an hour I came across an air force listening post. The very dark chaps wearing blue peaked caps made me think I was in enemy territory but they turned out to be Maltese. A message was sent to control and next morning I was taken to Mersa Matruh.

When he arrived in Egypt Carroll gave information that small parties of Australian and British troops were still at large round Ayia Galini. As

---

[6] Sgt S. L. Carroll, WX953. 2/11 Bn; later served in RAN. Of Claremont, WA; b. Geraldton, WA, 6 Jan 1915. (Carroll had had a varied career. In 1952 he wrote that "due to the depression" he had been in turn "shop assistant, telegraph messenger, and linesman, traveller, grocer, truck-driver, seasonal worker in primary industries, gold miner". At the outbreak of war he had a carrying business in Southern Cross. Since the war, with the help of the Commonwealth Reconstruction Training Scheme he has become a school teacher.)

a result Lieut-Commander F. G. Poole, who had lived at Heraklion before the war, was landed in the area from a submarine late in July. He soon met Captain Jackson of the 2/11th who had led a party of five other officers and nineteen men of his unit to the south coast, and next evening the submarine—H.M.S. *Thresher*—took off this party and as many other Australian, New Zealand, British and Cypriot troops as could be gathered in the time.[7]

Poole remained on Crete when *Thresher* sailed, but it was arranged that a submarine would return on 18th August, by which time he was to collect another submarine-load of soldiers. Poole sent messages by trusted Greeks to several parties of troops learnt to be hiding in central Crete. To Sandover, whom his information caused him to mistake for an English archaeologist from Heraklion (who had in fact been captured at Ayia Galini), he sent the following cryptic (but effective) message: "Do you remember the young lady who swam naked to the Elafonisos Islands. The man who entertained you then is waiting to greet you now. Follow this guide, he can be trusted." Sandover reached Poole after an 11-hour journey and was instructed to bring any parties he could find to Prevali. There on the nights of the 18th, 19th and 20th August, more than 100 troops were taken off in the submarine *Torbay*. Altogether 13 officers and 39 other ranks of the 2/11th Battalion who had fought at Retimo escaped.[8]

Private Buchecker,[9] an Australian, and two New Zealanders, Privates Carter[1] and McQuarrie,[2] stole a boat on the night of the 15th-16th July, and sailed south-east and south until they reached Sidi Barrani on the night of the 19th. On 17th September Captain Adonis of the Greek Navy brought out a party of eleven, including five Greeks, two Scots, one Australian,[3] two Cypriots, and an "Austrian refugee" in a fishing boat which was intercepted by the destroyer *Kimberley* forty miles from Bardia on 20th September.

On 3rd July Captain Embrey of the 2/1st with Private Hosking,[4] 2/11th, and Gunner Cole,[5] 2/3rd Field Regiment, escaped from Maleme prisoners' camp and walked south into the hills. There they lived in an area where "every village had from two to five 'English' ", and planned escape. Embrey estimated that at this time about 600 Australians and 400 New Zealanders were living in villages in western Crete. Under 5th July

---

[7] They included Lt Greenway of the 2/11th, who later made three voyages from Egypt to Greece in caiques, where he helped to rescue several hundred soldiers and civilians, and one to Crete, where he rescued the Abbot of Prevali, who had fed the party to which Greenway belonged during their long period in hiding.

[8] One officer (Lt R. D. Hull) and fourteen other ranks of the 2/1 Bn who were in Crete reached Palestine in June. A second officer (Capt F. J. Embrey) escaped later. Three officers and 64 other ranks of the 2/7 Bn escaped from Crete.

[9] Sgt H. R. Buchecker, MM, VX4712; 2/7 Bn. Farm hand; of Merbein, Vic; b. Mildura, Vic, 25 Aug 1919.

[1] Pte B. B. Carter, MM; 27 NZ MG Bn. Farmer; of Pukekohe, NZ; b. Auckland, NZ, 23 Apr 1916.

[2] Pte D. N. McQuarrie, MM; 18 NZ Bn. Timberyard hand; of Ellerslie, NZ; b. 12 Jun 1918. Died of wounds, 2 Dec 1941.

[3] WX2253 Pte H. Nicol (of Bulong, WA), 2/11 Bn.

[4] Lt C. G. S. Hosking, WX399; 2/11 Bn; RAE Tp 1 Para Bn. Science student; of Subiaco, WA; b. Perth, WA, 1 Feb 1916.

[5] Gnr J. W. Cole, WX179; 2/3 Fd Regt. Milk carter; of Fremantle, WA; b. Fremantle, 27 Jun 1918.

Hosking's diary of this escape says: "Met Greek. Said 'Kalimera' (Good Day) in best Greek. Reply: 'Hullo, George' despite Greek clothing."

Embrey made many plans to escape but there were few boats and they well guarded. Late in July he met Lieut-Commander Vernacos, a Greek in the Royal Naval Volunteer Reserve. Vernacos who had been busy organising refuge for British troops in the villages now persuaded Embrey and two officers of the Notts Yeomanry to join him in an attempt to escape and organise British help for a revolution in Crete. After the failure of many plans these four sailed to Greece by night in a Greek caique and thence, after many privations, they reached Turkey on 4th September.

In the area of Neapolis at the south-eastern tip of the Peloponnese had gathered other parties of Australians, some of them from Crete, who wandered from village to village and sought a means of sailing to Africa or Turkey. One party, including Private Hosking and Gunner Cole above mentioned, and with Sergeant Redpath[6] as leader, decided to seize one of the fishing boats, which they had noticed sheltering in the bay of Agia Elias on the south coast of Greece. Accordingly one night three of them swam out 400 yards, detached the caique's dinghy and towed it ashore. Seven men then rowed out in the dinghy, woke the crew of the caique and "explained to them roughly the idea". The captain of this vessel deceived the Australians into allowing him to return to his home for stores and equipment and eluded them. The same men then repeated their tactics and captured a second caique. In this vessel they sailed from Greece on 10th October and landed west of Mersa Matruh on the 17th, having been bombed at by both British and German aircraft on the way.[7] By 1st September 317 Australians had escaped from Crete, including 23 officers.

Even after September resolute escapers were still trickling back to their units in the Middle East. One of these who wrote a particularly full account of his experiences was Lance-Corporal Welsh[8] of the 2/6th Battalion, who served in Crete in the 17th Brigade Composite Battalion. Welsh escaped from a prison camp at Skines in the hills south-west of Canea early in June. With another Australian he took a rowing boat and set out for Cyprus, but, 500 yards from the shore, they were attacked by two aircraft, which chased them to the shore and there destroyed the boat. Welsh returned to Skines and re-entered the prison camp without his absence having been noticed. Early in July some 3,000 prisoners including Welsh were shipped to Salonika and placed in a verminous and disease-ridden prison camp there.

About 13 July 1941 I made another attempt to escape, this time in company with many others (he wrote later). There were three main blocks of latrines and wash

---

[6] WO2 J. A. Redpath, DCM, MM; 19 NZ Army Tps Coy. Company manager; of Kerikeri Central, Bay of Islands, NZ; b. Christchurch, NZ, 2 Feb 1904.

[7] Other Australians in this party were Cpl E. N. Park (Manilla, NSW—later Lt. DSO), Pte I. A. McLaren (Paddington, NSW), 2/2 Bn; Pte R. J. Hipwell (Echuca, Vic), 2/7 Bn; Gnrs C. H. Jager (Caulfield, Vic), K. Murphy (Melbourne), F. D. Travers (Middle Brighton, Vic), 2/2 Fd Regt; and one other wounded Australian.

[8] L-Cpl I. D. Welsh, VX4460; 2/6 Bn. Poultry farmer's assistant; of Frankston, Vic; b. Launceston, Tas, 12 Aug 1917.

houses in the camp, and from each of these led a drain which discharged into a pit which was about 6-ft deep, 6-ft in diameter, and was covered by a 2-ft manhole with a concrete lid. From this pit a main sewer ran for about 200 yards, under the wire, and discharged into a small creek outside the wire. This sewer was about 2-ft 6-in. in diameter to start with, but got smaller as it ran outwards. A party had got out of the sewer earlier that night. Our party consisted of 30 and we decided to go at 11 p.m. divided into three smaller parties of ten each, allowing a few minutes intervals between parties. This . . . would give us some air in the sewer which was very foul with gas, and secondly searchlights played over the camp at intervals and there was more chance for smaller parties. My party of ten went first, and I led the party, followed by Hadwell,[9] and two other Australians. I crawled along on my hands and knees, but as the drain grew smaller I had to wriggle. Some of the men who had gone before me had discarded garments in the sewer, which made passage more difficult. The bottom of the sewer was running with liquid and the sides covered in filth. The whole of our 30 got into the sewer all right, but when I reckoned that I was only about 30 yards from the exit and under the wire the pipe bent a bit and I came upon the body of a Cypriot. He must have been overcome by the fumes in the drain and had collapsed and died; his head was half under. I tried to crawl past him, but this was impossible, then I tried to dislodge him or push him in front of me, but not being able to kneel up I could not do so. I told Hadwell that we would have to get back but he urged me to have another try. After violent efforts to dislodge him I failed, and then tried to dislodge the bricks of the sewer, but this only broke my nails. I was sweating hard and breathing heavily and thought for a moment that I was going to go out with the foul gas. It was, of course, pitch dark in the sewer. The people behind could not understand what was happening and were pushing to get on, although Hadwell had passed word back what was happening. Finally we told them that the Germans were in front of us, which was not true, but had the desired effect, and we all started back up the drain cray-fishing all the way because we were unable to turn around. Our pockets got filled with filth. Fifteen of the men got back all right, climbed out through the man-hole and dispersed to their quarters. Each man had to wait and dodge the searchlights. Unfortunately, as the fifteenth got out he let the heavy cement lid drop with a bang on the man-hole, the guard heard the bang and flashed his torch upon him, opened fire, called out the guard and rushed in and prevented us from getting out. Guards were sent to the other end of the drain to capture anyone escaping, and also were ordered to fire up it, and they did so. Luckily for us in the drain there was a bit of a bend, where the Cypriot was stuck, and most of the bullets lodged in his body and a few ricochetted on, but no one was hit. Next day when the Cypriot's body was removed I was told he had six bullets in him. The guards shouted to us to come out, or they would throw bombs down the man-hole. As each man emerged from the man-hole he was subjected to a brutal attack by the guards who hit, kicked or struck with the butts of their rifles at any portion of the body that opportunity offered to them. Getting out, my friend Snowy Hadwell slipped and fell back into the pit. The guards thought he was trying to get away and fired into the pit and a bullet wounded him in the right thigh. I helped Hadwell to get out of the pit and was then kicked on the leg with a jack-boot, and was unfortunate enough to be struck on the head with a rifle butt and passed out.

When I regained consciousness, which I think was about an hour later, I was lying on the floor in the guard room. A Cypriot who had been shot trying to run away, was lying on a stretcher screaming for water, the other twelve were lined up around the wall with their hands in the air, and guards were standing close to them pointing bayonets at their stomachs. A German officer, who was the Camp interpreter, and who wore a white uniform and a funny little dress sword, was abusing the guards and asking questions of the prisoners. He wanted to know how many had got out,

---

[9] Pte J. M. Hadwell, NX2404; 2/2 Bn. Farrier; of Byron Bay, NSW; b. Glen Innes, NSW, 8 Sep 1919.

where we were going to if we had succeeded in getting out, and above all, who was the ringleader of the attempt. He did not get any information from anyone.

After five days in hospital Welsh was interrogated by two Gestapo men who attempted in vain to discover who were the ringleaders among those who had tried to escape and whether the Australian medical officers were helping men to escape.

Welsh was still determined to get away. In August, having obtained a complete outfit of Greek clothing, he slipped out of the camp with a large working party of prisoners who were employed grooming horses. He hid in a forage store, removed his uniform, revealing his Greek workman's clothes, and walked out past the guard. In Salonika he went to the poorer part of the city.

> I thought my best chance of making a contact and not being given away, was to find some woman with a large family .... I saw a fat woman with a lot of children playing in the front garden .... I walked straight up to her and told her I was an Australian soldier. She whipped me into the house and sent for her husband, but I could not make myself understood very well. However they immediately gave me food and were most kind.

The Greeks led Welsh to a house where six other soldiers were hiding. Friendly Greeks guided Welsh and another Australian, Walter Sicklen,[1] of the 2/1st Battalion, south-east to Athos where they at length met a priest and obtained a boat to take seven escapers who had assembled there to Turkey. After several attempts to make the voyage had been defeated by stormy weather, they reached the Turkish island of Imbros, where the priest landed them and then set off for Athos to bring more prisoners over. In Turkey they joined thirteen other escaped prisoners. At Adana "the German Consul complained to the Turkish Government about the passage of British prisoners of war, but was reminded gently about German and Vichy escaped prisoners and soldiers who were in Turkey awaiting passports to Europe". On 10th October this group of prisoners crossed the Turkish border into Syria (which had meanwhile been occupied by British troops).

The total strengths of the British, New Zealand and Australian contingents on Crete on 20th May were: British 17,000, New Zealand 7,700, Australian 6,500. About 16,500 were embarked. The losses suffered by these contingents were:[2]

---

[1] Pte W. A. Sicklen, NX3921; 2/1 Bn. Boot finisher; of Paddington, NSW; b. Katoomba, NSW, 30 Jan 1916.

[2] So far as they can be ascertained, the losses suffered by Australian and New Zealand infantry and artillery units and United Kingdom infantry units were:

Australian:	Killed	Wounded	Prisoners		Killed	Wounded	Prisoners
2/1 Bn	43	64	511	16 Bde Composite Bn	4	9	97
2/4 Bn	22	33	24	17 Bde Composite Bn	3	13	198
2/7 Bn	27	60	431	2/2 Fd Regt	6	23	56
2/8 Bn	10	41	95	2/3 Fd Regt	20	30	126
2/11 Bn	53	126	423	7 LAA Bty	2	2	144
2/1 MG Bn	11	22	49				

	Killed	Wounded	Prisoners
New Zealand	671	1,455	1,692
British Army	612	224	5,315
Australian	274	507	3,102
Royal Marines	114	30	1,035
Royal Air Force	71	9	226

Thus the effort to hold Crete cost the British force about 15,900 men, of whom about 4,000 were killed or wounded; the Germans claimed also 5,255 Greek prisoners, and they released 14,000 Italians. The German *Fourth Air Fleet* reported the loss of 3,986 killed or missing, of whom 312 were air crew; and 2,594 wounded; 220 German aircraft were destroyed.[3] The German force employed totalled 23,000. The German troops who were killed were almost all highly-trained fighting men, more than 3,000 of them from the *7th Air Division*—a crippling loss to this skilled formation. The British soldiers who were captured belonged mostly to base units; in fighting units the heaviest loss was the Australian—three infantry battalions as well as parts of other fighting units. For gallantry on Crete the German mountain troops were awarded 5,019 Iron Crosses of various grades, and 971 War Service Crosses.

Could Crete have been held? It is now evident that from November onwards useful time was lost because of the failure of the higher staffs to define a policy and appoint a senior commander who would remain on the island and carry that policy out. In 1941 an Inter-Services Committee was appointed to report on the campaign. Although the evidence before it was not comprehensive, some of its judgments remain valid. "Six months of comparative peace," it decided, "were marked by inertia for which ambiguity as to the role of the garrison was in large measure responsible .... There was a marked tendency at one time to regard Crete as a base for offensive operations against the Dodecanese without any apparent regard to the advisability of being able to operate from a secure base."

It was axiomatic that Crete would be attacked only if the enemy commanded the air, in which case sea communications would be precarious. It was desirable therefore that large supplies should be stored on the island before strong air attack developed. A garrison preparing to meet airborne attack could have been given one telling advantage over its adversary—possession of heavy weapons which could be landed in quan-

New Zealand:	Killed	Wounded	Prisoners	United Kingdom:	Killed	Wounded	Prisoners
Div Cav Regt	10	50	7	2/Yorks and Lancs	58	6	115
18 Bn	108	157	71	2/Black Watch	65	14	93
19 Bn	65	117	85	1/Welch	115	2	453
20 Bn	86	179	32	1/Rangers	23	18	249
21 Bn	36	65	44	1/Argylls	21	1	223
22 Bn	64	144	94	2/Leicesters	73	25	46
23 Bn	56	187	56	MNBDO (Royal Marines)	114	30	1035
28 (Maori) Bn	73	147	26				
27 (MG) Bn	18	29	75				
4 Fd Regt	17	37	68				
5 Fd Regt	20	65	194				

In the United Kingdom list, and to a less extent in the Australian list, many of the wounded are included as "prisoners". The United Kingdom artillery units lost 188 killed or died of wounds.

[3] It is likely that lightly wounded were not included in the German casualty figures. It appears that all German prisoners taken on Crete were released except 17 officers taken to Egypt.

tity from ships, whereas the enemy would have to depend on such weapons and ammunition as aircraft could carry. If the tank, artillery and infantry units retained on the island had been fully equipped with efficient heavy weapons—tanks, guns and mortars—the initial German attack would probably have been beaten in every sector. To have provided this equipment would have necessitated boldly denuding units in reserve in Egypt and Palestine; a middle way was followed of sending to Crete a few tanks, but not enough to be effective, and some captured guns most of which were incomplete and all inferior.[4] Crete was lost.

The problem of supply which was certain to become acute sooner or later could have been greatly lessened by removing from the island all except strong and fully-equipped or re-equipped units. The eventual removal of about 16,000 troops in four nights demonstrated that the embarkation of all ill-armed or inessential detachments could have been carried out much earlier by employing similar methods.

General Freyberg's position was unenviable. Greater foresight on the part of Wavell and his staff would have placed on Crete a commander and staff who, at least since the decision to send a force to Greece, might have devoted themselves to planning the defence of the island, and incidentally to the problems of withdrawal from Greece to Crete. But Freyberg had not been on Crete until he landed on the 29th April, weary after commanding the rearguard in the Peloponnese; he inherited no comprehensive plan; he had to improvise a staff (and by so doing depleted the staff of his old division); at the outset a large number of his men lacked even light weapons and personal gear. When the attack opened his troops, though in good heart, were still often poorly equipped, particularly his artillery. He had no motor road to a port on the south coast, and Suda Bay was a dangerous harbour, to be entered only at night by fast ships, of which few could be spared.

Once an airfield was firmly in German possession there was no longer any hope of defending Crete. A swifter and stronger counter-attack by the reserve on the night of the 20th or 21st might have recaptured the Maleme field. This would have prolonged the resistance of the garrison; but whether it would have caused General Lohr to cut his losses and accept defeat can only be guessed.[5] If he was resolved to order his troops to hold their ground and his air force to isolate the British garrison, he was sure to win eventually—if only because the garrison's supplies would be exhausted and the navy would be unable to afford the losses involved in preventing invasion by sea. In the fight for Crete the Mediterranean Fleet lost the

---

[4] In the *Army Quarterly*, Jul 1947, Brig Brunskill set out the following essentials for holding Crete:
"(a) Four months'—preferably six months'—supplies of all natures, including weapons and equipment for the troops from Greece.
(b) A road right through to Sfakia, which could have been put through by a field company in a month to six weeks with some road-making equipment.
(c) The following additional troops:
One additional infantry brigade fully equipped with weapons and transport;
One divisional artillery;
100 more R.A.S.C. lorries (we had only 27)."

[5] In a report Maj-Gen Ringel of the *5th Mountain Division* wrote: "The enemy's stubborn defence could have led to the defeat of our attack if he had grasped the situation at the very first and made use of all his available troops and resources."

cruisers *Gloucester, Fiji* and *Calcutta,* and the destroyers *Juno, Greyhound, Kashmir, Kelly, Hereward,* and *Imperial.* Two battleships, an aircraft carrier, two cruisers and two destroyers were damaged so severely that they could not be repaired at Alexandria; three cruisers and six destroyers were less severely damaged. About 2,000 naval men were killed. In addition, during the operations in and round Greece and Crete from 6th March to 2nd June 315,000 tons of British and Allied merchant shipping were lost. Lohr's aircraft losses could easily be replaced, but each British naval ship sunk or damaged gravely reduced the narrow margin by which Admiral Cunningham held the eastern Mediterranean. (In addition, from 23rd to 27th May, the German battleship *Bismarck* was at large in the Atlantic; on the 24th she had sunk the *Hood* and damaged another British capital ship.)

However, the disastrous losses suffered by the German airborne division in Crete dissuaded Hitler from ordering a similar attack on Cyprus, then slenderly held by less than a brigade.

The German decision that they should not attempt airborne attack on Cyprus was promptly taken. A proposal to capture it with a seaborne force sailing by night from the Dodecanese was substituted, but was never carried out. It can justly be said that the resolute resistance offered by the garrison of Crete saved Cyprus from a similar attack, which must have succeeded. The garrison of Cyprus then comprised the 7th Australian Cavalry Regiment (Lieut-Colonel Logan[6]), 1/Sherwood Foresters, "C" Special Service Battalion (commandos), a battalion of Cypriots and a troop of field artillery.

Cyprus remained a source of acute anxiety to the British leaders for the following three weeks, however. On 6th June General Blamey reported to the Australian Government that the estimated scale of attack on Cyprus was by 450 German transport aircraft, which could land 7,000 to 8,000 troops in 48 hours; and that the force required to ensure the safety of the island should include four infantry brigades, two regiments of light tanks and one squadron of heavy tanks, and supporting units. "Position is one of acute anxiety to Middle East Commanders," he added, "but no prospect increasing garrison for next two to three months."

When he received this cable, the Australian Prime Minister, Mr Menzies, sent a message to the High Commissioner in London, Mr Bruce, on the 8th June that "another forced evacuation, particularly if accompanied with great losses, will have serious effect on public opinion in America and elsewhere, whilst in Australia there are certain to be serious reactions which may well involve the Government". He offered the opinion that there were two alternatives: either to garrison Cyprus with a sufficiently strong force or to abandon it.

Soon, however, the fears about Cyprus were submerged in other anxieties, and, in a fortnight after Menzies' cable, the invasion of Russia would begin.

---

[6] Lt-Col E. P. Logan, NX12339. CO 7 Cav Regt 1940-42. Company director; of Lindfield, NSW; b. Mosman, NSW, 26 Dec 1903. Killed in action 19 Dec 1942.

It was perhaps fortunate from a British point of view that the German forces persisted with the attack on Crete and took the island without great delay, accepting the heavy losses which dissuaded them from undertaking a similar attack on Cyprus. If the airborne invasion of Crete had failed and a struggle had developed between a German air force on the one hand and the Mediterranean Fleet and air force on the other, the one loyally attempting to supply and support the garrison of Crete, the other determined to isolate it, Britain would probably have been by far the heavier loser in a costly campaign of attrition. As it was, Admiral Cunningham described the twelve-day battle for Crete as "a disastrous period in our naval history".

CHAPTER 15

POLITICAL DECISIONS

THE failures and reverses of April and May had reduced the number of effective fighting formations at General Wavell's disposal almost by half. In March he could deploy ten divisions—the 2nd Armoured; 1st Cavalry; 6th (British); 6th, 7th and 9th Australian; 4th and 5th Indian; New Zealand; 1st South African. Five of these had now either been broken up into small groups (as the 6th British and the Cavalry) or had lost their heavy weapons and were in need of rest and reinforcement (as the 6th Australian and the New Zealand). Of the divisions which remained, the 9th Australian was now besieged in Tobruk, the rearmed 7th Armoured (not included above), the 1st South African, and the 4th Indian were in process of concentrating on the Western Desert front, and the 5th Indian and the small British-African divisions were engaged in mopping-up in Abyssinia. The only substantial and ready reserve was the 7th Australian Division, in position about Mersa Matruh.

Admiral Cunningham's Mediterranean Fleet had been reduced even more calamitously than Wavell's army by its losses off Greece and Crete. He now had only two battleships, three cruisers, and 17 destroyers fit for action. With this force he had to run supplies into Tobruk and Malta in the face of a great enemy superiority in the air, and do what he could to interrupt the shipping of Axis supplies and reinforcements to North Africa. Late in May he sent a strong appeal to London for air reinforcements on a large scale, so that the R.A.F. and the Fleet Air Arm could sink enemy ships in substantial numbers, and also give the army enough support to enable it to advance in North Africa.

After its losses in Greece the British air force in the Middle East possessed only about 200 serviceable aircraft, excluding obsolescent types, with which to carry out tasks over Malta and the eastern Mediterranean, Crete, North Africa, Italian East Africa, Aden and the Red Sea, Palestine, and perhaps Syria and Iraq. Against these the Germans had more than 1,200, the Italians more than 600; if only half of the enemy aircraft were always ready for immediate action, 900 were pitted against 250 British, of which about 50 were obsolescent machines.[1] The enemy could reinforce his squadrons quickly from stations a day or two away, whereas British replacements had to be flown either through the dangers of the Mediterranean, refuelling by night at Malta, or over the sea to West Africa and thence some 3,700 miles to Cairo.

There was thus an urgent need for heavy equipment to rearm veteran divisions and for air force squadrons, and for the rapid repair or reinforcement of the damaged naval vessels with which Alexandria was crowded. If these were provided and no new commitments added, it should be

---

[1] We know now that a considerable proportion of the German air force in the eastern Mediterranean was then being made ready for transfer to the Russian front.

possible to concentrate a force of formidable strength for a renewed thrust towards Tripoli. In May, however, even before the German attack on Crete opened, it had been made evident to the Commanders-in-Chief in the Middle East that a new task would soon be added—a march into Vichy-French Syria.

In the early months of 1941 the political background of General Wavell's command had become so complex that, in April, he reached the conclusion that British political policy in the Middle East could no longer be efficiently directed from London and asked, through the Chiefs of Staff there, for "the appointment of an authority in the Middle East who could decide upon political policy in relation to strategy without the delay in referring home". No doubt this opinion had been influenced by the speed with which decisions had been obtained during Mr Eden's visits. One political complication embarrassing Wavell was the activity of General de Gaulle who, in April, had communicated direct to Mr Churchill a proposal that Free French forces should take military action against Syria—a frivolous suggestion since the Free French forces in Palestine early in May consisted of only five battalions and a section of artillery, whereas General Henri Dentz, the Vichy Government's Commander-in-Chief in Syria, was believed to command some 28,000 well-trained and well-armed men. Nevertheless such a proposal was likely to be listened to sympathetically by Churchill, who had great hopes of the de Gaullist movement;[2] and de Gaulle had the support of General Catroux (his deputy in the Middle East), Sir Miles Lampson, and General Spears,[3] the influential British liaison officer at Free French headquarters.

About the end of April General Dill had informed Wavell that, in view of the danger of German airborne attack on Syria, the Foreign Office was about to warn Dentz of such a possibility and ask him what preparations he was making for defence. He asked Wavell what troops he could spare to assist Dentz against the Germans, adding that it was inadvisable to use the Free French unless requested. In reply to the British inquiry Dentz said that he would resist German encroachment, but that he must obey whatever instructions he received from his Government. Wavell, for his part, informed Dill, on 28th April (the embarkation from Greece was then in progress), that he had only one cavalry brigade group available.[4]

---

[2] As early as Nov 1940, Churchill had written to Lord Halifax (the British Foreign Secretary): "We shall most certainly have to obtain control of Syria by one means or another in the next few months. The best way would be by a Weygand or a de Gaullist movement, but this cannot be counted on, and until we have dealt with the Italians in Libya we have no troops to spare for a northern venture." (*The Second World War*, Vol II, p. 611.)

[3] Maj-Gen Sir Edward Spears, KBE, CB, MC. Head of Brit Mission to Gen de Gaulle 1940-41; First Minister to Republics of Syria and the Lebanon 1942-44. B. 7 Aug 1886.

[4] On 4th June Churchill sent Wavell a minute in which he complained, in effect, that he was failing to maintain enough fighting formations with the men and weapons which had been sent to him. Churchill pointed out that Wavell then had 530,000 soldiers, 500 field guns, 350 anti-tank guns, and 450 heavy tanks yet was "evidently hard put to find a brigade or even a battalion".
He then informed Wavell that he was sending out General R. H. Haining as "Intendant-General" to assist Wavell by performing for him many of the duties done in England by the War Office and the Ministry of Supply.
It is improbable, however, that Wavell could have maintained substantially more fighting formations with his 530,000 men and 500 field guns. If the two British-African divisions in Abyssinia, the 6th British and the cavalry division are included he had thirteen divisions either

Wavell was instructed that, if Dentz resisted German invasion, all available help should be given to him; if he failed to resist, Wavell and his colleagues should take "any military action deemed practicable"; in the event of a German invasion the air force should strike at once. General de Gaulle was being kept informed, but Wavell should decide whether Free French troops were to be employed.

At the request of General Catroux, de Gaulle's deputy in the Levant, a conference was held in Cairo on 5th May to discuss the situation in Syria. Catroux said that he did not believe that Dentz's troops would resist a German attack and urged that, if the Germans landed, he should move into Syria with a force of six Free French battalions which would soon be ready. The Chiefs of Staff approved this proposal. The British leaders now knew from their representatives and agents that Dentz had been instructed to allow German and Italian aircraft to fly over Syria, but to fire on British aircraft. On 9th May Churchill sent a cable to Wavell in the course of which he said:

In face of your evident feeling of lack of resources we can see no other course open than to furnish General Catroux with the necessary transport and let him and his Free French do their best at the moment they deem suitable, the R.A.F. acting against German landings.[5]

On 12th May it was reported from Damascus that German aircraft were alighting in Syria. The Middle East Air Force, now commanded by Air Marshal Tedder, who had replaced Air Chief Marshal Longmore, was authorised to act against these aircraft, and on the 14th and 15th May British aircraft bombed the Damascus airfield. The Rayak and Palmyra fields were bombed on the 18th and 19th.

A tangle of political complications was likely to result from the outbreak of fighting between Britain and Vichy France and it was largely in anticipation of such crises that Wavell had asked for the appointment to Cairo of a leader empowered to make political decisions.

From the 16th century onwards France had obtained a cultural and commercial ascendancy over the Ottoman Empire. This gained steadily in strength as that Empire sickened and its outlying provinces acquired partial or complete independence. French became the second language of the nearer Arab lands; so far as the Near East adopted European customs they were derived chiefly from France; the cultivated Egyptian or Levantine regarded Paris as the centre of European culture and commerce. Despite the growth of British influence since the middle of the 19th century, France and the French retained very considerable financial and industrial concessions, and gained new ones, and French schools and missions grew and multiplied. After the war of 1914-1918, however, and the negotiations which followed, Britain, partly by force of arms, partly

---

in the field or resting and re-equipping. Large static garrisons had to be maintained for anti-aircraft defence, security duties and guarding prisoners. In the circumstances, a ratio of 40,000 men to each fighting division does not seem unduly high.

[5] Quoted in Churchill, Vol III, p. 289.

(Australian War Memorial)
Troops from Crete disembarking at Alexandria, June 1941.

A group of Australians who escaped from Crete in a barge and sailed to Egypt.
Back row: Ptes A. C. Jackson, R. N. Doran, Dvr J. L. Smith, Pte E. J. Host.
Front row: Ptes J. A. Gorton, Harry Richards, L-Cpl G. J. McMillan, Pte J. C. Thompson.

Ras Naqoura, the rocky promontory on the border of Syria and Palestine.

(*Australian War Memorial*)

Air Commodore L. O. Brown; Maj-Gen J. D. Lavarack; Lt-Gen H. Maitland Wilson; General Catroux.

(Maj-Gen J. E. S. Stevens)

The crater in the coastal road, near Iskandaroun.

(Australian War Memorial)

The bridge built by Australian engineers over the Litani near Merdjayoun, with a view of the demolished bridge in the background. June 1941.

(Australian War Memorial)

Lieutenant Connor's party outside Fort Khiam, 9th June. *Left to right*: Cpl R. K. Campbell; Sgt A. M. Sweetapple; Lt G. B. Connor; Pte J. J. Wayte.

(Maj-Gen J. E. S. Stevens)

Maj-Gen A. S. Allen; Brig F. H. Berryman and Brig A. R. Baxter-Cox. Syria, June 1941.

as a result of her strong support for Arab nationalism, partly by diplomacy, emerged as the dominant European Power in the Middle East, and French power and prestige declined. The settlement with the new Turkey at the Treaty of Lausanne was a bitter disappointment to Frenchmen of most parties; and, after 1924, French and British policy took radically different directions. Britain made fairly rapid steps towards the emancipation of the Arab countries she dominated whereas (in the words of a Frenchman) "anxious to educate the people (much more than Great Britain), to create an elite, a highly-educated class, in order to ensure a good administration, French progress was undoubtedly very slow, too slow".[6]

In Syria and Lebanon, where France ruled some 3,300,000 people under a mandate from the League of Nations, there was a patchwork of religious and cultural communities, Islamic, Christian and Jew. Under French rule the mandate was divided into four zones: Syria, predominantly of the Sunni sect of Islam; Lebanon, where there was a Christian majority; Latakia with a majority of Alawis whose religion is an amalgam of Islamic, Christian and pagan; and the Jebel Druse peopled by a semi-Islamic warlike sect from which their mountain stronghold takes its name. In Syria and the Jebel Druse there was, from the beginning of the French mandate, much discontent based on nationalistic feeling and fed by a conviction that the French officials were often corrupt, arbitrary and oppressive. Discontent flared into civil war in 1925 and involved the French and the insurgents in military operations which lasted until 1927. In the succeeding eleven years Syrian and Lebanese political awareness increased and disagreements with the French Government multiplied until, in July 1939, the High Commissioner dissolved the infant Syrian Chamber of Deputies and replaced it by an appointed Council of Directors. At the outbreak of war in Europe the relatively placid Lebanese Chamber was also dissolved, and certain extreme nationalist parties were suppressed and their leaders imprisoned. The strategical importance which the French Government attached to Syria was indicated by the appointment of General Weygand, after Marshal Pétain the most highly esteemed of French commanders, as Commander-in-Chief in the Levant.

Most Syrian and Lebanese leaders expressed their willingness to support France and her allies in the war, but the people appear to have been apathetic and cynical.

> Except among the Francophil elements, people tended to think that, although the belligerents might invoke the noblest of principles to justify their taking up arms, in reality all were equally moved by self-interest, and that from the point of view of the exploited nations of the East there was nothing to choose between the oppression exercised in the name of democracy and that exercised in the name of Fascism. This tendency was encouraged by the efforts of the competing propaganda services, each of which purported to unmask the true face of the other party.[7]

When, in June 1940, General Mittelhauser declared that the terms of the armistice with Germany would be observed in Syria, the British Govern-

---

[6] Robert Montagne, in *International Affairs*, Jan 1947.
[7] A. H. Hourani, *Syria and Lebanon* (1946), pp. 230-1.

ment announced that it would not allow Syria to be occupied by a hostile Power. A minority among the civil and military officers wished to continue the fight against Germany, and some of these made their way to Palestine. Gradually, those officials believed to have pro-British sympathies were replaced; in November 1940 the post of High Commissioner was given to General Dentz who, as a junior officer, had served in Syria in the 'twenties on the staff of Weygand, and of General Sarrail when that commander took the repressive steps which led to the rebellion of 1925.[8] He had been Deputy Chief of the General Staff from 1934 to 1939 and Military Governor of Paris when it was surrendered in June 1940.

The majority of politically-conscious Syrians, already apathetic about the European war, felt humiliated to be subject to a defeated nation; and after the withdrawal of France from the League of Nations they considered the legal basis of the mandate to have disappeared. Early in 1941 there were strikes and demonstrations in Syrian towns in protest against the shortage of food and consequent profiteering. Nationalist leaders took over the direction of this unrest. In April Dentz broadcast a conciliatory statement forecasting the formation of an Advisory Assembly and economic reforms; he then appointed "Ministries" in both Syria and Lebanon. Meanwhile, in anticipation of possible military operations in Syria, British agents were wooing the Syrian Arabs; since February, on instructions from London, Mr Kirkbride,[9] the British Resident in Transjordan, had been secretly in touch with the Jebel Druses, and Major Glubb,[1] of the Arab Legion, with the Syrian tribes.[2]

Henceforward, General Dentz's actions can be understood only if seen against the background of the changing moods and policies of his own government at Vichy and of Hitler and his staff. The leading figures in the Vichy Government were bitterly antagonistic to Britain, and likely to remain under German influence, not only because they considered that they would gain by a German victory but because, in common with strong forces in the French upper classes and the army, they believed that France's salvation lay in the establishment of a totalitarian state on the German model. This did not mean, however, that their nationalism was dead or that all of them wished France to be completely subordinated to Germany; and, in the late summer of 1940, when it began to appear that Britain would not immediately be defeated, Pétain and some of his Ministers gave evidence

---

[8] Dentz had been succeeded as senior Intelligence officer in Syria by Colonel Catroux now Free French leader in the Levant.

[9] Sir Alec Kirkbride, CMG, OBE, MC. Brit Resident in Transjordan 1939-45. B. 19 Aug 1897.

[1] Lt-Gen J. B. Glubb, CMG, DSO, OBE, MC. OC Arab Legion, Transjordan since 1939. B. Preston, Lancs, Eng, 16 Apr 1897.

[2] Brigadier Glubb wrote, in *The Story of the Arab Legion* (1948), p. 307: "For eleven years I had worked in Transjordan and dealt with many problems and disputes along the Syrian frontier. Throughout this time Transjordan, the Arab Legion, Peake Pasha and myself had been constantly accused by the French of intriguing against them. Nothing we could do affected their firm conviction of our treachery. No modification in this situation resulted from the fall of France . . . . We still abstained scrupulously from interference in Syria. The French still believed that we were busy intriguing. Then suddenly, in February 1941, we received secret instructions from England reversing the situation. We were told to place ourselves in touch with the people of Syria, with a view to possible resistance to the Germano-Italo-Vichy Government. Money was placed at our disposal for this purpose. It was agreed that Kirkbride should deal with the Druses and I with the Syrian tribes."

of a determination to resist further German encroachments. In October Weygand was sent to North Africa to organise resistance with the object of robbing both Germany and Britain of the excuse of having to occupy French North Africa to prevent the other from doing so. British efforts (through United States channels) to persuade the Vichy Government to go to North Africa and continue the struggle against Germany won no success. Indeed, while these negotiations were in progress, Pétain, determined to keep a foot in each camp, met Hitler at Montoire on 24th October and was persuaded into an agreement to give help to the German arms. This agreement stated that "the Axis Powers and France have an identical interest in seeing the defeat of England accomplished as soon as possible. Consequently, the French Government will support, within the limits of its ability, the measures which the Axis Powers may take to this end . . ."

During the winter of 1940-41, however, Pétain became less enthusiastic about a German victory. In December, M. Laval, the most pro-German of his leading Ministers, was arrested, and the efforts of United States envoys to detach Vichy from German dominance won some success. In May United States policy was to humour the Vichy Government to the utmost. The British leaders, tied as they were to the support of de Gaulle, disappointed at the failure of earlier efforts to win Vichy over, and anxious about the growth of German infiltration in North Africa, disagreed with the United States policy, being convinced that they had little to hope for from Pétain, from his lieutenant, Admiral Darlan, or from Weygand in North Africa. Nevertheless, as a concession, they allowed a limited number of ships bearing American wheat to go through the blockade to Marseilles.

The British policy of taking firm action against the Vichy Government was acceptable to a variety of influential leaders in the Middle East. For their information about Syrian conditions the British political and military staffs depended on officials with long service in the area and on the de Gaullists. It was not surprising that, as a rule, these British officials had been influenced by the keen rivalry between Britain and France in the Arab world. There was much in the French record (as in the British) that could be criticised; and this could be put forward as an indication of weakness and a reason why the conquest of Syria was not only a necessity, but would be relatively easy. The French officers, it was declared, were ill-paid and often corrupt, and their rule had been harsh; the population would not be sorry to see them go. The de Gaullists, adding their counsel, insisted that the French military leaders needed only to be provided with a pretext for surrendering. Both these groups of advisers were not unbiased.

On the other hand Wavell's Intelligence staff estimated the French army of Syria at about 28,000 metropolitan and colonial troops—highly trained and well-equipped regulars, mostly Negroes and Arabs—plus 25,000 Lebanese and Syrian troops, and a considerable force of gendarmeries who included a leavening of French officers and N.C.O's. Estimates of the number of German troops and agents in Syria ranged from an innocuous 200 to an ominous 3,000. General Wilson's staff considered that, at this stage, there were probably about 300.

The existence of this considerable army of regulars in Syria was the hard military fact which confronted Wavell, yet he was beset by political authorities who seemed convinced that he had only to throw his cap into Syria and walk in after it unharmed. Churchill had told him on the 9th May that he could see no other course open than to send in General Catroux. In military terms "General Catroux" connoted perhaps six battalions, including four of Senegalese mercenaries, and two batteries of 75-mm guns. On the 10th May General de Gaulle had complained to Wavell, by telegram, of delay in concentrating Free French forces for action in Syria. On the 18th, Catroux, keen to march into Syria, informed Wavell that the Vichy forces were withdrawing into the Lebanon preparatory to handing Syria over to the Germans; if this was so, it would leave the road to Damascus open, and Catroux asked leave to advance on that city. Wavell doubted Catroux's information and deferred a decision. Within a few hours Catroux's report was shown to be erroneous, when General Dentz made a broadcast stating that the British Government had accused France of "not having forcibly repelled German aircraft flying over Syria, some of which were forced to make landings", and declaring that his army was "ready to reply to force with force".

The Chiefs of Staff in London decided that Catroux should be allowed to move his troops to the frontier opposite Deraa and to advance into Syria if the reactions of Arabs and Vichy French were favourable. Consequently, on the 20th (the German attack on Crete opened that day), Wavell bowed to what seemed the inevitable. He instructed General Maitland Wilson, now commanding in Palestine and Transjordan, to prepare a plan for a combined British-Free French advance to Damascus, Rayak and Beirut, and warned the 7th Australian Division (General Lavarack) to make ready to move to Palestine.

Wavell plainly told the Chiefs of Staff in London, however, that at that stage a Free French entry into Syria, which they had approved, was bound to fail. He added that, if military policy in the Middle East was to be dictated by de Gaulle and Catroux, it were better to relieve him of his command.

The situation that had arisen in the month since Wavell had proposed that a political authority be appointed in the Middle East had underlined the wisdom of his suggestion. The ill-equipped garrison of Crete was under attack, Tobruk besieged, the force in the Western Desert dangerously weak, the revolt in Iraq still simmering. Yet, against Wavell's advice, Churchill and the Chiefs of Staff in London had approved in principle an invasion of Syria by a Free French force almost wholly lacking in artillery and transport and only one-fifth as strong numerically as the well-armed regulars commanded by Dentz.

Churchill himself replied to Wavell's protest. In a cable sent on the 21st he told Wavell that he was

> wrong in supposing that policy . . . arose out of any representations made by the Free French leaders. It arises entirely from the view taken here by those who have the supreme direction of war and policy in all theatres. Our view is that if the

Germans can pick up Syria and Iraq with petty air forces, tourists, and local revolts we must not shrink from running equal small-scale military risks . . . . For this decision we of course take full responsibility, and should you find yourself unwilling to give effect to it arrangements will be made to meet any wish you may express to be relieved of your command.[3]

Meanwhile, no sooner had the Chiefs of Staff agreed to Catroux's request that he be allowed to assemble his force for what he declared would be an easy advance to Damascus, than Catroux received information that caused him to alter his mind.

On 21st May (wrote Wavell) General Catroux, who had gone to Palestine to meet a French officer from Syria, cabled admitting that his information was entirely incorrect; that, far from withdrawing into the Lebanon, the French were moving troops south of Damascus and taking up positions to defend the routes to that city. He said that nothing but a large force could attempt the occupation of Syria. Meanwhile I had been receiving telegrams from General de Gaulle in West Africa, couched in imperative language, enquiring why the Free French troops were not already on the march to Damascus. This incident illustrates the difficulties there sometimes were in dealing with the Free French.[4]

The officer from Syria was Colonel Collet, commanding the Vichy forces in the Hauran province west of the Jebel Druse, who, also on the 21st, crossed into Palestine with seven of his ten squadrons of Circassian cavalry. (Of these, however, only some 350 men elected to remain in Palestine, the others returning to Syria.) Collet immediately convinced Catroux that Dentz was preparing to defend Syria, and that action by the Free French alone would be futile. On the 22nd Wavell again explained to General Dill that he did not wish to move into Syria until he could do so effectively, and declared his dislike of "political adventures" and "Jameson raids". He added, however, that, after having consulted Cunningham, Tedder and Blamey, he was moving reinforcements to Palestine.

Three days later, after a visit to Basra to confer with the Commander-in-Chief in India, General Auchinleck, Wavell reported to the War Office that he was preparing a plan for a combined advance into Syria with the 7th Australian Division (only two brigades), the Free French contingent, and units of the 1st Cavalry Division—a total force of about a division and a half, but with practically no armour. The objective was a line Damascus-Rayak-Beirut. He said that he considered this force was too small, and that two infantry divisions and an armoured division, or at least an armoured brigade, were needed for the operation.

The Defence Committee in London considered Wavell's proposal on the 27th. Next day Wavell was instructed that defeat in Crete must be accepted, that the first objective must be success in the Western Desert, but Syria must be occupied before the German Air Force had recovered from its losses in Crete. The Turks would be invited to occupy Aleppo.[5] It was left to Wavell to fix the date of the invasion, but it was to be as

---

[3] Quoted in Churchill, Vol III, p. 290.
[4] Wavell, *Despatch on Operations in the Middle East from 7th February 1941 to 15th July 1941*.
[5] On 18th June Turkey made a pact of friendship with Germany.

soon as he was "reasonably prepared". Wavell replied that 7th June was the earliest possible date.

General de Gaulle arrived in Jerusalem on the 29th May accompanied by Major-General Spears.

> Spears . . . came to see me first (wrote General Wilson[6]) and impressed on me the importance with which H.M. Government regarded de Gaulle and that one should defer to his wishes as much as possible. He explained to me his mission and the role of his political officers which was to ensure British control as a military necessity; his advice as to the treatment of the French in Syria was that the senior officers, junior officers and other ranks should all be segregated from each other and that the latter should be well fed and given wine and coffee; while we were advancing the French should be shouted at to get out of the way and let us get at the Germans! That evening de Gaulle came and saw me in my office; he stressed the psychological aspect of the operation; there were a vast number of French soldiers who disliked the idea of fighting the British or the Free French; with the Syrian professional army it was a question of honour, if instructed to hold a position they would have to defend it; it would be better to give it a pretext not to fight or to fight as little as possible—the best pretext would be to be extremely strong; the taking of Beirut would have a lot of influence to discontinue resistance as everyone was accustomed to receive orders from there; that aviation attack was preferable to artillery bombardment and would probably offer a better pretext. All these opinions could have little influence on the strength of the force as Wavell was stretched to the utmost to provide what we had.

To what extent had the Australian Government been consulted about the new project, in which a largely Australian force was to be employed? On the 18th May Blamey cabled to the Australian Government that it might become necessary to send the 7th Division to Palestine because of developments in Syria. It will be recalled that Wavell warned Lavarack on 20th May to be ready to move the 7th Division to Palestine, and on the 25th he informed the War Office that he was planning an advance into Syria using the 7th Division and other troops.

On the 24th May the Australian High Commissioner in London, Mr Bruce, had sent a cable to Mr Menzies emphasising the need to prevent the Germans from establishing themselves in Syria and suggesting that Menzies might wish to send a cable to Mr Churchill supporting this view. Before the Australian War Cabinet had considered this suggestion, Bruce, on the 27th, sent a second message stating that he understood that the Defence Committee was considering a plan for the immediate entry into Syria. In fact, on that day, the Defence Committee decided to give Wavell definite orders to invade Syria. On the 29th the Australian War Cabinet decided to ask General Blamey to give an appreciation of the position in the Middle East, including "the possibility of denying the use of Syria to the Germans", and on the same day, in a message to Churchill, Menzies said:

> Is it not possible to make some attempt at occupation of Syria by British forces? No doubt there has been some reluctance to do this because of the possible effect upon American public opinion. But I am assured by Casey on good authority in

---
[6] *Eight Years Overseas*, pp. 111-12.

Washington that American opinion would applaud aggressive British action. Anything would appear to be better than allowing Germany to make her foothold in Syria sufficiently strong to enable a jump forward to be accomplished.

For nine days before this cable was sent the planning of such an operation, to be undertaken largely by Australian troops, had been in progress. On the 30th Blamey's appreciation arrived in Australia. In it he said that it had become necessary to attempt to secure control of the Syrian air bases as soon as possible, and outlined the plan of attack. He said that the force available comprised two cavalry brigades, the 7th Australian Division less one brigade, one Indian brigade, and the Free French Division. (As will be seen below, the cavalry brigades were not ready for action, and the Free French contingent was not a division in the sense in which the word would be understood in Australia.)

On 31st May Churchill informed Menzies that Syria would be occupied as early as possible. On 4th June the Australian Ministers had not been informed of the proposed date of the invasion and, in a cable to Churchill, Menzies said that they were concerned about the delay in the movement into Syria. Late on the 7th Menzies learnt both from Churchill and Blamey that the attack would begin next morning. On the same day Churchill gave this information also to President Roosevelt.

Thus the Australian Government was not directly consulted about the invasion of Syria and was not informed about the planning until several days after the invasion had been ordered. On the other hand, in his message of the 29th May, Menzies had made it clear that his government favoured an attempt to occupy Syria. Anxiety about the fate of Australian troops included in the small garrison of Cyprus may have influenced the Australian Ministers in urging an invasion of Syria.

Was there in fact a danger that German forces might establish themselves in Syria, and had an advance-guard already arrived? The terms of the armistices between France on the one hand and Germany and Italy on the other provided that Italy was to determine the extent of, and supervise the partial demobilisation of French Colonial forces. An Italian Armistice Commission had arrived in Syria in August 1940, and by November the French regular forces there had been reduced to some 28,000.

After his talks with Pétain at Montoire Hitler decided that the best way to ensure that Britain or the de Gaullists did not occupy any more French colonies would be to enable Vichy France to defend them. The German and Italian staffs considered that the French army in Syria should be increased to three divisions by reinforcing it with some 10,000 Moroccan troops; but the problem of getting them there remained unsolved.

Darlan, the French Foreign Minister, went to Paris on 3rd May at the invitation of Abetz, the German representative there, and it was then that it was agreed to make munitions stored in Syria available to the Iraqi forces and to allow German and Italian aircraft to refuel in Syria.

Five days later Darlan ordered Dentz to allow the Germans to use what facilities Syria offered and to resist any attempt by the British to retaliate, and, as mentioned above, a German Foreign Office official, Rudolph Rahn, arrived in Syria on the 9th to organise supplies to Iraq. The German leaders were so pleased by the agreement with Vichy that on the 11th and 12th May Darlan was allowed to see Hitler at Berchtesgaden, where Hitler told him that if France defended her colonies she would be allowed to retain them after the war, but if Germany had to defend them for her she would take them away. The general agreement that Darlan had made at Paris was expressed in an undertaking which Darlan signed containing a detailed statement of the help to be given to Germany in Syria and North Africa. He agreed to sell to Iraq three-quarters of the military gear kept in store in Syria under the terms of the Armistice of July 1940; to refuel German and Italian aircraft in Syria; to allow the German forces to use the Aleppo airfield, and the Syrian ports and railways; and to transmit all intelligence about British forces and plans in the Near East to the German High Command. The Germans agreed to allow the transfer from France to Syria of eighty-four field, anti-aircraft and anti-tank guns and three batteries of heavy anti-aircraft guns, and some troops from North Africa. The agreement provided also that, in North Africa, France would allow the German forces to use the port of Bizerta, would sell trucks and guns to Germany and allow German ships and aircraft to use Dakar as a base.

When Pétain was warned by his colleagues that the concession regarding Bizerta and Dakar would probably provoke the strong disapproval of the United States, and perhaps war with Britain, he summoned Weygand, who protested strongly against the Darlan agreement; and on 6th June it was agreed that there should be a complete re-examination of Franco-German relations.[7] (The French Government was, of course, unaware that the North African undertakings had been robbed of military importance by the fact that the German Army was no longer free to undertake a large-scale African campaign. The German attack on Russia was being prepared, and on 6th June Hitler was finally to fix the 22nd as the day on which his armies would march across the Russian frontiers.)

On 25th May Hitler informed his staff that arms and aircraft should be sent to Iraq but whether it would be possible afterwards "to launch an offensive against the Suez Canal and eventually oust the British finally from their position between the Mediterranean and the Persian Gulf" could not be decided until the operations against Russia were complete.

At his trial in 1945 Dentz declared that late in April he had assured the British Consul-General at Beirut that there need be no anxiety lest he allow Germans to use Syrian airfields; they were well guarded. On the 6th May, however, Dentz received the order from Darlan to allow German aircraft to land and refuel; and on the 9th and the 11th a total of four

---

[7] In his memoirs (p. 963) Cordell Hull, the United States Secretary of State, described this as "one of the most fateful discussions of the war". "What could well have been an insurmountable crisis in our relations with Vichy was averted."

German machines wearing Iraqi colours landed at Syrian airfields. A few days later thirty-three German mechanics reached Aleppo, and in the course of the Iraq campaign 120 German aircraft passed through, coming and going. As for sending arms to the Iraqi, Dentz said afterwards that he dispatched not 24 guns, 800 machine-guns and from 30,000 to 40,000 rifles as he had been instructed to do, but eight guns without sights and 354 old machine-guns.[8] Late in May, when it was evident that the Iraq rebellion had failed, Dentz appealed to Darlan to order the withdrawal of the German missions, and by 6th June the last German aircraft and the last German officers and mechanics—the thirty-three men had not been increased—departed from Syria, and General Jennequin, who commanded the French air force in Syria, informed the United States Consul-General that this had been done.

The withdrawal of the German party had been ordered by the German High Command lest it provide a pretext for a British invasion of Syria. Hitler's Chief of Staff, General Keitel, had reported to General Cavallero, the Italian Chief of the General Staff, on 2nd June that these orders had been given. "The only people to stay were Intelligence officers whose presence would be camouflaged," he added. The policy given to Rahn was to do all he could to deprive the British of a pretext for invading Syria and to increase antagonism between the British and the French. Major Hansen, a Germany army officer who had gone to Syria with Rahn, reported early in June that a German operation based on Syria would need long preparation and could not begin before the middle of October; until then everything possible should be done politically to prevent British forces from entering.

Dentz had received definite instructions from Vichy that he was to oppose any British attempt to enter Syria—British but not German forces were to be treated as hostile. At his trial, where it was soon made plain that any plea that he was a soldier acting under orders would be ineffective, Dentz defended the policy of resistance. He claimed that only if he resisted, and threw some vigour into the fight, would the Germans be persuaded not to overrun unoccupied France and the North African colonies on the ground that the French could not defend them. "It has been said that I defended Syria for Hitler," he declared. "It is not true. I defended, in Syria, France and North Africa against seizure by Germany .... It was that which guided my conduct. That was the reason for the attitude I adopted from the outset."

It was a strange situation. The British Government had insisted that its local commanders must invade Syria before the Germans gained control of it, but (although they did not know it) they had done so at a time when very few Germans remained in Syria and the main line of German policy in the Levant was to avoid providing Britain with any pretext for invasion.

---

[8] The report of Rahn, the German agent in Syria who organised the dispatch of these weapons, does not explain precisely how many were eventually sent. He mentions a first consignment of 4 guns, 200 machine-guns and 15,500 rifles, but implies that there were later consignments.

Before this stage was reached, Axis policy in this zone had been marked by procrastination and misfortune. At the outset the German leaders had set about disarming the French forces in the colonies. When this had been half done, they decided that they had made a mistake and that the best way to keep those colonies out of British hands was to enable the Vichy French themselves to defend them. It was then too late, however, to rebuild the French Colonial armies they had half dispersed. When, in September, the principal Arab Nationalist leader had approached the German Government for arms and gold, it cold-shouldered him; but in January, after valuable months had been lost, it changed its mind. When the *coup d'état* in Iraq occurred the German leaders had no plan for intervention and the operations in Iraq were well under way and Iraq's hopes were fading before their agents got to work. The commander of the little air force they sent to Iraq was shot down by Iraqi gunners when his machine appeared over Baghdad and, within a few days, all but two of the German aircraft flown in were unserviceable. Meanwhile several trainloads of French arms were sent into Iraq. They arrived too late to be of use to the Iraqis, and it seems probable that the French, who loved the Arabs even less than they loved the Germans, saw to it that the arms sent were of little value to the Iraqis. Nevertheless these trainloads of arms did not return to Syria, where the French would have been able to make use of them.

Dentz and his followers in Syria were under the supervision of an Italian Commission which they despised. Their government had commanded them to cooperate discreetly with the Germans whom they detested and who had laid their country low. They were threatened with possible attack by the forces of Britain, the ally who (so they believed) had failed them in Europe in 1940 and for a generation had intrigued against them in the Levant; and by the forces of de Gaulle whom the followers of Pétain regarded as a rebel against the Government of France.

CHAPTER 16

THE SYRIAN PLAN

THE task which Wavell had been required so unwillingly to undertake was to attack and overrun a region of tangled mountains and wide desert land garrisoned by an army considerably larger and in important respects better equipped than any the invaders could put against it—at least within the following few weeks. The Syrian mandate extended some 300 miles from north to south and from east to west, but militarily the vital region was the south-western corner bounded by the frontier on the south, and, on the north, by the railway from Beirut, the capital of the Lebanon and the site of the French General Headquarters, through Rayak, the principal airport, to Damascus, capital of Syria proper. In that area were two of the three main cities and nearly half the population. Its western half is a zone of rugged mountains and steep-sided upland valleys. One geographer has compared the relation of these mountains to Palestine as being similar, from a military point of view, to that which the mountains of Afghanistan bear to India; and the ancient fortress of Banias at the foot of towering Mount Hermon as being comparable with Peshawar near the entrance to the Khyber Pass.[1] The mountains of Lebanon are not on the Afghan scale, but an invader from Palestine faces somewhat the same problems as an Indian invader of Afghanistan.

Three main routes, two served by more than one road, led from Palestine into Lebanon and south-western Syria. On the west a road wound along the narrow coastal ledge at the foot of the Lebanons or was tunnelled through the cliffs. A parallel road, later forking into two, travelled from Banias in Palestine along the upland valley between the Lebanon on the west and the still higher range of Hermon and the Anti-Lebanon on the east. Along this valley flows the Litani River until, near the frontier, it turns west and enters the sea between Tyre and Sidon. Farther east, pinched between the eastern range and the difficult lava-strewn Jebel Druse, a third road (and from Transjordan a fourth) led through the low desert and steppe land and joined at Damascus. Thus geography imposed on the commander of an army invading Syria from Palestine three possible lines of advance—(i) through a defile between sea and mountains, (ii) along a winding mountain road, or (iii) over an area of broad desert highways. The coastal route travelled through a region of olives, mulberries and bananas; the central roads through denuded mountain country with wheat and vines in the valleys and on terraced hillsides; the eastern through desert and wheat land with occasional oases, of which Damascus is one.

The Vichy French army was believed to include six regiments of regulars, including one of the Foreign Legion, one of mixed colonial and metropolitan troops, and four of African natives. There were also about 9,000

---

[1] G. A. Smith, *Historical Geography of the Holy Land*, (1894).

cavalry, some units being horsed and others equipped with tanks or armoured cars, ninety field and medium guns, and some 10,000 Levantine infantry of doubtful value. Thus, leaving out of account the Levantine troops, there was the equivalent of two strong infantry divisions and a half-division of tanks, armoured cars and cavalry—35,000 regulars in all, including some 8,000 Frenchmen. Under Dentz, General de Verdilhac was deputy commander-in-chief; the three principal area commanders were General Delhomme at Damascus, Colonel Beucler at Beirut, and Colonel Rottier at Aleppo. General Jennequin commanded the air force.

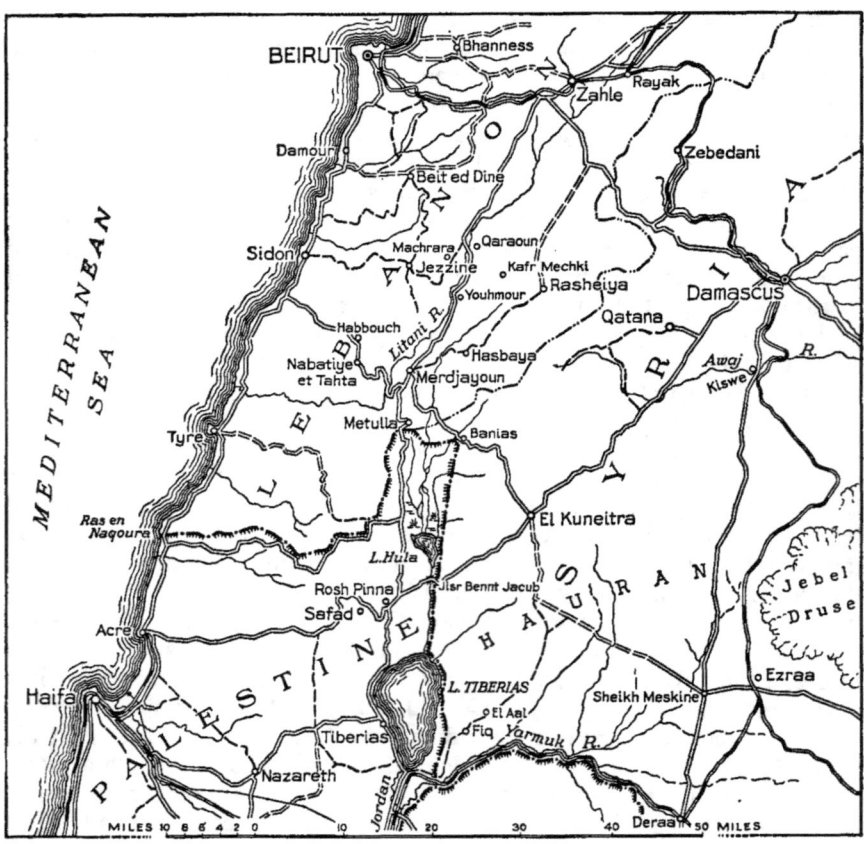

The main components of the invading force were to be the 7th Australian Division, hitherto untried in battle but strenuously trained since its formation in April and May 1940; the veteran 5th Indian Brigade, recently withdrawn from Abyssinia;[2] and the Free French contingent, which was in process of being organised into six battalions, two batteries of 75's,

---

[2] This brigade had arrived at Mersa Matruh from Abyssinia on 12 April, and moved to Palestine in the third week of May.

one tank company, and Colonel Collet's cavalry detachment. The air force made available by Air Marshal Tedder to support the invasion consisted of two fighter squadrons and a half (including No. 3 R.A.A.F.), two bomber squadrons and one army cooperation squadron. These were commanded by Air Commodore L. O. Brown[3] and possessed some 70 first-line aircraft; the French had nearly 100, including 60 fighters.[4] While the military operation was being planned part of the British air force had continued almost daily to bomb Syrian airfields.

To support the advance on the coastal plain and protect it against interference by the French naval force, which included two 3,000-ton destroyers and three submarines, Admiral Cunningham allotted, at the outset, two cruisers and four destroyers under Vice-Admiral King of the 15th Cruiser Squadron. A second naval force—the landing ship *Glengyle,* cruiser *Coventry,* and two destroyers—was to be available to land troops on the Syrian coast. Thus all the serviceable cruisers and six out of about 17 serviceable destroyers were allotted to the Syrian operation.

Since April the 7th Division had been improving and manning the Matruh fortress, where it had gained in experience and physical fitness, and had been under fairly frequent air bombardment. In the past six months it had been chopped and changed. Of its two brigades, the 21st had belonged to the division from its formation; the 25th had been formed in England in the critical months of 1940. One battalion of the 25th—the 2/32nd—had, on 3rd May, been sent to Tobruk to complete the 24th Brigade, whose third battalion, the 2/25th, had just arrived in Egypt, armed only with rifles. A week later, having received its automatic weapons, the 2/25th joined the 25th Brigade. General Lavarack's divisional cavalry regiment was the 6th, the 7th being in Cyprus. He had all three of his artillery regiments. Thus, if he could borrow an infantry brigade, his division, already reinforced with units from two other divisions, would be at full strength.

While General Lavarack was in Cairo receiving his instructions, he saw General Blamey and discussed the further reinforcement of the depleted 7th Division by units of the 6th Division and Corps troops. Blamey, though now Wavell's Deputy Commander-in-Chief in the Middle East, was still commanding the A.I.F. and still in direct control of I Australian Corps, the staff of which was then collected at Deir Suneid in Palestine, resting after Greece and Crete.

Part of the 6th Division was then (late in May) in action in Crete, but part was resting and re-training in Palestine and was a pool from which the 7th Division's shortage of infantry might be made up. At length it was decided that the 2/3rd and 2/5th Battalions would be placed under Lavarack's command. Five of the nine battalions of the 6th were in Crete (though parties that had become detached from some of them were in

---

[3] Air Vice-Marshal Sir Leslie Brown, KCB, CBE, DSC, AFC. AOC Levant 1941-42, 84 Gp 1943-44; Comdt Sch of Land/Air Warfare RAF 1944-49. Regular airman; of Durban, Sth Africa; b. Pietermaritzburg, Sth Africa, 11 Jul 1893.

[4] A Fleet Air Arm squadron on Cyprus and long-range bombers from the Delta area were also to assist.

Palestine). Of the remaining four battalions—2/2nd, 2/3rd, 2/5th and 2/6th—enough officers and men had been left in Crete to form the 16th and 17th Composite Battalions; and the 2/2nd and 2/6th had lost heavily at Pinios and at the Corinth Canal respectively.[5] The 2/3rd and 2/5th alone possessed a nucleus strong enough to make it reasonable to expect them to be ready for action within, say, a month.[6]

When General Lavarack met General Wilson at his advanced report centre at Sarafand in Palestine on 22nd May Wilson told him that Wavell and he had agreed that the main effort of the invading force should be towards Beirut along the coast road, and only subsidiary drives should be made from Metulla. Elaborate measures were to be taken to conceal the British intention and the preliminary movements. The 7th Division would be named "Aust Exporter Division" and Australian troop movements in northern Palestine would be explained as merely the relief of the 6th Division's units there. Other measures were taken to conceal the new plan. Senior officers were instructed not to visit Jerusalem or Haifa; no leave was to be given; Australians who moved forward to within sight of the French were to wear caps or topees not Australian hats.

Two days later at another conference at Sarafand Wilson emphasised that there should be as great a show of force as possible. When he said again that the main line of advance would be along the coast road Lavarack expressed the opinion that the right column had the greatest hope of success; but Wilson said that Wavell and he had agreed to make the main effort on the left. However, at the next conference, on the 26th, when Lavarack again said that he thought the right column would make faster progress, Wilson agreed that this was "a likely development". At the conference on the 24th Wilson had said that he thought the invasion might begin on the night of the 31st, but two days later he said that date —a week ahead—would be too early. Lavarack's division was still at Matruh; even his advanced headquarters had not yet arrived in Palestine; details of the force available were still so obscure that precise planning was yet impossible.

---

[5] From southern Greece embarked only seven officers and 180 men of the 2/2nd who thought they were all that was left of the battalion; but during May the arrival of groups of escapers from Greece, including Colonel Chilton, and the addition of 250 reinforcements brought the strength to 540, and in June the addition of the men from Crete swelled it to 640.

[6] At 12 May it was estimated that the men of the infantry battalions of 6 Div were divided between Crete and Palestine thus:

Bn	Crete	Palestine	Bn	Crete	Palestine
2/1	620	72	2/7	647	53
2/2	189	356	2/4	554	22
2/3	129	484	2/8	386	207
2/5	74	569	2/11	688	6
2/6	215	327			

The division had gone to Greece 12,486 strong. It was estimated that on 12 May 6,178 were in Crete, 4,258 in Palestine, and 2,050 had been lost in Greece.

The re-forming of the 2/1st Battalion after the main body of the battalion had been lost in Crete may be taken as typical. Early in June the 2/1st comprised about 70 men in Palestine. The two other battalions of the 16th Brigade each contributed to it 100 experienced men, including a quota of non-commissioned officers (Colonel Chilton of the 2/2nd wisely allowed Major Edgar of the depleted 2/1st to choose his own N.C.O's from the 2/2nd.) Some original officers of the 2/1st were brought back from other appointments, and the battalion was brought up to strength with about eighteen officers and 500 men from the reinforcement battalion. Thus of the officers and men of the re-formed battalion about one-third had been in action. At first some of the men transferred from the other battalions wore miniature colour patches of their old units above their new patches, an indication of the deep-seated attachments that had developed.

Lavarack considered that the senior staffs were approaching the problem with undue optimism. An outline plan prepared by Wavell's planners declared that "the success of the operation largely depends on lack of resistance, or at least acquiescence by the French", and was based on a conviction that, when attacked, the French would withdraw "into the Lebanon, thereby leaving the rest of the country open to invasion"—an ambiguous statement since it was against the Lebanon that the main part of the invading force was being concentrated. The planners' proposals included "a rapid move along the coastal road to Beirut by armoured cars and motorised infantry with the object of seizing all important control points and high officials in Beirut before dawn".

On the 28th Wilson was still unable to tell the divisional commander exactly what units would be in his force; and only a few copies of an Intelligence handbook providing information about the Syrian roads, towns and people and the defending army were available. The only maps were on a scale of 1 to 200,000, whereas maps on a scale of 1 to 25,000 or 50,000 are desirable for warfare in tangled mountain country. Wilson informed Lavarack that no heavy tanks or heavy anti-aircraft artillery would be ready until the middle of June and asked when he would be able to attack without them. Lavarack said that he hoped at least a battery of light anti-aircraft guns would be available; he thought the attack should begin early, and that he would be ready by 3rd June. Wilson said that other units would not be ready until the 5th; and the attack could not begin before that date. Even more disturbing than this evidence that some of the preparations were moving slowly was the news that the French knew that an attack was imminent.

Commanders of the invading force were informed that French-speaking officers and Free French officers would be attached to their formations on a scale of one to a battalion, and that these would approach French posts with a white flag and a megaphone and call upon the occupants to surrender and join de Gaulle. The Australian commanders were not impressed by these proposals and most of them appear not to have taken them very seriously. Day by day the British agents on the frontier, mostly Jews, brought in information that the posts were being reinforced. British officials who had crossed the frontier on friendly visits had seen the French siting guns and digging in round the Merdjayoun area; and a few days before the invasion was to open new French troops appeared at the frontier posts and all fraternisation ceased.[7]

In the early days of June, in an atmosphere of haste and some uncertainty, the plan took final shape. The French commander was moving troops towards the frontier. It was believed that he had five battalions and four squadrons of cavalry forward in the coastal sector, perhaps three battalions and some tanks in the centre, and two battalions with several

---

[7] At a conference on 31st May Lavarack raised the question of the danger of attack on his right flank across the Jordan from the Kuneitra area and suggested that the area should be occupied in anticipation of such an attack. Because he did not consider the precautions taken to be adequate Lavarack picketed the Jisr Bennt Jacub and the slopes of the hills east of the Jordan and north of Lake Hula.

cavalry and motorised squadrons in the desert zone. At a conference on 4th June the time of the attack was fixed—2 a.m. on the 8th. At earlier conferences the main outlines of the plan had already been made known to the formation commanders.[8]

Wilson wrote afterwards: "The main objective was Beirut; the shortest approach was along the coast but the road could be easily blocked. I decided, therefore, to advance three-headed on a wide front."[9] The first phase of the attack was to be the capture of Damascus, Rayak and Beirut —the two capital cities and the main air base on the road linking them; the second phase an advance to Palmyra, Homs and Tripoli. On the left would be one reinforced brigade of the 7th Australian Division; in the centre another reinforced brigade of that division; on the right the 5th Indian Brigade Group and the Free French contingent. The Australian column on the left was to advance along the coast road to Beirut, the column in the centre through Metulla and Merdjayoun to Rayak; the Indian brigade was to advance into the Hauran, the high wheat lands east of Lake Tiberias and the upper Jordan, and with one column occupy Deraa, Sheikh Meskine, and Ezraa, with a detachment Fiq and El Aal, and with a left column Kuneitra. Thus it would form a bridgehead through which General Legentilhomme's French brigade would advance through Kiswe to Damascus, while Colonel Collet's cavalry (300 strong) rode north through Fiq to Kuneitra. To the consternation of the enthusiastic Glubb Pasha the invasion was planned without a role being given to his little Arab Legion in Transjordan—about equal in strength to a British cavalry regiment.

---

[8] On the day of the invasion the force nominally included:
  7 Aust Div (Maj-Gen J. D. Lavarack)
    21 Bde (2/14, 2/16, 2/27 Bns)
    25 Bde (2/25, 2/31, 2/33 Bns)
    Divisional troops, 6 Div Cav   2/2 A-Tk Regt
                       9 Div Cav   2/3 Bn
                       2/4 Fd Regt   2/5 Bn
                       2/5 Fd Regt   2/3 MG Bn
                       2/6 Fd Regt   2/2 Pioneer Bn
    Additional troops under command:
      The Greys and the Staffs Yeomanry (forming one composite mechanised regt)
      One sqn, The Royals (armoured)
      57 LAA Regt
  5 Indian Bde Group (Brig W. L. Lloyd)
    5 Indian Bde (1/Royal Fusiliers, 3/1 Punjab, 4/6 Rajput Rif)
    1 Fd Regt
    One bty RAA
    Two tps LAA
  Free French Division (Gen Legentilhomme)
    Bde d'Orient (1 B.M. Bn, 2 B.M. Bn, Foreign Legion)
      One bty arty (4 75-mm guns)
      One tank coy (nine tanks)
      One anti-tank coy
      Coy Marine Fusiliers
    Circassian Cavalry (300 strong)
      Force Troops

Engineer, signal and service units have been omitted. In addition to its own two field companies of engineers (2/5 and 2/6) the 2/9 Fd Coy was attached to 7 Div. Although 2/3, 2/5 Inf, and 2/3 Machine Gun Bns and 9 Div Cav were included in the order of battle, they were still incompletely equipped. The two infantry battalions were not to receive an adequate allocation of vehicles until 17 June.

Three battalions of Senegalese and a second battery were to be added to the Free French Division eventually enabling a second brigade to be formed.

[9] Lord Wilson, *Eight Years Overseas*, p. 113.

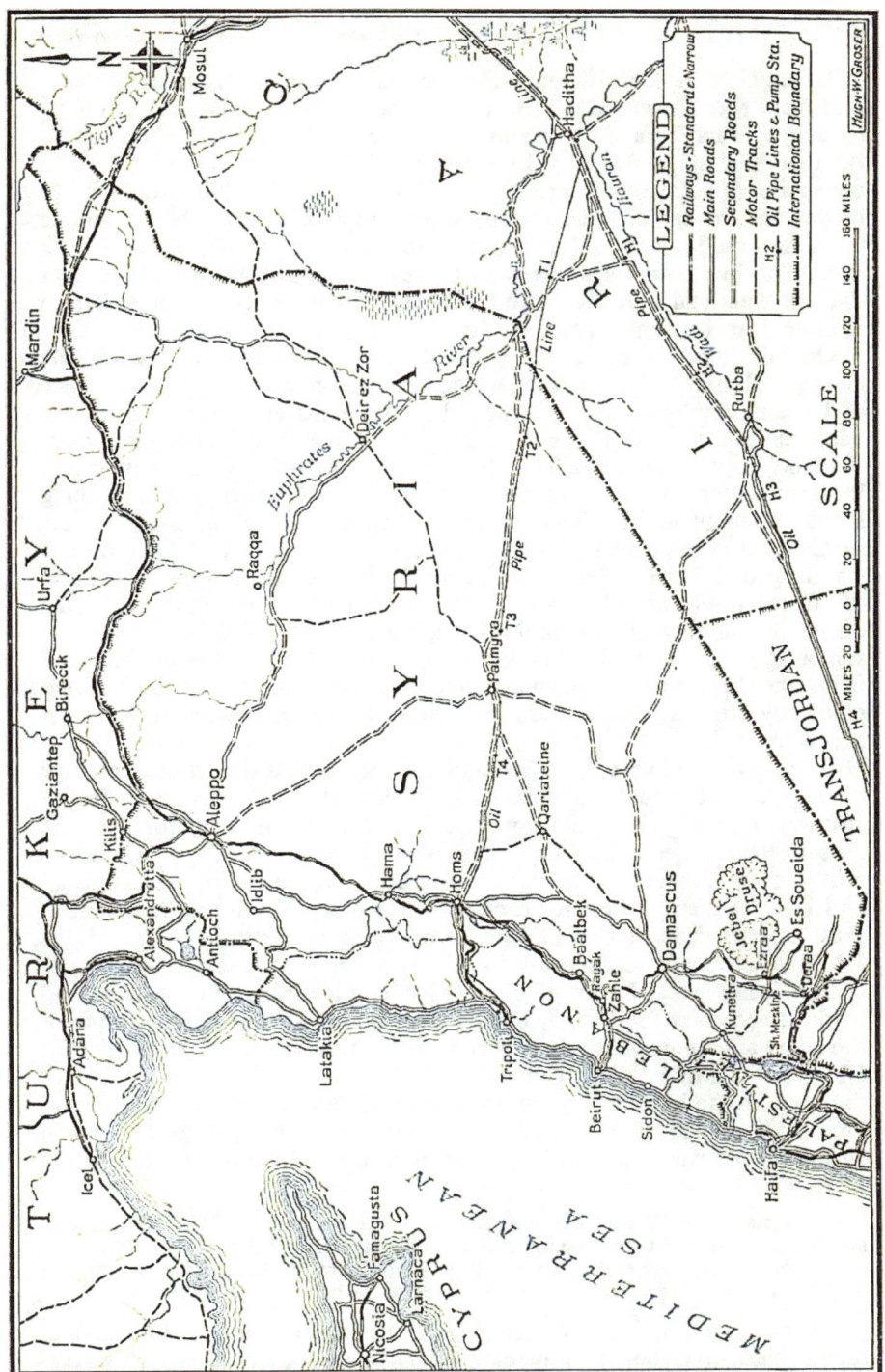

Lavarack gave his division three successive objectives: the first was a line from Merdjayoun along the road to Sidon; the second a line joining Rasheiya, Machrhara, Jezzine and Sidon; the third the Rayak-Beirut road. At that final stage the 21st Brigade would be in Beirut and the 25th occupying the Rayak aerodrome. The first task of the 25th would be to move forward on foot and occupy the Merdjayoun area whence mobile columns would advance along the two roads leading thence to the Rayak area. The two battalions borrowed from 6th Division were to take over the prisoners and police captured territory. An independent force was to operate from Iraq against eastern Syria.

On 5th June Lavarack was given definite instructions (of which the Corps staff already had warning) that when the first stage of the advance had been completed, that is, when the line Damascus-Rayak-Beirut had been reached, he would take command of I Australian Corps and control the whole operation, Brigadier Allen of the 16th Brigade succeeding him in command of the 7th Division. At that time General Blamey, being Deputy Commander-in-Chief in the Middle East, had his headquarters in Cairo, and the senior officer at I Corps headquarters at Deir Suneid was Brigadier Rowell. Before 5th June, Rowell, fearing lest, as in Greece, the Corps would be called upon to take command in the field not at the outset but in the midst of operations, pointed out to General Wilson's senior staff officer that the Australian Corps should be given command from the beginning, contending that command could not be exerted efficiently from a headquarters in Jerusalem, but the proposal was not accepted.

It appears that Wilson and his staff considered that the Corps' shortage of vehicles and signal equipment as a result of losses in Greece was a strong reason why it should not take command of the field force at the outset. Nevertheless, the Corps staff was moved forward to Nazareth—partly in vehicles lent by the Palestine Police—on the eve of the campaign and was complete, except for a corps commander. From the beginning it sent out its liaison officers and heads of services, particularly among the 7th Division, so as to be ready to take over when the time came.

The decision that I Australian Corps should again go into the field had made it necessary for Blamey to appoint a successor to himself in one of the three appointments he now occupied. He was Deputy Commander-in-Chief in the Middle East; Commander of the A.I.F., which was part of the force in the Middle East; and, since no successor had been appointed, *de facto* Commander of I Australian Corps, which was part of the A.I.F. In the second week of May he had written to the Minister for the Army, Mr Spender:

> I understand from Press wires that you desire me to continue GOC AIF. It does not appear that the two appointments are incompatible. They are in fact complementary to a considerable degree. It will not however be possible for me to continue in command of the Australian Corps as such.

At the same time he informed the Prime Minister that he intended to recommend that General Lavarack be appointed to command an Australian Corps (7th and 9th Divisions) and General Freyberg an Anzac Corps (6th and New Zealand Divisions).[1] It was appropriate that General Lavarack should thus be promoted to a senior command. In order to obtain an active command in the field he had accepted appointment to the 7th Division with the rank of major-general although he was a lieut-general in the Australian Staff Corps and for four years had been Chief of the General Staff in Australia. This loss of rank placed him under British generals who had hitherto been junior to him—an experience that he shared with most Dominion generals who served under British and American commanders. He had been disappointed at being transferred from command of the force in the Western Desert in April and replaced by a relatively junior British officer, General Beresford-Peirse (who, how-ever, had had useful desert experience as commander of the 4th Indian Division). The staff of his division, which contained rather more regular officers than General Mackay's 6th Division did, was led by Colonel John Austin Chapman,[2] who, when war broke out, had been on loan to the British Army as an instructor at the Staff College at Camberley; his artillery commander was Brigadier Berryman who had been Mackay's senior staff officer in the Western Desert.[3] Berryman was a confident and highly-qualified staff officer who had served in the artillery in France in 1916-1918 and in general staff appointments between the wars. At this stage he was the most widely experienced of Lavarack's three Australian brigadiers.

The axes of the division's advance were so widely separated that the brigade commanders would inevitably bear a heavier responsibility and control larger bodies of attached troops than in an attack on a narrower front. The senior of them was J. E. S. Stevens, a militia officer who had served in the Signal Corps, both in France in the previous war and at home in the militia, until 1935, when he was appointed to command an infantry battalion. His first appointment in the Second A.I.F. had been to command the signallers of the 6th Division. Short and slight in stature, waspishly aggressive and persistent in action, Stevens was picked out of the 6th Division by Lavarack in 1940 and given the task of forming and commanding the 21st Brigade in the 7th. At the time of his appointment he was by several years the youngest brigade commander in the force; in 1918 he had been a subaltern of 22 whereas his fellow brigadiers of 1940 had then been infantry or staff officers of higher rank and wider experience.

Brigadier Baxter-Cox's[4] 25th Brigade had already had two com-manders when he was appointed to it in March 1941—Stevens had then

---

[1] Details of this proposed reorganisation are given in Chapter 28.

[2] Maj-Gen J. A. Chapman, CB, DSO, VX13844. (1st AIF: Maj 30 Bn and BM 8 and 15 Bdes.) GSO1 52 Brit Div Sep-Nov 1939, 7 Aust Div 1940-41; DA & QMG Adv LHQ 1942-44; Deputy CGS 1944-46. Regular soldier; b. Braidwood, NSW, 15 Dec 1896.

[3] The principal appointments to the Staff of the 7 Div in June 1941 were: *GOC* Maj-Gen J. D. Lavarack; *GSO1* Col J. A. Chapman; *GSO2* Maj R. G. Pollard; *Snr LO* Maj C. H. Grace; *AA & QMG* Col V. C. Secombe; *DAAG* Maj N. W. Simpson; *DAQMG* Maj L. G. Canet; *ADMS* Col F. K. Norris; *Legal Staff Offr* Maj F. B. Gamble; *DADOS* Lt-Col C. R. Speckman; *DAPM* Capt N. W. Faulkner; *CRA* Brig F. H. Berryman; *CRE* Lt-Col R. J. H. Risson; *CO Sigs* Lt-Col B. T. R. Chadd; *CO ASC* Lt-Col P. S. McGrath.

[4] Brig A. R. Baxter-Cox, CBE, WX1573. (1st AIF: Lt 4 Bn.) CO 2/16 Bn 1940-41; Comd 25 Bde 1941; Mil Sec LHQ 1943-46. Architect; of Perth, WA; b. Cue, WA, 7 Sep 1898.

been training his brigade for nine months. In 1918 Cox had been a 2nd-lieutenant in France. He was an architect by profession and had served with the engineers and later the infantry between the wars. In 1940 he was transferred from the command of a militia brigade in Western Australia to form the 2/16th Battalion.

The third brigade commander in the force taking part in the initial assault, W. L. Lloyd, whose 5th Indian Brigade was operating independently on the right, was a tested Indian Army officer with recent experience, in the Western Desert and Abyssinia, of hard fighting in country of the kind that now faced his battalions.

Brigadier Stevens' problem in the coastal sector was greatly complicated by the likelihood that the defenders would demolish the roads and bridges ahead of him, and particularly the road a few miles north of Ras en Naqoura where it ran along a steep cliff face, and the bridge over the Litani which flowed into the sea 17 miles from the frontier. It was decided to send in a small party of infantry and engineers ahead of the main force to prevent the demolition of the coastal road beyond Iskandaroun on the steep Naqoura headland, and to land a British commando battalion under Colonel Pedder,[5] on the far side of the Litani at dawn on the day of the invasion to save the bridge over that river.

From the sea at Ras en Naqoura eastwards to the eastern limit of Stevens' 25-mile sector the frontier followed a line of lofty, rugged hills into which the only entrance for motor vehicles was the coast road. There were, however, two lateral roads one south and one north of the frontier, and, at El Malikiya more than 20 miles from the coast, they approached to within 1,000 yards of one another. If this gap could be bridged it would be possible to reach Tyre, which lay north of the possible demolition at Iskandaroun, along a road that wound through the hills through Bennt Jbail and Tibnine.

Along the heights between the upper Jordan Valley and the coast the French had a line of widely-spaced blockhouses—at Aitaroun, Bennt Jbail, Ain Ebel, Yaroun, Remeiche, Aita Chaab, Ramiet, Jereine, Alma Chaab and Labouna. Stevens decided that he would seize these posts, and as quickly as possible cut a road from El Malikiya to the French frontier road so as to make a second gateway into the coastal zone.

He divided his force into two main columns. The strongest of these under Lieut-Colonel MacDonald[6] of the 2/16th, which Stevens then considered the best of his battalions, and including that battalion, two troops of armoured cars, the carrier troops of "A" Squadron of the 6th Divisional Cavalry, and about half his artillery and engineers, was to move on Tyre along the difficult inland road through Bennt Jbail and Tibnine. Farther west the 2/14th Battalion was to seize the frontier posts; and this done,

---

[5] Lt-Col R. R. N. Pedder; CO "C" Special Service Bn 1941. Regular soldier; b. Woolston, Hants, Eng, 20 Jul 1904. Killed in action, 9 Jun 1941.
[6] Col A. B. MacDonald, SX4539. CO 2/16 Bn 1941; various training appts incl DDMT LHQ 1945. Regular soldier; of Walcha, NSW; b. Walcha, 13 Apr 1898.

a column led by Lieut-Colonel Moten[7] of the 2/27th and including the light tank troops of the cavalry squadron and a share of artillery and engineers, was to advance along the coast road if it could, but, if that road was so damaged as to be impassable, Stevens might order it to follow MacDonald's column through Tibnine, thus by-passing the demolitions on the coast. A subsidiary column would be formed by the Cheshire Yeomanry, a horsed cavalry regiment allotted to Stevens, which he ordered to move through the hills by way of Tibnine and Srifa to Kafr Sir on the Litani, where it would be in a position to outflank the enemy positions near the mouth of that river should the advance be held up there. The coastal column was to be supported by the guns of the naval squadron.

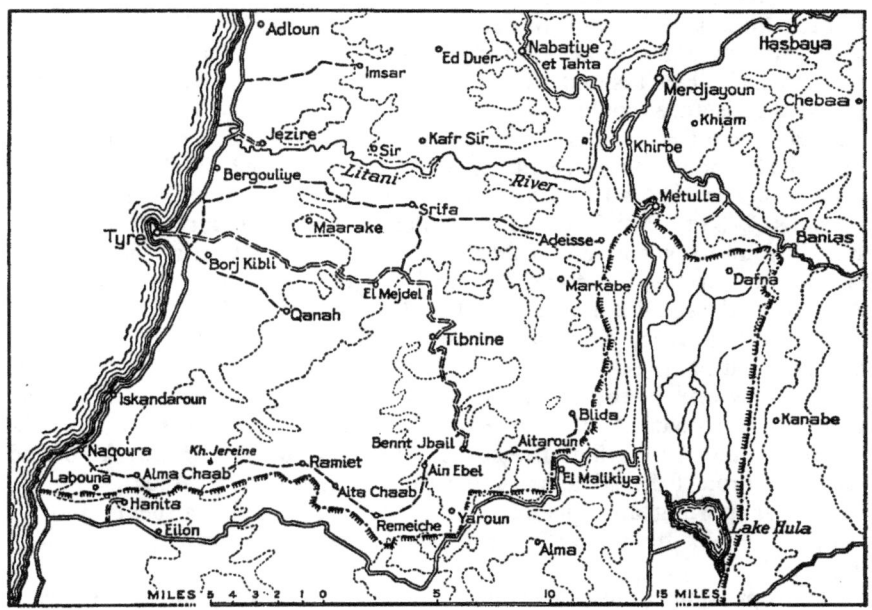

In the 25th Brigade's area the main approach to the frontier was along the road travelling due north to Metulla between the Hula marshes on the east and the Lebanons on the west and, from Rosh Pinna northwards, visible from Syrian territory. Thus Cox's first problem was to move his force forward into the Metulla salient and take the frontier posts overlooking his line of advance from east and west. With this object he decided to assemble his attacking troops on the lateral road to Dafna. Thence they would capture the posts on the high ground overlooking them and occupy a line through Chebaa, Hasbaya, Merdjayoun to Nabatiye et Tahta. This done, the group would divide into two columns each containing a battalion and a proportion of the mechanised cavalry, artillery and other troops. One

---

[7] Brig M. J. Moten, CBE, DSO, SX2889. CO 2/27 Bn 1940-41; Comd 17 Bde 1941-45. Bank officer; of Woodville, SA; b. Hawker, SA, 3 Jul 1899.

column would advance along what was named Route "A", through Hasbaya, the other on Route "B" along the eastern edge of the Litani gorge to Qaraoun, where the road crossed the river and continued to Zahle. It was known that the road was heavily mined and strongly defended in the defile at Youhmour; consequently the plan provided that the armoured detachments on the left hand column should in fact move as far as the Kafr Mechki lateral track with the right hand column and there swing west and come in on the main road behind the enemy force defending the defile. This would complete the second phase of the operation. The right-hand column would then advance along the good road to Zahle, cut the Damascus road and attack the Rayak airfield.

The ground over which the initial attack in this sector was to be made offered little cover except for occasional copses and boulders, but for the first few hours the attackers would be covered by darkness, and their leaders had been assured that once the shell of the defence had been cracked resistance would end.[8] The first objective of the 2/33rd Battalion (Lieut-Colonel Monaghan[9]) on the right, with a battery of field artillery and detachments of anti-tank artillery and engineers under command, would be a line from Chebaa to Khiam; of the left column, Lieut-Colonel Porter's 2/31st Battalion, with similar artillery support, a line from Merdjayoun to Nabatiye et Tahta. On the left a squadron of the Cheshire would protect the left flank by moving along the road from Blida to Adeisse and establish touch with the 21st Brigade. There was to be no preliminary artillery fire; the initial attack was to rely for success on surprise and darkness.

The first task of the eastern column was to secure the Hejaz railway east of the Jordan. At the same time a defensive flank was to be established by the 5th Indian Brigade from Deraa to Sheikh Meskine and Ezraa to protect the advance by the Free French to Damascus.

The supporting air squadrons were to bomb enemy airfields and oil supplies, attack his forward troops, and protect their own troops against air attack.

The opposing armies were approximately equal in numbers. In skill, physical fitness and weapons (except that the French possessed a strong force of good tanks—a very potent asset) there was, on the face of it, little to choose between them. By dividing his force into three columns each of approximately equal strength General Wilson reduced the likelihood of achieving a marked success in any one sector. If the defenders proved half-hearted, simultaneous attacks in all sectors might the more quickly overcome their will to fight; but if the defenders proved resolute such dispersal of force would decrease the attackers' chances of achieving a swift victory.

---

[8] Lieut-Colonel Porter (2/31st Battalion) and his company commanders went a little distance into French territory before the invasion opened and sketched some of the country ahead. Porter was flown over the area and made some useful observations before the aircraft was chased home by French fighters.

[9] Brig R. F. Monaghan, DSO, QX6152. CO 2/2 A-Tk Regt 1940-42; (Admin Comd 2/33 Bn, 2/2 Pnr Bn in 1941); Comd 29 Inf Bde 1942-45. Regular soldier; of Brisbane; b. Goulburn, NSW, 28 Nov 1898.

CHAPTER 17

THE FIRST DAY

THE assaulting troops, with their vehicles, moved into position close to the Syrian frontier on the nights of the 5th-6th and 6th-7th June. Throughout the 7th they lay under cover. It was the first time in this war, or the one before, that British troops had hidden, like Germans, near a peaceful frontier ready to make a surprise invasion.

> Our particular selection (wrote one soldier) was bounded on one side by the outskirts of an infantry battalion, on another by an anti-tank company, and at the rear by a low stone wall used by the local vendors to display their wares, where one could buy anything from a boiled egg to a bottle of cheap wine. The olive trees were dispersed widely enough to allow vehicles to move in almost any direction through the grove. The trees were low but capable of concealing the bonnets of vehicles, and were a useful shelter from the sun and reconnaissance planes during the day. Generally the practice upon arrival in the area was to run the bonnets of the non-essential vehicles beneath the olive trees, sweep away the wheel marks, and thenceforward restrict movement of vehicles to the roads through the area. Near Er Rama the men camped on the red brown soil (it had occasional rocky outcrops) beneath the trees or in the shelter of the trucks, singly or in twos and threes according to their inclinations, provided they were within the company area. The night was mild, a covering blanket ample. One ill-conceived method of concealing the presence of Australians in the olive groves at Er Rama was an instruction to distort the familiar shape of our slouch hats so to render them unrecognisable; but while it provided opportunities for the company humorists, as a measure of deception it was a dismal failure from the start. To the Wogs we were "Ostralees" when we arrived and "Ostralees" when we left.
>
> For most of us the 7th of June was a day of rest. All our preparations for invasion had been completed. There was some last-minute checking of personal equipment, but for most it was a day for playing cards or draughts, reading, writing or merely talking. Men strolled around in shorts and shirts from group to group, occasionally pausing to fill a bottle at the water-tank, or sauntered over to other camps to see their mates. In other lines there were some simple but oddly moving church services during the day. Towards dusk, when it was usual to change into slacks and roll down shirt sleeves, a group of us gathered round the tailboard of a truck to swap yarns and discuss prospects for tomorrow. We were to move off before midnight and none but the most phlegmatic considered it worthwhile to sleep. A few were inclined to scoff at any predictions of a pushover, and regarded the projected slouch hat invasion as a prize piece of colonial impertinence. One said "All we've got to do tomorrow is walk in, wave our hats to the Frogs, and walk on."

Most were full of confidence, yet this untried division was deeply conscious that it was faced with a test like that which its sister divisions had already passed through—the test which would prove that it was as good as the old A.I.F. "All through," wrote an historian of the 2/16th, "there was a grim determination to live up to the great fighting record of the old Sixteenth whose history had been widely read throughout the unit."

On the morning of the 7th Brigadier Stevens assembled his unit commanders for a final conference. That day he learnt that the landing of the commando battalion would probably be impossible on the 8th because of bad weather.

At 9.30 that night, four hours and a half before zero, the first troops had crossed the frontier. They were two small parties of rubber-shod men of the 2/14th Battalion and 2/6th Field Company, one of which was to cut the telephone wire leading from Ras en Naqoura to the post at the point in the road near Iskandaroun where the French had placed demolition charges, while the other overcame the guards at that point and removed the charges. Australian and Palestinian guides led the men to a Jewish farm colony at Hanita, where they were well fed in the communal dining room, and thence across the enemy frontier where it was unguarded and over the thorny hills. It was cloudy and fairly dark. One group, under Captain Gowling,[1] branched off towards the road just north of the Ras; the other (Lieutenants Kyffin,[2] Allan[3] and Cowdery[4] and fifteen men, including three Jewish guides and one Arab) went on until, about 3.30 a.m., after fifteen miles, they reached the road just north of the point near Ras el Bayada where they had been told the charges were. Kyffin left Lance-Corporal Wardley[5] and three men to halt any vehicles coming from the north and led the remainder of the party southwards. Stealthily, and in the darkness, they examined various bridges and culverts and found that they were not mined. At one of these Allan was left with three men to block the road while Kyffin went on with the remainder to search still farther south for the mined road. About 5 a.m., when they were north of Iskandaroun, they were fired on from a strong-post built of stone. The Australians rushed the post and took it, and were rounding up prisoners when Allan, who had heard the firing, arrived with his men.

A long, grim fight began which attracted one group after another of French reinforcements. A party of Kyffin's men attacked some French troops in a near-by orchard where a machine-gun was silenced by Private Henderson[6] who attacked it with grenades; and a mortar was captured. Two of the Jewish guides were wounded. Kyffin's men, still under fire from the orchard, mounted the mortar and a captured Hotchkiss gun on the roof of the post, and soon were exchanging brisk fire with a French column moving along the road from the north to meet the invader. Some trucks in this column were halted and their crews taken prisoner. Next appeared two armoured cars. A shot from the captured mortar stopped the leading car, the driver was killed and the crews of both cars surrendered. Twelve horsemen then arrived and, when fired on, scattered into the hills.

---

[1] Capt H. R. Gowling, VX14107; 2/14 Bn. Joiner; of Wangaratta, Vic; b. St. Kilda, Vic, 3 Mar 1912.

[2] Capt P. J. Kyffin, MC, VX14660; 2/14 Bn. Labourer; of Richmond, Vic; b. Seymour, Vic, 4 Mar 1909.

[3] Maj W. G. Allan, VX12013; 2/14 Bn. Carpenter; of South Melbourne; b. South Melbourne, 20 Sep 1914.

[4] Maj G. D. Cowdery, NX12630. 2/6 Fd Coy 1940-42; HQ RAE 7 Div 1942-43; OC 4 Fd Coy 1944-46. Surveyor; of Drummoyne, NSW; b. Kempsey, NSW, 8 Mar 1920.

[5] Lt W. J. Wardley, VX21974. 2/14 Bn 1940-42; Indian Army after 1943. Student; b. London, 25 Mar 1920.

[6] Cpl G. F. Henderson, MM, VX15513; 2/14 Bn. Contractor; of Mildura, Vic; b. Merbein, Vic, 25 Jan 1917.

Wardley and his three men (two were Palestinians) were summoned from the northern post to reinforce the men on and round the blockhouse, which half the men manned while the remainder were still engaged against the Frenchmen holding machine-gun posts in the orchard.

It was about 7 a.m. when a loud explosion was heard south along the road; and both parties, Kyffin's to the north and Gowling's to the south, guessed that the road had been blown somewhere on the cliff face north of Naqoura. The demolition they had tried to prevent had been carried out.

After separating from Kyffin, Gowling with a platoon and four Palestinian guides, had reached the road a mile north of Naqoura just before 1 a.m. He found and cut the telephone wire and took up a position astride the road, which his men blocked with boulders. It was quiet until 4.30 when firing broke out round Naqoura and the waiting men knew that their battalion had reached that village. A few minutes later one of the Australians captured a Frenchman who said that he had been sent from Naqoura to give the alarm, because the telephone was dead—as Gowling had intended. Others—French customs officials and African cavalrymen—arrived from the south and were rounded up; at length Gowling held sixty-five prisoners and a captured car. He sent Sergeant Dredge[7] and three others in this car towards Iskandaroun, where they came under fire and Dredge and Private Constable[8] were wounded. This party was exchanging fire with the French troops there when the road was blown up.

Although Kyffin's party had been wrongly informed that the road was mined north not south of Iskandaroun[9] and had failed to prevent the demolition, the patrol had succeeded in clearing the road for some distance north of the demolition and had captured some thirty prisoners, a number of weapons, six vehicles including one armoured car, and more than thirty horses abandoned by African cavalrymen. Only one of their men had been killed—Corporal Buckler[1], who had evidently been shot while moving out alone into the orchard to attack a machine-gun there.

At 2 a.m. the main advance had begun. It will be recalled that the task of taking the three westernmost French posts and forming a bridgehead through which Colonel Moten's column could advance along the coast road was given to the 2/14th.[2] On the extreme left a platoon of that battalion advanced from the British Customs post south of Naqoura at 3 a.m. After moving forward in the darkness astride the road for about

---

[7] Lt R. A. Dredge, VX14628; 2/14 Bn. Photographic employee; of Brighton, Vic; b. Coburg, Vic, 7 Mar 1917.

[8] Pte G. N. Constable, VX27896; 2/14 Bn. Farmer; of Warracknabeal, Vic; b. Brunswick, Vic, 21 Oct 1905.

[9] It was unlikely that the enemy would have cratered the road at the point indicated to the Australian patrol because that point (near the Wadi Blida) was by-passed by a track through the foothills suitable for motor vehicles.

[1] Cpl H. A. Buckler, VX48590; 2/14 Bn. Bank officer; of Coff's Harbour, NSW; b. Coff's Harbour, 12 Jun 1916. Killed in action 8 Jun 1941. His brother (Maj S. H. Buckler) was adjutant of the battalion.

[2] Throughout the opening phase of the campaign, because the main weight was thrown in on the left, the action will be described from left to right instead of from the opposite direction in the orthodox fashion.

one mile the leading scouts, Privates Wilson[3] and Curson,[4] encountered two French sentries whom they shot. It was 5 o'clock before they reached the wired post at Naqoura another two miles ahead, where the French opened fire. Lieutenant Ayton[5] sent one of his sections to each flank and kept one on the road. For about five minutes the Australians exchanged fire with the garrison, which appeared to be using two machine-guns and about twenty rifles. Then, after firing a few mortar bombs, the centre section charged and drove the Frenchmen from the post and the village beyond, killing five men and capturing about twelve. Later a troop of Spahis opened fire from the village, but were driven off.

Stevens, restlessly moving from point to point in a carrier, ordered that a platoon of the 2/27th be sent forward to discover the condition of the road. Lieutenant Rudd's[6] was dispatched, with six light tanks, two anti-tank guns and some engineers under command. Rudd passed through Naqoura about 6.30 a.m. and attacked a strong group of enemy troops covering the road. The 2-pounder guns went into action near the beach while the tanks advanced on the right of the road to within 300 yards of the enemy and engaged him with machine-guns. The infantry dribbled forward along the higher ground farther inland and after a sharp fight drove the enemy back. Five of the defenders were killed and two wounded.

East of the coast the hill country was so tangled that in the case of Lieutenant Farmer's[7] platoon that was to take the Labouna post the Jewish guide lost his way and the platoon did not reach the neighbourhood of Labouna until 5.30, three hours late.

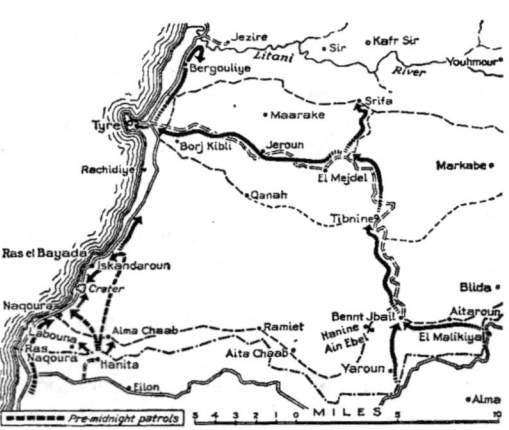

Advance of 21st Brigade, 8th June

There it met an enemy patrol of six to ten men and, after an exchange of fire in which one man was wounded, charged with fixed bayonets and drove the enemy off. Labouna itself was occupied without incident. Farther east Captain Noonan's[8] company of the 2/14th rushed a French sentry

---

[3] Pte R. I. Wilson, VX15892; 2/14 Bn. Station hand; of Rowsley, Vic; b. Bacchus Marsh, Vic, 10 Jul 1919.

[4] Pte G. Curson, VX22201; 2/14 Bn. Labourer; b. Hull, Eng, 10 Dec 1903.

[5] Maj P. J. Ayton, VX14618; 2/14 Bn, and Movt Control. Shipping clerk; of Murrumbeena, Vic; b. Hawthorn, Vic, 16 May 1918.

[6] Lt L. K. Rudd, SX2923; 2/27 Bn. Gas salesman; of Bridgewater, SA; b. Bridgewater, 17 Aug 1916. Killed in action 14 Jun 1941.

[7] Capt J. G. Farmer, VX14657; 2/14 Bn. Air traffic officer; of Pascoe Vale, Vic; b. Wedderburn, Vic, 9 Oct 1917.

[8] Maj B. S. Noonan, VX14120. 2/14 Bn 1940-42; 19 Bn 1942-44. Public servant; of Mont Albert, Vic; b. Carlton, Vic, 29 Jul 1909.

post and, with some difficulty, found the village of Alma Chaab and captured it after an exchange of fire in which Sergeant Lawley[9] was killed and another man wounded. By 7 a.m. all three posts had been taken; but the brigade commander still did not know whether the road had been cratered ahead of him.

In the tangled country 20 miles to the east, Lieut-Colonel MacDonald of the 2/16th, to secure his bridgehead, sent in two companies of infantrymen, one, Major Caro's,[1] to Aitaroun and another, Captain Horley's,[2] to Yaroun; both were to converge on the village of Bennt Jbail.[3] Horley was then to clear Ain Ebel. Meanwhile an advance-guard under Major Potts,[4] including a squadron of the 6th Australian Cavalry, two armoured car troops of the Royals, a company of the 2/16th and detachments of artillery and engineers, would wait at El Malikiya while a company of the 2/2nd Pioneers made a road able to carry vehicles thence to Aitaroun. When this road had been made Potts' force was to move along it to Tyre and on, by the coast road, to Beirut—if possible.

Caro's company took Aitaroun without opposition, capturing four unwary men in a police post there, and, moving through the hills towards Bennt Jbail, encountered a French post equipped with machine-guns. Lieutenant O'Neill[5] led his platoon forward and captured the posts, losing one man killed[6] and one wounded—Corporal Holmes[7] who continued to lead his men until the fight was won. Caro arrived at Bennt Jbail to find that Horley's company, having taken the sentries at Yaroun unawares, had marched on to Bennt Jbail where there had been a sharp fight in which the West Australians dispersed about seventy Spahis, killing several of them.[8] Ain Ebel was found to have been abandoned by the enemy.

Working furiously, a company of the 2/2nd Pioneer Battalion quickly made the track linking the Palestine road at El Malikiya with the Syrian at Aitaroun and, about 4 a.m., Potts' advance-guard crossed the frontier. About 6.30 Lieutenant Mills, an outstanding leader in the 6th Australian Cavalry during the operations in Cyrenaica, with thirteen carriers of his own regiment, followed by a platoon of Captain Johnson's[9] company of the 2/16th in trucks, led the spearhead of Potts' force through Bennt

---

[9] Sgt R. H. Lawley, VX18464; 2/14 Bn. Storeman-driver; of Brunswick, Vic; b. Bendigo, Vic, 24 Nov 1904. Killed in action 8 Jun 1941.
[1] Lt-Col A. E. Caro, WX3373; 2/16 Bn (CO 1942). Accountant; of Nedlands, WA; b. Maylands, WA, 29 Jun 1905.
[2] Capt D. G. Horley, WX1588; 2/16 Bn. Barrister and solicitor; of Northam, WA; b. Coalville, Vic, 23 Oct 1907. Killed in action 13 Jun 1941.
[3] Before these companies moved Cpl J. R. MacKenzie (Northam, WA) and two others crossed the frontier and cut the telephone lines north of Bennt Jbail.
[4] Brig A. W. Potts, DSO, MC, WX1574. (1st AIF: Capt 16 Bn.) CO 2/16 Bn 1941-42; Comd 21 Bde 1942, 23 Bde 1942-45. Farmer; of Kojunup, WA; b. Peel, Isle of Man, 16 Sep 1896.
[5] Capt J. H. O'Neill, WX2731; 2/16 Bn. Bank clerk; of Subiaco, WA; b. Northam, WA, 30 May 1920. Died of wounds 5 Dec 1942.
[6] Pte P. E. Connolly (of Dalwallinu, WA).
[7] Sgt A. R. Holmes, WX2816; 2/16 Bn. Storeman-truck driver; of Perth, WA; b. Midland Junction, WA, 20 Mar 1910.
[8] Lt E. T. J. Barnett (of Perth, WA) and three others were wounded here.
[9] Capt I. Johnson, WX1592; 2/16 Bn. Farmer and engineer; of Carnamah, WA; b. Claremont, WA, 17 Jan 1906. Killed in action 9 Jun 1941.

Jbail to Tibnine, a picturesque town with an old Turkish castle. There they caught up and drove off what were left of the Spahis whom Horley's company had expelled from Bennt Jbail earlier on. There was a pause in Tibnine while the friendly mayor of the town telephoned his colleague in Tyre and, after talking with him, informed the advancing troops that they would be welcome there. After waiting for two troops of the armoured cars of the Royals to join the vanguard, Mills moved on. Between Tibnine and the coast Mills' vanguard had a series of skirmishes, but the enemy were too dispersed to resist effectively and, just before 2 o'clock, his leading cars and carriers drove up to the cross-roads outside Tyre, where they saw a British naval force standing off the port and French aircraft bombing it.

The naval squadron had neared the coast about 6.45 a.m. "Occasional troops and lorries which could not be identified as friend or foe were seen but the extent of the army's progress could not be established." The demolition of the road north of Iskandaroun was seen at 7 a.m. The destroyer *Kimberley* shelled French positions near the Litani Bridge for half an hour.

On land the armoured cars of the Royals, now in the lead, moved north along the road and met no enemy troops, except some Spahis, some of whom they captured while others rode off into the hills, until they were halted by a road-block just south of the Litani. Some men dismounted from the cars and were dismantling the road-block when the French opened fire from the north bank of the river with field and anti-tank guns and mortars, whereupon the Royals briskly withdrew, leaving two damaged cars behind. Lieutenant Dent's[1] troop of the 6th Australian Cavalry (reduced to one carrier), which had followed the cars, also ran into the French fire; with the surviving cars the carrier turned off the road to the shelter of the wadis where the guns continued to shell them. Two guns of the 2/4th Field Regiment, which were with the advance-guard, deployed and opened fire from positions near Bergouliye. Soon only one of the armoured cars was still undamaged, and it remained in the doubtful shelter of the wadi while Dent's carrier withdrew with French shells chasing it. The carrier broke down; Dent sent his driver, Trooper Jubb,[2] back with a message and, after waiting in vain for a reply, went back himself leaving the remaining member of his crew, Corporal Britten,[3] to mount guard over the disabled carrier with the Bren gun. He remained there, all night, a one-man outpost. That evening patrols of the leading company of the 2/16th moved to within 800 yards of the river and reached the conclusion that no French troops were south of it.

---

[1] Maj J. Dent, NX192. 6 Cav Regt; and HQ 25 Bde. Grazier; of Cootamundra, NSW; b. Strathfield, NSW, 3 Mar 1912.

[2] Tpr N. Jubb, NX515; 6 Cav Regt. Plumber; of Concord, NSW; b. Mt. Victoria, NSW, 27 Dec 1912. (Jubb lost his way and was captured.)

[3] Capt C. B. Britten, NX544; 6 Cav Regt. Articled clerk; of Parramatta, NSW; b. Parramatta, 1 Nov 1914.

While the advance-guard of MacDonald's column was thus pressing on roundabout through the hills to within sight of the Litani, known to be the main enemy line of resistance, Stevens' chief anxiety had been to learn whether or not the road had been cratered at Iskandaroun, and whether the coastal column could advance. As the hours passed and no news came back, he decided to order the companies of the 2/14th which had overcome the frontier posts to continue the advance and, for the present, not to send on Colonel Moten's fully-motorised column, ready with its waggons loaded. It might be held up at a demolition and have to halt and return across the frontier again, with the confusion such an about-turn on a narrow road would cause. Therefore, early in the morning, the 2/14th advanced to the demolition with the tank troops of the squadron of the 6th Cavalry (as distinct from the carrier troops Mills was leading through the hills) and a section of anti-tank guns. When the leading troops reached the French crater they found that the face of the cliff had been blown off, making a gap in the road 100 feet long and 30 feet deep.[4] At 9.45 Stevens arrived there in a carrier. About noon an anti-tank gun was man-handled across and then towed forward by a captured truck. A section of the 2/6th Field Company, under Lieutenant Harper,[5] began to repair the road by blowing spoil down from the cliff above the crater, but it was not until 5 a.m. on the 9th that Moten's vehicles were able to cross. Meanwhile a company of the 2/14th marched along the cratered road on foot.

In the hills on the right, the main body of MacDonald's column had followed Potts' force—its vanguard—through Bennt Jbail. A few miles south of Tibnine it had been delayed just before 9 a.m. while a deviation was cut round an 80-foot crater and a minefield cleared, a task which took the engineers four hours. (Potts' advance-guard had man-handled their trucks past this crater.) About 5 o'clock in the afternoon the column reached the main coast road and joined the 2/14th. One company of the 2/14th, Captain Howden's,[6] which was with MacDonald's column, took control of Tyre, where it was given "a great ovation by the populace".[7] Stevens, who had crossed the Iskandaroun crater on foot, was at the Tyre cross-roads when the 2/16th arrived.[8] Meanwhile the mounted men of the Cheshire were making progress slowly through the precipitous country between Tibnine and Kafr Sir.

Thus, at the end of the day, Tyre had been occupied, and contact made with the enemy's main line along the Litani; but it was evident that he

---

[4] About ten Spahis under a white sergeant-major were fired on here and surrendered. The sergeant-major asked why the Australians had used force first instead of sending forward a party to ask for surrender. He had been in the French Rugby football team which had played the AIF at Beirut in 1940.

[5] Maj C. H. D. Harper, MC, NX34748; 2/6 Fd Coy. Shire engineer; of Donald, Vic; b. Richmond, Vic, 28 Jul 1906.

[6] Lt-Col W. S. Howden, DSO, VX14047. 2/14 Bn 1940-42; CO 2/8 Bn 1943-45. Bank officer; of Caulfield, Vic; b. Caulfield, 7 Dec 1906.

[7] Earlier, about 2.15 p.m., the Intelligence officer of the 2/16 Bn, Lt N. M. Symington (of West Perth, WA), and an officer of a British regiment, attached as an interpreter, with three carriers, had driven into Tyre. The only armed men they found were eight gendarmes.

[8] After the Australian efforts on the opening night to seize bridges and stretches of road that had been mined the enemy henceforth made a practice of carrying out demolitions well before any attacking troops could conceivably reach them.

intended to fight hard and that there would be no swift occupation of Beirut by a force which had only to brush aside token resistance.

It will be recalled that Brigadier Cox's brigade was divided into two columns for the first phase of its advance to Rayak. On the right was Moncolumn, commanded by Lieut-Colonel Monaghan and including chiefly his 2/33rd Battalion, of which he had taken command only a few days before, and detachments of cavalry, artillery and others. Its task was to cut the road from Kuneitra to prevent an enemy advance from that direction, advance into the Hasbaya area on the right and through Khiam on the left.

On Cox's left was Portcolumn, commanded by Lieut-Colonel Porter of the 2/31st Battalion, and including in addition to that battalion "C" Squadron of the 6th Cavalry, a six-gun troop of the 2/6th Field Regiment, and four 2-pounders and two Solathurn anti-tank guns of the 2/2nd Anti-Tank Regiment. The cavalry squadron had three light tanks and six machine-gun carriers. The task of this column was to capture a line from Merdjayoun to Nabatiye et Tahta. This line was to form the base for a subsequent advance along "Route B", one of two roads leading north to the vital Damascus-Beirut highway. Farther left a squadron of the Cheshire Yeomanry had the task of advancing through Blida and Adeisse to the main bridge over the Litani River about 5,000 yards south-west of Merdjayoun, and if possible establishing touch in the mountain barrier with the 21st Brigade at Habbouch.

At 2 o'clock Monaghan's infantry moved forward in the darkness. The men carried two days' rations, and wore steel helmets, shorts or slacks. Monaghan, in deference to the higher commanders' opinion that the French might surrender the more easily if they saw men wearing felt hats, gave an order that "felt hats will be worn as often as the occasion permits".

One company of the 2/33rd, Captain Bennett's,[9] had been given the task of moving across the frontier under cover of darkness, clambering through the Anti-Lebanon, occupying Ferdisse, cutting the road just west of it, and outflanking the defenders 12 miles to the north of his starting point at Metsudat. If Bennett's company succeeded in accomplishing its march through the mountains, its efforts would not be felt until a later phase of the advance.

Major Wright's[1] company, which was given the task of capturing frontier posts from Banias to El Morheur and blowing up the bridge south-east of Banias as a precaution against a possible French flanking attack from Kuneitra, took Banias late in the morning and early in the afternoon reported to Monaghan that the bridge had been demolished and all was quiet.

---

[9] Maj G. W. Bennett, MC, WX335; 2/33 Bn. Pastoral overseer; of Port Hedland-Marble Bar, WA; b. Subiaco, WA., 4 Nov 1912.
[1] Maj H. E. Wright, VX13927. HQ 21 Bde; 2/33 Bn; 37/52 Bn. Solicitor; of Toorak, Vic; b. Malvern, Vic, 14 May 1912.

8 June FORT KHIAM

The task of taking the frontier posts farther to the left, in the area of Rhadjar and Arab el Loueize, was given to Captain Cotton's[2] company, which left its assembly area at Abd el Kamh at 2 a.m., marched for half an hour after crossing the border without meeting opposition but, about 3 a.m., encountered a French post. After a mêlée in which one Australian (Lance-Corporal Webb[3]) was killed and three Frenchmen wounded, the remainder of the garrison — about twenty-five men, mostly Senegalese—surrendered.

Lieutenant Connor's[4] platoon of this company had been given the task of capturing intact the Jisr Abou Zeble, a bridge carrying the Banias - Merdjayoun road over the Hasbani, and of investigating other points where trouble might occur. He divided his platoon into four patrols each with a definite objective, and himself led the patrol that had to save

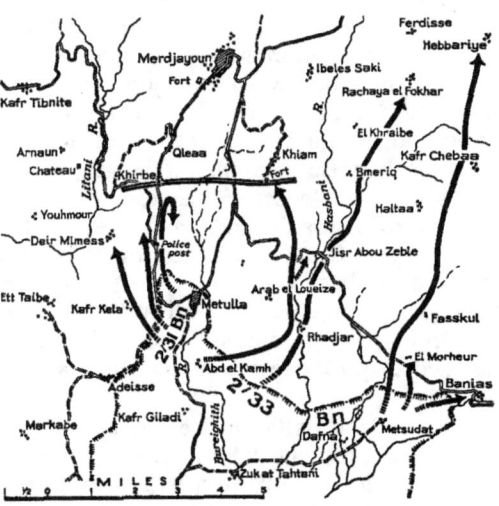

the bridge. This patrol—Connor and four—reached the bridge at 4 a.m., drove off about twelve French infantry and some cavalry, and occupied the area. The bridge was undamaged. Although it had not been blown there was, however, a large crater in the road farther towards Khiam. Captain Ferguson's[5] company of this battalion moved forward under fire along the valley leading past Khiam on the south-east but was held by heavy fire from Khiam and Bmeriq.

At 11.30 a.m. Monaghan ordered Cotton's company to capture Fort Khiam, which stood on a hill just south of the village itself, and about midday it attacked. The French held their fire and it was not until the Australians were about 300 yards away that they opened with field guns, mortars and small arms. Cotton's men were well dispersed and moved on, suffering only one casualty, until they were only 50 yards from the square building which resembled the forts they had seen in American films about the French Foreign Legion. Thence the Australians poured fire at the French weapon posts until they had silenced the machine-gun in one of the bastions. Connor ran forward, cut his way through the barbed wire

---

[2] Lt-Col T. R. W. Cotton, DSO, MC, WX299; CO 2/33 Bn 1943-45. Farmer; b. Dover, Eng, 14 Nov 1907. (Cotton had enlisted as a private in the 2/11 Bn in 1939.)

[3] L-Cpl T. Webb, SX155; 2/33 Bn. Station hand; of Adelaide; b. Oldham, Lancs, Eng, 28 Sep 1911. Killed in action 8 Jun 1941.

[4] Capt G. B. Connor, NX34870; 2/33 Bn. Student; of Roseville, NSW; b. Lugarno, NSW, 8 Nov 1919.

[5] Capt J. B. Ferguson, VX11997; 2/33 Bn. Engineer; of Melbourne; b. Adelaide, 31 Aug 1915. Missing, believed killed, 7 Sep 1943.

round the fort and reached the wall where five men joined him. He climbed the wall, ran into a long barrack room, and fired at the occupants with his sub-machine-gun. A machine-gun crew shot at him from an opposite corner of the fort, whereupon he took refuge in the thick-walled bastion where he was joined by three men—Sergeant Sweetapple,[6] Corporal Campbell[7] and Private Wayte[8]—who had followed him over the wall. Soon the little party, its ammunition now exhausted, was joined by a French non-commissioned officer and two medical orderlies who explained that they wished to join the de Gaullists. Until Connor's voice was heard calling through a firing slit Cotton did not know what had happened to him and his men, except that they were in the fort and there was much noise therein. At length, with the help of the men outside, Connor's party loosened the stonework of the wall and made a hole large enough to climb through, and they and the Frenchmen emerged, after having spent five hours in the fort. Cotton now decided to attack through the broken bastion with support from his mortars. He put some men through the hole in the wall, but the French—there were nearly 100 in the fort—fired vigorously from other parts of the building and Cotton decided to postpone the attack until next morning.

The 2/31st Battalion was to advance with three companies forward, two moving through Khirbe and the other to Kafr Tibnite past the Litani bridge (which a patrol under Sergeant Davis,[9] having crossed the frontier the previous night, was to have saved from demolition). The main French positions covering Khirbe and the Chateau de Beaufort, a Crusader's castle, were superbly situated from the defenders' point of view; the Australian attack on the left was made up steep bare slopes, and on the right too there was little cover.

The leading Australian companies moved off from a taped start-line just north of Metulla a few minutes after 2 a.m. Captain Houston's[1] on the right found only one man in the police post on the frontier, and he in bed. In the darkness Houston's men began moving along the ridge leading to Khirbe. A Free French liaison officer who was with them marched forward into the village holding a white flag. His fellow-countryman in command at Khirbe rejected a proposal that there should be no resistance and the envoy began to march back again. Before he had reached the Australian lines a shot fired from Khirbe hit and wounded him, and heavy fire from field guns, mortars and machine-guns was brought down on the leading Australians, now advancing through open fields. The Australians were only 200 yards from well-sited French pill-

---

[6] Lt A. M. Sweetapple, WX96; 2/33, 28 Bns. Clerk; of Belmont, WA; b. Perth, WA, 25 Nov 1919.
[7] Cpl R. K. Campbell, NX41331; 2/33 Bn. Station hand; of Narrabri West, NSW; b. Warialda, NSW, 7 Apr 1915. Killed in action 14 Sep 1943.
[8] Cpl J. J. Wayte, NX41301; 2/33 Bn. Labourer; of Armidale, NSW; b. Armidale, 17 Jun 1919. Died of wounds 26 Sep 1943.
[9] Lt M. H. Davis, QX2123; 2/31 Bn. Civil engineer; of Townsville, Qld; b. Foster, Vic, 28 Dec 1904. Killed in action 10 Jul 1941.
[1] Capt J. R. Houston, NX34788; 2/31 Bn. Sales manager; of Strathfield, NSW; b. Rutherglen, Vic, 22 Aug 1903. Killed in action 18 Jun 1941.

boxes and mortar pits and any movement attracted heavy fire, but they continued to advance. Houston's second-in-command, Lewington[2], was wounded. One of the platoon commanders, Lieutenant Kelly,[3] was killed leading his men forward to the enemy's wire, and in the course of the morning eight of his men were killed or wounded. Soon it was apparent that any further attempt to edge forward would lead to disastrous casualties and the men sought cover. On the left Captain Byrne's[4] company advanced without incident, until a little after 4.30, when it too was pinned down. In the next few hours it lost thirteen or fourteen men and made no progress. Captain Brown's[5] company, advancing on the left towards Deir Mimess, was pinned down and Brown wounded. Thus the battalion was halted on open ground and casualties were mounting. Sharp artillery fire was brought down on the French positions by the 2/6th Field Regiment; while its shells were falling, parts of the Australian line were withdrawn to better cover but were still under searching fire. So far from the French defence being a thin shell on the frontier which the infantry could crack by a brisk night attack, it was a well-prepared position so far north of the frontier that the advancing Australians had not come in sight until light was breaking. The French had shrewdly held their fire until the attackers were almost on top of them and they were the more likely to inflict crippling losses.

Porter had planned to use his remaining company in an attack with artillery support at 10 a.m. but, now realising the strength of the enemy, he cancelled this project, having decided that the only hope of success lay in a deliberate attack supported by at least a regiment of artillery. About 10.30 the three light tanks of the 6th Cavalry[6] in support of Porter's column were led forward by Lieutenant Lapthorne.[7] They silenced three French machine-gun posts but drew the fire of every French weapon within range. Lapthorne's tank was hit and he was killed; a second tank was hit and disabled, its commander, Corporal Hicks,[8] being fatally wounded; and the third tank (Sergeant Groves[9]), after driving forward and rescuing the wounded, withdrew. Byrne's company then withdrew about 400 yards south along the Litani valley under heavy mortar fire; Houston's remained until dusk and then was withdrawn after having hung on all day in the position it had reached at dawn. At the end of the day

---

[2] Capt A. J. M. Lewington, NX12285; 2/31 Bn. Accounting clerk and wool classer; of Lindfield, NSW; b. Townsville, Qld, 18 May 1913.
[3] Lt C. C. Kelly, QX6096; 2/31 Bn. Jackeroo; of St Kilda, Vic; b. Longreach, Qld, 7 Oct 1919. Killed in action 8 Jun 1941.
[4] Lt-Col J. H. Byrne, QX6010. 2/31 Bn; CO 42 Bn 1944-45. Manufacturer; of Brisbane; b. Maryborough, Qld, 22 Oct 1913.
[5] Capt T. Brown, QX6009; 2/31 Bn, and trg appts. Clerk; of Kedron, Qld; b. Brisbane, 11 Feb 1917.
[6] The squadron of 6 Cav Regt consisted of two troops each with three light tanks and four each with three carriers.
[7] Lt H. D. Lapthorne, SX1450; 6 Cav Regt. Salesman; of Toorak Gardens, SA; b. Adelaide, 16 Jan 1916. Killed in action 8 Jun 1941.
[8] Cpl L. R. Hicks, SX1280; 6 Cav Regt. Gardener; of Clare, SA; b. Lameroo, SA, 9 Apr 1917. Killed in action 8 Jun 1941.
[9] Lt M. D. Groves, SX1309; 6 Cav Regt. Engineer; of Magill, SA; b. Peterborough, SA, 29 Dec 1917.

little had been gained beyond finding the enemy's defences, sampling his strength, and learning that hard fighting lay ahead. The battalion's line ran east and west through the police post about two miles south of Khirbe.

Meanwhile, on the extreme right flank, Brigadier Lloyd's 5th Indian Brigade Group had moved across the frontier at 2 a.m. in four columns each in motor vehicles. The left column, comprising the 1/Royal Fusiliers, some field artillery (including the 9th Australian Battery) and other troops, passed the frontier just east of the Jordan at 4.15 a.m. and at 5 o'clock was at Kafr Naffakh where the infantry left their vehicles and advanced on foot towards Kuneitra. An hour later the advance-guard came under fire from Tel Abou Nida, a hill about two miles south-west of the town, and two emissaries—a British and a French officer—went forward to demand surrender and fire ceased. When these returned about 9.30 they said that they had received the impression that the younger officers wished to join the Free French but that the commander was determined to resist, and in any case would have to refer to General Dentz at Damascus. Later in the morning the envoys went forward again and a truce was agreed upon to enable the civilians to leave the town. It was evident that the French were trying to gain time; the invaders for their part took advantage of the delay to move their artillery observers forward, and the envoys discovered that the garrison consisted of a battalion of Senegalese and six armoured cars carrying light guns. At length a French officer came out and, like a herald in a mediaeval war, announced that hostilities would begin again at midday; and at that hour the guns opened fire. After a sharp concentration of artillery fire the infantry attacked and occupied Tel Abou Nida, with little opposition. Next morning it was discovered that the French had abandoned Kuneitra in the night, and the British troops entered it before dawn on the 9th, and took prisoner six "white" French machine-gunners.[1]

A platoon of the Rajputana Rifles under Captain Adam Murray[2] was given the task of preventing the destruction of the railway viaduct at Chehab (the bridge which T. E. Lawrence tried without success to destroy in 1918 during Allenby's offensive). Murray and a havildar crawled into the French sentry post in the darkness and shot the occupants while the remainder of the platoon rushed the guard post on the viaduct and saved the bridge, in which charges had been laid. Meanwhile a detached company of the Fusiliers had occupied Fiq with little opposition.

The third and fourth columns, one commanded by Lloyd himself and including the 3/1st Punjab and the other by Colonel Jones[3] of the 4/6th Rajputana Rifles, had surrounded Deraa by 6 a.m. after having met little opposition. A flag of truce was sent into the town with a demand for

---

[1] The Australian battery (Maj W. J. Courtney, of Sydney) left Kuneitra on the 9th to rejoin its regiment having had "a most valuable introduction to active service even though, in the words of the battery commander, it was mostly in the nature of a Gilbert and Sullivan opera because of the parleys, the envoys, and the flags of truce going to and fro".

[2] Lt-Col A. T. Murray, MC. 4/6 Rajputana Rifles; BM 11 Ind Bde. Regular soldier; of Belfast, N. Ireland; b. Belfast, 16 Dec 1916.

[3] Brig L. B. Jones, DSO. CO 4/6 Rajputana Rifles. Regular soldier; b. 17 Oct 1897.

surrender. When the car carrying the party was fired on and hit by a shell which did not explode the envoys bravely continued on foot, but their demand for surrender was rejected. Thereupon at 7.30 the artillery opened fire. After a brief bombardment the two Indian battalions attacked and by 8.30 a.m. had occupied the town, with few casualties. The Rajputana with a battery of artillery then drove on towards Sheikh Meskine where they arrived late in the afternoon after having met some opposition from armoured cars and having been bombed by aircraft on the way. An attack on the town failed in the face of machine-gun and artillery fire but late in the afternoon, after a hard fight, high ground dominating the town from the west was occupied.

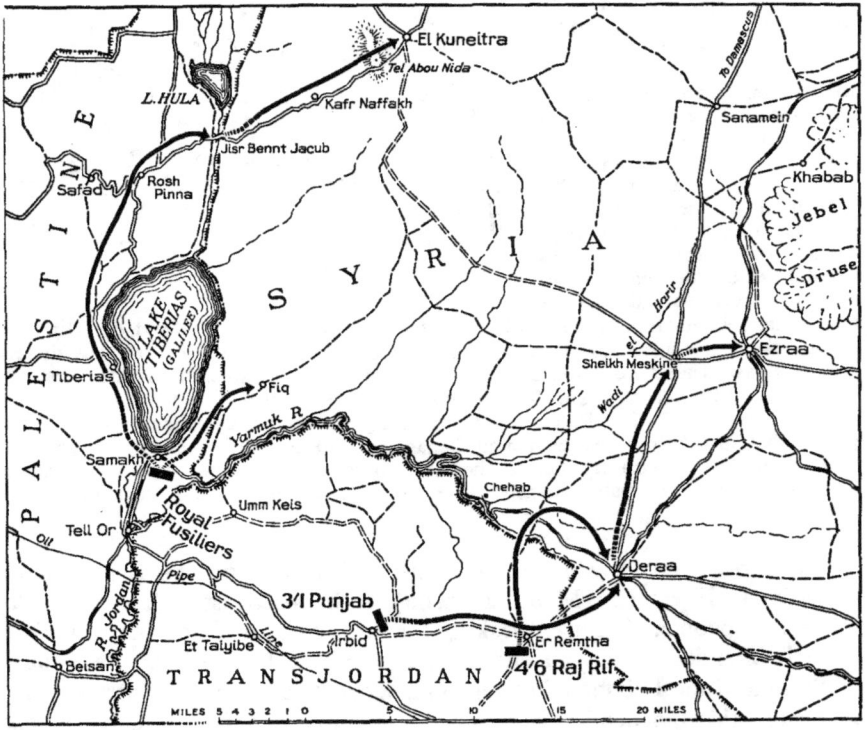

Early on the morning of 9th June, the Rajputana occupied Sheikh Meskine and Ezraa, which the enemy had abandoned during the night, and at 10 a.m. the Free French contingent passed through on its way to Damascus, leaving the Indian brigade to guard the desert flank, at Kuneitra, Sheikh Meskine and Ezraa, while they took up the pursuit. The Indian brigade had done its job swiftly and had captured thirty officers and some 300 men.[4]

---

[4] On the evening of the 8th General Blamey sent a brief message to the Minister for the Army reporting the first day's progress, stating "troops participating British, Free French, Australian

The French Army in Syria included all or part of seven regiments of regular infantry—the *6th Foreign Legion, 1st Moroccan, 16th Tunisian, 17th Senegalese, 22nd Algerian, 24th Colonial* and *29th Algerian.* There were 18 battalions in all, four of them belonging to the Foreign Legion.

There were two regiments of *Chasseurs d'Afrique* each armed with 45 twelve-ton tanks ("Renault 35") armed with a 37-mm gun and a machine-gun; 150 locally-adapted armoured cars, some armed with 37-mm guns and some with machine-guns; 30 batteries of artillery. In addition there were eleven battalions of Levantine troops of doubtful reliability.

On the day the invasion opened a force of Spahis (Algerian troopers) and part of one of the Algerian regiments was deployed in the coastal sector and part of an Algerian regiment at Khirbe

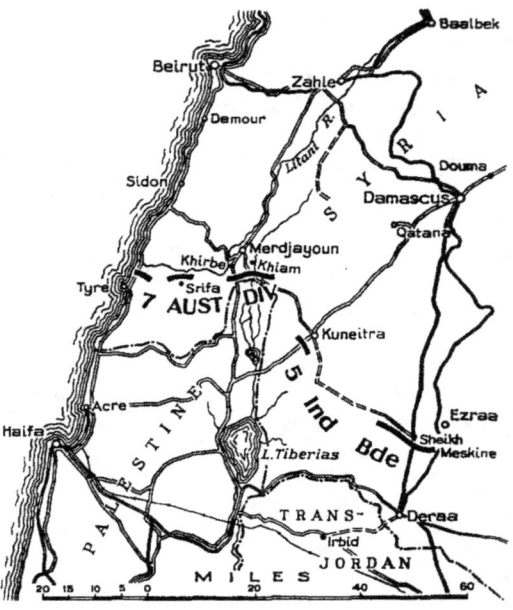

Dusk, 8th June

and Khiam. From Banias eastwards the *17th Senegalese Regiment* and detachments of tanks and armoured cars were deployed. One company of the *1/17th* was driven from Banias. The *II Battalion* escaped with difficulty from Sheikh Meskine, having been reduced to 350 men. The *III Battalion* was at Kuneitra.

In a report to Berlin, Rahn, the German agent, declared, evidently with some pride, that just before the campaign began he had persuaded Dentz to transfer units from the Turkish frontier to the area south of Damascus, and at the same time to advance his main defensive line from Kiswe to a line Kuneitra-Soueida-Ezraa.

As soon as the invasion began General Catroux and the British Ambassador in Egypt (Sir Miles Lampson) each broadcast a declaration to the Syrian people. Catroux, speaking for de Gaulle, declared that the Free French intended to put an end to the mandate, to proclaim the people of Syria and the Lebanon free and independent, and to negotiate a treaty to ensure this independence. Lampson said that the British Government associated itself with this assurance of independence, and that, if the people of Syria and Lebanon joined the Allies, the blockade would be lifted, and they would enter into immediate relations with the sterling *bloc,* and thus gain "enormous and immediate advantages from the point of view of . . . exports and imports".

---

and Indian" and concluding "request minimum publicity of details". The order in which the troops were listed may have created an impression that the Australian and Indian forces had provided contingents to augment a mainly British and Free French force. In fact, of the battalions and cavalry regiments, twelve were Australian, two Indian, three British, and three Free French; of the field artillery and anti-tank regiments, four were Australian and one British.

At the end of the first day, however, it seemed evident that Syria would have to be won by military not political operations. The French had shown that they would resist. Consequently, since the French deployed 18 good battalions of regulars against 9 good Australian, Indian and British battalions, and 6 Free French battalions of doubtful quality, the "armed political inroad" which Churchill had advocated was likely to develop into a hard-fought campaign.

CHAPTER 18

ACROSS THE LITANI

ON the evening of the 8th Brigadier Stevens, commanding in the coastal sector, faced a problem very like the one that had confronted him the day before. His engineers had repaired the road at Iskandaroun, but the Litani bridge lay ahead—another frontier to cross. He now knew that the sea had been too rough to permit the landing of the commando battalion early on the 8th, and that a second attempt to land them would be made on the 9th. He had been instructed that, if his own men crossed the Litani before 4 a.m. on the 9th, they were to fire four Very lights to warn the commandos, then out to sea, not to land; if no lights were seen, the commandos would come ashore at 4.30 a.m. and try again to save the Litani bridge.

On the afternoon of the 8th Stevens had ordered Lieut-Colonel Mac-Donald of the 2/16th Battalion to launch an attack at 5.30 a.m., but only if the commandos had been unsuccessful. MacDonald allotted the task of saving the bridge to Captain Johnson's company to which a fourth platoon was attached to carry canvas boats forward in case they were needed. A second company was to follow Johnson's across the river, and a third (Major Caro's) was to move out to the coastal flank to give supporting fire for the commandos—if they landed.[1]

What had happened to the commandos? The unit (twenty officers and 400 men) had sailed from Port Said in the transport *Glengyle* on the 7th, with a naval escort, and arrived off shore about four miles west of the Litani before 1 a.m. on the 8th. Assault landing craft were lowered and filled with troops. In the moonlight a heavy surf could be seen, however, and the naval commander decided that the craft would capsize before they were beached. The men re-embarked in *Glengyle,* which returned to Port Said. At 3.15 a.m. on the 9th *Glengyle* was again off the Litani escorted by a cruiser and two destroyers. For the landing the commando unit was divided into three groups: one under Major Keyes[2] was to lead the attack on the position north of the river; a second (Captain More[3]) was to cut off this area from the north; the third formed a reserve. Unhappily a sandbank obscured the mouth of the river and, at 4.50 a.m., Keyes' group landed half a mile south instead of north of the river and south of the flanking company of the 2/16th. Nevertheless they advanced to the attack.

The river was from 30 to 40 yards wide and flowed fast between steep banks lined with poplars. The road travelled round the foot of the hills about 1,000 yards from the coast and crossed the river on an arched stone

---

[1] This and later accounts of the operations of the 2/16 Bn are partly based on that battalion's excellent regimental history, not yet published, and partly on interviews and correspondence with participants.

[2] Lt-Col G. C. T. Keyes, VC, MC. OC "C" Special Service Bn 1941. Regular soldier; b. Aberdeen, Fife, Scotland, 18 May 1917. Killed in action 18 Nov 1941. (Son of Admiral of the Fleet Lord Keyes.)

[3] Lt-Col G. R. M. More, MC. "C" Special Service Bn; 7 Armd Div. B. Athens, 3 Nov 1918.

bridge. North of the river the road travelled through flat land planted with fruit trees and corn for about 500 yards. This flat land was dominated, north of the river, by a steep hill about 500 feet in height into which the main French defences were dug.

A few seconds before the attack by the 2/16th Battalion towards the bridge was to begin, a scout, who had been sent out to reconnoitre, shouted the news that the bridge had just been blown up. Thereupon the plan, whereby one platoon would rush the bridge covered by the fire of another, had to be scrapped. The only course was to cross in the boats. The men of the leading company took what shelter they could from heavy enemy fire which opened as soon as the bridge was blown —chiefly among the headstones of a graveyard near the river bank. In a few minutes the boat-carrying parties arrived. Johnson decided that the river was flowing too fast—about five knots—to paddle the boats over, and Captain Hearman,[4] his second-in-command who was in charge of the boats, a man of uncommon physical strength and great confidence, ordered the men to cut the painters from the boats and to cut telephones wires from the poles along the road and

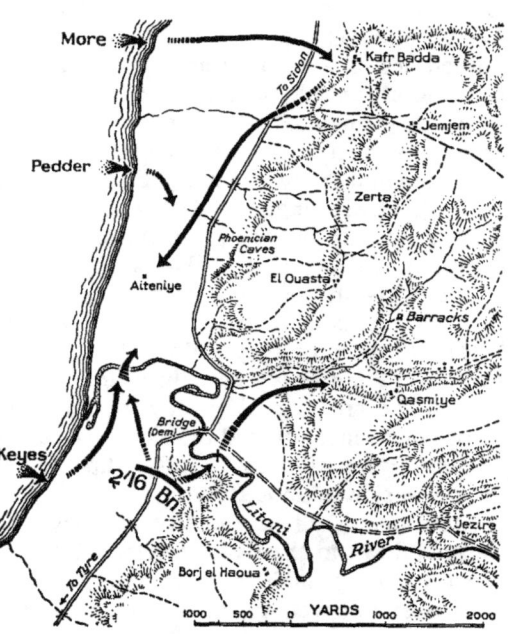

The crossing of the Litani river

knot them into a long rope. With this rope Corporal Haddy,[5] who declared that he was the strongest swimmer, waded into the Litani, and, though hit by a fragment of a mortar bomb, swam on and struggled to attach the rope to a tree on the opposite bank. Seeing that Haddy was becoming weak Lance-Corporal Dusting[6] swam across to help him, while Hearman collected volunteers to take the first boat over. Corporal Walsh[7] and eight men of Lieutenant Sublet's[8] platoon manned the boat—Privates

---

[4] Maj J. M. Hearman, WX1593; 2/16 Bn. MLA in WA since 1950. Farmer; of Donnybrook, WA; b. London, 10 Nov 1910.

[5] Lt A. C. Haddy, WX3636; 2/16 Bn. Maltster; of Perth, WA; b. Laverton, WA, 16 Jun 1912. Killed in action 7 Dec 1942.

[6] Cpl H. W. Dusting, WX5635; 2/16 Bn. Labourer; of Woodanilling, WA; b. Katanning, WA, 15 Dec 1917. Killed in action 30 Aug 1942.

[7] L-Sgt B. W. Walsh, WX4268; 2/16 Bn. Labourer; of Boulder, WA; b. Boulder, 26 May 1917. Killed in action 30 Aug 1942.

[8] Lt-Col F. H. Sublet, DSO, MC, WX1598. CO 2/16 Bn 1943-45. Public servant; of Victoria Park, WA; b. Meekatharra, WA, 13 May 1910.

"Pud" Graffin,[9] Len O'Brien,[1] Alf Ryan,[2] "Chook" Fowler,[3] "Bobby" Wilson,[4] "Blue" Moloney,[5] "Chummy" Gray[6] and Frank Moretti.[7] All of them, like the remainder of the platoon except the commander and his sergeant, McCullough,[8] had come from Kalgoorlie, and had been to school together. They had never been in a boat before and each was laden with all his gear and 300 rounds of ammunition. With difficulty the men persuaded Hearman not to enter the boat; there was very little freeboard, and the addition of so heavy a man, they thought, might have sunk it. Once they were out in the stream the machine-gun fire went over their heads, although mortar bombs were bursting on the water. They were hauled across without casualties. They landed on the north bank, spread out and advanced, bombing French posts concealed in bamboo thickets.

As the remainder of Sublet's men crossed, mortar bombs were falling among the men on the south bank. One bomb killed Johnson and wounded Hearman and the two remaining platoon commanders, N. B. G. Meecham[9] and W. G. Symington.[1] Although he was hit in four places, Hearman carried on until he was hit again. Sublet, the only surviving officer in the company, then—about 6.30—had his whole platoon plus a few other men of the boat-carrying party on the north bank, whence they moved briskly through the bamboo and into orchards beyond, driving the defenders before them until they held a bridge-head about 400 yards in depth. Because of the heavy casualties among officers, and because the French fire on the crossing place now became intense, there was a long delay before more men crossed to join Sublet. A second platoon of this company under Sergeant Phillips[2] crossed first increasing the number of men on the north side to about fifty.

MacDonald had now ordered Horley's company forward, and the men charged down to the river at the double through the mortar and machine-gun fire. Using Sublet's boat Horley led the way with six men, and the remainder followed six at a time until seventy were across. Soon after-

---

[9] Pte A. B. Graffin, WX4234; 2/16 Bn. Miner; of Kalgoorlie, WA; b. Kalgoorlie, 2 Feb 1914.

[1] Pte L. C. O'Brien, WX4206; 2/16 Bn. Mine bogger; of Kalgoorlie, WA; b. Kalgoorlie, 13 May 1916. Killed in action 4 Sep 1942. (Thus Haddy, Dusting and two of the nine men in the boat were killed in the Papuan Campaign of 1942.)

[2] Pte A. Ryan, WX4265; 2/16 Bn. Labourer; of Kalgoorlie, WA; b. Boulder, 19 May 1915.

[3] Pte E. Fowler, WX4185; 2/16 Bn. Labourer; of Fimiston, WA; b. Croydon, Eng, 14 Mar 1910.

[4] Pte R. J. Wilson, MM, WX4272; 2/16 Bn. Miner; of Kalgoorlie, WA; b. Kalgoorlie, 21 Aug 1916.

[5] Lt B. W. Moloney, MM, WX4210; 2/16 Bn. Miner; of Kalgoorlie, WA; b. Bullfinch, WA, 23 Sep 1915. Killed in action 20 May 1945.

[6] Capt A. H. Gray, WX4177; 2/16 Bn, 19 MG and 11 Bns. Mine bogger; of Kalgoorlie, WA; b. Beverley, WA, 7 Sep 1910.

[7] L-Cpl F. Moretti, WX4195; 2/16 Bn. Miner; of Kalgoorlie, WA; b. Kanowna, WA, 18 Apr 1918. Died 12 Oct 1943.

[8] Capt K. McCullough, WX4335; 2/16 Bn. Timber worker; of Jardee, WA; b. Kalgoorlie, WA, 3 Apr 1913.

[9] Capt N. B. G. Meecham, WX2738; 2/16 Bn. Company director; of Cottesloe, WA; b. Katanning, WA, 13 Dec 1912. His brother, Lt R. N. G. Meecham (of Cottesloe), a platoon commander in Horley's company, had been wounded a few minutes before.

[1] Maj W. G. Symington, WX1597; 2/16 Bn. Clerk; of Cottesloe, WA; b. Chatswood, NSW, 4 Feb 1916.

[2] Sgt A. M. Phillips, WX2746; 2/16 Bn. Butcher; of Geraldton, WA; b. Sandstone, WA, 7 May 1915.

wards two French destroyers stood close inshore and shelled the Australians north and south of the river until guns of the 2/4th Regiment began to reply, whereupon they threw out a smoke screen and hurriedly departed.

The French destroyers were the *Guépard* and *Valmy*. Admiral King led his squadron in search of them but they had gone when it arrived. He left four destroyers off the coast and, in the afternoon, these saw the *Guépard* and *Valmy* off Sidon. In a running fight the British destroyer *Janus* was hit and the faster French ships made off to the north.

While Sublet's men, who had come under the naval fire, engaged French posts forward of the bridgehead, Horley sent his platoon commanders back to MacDonald to report how matters stood and ask for artillery and mortar fire to support a flanking attack by his company. (By this time Signalman Bright,[3] working under fire, had got telephone lines across the river.) Captain Gaunt,[4] with Lance-Bombardier Murphy[5] and three other men of the 2/4th Field Regiment, had established an observation post overlooking the river, and effective fire was directed against enemy positions. Early in the afternoon, after an artillery concentration lasting ten minutes, Horley's two platoons across the river—Lieutenant Atkinson's[6] and Lieutenant Elphick's[7]—attacked with swift success. The supporting artillery fire, by six 25-pounders, was very accurate, and in spite of the fact that the advance was over ploughed land offering no cover and against well-wired enemy posts, there were few casualties. One of those who were hit was Private Colless,[8] who was severely wounded while cutting the wire in front of the French positions but finished his job. Corporal Wieck[9] and Corporal Duncan[1] went forward and cut the wire blocking their sections. In twenty-five minutes the West Australians had overrun the enemy positions (they were manned by Algerians) on the ridge dominating the river, killed about 30, taken 38 prisoners and captured 11 machine-guns at a cost of 3 men wounded.

Encouraged by this success Horley decided to work left along the ridge against the French posts with which Sublet's men were exchanging fire. After a brief artillery bombardment his men again advanced and captured these posts, taking twelve more prisoners, a 75-mm field gun,

---

[3] Cpl F. G. Bright, DCM, WX4186; 2/16 Bn. Plumber; of Fimiston, WA; b. Kalgoorlie, WA, 19 Sep 1916.

[4] Maj D. C. Gaunt, MC, VX14105; 2/4 Fd Regt. Audit clerk; of Regent, Vic; b. Footscray, Vic, 1 Oct 1911.

[5] S-Sgt R. P. Murphy, VX18535; 2/4 Fd Regt. Proof reader; of St Kilda, Vic; b. Christchurch, NZ, 29 Aug 1909.

[6] Maj W. M. Atkinson, MC, WX2846. 2/16 Bn 1941-43; 1 Aust Para Bn 1944-45. Shopkeeper; of Merredin, WA; b. Cottesloe, WA, 1 Mar 1911.

[7] Lt W. T. Elphick, WX4545; 2/16 Bn. Law clerk; of Mt Lawley, WA; b. Bunbury, WA, 10 Jul 1914.

[8] Pte O. W. Colless, WX1952; 2/16 Bn. Clerk; of Fremantle, WA; b. Kalgoorlie, WA, 15 Mar 1910. Died 27 Jul 1949.

[9] Cpl S. Wieck, WX3685; 2/16 Bn. Cartage contractor; of Mt Lawley, WA; b. St Peters, SA, 24 Jan 1914.

[1] Lt W. J. Duncan, WX3280; 2/16 Bn. Warehouse assistant; of North Perth, WA; b. Perth, 4 Jul 1919.

and two machine-guns. One of the prisoners declared that a fresh company of his battalion of the *22nd Algerian Regiment* was on the next ridge, whereupon Horley and Sublet (whose platoons were now led by sergeants or corporals, among whom McCullough had been "an inspiration") placed their men ready for a possible counter-attack. It was then 4 o'clock in the afternoon.

In the meantime, on the flat coastal strip on the left, Keyes' group of commandos had advanced to the river where they came under intense fire. Men of Caro's company of the 2/16th set out to carry boats forward to them. In the heavy fire, which had caused severe losses—about 25 per cent—among the commandos and the boat parties, only one boat reached the bank, and with it a gallant lance-corporal, Dilworth,[2] and Private Archibald[3] ferried two boat loads of commandos and Australians across. There, about noon, they captured a strong redoubt commanding the river and took thirty-five prisoners. By the middle of the afternoon Keyes and his men and one of Caro's platoons were across. About 4 p.m. Stevens sent Captain Longworth,[4] a forward observation officer of the 2/4th Field Regiment, to Caro with orders that Caro should attack and capture the high ground on the right of the coast road just north of the river, with artillery support directed by Longworth. After seeing Caro, whose men were now extremely fatigued, Longworth agreed, as an initial move, to take his party across the river to support the force already on the other side.

> On our way to the mouth of the river (wrote Longworth) we passed what remained of portion of the gallant S.S. Battalion which had been met by a murderous hail of steel and H.E. from French 75's, mortars and heavy machine-guns. Their dead literally littered the beach.[5]

On the other side of the river Longworth found Keyes "nonchalantly perched . . . in full view of the enemy", and his signallers strove, at first without result, to speak to their guns by wireless. Caro had now brought the remainder of his company across the river; about 5.30 p.m. Longworth's signallers got through to their command post, and later learnt that a general attack, with artillery support, was to be made at 9.30 p.m.

Colonel Pedder's commando group, of which Keyes' group was a part, had landed about a mile and a half north of the river in the midst of well-sited French positions. After confused fighting in which Pedder and two other officers were killed, one party surrendered; another, having captured prisoners, worked its way back to the Litani to join the Australians. More's group, after landing two and a half miles north of the river, was

---

[2] WO2 C. E. J. Dilworth, WX5648; 2/16 Bn. Bank clerk; of Katanning, WA; b. Ealing, Eng, 19 Sep 1907.

[3] Cpl T. Archibald, WX4387; 2/16 Bn. Timber worker; of Manjimup, WA; b. Wallsend-on-Tyne, Eng, 28 Jan 1907.

[4] Maj L. E. Longworth, VX14109; 2/4 Fd Regt. Bank clerk; of Brighton, Vic; b. Warrnambool, Vic, 30 Mar 1912.

[5] Quoted in R. L. Henry, *The Story of the 2/4th Field Regiment* (1950), p. 100.

engaged in confused fighting round Kafr Badda and finally surrendered at Aiteniye early on the 10th. The commando landing had experienced bad luck, but also it was ill-arranged. Stevens had seen Pedder for only a few minutes at Nazareth and they had then had no time to coordinate their plans, and each was left with a feeling of uneasiness. The position was now such as to cause Stevens some anxiety. The only link with the half-battalion on the north side of the river was the flimsy ferry, and the engineers could not bridge the stream except under cover of darkness. At 6.45 p.m. Stevens issued orders (referred to above) that from 9.30 the 2/16th, with a company of the 2/27th, should clear the high ground ahead of its leading companies, while his engineers built a bridge of folding boats across which the remainder of the 2/27th would cross, occupy the ground north-east of the road and push on as opportunity offered.

In the meantime Horley had been pressing on. About 6 p.m. a third company of the 2/16th, hitherto covering the crossing from high ground overlooking the south bank, began to cross. Its commander, Captain Hopkinson,[6] had been wounded early in the morning, and Captain Mackenzie[7] now led it. When it reached the north bank Horley sent it into a new advance whose aim was to overcome the French posts on the western side of the ridge. The men moved off at 7.30, but were soon stopped by heavy machine-gun fire which killed one man and wounded a platoon commander, Lieutenant Langridge;[8] but Horley himself and Corporal Sadleir[9] stalked to the rear of the French machine-gun post and captured the six men manning it. By dark the attackers had reached the top of the ridge at a point about 500 yards south of "the Barracks", a large building right of the road, having taken seventy prisoners including five officers.

Unfortunately at this stage the telephone failed with the result that Horley could not inform MacDonald where he had got to. He knew that, at 9.30, the artillery would fire on the heights in preparation for an attack on a position he already partly occupied, and yet he had no means of stopping that fire. Consequently he withdrew his leading men to the foot of the hill, intending to reoccupy the slopes next morning. He then hastened back to the headquarters of his battalion, where he was told that the planned attack must go on. In the confusion, and with such flimsy communications, the extent of the success of the men across the Litani was probably not fully appreciated by those on the south bank. Soon afterwards British ships mistakenly bombarded the ridge, necessitating a further withdrawal of Horley's force.[1]

---

[6] Maj W. Hopkinson, WX3374. 2/16 Bn and training appts. Public servant; of Cannington, WA; b. Leeds, Eng, 22 Apr 1909.

[7] Maj R. B. Mackenzie, WX1595. 2/16 Bn and Comb Ops. Public servant; of Nth Cottesloe, WA, b. Swanbourne, WA, 21 Dec 1912.

[8] Capt B. D. N. Langridge, WX1599; 2/16 Bn. Bank clerk; of Inglewood, WA; b. North Perth, WA, 10 Feb 1919. Killed in action 8 Sep 1942.

[9] Cpl J. C. Sadleir, WX4228; 2/16 Bn. Miner; of Maylands, WA; b. Kanowna, WA, 8 Oct 1902. Killed in action 13 Jun 1941.

[1] It was not until two days later that a naval liaison officer attached to the 7 Div joined Stevens' headquarters, thus making close coordination possible. (Nevertheless on the 8th Stevens' units had sent visual signals to the squadron offshore suggesting tasks which were successfully carried out.)

At 9.30 the planned artillery fire descended on the high ground beyond the river; in half an hour the guns fired 960 rounds. On the right Horley's force reoccupied the positions it had gained early in the day. On the left Major Isaachsen's[2] company of the 2/27th had been brought forward, and the men ferried across the river six at a time in the single folding boat that was available. When two platoons were across they attacked into sharp mortar and machine-gun fire. After a prolonged fight a whole company of Algerians surrendered to the South Australians, who rescued some twenty of the commandos. In the "Phoenician Caves", dug into the cliffs above the road about a mile beyond the river, large quantities of food, weapons and ammunition were found. The river was bridged during the night by engineers of the 2/6th Field Company under Lieutenant Watts[3] helped by eighty infantrymen working as labourers. At 5 a.m. on the 10th, men and vehicles of the 2/27th began to cross this pontoon bridge, 400 yards east of the demolished stone bridge.

Stevens' orders for 10th June were that the 2/27th should advance along the main road with Lieutenant Mills' squadron of the 6th Cavalry probing ahead, while the 2/16th cleared the hills on the right. The Cheshire was still moving forward in the rugged hills farther inland from Srifa towards Kafr Sir which they entered, after a skirmish, that day. Mills' carriers crossed the pontoon bridge at 6 a.m. and whirred north. One troop was sent inland along the road to Imsar, while another led the advance along the main road. This troop met and dispersed a party of Spahis with a line of pack mules, and then came under fire from French armoured cars which were driven off with anti-tank rifles. By 10 a.m. the carriers were among the buildings south-west of Adloun and had been fired on by light guns and their crews had sighted two tanks. Mills brought forward a 2-pounder to deal with the tanks but, when they did not return the fire, he drove forward and found that four French tanks lay abandoned though apparently in good condition. However, when a troop drove forward to locate a gun which had fired from a position between the road and the sea, the leading carrier unwittingly ran to within a few yards of the anti-tank gun and a machine-gun and two members of the crew were killed and the third wounded and captured. Sergeant Stewart[4] in the next carrier astern poured about 2,000 rounds into the French position from his Vickers gun, and, pursued by shells, the surviving carriers withdrew.

Lieutenant Glasgow's[5] troop of three carriers which had turned off towards Imsar met fifty white French troops with two idle field guns at Kafr Badda, only half a mile from the main road. After the cavalrymen

---

[2] Lt-Col O. C. Isaachsen, DSO, SX2915. 2/27 Bn 1940-42; CO 36 Bn 1942-45. Barrister and solicitor; of Malvern, SA; b. Mannum, SA, 5 Jun 1911.

[3] Capt R. H. Watts, MC, NX12290; 2/6 Fd Coy. Architect; of Manly, NSW; b. Croydon, NSW, 24 Oct 1916. Died while prisoner of war, 14 Jul 1943.

[4] Capt G. F. Stewart, MC, NX579. 6 Cav Regt; 2 NG Inf Bn. Bank clerk; of Beecroft, NSW; b. Manly, NSW, 9 Mar 1914.

[5] Lt-Col D. D. Glasgow, QX6070. 6 Cav Regt; CO 1 Army Tk Bn 1943-45. Bank clerk; of Ascot, Qld; b. Gympie, Qld, 21 Aug 1915.

had fired a few bursts the enemy gave up the fight, half of them making off and half surrendering. When the captives had been handed over to provosts, Glasgow drove back along the road and overtook the remainder of the Kafr Badda party, but could not capture them because they ran for the shelter of rocky hills where carriers could not follow. Thence the carriers continued to Imsar, where the head man of the village said that the French had departed the evening before.

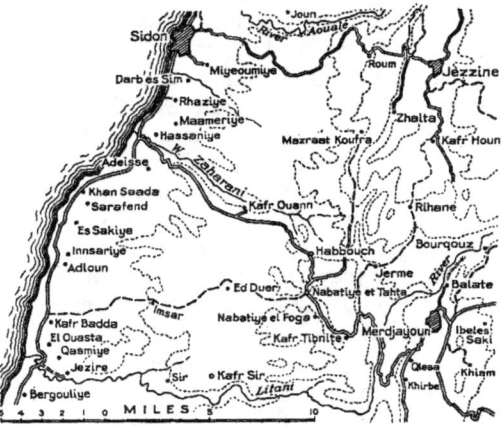

In spite of such evidence as the cavalry had seen of a withdrawal north of the Litani, the French posts during the morning were still holding out firmly in the hill positions just east of the coastal road, south of the cavalry patrols, and both the 2/16th and 2/27th were meeting opposition and suffering casualties. (Sublet was wounded here.) The enemy was still in strength particularly at El Ouasta, where a patrol reported that the enemy had thirteen machine-guns emplaced, and whence the 2/16th was being enfiladed. However, this area was heavily shelled both by the field artillery and by the ships off shore and at length the enemy abandoned it. At the end of the day the enemy had been cleared from the coastal plain as far as a line astride the road south-west of Adloun, but was evidently in some strength there and at Innsariye; the lateral track had been explored as far as Imsar; and the British horsed cavalry were at Kafr Sir and that day made contact with the 21st Brigade at Qasmiye.

After the battle the West Australians reached the conclusion that if they had been holding the strong natural defensive line of the Litani and the French attacking it, the attack would have failed. Their achievement was one on which they could look back with justifiable pride. Despite the demolition of the bridge and the failure of the ill-planned and costly landing by the commandos, the coolness and enterprise of their leaders and the skill and dogged courage of the men had forced a crossing and breached cunningly-concealed, well-manned enemy positions armed with many mortars and machine-guns. A weakness that was discerned in the French defence here and later was their failure to deny the attackers the approaches to the obstacle they were defending and adequately to defend the area on the seaward side of the road, probably for fear of naval bombardment.

In the Merdjayoun sector the deadlock persisted. On the afternoon of the 8th, having learnt that the 25th Brigade was meeting determined and skilful opposition, Lavarack had offered Cox from his divisional reserve the remainder of the 2/25th Battalion, of which Cox already held two companies, and suggested that at dawn on the 9th he use this reinforcement, with the 2/33rd Battalion, in an effort to take Merdjayoun from the east. There was little time, however, to bring up the new battalion and organise an attack so soon. The 2/25th had assembled in the Dafna area, whence one company had already gone forward to Metulla on the night of the 8th-9th; next morning, with two companies, it moved up to the right of the 2/33rd south of and 1,000 feet below Ibeles Saki.

Meanwhile early on the 9th Cotton's company had advanced against Fort Khiam, after a sharp artillery concentration ordered by Brigadier Berryman, Lavarack's artillery commander, and found it abandoned. Cotton moved past the fort into the village, but was held at the northern end until about 5 p.m. when French shells set fire to haystacks in a threshing area there just behind his leading men, causing such heat and smoke that they withdrew to the southern end of the village. Throughout the day the 2/31st was still held by enemy fire from Khirbe and west of it.

It was on the morning of the 9th that the first news arrived at Porter's headquarters of Sergeant Davis' patrol, whose task, it will be recalled, had been to save the bridge over the Litani south-west of Merdjayoun. The patrol itself did not arrive until that evening. At midnight on the 7th Davis, with four riflemen, two engineers and two Palestinian guides had set out from Metulla. After having climbed into French territory across country for more than three hours without being detected, the patrol passed a telephone line, which Davis cut. Twice they were close to French posts or sentries but were not detected. When they were only a few hundred yards from their objective one of the guides accidentally pulled the trigger of his revolver and wounded himself in the hip, but evidently this shot was not heard by the French. The wound was dressed, and the Palestinian marched on. "I go on," he said, "show you the bridge. You (he made the motions of bayonetting), *then* I lie down."

At 4.30 a.m. the patrol reached a small bridge over the Litani river about 400 yards south of the main bridge. Here a dog began to bark, and a sentry walked on to the road. The Australians flattened themselves on the ground. Davis decided to overpower the sentry without opening fire. However, when he and his men were about 10 yards away, the Frenchman called out loudly, slipped a round into his rifle, and after standing with it at his shoulder for a few tense seconds with visibly trembling hands, fired at the advancing Australians, who were then only two or three yards away. His shot missed. Almost simultaneously Lance-Corporal Hopkins[6] fired, and then five others. The sentry staggered across the road, and, with two other French soldiers who had run out to join him, disappeared in a gully.

---

[6] L-Cpl F. W. McVicar, NX97777. 2/31 and 2/5 Bns. (Served also as QX11522 L-Cpl N. H. Hopkins.) Of Cowra, NSW; b. Cowra, 30 Jun 1921. (It appears likely that McVicar, who was killed serving with the 2/5 Bn at Mt Tambu, New Guinea, on 24 July 1943, mis-stated his name and occupation in order to evade manpower regulations. Records disclose his occupation to have been variously stated as prospector, lorry driver, wireworker and electric welder.)

After a brief exchange of shots, Davis led his men charging with fixed bayonets towards a rough shelter which served as a guard hut on the eastern end of the main bridge. In the doorway of the hut were two French soldiers in pyjamas hastily thrusting a magazine into a light machine-gun. They surrendered, and Davis with one man ran across the bridge to a blockhouse at the other end of it where two more men hurried out and surrendered after Davis had tossed in a grenade.

Davis and the two engineers found the wire that led to the demolition charges in the bridge, disconnected it, and threw wire and detonators into the river. He then led the patrol, with its four prisoners, and with a captured machine-gun and five captured rifles, to the side of a steep hill overlooking the bridge from the west. It was now a little after 5 a.m. Davis' plan was to hold high ground from which to launch an attack on the bridge when his battalion approached. By this time the invasion proper had begun. Lying on the hillside they could hear the whistle of shells, the continuous rat-tatting of machine-gun fire, the drone of aircraft engines. In the valley below they could see "countless civilians" hastily moving north away from the battle, and French troops moving south towards it. To mislead the French below into believing that he had a considerable force, Sergeant Davis, a born soldier, made his men crawl from one rock or bush to another and allow themselves to be seen now and then. By 6.30 a.m. fifty-seven French vehicles were lined up along the road. These vehicles turned and departed. About 7.30 a.m. the French stationed eight men on the ridge east of the river, evidently to defend the bridge against attack by Davis' patrol, and later more French troops were moved on to the high ground above the bridge. At 3 p.m. the French demolished the small bridge and at 4 p.m. the main bridge.

About an hour after the last explosion an Australian soldier appeared on the road below Davis' party, walking unconcernedly along with an anti-tank rifle on his shoulder. Davis hurried down to the bank to speak to him. It was Corporal Feltham,[7] of Davis' battalion, who had been hit on the head in front of Khirbe the night before, had become separated from his unit, and was now, he thought, marching forward to rejoin it. Davis told him he was far behind the French lines and called to him to go downstream to find a crossing. At dusk Davis moved his men, and his prisoners, to a point on the hills about three-quarters of a mile below the bridge. Next morning they crossed the river and moved south along the main road. At length they saw Feltham, now with five other Australians on the other side of the river. One of Davis' men swam the river carrying 50 or 60 feet of the heavy gauge telephone wire which Davis had cut two nights before. It was secured to a tree and, using it for support, Feltham and his men crossed. The imperturbable Feltham reported that, after having failed to find a ford across the river the previous day, he had spent the night on its banks and eventually found his way back to his battalion, and there obtained permission to lead out a party to rescue

---

[7] Cpl E. J. A. Feltham, DX104; 2/31 Bn. Regular soldier; of Hobart; b. Hobart, 5 Feb 1917. Killed in action 24 Nov 1943.

Davis and his party and guide them home. Together the Australians, still with their prisoners, made their way along the Litani, across the northern slope of the hill on which Deir Mimess stands (where they came under some mortar and machine-gun fire) and onwards, round the edge of the battle, to the road junction where Colonel Porter had his headquarters.

The events of the 9th had emphasised the difficulties faced by Cox's brigade: his battalions were on ground that offered little cover, and at night from 11 o'clock onwards the moon was bright. A handful of infantry tanks could have carried the attack forward, but his light tanks were very vulnerable to the fire of French anti-tank guns. On the other hand the French possessed a force that seemed as strong as his own and were in prepared positions well supported by artillery. Their posts were carefully sited to give enfilade fire and were defiladed from the front. Scattered over the area were small cairns of stones erected to mark the range for the French gunners and mortarmen. Even to send food to the forward infantry companies was laborious and dangerous.

Lavarack had watched Berryman's effective artillery concentration which had subdued the garrison of Fort Khiam and, that afternoon, he withdrew the 2/6th Field Regiment from Cox's command and placed Berryman, with the 2/6th and 2/5th Regiments under his control, in support of Cox's infantry for a set-piece attack on Merdjayoun, not next day but on the 11th, to give time for systematic preparation.

On the 10th one attempt seriously to test the enemy's strength was made, and that on Porter's front. Early in the afternoon, at Berryman's suggestion, a detachment of the 6th Cavalry consisting of one light tank and six carriers under Lieutenant Millard was ordered to advance towards Khirbe to draw their opponents' fire. The plan was that Lieutenant Florence[8] should lead a troop of three carriers along the road on the Khirbe ridge until the ground allowed him to deploy, while Millard led his carriers forward and deployed on Florence's right, and Sergeant Groves gave supporting fire from a light tank hull-down near an observation post whence artillery fire could be directed against the French when they revealed themselves.

Without opposition Florence's troop reached the foot of the hill on which Khirbe stands. Millard's carriers were deploying when the French opened with machine-guns, mortars and an anti-tank gun. In the first burst Corporal Oswell,[9] Millard's wireless operator, was wounded in the arm and could not send out his orders. Millard gave the hand signal to retire. Florence's troop retired under heavy fire while Millard shot at the French positions with his Vickers gun. As he turned to run back to a more sheltered position the track of Millard's carrier was blown off by a mortar bomb. Under hot fire Millard and his crew dashed for the cover of a low stone

---
[8] Capt J. M. Florence, VX13847. 6 Cav Regt; "Z" Special Unit 1945. Farmer; of Rupanyup, Vic; b. Ballarat, Vic, 11 Feb 1912.
[9] Lt J. L. Oswell, VX543. 6 Cav Regt; 1 Armd Regt. Bank clerk; of Canterbury, Vic; b. Kerang, Vic, 28 Dec 1917.

(Australian War Memorial)

A 2/6th Field Regiment troop command post at Merdjayoun, June 1941. The Gun Position Officer, with megaphone, is Lieutenant J. W. Hutton.

Fort Merdjayoun.

(2/5 Fd Regt Association)
Looking north-east from Merdjayoun. A portion of Route "B" can be seen on the left.

(Maj-Gen S. H. W. C. Porter)
A sketch captured in an enemy post at Khirbe, looking towards Metulla, and illustrating the fields of fire enjoyed by the French.

wall. The driver, Corporal Limb,[1] ran back to the damaged carrier, manned the wireless and tried to call for artillery support but the set had been put out of action by the explosion. The Australian artillery had rapidly and accurately begun shelling the positions round Qleaa and Khirbe knocking out the French anti-tank gun.

Seeking to rescue the crew of the disabled carrier Florence drove his own one forward down the road leading to the village. He ran the last 100 yards down the centre of the road towards the abandoned carrier (which was still under heavy fire) brandishing and firing his revolver and calling out to the crew. Finding it abandoned he returned to his carrier, while Sergeant Martin,[2] who had driven his carrier behind a rise, advanced the last couple of hundred yards across open ground under fire to the wall where Millard and his men had now been sheltering for an hour and a half. He guided Millard and his crew, including the wounded Oswell, along the wall to a position whence it was possible to reach cover by making only a short concerted dash across the open. All but two of Millard's six carriers were hit and six men out of the eighteen in the carrier crews were wounded. At 9 p.m. Cox informed Millard that he wished him to adhere to an earlier order to support the infantry attack planned to begin at 2 o'clock next morning. Millard pointed out that he now had only one tank and one carrier fit for action, and eventually was released from the task.

It will be recalled that on the night the invasion began the right company of the 2/33rd (Captain Bennett's) had been sent through the hills to occupy Ferdisse. Since then it had been out in the blue; little was learnt about Bennett's company by battalion headquarters, and Bennett knew less of how the battle was going round Khiam and Merdjayoun. On the first night Bennett and his men had difficulty in finding the track to Chebaa and it was not until daylight that they were sure where they were. All that day, without seeing a French soldier, they marched into Syria over the rock-strewn hills, and came within sight of Hebbariye some hours after nightfall. The plan was that Bennett's company would take four hours to reach Hebbariye; in fact it took twenty-four. Outside the village Bennett met some native Syrians who had lived in America, and they told him that French cavalry had been in Hebbariye that night but evidently did not know of his presence in the area. Bennett's scouts probed round the village in the dark, and, at 8 a.m. on the 9th, he moved off to occupy Ferdisse, and in accordance with his orders establish his company astride the main road to the west of it.

Approaching Ferdisse his men were fired on by a machine-gun sited to the north of the village, so Bennett decided to move on with two of his platoons, leaving one covering his rear in the Hebbariye area. The two platoons advanced into Ferdisse under fire, and then Bennett ordered his

---

[1] Lt T. M. Limb, WX1142; 6 Cav Regt. Motor mechanic; of Bayswater, WA; b. Bayswater, 21 May 1917.
[2] Sgt B. S. Martin, SX1190; 6 Cav Regt. Truck and tractor driver; of Renmark, SA; b. Adelaide, 2 Mar 1911.

remaining platoon forward over the hill south of Ferdisse. As they reached the summit they saw a dozen Frenchmen with machine-guns loaded on pack mules moving south towards Ibeles Saki. Still under fire from distant French machine-guns Bennett moved his men towards the main road and established them on the high ground each side of the track just short of its junction with the main road.

Next day (the 10th) Bennett still faithfully awaited the arrival of the rest of his battalion, which was in fact four miles away to the south. A French force, which he estimated to be a company, came leisurely down the main road from Hasbaya, deployed and attacked the platoon dug in on the northern side of the track. Three attacks were made, one at 10 a.m., another at midday and a third at 4 p.m. Each time Lieutenant Copp,[3] a cool and skilful young regular soldier, let the advancing Frenchmen—all white troops—attack up hill until they were within 50 yards of his posts, then opened fire and drove them back leaving dead and wounded men behind. As the final French attack was sent in, a body of about fifty horsed cavalry attacked Bennett's rear at Ferdisse (evidently having come over the hills from Hasbaya). They were within 200 yards of his men round the village and had dismounted before they were seen by a section posted just south of the houses. This section opened fire and routed the Frenchmen, some of whose horses bolted and went thundering along the valley towards Bennett's main position.

Next morning (11th June) Bennett's force was subjected to two more attacks from the main road. In the course of one of these the French forced an entry into Ferdisse, cutting off his only supply of water and capturing his six wounded men and the stretcher-bearer who was with them. The rear platoon stayed where it was, overlooking Ferdisse from north and south. Bennett now had French troops on the main road in front of him and in the village behind him. At this stage a Syrian came to his headquarters and announced that the French commander wished to see him. Bennett sent back a message that if the French commander wished to see him he could come to his headquarters, and under escort. There was no reply.

On the fourth day (the 12th) there were no attacks on Bennett's beleaguered company, though the French surrounding him fired at intervals during the day and horsed cavalry patrols probed round his area. About 11.45 one horseman—an African native—rode, perhaps unknowingly, right into Copp's position. Copp allowed him to come close and then shot the horse. Corporal Marshall[4] ran out to capture the rider, but the native resisted and a fierce wrestle began while the Australians cheered their champion. Marshall broke away, whereupon his opponent advanced on Private Norris[5] who shot him.

---

[3] Maj W. D. Copp, MC, VX11589; 2/33 Bn. Regular soldier; of Rutherglen, Vic; b. Corowa, NSW, 24 Nov 1918. (Served also as H. D. Cullen.)

[4] Cpl G. E. D. Marshall, QX7446; 2/33 Bn. Labourer; of Burleigh Heads, Qld; b. Inverell, NSW, 26 Jul 1911.

[5] Pte F. A. Norris, QX7073; 2/33 Bn. Dairy farm hand; of Mullumbimby, NSW; b. Portsmouth, Eng, 29 Aug 1909.

12-13 June THE DESERT FLANK 373

Bennett had now held his position overlooking the road for four days. He had no news from battalion headquarters since he had spoken to them by wireless from Hebbariye on 8th June, though he had sent three runners back.[6] When he set out his men had had twenty-four hours' rations and full water-bottles, but since 9th June, and it was now the 12th, the men had had nothing to eat but a little local "mungaree".[7]

Bennett decided to retire on to the remainder of his battalion after dark that night. He instructed Copp and Dwyer[8] to take their platoons southwards across country, moving separately on compass bearings, while Lieutenant Marshall's[9] covered the withdrawal. Thus while Copp and Dwyer steered their way southwards on parallel courses, Marshall "somehow managed" to march out along the track on which he had come; and Bennett and his headquarters went through Rachaya el Fokhar and Kheibe. The moon was just rising as the headquarters party set off. As Bennett crossed the track a French patrol came along the road and sat down a few yards from him and his batman. The Australians sat quietly for a while, then crept up the hill among the rocks, unobserved. The headquarters party camped below Rachaya el Fokhar that night, marched all next day and, after dark, reached Monaghan's headquarters where they found that the three platoons had arrived during the day. All Bennett's men returned safely except the six wounded men and stretcher-bearer captured in Ferdisse. Monaghan's use of this company had been very bold—perhaps too bold in view of the rawness of the troops and the lack of signal communication. Bennett was given a task that would have better fitted a whole battalion.

On the desert flank Colonel Collet's cavalrymen, having followed the 5th Indian Brigade to Sheikh Meskine, advanced into the volcanic boulder country to the east where horses were more useful than vehicles, and on the 10th reached Najha on the Nahr el Awaj where he captured some prisoners. He then encountered a force of Senegalese infantry with armoured cars and tanks, and fell back about six miles to a good defensive position. There he was attacked on the 11th but, with his one anti-tank gun, succeeded in checking the enemy.

The leading troops of the main Free French column went through Sheikh Meskine on the morning of the 9th, the vanguard consisting of marines and Senegalese; Lloyd lent them a battery of the 1st Field Regiment and a troop of light anti-aircraft guns to compensate for their shortage of artillery. By nightfall General Legentilhomme had occupied Khan

---

[6] On 8 June battalion headquarters had ordered Bennett to send an officer back to confer with the Intelligence officer, and gave as the meeting place the map reference of Ibeles Saki when actually Khiam was intended. Both Lt J. K. Bryce (of Frankston, Vic), Bennett's second-in-command, and Pte N. V. Birrell (of Homebush, NSW) reached battalion headquarters safely, Birrell, however, making the journey over the hills in Arab clothing. Afterwards Birrell said to Bennett: "I wouldn't have got through if I hadn't been able to speak Arabic." Bennett asked him how much Arabic he knew. "Oh, only 'Sayeeda George'," said Birrell.

[7] However, they refilled their bottles from a water main which they pierced with a shot from an anti-tank rifle.

[8] Lt H. G. Dwyer, NX34866; 2/33 Bn. Clerk; of Roseville, NSW; b. Sydney, 4 Oct 1905.

[9] Maj E. S. Marshall, NX70757; 2/33 Bn. Accounts clerk; of Mosman, NSW; b. Adelaide, 2 Sep 1918.

Deinoun and Deir Ali and was in touch with the Vichy outposts. There he awaited reinforcements during the 10th; and on the 11th, with a Senegalese battalion, attacked towards Kiswe which was defended by Moroccans about equal in strength to the attackers.

General de Verdilhac was greatly disturbed by the rapid Free French advance towards Damascus and decided to give battle on the Nahr el Awaj position. He ordered the *6th Chasseurs d'Afrique* with their tanks and the *II/6th Foreign Legion* into that area on the 9th, and on the 11th added the *7th Chasseurs d'Afrique* and the *I/6th Foreign Legion.* Thus by the 12th six battalions including two of the Foreign Legion, the most valued infantry, and most of the tanks were in the area between Mount Hermon and the desert. Three additional battalions, mainly Tunisian, were in the Jebel Druse area.

The enemy force defending the Litani area appears to have included part of the *24th Colonial Regiment,* sent south from Tripoli, and companies of the *22nd Algerian* and the *6th Foreign Legion,* supported by seven batteries of artillery. De Verdilhac sent the *IV Battalion* of the Foreign Legion to the coastal sector on the 10th.

Indeed, in the opening days, de Verdilhac deployed in each sector a force stronger in infantry than that of his opponent; in addition he had a substantial reserve of armour; and, whether he chose to defend or attack, the terrain would favour him rather than the invader.

CHAPTER 19

PRESSING ON: TO SIDON, MERDJAYOUN AND JEZZINE

THREE days had passed and the Syrian expedition, instead of a fast-moving three-pronged thrust against a half-hearted enemy, had resolved itself into a hard campaign against resolute and skilful troops. On the right the Free French had been held but were now being reinforced from Lloyd's Indian brigade which had been guarding their rear; in the centre the advance had bogged down within sight of the frontier; on the left progress had been faster but, to judge by the events of the previous days, a series of exacting fights lay ahead against an enemy who would put up a capable defence at well-chosen positions in the long defile between sea and mountain.

It will be recalled that in that sector, at nightfall on the 10th, the 2/27th Battalion, after a sleepless night and a long advance from the Litani, was astride the road just south of Adloun and Innsariye. The thrustful Brigadier Stevens had ordered Lieut-Colonel Moten, its commander, to attack the Innsariye position at midnight, giving the French no rest. The men of the 2/27th were hungry, and thirsty, and as they waited for the attack to open they sucked the juice of green tomatoes growing in the gardens. The guns fired for half an hour from midnight and then the two leading companies advanced, each with two platoons forward.

Captain McPhee's[1] was on the right of the road; Captain Woore's[2] astride the road and extended well to the left. Captain White's[3] was to follow McPhee's, pass through it and advance to the final objective—a position beyond a row of Phoenician caves cut into the cliffs just west of Adloun. After having advanced about 500 yards the leading companies suddenly came under severe fire at close range. McPhee's lost four men killed and six wounded, including the commander. On the left Woore, too, was wounded as he called his men forward. Fire was coming from French positions on either side of the road and particularly from round the cavalry carrier disabled the previous day. A grenade thrown into a building containing a store of petrol set fire to it and it illuminated the whole area brightly; the right company turned towards it "like moths to a candle".

A patrol led by Captain Johnson[4] moved forward on the western flank and returned with news that eight light tanks were warming up their engines. This disturbing report was telephoned to Stevens, who ordered

---

[1] Lt-Col D. R. McPhee, OBE, SX3707; 2/27 Bn and Movt Cont. Brewery representative; of Trinity Gardens, SA; b. Adelaide, 28 Dec 1907.
[2] Maj T. G. Woore, MBE, SX2928; 2/27 Bn; and Mil Sec Branch 1943-45. Industrial chemist; of Adelaide; b. Mt Morgan, Qld, 25 Nov 1909.
[3] Maj D. A. H. White, VX36378; 2/27 Bn. Grazier; of Kigwigal, NSW; b. Burwood, NSW, 4 Dec 1909.
[4] Maj R. L. Johnson, DSO, SX2925; 2/27 Bn. Solicitor; of Prospect, SA; b. Adelaide, 15 Mar 1916.

Major Rau,[5] commanding the 2/4th Field Regiment, to have two of his 25-pounders and four 2-pounders ready by 3.15 a.m., and take them forward himself. At that time Stevens collected this reinforcement and led it to a point 1,000 yards behind the infantry, where the advanced headquarters of the 2/27th was, and after discussion with the adjutant (in Moten's absence forward), Rau, hurrying forward in his pyjamas with a greatcoat over them, took one of the field guns along the road, and in the moonlight it opened fire at short range. The tanks made off, but the infantrymen pointed out a stone house only 200 yards away near the abandoned carrier whence an anti-tank gun and a machine-gun were firing. By arrangement Rau fired twelve rounds into the building, whereupon an infantry section which had crept near the house, having counted the rounds, charged. Inside the battered building were found four dead Frenchmen.

It has been mentioned that a third company (Captain White's) was to advance over the heights on the right and pass through McPhee's to the final objective. When the house caught fire White's company (accompanied by Moten and his headquarters) swung right to keep outside the illuminated area, advanced silently round the eastern end of the first objective and, not finding McPhee's company there, pushed on to its own objective without opposition. Thence small patrols were sent out in all directions to find the other companies. At length Moten learnt that they were held up and heavily engaged on either side of the road 1,200 yards behind him. It was then 3.30 a.m.—

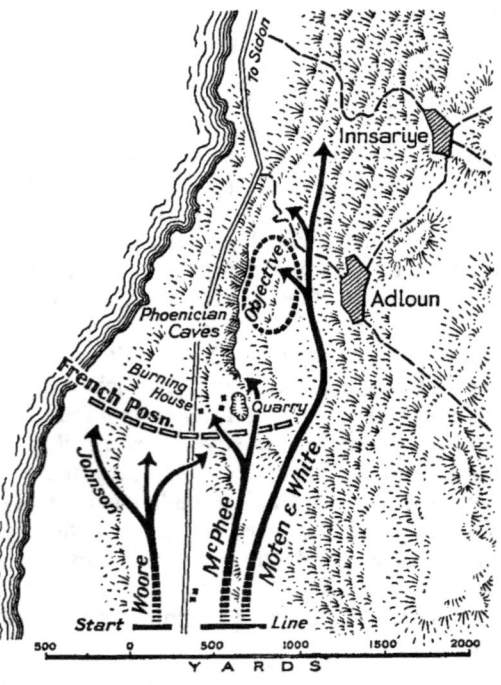

Moten, seeing an opportunity of encircling the enemy force, ordered White to advance to high ground overlooking the side road to Es Sakiye, while, with the pioneer platoon and his headquarters, he took up a position above the coast road to block the escape of the French who were fighting his rearguard companies. At dawn these French troops surrendered; soon

---

[5] Col W. L. Rau, DSO, VX14472. CO 2/4 Fd Regt 1941-42; Aust Senior Mil Liaison Offr, GHQ SWPA 1943-44. Manufacturer and orchardist; of Moorooduc, Vic; b. Richmond, Vic, 31 Jan 1900.

afterwards Moten walked south along the coast road to visit the rear companies.

At daylight on the 11th the 2/14th Battalion, with the cavalry squadron, was ordered to continue the advance. At dawn the cavalrymen moved forward; they met no opposition until, just beyond the Es Sakiye road junction, they came under the fire of a group of enemy tanks supported by anti-tank guns. Lieutenant Mills placed three of his light tanks behind a ridge, in reserve, then led some carriers forward. Taking from the crews of these carriers Sergeant Cramp,[6] Sergeant Edwards[7] and Trooper Killen,[8] between them carrying an anti-tank rifle, Bren gun, sub-machine-gun and rifle, he worked his way to the crest of a ridge overlooking the French position, which was round a road cutting at its foot. There a duel began between Edwards with the anti-tank rifle and the French tank and anti-tank gunners, and eventually the tanks withdrew out of sight. Mills and his men concentrated fire on an anti-tank gun sited above the cutting and killed or dispersed the crews. Thinking he had disposed of the enemy Mills went forward down the ridge with Killen, but saw a party of Frenchmen dug in between him and the cutting. While climbing down the terraces he suddenly found that he was standing over another

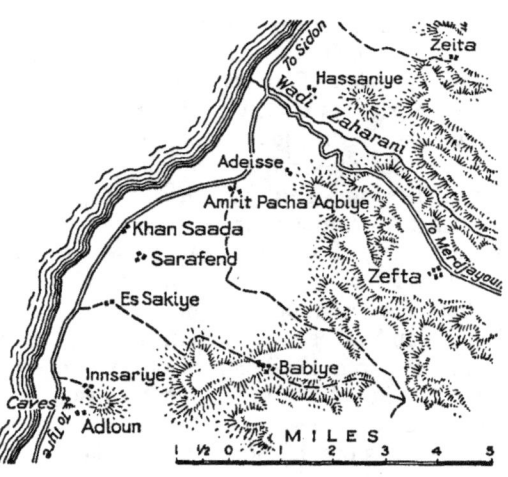

trench full of Frenchmen. His sub-machine-gun jammed, but the French dared not fire for fear of hitting their own men and, at this critical moment, Cramp, who was following, attacked the other enemy group and both parties surrendered. Between them Mills, Cramp and Killen captured forty-five prisoners of the Foreign Legion, five machine-guns, two mortars, and the two anti-tank guns, which were undamaged and plentifully supplied with ammunition.

It was then mid-morning and the 2/14th was now close behind, advancing astride the road and on the slopes east of it. The cavalrymen having dealt with the French rearguard, there was little opposition, except on the right where the 2/14th killed nine and captured forty-five. By the middle of the afternoon the infantrymen had taken a total of nearly 100 prisoners and passed through Es Sakiye, Sarafend and Khan Saada. Beyond Khan

---

[6] Capt R. T. Cramp, MM, NX8680; 6 Cav Regt. Station hand; of Cowra, NSW; b. Sydney, 6 Aug 1912.

[7] Lt R. A. Edwards, NX8679; 6 Cav Regt. Dairy farmer; of Exeter, NSW; b. Sussex, Eng, 24 Jul 1906.

[8] Tpr T. D. Killen, NX11657; 6 Cav Regt. Farmer; of Leeton, NSW; b. Sydney, 15 Sep 1915.

Saada the advancing infantry learnt from the cavalrymen scouting ahead that enemy machine-gun posts and five tanks had been seen about two miles beyond in the Wadi Zaharani. It was evident that he intended to fight for the junction of the coast road with the lateral road to Merdjayoun, which travelled along the southern slopes of the Zaharani gully.

Brigadier Stevens ordered Lieut-Colonel Cannon,[9] the commander of the 2/14th Battalion, to continue the advance and cut this road. Cannon's plan was to use his inland company, Captain Noonan's, with another, Captain Silverman's,[1] to cut the side road while a third company, Captain Howden's, made a diversionary attack astride the main road. Silverman's company, however, was unable to reach the area in time. It was then decided that this company should attack west of the coast road—with Captain Howden's on its right—a radical change of plan.

As soon as the troops began to move forward across the flat ground, on which young crops were growing, they came under severe machine-gun and mortar fire. This combination forced Howden's company on the right into the partial protection of the rocky slopes east of the road. On the left Lieutenant Kyffin led his platoon wide to the west and thence to within 50 yards of the bridge over the Zaharani, while Ayton's platoon, moving through banana fields, reached a point 100 yards from the bridge, where the men lay under sharp mortar fire. At 6.15 out of the smoke and dust ahead emerged six enemy tanks which formed up in a semi-circle round the leading infantry and bombarded them with shells and machine-gun bullets at short range. Cannon sent orders to Silverman to withdraw. But Silverman had been wounded; and Ayton and six of his men had already been hit. Both leading platoons withdrew, Corporal Staley[2] leading out Ayton's, in which the sergeant, Buxton,[3] stayed behind to assist the wounded and was himself hit. Fire from anti-tank rifles halted the enemy tanks but did not appear to damage them.

Stevens ordered Moten's 2/27th to take over the task of advance-guard from the 2/14th on the morning of the 12th. Moten went forward about 3.30 a.m. and at daylight, as he was setting out to reconnoitre the right flank, he met Captain Buckler,[4] the adjutant of the 2/14th, who suggested that there was a likely approach to the flank of the enemy's position to the east of Noonan's company. Thus at 11 a.m. Major Isaachsen's company struggled through the hills and across the river under sharp fire, while Johnson's advanced through Adeisse, across the river (where Johnson was wounded), and on to Hassaniye and Maameriye taking about forty prisoners and a number of mortars and machine-guns.

---

[9] Lt-Col W. G. Cannon, VX13432. (1st AIF: Gnr 6 FA Bde.) CO 2/14 Bn 1940-42. Public servant; of Hawthorn, Vic; b. Bairnsdale, Vic, 7 May 1896.

[1] Lt-Col J. S. Silverman, VX8325; 2/14 Bn; and Amenities Service 1943-45. Salesman; of Melbourne; b. Adelaide, 16 Apr 1906.

[2] Cpl E. R. Staley, VX18222; 2/14 Bn. Sharebroker; of Toorak, Vic; b. Midway, near Swadlincote, Derbyshire, Eng, 16 Jul 1901. Killed in action 24 Jun 1941.

[3] Lt D. R. Buxton, VX16934. 2/14 and 19 Bns; 1 Aust Cdo Bn. Salesman; of Brighton, Vic; b. Melbourne, 12 Feb 1917.

[4] Lt-Col S. H. Buckler, VX13637. 2/14 Bn and staff appts. Regular soldier; of Coff's Harbour, NSW; b. Coff's Harbour, 12 Feb 1919.

Meanwhile, on the coastal flats, the French tanks had been driven back by artillery fire; and the carrier platoon of the 2/27th, after a long exchange of fire with the French posts north of the Zaharani, advanced along the beach, and from the flank attacked the French holding the bridge taking about sixty prisoners, and held it until Lieutenant Rudd's platoon arrived over the hills from the north-east. In the afternoon the prisoners were increased to about 200.

Where the Victorians' frontal attack across flat ground on the coastal plain had failed, the 2/27th's, on the flank and thrown in immediately the first attack was held, had been completely successful, and another obstacle on the advance to Beirut was cleared. By dusk on the 12th the cavalry patrols and Lieutenant Fawcett's[5] carriers of the 2/27th had moved three miles forward through Rhaziye until they came under sharp artillery fire. Stevens, as at Adloun, thrust two field guns forward with the infantry to defeat French tanks if they appeared. They came under well-directed French artillery fire, and in a duel over open sights, the section commander[6] and a gunner were killed and five men wounded, and one gun was disabled; the other gun was withdrawn.[7]

Wishing to spare Sidon with its ancient mosque and Crusaders' castle, Brigadier Stevens was giving orders that an attempt be made to parley with its defenders when the French artillery opened fire. Stevens ordered his gunners to reply.[8] Like Tyre and other Phoenician towns, Sidon was built on a little promontory which shields a small natural harbour. Into the town was crowded a population of about 12,000, and thus it was the largest town by far that the invading force had yet seen in Syria or the Lebanon. North and south of the town, for five miles in all, the coastal plain was about a mile in width and planted with orange, apricot and banana orchards which were often surrounded by stone walls about nine feet high. After crossing the Sataniq, two miles south of the town, the main road ran close to the sea for more than eight miles and was open to bombardment by the naval vessels that were now off shore asking the leading troops to give them targets. This was more attractive country than any this column had hitherto seen in Syria.

> Fairy-like villages dotted the landscape (wrote the historian of the 2/4th Field Regiment). Tall cyprus trees, red roofs, yellowy walls, pale blue shutters, trees, orchards, shrubs and churches blended into a peaceful scene . . . . A persistent wog, selling 'eggasis' and tomatoes, helped gleefully to manhandle the guns into the position. He could not be discouraged to leave us alone.[9]

---

[5] Lt-Col G. H. Fawcett, SX6219. 2/27 Bn; Trg and staff appts. Regular soldier; of Hurstville, NSW; b. Oakey, Qld, 5 Nov 1911.

[6] Lt A. L. Doolette (of Elwood, Vic).

[7] Brig Stevens was slightly wounded here by shell splinters. Late that afternoon (the 12th) a squadron of French aircraft flew along the main road firing its machine-guns. It concentrated its fire on a column of 103 prisoners whom the carriers of the 2/27 had taken earlier in the day, killing ten, and wounding an Australian officer (Lt A. Treloar—2/14 Bn—of Canterbury, Vic) and five of the six men guarding them. A Bofors crew shot down one of these aircraft which crashed in the 2/27 positions, killing and wounding several more men.

[8] In the evening the naval squadron received a request to bombard Sidon but the commander declined because he "had no authority to fire on non-military targets".

[9] R. L. Henry, *The Story of the 2/4th Field Regiment*, p. 135.

Brigadier Stevens decided to give the task of taking Sidon to the 2/16th, which had been in reserve for four days. The West Australians were to move through the 2/27th on the morning of the 13th, advance past the town and occupy the line of the Wadi Abou Zare two miles beyond it. Two companies of the 2/27th which had advanced to Darb es Sim during the night of the 12th-13th were to picquet the approaches from the east but during the 13th were still unaware of their role because efforts to establish contact with them failed; the cavalry squadron was to protect the right flank of the 2/16th. The task of the 2/16th entailed an advance of about seven miles in daylight on a wide front and through open country. Lieut-Colonel MacDonald decided to attack with two companies forward and two following at about 1,000 yards to mop up. The troops were to advance in open formation.

The leading companies—Captain Horley's on the right and Major Wain's[1] on the left—moved from the start-line at 10 a.m. behind a series of concentrations fired by the 2/4th Field Regiment. After advancing about two miles without serious opposition, Wain's company encountered a series of machine-gun posts just south of the Wadi Sataniq, a dry creek half way between their start-line and Sidon. These were outflanked and the enemy withdrew. The company then re-formed and advanced through the gardens until they were about one mile from the town, where they again came under sharp fire. Wain himself led forward a patrol, including Sergeant McCullough and one section, and overcame a post, taking seven prisoners, while the remainder of the company, mopping up posts among the orchards, took 40. About 12.30 two French tanks appeared, but after firing without much effect, they withdrew and the advance was resumed until a point due east of the centre of the town had been reached. Enemy troops encountered here made off after a short fight, and by 3 p.m. the company was only a few hundred yards from the objective—the Wadi Abou Zare—but was out of touch with the company on its right. Wain now found that his company was out by itself with an open flank and decided to extricate it from an unhealthy position. The company withdrew to Sakhet ez Zeitoun, south of Sidon, where it got into touch with its supporting company (Major Caro) about 5.30.

The reason why Horley's company on the right had been far out of touch when Wain reached the limit of his advance was that, as that company, with Captain Inkpen's[2] following, approached the outskirts of Sidon, several French tanks appeared and made a determined attack. Soon they were circling and firing on the West Australians who, seeking cover, split into small groups. Horley was killed and the company disorganised. The tanks advanced and attacked the supporting company, killing also its commander—Inkpen—and forcing some groups of men into the foothills on the east.

---

[1] Col W. J. Wain, DSO, WX1576. (1st AIF: Lt 15 MG Coy.) 2/16 Bn 1940-41; CO 2/43 Bn 1941-43. Works manager; of Nedlands. WA; b. Perth, WA, 7 Aug 1898.

[2] Capt F. M. B. Inkpen, WX1591; 2/16 Bn. Clerk; of Bunbury, WA; b. Midland Junction, WA, 29 Dec 1915. Killed in action 13 Jun 1941.

Captain Mackenzie, now commanding what remained of this company, led a fight in which efforts were made to drive the tanks off by throwing grenades and hitting them with anti-tank rifle fire, and with machine-gun fire aimed at the slits. All three methods of attack were ineffective. At this stage Mackenzie's company comprised only a sergeant and 17 others. At length, about 6 p.m., he and his men broke away and reached the main

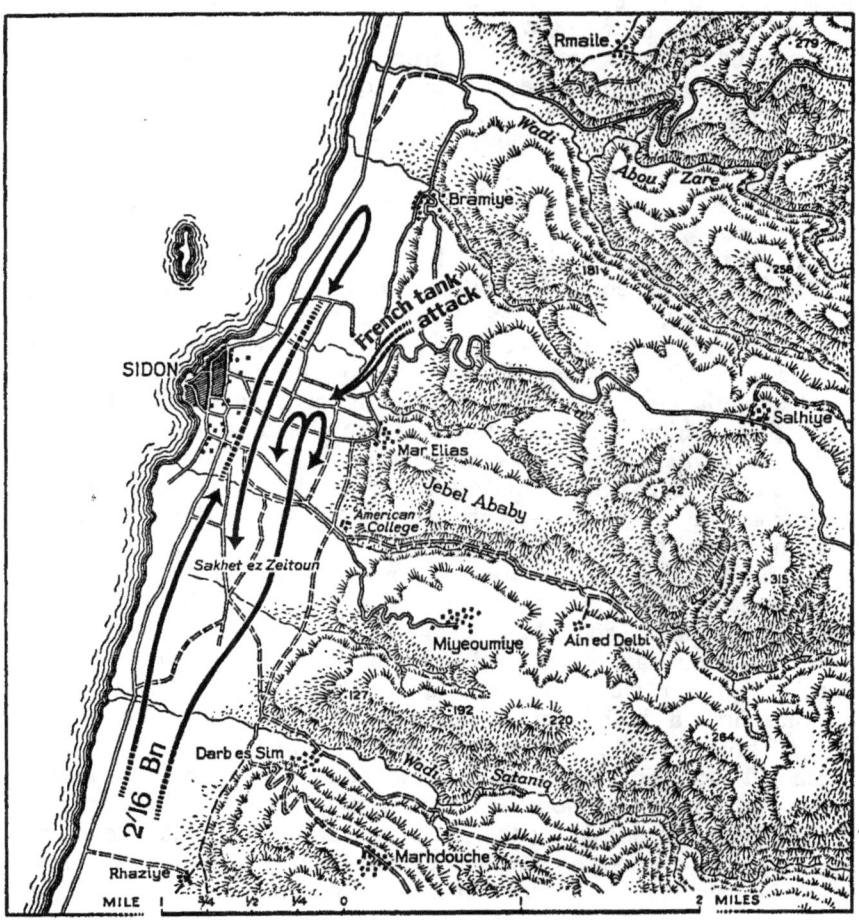

road, on to which the tanks would not venture for fear of fire from the supporting field guns. Lieutenant Mills, of the cavalry, who was ordered to deal with the attacking tanks, led forward a field gun and two anti-tank guns. The anti-tank guns were fired at 800 yards, but at that range their hits had no apparent effect and one gun was knocked out. Mills then led the 25-pounder forward to engage the tanks in the open from about 1,300 yards, but the commander of the gun detachment—Lieutenant Marsden[3] —was wounded, the tractor damaged by cannon fire, and at length the gun was withdrawn. Two trucks carrying sticky bombs (which when thrown stuck to the side of the target and then exploded) and the battalion's reserve of ammunition were sent towards the infantry about 1.30 but a shell from a tank hit one and it exploded; the other was brought back. Mills then asked four of his carrier commanders whether they would go forward to draw the French tanks into the open where the guns could deal with them. Lieutenant Wray,[4] Sergeant-Major Baldock[5] and Sergeants Stewart and Edwards drove their carriers forward through the river bed to the first orange groves beyond, and urged the infantrymen there—of Caro's company—to hurry back while the carriers covered their retreat. The infantrymen ran back. The carriers fired their Vickers guns furiously into the French positions until the French tanks appeared, when the carriers withdrew under fire from anti-tank guns, picking up infantrymen as they went.

Later in the afternoon Lieutenant Lucas[6] was sent forward with two guns of the 2/4th Regiment to deal with the tanks which had trapped Horley's company. One gun fired on five tanks at about 1,000 yards and drove them off, while the second was sited farther back to cover a withdrawal, if necessary. After this shoot Lucas' forward gun detachment pulled their gun behind the crest of the ridge on which it was sited and man-handled it to another position from which it opened fire as soon as tanks reappeared. This manoeuvre was repeated during the remainder of the day. Throughout the day French aircraft made a series of attacks—the heaviest so far experienced in this sector—on the guns of the 2/4th Regiment and the headquarters of the attacking battalion.

As mentioned above, the two leading companies of the 2/27th, very weary because they had had little rest since crossing the frontier five days before, were on the south bank of the Sataniq where it cut through the hills well to the east of the road. (On the 12th Moten had reached the conclusion that it would be best to avoid a frontal attack and instead to advance through the hills to Miyeoumiye and descend on Sidon from the east.) Throughout the morning his leading companies had been out of touch and out of sight in the deep gullies, and it was not until the afternoon that a patrol from battalion headquarters found exactly where they were. Finally Stevens ordered that the rest of the battalion should move on to the steep ridge overlooking the Sataniq from Darb es Sim and thence attack on to the heights east of Sidon. At 4 p.m. the remainder of the battalion moved into the hills from Hassaniye and about 5 p.m. turned north towards Darb es Sim. It was a gruelling march in single file over rugged country, and in darkness until about midnight when the moon rose. Except

---
[3] Capt E. C. H. Marsden, VX39363; 2/4 Fd Regt. Bank clerk; of Brighton, Vic; b. Huntingdonshire, Eng, 9 Mar 1918.
[4] Maj C. H. W. Wray, NX12264; 6 Cav Regt. Farmer; of Maclean, NSW; b. Maclean, 14 Nov 1915.
[5] Capt R. G. Baldock, QX673. 6 Cav Regt 1939-42; 2/6 Armd Regt 1942-44. Pastoralist; of Cecil Plains, Qld; b. Bombay, India, 5 Jan 1913.
[6] Capt L. Lucas, WX921. 2/4 Fd Regt; RAA III Corps; 2 Fd Regt. Mine worker; of Bendering, WA; b. Cassilis, Vic, 6 Sep 1906.

for an hour's rest at 11 p.m. the column moved steadily on, pausing only when, on several occasions, enemy aircraft attempted to bomb it. The infantrymen reached Darb es Sim at 4 a.m. on the 14th, almost exhausted, but relieved the leading companies, which were withdrawn to prepare to attack across the Sataniq that morning.

The start-line for the attack—to open at 9.30 a.m.—was the ridge on the opposite side of the Sataniq from Darb es Sim. The objective was Miyeoumiye where a large building with a tiled roof was a conspicuous landmark.[7] By the time Isaachsen's company had clambered up to the start-line the men were limp with fatigue and one of the four officers collapsed and was left behind. After resting for twenty minutes the company, about 5 p.m., began to advance towards the objective, 1,500 yards away as the crow flies and across a steep-sided wadi 200 feet deep. The thin line of attackers came under fire from mortars and heavy machine-guns as soon as they moved. Lieutenant Crafter's[8] platoon on the left went to ground after losing men while climbing down the eight-foot terraces. Sergeant Macpherson's[9] platoon, however, jumped and ran fast down the terraces, reached the wadi without loss, and veering away from the heaviest of the fire, which was coming from a blockhouse forward of the "Monastery", swung right along the shelter of the wadi, climbed the northern face and entered the village from the east.

The defenders were obviously surprised by the appearance of a party (Macpherson had only seventeen men) advancing upon them from the east, and twenty-four of them, all Europeans, promptly surrendered. Macpherson found about forty pack-mules among the terraces which suggested to him that the French had been preparing to withdraw. He quickly deployed his little party for the next move. He sent one section towards the "Monastery" to take up a defensive position and cover the Jebel Ababy, a high ridge to the north, dispatched a runner to his company headquarters,[1] and sent a section under Private Morris,[1] a noted marksman, into the village where they took the surrender of ten more prisoners.

After having left his third section on the east of the village to cover the lower ground on that side Macpherson took a patrol along the streets towards the "Monastery". This patrol killed four foreign legionaries but, at the southern edge of the village, came under heavy fire from the south —in fact from the two companies of their own battalion which were, as they believed, giving supporting fire. Macpherson was now certain that the attack on his left had failed and that it was not known that he was in Miyeoumiye. His small party now held thirty-six prisoners. At 9 p.m. he sent off half of his platoon towards the Sataniq; he followed with the rest half an hour later. With a loss of one man wounded this skilful young tactician had gained the objective, killed or taken prisoner forty of the

---

[7] It was thought to be a monastery, but was in fact a military barracks.
[8] Maj J. G. Crafter, SX4516; 2/27 Bn. Regular soldier; of Wayville, SA; b. Port Augusta, SA, 28 Jun 1914.
[9] Lt W. N. Macpherson, SX2775; 2/27 Bn. Clerk; of Westbourne Park, SA; b. Adelaide, 9 Jun 1915.
[1] Pte J. Morris, SX4164; 2/27 Bn. Trucker; of Broken Hill, NSW; b. Kington, Herts, Eng, 6 Apr 1909. Killed in action, New Guinea, 1942.

enemy and returned. "We'll have to keep together," Sergeant MacDonald[2] had said to him in the moment of triumph at Miyeoumiye towering over the diminutive Sergeant Macpherson, "with your brains and my brawn we'll go a long way."

On the left wing the attack by the weary troops of Isaachsen's other two platoons had been quickly broken. The line walked straight into accurate machine-gun fire from the "Monastery" across the deep gully. Before the men had advanced 100 yards down the terraces Isaachsen and Lieutenant Crafter had been wounded and Lieutenant Rudd killed. Some of the remaining men advanced into the wadi and beyond, at which stage Lance-Sergeant H. V. Smith,[3] their leader, was wounded. Others found what cover they could among the olive trees on the terraces. At dark all withdrew. In the course of the day the company lost twenty-three men.

The company next to the left had been unable to advance because of the heavy fire and the nature of the ground. During the night, however, a patrol under Corporal Jose[4] reached the village. Meanwhile Captain Lee's[5] company still farther to the left reached Hill 127, where they found that the French were strongly holding high ground ahead. By moving well to the east, Lee reached his objective at 1 p.m. but attempts to move down the face of the hill drew heavy fire from mortars and machine-guns about 1,100 yards away, too far for effective reply by the Brens. The men were very tired and the company did not advance farther. While the companies on the right were making their attack the men of the left company crawled over the sky-line and, under mortar bombardment, fired at long range on the French positions on which the other companies were advancing.

During 14th June the 2/16th Battalion was still in the gardens south of Sidon. At 4.30 p.m. the French counter-attacked with about eight tanks and infantry, which advanced, as on the previous day, from behind the American College. Brigadier Stevens saw the opening of the attack from the artillery observation post; artillery fire was brought down immediately at about 4,000 yards, and two tanks were hit and the attack broken.

At first it seemed that nothing had been achieved by the hard fighting on the 13th and 14th but, during the morning of the 15th, acting on Macpherson's information that the enemy had abandoned Miyeoumiye, Moten moved the 2/27th Battalion forward into that village and on to the "Monastery" (which had been French headquarters) without opposition. It was soon apparent that there had been a considerable French withdrawal. By 9 a.m. the left company of the 2/27th had sent a patrol to

---

[2] Capt G. G. MacDonald, SX3238; 2/27 Bn. Jackeroo; of Nth Walkerville, SA; b. Adelaide, 8 Apr 1919.

[3] L-Sgt H. V. Smith, SX2963; 2/27 Bn. Transport driver; of Blackwood, SA; b. London, 6 Jul 1910.

[4] Lt R. Jose, SX3336. 2/27 Bn; 2/15 Bn 1945. Farmer; of Murray Bridge, SA; b. Lameroo, SA, 21 Oct 1918.

[5] Lt-Col A. J. Lee, MC, SX2917. 2/27 Bn 1940-43; 2/16 Bn 1943-44; CO 2/9 Bn 1944-45. Company director; of Glenelg, SA; b. Adelaide, 30 Jul 1912.

Mar Elias and found it clear of the enemy. At 1.30 p.m. the American College was found to be empty of troops. Moten suspected that Sidon itself had been abandoned, and Sergeant Johns[6] removed his steel helmet and equipment, mounted a captured motor-cycle, and rode into the town and up the main street. His cycle then broke down, but he forced two Syrians to guide him out. As soon as he returned Moten, at 11.15 a.m., entered the town with a few men of his headquarters, demanded and saw the mayor, who said that the French had withdrawn in the night, and appealed to him to stop the shelling—the naval ships were firing on the northern outskirts, the field guns on the southern. Thereupon Moten commandeered a taxi and drove back to Stevens' headquarters to report.

Stevens entered the town and at 4 p.m. formally took it over from the mayor and proclaimed martial law.

Other Australians on the left had already discovered the abandonment of the town. A cavalry patrol (of the fresh 9th Australian Cavalry Regiment[7] which had replaced the 6th on this sector) was convinced of it at midday, and soon afterwards Lieutenant Harper[8] of the 2/16th Battalion moved in. At 3 o'clock the 2/16th, weary and in torn and muddy clothing, marched through the streets, left a company in the town, and moved on to a position on the south side of the Wadi Abou Zare.

It soon became evident that the French had not only abandoned Sidon but made a long withdrawal. Cavalry patrols found the coast road clear as far north as Ras Nebi Younes, and the lateral roads north of Sidon un-

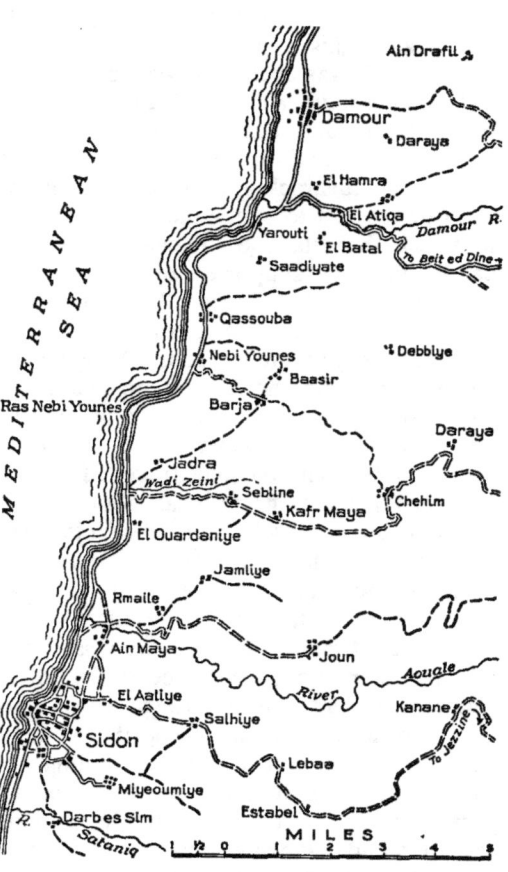

---
[6] Lt R. D. Johns, MM, SX3078; 2/27 Bn. Bank clerk; of St Peters, SA; b. Glenelg, SA, 8 Oct 1920.

[7] The 9 Cav Regt arrived at Suez from Australia without equipment on 14 May. Partly equipped it joined the 7 Div in Syria twenty-five days later. One squadron joined the 21 Bde south of Sidon, another the 25 Bde on the day of its advance to Jezzine, and, on the 15th, patrolled the lateral road from Jezzine to Sidon.

[8] Lt T. Harper, WX2952; 2/16 Bn. Builder; of Nedlands, WA; b. Maylands, WA, 22 Dec 1912. Died of wounds, 7 Jul 1941.

occupied as far as Salhiye, Jamliye and Sebline. That night the weary infantrymen washed, ate a hot meal and had their first genuine rest for several nights. Their advance was going relatively well, but events on each of the other sectors were to bring it to a prolonged halt.

It will be recalled that on 10th June orders were issued for a renewed attack in the Merdjayoun sector by the 2/25th against Ibeles Saki and by the 2/31st against Merdjayoun, the 2/31st to be supported by a barrage provided by the 2/5th and 2/6th Field Regiments, under Brigadier Berryman's direction.

On the 10th the 2/25th had advanced along the narrow gorges until it was close to the steep-sided Ibeles Saki plateau. At dawn on the 11th its leading company began to move up the abrupt slopes towards the village but, finding this approach impossible, swung round to the north of the place, and it was eventually occupied by Lieutenant Butler's[9] platoon with but one casualty. Arms and ammunition and, more valuable still, twelve mules with pack-saddles were captured in the area; and from it the 2/25th dominated the roads leading north from Merdjayoun.

General Lavarack and General Allen (a close observer because he was soon to succeed to command of the division) came to Cox's headquarters to watch the attack on Qleaa and Merdjayoun—the first attack in the campaign to be supported by so strong an assembly of guns. The plan of Lieut-Colonel Porter of the 2/31st was to attack astride the Khirbe ridge with two companies forward. When Khirbe had been reached the rear companies were to pass through and advance to Merdjayoun. The barrage covering the 2/31st opened at 2.30 a.m. on a front of 1,120 yards—one gun to 28 yards—and, because the country was rough and not reconnoitred, moved forward 100 yards at relatively long intervals of four minutes. The barrage travelled to a depth of more than two miles, each of forty guns firing in all about 130 rounds. The advancing infantry followed up so closely that, as a rule, the shells fell only some 30 yards in front, and often they had to halt and wait for the barrage to move on. Major Cruickshank,[1] a fine young regular soldier leading the right-hand company, was killed at the French wire. Soon the leaders were among abandoned French positions and saw men moving off ahead of them, although some posts continued to fire after the advance had passed them. The leaders had passed through Qleaa and were at the cross-roads soon after 5 o'clock, with the supporting companies following closely to avoid French mortar bombs which were falling well behind the foremost platoons. These companies met the fire from enemy posts which the leaders had passed by. In Khirbe, for example, at dawn there was a sharp fight with grenades and bayonets between one company and the French garrison. Fifty-six prisoners were taken.[2]

---

[9] Maj W. G. Butler, MC, QX6349. 2/25 Bn; BM 7 Bde 1945. Grazier; of Longreach, Qld; b. Southport, Qld, 3 Oct 1912.

[1] Maj R. M. Cruickshank, QX6055; 2/31 Bn. Regular soldier; of Hobart; b. Hobart, 16 Jun 1913. Killed in action 11 Jun 1941.

[2] The 2/31 lost 16 killed and 34 wounded in the day.

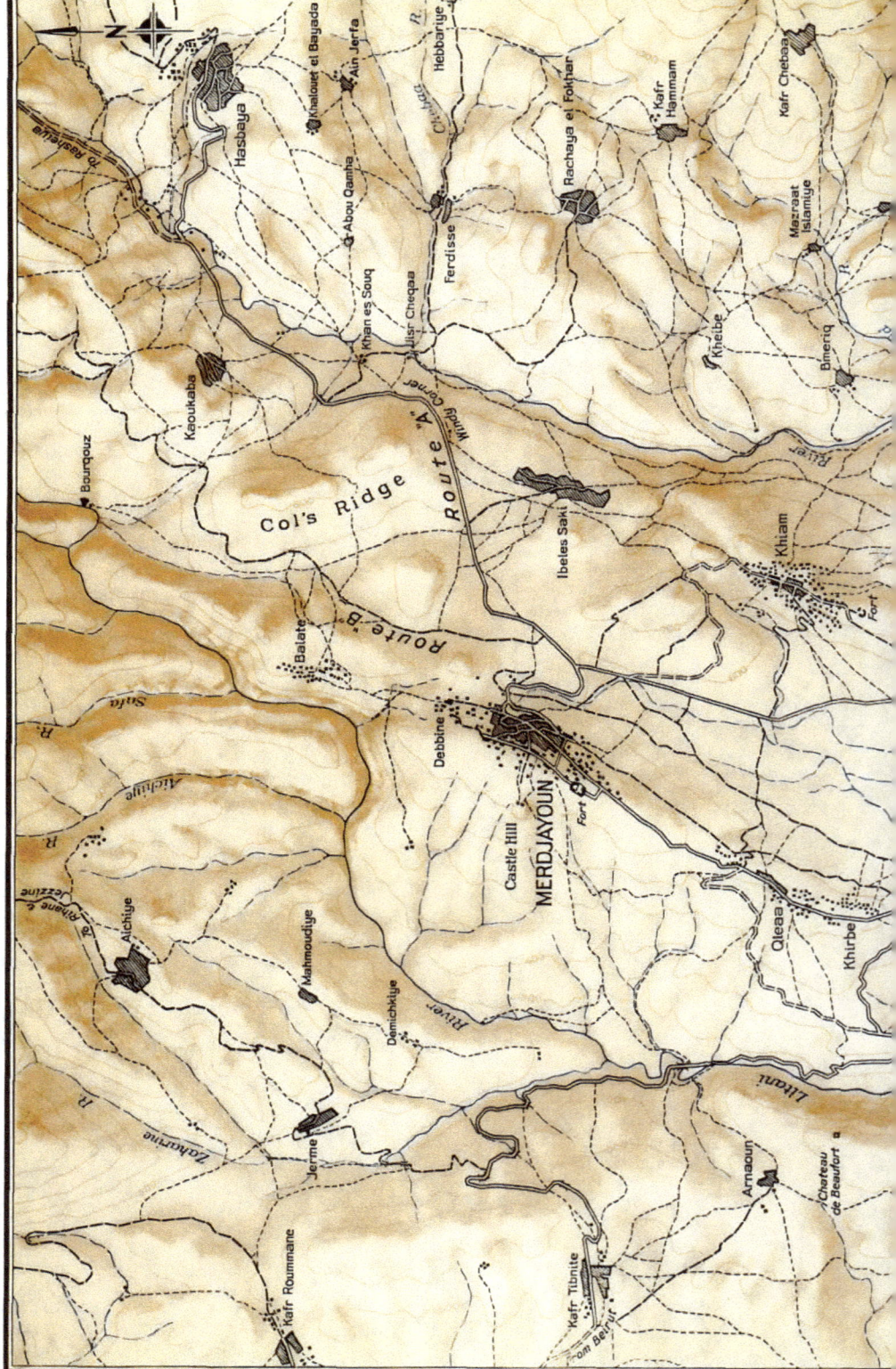

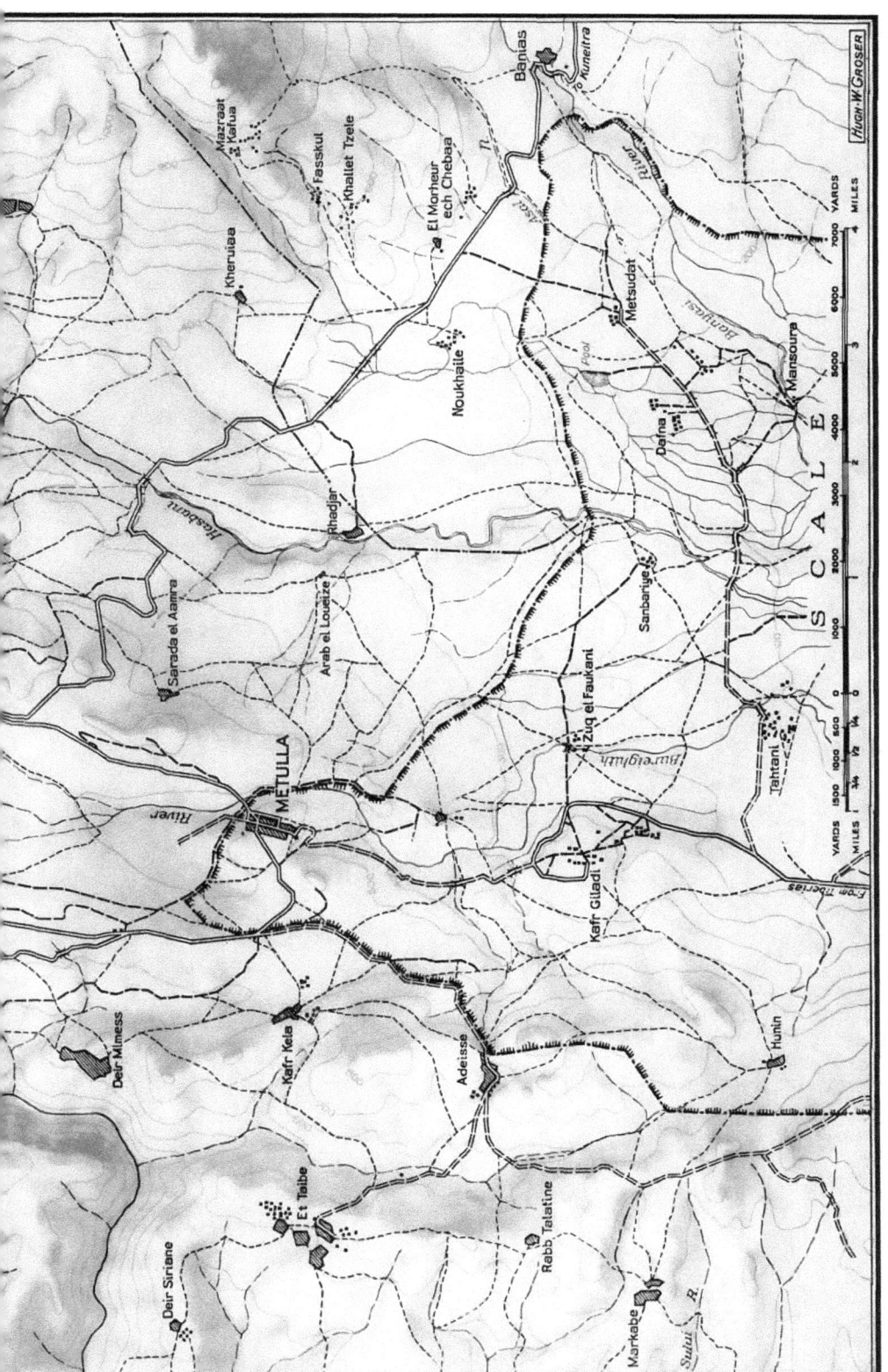

The second phase of the advance was to open at 1 p.m. and carry the battalion to Merdjayoun on which shells were then falling. However, Lieut-Colonel Daly[3] of the 2/6th Field Regiment suggested that he should parley with the French, and about 12.35 set out in a carrier flying a white flag. At 12.55 he had not reached the fort and, knowing that the guns of his own and the 2/5th Regiment were to open fire at 1 p.m., he withdrew. In the meantime, Lieut-Colonel O'Brien[4] of the 2/5th, after consulting Porter, cancelled the fire plan. Porter set off to warn his left company of the change of plan, but it had already begun to advance. He met Daly and they followed the infantry to the fort, which had in fact been abandoned. Out of hiding places in Merdjayoun appeared civilians waving white flags; they announced that the French had gone. The road to Merdjayoun was heavily mined; engineers led by Lieutenant Flint[5] and Sergeant Giles[6] advanced with the leading infantry, removing these mines.

The principal townspeople welcomed the new arrivals—Brigadier Berryman closely followed by General Allen and Brigadier Cox had now overtaken Porter—and formally surrendered the town, a modern place most of whose people were Christians of the Orthodox Church. The leaders were showered with rose petals as they strode along the narrow streets. As they reached the centre of the town the flag of Lebanon broke at a mast-head. In the fort the troops found medical supplies (in a very unclean hospital), much food, officers' baggage piled in a kit store and some obsolescent weapons, but no troops were seen.

On the evening of the 11th the 2/25th were in position north of Ibeles Saki, the 2/33rd north of Khiam, the 2/31st at Merdjayoun. Late in the afternoon a platoon of Flint's engineers reached the bridge over the Litani south-west of Merdjayoun where it carried the lateral road to a point on the coast south of Sidon. Not only had the bridge been demolished but half a mile short of the river a crater 96 feet in width had been blown and a track had to be cut into it before the sappers' vehicles could move forward. However in the middle of the Litani stood a huge boulder, and, using it as a central pier, the engineers began to build a bridge of two 32-foot sections joined at the boulder.

On the 12th General Lavarack decided that, because the Merdjayoun area offered such advantages to a determined defender and progress was slow, he would thrust his 25th Brigade swiftly northward along the winding track to Jezzine. From Jezzine ran a lateral road to Sidon, and thus the 25th Brigade could support Stevens' advance on the coast. Only the 2/33rd Battalion, the cavalry and a battery of artillery would remain at

---

[3] Brig R. Daly, NX377. CO 2/6 Fd Regt 1940-42; CRA 6 Div 1942-43. Secretary; of Randwick, NSW; b. Alectown, NSW, 23 Feb 1902.

[4] Maj-Gen J. W. A. O'Brien, DSO, VX15127. CO 2/5 Fd Regt 1941-42; Dir of Arty LHQ 1942-43; DMGO (Army Eqpt) LHQ 1943-44. Consulting engineer; of Glen Iris, Vic; b. Melbourne, 13 Jun 1908.

[5] Maj C. F. Flint, VX13917. 2/5 Fd Coy; OC 2/3 Indep Fd Sqn RAE 1943-45. Regular soldier; of Hobart; b. Hobart, 31 Aug 1919.

[6] Capt A. V. Giles, DCM, NX14674; 2/5 Fd Coy. Radio technician; of Willoughby, NSW; b. Mosman, NSW; 27 Dec 1917.

Merdjayoun, the infantry in a defensive role, the cavalry probing forward along the two routes, "A" and "B", forking north-east of the town.

On the night of the 11th Lieut-Colonel Todd[7] of the Scots Greys, the senior cavalry officer, had been ordered to pursue the enemy believed to be withdrawing towards Zahle. Todd's force was to divide and move along Routes "A" and "B", the force on "A", under Major Morrison[8] of the 6th Australian Cavalry, consisting of three light tanks, some carriers and two guns, the force on "B", similarly constituted, under Major Macarthur-Onslow. The cavalrymen were excited at the prospect of a pursuit of the kind they had experienced in Libya. However, just after they divided, the columns were sharply attacked by six French aircraft,[9] and later Morrison's force was halted at a point in the road where a cliff face had been blown down on to it. It took four hours until midday to repair this gap, and then—to the surprise of the cavalrymen, engineers and others who had been working there all the morning—when a carrier began to cross, a hail of shells and bullets fell on the area, and blew the tracks off the advancing vehicle.

Meanwhile Onslow's column, after moving without incident to the point where the road swings right at Balate Ridge, had also run into accurate artillery and mortar fire which hit a carrier. Efforts were made to shell the enemy but it soon was apparent that from the heights north of Bourqouz he dominated the area. Todd still cherished an intention to attack again next morning with the carriers forward, but Onslow was convinced that such a move would be impossible. The sharp resistance on the 12th and 13th north of Merdjayoun and the fact that on the 13th he began harassing Merdjayoun with occasional shell-fire showed that the enemy intended to hold his excellent positions on the roads leading north. On the 12th French aircraft made several strafing runs along the main road. That day, about 2.30 p.m., the bridge over the Litani was finished, and a carrier patrol travelled along the lateral road linking the 21st and 25th Brigades.

Only one road travelled from Merdjayoun to Jezzine, and the map showed that it wound round a series of steep-sided mountains from which an enemy might attempt delaying actions. A patrol of the Cheshire Yeomanry had travelled about 500 yards along the road and reported that it would carry traffic at its southern end. Cox's plan was to send an advance-guard consisting of the 2/31st plus strong detachments of cavalry, artillery and engineers along the road with three successive objectives: the high ground south of Rihane, the Kafr Houn ridge, and finally, Jezzine itself. At the same time a squadron of the Cheshire was to move north

---

[7] Brig G. H. N. Todd, MC. CO RS Greys 1939-42; Comd 1 Armd Bde 1942, 50 Tk Bde 1944-45. Regular soldier; b. Newton, Lincolnshire, Eng, 4 Jul 1897.

[8] Lt-Col S. A. Morrison, VX126. 6 Cav Regt; Comd 4 Mot Regt 1943-44. Accountant and grazier; of Bairnsdale, Vic; b. Bairnsdale, 1 Sep 1906.

[9] This attack fell most heavily on a company of the 2/25 Bn which was occupying the Debbine defile north of Merdjayoun.

through Zhalta to the Jezzine-Sidon road and establish touch with the 21st Brigade. The main body of the brigade was to follow.[1]

At 9 p.m. on the 13th the 2/31st Battalion led by a troop of the 9th Australian Cavalry set off along the winding, narrow road to Jezzine. Three-ton trucks, drawn from a British transport company, carried the troops. The convoy drove all night without lights. At times the trucks had to back three times before they could get round the sharp corners and the guns had to be unlimbered and man-handled. Sometimes the trucks bogged in the mountain streams; one overturned. There was a delay of two hours at the turn from the Sidon road where no guide had been placed, and part of the convoy continued towards Sidon and had to be recalled. Just south of Jerme was a bend so sharp that the engineers had to work on it for two hours before heavy vehicles could pass; the tail of the advance-guard was still struggling round it when there arrived the head of the main column, which had set off at 1 a.m. It was unwise to attach an advance-guard of mechanised cavalry to a column advancing along a mountain track—in effect a defile. It lacked mobility and lengthened the convoy, blocking progress each time a tracked vehicle broke down. Once Porter ordered that a halted tank be pushed over the side of the road.

By daybreak on the 14th the column had reached Kafr Houn, where native women were standing in the street cheering the new arrivals. Here the head of the column was fired on by riflemen in the hills beyond and, after debussing, the companies marched forward towards Green Hill, dominating Jezzine, where the cavalrymen, who were scouting ahead, had reported strong enemy positions.

About 3 miles south of Jezzine, Porter was shot through the thigh but insisted that he was not seriously hurt and carried on. He sent a platoon to locate the enemy and, after hearing its report and discussing the situation with Berryman, commanding the artillery, decided to attack with two companies forward. A troop of field guns (Captain Thomas[2]) and the battalion's mortars were in close support, the guns being deployed only 1,000 yards from the enemy's position.

The attackers formed up under mortar and artillery fire on a rocky outcrop facing Green Hill. The hill below them and the face of Green Hill were terraced every ten yards or so, the terraces being up to three feet high. Vines and scattered trees covered the slopes. The attack began at 6 p.m. "As the guns opened up the men surged down the hill like ants." They jumped down the terraces, so well dispersed, moving so fast, and making such skilful use of what cover offered that Captain Robson's[3] company reached the road without a casualty, though under rifle and machine-gun fire and completely exposed.

---

[1] The force included: 2/25 Bn, 2/31 Bn, one sqn 9 Cav, 2/5 Fd Regt, less one bty, 2/6 Fd Regt, and detachments of engineers, anti-tank guns, machine-guns and others. Brig Berryman commanded the artillery, only one battery (the 10th) now remaining at Merdjayoun.

[2] Maj C. C. Thomas, NX12260. 2/6 Fd Regt 1940-42; BMRA NG Force 1942-43, 6 Brit Airborne Div 1944-45. Bank clerk; of Gordon, NSW; b. Bendigo, Vic, 17 Aug 1911.

[3] Lt-Col E. M. Robson, DSO, NX349. CO 2/31 Bn 1943-45. Solicitor, and MLA NSW since 1936; of Rose Bay, NSW; b. Ashfield, NSW, 7 Mar 1906.

The success was aided by the fact that Porter had instructed Lieutenant Hammon,[4] the enterprising commander of the machine-gun platoon attached to his battalion, to disregard conventional methods of fire control and let each gun fire independently on enemy posts as they revealed themselves on the opposite slope. Almost as soon as each opposing machine-gun fired it was silenced by the Vickers guns. The French fought for the hill. Private Luff[5] in Houston's company saw a section in the platoon on his left held up by a machine-gun just in front. He stalked to the rear of the French position and killed the five Frenchmen in the post with rifle and bayonet. The attacking companies lost four men killed and eight wounded.

At the bottom of the hill was a flat area about 100 yards across, swept by the fire of machine-guns evidently firing on fixed lines. The men sprinted across it—casualties were heavier there—and climbed to the summit overlooking Jezzine itself. As the leading companies reached the top they saw eight to twelve French cavalrymen on the road below mounting their horses. The Australians fired at them with Brens and rifles, at about 800 yards' range, as they cantered away.

Porter decided to follow up his success, though his men had been without food or sleep for twenty-four hours, and so ordered the two rear companies to pass through the forward ones and push on to the town. The final advance to Jezzine was down a cliff face so steep that the men had to scramble all the way, swinging down the terraces with the help of vines and the branches of trees, and often falling. There was no opposition now. When, about 8.30 p.m., the troops entered the town riderless French cavalry horses were roaming round the streets. The ever-active Berryman was with the leading Australian platoon (Sergeant Gardner[6]). The townspeople offered bread and drinks of water to the weary troops and at the police headquarters wine and more food was provided. That night the companies consolidated on the heights east of Jezzine and across the roads leading north and west, and patrols found the French rearguards astride the road. During the night a hot meal was sent forward to the weary and hungry infantrymen.[7] Because of the congestion the 2/25th Battalion remained in bivouac at Jerme. The Cheshire reported that on the 13th they had gained Mazraat Koufra, but on the 14th that they had been unable to reach Zhalta.

Meanwhile, east of Mount Hermon, General Legentilhomme had continued his attacks on the Vichy positions at Kiswe. Some progress was made on the 12th but when reports arrived that Vichy tanks were moving

---

[4] Capt J. D. C. Hammon, MBE, VX46251; 2/3 MG Bn. Salesman; of South Yarra, Vic; b. Invercargill, NZ, 3 Mar 1914.

[5] Pte S. P. C. Luff, QX14581; 2/31 Bn. Labourer; of Wynnum, Qld; b. Hastings, NZ, 22 Apr 1906. Died of wounds 12 Jul 1941.

[6] Capt L. G. Gardner, DX124; 2/31 Bn. Regular soldier; of Footscray, Vic; b. Kensington, Vic, 5 Jan 1917.

[7] The enemy had had at Jezzine 1½ companies of infantry and 2 squadrons of cavalry with additional mortars and heavy machine-guns. After the campaign General Dentz told General Lavarack that he had intended to occupy Jezzine in strength on the 15th—one day too late.

round the right flank Legentilhomme ordered his troops to stand firm on the Jebel Maani and Jebel Badrane; later in the day he was wounded. General Wilson, who was at Irbid that day conferring with General Wavell, doubted that a counter-attack was developing. He put the 5th Indian Brigade under Free French command to renew the attack, and made the little Transjordan Frontier Force[8] responsible for protecting the lines of communication as far as the southern edge of Sheikh Meskine. Soon afterwards it was discovered that the alarm of the Free French was unfounded; the tanks seen to the east of them belonged to their own Colonel Collet. However, when Brigadier Lloyd went forward on the 13th he decided that the enemy's positions at Kiswe were so strong that only a carefully-organised attack with artillery support would take them. He returned to the field ambulance at Deraa to discuss this proposal with the wounded Free French leader, who agreed that further attack, under Lloyd's command, should be postponed until the 15th.

As a preliminary, on the 13th, the Indian brigade moved forward, though leaving its English battalion—the 1/Royal Fusiliers—at Kuneitra. One company of this battalion with two armoured cars pushed forward towards Sassa, half way between Kuneitra and Damascus. There they encountered a strong French force and fell back. This enemy force was well situated, since it might counter-attack either towards Kuneitra, or, moving east, cut the Deraa road behind the force approaching Kiswe.

In the first week of the campaign the R.A.F., though at the outset inferior in numbers to the French air force, had successfully carried out its tasks: close support of the forces on the ground; protection of the naval squadron; attacks on airfields, ports and oil tanks. On the first day No. 3 Squadron R.A.A.F. (now commanded by Squadron Leader Jeffrey[9]) had shot up six French aircraft on the ground at Rayak, and Blenheims had bombed oil tanks at Beirut. From the 9th onward No. 3 Squadron flew frequent patrols over the naval squadron, and, on the 14th, eight Tomahawks led by Jeffrey shot down three out of eight German Ju-88's which were attacking it.[1]

The stubborn French resistance on each sector had been causing great concern in London, and General Dill proposed to General Wavell, first that mobile columns from Iraq be sent into Syria—a project Wavell had already decided on—and that bombers from Egypt be used to add weight to the attack. On the 12th Wavell had informed Dill that although progress was slow "as I warned you it would be if the French resisted", it might be considered satisfactory in view of the difficult terrain and inadequate force.

---

[8] This force, the regular army of Transjordan, was about 700 strong and led by British officers. In Transjordan was also the Arab Legion—a police force of some 1,600 men.

[9] Gp Capt P. Jeffrey, DSO, DFC. Comd No. 3 Sqn RAAF 1940-41; W Ldr 234 Wing RAF 1941; Comd 75 and 76 Sqns 1942, 1 Fighter Wing 1943-44. Regular airman; of Sydney; b. Tenterfield, NSW, 6 Jul 1913.

[1] A more detailed account of air operations in Syria will appear in J. Herington, *Air War Against Germany and Italy, 1939-1943*.

To strengthen that force he ordered the 16th British Brigade Group from Egypt to Syria. The units of this brigade had already been in action in the Western Desert and some of them in Crete. The addition of the 16th Brigade would bring the Allied force to a strength approximately equal to the one which the defenders possessed.

CHAPTER 20

THE FRENCH COUNTER-ATTACK

Two deep salients had now been driven into Syrian territory, the point of the eastern thrust being just south of Kiswe and 25 miles from Damascus, the blunt end of the western resting at Jezzine and Sidon, some 30 miles from Beirut. In the Merdjayoun sector, however, the advance had moved fewer than 10 miles beyond the frontier, and thus, between Jezzine and Damascus, the enemy still held a deep wedge of territory embracing the Litani Valley, Mount Hermon and its foothills.

In the eastern sector the Vichy forces defending Damascus on the line of the Nahr el Awaj were in a very strong position. East of the road they had good cover for infantry and tanks in gardens and among houses behind which rose the steep boulder-strewn Jebel el Kelb and Jebel Abou Atriz on which the defenders were strongly sited. West of the road stood the Tel Kiswe, Tel Afair, and Jebel Madani, which commanded both the Deraa and the Kuneitra roads. Most of the undulating lower country was scattered with lava boulders which made it impossible for wheeled vehicles to leave the roads, and even impeded the movement of infantry, who cut their boots to pieces in a few hours of marching over the stones.

It will be recalled that, on the 14th Brigadier Lloyd had replaced the wounded General Legentilhomme in command of the British and Free French forces; Colonel Jones took over the Indian brigade. Lloyd's plan of attack provided that the Indian brigade, plus the Free French battalion of marines, should attack west of the road before dawn on the 15th and occupy Moukelbe, Tel Kiswe and Kiswe village, whereupon, about 8 a.m., Colonel Casseau's Free French brigade on the right was to advance and take Jebel Abou Atriz and Jebel Kelb.

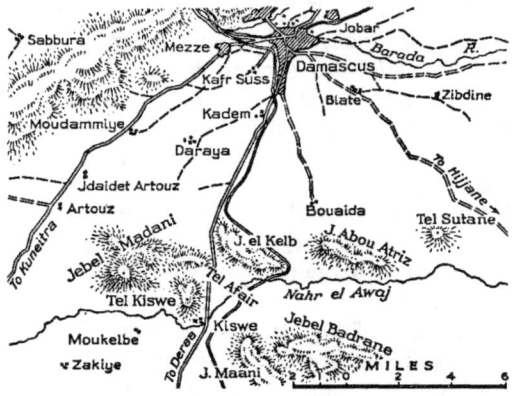

It was believed that a Vichy Moroccan and Tunisian battalion were in and round Kiswe and two Foreign Legion battalions at Tel Kiswe and Moukelbe; thus the defenders outnumbered the attackers. In addition, conflicting sentiments were taking the heart out of the French mercenaries. Casseau had two Senegalese battalions and one Foreign Legion, and they now faced Senegalese and Foreign Legion battalions on the Vichy side. Their enthusiasm was visibly waning.

At 4.30 a.m. the 3/1st Punjab Battalion, with a company of the 1/Royal Fusiliers on its left, moved out to attack Kiswe village, carrying thirty wooden ladders with which to cross an anti-tank ditch 13 feet wide and about the same in depth. The guns of the 1st Field Regiment fired on Tel Kiswe and the enemy positions below it as the Indians advanced in the darkness, and, just before 6 a.m., the infantry crossed the wadi east of the village, and confused fighting began in the gardens and houses. The flanking company of the Indian battalion wheeled and helped to attack the village. By 8.30 the French were beaten. A determined attack in the darkness, though made without tanks across an area that offered little cover and against an enemy twice as strong, had succeeded. Luck played a part, because the attackers arrived just as the French were carrying out a relief and many weapons were loaded on lorries. At once the Rajputana began to move forward through the Punjab to attack Tel Kiswe. In little more than an hour the Rajputana, veterans of Keren, had taken the hill, and by 11.30 the French marines and the Fusiliers on the left had taken Moukelbe. Four Vichy French battalions had been forced out of their positions and the enemy flank had been broken.

On the right, however, the Free French attack failed. The Jebel el Kelb was taken, but flanking fire from the Abou Atriz prevented further progress, and, on the far right, Colonel Collet's cavalrymen were held by artillery fire and tanks.

Meanwhile Lloyd received disturbing news from his rear. From Ezraa on the railway and near the road, 35 miles behind, came a report that on the afternoon of the 14th a column of two companies of Tunisians with ten armoured cars and some artillery had recaptured the town, driving out the two squadrons of the Transjordan Frontier Force, which took up a position across the Ezraa-Sheikh Meskine road. From Kuneitra came news that a strong force was advancing against that town from the north-east. About 2.30 a.m. on the 15th this force, including about ten armoured cars, had moved out from Sassa and driven off the company of the 1/Royal Fusiliers, which, with a few carriers and two armoured cars, as mentioned above, had been sent forward from Kuneitra and was in position four miles south of Sassa. During the day the enemy appeared to be sending south towards Kuneitra large bodies of infantry, tanks and cavalry. The Indian and Free French force had merely blocked the Kuneitra-Damascus road and advanced on Damascus along the circuitous route through Kiswe, leaving the Vichy French force astride the Kuneitra road to its own devices. It now appeared that this force, and their garrison in the Jebel Druse, which had also been by-passed, had sallied out to cut both roads behind the invader.

Promptly Lloyd sent a column consisting of two companies of Free French troops and some British guns under Colonel Genin towards Sheikh Meskine to hold that road.[1] Confirmation that Kuneitra was seriously threatened was provided by a French deserter who declared that the

---

[1] Seven Tomahawks of No. 3 Squadron RAAF attacked enemy vehicles near Sheikh Meskine at noon on the 15th.

enemy intended to attack the town on the 15th using two battalions of infantry and a force of tanks.

The thrust towards Kuneitra was part of a larger move. On 14th June most of the troops in the Merdjayoun area were combined under Lieut-Colonel Monaghan, his command including his own battalion (the 2/33rd), the 6th Australian Cavalry, the 10th Field Battery, and appropriate detachments of anti-tank artillery and engineers. In addition there were two units in the area that were directly under General Lavarack's command, namely the Scots Greys (Colonel Todd), round Merdjayoun, and the 2/2nd Pioneers whose headquarters were near the Litani crossing with some of the companies at work elsewhere. Thus, for the time being, there were three separate forces in the Merdjayoun sector.

The war diary of the 7th Division states that on 14th June

GOC visited Lt-Col Monaghan [and] gave permission for Lt-Col Monaghan to use one coy in a small attack on Poste Christofini, east of Hasbaya, with the general intention of eventually seizing Hasbaya, which is . . . rather a thorn in our side. Instructed Lt-Col Monaghan that his main function is to be to protect the right flank and rear of the Div during its advance north . . . . In discussion with Lt-Col Monaghan G.O.C. agreed that his defence should not be passive, and that he should take every reasonable opportunity of harassing the enemy, always subject to the performance of his main task, the protection of the division's right flank and rear.

In the event, however, Monaghan decided that day to leave only one company of his battalion forward of Khiam in a defensive role while, with the remaining three, he made a wide flanking advance over the foothills of Hermon into the Hasbaya area to cut the road behind the enemy's leading forces—the task given to a single company on the first day of the invasion. Accordingly, on the night of the 14th-15th, the three companies set off through the mountains aimed respectively at Fort Christofini, Hebbariye, and Ferdisse. To guide them through the mountains they still had no better map than a sheet on a scale of one inch to 3.16 miles, in which the tangled area between Ibeles Saki and Hasbaya could be covered by a largish postage stamp.

Captain Bennett's company was on familiar ground, having engaged in the similar enterprises during the opening days of the campaign. The villagers now knew the Australians, and were friendly and helpful, and told them, as they passed through Rachaya el Fokhar, that the French were occupying Christofini, their objective. On the morning of the 15th Bennett established his company and its six mules near Hebbariye and sent patrols forward towards Christofini; these learnt from villagers that French cavalry had recently been using the picturesque fort there, groups of up to fifty at a time entering or leaving it. Bennett decided to probe forward during the night and attack next day—the 16th. (It seems probable that the French had actually abandoned the fort after it was shelled early on the 15th.)

Major Buttrose's[2] objective was Hebbariye. He set out with donkeys carrying the heavy weapons and ammunition, but the country was too steep for them, and the men themselves carried the loads, leaving the animals behind. At Rachaya el Fokhar an Arab who had lived in America offered to guide the men down the face of the cliff into Hebbariye and they arrived there at 11.30 a.m. and took up a position above the village. At 3 o'clock a friendly Arab told the Australians that the French knew where they were. Buttrose promptly moved his company to a new position below the village, a precaution soon justified by the fact that shells began falling in the area that he had abandoned. He could not reach Monaghan by wireless, but was in touch with Captain Cotton's company. It had entered Ferdisse at 1 p.m., established touch with a patrol of the 6th Cavalry, and met no opposition until 3, when about a platoon began attacking from the direction of Hasbaya. Just at that time the French field guns began briskly shelling the British positions north of Merdjayoun, five miles to the west and far below.

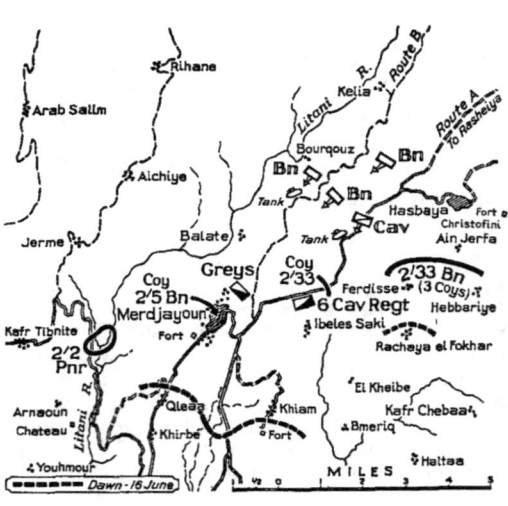

It will be recalled that, just north of Merdjayoun, the road turns south in a long narrow loop, climbs round the foot of the Balate Ridge and, turning north again, forks into Routes "A" and "B". On the afternoon of the 15th when the French guns opened fire, the one remaining company of the 2/33rd was astride Route "A" at "Windy Corner", under the command of Major Onslow of the 6th Cavalry, who had his two squadrons

---

[2] Brig A. W. Buttrose, DSO, SX1434. CO 2/33 Bn 1942-43; 2/5 Bn 1944-45. Wool expert; of Woodville, SA; b. Glenelg, SA, 18 Nov 1912.

in the same area. Between the road and Ibeles Saki were a platoon of machine-gunners (Lieutenant Clarke),[3] two anti-tank guns and the 10th Field Battery, one of whose observers, Captain Brown,[4] was on the slopes overlooking "Windy Corner" from the south, while the other (Captain Hodge[5]) overlooked Route "B" from a post on the south end of Balate Ridge. Hodge's task was to support the Greys, who were astride the road some distance north of him. At 3 p.m. a rapid concentration of shells fell on Balate Ridge and round it, and, half an hour later, ten French tanks and about fifty cavalrymen appeared on Route "B" and deployed across the valley, while what appeared to be two companies of infantry assembled on the north end of Balate Ridge and set up machine-guns there. About 4.30 p.m. tanks attacked along both routes.[6] As they came round "Windy Corner" they were hotly engaged by the anti-tank gunners and machine-gunners from the Ibeles Saki slopes. The gunners hit and disabled the leading tank and two others retired hastily round the corner and concentrated their fire on the machine-guns. At the same time French troops on "Col's Ridge",[7] towering above the road on the northern side, opened heavy fire with mortars and machine-guns on gun positions of the 2/5th 200 feet below them and about 1,200 yards away.

On Route "B", where the French were attacking in greater strength, supported by intense artillery, mortar and machine-gun fire, the Greys had now begun to withdraw down the road while the French tanks drove forward under hot bombardment from field and anti-tank guns. Eleven tanks attacked here. In quick succession four were put out of action; the remainder withdrew round the bend in the road. Meanwhile the enemy infantry were steadily advancing. At Route "A" two anti-tank guns were overrun; at Route "B" after a second duel with the enemy tanks the guns were withdrawn. The line to Hodge's observation post was cut and a gunner sent back to find what was happening returned with the news that the Greys had gone back. Hodge and his team then withdrew covered by a troop of carriers which drove up the Debbine Valley to help him out.

There was now a general withdrawal along the whole front. On the right the tanks had been held thus far but the situation seemed dangerous. Monaghan instructed Onslow to coordinate the retirement of the troops in the forward area, and then went to Todd and suggested that the Greys should hold the high ground immediately north of Merdjayoun while Monaghan held Khiam and organised a counter-attack by his companies round Rachaya el Fokhar.

---

[3] Maj A. J. Clarke, SX10327; 2/3 MG Bn; RAE Water Tpt 1942-45. Public servant; of Wau, NG; b. Euroa, Vic, 14 Apr 1901.

[4] Maj T. B. Brown, NX12459. (1st AIF: 1 Div Arty.) 2/5 Fd Regt. Electroplater; of Sydney; b. Nowra, NSW, 24 Dec 1897.

[5] Maj F. W. Hodge, MBE, NX12317; 2/5 Fd Regt. Insurance officer; of Sydney; b. Sydney, 6 Mar 1906.

[6] In *Guns and Gunners: the Story of the 2/5th Australian Field Regiment in World War II* (1950), the author, Maj-Gen (then Lt-Col) J. W. O'Brien, says that "vigorous enemy fire" began at 4 p.m. A majority of the units present, however, report the French fire as beginning at 3 p.m. and becoming intense perhaps an hour later.

[7] Named after Capt Colin Morris (Artarmon, NSW) of the 2/5 Fd Regt, who was killed in action on 13 June.

Attached to Todd's force was Lieutenant Mayberry's[8] recently-arrived company of the 2/5th Battalion, which had two platoons in Merdjayoun and one in Nabatiye et Tahta. At 4.30 p.m. Todd ordered Mayberry to take up a defensive position on the Balate Ridge; but at 5.15, as the company was moving through the north edge of the town, Todd's second-in-command told Mayberry that a squadron of the Staffordshire Yeomanry (attached to the Greys) was on that ridge, and ordered him to go through Debbine and on to the ridge west of the Balate to relieve a troop of Australian cavalry. However, this troop was met withdrawing south of Debbine, and Mayberry took up a defensive position north of that village.

The French continued to press the attack. At 7.15 p.m. about two companies of French infantry, following intense artillery and machine-gun fire, drove the squadron off the Balate Ridge and it withdrew to Merdjayoun. At 8 p.m. Mayberry who now, though not being pressed, was 700 yards north of the leading enemy troops, withdrew to Merdjayoun, where he was instructed to join a troop of the Greys, which, with two anti-tank guns, had orders to hold a road-block in the town until 2.45 a.m. on the 16th, while the regiment prepared and occupied defensive positions at Qleaa.

Early in the afternoon alarm had begun to spread among bodies of troops behind the forward positions. Reports were rapidly circulated that "the tanks had broken through", and were in Merdjayoun and approaching Ibeles Saki. An Australian artillery officer saw a troop of the Greys return to their vehicle park and find their vehicles gone, whereupon a "wave of panic set in among some of the men and control, both mass and individual, was lost". Four vehicles of the 2/5th Field Regiment "which had not received orders from the battery in the confusion, had got mixed up in a wild stampede through Metulla, and from there on every order received en route was to keep going and to get the roads clear, whilst on arrival at Rosh Pinna wild stories of tanks on the Metulla road were current and no vehicle was permitted to go forward. Eventually, after wandering for two days, during which Nazareth and Er Rama were visited to obtain orders, the little convoy of four trucks returned to the battery".

At 4.45 it was decided to withdraw the field guns a troop at a time to the Qleaa road junction. One troop moved out safely through Merdjayoun to a position near Qleaa and continued firing. Drivers bringing up ammunition found a canteen at the Police Post abandoned and brought forward to the gun teams not only ammunition but cases of beer and cigarettes. However, at 5.15 p.m., when tanks were advancing astride Route "A" and French machine-guns were firing from the slopes northeast of Ibeles Saki, four guns were still in the battery position near Ibeles Saki. Infantrymen were moving past exclaiming that tanks were coming and, when a driver informed Major Humbley,[9] the battery com-

---
[8] Lt-Col W. M. Mayberry, DSO, VX3272. 2/5 Bn; CO 58/59 Bn 1945. Jackeroo; of Jerilderie, NSW; b. London, 10 Mar 1915.
[9] Maj A. S. Humbley, NX12315; 2/5 Fd Regt. Wholesale stationer; of Pymble, NSW; b. Drummoyne, NSW, 8 Dec 1909.

mander, that tanks were on Route "A", he decided that the guns must be withdrawn directly along the terraced wadi leading south to Khiam. Captain Evans[1] was sent back to find a route, but, before he returned, the French troops were reported to be close, and Humbley ordered that the guns be taken out. Under machine-gun fire from Ibeles Saki the column of trucks and guns moved off and bumped their way along the wadi. Three vehicles, disabled by the rough going, were abandoned. Farther on, in an effort to avoid the difficult country, a leading driver began to make a detour, but it led the column to a series of three stone terraces where runways were furiously cut with picks and shovels and the guns themselves hauled up the slope with winches. Lieutenant Gilhooley[2] brought the rear gun into action and fired at the French on Col's Knoll—the southern end of Col's Ridge—over open sights. While most of the vehicles and guns were bunched on the second terrace, which was about 30 yards wide, a French bomber appeared at about 200 feet, banked and sped towards the crowd of struggling vehicles, but, as it began to dive, a British Bofors gun team 500 yards to the west opened fire and in a few rounds hit the aircraft which crashed, its bombs detonating with a roar.[3] The gunners stopped work to give three cheers, then went back to their job of coaxing their vehicles up the last terrace wall. From the top of the hill the guns were driven back to the Khiam-Banias road junction. There Onslow told Humbley that the Bofors gun was still forward, and one gun was made ready for action while the Bofors gun and crew came in. At dusk the troop of field guns at Qleaa withdrew to Metulla.

Meanwhile at Merdjayoun, about 7.30 p.m., Captain Hodge had been assured by a major of the Greys that there were no longer any British troops on the ridge in front. The Greys were then moving fast through Merdjayoun.

> Some little time earlier than this (said the diarist of the 2/5th Field Regiment) Lieutenant Nagle[4] . . . went forward on foot and found both British and Australian troops moving south through the town, but no one seemed to have any idea of what was happening except that the French were coming. He endeavoured to rally these troops telling them that the guns would support them but the majority seemed to have no other idea than to get back, although there was some talk of a plan to hold the east side of Merdjayoun. Eventually Nagle got to the south end of the town and held up a trooper carrying his Bren gun to the rear and on ordering him to stay or give up his gun the Bren was handed over without ado.

As frequently happens when alarm spreads throughout a force, particularly if caused by reports of tanks breaking through, stolid parties of infantry, cavalry and artillery were in forward positions unaware of the excitement behind them. At dusk the French attack had in fact halted,

---

[1] Lt-Col F. R. Evans, NX12273. 2/5 Fd Regt and Staff appts. Regular soldier; of Brisbane; b. Melbourne, 10 Sep 1913.

[2] Lt G. J. E. Gilhooley, NX56439; 2/5 Fd Regt. Clerk; of Burwood, NSW; b. Hunter's Hill, NSW, 11 May 1916. Killed in action 27 Aug 1942.

[3] This gun belonged to a troop of 171 Light Anti-Aircraft Bty under Lt G. A. Baylis which had protected the withdrawal of the field guns and behaved gallantly throughout.

[4] Maj J. F. Nagle, VX1143. 2/5 Fd Regt 1940-43; 1 Para Bn 1944. Barrister; of Sydney; b. Albury, NSW, 10 Jul 1913.

nor could the tanks have continued to move in such country in the dark. The rearguard at Merdjayoun remained in position. Mayberry's company, carriers of the 6th Cavalry and anti-tank guns of Major Rickard's[5] battery of the 2/2nd Anti-Tank Regiment, were still north of the town. At 2.30 a.m. Mayberry sent a patrol forward and it went 500 yards and saw no sign of the enemy. At 2.45 a.m., in accordance with its orders, the little rearguard abandoned Merdjayoun and moved back to Qleaa, where the squadron of the Staffordshire Yeomanry was in position on the right and a squadron of the Greys on the left. The Victorians took up a position in the centre, astride the road. It was not until 10.30 a.m. on the 16th that the first French tanks appeared, and then only two, one of which was hit and destroyed by the anti-tank guns; the other retreated.

Meanwhile, as part of the general withdrawal, Captain Peach's[6] company from "Windy Corner" had withdrawn to Khiam where it took up a position at the fort. Vickers gunners of the 6th Cavalry were on his left at the Banias-Merdjayoun road junction.

This double-pronged counter-attack, with its immediate threat to the communications of all the invading forces east of the Lebanons, transformed the situation. Few reserves were available to meet it. General Wilson called upon the 7th Australian Division to furnish anti-tank guns and ammunition to help the defence of Kuneitra and ordered the 2/Queen's (the leading battalion of the 16th British Brigade) to Deraa. The reserves of the 7th Division consisted of the headquarters and two companies of the 2/3rd Machine Gun Battalion and the headquarters and one battery of the 2/2nd Anti-Tank Regiment at Er Rama. In addition the 2/2nd Pioneer Battalion, which might be employed as infantry, was engaged in engineer work in the 7th Division's area—one company on the road leading inland from Tyre, one with the 25th Brigade, and two on the Jezzine road.

With his two brigades Lavarack was responsible for 37 miles of front, measured through the forward posts. The counter-attack at Ezraa, Kuneitra and Merdjayoun offered a threat to the roads serving his right-hand brigade, because the enemy, already astride the communications of the force attacking towards Damascus, might move from Kuneitra either towards Banias or Rosh Pinna. He decided therefore to send the depleted 2/3rd Machine Gun Battalion, with the remaining anti-tank battery, to hold the crossing over the Jordan at Jisr Bennt Jacub (bridge of the daughters of Jacob) and to dispatch a proportion of the anti-tank and machine-guns north towards Metulla. The 2/2nd Pioneers were ordered to prepare the Litani bridge west of Merdjayoun for demolition and to protect the crossing. These decisions disposed of his only reserves; further reinforcement of the hard-pressed force at Merdjayoun could be achieved

---

[5] Lt-Col A. L. Rickard, DSO, MC, NX438. (1st AIF: Maj 12 FA Bde.) 2/2 A-Tk Regt; CO 103 A-Tk Regt 1942-44, 106 A-Tk Regt 1944, 2/1 A-Tk Regt 1944-45. Of Wahroonga, NSW; b. Sydney, 18 Sep 1895. Died 9 Mar 1949.
[6] Maj C. N. B. Peach, NX12294; 2/33 Bn. Company director; of Bexley, NSW; b. Arncliffe, NSW, 1 Mar 1913.

only by transferring units already engaged at Jezzine or on the coast. Lavarack ordered that the 2/25th Battalion, the 2/5th Field Regiment (one of whose batteries was already with Monaghan) and a troop of the 2/6th should move from Jezzine to the Merdjayoun sector. This left only one battalion, the 2/31st, in Cox's 25th Brigade at Jezzine, whereas at Merdjayoun a force considerably stronger than a brigade was now assembling. General Lavarack instructed Brigadier Berryman, his artillery commander, and the most experienced of his three brigadiers, to take command of all troops in the Merdjayoun sector west of the Litani and organise a defensive position facing east to cover the right rear of the 25th Brigade.

Orders to concentrate at the Litani crossing reached the scattered companies of the 2/2nd Pioneer Battalion late on the night of the 15th-16th. One company, which had been repairing the road near Jerme, set out on foot about 11 p.m. and marched to the crossing, arriving just before dawn. The others began marching but were picked up by trucks. All were very weary next morning.

The order to guard the Jordan crossings reached Lieut-Colonel Blackburn[7] of the 2/3rd Machine Gun at 6.30 p.m. on the 15th, and he hastened forward from Er Rama to reconnoitre, driving as fast as he could without lights over a twisting road crowded with vehicles. As he descended into the Jordan Valley a thick mist was enveloping road and river. He reached the bridge about midnight and found some British horsed cavalry guarding it. Half an hour later an officer arrived from Lavarack's headquarters with orders that Blackburn send a company to occupy a defensive position on one of the two main roads leading into Palestine. Blackburn drove along the valley with this company, saw it placed in position, and arrived back at the Jordan bridge at daylight. During the night two troops of the 2/2nd Anti-Tank Regiment arrived at the Jordan bridge. The little force busied itself preparing for the defence of the crossing, and the bridge was made ready for demolition.

Brigadier Berryman received his orders at Jezzine about midnight on the 15th. He sent Lieut-Colonel O'Brien of the 2/5th Field Regiment to the Merdjayoun sector to discover the situation there. He himself left Jezzine at 1 a.m. on the 16th, and at 6.30 a.m. met Lieut-Colonel Wellington[8] of the 2/2nd Pioneers at the Litani crossing. Although his responsibility was confined to the area west of the Litani, Berryman took the initiative of ordering Wellington to send one company to take up a position on the ridge between Merdjayoun and Qleaa where the Greys were already in position; and he ordered that the Greys were to hold on.

Meanwhile, at 3.45 a.m. on the 16th, the French Force advancing south astride the Damascus road attacked Kuneitra, now held by the

---

[7] Brig A. S. Blackburn, VC, CBE, SX6962. (1st AIF: Capt 10 Bn.) CO 2/3 MG Bn 1940-42; Comd Blackforce in Java, 1942. Solicitor; of Adelaide; b. Woodville, SA, 25 Nov 1892. (As a private at the Anzac Landing, on 25 Apr 1915, Blackburn and a companion reached a point farther inland than any other soldiers whose names are known.)

[8] Col N. F. Wellington, DSO, MC, VX12732. (1st AIF: Capt 21 Bn, BM 16 Brit Bde 1918.) CO 2/2 Pnr Bn. Town clerk; of Essendon, Vic; b. Mount Pleasant, Vic, 4 Apr 1889. Died 1952.

Fusiliers less a company. The defenders estimated that more than 1,500 French troops with eleven tanks, ten armoured cars, and one or two field guns opposed the garrison—about 570 British infantry supported by one Italian 20-mm gun.[9] By 6 a.m. the French tanks were cruising in the streets; the Breda gun was broken and the tanks were impervious to the anti-tank rifles and Molotov cocktails of the defending infantrymen, and overwhelmed one section post after another. At 11.30 a.m. the commanding officer collected the survivors in three stone houses.

> The siege started, the enemy sniping strongly from tanks and houses (wrote the historian of the Royal Fusiliers). Spirited replies from Bren gunners reduced the numbers of enemy snipers . . . the tanks roamed exactly where they liked and cruised round the battalion area shooting up the trenches, into doors and windows and at all trucks . . . . Tank-hunting squads, mostly M.T. drivers, drew grenades from the battalion reserve S.A.A. truck . . . and continued their hopeless hunt . . . .
> At about this time Corporal Cotton, D.C.M., distinguished himself for the last time. He withdrew to the area of battalion headquarters at about 1230 hours. With Second Lieutenant Connal and one Fusilier, he carried back a Hotchkiss machine-gun he had captured a week before, together with 1,300 rounds. With this he continued in action for half an hour, but when the gun broke down he took an anti-tank rifle and went to attack the tanks single-handed. He drew their fire and was eventually killed by a round of high-explosive . . . . There were many other gallant deeds that day. Towards the evening it looked as if the enemy infantry had withdrawn, as there was a lull. At 1820 hours a French officer approached in an armoured car, waving a white handkerchief, and came to battalion headquarters with a Fusilier prisoner. The officer explained that the battalion was surrounded by a vastly superior force of tanks and other armoured fighting vehicles. He hoped they would surrender now, as he hated shooting Englishmen. The Commanding Officer demanded half an hour to decide. After consultation with the second-in-command and Regimental Sergeant-Major, he decided that to give in was the only alternative to the massacre of the remainder of his men . . . . As he went over to speak to the French Commander, he saw eleven medium tanks behind the nearest group of houses. At 1900 hours he surrendered, with thirteen officers and 164 other ranks . . . .[1]

Later in the evening the fourth rifle company of the battalion with a 25-pounder gun approached down the Sheikh Meskine road from Kiswe, but withdrew after the gun had fired all its ammunition.

Late in the afternoon of 16th June news had reached Blackburn that the Fusiliers were hard pressed and short of ammunition. He ordered Captain Kennedy[2] to take a small force forward to Kuneitra in three trucks and with two anti-tank guns with the object of luring the French tanks out and destroying them.[3] Soon after this party had set out Captain Houghton of the Cheshires, who had joined Blackburn as a liaison officer from General Wilson's headquarters, issued instructions to Blackburn that he was to send forward two armoured cars, one company of machine-

---

[9] Actually there were 27 medium and 12 light tanks, about 12 armoured cars, two field guns and mortars.

[1] C. N. Parkinson, *Always a Fusilier* (1949).

[2] Capt J. Kennedy, TX2084; 2/3 MG Bn. Manager; of Hobart; b. Hobart, 18 May 1912.

[3] At this stage one company of the 2/3 MG Bn was with the 21 Bde, one company divided between Jezzine and Merdjayoun, one company less a platoon in the Metulla area, the headquarters of the battalion with one company plus one platoon with Blackburn at the crossings over the Jordan.

(Australian War Memorial)

The surrender of Damascus, 21st June 1941. General Catroux, followed by General Legentilhomme, taking the salute from a guard of honour of Free French Marines.

(Cpl H. A. Norcott, 2/3 Bn)

Looking west along the Barada Gorge. The site of the 2/3rd Battalion road-block on the Damascus-Beirut road.

Looking north from Jezzine along the Wadi Jezzine. The high feature is Hill 1284.

(*Lt-Col R. A. C. Muir*)

gunners and two anti-tank guns to take 60,000 rounds of ammunition to the Kuneitra garrison. Houghton said he was speaking with the direct authority of General Wilson's headquarters. Blackburn questioned these orders, saying that he had received no such orders from General Lavarack. Houghton was insistent that "his instructions were to be acted upon". However, at 7.15, Captain Kennedy's party returned, together with a patrol from the Yorkshire Dragoons and five men who had "escaped from Kuneitra", and Blackburn suspended the move of the company towards Kuneitra. Towards midnight, however, the orders from Wilson's headquarters were confirmed.

At Kiswe Lloyd did not allow the threat to his rear to upset his plan. He ordered the Indian brigade to advance on Jebel Madani, and they did so during the night of the 15th-16th. Soon after dawn on the 16th the Punjab had driven the French from the heights and could see the minarets of Damascus, nine miles away; the Rajputana, whose positions on Tel Kiswe had been taken over by a Free French battalion, had passed through and seized a line from Jdaidet Artouz along the Kuneitra road for two miles to the south. There the French marine battalion joined them, and in the afternoon they were heavily attacked by tanks and strafed by fighter aircraft, suffering heavy casualties.

By sending these battalions across to the Kuneitra road Lloyd had improved an extremely awkward situation. The French at Ezraa threatened the Deraa road along which he was operating and on the alternative road there were French troops between him and Kuneitra. By occupying Artouz, however, he had in his turn cut the road behind the French force at Kuneitra; and, in the afternoon, he received news (incorrect at that time) that Ezraa had been recaptured.

In the Merdjayoun sector on the 16th a brief but successful action was fought on the remote right flank. About 11 p.m. on the 15th a messenger reached Major Buttrose's company of the 2/33rd at Hebbariye with news of the fight at Merdjayoun and orders from Colonel Monaghan to withdraw forthwith to a position astride the Bmeriq-Banias road. The messenger then set off to deliver a similar order to Captain Bennett at Fort Christofini. Buttrose's company began to retire about midnight and by 6 a.m. on the 16th reached Rachaya el Fokhar just ahead of some squadrons of Vichy French Circassian cavalry which had advanced along the track leading into that village from the west. The Australians quickly took up a position round the village and poured fire into the French as they advanced towards them on foot, and did specially effective work with a 2-inch mortar. Meanwhile, about 7.30 a.m., the runner had reached Bennett with orders to withdraw. At 1 p.m., as he was moving his company along the track to Rachaya, Bennett came over the top of a hill and saw Buttrose's fight in progress below him about 1,000 yards away. Some 200 French cavalrymen on the right, as he faced south, were then advancing up the terraces to attack Buttrose's company.

Bennett decided to advance down the hill against the French flank. Lieutenant Copp's platoon fixed bayonets and charged, then Marshall's platoon charged on his right, while Dwyer's men, farther to the right, established themselves overlooking the track along which the French would have to withdraw to Ferdisse. Copp's platoon advanced among the French with Tommy guns and bayonets, and the enemy ran. Buttrose's company joined in the chase, and his mortars and Dwyer's Bren gunners poured fire into the fugitives. More than fifty French troops were killed. Both companies then took up defensive positions on the high ground west of Rachaya until, about 5 p.m., orders came from Monaghan to withdraw to Bmeriq. They did so and took up positions there that night. Thirty-two French cavalry horses, fine Arab stallions, were captured in the fight at Rachaya. The battalion used them to mount its messengers and for officers' chargers.[4]

At Khiam fort early in the afternoon about a company of French troops attacked Peach's company from both flanks. The French were not using tanks, but they attacked with vigour and Peach withdrew to a position 300 yards south of the fort. Here Cotton's company, having marched back from Ferdisse, joined him, and both took up a position in a ravine, where they remained until, in the evening, Monaghan ordered them to fall back to a line about one mile and a half south of the fort.

Farther to the left the Greys and Lieutenant Mayberry's company of the 2/5th were astride the road north of Qleaa, with a company of the 2/2nd Pioneer Battalion on its way to reinforce them. There the enemy had been singularly inactive since 10.30 in the morning when the advance of his two tanks had been stopped.

Brigadier Berryman decided that the best way to check the enemy in the Khiam area would be to attack at Merdjayoun. On the 16th General Lavarack visited him, extended his command to include all the troops in the Merdjayoun area and approved his plan to attack Merdjayoun on the 17th, using the 2/2nd Pioneers and 2/25th Battalion. Meanwhile Berryman allotted a lavish supply of ammunition to the guns intending to compensate for his lack of tanks by generous use of artillery. Berryman's force now included three battalions, 22 field guns, the Scots Greys, and part of the 6th Cavalry.[5] In fact the French counter-attack had, in less than twenty-four hours, attracted to this area the strongest force—though a motley one—on any of the three sectors west of the Damascus front.

The counter-attack fell also on the 25th Brigade at Jezzine, but less forcibly. The swift move along the tortuous mountain road had placed

---
[4] Finally these horses were handed over to the 6th Cavalry Regiment to mount a troop known as the "Kelly Gang".

[5] It included:
    Scots Greys
    6 Aust Cav (less two squadrons)
    2/33 Bn, 2/25 Bn
    2/2 Pnr Bn (plus one coy 2/5 Bn)
    One coy 2/3 MG Bn
    2/5 Fd Regt (plus one tp 2/6 Fd Regt)
    8 Aust A-Tk Bty
    One Tp 57 LAA Regt
    One Sec 2/5 Fd Coy

this brigade on the flank of the 21st Brigade; and, on the morning of the 15th, patrols travelled along the Sidon-Jezzine road and found it clear of the enemy. Jezzine was a pleasant mountain town, lying in the centre of a tobacco-growing area. From it a good road wound north to the larger town of Beit ed Dine. To the east the lofty Jebel Niha towered between the Jezzine Valley and the valley of the Litani; whereas at Merdjayoun the brigade had been on the eastern slopes of the Lebanon, it was now on the western. From a point a few miles south of Jezzine a winding track led through the mountains to Machrhara, the terminus of a first-class road from the Zahle district, and thus provided a route by which the enemy might attempt to cut across the Australians' slender line of communication. The road leading north was cut into the side of the range and dominated on the east by a series of hills which came to be known by their altitudes as marked on the map (in metres)—the "1199 Feature", the "1284 Feature" and the "1332 Feature". On the west the land fell away steeply, sometimes in sheer precipices into a deep gorge. Indeed, the line of advance offered every advantage to the defender. Cox's force at Jezzine now comprised only the 2/31st Battalion and supporting detachments; its second battalion, the 2/25th, and some of the artillery having been recalled to reinforce the hard-pressed force at Merdjayoun. On the 15th the 2/31st had its leading companies forward on the high ground overlooking the town from the north, and astride the Machrhara road. The Cheshire was holding the road leading west to the coast.

Early on the 15th the infantry north of Jezzine saw trucks and horsed cavalry moving far ahead of them and reached the conclusion that the enemy was reorganising for a counter-attack. In the evening, a few hours after Cox had learnt of the counter-attack at Merdjayoun, Captain Thomson's[6] company, which was forward just north of Hill 1199, was attacked by what appeared to be a company and a half of infantry and a squadron of cavalry with three field guns. One French gun was dragged round the sharp bend of the road and fired over the heads of the men in the forward positions. Within ten minutes hard and accurate artillery fire was brought down on the French and they withdrew before their infantry had fired a shot.

At dawn next morning, the 16th, an enemy patrol approached along the road from Machrhara. Here Captain Houston's company was well concealed astride the road at the foot of towering Mount Toumat. Houston was a cool and deliberate soldier, and Porter had instructed him, if he was attacked by a small enemy detachment, to hold his fire and capture a prisoner. He held his fire until the enemy column was only 200 yards away and then opened with a 2-pounder gun (of the 7th Anti-Tank Battery) and small arms. The gunners hit the leading armoured car, then the rear one and the one in the middle in quick succession. The crews ran, leaving behind the three wrecked cars (which thenceforward formed

---

[6] Capt C. L. Thomson, QX6042. 2/31 Bn; 2/1 A-Tk Regt. Merchandise manager; of Clayfield, Qld; b. Sydney, 21 Nov 1912.

a useful road-block) and two undamaged motor-cycles. Sergeant Sheppard[7] and Private Murray Groundwater[8] clambered over high ground and headed off and captured seven men. During the day an officer in a motor-car and another armoured car drove up to the road-block and were captured. At this stage Houston reported that he was "running out of parking space".

A similar thrust, equally costly to the enemy, was made along the northern road later in the morning by French horsed cavalry which were caught under artillery and machine-gun fire and lost almost every man and horse. Throughout the day French artillery fired on Jezzine and the exposed mile of road to the south of it. Trucks carrying rations forward over the difficult mountain road had not arrived and some companies had had to eat their iron rations; a little food was requisitioned from the townspeople who gave it willingly and added two sheep ready-cooked.

At 3.15 a.m. on the 17th, Colonel Blackburn, in accordance with General Wilson's order, dispatched one company of his machine-gunners, under Captain Gordon,[9] two lightly-armoured cars belonging to the Palestine Police, and two anti-tank guns towards Kuneitra, 25 miles away. The plan was to move forward in three bounds on the last of which the machine-gunners would occupy a covering position while the armoured cars attempted to enter the town.

On the way Gordon met an officer of the Fusiliers, who told him that the French were holding Kuneitra strongly with a force of tanks, armoured cars, infantry, artillery and cavalry, and that they had outposts on the hills between the town and the little force advancing against them. At 6 a.m. another officer of the Fusiliers was met who said that his battalion had surrendered the previous evening at 6 p.m. to a force of "twenty-six tanks and armoured cars, a battery of artillery and 1,200 to 1,500 infantry and cavalry". He added that "only 160 Fusiliers were left, seventeen of them officers". Gordon decided that it was useless to attack such a force as the French evidently possessed with a company of machine-gunners, two armoured cars and two 2-pounder guns, and took up a defensive position astride the road on a ridge overlooking the town; thus at least he could block the route to Palestine. From an observation post on this eminence he saw three armoured fighting vehicles on the far side of the town. Some cavalry and two armoured fighting vehicles approached the machine-gunners' position. Fire was opened by the machine-gunners with the object of drawing the tanks within effective range of the anti-tank guns; but immediately the French armoured fighting vehicles returned to the town, and the cavalry went to ground until the British armoured cars drove forward and scattered them. Three more tanks were then seen

---

[7] Lt R. Sheppard, NX22082; 2/31 Bn. Clerk; of Woonona, NSW; b. Woonona, 2 Dec 1918. Killed in car accident, 4 Feb 1949.

[8] Pte M. Groundwater, MM, QX2077; 2/31 Bn. Oil company employee; of Ingham, Qld; b. Townsville, Qld, 4 Feb 1920.

[9] Lt-Col R. R. Gordon, DSO, VX17441; CO 2/3 MG Bn 1944-45. Railways administrative officer; of Essendon, Vic; b. Essendon, 13 Mar 1907.

in the town of Moumsiye opposite the Australian positions, and the machine-gunners saw artillery moving northward along the Sheikh Meskine-Kuneitra road, but could not determine whether they were enemy guns or not. When these guns were close to the village, however, the French opened fire on them—they were British. The British artillerymen went into action, the French tanks retired, and Gordon sent his armoured cars over to the newly-arrived guns to point out his position.

A 9 a.m. Gordon received a message that two battalions of infantry were coming out to support him. At 5 p.m. one battalion—the 2/Queen's —arrived. Its commanding officer took charge of the force and planned an attack which began at 7 p.m., with the Australian machine-gunners and anti-tank gunners giving supporting fire from the left flank and the armoured cars following the infantry into the town. Using long range ammunition the machine-gunners fired on the French field guns and their forward defences. The infantry advanced and retook the town, losing only one man.

> Kuneitra was a remarkable sight (wrote Blackburn afterwards). In 48 hours it had been successively 1. held by a British force, 2. attacked for nearly 24 hours, 3. held by the enemy for nearly 24 hours, 4. twice bombed by our aircraft, 5. shelled by our artillery, 6. attacked and recaptured by our forces. In the centre of the town was a French tank burning and nearly red hot. Along the streets and roads were overturned lorries, British and French, three smashed armoured cars, dead horses, piles of ammunition, papers, clothes, shells, guns, rifles and several ordinary cars riddled with bullets. In spite of this most of the shops were open. Australians—those off duty—were wandering along the streets buying. Locals were calmly cleaning up, sorting their belongings, shopping, and seeming indifferent to the war.

During the 16th and 17th the force at Sheikh Meskine had been hard pressed. At dawn on the 18th Colonel Genin attacked Ezraa with one company, but in the fight it was surprised by tanks and scattered and Genin was killed. Thereupon Major Hackett,[1] a young Australian serving in the British regular army, led forward in trucks a force of fewer than 100 men—half a company of Senegalese, twelve Royal Fusiliers, two carriers and one anti-tank gun. These men made a determined assault, gallantly supported by their one small gun, manned by Corporal A. Clarke, and recaptured the town, taking 168 prisoners, three light guns, sixteen machine-guns, a mortar and a field gun. Hackett lost fourteen men; in the five days of fighting round Ezraa 71 Allied and probably about 120 enemy troops were killed or wounded.

Throughout the 17th June Lloyd's Indian battalions pressed on, reaching Artouz, but the Free French on the Jebel el Kelb made no move. Lloyd decided that on the night of the 18th-19th he would make a surprise attack towards Mezze and cut the Damascus-Beirut road. Meanwhile his battalions would rest.

---

[1] Brig J. Winthrop Hackett, DSO, MBE, MC. Transjordan Frontier Force 1937-41; Comd 4 Parachute Bde 1943-45. Regular soldier; b. Perth, WA, 5 Nov 1910.

As mentioned above, Brigadier Berryman had decided, on the 17th, to recapture Merdjayoun. His plan[2] was that, in the early morning, the 2/25th, which had reached Jerme early on the 16th and that afternoon had begun moving through the hills towards Merdjayoun, should march across the Litani and attack towards Merdjayoun from the north-west, and cut the road into Debbine. At dawn a company of the 2/2nd Pioneer Battalion was to attack from the direction of Qleaa, supported by artillery and machine-gun fire, and a second Pioneer company was to follow through and exploit the success of the first.

The orders gave an imposing task to both battalions. The pioneer battalion, though a year old, had arrived in the Middle East only in May and had done no advanced training as an infantry unit, nor was it fully equipped or organised to fight as an infantry battalion. It had only one light automatic and one sub-machine-gun to a platoon, no mortars, no Intelligence section, and a signal section of only seven men. Now one of its companies had the task of attacking with patrols over country which (as the 25th Brigade had learnt) was easy to defend, and familiar to the French, and in which was deployed an enemy force possessing tanks and strong enough to have carried out a sweeping counter-attack. The advance by the 2/25th towards "the first b in Debbine" entailed a march, partly in the dark, over tangled mountain country, through the gorge and the swift-flowing stream of the Litani, to the steep ridge on which lay Merdjayoun.

The leading pioneer company (Captain Aitken[3]) was to move behind a barrage some 400 yards wide and lifting 100 yards every five minutes, and advance to a depth of 600 yards to the fort at the southern end of the town. The walls of the fort were about 15 feet high and so thick that 25-pounder shells did them little damage. The two forward platoons of the leading company followed the barrage closely on the left of the road. Soon they were under hot fire from machine-gunners and riflemen well concealed among the stone walls which criss-crossed the area, and machine-gunners firing through slits in the walls of the fort. They lost

---

[2] The order read:
RAA EXPORTER OP INSTN NO. 3
16th June 41.
1. 2/25 Bn less 1 Coy and 1 Coy 2/2 Pnr Bn will attack Merdjayoun.
2. 2/25 Bn will cross R LITANI and attack in SE direction towards the first B in DEBBINE with the object of cutting the Rds running out of the NE of the town. After cutting these routes patrols will enter town from NORTH.
3. 1 Coy 2/2 Pnr Bn will attack fort with patrols from SW on left of Rd KHIRBE-MERDJAYOUN.
4. Tps will use rocky slopes as a measure of protection against tanks and will NOT halt on rds.
5. 9 and 10 Fd Btys will support attack Z to Z plus 30 barrage across front of fort starting 300 yds SOUTH and moving to a depth of 600 yds lifting 100 yds in 5 mins. Rates 10 Bty 2 rpgpm, 9 Bty 1½ rpgpm.
6. GREYS and 6 AUST CAV will support attack by fire.
7. 2/25 Bn will ford LITANI at Zero.
8. ZERO NOT before 1300 hrs.
9. From Zero plus 9 Fd Bty will support 2/25 Bn and 10 Fd Bty 1 Coy Pnr.
Issued to Reps at 1300 hrs.
J. G. Wilton, Maj.
BMRA Aust Div
Exporter.

[3] Lt-Col E. F. Aitken, VX15141; CO 2/2 Pnr Bn 1945. Traveller; of St. Kilda, Vic; b. Kensington, Vic, 31 Jan 1913.

men rapidly, but the survivors reached a point about 30 yards from the fort. A supporting company following 50 yards behind the first was pinned down. When it was light, both companies were lying out under searching fire from the slopes ahead of them. Soon French tanks emerged from Merdjayoun and captured thirty-eight of the survivors (the Pioneers had no effective anti-tank weapons), including Lieutenant Summons[4] of the leading company, and Lieutenant Pemberton[5] of the supporting company. Later Captain Aitken became a prisoner. For the remainder of that hot day those who were left lay behind such cover as they had been able to find and tried to drive the enemy outposts back to the fort. A captured anti-tank gun and a captured 81-mm mortar were brought forward to assist. At dusk the survivors of the leading companies straggled back and the line was stabilised about 800 yards from the fort, where the tanks could not advance without coming under fire from anti-tank guns of the 8th Anti-Tank Battery north of Qleaa. The two companies of Pioneers had lost 27 killed, 46 wounded, and 29 prisoners.

Meanwhile, at 10 p.m. on the 16th, the 2/25th had begun to move across the Litani valley. In single file they stumbled and slipped down the hillside, and in the early hours waded the swift-flowing river breast high and arrived wet and weary on the opposite bank. By dawn they had advanced some distance up a valley leading to the Merdjayoun plateau, but it was three hours after dawn before they reached the upper slopes. All chance of surprise had now been lost and the battalion was halted far short of its objective.

In the Jezzine area, as a result of the events of the 16th, Cox, who had moved his headquarters back to Kafr Houn, decided that he could defend Jezzine, but could not advance with so small a force. Soon after dawn on the 17th the enemy made it plain that he held the initiative. He launched a strong attack with apparently a whole battalion against Robson's and Thomson's companies on the heights east of the Beit ed Dine road. The attackers reached a copse south of Hill 1332 and were held there under heavy fire from Thomson's company. Robson, on the right, about 8.30 a.m. led his men by a circuitous route until he was only 75 yards from the French position, and then charged with two of his platoons, their bayonets fixed, while the third gave covering fire. After a sharp hand-to-hand fight in which three Australians were killed and several wounded, the survivors of the French—two officers and sixty-five men, mostly Senegalese—surrendered. The prisoners were weary and dejected. They said that they had marched for four days before the attack and were very hungry; they were obviously fatigued and utterly weary of war. Nevertheless, despite this set-back, the enemy continued to press forward all day and threatened to outflank the two companies by moving round them on

---

[4] Lt W. I. Summons, VX14642; 2/2 Pnr Bn. Student; of Camberwell, Vic; b. Melbourne, 6 Apr 1920.
[5] Capt J. M. Pemberton, VX38875; 2/2 Pnr Bn. Hatter; of Essendon, Vic; b. Beechworth, Vic, 7 Jun 1905.

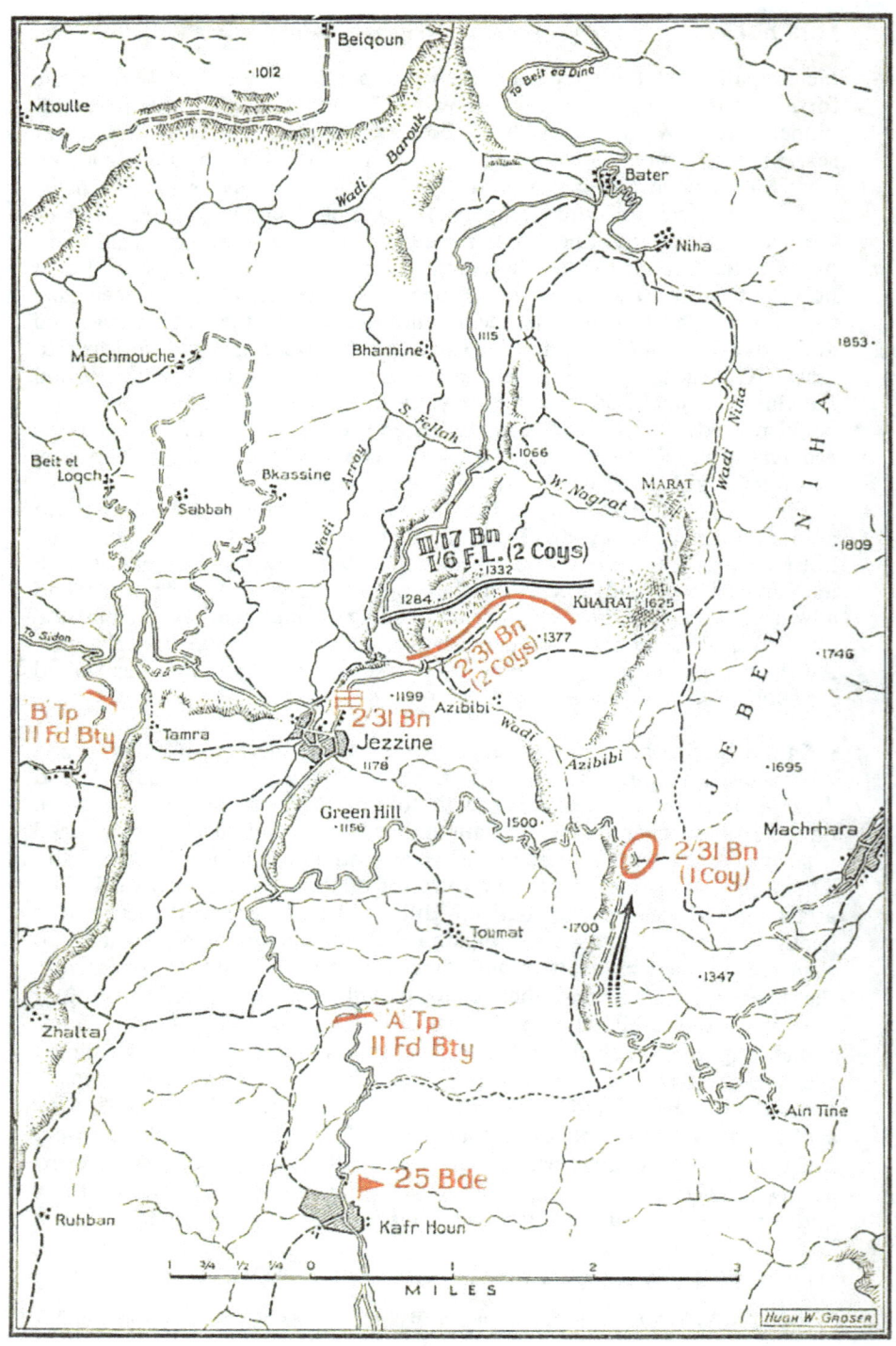

Soon after dawn, 17th June.

the east. Pack animals carried their supplies over the rugged range. Robson's company thrust forward and occupied Hill 1332 but was forced back to the copse by searching mortar fire and infantry attack, and eventually withdrew to a position well south of the hill. Thomson's company held astride the road under constant mortar fire. Meanwhile Porter had hurried the company which had been on the Machrhara road (leaving one platoon and the anti-tank guns there) to Hill 1377 whence it harassed the attackers with machine-gun fire; and by 4 p.m., though the enemy continued to mortar and machine-gun the forward positions, his thrust had been halted with considerable loss. At the end of the hard day the Australians were weary, hungry and cold—they wore only shirts, and shorts or trousers. On Hill 1377 they collected food from the French dead in front of their positions, and their stretcher-bearers collected the enemy wounded; the Australians shared their water with these though very short of it themselves.

That night the French artillery shelled the Australian posts at frequent intervals, and when light came, enemy infantry were seen concentrating on the high ground east of the road and showing signs of renewing their costly attacks. Porter ordered Houston's company to drive them off Hill 1332 whence they dominated the Australian positions. The advance began at 10.50 a.m. from a position near the copse, with artillery support. When his men were about 100 yards from the French on Hill 1332, Houston, in accordance with a prearranged plan, sent up a Very light signal to the artillery to cease fire, and charged. His line was only 50 yards from the French posts before they retaliated with withering machine-gun fire. Houston, a fine leader, Lieutenant Coakley[6] and five others, were killed and twenty-two wounded.

This was an unhappy end to the successful repulse of the counter-attack in this sector, but the enemy had lost far more heavily than the Australians. Cox's depleted force had held its ground. Some of the 2/31st's success then and later was due to the fact that the battalion had been formed in England largely from artillery and other technical troops, and contained officers and men who were expert with the wireless telephones they had obtained there, and officers able competently to direct artillery fire. This produced particularly close cooperation with the field battery (Major Reddish[7]).

Late in the afternoon as this long fight was ending six bombers, escorted by fighters, dropped about twenty bombs on Jezzine. Several hit the three-storeyed Hotel Egypt where the 2/31st's ration store and kitchen were installed. Forty men were buried in the wreckage, of whom seventeen, including three company quartermaster-sergeants who were collecting rations, died; ten others were sent to hospital. The terrified townspeople

---

[6] Lt J. B. Coakley, NX12470, 2/31 Bn. Public servant; of Mont Park, Vic, and Canberra; b. Ivanhoe, Vic, 5 Dec 1918. Killed in action 18 Jun 1941.

[7] Brig J. Reddish, DSO, NX105. CO 2/6 Fd Regt 1942-43; CRA 6 Div 1943-45. Accountant; of Drummoyne, NSW; b. Croydon, NSW, 19 May 1902.
Lt C. C. Thomas of the 2/6 Fd Regt frequently distinguished himself here as an intrepid artillery observer.

fled to refuge in caves in the surrounding hills. Some were carried away to other villages in army vehicles, and the force had to find men to police the town against the Arabs who crowded in from the outlying areas looking for loot.

What had been the objectives of the French counter-attacks? On the 13th General de Verdilhac had ordered that offensive reconnaissance be made in front of the Nahr el Awaj positions. To that end a patrol comprising an armoured car troop and a lorried troop of the *1st Spahis* was ordered to move out from Sassa. It reached the neighbourhood of Kuneitra where it was fired on and withdrew. On the 14th, however, Verdilhac decided to attempt counter-attacks on a larger scale with the object of so disorganising the invading army that it would be possible to divert some of his forces to meet an expected British attack from Iraq. Verdilhac had now used thirteen of his eighteen regular battalions; others were dispersed on defensive tasks; his reserves were almost exhausted. A column, including the *7th Chasseurs d'Afrique*, a company of Senegalese and a few guns, was ordered to take Kuneitra, if weakly held, and advance to Banias and Jisr Bennt Jacub; a weaker patrol was to advance on Sanamein; and a third, with armoured cars and lorried infantry, to advance from Hijjane to take Ezraa and Sheikh Meskine and cut the Deraa-Damascus road. At this stage three battalions—*III/29th Algerian, V/1st Moroccan* and *1/17th Senegalese*—were deployed on the Nahr el Awaj protecting Damascus.

At Kuneitra the mobile column (under Colonel Lecoulteux) after fierce fighting took the town, with 470 prisoners, including 18 officers. However, because of the failure of the column which was to take Sanamein (which was found "strongly held"), Colonel Keime, in command of all the raiding columns, ordered Lecoulteux to withdraw his main force to Sassa, leaving a detachment of one company of infantry and some armoured cars to hold Kuneitra until heavily attacked, when it was to retire. Meanwhile, as a result of Lloyd's continued attack, and the loss of Kiswe, the threat to Damascus became so pressing that Verdilhac reinforced the area with two fresh battalions—*I/29th* and *III/24th Colonial*. He replaced the commanders of two of the three battalions at Kiswe and appointed Colonel Keime to replace General Delhomme in command of the whole South Syrian Force. Keime placed his newly-arrived battalions in the Artouz-Mezze area.

At Merdjayoun the counter-attack was made by three African battalions (evidently the *I/22nd Algerian, II/29th Algerian* and *II/16th Tunisian*), with some twenty tanks. Two of the battalions attacked from an east-west line astride Routes "A" and "B" and the third moved along the axis of the advance in their rear. Cavalry guarded the eastern flank round Hasbaya. The final objective was a line just south of Khirbe and Fort Khiam, whence the eastern battalion was to exploit towards Banias, the west towards Metulla. By the 21st the *III/6th Foreign Legion* was also in this area.

The advance to Jezzine attracted enemy reinforcements from the Damascus area: the *II/17th Senegalese Battalion* and companies of the *I/6th Foreign Legion*. At the end of this phase there appear to have been two battalions in the Jebel Druse, five in the Damascus area, three at Merdjayoun, one and a half about Jezzine, and five or six in the coastal sector.

The French counter-attack on the inland sectors had the indirect effect of halting the 21st Brigade on the coast: on the 17th June General Lavarack ordered Brigadier Stevens to stand fast and adopt an "aggressive defence" until the position at Merdjayoun had been cleared up. That evening Brigadier Cox informed General Lavarack that he was opposed by three French battalions and a half—an over-estimate—and, if he did not receive reinforcements, would have to withdraw. General Lavarack ordered him to hold on; Brigadier Stevens was told not to advance farther until the position of the 25th Brigade had been stabilised; later that night Stevens was instructed to reinforce Jezzine with his 2/14th Battalion and detachments of artillery. At 1 a.m. the following morning Lavarack informed General Wilson of these steps and asked that he be given the 2/3rd and 2/5th Battalions. Wilson allotted him instead the 2/King's Own of the 16th British Brigade. Lavarack ordered it to join the 21st Brigade to replace the 2/14th. The 2/3rd and 2/5th, as mentioned above, had been included in the order of battle of the 7th Division from the outset, and one company of the 2/5th had fought at Merdjayoun. The 2/King's Own would be the second battalion of the 16th British Brigade to arrive forward, the first having been the 2/Queen's which recaptured Kuneitra.

In the middle days of June the sea and air battle off the Syrian coast became more intense. On the 15th French aircraft bombed and severely damaged the British destroyers *Isis* and *Ilex*. Next day aircraft of the Fleet Air Arm, based in Cyprus, sank the French destroyer *Le Chevalier Paul,* believed to be running arms into Syria. On the 17th a French sloop appeared off Sidon, came close inshore and shelled and machine-gunned the gun positions of the 2/4th Field Regiment north of that town. In accordance with orders not to disclose gun positions to enemy warships, the troops took cover until the sloop began to move out to sea. Then seventeen guns opened fire at about 4,000 yards and maintained it until the ship was out of range, achieving some direct hits.

The plan of campaign had provided that when the attacking force reached the Beirut-Damascus road—the first and main objective—General Lavarack would hand over his division to General Allen, take command of I Australian Corps, and assume control of the operations in Syria and the Lebanon. After ten days of fighting the objective had not been reached, but there were good reasons for transferring command of the forces in the field to a leader who would have a smaller sphere of respon-

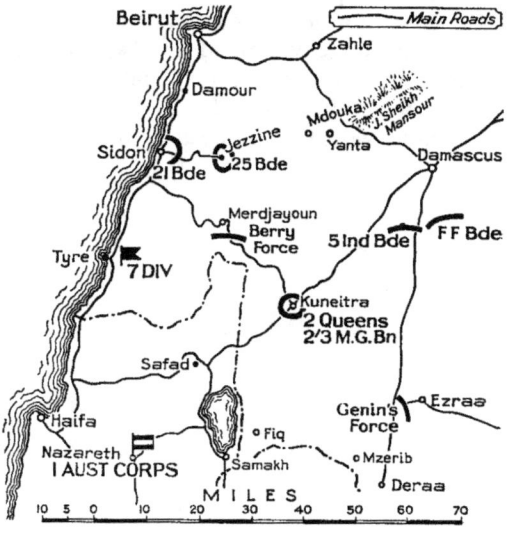

sibility than General Wilson had. Wilson's main headquarters were in Jerusalem (at the King David Hotel), and his area included all Palestine and Transjordan. At 9 a.m. on the 18th Lavarack handed over the 7th Division to Allen, and took over I Australian Corps Headquarters, which had been established at Nazareth since the beginning of the campaign awaiting the order to assume command.

All troops in Syria except "Habforce", a column which, on the 13th had been ordered to advance into Syria from Iraq, thus came under Lavarack's command—namely the 7th Australian Division, the 5th Indian Brigade, the 1st Free French Division, and the lines of communication. At a conference that morning Wilson instructed Lavarack to regard the operations against Damascus as of secondary importance and concentrate his main effort against Beirut. He ordered that the 16th British Brigade, which had one battalion at Kuneitra, one at Rosh Pinna, and the third on its way to the coastal sector, be incorporated in Allen's division, which was to prepare for an advance on Beirut. That evening General Wilson broadcast a message to General Dentz calling on him to declare Damascus an open city and withdraw his troops from it; but without result.

General Lavarack and his staff thus took over a problematical situation. In three sectors the French were either attacking or else had soundly defeated recent Allied attacks; and on the coast the advancing column had been ordered to halt. The 5th Indian Brigade had lost heavily and the Free French troops were in low spirits. Practically all reserves had been committed, and two hard-pressed sectors had been reinforced at the expense of others. However, by collecting the scattered units of the 16th British Brigade, a reinforcement could be provided for the Sidon-Jezzine salient, on which Wilson ordered the new field commander to concentrate his main strength—a return to the original plan. That afternoon General Lavarack informed General Allen that the Merdjayoun sector would be placed under the command on Major-General Evetts, now leading the 6th British Division, so that Allen could concentrate the 7th Australian Division west of the range for a decisive thrust towards Beirut, against which the main effort would now be directed.

CHAPTER 21

DAMASCUS FALLS

CONVINCED that the best means of countering the French forays across his lines of communication would be to press on to Damascus, Brigadier Lloyd had issued orders for a renewed attack before he knew even that Kuneitra had been recaptured from the enemy. On his right the Free French contingent was to advance along the Deraa road to Kadem, as a first step towards entering Damascus from the south. On the left the 5th Indian Brigade, on the night of the 18th-19th, would move on foot along the Kuneitra road to Mezze and cut the road from Damascus to Beirut, now the defenders' main lateral artery. The French marines and two detached companies of the Indian brigade were to form a defensive flank from Artouz to Jebel Madani. The enterprise to which Lloyd committed the main body of the Indians was bold in the extreme, and typical of the irrepressible leader who conceived it. The Indian brigade had lost its British battalion at Kuneitra; on the 17th when he gave the order the enemy was astride one of the two roads behind him, and was close to the other; his remaining battalions were below strength as a result of casualties and detachments; they were fatigued and were outnumbered by the defenders. Notwithstanding, Lloyd proposed to make a night advance of about 12 miles, and seize a vital position for which the enemy would certainly fight hard. But if all went well—and Lloyd was evidently one of those who assumed that a determined stroke would win success—the French would have only one line of retreat, namely the road leading north-east to Homs.

Lloyd's order was elaborated by Colonel Jones, whose detailed plan provided that one company of the Punjab, the leading battalion, would deal with any opposition encountered on the way and that when his column reached the road just south of the heights overlooking Mezze from the south-west, another company of the Punjab would seize them. When Mezze was entered, the Rajputana would block all roads into the area and hold on.

The Indian column began to move at 8.30 on the night of the 18th, the men on foot following a route just west of the road with their twelve vehicles on the road itself. While the battalions were moving off in pitch darkness the area was heavily shelled and some men lost their way. At 10 p.m. the column came under heavy fire from Mouadammiye, which was set among many trees. Throwing grenades and shouting to one another so as to keep in touch in the darkness, the Sikh company of the Punjab attacked, while the main column marched on, keeping level with the flashing of grenades on their right. The Sikhs encountered and set fire to several tanks, useless in the darkness. There was a long fierce fight in the woods and only some 270 men reached the far edge, but the attackers had broken up a strong enemy post and the advance was able to continue.

By 11 o'clock the head of the column was through the enemy's first line. However, it was difficult for the leading men to keep in touch, and the trucks, outstripping the troops, ran into a French road-block guarded by an anti-tank gun. The gun opened fire and disabled some of the trucks, and the surviving vehicles were eventually sheltered in olive groves where they were pinned down by the fire of enemy guns. They did not rejoin the battalions. Meanwhile the infantry, overcoming some posts and by-passing others, moved on past the aerodrome and at 4.15 in the morning were at Mezze "after a 12-mile march, against opposition, over unreconnoitred country and in utter darkness . . . a military feat of outstanding brilliance".[1]

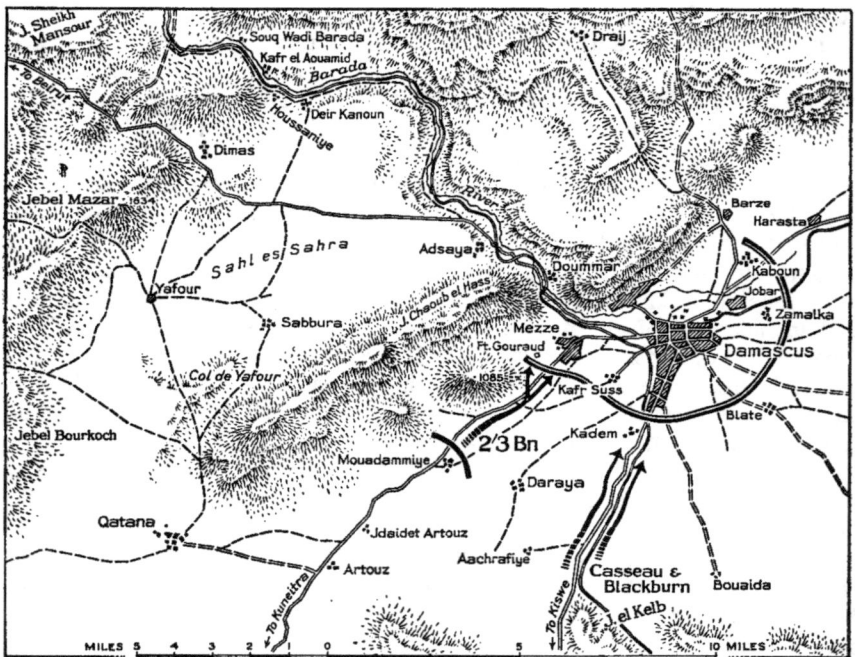

The attack on Mezze itself began at 4.30 a.m. Soon the Indians were fighting among the square white buildings, and for an hour a street battle was waged in which infantrymen with Tommy guns knocked out the crews of several field guns sited to fire along the road, and yet another tank was set on fire. A company of the Rajputana moved round the village and on to the Beirut road, set fire to a petrol dump, turned back a train, beat off an attack and caused some alarm in Damascus. When daylight came, however, they themselves were attacked by five tanks and retired to Mezze.

At that village the remainder of the brigade were busy preparing defence against an inevitable counter-attack by infantry and tanks. Road-

[1] W. G. Hingston, *The Tiger Strikes* (1942), p. 137.

blocks were built with timber, stones and wire. Brigade and the two battalion headquarters and a company of each battalion were established in and round a large square, two-storeyed house with a walled garden—Mezze House—on the northern edge of the village, and the wall was loopholed; the other companies took up positions in the village.[2] About 9 a.m. French tanks appeared and opened fire. The Indians' small arms kept off the enemy infantry but tanks, against which they had no effective weapon, cruised round the village firing through the walls and windows of the house. The village was shelled persistently.

All day the fight went on. At 4 p.m. one isolated company surrendered. Resistance was then concentrated in and round Mezze House; the house itself had become a hospital in which an increasing number of wounded were collecting. Medical stores were exhausted and wounded were bandaged with strips torn from sheets found in the building. The men were hungry and had no food, and ammunition was running short—because they had lost their trucks. Lieut-Colonel Greatwood[3] of the Punjab was mortally wounded. At 8.45 Jones sent a jemadar and two English officers to reach Lloyd's headquarters and report the situation. They crawled through a hole in the wall, swam a stream, clambered through a garden, over the roofs of several houses and through cactus hedges, and at 5.30 a.m., nearly exhausted, reached the headquarters of the force and made their report.

The Indian brigade had been one prong of a two-pointed attack, the other being formed by the Free French contingent on the Deraa road. The French attack on the 19th had failed completely. The Free French troops were tired and disheartened, so much so that General Legentilhomme told General Evetts, commander of the 6th British Division then coming in on the Damascus flank, that nothing would set his men moving again except the sight of British troops. Lloyd considered that the failure of the Free French attack on the night of the 18th-19th was "possibly the main cause of the heavy losses suffered by 5 Indian Infantry Brigade at Mezze". ("Heavy losses" was a euphemism; the brigade had been virtually extinguished.) "There is good reason to believe," he added, "that the Vichy French, threatened by the cutting of their line of retreat by the thrust at Mezze, had begun to withdraw from Damascus; but the failure of the Free French attack now allowed them to concentrate heavy forces against Mezze .... The Free French could not mount a new attack until the afternoon of 20th June after they had been reinforced by two British anti-tank guns and an anti-aircraft gun which drove off the three Vichy tanks which had been holding up the advance."

Early on the 20th, after the three officers from the force besieged at Mezze House arrived at his headquarters, Lloyd had sent the remaining

---

[2] The two companies of the Punjab that had been engaged at Mouadammiye, where enemy pockets still held out, and on the heights west of Mezze were unable to rejoin the rest of the brigade in Mezze itself, but were in the woods south-east of it where the company of the Fusiliers later joined them. A third company of the Punjab was at Jebel Madani.

[3] Lt-Col H. E. G. Greatwood. CO 3/1 Punjab Regt. Regular soldier; b. 11 Sep 1899. Died of wounds 22 Jun 1941.

companies of the Punjab and two companies of French marines with the 1st Field Regiment, all commanded by Major Bourke,[4] to relieve the beleaguered brigade. The gunners advanced boldly, sometimes ahead of the infantry, but, at the end of the day, they were still hotly opposed by French tanks and had not succeeded in reaching their objective.

The advance to Mezze had an influence on the conduct of the campaign that was out of proportion to the local gains or to its immediate effect on the defenders of Damascus; partly as an outcome of that advance a decision was made again to swing the main effort from one flank to the other. On the 19th General Evetts took command of all British troops east of the Merdjayoun sector and "control" of the Free French forces. Late on the 19th, General Lavarack, having learnt that further British troops might be added to his command, decided that some additional units at Damascus might turn the scale there, and asked General Wilson to alter his decision made the previous day to add the 16th British Brigade to the 7th Australian Division for the advance to Beirut, and re-allot it to the Damascus sector. Wilson agreed, but urged that the Damascus operations should be completed before the time arrived to thrust towards Beirut. At the outset Evetts' force was in four groups: one small contingent guarding the lines of communication from Deraa north to Kiswe; the 5th Indian Brigade advancing, with the Free French, on Damascus; the 16th Brigade with one battalion—2/Queen's—at Kuneitra and the 2/Leicesters at Rosh Pinna (the third battalion having been detached to the 21st Australian Brigade); and Lieut-Colonel Blackburn's force. Evetts' headquarters were at Rosh Pinna and those of Lloyd and Legentilhomme at Khan Deinoun, eight hours' drive away.

At 11 a.m. on the 20th Evetts sent a message to Lavarack that heavy fighting continued at Mezze, and added:

> We are optimistic of success but I wish to point out that should the action go against us the 5 Inf Bde will be seriously depleted in both personnel and material and reduced to approx one Bn. Other portion of 5 Inf Bde are just about to start operations to clear front of Free French forces in neighbourhood of Aachrafiye; if successful Free French will probably be in a position to advance towards Damascus. I still consider and am supported by [Legentilhomme and Lloyd] that it is essential to move up the 16 Inf Bde Gp as soon as possible by the Kuneitra-Damascus road. Hope you have been able to arrange this as any cessation of pressure on our part will in my opinion prejudice the whole success of the operation.

Lavarack promptly telephoned Brigadier Rowell, his chief staff officer, who was at General Allen's headquarters, informing him of the decision to divert the main effort temporarily to Damascus and to send the 16th British Brigade there. He asked him to find out whether Allen could hold his positions without the 16th Brigade (though he would retain one of its battalions—the 2/King's Own). A few minutes later, while waiting for a reply, Lavarack was telephoned by Wilson who said that General Catroux had given him a gloomy picture of the force attacking towards Damascus.

---

[4] Brig H. S. J. Bourke, DSO, OBE, MC. 1 Fd Regt 1939-42; CO 51 Fd Regt 1942; CRA 70 Div 1942-43, 2 Div (India) 1943-44. Regular soldier; b. Mussourie, India, 25 Aug 1900.

Lavarack replied that Evetts was confident but was asking for the 16th Brigade and he intended to let him have it provided Allen would spare it. Allen declared that by active patrolling he could hold his positions with two brigades; consequently his division was given a defensive role. That evening Lavarack informed Evetts that the central and coastal sectors had been denuded of infantry reserves to enable him to capture Damascus; but, as soon as he had done this, the 16th Brigade—and the Australian 2/3rd and 2/5th Battalions which he had also placed under Evetts' command—should be ready to move "elsewhere".

At length, by the night of the 20th, Evetts' force had been increased until it included two brigades (5th Indian and 16th British) and three additional battalions (2/3rd and 2/5th Infantry, and 2/3rd Machine Gun); and, for the time, attention was concentrated on the effort, already in full swing, to take Damascus.

Late on the 18th June, the day on which the Indian brigade had begun its bitter fight at Mezze, the 2/3rd Australian Infantry Battalion (Lieut-Colonel Lamb) had begun entraining at Majdal in Palestine for Deraa where it was to form a "stop" on the Damascus-Deraa road. A week earlier, one of the battalion's four rifle companies had been sent to Sidon for garrison duty, and, on the 18th, the battalion had transferred 100 men to help to re-form the 2/1st Battalion which had lost all but a handful of its men in Crete. As a result of these subtractions the 2/3rd possessed only 21 officers and 385 men, and some of these men had not fully recovered from privations in Greece and Crete.

The journey to Deraa took seventeen hours. From Haifa the men travelled in eight cattle trucks through the stifling heat of the Jordan Valley—the temperature at Samakh was 130 degrees—and on to Mzerib. There the grade was too steep for the engine to haul the train up in one piece and, consequently, the train was divided into two parts. When the engine was returning for the second section its brakes failed and it crashed into the trucks, injuring three men. At Deraa at dusk on the 19th the battalion boarded civilian buses and was joined also by its own few vehicles which had travelled from Julis by road. Thence the little column drove all night and, along a road that was broken in many places by bomb craters, little more than a walking pace could be achieved. Two of the trucks overturned during the 50-mile journey. At Khan Deinoun, where the column arrived in the early morning of the 20th, Lamb was informed that his battalion was to join the depleted 5th Indian Brigade, replacing the 1/Royal Fusiliers as the British battalion in that brigade. The leading Australians moved forward in trucks to Mouadammiye on the Kuneitra road at 11 a.m., and dispersed and dug in on the right of the road about one mile south of the aerodrome under sporadic shell-fire. Ahead of the Australians a battery of the 1st Field Regiment was firing—it was part of Major Bourke's column vainly trying to relieve the remnant of the Indian battalions in Mezze.

General Evetts was convinced that the Free French units were weary and disheartened; this day he wrote to Brigadier Rowell that they had "little or no desire to go on killing their fellow Frenchmen and it is doubtful whether they can be persuaded to advance even against feeble resistance". Evetts summoned Blackburn to his headquarters at Rosh Pinna and gave him orders to assist the Free French forward to Damascus. As a result, Blackburn, whose "battalion" comprised one company (Captain Gordon's), one platoon of another company and five anti-tank guns, advanced to Colonel Casseau's Free French force at the Jebel el Kelb. At Casseau's headquarters (where Brigadier Lloyd was urging Casseau to push on so as to relieve the pressure on his brigade at Mezze) Blackburn learnt that the Free French troops were very weary after eleven days of fighting in the heat and sand and had come to a standstill; the Vichy force had tanks and armoured cars and they had none. He told Casseau that his little force was fresh and eager and (which particularly pleased Casseau) that it possessed anti-tank guns. At Blackburn's urging Casseau agreed to advance at 5 o'clock that afternoon, whereupon Blackburn ordered Gordon to deploy his four platoons astride the road and inspire the French to attack boldly. Gordon promptly placed most of his company in the French line on the heights east and west of the road and sent one platoon forward 1,000 yards ahead of the French infantry on the road itself. So far as Gordon could discover the Free French advance was being opposed only by the fire of one field gun and a small force of infantry—perhaps a weak battalion.

Half an hour later Casseau's infantry, mostly Africans, began to advance, with Casseau himself driving his car slowly along the road level with the leading men. However, when the infantry drew up to the machine-gunners they halted, and it was not until Blackburn had sent his men to a new position 300 yards forward, and they opened fire again, that the Free French troops moved forward. In this fashion progress continued, the machine-gunners leading the tired and dispirited African infantry until they had advanced three miles and were on the outskirts of Damascus. Here there was stronger opposition from Vichy troops occupying a large building and sniping from among the trees in the plantations, and some Vichy tanks appeared. The advance was halted for the night, and Gordon's company withdrew to a position behind the infantry to form a reserve line in case the French troops were forced back during the night.

Meanwhile, in the afternoon of the 20th, Lloyd had ordered Lamb of the 2/3rd Infantry to attack over the high ground on the left of the road, that is to say on the left of the Indians and the gunners advancing towards Mezze. He did not then know that the Indians in Mezze had been overwhelmed. All night of the 19th-20th the Vichy French had continued to attack Mezze House and, from 1.30 p.m. on the 20th, they shelled it with field guns at point-blank range. An attack which followed this bombardment was driven off, but when it was over the Indians' ammunition was exhausted. The defenders could then hear the fire of their own troops to the south and, hoping to delay the attackers until help arrived, they sent out an emissary to ask for an armistice so that they could remove the wounded. However, when the French saw the white flag advancing, they assumed it meant surrender and rushed the building. News of this set-back reached Lloyd later in the day. It signified that the force astride the Kuneitra road consisted only of a handful of Indian infantry, some French marines (who had not succeeded in winning Lloyd's confidence) and part of the 1st Field Regiment. In fact the 5th Indian Brigade had now been reduced to little more than a few depleted companies of British and Indian infantry, and the newly-arrived Australian battalion, which was at less than half strength. Unperturbed, Lloyd decided to continue to attack, but with the Australian battalion spread more widely across his front. His new orders were that one company of Australians was to cut the Damascus-Beirut road, while the remainder of the battalion advanced on to the steep bare heights which overlook the Kuneitra road from the west.[5]

This ridge, one of the foothills of Mount Hermon, is a huge wedge thrusting towards Damascus from the south-west. On the east it falls steeply into the plain along which travels the Kuneitra road; on the north it forms the southern wall of the Barada Gorge along whose narrow floor run the road and railway to Beirut. On top of it the French had built a group of stone forts and had given them the names of distinguished soldiers — Andrea, Gouraud, Goybet, Vallier, Weygand, Guedeney, Sarrail.

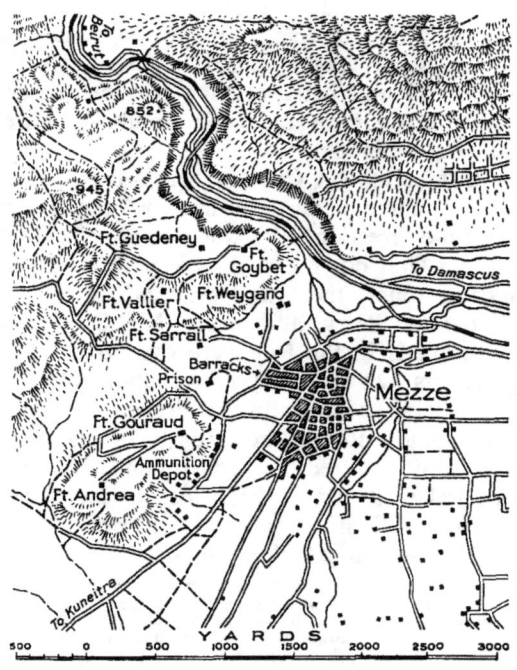

It was 5.30 p.m., and the Australian companies were already forming up for the attack arranged earlier in the day, when Lamb arrived with these new orders. The change of plan caused some delay and it was dusk before the companies set off. On the right Captain Parbury's,[6] which was given the task of cutting the Beirut road, moved

---

[5] On this and later days the enemy made fairly frequent air attacks on Allied vehicles. One Australian truck was hit this afternoon, one man being killed and two wounded.

[6] Lt-Col P. K. Parbury, DSO, MC, NX69. 2/3 Bn; CO 31/51 Bn 1944, 2/7 Bn 1944-45. Factory superintendent; of Wollongong, NSW; b. Sydney, 16 Sep 1910.

forward astride the tributary road leading to that objective and was soon out of sight. Of the remaining companies Major McGregor's was ordered by Lamb to take Goybet,[7] the northernmost of the forts, Captain Ian Hutchison's company to take Vallier, which lay south-west of Goybet, and the headquarters company to take Sarrail. Lamb had been informed at Lloyd's headquarters that the Indians held Gouraud and Andrea.

As they approached Goybet after a steep climb McGregor's men were met by fairly heavy fire and were pinned down. Hutchison, however, on his left, found Vallier empty, though there were signs of recent occupation. These included a litter of clothing and some blood-stained bandages, which the Australians took to be evidence of the effectiveness of the fire of the British artillery which had been shooting at the forts during the afternoon; and a rope made of sheets hanging over the northern wall, suggesting that the occupants had made off towards Goybet. McGregor sent a message to Hutchison asking for help, and Hutchison sent two platoons towards Goybet; in the darkness they could not find McGregor's company but only two wounded Australians who said that they thought the rest of the company had withdrawn.

Meanwhile the pioneers, carrier crews and the signallers of Lamb's headquarters company under Captain Mackinnon[8] had occupied Fort Sarrail where Lamb established his headquarters about 10 p.m. Thus, at midnight Hutchison's company was posted round Vallier, McGregor's was to the north, having failed to take Goybet, Lamb and Mackinnon were in Sarrail and had posted a platoon under Lieutenant Gall[9] about 800 yards from it on the road leading south-east. Parbury's company was still out of touch.

After midnight Captain Mackinnon led a patrol out from Sarrail and almost immediately ran into a French force that was moving in the opposite direction. Fire was exchanged. Mackinnon tried to move forward to join Gall but his men were held by the fire of the French troops who moved round them and attacked Sarrail. In the mêlée which followed Lieutenant Perry[1] and several N.C.O's[2] were wounded and eventually the Australians in the fort were overpowered and led off along the road as prisoners. On their way they encountered Gall's platoon, but the prisoners were between him and the French so that he could not fire, and at the same time another strong party of enemy troops appeared on the slope above and covered him; consequently Lamb, who was among the prisoners, ordered Gall and his men also to lay down their arms. Moving on, still in the half light, the party came upon a carrier manned by Indian troops. Lamb tried to tell the Indians that there were Australians in the party

---

[7] All of these "forts" except Gouraud (to the south, and which the enemy had abandoned) were described on the French map as "ouvrages" or outworks. The system faced northwards as if against rebellious attack from the direction of Damascus.

[8] Maj A. S. Mackinnon, NX325. 2/3 Bn 1939-42; HQ 7 Div 1942-44. Bank officer; of Sydney; b. Crow's Nest, NSW, 28 May 1907.

[9] Capt J. M. Gall, MC, NX12174; 2/3 Bn. Station overseer; of Moree, NSW; b. Inverell, NSW, 16 Mar 1915.

[1] Lt J. L. Perry, MC, NX4920; 2/3 Bn. Engineer; of Stanmore, NSW; b. Hobart, 13 Feb 1910. (Correct name J. L. McDermott.)

[2] Including WO2 E. P. Flynn (of Bellambi, NSW) and Sgt L. E. G. Buderus (Marrickville, NSW).

but they did not understand and opened fire killing two and wounding Lamb himself and one other. Thereupon French troops in Fort Weygand opened fire, revealing to the Australians that the French still held this fort, close to their headquarters area. When this firing ceased the wounded colonel and some of the other Australian prisoners were escorted into Weygand and the remainder were held some distance outside it.

Thus, though the forward companies of the 2/3rd had made some progress across the fortified ridge and held one of the "ouvrages", a French counter-attack coming in behind them had made prisoners of their commanding officer and most of his staff and headquarters company. Not all of it, however, was captured for Lieutenant Ayrton,[3] who had a small party in an outpost about 400 yards from Fort Sarrail, had not been involved, yet had been a distant spectator of what had happened, and at dawn, when Lieutenant J. E. MacDonald, whom Lamb had appointed as his liaison officer at brigade headquarters, arrived and was fired on by what he imagined to be his battalion's headquarters, Ayrton hailed him and told him what he knew. MacDonald hurried to brigade headquarters with the news that the staff of his battalion had been captured, and that he did not know where the rifle companies were.

When Parbury had set out the previous night along a road of which he knew little (for his map ended short of the road junction) except that it joined the Beirut road a mile or so ahead of him, he believed that the Indian battalions were holding out somewhere to the west of Damascus and was not surprised when he encountered no opposition on the first stage of his advance. Near the road junction, however, he came under fire from French troops in some buildings there, and from the heights on the left. The company vigorously engaged the enemy. Lieutenant Murdoch[4] and two men ran to one of the houses and threw in grenades, and Corporal Badans[5] did the same at another house. Scouting ahead, Parbury found a track which brought him to a point whence he looked down on a wide ribbon of road—his objective. He broke off the engagement and led his company forward along it.

Darkness had just fallen when the leading platoon reached the main road along which were rows of shops and houses. Warrant-Officer Mac-Dougal who led this platoon saw a light in one shop and the door being slammed. He raced across the road and pushed a bayonet through the door. An old Frenchman and his wife were the only occupants; no French troops were to be seen. Promptly the Australians cut down two telephone poles, placed them across the road, deployed along the sides of the road and awaited developments. Soon French vehicles began to arrive from the direction both of Damascus and of Beirut. In the darkness they pulled up at the road-block and the occupants were hustled out by the Aus-

---

[3] Capt E. N. Ayrton, NX5017; 2/3 and 4 Bns. Tram conductor; of Petersham, NSW; b. Bondi, NSW, 17 Sep 1913.

[4] Capt M. H. Murdoch, NX9504; 2/3 Bn. Insurance officer; of Stockton, NSW; b. Subiaco, WA, 7 Apr 1918.

[5] Cpl C. N. Badans, NX4805; 2/3 Bn. Labourer; of Wollongong, NSW; b. Orange, NSW, 9 Feb 1915.

tralians. There were occasional scrimmages, but generally the French were completely surprised. Soon Parbury and his ninety men had twenty-six vehicles jammed head to tail on the road, two cars across the railway line to block it, and held eighty-six prisoners, about one-fifth of whom were officers. The prisoners who were herded into a house and a shop beside the road were an embarrassment, and therefore Parbury, who was anxious both to be rid of them and to send back news of his progress, dispatched a trusted young sergeant, Copeman,[6] to the headquarters of the 5th Indian Brigade to ask for an escort. However, it was not until Copeman had returned with information that no men could be spared, and Parbury himself had gone back to headquarters to plead more vigorously, that an officer and four men (of the 1/Royal Fusiliers) went forward and escorted the prisoners back.

Firing could be heard to the east of the Australians and there was still some fire from the heights above them; this fire, Parbury considered, was likely to make it impossible for him to hold his road-block when dawn came and the French could see more clearly. Therefore he decided to leave one platoon (commanded by Lieutenant Murdoch) on the road, while he himself led the remainder of the men up the side of the ravine to drive the French off the summit. Parbury did not know that there were fortifications there.[7]

It took the Australians two hours to scale the slippery side of the steep cliff in the half light. As they were climbing, an armoured car appeared on the road from the Damascus side and opened fire on them until they turned their Bren guns on to it and drove it off. Eventually they reached a ledge near the summit, whence, 150 yards ahead, they could see a formidable fort and two pill-boxes, surrounded by barbed wire. MacDougal led an advance against one pill-box and found it unoccupied, but when the main fort was approached brisk fire broke out from it. In addition occasional shells were falling round the fort, evidently from the British guns to the south. The men were very tired after the long climb; they had been hungry when the engagement began and now had no rations left and very little water. They had not eaten a hot meal since they had entrained at Julis in Palestine, two days and three nights before, and they took cover to rest. It was at this stage that Hutchison's company appeared approaching Goybet from the south-western side.

When, about 7 a.m., Major Stevenson,[8] the second-in-command of the 2/3rd, had arrived at brigade headquarters from the rear where he had been organising the battalion's transport, Major Bourke, now temporarily in command at Lloyd's headquarters, gave him the disturbing news that

---

[6] Lt J. Copeman, MC, MM, NX4545; 2/3 Bn. Dairy farmer; of Picton, NSW; b. Ballina, NSW, 8 Dec 1919.

[7] At this stage Parbury sent a signal to brigade headquarters which Lt J. E. MacDonald, the Australian liaison officer there, remembers as: "A Coy is astride Damascus-Beirut road at map reference 19831751. Water rations and ammo almost depleted and troops becoming exhausted. Enemy on high ground dominate this position from both sides of road and at dawn position will become untenable. I intend to attack."

[8] Brig J. R. Stevenson, CBE, DSO, NX49. CO 2/3 Bn 1941-43; Comd 11 Bde 1943-45 (Merauke Force 1943-44). Parliamentary officer; of Lakemba, NSW; b. Bondi, NSW, 7 Oct 1908.

his battalion headquarters had been captured, Parbury's company was vaguely known to be somewhere in the direction of the Barada Gorge, and the regimental aid post was nowhere to be found (it was with Parbury). Bourke told Stevenson that the brigade commander wished Stevenson to capture Goybet as soon as possible, and it was agreed that an attack would be made after the artillery had fired on the fort from 9 to 9.30. Stevenson hoped that Parbury's company would be found by that time. Meantime he had sent out Corporal Hickson,[9] a gallant and capable member of his Intelligence section, who roamed about and by 9.15 had discovered two men lying wounded by the road and learnt the whereabouts of Parbury's company and of the imprisoned battalion headquarters. Stevenson decided that when Fort Goybet had been taken he would attack south along the ridge and release the prisoners in Weygand.

Stevenson ordered Hutchison to make the attack on Goybet. When Hutchison and his men were cautiously reconnoitring they encountered Parbury—not at the bottom of the gorge but on the summit of the ridge, also planning to attack the fort. At length the artillery[1] opened fire but, by the wrist watches of the infantry on the heights, the fire ceased ten minutes too early and, after waiting for it to continue, they attacked late, being in doubt whether to move forward or not. In the face of brisk fire Corporal Morgan[2] with two men climbed to within 30 yards of the walls and tried to throw grenades through the firing slits while the French machine-guns fired over his head. A gallant veteran of the war of 1914-18, Private Scott Orr,[3] was killed at the foot of the wall firing his Bren gun, and it soon became evident that the only way into the fort was through the gate. Morgan brought his men out and both companies began firing on the fort in preparation for a new attack, when, to their surprise, a French soldier emerged carrying a white flag. The nearest platoons of Australians rushed through the gate and took the surrender of about seventy-five European troops. Their commander, a captain, was dead and the only other officer, a lieutenant, wounded. The survivors said that they had surrendered because, seeing the leading Australian parties withdraw, they feared that the guns would open fire on them again. It was then about 10 a.m.

There was no need for Stevenson to carry out the second part of his plan—to face about and attack Weygand with the object of releasing the prisoners—because a company quartermaster-sergeant, Carlyle Smith[4] (an enterprising soldier whose nickname was "Beau Geste"), had already

---

[9] Sgt D. R. Hickson, NX5379; 2/3 Bn. Jackeroo; of Coonamble, NSW; b. Coonamble, 7 Sep 1919. Killed in action 24 Oct 1942.

[1] The arty fire was extremely accurate. Although, as one man described it later, "Goybet sat on top of a pinnacle and to fire at it with arty was like throwing a tennis ball at the knob on a flagpole", the guns made several direct hits.

[2] WO2 W. Morgan, MM, NX5458; 2/3 Bn. Station hand; of Brewarrina, NSW; b. Lakemba, NSW, 18 Oct 1916.

[3] Pte W. Scott Orr, NX13232. (1st AIF: 34 Bn.) 2/3 Bn. Grazier; of Five Dock, NSW; b. Homebush, NSW, 16 Mar 1897. Killed in action 21 Jun 1941.

[4] WO2 C. R. F. Smith, MM, NX5013; 2/3 Bn. Labourer; of Marrickville, NSW; b. Mudgee, NSW, 3 Aug 1911. Died 11 Dec 1946.

led out from Mezze a party of three armed with sub-machine-guns to accomplish this purpose. They had been in charge of a kitchen truck and had been held up by enemy fire. They crept upon and shot the unwary sentries who were guarding Lieutenant Gall and some of his men outside Weygand, whereupon Gall led five men at Weygand itself, captured it and released Lamb and the remainder of the prisoners. Thus, between 8 o'clock and 10, an extremely tangled situation was unravelled, and the heights overlooking Mezze and the gorge were in Australian hands.

Murdoch, however, with his "platoon" of nine Australians and three Free French, was still at the road-block at the bottom of the gorge. He had placed eight men under Corporal Norcott[5] on the left of the road facing towards Beirut, while he and Sergeant Copeman took up a position on the steep slopes overlooking the road on the northern side. Here they held the road for twelve hours against intermittent forays by tanks and armoured cars which attempted to break through both from the east and the west. Some twenty French troops who were supported by two tanks advanced from the large barracks that lay on the Damascus side of the barrier and made a brave attempt to clear the road. In the fight that followed, Copeman, from his position on the side of the gorge and having no better anti-tank weapon, threw three mortar bombs (which did not explode) on to the tanks, and he and Murdoch fired at the tanks' eye slits at a range of a few yards. The French attackers did not give up, however, until seven of them had been killed. Thenceforward attacks from Damascus ceased, though first an armoured car and later three tanks tried to break through from the western end of the gorge, but again without success. There was now a platoon of Australians in the gorge, a company in Goybet and another in Vallier. About 4 p.m. a company of Indian troops which had been placed under Stevenson's command arrived with anti-tank rifles, drove the French tanks away and took up a position 200 feet above the road-block on the northern side of the gorge.

A French report states that the counter-attack towards Mezze on the 19th was made by the *7th Chasseurs d'Afrique*, and freed the Damascus-Beirut road. The Chasseurs took 150 prisoners. However the Indian troops continued to infiltrate, and a second mopping-up of Mezze on the 20th was ordered, and an additional 150 prisoners taken. That night the French withdrew to a line from Fort Gouraud on the west through Kafr Suss, Zamalka and Kaboun. Thus they were on this line when the 2/3rd Australian Battalion attacked and cut the Beirut road. The final French counter-attack on Mezze, Forts Weygand and Sarrail was made by Colonel Plantard's *III/24th Colonial Regiment* with three companies. It advanced guided by a sergeant of the *III/6th Foreign Legion* east from Kafr Suss at 12.30 a.m. on the 21st; about 3 a.m. one company (Captain Bousin) was on the southern outskirts of Mezze, another (Captain Harant) in Mezze, and a third (Captain Martinet) in the vicinity. Harant (on whose report, captured later, this account is based) was surprised to find the Mezze gardens full of Indian and Free French troops, some of them sleeping. Confused fighting with rifles and grenades followed. Harant lost six men and tried to move to the right but met hot fire in that direction. "A frightful stench of death fills the lane, and a soft body is under my hand and knee at the foot of the wall," wrote Harant. "This terrifies me and I decide to

---

[5] Cpl H. A. Norcott, NX68315; 2/3 Bn. Printer; of Campsie, NSW; b. Newtown, NSW, 12 Jul 1919.

leave anything rather than stay near these bodies, to be killed with these dead without being able to reply . . . . We must therefore attack." Harant tried to urge his men on with shouts, "kicks and punches", with little success. He then veered to the right and attacked Forts Weygand and Sarrail. At 4.45 a.m. about thirty men entered Weygand, which was unoccupied; but near it they took thirty Australian prisoners and escorted them into the fort. About the same time another group took Sarrail after an exchange of fire in which one Frenchman was wounded, one Australian killed and three wounded. Fifty-nine Australians were captured "including a colonel and a captain".

When the Indian carriers attacked the French and their prisoners, several were killed including Sergeant Comte who had played a leading part throughout. After the attack there were, in the French force, only seven Europeans and twenty-two natives left unwounded. "From 8 a.m. onwards" British guns bombarded Weygand and at 11 a.m. Goybet also. About midday Goybet was taken and at 1.30 Australians entered Weygand where they captured seventeen Europeans and twenty-two natives.

Although the Australians holding the road-block in the Barada Gorge did not know it at the time, the reason why, after 11 o'clock, no further attempts were made to break through their barrier from the direction of Damascus was that, chiefly as a result of their success, Damascus had fallen.

In the morning of the 21st Colonel Casseau's force on the Kiswe-Damascus road had resumed its advance through the outskirts of the city. Vichy troops continued to fire from the barracks where they had held up the advance the previous evening, until Colonel Casseau ordered a gun forward to bombard it at a range of 1,000 yards. Farther forward his guns, firing from close behind the leading troops, demolished a concrete pill-box from which a damaging fire was coming. Gordon's company of Australian machine-gunners were now on the right near Kadem guarding against a possible counter-attack through the plantations beyond the railway, which was to the east of the road; and the Free French infantry were advancing on the left and in the centre.

About 11 o'clock Casseau, believing that all opposition had ceased, sent two armoured cars forward. They had not gone far before there appeared travelling towards them a procession of motor-cars led by one which was flying a white flag. Casseau and Blackburn drove forward and, after a long discussion in French which Blackburn could only pretend to understand, he and Casseau re-entered their cars and drove into the city, the mayor and his officials leading the way. They proceeded to the Town Hall where Casseau and Blackburn (as the senior British officer present) accepted the formal surrender of the city and the police force. There were polite speeches and then a formal luncheon.

About 4 p.m. a more picturesque procession led by General Legentilhomme entered the city in cars escorted by a detachment of Colonel Collet's Circassian cavalry, and was received by the Syrian Cabinet. On its way this cavalcade was passed by a platoon (Lieutenant Clennett's[6])

---

[6] Maj B. G. Clennett, TX2097; 2/3 MG Bn. Sawmiller; of Hobart; b. Hobart, 3 Nov 1920.

of Gordon's company which had been ordered to find its way through the city and take up a position on the northern side astride the road to Homs.[7]

That afternoon two companies of the 2/3rd Battalion were on the heights above the Barada Gorge and the third company (McGregor's with which the fighting troops of the headquarters company had now been combined to make one weak rifle company) was at the road-block on the Beirut road. Brigadier Lloyd's plan was now to make an immediate advance westwards astride the Beirut road and over the heights whose eastern end the 2/3rd were occupying, but Stevenson asked that his men, who were near the end of their endurance, be given a rest and some hot food, and make the attack next morning. Lloyd, a hard-driving leader whose clear planning and quick decision had quickly won the admiration of the Australians, agreed to this request, and the men had an afternoon and a night of comparative rest, and some hot meals. At 9 o'clock next morning the new attack was launched, Stevenson standing on top of Fort Goybet with a signaller who sent messages to the companies with an improvised flag. On the right a depleted company of Indians, advancing along the heights north of the road, covered that flank while McGregor's moved along the floor of the gorge until, beyond the railway crossing, it came under machine-gun fire. The men crossed the canal at this point using a swing contrived with rifle slings and, to avoid the enemy snipers posted along the gorge, climbed thence to a protected position on the heights on the northern side.

Parbury, in the centre, moved across the heights, losing some men as a result of hot fire from artillery, mortars and machine-guns both from positions forward of him and on the heights north of the gorge[8]—these were also holding up the Indians. At one stage this fire threatened to hold the advance but Private Donoghue,[9] a courageous and expert Bren gunner, worked his way forward and shot the crews of three French machine-guns at a range of 500 yards. From the objective on the heights south of Doummar Copeman led a patrol down the slopes towards that village, where he saw some armoured cars and gained the impression that the enemy, despite his intermittent artillery fire, was withdrawing his rearguard west along the Beirut road.

Hutchison on the left of Parbury, with an Indian second-lieutenant and twenty men on his left flank, had advanced sooner than Parbury and, using a covered approach, had advanced about a mile from Fort Vallier and seized two small pinnacles from which the artillery observer was able to direct effective fire against the French positions, while the infantry used their Brens at long range.

---

[7] "Its [the procession's] dignity was marred unfortunately . . . by the sudden appearance on the road of hordes of Australian vehicles crowded with Diggers all imbued with one ambition: to be first into Damascus. I still do not know where they came from, nor to whom, if anyone, they owed allegiance." Bernard Fergusson, *Blackwood's Magazine*, April 1943. This was almost certainly Clennett's platoon, carrying out its urgent task. Fergusson was a liaison officer at Free French headquarters.

[8] Cpl Lyndon Dadswell, the sculptor, was wounded here.

[9] Lt T. J. Donoghue, MC, MM, NX4957; 2/3 and 2/2 Bns. Electric motor driver; of Captain's Flat, NSW; b. Marrickville, NSW, 4 Jan 1918.

Thus the foothold on the heights was enlarged, but the position of the thin line of perhaps 400 men spread across a front of more than two miles was by no means secure. Throughout the day the French guns shelled Mezze repeatedly, setting fire to the ammunition dump there, and later hitting the 2/3rd's regimental aid post and killing some Indian patients. The shelling of the Kuneitra road was so frequent and so accurate (the French gunners were firing over ground which they knew intimately) that vehicles were compelled to use the roundabout route through Kiswe and, as he was moving from his northern company to his southern companies, Stevenson was wounded in the side by a machine-gun bullet, but carried on. The difficulty of distinguishing friend from foe and the fact that there were not enough troops to thoroughly mop up so wide an area added to the problems of the Allied troops, who included not only Englishmen, Australians and Indians, but Free French of several races and nationalities, wearing a confusing variety of uniforms. On several occasions Australians were (and still are) at a loss to know whether troops seen in their neighbourhood were Indian or Free or Vichy French, and more than once shots were exchanged with troops later believed to be friendly. In the course of the afternoon a skirmish took place on the outskirts of Mezze with two tanks which had been allowed to approach in the belief that they were Free not Vichy French.

It was the loss of the Beirut road rather than the pressure from the south that persuaded Colonel Keime to abandon Damascus. He ordered the establishment of road-blocks at Qatana and Doummar to prevent the advancing force cutting the road behind the French at Merdjayoun. The weary Damascus force of six battalions —*V/1st Moroccan, I* and *III/17th Senegalese, III/24th Colonial* and *I* and *III/29th Algerian*—withdrew westward through the mountains on the 21st and 22nd and concentrated in the area Souq Wadi Barada, Kafr el Aouamid, Houssaniye, Deir Kanoun—that is, round the Barada Gorge north of the Damascus-Beirut road, which emerges from the gorge about five miles west of Damascus. During this movement the eastern part of the Barada Gorge was held by a force of armoured cars and a company of the *24th Colonial Regiment*.

In the afternoon of the 22nd Lloyd and Stevenson surveyed the ground from the elevated Fort Goybet, and Lloyd told the Australian battalion commander that General Evetts' plan was to occupy a defensive line from Doummar, north of the road, along the Jebel Chaoub el Hass, the towering feature two miles in length and rising more than 600 feet above the level of the Barada River. Stevenson pointed out to Lloyd that his battalion consisted of only three depleted companies, 21 officers and 320 men in all, whereupon Lloyd, to lighten the Australians' task, decided that only patrols would be established on the Jebel and these would withdraw to the positions the main part of the battalion then held if the Jebel was attacked by the French. Thus, during the 23rd the line remained where it was, though patrols moved forward beyond Doummar.[1] In the

---

[1] One of these was made by the battalion's Intelligence sergeant, J. S. Mair (of Dulwich Hill, NSW) in a truck driven by Dvr A. E. Mount (of Marrickville, NSW). Mair, having seen tanks in Adsaya, drove along the road, dismounted, and began to "stalk" them with a Bren gun until a tank opened fire and wounded him. Mount carried him out under brisk fire and drove him away in the truck.

afternoon Lloyd informed Stevenson that his battalion was to be transferred to the 16th (British) Brigade, Brigadier Lomax,[2] now taking over the defensive line. (Thus the 2/3rd would replace in the 16th Brigade the 2/King's Own which was still in the Merdjayoun sector.) The brigade had occupied Qatana that day and was advancing northward to the Beirut road. The 2/3rd was to move along the Beirut road—that is to say, across the face of this advance—and join its new brigade about six miles to the west where a branch road travelled south to Yafour. To support him on this advance along a road still, perhaps, held by the enemy, Stevenson was given a battery of field guns, and placed two of them forward to deal with tanks. He asked for a loan of three captured tanks but these were refused; instead he was lent three carriers but was told they were "not to be used in battle".[3] That evening Stevenson learnt that Sabbura had been taken but not Yafour, and realised that his battalion would therefore arrive at the rendezvous before the remainder of the brigade.

The Free French were now deployed covering Damascus on the east and north, while Evetts' "division" (it consisted of little more than two British battalions, one Australian and the few survivors of the 5th Indian Brigade) faced north-west.[4]

At 5 a.m. on the 24th the Australian column had moved off in trucks along the Beirut road. The three carriers led, followed by a "tank-hunting" platoon whose only anti-tank weapons were a .5-inch rifle and a Very light pistol which the commander, Lieutenant Murdoch, carried. The Australians knew that the Leicesters were to advance towards the road from Sabbura, and the Queen's from Yafour and thus both were moving forward at right angles to their own line of advance. As the 2/3rd approached the rendezvous they encountered heavy shell-fire. After having deployed astride the road they came under small arms fire and replied until they discovered that they were exchanging it with the Leicesters.

With the commanding officer of the Leicesters Stevenson agreed that the 2/3rd would help to take eminences which the enemy was holding north of the road, which passes through a defile at this point, and would then move into reserve and remain at the rendezvous to block the road there. The enemy was shelling the road heavily and with accuracy—the heaviest fire that these Australians had encountered in three campaigns. With Parbury's company leading, the 2/3rd advanced astride the road, widely dispersed and moving fast to lessen the risk of casualties. The platoon on the south side of the road reached the hill which was its

---

[2] Maj-Gen C. E. N. Lomax, CB, CBE, DSO, MC. Comd 16 (Brit) Bde 1939-41, 26 Indian Div 1943-45. Regular soldier; b. Birmingham, Eng, 28 Jun 1893.

[3] That evening Wavell was at Lavarack's headquarters. Lavarack pressed once more for tanks. Wavell volunteered the opinion that an infantry-tank battalion would have been a better investment in Syria than in the Western Desert, but none arrived in Syria.

[4] Up to 22 Jun the losses in the bns of the 5 Ind Bde had been:

	Officers	Men
1/Royal Fusiliers	19	578
3/1 Punjab	15	214
4/6 Rajput	19	490

The two Indian bns were then formed into a composite bn.

objective with only one casualty, and then was attacked by two French tanks. The Australians north and south of the road set upon these tanks with a strange collection of weapons. Sergeant Hoysted[5] hit the tanks with smoke bombs from a 2-inch mortar, firing until they were only 10 yards from him. Murdoch fired at and hit the tanks with Very lights. MacDougal, who lay firing an anti-tank rifle, had his pistol and holster shot off by one of the tank's machine-guns. Private Donoghue lay behind a rock and fired at close range with his Bren. Evidently bewildered by this fusillade which, though it was incapable of harming the tanks, was extremely spectacular, the tanks retreated. The intense shelling continued, directed, the Australians decided, by observers from Jebel Mazar, which towered some 1,600 feet above the road about four miles to the south-west, and whence the observers could look down on the guns, men and vehicles below as if from an aircraft. The two British guns were put out of action, all but three men of their crews being killed or wounded, but not before they had dispersed a considerable force of French cavalry which was concentrating on the heights ahead of them.

Meanwhile, as an outcome of operations that will be described in the following chapter, the French had at last, on the night of the 23rd-24th, abandoned Merdjayoun. On the 24th, Lavarack agreed to a proposal by Evetts that he should press on to Zahle, secure the Rayak airfield, and cut off the retreat of the forces north of Merdjayoun—a difficult task which entailed mastering the heights dominating the Damascus-Zahle road.

Early in the afternoon Brigadier Lomax ordered Stevenson to withdraw his battalion to Adsaya except for one company which was to remain with the Leicesters; the Leicesters were to form a flying column which was to thrust along the main road as soon as Jebel Mazar was taken. The task of capturing Jebel Mazar, which Lomax believed unoccupied, was allotted to one company (Hutchison's) of the 2/3rd; the remainder of the battalion was to hold a defensive position. Despite the intensity of the shelling and the long period the battalion had spent under fire the casualties for the day were only ten, a result which the Australians attributed to their dispersion, and their swift movement over any country which offered no cover. Even these casualties, however, were a serious loss to the depleted battalion and Stevenson was compelled again to amalgamate two companies—Hutchison's and McGregor's—which together totalled only five officers and eighty-three men. Thus the battalion now had only two rifle companies instead of four and each of these was far below normal strength. That day, however, when General Lavarack had visited the battalion at Adsaya, Stevenson asked him to allow the company of the 2/3rd which was doing garrison duty in the coastal zone to rejoin the battalion, and Lavarack agreed.

In the evening of the trying advance along the Beirut road, and after only such rest as they were able to get during the truck journey through

---
[5] Sgt A. R. Hoysted, NX9686; 2/3 Bn. Clerk; of Mentone, Vic; b. Wangaratta, Vic, 24 Mar 1917.

Qatana, Hutchison's company debussed at Yafour and set off to scale Jebel Mazar. This spur of Mount Hermon, rising 1,600 feet above the surrounding country, commands a long stretch of the Damascus-Beirut road which skirts its northern edge, and overlooks to the east the relatively flat area round Qatana in which now lay the left flank of the 16th Brigade. As the French were proving, artillery observers on the summit of Mazar could direct fire accurately over most of the area through which the British force was advancing, from guns invisible to the attackers behind the lofty ridge.

Hutchison's company, with an artillery observer and a line party, left Yafour at 8.30 p.m. on the 24th led by a native guide. In the darkness the weary men climbed westwards. By 9.30 the guide had led the Australians to the top of a hill which, he said, was their objective. Hutchison and the artillery officer examined their map by striking matches and shielding the light with a blanket and decided that they were not on the summit. The map was on a scale of four miles to an inch, and thus was not detailed enough to guide troops making a night march up an unfamiliar mountain cut with wadis, but nevertheless Hutchison decided to make a second attempt. When daylight came he found that he was still 600 feet below the summit facing a steep, high bank, and that a number of his men were missing, having become lost in the darkness. He and his sergeant-major, Hoddinott, tried to find a way up the hill but failed, and then for two hours or so the men slept.

About 8 o'clock under a blazing sun the climb was resumed, but soon the leading sections came under fire from machine-guns and a heavy mortar and took cover. At that point, some 500 feet below the summit, the handful of Australians—now only thirty-five strong—built sangars for protection and waited for darkness. The heat was intense (though the snow could be seen on distant Hermon) and one of Hutchison's platoon commanders was overcome by it and collapsed. The men were short of water, which they drew from a creek nearly two-hours' journey away, and extremely weary after a day and a night with little rest or sleep.

Brigadier Lomax learnt nothing of the fate of the attackers until nearly 5 p.m. on the 25th, when it was reported that they were unable to reach the objective because of fatigue and lack of water. Later Stevenson asked for permission to relieve them with a new company—Captain Murchison's, which was fresh, having just arrived from Sidon. It was 110 strong—equal to the other two rifle companies of the battalion put together —and was thus a notable reinforcement. Lomax agreed to the proposal that it should renew the attack and Stevenson ordered Murchison to replace the weary company already on the upper slopes of the Jebel and advance to the summit in its stead.

Guided by the same Syrian who had misled Hutchison, the new company set out in the darkness, were led too far to the left and finally were told by the guide that he did not know where he was. By 5.30 in the morning (the 26th) they had reached the eastern edge of the ridge that runs southwards from the summit and where they expected to find the company they were relieving, but there was no sign of it there. Nevertheless Murchison decided to continue the climb to the summit, which, he had been told, was being used only as an observation post and would not be strongly held. The company set off in single file but, about 9 a.m., while still well below the top, the head of the column was halted by mortar and machine-gun fire from French troops who were among the rocks close ahead of them. The leading platoon, in which several men had been killed, withdrew. Its commander, Lieutenant Maitland,[6] fell and sprained his ankle and, with Corporal Spence[7] and several others who were covering the withdrawal, was taken prisoner.[8]

Soon after this set-back Murchison found Hutchison's company on the far side of the ridge up which he was advancing and, after discussing the situation, they decided that both companies would assemble there, and when it was dark Murchison's company, reinforced by a platoon of Hutchison's—actually the remnants of "B" Company under Lieutenant Brown[9]—would again attack towards the summit.

While the two company commanders were thus planning a third attack on Jebel Mazar, Lomax ordered the withdrawal of all three of his battalions to defensive positions—the Leicesters to the Beirut road, the Queen's to a ridge east of Yafour and the 2/3rd to Col de Yafour, in reserve, but Stevenson persuaded him to allow another attempt to take Jebel Mazar. At 7 p.m., as Murchison's company was preparing to advance over the ridge to join Hutchison, a sentry gave warning that the French were attacking. Their approach had been made stealthily and in a few moments fire was being exchanged at short range and grenades were being thrown. Murchison divided the company into two parts, led one at the enemy himself while his second-in-command, Lieutenant Dennis Williams, led the other. The Australians advanced, firing as they went, and forced the French in the direction of Hutchison, whose Bren gunners caught them unawares at a range of 30 yards. The survivors clambered back the way they had come leaving behind more than 20 dead and wounded and 12 prisoners out of a company of perhaps 100 men.

Murchison then led his company to Hutchison's position and, at 1 a.m. —it was now the 27th June and the first attack had begun on the evening of the 24th—the men began to climb in single file—the only possible formation on such a slope—towards a ridge on the left of Hutchison's position, which had been chosen as the "start-line" of their night attack. They left behind their packs and each man carried only his weapons, haversack, water-bottle and 150 rounds of ammunition. Because, when the sun rose, it would be very hot they wore only shorts and shirts and their steel helmets. As they were approaching this line Murchison who

---

[6] Capt F. J. V. Maitland, NX337; 2/3 Bn and Movt Control. Contractor; of Queanbeyan, NSW; b. Goulburn, NSW, 3 Dec 1914.

[7] Cpl J. H. Spence, NX4903; 2/3 Bn. Commercial artist; of Port Kembla, NSW; b. Cobar, NSW, 8 Dec 1909. (Correct name H. H. A. Nixon.)

[8] Cpl J. A. Begent (of Canberra) was killed here.

[9] Capt C. K. Brown, NX4867; 2/3 Bn. Solicitor; of Wollongong, NSW; b. Los Angeles, Calif, 7 Nov 1909.

was leading suddenly shouted "There they are!" The Australians advancing stealthily up the hill in the darkness were close below a French outpost, several of whose sentries they could see silhouetted against the sky on the two steep-sided knolls above them. The wind which was now whistling strongly had covered the sound of their approach, and Murchison could see the sentries peering forward. Immediately Murchison shouted orders to one of his leading platoons to charge the right hand knoll and the other the left. A fierce mêlée followed in which Brens, rifles and sub-machine-guns were fired, grenades were thrown and bayonets crossed. The French were on the higher ground but the Australians could see them against the sky-line yet could not be clearly seen themselves. One Australian grasped a Frenchman's rifle and pulled him stumbling down the slope. In five minutes Murchison, seeing that the Frenchmen had been overcome, called a halt. More than thirty prisoners were collected and six of the Frenchmen had been killed, several of them with the bayonet. Two Australians had been wounded.[1]

Leaving Lieutenant Gidley King[2] and fifteen men, though he could ill spare them, to take the prisoners back to Hutchison, Murchison led the remainder of his company on. The right wing of his advance now consisted of Brown's remnants of "B" Company which Hutchison had allotted to him—perhaps thirty men—his left of a platoon under Lieutenant Hildebrandt,[3] and his reserve of seven men of company headquarters under Williams. The ground was very broken and so steep that the men had to sling their rifles over their shoulders so that they could use their hands for climbing. Soon Murchison found that Williams' party was missing and then that Hildebrandt's could not be found. He continued the climb with only Brown's platoon. During a ten-minute halt most of the men fell asleep sprawling on the rocks; it was their second night of marching and fighting. About 400 yards from the summit, the noise of their advance still drowned by the howling of the wind, they saw a French machine-gun post against the sky-line. Again taking advantage of the fact that they could see the shadowy outlines of the Frenchmen while the Frenchmen could not see them, they stealthily climbed the hill until they were higher than the guns and then charged down on them from above. One gun was quickly overrun, but the second opened fire when the attackers were still 30 yards away. Murchison advanced towards it firing his pistol until, from his side, Private Melvaine[4] ran forward with his bayonet fixed. As the machine-gunner traversed his gun Melvaine seemed for a moment to be moving forward with tracer bullets flashing first on one side of him and then the other, but when, still unharmed, he was within a yard, the gunner —an African—leaped up and ran. Still under fire from more distant

---

[1] Cpl D. C. Adam (of Wangaratta, Vic) and Pte G. ("Abdul") Andrews (of Redfern, NSW).
[2] Lt G. B. Gidley King, NX12157; 2/3 Bn. Trustee officer; of Mosman, NSW; b. Goonoo Goonoo, NSW, 15 Mar 1912.
[3] Lt C. W. Hildebrandt, NX4883; 2/3 Bn. Draper; of Wollongong, NSW; b. Sydney, 29 Jun 1909. Killed in action 27 Jun 1941.
[4] Pte M. V. C. Melvaine, DCM, NX40814; 2/3 Bn. Prospector; of Uralla, NSW; b. Uralla, 22 Mar 1920.

machine-guns they climbed another 400 yards and there the hill began to level out, and the attackers knew they had reached the crest. There were no casualties during this final stage because the attackers could see the direction of the tracer bullets in the darkness and there were large boulders for cover.

The wind which had been fierce before was now a howling gale. Seeing that the French posts on his objective were only 100 yards ahead Murchison shouted to the thirty or so men who were with him to fix bayonets and charge. The men numbed with fatigue began to stumble forward into the French fire. Murchison cried out to them to yell as they had been taught to do and, with shouts and curses, they began to run forward; as they approached, the startled Frenchmen and Africans took panic and ran.

On the summit Murchison pulled out his Very pistol and fired a light into the sky as a signal of success to the men below. Surprised by this brilliant light some of the fleeing Frenchmen stopped and put up their hands in surrender. Five French dead were found and twenty prisoners were taken. Murchison considered that about 100 more escaped down the slope, and that in its three fights his company had driven a depleted French battalion off Jebel Mazar. It was then 4.30 and dawn was breaking.

The Australians found that Jebel Mazar was capped by two small knolls 200 yards apart. Murchison posted some of his men on one of them and some on the other, and they took up positions in the sangars and shallow connecting trenches the French had abandoned. He was inspecting the area in the half-light when he saw what he thought was a crumpled groundsheet lying on the hillside with a helmet beside it. But the helmet rose and below it appeared the head of a French officer who was sheltering in a small trench. Murchison thrust his pistol towards him.

"Ha!" said the Frenchman. "There are no Germans here."

"What of it?" said Murchison.

"Then why are you fighting?" asked the Frenchman.

"Because I've been told to," replied Murchison, adding after a little hesitation, "because you are collaborating with the Huns." And in this style there was a brisk argument on the rights and wrongs of the campaign. The French officer was the artillery observer who had been directing fire on the British positions below.

As the light increased the Australians were able to appreciate the value of the position they had taken. On the plain below them to the west they could see three French batteries, six tanks, troops moving about and many vehicles. But possession of Jebel Mazar was of small value without an artillery observer to direct the fire of the British guns on these targets, and the observing officer who was to have joined Murchison had not done so. At 7 o'clock this officer arrived. The targets were pointed out to him, but he told Murchison that he had left his wireless set 1,000 yards down the hill at the foot of the final steep slope. Murchison told him to go and get it and he set off down the hill leaving his pistol and an excellent oil compass behind him; but the Australians did not see him again.[5]

During the morning the parties who had lost touch in the night attack began to arrive. First Hildebrandt's platoon reached the summit. Later Williams and King appeared leading a larger party than they had set out with. Advancing in darkness over an unknown and rugged mountain and lacking even a compass Williams and his small party had lost touch. On the way they had encountered a strongly-sited French sangar from which two machine-guns opened fire. They returned to Hutchison's company where they collected some more men and led them forward carrying food and water. Next came an unexpected reinforcement—a Sergeant Mountjoy of the Queen's with seventeen men. Mountjoy, an imperturbable soldier, announced that he had been sent out to clear the ridge that runs north from the summit of Jebel Mazar, a ridge which the Australians, from their point of vantage, now estimated was occupied by perhaps a battalion of French troops and from which a brisk fire was being directed. Murchison told Mountjoy that he could try to capture the ridge if he liked but, if he stayed where he was, he would have a French battalion to the right, one to the left, and six tanks and much artillery forward of him. Mountjoy decided to remain with the Australians.

As soon as the light was clear enough, and before the whole company had arrived on the summit, the French opened a galling fire from positions 1,000 yards to the right and 1,000 yards to the left and, with medium machine-guns and field guns, from the front. During the first prolonged bombardment the French artillery observer who had been captured succeeded in escaping down the hill dodging for cover among the rocks, carrying with him full knowledge of the weakness of the force on the summit. At 7 a.m. the French began advancing up the hill from the Australian right. From then until midday five determined attacks were made by groups of French troops thirty to fifty strong, climbing up the hill using the boulders as cover, but they were not coordinated nor was there effective supporting fire by the artillery. After the first attack the Australians, already anxious lest they should exhaust their ammunition, waited until the attackers were 10 to 20 yards away and then destroyed the attack with a sharp, accurate burst of fire. In one of these attacks Private Atkinson,[6] whose comrade had just been shot through the head beside him, jumped out of his sangar with a bag of grenades and disdaining cover made a single-handed counter-attack on the French and drove them off. Early in the afternoon, however, a considerable number of Frenchmen were holding on among the rocks only 200 to 300 yards

---

[5] The artillery observer had set out from the Queen's with a mule train under Lieutenant F. A. Stanton, who wrote: "The foot of the last ascent . . . was as steep as the side of a house and I had no alternative but to off-load the ammunition and return to Hutchison, from where a runner was dispatched to Murchison by another route to tell him of the ammunition below him. The artillery officer continued on and endeavoured to take mule and wireless with him—an impossible task. Soon afterwards enemy troops advanced up the hill and probably captured ammunition, wireless set and F.O.O."

[6] Cpl C. C. Atkinson, DCM, NX4314; 2/3 Bn. Chef; of Blakehurst, NSW; b. Kogarah, NSW, 21 May 1915.

from the summit and snipers had worked their way into positions from which they could fire across the reverse slope of the hill.

About 2 p.m. a man carrying a white flag appeared on the southern end of the ridge and was conducted to Murchison by Hildebrandt. The envoy was one of the Australians who had been captured with Maitland and he carried a note addressed to Murchison by name and announcing that he was surrounded and if he did not surrender by 5 o'clock, he would be blasted off the hill by artillery and heavy mortars. Murchison scornfully sent the envoy back with a verbal reply: "If you want to get us off come and do it."

Murchison, though a leader of uncommon courage and coolness, was nevertheless impressed by the apparent hopelessness of his situation. He had no artillery observer and could reply to his attackers only with small arms fire from a dwindling supply of ammunition. His ammunition would have been exhausted already had it not been that his men had used three Hotchkiss machine-guns which the French had abandoned, and French rifles and grenades. His only signal gear—a heliograph—had been lost during the night. His men had little food and water. A French regiment was steadily encircling him; to the extent that they were firing across the eastern face of the hill, they had already done so. He had watched an attack on Hutchison's company and seen them driven off the hill far below—too far away for him to be of any help. However, he was not yet completely cut off for during the day runners had carried a few messages up to him and he had sent messages back. One of these increased his problem; it was a message from the brigadier saying "Congratulations. Hold on at all cost."

Soon after 5 p.m. the French tried to carry out their threat to blast the Australians off the summit, but their artillery fire was ineffective, either striking the cliff-like face of the hill below them or over-shooting the ridge and falling far behind. The mortars, on the other hand, lobbed their bombs accurately, soon began to cause casualties and drove the left platoon out of its position. This bombardment was followed by a half-hearted attack by infantry which was dispersed. Murchison could now see that the Queen's, to the east, were withdrawing, and that Hutchison's company, having been driven from its position by a strong French attack across the lower slopes of the Jebel, was no longer in sight. Murchison pondered deeply as to what he should do. He knew his battalion had no reserves with which to counter-attack. He knew also that the French had at least two battalions with ample artillery and mortars, whereas his men had very little water left and an average of only twelve rounds of rifle ammunition a man. On the other hand if he withdrew just as his battalion was preparing to attack that attack must fail; his presence on the summit would give such an enterprise its only hope of success. At length he decided that he would hold on until dark and, if he received no message by that time, and saw no indication that an attack was in progress, he would withdraw. He would climb down the steepest part of the hill, because that would be least likely to be held by the French, and he would count on the noise of the night wind to conceal the sound of his departure.

There were four wounded men, two of whom could not walk.[7] After darkness had fallen and no message had reached them the company began to assemble for the withdrawal. All were stealthily brought in except Hildebrandt and Corporal Wilson[8] and his section who could not be found despite much searching.[9] It had become bitterly cold for men wearing only shirts and shorts when, at 10.30, the survivors, assuming that Hildebrandt and Wilson had withdrawn by another route, set off in single file down the eastern slopes of Jebel Mazar, Williams and Mountjoy leading the way and Murchison bringing up the rear. Two of the wounded men were carried down the steep slopes by men who held them at the knees and armpits. The other wounded men, whose legs were sound, walked. At the last moment firing was heard near by and Private Everett,[1] anxious lest it meant that some of his mates had been left behind, went back to investigate. When he rejoined the company he had a wounded arm but had seen no sign of Australians on the summit. Mountjoy guided the company to his battalion's former position but there was nothing there but some abandoned packs. They marched wearily on to Yafour where they found nobody, and took refuge in two large caves and slept. At daylight—on the 28th—they found a truck belonging to the Queen's and with it drove back a mile or so and picked up one of the wounded who had been left there exhausted. The truck carried out the wounded, while the fit men slept that day and night and marched out at dawn next day, eventually rejoining their battalion.[2]

In the meantime Hutchison's company had been strongly attacked during the afternoon (as Murchison had seen) but, under the cover of a party skilfully led by Sergeant-Major Hoddinott, he had extricated the company and withdrawn it about 800 yards towards the east. About 4 o'clock Stevenson arrived with a party carrying 16,000 rounds of ammunition hoping to send it to Murchison. When he saw that this could not be sent forward across a plain swept by intense and accurate artillery fire he ordered Hutchison to hold fast until 9 p.m. to cover the withdrawal of the Queen's and the artillery and then to retire to Yafour. At the headquarters of the Queen's he asked the commanding officer, Lieut-Colonel Oxley-Boyle,[3] to lend him a company with which to try to hold on, but Oxley-Boyle pointed out that he had already lent a platoon, and Lomax was ordering him to withdraw to a defensive position. Both Stevenson and

---

[7] Lt Brown had been wounded by mortar fire. It was his second wound that day, but was not disabling, and he carried on.
[8] Capt R. Wilson, NX7855; 2/3, 2/15 Bns. Clerk; of Mt Kembla, NSW; b. Mt Kembla, 21 Dec 1919.
[9] Hildebrandt had placed Wilson and a group of men at an observation post and had omitted to inform Murchison what he had done. Hildebrandt himself was killed in the mortar bombardment (though this was not known to Murchison until later) and no one else knew where Wilson's section was. Wilson and his men remained in their post all night and in the morning found the hill-top occupied by the French, who made them their prisoners.
[1] Pte W. H. Everett, NX13572; 2/3 Bn. Sewing machine assembler; of Newtown, NSW; b. Sydney, 12 Nov 1918.
[2] In the action on Jebel Mazar the company lost 5 killed and 8 wounded, and 15 were missing.
[3] Brig R. F. C. Oxley-Boyle, DSO, MC. CO 2/Queen's 1940-42; Comdt ME OCTU 1942-43. Regular soldier; of Camberley, Surrey, Eng; b. Peckham, London, 4 Aug 1896.

Hutchison believed that Murchison's company had been overwhelmed and, even if they had considered there was a chance of saving it, the only force available to make the counter-attack was Parbury's depleted company, little stronger than a platoon, which could not have advanced to the foothills of the Jebel until darkness because of the well-directed artillery fire on the flat country west of Yafour. In the night Hutchison withdrew. Stevenson had ordered trucks to remain at Yafour until 3.30 a.m. because of the possibility, which he considered remote, of the missing company reappearing, but they had gone a few minutes before the survivors from Jebel Mazar arrived.

It had been a disappointing experience for the Australians who were convinced that if they had had an artillery observer in communication with the guns below them they could have not only held the summit but driven the French from the slopes beyond. The report of this action by the 16th British Brigade says: "Unfortunately essential parts of the O.P. wireless set had been lost on the way up and the O.P. was unable to make contact with the battery. Had this support been available there is little doubt that the objective would have been held."[4]

On Evetts' orders the 16th British Brigade had withdrawn out of the Sahl es Sahra, which was commanded by French guns, to a line from Deir Kanoun to Yafour; the remnant of the 5th Indian Brigade was on the Col de Yafour. The attack on Jebel Mazar was not resumed for ten days.

After Murchison's company had taken Jebel Mazar the French counter-attacked with a company of the *1/17th Senegalese*. This failed. At 2 p.m. a company of the *V/1st Moroccan* and a company of the *1/24th Colonial* counter-attacked. The war diary of the Southern Syrian Command says that "at the cost of many casualties and enormous efforts demanded by the nature of the ground these units reached a position 50 metres from the point. Night fell, and the situation remained unchanged owing to the exhaustion of both sides. Hardly any further progress was made with the operation for the recapture of Jebel Mazar during the night because of the uncertainty of our units as to the exact situation, the tiredness of our troops, the nature of the ground, and the cold".

Early in the morning a troop of Moroccan Spahis "although suffering some casualties . . . took seven prisoners". It was not until about 9 a.m. on the 28th that the French, now reinforced, discovered that the main body of the defenders had withdrawn; they reported taking ten more prisoners.

The French reached the conclusion that the force which had taken Jebel Mazar had been a special "storming party". "It is to be noted," stated an Intelligence report

---

[4] The Australian battalion's conduct evoked comment of a kind rarely encountered in military reports. Lomax wrote: "Throughout the operation all ranks 2/3 Aust Inf Bn displayed the very highest courage and determination and their dogged endeavour has very justly called forth the unstinted praise and admiration of all ranks of 16 Inf Bde." Of the earlier action on the heights west of Mezze, Lloyd had written: "The bn acted with the greatest gallantry and dash throughout, the initiative and keenness of the junior leaders being marked. The success . . . in spite of very reduced numbers and fatigue against an enemy in masonry forts, and on ground well known to him was remarkable and worthy of the highest praise."

The 2/3rd Battalion was relieved by two companies of the 1/Royal Fusiliers on the 30th and set off through Kuneitra and Banias for the coast to come under the command of Brigadier Savige of the 17th Brigade and take part in the attack on Damour. In Greece as in Libya the 2/3rd had fought in its own brigade, the 16th. In Crete in May parties from the battalion had formed a company of the "16th Composite Battalion", part of the "6th Composite Brigade". In Syria in June the 2/3rd had fought in the 5th Indian Brigade and the 16th British Brigade; and in July at Damour was to join the 17th Australian Brigade.

on this action, "that British storming parties number on the average about 50 men with well-trained officers and N.C.O's and plentifully supplied with machine-pistols and grenades. Men have been found with rubber-soled shoes."

Meanwhile the column advancing from Iraq had reached a deadlock similar to that at Jebel Mazar. On the 13th June Major-General Clark,[5] commanding Habforce (the 4th Cavalry Brigade and other units including the 1/Essex from Iraq and 350 men of the Arab Legion from Transjordan), had been ordered to move into Syria, occupy Palmyra, and thence advance and cut the road from Damascus to Homs. At that time Habforce was widely scattered at Mosul, Kirkuk, Baghdad and elsewhere, but its relief by the 10th Indian Division was about to begin. By the 17th the main body was concentrated at pumping station H3, some 140 miles south-east of Palmyra, while one regiment assembled at T1 on the branch pipe-line to Tripoli to mislead the enemy into believing that an advance would be made up the Euphrates. On the 18th Generals Wavell and Auchinleck agreed on a plan whereby two additional brigades, drawn from the 10th Indian Division, should advance into Syria from Iraq.

Habforce began its advance on the 21st with the object of capturing Palmyra that day. The main body of the 4th Cavalry Brigade (Brigadier Kingstone)[6] advancing from H3 included the Wiltshire Yeomanry and Warwickshire Yeomanry, each lacking one squadron.[7] South of the ruined city lies a great salt pan reported to be impassable by vehicles. High rocky ridges dominate it on the south-west, north and north-west where

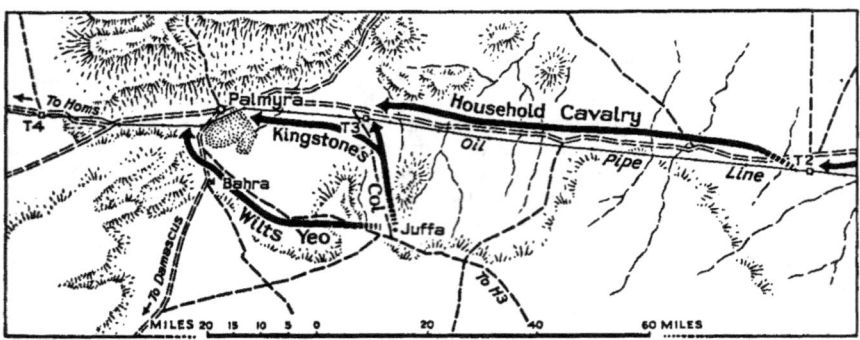

lies an ancient fortress called the "chateau". The garrison was known to consist of two companies of the Foreign Legion and a Light Desert Company. The plan was that the Wiltshire should seize the hills west of Palmyra and the chateau, while the Warwickshire moved east of it by way of T3 on the Iraq-Haifa pipe-line and attacked and entered from the

---

[5] Lt-Gen J. G. W. Clark, CB, MC. GOC 1 Cav Div; Ch Admin Offr Allied Force HQ Medit Theatre. Regular soldier; b. Wargrave, Berks, Eng, 12 May 1892. Died 16 May 1948.

[6] Brig J. J. Kingstone, CBE, DSO, MC. Comd 4 Cav Bde 1940-41. Regular soldier; b. Milton, Wilts, Eng, 26 Aug 1892.

[7] The whole force included also the Household Cavalry Regiment, the 1/Essex, 237 Bty RA (less two troops), one tp 239 Bty RA, detach No. 2 Armoured Car Coy RAF (nine cars) and 350 men of the Arab Legion.

north. The column of cars and trucks crossed the Syrian frontier at dawn. About 25 miles from Palmyra French bombers attacked, and some vehicles of the Warwickshire were hit, but by 1 p.m. the leading squadron was approaching the south-western edge of Palmyra, where machine-gun fire from the plantations checked it. The remainder of Kingstone's force advancing from Juffa, found T3 strongly held and was halted under repeated air attack. During the day Clark with the 1/Essex and the remaining artillery of the force from H3 and the Household Cavalry (Major Gooch[8]) from T1 arrived in the area. At T2, held by a detachment of the Foreign Legion, one of Gooch's squadrons was left to watch the station (whose garrison surrendered that afternoon) while the others advanced under attack by aircraft.

Next day Clark signalled to Jerusalem an urgent request for protection against the persistent attacks by French aircraft; nine Gladiators arrived at H3 later in the day but because there were no facilities for defence of a forward landing ground were withdrawn. The air attacks became heavier on the 23rd and 24th and so many vehicles were hit that supplies ran short.

A force led by Fawzi el Kawakji, the Arab nationalist leader, and reinforced by French armoured cars lay in wait for supply columns near T3, where one troop of the Warwickshire now watched the garrison. Here on the 24th six armoured cars approached the British troop and, when the yeomanry (who claimed that one vehicle was flying a white flag) emerged from their shelters, the cars opened fire and killed or captured twenty-two men. Later in the day a British convoy was waylaid and captured here. In this fight or the earlier one Fawzi el Kawakji was wounded. Brigadier Kingstone collapsed on the 24th his place being taken by Major Gooch.[9]

The attacking force continued doggedly to press forward round Palmyra. On the 28th they were greatly heartened by the spectacle of a bombing attack on the enemy and six French bombers being shot down by the escort of nine Tomahawks of No. 3 Squadron R.A.A.F. The 1/Essex captured the chateau that day, but the defenders of Palmyra itself still resisted strongly. Meanwhile the 10th Indian Division in Iraq, commanded by General Slim,[1] a rugged leader who had commanded a brigade of the 5th Indian Division in Abyssinia, was preparing an advance by two brigades along the Euphrates to Aleppo.

The day after the fall of Damascus, an event occurred which transformed the situation in every theatre of war. On the morning of the 22nd June German armies advanced into Russia. For a time the threat of substantial German intervention in Asia Minor would be remote.

---

[8] Col Sir Robert Gooch, Bt., DSO. Household Cavalry; OC The Life Guards 1943-46. Regular soldier; b. 6 May 1903.

[9] On 29 Jun Brig J. G. E. Tiarks took command.

[1] Field Marshal Sir William Slim, GBE, KCB, DSO, MC. Comd 10 Ind Inf Bde 1939-41; GOC 10 Ind Div 1941-42; Comd XV Indian Corps 1942-43, Fourteenth Army 1943-45; C-in-C Allied Land Forces SE Asia 1945-46; Ch of the Imp Gen Staff 1948-52. Governor-General of Australia since 1953. Regular soldier; of Bristol, Eng; b. 6 Aug 1891.

On the 24th Wavell had sent a summary of the Syrian situation to Dill. He said that the plan then was that Habforce should take or by-pass Palmyra and advance to Homs; the Free French secure the Nebek-Homs road. The 16th British Brigade was to take Rayak, the Australians to clear up the situation at Merdjayoun and advance on Beirut. He reported that another brigade of the 6th Division—the 23rd—was on its way to Syria from Egypt.

CHAPTER 22

MORE ATTACKS ROUND MERDJAYOUN

IN the Merdjayoun sector the invading column had advanced only a few miles beyond the frontier. After the failure on the 17th Brigadier Berryman walked through the country over which the 2/25th had made its abortive attack and arranged an artillery fire plan and fixed objectives for a second similar effort which he decided should be made on the 19th. He divided his position south of Merdjayoun into three sections: the right, on the foothills of Hermon, was manned by the 2/33rd (now commanded by Lieut-Colonel Corby[1]); the centre by the 6th Cavalry (under Major Onslow); the left, facing Merdjayoun itself, by the 2/2nd Pioneers, the Greys, and a company of the 2/5th Battalion (all under Lieut-Colonel Wellington). Each sector commander had a share of anti-tank guns.

Again the 2/25th Battalion, on the far left flank of these units, was to attack from the southern edge of the Litani gorge, its final objectives being, on the left, the cemetery, and on the right, a group of houses north of the fort. The Pioneers were to "demonstrate" from the south in order to distract the enemy's attention, and were to get in touch with the 2/25th and be ready to help it exploit its gains.

The Australian guns opened fire on the Merdjayoun fort (to delude the enemy) at 4.20, and after ten minutes were switched to the first objectives of the attacking infantry who were awaiting the order to move. Shells from the French guns, which quickly retaliated, burst among the Australians and wounded five men in Captain Marson's[2] company, which led the advance on the right; at 5 o'clock, when the infantry were due to advance, shells were still falling close to Marson's men and the companies did not move until 5.20.

The company on the left cleared a copse in which the French were strongly established and advanced into the town, breaking up into small groups to clear houses from which Frenchmen were firing. It was led by Lieutenant Stringer[3] until he was seriously wounded. In a sharp fight in the cemetery Lieutenant Barnett[4] and two of the five men with him were wounded. Lieutenant Hurford[5] was killed leading his men on.

On the right Marson's company fought its way forward. Lieutenant White's[6] platoon captured a blockhouse and about thirty prisoners; another

---

[1] Lt-Col J. A. Corby, VX14050. CO 2/33 Bn 1941-42, 34 Bn 1943, 41/2 Bn 1943-44. Bank manager; of South Yarra, Vic; b. South Yarra, 28 Dec 1898.

[2] Lt-Col R. H. Marson, DSO, QX6378; CO 2/25 Bn 1942-45. Dairy farmer; of Toogoolawah, Qld; b. Wiltshire, Eng, 21 Jun 1904.

[3] Lt J. R. Stringer, QX6371; 2/25 Bn. Manufacturers' agent; of New Farm, Qld; b. Wellington, NZ, 18 Sep 1909. Died of wounds 22 Jun 1941.

[4] Maj A. Barnett, MC, QX4914; 2/25 Bn. Insurance clerk; of Lismore, NSW; b. Taree, NSW, 18 Mar 1919.

[5] Lt W. C. Hurford, QX6353; 2/25 Bn. Grazier; of Brisbane; b. Toowoomba, Qld, 16 Feb 1912. Killed in action 19 Jun 1941.

[6] Lt A. E. D. White, QX6372; 2/25 Bn. Grazier and farmer; of Mt Berryman, Qld; b. Brisbane, 26 Feb 1909.

platoon commander, Lieutenant Jefferson,[7] and a number of his men were killed. There was scattered fighting among the houses. Then French tanks and armoured cars appeared in the streets. Against these there was no defence, and small parties of Australians were rounded up and captured. Four tanks moved on to the cemetery where Barnett's men were holding out. Captain Blundell,[8] Marson's second-in-command, hastened back to ask that another company be sent forward to assist, spoke eventually to his commanding officer, Lieut-Colonel Withy[9], by telephone and was allowed to lead into the fight two platoons that were in reserve. These reinforcements, under Lieutenants Crombie[1] and Miles,[2] drove off the tanks, and not only released most of Marson's men but captured several of the enemy and formed a strong position from which patrols were sent forward to help the scattered parties.

Meanwhile the artillery observers' line had been cut by shell-fire and the artillery team—Captain Clark,[3] Lieutenant Cutler[4] and Gunners Grayson[5] and Buckingham[6] (of the 2/5th Field Regiment)—and a few infantrymen who were with it were attacked by two of the tanks, which were followed by about fifteen French infantrymen. Cutler and Lance-Corporal Pratt[7] each opened fire on the tracks of the tanks with anti-tank rifles and saw their bullets hitting, but with no effect except to cause the tanks to lurch and seek shelter. Thereupon Cutler and Pratt exchanged their anti-tank rifles for a rifle and Bren gun and fired on the enemy infantry, who took cover behind a stone wall and replied. The tanks advanced again and opened fire with their turret guns. The second shot killed Pratt, fatally wounded Clark, and wounded Grayson. Cutler took up an anti-tank rifle and hit the tanks' turrets, but without effect. Then he fired and hit their tracks, whereupon tanks and infantry withdrew to shelter. Covered by the fire of their own infantry, the surviving Australians withdrew, carrying Clark, who was still alive.

Cutler was convinced that the enemy were unsure of themselves and that it would be wise to press on into the town where the attackers could find shelter from the tanks; Marson agreed. Cutler set up an observation post among rocks at the north-west corner of the town and was about to

---

[7] Lt M. F. Jefferson, QX6335; 2/25 Bn. Bank clerk; of Annerley, Qld; b. Dalby, Qld, 8 Feb 1912. Killed in action 19 Jun 1941.

[8] Capt P. L. Blundell, QX6368; 2/25 Bn. Grazier; of Stanthorpe, Qld; b. Brisbane, 13 Feb 1909.

[9] Lt-Col C. B. Withy, DSO, MC, QX6291. (1st AIF: Capt 1 Bn.) CO 2/25 Bn 1940-42. Coy manager; of Ascot, Qld; b. St Leonards, NSW, 30 Jan 1893.

[1] Capt W. M. Crombie, QX6414; 2/25 Bn. Station overseer; of Longreach, Qld; b. Brisbane, 12 Mar 1914.

[2] Capt W. N. Miles, QX6340; 2/25 Bn. Salesman; of Toowoomba, Qld; b. Toowoomba, 9 Jan 1916.

[3] Capt C. A. Clark, NX407; 2/5 Fd Regt. Master tailor; of Strathfield, NSW; b. Paddington, NSW, 15 Dec 1912. Died of wounds 19 Jun 1941.

[4] Lt A. R. Cutler, VC, NX12378; 2/5 Fd Regt. Australian High Commissioner in NZ 1946-52, in Ceylon since 1952. Public servant; of Manly, NSW; b. Manly, 24 May 1916. (For his gallantry here and later at Damour Cutler was awarded the Victoria Cross—the only Australian artilleryman in this or the previous war to have been so honoured.)

[5] L-Sgt G. N. Grayson, MM, NX24778; 2/5 Fd Regt. Clerk; of Bondi, NSW; b. Silverstream, NZ, 5 Mar 1907.

[6] Gnr B. Buckingham, NX24434; 2/5 Fd Regt. Of Manly, NSW; b. Grafton, NSW, 26 Mar 1909.

[7] L-Cpl V. G. Pratt, QX13849; 2/25 Bn. Farm hand; of Kilcoy, Qld; b. Kilcoy, 1 Jan 1919. Killed in action 19 Jun 1941.

order his guns to open fire when he saw Australians ahead at a house on "Castle Hill" and a patrol advancing towards enemy machine-gun positions some distance away. In reply to shouts the men at this house called that they were White's platoon, which had moved into this tank-proof country with their prisoners earlier in the morning, and that the patrol was from the 2/2nd Pioneer Battalion. This was encouraging news.

The Pioneers were, in fact, only a small party led by two veterans—Major Lang,[8] the second-in-command of the battalion (who had been a notable infantry subaltern in the previous war), and Captain Camm[9] (an air force observer in that war). When he received his order to make a feint from the south, Lang, mindful of the failure of the attack on the 17th, decided to concentrate on a patrol round the flank in the direction of the 2/25th's advance. The two officers, with about twenty men, later reinforced by a platoon, had made their way forward under cover of rocks and grass until they were only 300 yards from the fort, and could shout to the Queenslanders on Castle Hill. Thence they crept forward, came up to a French machine-gun post from the rear and captured it, and moving north of the fort captured a mortar and its crew. The mortar was fired by Private Robertson[1] who had been a mortarman in the militia. During a "sniping match" between Lang's party, using their own weapons and the captured mortar, and French troops in other houses, Lang was wounded. He was reputed to weigh 20 stone, and was carried out on a ladder by some of the prisoners whom White's men had captured. Later in the afternoon when French tanks appeared the Pioneers withdrew.

Some of the survivors of the attacking companies had moved back into Lang's area, some to a company which, from the outset, had been in a defensive position on the extreme left flank. By early afternoon the situation was stable and, if there had been any reinforcements, they might have attacked with success, but nearly all the fighting troops had been committed; and not long afterwards French reinforcements were seen advancing from Debbine.

About 4.30 p.m. Marson and Cutler led a patrol into the north edge of the town. They encountered only desultory machine-gun fire, and Marson returned and led another patrol in from a new direction, but it was stopped by sharp fire. About 7.30 two French tanks and a squad of infantrymen moved out of the town and set up posts between Cutler (who had scouted forward with Lance-Corporal Williams[2] of the 2/25th) and the remainder of his party. Cutler and Williams lay low until dark. Cutler then collected

---

[8] Lt-Col J. T. Lang, OBE, MC, QX6067. (1st AIF: Capt 53 Bn and Indian Army.) CO 2/2 Pnr Bn 1942-43; Comd Buna Base Sub Area 1943-44. Mechanical and electrical engineer; of Brisbane; b. Dunedin, NZ, 15 Sep 1896.

[9] Capt R. A. Camm, VX16147. (1st AIF: Pte 3 LH Regt; Lt No. 1 Sqn AFC.) 2/2 Pnr Bn. Poultry farmer; of Scottsdale, Tas and Kilmore, Vic; b. Zeehan, Tas, 29 Jan 1893. Killed in action 27 Jun 1941. (Camm's son, Pte R. Camm, was also a member of this battalion. He was lost at sea while a prisoner of the Japanese in September 1944.)

[1] Cpl H. S. Robertson, VX29954; 2/2 Pnr Bn. Commercial traveller; of West Brunswick, Vic; b. Toorak, Vic, 13 Jul 1921. Died 12 Sep 1944.

[2] Cpl J. Williams, QX10388; 2/25 Bn. Bread carter; of Toowoomba, Qld; b. Owestry, Eng, 31 Aug 1903.

the others of his party and led them through the enemy's lines to the 2/25th Battalion.

Also at 4.30 Berryman issued an order that during the night two platoons of the 2/2nd Pioneer Battalion were to "hunt down and put out of action enemy tanks and occupy Merdjayoun fort"; the 2/25th were to "locate and put out of action tanks found in their immediate vicinity", and, after the Pioneers had taken the fort, were to secure the town. To achieve this, forty sticky bombs were to be available to the Pioneers and twenty to the 2/25th. Berryman had decided that there were only five tanks at Merdjayoun and once they were destroyed the fight would be won. This order could not be carried out; sticky bombs could not be delivered to the 2/25th in the time available.

The companies of the 2/25th were now so scattered that, at nightfall, it was decided to withdraw to the western edge of the plateau. At dusk, when a platoon was digging in at the copse near Merdjayoun, the enemy attacked with a tank and machine-guns, the Australians were thrust back, and the telephone line which went through the copse to the leading companies was broken. They were out of touch until Lieutenants Robertson[3] and Dodd[4] with a corporal found a new way of approach. The survivors of the leading companies hung on to a perimeter position; within it the men not on guard collapsed in a sleep of exhaustion. Later the battalion was ordered to withdraw to the Litani. It had lost about 25 killed and 60 wounded. After the action 73 men were missing (including some later found to have been killed or wounded).

The attack had come close to success. The main causes of its failure appear to have been the numbing weariness of the attacking infantry, who had had little rest since their ordeal on the 17th and 18th; and the aggressive spirit of the defenders—particularly the Foreign Legion—who grasped every opportunity of regaining the initiative, and of the French tanks which had split up the leading company at a critical moment and against which the infantry had no effective weapon. Berryman, however, decided to make a third attack from a new direction.

The French in the Merdjayoun area were dependent on traffic along either Route "A" or Route "B", and because Route "B" was now under fire from the guns south of Jezzine, and the enemy had evidently ceased using it, Berryman now turned his mind to this right flank position. He decided to occupy the high ground round Ibeles Saki whence his guns could command also Route "A". Round Ibeles Saki the rock-strewn hillsides might protect his infantry from the tanks which had defeated them at Merdjayoun. On the 22nd June Generals Lavarack and Allen examined the ground and approved Berryman's plan.

---

[3] Maj A. C. Robertson, QX6352; 2/25 Bn. Share broker; of Toowoomba, Qld; b. Toowoomba, 5 Nov 1912. (Son of Brig-Gen J. C. Robertson who commanded the 9 Bn at Anzac and the 12 Bde in France in the previous war.)

[4] Maj R. W. P. Dodd, QX6337; 2/25 Bn. Theatre manager; of Toowoomba, Qld; b. Kerang, Vic, 17 Mar 1913.

On this flank the 2/33rd had been patrolling and had discovered not only that the impetus of the enemy's drive had been exhausted but that he was abandoning some of his gains. On the night of the 20th a patrol found that Fort Khiam was unoccupied, and on the night of the 21st that the French had abandoned Khiam village and Bmeriq.

On the eve of the planned attack on Ibeles Saki, Berryman ordered that a troop of horsed cavalry be formed by the 6th Cavalry to patrol the rugged hills of the Anti-Lebanon and protect his right. It will be recalled that, on the 16th, Captain Bennett's roving company of the 2/33rd had captured thirty-two good cavalry horses at Rachaya. In the ranks of the 6th Cavalry were many countrymen and some who had served at home in light horse regiments of the militia. From such men was formed a cavalry troop, at first of eighteen men but in a few days increased to forty, when saddles and packs arrived from Palestine; its unofficial title was the "Kelly Gang". On the night of the 22nd, a few hours after the horses had been taken over, Lieutenant Burt (a dairy farmer in civil life) led the force to Bmeriq and patrolled the area beyond; and, in the following days, the cavalrymen, then under Lieutenant Millard, rode through the country bounded by Bmeriq, Kafr Hammam, Kafr Chebaa and Mazraat Islamiye in the tangled mountains overlooking the Merdjayoun valley from the east.

The 2/King's Own had now been transferred from the 21st Brigade to Berryman's command; on the 22nd the 2/25th was transferred to divisional reserve and moved into a bivouac area at Kafr Roummane on the Merdjayoun-Sidon road. Berryman's plan for the new attack, on the 23rd, was that a company of the 2/33rd should capture the ridge just north of Khiam, then a company of the King's Own should capture "the Pimple"—the ridge between Khiam and Merdjayoun—after which two companies of that battalion were to capture Ibeles Saki itself. The artillery and the Pioneer battalion were to give the impression that the attack was aimed not at Ibeles Saki but Merdjayoun.

At 4.30 a.m. Buttrose's company of the 2/33rd Battalion, now only about 75 strong, attacked, the artillery and a platoon of machine-gunners giving effective support. The infantrymen stormed the hill, where evidently two companies of Algerians were firmly dug in and had an abundance of heavy weapons. There was hand-to-hand fighting; grenades were thrown and thrown back again, and bayonets were crossed. Sergeant Henderson[5] took a 37-mm gun, turned it against the enemy and fired it until he was shot through the head. In addition five heavy and nine or ten light machine-guns and three mortars were overrun.

About an hour later, when Buttrose's company had taken this feature, the Algerians counter-attacked but were driven off. In the afternoon and evening they attacked thrice more, once pushing right among the Australian positions so that grenades and bayonets were used again. The Australians lost eight men in the afternoon, and the company had little more than the strength of a platoon left. They held forty prisoners on the

---

[5] L-Sgt N. F. Henderson, NX8038; 2/33 Bn. Grazier; of Mungindi, NSW; b. Sydney, 6 Aug 1906. Killed in action 23 Jun 1941.

hill. It was impossible to take them back because the track was swept by machine-gun fire from Ibeles Saki; the prisoners were held on the rear slope where all were killed by French mortar fire. Throughout the action the enemy's artillery fire was fierce and accurate.

The attack on "the Pimple" was less successful. After coming under fire from the top of that hill, the King's Own established themselves about half way up the slope. Finally the commanding officer was instructed by Berryman to hold his positions with two of his companies and withdraw the other two with the object of renewing the attack next morning, Berryman being convinced that if the whole battalion was committed without a new fire plan there would be many more casualties but little hope of success. In the evening, on Berryman's instructions, Major Rickard and Lieutenant Cutler took a field gun forward and at dawn on the 24th Cutler placed it in position in front of the infantry on the left of the Pimple to fire on the French posts at point-blank range.

That morning at 4.30 a.m. the King's Own attacked again. Just before zero French mortar bombs fell among the rear companies. The riflemen, though regulars, were inexperienced in battle, and when the mortar bombs fell, believed their own artillery fire was falling short, and in the resultant delay failed to follow the barrage closely.[6] However, probably as a result of the artillery fire, the enemy offered little opposition. He appeared to have withdrawn most of his troops during the night in some haste, abandoning guns and mortars. By 9.40 a.m. patrols from the King's Own and the 2/33rd had entered Ibeles Saki.

Meanwhile, on the early morning of this attack, a patrol of the 2/2nd Pioneers, under Corporal Dunn,[7] which had been on the edge of Merdjayoun, had reported much noise near the fort. Informed of this his platoon commander, Lieutenant Tilney,[8] took his men forward and opened fire; there was no reply. Consequently Colonel Wellington ordered his two leading companies to advance under cover of a smoke screen laid down by the artillery. The Pioneers moved through the town without meeting any resistance. Many dead French troops were lying on the ground, and the Pioneers who had been killed in the attack on the 17th were found and buried. The only living enemy troops in the town were two wounded men of the Foreign Legion, one French and one Irish. The town was in chaos. Artillery fire had done much damage, but the French troops had done more. Verandah posts had been knocked down (by tanks, the Syrian inhabitants declared), goods in the shops had been smashed with axes and hammers.

Also on 24th June, Bennett, whose company was still being allotted the lonely tasks on the right flank, was ordered to take Kheibe. A platoon

---

[6] Cutler and later Rickard (probably the most experienced soldier in the vicinity) identified the fire as being from enemy mortars, and Cutler was sent to the King's Own to explain this to them.

[7] Cpl B. Dunn, VX23247; 2/2 Pnr Bn. Timber worker; of Albert Park, Vic; b. Burnie, Tas, 18 Jul 1913.

[8] Capt W. W. Tilney, MBE, QX4548; 2/2 Pnr Bn. Farmer; of Ipswich and Maleny, Qld; b. Brisbane, 22 Aug 1911.

entered the village without firing a shot, but was mortared and machine-gunned from a spur to the north-west. Thus, at the end of the day, the 2/33rd Battalion held Bmeriq, Kheibe, Ibeles Saki, Khiam Fort; the 2/King's Own held the Pimple; the 2/2nd Pioneers had companies in Merdjayoun and companies forward on the ridge north-east of the town; the Greys had a detachment near Bourqouz, a detachment at the Litani River bridge and the rest of the unit with the 2/2nd Pioneers; the 6th Cavalry were covering the roads and the valley between the Pimple and Merdjayoun.

Since the 17th Berryforce had now made four attacks; two of them had been carried out since General Lavarack had allotted General Allen a defensive role while the main weight was put into the Damascus operations. On the other hand possession of Merdjayoun was desirable as a defensive measure; and support for the aggressive policy Berryforce had followed was given by both Lavarack and Allen; and, on the 23rd while the Ibeles Saki attack was in progress, by Wavell. Wavell held a conference at Berryman's headquarters attended by Lavarack and Allen, and suggested that the offensive should be resumed "wherever possible"—a suggestion which, the diarist of the 7th Division reflected, "rather conflicted with the role which had been allotted to the division by I Aust Corps".[9]

The enemy now had his right on Col's Ridge, which dominated Routes "A" and "B", and his left on Hasbaya to protect his line of communication against a possible incursion through the Anti-Lebanon, where at first Australian infantry and now Australian horsed cavalry patrols had been active since the first day of the campaign. After a reconnaissance Berryman decided to test the enemy's strength by attacking Col's Ridge with a company of the Pioneers. Colonel Wellington gave this task to Captain Camm's company which was then established on the Balate Ridge to the west.

It was decided to attack from the north, thus striking the enemy's right flank and rolling it up. The Pioneer company moved forward from Balate at 2 a.m. on the 27th and were guided forward to the creek at the foot of the ridge.[1] At 4.5 a.m. artillery fire descended on the top of the ridge, then dropped to form a creeping barrage lifting 50 yards at a time which would lead the infantry to their objective. Camm's three platoons were lined up on a front of about 850 yards, Lieutenant Hamilton's[2] on the right, Angus'[3] in the centre and Houston's[4] on the left.[5] Bayonets fixed,

---

[9] At this conference Allen pressed upon Wavell the urgent need for more mortar ammunition.
[1] Lt-Col Wellington was wounded on the 26th while reconnoitring and Lt-Col Monaghan took command of the battalion late that afternoon.
[2] Maj H. M. Hamilton, VX15146. 2/2 Pnr Bn 1940-42; 20 Bde 1942-44. Bank officer; of South Melbourne; b. Wonthaggi, Vic, 17 Mar 1918.
[3] Lt J. A. Angus, VX14689; 2/2 Pnr Bn. Regular soldier; of East Malvern, Vic; b. Melbourne, 7 Sep 1915. Killed in action 27 Jun 1941.
[4] Lt R. G. Houston, VX15543; 2/2 Pnr Bn. Regular soldier; of Melbourne; b. Quorn, SA, 11 May 1907.
[5] The Pioneers were still not armed as heavily as infantry. For example, one platoon (of four sections) had a Bren in one section, a sub-machine-gun in another, a captured French light automatic in a third and only rifles in the fourth.

they advanced up the hill, apparently without being observed, until they were about 300 yards from the first objective—the saddle north of Col's Knoll. The advancing men met machine-gun and mortar fire, the machine-gun fire at first passing well over their heads. Then men began to fall, but a final rush carried the company on to the knoll.

Hamilton's platoon reached the objective at first light without casualties. It took two prisoners and killed a third Frenchman. Hamilton decided that he had met only outpost positions and the French strength was farther on. He was consolidating on top of the ridge, rather than on the reverse slope where the rocks allowed only a small field of fire, when he saw large parties of the enemy in front and on his left. A mortar fired on his right, causing two or three casualties. Private Pugh[6] stalked forward, shot the crew with a Thompson gun, threw parts of the mortar away and returned. On the top of the hill Hamilton went forward until he could see the French artillery "a mile away in a copse across a creek". His equipment was hit by bullets. He and some of his men fired at Frenchmen on the forward slope.

The French fire intensified and, as soon as the supporting artillery fire ceased, their infantry began to press forward covered by mortar and machine-gun fire. Camm, Lieutenant Angus and a number of others were killed, and Captain Nason,[7] who was with Hamilton's platoon, took command. Then Hamilton was hit through both legs. A corporal, Hann,[8] went forward to him and offered to carry him out but Hamilton ordered him to lead the platoon back; a strong counter-attack was developing from the left, ammunition was running short, and there was no means of bringing more forward. The survivors, only about twelve men, disappeared down the slope under sharp fire, escorting their two prisoners and leaving a group of five wounded men who lay and watched groups of men of the Foreign Legion picking up abandoned rifles and ammunition as they advanced. Lieut-Colonel Monaghan, realising that the attack had failed, called down defensive fire by the artillery. Thereupon Sergeant Warburton[9] led out the survivors of Angus' platoon, and Lieutenant Houston, seeing the others withdrawing, also moved back to the start-line, where the sergeant-major, Topfer,[1] had collected all the men he could, including wounded, to form a defensive line.

The ridge, which was the main French position, had been held by two French battalions which had withdrawn over the hill during the barrage, and, when it ceased, had advanced again. Of the company which went into the attack twenty-seven were killed, more than thirty were

---

[6] Pte H. B. A. Pugh, VX22587; 2/2 Pnr Bn. Bank teller; of Castlemaine, Vic; b. Dimboola, Vic, 20 Sep 1906.

[7] Capt C. H. T. Nason, MBE, MC, VX16136; 2/2 Pnr Bn. Grazier; of Wangaratta, Vic; b. Wangaratta, 18 Oct 1905.

[8] L-Sgt J. E. Hann, VX14976; 2/2, 2/3 Pnr Bns. Sawyer; of Ringwood, Vic; b. Ringwood, 24 May 1913.

[9] Sgt C. H. Warburton, MM, VX16232. (1st AIF: Cpl 3 Pnr Bn.) 2/2 Pnr Bn. Clerk; of Caulfield, Vic; b. Caulfield, 7 Aug 1896.

[1] Lt G. H. G. Topfer, VX14692; 2/2 Pnr Bn. Bank clerk; of Glen Iris, Vic; b. Lismore, NSW, 24 Aug 1914.

wounded, and others were taken prisoner. After dark Staff-Sergeant Peeler[2] (who had been awarded the Victoria Cross in 1917) led out a patrol which brought in four wounded men, but, after much searching, failed to find Camm's body.

On the night of the 27th-28th June and the following day the 2/King's Own relieved the forward companies of 2/33rd Battalion, which was placed in reserve. The Australian battalion had been fighting continuously for three weeks. Its strongest rifle company now had a strength of only 3 officers and 63 other ranks, its weakest 5 officers and 51 other ranks.

During the attacks at Merdjayoun the enemy force there was increased until, by the 21st, it included five battalions: *III/6th Foreign Legion, II/16th Tunisian, I* and *II/22nd Algerian,* and *II/29th Algerian.*

In the evening of 29th June Berryforce ceased to exist. Brigadier Galloway, the commander of the 23rd British Brigade (the same who had been General Wilson's chief of staff in Greece), took control of the troops in the area, and Brigadier Berryman returned to the command of the artillery of the 7th Division.[3] In the course of the next few days units of the 23rd British Brigade relieved most of the Australian units in the Merdjayoun area.[4]

The Australians who fought the long and often costly battle round Merdjayoun had held the pass which, if given to the enemy, would have let him into Palestine with disastrous consequences. They had also attracted to that sector a substantial part of the defending army and thus, to an extent, had eased the struggle in other sectors.

---

[2] S-Sgt Walter Peeler, VC, VX8345. (1st AIF: 3 Pnr Bn.) 2/2 Pnr Bn. Officer, Shrine of Remembrance, Melbourne; b. Castlemaine, Vic, 9 Aug 1887.

[3] The 2/9 Aust Fd Regt was included in the 23 Bde Gp.

[4] The casualties in the Australian battalions of Berryforce from 16 to 29 June, not including prisoners (who totalled 209), were:

	Officers	Men
2/25 Battalion	4	94
2/33 Battalion	2	61
2/2 Pioneer Battalion	14	125

CHAPTER 23
HARD FIGHTING AT JEZZINE

IN the long fortnight between the launching of the French counter-attack and the relief of the Australians at Merdjayoun the struggle for the heights commanding the road leading north from Jezzine had gone on. The French attacks on the 17th and 18th June had ended in a stalemate. On the Australian side two depleted and weary companies of the 2/31st were forward astride the French line of advance. One, only sixty-five strong, was on Hill 1377 holding a front of 1,500 yards, and one across the main road to Beit ed Dine and the ravine through which it ran. On the left the Cheshire Yeomanry were protecting Jezzine against a possible enemy advance through the mountains by way of Machmouche. The French, with two companies of the *II/6th Foreign Legion,* one battalion of Senegalese (the *II/17th*) and some African cavalry, held forward posts within rifle shot of the Australian positions, which they shelled and mortared intermittently, and their patrols moved both by day and by night in the rugged area between the Australian positions on Hill 1377 and the town. Through this country it took the Australian ration parties and their mules two hours and a half to reach the store at battalion headquarters and six hours to climb back again. One party, with three mules laden with bully beef and biscuits, had a skirmish with a French patrol and two mules were shot before the French were driven off. Despite such forays, however, the enemy showed no signs of renewing the attack, though his guns continued to shell the Australian area heavily.[1] Indeed, both the Australians and their adversaries were tired out, and, though still enterprising and aggressive, neither had the strength to do more than hold what they had.

It will be recalled that one effect of the French attacks at Jezzine and Merdjayoun had been a decision to reinforce Brigadier Cox's one-battalion brigade at Jezzine with the 2/14th Battalion from the coast. Lieut-Colonel Cannon of the 2/14th received orders late on the 17th to move to Jezzine with his battalion and a tail of supporting detachments.[2] This little force travelled along the precipitous road from Sidon to Jezzine on the 18th and, as it climbed into the mountains, saw for the first time the lie of the land their division was fighting over—the lofty, steep-sided heights of the Lebanon with its pine forests and terraced farm land, the steep descent to the west and now, far below them, the narrow coastal plain from which they had climbed, and the sea at its edge. After travelling either in trucks or on foot for a night and a day, the 2/14th went into position on the right of the 2/31st, on a line through the Wadi Azibibi. The Victorians had not been fully rested since their fighting on the coast, and the night-

---

[1] "Their ammunition supplies must have been inexhaustible," wrote the diarist of the 25 Bde. "It was amazing that their gun crews could stand up to the rate of fire demanded."
[2] These included: one tp, 2/4 Fd Regt, one section of the 170 LAA Bty, one gun of 5 A-Tk Bty, one pl of 2/3 MG Bn.

and-day move, a long march on the following night, and the sudden transference to high altitudes left them utterly worn out.

When describing this night the historian of the 2/14th Battalion wrote of "the perpetual fatigue which weighs down the infantryman between battles" (including as infantry those other soldiers who move and fight on foot).

> In battle (he declared) weariness slips away, but when the main need is over, dragging fatigue, the protest of the body against will-power, begins again. Mental and nervous reaction coupled with physical overstrain take their toll. In addition, many nights' sleep are lost altogether while the remainder are broken by sentry-go and patrolling. Even . . . the engineers . . . who frequently plod with the infantry . . . cannot fully comprehend this aching lassitude. It fills the infanteer's veins with mud and covers his brain with a fog through which he can see only the words "I must keep going". The airman or the sailor when the battle is over has the one his camp stretcher and the other his bunk (and Heaven knows they deserve them!). The infanteer drops in the mud or among the rocks, to be roused an hour or so later by an N.C.O. saying, "Your turn as sentry", or an officer saying, "We've got to go out on a patrol".[3]

The arrival of the 2/14th, however, gave Cox the power to attack again. How should he use it? To thrust through the precipitous country on the left was impossible; to advance along the road, overlooked by the enemy positions on top of the escarpment to the east, would demand tanks and air support; a move through the hills on the west would need pack-animals to carry mortars and machine-guns, and of these he had few. On this flank, however, a 5,000-foot mountain, Kharat, rose above the surrounding ridges and overlooked the escarpment, which in its turn commanded the road. Cox decided to employ part of the new battalion in a flanking attack by night from Kharat across the intervening valley against the French positions on the two main peaks—Hill 1332 and Hill 1284—on top of the escarpment.

Viewed from the south these hills presented a formidable obstacle. From the 2/31st Battalion's area round the Azibibi wadi

> the mountain rose 1,000 feet in a series of cliffs and rocky shelves. The bridle path that led up the face of this feature was steep and winding to the extent that even the peasants' donkeys employed to take supplies and ammunition to companies on Wadi Azibibi were rapidly exhausted. The crest of this mountain was covered by a succession of rocky terraces up to six feet high and had a backbone of rock running from Wadi Azibibi north to the blockhouse on the summit. Loose stones and boulders were strewn everywhere although few of them gave effective cover against mortar fire. Only one or two tracks to the blockhouse existed and as can be imagined these were completely ranged by the enemy.[4]

Two companies of the 2/14th were to assemble on the lower western slopes of Kharat on the night of the 21st-22nd and advance due west across the valley, in which young wheat was growing. The advance was to begin at 4 a.m. and the intention was that, at dawn, the two companies

---
[3] W. B. Russell, *The Second Fourteenth Battalion* (1948), p. 62. In fact on occasions the seaman no less than the soldier suffered lack of sleep. See, for example, Chapter 9, "Crete", of G. Hermon Gill, *The Royal Australian Navy 1939-1942* (in preparation).

[4] Report of 25th Brigade, Syria.

should attack Hill 1284 and that after that attack had succeeded one company should exploit towards 1332. The 2/31st which had a company astride the road and one on Hill 1377 would feign an attack on 1284 from the south.

The information which General Allen received of Brigadier Cox's plan late that night made him fear that there was to be no artillery support, and he cancelled it. Later it was learnt at Allen's headquarters that artillery support had been arranged, and at 10.15 p.m. Cox was informed that the attack might proceed, but it was then too late for the infantry to reach their positions that night and Cox postponed the operation. Later that night he was ordered to report to Allen next morning. He did so and from Allen's headquarters at 3 p.m. the next day—the 22nd—Cox telephoned to Bertram,[5] his brigade major, his final instructions for the attack. The artillery plan provided that the 2/6th Field Regiment would fire for ten minutes on 1284 and then lift to 1332 for twenty minutes, after which fire would again be concentrated on 1284.

That night the two attacking companies of the 2/14th set out through the mountain country for the distant start-line. At 3.50 a.m. the artillery opened fire and carried out its program. When daylight came, and after the night mist cleared, the men of the forward companies of the 2/31st gazed anxiously northwards over the valley towards the two heights the French had held so long. Soon after 5 a.m. their leaders reported to Colonel Porter that they could see no sign of the 2/14th. In fact the march through the fog and the rugged country had been so slow that the attacking companies had not linked at the start-line until long after the artillery fire on 1332 had ceased and the company commanders—Captains Landale[6] and Russell[7]—decided that it would be fatal to attack. Cox ordered that the attack should be renewed on the following day. In the meantime the cold and weary infantrymen—they still wore only the shirts and shorts that had sufficed on the warm coastal plain—assembled to the south of Hill 1377 to await a second night of marching, with an attack to follow.

Meanwhile Captain Robson, commanding the company of the 2/31st south of 1284, had sent out a fighting patrol of six sections to test the enemy's strength on that feature and if possible to push him off. The enemy withdrew and the patrol gained the hill to within 100 yards of the blockhouse. The French, however, had craftily withheld their fire until their enemy had declared his intentions and assembled on the summit; now they opened fire from hitherto concealed posts on the front and flanks, and their artillery was brought down on the southern face of 1284 and on Hill 1199, between it and Jezzine. Finally Robson decided to withdraw along the sheltered edge of the escarpment to the south-west. The with-

---

[5] Lt-Col G. A. Bertram, OBE, NX324. 2/2 Bn 1939-41; BM 25 Inf Bde 1941-42; GSO1 (Ops) Adv LHQ 1943-45. Regular soldier; of Willoughby, NSW; b. Barradipare, India, 12 Dec 1913. Killed in aircraft accident 5 Mar 1945.

[6] Maj W. G. A. Landale, VX14682; 2/14 Bn. Clerk; of Deniliquin, NSW; b. Melbourne, 17 Feb 1914.

[7] Maj W. B. Russell, VX14035; 2/14 Bn. School teacher; of Highett, Vic; b. Creswick, Vic, 3 Mar 1911.

drawal was gallantly covered by Lance-Corporal Ferguson[8] who fought off the enemy with his Bren mounted on a ledge 50 yards from their positions, and Private Murray Groundwater, who ran forward covered by Ferguson's fire, silenced an enemy post with grenades, and having seized a box of grenades, used them to defend the position against the advancing Frenchmen. Robson was wounded by a mortar bomb that afternoon.

By the end of the 22nd June less than nothing had been achieved, because the French had now been enabled to conclude that the Australians were bent on attacking. On the following night at 1 a.m. the two Victorian companies, on the east, again began marching forward to their start-line; this time the infantry were to give the signal for the artillery to open fire. They reached the start-line at 3.50 a.m., ten minutes before zero hour, and at 4 o'clock Landale fired two red Very lights into the sky to inform the artillery that he was ready—and thus perhaps indicated to the French the general direction from which the attack might be expected. Instantly the guns flickered on the southern horizon, and the infantry began scrambling fast down the lower slopes of Kharat. After they had advanced a few hundred yards, the French, who also had been sending flares into the sky and seemed uncertain of the exact direction of the attack, opened fire and men fell wounded. The leading platoons of Russell's company and one platoon of Landale's went on, but the men behind were held back under increasingly heavy fire from mortars and machine-guns. At dawn, however, the leading men of the forward company were at the foot of 1332, but there were only about forty of them—one platoon and part of another (Lieutenant Whittaker,[9] its commander, was killed at this stage). One platoon of Landale's company was moving up 1284 farther to the left.

Meanwhile Lieutenant Kyffin had led two of the remaining platoons forward. They reached to within 300 yards of a flanking platoon under Sergeant Ralph Thompson,[1] who, though wounded, continued to command. Kyffin and others were wounded. These men, exposed to fire from well-sited posts on three sides, fought on until, about an hour after daylight, their ammunition was exhausted. Among them Privates von Bibra[2] and Chris Walker[3] and a stretcher-bearer of Greek descent, Private Vafiopulous,[4] who was critically wounded while attending the fallen men, showed outstanding courage. At last the survivors—eleven in all and most

---

[8] Cpl W. C. Ferguson, MM, VX14585; 2/31 Bn. Labourer; of Mildura, Vic; b. Hopetoun, Vic, 8 Dec 1915.

[9] Lt R. K. Whittaker, VX14162; 2/14 Bn. Asst Shire Secretary; of Mildura, Vic; b. St Peters, SA, 2 Feb 1911. Died of wounds 24 Jun 1941.

[1] Capt R. V. Thompson, VX15269; 2/14, 2/15 Bns. Farmer and grazier; of Moorooduc, Vic; b. Frankston, Vic, 8 Dec 1917.

[2] Pte K. C. von Bibra, VX29109; 2/14 Bn. Journalist; of Harkaway, Vic; b. Launceston, Tas, 13 Dec 1910. Killed in action 24 Jun 1941.

[3] Pte C. M. Walker, VX25853; 2/14 Bn. Journalist; of Dandenong, Vic; b. Dandenong, 26 Mar 1901. Killed in action 24 Jun 1941.

[4] Cpl C. Vafiopulous (changed name by Deed Poll to Vapp), VX42431; 2/14 Bn. Canister maker; of Caulfield, Vic; b. Camberwell, Vic, 17 Feb 1920.

of them wounded—surrendered to the Senegalese, who were close around them.[5]

On the left Lieutenant Christopherson's[6] platoon had advanced fast under fire from well-sited machine-guns and mortars and from riflemen behind the rocks on the base of the steep hill. Low on the slopes of 1284 one man was killed and two wounded, one mortally. Where they fell Lance-Corporal Russell McConnell,[7] who ran back to help them, set up his Bren on low ground overlooked by French machine-gunners and fired back at them. This action drew the enemy's fire towards this lonely figure and away from the others who, led by the resolute Christopherson, were clambering quickly up the terraced hill finding cover among the growing wheat. Soon afterwards McConnell was killed carrying a fatally-wounded sergeant, Dossetor,[8] to cover.

Christopherson was only three terraces from the summit when, about 6.30, Captain Russell, who had accompanied this platoon, saw that the platoon that was to have followed them was not in sight (Landale had held the third platoon of his company on Kharat where it drove off a French patrol which moved on to Kharat from the north early that morning) and that he and his handful of men were isolated. He ordered Christopherson to move his platoon farther round the left flank of 1284 to lessen the effect of flanking fire from 1332. Later he decided that Christopherson's platoon could not continue the assault alone and ordered him to move out along a near-by wadi. In batches the men dashed for the cover of this wadi, and there Christopherson found to his dismay that of the twenty-five he had led into action only thirteen remained, and learnt for the first time that his sergeant was missing and others had been killed or wounded following him up the slope. He went back to discover whether he could see any more of his men but only one came in—a wounded corporal, Blair,[9] with news that another wounded man, Private Dower,[1] lay 50 yards behind. Christopherson took four men back and together they carried Dower to shelter. During the morning the survivors were drawn back southwards in dead ground toward Hill 1377.

Thus the attack across open country against a steep-sided ridge strongly held by a well-prepared enemy force ended in failure.

Meanwhile about 7.15 a.m. a runner had reached Lieut-Colonel Cannon from Russell's company with news that the attack was failing. Cannon

---

[5] The supporting troops on Kharat, about 1,200 yards away, could see the gallant fight of this platoon, and at length discerned figures in khaki shorts and others in grey trousers suddenly mingling and knew that the survivors had been captured. Von Bibra and Walker were killed about this time.

[6] Maj F. A. Christopherson, VX14038; 2/14 Bn. Bank clerk; of Ballarat, Vic; b. Port Augusta, SA, 4 Feb 1915.

[7] L-Cpl R. D. McConnell, VX15730; 2/14 Bn. Laundry spotter; of Windsor, Vic; b. Windsor, 31 Mar 1922. Killed in action 24 Jun 1941.

[8] Sgt O. R. C. Dossetor, VX15789; 2/14 Bn. Newspaper employee; of Sandringham, Vic; b. Brisbane, 2 Apr 1917. Killed in action 24 Jun 1941.

[9] WO2 D. A. Blair, VX15798; 2/14 Bn. Clerk; of South Yarra, Vic; b. South Yarra, 24 Sep 1918.

[1] Pte H. A. Dower, VX21917; 2/14 Bn. Labourer; of Bendigo, Vic; b. California Gully, Bendigo, 4 Apr 1920.

ordered a platoon under Lieutenant O'Day[2] to advance on to 1284 from the south to reinforce the attack. O'Day and his men passed through the left company of the 2/31st, whose forward post was on the lower slopes of the hill, and by 9.30 were climbing them. His instructions were to capture the French position on 1284, the same position which the 2/31st had been unable to hold on the 22nd, though O'Day knew nothing of that. Hill 1284 was in effect a small fortress consisting of machine-gun emplacements surrounded by a 6-foot rock wall enclosing an area 50 yards in diameter, and with a pill-box outside this wall, the whole perched on top of a high, steep hill whose western side was a precipice broken by occasional ledges. There O'Day was to remain, he was told, until the 2/31st reinforced him from the south and he was joined by the attacking companies of his own battalion from the north and west.

It took O'Day's thirty-two men two hours to climb the rocky slope, which was so steep that until they neared the top they were invisible to the French. Near the summit he sent a Bren gunner, Private Smith,[3] and two others to crawl round a narrow ledge leading up the western side of the hill, while he led the remainder on to a ledge 40 feet below the fort. The French were now firing down at them, but they charged forward among the rocks and took the pill-box, which was manned by only two Frenchmen.

The main body of the defenders were now firmly established in their rock-walled fort, with the Australians within a few yards of them on two sides, shooting from behind rocks, some of which were 15 feet high. For an hour the Australians and French (white troops, evidently of the Foreign Legion) fought it out with light machine-guns, rifles and grenades. A party of Frenchmen sallied out moving round a ledge under cover. Corporal Wilson,[4] one of three brothers in this platoon,[5] crept upon them and with grenades killed six men and drove the few survivors back into the fort. Corporal Lochhead[6] and Private Uren[7] moved close enough to the wall to kill the crew of a machine-gun with grenades, but not before Uren had been shot by the machine-gunners at a range of a few yards. After about an hour the Australians had almost exhausted their ammunition. One man whom O'Day sent back for more was wounded on the way; at 11.45 he sent back another. At 12 the French opened fire with a heavy mortar which searched the sheltered places behind the rocks, and at the same time some twenty Frenchmen, each carrying haversacks filled with grenades, ventured out on the right and, moving from rock to rock,

---

[2] Maj G. O. O'Day, VX14097; 2/14 Bn. Costing clerk; of Hawthorn, Vic; b. Brighton, Vic, 8 Aug 1919.
[3] Sgt W. R. D. Smith, VX13452; 2/14 Bn. Farm hand; of Sale, Vic; b. Corringham, Lincolnshire, Eng, 6 Jul 1911.
[4] WO2 W. J. Wilson, VX14612; 2/14 Bn. Tractor driver; of Camberwell, Vic; b. Stawell, Vic, 11 Jun 1912.
[5] Cpl W. J., Ptes C. R. and B. G., sons of Lt-Col B. Wilson, adjutant of 14 Bn, CMF (of Camberwell, Vic). All were wounded this day.
[6] WO2 J. A. Lochhead, VX15468; 2/14 Bn. Fruit grower; of Mildura, Vic; b. Mildura, 8 Sep 1913. Killed in action 29 Nov 1942.
[7] L-Cpl J. W. Uren, VX18015; 2/14 Bn. Insurance agent; of Geelong, Vic; b. Portland, Vic, 17 Jul 1913. Killed in action 24 Jun 1941.

began hurling their bombs. The Australians shot six of these men and the remainder withdrew into the fort; but O'Day's force was being steadily reduced. The well-aimed mortar bombardment against which the rocks gave no protection had wounded four of Corporal Wilson's men, and the remainder had fallen back to the pill-box; men in other sections had been hit, including Privates Avery,[8] who was wounded by a grenade in an affray in which he shot four Frenchmen with his "Tommy gun", and Deeley,[9] who had played an outstanding part in the attack.

Soon after midday O'Day decided that his position was hopeless. One third of his men had been killed or wounded; they had used their last grenade and one of the Brens had been damaged; there was no sign of reinforcements, and another party of enemy grenadiers, about thirty strong, had emerged from the sangar and was moving forward from rock to rock. O'Day first sent one of his sections (Corporal McLennan's[1]) to find the small group of the 2/31st on the lower slopes, but they had gone.[2] Next he sent out Wilson's section, now only four unwounded men, carrying the wounded. The seven men who covered the withdrawal maintained an accurate rifle fire on the French grenadiers, and after five of these had been hit and seen to fall the rest sought cover. Thereupon O'Day decided to withdraw while he could. However, 80 yards from the pill-box the little rearguard found three of their men lying wounded, including Corporal Wilson. Thereafter O'Day, Sergeant Mortimore[3] and Corporal Lochhead kept the enemy at bay, moving back from ledge to ledge down the terraced hill, while the others toiled ahead of them carrying the wounded. They reached the forward posts of the 2/31st Battalion at 2 p.m.

Meanwhile Private Smith and the two men with him were doggedly clinging to their ledge on the western face of the peak. Smith and Private Le Brun,[4] having sent the third man back, held the French off with their Bren until late in the afternoon when, having shot six Frenchmen, they slid down the hillside and clambered back to the 2/31st's position. Of O'Day's thirty-two men eighteen came out unwounded.[5]

If the attack westerly from Kharat had surprised the French and if the Victorians had been able to reach the top of the ridge in darkness it might have succeeded. But the French were well prepared for a blow from that quarter, and their Senegalese troops were on familiar ground and care-

---

[8] Lt A. R. Avery, MM, VX17772; 2/14 Bn. Nurseryman; of Prahran, Vic; b. Armadale, Vic, 7 Apr 1917.

[9] Cpl L. D. Deeley, MM, VX23597; 2/14 Bn. Moulder; of Melbourne; b. Clifton Hill, Vic, 24 Oct 1921. Killed in action 30 Aug 1942.

[1] Sgt T. A. L. McLennan, VX15497. 2/14 and 24 Bns. Labourer; of Heidelberg, Vic; b. Sea Lake, Vic, 21 Nov 1918. Killed in action 24 Jan 1944.

[2] In this section of only five men two had been killed and one wounded by French mortar fire.

[3] Lt H. E. Mortimore, VX16042. 2/14 and 39 Bns. Bread carter; of Red Cliffs, Vic; b. Warburton, Vic, 10 May 1914.

[4] Sgt K. W. Le Brun, VX14745; 2/14 Bn. Labourer; of Coburg, Vic; b. Brunswick, Vic, 29 Mar 1912.

[5] The sangar on 1284 was then held by a company of the *II/6th Foreign Legion*. When the 2/31st finally occupied the hill they found 21 graves and 15 dead bodies.

fully deployed; that so many survived out of fewer than 100 Victorians who reached the upper slopes facing Kharat was evidence only of the skill of the individual infantrymen in taking advantage of the cover offered by terraced hillsides and rock-strewn crests. General Allen had been anxious lest Cox should plan an attack with inadequate artillery support, yet the company officers who led the assaulting troops were convinced that artillery fire was not effective against good defenders on those steep, rock-strewn peaks; mortars, which could be used at short range and could search behind the rocks and below the terrace walls, were more useful weapons, and it was chiefly the French mortars, which seemed to possess inexhaustible supplies of bombs, that had defeated both recent efforts to hold a position on Hill 1284.

Brigadier Plant arrived at Jezzine on the afternoon of the 24th to replace Brigadier Cox in command of 25th Brigade. Allen was convinced that Cox was too ill to carry on. Cox was reluctant to leave his post, but subsequent medical examination revealed that he should be in hospital, and he was sent to one. Plant, a buoyant and cheerful leader who had seen long and distinguished service as a young infantry officer and brigade major in the previous war, took over a depleted force. The men of both battalions were very weary, though some dogged parties from the 2/14th had strength enough left to spend the night of the 24th and the following day searching the wheatfields for their dead and wounded.[6] The attacking companies of this battalion had lost about forty-eight men including ten killed, the loss falling mainly on Russell's company and O'Day's platoon. The men of the 2/31st, now numbering only 545, were also showing signs of extreme fatigue. "This is noticeable today when not noticeable yesterday," wrote a company commander (Lieutenant Hall[7]) on the 24th, "several are suffering from slight shell-shock."[8] The French were no less worn out, and, on the 24th, ten deserters from the Foreign Legion surrendered; they complained of the heavy casualties the Australian artillery fire was causing.

The Australians believed that the dejection of the enemy troops and the desertions were the results partly of a ruse. Having heard an unfamiliar voice speaking on the wireless telephone they decided that the enemy was listening in. Thenceforward Porter addressed each of his four company commanders as "adjutant" hoping that the enemy would conclude that he commanded four battalions and not four companies. The success of

---

[6] Sgt R. H. Dougherty (of Mordialloc, Vic) was a devoted leader of these rescue parties on which the French seldom fired though they came within range of their machine-guns.

[7] Maj K. S. Hall, DSO, SX4855; 2/31 Bn. Farmer; of Willunga, SA; b. Willunga, 19 Jun 1917.

[8] Later Capt H. B. Woolford (of Manilla, NSW), then medical officer of the 2/6 Fd Regt, wrote: "It was in the third week of the Syrian campaign that I remember observing fatigue most. My RAP was then at Kafr Houn . . . on the Jerme-Jezzine road, about six miles from Jezzine. I observed it particularly among men of the 2/14 Bn, 2/3 MG Bn and 2/5 Fd Coy, who were about or passing through that area. I think also it was at this time I observed the craving for sweets. Being right on the roadside we did a brisk trade in coffee and tea. I recollect that it was about that time that Lt A. W. Clarke of 2/6 Fd Regt called in to ask me if we had any chocolate or similar for himself and his men. I clearly remember his remarking that he had never before felt the urge to eat chocolate as he did then."

this subterfuge was perhaps confirmed afterwards when the French sector commander complained to Brigadier Plant: "What could I do with my three battalions against your four?"

General Allen instructed Brigadier Plant that it would be futile to attempt more attacks on the heights dominating the road and that he should blast the enemy off the rock-strewn summits with artillery fire and take command of the ground on his front by aggressive patrolling. "The country was as bad as Gallipoli and worse," said Plant later. "The hills were bigger; there were more boulders and, in the Kharat area, no scrub at all." The ruggedness of the country made it necessary to man more artillery observation posts than normal and these were often separated from the guns by deep valleys. Consequently the gunners were often near the end of their supplies of signal wire, and sometimes had to borrow it from the infantry. The 11th Battery at one stage had 35 miles of wire in use; often the distance of observation post to guns was more than 7,000 yards.

On the 26th June Allen informed Plant that he proposed soon to relieve the pressure on the Jezzine brigade by a thrust in an entirely new direction. He would send a small and mobile column from the coastal sector through the mountains by way of Aanout and Rharife towards Beit ed Dine. When the effect of this drive had become apparent, but not until then, Plant was to press on and join the 21st Brigade—at Beit ed Dine it was hoped. For this new thrust through the mountains on the left were chosen the Queenslanders of the 2/25th, who had fought first on the central sector, then on the coast, and now were to undertake an operation in the mountain spine between those sectors.

It will be remembered that on the 18th June General Lavarack had ordered the 21st Brigade not to advance any farther until the position at Merdjayoun had been stabilised. Consequently Brigadier Stevens' units confined themselves to aggressive patrolling. On the 19th, for example, his cavalry squadron (of the 9th Australian Cavalry) had been ordered to move forward, locate some land mines believed to be in the coast road near Ras Nebi Younes and push on to Sebline. At 8.35 a.m. these newly-arrived cavalrymen were at the Wadi Zeini and had reached a road-block of whose existence they had learnt from a prisoner picked up at Rmaile. Fifty yards beyond the block a French anti-tank gun, 150 yards away in a clump of cactus, fired on the leading Australian tank. The second shot penetrated the engine and later shots jammed the turret. Lieutenant Langlands[9] was killed but the driver and wireless operator crouched on the floor unharmed. Trooper Bryne[1] who was following Langlands in a carrier put his vehicle under cover and went forward carrying an anti-tank rifle with which he silenced the French gun. He then directed the fire of his squadron's tanks on to suspected enemy positions. After returning to

---

[9] Lt E. R. Langlands, VX14751; 9 Cav Regt. Merchant; of Horsham, Vic; b. Horsham, 18 Apr 1914. Killed in action 19 Jun 1941.

[1] Sgt J. Bryne, MM, VX33930; 9 Cav Regt. Clerk-salesman; of Hampton, Vic; b. Birmingham, Eng, 9 Jul 1914.

squadron headquarters to report what he had done he went forward again to help extricate the damaged tank.

Meanwhile a troop which was forward on the right had been firing on the enemy at 100 yards and less, driving them down into the wadi itself. Sergeant Carstairs[2] left his vehicle and, under fire, fetched tow ropes from this troop, returned to the road and with Bryne moved forward in a carrier and towed the damaged tank out. Nine shells had hit it, but the two surviving members of the crew were still unharmed. The cavalrymen directed artillery fire at the Frenchmen in the wadi forcing them to withdraw to the north-east abandoning their gun. The 2/16th Battalion, following the cavalry, attacked and took Jadra village overlooking the Wadi Zeini, where some forty prisoners were collected. That afternoon the 2/27th Battalion moved to the El Ouardaniye-Sebline-Kafr Maya area.

Mills' veteran squadron of the 6th Australian Cavalry, now equipped with four captured 11-ton French tanks, two British light tanks, and eight carriers, relieved the squadron of the 9th Cavalry on 20th June and patrolled forward on the coast road and inland along the Kafr Maya road. On the following day the 2/27th Battalion patrolled to Kafr Maya and Sebline. Such patrolling was continued for the following few days by the 2/16th astride the coast road on the Jadra ridge, the 2/27th strung out guarding the lateral roads and tracks for a distance of five miles to the south, and the Cheshire Yeomanry farther back astride the lateral roads from Jezzine and Merdjayoun. Thus, throughout this period, two of Stevens' three units were employed protecting his area against possible thrusts across his lines of communication from the Lebanons.

It was at this stage that General Allen, anxious about the evident presence of substantial French forces in Beit ed Dine and the other mountain towns along the winding roads that led south from it, decided to send the 2/25th into this country. These French forces formed a wedge between Plant's 25th Brigade north of Jezzine and the 21st Brigade on the coast. The success of this expedition would remove a threat to the 25th Brigade and would reduce the number of troops employed watching the roads leading east and west through the Lebanons between the Jezzine road and the coast.

On the 25th Stevens ordered the 2/27th and 2/16th Battalions to move forward to the El Haram ridge and to send out patrols thence to Er Rezaniye on the right and Es Seyar and Es Saadiyate on the left. At the same time, in accordance with Allen's plan, he ordered the 2/25th, which had arrived at Sidon from the Merdjayoun sector on the 24th, to clear the enemy from Chehim, Daraya and Aanout, to send patrols thence to El Mtoulle and Hasrout, and occupy Hill 832 overlooking Hasrout if it gave good observation to the north. This would close a lateral road to Beit ed Dine and remove the threat of a counter-attack from that direction. He instructed Lieut-Colonel Withy of the 2/25th to pay special

---

[2] Lt R. J. Carstairs, MM, VX16264; 9 Cav Regt. Law clerk; of Natimuk, Vic; b. Ararat, Vic, 31 Mar 1915.

attention to the southern flank where on two successive days patrols of the 6th Cavalry had seen enemy forces moving.

Late that afternoon the 2/16th, on the coast, with two companies forward, set out for its objective. They had a long march over country cut by several deep wadis and it was 11 p.m. before the left company reached the El Haram ridge, and 4 a.m. before the right company, which had rougher country to cover, was in position. There was some artillery fire but otherwise no opposition. On the right of the 2/16th one company of the 2/27th marched to El Haram itself, where it arrived at 8 p.m. after six hours and a half over very difficult country. It bivouacked near the village that night and, at dawn, began to move in. There was a little firing by a party of French troops but as the men of the 2/27th advanced

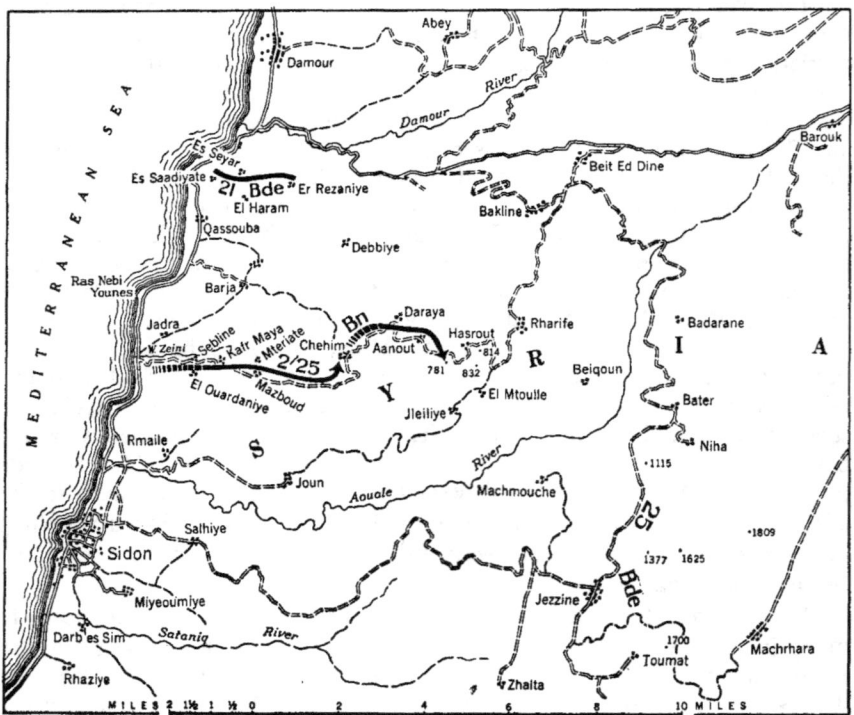

a patrol of the 2/16th arrived from the western side and between them they captured eight prisoners and a machine-gun. That evening the two leading companies of the 2/16th moved forward to the ridge through Es Saadiyate without opposition. The French guns shelled them at intervals during the night but caused no casualties.

For the expedition to Chehim and Aanout, Brigadier Stevens allotted Withy one anti-tank gun and a detachment of engineers of the 2/6th

Field Company. He arranged that after the 2/25th had occupied Chehim an artillery observer would be attached to the force with wireless communication to a troop of the 2/4th Field Regiment, whose guns could fire from positions on the coastal plain at targets in the hills, Chehim being only about five miles from the coast as the crow flies.

After its losses at Merdjayoun the 2/25th Battalion had been reorganised by distributing the men of one of the rifle companies among the other three. From Sebline after dark on the 26th two companies commanded by Captain Marson, an outstandingly cool and trusted leader, marched along the road through Kafr Maya to a point short of Mazboud and thence (by-passing Mazboud where a patrol of the Cheshires had been fired on) over the hills past Mteriate and along a ravine towards Chehim. The mules on which the mortars were loaded could not negotiate the rugged country and were left behind at Mteriate.

At dawn on the 27th the little column reached the road immediately south of Chehim. Lieutenant Macaulay,[3] who was leading, had just crossed the road with three men, when a burst of fire came from two armoured cars on the road to the north. When the rest of his platoon tried to cross men were hit. Marson sent another platoon (Lieutenant White's) under cover along the side of the hill where it reached a position north of the cars and engaged them, but they could not be damaged by bullets.

Macaulay decided that he could break the deadlock and with his three men—two "runners" and one Bren gunner—he moved around the slope overlooking the little town to the northern side, surprising and capturing a French signaller on the way. There, at 7 a.m., he and his men, undetected, piled stones across the road and he sited the Bren gun and his two riflemen on a terrace overlooking this road-block. Soon a French motorcyclist raced out of the town, pulled up at the wall of stones and surrendered. Then two armoured cars appeared on the road coming from the east, each with ten or more troops clinging on to the vehicles. The leading car stopped at the little wall of stones and a French officer sauntered up to it swinging a cane. Macaulay shouted to him to surrender but he ran back to the cars and the men deployed and began climbing the terraces towards Macaulay's post. The odds were too great; two of Macaulay's men were captured and he and the third man made off the way they had come, eluding the pursuers.

Meanwhile Marson and his two companies had surprised and knocked out the two armoured cars with sticky bombs and moved to the north-west of the town, whence he called down artillery fire on the town itself, using a telephone line that had been laid from battalion headquarters. As soon as the shells began to fall in the town two French cars drove off to the north-east carrying about twenty-five French troops with them. The townspeople were assembled in the market square where they wailed miserably until ordered back to their homes. By midday a patrol had found the road through Mazboud to be clear and Withy had sent four

---

[3] Capt T. B. Macaulay, MC, QX6341; 2/25 Bn. Salesman; of Rockhampton, Qld; b. Rockhampton, 12 Nov 1914.

carriers through to Chehim. The French retaliated with intermittent artillery fire, but later the 2/25th marched on to Daraya, and through Aanout to Hill 781 before meeting other opposition. There an advance-guard of carriers came under mortar and machine-gun fire from Hasrout, and for the time being the advance petered out. Thus the inland flank was secured and the force on the coast was moved forward to a line from which it could begin reconnoitring for an attack on Damour.

At Jezzine Brigadier Plant carried out the sage policy of pounding Hills 1284 and 1332 with artillery fire. This prolonged bombardment proved successful. On the night of the 28th-29th a patrol of the 2/31st found 1284 abandoned, although when the patrol began to establish itself the French sent over heavy mortar and machine-gun fire from positions farther north in the Wadi Nagrat, and on 1332, and the patrol withdrew. Next day Captain Muir[4] (of the brigade staff who had taken over Robson's company) led a fighting patrol of two sections forward under orders from Porter to make a mock attack and cause the enemy to reveal himself.[5] The patrol climbed to the boulder-strewn crest, and there orders were shouted as though for a battalion attack, Very lights were fired, and supporting sections fired heavily over the heads of the advancing men. The French opened fire, but Muir pressed on with fourteen men past 1284, which the French had abandoned, and on to 1332, which the patrol held until nightfall when it was relieved by another company. Hill 1284 bore evidence that persistent artillery fire had made it untenable. The rocky crest was scarred in a close pattern for many yards. Bodies of men spattered the stone emplacements, and shattered remains of arms and equipment were strewn everywhere.

Throughout the 25th Brigade's area patrolling became more vigorous and ambitious as the troops' spirits and strength were refreshed. On 28th June, for example, two fighting patrols of the 2/14th under Corporals Osborne[6] and Waller[7] climbed Kharat before dawn, took two machine-gun posts and captured nine Senegalese (of the *II/17th Battalion*). The battalion then occupied the reverse side of Kharat and, in the afternoon, a mortar detachment under Lance-Corporal Booth[8] engaged machine-gun posts on that mountain. Because the ground was too hard to place aiming posts and no suitable aiming mark could be found Private Douglas[9] stood up in the open and, stretching out his arms, was used as an aiming post.

---

[4] Lt-Col R. A. C. Muir, QX6236. 7 Cav Regt; BM 17 Bde 1941-43, and staff appts. Chartered accountant; of Brisbane; b. Perth, WA, 20 Jun 1910.

[5] This day Maj R. G. Pollard of the divisional staff took over command of the 2/31st from Lt-Col Porter, who had been wounded on 14 June, but had carried on. On the advice of his senior medical officer, Colonel F. K. Norris, General Allen now agreed that Porter should go back for treatment.

[6] WO2 W. J. Osborne, VX15655; 2/14 Bn. Farm hand; of Pootilla, Vic; b. Geelong, Vic, 2 Jun 1912.

[7] Cpl L. L. Waller, VX16413; 2/14 Bn. Printer; of Bairnsdale, Vic; b. Warragul, Vic, 29 May 1920. Killed in action 5 Sep 1942.

[8] Sgt C. E. Booth, VX15299; 2/14 Bn. Vigneron; of Taminick, Vic; b. Taminick, 5 Oct 1911.

[9] Pte C. H. Douglas, VX43676; 2/14 Bn. Printer; of Murtoa, Vic; b. Melbourne, 5 Jul 1907.

Later that afternoon the same detachment knocked out three machine-gun posts on the forward slopes of the mountain.

On the 29th about twenty-five men under Lieutenant Crook[1] of the 2/31st Battalion set out to raid Hill 1066. Crook took his men along the road to the Sagret Fellah whence they climbed up a goat track in single file and, on the open plateau on top, re-formed and attacked in extended order. The little force advanced 400 yards and took about thirteen prisoners before Crook decided to withdraw so as to be clear of the area before daylight.

The same day a patrol of the 2/14th under Lieutenant McGavin[2] attacked a blockhouse near Machrhara. After a long climb they moved forward, using the rocks as cover, to a point about 100 yards from the blockhouse and the machine-guns round it. There McGavin put down two of his sections to give covering fire while he and Lance-Corporal Burns[3] charged, McGavin shouting in French to come out. They reached the blockhouse unhurt, took ten prisoners there and were just emerging when a machine-gun opened fire from the cover of vines only twenty yards away. McGavin and Burns with their prisoners hurried back into the blockhouse while the rest of the platoon engaged the French machine-gun, whose crew surrendered when they saw that their comrades in the blockhouse were captured. By 6.30 p.m. McGavin was back in his platoon area with fourteen prisoners who said that they were from a Foreign Legion battalion recently at Damascus. The patrol suffered no serious casualty.

The 2/14th now learnt that they were to be relieved on 1st July and to return to their own brigade on the coast. By the 30th the brigade was holding posts from Toumat on the right through Kharat and Hill 1377 to Hill 1332—a front of 10 miles. Merely to live in the outposts on the 4,000-foot ridges along this line was a hardship, leaving out of account the intermittent bombardments and arduous patrolling.

Meanwhile a lively action had been fought on the right wing beyond Damascus where the Free French had thrust far to the north. On 30th June the force at Nebek consisted of the 2nd Free French Battalion supported by four British field guns and some anti-tank guns. The infantry was deployed astride the road north of Nebek. At 4.55 a.m. the enemy's guns began firing a heavy creeping barrage and at 5.35 seven tanks attacked from the east. They advanced very slowly but in two hours had reached orchards east of the village. Seven more tanks then appeared advancing down the main road, but were driven back by the artillery. The tanks on the east, now supported by lorry-borne infantry, pushed on to the south-eastern edge of the village, where, however, they came under fire

---

[1] Lt L. C. Crook, NX3800; 2/31 Bn. Chemical traveller; of Sydney; b. Sydney, 20 Aug 1917. Killed in action 8 Jul 1941.

[2] Capt A. S. D. J. McGavin, VX14106; 2/14 Bn. Student; of Black Rock, Vic; b. Calcutta, India, 25 Jul 1920. Killed in action 28 Nov 1942.

[3] Cpl P. Burns, VX12955; 2/14 Bn. Salesman; of Springvale, Vic; b. Melbourne, 20 Feb 1919. Killed in action 22 Nov 1942.

from anti-tank guns and one field gun; three tanks were destroyed, one captured and the remainder hastened away. Nevertheless the Vichy infantry dismounted and pressed on steadily and were near the village when, about 1 p.m., the Free French counter-attacked and drove them off. The defenders lost 8 men, the Vichy French left 40 dead and 11 prisoners.[4]

Farther east, Habforce, still under heavy attack by French aircraft, continued its attacks on Palmyra. On the 29th the defenders struck back and drove the Wiltshire Yeomanry from a ridge above the town; next day the 1/Essex counter-attacked and regained part of it, and on the 1st July observed the defenders withdrawing from the outlying gardens to the inner defences.

Firmly held at Palmyra and under frequent attack from the air the British force was being harassed also by French raiding parties based either on Seba Biyar to the south or Sukhna and Deir ez Zor to the north-east. On the 26th General Clark of Habforce gave Major Glubb and his Arab troops a task well suited to their temperament and experience: to take and hold Seba Biyar and Sukhna and thus protect his supply lines. On the 28th Seba Biyar was surrendered to Glubb's Arabs by a French warrant-officer who declared that he was a keen de Gaullist. Next day Sukhna was found to be empty of French troops; a squadron of the Household Cavalry was sent there to reinforce the Arabs. The origin of the raiding parties was revealed on 1st July

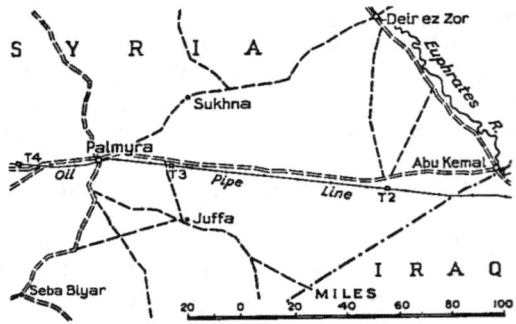

when a column of French vehicles unexpectedly approached along the Deir ez Zor road. The French deployed and attacked but were routed by an impetuous attack by Glubb's Arabs; eleven of the enemy were killed and eighty men and six armoured cars captured. It was found that this force comprised one of three French light desert companies of which two had now been virtually destroyed at Sukhna or Seba Biyar and one was in Palmyra. "After the action at Sukhna," wrote Glubb, with pardonable exaggeration, "the Syrian deserts were entirely cleared of enemy troops."[5]

---

[4] The Vichy force consisted of fourteen "R35" tanks, two infantry companies (one mixed and one of the *1/16th Tunisian*) and perhaps two batteries.
[5] J. B. Glubb, *The Story of the Arab Legion* (1948), p. 336.

French shells bursting south of Jezzine. *(Lt-Col R. A. C. Muir)*

A rocky slope near Jezzine. *(Australian War Memorial)*

The "Mad Mile" near Jezzine. *(Australian War Memorial)*

(Lt-Col R. A. C. Muir)
French mule teams caught by Australian shell fire near Bater.

CHAPTER 24

PREPARING A FINAL BLOW

SINCE the fall of Damascus on the 21st June there had been little progress in the three western sectors. Merdjayoun had been captured but the enemy had halted the attackers at a strong position just north of it. The heights beyond Jezzine had been abandoned by the French, but Beit ed Dine, the junction which Jezzine protected, still lay far ahead of the Australians. On the coast the depleted 21st Australian Brigade had thrust back one enemy outpost after another and cleared the lateral roads, but was still under orders not to undertake a major project.

Each day, however, the relative strength of the invading force, both material and moral, had increased. The French units were being whittled away by casualties and desertions; the Allied force was not only supported by a pool of replacements, but it now contained about twice as many units as it had when the invasion opened, if the formations advancing from Iraq be included. It was now able, while adequately securing the Jebel Mazar and Merdjayoun sectors, to concentrate more than a full division on the coast and in the Lebanons for a final blow at Beirut.

On 28th June, in accordance with General Wilson's orders, General Lavarack issued an instruction that the 7th Division, brought to near full strength by adding the 17th Brigade, should concentrate in the Jezzine and coastal sectors. The 17th Brigade was to consist of Brigadier Savige's headquarters, and the 2/3rd and 2/5th Infantry and 2/2nd Pioneer Battalions, but all three were far below full strength. Major-General Evetts, of the 6th British Division, would control the Merdjayoun and Damascus sectors, and at Merdjayoun his 23rd Brigade would relieve units of the 7th Division so that they could move west. His role would be to mislead the enemy into expecting attacks in the eastern sectors, and to protect Damascus and the road from Kuneitra to Sidon.[1]

---

[1] To carry out the moves involved in this redeployment presented a problem, particularly as all the battalions concerned were engaged against the enemy. The transfers of infantry, cavalry and artillery units of the 7 Div alone included:

2/33 Bn	Merdjayoun to Jezzine
2/3 Bn	Damascus to coast
2/5 Bn	Deraa and Merdjayoun to coast
2/14 Bn	Jezzine to coast
2/25 Bn	Lebanons to coast
2/King's Own	Merdjayoun to Damascus
2/2 Pnr Bn	Lebanons to coast
The Greys-Staffs Composite Regt	To Sheikh Meskine
6 Cav Regt	Merdjayoun to coast
2/5 Fd Regt	Merdjayoun to coast

The rearrangement of forces later involved also British yeomanry units of the 1st Cavalry Division. Its 4th Brigade comprised Habforce; units of the remaining brigades were scattered in Syria and Palestine. General Wilson decided to reassemble the 5th Brigade and give it the task of dealing with substantial enemy forces still in the inaccessible Jebel Druse, and protect the Deraa-Damascus route and the western part of the route from Haifa to Baghdad. The 4 Cav Bde Gp was to include: Greys-Staffs Yeo Composite Regt, Yorkshire Dragoons, Cheshire Yeo, Transjordan Frontier Force, Druse Legion. Its only artillery was to be one tp of the 2/1 A-Tk Regt.. At the request of Lavarack the Cheshire was retained by the 7 Div until its approach to Damour had been completed. The remaining brigade of the cavalry division—the 6th—was made responsible for the security of Galilee and Samaria in Palestine.

This was the third occasion on which a policy had been adopted of concentrating on a drive towards Beirut and treating the inland sectors as of secondary importance. When the invasion began it was made by three widely-separated columns of almost equal strength. The French counter-attack had had the effect—highly satisfactory to the French—of drawing troops away from the coastal sector where promising progress had been made, and from the reserves, to reinforce Damascus, Merdjayoun, and, finally, Jezzine. At Damascus and Merdjayoun a series of costly counter-attacks had followed. One of these—Lloyd's at Damascus—had provided a situation at once so promising and so precarious that, although General Wilson had decided on 18th June to concentrate against Beirut, General Lavarack next day persuaded Wilson to vary this decision by sending the 16th British Brigade to the eastern sector and thus enable him temporarily to concentrate on the Damascus operation. It was not until a week later that Lavarack reverted to the original policy, and for the reasons that had applied from the outset; namely, that operations on the coastal plain could be fully supported by the navy and R.A.F., that Beirut was the main French base and seat of Government, and that operations from Damascus and Merdjayoun, if successful, "would only clear up the situation in the Anti-Lebanon and would leave the problem of crossing the Lebanon still to be faced".

One British "principle of war" is that victory can be won only by offensive action, but to take the offensive at all times and in all places, the French theory of 1914, can be as disastrous as the opposite principle —the French theory in 1940. Lloyd's counter-attack at Mezze had virtually destroyed a brigade (his commander then possessed but four) and had failed to reach its objective. The attacks at Merdjayoun had cost the Australian division almost one-third of the casualties it suffered in the whole campaign. It is arguable that, in the light of knowledge then possessed, the return to the original plan of concentrating on a thrust towards Beirut should have come earlier; indeed the reasons eventually given for transferring the main effort to the coast were reasons which had been valid since before the invasion began. In his report Lavarack said that the recapture of Merdjayoun and its retention by adequate forces enabled consideration to be given to a resumption of the advance in the coastal sector; and it is true that as long as there was any doubt of his ability to hold the Merdjayoun area it was not advisable to advance the left flank farther along the coast road. In addition possession of Merdjayoun gave the invaders a short lateral road from the coast to the central sector.

Now Lavarack was determined that there would be no more diversions from the main objective, and took special steps to curb the ambitions of the only subordinate from whom such a diversion was likely to come—General Legentilhomme. Legentilhomme's task was to secure Damascus against possible counter-attack, but his desire might have been to make a spectacular and politically-advantageous advance into northern Syria.

On 2nd July Lavarack sent him a tactfully-worded instruction in which he said that

> while the Corps Commander does not desire unnecessarily to restrict your liberty of action in your interpretation of [your] task, he wishes to make it clear that, for the present, he does not approve of any advance in force beyond Nebek.

On the same day Lavarack wrote to Legentilhomme suggesting that the senior Australian liaison officer, Lieut-Colonel Rogers, should join Legentilhomme's staff, and that the other British liaison officers there should work under Rogers' instructions.

The enemy's positions on the Damour River, which now formed the greatest obstacle to an advance to Beirut, possessed far greater natural strength than any yet encountered on the coastal sector. North from the line of posts which the 21st Brigade occupied, the coast road travelled along a narrow shelf between the sea and a series of precipitous east-west ridges intersected by wadis until it reached the Damour River. This stream wound through a wide cleft in the coastal range. South of it the main road curved along the coastal ledge and then bent inland to a point about a mile from the sea where it crossed the Damour River on a stone bridge. Immediately north of the bridge a road branched off eastward along the bottom of the ravine, crossed to the south bank of the river about two miles inland, and then began to zigzag up the face of the range towards Beit ed Dine, climbing 3,000 feet in a bee-line distance of about six miles. North of the river the coastal plain, about half a mile wide, was thickly planted with orchards and banana groves. A stone-walled water channel about 20 yards wide ran east and west through the groves about a mile north of the river. Just beyond it lay Damour, a town of some 5,000 people. From the inland edge of this cultivated area the ridges rose steeply, sometimes climbing 600 feet within a little more than a mile from the orchards, but these ridges were lower than the heights overlooking the ravine from the south. For some two miles from the plantations the mountain ridges were almost bare, but from about the 1,000-foot contour upwards trees and scrub were thicker.

If Damour was taken Beirut would be comparatively easy to approach. General Dentz had announced that he would fight in the streets of Beirut, but it was a reasonable assumption that if that city fell the French would capitulate.

Restless under the restraint imposed by events on another front than his own, Brigadier Stevens, of the 21st Brigade, on 22nd June, had drafted a "note on future operations" which was to become the basis of the planning of the final battle, though it was radically amended when additional forces became available. In it he said that the first essential for an attack on Damour was to secure a line from which artillery fire could be directed against the French positions north of the Damour gorge—namely, the line of the ridge from Es Saadiyate to Es Seyar, then three miles ahead of his outpost line. He proposed, therefore, that one of his battalions should secure Barja, and that the other should move up the road past Es Saadiyate and seize the "143 feature" from which they could look down into the western end of the Damour Valley. When this had been achieved he considered that a battalion should be moved up the coast road and advance across the mountains through El Haram to El Labiye, whence it could look down into the Damour ravine from a ridge more than 800 feet high. He considered that, forty-eight hours after the El Labiye ridge had been occupied, a successful attack on the Damour line could be launched by his two battalions, one to obtain a bridgehead across the river on the coast road and the other to seize the El Hamra ridge immediately north of the river and the narrower ridge beyond it. He emphasised that the battalion on the left should not be committed to a fight in the orange and banana groves (as had happened at Sidon).

Such an operation could not be carried out, he decided, with his present resources, but he would need a third battalion to enable his 2/16th to be rested after it had gained the heights overlooking the Damour orchards. He would also need naval protection, protection from air attack, and certain equipment for mountain warfare, notably mules—at least sixty —and machine-guns and wireless sets that could be packed on their backs. In addition, it would be essential to guard the attacking force against a French move down the Beit ed Dine road, for the move forward would entail crossing a *fourth* lateral road leading into the rear of his positions from the towns the French still held in the southern Lebanons.

At that time there was little immediate prospect of obtaining these requirements. Indeed Stevens' brigade of two depleted battalions lacked even what was necessary comfortably to maintain its present positions. The waning spirits of the Foreign Legion helped to provide one need, when, on the 23rd June, twelve Spanish soldiers of the Foreign Legion deserted bringing a small mule train with them. The same day, when on a visit to Berryforce headquarters, Stevens saw General Wavell and told him that, despite repeated requests, he could get no bombs for his 3-inch mortars, although United Kingdom units were being supplied with them. Next day 320 bombs arrived for each Australian battalion. Batches of reinforcements arrived from Palestine in the next few days but not enough to build the battalions up to full strength. The 2/27th Battalion, for example, received 10 officers and 119 men. (At this time all but 7 of the 27 Australian infantry battalions in the Middle East were serving and suffering casualties, either in Syria or Tobruk; and of the seven, 3 (2/1st, 2/7th and 2/11th) had been captured in Crete and were then being re-created, and the remaining 4 (2/2nd, 2/4th, 2/6th and 2/8th) had had heavy losses in Greece and Crete, and were being gradually restored.)

The 21st Brigade continued to thrust forward, and by 28th June the forward posts were on a line through or ahead of Es Saadiyate-Es Seyar-El Festeqaniye-Er Rezaniye and patrols probing out from this line had met enemy troops only at one point—the 394-metre feature on the right which commanded a view into the Damour gorge and beyond it across the river as far as Daraya. On 27th June a patrol of the 2/27th was met by fire from three machine-guns on Hill 394, and one man failed to return.

In the new positions the infantry were now inviting fire from the French artillery beyond the Damour River and each day any movements seen by the French observers provoked sharp bursts of shell-fire. Brigadier Stevens told his battalion commanders that he had decided to "sit back from the river to avoid casualties" but to patrol vigorously. On 29th June, Lieut-Colonel Moten of the 2/27th, with his Intelligence sergeant, Burr,[2] reconnoitred the right flank, passing through Baasir, Baaqoun, Aaqliye and Er Rezaniye, where Captain Nicholls,[3] commanding an outlying company in that direction, reported that there was still enemy movement on Hill 394. Moten and Nicholls went forward and examined this valuable feature, commanding the Damour ravine, and as a result, Moten ordered Nicholls to send a strong fighting patrol out that night to seize the hill and hold it. Accordingly Nicholls set out from Er Rezaniye that evening with two platoons and, after an arduous march, arrived on the slopes of Hill 394 at midnight. One platoon under Lieutenant Mullighan[4] crept round to the eastern side of the hill and attacked up the steep escarpment. Five enemy soldiers (of the *II/6th Foreign Legion*) were taken completely by surprise and surrendered after having thrown a few grenades. Mullighan's platoon then dug in on the sheltered side of the hill, established an observation post on the summit and was shelled by the French from 5 a.m. to 9.15, while the other platoon marched back to Er Rezaniye. Moten told Stevens what had been done, and it was agreed that the men on 394 should keep out of sight on the south side by day and sit on top by night.

It now remained to reconnoitre river crossings, particularly on the right, because Stevens was determined to avoid a frontal attack and instead to gain the heights to the east of the Damour orchards. The French map showed a path winding down the escarpment from El Batal to the Beit ed Dine road. Four hundred yards to the west the road crossed the river and, just north of the crossing, a better-defined track zigzagged northward up to the village of El Boum. The only other track down the escarpment was one leading due east from Hill 394 down to a tributary wadi and along it to the Beit ed Dine road north-east of the observation post.

The night after the capture of Hill 394, Lieutenant R. G. Geddes[5] led a patrol of four by night down the track from El Labiye to the Damour River where they managed to approach to within 40 yards of French sentries who were guarding the concrete bridge there. The sentries were restless and appeared to suspect that there was a patrol near by, but

---

[2] Capt F. S. Burr, SX3995. 2/27 Bn; Staff appts. School teacher; of Murray Bridge, SA; b. London, 1 Aug 1901.

[3] Maj F. J. Nicholls, SX2920. 2/27 Bn; BM 6 Bde. Clerk; of Rose Park, SA; b. Rose Park, 20 Jan 1914.

[4] Lt T. D. Mullighan, SX3076; 2/27 Bn. Oil traveller; of Kensington Gardens, SA; b. Mount Gambier, SA, 4 May 1917. Killed in action 7 Jul 1941.

[5] Lt R. G. Geddes, SX3170; 2/27 Bn. Grazier; of Melrose, SA; b. Port Pirie, SA, 28 Apr 1916. Killed in action 6 Jul 1941.

Geddes and his party made their way back to El Labiye without being discovered.

The task of finding a crossing over the Damour below El Batal was then given to Lieutenant Sims,[6] a cool and determined young platoon commander of the 2/27th. He led his platoon out of El Haram at 8 p.m. on 1st July and reached El Batal after a three hours' march along the mule tracks. There he gave orders to each of his sections to fan out and search for the track marked on the map and to reassemble at El Batal four hours later. At least one French patrol was also out, because at 1.45 in the morning one of Sims' sections was ambushed north-east of El Batal; one of its men was killed and, when the platoon reassembled, the track had not been found. Thereupon Sims sent back all but a sergeant and a sapper and waited for dawn. After climbing round the side of the hill in the daylight for two hours these found a well-marked mule track. There, all day, they waited for darkness, but meanwhile they sketched the French positions on the El Atiqa ridge, 1,000 yards away across the ravine, where they could see individual men moving about. They had no rations left, and only half a bottle of water, and were hungry and weary when, at 9 p.m., darkness having fallen, they began cautiously to feel their way down hill. At 11 o'clock they reached the main road and dashed across it to the river, where they filled their water-bottles and ate leeks growing there—their first food for a day. As they moved along the banana-fringed river they saw several French soldiers at the north end of the bridge, but were able to creep close enough to it to see that it was not mined and wired ready for demolition. Near the bridge they found a good ford, silently crossed it, returned, and climbed quietly back up the track again, arriving home at 6 a.m. on 3rd July. Sims reported that the escarpment to the north was too steep to negotiate except along the El Boum track and that the track down to the river from Batal could be travelled by mules.

These were only two of a series of arduous night patrols down the steep, rock-strewn escarpment to the banks of the Damour. On the extreme right, for example, Lieutenant Skipper[7] led a patrol to the southern tributary of the river, and along it towards what appeared on the map to be a crossing about 500 yards east of the bridge, but he came to a point where the creek was pinched between cliffs so steep that he could go no farther. A patrol led by Lieutenant Katekar[1] explored the tangled country each side of the creek north-east of Aaqliye. As a result of patrols on this flank (in which Sergeant Jamieson[2] of the engineers played a leading part) it was decided that the best route to the El Mourhira hill up which the Beit ed Dine road climbed could be travelled by a company in four hours.

---

[6] Maj C. A. W. Sims, MC, SX9455; 2/27 Bn. Electrical fitter; of Wallaroo, SA; b. Sydney, 12 Jul 1916.

[7] Capt J. W. Skipper, SX2926; 2/27 Bn. Solicitor; of Walkerville, SA; b. Adelaide, 3 May 1914. Killed in action 29 Nov 1942.

[1] Maj H. J. Katekar, SX3079. 2/27 Bn; BM 6 and 26 Bdes. Solicitor; of Renmark, SA; b. Mile End, SA, 24 Aug 1914.

[2] L-Sgt R. T. Jamieson, MM, NX22103; 2/6 Fd Coy. Truck driver and mechanic; of Edith via Oberon, NSW; b. Oberon, 9 Jun 1917. Died while prisoner of war, 18 Nov 1943.

On the left the patrols of the 2/16th met more opposition, an indication that the French considered that the vital sector. On four nights from 30th June-1st July to 3rd-4th July patrols of the 2/16th, each accompanied by an N.C.O. of the engineers, Corporal Buderis,[3] explored routes leading down to the river, and at length Buderis found two points where the river could be forded. On the night of 3rd July, after an attempt to drive a French standing patrol out of an ancient two-storeyed blockhouse named Yerate had failed, Colonel MacDonald ordered a fighting patrol of two platoons with artillery support for the next night. This patrol, following the artillery fire, found the post empty, but next morning seven enemy soldiers walked up to Yerate and six of them were captured. On the night of the 4th-5th, also in the wake of concentrated fire from the guns of the 2/4th Field Regiment, Captain Hearman organised patrols from three companies (to make men in each company familiar with the ground) down the almost bare, terraced face of the 500-foot hill to the river, where they found a ford and saw a track leading from the river to the main road. A patrol under Corporal Harley[4] crossed the river and crept up to the banana plantation beyond. From prisoners MacDonald gained a fairly clear picture of the French defences. There were two main defended areas, one including the bridge and the delta and another behind the watercourse about half a mile to the north. The El Atiqa hill was also defended with posts which were placed so that they could fire to the front or could enfilade a force attacking through the plantations. Daily, from the 26th onwards, the naval squadron shelled this and other targets round Damour, including a battery at Abey, five miles inland.

Despite his limited resources Brigadier Stevens had achieved his objectives. He had gained the heights overlooking the French defences, but, to avoid casualties in his depleted battalions and to rest the men as much as possible, had kept most of his troops well back from the zone that was subject to French artillery fire. Although the French shelling was intermittent it was often heavy, up to 200 shells being fired in a single concentration, yet casualties had been very few. Stevens formed the opinion that the defenders were concentrated along a front of about a mile and a half of strongly-wired and well-dug-in defences astride the main road, and were holding the rugged heights to the east only lightly, depending on the extraordinary difficulty of the country and possibly also on the fact that an attack on the inland flank, necessarily slow-moving, would be open to a counter-attack from Beit ed Dine.

The plan which Brigadier Stevens now proposed to General Allen was to attack the enemy's left flank with one of his battalions, to attack the El Atiqa positions with another battalion, but in such a direction as to defilade it from the French posts in the orchards and banana groves west of the coast road, and to use two companies of his third battalion to

---

[3] Cpl T. A. Buderis, MM, NX18017; 2/6 Fd Coy. Carpenter; of Moree, NSW; b. Fielding, NZ, 22 Aug 1909.
[4] Lt K. N. Harley, WX5824; 2/16 Bn. Auctioneer; of Katanning, WA; b. Balaklava, SA, 29 Nov 1916.

guard his flank against counter-attack down the Beit ed Dine road, while the remainder exploited through the right-hand battalion to the north-west outskirts of Damour. He was confident that his infantry had been well enough trained during exercises in the Judaean Hills to attack by night over even such rugged mountain country as this.

This plan had been maturing while Stevens had only two battalions under command. On 27th June he had discussed it with his unit commanders, and on the 29th Allen had discussed it with him. Now Stevens had three battalions, and a second brigade was to join in the battle. Stevens proposed to Allen that they should box Damour in, the 21st Brigade forming two sides, the sea a third, and the 17th Brigade putting the lid on. Thus the role of the 17th Brigade would be to circle round through the hills on the right and cut the road leading northward out of Damour. Savige reconnoitred the area on the 30th June and 1st July and reached conclusions similar to Stevens'—a movement of his brigade round the right flank to block the road north of Damour.

At a conference at Allen's headquarters on 2nd July these plans had been approved in principle and it was decided that the attack would open on 5th or 6th July. To cover the left flank of the 21st Brigade when the 2/16th Battalion attacked El Atiqa, Allen decided to give Monaghan's 2/2nd Pioneers (less two companies) to the 21st Brigade. He also placed Stevens in control of an advance by the 2/25th Battalion and the rest of the 2/2nd Pioneers against Rharife in the Lebanons before the Damour battle opened. The object of this move was to assist the 25th Brigade to move forward from Jezzine toward Beit ed Dine, but at the outset control was given to Stevens because he was in a better position geographically to exercise it. It was learnt that sixteen medium and forty-four field guns would be available to support the attack on Damour along a front which, in the opening stages, would be about two miles in width.

Whereas three battalions had been deployed between Jezzine and the coast on 23rd June, nine battalions were in that area on 2nd July. The force then assembling was, however, considerably weaker than a listing of the units suggests. Each battalion of the 21st Brigade was below strength; in the 2/16th, for example, the strongest rifle company had ninety-nine officers and men, the weakest seventy-five. The 2/2nd Pioneers lacked the two companies which were under Colonel Withy's command in the Rharife sector. Savige's brigade was to carry out its attack with two battalions each about 300 strong; one of these, the 2/3rd, had just come from a series of strenuous fights at Damascus and Jebel Mazar, and contained men who in the previous six months had fought and marched in Libya, Greece and Crete and were suffering the effects of exposure and malnutrition. The Australian commanders knew, however, from the steady trickle of deserters from the French army that the enemy's troops were in a worse way.

North and east of Jezzine the main body of the 25th Brigade on 1st July was holding a line of posts covering Toumat, Kharat, and the road leading north from Jezzine. East of the gorge the 2/25th Battalion held Aanout. That day patrols of the 2/25th found that the enemy was holding Hasrout on the lateral road to Beit ed Dine, but had evidently abandoned the track leading through Jleiliye. On the night of 2nd July the enemy abandoned their positions in the Wadi Nagrat and moved back towards Beit ed Dine.

Stevens ordered that the advance on Rharife should be made by two columns, one comprising the 2/25th with artillery and engineers, and the other the 2/2nd Pioneers (less two companies) with cavalry, artillery, and other detachments. The first was to move along the Chehim road, the second along the Mazraat ed Dahr-El Mtoulle road. Both were to join round Hasrout and Hill 832 and advance together to Rharife.

Advancing from Mazraat ed Dahr to Jleiliye on 3rd July the leading company of the Pioneers was shelled; two section leaders were killed and several men wounded, but after the enemy had been bombarded by artillery—Monaghan had a troop of howitzers firing from the coastal plain under his command—and by the mortars of the Pioneers and the machine-guns of a detachment of 6th Cavalry, a company attack was launched at 4 p.m. Advancing near the village Captain Mitchell,[5] the company commander, was wounded. This caused delay and it was dusk before the village was occupied. Monaghan sent the other company on to take Mtoulle but it could reach only the southern edge of Mtoulle before dark.

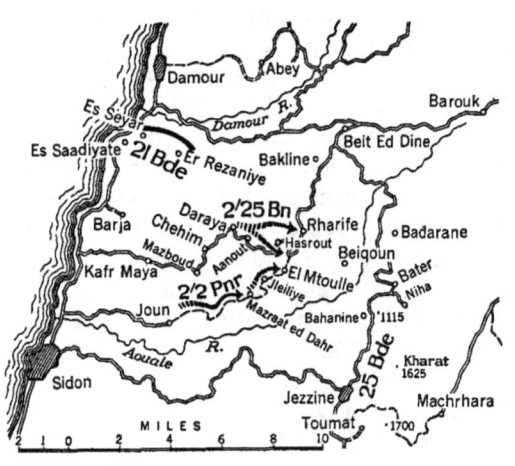

On the 2/25th Battalion's front the attack on Rharife was to be made by Captain Marson's company, which was to cut the road north of Rharife, and Captain Kerr's,[6] which was to capture the dominating plateau above Hasrout and occupy the town. A reconnaissance revealed that the enemy held the plateau, and after the plan of attack was outlined to all company officers from an observation post at Aanout, which overlooked the valley, and the steep 1,000-foot plateau beyond, Kerr's company left Daraya on the night of the 3rd-4th in strong moonlight. After very difficult going over intervening ridges, which made it a problem to keep direction, a halt was called at midnight in a copse at the foot of the plateau. The

---

[5] Maj W. H. Mitchell, VX15157. 2/2 Pnr Bn; Torres Strait Pnr Coy. Clerk; of Coburg, Vic; b. Melbourne, 11 Oct 1914. Died of injuries 23 May 1945.

[6] Maj R. J. L. Kerr, QX6404; 2/25 Bn. Bank officer; of Kingaroy, Qld; b. Rockhampton, Qld, 21 Sep 1903.

going had been too difficult for the mules carrying the mortars, and these were sent back to battalion headquarters.

The advance continued in single file at 1 a.m., but the leading platoon lost direction and had to be halted and reoriented. Fortunately, during this complication, the moon was blotted out by heavy clouds. The advance continued, but when moving up a defile almost at the crest the leading scout was set upon. He bayonetted his assailant, who gave out a bloodcurdling cry which awoke the defenders.

The French were occupying the crest in a semi-circle round the Australians, and for nearly an hour poured fire from four machine-guns and small mortars on to the attackers. Under telephoned orders from Lieut-Colonel Withy, Lieutenant Robertson was instructed to coordinate the attack of the leading platoons. Lieutenant Crombie's took up a position on the right flank and Lieutenant Miles on the left. As dawn approached Robertson ordered a bayonet attack. The fixing of bayonets evidently unnerved the French and, as the attackers advanced, they fled. By 5 a.m. Crombie had occupied all Hill 814 after brief engagements, and Miles had all Hill 832.

Lieutenant Cameron's[7] platoon captured the town of Hasrout, and established a road-block. During the morning the company was heavily shelled and machine-gunned, and an enemy counter-attack was seen being assembled on the southern side. However, Robertson directed artillery fire on the assembled French troops and they were dispersed. Some fifty French were seen running from the village towards Rharife.[8]

Meanwhile at 11.30 a.m. on the 4th the Pioneers opened an attack on Mtoulle. They encountered fire from field guns, mortars and machine-guns, but late in the afternoon had taken the village and were in touch with the 2/25th.

Marson's company had moved out at 4.30 p.m. on the 3rd through Daraya and advanced east and north-east through the mountains until they were fired on by about twelve Frenchmen who were in position on the west of a steep hill north of the track about a mile west of Rharife. By the time this enemy party had been manoeuvred off this hill it was dark. Marson took two platoons through Rharife where he found one Senegalese soldier who was taken prisoner. Unable to reach his battalion headquarters with his radio telephone, he fired a prearranged success signal with a Very pistol, and put the company in a defensive position on the road about 1,000 yards north of Rharife until the following morning, when he marched through the village again. On 4th July large numbers of French were withdrawing north-east from Mtoulle.

---

[7] Lt G. L. Cameron, QX7317; 2/25 Bn. Oil company representative; of Graceville, Qld; b. Brisbane, 10 Jul 1912.

[8] During the attack on 832 and 814, Pte A. Jackson (of Brisbane), a stretcher-bearer, was walking unarmed along an olive terrace when on the terrace below he saw two fully-armed French soldiers moving towards him. Jackson jumped down on to the lower terrace and seized one of the French soldiers' rifles, whereupon both of them surrendered. The company lost one killed and ten wounded. Cpl F. J. Mooney (of Brisbane) was killed by a grenade while leading his section against a French machine-gun position.

General Allen instructed Brigadier Plant to continue active patrolling and to take advantage of the enemy's withdrawal by advancing to Beit ed Dine. That day the 2/31st Battalion reported that there were no French troops in the Wadi Nagrat or Array, but that there were concentrations north of Kharat. A company of the 2/31st patrolled north along the road with the object of examining the ridge west of Marat by an advance from the north-west. The company occupied Hill 1115 but was forced off it by heavy fire, though not before it had taken fourteen prisoners, among whom was the artillery observation officer who had been directing fire on Jezzine and the roads leading into it. Thus on 5th July the 2/25th Battalion on the left was holding a line through Rharife, Beiqoun and Mtoulle, while the 2/31st, east of the gorge, was patrolling forward along the road leading north from Jezzine to Bater.

General Lavarack had ordered General Evetts' 6th Division to carry out aggressive patrols[9] in the Damascus and Merdjayoun sectors with the object of suggesting to the French that an attack was likely in those areas, and thus preventing them from transferring troops to the west. To add to the deception troops were moved by daylight in the Damascus area, but at night on the coast—a device that probably proved ineffective because the movements were reported to the French by agents in the villages.

By 3rd July the 6th British Division was deployed with its 16th Brigade astride the Beirut road from Deir Kanoun to Yafour, the depleted 5th Indian Brigade on the Col de Yafour, closing the gap north of Qatana, the North Somerset Yeomanry in the Chebaa area on the southern slopes of Hermon, and the 23rd Brigade at Merdjayoun and Khiam.[1] As a precaution against a possible attack on Damascus the 1/Royal Fusiliers manned the forts overlooking the Beirut road and the 9th Australian Cavalry (less two squadrons) was held in readiness to counter-attack.

At 6 a.m. on the 3rd the dogged little French garrison at Palmyra surrendered. It numbered only 165—six French officers, 87 Germans and Russians of the Foreign Legion, 48 air force men, and 24 of a desert company. Next day three N.C.O's and nineteen others of the Foreign Legion at T3 also capitulated. These 187 soldiers, mostly mercenaries, with air support, had sustained for twelve days the attacks of a force of four cavalry regiments (counting the Arab Legion as one), and an infantry battalion.

---

[9] On 2 July a daring patrol was made by a troop of 9 Cav to the Jebel Bourkoch. The squadron was then attached to the Indian brigade in the Qatana area. As it neared Bourkoch early in the morning it ran into heavy fire and its retreat was cut off. The remainder of the squadron, a squadron of Circassian horsed cavalry and a party of batmen, cooks, clerks and others from the headquarters of the regiment, hastened to their rescue. After a long exchange of fire the patrol, except for the officer commanding, Lt J. L. D. Ferguson (of Yarrawonga, Vic) and Sgt J. C. McEachern (of Mt. Gambier, SA) and a trooper, was soon able to withdraw; Ferguson and McEachern made their way back after dark, but the trooper was captured.

[1] 6 Div was supported by two British field regiments—the 1st and 4th—and one Australian (the 2/9th less a battery at Damour), and by the 5 Aust A-Tk Bty. The force in Syria was now exceptionally strong in field artillery, there being eight such regiments, five Australian and three British.

General Quinan's force in Iraq now included five infantry brigades, two more—the 17th and 24th—having arrived at Basra between 9th and 16th June. On 3rd June troops were flown into Mosul, and later in the month Major-General Slim of the 10th Indian Division was placed in command of all troops in northern Iraq.

General Wilson now instructed General Clark to cut the roads from Homs to Tripoli and Baalbek, working in conjunction with Free French companies from Nebek, gain touch with the 10th Indian Division about Deir ez Zor, and open communications with Damascus. The 1/Essex garrisoned Palmyra and the cavalry force concentrated at El Beida on the pipe-line 20 miles west of Palmyra. It was unlikely that these forces would now meet strong opposition to their occupation of eastern Syria; a fortnight earlier the defenders had withdrawn the bulk of the forces from eastern Syria into the Lebanon, leaving only isolated outposts in the desert.

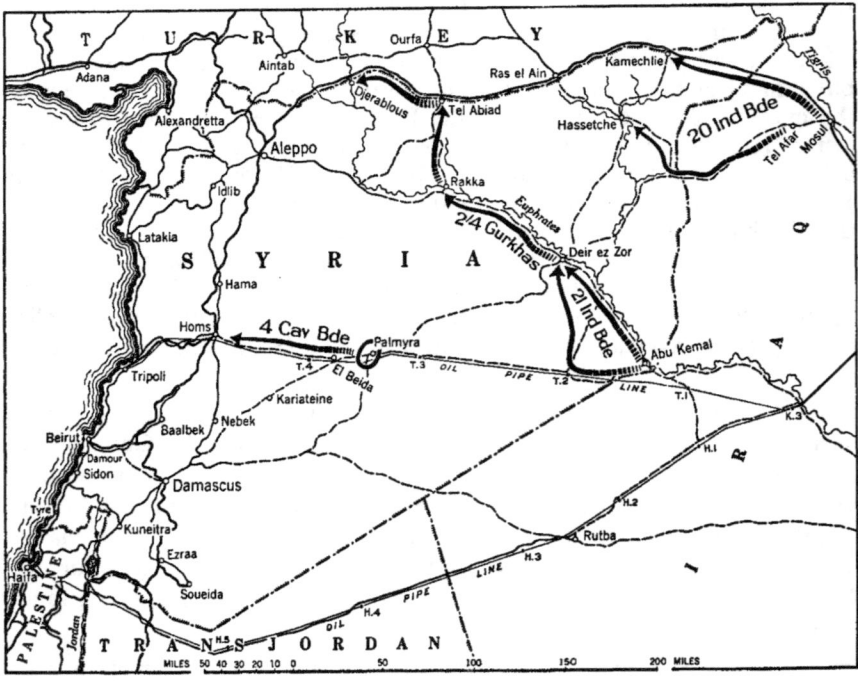

In spite of the small results achieved by the desert thrusts of Habforce up to 3rd July, the staffs in Cairo and London had continued to pin much faith on such manoeuvres. On the 3rd an appreciation prepared for the Chief of the General Staff in London stated that the plan was to maintain pressure "on a broad front from the Damascus area to the coast while Habforce moves on Homs via Palmyra and an Indian brigade from

Iraq will move on Abu Kemal and Deir ez Zor and ultimately on Aleppo . . . no early conclusion of the campaign should be expected".

The precise tasks allotted to Slim's 10th Indian Division advancing from Iraq were to move north from Abu Kemal and seize Deir ez Zor, to drive off any Arab irregulars such as those organised by Fawzi el Kawakji, and to prepare for a further advance along the Euphrates to Aleppo. Only one brigade group could be maintained on wheels forward of Abu Kemal, but this group—Brigadier Weld's[2] 21st Indian Brigade—included the 13th Lancers (armoured cars). In addition the 20th Indian Brigade, at Mosul, was to send out a battalion group to demonstrate against Deir ez Zor, and another column was to operate independently against Hassetche and Kamechlie in the remote north-eastern corner of Syria. The only direct air support available to these forces was from an improvised squadron of four Hurricanes and four Gladiators manned by semi-trained pilots, and four Blenheim bombers.

The 21st Indian Brigade entered Syria on 28th June. The main column (including two Gurkha battalions) advanced along the Euphrates while a flying column (13th Lancers and 4/13th Frontier Force Rifles) moved along the pipeline to T2 and thence on Deir ez Zor from the south. They were delayed by air attacks, dust, and shortage of petrol and water. On the 3rd a concerted attack was launched against the town which was soon taken, with about 100 prisoners, nine guns and fifty lorries. A number of the enemy escaped and many Syrian troops removed their uniforms and hid. The garrison had consisted of one Syrian infantry battalion, a light desert company, a light mechanised unit, and eleven guns. The French subjected the force at Deir ez Zor, as at Palmyra, to sharp air attack each day and by 6th July the last of the supporting Hurricanes was shot down.

> While the number of casualties inflicted were not many (states the report of the 10th Indian Division) the moral effect of the frequent bombing and machine-gunning from the air was serious. All units, British and Indian, were somewhat shaken by it and certain administrative units, which were composed of recently enlisted, only partially trained and often unarmed men, were for some days hardly able to carry on.

On 5th July the 2/4th Gurkhas occupied Rakka without opposition. Three days later information arrived that the enemy was withdrawing his outpost forces in the north-east corner westward along the frontier. The 2/4th Gurkhas were sent to Tel Abiad to cut them off but when they arrived there on 9th July the enemy had gone. A squadron of armoured cars and a platoon of infantry pursued the enemy as far as Djerablous, where the Euphrates enters Turkish territory. Meanwhile, the small garrison left at Rakka was strafed by aircraft, shelled by guns sited on the south side of the river, and severely attacked at night by Arab tribesmen. The northern columns—two Indian battalions operating from Mosul—occupied Kamechlie on the 7th and Hassetche on the 9th without opposition.

---

[2] Maj-Gen C. J. Weld, CIE, MC. Comd 21 Ind Bde 1940-42; OC Troops Cyprus 1942. Regular soldier; b. 4 Feb 1893.

In this operation the 10th Indian Division lost 25 killed, 50 wounded and 10 missing, more than half of these casualties being caused by air attack. Chiefly because of transport difficulties and the opposition of the French air force the proposed advance on Aleppo did not develop.

Meanwhile the final stage of the preparations for a weightier offensive —the assault on Damour—had been reached. The French force defending Damour and Beirut was believed now to consist of two battalions of the Foreign Legion, one of which contained only three weak companies; and five battalions of native Lebanese troops, each probably at about half strength. There were thought to be four batteries of 75's and two of medium guns, and some coast defence guns. The Australian staff had received information also that General Arlabosse, when inspecting the Damour defences, had mentioned that there were two supporting lines, one about Khalde, and one just south of Beirut extending inland through Aley to Bhamdoun. This last line was manned, it was believed, by two battalions of Lebanese troops and some squadrons of Spahis.

Allen's final instructions for the Damour attack (issued on 4th July) were that before the attack opened the 21st Brigade was to clear enemy patrols from the area south of the river and, on the first day, advance to a line Er Roumane—Four a Chaux—Point 212—the river mouth; and exploit to Kheurbet el Biar and Damour. The 17th Brigade was to concentrate about Dhar el Moughara and be ready at one hour's notice either to counter any threat outside the 21st's area or to carry on its attack. On the first day it was to move forward into the area vacated by the 21st.[3] The 25th Brigade, now brought to full strength by the transfer of the 2/25th Battalion to Plant's command, was ordered to press on towards Beit ed Dine, with the Cheshire Yeomanry operating in the mountains on its right flank.

Allen's instruction listed the targets to be bombarded by the navy on the two days before the attack and on "D-day"; and the role of the air squadrons. The air force's chief task was to give protection over the battle area, and particularly to protect the guns, and to bomb targets indicated by the army; its secondary task was to strafe troops on the roads to the French rear.[4]

On the 5th Stevens issued detailed orders to his battalions. They provided that as a preliminary operation a company of the 2/27th should destroy the enemy on the spur west of El Mourhira where it would be relieved by two companies of the 2/14th; the 2/16th would capture El Atiqa and exploit to the Nahr Daqoun; and the 2/27th would move across the river to El Boum and Four a Chaux and turn the enemy's flank. The 2/14th with two companies would then move through the 2/27th to the line of the Nahr Daqoun.

---

[3] Here it was to take over command of the 2/2 Pnr Bn, which was to occupy a defensive position astride the coast road after the 2/16th had advanced.

[4] In the final days of June air attacks increased in weight and from the night of the 25th-26th Beirut was bombed almost every night. On the 29th four Blenheims attacked the Residency at Beirut making twelve direct hits; Gen Dentz was absent at the time.

The 21st Brigade was to be supported by the guns of the 2/4th and 2/5th Field Regiments, two troops of the 2/9th Field Regiment and the 212th British Medium Battery—62 guns in all. These would concentrate on the enemy's infantry and artillery positions from 12.35 a.m. to 1.20 a.m., then from 1.20 until 4.40 a.m. protect the advance of the 2/16th Battalion to its forming-up position beyond the river. From 4.40 to 5.30 the guns would provide a barrage ahead of the 2/16th and lifting 100 yards every five minutes. Finally the 2/4th would support the 2/27th Battalion and the 2/5th the 2/16th Battalion, each battalion being accompanied by a forward observation officer.

The 17th Brigade's role, if ordered to continue the attack, was to advance through the right flank of the 21st until its left battalion, the 2/5th, was on a line from Deir Mar Jorjos to En Naame and the 2/3rd occupied the wooded plateau on the right covering the roads leading into the area from the east.

It was a plan that would demand uncommon fortitude and endurance from the infantry. On the left a steep and well-defined ridge overlooking the river was to be assaulted. On the right there was to be a flanking march by four battalions through extremely rugged country into which they could take only what they, and perhaps the mules, could carry on their backs.

CHAPTER 25

THE BATTLE OF DAMOUR

FROM midnight onwards on the night of the 5th-6th July the leading companies of 21st Brigade set off one by one towards their distant objectives across the Damour River. After they had disappeared down the side of the ravine into the darkness there was silence, until, at 12.35 a.m., the artillery—sixty guns—opened fire on the French positions beyond the river. Then the whole area seemed to spring into violent life. The watchers on the southern ridge could see the shells bursting along the opposite wall of the chasm and French signal flares sailing up. The rocky sides of the ravine multiplied the sound of the shelling. The watchers knew that it would probably be light before the first news would come back from the forward troops or their first signals be seen. The roughness of the country over which the flank attack was to be made prohibited all but the simplest forms of signalling gear, and all but the lightest of weapons.

Captain White's company of the 2/27th led the procession of four battalions which was to stumble and slide in single file down the goat-track, cross the Damour and clamber up to El Boum. It had left El Haram at dusk and marched for three hours to El Batal, where the men rested until midnight. Twenty minutes later the men set off through El Labiye and down the steep track. The leading platoon was commanded by Lieutenant Sims, the same who had found the crossing four nights before. He and his men were on the road at the bottom of the ravine when their own artillery opened fire. The explosions reverberated so loudly that the men in the gorge could not hear themselves shout and shell fragments began falling down the precipitous sides. Sims led the way not up the track but along a wadi just to the west of it where his men would be sheltered from the French artillery and from mortars which could be heard firing in El Boum. The wadi rose so steeply that, laden as they were with 60 to 70 pounds of gear and some labouring under anti-tank rifles, the men could climb only 100 yards in twenty minutes, and therefore Sims decided to move to the track, preferring the risk of French fire to the danger of injury from falling down the little precipices in the wadi. At the first glimmer of light the toiling climbers reached some concertina wire stretched across the track, about a quarter of a mile from El Boum. Enemy troops somewhere ahead were firing but evidently not at them. They went on until they were 100 yards from the edge of the village. There the exuberant Sims formed the platoon up across the track, bayonets were fixed and the men clambered over some terraces and charged into the village. There was nobody there except some Syrians peering anxiously out of half-opened doors and a few alarmed French troops who were seen in the distance hurrying out of the place on the eastern side, having abandoned several mortars which they had been firing from a quarry there. Sims' men

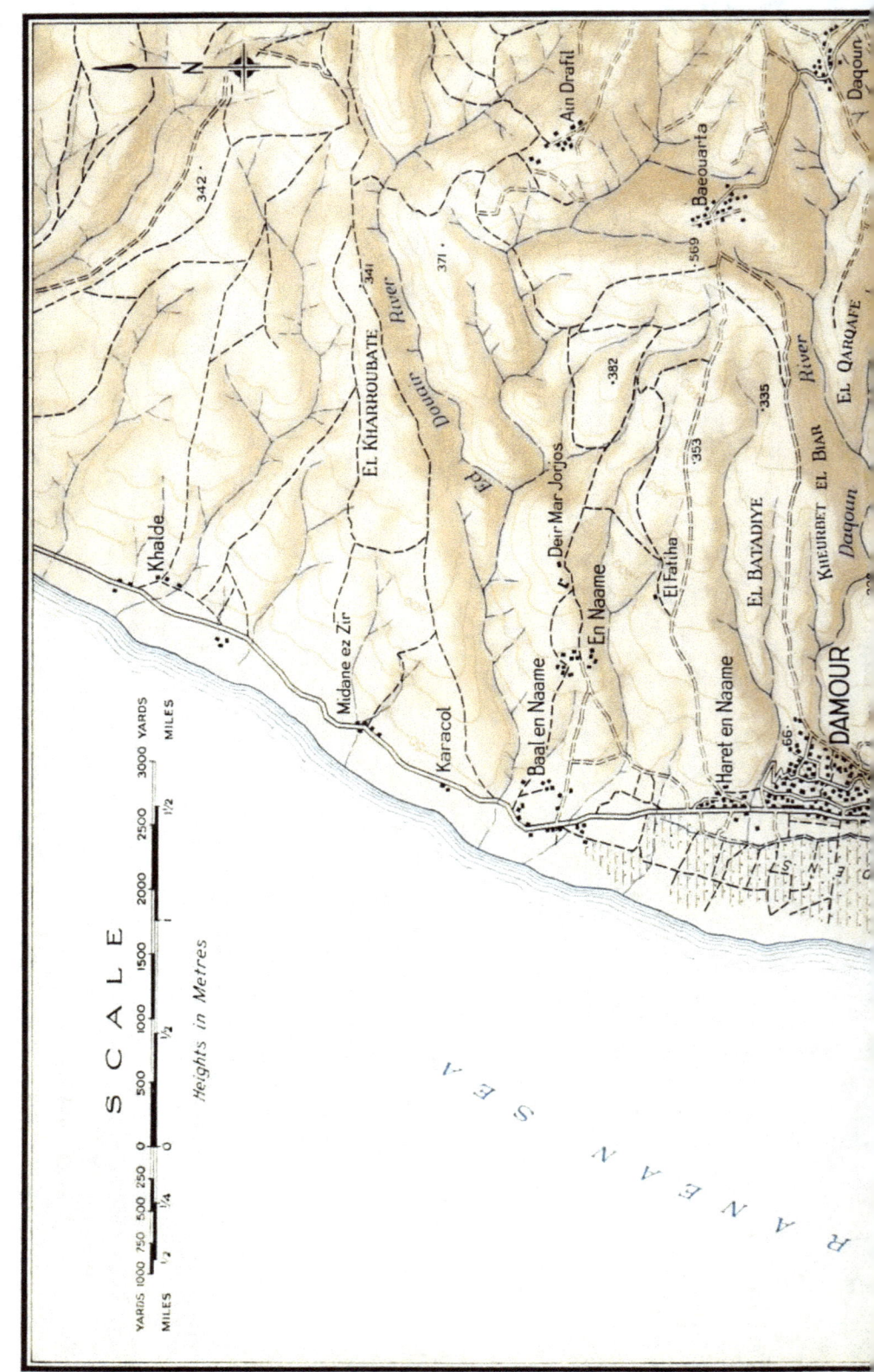

Midnight, 6th July 1941.

took up positions in the village and across the approaches from the east, north and west. About three-quarters of an hour later the remainder of their company arrived and were welcomed by loud shouts from the advance-guard announcing that Australians and not "Frogs" occupied the village.

The next company to move down the track was led by Captain Rice,[1] a high-spirited young regular. The column had been moving through El Batal when the barrage opened. Almost immediately shells began falling among them. The first killed Lieutenant Grant[2] and two others and seriously wounded Rice. He tried to struggle to his feet and lead the company on but was too weak and, when shells continued to fall, he ordered the men to disperse and seek cover. This command reached some of the company as an order to withdraw and the platoons became separated. Sergeant Macpherson gained touch with Colonel Moten's headquarters, reported what had happened and was ordered to collect the men and push on. Meanwhile Lieutenant Thomas,[3] the only remaining officer, was trying to reorganise the scattered sections when Captain A. J. Lee arrived leading his company, the next to move off. The shelling had now ceased. Lee told Thomas that his company would take over Rice's role and instructed him to follow as soon as he could and "have a go at the third objective" (which had been Lee's task). Lee led his men off into the darkness and about half an hour later Thomas set off with about twenty-five men, followed later by other small groups from this scattered company.

As this incident showed, the French artillery fire had been prompt and accurate. His gunners were concentrating on targets that had been carefully ranged. Among them, inevitably, were the artillery and infantry observation post on Hill 394. By 7 a.m. this area had been thoroughly pounded. "The wireless had been knocked out, water cans ruined and blankets and equipment torn to shreds."[4] Later the artillery observers moved lower down the forward slope of the hill.

Meanwhile, when Rice's company failed to arrive at El Boum by 7 a.m., White decided to advance without waiting for it. He spread his company out along the east-west track beyond El Boum and moved off. There was no opposition at the eastern end of the track but at the western end, near Hill 250, the infantrymen encountered a strong French post—a group of sangars manned by Senegalese with French officers, and some Foreign Legionaries. Pressing forward Lieutenant R. G. Geddes and Corporal Martin[5] were killed and others were wounded; the post was still resisting when Lee's company arrived. This company gave additional supporting fire—particularly with mortars which scored direct hits on the sangars—

---

[1] Maj D. G. Rice, SX4541. 2/27 Bn and Staff appts. Regular soldier; of Sandy Bay, Tas; b. Mosman, NSW, 3 Jan 1915.

[2] Lt J. L. Grant, SX3491; 2/27 Bn. Theological student; of North Adelaide; b. Adelaide, 18 Apr 1920. Killed in action 6 Jul 1941.

[3] Lt S. E. Thomas. SX3124; 2/27 Bn. Clerk; of Glenelg, SA; b. Adelaide, 15 Jul 1916. Killed in action 7 Jul 1941.

[4] Henry, *The Story of the 2/4th Field Regiment*, p. 162.

[5] Cpl A. K. M. Martin, SX4008; 2/27 Bn. Sheep breeder; of Terowie, SA; b. Terowie, 29 Feb 1916. Killed in action 6 Jul 1941.

and after ten minutes a white flag was raised. The attackers began to advance but a French machine-gun opened fire and two Australians were wounded. The Australians fired again, and after five minutes the enemy stood up, one waving a white flag.[6]

Lee then moved on to take the next objective (a line through Er Roumane). There his company was fired on by three machine-gun posts from lower ground ahead. He spread his platoons over a wide front, decided that the enemy "now being surrounded would move out at dusk" and, in anticipation, fired the success signal. Later he sent a platoon to hold the towering Hill 560 on his right.

At 1.30 Moten arrived at the river crossing on the way to establish a new headquarters at El Boum. From the river (where Stevens had posted his brigade major, Finlay,[7] to keep him informed about events on that important flank) a telephone line had been laid to El Boum, and on it Moten spoke to Nicholls, whose company, having finished its task on the right flank (described below), had marched across country to El Boum where it had arrived at 8 a.m. Nicholls gave him an account of what had happened on the right and Moten ordered Nicholls (there being still no news of Rice's company) to march on through Lee's company and take the final objective. Nicholls' company marched on, was delayed at the Er Roumane position until it was discovered (as Lee had anticipated) that the French had withdrawn, and then moved on, establishing themselves on the feature overlooking Daraya from the east (the 512 metre hill) at 10.35 p.m. Thus before midnight on the 6th the 2/27th was firmly holding the corridor through which the 17th Brigade was to advance to cut the road leading northward out of Damour.

The rearmost company (with the remnants of Rice's company, now about fifty men) was holding a wider front than the orders had demanded. Each of the two forward companies was on the high features to the east of their axis but neither was yet occupying ground as far west towards Damour as the plan had proposed.

Though it had met little opposition, the march of the leading company on the right—Nicholls'—was an impressive demonstration of the stamina of the men and their skill in mountain country. They had reached the wooded area above the Damour tributary at 10 p.m. on 5th July, had marched down into the tributary, climbed up 800 feet on the other side, taken part in an action there, marched down again to the floor of the Damour gorge north of the Beit ed Dine road, made a hand-and-foot climb up the far side rising 1,000 feet to El Boum, and thence, after a few hours' rest, had taken over another company's role and moved across four wadis and four steep ridges to Daraya, whence one of the platoons had climbed a 1,500-foot eminence overlooking that village. In a bee-line they were a little more than three miles from their starting point; in terms

---

[6] Later a French machine-gunner said that after the white flag had gone up his team had been forced to fire by an officer who threatened to shoot them if they did not. Seventeen men were captured, eleven were found dead, and some escaped towards El Hamra.

[7] Col C. H. Finlay, OBE, NX73. 6 Cav Regt 1939-41; BM 21 Bde 1941, 26 Bde 1942; CO 2/24 Bn 1942-43; CO Z Special Unit 1944-45. Regular soldier; b. Sydney, 6 Oct 1910.

of human effort they had done all that fit and confident men could do in twenty-four hours.

The three companies of the 2/16th which were to attack El Atiqa assembled on the south side of Hill 168 before midnight. Colonel MacDonald sent Major Potts forward to the river crossings. Captain Robinson's[8] company was to cross the river to the right, Major Caro's to the left, and both were to advance against El Atiqa. Captain Hearman's company was to follow Caro's across the river, form up on the main road and attack westward through the plantations. As Caro's company was leaving the assembly area French shells fell round them and one platoon lost touch with the remainder of the company. When the supporting guns opened fire and the detonations began to reverberate in the rocky gorge the infantry moved down the slope towards the river. Well before dawn, the three companies (less the platoon mentioned above) were across the river and on their start-line—the Beit ed Dine road. Potts replaced the missing platoon in Caro's company by transferring one from Hearman's. At 4.40 a.m. the barrage lifted to a line higher up the El Atiqa ridge and became more intense; immediately the French, as though they too had been awaiting this signal, opened fire with artillery, mortars and machine-guns. The El Atiqa position blazed with the flashing of guns and bursting shells and the noise was stunning. For the watchers (and particularly MacDonald who had suffered some misgivings about this frontal attack on an area that was dangerously wide for his weak companies) this was the beginning of an anxious wait for perhaps an hour or more until news came back from across the river. After an hour and ten minutes the barrage ceased. Observers at Yerate saw flares and took them for their troops' success signal —in fact they were S.O.S. signals fired by the French.

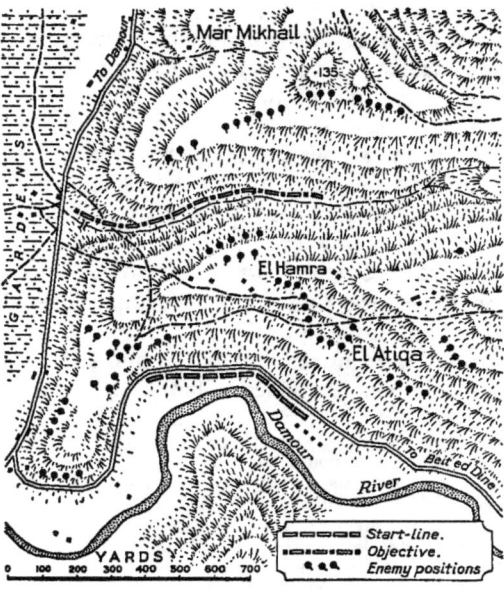

The advancing troops had climbed only a short distance from the road when they ran into intense fire from well-sited posts, and the attack developed into a series of small fights in which platoon became separated

---

[8] Maj A. Robinson, DSO, WX1589; 2/16 Bn. Hotel keeper; of Geraldton, WA; b. Prescot, Lancs, Eng, 13 Apr 1906.

from company and section from platoon. On the right Robinson's company overran one post, then came under heavy and accurate fire from another. In the platoon on the right Lieutenant O'Loughlin[9] and his sergeant, Dickson,[1] were both killed and the advance was halted. Lieutenant Madigan[2] led his platoon across to assist but it too was pinned down. Some men of O'Loughlin's platoon trickled down the slope, some joined Madigan, whose men, though unable to advance, resolutely held their ground all day exchanging fire with the enemy posts from whatever cover they could find, and became a collecting point for men who had lost their platoons and for French prisoners, of whom forty were assembled there during the day.[3] Eventually Madigan took up a position in a cave which had been used by the French as a storeroom.

Meanwhile the remainder of the company, now less than half the number that had gone into the attack, had pushed on until they came under fire from the farther ridge of Mar Mikhail. All efforts to find a covered approach to these posts failed, and casualties reduced what remained of the company to the strength of a platoon.[4] Fire was concentrated on these men from one French post after another until six had joined in. Believing that some of the fire was coming from the neighbouring company of his battalion Lieutenant Stapledon[5] stood up to signal to them and was fatally wounded by a burst of enemy machine-gun fire. The survivors trickled back into the wadi at the foot of Mar Mikhail, while Madigan's party gave covering fire from the southern side. The ground between them and Madigan's position was swept by fire and eventually they moved left across the line of the centre company's planned advance. After picking up some scattered men of that company and some prisoners, Captain Robinson established the party in a house near the junction of the main road and the road to Beit ed Dine, where some men of both the other attacking companies had already collected, including one officer who was severely wounded.[6]

Caro's company, to which some of these men belonged, moved briskly to the top of the El Atiqa ridge, through a barbed wire obstacle there and moving to the right gained a foothold on the Mar Mikhail ridge. There they ran into heavy fire and Lieutenant Rose[7] was fatally wounded. His platoon, convinced that their own shells were falling in the area,

---

[9] Lt C. E. O'Loughlin, WX2808; 2/16 Bn. Salesman; of Inglewood, WA; b. Brookton, WA, 7 Jan 1915. Killed in action 6 Jul 1941.

[1] Sgt T. J. M. Dickson, WX2643; 2/16 Bn. Storeman; of Cottesloe, WA; b. Esperance, WA, 31 Jun 1907. Killed in action 6 Jul 1941.

[2] Capt E. B. Madigan, MC, WX11020; 2/16 Bn. Signwriter; of West Perth, WA; b. Northam, WA, 14 Mar 1910.

[3] They included a French doctor with two stretcher-bearers who did admirable work collecting both French and Australian wounded under fire. One stretcher-bearer was killed attempting to rescue a wounded Australian.

[4] Lt T. Oversby (of Leederville, WA), the second-in-command of the company, and the CSM, WO2 F. L. Martin (Cottesloe, WA), were killed here.

[5] Lt H. D. Stapledon, WX3246; 2/16 Bn. Barrister and solicitor; of West Perth, WA; b. Claremont, WA, 8 Jul 1904. Killed in action 6 Jul 1941.

[6] Lt R. J. C. Reid.

[7] Lt R. N. Rose, WX2811; 2/16 Bn. Farmer; of Burekup, WA; b. Bunbury, WA, 20 Oct 1914. Died of wounds 7 Jul 1941.

moved back into the comparative shelter of the wadi. The two platoons on the left—Sergeant Salom's,[8] which was leading, and Lieutenant Harper's —met heavy fire on the El Atiqa ridge itself. In a successful attack on a strong post both Harper and Salom were wounded, Harper fatally, but Caro established the survivors on the ridge.

Lieutenant Cutler was with Caro's company as artillery observation officer. In the advance Cutler

became involved in the infantry fight, and captured eight Frenchmen from three machine-gun posts. The enemy in the first nest were persuaded to surrender by the sight of this six-feet-four-inches of elongated Aussie jumping right into their midst. Those in the second nest were talked into it by Cutler's limited French. A grenade dropped into the third plus the assistance of a Bren-gunner from the battalion, caused its occupants to make an instant decision on the subject.[9]

The infantry's wireless would not work in such hilly country and Cutler offered to go back to the river to a pre-arranged rendezvous with Lieutenant Macmeikan,[1] of his regiment, and carry a telephone line forward so that he could bring artillery fire down on the enemy posts. On the way, however, he was severely wounded in the leg.[2] There was no artillery link with the forward companies of the 2/16th until Macmeikan established a post about 300 yards north of the demolished bridge on the morning of the 7th.

Hearman's company, which had followed Caro's across the river, also met heavy fire soon after it began moving up from the road at zero hour. Gallantly guided by Warrant-Officer Burbidge[3] and Sergeant Gray, the right-hand platoon took one French post and was moving on when both Gray and Burbidge and then Lieutenant Reid[4] were wounded and the attack faded. The remainder of the company, farther to the left, had been pinned down by enemy fire. It withdrew and reorganised among the trees just north of the river. Hearman, with the thirty of his company who remained, tried to move left then right, but in each direction ran into severe fire. Three signallers, Corporal Bremner[5] and Privates Hickey[6] and Bright, worked their way forward with a telephone line, reporting what they could see of the progress of the fight to MacDonald as they went.

---

[8] Lt A. L. Salom, WX3567; 2/16 Bn. Farmer; of Brunswick Junction, WA; b. Perth, WA, 7 Jan 1906.

[9] J. W. O'Brien, *Guns and Gunners, The Story of the 2/5th Australian Field Regiment in World War II*, p. 122.

[1] Capt T. K. L. Macmeikan, VX1055; 2/5 Fd Regt. Clerk; of Malvern, Vic; b. Murrumbeena, Vic, 29 Jun 1918.

[2] Cutler lay isolated and exposed for some hours until some of his prisoners carried him to the road. There, next morning, Lt Macmeikan found him and had him taken to Yerate. When the regimental medical officer, Capt A. M. Johnson (of North Sydney), was attending him, shell-fire descended on the building, a shell burst in an open doorway and wounded several men. Johnson had Cutler placed on a truck which was driven, under sharp fire, to the main dressing station where Cutler's leg was amputated.

[3] WO1 T. Burbidge, DCM, WX2834. (1914-18: 2-Lt 8/Norfolk.) 2/16 Bn. Contractor; of Toodyay, WA; b. London, 19 Jan 1896.

[4] Capt R. J. C. Reid, WX3859; 2/16 Bn. Shipping clerk; of Perth; WA; b. West Perth, WA, 27 Apr 1917.

[5] Lt L. D. Bremner, WX3865; 2/16 Bn. Railway fireman; of North Perth, WA; b. Kalgoorlie, WA, 19 Aug 1911.

[6] Pte J. H. Hickey, WX8255; 2/16 Bn. Miner; of Kalgoorlie, WA; b. Albany, WA, 9 Apr 1913.

By 11 a.m. they reached Hearman who gave MacDonald an account of the morning's fighting. Its position clearly seen by the enemy, and under intermittent machine-gun fire and frequent mortar bombardments, Hearman's company held on until 4 p.m. when he was wounded by a splinter from one of the shells now being fired into the orchard area by the supporting British naval vessels. Before he left he ordered Captain Anderson,[7] his second-in-command, to withdraw the remnants of the company to the south side of the river when darkness fell.[8] Anderson did so.

At zero a small party from MacDonald's remaining company had been sent to the delta to clear the enemy out of it. They had reached wire entanglements on the north side when the enemy opened fire. When Sergeant Dungey,[9] Corporal Charlesworth[1] and Private Ross[2] went forward to cut a way through the wire the first two were killed and Ross severely wounded; the rest withdrew. At 8 o'clock the remainder of the company went forward to give covering fire for the attack which (if all had gone well) Hearman's company was to have made on the orchard area. It was still believed that Hearman's company had reached its first objective and would soon be advancing west into the orchards. However, when the supporting company reached the river it met heavy fire and suffered casualties. Finally, the attack on the orchards having failed, it was sent back to Yerate. Before the company withdrew, Corporal Wieck and Private Douglas[3] crossed the delta under fire and carried in the brave Ross.

During the day the telephone lines to Colonel MacDonald's headquarters had been broken again and again by shell-fire, and by the tracks of carriers moving on the road. It was not until Hearman spoke to him that he had been able to gain even an approximate picture of the situation at El Atiqa. It seemed to him then that the attack had failed but soon he learnt that the 2/27th on the right were advancing to their third objective. In mid-afternoon Brigadier Stevens ordered Colonel MacDonald to consolidate and give up no ground, and to protect his left flank along the El Atiqa spur at a distance of 400 yards from the road. After midnight, he ordered, patrols should be sent into the orchards to find and destroy the machine-gun posts there. One company was to be placed astride the coast road beyond Yerate to guard against counter-attack.

Thereupon, when Captain Anderson arrived at battalion headquarters with the remnants of his company, they were trucked back along the road to the river crossing and, in the darkness, climbed the El Atiqa ridge and took up a position there; in the late evening, Captain Mac-

---

[7] Lt-Col A. J. Anderson, DSO, WX1590. 2/16 Bn, 39 Bn; CO 24 Bn 1944-46. Gold refiner; of Fimiston, WA; b. Boulder, WA, 19 Nov 1912.

[8] During the day the cruisers *Ajax*, *Perth* and *Carlisle* and six destroyers gave supporting fire.

[9] Sgt P. B. Dungey, WX2945; 2/16 Bn. Pastoralist; of South Perth, WA; b. Lancefield, WA, 12 Jun 1909. Killed in action 6 Jul 1941.

[1] Cpl A. E. Charlesworth, WX4658; 2/16 Bn. Master builder; of Victoria Park, WA; b. Carlton, Vic, 28 Sep 1909. Killed in action 6 Jul 1941.

[2] Pte C. F. Ross, WX5792; 2/16 Bn. Farm labourer; of Bayswater, WA; b. Glasgow, Scotland, 19 Nov 1913. Died of wounds 8 Jul 1941.

[3] Sgt E. F. R. Douglas, WX4307; 2/16 Bn. Orchard hand; of Collie Cardiff, WA; b. Meerut, India, 6 Dec 1905.

Kinnon's[4] company with some twenty men who had trickled back in the disorganisation of the other companies, and with a section of the 2/3rd Machine Gun Battalion, crossed the river and formed a defensive line north of the demolished bridge. Thus, during the night, what was left of the three attacking companies of the 2/16th Battalion were reorganised and dug in along the El Atiqa ridge with the reserve company holding the bridge-head behind them. They were more or less on the line that was held at dusk, from Robinson's position in the house on the main road, through Caro's thinly-held line on the ridge to the lonely outpost Madigan had established in the cave-storeroom on the right. The 2/16th had been set a very hard task—a frontal attack against a skilful enemy well dug in in a dominating position—but, at heavy cost, they established a bridgehead on the El Atiqa ridge across the Damour and pinned down the main French forces.[5]

Meanwhile, at the eastern extremity of the attacking line an isolated fight had been going on all day on the 1,500-foot ridge up which the road wound towards Beit ed Dine, and along which it was feared that the French might launch a flank attack on the Australian force, and use tanks and armoured cars, which could travel along that road from Beirut.

At 10 p.m. on 5th July Nicholls' company of the 2/27th (whose later advance to Daraya has already been described) was in the wooded area between Ed Dalamiye and the Damour tributary. At 8 p.m. Russell's company of the 2/14th and Captain Rhoden's[6] were at Kramdech, both companies being under Rhoden's command for the operation; they had moved forward toward the tributary, the infantry column being followed by a string of mules carrying the mortars and mortar bombs, and by signallers reeling out mile after mile of telephone wire.

Russell's company clambered north-east across the ridges in the darkness and at 3.15 was on the Beit ed Dine road where it travelled, a mere ledge, across the face of the 567-metre ridge. Here the men built a rough wall of stones to block the road and waited for dawn. At the first glimmer of light Lieutenant Treacy,[7] with twelve men, was sent up the slope of Hill 567 to discover whether it was occupied. They came under fire from a strong French post, not on the summit at which Treacy was aiming but on the saddle between it and a twin knoll to the west; they withdrew leaving two men in the hands of the French. Russell thereupon organised an attack with his three platoons, Treacy's to climb to the western knoll while Lieutenant Bisset[8] moved on to Hill 567 with two

[4] Maj W. A. MacKinnon, WX1594; 2/16 and 11 Bns. Accountant; of Nedlands, WA; b. Huntly, Aberdeenshire, Scotland, 7 May 1911.

[5] In the whole battle the 2/16th lost 27 killed or died of wounds and 74 wounded, nearly all of them on this day and in the three forward companies, which had gone in with a total strength of only 263. Five wounded and two unwounded men were taken prisoner by the French. Each of the three forward companies had lost three officers or sergeants-commanding-platoons.

[6] Lt-Col P. E. Rhoden, OBE, VX14250. CO 2/14 Bn 1943-45. Solicitor; of Essendon, Vic; b. Essendon, 23 Dec 1914.

[7] Capt M. A. Treacy, MC, VX15489; 2/14 Bn. Shop assistant; of Mildura, Vic; b. Nathalia, Vic, 24 Nov 1915. Killed in action 29 Nov 1942.

[8] Lt T. H. Bisset, VX14631; 2/14 Bn. Clerk and jackeroo; of Surrey Hills, Vic; b. Albert Park, Vic, 30 Jun 1910. Killed in action 30 Aug 1942.

platoons; the French defeated this attempt by rolling grenades down the slope. At 8.30 a.m. three armoured cars appeared from the direction of Beit ed Dine, and drove to within 200 yards of the road-block. Here a party of Russell's men were stationed and, as the cars arrived, Corporal Daley[9] stood up and threw a sticky bomb at the leading one. It failed to stick and exploded harmlessly on the road, but the cars hastily retreated about 2,000 yards along the road, halted, and began firing their 2-pounder guns. Encouraged by this support the enemy infantry sallied forth to drive the Australians off the road, but were beaten back with small arms and mortar fire, whereupon Russell's men attacked again at 9.15 a.m., supported by mortar fire, and gained a foothold on the upper slopes of Hill 567. A third attack, at 12.30, drove the French off the peak.

The fight continued, the French counter-attacks becoming stronger as the enemy force, which, at the outset, had consisted of about a platoon of Senegalese with French officers and N.C.O's, was strengthened by the addition of men who were being driven along the tops of the ridge by Rhoden's company at the western end of the El Mourhira spur. This company with Nicholls' company of the 2/27th had secured its objective before dawn and without opposition. The South Australians had then marched away to the north while Rhoden moved east along the spur to link with Russell, having built an obstacle on the road where it joins the secondary road between it and the Damour tributary.

Finally at 5.30 p.m. the French, now apparently about two platoons strong, made their best-organised attack on Russell's company, using smoke to conceal their advance but shouting as they came. This attack reached to within 40 yards of Treacy's platoon on the summit before it broke; one French officer and nineteen others were lying dead within sight of the defenders, but the well-dispersed Australians had no casualties. After another less determined effort by the enemy had failed, the two companies linked; the French withdrew, and did not again dispute possession of El Mourhira.[1] As soon as daylight had come the value of these heights had been apparent; they commanded a view not only of two miles of the road from Beit ed Dine—the only road along which vehicles could possibly carry reinforcements to the French—but also of the country over which the main attack by the 2/27th was moving north.

As soon as Brigadier Stevens received news of the good progress of the 2/27th he decided to use the remainder of the 2/14th, which was his reserve, to move through the corridor the 2/27th formed and advance to the line of the Wadi Daqoun north of Daraya. He gave Lieut-Colonel Cannon orders to this effect at midday on 6th July and at 3 p.m. the battalion (less the two companies on El Mourhira) set off from the Wadi Qassouba by way of Er Rezaniye to El Boum where they began to arrive

---

[9] Cpl W. Daley, VX17614; 2/14 Bn. Rigger; of Dareton, NSW; b. Emerald, Vic, 6 Mar 1908.

[1] Russell's company (which had lost only two men killed and two wounded in the day) remained on the El Mourhira feature until the Armistice, generally on short rations because all supplies had to be carried for many hours over rough country. All water had to be brought up from the river 1,500 feet below them. They managed, however, to buy bread from the few villagers in houses near the road.

half an hour after midnight. At 2.50 p.m. Colonel Chapman, Allen's G.S.O.1, asked Brigadier Savige whether his 17th Brigade could securely advance to El Boum by day, setting off that afternoon; but Stevens urged upon Savige, who consulted him, that it would be unwise to attempt the descent to the river in daylight in full view of the French artillery, and Chapman agreed.

Consequently, while the 2/14th was arriving at El Boum, the 2/3rd—the leading battalion of Savige's brigade—began filing down to the river, and the 2/5th was preparing to follow. Soon half the 2/14th, then the 2/3rd, and then the 2/5th would be strung out along the corridor. Savige decided to hold the 2/2nd Pioneers in the coastal area. The orders given to the leading battalions of the 17th Brigade were to form up on the track from the crossing to Hill 498, to move thence to a start-line on the Wadi Daqoun (assuming the 2/14th had secured it), and thence to advance to the objective, which was a line from the coast, through Deir Mar Jorjos to the high hills on the east, probably including Hill 569. To perform these orders would demand uncommon stamina and fortitude. As companies of the 21st Brigade had found, simply to reach Daraya in one more or less continuous march, much of it by night, was a considerable feat. For the 17th Brigade the march to the Wadi Daqoun beyond Daraya was to be simply the move to the start-line; after that their main task would begin.

The fact that the 2/3rd and 2/5th were to go so far into hills through which even mules might not be able to follow made it necessary to give the men a heavy load.[2] Each carried forty-eight hours' rations, not less than fifty rounds of ammunition (some carried up to 300), two grenades, one sticky bomb, a blanket and a full water-bottle. Mules were to carry reserves of ammunition and one "No. 11" wireless set for each battalion; the brigade signal section was to run a telephone line to each battalion. No artillery observing officers were to accompany the infantry; it was left to the commanding officers to signal for artillery support either by wireless or by telephone, or, if these failed, by signal lamp to the observation post on Hill 394; this had soon become the best source of information—sometimes the only one—on the inland flank.

From El Labiye onwards the cliff leading down to the river crossing was so precipitous and a shower of rain had now made it so slippery that the men of the 2/3rd often found themselves sliding down on their backsides. A drizzle of rain added to the difficulty. Half way down, the track, which had been a target all the previous day, disappeared in shale caused by the shelling; and equipment lay around marking the trail of the 2/27th Battalion on the previous night. The mules were left at this point.

When the head of the 2/3rd Battalion arrived at the Beit ed Dine road soon after 3 a.m. on the 7th an officer of the 2/27th Battalion pointed out the line of signal wire leading to the battalion's headquarters at El Boum. Bishop, Savige's brigade major, accompanied the battalion to this

---

[2] The two coys of the 2/14th had decided before they began to descend to the river that the country was too rugged for mules and had left their animals at Er Rezaniye.

point but there he left it, first requesting Major Stevenson, commanding the 2/3rd, to move to the left of his battalion when he reached the forming-up place so as to be close to Lieut-Colonel King, commander of the 2/5th, who was to coordinate the advance of the two units.

The leading party of the 2/3rd lost track of the signal wire, which had been buried in loose earth dislodged by the shell-fire. After searching for it for fifteen minutes Stevenson led the men straight up the hill, near the summit of which they found the track again. It was now becoming light. The leading company reached El Boum at 5.30 a.m., but it was about 8.30 before the entire battalion had arrived and stragglers had been collected. Eight men were missing, as was the Intelligence officer who had been injured crossing the river. After breakfast and one hour's rest the battalion was ready to move at 8.45 a.m., but it was not until 9.50 that Stevenson was able to find King, and a conference was held.

King's battalion had the same difficulty as the 2/3rd in clambering down the narrow track to the river in single file. "This plus the fact that the Cypriots in charge of the 2/3rd Battalion's mules stopped for no reason at all (says one account) caused many unnecessary halts . . . . In the dark, with mules dispersed through the column almost continuously tangling both themselves and the troops among the signal wires, it was an impossible trip." King ordered that all mules be put off the track.

Where the track to El Boum reached the top of the first series of steep rises King found some stragglers (of the 2/3rd) asleep. From here King, who had sprained his ankle two days before and was in acute discomfort, went forward to El Boum to find Stevenson. His troops, now very weary, reached El Boum between 7.45 and 8.45 a.m. There King decided that the proposed forming-up place, which followed the line of the steeply-faced ridge overlooking the Wadi Zouade, was not suitable and fixed a new line running east-west through El Boum where the 2/3rd Battalion formed on the right and the 2/5th on the left.

At 10 a.m., just after King's conference with Stevenson, a mule train arrived with one of the wireless sets and King was able to inform Savige of his progress.[3] Blankets and other gear that could be dispensed with were placed in a dump and, at 10.30 a.m., the battalions began to advance due north each in diamond or arrowhead formation with 500 yards between companies, 200 yards between platoons and the men in single file. The 2/3rd Battalion on the right reached Daraya at 12.30 and there found Nicholls of the 2/27th who told Stevenson that he had patrols on Hill 560 (which rose high on their right rear) and that a company of the 2/14th had crossed the Daqoun and swung towards Damour. Machine-gun fire was coming from the ridges ahead.

To return to the right flank: the 2/3rd Battalion had lost touch with the 2/5th after leaving the forming-up position beyond El Boum. "The map (says its report) failed to reveal the true nature and the steepness of the wadis." It was late in the afternoon before the battalion was in position

---

[3] The 2/3rd had no W.T. but was communicating with the observation post on Hill 394 (where Bishop was now stationed) with a lamp.

on the "start-line" beyond the Wadi Daqoun; one company set off to occupy the steep El Qarqafe feature on the right and the other three companies were ordered to occupy the Kheurbet el Biar ridge (along the southern slopes of which a company of the 2/14th Battalion had advanced down to Damour earlier in the day). King arrived soon after this advance began and said that, because of the number of points from which enemy machine-gun fire was breaking out, he wished to postpone any attack until next morning—the 8th—when he would ask for artillery support.

Soon Captain Hutchison's company of the 2/3rd had climbed the pine-clad Qarqafe razor-back, where French shells which were arriving spasmodically lit the trees and the men had to fight a bush-fire. In the centre Captain Murchison's company occupied Hill 335 about 3 p.m. Later Stevenson received from brigade headquarters a signal timed an hour earlier warning him that a French battalion was on his right flank an hour and a half away. He informed Lieutenant Clarke of the 2/3rd Machine Gun Battalion who had a platoon in position on the south side of the wadi. In due course, about 100 enemy troops appeared and began to unload mules under the pines east of Hill 512. Clarke held his men's fire until the French were 600 yards away then fired "with devastating effect" on the troops and on their mule train. The battalion's 3-inch mortar opened fire on the French and completed the job of dispersing them and their mules.

At 5.45 p.m., Savige, anxious not to lose the effect of surprise by delay which might enable the enemy to counter this move on the flank, ordered King to begin his advance to Deir Mar Jorjos that evening. "Tired men who had won through," Savige said, "were better than dead men killed in storming occupied positions." King agreed and the weary men of the 2/5th moved off again, now with three companies forward and in line and one company following, all moving in single file across the wadis but resuming normal formation as soon as each wadi had been crossed. The battalion crossed the steep Wadi Daqoun in fading light and in the darkness the pace became slower and slower. At each halt men would fall asleep, and it took much time to make sure they were all awake when the march had to be resumed. After the 2/5th had passed through the 2/3rd, Stevenson decided that it would be unwise to continue his advance in the dark, in case fire fights developed with the 2/5th Battalion, moving northward along what would also be his line of advance.

In the meantime the two companies of the 2/14th which had passed through Daraya at 8.30 a.m. that day ahead of the battalions of the 17th Brigade had been advancing westwards, one company (Captain Noonan's) along the ridge north of the Wadi Daqoun, and the other (Captain Arthur's[4]) along the ridge south of it. This was in obedience to Stevens' plan that they should swing into Damour from the east and gain touch with the 2/2nd Pioneers there. After Noonan's company had moved 200

---
[4] Capt W. H. Arthur, VX43377; 2/14 Bn. Carrier; of Shepparton, Vic; b. Mooroopna, Vic, 22 Feb 1910.

yards along the ridge one of the two leading platoons found two enemy soldiers who surrendered. The weary men marched on without opposition until they reached a point about 400 yards from the edge of the town. There they rested for two hours.

Arthur's company on the ridge south of the wadi had been ordered by Cannon to advance along the Daraya ridge to Hill 225 from which, the map showed, a view could be obtained far to the south and north and over Damour town on the west. He sent one of his platoons (nineteen strong) along the northern slope of the ridge, another (twenty strong) along the ridge and held his third platoon (one corporal and three privates) as a reserve. When they were 400 yards from the hill machine-gun fire broke out from French troops who were holding it. The men on the ridge went to ground, but Arthur ordered his platoon on the right to move to higher ground and give covering fire. At the same time he sent his "reserve" to the left where they too were pinned down by fire from four machine-guns posted round the hill. Arthur sent a message back to Daraya asking for mortars and received instead two Vickers guns of the 2/3rd Machine Gun Battalion. These arrived late in the afternoon, the gunners quickly found the range and so disorganised the French and Senegalese defenders that the infantrymen were able to press forward. At the same time the French found themselves being attacked by other Australians coming from the direction of Hill 104 at the south-western extremity of the ridge. These belonged to a strong patrol led by Lieutenants Katekar and Mullighan of the 2/27th which Nicholls had sent in that direction. Finding it held by French troops whose machine-gun fire pinned his men down on the bare ridge, Katekar sent back a runner, Private Burzacott,[5] who pointed out the enemy's positions to Captain Samson[6] who was forward observing for the 2/4th Field Regiment. Samson brought down accurate artillery fire until the watchers could see French soldiers running, clearly silhouetted against the drifting smoke. Katekar's patrol then moved along the ridge towards Hill 225, where at dusk the French defence, now pressed from three sides, began to disintegrate.

Meanwhile, in Arthur's area Sergeant Thomson[7] and seven men, stalking forward on the right in the dim light, surprised two Frenchmen and sixteen Senegalese who surrendered. A little later, when it was dark, in a skirmish on Hill 225 itself, Thomson and Private Kramme[8] were hit with bullets at short range. About the same time Katekar's patrol moving up towards Hill 225 from Hill 104 also came under fire in the darkness and Mullighan and one other were killed. But by midnight the whole feature had been cleared of the enemy, 18 of whom had been killed, and 28, mostly Senegalese, taken prisoner. Six machine-guns, 10,000 rounds

---

[5] Sgt W. R. Burzacott, SX4484; 2/27 Bn. Labourer; of Naracoorte, SA; b. Naracoorte, 18 Jan 1918.

[6] Lt-Col B. E. G. Samson, VX14098. 2/4 Fd Regt 1940-42; CO 13 Fd Regt 1943-44, 2/11 Fd Regt 1945. Bank clerk; of Glen Iris, Vic; b. Melbourne, 2 May 1911.

[7] Lt A. W. Thomson, VX15794; 2/14 Bn. Clerk; of Kew, Vic; b. Ivanhoe, Vic, 6 May 1918.

[8] Pte J. H. Kramme, VX16372; 2/14 Bn. Farm labourer; of Mossiface, Vic; b. Melbourne, 29 Jul 1918.

of ammunition, 300 grenades and other equipment were found abandoned by the French, whose strength at the outset was estimated at 150.

> It was indeed a triumph (Arthur reported) and everyone though worn and hungry was very happy and bucked up.

Noonan's company which we left on the northern side of the Wadi Daqoun only 400 yards from the outskirts of Damour itself could hear intense fire being exchanged on the other side of the wadi to the south-east, yet they had met no enemies; evidently the way into the town was open. Lieutenant McGavin, one of Noonan's platoon commanders, urged him to advance into the town, arguing that at least there would be good water there, perhaps food, for they were on short rations. Eventually Noonan decided to hold his headquarters and one platoon where they were and send two platoons into the town. As the infantry advanced cautiously along the streets shots were exchanged with a party of Frenchmen, whereupon the Australians occupied some sturdy stone buildings. Soon a French N.C.O. led a party of ten white troops searching along the street. The Australians waited until these were so close to them that they could not miss, then fired, killing or wounding every man.

About 4 p.m. parties of Senegalese, pressed from the east by Arthur's company and the south by Katekar's men, began to trickle straight into Noonan's company. First came a handful of Senegalese who surrendered when fired on. Twenty minutes later more Senegalese, commanded by a French officer, began to crowd down the hillside opposite Noonan's men. There were more than 100 of them closely bunched together. Sergeant Mott[9] waited until they were only 300 yards away and then fired a burst over their heads and shouted "Surrender!" at the top of his voice. The Senegalese ran for cover but the hillside was bare and the Australians were in secure positions that had been dug by the French. There was some more firing, the French officer was hit, and ninety-two Senegalese, some of whom had been wounded on Hill 225, surrendered. Later in the afternoon more parties of Senegalese appeared but, apparently warned by the sound of firing from Damour, veered to the east. Hungry, thirsty and weary, Noonan's men packed their prisoners (who outnumbered them) into a house on the edge of Damour, established themselves in other houses, all empty of both people and food, and, somewhat anxiously, waited for the battle to catch them up. All night they could hear vehicles driving into the town from the north. The French knew they were there and their own gunners did not, with the result that the neighbourhood was shelled intermittently by both sides.

Few moves were made on the 2/16th Battalion's front on the 7th. Dawn patrols discovered that during the night the enemy had withdrawn from his remaining positions on the El Atiqa ridge. Patrols entered the banana plantations, and cleared them to a line level with the ridge. The river

---

[9] Capt M. L. Mott, VX15274; 2/14 Bn. Sub-manager of newspaper; of Albury, NSW; b. Albury, 9 Jun 1915.

was bridged this day and vehicles began to cross at 2.30 p.m. During the afternoon three tanks and two companies of the 2/2nd Pioneers moved into the plantation area.

During daylight on the 7th the eastern side of the 2/27th's corridor was not attacked, and it was apparent that the French had stationed no troops on or near the eastern heights overlooking the route from El Boum to Daraya. The protection of the route against attack from the east was the task of a line of three large standing patrols each of which occupied one of the hills that rose steeply from the ridge in which the southern group of parallel wadis that ran down towards the Damour plantations had their source: the remnants of one company of the 2/27th were placed on Hill 498, another company whose headquarters were near Er Roumane had a platoon on the slopes of Hill 560, the next main feature to the north, Nicholls, at Daraya, had placed a patrol on Hill 512. Hill 560, a pine-clad eminence with a flat top from which the sides fell almost sheer for 100 feet, dominated the area. A good track linked to the road from Kafr Matta and Abey led from the east to its foot, then forked round it, sending one branch to Er Roumane and the other, deviously, to El Boum.

At 1.45 p.m. on the 7th July Moten sent his Intelligence officer, Lieutenant Dean,[1] to Hill 560 to see whether, from that eminence, he could plot the position of enemy guns that were shelling the battalion's area from somewhere to the north-east. Late that night Dean sent back news that the enemy was digging in on the eastern slopes of Hill 560. This was a serious matter, because thence the French could observe the whole of the corridor; indeed they could place much of it under long-range fire from machine-guns. Immediately Moten ordered Captain A. J. Lee at Er Roumane, in whose area Hill 560 lay, to drive the enemy off the hill. One platoon of Lee's company would attack from the west while another platoon which Moten put under Lee's command would attack from the south. Lee's force reached the slopes of Hill 560 about midnight but encountered heavy fire from mortars and machine-guns. Lee then organised a second attack using three platoons, and also a depleted platoon under Sergeant Cowan,[2] which had been sent out from El Boum to locate the patrol on Hill 498, had come into Lee's area and was co-opted to join in the fight. Still in the darkness this force attacked up the slopes of Hill 560, arrived within 180 yards of the French positions and there held on, expecting that the French, so closely pressed, would surrender when daylight came. They were not surprised when a French officer came forward and began to parley. However,

it was a ruse (wrote a diarist) enabling the enemy to crawl to a ledge overlooking our men and launch a dastardly attack with grenades, the officer disappearing behind a rock.

---

[1] Capt A. C. Dean, SX2643; 2/27 and 39 Bns. Regular soldier; of Adelaide; b. Parkside, SA, 26 Jun 1915. Killed in action 8 Aug 1942.

[2] Maj R. W. T. Cowan, SX4337; 2/27 Bn and Aust Int Corps. University tutor; of Lucindale, SA; b. Adelaide, 10 Apr 1914.

News came back that not only were the attacking troops—a collection of platoons and patrols from three companies—held on the slopes of 560 but that Lee's headquarters west of Er Roumane were under attack by fifty or sixty French troops with mortars who were advancing from the east round the north of the hill, and that he was hard pressed and suffering casualties.

Moten, learning of the strength of the French position, sent forward the few who remained of Lieutenant Thomas' company. This small reinforcement—one of the platoons contained only six men—was held all day by French fire south-west of Er Roumane on the way to Hill 560 having run into the French attack on company headquarters.[3] Lieutenant Sims was next sent forward with a platoon to join in the fight. The French near Er Roumane kept up their pressure for six hours, Lee keeping them at bay with the help of a section of Vickers machine-guns and some mortars of the 2/5th Battalion whose teams, fortunately for him, were labouring along well behind the advance of their own unit.

Thus, at midday, nearly all Moten's troops were committed. Of the three rifle companies which were south from Daraya all but two sections were in the fight either on the upper slopes of 560 or on the lower slopes between Point 278 and Er Roumane. In mid-afternoon Captain White took the remaining two sections forward with orders to take command of the whole action. Later the force attacking Lee's headquarters area, now 150 to 200 strong, was seen moving back out of range to the north-east. Although this thrust had pressed Lee hard the attackers had been in a very uncomfortable situation in that they were overlooked by part of Nicholls' company along the Daraya ridge about 500 yards to the north and were under fire all day from that direction.

French prisoners were taken, and these said that the counter-attack was being made by three companies of the *1/6th Foreign Legion* and a company 200 strong of the *29th Algerians*. The Algerians had arrived from France by way of Germany, Yugoslavia and Greece five days before.

As soon as it was dark yet another attack was made on Hill 560. White decided to withdraw his men to the terraced southern slopes and seek artillery support. Learning of this from a runner Moten went forward with an artillery officer. He arrived at the company positions at 5 a.m. on the 8th and, suspecting that the French might have withdrawn after such a mauling, ordered that patrols be sent forward. The hill was unoccupied, and many French dead were lying there. The victors too had lost heavily and each company had now little more than the strength of a platoon. White's company, for example, was only forty-five strong when the fight was over.

At dawn on the 8th the 2/3rd Battalion was on the Kheurbet el Biar ridge; soon after it was light, French artillery and mortar fire began falling along it. Enemy gun positions could be seen through the gap in the hills cut by the Wadi Daqoun, but the 2/3rd had no means of bringing its own

---

[3] Lt Thomas was killed here.

artillery fire to bear on them. At 6 a.m. Captain Parbury reported that he could see Australians at Deir Mar Jorjos on the northern sky-line. The battalion immediately moved forward to occupy the heights on the east which were its objective. When they had reached El Batadiye, Stevenson ordered Parbury to send a patrol to Hill 569, a commanding feature about 2,000 yards to the right.

Lieutenant Murdoch's platoon, to which Parbury gave this task, had climbed only half way up that hill when it was pinned to the ground by machine-gun fire, whereupon Stevenson ordered Parbury to capture the hill and if possible some guns firing somewhere east of it. Parbury's men were not only weary but thirsty, because they had not found any water to refill their bottles, and the mules carrying cans of water had not been able to cross the steep Daqoun; they thought the battle was won and did not relish the prospect of a long climb and an attack at the end of it. He led the men towards Hill 569 along a wooded ridge leading from the wadi. Without having met opposition he occupied the southernmost of two knolls forming the summit, and thence, about 500 yards to the east, saw five field guns on the outskirts of the village of Baeouarta. These were the guns that had been harassing the battalions along the corridor from the outset. Parbury ordered one platoon to cover the guns and the northern knoll, and another under Warrant-Officer MacDougal to capture it (it was bare, whereas the southern was wooded). MacDougal and his men advanced along the saddle and had climbed almost to the top of the 400-foot slope when heavy machine-gun fire came from round the guns. With bullets striking the hill round them, the attackers rushed the knoll, while the supporting platoons fired on the gun positions, which were accessible from Hill 569 only along a narrow track on a steep-sided ridge. It was then 2 p.m., and until dark a fire-fight continued between Parbury's company (which Murdoch then joined) and the enemy round the battery. The men had little water left. Late in the afternoon of the 9th Parbury's company attacked and, without loss, took the five guns and occupied the village.[4]

The 2/5th Battalion had reached the wadi south of Deir Mar Jorjos after midnight on the 7th-8th. The forward companies were engaged by machine-guns and rifles but soon silenced them. One company as it moved across the wadi met some opposition, but overcame it, capturing three prisoners and overrunning four 75's and eight medium machine-guns. At 3 a.m. on the 8th Deir Mar Jorjos was occupied and Captain Rowell's[5] company moved out to secure the high ground forward of En Naame. A fighting patrol which entered the village captured a French colonel of the Foreign Legion and his staff. This company remained among the trees and buildings at En Naame, two others were at and round Deir Mar Jorjos, and the fourth rifle company and headquarters company were

---

[4] An outstanding leader in this company was Pte Hector Mackay (of Curran, NSW), acting as a section leader, an old soldier reputed to be over 60, and an expert rifleman.

[5] Maj F. A. Rowell, VX159. 2/5 and 58/59 Bns; 7 Bn 1944-45. Bank clerk; of Canterbury, Vic; b. Canterbury, 19 Aug 1919.

The Wadi Damour. (2/5 Fd Regt Association)

(2/5 Fd Regt Association)
Lieutenant A. R. Cutler being carried towards Yerate by French prisoners. The medical officer of the 2/5th Field Regiment, Captain A. M. Johnson, is on the right. French shells are straddling the road to the rear.

(*Australian War Memorial*)

Shell fire covering the advance toward the wireless mast at Khalde.

south of it. By this time the infantry signallers had run out of wire, but by about 8 a.m. Captain Samson, of the 2/4th Field Regiment, had managed to bring his line through—it was now 15 miles long—and with it King was able to speak to Savige and report his position.

Soon after dawn on the 8th the French provided evidence of having recovered from the first shock that followed the arrival of Australian troops so deep behind their positions. Mortar bombs began falling among Rowell's company, from mortars sited on the ridge north of Deir Mar Jorjos. At 12.30 p.m. the headquarters company was brought forward to replace Rowell's, which was sent down the steep slopes to the main road to establish a road-block near the point where the track from En Naame meets the Beirut road. Seventy-five yards from the road, however, Rowell saw enemy troops in position under a bridge. He decided that one platoon should storm the bridge while the other two platoons gave covering fire.

> I had orders from the company commander to shoot my way through (reported the commander of the leading platoon, Lieutenant Leask[6]). I picked out a corporal (Matthew[7]) and two Tommy-gunners for the job and later, on the corporal's suggestion, added a Bren gun. In order to make as little movement as possible I did not view the enemy position but sent the corporal forward to look round the corner through a periscope. The corporal put forward a plan of attack which I adopted, and then he, two Tommy-gunners, a Bren gunner and myself stormed the position which was 75 yards along the wadi from the corner. The corporal threw a grenade while advancing, and as we neared the bridge and the dust had cleared, the last of the enemy could be seen disappearing to the rear.

From the observation post on Deir Mar Jorjos, however, Colonel King could see the enemy gathering for a counter-attack and ordered the artillery to put down a concentration. "The enemy broke and fled," wrote the battalion's diarist. "It is thought that this action led to the collapse of Damour."

In fact the town of Damour was now being pressed hard from three directions. The 2/5th had closed the road leading out of it to the north, the 2/14th was in the north-eastern outskirts, and the 2/2nd Pioneers were moving up from the south. It was difficult to coordinate these groups and there was a particular danger that artillery fire brought down in support of one of them might fall on another. Early in the afternoon, Brigadier Stevens informed Brigadier Savige that his troops would be withdrawn from the gardens south of the town while both town and gardens were bombarded. At 1.55 p.m. Savige passed this information on to Colonel King. Savige gathered from reports received from the 2/5th that part of that battalion was in the north-east corner of the town (actually the men who were there belonged to the 2/14th), and at 3.25 asked that the northern end of Damour be not bombarded. At 5 p.m. Colonel Chapman visited Brigadier Savige's headquarters with orders from General Allen

---

[6] Capt J. C. Leask, VX7043. 2/5 Bn 1940-42; Directorate of Engr Eqpt (Small Craft Sec) 1943-45. Shipping clerk; of St. Kilda, Vic; b. Melbourne, 12 Feb 1918.

[7] Lt D. H. Matthew, VX5316. 2/5 and 15 Bns. Grocer; of Swan Hill, Vic; b. Kyneton, Vic, 18 May 1915. Died of wounds 1 Sep 1943.

that when Damour fell the 21st Brigade would become responsible for the area south of the Wadi Daqoun, and the 17th responsible for the area north of it; the proposed role of the 17th would be to gain contact along the coast road, starting from 24 to 48 hours after the fall of Damour, while the 21st advanced east through Abey.

At 7.30 p.m. enemy movement from the north-east of the 2/5th Battalion was reported; Rowell's company was withdrawn from the roadblock, and the battalion occupied an arc from En Naame on the left, through Deir Mar Jorjos to Hill 230, south-east of it.

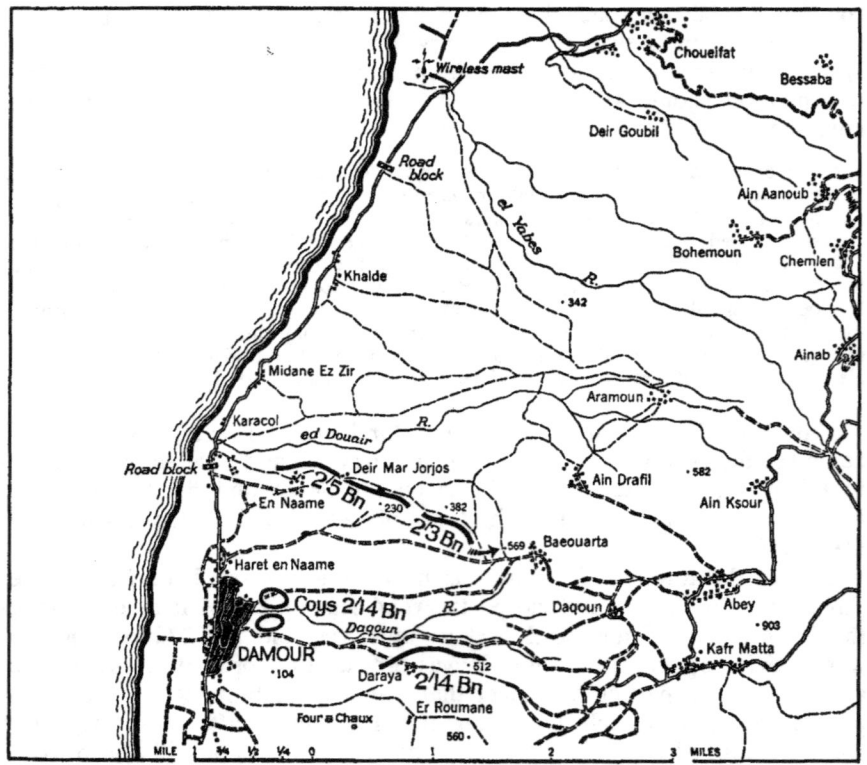

Nightfall, 8th July

During this day Noonan's company and Arthur's of the 2/14th Battalion had remained in or near the eastern outskirts of Damour, the one north the other south of the Wadi Daqoun. In the morning battalion headquarters was still not in touch with Noonan. Warrant-Officer Tipton[8] led a patrol across the Wadi Daqoun to find him but failed, though he located both the 2/3rd and 2/5th Battalions, and found the body of

---

[8] WO1 L. E. Tipton, VX14386; 2/14 Bn. Motor driver; of Nth Carlton, Vic; b. Carlton, Vic, 25 Jun 1911.

Lance-Corporal White[9] of Noonan's company, who had been sent back the previous day to locate his rear platoon and had not returned. Later in the morning, however, a runner from Arthur's company south of the Wadi Daqoun reached Noonan with the news that Arthur was in contact with battalion headquarters. At midday Arthur himself arrived, with a ration party, and, after a day during which there was spasmodic firing, instructions arrived at Noonan's headquarters that Arthur should move his company westward and Noonan should move to the south. This order was cancelled an hour later, to Noonan's great relief because, as he wrote afterwards, "the enemy was still between us and the troops to the south and I feared we would come into conflict with our own troops".

During the 8th the 2/16th improved its positions on the Mar Mikhail and El Atiqa ridges. That morning Lieutenant Boyd's[1] troop of the 6th Cavalry forded the Damour River and joined the three tanks of his regiment and the two companies of the 2/2nd Pioneers which had crossed the river the previous day. The Pioneers had pressed on and were now about a mile north of the river. Corporal Shannon,[2] on this day as on the 7th, had led fighting patrols forward with great gallantry. The attackers could now make no further progress through the banana groves, however, because of heavy mortar and machine-gun fire from a line of strong-posts along a gully cutting through the plantations here. The tanks could not advance because the road was covered by French 75's. During the morning Captain Mills, commanding the cavalry squadron, intercepted a message from the brigade commander to Colonel Monaghan of the Pioneers asking him why he was not making progress, and Monaghan's reply that he was so far forward that he was ahead of the cavalry. Thereupon Mills indignantly sent three tanks forward. The two tank troops of this squadron of 6th Cavalry were commanded by twin brothers—Duncan[3] and Gordon[4] Glasgow—who resembled each other closely. Monaghan ordered the troop which came forward to investigate the road into Damour, believing wrongly that he was employing the same troop commander as had made a reconnaissance the day before, had been fired on by a 75-mm gun in a stone building on the right of the road at the southern edge of the town, and was therefore well aware of the position of the gun. Unwarned of the probable presence of this gun, however, Sergeant Gordon Glasgow nosed his tank round a bend in the road and was suddenly fired on by the 75 only 300 yards away. The first shot blew off a track. The second tank of the troop which was following came up to help

---

[9] L-Cpl R. S. White, VX16025; 2/14 Bn. Motor body trimmer; of Ivanhoe, Vic; b. Burnley, Vic, 20 Mar 1920. Killed in action 7 Jul 1941.

[1] Capt D. G. Boyd, NX12295. 6 Cav Regt; 2/9 Cdo Sqn. Articled law clerk; of Peak Hill, NSW; b. Belfast, N. Ireland, 3 Aug 1911.

[2] Cpl T. A. Shannon, MM, VX42260; 2/2 Pnr Bn. Farmer; of Tallangatta, Vic; b. Melbourne, 8 Jun 1900. Drowned at sea while prisoner of war 24 Jun 1944.

[3] Capt Duncan Glasgow, QX364. 6 Cav Regt and staff appts. Clerk; of Brisbane; b. Blackall, Qld, 8 Jul 1918.

[4] Capt Gordon Glasgow, QX363. 6 Cav Regt and 2/1 Armd Bde. Shipping clerk; of Ascot, Qld; b. Blackall, Qld, 8 Jul 1918.

Glasgow whose gunner continued firing till his tank was hit again and set alight. Glasgow and his crew thereupon abandoned the tank and escaped while the gunner of the second vehicle gave covering fire. Lieutenant Macmeikan of the 2/5th Field Regiment saw the flash of the gun, and engaged and silenced it with artillery fire.

About 2 p.m., because little progress was being made, Stevens (as mentioned above) decided to withdraw Monaghan's Pioneers and the tanks and carriers and bombard the area. The French, however, shrewdly advanced as the Pioneers withdrew and most of the shells went over their heads; the ground lost was not regained that day, but a section of 4.5-inch howitzers was sent across the river to support the Pioneers. Captain Nason's company of the Pioneers attacked about 1 a.m. on the 9th, retook the ground that had been lost and, in the face of some rifle and machine-gun fire, advanced "well into the town". At 4 a.m. a troop of the 6th Cavalry went right through Damour. The town had fallen.

It soon became apparent that the French had made a large-scale withdrawal and, during the night, had abandoned every position for which they had been fighting so resolutely since the battle began. In and round Damour "stacks of unlaid mines were beside the road". By 7 a.m. the 2/2nd Pioneer and 2/16th Battalions had made contact with Noonan's men on the north-east outskirts of Damour, and the 6th Cavalry with some of the Pioneers had advanced north to Karacol and had patrolled to the ridge beyond it.

In the 2/5th Battalion's area two companies now occupied the road-block and awaited orders from Colonel King who had gone along the Beirut road to see the positions taken up by the 2/2nd Pioneers forward of his companies.

During the night Brigadier Savige's staff learnt from a native that Abey and the line of high features on the east had been abandoned by the enemy and informed General Allen of this.

Early on the 9th Brigadier Berryman, who had now returned from command of the Merdjayoun sector to his post as commander of the 7th Division's Artillery, and Colonel O'Brien of the 2/5th Field Regiment drove through Damour to three and a half miles north of it reaching a point where two tanks of the 6th Cavalry under Lieutenant Ryrie had been halted by a road-block. Berryman ordered the Pioneers and the left company of the 2/5th to occupy a position astride the road, and then telephoned to the headquarters of the division to say that he had instructed the 2/5th Battalion to push on. Chapman pointed out that the 17th Brigade was not to advance to the second objective until the general ordered it. He would arrange for the Pioneers to come under the command of 17th Brigade, since they had advanced beyond Savige's own battalions. Guns of the 2/5th Regiment had now dashed northward through the town. The leading guns were deployed about Karacol under sharp fire from French guns, and engaged the forward French troops over open sights. Later they shelled the southern outskirts of Beirut at extreme range.

"Things were now getting a bit mixed," wrote Savige later. In accordance with the arrangement outlined on the 8th, Savige was instructed to take over the area north of Damour and "straighten the matter out".[5] The two forward troops of the 6th Cavalry, a battery of the 2/5th Field Regiment, a troop of the 2/2nd Anti-Tank Regiment and other detachments were put under Savige's command, and he was instructed to relieve the 2/2nd Pioneers and put them in an area where they could obtain some rest.

Later in the afternoon, in obedience to the order to Stevens' brigade to take Abey and Kafr Matta while Savige's moved towards Beirut, a fighting patrol of the 2/27th Battalion under Sergeant Martin[6] moved into the Daqoun area and into Abey and found that the French had just abandoned both places. The 2/14th Battalion, now concentrating at Daraya, was ordered to occupy Abey, Kafr Matta and the dominating Hill 903 which lay between them, and then to move on to the road junction and "block all the roads to the north and south".

Savige went through Damour, found King, and, about 4.30 p.m., ordered him to relieve the Pioneers and use the cavalry to maintain contact with the enemy; he then returned to divisional headquarters to have his role clarified. Meanwhile, King established his headquarters on the road, and one of his companies relieved the Pioneers astride the road farther north. It was found that troops in this position could not protect the artillery and King ordered a night advance to a line from about Khalde on the left south-east across the hills for about two miles.

This forward move was completed by 4.20 a.m. on the 10th. The 2/5th was merely the skeleton of a battalion, none of the three forward companies exceeding forty-four men. There was only enough signal wire to lay a line to the centre company with a branch line to the company on the left.

Savige called on King that morning and instructed him to occupy the ridge overlooking Khalde from the east and patrol forward towards the next French road-block, about three-quarters of a mile south of a conspicuous wireless mast. The forward troops now had the support of the whole 2/5th Regiment and a troop of 6-inch howitzers of the 7th British Medium Regiment. King made a plan whereby some of these guns would concentrate on the wireless mast round which French guns were grouped, while others would put down a barrage 500 yards in front of the leading troops until zero hour and then would lift in 100-yard bounds every two minutes until all the guns were concentrating on Khalde. The French artillery fired heavily on the Australian positions during the day.

The attack began at 3.30 p.m. By 3.48 the leading company, despite mortar fire from the ridge on the right, had advanced 500 yards. The enemy's artillery fire became more intense, but at 4.15 all companies of the battalion were advancing, and a few minutes later the leaders

---

[5] 17th Australian Infantry Brigade, Report on Operations in Syria, July 1941.
[6] Lt E. T. Martin, SX3082; 2/27 Bn. Farmer; of Balhannah, SA; b. Balhannah, 2 Apr 1917. Killed in action 9 Oct 1943.

reached the French road-block and came under machine-gun fire from a blockhouse there. The road-block was made of "dragons' teeth" with stones piled on top, and a few yards behind it was another similar block. On the ridge to the right a platoon was held by mortar and machine-gun fire for two hours and a half. Tanks and carriers of the 6th Cavalry moved forward at this stage, and by 6.30 had cleared the road for 400 yards forward of the road-block.

Next morning (11th July) enemy fire dwindled and eventually ceased. At 1 p.m. King went forward to the road-block and ordered that a patrol from the company there probe forward for about 1,000 yards. The patrol returned and reported that it had not met any enemy. King then sent patrols forward from each company. All of these encountered the enemy; it was apparent that the patrol which had previously reported not meeting any enemy had been allowed to pass forward and back through his posts, which remained concealed and withheld their fire. About this time a squadron of enemy tanks paraded in full view on the sand dunes

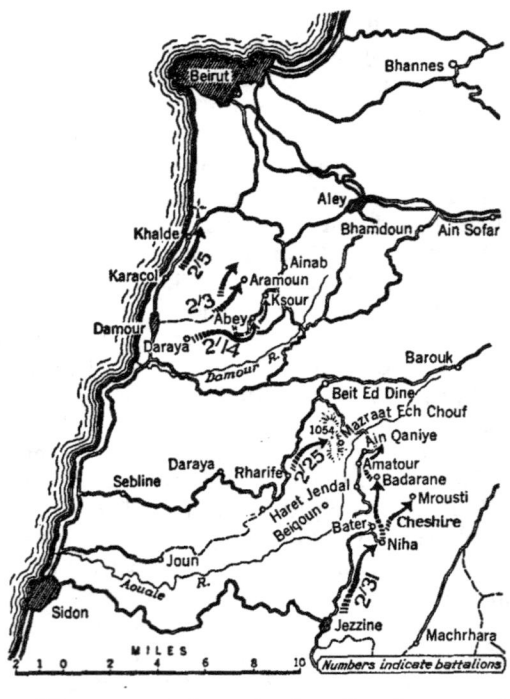

just beyond the wireless mast. King reported to Savige that he was in contact with the enemy's main defences; he was ordered to stay in position for the night and told that a coordinated attack would be planned for the next morning.

Savige had ordered the 2/3rd Battalion, in the hills on his right, to occupy dominating ridges round Aramoun and north of it. Early on the 11th this battalion had moved forward. Already they were so far into the hills that it was either difficult or impossible to carry rations to the forward positions; Captain Murchison's company, for example, had no army rations for three days but lived by shooting and cooking goats and acquiring horse meat from the villagers. Hutchison's, Murchison's and Parbury's companies made the advance to the wooded heights in the area of Aramoun, commanding the road from Abey. Murchison's company reached its objective beyond Deir Mar Jorjos without incident. Parbury occupied Aramoun and the heights to the west without opposition, but could hear heavy firing in Hutchison's area on his left. Hutchison's company—now only about thirty strong[7]—came under sharp fire when due west of Aramoun. They withdrew and set up a mortar which duelled with French machine-guns on the opposite hill.

Meanwhile, farther inland the 2/14th Battalion, on the morning of the 10th, had begun moving towards Abey (already found unoccupied by a patrol of the 2/27th) and Kafr Matta. One company moved from Daraya to Daqoun, established a road-block there, and marched on to Abey. Passing through Daqoun it found four 155-mm guns and 200 rounds of ammunition. After dark Lieutenant Nye[8] led a patrol to Ain Ksour and reported it unoccupied. In the early hours of the next morning the battalion occupied Ain Ksour.

While the battle was being fought at Damour there had been steady progress and some severe fighting by the 25th Brigade on the Jezzine flank. On the 6th the 2/31st followed the enemy as he withdrew north along the road to Beit ed Dine and early on the 7th were north of Niha and on the heights north of Bater; and a patrol of the Cheshire Yeomanry had passed through Mrousti and taken some prisoners there. A Swiss prisoner of the Foreign Legion said that the main French force had withdrawn from Bater because the Australian artillery had made it too difficult to bring supplies into the town. On the 6th Brigadier Plant ordered Colonel Withy's battalion group on his left to clear the enemy from the Beiqoun-Mazraat ech Chouf area. Withy gave Captain Marson's company of the 2/25th Battalion the task of advancing from Rharife and occupying the heights overlooking Mazraat ech Chouf.

Marson's plan was to place one platoon to cover his road-block north of Rharife while the other two, with artillery support directed by Lieutenant Johnson,[9] of the 2/6th Field Regiment, who was to establish an observation post on Hill 1054, moved along the ridges from Rharife to Mazraat. One of these (Lieutenant Macaulay's) was to move along a track to Hill 1054; the other (Lieutenant Farquhar's[1]) was to move along a gully farther south and then turn south-east and occupy an eminence south of 1054. At 3 p.m. on the 8th, when Farquhar and Macaulay were about half way to their objectives, the enemy opened fire from a hill to the north. Johnson crawled forward into the open and brought down very accurate fire on the French positions, but in spite of it, African troops began to attack Farquhar's platoon. They were checked, however, but the right section of Farquhar's platoon became confused and began to trickle back. Marson sent Macaulay's platoon forward to steady the position. Macaulay led his men on, but they came under fire from the south.

---

[7] Lt F. A. Stanton's platoon consisted of himself and eight men. "As a matter of interest, five of the nine were over thirty. We had had a gruelling week, and everyone was completely done in."

[8] Lt C. C. P. Nye, VX14096; 2/14 Bn. Railway employee; of Ormond, Vic; b. Port Melbourne, Vic, 1 Nov 1916. Killed in action 8 Sep 1942.

[9] Lt A. T. Johnson, MC, NX34979; 2/6 Fd Regt. Electrical engineer; of Longueville, NSW; b. Geraldton, WA, 26 Mar 1916.

[1] Maj E. A. Farquhar, QX6443; 2/25 Bn. Insurance officer; of Brisbane; b. Sydney, 25 Apr 1907.

It was now 7 p.m.; Macaulay had lost two men killed and two wounded, and the company was under fire from both flanks. At dark Marson went forward and withdrew Macaulay's platoon. Thus the French held the high ground at Mazraat ech Chouf whence they had good observation of the Rharife area, and directed artillery fire on the area generally and on the Mtoulle-Rharife road in particular.

Farther east the company of the 2/31st Battalion on Hill 1069 north of Bater was heavily attacked twice on the 8th July, and each time the attack was repulsed. The first came in the morning. The French caught the Australians unawares and the first they knew of the attack was a shower of grenades; grenades were thrown back. Five French were killed and the attack faded, but not before Lieutenant Crook and Private Breakspear[2] were killed and several men wounded, leaving the company only about twenty strong. The survivors appealed for help ("Did you see the picnic we were having? Can you give us any support?" they signalled to the company on the higher ground behind them), and about 4.30 Lieutenant Evans'[3] platoon of eighteen men came from that company on Hill 1203. The French next tried to circle round their left flank, but were driven off.

That day (the 8th) Captain Millroy's[4] company of the 2/25th Battalion was ordered to make the battalion's second attempt to drive the French from their position on Hill 1054. After an artillery barrage which opened at 3.30 a.m. Millroy led his company forward at 4 a.m. Nothing happened until the attackers were approaching the objective. Then the French opened fire from 50 yards away with machine-guns. One platoon went to ground below a 5-foot wall, and then withdrew—it was still dark. Millroy was wounded here and Lieutenant Butler took command. When daylight came it showed some sections of both platoons to be out in the open in full view of the enemy on Hill 1054. These sections were unable to move, and the company just held its ground, returning the fire of the enemy troops who were in well-prepared positions among the rocks, whence they were using accurate machine-gun fire on fixed lines.

Soon after light Butler found Marson and they decided to attack in the afternoon, after the men had eaten and after an artillery program had been arranged. Butler's company, with two platoons forward, would attack from a position on the ridge about half a mile from the objective

---

[2] Pte H. W. Breakspear, QX12371; 2/31 Bn. Farmer; of Gracemere, Qld; b. Croydon, Eng, 12 Apr 1915. Killed in action 8 Jul 1941.

[3] Capt A. Evans, WX3382; 2/31 Bn. Accountant; of South Perth, WA; b. Boulder City, WA, 5 Feb 1916.

[4] Maj A. J. Millroy, QX6418; 2/25 Bn. Company director; of Rockhampton, Qld; b. Rockhampton, 8 Jul 1904.

with Marson's depleted company on the right. Meanwhile Lieutenant Tilney's platoon of the 2/2nd Pioneer Battalion had advanced towards 1054 from the right until it was 250 yards from a group of enemy machine-gun posts. A long fight ensued in the course of which Tilney, Corporal Mucklow[5] and two Bren gunners silenced three machine-gun posts. Meanwhile a second platoon of Pioneers had moved forward along the edge of the gorge on Tilney's right. Tilney informed Butler by runner that he had taken the posts that had been ahead of him and it was arranged that the Pioneers should attack on the flank of the 2/25th. At 2.40 the artillery opened fire. After a fifty-minute bombardment the line of attackers moved forward with fixed bayonets and advanced 150 yards before the French opened a heavy but erratic fire with machine-guns and rifles. Some of the fire was from the right, so Marson ordered one of his platoons to swing in that direction to deal with it while the remainder, about seventy men, charged, firing from the hip and shoulder.

> When they were 100 yards from the enemy he started to run. This was the end. Our boys started cooee-ing and cheering as they ran after them and a considerable amount of effort was needed by officers to prevent them from overrunning down the north-eastern end of the hill. It was a remarkable sight . . . . Unfortunately the F.O.O. had no wire and was unable to follow us through, otherwise we could have taken a heavy toll as the enemy evacuated Mazraat ech Chouf with vehicles, on foot, with pack teams that had been hastily saddled. It was a scene of confusion but out of effective L.M.G. range.

Thus Mazraat ech Chouf and the heights overlooking it were taken.

Before the firing ceased in Syria there was one more fierce fight in the central sector. Lieutenant Stable's[6] company of the 2/31st Battalion, now only about sixty strong, was ordered to take the high ground overlooking Amatour and Badarane. A troop of the 6th Cavalry and the carrier platoon of the battalion were sent forward to help the infantry, but a broken bridge at Haret Jendal prevented them from taking part.

The country over which the attack was to be made was as difficult as any the battalion had met. A steep-sided wadi 800 feet deep separated the attackers from the objective, which rose another 600 feet on the far side of the wadi in a series of terraces four or five feet high. Merely to climb the hill was no small feat. The company's platoons were led by three outstanding soldiers—Lieutenant Hurrell[7] and Sergeants Davis and Sheppard.

It was a bright night with a half moon. Guided by a native, the company set out from Niha, more than three miles from the objective as the crow flies and more than twice as far as the mule plods. It began its march at 9 p.m. on the 9th and climbed down gorges and up precipices

---

[5] Sgt C. W. Mucklow, VX18985; 2/2 Pnr Bn. Truck and tractor driver; of Nathalia, Vic; b. Leamington, Eng, 12 Jul 1907. Died while prisoner of war 29 Jan 1944.

[6] Maj N. S. Stable, QX164. 2/31 Bn; Legal Services 1942-45. Barrister; of Brisbane; b. London, 22 Oct 1909.

[7] Capt L. T. Hurrell, NGX22; 2/31 Bn. Agriculturalist; of Keravat, New Britain and Cobargo, NSW; b. Comboyne, NSW, 23 Dec 1914. Killed in action 4 Dec 1942.

followed for a while by four mules carrying ammunition and rations. These animals and their drivers were left behind, however, in the first two hours.

The steep gullies were all so alike that, in the dark, it was hard to maintain direction. At 2.30 a.m., when the attackers were about 400 yards from Badarane, heavy fire broke out from four or five machine-guns which seemed in the darkness to be about 250 yards ahead. The fire was on fixed lines and the attackers could see that it was going over their heads and landing behind them.

Stable edged his men to the left of the Badarane heights, which were covered with olive trees 20 to 30 feet apart, and then, with Davis' and Hurrell's platoons leading and Sheppard's following, he sent in an attack. The weary men clambered uphill over terraces two to three feet high, firing as they went. The only delay was on the right, where the advance was held by intense fire until a quiet, cool West Australian, Private Gordon,[8] crept forward with rifle and bayonet to within a few yards of a stubborn French post, then charged, and bayonetted the four men who manned it.

On the left the gallant Davis—outstanding among young leaders in this battalion—was killed, and others with him. Of the forty-three men who went into the remote attack thirteen were killed or wounded before it was over, but forty to fifty dead Senegalese were counted on the ground, and a larger number of wounded men were taken prisoner—there were probably 200 of the enemy in prepared positions on the Badarane heights when the attack was launched. It was 5 a.m. before the fight was over and the Australians had established themselves at Badarane in the posts they had won. The Bren gunners and riflemen had fired heavily and there were only about fifty rounds of ammunition for each man.

At 5 a.m. Stable sent a wireless message to Major Pollard[9] at battalion headquarters to say that he was on the objective but had little ammunition or food. Two hours passed before a reply came back ordering Stable to destroy any enemy equipment that could not be carried and withdraw to battalion headquarters. While they were wrecking the French machine-guns and gear, the men found many water-bottles and one-gallon kegs filled with brandy—not uncommon in positions occupied by Senegalese troops. These were destroyed, and with them a large wireless set that had been used by a French artillery observation officer. While this work was going on one of Sheppard's corporals came to him and said: "There are Frogs moving round on the left." Sheppard looked and agreed. He estimated that there were at least twenty, and probably more behind them.

Hurrell's platoon retired while the remainder of the company covered it, waiting until the French were within 100 yards before they opened fire. The French took cover and after a brief exchange of fire the Australian

---

[8] Sgt J. H. Gordon, VC, WX2437; 2/31 Bn. Farmer; of Gingin, WA; b. Rockingham, WA, 7 Mar 1909. (Gordon was awarded the Victoria Cross for this action.)
[9] Col R. G. Pollard, DSO, NX70398, Acting CO 2/31 Bn in Jun-Jul 1941; GSO1 6 Div 1942-43, and various staff appts; Dep Dir Mil Ops LHQ 1945. Regular soldier; b. Bathurst, NSW, 20 Jan 1903.

rearguard began to withdraw. The men were desperately tired. Between the time that his corporal had reported that the French were advancing and the opening of the last fight, Sheppard himself had fallen asleep three times. The little company filtered back the way it had come. As they had no stretchers, they carried their wounded in pullovers threaded over rifles with bayonets fixed. The pullovers sagged so much that it was like carrying a man in a bag. Under fire from French rifles and Hotchkiss guns, the thirty men clambered down the terraces and along a wadi to the Jezzine-Beit ed Dine road. It was the last fight in this sector and one of the fiercest.

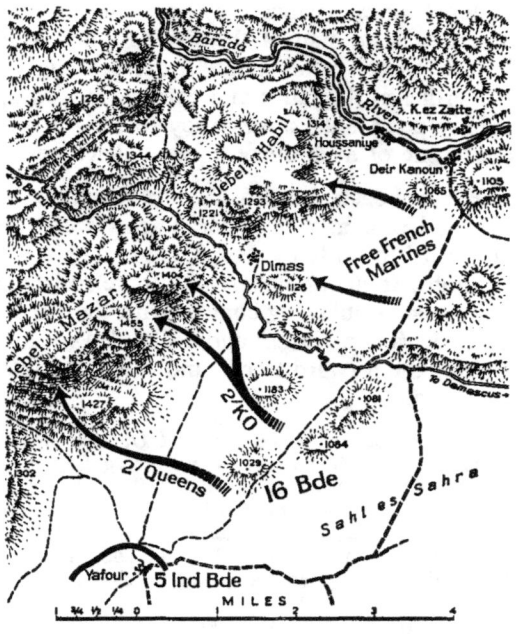

It will be recalled that on the 30th the 23rd British Brigade had taken over at Merdjayoun and all British troops from that sector eastwards came under the command of General Evetts, who also exerted control of the Free French.[1] On the night of the 9th-10th the French forces north of Merdjayoun began a general withdrawal. Next day, when the 23rd Brigade advanced on the 11th towards the Bekaa (the long narrow valley, stretching 70 miles southward of Homs) no enemy was found; progress was slow because the French had left many demolitions and booby traps along the route.

Evetts planned an attack on Jebel Mazar, to be made on the 10th July by his 16th Brigade, now complete, and the French Marine Battalion. The attack which opened at 2 a.m. made some progress in the hours of darkness and was continued the following night. However, by the 11th the summit was still held by the enemy and the positions of the British troops on the crests of the ridge were precarious. Evetts was contemplating ordering a withdrawal when he received reports of an armistice and ordered his men to hold on. It happened that the French commander had decided to withdraw, and by midnight the 16th Brigade was on top of Jebel Mazar.

---

[1] As from 10 July Lavarack placed 23 Bde directly under his own command so as to free Evetts of responsibility for the Merdjayoun sector during the preparation and the battle for the capture of Jebel Mazar.

To exploit the assault on Jebel Mazar, Evetts had formed a pursuit force led by Lieut-Colonel Bastin[2] of the 9th Australian Cavalry and including that regiment (less one squadron), the 2/Queen's, and detachments of artillery, machine-gunners and others, and four Free French tanks. When the advance of the Free French marines on the right was held up, Evetts detached Major Newton's[3] squadron of the 9th Cavalry, the tanks and other detachments, to help them take Jebel Habil. They moved at midday on the 10th, arrived at Dimas at 1 p.m. and came under sharp fire from artillery and small arms, particularly from the summit of Jebel Mazar (which they had believed to be held by their own infantry). There was no sign of the Free French at Dimas, but Newton's column, in the gorge, came under fire from high ground east, west and north. Nevertheless the tanks and carriers moved up and down the road engaging enemy posts until dusk. They lost eight men killed and twelve wounded, every one of their thirty-three vehicles being hit.

Farther east, the 4th Cavalry Brigade (of Habforce) on the 6th and 7th had sent armoured-car patrols westward. The whole brigade set off westward towards the Homs-Damascus road on the 11th, moving in three columns. It met and overcame some resistance and reached the road south of Homs, establishing contact with the Free French brigade there.[4] On the 12th Brigadier Tiarks[5] and his staff were attacked by armoured cars while visiting the forward troops and the staff captain and two other officers were captured.

It seems that when the battle of Damour opened the equivalent of seven French battalions, including two of the Foreign Legion, faced the 7th Australian Division at Damour and Jezzine; and a force of similar size, including one battalion of the Foreign Legion, faced the 6th British Division at Merdjayoun and Jebel Mazar. There were two in the Jebel Druse. All these battalions were greatly depleted (as were most of those on the other side), and some reduced by the detachment of companies. When the fight ended the strength of the Vichy battalions seems to have ranged between 250 and 450.

Two French units—the *7th Chasseurs* and *II/29th Algerian*—were withdrawn from the eastern sector during the course of the Damour battle, leaving three battalions and a cavalry regiment astride the Damascus-Beirut road. The diarist of the South Syrian force said that the first renewed attack against Jebel Mazar was driven back with a loss to the British of 194 prisoners, as a result of "the vigorous resistance of troops who knew the ground thoroughly, the coolness of unit commanders who maintained resistance even when surrounded and the heavy, well-timed support of artillery". A second British attack "had barely begun when it came to a standstill". A renewed attack on the 11th was "held in check", but the French losses were so heavy, specially in the *1/17th Senegalese* astride the Beirut road, that at 6.30 p.m. General de Verdilhac ordered a withdrawal that night to a line along the Jebel Sheikh Mansour, Yanta, Mdouka. The *1/17th* and the *1/24th Colonial* were again attacked while withdrawing. The *V/1st Moroccan* and the *1st Moroccan Spahis* "broke off without difficulty". No account has been obtained of the French operations at Damour.

---

[2] Lt-Col H. E. Bastin, MC, VX29296. (1st AIF: Maj 7 Bn, and Indian Army.) CO 9 Cav Regt 1940-42, 2/7 Cav (Cdo) Regt 1943-44. Grazier; of Buangor, Vic; b. Richmond, Vic, 17 Jun 1895.
[3] Maj T. H. Newton, SX2721. (1st AIF: 3rd Mech Tpt Service.) 9 Cav Regt 1940-42; 2/9 Cav (Cdo) Regt 1943-44. Motor parts representative; of Mount Gambier, SA; b. London, 4 May 1900.
[4] One squadron of the 9th Australian Cavalry was now attached to the Free French at Homs.
[5] Brig J. G. E. Tiarks; Comd 4 Cav Bde 1941-42. Regular soldier; b. 28 Dec 1896.

All day on 11th July rumours circulated among some forward units that an armistice was likely. At 7 p.m. the staff of the 7th Division were warned that an order to cease fire might be expected, and at 8.15 a definite announcement came that fighting would stop one minute after midnight. It was difficult to get the news forward to the outlying companies. The orders were flashed to the forward companies of 2/3rd Battalion, for example, by Lucas lamp from Hill 569 and reached them after 10 p.m.—it would have taken four hours for runners to reach these companies. Evidently the French had equal difficulty in informing their forward troops of the decision, because their artillery fire continued at intervals along the inland sector till 3 a.m. in some places, and a company of the 2/14th Australian Battalion which was covering the road south of Ainab was fired on by machine-guns at 8.30 next morning, but took no action. Half an hour before these machine-guns opened fire the French envoys, led by General de Verdilhac, had passed through the 2/5th Battalion's lines to General Allen's headquarters.

General Dentz had reached the conclusion more than a fortnight earlier that his forces should capitulate. Indeed, on 22nd June, he told Rudolph Rahn, the German agent, that his army would collapse in two or three days, but the successful defence of Palmyra and news that four new battalions were arriving from France raised his spirits.[6] On the 26th, however, he sent two staff officers to Vichy to point out again that further resistance would be futile. By this time Dentz had transferred his headquarters to Aleppo, where Rahn joined him. At Vichy on the 28th Marshal Pétain and Admiral Darlan agreed that resistance in Syria should cease; but Dentz did not learn of this decision until ten days later. On the 29th, as mentioned above, British bombs half-destroyed his residence at Beirut, the British staff not knowing that Dentz had vacated it. Some of his officers urged him to order that the home of the High Commissioner in Jerusalem be bombed, but (Dentz said later) he was not willing to authorise the bombing of the Holy City.

At this stage the Australian commander had begun to take part in the negotiations for an armistice. Lavarack on 30th June obtained Wilson's approval to the sending of the following message to Dentz through the United States Consular Service:

> The Commander of the Australian Forces in Syria, General Lavarack, feeling that to both Frenchmen and Australians the idea of comrades of the last war fighting against one another is repellent and distasteful and a useless waste of good men, suggests that he send an envoy by air to Rayak or to some other mutually convenient airport to meet the representative of General Dentz and to deliver to him a message from General Lavarack which may lead to a solution of the unpleasant conditions which today exist and thus avoid unnecessary bloodshed.

When he learnt that Dentz's residence in Beirut had been bombed the day before, Lavarack considered that this action had stultified his message,

---

[6] It appears that only detachments of these units reached Syria, and the remainder were still in Salonika when the fighting ended.

and that some confusion was being caused between a request which Wilson had made to Dentz to declare Beirut an open city and the indications from Vichy that an armistice was being sought. The fall of Palmyra on the 3rd, opening the route to Aleppo, impressed Dentz again with the futility of further fighting, and on the 8th, as soon as he learnt of his Government's decision, he visited the United States Consul at Beirut, Mr Cornelius van Engert. Next day van Engert placed before Dentz the conditions under which the British commander would agree to a cease-fire. Dentz informed the consul that he would accept, and wished to cease hostilities at midnight on the 11th, but with the reservation that he would treat only with the British High Command and not the Free French. The news of this offer sped to the British and Dominion Governments, and in Australia was unwisely made public. General Lavarack was incensed and, on the 11th, addressed the following letter to General Blamey:

> On 9 Jul 41 at 0915 hrs L.T. the B.B.C. in a news bulletin announced that Sir Frederick Stewart, Minister for External Affairs in Australia, had stated in Sydney that General Dentz had asked for an armistice to discuss the cessation of hostilities. It would now appear that this announcement, if not premature, was at least injudicious, since the tenor of Mr Churchill's somewhat guarded announcement later in the day made it appear that his hand had been forced by Stewart's statement. With this added publicity every man in the Force now operating in Syria was in possession of the information, in some form or another, by the morning of 10 Jul 41.
> 2. The reaction of the troops to the news in relation to their fighting capacity can, at the best, be only speculative. But it is not unreasonable to assume that with the knowledge of the possibility of an early armistice the troops would be disinclined to produce that small amount of extra effort which so often means the difference between success and failure. No man is likely to risk his life unnecessarily if he feels the campaign is virtually over.
> On the enemy side the same motives probably do not apply. Conscript armies are not expected to think for themselves, while those of Dictator countries only receive information from a State-controlled Press and radio service. In the case of the Vichy troops now opposing us in Syria the men merely follow their individual officers, and presumably have no knowledge of any such application by General Dentz.
> 3. A study of the operations on 10 Jul 41 is interesting when taken in relation to the above assumption. The enemy on all fronts put up a most spirited resistance and was fighting back. Our progress on the other hand was slow. If it is accepted that both sides were equally tired and battle worn, the inference is that the rather disappointing progress this day was due more to lack of push on the part of our troops than to any high resolve on the part of the enemy.
> 4. This deduction is not intended as a reflection on the units of the AIF engaged in this campaign who have fought splendidly in most trying and difficult conditions. But it is put forward to emphasise the danger which a similar premature announcement might have in the future if our opponents were the Germans.
> 5. It cannot be too strongly urged that all armistice negotiations should be kept secret until the latest possible moment, and it is submitted that the matter should be taken up with the Prime Minister with a view to the prevention of any such similar indiscretion in the future by a member of his Cabinet.

Early on the 11th Lavarack also sent a signal to Wilson urging that he should "make a concrete proposal for Dentz to dispatch envoy at time and place to be definitely stated to negotiate purely military armistice". Later that morning he spoke to Wilson on the telephone and informed him that on the coastal sector the enemy was "still resisting and trying to counter-attack everywhere", and that the 6th British Division might have to evacuate Jebel Mazar. Wilson said that he proposed to tell Dentz that unless Beirut was declared an open town by the next night it might become necessary to bomb and shell it. Lavarack replied that there was no certainty that his artillery would be close enough to shell it, but he would do his best.

Wilson wirelessed to Dentz that the British Commanders-in-Chief could accept no reservations concerning plenipotentiaries, and unless Dentz's plenipotentiaries presented themselves with a flag of truce at the British outpost on the Beirut-Haifa road at or before 9 a.m. local time on the 12th hostilities would be resumed at that hour. Two hours later Dentz replied by wireless:

> Please listen at 1800 hrs local time . . . when I shall address in plain language the General Officer Commanding-in-Chief the Middle East through Vice-Admiral Godfroy[7] as intermediary . . . . I shall also reply to the memorandum of His B.M's Government concerning the cessation of hostilities.

At the appointed hour Dentz wirelessed that he was prepared to engage in discussions on the basis of a memorandum handed to him that day by the United States Consul on behalf of the British Government, and proposed to suspend hostilities at 12.1 a.m., local time, on the 12th July. He asked where he might send an envoy plenipotentiary, it being understood that "the French Government does not authorise him to treat with the representatives of any allied power whatsoever but only with the representatives of the British High Command".

The political and military leaders in Cairo "took into account the opinion of the American Consul at Beirut that Dentz was entirely insincere and might be playing for time in the hope of a last-minute rescue by the Germans",[8] rejected this condition and summoned Dentz to send his plenipotentiaries to the British outpost on the Damour-Beirut road at or before 9 a.m. on the 12th, or hostilities would be resumed. At 7.55 p.m. Lavarack was informed that all troops were to cease fire at one minute after midnight.

Next morning the French envoys arrived at the Australian outpost on the Beirut road and were taken to Acre where they were met by Generals Wilson, Lavarack and Catroux and representatives of the navy and air force.

> Taking it on the whole the discussions went smoothly (wrote Wilson later) though at one moment I did threaten to start the war again, while at times Generals Catroux and de Verdilhac were engaged in heated argument . . . . When it came to initialling the drafts the Press were allowed in and brought with them all the equipment for taking pictures of the proceedings. In doing so, an Australian photographer who was somewhat over-refreshed got himself tied up in a flex of one of the lamps and in his struggles to get free succeeded in fusing not only the lights in the barracks but also those within a three-mile radius. The final scene was

---

[7] Godfroy commanded the French squadron immobilised in Alexandria.
[8] C. J. E. Auchinleck, *Despatch on Operations in the Middle East, 5 July 1941-31 October 1941.*

enacted by the light of hurricane lamps and that of a motor-cycle wheeled into the room. The climax of the day came when it was found that a souvenir hunter had taken the gold-leaved kepi of General Catroux.[9]

Afterwards General Catroux wrote a genial account of the incident of the kepi:

> An amusing mishap occurred after my arrival at the St Jean d'Acre barracks where our meeting was to be held. The camp was occupied by Australians who, as is well known, besides being fine fighters have an instinctive belief in freedom of action. They are keen on bringing back souvenirs to their distant native land from their travels or military campaigns. I was imprudent enough to leave in my motor car my "oak leaf kepi", the gold embroidery on which fascinated some son of Australia. It was a fine "souvenir" to carry off. Perhaps it was still more valuable; it might even be the kepi belonging to General Dentz, and that would add to the value of the trophy. The Australian could not resist the temptation and my headgear was missing when I returned to my car. Need I say that the camp commandant was all the more upset because he well knew that he would not get my kepi back. I reassured him by dissuading him from attempting a search, and said to him that I had commanded fellows very like his Australians—I meant the Foreign Legionaries—and knew by experience that what was taken by them was taken for good. The incident delighted Wilson, and made Lavarack smile. Lavarack was commander of the Australians and well knew what his soldiers were likely to get up to. When the incident became known to the Vichy delegation the whisper went round that I was a deserving victim of the bad company I kept.[1]

The agreement provided for the occupation of the country by Allied forces, the grant of full honours of war to the French forces, who would retain their individual arms but stack all other weapons under Allied control. At 1.30 a.m. on the 13th de Verdilhac returned through the Australian lines.

At midday on the 15th the units of I Australian Corps moved forward to occupy key points in Syria and Lebanon.

The column which led the way along the coast road—the 2/5th Battalion with detachments of cavalry and artillery—was bound for Latakia and was instructed to by-pass Beirut, into which a ceremonial entry was to be made next morning. The 2/16th Battalion and a squadron of the 6th Australian Cavalry entered the town that day and were welcomed with cheers by an excited crowd of Syrians, who evidently regarded the arrival of the newcomers as heralding their political independence. Meanwhile the main column of the 7th Division had sped northward to Tripoli and Latakia. At 10.30 a.m. on the 16th July the Allied leaders, including Generals Wilson, Catroux, Lavarack, Allen and Evetts made a ceremonial entry into Beirut escorted by 24 Bren carriers and a troop of field guns.

---

[1] Catroux, *Dans la bataille de Méditerranée* (1949), p. 150. In fact only four Australians were present and it is most improbable that any of them took General Catroux's kepi.
[9] Wilson, p. 119.

General de Verdilhac arriving for the signing of the Armistice, Acre, 12th July 1941.

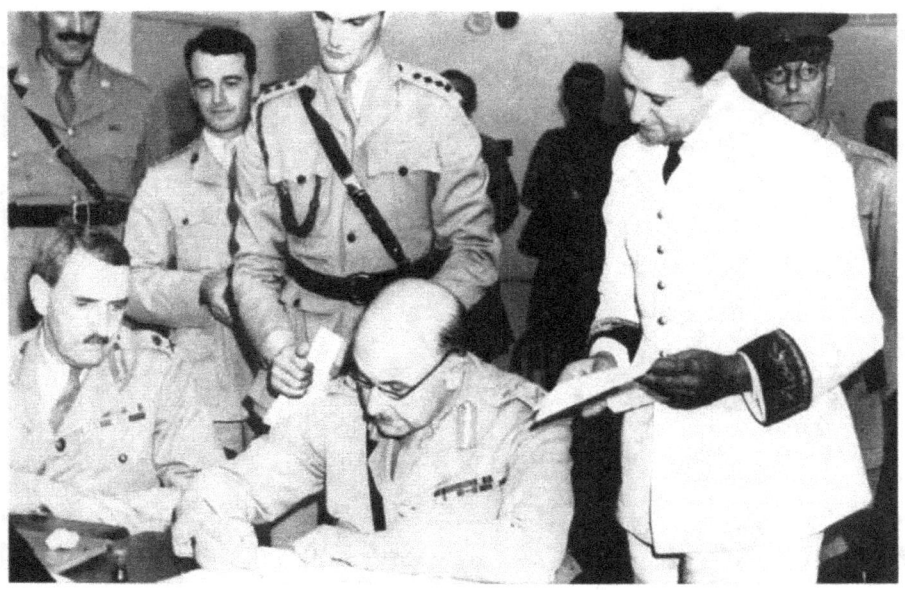
(Australian War Memorial)
General Wilson signing the armistice agreement. General Lavarack is on his right.

Brig J. E. S. Stevens and Maj-Gen A. S. Allen, Acre, 12th July 1941.

The entry into Beirut, 15th July 1941.

(I Aust Corps War Diary)

(*Australian War Memorial*)

Australian ski troops training in the Lebanons.

(*Australian War Memorial*)

The 2/33rd Battalion leaving the transit camp at Suez to embark with other units of the 25th Brigade Group on U.S.S. *Mount Vernon*. This was the first transport to land units from the Middle East in Australia.

(*2/5 Fd Regt Association*)

Men of the 2/5th Field Regiment on board the *Nieuw Amsterdam*, which carried the 18th Brigade Group from Suez to Bombay in February 1942.

CHAPTER 26

ADMINISTERING THE ARMISTICE

AFTER the capitulation, the territory from the Damascus-Beirut road northwards was placed under the control of I Australian Corps. The 7th Australian Division would occupy the coastal zone and the western slopes of the Lebanon watershed; the Free French Division an area east of the watershed of the Anti-Lebanon and including Damascus and Nebek; the 6th British Division the area between the Lebanons and the Anti-Lebanons, and the desert area surrounding the Free French zone and including Homs, Hama and Palmyra; Habforce, now placed under General Lavarack's command, was to occupy north-eastern Syria west of the Euphrates. The area beyond the Euphrates in the far north-east was occupied by the 10th Indian Division.

The Syrian armistice agreement—the Acre Convention as it was named—contained two provisions that were later to come into dispute: first that Allied prisoners, including those transferred to France, were to be set free, the British authorities reserving the right to hold as prisoners an equal number of French officers of similar rank until the Allied prisoners had been released; secondly, that the alternatives of joining the Allies or being repatriated were to be left to the free choice of the individual Vichy Frenchman, all who wished being repatriated.

To the convention had been added a confidential protocol in which General Wilson and General de Verdilhac agreed that there should be "no personal contact between French and Allied individuals in order to influence the free choice of French military personnel"; that the Allied authorities might use pamphlets, wireless and loud speakers "for dissemination of their point of view"; but that "the choice of alternatives" should be made without any sort of pressure, and the assistance of British officers might be invoked by the French (meaning Vichy French) authorities if considered necessary.

The supervision of the Acre Convention was entrusted to a commission of control headed by Major-General Chrystall,[1] a former commander of the Transjordan Frontier Force. It included Lieut-Colonel Fiennes;[2] a representative of General Catroux, and two representatives of General de Verdilhac, with a third British officer as secretary. The commission was to establish its office in the Beirut area. Under it were created a number of committees to supervise various departments of its work; one was to deal with problems concerning prisoners and was presided over by Colonel Blackburn, a South Australian lawyer in civil life, whom we last met leading the advance into Damascus.

---

[1] Maj-Gen J. I. Chrystall, CBE, MC. Comd TJFF 1936-40, 6 Cav Bde 1940-41; President Syrian Commission of Control 1941. Regular soldier; b. 6 Oct 1889.

[2] Lt-Col Sir Ranulph Fiennes, DSO. CO Royal Scots Greys 1941-43. Regular soldier; of Studland Bay, Dorset, Eng; b. London, 12 Nov 1902. Died 24 Nov 1943.

The situation in Syria after the armistice was peculiar and delicate. Five distinct groups were involved—British, Vichy, Free French, Syrian, and Australian—each with its own aims and ambitions. The most powerful group was headed by Mr Oliver Lyttleton[3] (who had recently been appointed Minister of State in the Middle East) and General Auchinleck, and represented British political and military strength in the Middle East. It had entered into a confidential agreement with the Vichy army, its recent enemy, to protect that army against the probable efforts of the Free French, its allies, to use pressure to persuade Vichyites to join General de Gaulle. The British objective was to remove General Dentz's army from Syria rapidly and without disturbance.

General de Gaulle and General Catroux, on the other hand, were chiefly interested in establishing their prestige and authority in Syria, and, as a means to that end, in persuading as many Vichyites as they could to join them. They hoped thus to form two full divisions, equipped with French arms, in place of their half-division lacking in artillery and other technical equipment.

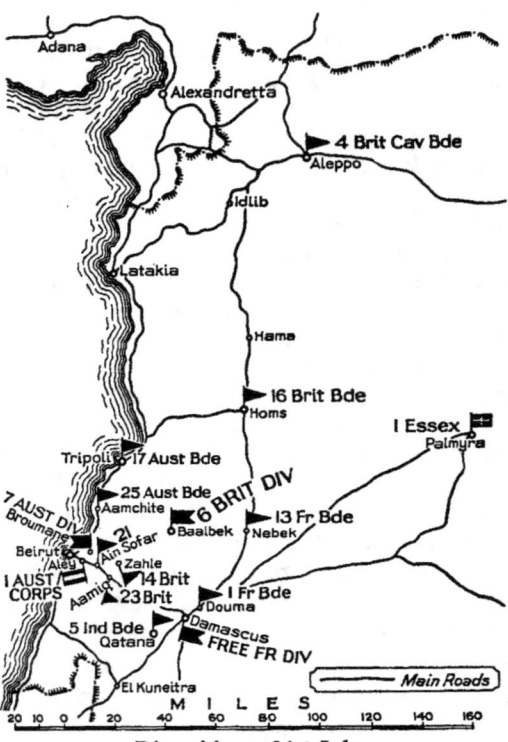

Dispositions, 31st July.

The third group — the Vichyite leaders and practically all their men—detested the de Gaullists and wished to return to the relative peace and security of France.

The army occupying most of Syria (the fourth group) was principally Australian and led by an Australian general. In common with the British, the Australian leaders were anxious to see the terms of the convention carried out smoothly, but they were uninterested in a variety of political considerations that the British leaders could not ignore. They had a warm fellow feeling for the Vichyites—at the armistice General Lavarack had ordered that "all possible courtesy and consideration" be shown to a defeated enemy who had "put up a very gallant defence".[4] They felt

---

[3] Capt Rt Hon Oliver Lyttleton, DSO, MC. President of Board of Trade 1940-41; Min of State and Member of War Cabinet 1941-42; Min of Production and Member of War Cabinet 1942-45. B. 1893.

[4] I Aust Corps Intelligence Summary, 13 Jul 1941.

a little coolness towards the Free French, whom they considered had misled them before the campaign and played an undistinguished part during it.

The fifth group comprised the Syrian peoples. They had welcomed the British troops with some enthusiasm but impressed the Australians as being doubtful whether the change of government would hasten the time when they would gain independence of European rule.

It was inevitable that in such circumstances political problems should soon arise. On 21st July General Wilson informed his subordinate commanders that General Catroux had asked for a wider distribution of Free French troops so as to place his units not only in Damascus but in Beirut, Tripoli, Aleppo and Homs. Wilson added that, although he had agreed to allow two French battalions to go to Beirut, he would permit no other changes until the repatriation of the Vichyites had been completed "because of the danger of clashes between the two". Nevertheless other Free French units were in fact moved; and on 30th July Lavarack ordered the commander of the Free French Division not to act on orders from anyone else without Lavarack's sanction. Two days later, when Wilson called for fuller information about the general situation, Lavarack replied:

> Situation satisfactory. Large numbers French would join British but marked hostility to Free French. Security situation deteriorating owing growing hostility to French taking control. This reduces security for which we invaded Syria. French equipment particularly anti-tank and anti-aircraft and tanks available replace and fulfil deficiencies in troops under my command reserved for Free French future needs. Such material could be used for training now and if necessary returned Free French when fighting troops otherwise equipped. Wide scattering Free French troops for political reasons is tactically and administratively unsound in area seized for our own protection. In general Vichy apparently carry out terms of convention though most officers appear admire Nazi whilst faithful Pétain. Direct Free French political interference occurring and has caused military move to Soueida of Free French troops under my command without my knowledge. Under orders General Catroux Sûreté arrested Captain Bordes while acting correctly on parole under Australian arrest. Release secured but Colonel Barter[5] says Free French intend re-arrest in spite full explanation situation.

On 3rd August Lavarack reported that "despite two telegrams and personal interview with Corps Commander, Legentilhomme still fails acknowledge receipt written order", and that the Free French alleged that, operations having ceased, their civil administration was paramount. On the same day he wrote to General Blamey that the Free French were acting on orders from Catroux on "the openly-admitted grounds of showing that the Free French and not the British control Syria". He added that the relations of his force with the Vichy French were "correct but cordial", the Vichy French having more than carried out their side of the convention, but there had been breaches of the convention by the Free French. He considered that cooperation between the two French groups was practically impossible, that they were trying to delay the repatriation

---

[5] Lt-Col A. R. Barter who is mentioned earlier as a liaison officer with the Greek Army.

of the Vichyites, were no less unpopular with the Syrians than the Vichyites, and their assumption of control was leading to a deterioration in the local security problem.

> I would be most pleased (he concluded) if you could find time to come here quickly so as to see for yourself . . . . In Australia the political repercussions . . . might be serious if our troops are denied equipment which they need and which they helped to capture and if military security . . . is destroyed . . . for political motives between Great Britain and Free France.

In short the Australian commander wanted two assurances: first that the Free French should stay put and not complicate a touchy police task, and second that his corps should be able to replenish its equipment from the stores it had captured, the better to carry on with the fight against Germany. General Lavarack quoted a report by Colonel Blackburn in which Blackburn pointed out that, in spite of the protocol to the Acre Convention, Free Frenchmen were about to try personally to persuade Vichyites to join de Gaulle, that there was to be no free choice among civilians, that officers' personal arms were to be confiscated and certain senior officers were not to be repatriated until the very end. Blackburn said that the Vichyites trusted the Australians and, if the convention was broken, the Australians concerned would be branded with dishonour in the eyes of the Vichy army. He therefore suggested that Australians be no longer employed supervising the choice of Vichy French whether to join de Gaulle or not.

De Gaulle had objected to the terms of the armistice on the grounds that they did not provide sufficient opportunity for his subordinates to rally the French to his cause, and did not sufficiently safeguard the political position of Free France in Syria. His protests led to discussions with Mr Oliver Lyttleton at which it was agreed that civil authority in Syria should be in the hands of the Free French, but the French forces would be under the command of General Auchinleck for operational purposes, and in the British military zone the civil authorities would carry out the wishes of the military commander. It was agreed also that the confidential protocol to the Acre Convention be cancelled; that is to say, the Free French were to be allowed to enter Vichyite camps. Lavarack's response was to order, on 6th August, that no British or Australian troops under his command should take part in "such entry or propaganda" nor be used to enforce it.

The question of the disposal of Vichy equipment was still unresolved. At a conference on 8th August attended by General Wilson, Major-General Spears,[6] General Catroux and others it was underlined that all French war material belonged to the Free French, but that after they had satisfied their immediate needs they should supply the British army with anything it asked for. The Free French were to police the districts in which Vichy troops were concentrated. It was decided that after the Vichyites had been embarked, two British corps would be in position in

---

[6] To obtain cooperation between the British Minister of State and General Wilson on the one hand and General Catroux on the other a mission headed by General Spears was set up on 2 August.

northern Syria, one west and one east of the Anti-Lebanon, with the French troops in reserve between Beirut and Damascus, and occupying most of the principal towns—Beirut, Aleppo, Damascus, Homs, Tripoli and Soueida—each with one battalion. When General Catroux asked for information about the British order of battle General Wilson was hesitant "in view of the present unsatisfactory state of affairs as regards security", but finally agreed that it should be shown to Catroux and one other French general and to them only.

That day General Lavarack obtained an interview with Mr Oliver Lyttleton, who said that he had taken steps to ensure that General de Gaulle modified his intolerant attitude towards British control in Syria and the British forces, and that the supremacy of the British military command had been made quite clear. Lavarack protested against the denouncing of the confidential protocol, and added that Australians felt keenly that their honour was involved. Lyttleton said that there was ample justification for denouncing the whole convention if it was desired. As a result of conversations between Free French officers and British members of the Spears Mission it was agreed, on the 12th, that three days' notice was to be given of any moves by Free French into the Australian Corps area, which was defined as all Syria north of the Damascus-Beirut road but not including those towns. Meanwhile on the 7th August Mr Lyttleton and General de Gaulle exchanged letters in which Lyttleton gave an assurance that Britain had no interest in Syria and Lebanon except to win the war; but pointed out that both Free France and Britain were pledged to the independence of Syria and Lebanon. De Gaulle noted that Great Britain admitted "as a basic principle the pre-eminent and privileged position of France" in Syria and Lebanon.

Meanwhile the repatriation of French troops proceeded. Eight convoys, three hospital ships and one "gleaner" ship sailed for France between 7th August and 27th September carrying 37,500 people, of whom some 5,000 were civilians and the remainder troops. Of 37,700 Vichy soldiers only 5,668 chose to join the Free French forces.[7] General Catroux had anticipated forming a second French division. In fact he did not receive enough volunteers to bring his one division to full strength and, late in August, the "1st Free French Division" ceased to exist and the French army in Syria was divided among three "district commands" with headquarters at Aleppo, Damascus and Beirut.

While these problems were still unsettled a new difficulty arose in the relations between British authority in Cairo and Jerusalem and the Australian commanders on the spot in Syria. Some British, Australian and Indian prisoners of war—thirty-nine officers and thirteen N.C.O's—had

---

[7] In *Journey Down a Blind Alley* (1946) Mary Borden (the wife of General Spears) said that many of these remained "not to take part in the war, but because they had business interests in Syria and the Lebanon". The small appeal of the de Gaullist movement in the early years is illustrated by the fact that in 1940 the strength of the Free French contingent in Britain was only 2,000.

been sent to France, and eighteen were in Italian hands at Scarpanto in the Dodecanese. The Allied members of the Control Commission demanded of General de Verdilhac that they be returned by 5th August and declared that, if this was not done, fifty senior Vichy officers would be detained.

Consequently General Allen was instructed that Brigadier Savige should arrange for General Dentz to go to General Lavarack's house, and that two colonels should similarly arrest Generals Arlabosse and Jennequin at the same hour. With these instructions were delivered three pairs of letters, signed by General Chrystall, which were to be handed to the French generals if necessary. The first letter of each pair stated that the time limit for the return of the Allied prisoners had expired and requested each general within one hour to accompany the officer presenting the letter, taking with him an A.D.C., two servants, and "bedding, baggage and sufficient food for twelve hours"; because of failure to return the prisoners, the terms of the armistice could be considered null and void. The second letter (to be used if the general concerned refused to accompany the officer sent to detain him) stated that that officer was to use force to compel him to do so. Allen was instructed that "besides tne officers in charge and an interpreter, three other officers shall accompany each party in case it is necessary to use force on the officer concerned whose rank requires that he shall not be man-handled by other ranks". Allen was not happy about these proposals, and was convinced that the task could be carried out with no show of force; indeed that a show of force might lead to bloodshed. Allen summoned Savige and Plant (in whose area General Arlabosse lived) and obtained their agreement that armed parties were not necessary. He sought an interview with Lavarack and asked for a free hand as to method, and Lavarack agreed.

Savige then obtained Allen's permission to substitute an Australian subaltern who spoke French for Lieut-Colonel Fiennes of the Commission of Control who had been sent forward to assist him. (Savige did not speak French and therefore felt himself greatly dependent on his interpreter.) He also chose Lieut-Colonel Stevenson of the 2/3rd to deal with General Jennequin. Fiennes, when he arrived, protested strongly that his orders were to accompany Savige at "the ceremony of arresting Dentz"; and, when Savige refused, Fiennes asked to be allowed to telephone his superiors. Savige forbade this and gave Fiennes a written statement that he had decided that Fiennes should instead accompany Stevenson to detain Jennequin.

At 3.45 on the afternoon of the 7th Savige, accompanied by a British officer as interpreter, called upon Dentz, who had been suffering from an attack of fever said to be dengue, and presented the first of the two letters to him. Dentz expressed indignation both at the arrest and at the order that he carry bedding and rations. Savige did his best to blunt the edge of this indignity by explaining that there might be a breakdown on the long night journey to Jerusalem and that, in fact, he had brought a hamper of food for Dentz's use. Dentz then said that he felt the need of a night's rest because of his illness and would be available for the journey at 9 o'clock next morning. Savige countered this proposal by suggesting that his own senior medical officer (Lieut-Colonel Lovell[8]) examine Dentz in the presence of Dentz's own medical officer. This was done, and at length Lovell expressed the opinion that Dentz was able to make the journey without risk. Dentz still refused. Savige, determined to do all he could to avoid presenting the second letter, asked the general to reconsider the decision in the light of his rank and dignity. This nonplussed the old French general who rose from his reclining position on the couch and said "Yes, you are right; how long will you allow me to get ready?"

At 9.30 that night Savige and Dentz, who rode in his own car driven by his own driver without an escort sitting with him, arrived at the headquarters of General Lavarack. Lavarack was out, but next morning received Dentz, and "was most charming in his attitude towards [him], which had a most appreciable effect on the general". It was agreed that Dentz was unfit to travel farther immediately. Next morning, as Savige and Dentz departed, a guard paid compliments to the French general.

General Jennequin was away from Beirut when the officers arrived to detain him. Road-blocks were established across the routes along which he might escape but he was eventually found in Tripoli, and at length, though at first he objected, he was escorted to Jerusalem by Colonel Stevenson. General Arlabosse was at Djournieh. Brigadier Plant, who was on very good terms with him, found him understanding, and Plant escorted him to Lavarack's headquarters. When they arrived at Jerusalem Dentz and his colleagues, thirty-five in all, were placed in quarters guarded by armed sentries.[9]

The Allied prisoners (including four Australians) had arrived at Toulon on 4th August, having been flown to Athens, taken by sea to Salonika and thence by railway. It was not until 9th August that they were placed aboard a ship travelling to Beirut, where it arrived on the 15th; the prisoners from Scarpanto did not return until the 30th. In September Dentz and his senior officers were allowed to leave for France.

What had been the attitude of the people of Syria and Lebanon towards the invading and the defending armies? Most of them sided actively with neither one nor the other, but patiently waited for the battle to pass by, and adopted a friendly policy to whichever side occupied their town or village—a policy no doubt deeply ingrained in the people of a country which had been for centuries a battleground. Arms, probably abandoned on the battlefield or by fleeing French troops, were found in some homes; during the campaign there was some traffic through both British and French lines; there were reports that civilians were observing for French artillery and cutting British telephone lines, but no evidence of substantial

---

[8] Col S. H. Lovell, NX451. CO 2/4 Fd Amb 1940-42; ADMS 5 Div 1942-43; CO 103 AGH 1944. Surgeon; of Bellevue Hill, NSW; b. Sydney, 22 Sep 1906.

[9] General Garnier succeeded to the command of the Vichy troops. On 9 Aug General Allen sent Maj C. H. Grace (of Sydney) of his staff to convey his compliments to Garnier.

sabotage; some of the inhabitants were more friendly than others; a few seemed hostile; the gendarmerie were almost always cooperative. General Dentz averred at his trial in 1945 that throughout the campaign there was no rioting, and no telephone line of his was cut nor railway line damaged.

CHAPTER 27

DEBITS AND CREDITS

IN the five weeks during which the Syrian campaign had been fought the whole shape of Hitler's war had changed. With the invasion of Russia any immediate prospect of a German offensive in the Levant vanished. A week before that invasion opened the British and Indian force in the Western Desert had attacked with the object of defeating the German armour on the Egyptian frontier and relieving Tobruk.[1] All went well on the first day, but on the second and third General Rommel, having brought forward tanks from Tobruk, counter-attacked and compelled the British force to withdraw, after losing many of its tanks.

This failure was "a most bitter blow" to Mr Churchill, and, on the 21st June—the day Damascus fell—General Wavell learnt from his Prime Minister that he was to change places with the Commander-in-Chief in India, General Auchinleck. Auchinleck had won a reputation as an able and forceful soldier, particularly during his service in India between the wars. He had commanded the Allied forces in northern Norway in May and June 1940; and, later, as commander in India, had gained acquaintance with some of the problems on the outskirts of the Middle East command. Wavell's biographer has recorded that Wavell's chief of staff, Lieut-General Arthur Smith, received the telegram announcing the transfer shortly after midnight. He took it to Wavell early the next morning. Wavell was shaving. Wavell read it quietly, and then remarked: "I am sure the Prime Minister is right. You will find a new man with new ideas will be a good thing."[2]

Afterwards Churchill wrote that he held Wavell responsible, in part or wholly, for the loss of Benghazi "which had undermined and overthrown all the Greek projects on which we had embarked";[3] for the failure in Crete; and for the defeat in the Western Desert. He said also that he was displeased by Wavell's opposition to the reinforcement of Iraq from the Middle East, and to the plan to invade Syria.

The loss of Benghazi, however, had been chiefly a consequence of denuding Cyrenaica so as to send an expedition to Greece. As a result of the loss of Benghazi, Wavell retained in the Western Desert for two months one Australian division earmarked for Greece. It is hard to accept the assumption that if that division had been sent to Greece (where it could not have arrived until the campaign was at least ten days old and defeat had been accepted) the Allies would have achieved "the Greek projects on which we had embarked, with all their sullen dangers and glittering prizes in what was for us the supreme sphere of the Balkan war".[4]

---

[1] These operations will be described in the next volume of this series.
[2] R. J. Collins, *Lord Wavell* (1948), p. 436.
[3] Churchill, *The Second World War*, Vol III, p. 308.
[4] Churchill, p. 308.

Among his colleagues and subordinates in the field Wavell's reputation was undimmed. Admiral Cunningham, now the only remaining member of the original triumvirate, wrote later that he was "desperately sorry" about the departure of this fellow commander whom he considered "one of the great generals thrown up by the war, if not the greatest".[5]

Wavell's earlier operations against the Italians, boldly undertaken with forces far inferior to theirs in numbers and equipment, had been brilliantly successful. He loyally accepted responsibility for the faulty estimate of the enemy's strength before the loss of Cyrenaica. He had supported the Greek venture, of which the loss of Crete was merely a consequence, but had done so with some misgivings. He undertook the operations in Iraq and Syria only after considerable pressure from London. So far as Iraq was concerned events proved that he was wrong to hesitate. As for Syria, fairly substantial evidence that Germany was not planning an early offensive in the Levant was provided at the time by her belated and insubstantial aid to Rashid Ali in Iraq; and it was to anticipate such an offensive that the invasion of Syria was undertaken.

In May the British Prime Minister did not know for certain that the Germans were concentrating for an early invasion of Russia but he thought they were doing so and had attempted to warn Stalin of the coming onslaught early in April.[6] There was a possibility, however, that the eastern Mediterranean was also an objective, and Churchill's instinct was to anticipate Hitler and seize the initiative. This policy had not succeeded in Greece because he lacked land forces strong enough to withstand the Germans on the Continent. The attack on Syria, like the expedition to Greece, was carried out only by withdrawing formations from the Western Desert. The outcome was that both the Syrian and the Western Desert offensives were undertaken simultaneously with insufficient forces. In consequence the Syrian campaign was unduly prolonged and costly, and the Western Desert offensive failed. Two senior officers of Wavell's staff, Lieut-General Smith and Lieut-Colonel (later Major-General) de Guingand, writing after the campaign, expressed the opinion that the Government was right in pressing Wavell to invade Syria. "We were ordered from home to carry out the advance into Syria not so much as a military operation as 'a political gesture'," said General Smith. "An odd way to wage war, but events proved the British Government to be right."[7] One outstanding event, however—the German invasion of Russia—showed the Syrian offensive to have been premature. There would have been time to undertake it later with adequate forces.

Moreover, if it was primarily "a political gesture" the political factors were somewhat misjudged. The political advisers on the Allied side failed to estimate correctly the feelings of the Vichy French. The Free French, wishing to ensure that the invasion took place, under-estimated the probable resistance. Naturally the Free French were anxious to take a leading

---

[5] Cunningham, *A Sailor's Odyssey*, p. 402.
[6] Churchill, pp. 319-22.
[7] *Journal of the Royal United Service Institution*, Feb 1943.

part in the operations so as to enhance their prestige and be on the spot to assert their political interests; but it seems that the presence of the hated de Gaullists as much as any other factor ensured a bitter resistance by the Vichy leaders, who regarded them as renegades. France was in a state of civil war and the two groups were divided by all the rancour and recrimination that civil war breeds.

The presence of the Free French contingent also complicated control, because it was not placed fully under a British commander, but acted in "cooperation"—always an unsatisfactory procedure, and particularly with a force built up largely of more or less mercenary African troops and foreign legionaries.

The hotch-potch of political and military considerations was reflected in the news which went to the outside world. A political as well as a military censor was given supervision of reports of the campaign. The first communiqué issued at Cairo stated that "only slight and often no resistance" had been met; the censors were instructed from Wavell's headquarters that they must delete references to fighting. The Australian army censor, Major Fenton,[8] would not apply this instruction to reports for Australian newspapers, and General Lavarack's chief Intelligence officer informed Middle East headquarters that Lavarack was worried about the effect on his troops of B.B.C. broadcasts that the French were not resisting. This situation—the result of the inexperience of officers and civil officials—caused some London correspondents, having discovered what was happening, to advise their newspapers to have Australian dispatches about Syria cabled back from Australia to London, and this was done.

The fiasco of the British press censorship in the early stages of the campaign, and the vigorous protests, particularly of the American correspondents, against the general working of the public relations system led to changes in the censorship staff and the appointment as Cairo "spokesman" of the enterprising Major Randolph Churchill,[9] Mr Winston Churchill's son, who was serving in a commando unit in the Middle East.

It was on Randolph Churchill's advice that his father at last, in June, granted General Wavell's request, made in April, for the appointment of a senior political authority to Cairo. "Why not send a member of the War Cabinet here to preside over whole war effort?" Randolph Churchill cabled on 7th June. On the 29th the Prime Minister informed General Wavell that Mr Oliver Lyttleton, formerly President of the Board of Trade, would leave London by air next day to become Minister of State in the Middle East.

The larger part of the task in Syria had been borne by Australian troops. Early in July General Auchinleck sent to the War Office a statement of the

---

[8] Lt-Col A. G. Fenton, MBE, NX484. Censorship Liaison Officer, GHQ, ME 1940-42, ADPR First Army and NGF 1942-43, LHQ 1944. Journalist; of Newcastle, NSW; b. North Sydney, NSW, 28 Jul 1905. Killed in aircraft accident New Guinea 27 Jan 1945.

[9] Maj R. F. E. S. Churchill, MBE; 4 Queen's Own Hussars. MP 1940-45. Lecturer and journalist; b. 28 May 1911.

strength of each national contingent employed in Syria to the end of June: Australian, 18,000; United Kingdom, 9,000; Indian, 2,000; Free French, 5,000.

The total Allied losses were approximately: British and Indian, 1,800; Australian, 1,600; Free French, 1,300. All of the Australian losses thus listed, however, were killed and wounded; about 1,200 of the British and Indian troops, and about 1,100 of the Free French who were lost were taken prisoner. The battle casualties in the 7th Australian Division were: 37 officers and 379 other ranks killed, 87 and 1,049 wounded. In addition 3,150 sick men passed through the two Australian field ambulances, including 350 suffering with malaria.[1] If the campaign had lasted a few weeks longer malaria would have caused serious losses.

As a result of the censorship policy described above, the Australians, most of whom were in action for the first time, felt aggrieved that so little was printed about the campaign both during it and afterwards—a feeling that is evidenced not only in contemporary records but in regimental histories produced after the war.[2]

In August the Vichy French stated that their losses were 521 killed, 1,037 missing, 1,790 wounded and 3,004 prisoners. It appears that these figures do not give a true account of the numbers who deserted from the Vichy forces, because, according to British figures, these totalled 8,912. At the cease-fire the strength of the Vichy army was from 24,000 to 25,000. At his trial General Dentz said that 1,092 Vichy officers and men had been killed in Syria. If the dead numbered 1,092 the wounded probably totalled between 2,200 and 2,500. Such figures are not inconsistent with the total of 3,348 killed, wounded and missing quoted above.

In the light of later knowledge it is easy to criticise the conduct of the operations, particularly on the ground that there was failure to concentrate against one main objective. The relative weakness of his force, however, placed each senior commander—first Wilson and then Lavarack—in an

---

[1] The battle casualties in the Australian battalions and cavalry regiments were:

	Officers	Other Ranks		Officers	Other Ranks
21 Bde—			25 Bde—		
2/14 Bn	7	101	2/25 Bn	8	131
2/16 Bn	22	240	2/31 Bn	14	227
2/27 Bn	16	138	2/33 Bn	5	98
Total	45	479	Total	27	456
17 Bde—			6 Cav Regt	3	30
2/3 Bn	7	87	9 Cav Regt	5	14
2/5 Bn	2	39	2/3 MG Bn	1	41
2/2 Pnr Bn	14	161			
Total	23	287			

The 2/4, 2/5 and 2/6 Fd Regts and 2/2 A-Tk Regt together lost 11 officers and 83 other ranks. In this campaign, as in Greece and again in Crete, the one West Australian battalion engaged—the 2/11 in Greece and Crete, the 2/16 in Syria—had the heaviest battle casualties of any Australian unit.

[2] The desire to correct the "soft-pedalling" (as one regimental historian describes it) may be one reason why, up to April 1952, the only full-scale regimental histories published by Australian units which served in the Middle East had come from units of the 7th Division: 2/14 Bn, 2/4 Fd Regt, 2/5 Fd Regt. Histories of the 2/16 Bn and 2/2 Pnr Bn were then in typescript. It happened also that in its succeeding campaigns in New Guinea in 1942 and early 1943 the 7th Division, although it played a larger part than any other Australian or American formation, remained anonymous.

unenviable situation. The French were well led, skilful, and were fighting in country which they knew intimately and in which the defender had every advantage. In addition—a fact that could never be forgotten in the early weeks—they possessed some 90 medium tanks, whereas the attackers had none, except those they captured and could put into working order. In consequence, until the French tank force was disabled, the enemy had the means of launching counter-attacks across the vulnerable lines of communication of the whole invading force, and perhaps of marching across the Jordan into Palestine, which had been largely denuded of equipped troops. The French counter-attacks on the 15th and the following two days achieved greater dislocation than their strength merited, or—after the opening day—the French leaders themselves expected. This was because of fear lest a further short advance might cut vital roads behind the invading force.

Because the invading force had no tanks and was ill-equipped with ammunition for its mortars—invaluable weapons in the mountain country—the campaign soon resolved into a slogging match in which infantry supported chiefly by 25-pounder field guns again and again attacked well-trained regular forces supported by tanks, artillery and mortars.

It seems probable that the Allied failure to concentrate on a single objective until a late stage was partly the result of the unhappy arrangement (criticised by Brigadier Rowell before the invasion opened) whereby, until 18th June, operations were controlled from Jerusalem by General Wilson and a staff preoccupied with political and administrative problems and too remote from the battlefields to exercise close command in the field. In each of the campaigns with which this and the previous volume are concerned errors in the allocation of command had been made. In Libya the system whereby General Wilson, as commander of British Troops in Egypt, had been interposed between General Wavell and the field commander, General O'Connor, had proved unsatisfactory. In Greece General Wilson had found it necessary eventually to hand control of the field force to General Blamey. In Crete there had been failure at an early stage to appoint and retain a senior commander to concentrate on the problem of defending the island; the weary General Freyberg took over only when invasion was imminent.

In Syria the invading force had certain important physical advantages: command of the sea and, in the later stages, of the air; a slowly increasing pool of men and equipment on which to draw; more and better artillery boldly used—though the Frenchman's excellent heavy mortar largely offset the Australian guns in the mountain fighting; and the French were always plentifully supplied with ammunition.[3]

---

[3] General Lavarack referred to "two factors of the highest importance which contributed to the British victory . . . the bombardments provided in the coastal sector by the Royal Navy, and our superiority in the air". "The naval bombardments," he added, "caused a great deal of destruction of enemy transport and AFVs on the coast road, engaged (frequently with good effect) the enemy's gun positions, and, last but not least, caused a considerable deterioration in morale against troops exposed, without hope of retaliation and little of protection, to the gruelling

The invaders had a superior spirit. The French and colonial troops drew their determination from their professional pride as soldiers (many thought the British despised them for their defeat in France), from their hatred of the de Gaullists, and their resentment against the British for attacking them, and particularly for attacking them on the ground that they were harbouring Germans; but the British and Indian invaders were impelled by a stronger pride and devotion than such private animosities could produce; and the Australians in particular revealed greater staying power than the French.

Tactically the Australian division learned important lessons. Like the 6th Division in Greece it gained experience of mountain warfare which was to prove of great value in a critical operation in the following year. Leaders and men learnt the need in such country of securing the ridges, the danger of defiles, and the necessity for attacking defiles from a flank; the use of cover on rocky slopes; the value of mortars in tangled, steep-sided hills where field artillery was unable to operate with full effect. In addition, they learnt how to fight tanks with guns—holding the fire of the anti-tank gun until the tanks were within a few hundred yards, and employing one or two field guns forward with the infantry. The frequent possibility of ambush in mountain passes was seen and practised.[4]

Except in the Palmyra area and along the Euphrates, where the French air force achieved notable success, neither it nor the British air force was able to deploy sufficient power to greatly influence the battle below. At Palmyra, however, the Vichy aircraft provided a particularly illuminating illustration of the extent to which determined and repeated air attack may turn the scales in the land fighting. Efforts were made during the campaign to improve liaison between army and air force. For the Damour battle one fighter squadron (No. 3 R.A.A.F.) and one bomber (No. 45 R.A.F.) were placed in close support of the 7th Division. However, this experiment in obtaining quicker air support was only partly successful. Targets were hard to find in such rugged country, the delay between asking for support and the appearance of the aircraft over the target was from two hours to two and a half, and the number of aircraft available was too small to exert an important influence on the outcome of even minor engagements.

The country and enemy action made tactical reconnaissance and artillery difficult (stated the report of the 7th Australian Division). Enemy guns were well concealed and invariably difficult to locate. On several occasions the area in which enemy

---

flank fire from the sea." (Report on operations—I Australian Corps—in the Campaign in Syria, June-July 1941.)
The expenditure of ammunition by the Australian artillery regiments was: 2/4 Fd Regt 40,142, 2/5 Fd Regt 48,720, 2/6 Fd Regt 52,699, 2/2 A-Tk Regt 623, 2/9 Fd Regt 2,224.

[4] Concerning mountain warfare *Field Service Regulations*, Vol II, 1935, had said: "The principal centres of life and cultivation and the principal supplies of water lie in the valleys; whereas the high ground has the advantage . . . in observation and command, and therefore in facilities for attack and defence. In other words, strategically the valleys are more important, tactically the heights and the passes or defiles between one valley and another, as these are likely scenes of combat . . . tactical movement either in attack or retirement should always be along spurs or ridges rather than in the depressions between them."
This lesson was slowly re-learnt in each sector in Syria (and, since we rarely learn from history, learnt again by American troops in Korea in 1950).

guns were located was known, yet they could not be definitely pin-pointed from the air. When our planes were over the area the enemy artillery there remained silent. The difficulty of locating guns is best illustrated by the experience of one pilot who, knowing the exact location of our own guns, was not able to spot them until he was down to about 200 feet. It can be said that artillery reconnaissance, which was limited, was not really a success. It is considered that the Hurricane is too fast for this type of air cooperation. Tactical reconnaissance was provided throughout and obtained useful information, but owing to the nature of the country this information was chiefly confined to reports on roads.

Perhaps the most valuable contribution made by the air force in the coastal area was that, by protecting the naval squadron, it enabled it to continue its bombardment of the enemy on land. This bombardment hampered the French supply columns and depressed the spirit of their troops. The British fighters reduced French air attack in the coastal and mountain sectors to such an extent that it did not seriously impede movement on the roads; so successfully was this done that the report of the 7th Australian Division said that "lack of strong enemy air [force] has probably lulled this division into a false sense of security".

The campaign was won chiefly by the infantrymen's determination, physical strength and endurance. In those sectors where at length the fight resolved itself into an affair of attrition, the attackers eventually surpassed the defenders. After the fighting the French leaders volunteered that the Australian troops had proved more rugged than their own. One report quotes a French colonel as saying, "Until I saw your infantry crossing the Damour River and fighting in the mountains, I believed the Foreign Legion were the toughest troops in the world." The 5th Indian Brigade, the most experienced troops in Syria—excepting perhaps the 2/3rd and 2/5th Australian Battalions—had fought magnificently, as they and other Indian regular formations had done in the Western Desert and Abyssinia.

At the end the fighting men on each side were probably equally fatigued. Those infantrymen who had been in the three earlier campaigns in which Australians had fought considered that the Syrian operations were more exhausting than those in Libya or Greece; and in few later campaigns did diarists in infantry, cavalry and artillery so constantly refer to fatigue, mental and physical, to a consequent prevalence of "slight shell-shock", and the weeding out of those who were less fit in mind and body. It had been a costly and wearing campaign, bitterly fought out against the troops, mostly mercenaries, of a former ally. On the credit side was some strengthening of the strategical position in the Middle East, and the experience gained, particularly by an Australian formation which was soon to play a decisive part in a more critical campaign in another hemisphere.

CHAPTER 28

ON THE NORTHERN FLANK

WHEN the Syrian campaign opened it was only in the Middle East that German and Italian troops were in action; in the Western Desert they had been halted, but in Greece and Crete a victorious German army and air force seemed to be poised for a new thrust eastward into Asia. When the Syrian campaign ended, however, three-quarters of the German Army—nearly 150 divisions—was locked in a struggle with Russia. The Middle East, for nearly a year the centre of the conflict, had moved into the background.

As we have seen, in the second quarter of 1941 Hitler was engrossed with the coming campaign in Russia, and he allotted only token support to the revolt in Iraq, and agreed to the airborne attack on Crete with but moderate enthusiasm. In May and early June, however, it was natural that British leaders should be anxious lest the Germans attack Cyprus and Syria. Indeed, confident that Russia would swiftly be defeated, the German staffs in July issued preliminary instructions for operations that were to follow—a three-pronged thrust through Libya, Turkey and Persia. The British staffs also believed that Russia would rapidly be overcome and the victorious German armies might soon be advancing through the Taurus and the Caucasus towards Suez and the Persian Gulf. By the end of August, however, it seemed that Germany's success was now to be less swift than in Poland or France. In the north the Russians still held Leningrad; in the centre the German advance towards Moscow had come to a standstill; only in the south, where the German army had isolated Odessa and reached the Dnieper, was it making notable progress. It seemed that Russia would not be overthrown as easily as German and British—and American—leaders had expected. "In general," said a British Intelligence summary of 24th August, "there is as yet no sign that Russian resistance is anywhere nearing a collapse.... The further developments in the German plan are now unfolding. The present phase appears to be a desperate drive, before autumn sets in, to reach Rostov and thus isolate the Caucasus. This would deprive Old Russia of some 80 per cent of her oil supply and seriously weaken her ability to carry on a long campaign."

Meanwhile, during the first half of 1941, Britain's own strength had greatly developed. Her own and the Dominion factories had vastly increased their output, and Lend-Lease supplies from the United States (which in March President Roosevelt had proclaimed to be "the arsenal of democracy") were being delivered in mounting volume. It was predicted that American factories would produce 17,000 aircraft during 1941, of which three-quarters would go to Britain. A measure of the growth of the British Army is that it now contained seven armoured divisions, and Canada and Australia were each forming one. In August Roosevelt and Churchill met in mid-Atlantic, and afterwards announced the Atlantic Charter, which stated the common principles on which the two leaders based "their hopes for a better future for the world".

In the Middle East an immediate effect of German preparations for the invasion of Russia had been the withdrawal of German aircraft, particularly from Sicilian airfields whence Malta had been sorely blitzed during the early months of the year. Air Marshal Tedder reacted swiftly, and by the end of June had established a considerable air force on the island with the intention of making severe attacks on the German-Italian sea route to Africa.

The new military commander, General Auchinleck, when he arrived in July, took over an army considerably stronger than Wavell's had been in the critical early months of the year, despite the heavy losses of April and May. That army now included one armoured division and nine infantry divisions (most of which, however, held far less than their quota of vehicles and other equipment). A second armoured division—the 10th —was being formed, and an infantry division—the 50th (Northumbrian), re-formed after its losses in France—was arriving. It would be the first United Kingdom infantry division to reach the Middle East since the outbreak of war. The decisive defeat of the Italians in Abyssinia, where only one strong centre of resistance remained, enabled strong forces to be switched to the Western Desert. In May, June and July the 1st South African and 4th and 5th Indian Divisions were transferred north (as we have seen, a brigade of the 4th fought in Syria), leaving the two small African divisions, chiefly of native infantry, to complete the conquest of Abyssinia.

Some of the burden of responsibility that Wavell had carried was removed from Auchinleck's shoulders by the arrival of Mr Oliver Lyttleton as Minister of State to coordinate British activities, political, military and economic, in the Middle East. Lyttleton presided over a Middle East War Council, mainly concerned with political problems, and a Middle East Defence Committee, on which the three Commanders-in-Chief sat to deal with major military questions.

After the Syrian campaign Auchinleck considered that he must reckon with the possibility of a German attack through Turkey or the Caucasus in September or October. On 18th June the control of operations in Iraq had been returned to the Commander-in-Chief in India (who for the following fortnight had been Auchinleck himself) and consequently Auchinleck's present responsibility in this area was limited to the western part of the Turkish frontier[1]—thus in yet another respect his task was lighter than Wavell's.

While Auchinleck was attempting to build up his force in Syria new demands arrived from farther east. The British and Russian Governments

---

[1] The Syrian "duck's bill" east of the Euphrates was included for military purposes in the Iraq command.

were disturbed at the presence of active groups of Germans and Italians in Persia whose ruler, Riza Shah, in his efforts to free his country of the influence of Russia and Britain, had encouraged German and Italian firms and technicians, and at the same time had drawn closer to Turkey, Iraq and Afghanistan, whose rulers shared his desire to avoid European entanglements. In Persia were oilfields and refineries on which Britain greatly depended, and the road and railway from the Persian Gulf was the only route along which Russia might receive Allied supplies from the south. When the British and Russian Governments sought the expulsion of German and Italian citizens from Persia, Riza Shah refused to reverse his settled policy at the demand of traditional enemies. Finally, on 24th July, General Wavell was informed that the British Government had approved "the application of Anglo-Soviet diplomatic pressure backed by a show of force on the Iranian Government in order to secure the expulsion of Axis nationals from their country; should diplomatic pressure fail force was to be used".[2] General Wavell instructed General Quinan to concentrate forces on the frontier ready to advance in the second week of August.

Since the opening of the invasion of Russia Quinan's main task, like Wilson's in Syria and Palestine, had been to prepare against a possible German advance from the north; he had been instructed to develop facilities in Iraq for a force of up to ten divisions and thirty air squadrons, and to have forces ready to safeguard the oilfields.

For the present, however, in southern Iraq Quinan had little more than one division, the 8th Indian, one of whose brigades did not arrive from home until the 10th August. Next day the 9th Armoured Brigade (formerly the 4th Cavalry Brigade of Habforce—despite its new title it had no armour) arrived at Kirkuk and Khanaqin where the 2nd Indian Armoured Brigade (with little armour) was already assembled. The 10th Indian Division (Major-General Slim) in north-eastern Syria was also transferred to Quinan's command. Riza Shah on the other hand possessed an army of about ten small divisions varying in strength from 5,000 to 7,000, with some 524 guns and 280 aircraft. About half the army was believed to be facing the Iraq and half the Russian frontier.

An Anglo-Soviet ultimatum was presented to Riza Shah on 13th August; the reply was considered unsatisfactory and, after some delays, orders were given for a combined advance into Persia on the 25th August. That day, in the early hours, a brigade of the 8th Indian Division landed at Abadan, from naval craft, found most of the Persian troops asleep, and by 5 p.m. had captured the refinery; next day the whole island was occupied. On the 25th a naval force, including the cruiser *Enterprise,* aircraft carrier *Hermes* and the oiler *Pearleaf,* escorting two companies of the 3/10th Baluch Regiment on board the Australian armed merchantman *Kanimbla,* occupied Bandar Shapur, port and terminus of the railway from Tehran to the Persian Gulf. Soon the oilfields had been occupied

---

[2] A. P. Wavell, *Despatch on Operations in Iraq, East Syria and Iran, 10 Apr 1941 to 12 Jan 1942.*

and Slim was advancing on Kermanshah. On the 28th the Persian army surrendered. In the four-days' operation, the Indian-British force lost twenty-two killed (including sixteen Indians) and forty-two wounded.

Quinan decided to occupy the line Hamadan-Kermanshah-Shahabad, and to post a force at Ahwaz, thus guarding both oilfield areas, and to withdraw all troops not required for this task into Iraq; because of his shortage of vehicles he was unable to maintain troops forward of Hamadan.³

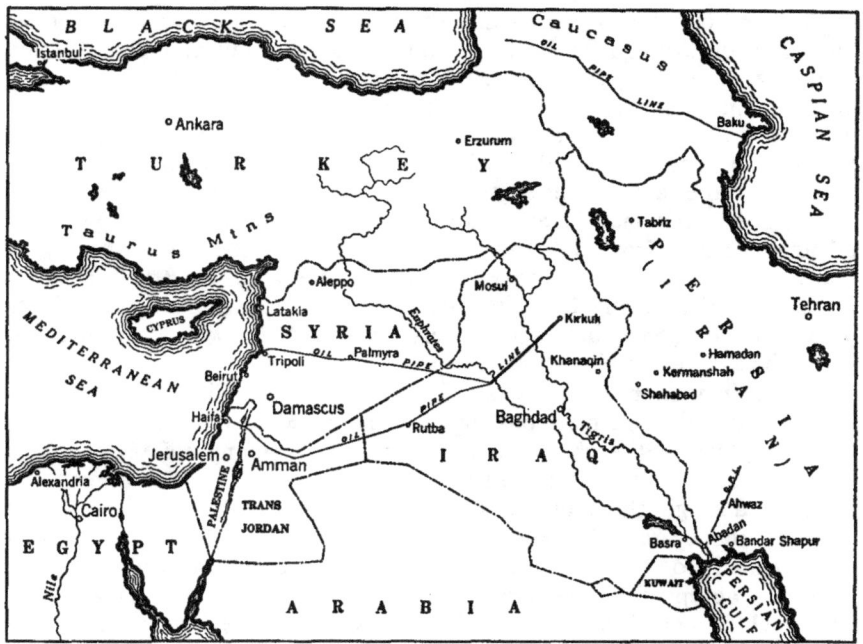

In spite of the danger of a German march through Turkey it had been decided that as soon as Syria had been occupied the main effort in the Middle East should be concentrated on driving the enemy from North Africa, and that the northern flank must be occupied by a minimum force. At the same time the advance into Syria was considered to have given added importance to Cyprus, garrisoned since 5th May largely by the 7th Australian Divisional Cavalry Regiment.⁴ It will be recalled that because of their losses on Crete the German leaders decided that they would not attempt an airborne invasion of Cyprus, but suggested to the Italians a seaborne attack by night from the Dodecanese. Nothing came of this

---

³ The 5 Indian Div (less a brigade) was sent into northern Iraq but did not reach the Persian frontier until after the surrender. It remained until the 6 Div arrived from India to replace it, and returned to Auchinleck's command in October.

⁴ This regiment, some 450 strong, was equipped with 15 light tanks, 14 carriers and 12 anti-tank guns mounted on trucks.

suggestion. The German leaders believed in June that the island's garrison would soon be reinforced. In fact, in July Auchinleck decided to send to Cyprus the 50th Division, then arriving from England, and to replace the 7th Australian Cavalry with an Hussar regiment. This movement was completed on the 29th August.

By mastering Syria and Iraq Britain had advanced the ground on which she might have to defend the Canal and the Middle East oilfields by 300 to 500 miles. On the eastern flank the German attack might come, by exploitation of a victory in Russia, through the Caucasus and into Persia and Iraq, or through Turkey. On either route an invading force would be severely limited by the small capacity of the Turkish roads and railways. Once he had reached the Syrian frontier the enemy would have three main lines of advance: the coastal road through Latakia, Tripoli and Beirut, the route east of the Lebanons through Aleppo and Damascus, and the route along the Euphrates, south-east to the Persian Gulf. Auchinleck's first task in Syria was to plan a defence against an army advancing south from the Taurus mountains; in addition he had to be ready to send a force into Turkey if she was attacked, the British attachés in that country having been instructed by their Government to tell the Turks that by December at the latest an Allied army of four divisions would be available to help them.

Whatever opinion the British staffs held about the ability of the Russians to withstand the German onslaught, they could derive much comfort from the fact that each week during which Germany failed to win a decisive victory made it the more unlikely that she would attempt an advance through the mountains of Turkey in 1941. On 15th August General Blamey told the Australian Government that he considered that it was already too late for the Germans to attack before the spring of 1942.

It was accepted by the British commanders that if a German army advanced through Turkey and the Turks resisted the best course would be to move a British force northward and occupy the mountain passes of southern Turkey. On the other hand the Turks might let the Germans through, or might not permit a British advance into their territory; or it might be impossible to bring adequate British forces forward in time to meet the enemy in the passes. Once an invading army reached the plain of northern Syria it would be in country through which armoured formations could move with ease, and it had to be assumed that the German force would be stronger in armour than the British. Consequently General Wilson decided that the solution to his tactical problem was to prepare a main defensive line through the rugged country of southern Syria. This line travelled from Tripoli, past Baalbek and south-east to the lava-strewn country of the Jebel Druse and Transjordan.

The defence plan pictured the use of mobile forces based on a series of fortresses astride the main routes. The northernmost fortress would be round Tripoli and manned by one division. The others would be on or south of the Damascus-Beirut road. One, manned by two divisions, would be in the area Zebedani-Dimas; another with one division in the Djedeide area; another round Merdjayoun; the Free French would be in the Ain Sofar area on the Beirut-Damascus road. It was estimated that a total of two armoured and five infantry divisions would be required for the combined Syria-Iraq area.

There was little prospect of four full divisions being available for the Syrian area in the near future, but in the meantime the formations in Syria could begin the work of siting, surveying and digging a defence system for an army of that size. At the end of July the garrison consisted chiefly of I Australian Corps (with headquarters at Aley). Under its command were the 7th Australian Division in the Tripoli area; the miniature Free French Division and 5th Indian Brigade round Damascus and Nebek; the 6th British Division at Baalbek with its brigades at Zahle, Homs and near Aamiq on the western wall of the Bekaa; and the 4th Cavalry Brigade at Aleppo. Outside this defence scheme was the 10th Indian Division which occupied that part of Syria east of the Euphrates,[5] and thus stood astride the line of advance from Turkey to the Persian Gulf.

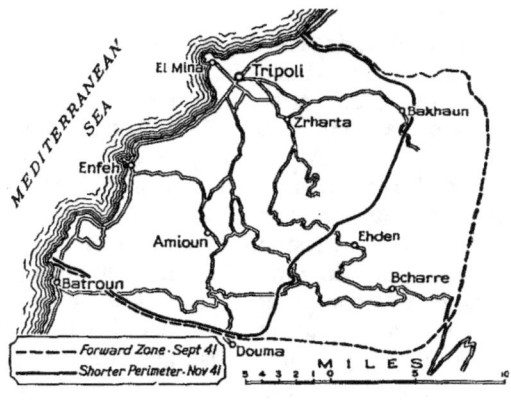

In the western zone, only the 7th Australian Division was complete in itself, but the 6th British Division's lack of cavalry, artillery, engineers and machine-gunners was remedied by attaching to it a number of Australian units: the 9th Divisional Cavalry, 2/9th and 2/11th Field Regiments, the 2/1st Anti-Tank Regiment, 2/15th Field Company, and two companies of the 2/3rd Machine Gun Battalion. The 2/9th and 2/11th Artillery Regiments were "corps troops" and thus could be spared without depriving any Australian division of its guns. The reforming of a division of British regular infantry supported chiefly by Australian technical troops underlined the wisdom of including a full allocation of corps troops in the A.I.F.—and the error of retaining in the Middle East large numbers of British regular battalions without sending there the artillery and other technical units needed to form them into effective fighting formations.

In the Tripoli area preparations were based on the assumption that the roads and railways leading from Turkey would support an enemy force of eleven divisions plus airborne troops. It was considered that the principal attack would be made along the axis Aleppo-Homs-Damascus-Lake

---

[5] Early in August the 5 Indian Bde, with HQ at Deir ez Zor, took over the Djezireh area, and the 23 Bde relieved the 4 Cav Bde at Aleppo to enable it to move to Iraq.

Tiberias, with a wide flanking movement through Palmyra; but that it was possible that the enemy might advance also along the coast. The Tripoli fortress was therefore to be prepared for all-round defence; General Allen considered that the performance of this task (in addition to the maintenance of a mobile force for counter-attack) would require two infantry divisions and one armoured. His division set out to construct a fortress area for a force of that size. Hope that a larger force would be allotted to the Tripoli area was dispelled, however, in October when General Auchinleck inspected the defences and informed General Allen that no troops would be added except possibly one tank battalion. Thereupon General Allen amended his plan to provide a shorter perimeter.

General Blamey disagreed with General Auchinleck's plans for the defence of Syria. He considered that the "box" plan was static and fundamentally unsound and, in particular, that his troops digging these defences were being converted into mere labourers. He arranged with General Wilson that they should dig only two days a week and train on the other days. General Auchinleck, however, countermanded this arrangement. General Blamey protested strongly. At length a considerable force of civilian labourers was added.

Blamey's protest on this occasion was symptomatic of a strong and fundamental difference of opinion with first Wavell and then Auchinleck. Blamey was convinced that the Middle East commanders had been unwise in frequently breaking up established corps and divisions and as frequently having to improvise new *ad hoc* formations. It was the period of "Jock columns"—brigade groups, or battalion groups, or even company groups—which had been appropriate enough in the kind of guerilla warfare which had preceded the Western Desert offensive in December 1940, but which, in Blamey's opinion and that of other Dominion soldiers, were now of small value in themselves and a menace to sound tactical doctrine.[6]

At this time the doctrine which General Blamey criticised was receiving commendation from Mr Churchill. On 3rd July Churchill wrote to the Secretary for War and the Chief of the Imperial General Staff: "It is highly questionable whether the divisional organisation is right for armoured troops. A system of self-contained brigade groups . . . would be operationally and administratively better . . . . However, where divisional formations have grown up and have been clothed with armed reality the conditions of war do not permit the disturbance of a change . . . ."[7] Blamey expressed his opinion in the course of a cable to the Minister for the Army on 3rd August:

> Outstanding weakness in past of Middle East has been failure to maintain organisation, even disregard of provisional organisation. If we have to meet Ger-

---

[6] "This was the era of the Brigade Group and the 'Jock' column. It has been said that at the Somme in 1916 British tactical doctrines reached their lowest depths, and it seemed to me that Libya '41, or the Winter Battle, or Auchinleck's offensive, or 'Crusader', as it was variously called, was fought with an equally total disregard of what one had understood to be the principles of war—with two exceptions . . . surprise . . . and maintenance of the objective." (H. K. Kippenberger, *Infantry Brigadier* (1949), pp. 81-2; see also p. 138.)

[7] Quoted in Churchill, Vol III, p. 711.

mans in Turkey or Syria next spring essential organisation in army corps be foreseen and provided now. It is urged that for Australian Corps this should include air forces.

Events were to demonstrate that Blamey was right, but a year would pass and a new commander-in-chief and a new field commander would arrive in the Middle East before the principles he advocated would be adopted.

Blamey's tactical doctrine ran parallel with his responsibility for realising the hope of the Australian Government that its oversea force should be grouped together under its own commander. By August, although single Australian divisions or brigades had fought in North Africa, Greece, Crete and Syria, and Australian Corps commanders had directed the field force in two of those campaigns, no two Australian divisions had been in action together. At the beginning of that month the 9th Division and a brigade of the 7th was besieged in Tobruk; some Australian units were in the Western Desert of Egypt; one unit was in Cyprus; the 6th Division was in Palestine; the 7th, brought up to strength with units of the 6th, in Syria, where several Australian units were now included in a British division. The 8th Division, less one brigade, was concentrating in Malaya. Each effort to assemble the corps had been defeated by the need hurriedly to send improvised forces to meet some new emergency.

At least as early as November 1940 General Blamey had a clear picture in his mind of the eventual size and shape of the Second A.I.F. On the 15th of that month, having read an announcement by the Chief of the General Staff, General Sturdee, that the four infantry divisions would be Australia's complete army effort, he wrote a long and wise letter to Mr Menzies in which he expressed the hope that this announcement had not been sponsored by the Government. "The reason given in the version that reached here," Blamey added, "was the limitation of manpower having regard to other demands . . . . I think Harold Holt [Minister for Labour and National Service] will find that this is not by any means the limit of our capacity in manpower. The details worked out by the Manpower Committee in my time there would correct this, and I am sure Sir Carl Jess has had it more completely worked out ere this.

"Looking forward I think we may take it for granted that when the armies clash ultimately in this war, the conditions of long drawn out attrition of the last war, with the consequent slow wastage in manpower, are not likely to be repeated. With modern armoured formations it is difficult to see long drawn out lines protected by wire, pill-boxes, etc., facing one another for long periods. The conditions of the present war will not give time enough to build suitable works—it can only be done in peace time as was the Maginot Line.

"It would seem that our whole aim as far as the army is concerned should be to have ready, when the time comes, the maximum of power for the series of land struggles that must determine the issue.

"Wishful thinking leads many into the error of believing that the war will be won by a combination of the blockade and air attack. Powerful as the blockade may be, it will take a long time before its effect is fully felt unless history's teaching is false. The Germans are endeavouring to make its stranglehold less effective this time by playing up to Russia. We may be sure that their eyes are on the metal and food supplies of the Ukraine, and the oil of the Caucasus, in whatever propositions they are putting to Russia during Molotov's present visit to Berlin.

"The Germans, too, have come to see that the air war can never finally determine the issue. They have learned this from the steadily increasing effectiveness of London's defences. The German air force is being driven ever higher into the upper air and bombing becomes increasingly haphazard in its results. These limitations will gradually become more obvious, and the bombing of a large fixed area like London, or of vessels lying in the harbour, should not deceive us. As time goes on the Germans will protect their own production centres more and more effectively. While there can be little doubt that the RAF saved England from invasion and while meticulous care is taken to ensure that results of air conflicts are not exaggerated, personal experience during the last war makes me doubtful as to the results claimed from our bombing of German production centres. The claims of young and optimistic pilots as to destruction by night in Germany are not so subject to check as they are in air battles over England.

"For these reasons I am sure that there is only one wise policy for us, and that is to endeavour to develop our maximum striking power with all possible rapidity ready for the clash that must come. It is a question of numbers, organisation and equipment after the attrition period, i.e., the period of naval blockade and air destruction. The time will come to force the issue on land, and it does not seem possible that British military force alone without active American assistance can develop sufficient strength to overwhelm the Germans.

"It would seem that ultimate victory depends upon two prime factors; the first is the entry of America into the actual field, and the second the development, while time permits, of the armed forces of the Empire to their maximum strength for the struggle.

"If international developments, for example in the Balkan countries, do not force us into the extremely dangerous position of participating piecemeal in land warfare, we must spend all our energies between now and the summer of 1942 in preparation. I would press the point that we should determine our maximum possible effort now and plan for it.

"From this view I would stress that four divisions do not by any means represent Australia's maximum, and nothing else will save us. I would urge that consideration be given to building this force up by the addition of at least two armoured divisions as soon as practicable.

"It will take time to accomplish, and therefore it should be begun systematically now. The men are the best material in the world for the task. The equipment could be planned for, and if it could be made available before the end of the next northern summer, it would allow a few months for training.

"Our A.I.F. is organised as a Corps of four infantry divisions. It can only be a completely self-contained force if it has its due proportion of armoured formations, and both for this war and looking to our national future, we should be a force fully organised.

"New Zealand has already recognised the realities of the position and her expeditionary force will now consist of one division and one armoured brigade.

"We have stuck to the infantry divisions probably because the AIF of the last war was composed of infantry divisions. Is it not the effect of looking backward? Surely it is time for a little forward thinking!"

On the 1st January 1941 the Government, having in July approved plans for making tanks in Australia, had authorised the formation of one armoured division as part of the A.I.F.[8]

Before the invasion of Syria a plan had been on foot not only to collect the Australian force together but to form in effect an Anzac Army. The grouping of the 6th Division with the New Zealand Division to form the "Anzac Corps" in Greece had awakened a desire for a closer association between Australian and New Zealand forces. In addition General Blamey felt that the welding of the formations would add strength to the whole military organisation in the Middle East. The project had been discussed by Generals Wavell, Freyberg and Blamey, and on 7th May, soon after Blamey's appointment as Wavell's deputy, the Australian and New Zealand Governments were informed by the Dominions Office that Wavell "would welcome the suggestion which had been made" that an Anzac Corps consisting of the 6th Australian and the New Zealand Divisions should again be formed, and placed under the command of General Freyberg. General Blamey cabled his approval of this proposal, which he elaborated by recommending that the 7th and 9th Australian Divisions be formed into an Australian Corps under General Lavarack.[9] He explained that the tentative policy was to group pairs of infantry divisions into corps and attach armoured formations to them according to tactical requirements.

The Australian War Cabinet deferred a decision until Mr Menzies returned from London, and in the meantime asked General Blamey how many additional troops would be required to carry out the project, adding that difficulties were being encountered in Australia in finding men both for the munitions program and the fighting forces. Blamey's proposal evidently suggested to the Ministers that he had in mind an Anzac Army[10] consisting of two infantry corps to which British armoured formations would be attached if needed. "Is it intended," Blamey was asked by the

---

[8] Maj-Gen J. Northcott was appointed to command it on 1 Sep 1941.

[9] General Blamey's proposal, first made in July, that the 9 Div be withdrawn from Tobruk so that it might be rested and the Australian Corps concentrated is discussed in Vol III of this series.

[10] This conception existed also in the minds of the rank and file. On 24 July (news of the formation of an Australian armoured division having arrived) an infantryman wrote in a letter home: "Without being clannish, I think it would be a welcome experiment to have an Australian or Anzac Army complete with armoured division and R.A.A.F. under a single command."

Minister for the Army, "to set up any additional headquarters establishment which would form an additional Australian commitment such as an Army Headquarters to control both . . . corps?"

Blamey replied on 30th May that the geographical separation of the divisions and lack of equipment for troops from Greece would make it impossible to concentrate the Australian and New Zealand divisions in one area as a complete force "for many months". For the present his proposals aimed only at having the available divisions grouped into corps. He then elaborated his suggestion: The Anzac Corps would include an Australian and a New Zealand division and 19,462 corps troops, of which 8,096 would be from New Zealand; the Australian Corps would be similarly constituted, but all Australian. In addition Australian base troops totalling 13,251 would be needed. Blamey listed the additional Australian units that would be required to provide corps troops for both corps, allowance being made for the provision of certain units by New Zealand. They included five artillery regiments (medium, anti-aircraft and survey) and a number of engineer, signals and service units with a total strength of 9,612; he suggested that all additional fighting troops be available by 1st December, all service units by 1st February. Each year 39,218 reinforcements would be required for the expanded Australian force in the Middle East—45 per cent of its total strength of 87,152. There were then 77,660 Australian troops in the Middle East,[1] 10,017 in Malaya and the islands, and 44,279 of the A.I.F. in Australia or at sea (including the armoured division and part of the 8th).

The adoption of Blamey's proposal would have produced a force resembling the Australian-New Zealand contingent of 1916, when an Australian and an Anzac corps were formed comprising five Australian divisions and one New Zealand. Then Australia and New Zealand provided few of their own base and corps troops; on the other hand the population of each country had increased by about 40 per cent since 1916.

In May 1941 the shape of the A.I.F. was being discussed also by Mr Menzies and the Chiefs of Staff in London. Menzies had asked the Chiefs of Staff to indicate the strength of the overseas force at which they considered that Australia should aim. In reply it was recommended that a fifth Australian division should be raised (making one armoured and five infantry divisions), which with the New Zealand Division would complete an Anzac Army of two corps each of three divisions; and that Australia should provide a number of ancillary units. The Chiefs of Staff stated that Australia, in common with other Dominions, was, broadly speaking, providing complete divisions, while corps and base units were being provided from British sources (a statement that, although true concerning base units, might in the ministers' minds somewhat have exaggerated the proportion of corps troops which Britain was providing in the Middle East, where Australia was maintaining her due quota of them).

---

[1] Australians then available in the Middle East (disregarding possible losses in Crete) were: Anzac Corps: 6 Div, 10,312; Corps troops to be allotted to Anzac Corps, 1,937. Aust Corps: 7 Div, 13,140; 9 Div, 12,122; Corps troops, 16,678. Base and L of C units, 7,806; reinforcements, 10,496; non-effectives, 5,169. Total 77,660.

At this time the strength of a division was 17,500; the proportion of army, base and lines-of-communication troops to each division was 12,500. The proposal was made in London that, for each infantry division, Australia should furnish 3,500 of the 12,500 base troops, in addition to reinforcements and 6,000 corps troops, Britain providing the remainder; and that for the armoured division Australia should provide (in addition to the division of 14,000 men) 14,000 corps, army, and base troops. Thus, allowance being made for first reinforcements, the initial needs of each new division would be 29,000 men.

Menzies had been informed in London that the ultimate composition of the army in Britain was to be thirty-two divisions (including four Canadian). Until the autumn of 1941, only two of these divisions could be spared for service overseas—the 50th to the Middle East, the 5th to Northern Ireland. In the winter two more British divisions would be sent to the Middle East, if they could be spared from the defence of Britain and were not needed elsewhere. By the spring of 1942 there might be seventeen infantry divisions in the Middle East—six Indian, four (including the 8th) Australian, four British, two South African and one New Zealand.[2] Acceptance of the British proposals would have necessitated increasing the A.I.F. to 229,000 during the remainder of 1941.

Meanwhile the New Zealand authorities had considered the administrative problems involved in the initial proposal to re-form the Anzac Corps. On 25th June General Freyberg informed Army Headquarters at Wellington that the New Zealand Prime Minister, Mr Fraser, then in Egypt, had discussed the proposal with Generals Wavell and Blamey and himself and all favoured it. "It only requires the Commonwealth Government's agreement to bring it into existence," he added.[3]

When, after Menzies' return, the Australian War Cabinet considered Blamey's larger proposals, it decided that they should not be adopted until a complete review of manpower had been made. It had resolved to maintain the militia at 210,000; it was committed to raising a further 12,000 men to complete the armoured division; the Chief of the General Staff, Lieut-General Sturdee, considered that for some time ahead 7,000 a month would be needed to maintain units in the Middle East and 400 a month to maintain units in Malaya. In April, however, only 4,746 recruits had entered the A.I.F., and though the rate of enlistment increased (for example 4,467 were accepted in the fortnight which ended on the 10th May), the Cabinet decided on 2nd July that for the present the existing divisions of the A.I.F., including the armoured division, were all that

---

[2] In April 1941 the establishments of the forces raised in each Dominion for oversea service numbered:

Australia	92,661
Canada	87,485
New Zealand	30,313
South Africa	48,200

In addition Australia and Canada had each authorised and were raising an armoured division, which would increase their total establishments to: Australia, 108,156; Canada, 102,337.

[3] *Documents Relating to New Zealand's Participation in the Second World War 1939-45*, Vol II, p. 14.

Australia could maintain in view of her other commitments—particularly to the Empire Air Training Scheme.

The Army staff in Australia based their calculations on higher casualty rates than the force had in fact suffered (or was to suffer) in the Middle East. In April there were 6,000 unallotted reinforcements in the Middle East, 7,300 were ready to embark from Australia in April, and 14,500 in May. Thus enough men were available to make possible the expansion which Blamey planned, and volunteers were coming forward in more than sufficient numbers to provide the reinforcements that he had asked for— 39,000 a year, compared with Sturdee's estimate of some 84,000. Indeed, in May they had enlisted at a rate equivalent to more than 100,000 a year.

The increase in recruits, so marked in May, and probably an outcome of the heavy fighting in April—news of such fighting usually caused a rush of recruits determined to help their fellows overseas—did not continue in June and July; in August, Sturdee, still basing his calculations on a far higher casualty rate than Blamey expected, informed the War Cabinet that the intake was not enough to maintain the A.I.F. and, unless it increased, a reduction of the number of divisions would have to be considered.[4] On the 13th August, the War Cabinet decided specifically that Australia could not agree either to the formation of two corps (of three Australian divisions and one New Zealand) in the Middle East or to the War Office's proposal that Australia should maintain a corps of five infantry divisions, one armoured division and an armoured brigade, with ancillary troops. It decided that it would endeavour to increase the size of its existing divisions in accordance with recent changes in the British establishment (this would entail adding 7,000 to the strength of the whole force) but that it might later be necessary to abolish one of the infantry divisions in the Middle East and maintain there a corps of one armoured and two infantry divisions.[5]

In accordance with this prediction and because recruiting still lagged, the new Ministry of Mr Fadden[6] on 17th September decided to convert the force in the Middle East into a corps of three divisions less one brigade group, but including an Army tank brigade, and to maintain only the armoured portion of the armoured division—the tank regiments but not the artillery, infantry and other units which such a division included. While that division remained in Australia these were to be sup-

---

[4] In August, however, possibly as a consequence of the fighting in Syria, the number of recruits rose to more than 7,000. The figures were: April, 4,746; May, 9,875; June, 5,762; July, 5,910; August, 7,622; September, 4,453.

[5] In August Blamey expressed a desire to leave his appointment as Deputy Commander-in-Chief in the Middle East and resume command of the Australian Corps but War Cabinet decided that because he had been appointed "to ensure Australian participation in the higher direction of the Middle East Campaign" he should continue. On 24 Sep he was promoted from the rank of lieut-general to that of general, a rank hitherto attained in the Australian Army only by Chauvel, Monash and White. The promotion was not given by the Australian Government until Blamey had pointed out on several occasions from June 1941 onwards that he was handicapped by not possessing equal rank to that of field commanders and others in the Middle East.

[6] On 29th August Menzies had returned his commission to the Governor-General and that day Fadden was commissioned to form a Ministry.

plied by the militia; if it went to the Middle East they would be provided by breaking up one of the infantry divisions there. The decision was confirmed by the new Ministry led by Mr Curtin which took office on 7th October.

It is doubtful whether either Cabinet realised the full gravity of its decision—and improbable that Cabinets which included a quota of men who had seen extensive service in the old A.I.F. would have agreed to it. In 1918 the breaking-up of Australian units for lack of reinforcements had led to mutiny, and it would be impossible to carry out the Ministers' new plan without breaking up units with fine records and an intense *esprit de corps,* and converting others.

In the opinion of General Blamey the proposed reductions were not necessary. By October the divisions in the Middle East were at full strength or near it. There were reinforcements ready in the training units. Only one division—the 9th—was in action and it was soon to be relieved. In Australia were some 36,000 men of the A.I.F.[7] As mentioned above, Sturdee, in his advice to the War Cabinet a few months before, had said that 84,000 men would be needed each year to maintain the A.I.F. at its existing strength; Blamey that 39,000 a year would be enough. In fact, in the six months from April to September 38,300 men enlisted—nearly enough to meet Sturdee's estimate of the requirements, and enough, according to Blamey's estimate, to maintain for a year the expanded force which he had recommended. By December all units in the Middle East had been brought to full strength and there were still 16,600 men in the reinforcement pool.

At his own suggestion General Blamey was brought to Australia to confer with the new Curtin Ministry. He left Egypt early in November and at a meeting of the War Cabinet on the 26th he pointed out bluntly that he had not been consulted before the Ministers' decision had been made and that he opposed it. He said that disbandment or conversion of units would damage morale, that there was no need for the A.I.F. to maintain an armoured brigade, that the units needed to complete the armoured division should be raised either in Australia or the Middle East from reinforcements or by allotment of corps units, that the estimated scale of reinforcements was too high, and that there were enough reinforcements in the Middle East to ensure that the corps could be maintained during operations in the spring of 1942. A table of figures presented to the Cabinet predicted that enough volunteers would be received to maintain the A.I.F. until late in 1942 when a shortage might occur. The Ministers reversed their decision, resolved that no change be made in the A.I.F. organisation, and that the armoured division be completed with A.I.F.

---

[7] In October the number of soldiers on full-time duty in Australia were:

Permanent forces	5,084
Militia	61,396
Garrison battalions	11,050
A.I.F.	36,357
Total	113,887

units. It recorded, however, that "ultimately" the number of infantry divisions would have to be reduced.[8]

Meanwhile on 20th September the New Zealand Government was still awaiting the Australian Government's views on the re-establishment of the Anzac Corps. That day Freyberg cabled to his Prime Minister that the corps could not yet be formed because the 6th Australian Division was not yet re-equipped and trained and the 9th was in Tobruk.

The visit to Australia gave Blamey an opportunity of advising the Ministers on a subject that might soon become urgent. Although in most respects Turkey was observing a careful neutrality, British and Turkish staff officers (as mentioned above) had been discussing what action should be taken if the Germans attacked Turkey, as well they might. It was now considered certain that the Turkish leaders would keep out of the war as long as they could, but would resist invasion. If forces were sent to Turkey to help her meet a German invasion, it was almost certain that they would include Australian divisions now in Syria. Consequently, on 11th October, General Blamey had taken steps to warn his Government of the new possibility. He advised that, if asked to agree to the dispatch of the A.I.F. to Turkey, the Government should make its agreement subject to the conditions that there should be a properly-devised plan and time to carry it out, properly-organised lines of communication and "a realistic order of battle and not one made up on paper, consisting largely of units that never existed, as was done for Greece". Blamey told the Advisory War Council, at a meeting which he attended in November, that he considered that Germany would wish to by-pass Turkey and would favour an attack by way of the Caspian and the Caucasus, cutting off India. On Blamey's advice Curtin agreed that the A.I.F. might be moved into the Taurus mountains, provided that the operations had been adequately planned and prepared.

Meanwhile in Syria the garrison had increased in size, and the troops had continued surveying, digging and wiring defensive positions in preparation for this possible German incursion from the north. In September the X Corps headquarters moved into Syria. That month the 18th Brigade having been withdrawn from Tobruk rejoined the 7th Division. In October the 6th Australian Division, restored and re-equipped after its losses in Greece and Crete, and now commanded by General Herring, General Mackay having been recalled to Australia to command the Home Forces, replaced the 6th British Division (which, in its turn, re-named the "70th Division", was to replace the 9th Australian Division in Tobruk). On 1st November the "Palestine and Transjordan" Command ceased to exist and General Wilson became commander of a new Ninth Army, embracing all troops in Syria and Lebanon, and with its headquarters at Broumane in the mountains above Beirut. The new army was chiefly Australian, and on 5th November twelve Australian officers, including a lieut-colonel of

---

[8] On 18 Nov the War Cabinet had reaffirmed, however, that in view of the situation in the Far East, it would not agree to a request by Blamey that the 8 Div be sent to the Middle East.

the general staff (Barrett[1]), of the signals (Kendall) and the medical service (Saxby[2]), were appointed to its headquarters, and five to Palestine Area headquarters. The new army was a top-heavy organisation, with headquarters enough to control three times as many fighting formations as it possessed—an arrangement perhaps justified by the probability that if Syria was invaded several more divisions would be hurried into that country.[3]

In Syria there was a new outbreak of complaints about Australian indiscipline. Ten days after the cease-fire General Auchinleck received a copy of a note written by General Spears in which he said:

> The Australians are already greatly feared by the natives. Their behaviour, with the exception of some specialised units which are well disciplined, would be a disgrace to any Army. They are alleged to have stolen Vichy officers' wedding rings and to have deprived prisoners of their water-bottles. At Mezze aerodrome, by way of contributing their quota to the efficient conduct of the war, they stole and smashed vital parts of the Air France wireless installation which was the most efficient and most powerful post on French territory between France and Indo-China.

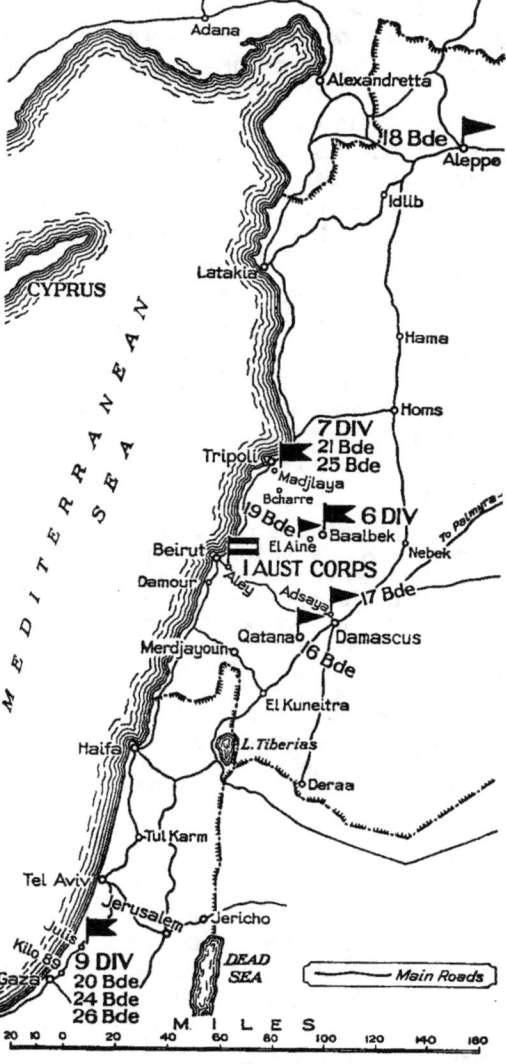

Location of A.I.F., December 1941

---

[1] Col J. E. Barrett, OBE, WX1554. DAAG 6 Div 1940; I Corps 1940; DDMT CGS Bch LHQ 1943-45. Regular soldier; of Perth, WA; b. Perth, 27 Sep 1898.

[2] Col N. H. W. Saxby, OBE, NX186. CO 2/3 Fd Amb 1941; ADMS 3 Div 1942-43; ADGMS Adv LHQ 1943-44; ADMS 5 Div 1944-45, 6 Div 1945. Medical practitioner; of Kogarah, NSW; b. Ashfield, NSW, 31 Dec 1907.

[3] As part of the defensive preparations the Australian engineers built railways, roads, bridges, defensive works and camps in Syria. This work, which continued during 1942, will be described in the next volume of this series.

Auchinleck passed this on to Blamey, and at length it was investigated and reported on by Colonel Rogers, the senior liaison officer of I Australian Corps who had happened to be liaison officer with the formations on the Damascus front from 17th June to 16th July. Rogers made a careful inquiry and reached the conclusion that the accusations were unfounded, also, in one respect, "grossly libellous, mischievous and irresponsible". Only two specific charges had been made against Australians since the campaign began: one of assault and robbery by an Australian and an English dispatch rider in company; and the other a charge not yet substantiated of theft of some equipment from Rayak and Aleppo airfields. On the other hand false rumours about Australian indiscipline had been numerous. He pointed out that as soon as it became evident that Australians were coming into disrepute in Damascus, and unjustly, Colonel Bastin, commander of the 9th Australian Cavalry, the largest Australian unit in the area, stopped all leave to that city, and was the first Allied commander to do so.

On 11th October General Wilson wrote the following letter to General Blamey:

> I regret to say that I have had many cases brought to me recently of brutal assaults by Australian soldiers, either against other soldiers (British or French), police (military or civil) or civilians. I am taking this up with your Commanders as I feel that exemplary punishments will have to be given to put a stop to it, and I am asking your Commanders to let it be known that in future all cases of assault must be tried by General Court Martial. Perhaps if they get a whack of penal servitude with the first two years to be done in the Middle East it might have a deterrent effect.
>
> I will not bother you with the details, but in some cases it has been due to neglect of picquets accompanying leave parties. Trouble has, however, occurred in Beirut, Damascus and Jerusalem. I thought you had better be aware of what is happening, and would be very glad of any advice you can give me as to how to deal with it.

Blamey replied recalling how earlier accusations against Australians had been proved baseless and adding: "It is a very convenient form of excuse for any happening to lay it on to broad Australian shoulders. But when it is not in accordance with fact it does an immense amount of harm to the relations between the various Empire forces." He concluded: "I am afraid that the question of discipline of the A.I.F. is entirely one for my action"; and enclosed a copy of relevant passages from his instructions from the Government.

In reply Wilson sent Blamey a list of two cases of fracas in cafés in Jerusalem, one involving two and the other seven Australians, and a note of a charge pending against an Australian who on 29th September had allegedly attacked a lieut-colonel and a nursing sister as they were leaving a hotel in Damascus.

A report which Blamey obtained from Corps headquarters stated that since the end of the operations in Syria, two months before, the following charges had been made against men of the Corps and its two divisions: assaults on other troops, 17; on police, 4; on civilians, 27. In 15 cases the guilt of an Australian had been established; 33 cases were awaiting investigation or decision.[4]

As winter approached, General Blamey, who had ski-ed in Australia, persuaded General Allen that ski troops should be trained to operate in the Taurus mountains soon to be snow-covered; he considered also that ski-ing would provide a pleasant recreation during this period of garrison service. There were at corps headquarters several officers who were accomplished ski-runners, among them Major Savage,[5] of the Signals, who was also a leader of the bush-walking movement in Australia. In October he was instructed to prepare plans, and the following month was appointed to form and conduct a ski school. When instructors were sought, hundreds of enterprising soldiers applied but few had reasonable qualifications. Savage proposed that outstanding Australian skiers (including Captain Mitchell,[6] serving in Malaya with the 8th Division, and Sergeant Jack Thomas[7]) be flown to Syria. When this proposal failed, he obtained, from the Spears Mission, Major James Riddell, who had ski-ed for Britain at the Olympic Games of 1936; Lieutenant E. D. Mills[8] of the 6th Cavalry Regiment who was a Tasmanian langlauf champion; Bombardier Stogdale,[9] who had won Australian championships; Sergeant Abbottsmith,[10] a former instructor at Mount Kosciusko, and others.

---

[4] In the re-training of the 6 Div Gen Mackay had taken steps to convince it that attack from the air on a trained military formation was ineffective. He feared that some of his men had decided that they were inferior to the Germans as fighters, and that the air attacks in Greece had contributed to this feeling. In an instruction written early in May he said that air bombing had exerted no material effect on the operations of the Anzac Corps; the damage done compared with the number of bombs dropped was infinitesimal; and most of the casualties caused by machine-gunning from the air could have been avoided if vehicles had not bunched. He ordered commanding officers to organise close-order drill, bayonet training, games and swimming as the most effective methods of restoring the men's minds and bodies, and to institute musketry courses when ammunition became available.

In this re-training period Mackay also circulated a statement about "two-up". On 18th Jul he sent a letter to all commanding officers of his division lamenting that the playing of that game was increasing and instructing them to suppress it. He said that he had been informed that three permanent schools at the Soldiers' Club at Tel Aviv were being conducted by the same group of managers, who had been able to prevent others from opening rival schools. The promoter took no risks but took 4/- in the £1 from the ring "besides what he might cadge from the tails round the ring, or rob from a man too drunk to count the change". Mackay pointed out that men who had lost their pay at the two-up schools were begging money in the streets. He enclosed a copy of an eloquent letter from a private soldier describing the drunken brawls that broke out round two-up schools, and his observation of the rate at which the players lost and the promoters won. He had seen one promoter win £10 in three hours; one soldier lose £10 in an hour.

There was much truth in these observations. On the other hand it should be recorded that good soldiers as well as bad conducted two-up schools. At Tel Aviv and other leave centres and in the transit camps it was likely that the same groups of promoters would be found. (They worked in pairs, one to handle the money and one to do the "spruiking".) In unit lines, however, the men who ran the games sometimes had wives and families, were making large allotments from their pay to them, and depended on the regular income derived from promoting two-up schools for a few extra perquisites. Generally each school was governed by a strict set of rules. The Australian soldier came from a community where gambling on horse races was a principal hobby of a large proportion of men and women; in the army two-up provided some of the excitement which punting had provided at home.

[5] Col R. W. Savage, OBE, NX34963. Comdt I Aust Corps Ski School 1941; CSO Second Army 1944-45, First Army 1945. Accountant; of Concord, NSW; b. Concord, 30 Sep 1906.

[6] Capt T. W. Mitchell, VX43577; HQ 8 Aust Div. MLA in Vic since 1947, Attorney-General and Solicitor-General 1950-52. Pastoralist; of Towong Hill, Vic; b. Towong Hill, 11 Nov 1906.

[7] Sgt J. V. Thomas, NX56505; 2/12 Fd Amb. Clerk and ski instructor; of Punchbowl, NSW; b. Woollahra, NSW, 16 Sep 1915. Lost in sinking of the hospital ship Centaur, 14 May 1943.

[8] Maj E. D. Mills, TX2023. 6 Cav and 2 Cav Regts. Pastoralist; of Longford, Tas; b. Longford, 6 Mar 1912.

[9] Bdr G. E. D. Stogdale, VX30699; 2/11 Fd Regt. Traveller; of Melbourne; b. Melbourne, 19 Jan 1910.

[10] Sgt J. Abbottsmith, NX60422. 24 Fd Pk Coy, 2/1 LAA Regt. Ski instructor-carpenter; of Bega, NSW; b. Tamworth, NSW, 16 Aug 1918.

With much difficulty equipment was obtained—ski-ing was a comparatively new sport in the Lebanon—and a Mount Kosciusko manual was reprinted. The school took over a hotel and barracks above Bcharre in the Lebanons at 6,500 feet, and there an initial class of some seventy officers and men were trained; it included artillery officers and signallers whose task would be to occupy observation posts above the snow line.

The intention was to form a ski company of about 200 men for each Australian division.[11] Their role would be to patrol, on skis in winter and as mountain troops in summer, the lofty mountains between the 7th Division round Tripoli and the 6th round Baalbek and Damascus. The snow which blanketed Syria and the Lebanon that winter was said to be the heaviest for thirty years, and for three weeks no vehicles were able to reach the school. Injured men were taken to hospital on sleighs made of galvanised iron sheets turned up in front—Major Savage remembered having read of such sleighs being used by the Australian light horse in the sand of Sinai in 1916.[1] Hard training and many experiments were carried out, but before the course was completed the men were ordered to rejoin their units.

Throughout the A.I.F. lack of equipment was not now a serious problem. No longer was it desirable for units partly to equip themselves at the expense of the enemy; indeed it was no longer permissible. A postscript to the period of persistent shortages is provided by a file of letters concerning an incident in the history of the 2/16th Battalion. It was reported to headquarters in Jerusalem that on the 6th October two aircraft flying over the area of the 2/16th in Syria had been fired on by a Breda heavy machine-gun; the aircraft were British. Brigadier McConnel,[2] chief of staff of British Forces in Palestine and Transjordan, sternly asked I Australian Corps to explain whether that battalion or any other battalion had Breda machine-guns and by what authority. At length the enquiry reached Colonel Potts of the 2/16th who explained that aircraft, flying low, failed to give recognition signals and were engaged—with two Bredas which men of his battalion had assembled from parts salvaged at Mersa Matruh in April and May, and had used with good effect against enemy aircraft in the Syrian campaign. Might not they be retained? Brigadier Stevens supported the request, as did General Allen. Lieut-Colonel Elliott on Corps staff was sympathetic. The correspondence had then occupied twenty days. In the meantime the Ninth Army had come into being. Its chief of staff was Brigadier Baillon,[3] who had been on exchange to the

---

[11] The senior company officers were to be: 6 Div, Capt W. G. A. Baines (of Haberfield, NSW); 7 Div, Capt T. R. W. Cotton; 9 Div, Capt J. S. Cumpston (of Canberra).

[1] H. S. Gullett, *Official History of Australia in the War of 1914-18*, Vol VII (1923), p. 105. This volume had been widely read in 1940 and 1941, particularly because it described operations round Gaza and in Syria in country familiar to the Second A.I.F.

[2] Maj-Gen D. F. McConnel, CB, CBE, DSO. BGS Brit Forces in Palestine and Transjordan 1939-41; GOC Pal and Transjordan, 1941-44. Regular soldier; of Colmonell, Scotland; b. Colmonell, 9 Jun 1893.

[3] Maj-Gen J. A. Baillon, CB, CBE, MC. (1914-18; Capt S Staff Regt.) GSO1 Brit Tps in Sudan 1940-41; BGS Ninth Army 1941-42; CGS Persia and Iraq 1942-43; CGS ME 1943-45. Regular soldier; b. London, 6 Oct 1895.

Australian Army when war began, and had come to the Middle East as a major on the staff of the 6th Division. Baillon's reply, though recognising the "initiative and enthusiasm shown by 2/16th Australian Infantry Battalion" was firm; the guns must be returned to Ordnance. It marked the end of a phase.

In October and November the German advance in Russia continued, although more slowly. They pressed nearer to Moscow, took Kharkov, entered the Crimea. To the men digging and training in Syria the possibility that they would next meet a German army advancing from the mountains of Asia Minor seemed not remote. In mid-November came encouraging news from their old battleground in the Western Desert. The Eighth Army (more imposing title of what had formerly been "Western Desert Force") under General Cunningham attacked towards Tobruk. Bardia was retaken and Tobruk relieved. Almost on the same day Gondar, the last main stronghold of the Italians in Abyssinia surrendered. By the end of November it was evident that the German advance in Russia had been checked and the Russians would have a winter during which to recover. The outlook in Russia and the Middle East was relatively bright when, on the 8th December (Australian time), the news sped round the world that the Japanese had attacked Hawaii, Malaya, and the Philippines.

One immediate outcome of Japan's entry into the war was a request from General Sturdee in Australia that certain senior officers be sent back from the Middle East to fill key appointments in Australia. Two valued leaders, General Mackay and Brigadier Rowell, had already been sent home to pass on experience gained on active service. In the course of the discussion about the reinforcement of the A.I.F. General Blamey had advised in October that Brigadiers Savige and Murray should return to conduct a recruiting campaign. On 11th December General Sturdee asked also for Brigadiers Plant (25th Brigade), Vasey (19th Brigade), Clowes (C.R.A. of I Corps), Robertson (commanding the Reinforcement Depot), and a group of senior technical officers and others. The four brigadiers (four of the five regulars who had commanded infantry brigades, or corps or divisional artillery, in action in the Middle East) were promptly sent, as were Savige and Murray.[4]

Soon the question of sending reinforcements from the Middle East to the Far East was being keenly discussed; and on the 3rd January a message arrived at Canberra from the Dominions Office stating that two divisions and one armoured brigade were being sent to Malaya, and two divisions to the Netherlands Indies. Two of the four were to come from the Middle East, to be replaced later from England; it would be of the greatest assistance if the Australian Government would agree that the divisions sent to the Netherlands Indies should be Australian. On the 6th the Australian Government informed the British Government that it agreed

---

[4] The remaining regular officer in this category was Brig Berryman, BGS of the Corps.

to the sending of the 6th and 7th Divisions, with the corps headquarters, corps troops and base units to the East.[5]

The men of the A.I.F. in the Middle East seem not to have been greatly stirred by the Japanese attack. Relatively few of the unit war diaries recorded it. One battalion historian wrote that it was "not treated seriously at that time", another that the Japanese problem then had "no sense of urgency for us"; there seem to have been few who considered that Australia itself might soon be threatened.

The day following that on which the Australian Cabinet agreed that a corps of two Australian divisions be sent to the Far East the 9th Division was ordered to relieve the 7th in Syria, and on the 15th January the advanced headquarters of the 7th moved from Tripoli in Syria to Julis in Palestine. Between the 21st and 28th small parties of officers, including Generals Lavarack and Allen set off by air to Java. The Corps which was to follow totalled 64,151. The 6th Division was 18,465 strong, the 7th 18,620; there were 17,866 corps troops and 9,200 base and lines of communication troops. From the 30th January onwards this force set out in a procession of convoys for the Far East.

---

[5] See *Vol. IV* of this series.

CHAPTER 29

THE END OF A PERIOD

THE departure of an Australian Corps from the Middle East marked the end of a phase; henceforward Australia's principal effort was to be directed against an enemy nearer home. The events of the two years now ended should provide an answer to the questions whether the military policies of her political leaders had been wise, and how the army of volunteers that they had created had responded to the test.

Both policy and army had been created in controversy between two main groups. In the wisdom that comes after the event it cannot be said that the measures which either group was prepared to take were adequate for Australia's safety. On the one hand were those who were convinced that the British Commonwealth could not survive unless it stood united, yet were satisfied with a token contribution to a common plan of defence to which, in peace, the United Kingdom provided nine-tenths of the men and materials (a proportion she could not maintain in a total war) and of which she took full direction. On the other were those who were averse from engaging in the defence of British "imperialism" (meaning that complex of political and commercial policies on which Britain's oversea trade largely depended) and wished to leave the defence of Australia to her own indignant citizens fighting an invader on and round Australian shores. The solution found by Australia's leaders in 1939 and 1940 was a compromise between the views of these two main groups.

It is now evident that it was within the ability of either the Indian or the Australian Army, promptly mobilised and supported by the modest air and armoured forces that Britain was maintaining in the Middle East, to expel the Italians from Africa within a few months of their entry into the war. Both Australia and India had armies readier for battle and, in most respects, as well armed as Italy's in Africa. The Indian Army, however, seems to have been regarded at first only as a pool from which the British regulars might be relieved, rather than as an individual army which, with the support of British armour and artillery, might fight its way to Tripoli. An equally powerful weapon lay in the hands of the Australian leaders—the divisions of high-spirited volunteers in the militia. To have appealed to them to go out against the European enemies would, if they responded, have been more likely to deter the probable Japanese aggressor close at hand than local half-measures would do. In Australia in 1939 such an appeal for an all-out effort was not considered; one political party wished to limit Australia to a token contribution, the other was opposed to sending away any troops at all. On the other hand contemporary evidence provided by men then in the militia, and later inquiry among them, suggests that they would have leaped at the opportunity. Most of them had volunteered after the Munich crisis in response to the very threat that had now become a reality.

The Australian leaders were influenced also by a widely-shared conviction that the war would be decided chiefly by aircraft, and that large armies would not be employed. In addition, to have sent a large force overseas would have entailed denuding Australia of military equipment that might be needed to meet attack by Japan. This combination of factors was decisive in preventing the Australian Ministers from promptly sending to Europe and the Middle East contingents comparable in size with those which their country had proudly maintained there in 1918.

The Australian Government's compromise was to leave the militia army at home unmobilised, and raise a small separate force of volunteers for the German war. The military leaders pressed so persistently for an increase of that force, and after the fall of France the citizens volunteered in such numbers, that it grew until it was able to play a leading role overseas. (Fortunately the circumstances of the war gave time for its training and its full equipment.) Without the Australian contingent, British operations in the Middle East would have been forced into a very different shape. It was the divisions from India and the Dominions south and east of Suez that enabled the British Commonwealth to hold the vital ground in the Middle East in 1941, and of those contingents the Australian (armed chiefly from British factories) was, until late in 1941, the largest.

To what extent had this experience solved the problem of obtaining effective cooperation between contingents from the independent nations that formed the British Commonwealth? In the Middle East in 1941 were British, Indian, Australian, South African and New Zealand forces. Between the British and the Indian Armies there was no difficulty. India did not possess political independence and the British and Indian Armies were virtually one. For their part, the Dominion politicians, probably without reflection, accepted the time-honoured system of delegating command to British generals, yet reserved to their own commanders administrative control and the right of appeal. This was a solution favoured not only by United Kingdom but by some Dominion soldiers, and its adoption in war was made easier both by the employment of common systems of training and equipment in peace (a considered policy) and by the mere habit of the Dominion governments and their officers of looking to Britain in peace to define policies and plans.[1]

This peculiar system worked fairly well—remarkably so considering the dissimilarities in temperament between the British political and military leaders on the one hand and those of the Dominions on the other—but

---

[1] In a discussion of this question in the *Army Quarterly* of Jan 1925 Lt-Col (later Lt-Gen) Wynter had outlined a doctrine on which he considered cooperation between British Commonwealth forces could effectively be based. Unified strategical control, he said, could be ensured only by all the States delegating authority to one of them, which would normally but not always be the mother country. The State concerned would naturally wish to employ a chief commander responsible to it alone. He discussed the problem involved in appointing to a subordinate command an officer not belonging to the delegate State. (The appointment of General Blamey to command the corps in Greece later provided an example.) Wynter would not admit that the commander of the troops of any subordinate partner State should refer to and take directions from his own government concerning operations; on the other hand he considered that maintenance of the identity of the forces by each State, and its own policy of appointment, promotion and pay must be insisted on.

it had notable deficiencies. As we have seen, the Australian Government was not always promptly informed about forthcoming operations in which its troops would play a main part.[2] The senior British commanders in the field in 1940 and 1941 sometimes failed to take the leaders of their Dominion contingents fully into their confidence, or to fully comprehend their special status and responsibilities. At this level this faulty liaison could have been anticipated and avoided by thorough instruction in the problem of Dominion contingents at the staff colleges between the wars. In view of the probability that, in war, the Dominion contingents would total perhaps one-third of the forces of the British Commonwealth, the subject was important enough to have justified measures aimed at preparing future commanders-in-chief to meet this aspect of their task with better understanding. The problem recurred persistently in the period covered by this volume; yet, when reporting to the Australian Advisory War Council in November 1941, Blamey could justly say that the British commanders still "had difficulty in recognising the independent status of the Dominions and their responsibility for the control of their own forces".

At the same time, even as late as June 1941, the Ministers and the Staff in Australia considered that General Blamey himself was providing them with inadequate information about their army overseas, and, by implication, Blamey agreed that this was so. On 22nd June Colonel Hopkins,[3] who had been sent to the Middle East to observe developments in armoured warfare, spoke to General Blamey on behalf of the Chief of the General Staff at home and pointed out that the information available in Australia about organisation and tactics in the Middle East was not up to date. Ministers sought additional information and wanted the cables it was receiving from overseas interpreted, he said, but Army Headquarters lacked enough knowledge to supply these needs. Information about tactical methods and new equipment, needed to ensure that training in Australia was on sound lines, was not being received. As a result of this conversation Blamey, within a few days, began sending a periodical liaison letter to the Secretary of the Department of the Army. It was in the first of these that he explained the dispersion of the force he commanded: that on the 5th July the 9th Division and a brigade of the 7th were in Tobruk, two field regiments and a machine-gun battalion in the Western Desert, the 6th Division less some of its units in southern Palestine, I Corps, the remainder of the 7th Division (including the 17th Brigade), the 6th and 9th Cavalry Regiments in Syria, the 7th Cavalry in Cyprus.

---

[2] The Australian Cabinet and Opposition learnt of one proposed operation of great importance as a chance result of recalling General Blamey for consultations in November 1941. Blamey reported that the British Government had decided to invade Sicily in October with three divisions—in his opinion too small a force. The Commanders-in-Chief in the Middle East opposed the plan and it was abandoned. Blamey said that "his knowledge of the proposed operation was obtained by virtue of his appointment as Deputy Commander-in-Chief and he would not have been consulted as GOC, AIF; but he would have informed the Commonwealth Government if it had decided to carry out the attack". (See also Churchill, Vol III, pp. 479-80; and Cunningham, pp. 417-18. Churchill writes that four divisions were to be employed, and were to come from England.)

[3] Maj-Gen R. N. L. Hopkins, CBE, NX392. (1st AIF: Lt 6 LH Regt 1918.) CO 7 Cav Regt 1940; GSO1 1 Armd Div 1941-42; DMO LHQ 1942; BGS HQ NG Force 1942-43; LO between LHQ and 7 Amphibious Force US Navy 1943-44. Regular soldier; b. Stawell, Vic, 24 May 1897.

Another deficiency inherent in delegation of command to the senior member of the British Commonwealth was that the drawing of senior commanders and staffs from the United Kingdom contingents led to a waste of talent and tended to build up staffs with a somewhat parochial outlook, especially as the United Kingdom drew its higher commanders and staffs almost entirely from its not-large professional officer corps. Special and valuable contributions which Dominion officers could make to the higher management of operations in terrain and climates different from those of Western Europe but commonplace to Dominion officers were largely lost. For example, to most Europeans the weather, dust and drought of North Africa were strange and forbidding, but to many South Africans and Australians these conditions were familiar, and their everyday experience had provided answers to many problems of transport, engineering, and mere living in such conditions.

The example, in 1916, of handing the command of operations in East Africa to South African leaders—first Smuts then Van Deventer—provided a precedent that might have been followed in the Middle East in 1940 and 1941. The fact that, until the spring of 1941, no suggestion was made that one or other of the immediately subordinate commands in the Middle East should be held by an officer who was not of the British or Indian regular service is significant of the degree to which the principle of delegation to the senior partner had been accepted by the Dominions and assumed at the British War Office. There was no written statement of the principle, nor does it appear to have been discussed on the political level until early in 1941. Indeed, so little attention had been given in Australia in peacetime to the problem of command of an oversea force that when it became necessary to draw up a statement of the powers of a general officer commanding an Australian expeditionary force, the army staff asked the Director of the Australian War Memorial to search the archives for a copy of General Bridges' charter of 1914.[4]

Thus, in 1940, Generals Blamey and Freyberg were, with the possible exception of Wavell, the most accomplished and experienced senior soldiers in the Middle East; General Lavarack, though junior to these in 1918, had for some years held the highest appointment in the Australian Army; yet only in emergencies were these employed in senior command. Blamey had the conduct of the withdrawal in Greece handed to him when it was about to begin, Freyberg the defence of Crete. First in the Western Desert and, later, in Syria another commander of a Dominion formation, Lavarack, took over at a critical stage.

The eventual appointment of Blamey as Deputy Commander-in-Chief in the Middle East created a special problem—foreseen by Wynter in the article quoted above. Experience had shown that there might be conflict of opinion between the Commander-in-Chief and the Commander of a

---

[4] The Director pointed out that the original powers of a GOC, AIF, had been published in the *Commonwealth Gazette* of 19 Sep 1914 and in *Military Orders* of that month.

Dominion contingent.[5] As Deputy Commander-in-Chief Blamey had a dual responsibility—to the United Kingdom and to the Australian Governments. It was desirable that suitable Dominion officers should be employed in higher posts, but when so employed, should they not have been relieved of their responsibilities as commanders of Dominion contingents? Would it not have been wiser of the Australian Government, when agreeing to the appointment of Blamey as Wavell's deputy, to have given command of the A.I.F. to another Australian? (Later in another area and with another Australian Service the same problem will arise again.)

The errors in the higher conduct of the operations in the Middle East in 1941 were those of political leaders and their advisers in London 3,000 miles away rather than of the senior commanders on the spot. At the outset Wavell's management of his resources had been both bold and economical. It was essential to deny the Middle East to the enemy and to prevent him from gaining access to the Indian Ocean. On the ground, by bold yet carefully-judged use of limited forces, Wavell succeeded in destroying a large Italian army in North Africa and another in Abyssinia. For the defeats that followed, in the Western Desert, Greece and Crete, the responsibility rests chiefly with the resolve of Churchill's Cabinet to send an expedition to the Balkans—a decision in which Wavell concurred, although evidently with reluctance. It was not unnatural that, after the disastrous expeditions to Greece and Crete, Wavell should have been hesitant about undertaking operations against Iraq and Syria. Eventually a campaign against Iraq became unavoidable, and it cost little; but, if the British leaders had been able to see into the future, a Syrian campaign might have been undertaken later and its results achieved without much cost. The transfer of Wavell to India at this stage is open to criticism on grounds of fairness and perhaps even of some of the finer points of honesty.

In the Australian force the campaigns of 1941 had shown the worth of the leaders chosen in 1939 and 1940, and incidentally that citizen soldiers could succeed in senior commands. Lavarack having been promoted, and Wynter invalided to Australia, the three divisional commanders were now, in December 1941, militiamen. Two of them, Morshead and Allen, possessed an experience of front-line warfare then rare among generals in any army, Allied or enemy, having commanded battalions in the field in World War I and brigades and divisions in World War II.[6] Of the nine infantry brigadiers all but two (Boase, who had succeeded Allen in command of the 16th, and Wootten of the 18th—a retired regular) were non-professional; two (Martin, now commanding the 19th, and Eather, the 25th) were militiamen too young to have served in the earlier war. When Japan attacked, few who had served in 1914-18 as regimental officers

---

[5] This was exemplified particularly clearly in the difference of opinion between Generals Auchinleck and Blamey concerning the withdrawal of the Australians from Tobruk, which is discussed in the next volume of this series.

[6] Allen had commanded in battle a platoon, a company, a battalion, a brigade and a division. It is probable that very few soldiers in any army could then claim a similar experience.

remained with their units; the commanding officers were generally militiamen in their late 30's and early 40's.[7] Any general conclusions about the ability of a militia to produce senior commanders should take into account, however, that the Australian militia of 1939 was exceptionally fortunate in possessing a considerable quota of leaders then only in their 40's who had been tested and schooled in four years of hard fighting with the old A.I.F. and as youngsters had risen to senior rank in it; their juniors had been trained by them and their highly-qualified professional colleagues. In many respects the new A.I.F. began where the old one left off.

The problem of selecting men for first commissions—the leaders of the future—had been keenly discussed in the Australian force in the last eighteen months without a fully-acceptable agreement being reached between the regimental officers on the one hand and the senior staffs on the other. It was generally accepted that these officers should be chosen with great care because it would be a long war, and from men commissioned in 1940 and 1941 would be drawn senior leaders of the future. The Australian units had arrived in the Middle East with a full quota of officers plus their "first reinforcements", most carefully picked from the big pool available in the militia and a few from the ranks. For training selected men a proportion of vacancies at the British Officer Cadet Training Unit at Cairo was accepted by General Blamey as by other Dominion commanders, but when the Australians graduated they were not immediately commissioned (as were graduates of all other contingents) if there was no vacancy for them in a unit. The prospect of promoting men from the ranks was further reduced when, in September and October 1940, three batches of reinforcements had arrived from Australia, including twenty-one officers for each battalion—whose full quota was only thirty-two. Lieut-Colonel Wardle,[8] the British commandant of the Officer Cadet Training Unit and an enthusiastic and original trainer of soldiers, approached both Wavell and, informally, Blamey's staff, to protest against failure to commission Australian graduates immediately. He pointed out that they included, for example, one cadet, Adler,[9] who had topped his class and was "one of the best cadets we have had as yet from anywhere", and others whom he would gladly accept as instructors in his school. It was a singular situation. In 1916-18 virtually all Australian officers had come from the ranks of fighting units and this policy was, in the Australian force, achieving outstanding success at a time when, in the British Army, officers were still being chosen from the "officer-producing classes" regardless of front-line experience. Yet in 1941 Wardle, a British regular soldier, was urging a Dominion commander to commission

---

[7] The force had not then suffered the heavy losses which, in 1915-18, had caused outstanding leaders to become commanding officers in their early 20's. On 7th December 1941 R. L. Sandover, 31, and I. N. Dougherty, 34, were the youngest battalion commanders.

[8] Lt-Col M. K. Wardle, DSO, MC. Comdt OCTU Cairo 1940-42. Regular soldier; b. 17 Feb 1888. (Author of *Foundations of Soldiering*, 1936.)

[9] Lt A. W. L. Adler, NX1349; 2/2 Bn. Production superintendent; of Newcastle, NSW; b. London, 14 Apr 1909.

his able and fully-trained N.C.O's.[1] The expansion of the A.I.F. after that time made it easier to find posts for Officer Cadet Training Unit graduates, and Blamey ordered that they be commissioned and posted either to units or to the reinforcement depot. He told Wavell that in future he would accept 72 vacancies a year—still a small number in relation to the groups of reinforcement officers regularly arriving.

In these circumstances Australian commanding officers, though impressed by the quantity and quality of the potential leaders in the ranks, saw little prospect of obtaining commissions for more than very few of them. At the beginning of 1941 there were more infantry subalterns in the reinforcement depot than in the battalions, yet the annual intake of infantry N.C.O's into the officer training unit represented fewer than three a battalion. On the other hand, commanding officers considered that as a general rule the reinforcement officers, selected and trained in Australia, had less ability and less military knowledge than many of their own N.C.O's.

> Reinforcement officers generally have proved a disappointment [wrote one commanding officer]. It is felt that man for man they are on the average as good material as the original battalion officers but (i) the weaker members of the original officers have been weeded out during fifteen months' hard training, boarded, declared unfit or transferred to non-combatant appointments, (ii) reinforcement officers started in the battalion with an enormous psychological disadvantage in lack of training and lack of experience.

This commander added that the high standard of N.C.O's directly promoted or trained by the Officer Cadet Training Unit threw the weakness of the average reinforcement officer into relief; he proposed that all new officers should come from the ranks of the unit, except for outstanding militia officers or other outstanding first appointees. In one battalion eighteen lieutenants joined as reinforcement officers in 1941 and nine N.C.O's were promoted from the ranks. Of the nine all were capable officers, some outstanding; between them they had won or would later win six decorations. Of the eighteen reinforcement officers, fewer than one-third succeeded as regimental officers.[2]

---

[1] "On the whole the leading of the Canadian and Australian officers and N.C.O's was superior to that of the British regimental cadres, and no doubt for the reason that they had been selected for their practical experience and power over men and not for theoretical proficiency and general education." Brig-Gen Sir James E. Edmonds (Editor), *Military Operations France and Belgium 1918*, Vol IV (1947), p. 515.
Wardle wrote in 1952 that the Australians at the OCTU were "an uncommonly fine lot" and added: "Among the many teething troubles at the start, I found Australian H.Q. by far the most helpful, and the least bound by red tape, of the five nations whose men came to OCTU."

[2] The force contained in the ranks a considerable number of men qualified by education, civil experience and character for commissioned rank. Some declined to seek promotion until they had tested themselves in action. In November 1940, in Egypt, one such man (in the 16 Bde) had written in a letter: "There has been a rush for commissions in the last few months, but I felt that I would prefer some front-line experience first. It is a responsible job and I would hate to realise too late that I was not cut out for it . . . . It is one thing to go all out for a job in civil life, but in this game you are dealing with human lives, not necessarily your own." Of three similar men in the 2/14 Bn, all killed at Jezzine on 24 Jun 1941—Cpl E. Staley (a member of the Melbourne Stock Exchange) and Ptes Chris Walker and Kenneth von Bibra (both senior newspapermen)—the regimental historian wrote: "They . . . had refused commissions in the non-fighting part of the army, preferring to enlist as privates in the infantry. Any one of the three could have commanded the battalion with distinction had they been spared to do so. Their quality influenced all whom they met." (W. B. Russell, *The 2/14th Battalion*, p. 70. Russell, in June 1941, was a company commander in this battalion.) Events were to show that there were enough potential officers in the divisions enlisted in 1939 and 1940 to provide good leaders for a force five times as large.

The discussion of this problem and the policies that emerged—a problem peculiar to the British Dominions where class distinctions were less clear than in Europe or the United States—incidentally illustrated a fundamental flaw of the Australian military system of the time. This was the division of the officers into two groups: a small but highly-trained professional staff corps, many of whose leading members had had little real regimental experience either in peace or war, and a corps of devoted amateur regimental officers in the militia. The militiamen drew their knowledge and traditions principally from the experience of the old A.I.F., having served in it or been taught by men who had; and they had usually studied the history of the first A.I.F. to discover what warfare meant. On the other hand the professional officer's experience of the first A.I.F., if he was old enough to have had any, was sometimes overlaid by twenty years of study of British manuals and training at British schools. With some officers, including men of seniority and influence, the tendency to admire and copy British military tradition reached the extreme of derogating the Australian tradition; a peculiar outcome, since in the nineteen-forties the British official historian of the campaigns in France was holding up to British soldiers the Australian Corps of 1918 as a model.[3] It is strange, in the correspondence concerning the problem of selecting new officers, discussed above, to read one senior Australian staff officer quoting a British general staff memorandum of 1919 on the subject, evidently without any appreciation of the fact that the British and Australian officer-finding problem in 1918 had been fundamentally different—even to the extent that the Australian force, which in 1918 was overflowing with "officer material", was contributing contingents of officers to the British Army, while the British Army was scraping the bottom of the bucket. In the available staff letters and memoranda of 1940-41 on this subject there is no reference to the old A.I.F.[4]

In the minor fields of amenities, historical records and publicity the Australian force in 1941 had achieved original and effective results. The Comforts Fund had greatly extended its work. Through its commissioners[5] and the amenities officers now attached to each brigade the steady flow of comforts and sporting gear collected in Australia or bought with money subscribed there had been distributed to the men, and a chain of first-rate leave centres had been established. In Jerusalem early in 1940

---

[3] For example, in the final volume of the British Official History of military operations in France and Belgium, 1914-1918, the historians (Brig-Gen Sir James Edmonds and Lt-Col R. Maxwell-Hyslop) after having given high praise to the military qualities of the Australian Corps in France in 1918, pointed out that the Australians "enjoyed certain advantages denied to the British troops". One of these was that their men, when wounded or sick, were sent eventually to their own depot and so back to their own units; the staffs at the British depots did not take the trouble to sort convalescent reinforcements and, not understanding a soldier's love of his unit as his war home, and the craving for the society of old comrades, dispatched these old soldiers to the first unit which required its ranks refilled. The others were the retention of the four-battalion brigade and the fact that the divisions were kept together as a corps.

[4] In view of the later developments in "psychological testing" the following statement from one memorandum is interesting as revealing the general opinion of that time: "Any officer who has reached field rank should be able, even after a ten minutes interview, to form a sound opinion as to whether a man has, at that time, the qualifications that fit him to be trained as an officer"

[5] In December 1941 the commissioners in the Middle East were: Lt-Col E. Gorman, Maj A. J. L. McDonnell, Maj H. T. Curtis, Maj R. Paxton, Maj H. E. Hovendene.

the Hotel Fast had been acquired and renamed the Australian Soldiers' Club; at Tel Aviv was a tea shop sponsored by the Fund and conducted by a number of Australian women living in Palestine. (In view of the good work Australian women did in Palestine and Egypt it might have been advantageous if the Australian Ministers had contrived to delay their decision—eventually inevitable—to prevent Australian wives travelling to the Middle East.) When the 6th Division moved to Egypt the Atlantic Hotel in Alexandria had been taken over by the Fund and converted into a soldiers' club. Colonel Eugene Gorman had entered Beirut with the first troops, and promptly and on his own responsibility had taken over the Hotel Metropole and established it as a soldiers' club. There were in addition the recreation huts maintained in the camps, run in conjunction with the Salvation Army and Y.M.C.A. At the leave hotels men could obtain an inexpensive room, bath, meals and drinks, and army post offices and pay offices were installed.

A department in which an Australian force had a special tradition to maintain was that of historical records. From 1914 onwards the first A.I.F. had been accompanied by an official correspondent, C. E. W. Bean, with whom there was an understanding that he would write the history of the force after the war. In 1917, largely through his activity, a war records section had been established, and a war memorial which would house the written records and the relics of the A.I.F. had been conceived. In 1941 the War Memorial building at Canberra was opened. In 1940, as a result of the efforts of the Minister for Information (Sir Henry Gullett) and the permanent head of his department (Major Treloar[6]), General White had included a war records section in the oversea administrative headquarters of the A.I.F. Each of the three men had intimate knowledge of such a section's needs and requirements. Gullett had been one of Bean's assistants in 1917-18, had written a volume of the official war history, and for some months had been Director of the Australian War Memorial; Treloar in 1917 had founded the Australian war records section and for twenty years had been Director of the War Memorial; White had been closely concerned with the formation of the war records section of 1917 and of the War Memorial.

Captain Howard,[7] novelist and journalist, was placed in charge of the new section. In the Middle East in 1940 a cinematographer and a photographer were added, and General Blamey appointed as a war artist Ivor Hele,[8] a young painter who was serving in the A.I.F. At the same time there were then in England or the Middle East two official correspondents,

---

[6] Lt-Col J. L. Treloar, OBE, VX39804. (1st AIF: 1 Div HQ and O i/c War Records Sec.) OC Mil Hist Sec 1942-46. Director, Aust War Memorial, Canberra; b. Port Melbourne, 10 Dec 1894. Died 28 Jan 1952.

[7] Lt-Col F. J. Howard, VX12841. Hist Rec Offr, HQ AIF ME 1940-41; LO Press Relations GHQ SWPA 1942-43; ADPR NG Force 1943-44. Journalist; of South Yarra, Vic; b. London, 17 Oct 1904.

[8] Capt I. H. T. Hele, SX7174; Mil Hist Sec. Artist; of Aldinga, SA; b. Edwardstown, SA, 13 Jun 1912.

Kenneth Slessor[9] and Ian Fitchett;[1] and a group of photographers representing the Department of Information and led by Frank Hurley,[2] an army photographer in the previous war.

Early in 1941 Treloar persuaded the Ministers to allow him to join the A.I.F. in the Middle East as liaison officer for the Department of Information and the War Memorial. This was agreed to, and after arriving in the Middle East Treloar persuaded General Blamey that, with Howard's men as a nucleus, a larger section should be formed consisting of a headquarters and "field teams" (comprising an officer commanding, photographer, cinematographer, clerk and batman-driver) attached to each division; and that more artists be chosen from those serving in the A.I.F. Treloar proposed that the photographers of the Department of Information be incorporated, but this was resisted by Hurley. Thereafter the two groups existed side by side: one an army section concerned primarily with historical records, the other a group of civilian journalists and photographers concerned with producing news and photographs for immediate publication. At Blamey's request, Treloar, though his duties were mainly historical, exercised supervision over certain internal news services within the army, including *A.I.F. News,* an A.I.F. broadcast from Jerusalem, the supply of news to Army Headquarters in Melbourne, and the annual production of an illustrated book written by the troops and following the lines of *The Anzac Book* of 1916. On this account the section was named the "Military History and Information Section".

In 1941 the Australian force had also established a workmanlike system for the movement of war correspondents and the censorship of their dispatches. At Wavell's headquarters there was a public relations branch equipped with a modest number of men and vehicles to establish camps for correspondents and to transport them and their copy. After the first Western Desert offensive opened it became apparent that the Australians would need their own vehicles so that they could follow the force with which their interest chiefly lay and not to be tied to the larger group of British and American reporters. An ideal system would have been to provide each member of so small a group of correspondents and photographers with a vehicle and a driver so that all could disperse and between them cover the campaign as widely as possible, bringing their reports to a central camp whence they could be hurried to the censors and the cable office at Cairo. Instead, enough vehicles were allotted to move correspondents and photographers in three groups—the correspondents in one, the photographers in another, and the Australian Broadcasting Commission's Field Unit in a third. As the Australian force moved forward, press camps were set up by an Intelligence officer and former

---

[9] Kenneth Slessor; Official War Correspondent AIF 1940-44. Author and journalist; of Sydney; b. Orange, NSW, 7 Mar 1901.

[1] Ian Fitchett. Sgt 2/4 Bn 1939-40; Official War Correspondent with AIF 1940-42. Journalist and solicitor; of Sydney; b. Terang, Vic, 10 Sep 1908.

[2] Capt F. J. F. Hurley, OBE. Official photographer with 1st and 2nd AIF. Explorer and photographer; of Sydney; b. Sydney, 1890.

journalist, Captain Wilson.³ Copy was often delayed in the Libyan campaign (even lost entirely, on the steadily-lengthening journey to Cairo) and lack of vehicles limited the independent movement of correspondents, but otherwise a relationship was established between correspondents and the leaders and men of the army that was of a kind that might reasonably be expected only at the end and not at the beginning of a war. "Conducting Officers", imposed when the Middle East public relations branch was in control, were dispensed with, and the correspondents moved freely in a force of which they had become a part during the training period in Egypt and Palestine. Some of the senior officers—particularly among the professional soldiers—had not at first overcome the fear of the Press, acquired in the isolated and frustrated period between the wars, but most of them soon became trustful and cooperative, and the correspondents reciprocated. It became evident that such excellent relations could be preserved wherever the band of correspondents was not unwieldy in size and had acquired enough knowledge of the army and of warfare to avoid irritating or embarrassing a commander.

The Australian correspondents' interests at the base in Cairo were well watched as a result of a wise move by Blamey's senior Intelligence officer, Lieut-Colonel Rogers, who established an Australian censor there. The ideal field censor is a trained Intelligence officer who has also handled news on a city paper. Few of the British censors had had first-grade newspaper experience and most had little experience of military Intelligence. On the other hand the Australian censor, Major Fenton, had been a senior newspaperman and since 1939 had served as an Intelligence officer in Australia or Palestine. He made it his task to ensure the quick release of Australian news from an office where hitherto the overworked censors, responsive to pressure by the groups which in their opinion carried the greatest weight, had given preference first to the big news agencies and secondly to the Fleet Street papers.

The presence of an Australian was necessary also to protect Australian news against a rigid application of Middle East regulations by Englishmen who were unaware of Australian needs; only a man who knew the Australian Army could decide when the use of a soldier's name or State, or some passing reference, might divulge useful information to the enemy, or detect an ill-considered remark which might do harm at home (thus the South Africans eventually installed a censor who understood their colour problem and the anti-war movement in South Africa). The British censors, who had been under intermittent fire from both the British correspondents and the Americans, warmly welcomed the presence of an experienced newspaperman in their office in Cairo.⁴

Normally the first news in English which the world received of events on Middle East fronts was a carefully-worded communiqué supplemented

---

³ Lt-Col E. H. Wilson, VX27463. GSO1 (Int) Directorate of Mil Int 1943-44, NG Force 1944, II Corps 1944-45. Journalist; of Hawthorn, Vic; b. Mt Gambier, SA, 17 Mar 1906.

⁴ In Greece, British military censorship was carried out admirably by two former newspapermen, Fenton and Maj E. Peter Lovegrove, an able and clear-headed English journalist.

by a report written by the so-called "second eleven" of correspondents in Cairo who had listened to the comments of the "spokesman" on the day's events—the "first eleven" were farther forward. There was a failure at this stage to appreciate that an official spokesman must be fully in the confidence of a commander and his staff as to current and future operations. Lacking such knowledge, a spokesman, under sharp questioning, may release information which should be confidential, or may inadvertently earn the command a reputation for lack of honesty, when in fact he has merely been ignorant and insufficiently trusted by his seniors. In British commands this task was usually given to officers recalled from the reserve. There has been a reference in the preceding volume to the short-lived policy of Middle East headquarters of describing Australians, South Africans and New Zealanders in communiqués as "British Imperial troops" —a practice that seems to have been adopted under pressure from London and ceased during the Syrian campaign.

In the words of one close Australian observer: apart from a natural desire to cover defeats and emphasise success "there was never (in Cairo at this stage) any deep-laid plot to deceive".

By the end of 1941 the Australian Imperial Force in the Middle East had acquired some of the characteristics of a long-service regular army. The men were all volunteers, and were proud of that fact and of the units and formations to which they belonged; indeed many had developed a far stronger loyalty and affection towards their units than had been inspired by any institutions at home—outside their families. They had been singularly unperturbed by the Japanese onslaught; relatively few seem to have foreseen their transfer to the Far East; and it seems probable that the bitter and misconceived rebukes, which some of them received in letters from Australia for skulking in Palestine and Syria while Japanese threatened their homes, were partly the outcome of their own patent unconcern at the addition of the Japanese to the lengthening list of their opponents. Allied to this was a steadily-increasing pride in their achievements and confidence in their own ability to cope with whatever faced them, a quality no doubt acquired rapidly by a force of colonial volunteers. To them war had become a technical accomplishment, its risks calculated, its results predictable.

Moreover they had demonstrated the wisdom of defending Australia by sending an expeditionary force against Germany (and her Italian and French allies). The eastern Mediterranean and the Middle East, which, if held by the Germans, would have enabled them to combine their operations with those of Japan, were still under Allied control, and from that area would soon be sailing east a tried force of some 64,000 men, well-armed, confident and expert, under tested leaders, ranging from those who had handled corps and divisions in the field to youngsters who had fought against Germans, Italians and Frenchmen, in desert and snow, mountain and plain.

APPENDIX

ABBREVIATIONS

A—*Assistant.*
A/—*Acting.*
AA—*Anti-aircraft.*
AA&QMG—*Assistant Adjutant and Quartermaster-General.*
Adm—*Admiral.*
AFV—*Armoured fighting vehicle.*
AGH—*Australian General Hospital.*
AHQ—*Army Headquarters.*
Amb—*Ambulance.*
AOC—*Air Officer Commanding.*
APM—*Assistant Provost Marshal.*
Arty—*Artillery.*
ASC—*Army Service Corps.*
A-Tk—*Anti-tank.*

Bde—*Brigade.*
Bdr—*Bombardier.*
BGS—*Brigadier, General Staff.*
BM—*Brigade Major.*
Bn—*Battalion.*
BRA—*Brigadier, Royal Artillery.*
Brig—*Brigadier.*
Bty—*Battery.*

Capt—*Captain.*
Cav—*Cavalry.*
CBO—*Counter-Battery Officer.*
CCMA—*Commander, Corps Medium Artillery.*
Cdo—*Commando.*
Cdr—*Commander.*
CE—*Chief Engineer.*
CGS—*Chief of the General Staff.*
C-in-C—*Commander-in-Chief.*
CO—*Commanding Officer.*
Col—*Colonel.*
Comb—*Combined.*
Comd—*Command, Commanded, Commander.*
Comdre—*Commodore.*
Coy—*Company.*
Cpl—*Corporal.*
CRA—*Commander, Royal Artillery (of a Division).*
CRE—*Commander, Royal Engineers (of a Division).*
CSO—*Chief Signals Officer.*

D—*Deputy, Director, Directorate.*
DAAG—*Deputy Assistant Adjutant-General.*
DADOS—*Deputy Assistant Director of Ordnance Services.*
DDMS—*Deputy Director Medical Services.*
DDMT—*Deputy Director Military Training.*
DDS&T—*Deputy Director of Supply and Transport.*
Det—*Detachment.*
Div—*Division.*
DMI—*Director of Military Intelligence.*
DMO—*Director of Military Operations.*
Dvr—*Driver.*

Engrs—*Engineers.*

Fd—*Field.*

Gd—*Guard.*
Gen—*General.*
GHQ—*General Headquarters.*
Gnr—*Gunner.*
GOC—*General Officer Commanding.*
Gp—*Group.*
GSO1—*General Staff Officer, Grade 1.*

HQ—*Headquarters.*
Hy—*Heavy.*

Ind—*India, Indian.*
Indep—*Independent.*
Inf—*Infantry.*
Int—*Intelligence.*

L-Cpl—*Lance-Corporal.*
LH—*Light Horse.*
LHQ—*Land Headquarters.*
LO—*Liaison Officer.*
L of C—*Lines of Communication.*
Lt—*Lieutenant.*

Maj—*Major.*
MD—*Military District.*
ME—*Middle East.*
Med—*Medium.*
MG—*Machine-Gun.*
Mil—*Military.*

NCO—*Non-Commissioned Officer.*
NG—*New Guinea.*
NT—*Northern Territory.*
NZ—*New Zealand.*

OCTU—*Officer Cadet Training Unit.*
Ops—*Operations.*
Ord—*Ordnance.*

Pdr—*Pounder*
Pk—*Park.*
Pnr—*Pioneer.*
PR—*Public Relations.*
Prov—*Provost.*
Pte—*Private.*

R—*Royal.*
RAAF—*Royal Australian Air Force.*
RAE—*Royal Australian Engineers.*

RAF—*Royal Air Force.*
Regt—*Regiment.*
RHA—*Royal Horse Artillery.*
RTR—*Royal Tank Regiment.*

Sgt—*Sergeant.*
Sig—*Signalman, Signals.*
Spr—*Sapper.*
Sqn—*Squadron.*
Svy—*Survey.*

Tk—*Tank.*
Tpr—*Trooper.*
Tps—*Troops.*
Trg—*Training.*

VDC—*Volunteer Defence Corps.*

WO—*Warrant-Officer.*

INDEX

AACHRAFIYE (Sketch p. 416), 418
AAL, EL (Sketch p. 334), 338
AAMIQ (Sketch p. 516), 535
AANOUT (Sketches pp. 462, 475), 460, 461, 464, 475
AAQLIYE (Map p. 482), 471, 472
Aba, British hospital ship, 214*n*
ABABY, JEBEL (Sketch p. 381), 383
ABADAN (Sketch p. 533), 532
ABBOTTSMITH, Sgt J., 547
ABD EL KAMH (Sketch p. 353), 353
Abdiel, British mine-layer, 239, 243, 244, 251*n*, 305
ABDUL ILLAH, AMIR, 199
ABETZ, Otto, 329
ABEY (Sketches pp. 462, 504), 473, 496, 500, 502, 503, 504, 505
ABOU ATRIZ, JEBEL (Sketch p. 393), 393, 394
ABOU NIDA, TEL (Sketch p. 357), 356
ABOU ZARE, WADI (Sketch p. 381), 380, 385
ABU KEMAL (Sketch p. 478), 479
ABYSSINIA, 7, 320, 321*n*, 334, 342, 441, 529, 555, 562; Italian defeat in, 197; British army strength in, 531
ACRE CONVENTION, 513-14; administration of, 515-22
ACROPOLE PALACE HOTEL, 24, 155; site of Lustre Force HQ, 33
ADAM, Cpl D. C., 434*n*
ADANA, 315
ADEISSE (Sketches pp. 343, 377), 344, 352, 378
ADEM, EL, 9
ADEN, 320
ADHELE (Map p. 258), 256, 262, 265, 274
ADHELE, WADI (Sketch p. 256), 257, 258
ADLER, Lt A. W. L., 556
ADLOUN (Sketches pp. 367, 376), 366-7, 375-7, 379
ADONIS, Capt, 312
ADRIATIC SEA, 48, 76
ADSAYA (Sketch p. 416), 429*n*, 431
AEGEAN SEA, 1, 39, 48, 184
AEGINA ISLAND, 230
AFAIR, TEL (Sketch p. 393), 393
AFGHANISTAN, 333; relations with Persia, 532
AGEDABIA, 30; Germans recapture, 37
AGHEILA, EL, 37
AGHYA PRISON (Map p. 218; Sketch p. 245), 224, 225, 230, 237, 242, 243, 244, 245, 247, 254
AGHYA RESERVOIR, 226, 232
AHWAZ (Sketch p. 533), 533
A.I.F. News, 560
AIKENHEAD, Brig D. F., 60
AINAB (Sketch p. 504), 511
AIN EBEL (Sketches p. 343, 348), 342, 349
AIN KSOUR (Sketches p. 500, 504), 505
AIN SOFAR (Sketch p. 516), 535
AIRCRAFT, influence on ground operations, 195-6, 547*n*; role in war, 538, 552. British: deliveries to M.E., 8; strength in M.E., 18*n*, available for defence of Crete, 208-9, for invasion of Syria, 335. *Types*: Blenheims, 22*n*, 83, 200, 206-7, 214, 247*n*, 266, 391, 479; Fulmars, 214, 220; Gladiators, 5*n*, 22*n*, 207, 214, 220, 280, 441, 479; Hurricanes, 5*n*, 10, 11*n*, 22*n*, 37, 80, 133, 149, 207, 214, 220, 247*n*, 287, 479, 529; Lysanders, 37; Marylands, 247*n*; Sunderlands, 301, 302; Tomahawks, 391; Wellingtons, 200. German: strength in Balkans, 18*n*; strength at invasion of Crete, 228, losses, 316. *Types*: Heinkels, 201; Junkers, 80, 304; Messerschmitts, 80, 304; Stukas, 86, 126*n*, 292
AIRFIELDS, Cretan, 203, defence of, 220; *Greek*, 150, 153, 163, 168, 228; *Syrian*, 333, 335, 338, 344, 391; German use of, 322, 329, 330, 331
AIR RECONNAISSANCE, at Matapan, 23
AITA CHAAB (Sketch p. 343), 342
AITAROUN (Sketch p. 343), 342, 349
AITENIYE (Sketch p. 361), 365
AITKEN, Lt-Col E. F., 408, 409
Ajax, British cruiser, at Matapan, 23; in evacuation of Greece, 176, 179; in battle of Crete, 233, 239, 291; at Damour, 488*n*
AKLADI (Sketch p. 147), 139
AKROTIRI PENINSULA (Map p. 218), 218, 226, 238
ALAMANAS BRIDGE (Sketch p. 147), 141, 153
ALAWIS, THE, 323
ALBANIA, 4, 6, 14, 29-30, 35, 48, 50, 51, 58, 70, 112, 203, 212; Greek offensive in, 1-2, 15, strength in,

ALBANIA—*continued*
192; proposed withdrawal of Greek troops from, 12, 16; British air support in, 22-3; Italian offensive in, 25; proposed Greek-Yugoslav offensive, 26, 27, 40, 41, 43; Greek withdrawal, 46, 54, 76-7, 80, 93
Alcides, Norwegian tanker, 188
ALCOHOL, 105, 206, 258
ALDRIDGE, Gnr J., 121, 122
ALEPPO (Map p. 339; Sketch p. 478), 327, 330, 331, 441, 479, 480, 511, 512, 517, 519, 534, 535, 546
ALEXANDRETTA, 188
ALEXANDRIA (Sketch p. 298), 17, 23, 30, 31, 151, 170, 174, 177, 202, 211, 227, 238, 239, 243, 251*n*, 291, 292, 298, 302, 305, 306, 311, 318, 320, 513*n*, 559
ALEY (Sketch p. 504), 480, 535
ALIAKMON-OLYMPUS LINE, *see* OLYMPUS-ALIAKMON LINE
ALIAKMON RIVER (Map p. 34; Sketches pp. 4, 75), 3, 4, 8, 29, 32, 34, 40, 46, 54, 55, 56, 58, 66, 68, 71, 73, 74, 75, 76, 77, 81, 82, 83, 85, 86, 90, 92, 93, 94, 158, 165*n*; 19th Brigade crossing, 87-9
ALIKAMBOS (Sketch p. 296), 307
ALIKIANOU (Map p. 218), 221, 224, 230, 243, 244, 246, 254
ALLAN, Maj W. G., 346
ALLEN, Maj-Gen A. S., 31; in Greece, 55, 85, 97, 98, 99, 102, 106, 125, 126*n*, 136, 138, 139, 145, 152, 153, 164-5, 171, 172, 173, at Pinios, 107, 115, 117, 119, 121, 122, 127; selected to command 7th Division, 340, 413-14; in Syria, 386, 387, 418, 419, 446, 449, 454, 459, 461, 464*n*, 491, 499, 502, 511, 514, 521*n*, 547, 548; policy at Jezzine, 460, 477, and plan for attack on Damour, 473-4, 480, arrest of French officers, 520, and Tripoli fortress, 536; transfer to Far East, 550; experience, 555
ALLEN, Lt-Col J. M., 223, 251
ALLENBY, Field Marshal Viscount, 356
ALMA CHAAB (Sketch p. 343), 342, 349
ALMIROS, 109
AMATOUR (Sketches pp. 504, 506), 507
AMBELAKIA (Map p. 106; Sketch p. 127), 107, 114
AMBROSIO, General, 50-51
AMENITIES, A.I.F., 558-9
AMERICA, *see* UNITED STATES
AMERICAN COLLEGE (Sketch p. 381), 384, 385
A.M.E.S. RIDGE (Map p. 282), 285, 286
AMFIKLIA (Sketch p. 147), 138, 139
AMFISSA (Sketch p. 156), 140, 142, 149, 156
AMINDAION (Map p. 66; Sketch p. 67), 30, 35, 43, 57, 66
AMIRIYA, 30, 31
AMMUNITION, shortages at Retimo, 257; *artillery*, expenditure in Syria, 527*n*; *mortar*, at Retimo, 269, in Syria, 470, 527
ANDERSON, Lt-Col A. J., 488
ANDERSON, WO2 D.A., 269
ANDERSON, Capt J. R., 146-7
ANDERSON, Col R. C. B., 287
ANDERSON, Lt-Col R. R., 61
ANDREA, Fort (Sketch p. 421), 421, 422
ANDREW, Brig L. W., VC, 222, 223, 236
ANDREWS, Pte G., 434*n*
ANGLO-IRANIAN OIL COMPANY, 200
ANGORA, 6
ANGUS, Lt J. A., 449, 450
ANKARA, 11, 12
ANO KALIVIA (Sketch p. 156), 158
ANSTIS, Cpl A. F., 308
ANTI-LEBANON, 333, 352, 449, 468, 515, 519
ANTIPSARA, 67*n*
APEX HILL (Map p. 282), 286, 287, 289, 293
ARAB EL LOUEIZE (Sketch p. 353), 353
ARAB LEGION, 324*n*, 338; strength of, 391*n*; at Palmyra, 440, 466, 477
ARABS, THE, 201, 326, 346, 412; National movement, 198, 202; relations with French, 322-4, 325, 332
ARAMOUN (Sketch p. 504), 504, 505
ARCHIBALD, Cpl T., 364
ARGOS (Sketch p. 145), 149, 150, 152, 161, 162, 163, 164, 166, 167, 168, 169, 173*n*, 175, 178, 179, 184
ARGOS ORESTIKON (Sketch p. 78), 76, 92
ARKHANIA (Sketch p. 288), 287

566   INDEX

ARLABOSSE, General, 480; arrest of, 520, 521
ARNOLD, Maj M. G. de L., 108, 126
ARRAY, WADI (Map p. 410), 477
ARTHUR, Capt W. H., 493, 494, 495, 500, 501
ARTILLERY, in Greece: 37, 44, 47, 123, 145-7, 153; destruction ordered, 144; value of, 196. In Crete: 215, 216-17, 218, 219, 223-4, 242, 256, 279; strength in M.E., 321n, deficiencies, 535. In Syria, 386, 404, 436n, 439, 443, 459, 460, 503, 527; strength at Damour, 474, 481; strength in regiments, 477n. *Anti-aircraft:* Greece, 165n, 166; in Crete, 219, 220, 221, 279, 280; strength, 204. French: in Syria, 452, 473, 480, 483. Persian: 532
ARTOUZ (Sketches pp. 393, 395), 403, 407, 412, 415
ASFENDHON (Sketch p. 296), 307
ASKIFOU (Sketch p. 296), 295, 297, 298, 299
ASSYRIANS, 200
ATALANDI (Sketch p. 147), 103, 151, 155
ATHENS (Map p. 34; Sketch p. 175), 2, 3, 6, 12, 13, 14, 17, 21, 22, 24, 25, 26, 27, 29, 30, 31, 32, 34, 35, 36, 37, 40, 44, 58, 65, 67n, 71, 78, 79, 80, 81, 83, 93n, 104, 106, 111, 112, 125n, 131, 132, 133, 140, 141, 143, 144, 149, 150, 151, 152, 153, 155, 158, 162, 163, 167, 168, 169, 175, 176, 177, 179, 182, 183, 184, 189, 195, 230, 521; Conference at, 9-11; Germans enter, 170
ATHOS, 189, 315
ATIQA, EL (Map p. 482; Sketch p. 485), 472, 473, 474, 480; capture of, 485-6, 488-9, 495, 501
ATKINSON, Cpl C. C., 436
ATKINSON, Spr J., 148
ATKINSON, Maj W. M., 363
ATLANTIC CHARTER, 531
ATLANTIC OCEAN, 318, 531
ATOCK, Pte J. K., 306
ATROCITIES, in Crete, 240, 255, 286, 290
ATTICA, 14, 162
AUBREY, Lt-Col A. W., 150n
AUCHINLECK, Field Marshal Sir Claude, 327, 440, 513n, 533n, 555n; C-in-C India, 199; administration of armistice in Syria, 516, 517, 518; appointed C-in-C M.E., 523, 531; states strength of national contingents in, 525-6; defence of Syria, 534, 536; and Australian discipline, 545-6
AUSTIN, Maj G. W., 138
AUSTIN, Maj H. McP., 61
AUSTRALIA, 7, 70n, 169, 341, 518, 525, 547, 557, 561; naval aid promised, 15; and Greek campaign, 16, 18, 194; war effort, 537, 538; and Overseas force, 540, 541-3; Blamey's visit, 543-4; Defence policy, 551-2, 562
AUSTRALIAN AIR FORCE, No. 3 Squadron, 335, 391, 394n, 441, 528-9
AUSTRALIAN ARMY, 554; officering of, 542, 544, 549, 558; strength in Australia, 543n; liaison with AIF overseas, 553, 560; see also AUSTRALIAN IMPERIAL FORCE
AUSTRALIAN BROADCASTING COMMISSION, 560
AUSTRALIAN COMFORTS FUND, in Middle East, 558-9
AUSTRALIAN GOVERNMENT, consultation with Great Britain, 14-15, 16-21, 194, 328-9, 553; Blamey's advices on Greek campaign, 19, 27, on Crete, 210, 215, on Cyprus, 318, on Syria, 328, on possible employment of AIF in Turkey, 534, 544, during visit to Australia, 553; Anzac Corps proposals, 70n, 539-40, 541-2; and direction of Middle East campaigns, 21-2, 151, 542n, 555; premature release of armistice negotiations in Syria, 512; and organisation of A.I.F., 537, 539, 541, 542-4; and reinforcement of Far East, 549, 550; A.I.F. wives, 559
—ADVISORY WAR COUNCIL, 19; Blamey's discussions with, 20n, 544, 553
—ARMY, DEPARTMENT OF, 553
—BOARD OF BUSINESS ADMINISTRATION, 129n
—DEFENCE DEPARTMENT, 151
—INFORMATION, DEPARTMENT OF, 560
AUSTRALIAN IMPERIAL FORCE: First, 548; "Australianisation" of, 21; at Gallipoli, 69-70; breaking up of units, 543; officering of, 557n; British praise of, 558; War Records Section, 559. Second, strength and distribution, in Greece, 182-3, in Crete, 213-4, in Syria, 525-6, in Middle East, 540, 543; employment of, 470, 537, 553; relations with French, 468-9, 516-19, compared to, 528, 529; Press censorship, 525, 526, 560-62; organisation of, 535, 537, 538-9; proposed expansion, 539-42, reduction, 542-4; proposed employment in Turkey,

AUSTRALIAN IMPERIAL FORCE—*continued*
544; discipline, 545-7; equipment, 548-9; reactions to Pacific War, 550; cooperation with British Army, 552-55; officering of, 555-8; amenities in Middle East, 558-9; quality and characteristics, 562
—HQ AIF Middle East, 211; creation of Rear Echelon, 22
—I AUST CORPS, 8, 211; staff of, 22, 34n; in Greece, 23, 30, 36, 44, 54, 55, designated Anzac Corps, 70; Lavarack proposed as commander, 340-41; controls operations in Syria, 413-14, 449; occupation of Syria, 514, 515, 517, 518, 519, 535, 546, 548; dispersal of, 537, 539n, 553; movement to Far East, 549-50, 551
—ANZAC CORPS, Australian proposals, 70n, 341, 539-42, 544; creation of, 69-70; in Greece, 71, 77, 79n, 81, 83, 90, 94, 95, 96-7, 102, 103, 110, 128-30, 133, 139, 143, 144, 145, 149, 151, 152, 178n, 183, 184, 195, 547; achievements, 196
—"AUSTRALIAN CORPS", proposed formation of, 539-42
—DIVISIONS: re-organisation of, 7; 1st Armd, 530-31, 538, 539, 540, 541, 542-3. 6th Inf, 549, 559; earmarked for Greece, 7, 17, 18n; embarks, 23, 32-3, 36, 37; staff, 36n; in Greece, 43, 70, 71, 72, 76, 82, 83, 93, 99, 104n, 109, 110, 111, 135, 138, 148, 160, 528, air attacks on, 128-9, 547n, embarkation, 150-51, 152, 153, losses, 183n, 261; in Crete, 210, 256n, strength, 315, losses, 315n, 336n; in Palestine, 320, 537, 540n, 553, re-formation of, 335-6, 547n; in Syria, 340, 544, 548; and Anzac Corps proposals, 341, 539; earmarked for Far East, 550. 7th, brigades of, 7; earmarked for Greece, 7, 17; priority of dispatch, 18n; retained in Egypt, 37, 38, 39, 70, 93, 197, 320; earmarked for Syria, 326, 327, 328, 329; strength and composition, 334-5, 338; plans for advance, 336, 340; staff, 341-2; in Syria, 345, 385n, 395, 400, 418, 449, 451, 510, 511, liaison with navy, 365n, 529, reinforcement of, 413, 467, casualties, 526; Allen becomes G.O.C., 413-14; effect of Press censorship, 526; lessons of campaign, 528-9; occupation of Syria, 514, 515, 529, 535, 537, 544, 548; proposal to place in "Australian Corps", 341, 539; strength of, 540n; earmarked for Far East, 550; dispersal of, 553. 8th, 537, 540, 541, 544n, 547; brigades of, 7. 9th, brigades of, 7; in Cyrenaica, 7, 37, 197, artillery strength, 216; at Tobruk, 320, 537, 553, relief of, 539n, 544, 555n; and proposed "Australian Corps", 341, 539; strength, 540n; relieves 7th Division in Syria, 550
—ARTILLERY, 219, 338n; strength in, 216; at Damour, 502. 2/3rd LAA Regt, Crete, 204, 213n, 280; losses, 292n, 315n. *Anti-Tank Regts:* 2/1st, in Greece, 33n, 35, 76n, 79, 90, 107n, 121-2, 144, 153n, 164n, at Vevi, 43, 44, 57, 60, 63, losses, 64, 183n; in Syria, 467n, 535; 2/2nd, in Syria, 338n, 352, 397, 400, 401, 404n, 405, 409, 452n, 503, casualties, 526n, ammunition expenditure, 527n. *Field Regiments:* 2/1st, in Greece, 33n, 82, 111, 135n, 145, 153n, 164, 173, at Kalamata, 178, losses, 183n, escapes, 189; 2/2nd, in Greece, 75, 102, 111n, 145, 164n, at Brallos, 145-7, 148, 156, 157, losses, 147, 183n; in Crete, 211, 216, 217, 218, 219, 226, 238, 243n, 250, 297n, 313n, strength, 214n, escapes from, 308, losses, 315n; 2/3rd, in Greece, 33n, 75, 82, 89, 144, 176, at Vevi, 43, 64, at Elasson, 102, 123, 124, losses, 183n; in Crete, 211, 219, 226n, 232, 242, 263, 276, 297, 299, 300, 304, 305n, strength, 214n, 256n, New Zealand opinion of, 232n, escapes, 310, 312, losses, 315n; 2/4th, 216, 338n; in Syria, 350, 363, 364, 376, 379, 380, 382, 452n, 463, 473, encounter with French Navy, 413, at Damour, 481, 494, 499, casualties, 526n, ammunition expenditure, 527n. 2/5th, 216, 338n; in Syria, 356, 389n, 467n, 481, at Merdjayoun, 370, 386, 387, 395, 397, 398-9, 401, 404n, 408n, 444, at Damour, 487, 502, 503, casualties, 526n, ammunition expenditure, 527n. 2/6th, 216, 338n; in Syria, 352, 355, at Merdjayoun, 370, 386, 387, 404n, at Jezzine, 389, 401, 411n, 454, 459n, 460, 505, losses, 526n, ammunition expenditure, 527n. 2/7th, 216, 310. 2/8th, 216. 2/9th, in Syria, 451n, 477n, 481, ammunition expenditure, 527n, 535. 2/11th, 535. 2/12th, 216
—CAVALRY REGIMENTS: 6th, 335, 338n, 547, 553; in Syria, 342, 349-50, 351, 366-7, 377, 380, 381-2, 385, 461, 462, 467n, 475, 507, 514, Merdjayoun area, 352, 355, 370-1, 387, 388, 395, 396-7, 398,

INDEX 567

AUSTRALIAN IMPERIAL FORCE—continued
400, 404, 408, 443, 449, squadron organisation, 355n, Kelly Gang, 404n, 447, Damour, 501-2, 503, 504; casualties, 526n. 7th, in Cyprus, 318, 335, 553, strength and equipment, 533, relief, 534. 9th, 338n, 535, 546, 553; history, 385n; in Syria, 385, 389, 460-1, 477, 510, casualties, 526n
—ENGINEERS, in Greece, 42, 74, 76, 88, 99, 110, 128-9, 134-5, 138n, 149, 153, 164n; in Crete, 217, 218, 219; in Syria, 342, 360, 389, 545n; *Field Companies*: 2/1st, in Greece, 48, 73-4, 76n, 88, 107, 145, 148, 157. 2/2nd, in Greece, 79, 125-6, 173n. 2/5th, 338n; in Syria, 387, 404n, 459n. 2/6th, 338n; in Syria, 346-7, 351, 366, 462-3, 472, 473. 2/8th, 144; in Crete, 211, 214n, 256n, 262. 2/9th, 338n. 2/15th, 535
—INFANTRY: *Brigades*: divisional reorganisation, 7; **16th**, 30-32, 340, 555; in Greece, 36, 37, 41, 46, 54, 55, 56, 58, 72-4, 76, 80n, 82, 85-6, 94, 136, 138, 142, 145, 150, 152-3, 162, 168, 171-5, 178n, 181n, at Pinios, 97, 115-19, 126n; re-formation, 336n; *see also* **Allen Force**. **17th**, 30, 36, 74n, 553; in Greece, 79, 106, 141, 145, 150, 152-3, 158, 162, 168, 171-5, 178, 181n; in Crete, 212; at Damour, 467, 474, 480, 481, 484, 490-3, 497-500, 502, 503-5; casualties, 526n; *see also* **Savige Force**. **18th**, 7, 190, 555; ordered to Tobruk, 37; rejoins 7th Division, 544. **19th**, 30, 549, 555; in Greece, 36, 74, 75, 76, 79, 81, 82, 87, 99n, 102, 135, 145, 152, 162, 163-4, 173n, 181, at Vevi, 41, 43, 44, 47, 58, 59-65, 74, crosses Aliakmon, 87-9, at Brallos, 140, 141, 143, 149, 155-8, 255; in Crete, 211, 219, 242, 246, 247, 249-50, 253, 255, 295, 296, 298-9, 300, 303, 304, at 42nd Street, 250, 251-3, embarks, 305-6. **20th**, 7. **21st**, 7, 335, 341; battalions, 338n; in Syria, 340, 342-3, 344, 345-52, 367, 385n, 388, 389, 402n, 405, 412-13, 447, 460-62, 467, 469, at Damour, 469-74, 480-81, 482-91, 500, 502, 505; liaison with navy, 365n; casualties, 526n. **22nd**, 7. **23rd**, 7. **24th**, 7, 22, 335. **25th**, 549, 555; transferred to 7th Division, 7; commander of, 341-2, replaced, 459; battalions, 335, 338n; in Syria, 340, 343-4, 352-6, Merdjayoun area, 367-73, 386-7, 408, Jezzine area, 385n, 387, 388-90, 400, 404-6, 409, 452n, 461, 464-5, 474, 480, 505-9, strength at, 401; casualties, 526n; *see also* **Berryforce**. **26th**, 7. **27th**, 7. Allen Force, 99, 106n, 107n, 127, 145, 150, 152-3, 161, 162, 164-5, 171-5. Berryforce, 443-46, 446-9, 449-51. Savige Force, 81, 82, 90, 99, 103, 106n, 109-11, 125-6, 134-5, 137n; misunderstanding with 1st Armd Brigade, 104
Battalions: battle fatigue in, 453; employment in Middle East, 470; compared to Foreign Legion, 529; 2/1st, 31, 33n, 190, 470; in Greece, 73, 74, 85, 86, 97, 98, 100, 111n, 134, 145, 164n, 175, at Brallos, 140-1, 148, 149, 155-6, 157, 158, casualties, 183n, escapes, 315; in Crete, 211, 213, at Retimo, 218, 219, 232, 234, 258-60, 261-4, 265, 266, 267, 273, 274-6, strength and equipment, 214n, 256-7, escapes, 278, 312, casualties, 275n, 315n; re-formation of, 336n, 419. 2/2nd, 31, 33n, 236n, 313n, 470; in Greece, 41, 42, 73, 74, 85-6, 97, 138-9, 142n, 153n, 172, at Pinios, 107, 108, 113-14, 115-16, 117, 118-19, 120, 122, 127, 134; casualties, 115, 122n, 183n; escapes, 67n, 185, 186-8, 189, 336n; in Crete, 214n; distribution between Crete and Palestine, 336. 2/3rd, 31, 33n, 335, 336, 338n, 413; in Greece, 73, 74, 85, 97, 98, 119n, 138, 139, 142n, 153n, 186, at Pinios, 107-8, 114, 116, 117, 118, 119, 120-21, 127, 134, casualties, 122n, 183n; in Crete, 214n; in Syria, 419, 420-26, 427, 428-9, 511, 520, 529, at Jebel Mazar, 429-39, at Damour, 467, 474, 481, 491-2, 493, 497-8, 500, 504-5; casualties, 438n, 526n. 2/4th, 33n, 470; in Greece, 75-6, 88, 89, 111, 135, 145, 164n; at Vevi, 44, 47, 48, 53, 56, 57, 59, 62-4, 66, at Sotir, 66-7, 68, at Brallos, 140, 141, 146, 148, 156, 157; casualties, 64, 183n; in Crete, 211, 213, 219, 281, 283, 286, 287, 289, 290, 292n, strength, 214n, 279, 280n, 336n, casualties, 315n. 2/5th, 33n, 336, 338n, 368n; in Greece, 79, 82, 90, 92, 97, 111, 118, 119, 125, 126, 135, 140, 141, 142, 149, 153n, 164, 173, 178n, casualties, 134, 183n; in Crete, 181, 214n; allotted to 7th Division, 335, 413; in Syria, 419, 467, 511, 514, 529, at Merdjayoun, 398, 400, 404, at Damour, 481, 491, 492, 493, 497, 498-9, 500, 502, 503-4, casualties, 526n. 2/6th, 33n, 336, 470; in Greece, 79, 82, 90,

AUSTRALIAN IMPERIAL FORCE—continued
106, 111, 134, 135, 141, 142, 150, 153n, 163, 173, 178n, at Lamia Pass, 136-8, at Corinth, 161-2, 164, 165, 166-7, casualties, 167, 183n; in Crete, 214n, escapes, 313-15. 2/7th, 33n, 313n, 336n, 470; in Greece, 79, 82, 90, 106, 111, 135, 141, 142, 150, 153n, 172, 173, 175, 178n, at Lamia Pass, 137, 138, casualties, 183n; in Crete, 211, 213, 218, 219, 234-5, 236, 242, 248, 253, 295, 296, 297, 299, 300, 301, strength, 214n, 241n, at 42nd Street, 250, 251-3, at Sfakia, 302, 303, 304-5, 305-7, escapes, 308-9, 312n; casualties, 252, 315n. 2/8th, 33n, 336n, 470; in Greece, 44, 75, 76, 89, 111, 135, 140, 141, 142n, 145, 153n, 155, 157, 158, 164n, 173, 175, at Vevi, 47, 48, 53, 56, 57-8, 59-62, 64-5, 71, casualties, 183n; in Crete, 211, 213, 218, 219, 226, 234, 238, 242, 246, 248, 253, 295, 296, 297, 299, 300-1, 302, 303, 305, 307, strength, 214n, 241n, at 42nd Street, 251, casualties, 315n. 2/11th, 33n, 44, 190, 336n, 470; in Greece, 79, 90, 97, 118, 119, 125, 126, 134, 145, 164, at Brallos, 140, 141, 148, 155, 156-8, 159, casualties, 183n; in Crete, 211, at Retimo, 213, 218, 219, 234, 257-8, 260, 262-3, 264-5, 266, 267-71, 272, 273-5, 276, 277, strength and equipment, 214n, 256n, 257, escapes, 278, 309-13, casualties, 275n, 315n, 526n. 2/14th, 338n, 557n; in Syria, 342, 346-7, 347-8, 348-9, 351, 377, 378, 379, 413, 467n, 511, at Jezzine, 452-3, 454, 455-9, 464-5, at Damour, 480, 489-91, 492, 493-5, 499, 500-1, 502, 503, 505, casualties, 526n. 2/16th, 338n; in Syria, 342, 345, 349-50, 351, 367, 384, 385, 461, 462, 470, 473, 514, 548-9, at Litani River, 360, 361-4, 365-6, 367, at Sidon, 380-2, at Damour, 474, 480, 481, 486-9, 495-6, 501, 502, casualties, 526n. 2/25th, allotted to 25th Brigade, 335, 338n; in Syria, 389n, 390, 447, 460, 480, Merdjayoun area, 368, 386, 387, 388n, 401, 405, 408, 409, 443-4, 445-6, advance to Rharife, 461, 462-4, 467n, 475-6, 477, at Mazraat ech Chouf, 505-6, 506-7, casualties, 446, 451n, 526n. 2/27th, 338n; in Syria, 343, 348-9, 365, 366, 367, 375-7, 378-9, 380, 382-5, 461, 462, 470-2, 480, at Damour, 480, 481, 482-5, 488, 489, 490, 491, 492, 494, 495, 496-7, 503, 505, casualties, 384, 526n. 2/28th, 190. 2/31st, 190, 338n, in Syria, 344, 352, 354-6, patrols, 368-70, Merdjayoun area, 386, 387, Jezzine area, 388-90, 405-6, 409-12, 452, 453, 454-5, 457, 458, 459-60, 464, 465, 477, 505, 506, 507-9, casualties, 526n. 2/32nd, 335. 2/33rd, 338n; in Syria, 344, 467n, Merdjayoun area, 352, 368, 371-3, 387, 395-6, 400, 403-4, 443, 447-8, 449, strength, 451, casualties, 451n, 526n. 16 Bde Composite, in Crete, 218, 219, 226n, 336, 439n, strength, 214n, casualties, 315n. 17 Bde Composite, in Crete, 218, 219, 226n, 336, strength, 214n, escapes, 313, casualties, 315n. Composite Battalion, at Tolos, 179. Reinforcement Battalion, at Tolos, 171, 178
—MACHINE GUN BATTALIONS: 2/1st, 33n; in Greece, 76n, 79, 86, 87, 89, 90, 135n, 137, 138, 141, 144, 153n, 156, 164, 175, 178n, casualties, 183n; in Crete, 211, 213, 236, 256n, 258, 259, 276, 300, strength, 214n, escapes, 310, casualties, 315n. 2/3rd, 338n; in Syria, 390, 397, 404n, 452n, 459n, 535, Damascus area, 400, 401, 402, 403, 406-7, 419, 420, 427-8, Damour, 489, 493, 494, casualties, 526n
—MEDICAL: *Field Ambulances*: 2/1st, 170; 2/2nd, 79, 173; 2/7th, 164n, 234, 256n. *General Hospitals*: 2/5th, 161, 164, 182; 2/6th, 182n. Nurses, evacuation from Greece, 164
—MILITARY HISTORY AND INFORMATION SECTION, 559-60
—ORDNANCE: *2/2 Field Workshop Company*, 160
—PIONEER BATTALIONS: 2/1st, 190; 2/2nd, 338n; in Syria, 349, 467, 474, 475, 476, 507, Merdjayoun area, 395, 400, 401, 404, 408-9, 443, 445, 446, 447, 448, 449-51, at Damour, 480, 491, 493, 496, 499, 501, 502, 503, organisation and equipment, 408, 449n, casualties, 409, 451n, 526n
—PROVOST COMPANIES: 6th, 150, 151, 165; 7th, 133
—SERVICE CORPS: 256n. *1 Aust Corps Petrol Company*, 178n
—SIGNALS: 164n; *1 Aust Corps Sigs*, 136n, 153, 178n; *6 Div Sigs*, 341
—SKI TROOPS: 547-8
AUSTRALIAN SOLDIERS' CLUB, 559
AUSTRALIAN WAR MEMORIAL, 554, 559, 560
AUSTRIA, 49, 50, 51, 57n, 71

INDEX

AVERY, Lt A. R., 458
AVLIANNA (Sketch p. 73), 73, 74
AWAJ, NAHR EL (Sketches pp. 374, 393), 373, 374, 393, 412
AXIOS (VARDAR) RIVER (Map p. 34; Sketch p. 4), 10, 34, 35, 41, 42, 52, 70
AYIA DEKA (Sketch p. 288), 288
AYIA GALINI (Sketch p. 203), 275, 310, 311
AYIA KONSTANTINOS (Sketch p. 147), 145, 158
AYIA MARINA (Sketch p. 147), 139
AYIA MARINA (Map p. 218), 242
AYIA MARINA (South of Suda; Map p. 218), 242, 249, 254
AYIA ROUMELI (Sketch p. 203), 226n
AYIA TRIAS (Sketch p. 147), 141, 148
AYIOS DIMITRIOS (Sketch p. 84), 101, 109, 123, 124
AYRTON, Capt E. N., 423
AYTON, Maj P. J., 348, 378
AZIBIBI, WADI (Map p. 410), 452, 453

BAALBEK (Sketch p. 478), 478, 534, 535, 548
BAAQOUN (Map p. 482), 471
BAASIR, 471
BABALI (Map p. 282), 284, 286, 287, 290
BABALI HANI, see BABALI INN
BABALI INN (Sketch p. 296), 253, 255, 295, 296
BADANS, Cpl C. N., 423
BADARANE (Sketches pp. 504, 506), 507-8
BADRANE, JEBEL (Sketch p. 393), 391
BAEOUARTA (Map p. 482), 498
BAGHDAD (Sketches pp. 198, 199), 198, 200, 201, 332, 440, 467n
BAILLIE-GROHMAN, Rear-Adm H. T., 131n, 133, 143, 177, 179
BAILLON, Maj-Gen J. A., 548-9
BAINES, Maj W. G. A., 548n
BAKER, Cpl A. A., 113
BAKRAINA (Sketch p. 127), 127
BALATE RIDGE (Map p. 386), 388, 396, 397, 398, 449
BALDOCK, Capt R. G., 382
BALKAN STATES, 14, 205; Italian ambitions in, 1; British plans for front in, 5, 6, 15, 191, 192, 193, 555, Blamey's warning, 538; German commitments, 48
BALLANTINE, Maj R. L., 128-9
BAMFORD, Lt-Col H. O., 171, 179n
BANAT, THE, 48
BANDAR SHAPUR (Sketch p. 533), 532
BANIAS (Map p. 386; Sketch p. 334), 333, 352, 353, 358, 399, 400, 403, 412, 439n
BARADA GORGE (Sketch p. 416), 421; road-block in, 423-4, 425, 426, 427; operations round, 428-9
BARCS (Sketch p. 51), 71
BARDIA, 2, 210, 234, 312, 549
BARDIA, WADI (Map p. 258), 256, 259, 261, 262, 276
Barham, British battleship, 202
BARHAM, Maj K. H., 62, 63, 64
BARJA (Sketch p. 462), 469
BARNES, Gnr C. E., 189
BARNETT, Maj A., 443, 444
BARRETT, Col J. E., 545
BARROWCLOUGH, Maj-Gen H. E., 109, 122, 148, 155, 168
BARTER, Brig A. R., 91, 92, 517
BASRA (Sketch p. 198), 198, 199, 200, 327, 478
BASSETT, Maj B. I., 245
BASTIN, Lt-Col H. E., 510, 546
BATADIYE, EL (Map p. 482), 498
BATAL, EL (Map p. 482), 471, 472, 482, 483
BATER (Map p. 410; Sketch p. 504), 477, 506
BAXTER, Pte B. A., 252
BAXTER-COX, Brig A. R., estimate of, 341-2; in Syria, 352, 368, 371, 386, 387, 388, 401, 409, 411, 452, 453, 454, 459, problems of, 343-4, 370, 405, 412
BAYADA, RAS EL (Sketch p. 348), 346
BAYLIS, Lt G. A., 399n
BAYLISS, Lt H. E., 269
BAYLY, Maj C. W., 268
BAYONETS, use of, 252-3, 348, 434, 435, 476, 508
BCHARRE (Sketch p. 545), 548
BEAMISH, Air Vice-Marshal G. R., 206, 207, 220, 247
BEAN, C. E. W., 559
BECHET (Sketch p. 4), 49
BECKER, Lt, 285
BEDDING, Maj T. G., 218, 227, 240
BEDELLS, Lt J. G., 267, 270n
BEDELLS, Maj T. C., 310

BEIDA, EL (Sketch p. 478), 478
BEIQOUN (Sketches pp. 504, 506), 477, 505
BEIRUT (Map p. 339), 326, 327, 328, 330, 333, 334, 336, 337, 338, 340, 349, 351n, 352, 379, 391, 393, 407, 413, 414, 416, 418, 421, 423, 424n, 426, 428, 429, 430, 432, 433, 442, 467, 468, 469, 477, 480, 489, 499, 502, 503, 513, 515, 517, 519, 521, 534, 535, 544, 546, 559; bombing of, 480n, 511, 512; entry into, 514
BEIT ED DINE (Sketches pp. 462, 475), 405, 409, 452, 460, 461, 469 et seq, 477, 480, 484, 485, 486, 489, 490, 491, 505, 509
BEKAA VALLEY, 509, 535
BELGIUM, 558n
BELGRADE (Sketch p. 51), 12, 13, 25, 26, 48, 50, 51, 71, 94
BELL, Lt-Col A. T. J., 143, 158, 304
BENGHAZI, 4, 5, 16, 523
BENNETT, Maj G. W., 352, 371, 372, 373, 395, 396, 403-4, 447
BENNT JBAIL (Sketch p. 343), 342, 350, 351; capture of, 349
BERCHTESGADEN, 24, 330
BERESFORD, Capt B. D., 235
BERESFORD-PEIRSE, Lt-Gen Sir Noel, 341
BERGOULIYE (Sketch p. 348), 350
BERITIANA (Sketch p. 296), 295
BERLIN, 14, 50, 358
BERNARD, Lt S. E., 252
BERRY, Pte H. L., 300n
BERRYMAN, Lt-Gen F. H., 549n; estimate of, 341; in Syria, 368, 389, 390, 451, 502, at Merdjayoun, 370, 386, 387, commands at, 401, 404, 408, 443, 446-7, 448, 449
BERTRAM, Lt-Col G. A., 454
BERTRAND, Maj G. F., 150n
BESSELL-BROWNE, Maj I. J., 273
BEUCLER, Colonel, 334
BHAMDOUN (Sketch p. 504), 480
BIRRELL, Pte N. V., 373n
BISHOP, Brig J. A., 161, 491, 492n
Bismarck, German battleship, 318
BISSET, Lt T. H., 489
BIZERTA, 330
BLACKBURN, Brig A. S., VC, 401, 402, 403, 406, 407, 418, 420, 427, 515, 518
BLACKBURN, Lt-Col C. A. D'A., 225
BLAIR, WO2 D. A., 456
BLAMEY, Field Marshal Sir Thomas, 44, 55, 76, 81, 83, 103, 104, 108, 109n, 129, 139, 143, 144, 145, 149, 150, 152, 215, 244, 298, 301, 327, 335, 512, 527, 552, 561; priority of dispatch of A.I.F. to Greece, 7; Menzies visits, 8; views on Greek expedition, 17-19, 27, 28, 192, 193, degree of consultation and responsibilities, 18-20, 194; raises question of leadership of Lustre Force, 21; proposed for higher command, 21-2, as Deputy C-in-C Middle East, 151, 340, 542n, 554-5; establishes Rear Echelon A.I.F., 22; reconnoitres Vermion-Olympus line, 34-5; opens headquarters in Greece, 36; protests at retention of 7th Division in Egypt, 37-9; presses for withdrawal of N.Z. Division to Olympus passes, 40; and Olympus-Aliakmon line, 43, 46, 54, 56, 58, 73, 79, 87-8; designates I Aust Corps Anzac Corps, 69-70; and Thermopylae line, 80, 82, 98-9, 140; reinforces Pinios Gorge, 95, 96-7; learns of decision to embark, 133, departs, 151, 168; evacuation of nurses, 164n; and Crete, 210, 303; and Cyprus, 318; and Syria, 328, 329, 357n, criticises defence plan, 536; organisation of A.I.F., 340-1, 536-7, 538-9, 539-41, 543-4; and German threat to Turkey, 534; visits Australia, 543-4, 553; A.I.F. discipline, 546-7; return of senior officers, 549; seniority and experience, 554; commissioning of O.C.T.U. graduates, 556-7; A.I.F. Records Section, 559, 560
BLIDA (Sketch p. 343), 344, 352
BLIDA, WADI, 347n
BLOCKADE, NAVAL, of Europe, 325, 538
BLOMBERG, Maj von, 201
BLUCHER, Lt Count, 285, 286n
BLUNDELL, Capt P. L., 444
BLUNT, Brig J. S., 177, 215
BMERIQ (Sketch p. 353), 353, 403, 404, 447, 449
BOASE, Lt-Gen A. J., 555
BOEHME, General, 50, 51, 52, 94, 126
BOLTON, Capt W. B., 252, 300

BOMBING, 195-6, 547n
Bonaventure, British cruiser, 23
BOND, Capt R. L., 299
BOOTH, Sgt C. E., 464
BORDEN, Mary, 519n
BORDES, Capt, 517
BOSGARD, Capt A. K., 186
BOSNIA, 94
BOULTER, Capt T. A. M., 188, 189
BOUM, EL (Map p. 482), 471, 472, 480, 482, 483, 484, 490, 491, 492, 494
BOURKE, Brig H. S. J., 418, 424, 425
BOURKOCH, JEBEL (Sketch p. 416), 477n
BOURQOUZ (Map p. 386), 388, 449
BOUSIN, Capt, 426
BOWSER, Col C., 36n
BOWYER-SMYTH, Capt Sir Philip, 180
BRALLOS PASS (Sketches pp. 82, 147, 156), 80, 83, 129, 134, 136, 138, 139, 183, 255; dispositions, 140-41, 142, 148, 149, 153; Vasey's orders, 143; artillery engagement at, 145-7; rearguard at, 155-8; German account, 158-9
BRAND, WO2 D., 157-8
BRAUCHITSCH, Field Marshal Walther von, 50, 51
BRAUER, Colonel, 284, 285, 286, 292, 293
BREAKSPEAR, Pte H. W., 506
BREMNER, Lt L. D., 487
BRIDGEFORD, Lt-Gen W., 34n
BRIDGES, Maj-Gen Sir William, 554
BRIGHT, Cpl F. G., 363, 487
BRITAIN, GREAT, 111, 132, 210, 335, 518, 547, 559; and Greece, 1, 2, 3, 5-6, 8, 9-10, 190-1, 192, 193, 214; relations with Turkey, 11, 534, with Yugoslavia, 13, 15, 24, 25, 26-7, 28; Dominion consultation, 14-15, 16-21, 194, 328-9, 553; and Iraq, 197, 199; relations with Arabs, 322-4; and Syria, 323-4, 331, 513, 524; relations with French, 324-5, 326, 330, 515, 516, 517, 519; Lend-Lease aid to, 530; reinforcement of Middle East, 8, 531, 541; and Persia, 531-3; Middle East strategy, 533, 534, 551, 555; reinforcement of Far East, 15, 549; proposed invasion of Sicily, 553
BRITISH AIR FORCE, 6, 319, 538; in Greece, 1, 9-10, 17, 44, 70, 83, 133, 149-50, 152, in close support in Albania, 5, strength and distribution, 18, 22-3, 28, 37, withdrawn to Athens airfields, 83, personnel strength, 181n, 183, losses, 183, relations with army, 195; strength in Middle East, 8, 320; in Crete, 219, 220, 231, 232, 242, 247n, 265n, 266, 302, strength and dispositions, 206-7, 214, losses, 316; in Iraq, 200, 201; at Malta, 531; in Syria, 322, 335, 344, 391, 441, 468, 479, 480, 527, 528-9
—AIR MINISTRY EXPERIMENTAL STATION: *No. 220*, 283
—ARMOURED CAR COMPANIES: *No. 2*, 440n
—FLYING TRAINING SCHOOLS: *No. 4*, 200
—SQUADRONS: *No. 11*, 22n; *No. 30*, 22n, 206-7, 214; *No. 33*, 22n, 207, 214; *No. 37*, 22n; *No. 38*, 22n; *No. 45*, 528-9; *No. 80*, 22n, 207, 214; *No. 84*, 22n; *No. 112*, 22n, 207, 214; *No. 113*, 22n; *No. 203*, 207; *No. 208*, 22n; *No. 211*, 22n; *No. 230*, 214; *No. 244*, 214
—WINGS: *Eastern*, in Greece, 22n, 80; *Western*, 22n
BRITISH ARMY, 1, 2, 523; strength and employment in Middle East, 6-7, 320, 321n, 531, 540-1, 551, allotment of commands, 21-2, 151, 527, 554-5; in Greece, strength, 17, 28, 182, 192, losses, 183, consultation with Greeks, 194-5; staff talks with Yugoslav Army, 24-5, 26-7, 28; relations with R.A.F., 195; in Iraq, 198; in Crete, 203-5, 312, strength, 213-14, 315, losses, 315n, 316; artillery and engineer shortages in, 216, 535; in Syria, 515, 516, 518-19, 528, 534-6, strength, 526; press censorship, 525, 526; tactical doctrines, 536-7; officering of, 556, 557n, 558; cooperation with Dominion contingents, 552-5
—ARMIES: *Eighth*, 549; *Ninth*, 544-5, 548
—COMMANDS: *British Troops in Egypt*, 527; *Middle East Command*, 302, 303; *Palestine Area*, 545; *British Troops in Palestine and Transjordan*, 326, 544, 548
—CORPS: *X*, 294

BRITISH ARMY—*continued*
296, 297, 299, 304, 305; *Lee Force*, 99; *Lister Force*, 180; *Lustre Force*, 24; selection of commander, 21-2; assembly in Greece, 30-33, shortages, 36-7; decision to embark, 131-3; departure of senior officers, 151-2, 155; strength in Greece and number embarked, 181n; *Pemberton Force*, 180; *Transjordan Frontier Force*, 201, 391, 394, 467n, 515; *Western Desert Force*, 151, 549
—GROUPS: *W Group*, in Greece, 43, 56, 77, 80, 90, 129n, 139, 143, 145, 155, 158, 160, 177, planned deployment, 36, splitting of headquarters, 37, command problems, 44, 54-5, cooperation with Greek Army, 65, 76-9, 81, orders to 1 Armd Bde, 103, 104, embarkation from Greece, 143-4, 162-3, precipitate closure of headquarters, 168
—DIVISIONS, ARMOURED: increases in, 530-31. *2nd*, 7, 8, 37, 70, 93, 197, 204, 320; *7th*, 7, 320; *10th*, 319
—DIVISIONS, CAVALRY: *1st*, 320, 327, 467n
—DIVISIONS, INFANTRY: establishment, 541. *5th*, 541; *6th*, 7, 320, 321n; in Syria, 414, 417, 442, 467, 477, 510, 513, 515, 535, becomes 70th Div, 544; *50th*, 8, 531, 534, 541; *70th*, 544
—BRIGADES, ARMOURED AND CAVALRY: *1st*, 17, 23, 211; composition of, 30; in Greece, 32-3, 34, 35, 42, 58, 72, 74, 77, 79, 82, 87, 89, 110, 111, 143, 152, 162, 165, 168, 169, 170, 175, 176, 181n, at Vevi, 44, 46, 47, 53, 59, at Proasteion, 66-9, placed under command Anzac Corps, 81, misunderstanding with Savige Force, 103-4, tank and equipment losses, 69, 90, tank strength, 141; *3rd*, 197; *4th Cavalry*, at Habbaniya, 201; in Syria, 478, 510, 535, at Palmyra, 440-1, composition of, 467n; becomes 9th Armd Bde, 532; *5th Cavalry*, 467n; *6th Cavalry*, 467n; *9 Armd*, 532
—BRIGADES, INFANTRY: *14th*, in Crete, 203, 204, 206, 210, 211, 212, 213, 219, 280n; *16th*, 210; in Crete, 215, 238; in Syria, 392, 400, 413, 414, 418-19, 430, 432, 439, 442, 509; *23rd*, 535n; at Merdjayoun, 451, 467, 477, 509; *Composite Brigade*, in Crete, 248, 249, 250, 251
—REGIMENTS, ARMOURED AND CAVALRY: *Cheshire Yeo*, in Syria, 343, 344, 351, 352, 366, 388-9, 390, 402, 405, 452, 461, 463, 467n, 480, 505; *Household Cavalry*, 440n, 441, 466; *3rd Hussars*, 225, 280n, 299, 300, 307; *4th Hussars*, 30n, 33n, 42, 67, 68, 90, 141, 143, 149, 152, 161, 162, 165, 166, 167, 169, 171, 177n, 178, 180, losses in Greece, 183n; *North Somerset Yeo*, 477; *Notts Yeo*, 313; *Royals*, 338n, 349, 350; *3rd Royal Tank*, 30n, 33n, 35, 43, 57, 67, 68, 79, 135n, 141, 143, 152, 163, 171n, 178, losses in Greece, 90, 183n; *7th Royal Tank*, 256n 280n; *Scots Greys*, 338n, 388, 395, 397, 398, 399, 400, 401, 404, 408n, 443, 449, 467n; *Staffs Yeo*, 338n, 398, 400, 467n; *Warwickshire Yeo*, 440, 441; *Wiltshire Yeo*, 440, 466; *Yorkshire Dragoons*, 403, 467n
—REGIMENTS, ARTILLERY: *Anti-aircraft*: 2nd Hvy, 33n, 163; 151 Hvy Bty, 204; 234 Hvy Bty, 204; 52nd Light, 204; 57th Light, 338n, 404n; 122 Light Bty, 165; 156 Light Bty, 204, 280n; 159 Light Bty, 204; 170 Light Bty, 452n; 171 Light Bty, 399n. *Anti-tank*: 102nd, in Greece, 30n, 33n, 68, 69, 77, 89, 90, 141, 149, 170, 176-7, losses, 183n; in Crete, 212, 216, 219, 226n, 248, 250, 251. *Royal Horse Artillery*: 2 Regt, in Greece, 30n, 33n, 43, 57, 59, 60, 62, 64n, 67, 68, 90, 141, 155, 170, losses, 183n; 106 Regt, 183n, 212, 216, 219, 232, 243n, 257, 282. *Field Regiments*: 1st, 338n, 373, 394, 418, 419, 421, 477n; 4th, 477n; 237 Bty, 440n; 239 Bty, 440n. *Medium Regts*: 7th, in Greece, 33n, 86, 183n; in Crete, 210, 212, 213, 216, 219, 279, 280n, 283, 286; at Damour, 503; 64th, in Greece, 33n, 35, 43, 44, 53, 64, 79, 86, 123, 141, 183n; 212 Bty, 481; 234 Bty, 280n, 283
—REGIMENTS, INFANTRY: 196; *1/Argyll and Sutherland Highlanders*, in Crete, 215, 219, 241, 243, 244, 287, 288-9, 290, 293, 310, casualties, 315n; *2/Black Watch*, in Crete, 206, 219, 279, 280n, 281-2, 284, 285, 286, 289, 292, 310, casualties, 315n; *1/Essex*, 201, 440, 441, 466, 478; *2/King's Own*, in Syria, 413, 418, 430, 447, 448, 449, 451, 467n; *2/Leicester*, in Crete, 215, 219, 220, 279, 280, 283, 284, 286, 287, 288, 289, casualties, 315n; *in Syria*, 418, 430, 431, 433; *2/Queen's*, 215n; 237, 238, 251n; in Syria, 400, 407, 413, 418, 430, 433, 436, 438, 510; *1/Rangers*, in Greece, 30, 33n,

BRITISH ARMY—continued
65n, 69, 104, 141, 148, 162, 169, 170, 176, at Vevi,
44, 47, 48, 53, 56-7, 58, 59, 60, 61, 62, 64, at Sotir,
67, 68, casualties, 183n; in Crete, 212, 219, 226,
238, 243, 244, 248, 250, 251, 265, 266, 267, casualties,
315n; 1/Royal Fusiliers, 338n; in Syria, 356, 391,
394, 402, 406, 417n, 419, 424, 439n, 477, casualties,
430n; 1/Sherwood Foresters, 318; 1/Welch, in Crete,
213, 218, 219, 225, 226, 238, 247, 248, 249, 250, 251,
308, casualties, 315n; 2/York and Lancaster, in
Crete, 219, 279, 280n, 283, 284, 286, 287, 288,
casualties, 315n
—BASE SUB-AREAS: 80, 180, 143; 82, 143; *Athens*,
150
—ENGINEERS: 88, 165. *Field Companies*: 42nd,
280n, 300; 292nd, 103; 580th Army Troops Coy, 74
—MEDICAL: *189 Fd Ambulance*, 280n; *7 Gen
Hospital*, 221, 225; *26 Gen Hospital*, 161, 182;
Nurses, evacuation from Greece, 164
—MILITARY MISSIONS: 12, 30, 44, 132n
—ORDNANCE: 266
—PIONEER CORPS: 150, 172
—SEARCHLIGHT UNITS: *304 Battery*, 204
—SPECIAL SERVICE BATTALIONS: 16n; "*A*" *Battalion*,
in Crete, 243, 251, 297; "*C*" *Battalion*, 318; in
Syria, 342, 346, 360, 364-5, 367; "*D*" *Battalion*, 253
BRITISH BROADCASTING CORPORATION, 189, 272, 512,
525
BRITISH COMMONWEALTH, and Greek Campaign, 192,
194; integration of forces, 551-2, 553, 554-5
BRITISH GOVERNMENT: 25n; Eden-Dill Mission to
Middle East, 9-14; appointment of Minister of
State to Middle East, 525
—WAR CABINET, 151, 214; dominance by Prime
Minister, 15, 193-4; Defence Committee, 327-8
—DEPARTMENTS: Admiralty, 298, 305; Foreign
Office, 214, 321; War Office, 4-5, 170n, 202, 204,
209, 321, 322, 326, 327, 328, 525, 536, 540, 541,
542, 554-5
BRITISH NAVY, 150, 220, 313; in Greece, 44; pre-
campaign assurances, 20-1
—MEDITERRANEAN FLEET, 9; at Matapan, 23; in
evacuation of Greece, 160-1, 163-4, 170-1, 172-3,
174-5, 176, 177, 179, at Kalamata, 180-1, losses,
175; bombards Tripoli, 202; in Battle of Crete,
227, 228, 233, 238-9, 291-2, 294, 297-8, 299-300,
301, 302, 305-6, losses, 239, 317-18, strength, 305,
320; supports Syrian invasion, 335, 350, 365, 367,
379n, 391, 413, 468, 473, 480, 488, 527, air force
protection, 529. *7th Cruiser Squadron*, 239; *15th
Cruiser Squadron*, 335
—FLEET AIR ARM, 320; in Greece, 22-3; in Syria,
335n, 413. *No. 805 Squadron*, 207, 214
—MOBILE NAVAL BASE DEPOT ORGANISATION, in
Crete, 204, 212. 213, 215, 219, losses, 315n
—ROYAL MARINES, in Crete, 204, 226, 231, 238,
243n, 248, 250, 280n, 299, 300, 302, 303, 304, 305,
308, casualties, 315, 316
BRITISH HISTORICAL SECTION, 193n
BRITTEN, Capt C. B., 350
BROCK, Capt B., 186
BROUMANE (Sketch p. 516), 544
BROWN, Pte C., 268
BROWN, Capt C. K., 433, 434, 438n
BROWN, Gnr E. S., 147
BROWN, Air Vice-Marshal Sir Leslie, 335
BROWN, Capt T., 355
BROWN, Maj T. B., 397
BRUCE, Rt Hon Viscount, 318, 328
BRUNSKILL, Brig G. S., 22, 29-30, 33n, 144n, 210, 317n;
coordination of command in Greece, 44
BRYCE, Lt J. K., 373n
BRYNE, Sgt J., 460, 461
BUCHECKER, Sgt H. R., 312
BUCKINGHAM, Gnr B., 444
BUCKINGHAM, L-Cpl J. R., 74
BUCKLER, Cpl H. A., 347
BUCKLER, Lt-Col S. H., 347n, 378
BUCKLEY, Lt-Col A. A., 114, 115, 116, 117, 118, 186,
190
BUDERIS, Cpl T. A., 473
BUDERUS, Sgt L. E. G., 422n
BULGARIA, 2, 3, 5, 8, 10, 11n, 13, 25, 26, 39, 191, 192;
Germans enter, 12, 49, strength in, 18n, 27, 37,
184; becomes German dependency, 24, territorial
promises, 48
BULL, Maj M. A., 302

BURBIDGE, WO1 T., 487
BURCKHARDT, Capt, 285
BURNS, Cpl P., 465
BURNS, Tom, 174n
BURR, Capt F. S., 471
BURROWS, Brig J. T., 236
BURSTON, Maj V. C., 297, 299, 302, 305
BURT, Lt S. F., 447
BURZACOTT, Sgt W. R., 494
BUTLER, Maj W. G., 386, 506, 507
BUTTERCUP FIELD (Map p. 282), 281, 283, 285
BUTTROSE, Brig A. W., 396, 403, 404, 447
BUXTON, Lt D. R., 378
BYRNE, Lt-Col J. H., 355

CADIRI (Sketch p. 296), 296
CAIRO, 6, 8, 9, 18, 20, 32, 83, 195, 197, 207, 210, 211,
214, 215, 244, 254, 271, 290, 298, 301, 303, 320,
322, 335, 340, 478, 513, 519, 525, 556, 560; press
censorship at, 561-2
Calcutta, British cruiser, 160, 298; loss of, 318
CALDWELL, Lt-Col W. B., 115, 116, 117, 118, 127
CALING, Cpl G. J., 41n
CAMERON, Lt G. L., 476
CAMERON, Pte K. D., 120
CAMM, Pte R., 445n
CAMM, Capt R. A., 445, 449, 450, 451
CAMOUFLAGE, 258
CAMPBELL, Pte C. C., 67n
CAMPBELL, Brig I. R., 86, 149, 234, 238, 243, 254, 259,
260, 261, 262, 263, 264, 265, 266, 267, 269, 271,
272, 277, 278, 279, 310; placed in command at
Retimo, 256; disposes force, 257-8; proposes
surrender, 273-5
CAMPBELL, Sir Ronald, 12
CAMPBELL, Cpl R. K., 354
CAMPBELL, Col T. C., 222
CANADIAN ARMY, 531; establishment of Overseas
force, 541; officering of, 557n. Canadian Kent
Corps Troops, 42
CANBERRA, 549, 559
CANEA (Map p. 218), 203, 206, 207, 208, 210, 212,
214, 217, 221, 224, 227 et seq, 238, 239, 240, 241,
243, 244, 248, 249, 250, 251, 254, 255, 258, 265,
266, 267, 279, 313; population, 202; dispositions
at 218, 219, 226n
CANET, Col L. G., 341n
CANN, Maj S. B., 73, 128
CANNON, Lt-Col W. G., 378, 452, 456, 490, 494
CAPE OF GOOD HOPE, 8
Carlisle, British cruiser, 170, 238, 239, 488n
CARO, Lt-Col A. E., 349, 360, 364, 380, 382, 485, 486,
487, 489
CARROLL, Maj K. A., 161, 162
CARROLL, Sgt S. L., 311
CARSON, Sgt A. L., 120
CARSTAIRS, Lt R. J., 461
CARTER, Capt A. G. G., 265n
CARTER, Pte B. B., 312
CASEY, Rt Hon R. G., 328
CASPIAN SEA, 544
CASSEAU, Colonel, 393, 420, 427
CASTELLORIZO ISLAND, 16
CASTLE HILL (Map p. 386), 445
CASUALTIES, medical cooperation in treatment of,
265, 266n, 269, 270n, 290, 486n; *Australian*, in
Greece, 122n, 134, 167, 183; in Crete, 252, 266n,
275, 283, 292n, 315n, 316; in Syria, 363, 384, 386n,
390, 409, 411, 438n, 446, 451n, 458, 468, 476n,
489n, 508, totals, 526; *British*, in Greece, 183; in
Crete, 315n, 316, 318; in Syria, 407, 526; in Persia,
533; *French*, in Syria, 407, 526; *German*, at Servia,
87, 93; at Pinios, 127; at Thermopylae, 159, at
Corinth, 167; total in Greece, 182; in Crete, 240,
252, 255, at Retimo, 275, at Heraklion, 285, 286;
totals, 316, in attempted seaborne invasion, 233;
Greek, at Kastelli, 227, 240; *Indian*, in Syria, 430n,
480, 526; in Persia, 533; *New Zealand*, in Greece,
87, 97, totals, 183; in Crete, 222, 252, totals, 315n,
316
CATROUX, General G., 321, 324n, 358, 418, 513, 514,
515, 516, 517, 518, 519; urges Free French advance
on Damascus, 322, 326-7
CAUCASUS, 530, 531, 534, 538, 544
CAVALLA (Sketch p. 39), 51
CAVALLERO, General, 331
CEMETERY HILL (Sketch p. 245), 230, 232

INDEX

CEMETERY RIDGE (Heraklion), 289
CENSORSHIP, in Middle East, 525, 526, 560-2
CESME (Sketch p. 187), 186, 188
CESMES (Map p. 258), 264
CHADD, Col B. T. R., 341*n*
CHAKMAK, Marshal, 11*n*
CHANNELL, Capt D. R., 259, 261, 263, 276
CHAOUB EL HASS, JEBEL (Sketch p. 416), 429
CHAPMAN, Maj-Gen J. A., 341, 491, 499, 502
CHAPPEL, Maj-Gen B. H., 204, 219, 283, 286, 290, 293-4; placed in command at Heraklion, 213, problems, 279-80
CHARLESWORTH, Cpl A. E., 488
CHARLIES, THE (Map p. 282), 279, 281
CHARRINGTON, Brig H. V. S., 33, 35, 59, 66, 68, 69, 74, 89, 90, 103, 104, 141, 148, 162, 170, 176, 177
CHATEAU DE BEAUFORT (Sketch p. 353), 354
CHAUVEL, General Sir Harry, 542*n*
CHEBAA (Map p. 386; Sketch p. 343), 343, 344, 371, 447, 477
CHEHAB (Sketch p. 357), 356
CHEHIM (Sketch p. 462), 461, 463, 464, 475
CHESTER, Maj R. R., 88, 89
CHILTON, Brig F. O., 42, 85, 97, 106-7, 113, 115, 116-17, 118-19, 186, 187-8, 190, 336*n*
CHIOS ISLAND (Sketch p. 4), 52, 185, 186, 188
CHRISTOFINI, FORT (Sketch p. 396), 395-6, 403
CHRISTOPHERSON, Maj F. A., 456
CHRYSTALL, Maj-Gen J. I., 515, 520
CHURCHILL, Maj R. F. E. S., 525
CHURCHILL, Rt Hon Sir Winston, 7, 8, 9, 13, 18, 328, 359, 512, 531; aid to Greece, 2, 6, 14*n*, 19; promises naval reinforcement of Pacific, 5; in British War Cabinet, 15, 193-4; seeks assurances before committing Dominion troops to Greece, 16, 17; hopes of Balkan front, 25, 27, 192, 555; and evacuation of Greece, 112-13, 131-2, 132-3; orders naval bombardment of Tripoli, 202; defence of Crete, 203, 207, 220, 241, proposes Freyberg as commander, 208; equipment of force, 210, 215; and de Gaullist movement, 321; approves proposed Free French advance into Syria, 322, 326-7; informs Menzies of decision to invade Syria, 329; transfers Wavell to India, 523-4, appoints Minister of State to Middle East, 525; organisation of British Army, 536; and proposed invasion of Sicily, 553*n*
CIANO, Count, 11*n*
CINCAR-MARKOVIC, M, 25
CIPHERS, in Crete, 242-3, 254
City of London, British transport, 173*n*, 174
Clan Fraser, British transport, 40
CLARK, Capt C. A., 444
CLARK, Lt-Gen J. G. W., 440, 441, 466, 478
CLARKE, Cpl J. W., 407
CLARKE, Maj A. J., 397, 493
CLARKE, Lt A. W., 459*n*
CLARKE, Lt F. L., 266
CLEAVER, Lt E. H. R., 259
CLENNETT, Maj B. G., 427, 428*n*
CLIFTON, Brig G. H., 99, 149, 177
CLOWES, Lt-Gen C. A., 34*n*, 95-6, 97, 549
COAKLEY Lt J. B., 411
CODES, German, at Retimo, 260, 264, at Heraklion, 283-4
COL DE YAFOUR (Sketch p. 416), 477
COLE, Gnr J. W., 312, 313
COLES, Pte G. T., 63
COLLESS, Pte O. W., 363
COLLET, Colonel, 327, 335, 338, 373, 391, 394, 427
COLLINS, Maj-Gen R. J., 523*n*
COLOUR PATCHES, 336*n*
COLQUHOUN, Capt C. T., 108
COL'S KNOLL, 399, 450
COL'S RIDGE (Map p. 386), 397, 399, 449
COLVIN, Lt-Col F. B., 243, 305, 307
COMMUNISTS, 24, 186
COMTE, Sgt, 427
CONKEY, Maj H. S., 57, 62
CONNAL, Lt, 402
CONNOLLY, Pte P. E., 349*n*
CONNOR, Capt G. B., 353-4
CONRAD, General, 228
CONSTABLE, Pte G. N., 347
CONSTANTA (Sketch p. 4), 49
COOMBES, Lt-Col C. J. A., 59, 60, 61
COOPER, Capt L. C., 301

COPEMAN, Lt J., 424, 426, 428
COPLAND, Maj J. S., 62, 63, 64, 67
COPP, Maj W. D., 372, 373, 404
CORBY, Lt-Col J. A., 443
CORINTH (Map p. 34), 162, 163, 164, 169, 173*n*, 177*n*, 183, 188, 197, 228, 275, 336; Isthmus force, 153, reinforcement of, 163; dispositions at, 161-2, 165-6; action at, 166-7; effect on embarkation plans, 168
CORINTH, GULF OF, 140, 142, 149, 166, 169
Costa Rica, Dutch transport, 173*n*, 174-5, 211
COTTON, Cpl, 402
COTTON, Lt-Col T. R. W., 353, 354, 368, 396, 404, 548*n*
COULAM, Pte C., 167
COURAGE, Lt-Col J. H., 160, 170, 179
COURTNEY, Lt-Col W. J., 356*n*
Coventry, British cruiser, 164, 298, 335
COWAN, Maj R. W. T., 496
COWDERY, Maj G. D., 346
COX, Brig C. H. V., 289
COYLE, Capt G., 116
CRAFTER, Maj J. G., 383, 384
CRAIG, Lt N. W., 259, 262
CRAMP, Capt R. T., 377
CRAWFORD, Capt A. A., 126
CRAWFORD, Capt A. D., 53*n*, 64
CREMOR, Brig C. E., 156, 157, 218, 219, 297*n*
CRETAN POLICE, 256*n*, 263, 276, 277, 278
CRETE, 6, 22, 23, 65*n*, 113, 139, 152, 174, 179*n*, 182, 185, 186, 188, 189, 201, 320, 321, 326, 327, 335, 392, 419, 470, 523, 524, 530, 533, 537, 540*n*, 544, 554, 555, 562; Greek Government established, 153, 207; strategic value, 197; topography, 202-3; British garrison, 1, 203-4, 209-10, 210-14, 217-19, 527, reinforcement of, 202, 205-7, 215, 243, 287; Freyberg assumes command, 208-9, strength of contingents in. 210, 214, 315, 336, supply of, 217, 237, 239; campaign in, 221-329; attempted seaborne invasion, 233; decision to evacuate, 254; escapes, 307-15; casualties, 315-16; naval losses, 318, 319; German strength and losses, 316; *see also* HERAKLION; MALEME-SUDA; RETIMO
CRIMEA, 549
CRNA RIVER (Map p. 34; Sketch p. 45), 47, 53
CROMBIE, Capt W. M., 444, 476
CROATIA, 48, 94
CROOK, Lt L. C., 465, 506
CRUICKSHANK, Maj R. M., 386
CULLEN, Maj H. D.; *see* COPP, W. D.
CULLEN, Lt-Col P. A., 185, 186, 190
CUMPSTON, Capt J. S., 548*n*
CUNNINGHAM, Admiral of the Fleet Viscount, 83, 151, 239, 318, 319, 327, 553*n*; views on Greek expedition, 9, 193, and embarkation of force, 20-21, 151, 181; takes up Italian challenge at Matapan, 23; bombardment of Tripoli, 202; dispositions to meet threat of seaborne invasion of Crete, 227; and evacuation of Crete, 298, 303, 305; appeals for air reinforcement of Mediterranean, 320; allots naval forces for Syrian campaign, 335; estimate of Wavell, 524
CUNNINGHAM, General Sir Alan, 21, 549
CUNNINGTON. Cpl E. A., 273, 274
CURSON, Pte G., 348
CURTIN, Rt Hon J., 19; becomes Prime Minister, 543
CURTIS, Maj H. T., 558*n*
CUTLER, Lt A. R., VC, 444-6, 448, 487
CVETKOVIC, M., 25
CYPRIOT PIONEERS, 492; in Greece, 137, 161, 165, 178, 180, strength and losses, 182-3; in Crete, 213, 253, 304, 312
CYPRUS, 208, 313, 319, 329, 530, 537, 553; garrison of, 318, 335, 533-4; Fleet Air Arm based on, 335*n*, 413
CYRENAICA, 7, 8, 9, 14*n*, 30, 41, 106, 193, 234. 349; British offensive in, 2, 4, halted, 6; German offensive, 16, 37, 197, 202; effect of aid to Greece on, 193, 523, 524
CZECHOSLOVAKIA, 24
CZERNAWODA (Sketch p. 4), 49

DADION, Greek airfield, 228
DADSWELL, Cpl L., 428*n*
DAFNA (Map p. 386), 343, 368
DAKAR, 330
DALAMIYE, ED (Map p. 482), 489

572 INDEX

D'ALBIAC, Air Marshal Sir John, 26, 112, 131, 207; employs air force in close support in Albania, 5; strength of air force allotted for Greek campaign, 22, 37, opposes establishment of joint headquarters in single building, 33n, withdraws air force to Athens airfields, 83, orders withdrawal of air force to Crete, 149-50; commands air force in Palestine and Transjordan, 200
DALE, Maj R., 90
DALEY, Cpl W., 490
DALMATIA, 94
DALY, Brig R., 387
DAMASCUS (Map p. 339; Sketches pp. 393, 416), 201, 333, 334, 338, 344, 352, 374, 413, 414, 430, 432, 441, 446, 449, 465, 467, 468, 474, 478, 510, 515, 517, 519, 523, 534, 546, 548; airfield at, 322; proposed Free French advance on, 326-7; Allied advance to, 356-8, 390-91, 400, 403, 406-7, 415-18, 419-27; capture of, 427-9; French counter-attack, 393-5, 401, 412; Allied dispositions, 477; *see also* BARADA GORGE; MAZAR, JEBEL
DAMOUR (Map p. 482; Sketches pp. 500, 504), 439n, 477n, 513; policy at, 412-13, 418-19; advance to, 460-2, 464, 469-74; defences at, 473, 528-9; orders for capture, 480-1; battle of, 482-505, casualties, 489n, French account, 510
DAMOUR RIVER, 469, 470, 471, 472, 482, 501, 529
DANUBE RIVER (Sketch p. 51), 48, 49
DAPHNI, 31, 178n
DAQOUN (Map p. 482), 503, 505
DAQOUN, WADI (Map p. 482), 480, 490 *et seq*, 495, 497, 498, 500, 501
DARAYA (Damour area; Map p. 482), 470, 484, 489, *et seq*, 496, 497, 505
DARAYA (Rharife area; Sketch p. 462), 461, 464, 475, 476
DARB ES SIM (Sketch p. 381), 380, 382, 383
DARLAN, Admiral, 325, 329-30, 331, 511
DAVIS, Lt M. H., 354, 368-70, 507, 508
DAWSON, Lt-Col R. B., 299
DAWSON, W. D., 227n
DAY, Lt G. M., 308
DEAN, Capt A. C., 496
DEAN, Capt H. A., 161, 165, 166
DEBBINE (Map p. 386), 388n, 398, 408, 445
DEBBINE VALLEY, 397
Decoy, British destroyer, 164, 180, 226n
DEELEY, Cpl L. D., 458
Defender, British destroyer, 173n, 174, 180, 298
DE GAULLE, General Charles, 321, 322, 332, 337, 358, 466; and invasion of Syria, 325, 326, 327, 328; ambitions in Syria, 516, 518-19, fails to rally Vichy French troops, 525, 528
DE GUINGAND, Maj-Gen Sir Francis, 10n, 11n, 524
DEIR ALI (Sketch p. 374), 374
DEIR EZ ZOR (Sketches pp. 466, 478), 478, 479, 535; capture of, 466
DEIR KANOUN (Sketch p. 416), 429, 439, 477
DEIR MAR JORJOS (Map p. 482), 481, 491, 493, 498, 499, 500, 504
DEIR MIMESS (Map p. 386; Sketch p. 353), 355, 370
DEIR SUNEID, 335, 340
DELHOMME, General, 334, 412
DELPHI PASS (Sketches pp. 82, 147), 80, 142, 149, 158, 164
DELVES, Lt W. P., 261
DE MEYRICK, Lt J. J., 63, 67
DEMOLITIONS, *British*, in Greece, 74, 83-4, 103, 106, 109, 110, 125, 126, 136-7, 138n, 149, 157, 165, 166, efficacy of, 84n, 142, 196; in Crete, 297. French, in Syria, 347, 351, 387
DENT, Maj J., 350
DENTZ, General Henri, 327, 334, 356, 358, 390n, 469, 480n, 514, 516, 522, 526; attitude to German encroachment in Syria, 321-2, 326, 330-1, 332, becomes High Commissioner, 324; defends policy of resistance to British advance, 331; and armistice negotiations, 414, 511-13; arrest of, 520-21
DERAA (Map p. 339; Sketch p. 357), 326, 338, 344, 391, 393, 400, 403, 412, 415, 418, 419, 467n; capture of, 356-7
DESKATI (Sketch p. 78), 47, 99n, 102, 128
DHAR EL MOUGHARA (Map p. 482), 480
Diamond, British destroyer, 171
DICKSON, Sgt T. J. M., 486
DICTE, MOUNT, 279
Dido, British cruiser, 233, 291, 292

DIFFEY, Maj S. C., 61
DILL, Field Marshal Sir John, 18, 151, 209, 442; accompanies Eden on Mission to Middle East, 6; at Athens Conference, 9-11; urges withdrawal of Greek forces from Eastern Macedonia, 12; views on Greek expedition, 14n, 15, 16, 17, 193; confers with Yugoslav leaders, 26, 27; and invasion of Syria, 321, 327, proposes employment of mobile columns from Iraq, 391
Dilwarra, British transport, 173n, 174
DILWORTH, WO2 C. E. J., 364
DIMAS (Sketch p. 509), 510, 535
DISCIPLINE, A.I.F., in Greece, 129-30, 151, 165, 171-2, 172-3, 174; in Crete, 212, 297, 306-7; in Syria, 545-7
DISHER, Brig H. C., 36n
DITTMER, Brig G., 224, 236, 251, 252n
DJEDEIDE, 535
DJERABLOUS (Sketch p. 478), 479
DJEZIREH, 535n
DJOURNIEH, 521
DNIEPER RIVER, 530
DODD, Maj R. W. P., 446
DODECANESE ISLANDS, 4, 16, 31, 186, 197, 293, 316, 318, 520, 533-4
DOIRAN (Map p. 34), 26, 27, 29, 34, 41, 42
DOIRAN, LAKE, 27, 40
DOIRAN-NESTOS LINE (Sketch p. 4), 4, 27; Papagos urges manning of, 25, 34; German attack on, 39-40
DOLIKHE (Sketch p. 55), 47
DOMENIKON (Sketch p. 124), 99n, 123
DOMINIONS, 530, 558; consultation with Great Britain, 14-15, 16-21, 132-3, 194, 328-9; attitude to Greek campaign, 191, 192; system of cooperation between, 552-5
DOMOKOS (Sketch p. 82), 97, 99, 105, 106, 129, 138n; rearguard at, 82, 90, 111, 134, 135, 136-7
DONALDSON, Pte A. T., 269
DONOGHUE, Lt T. J., 428, 431
DOSSETOR, Sgt O. R. C., 456
DOUGHERTY, Maj-Gen I. N., 48, 62, 63, 67, 88, 287, 289, 556n
DOUGHERTY, Sgt R. H., 459n
DOUGLAS, Pte C. H., 464
DOUGLAS, Sgt E. F. R., 488
DOUMMAR (Sketch p. 416), 428, 429
DOWER, Pte H. A., 456
DOWSETT, L-Cpl A. E., 268
DRAMA (Sketch p. 45), 52
DRAVE RIVER (Sketch p. 51), 50, 51, 71
DREDGE, Lt R. A., 347
DRUSE LEGION, 467n
DUFF, Brig C. S. J., 101, 102
DUNCAN, Lt-Col A., 250, 251
DUNCAN, Lt W. J., 363
DUNCAN, Capt W. N., 60
DUNDAS, Lt K. I., 273
DUNGEY, Sgt P. B., 488
DUNKIRK, 173
DUNLOP, Lt-Col E. E., 164n
DUNLOP, Maj J. W., 118
DUNN, Cpl B., 448
DUNN, Pte R. K., 120
DUNZ, Capt, 285
DURRAZO (Sketch p. 39), 23
DUSTING, Cpl H. W., 361, 362n
DWYER, Lt H. G., 373, 404
DYKE, Brig L. G. H., 218n

EAST AFRICA, 320, 554
EAST BEACH (Map p. 282), 281
EAST HILL (Map p. 282), 283, 284, 286, 287, 292
EAST WADI (Map p. 282), 281, 283, 284, 285, 286
EATHER, Maj-Gen K. W., 555
EDEN, Rt Hon A., 17, 18, 132, 321; warns of German threat to Balkans, 2; visits Middle East, 6; at Athens conferences, 9, 10n, 11n, 12; consults Turkish leaders, 11; urges Yugoslavia to join Allies, 13, 26; advocates expedition to Greece, 16
EDESSA (Map p. 34; Sketch p. 4), 3, 10, 27, 29, 30, 33, 35, 36, 42, 43, 70, 94
EDGAR, Brig C. R. V., 138, 336n
EDMONDS, Brig-Gen Sir James, 557n, 558n
EDWARDS, Lt A. D., 135
EDWARDS, Lt R. A., 377, 382
EGGER, Lt, 285

INDEX

EGYPT, 2, 3, 7, 15, 22, 30, 32, 71, 125n, 133, 151, 191, 194, 197, 200, 205, 206, 207, 208, 211 *et seq*, 232, 261n, 278, 287, 292, 293, 302, 307, 308, 309, 311, 312, 316n, 317, 322, 358, 391, 392, 442, 537, 541, 543, 557n, 559, 561
EKHINOS (Sketch p. 45), 39, 40, 52
ELAFONSIS ISLANDS, 312
ELASSON (Map p. 34; Sketch p. 124), 35, 36, 40, 44, 67n, 82, 83, 84, 99, 105, 109, 113, 128, 143, 158, 232n; rearguard at, 99n, 101-2, 122, 123-4
ELATIA (Map p. 106; Sketch p. 96), 97
ELEUSIS (Sketch p. 145), 150, 151, 164-5, 169, 228
ELEVTHEROKHORION (Map p. 38), 102
ELIA (Sketch p. 127), 108
ELLIOTT, Brig C. M. L., 34n, 548
ELPHICK, Lt W. T., 363
ELVY, Pte C. J., 268
EMBREY, Lt-Col F. J., 156, 157, 158, 263, 265, 267, 312-13
EMPIRE AIR TRAINING SCHEME, 542
ENGERT, Cornelius van H., 512
ENIPEUS RIVER (Sketch p. 136), 128
Enterprise, British cruiser, 532
EPIRUS, 14, 76, 131, 132, 140, 142, 156, 158, 183, 195; Greek surrender in, 133, 142
EQUIPMENT, problems of supply between Allies, 77; *Aust*, 107, 548-9, use of captured French equipment, 517, 518; *British*, destruction in Greece, 144-5, 170, 172, 173, compared to German, 196; shortages in Crete, 205-6, 210, 212, 215, 218, 220, 256n, 280n; *French*, supply to Iraq, 330, 331, 332; *Greek*, 5, 33, 41, 42, 54, 81, 207, 218
ERBIL (Sketch p. 198), 201
ERITHRAI (Sketch p. 175), 155, 158; covering force at, 144, 148, 162, 168, 169, 232n
ER RAMA, 345, 398, 400, 401
EUBOEA ISLAND (Map p. 34), 140, 141, 142, 148, 186, 189, 190
EUPHRATES RIVER (Map p. 339; Sketch p. 199), 200, 201, 440, 441, 479-80, 515, 531n, 534, 535
EUROPE, 552, 554, 558
EVANGELISMOS (Map p. 106; Sketch p. 127), 107, 115, 117, 118, 122, 127
EVANS, Capt A., 506
EVANS, WO2 F. P., 116
EVANS, Lt-Col F. R., 399
EVERETT, Pte W. H., 438
EVETTS, Lt-Gen J. F., 254, 298, 414, 417, 418-19, 420, 429, 430, 431, 439, 467, 477, 509, 510, 514
EZRAA (Sketches pp. 334, 395), 338, 344, 357, 358, 394, 400, 403, 407, 412

FADDEN, Rt Hon Sir Arthur, 15, 16, 19, 25; becomes Prime Minister, 542
FAIRBAIRN, Lt T. C., 86
FALCONER, Brig A. S., 217
FALLA, Capt J. St H., 88, 289
FALLUJA (Sketch p. 199), 201
FAR EAST, 544n; reinforcement of, 549-50, 562
FARMER, Capt J. G., 348
FARNINGTON, Maj C. J., 34n
FARQUHAR, Maj E. A., 505
FARRAN, Maj R. A., 246
FASCISM, 323
FATIGUE, in Syria, 453, 459, 529
FAULKNER, Col N. W., 341n
FAWCETT, Lt-Col G. H., 379
FELTHAM, Cpl E. J. A., 369-70
FENTON, Lt-Col A. G., 525, 561
FERDISSE (Sketch p. 396), 352, 371-3, 395, 396, 404
FERGUSON, Capt J. B., 353
FERGUSON, Lt J. L. D., 477n
FERGUSON, Cpl W. C., 455
FERGUSSON, B., 287n, 428n
FESTEQANIYE, EL (Map p. 482), 470
FIENNES, Lt-Col Sir Ranulph, 515, 520
Fiji, British cruiser, 215, 238, 318
FINLAY, Col C. H., 484
FIQ (Sketch p. 334), 338, 356
FITCHETT, Ian, 560
FITZHARDINGE, Capt J. B., 310
FITZSIMONS, Pte D. W., 268
Fiume, Italian cruiser, 23
Flamingo, British sloop, 173n
FLASHMAN, Capt J. A. F., 121
FLEET AIR ARM; see BRITISH NAVY
FLEMING, Lt-Col A. P., 61

FLINT, Maj C. F., 387
FLORENCE, Capt J. M., 370-1
FLORINA (Maps pp. 34, 66), 26, 27, 29, 34, 35, 36, 42, 43, 46, 54, 56, 67n, 70, 72, 76, 77, 81, 94, 104, 158
FLYNN, WO2 E. P., 422n
FORBES, Maj A. M., 297, 299, 305
FORD, Maj F. J. V., 261, 263, 273, 310
Formidable, British aircraft carrier, 23, 227
FORRESTER, Lt-Col M., 224, 237
FORSTER, Major, 255
FORTY-SECOND STREET; *see* MALEME-SUDA
FOUR A CHAUX (Map p. 482), 480
FOWLER, Pte E., 362
FRANCE, 8, 11, 45, 49, 52, 57n, 132, 497, 515, 520, 530, 531, 545, 552, 558n, 562; relations with Axis powers, 322, 324-5, 329-32, with Arabs, 322-3; rule in Syria, 323-4; relations with Britain, 324-5, 326, 328, 332; Free French movement, 321, 519n, 524-5, 528; and cease-fire in Syria, 511-13
FRANGOKASTELLI (Sketch p. 203), 304
FRASER, Pte J. R., 268
FRASER, Lt-Col K. W., 100
FRASER, Rt Hon P., 20, 210, 215, 301, 303n, 541
FREE FRENCH DIVISION, proposed employment in Syria, 321-2, 326, 327, earmarked for invasion, 329; strength and composition, 334-5, 338n, 359, 526, role, 338, 344; in Syria, 430, 442, 465-6, 478, 509, 510, 512, 525, 528, advance to Damascus, 357, 373-4, 375, 390-1, 393, 394, 403, 407, 414, 415, 417, 418, 420, 421, 427; and administration of Acre Convention, 515-16, 517, 518, 535; relations with A.I.F., 468-9, 517-19; disbandment, 519; *see also* FRENCH ARMY
FRENCH AIR FORCE, 331, 391; strength in Syria, 335, attacks on British Navy, 350, 413, on troops, 379n, 388, 421n, 479-80, 528; at Palmyra, 441, 466
FRENCH ARMY, in Syria, 328, 329, 524, 527; strength and dispositions, 325-6, 333-4, 358, 374, 390, at Damascus, 393, 426-7, 429, objectives of counter-attack, 412, at Jebel Mazar, 439-40, 510, at Nebek, 466, at Damour, 474-80, surrender of, 511; Free French recruitment, 515-19; arrest of officers, 520-1; casualties, 526; *see also* FREE FRENCH DIVISION
—REGIMENTS: *22nd Algerian*, 358, 364, 374, 412, 451; *29th Algerian*, 412, 429, 451, 497, 510; *6th Chasseurs d'Afrique*, 358, 374; *7th Chasseurs d'Afrique*, 358, 374, 412, 426, 510; *24th Colonial*, 358, 374, 412, 426, 429, 439, 510; *6th Foreign Legion*, 338, 358, 374, 412, 426, 440, 441, 446, 448, 451, 452, 458n, 471, 477, 497, 510, 529; *1st Moroccan Spahis*, 348, 349, 358, 412, 429, 439, 510; *17th Senegalese*, 358, 412, 429, 439, 452, 464, 510; *16th Tunisian*, 358, 412, 451, 466n
FRENCH NAVY, 513n; in Syrian campaign, 363, 413
FREYBERG, Lt-Gen Lord, 40, 69, 82, 95, 97n, 98-9, 101, 109, 139, 141, 143, 148, 150n, 154, 155, 162, 167, 177, 203n, 212, 221, 225, 231, 232, 234, 237, 242, 243, 244, 249, 250, 251, 253, 260, 263, 265, 266, 267, 271, 272, 278, 290, 293, 295, 527; consultation with Wavell before Greek expedition, 17, 18-19, 20; seniority, 21, 554; reconnoitres Vermion-Olympus line, 33-5; and Anzac Corps proposals, 70n, 341, 539, 541, 544; at Pinios, 117, 119; during air attacks, 129, 135; orders units to retain all fighting equipment until embarkation, 145; disregards order to embark from Greece, 152; takes command in Peloponnese, 163, 168; embarks, 179; takes command in Crete, 208-9, 317, staff, 210-11, disposes Creforce, 213, 220; and Greek Government, 214-15; cables Creforce requirements, 215-16; cables reports on fighting to Wavell, 227, 241, 247-8, 254; embarks, 300-2
FRIENDS AMBULANCE UNIT, 174n
FROWEN, Brig J. H., 210

GALATAS (Map p. 218; Sketch p. 245), dispositions at, 218; operations round, 221, 224-6, 230, 231, 237, 243, 244, 245-7, 254
GALILEE, SEA OF (Sketch p. 357), 467n
GALL, Capt J. M., 422, 426
GALLASH, Capt F. E., 265n
GALLIPOLI, 69, 70n, 188; compared to Syria, 460
GALLOWAY, Lt-Gen A., 22, 35, 46, 79, 204, assumes command at Merdjayoun, 451
GAMBIER-PARRY, Maj-Gen M. D., 204
GAMBLE, Col F. B., 341n

574 INDEX

GAMBLING, in A.I.F., 547n
GARDIKAKI see OITI
GARDINER, Pte L. N., 68n
GARDNER, Capt L. G., 390
GARNIER, General, 521n
GARRETT, Brig A. R., 34n, 79, 91, 92
GARRETT, Maj R., 238, 308
GATELY, Capt J. C., 59
GAUNT, Maj D. C., 363
GAVDHOS ISLAND (Sketch p. 203), 309
GAYDHAPOULA ISLAND, 308
GAZA, 188, 548n
GEDDES, Lt R. G., 471, 472, 483
GENEVA CONVENTION, 215, 219n, 225n
GENIN, Colonel, 394, 407
GENTRY, Maj-Gen W. G., 208
GEORGE, King of Greece, 5, 13, 112, 131, 150, 153, 212, 214-15, 226
GEORGIOUPOLIS (Sketches pp. 203, 296), 218, 226, 232, 234, 235, 254, 296
GERANIA (Map p. 38), 35, 36, 44
GERICKE, Captain, 240
GERMAN AIR FORCE, 4, 16, 240, 319, 327, 531; strength available for Greek campaign, 17-18, 37; attacks Piraeus, 40-1, 161; ordered to destroy Belgrade, 48; in Greece, 74, 80, 81, 83, 86, 90, 105, 115, 119, 120, 123, 125, 128, 129, 132, 133, 134, 135-6, 148, 149-50, 156, 162, 166, 176, attacks on shipping, 164, 171, 174, fails to exploit success, 130, tactical value, 195-6, 547n; in Iraq, 201, 332; in Crete, 242, 244, 265-6, 280-1, 292, deception of, 264, 283-4; strength in Mediterranean, 320; and use of Syrian airfields, 322, 329, 330, 331; role in war, 538
—FOURTH AIR FLEET, 227, 316
—CORPS: *VIII Air*, 227-8; in Crete, 233, 284, 285; *XI Air*, 219, 227-8; in Greece, 239, 284, 285, 292, 293
—DIVISIONS: *7th Air*, composition, 228; in Crete, 229, 292, losses, 316; *22 Airborne*, 219; composition, 228-9
—GROUPS: *Centre*, 228, 229; *East*, 228, 229; *West*, 228-9
—REGIMENTS, 56, 139, 142, 197; at Corinth, 165-7, 179, numbering of companies, 276n. *1st Assault*, composition, 228; in Crete, 229, 230, 233, 244, 247, 254; *1 Parachute*, in Crete, 284-6, 292-3; *2nd Parachute*, at Corinth, 166-7, in Crete, 229, 233, 243, 275, 276, 277, 284-6; *3rd Parachute*, in Crete, 229, 230, 240, 244, 254, 255, 276
GERMAN ARMY, 1, 3, 5, 10, 11, 14n, 188, 191, 195, 330, 331, 345; strength in Balkans, 2, 27, 37, 184, available for Greek campaign, 6, 17, 27-8, 49-50, 94, 184, 192; enters Bulgaria, 12, 13; takes offensive in Libya, 37, 197, 523; organisation of S.S. formations, 57n; time-table for invasion of Russia, 192-3; invades Russia, 441, 530, 549
—ARMIES: *Second*, composition of, 49-50; in Yugoslavia, 51-2, 71, 184; *Twelfth*, 39, 52n, composition, 48-50, in Greece, 94, 192, losses, 182
—GROUPS: *First Armoured*, 49, 51, 70
—CORPS: *XI Armoured*, 49n; *XIV Armd*, 49n; *XVIII Mountain*, 49, 50, 51, 52, 94; *XXX Infantry*, 50, 51, 52; *40 Motorised*, 50, 51, 52; in Greece, 70, 94, 142; *41 Motorised*, 49, 50, 52; *46 Armoured*, 49, 50, 71; *49 Alpine*, 49, 50; *51 Infantry*, 49, 50
—DIVISIONS, ARMOURED: *2nd*, 50; in Greece, 70, 94, 126, 127, 128, 142, 143, 158, 184; *5th*, 49, 70; in Greece, 94, 126, 128, 142, 143, 158, 180, 183-4; *8th*, 49, 71, 94; *9th*, 50, 52; in Greece, 70, 71, 93, 94, 126, 128, 143, 184; *11th*, 49, 94; *14th*, 49, 71, 94; *16th*, 50, 71
—DIVISIONS, INFANTRY: *22nd*, 227n; *46th*, 50, 184; *50th*, 50, 52, 184; *72nd*, 50, in Greece, 45, 52, 158, 184; *73rd*, 50; in Greece, 70, 94, 126, 183, 184; *76th*, 50, 184; *79th*, 49; *101st*, 49; *132nd*, 49; *164th*, 50, in Greece, 52, 184; *183rd*, 49; *198th*, 49, 184; *294th*, 49; "Graf Strachwitz" (Bulgarian), 49
—DIVISIONS, MOTORISED: *16th*, 49; *60th*, 49; S.S. Leibstandarte "Adolf Hitler", 50, 52; in Greece 57, 67n, 70, 71, 93, 126, 133, 142, 183, 184; S.S. "Reich", 49
—DIVISIONS, MOUNTAIN: *1st*, 49; *4th*, 49; *5th*, 50, 52; in Greece, 94, 126, 142, 143, 184; in Crete, 228, 233, 240, 255, 264, 292, 317n; *6th*, 50; in Greece, 52, 70, 79, 126, 142, 143, 158, 184, 228, 255
—REGIMENTS, ARMOURED: *3rd*, 126; *31st*, 277, 33rd, 71

GERMAN ARMY—continued
—REGIMENTS, INFANTRY: *11th*, 93; *125th*, 50, 52; "Grossdeutschland", 49; "Hermann Goering", 49
—REGIMENTS, MOUNTAIN: *85th*, in Crete, 239, 240n, 243, 246, 255, 297; *100th*, in Crete, 233-4, 239, 240, 243, 244, 247, 254, 255, 297, 307; *131st*, 127; *141st*, in Greece, 158-9; in Crete, 254, 255, 297; *143rd*, 126, 127
—UNITS: *55th Motor Battalion*, 159; *95th Engineer Battalion*, 240; *112th Reconnaissance Unit*, 126, 127
—see also GERMAN AIR FORCE
GERMANY, 1, 15, 16, 25, 49, 111, 182, 189, 197, 219n, 497, 518, 528, 562; and Greece, 2, 3, 5, 6, 9, 14, 133n; plans invasion of Russia, 6, 189, 441, campaign in, 523, 534, 538; relations with Turkey, 11, 327n, 534, 544, with Yugoslavia, 12, 24-5; and revolt in Iraq, 198, 199, 201-2; Middle East strategy, 201, 530, 531, 533-4; relations with French, 323-5, 329-30, 332; influence in Syria, 326, 327, 328, 331, 435; and Persia, 532
GIBBINS, Capt G. W., 118
GIBSON, Lt-Col J. T., 251
GIDLEY KING, Lt G. B., 434, 436
GILES, Capt A. V., 387
GILHOOLEY, Lt G. J. E., 399
GILL, G. H., 453n
GILMOUR, Maj P. R., 110
GILMOUR-WALSH, Lt A. H., 262
GITHION (Sketch p. 145), 163
GIURGIU (Sketch p. 4), 49
GLASGOW, Capt D., 501
GLASGOW, Lt-Col D. D., 366, 367
GLASGOW, Capt G., 501, 502
Glenearn, British transport, 161, 170
Glengyle, British transport, 160, 170, 174, 215, 298, 299, 335, 360
Glenroy, British transport, 238, 239, 243, 251n
Gloucester, British cruiser, 23, 31, 215; loss of, 238, 318
GLUBB, Lt-Gen J. B., 324, 338, 466
GLYPHADA (Sketch p. 175), 141
GODFROY, Vice-Admiral R. E., 513
GOERING, Field Marshal Hermann, 227
GONNOS (Map p. 106; Sketch p. 96), 99, 106, 107, 108, 113, 122, 126
GOOCH, Col Sir Robert, 441
GOOCH, Brig T. N., 153
GOODWIN, Capt H. K. H., 304, 305, 307n
GOOK, Capt W. W., 267, 268, 269
GORDON, Sgt J. H., VC, 508
GORDON, Maj R. K., 165
GORDON, Brig R. R., 406, 407, 420, 427, 428
GORMAN, Brig E., 558n, 559
GOSLETT, Lt-Col D. L. B., 97
GOURAND, FORT (Sketch p. 421), 421, 422, 426
GOWLING, Capt H. R., 346, 347
GOYBET, FORT (Sketch p. 421), 421, 422, 424-9
GRACE, Lt-Col C. H., 341n, 521n
GRAFFIN, Pte A. B., 362
GRAFFIN, Pte F., 260n
GRANT, Lt-Col J. L., 60
GRANT, Lt J. L., 483
GRAVIA (Sketch p. 147), 138, 140, 156, 157, 158, 159
GRAY, Capt A. H., 362, 487
GRAY, Capt A. W., 173, 180
GRAY, Brig J. R., 86, 244
GRAYSON, L-Sgt G. N., 444
GRAZ, 49, 51
GREATWOOD, Lt-Col H. E. G., 417
GREECE, 4, 18, 22, 27, 34, 197, 204, 205, 207, 208, 210, 211, 212, 215, 217, 227, 228, 232n, 234, 235, 236n, 275n, 279, 284, 285, 300, 306, 317, 320, 321, 335, 340, 419, 439n, 470, 497, 523, 526n, 527, 529, 530, 537, 539, 540, 544, 547n, 552, 554, 555, 561n; invokes British support, 1, British aid to, 3, 7, 8, 9-10, 11, 191-2, British Mission to, 12-14; German threat to, 2, 5, 14, 16; affirms decision to resist German attack, 5-6; and Yugoslavia, 26; communications system, 29-30, 35; campaign in, 39-196, embarkation planning, 20-21, 28, 81, 83, 105, 112-13, 131-3, 143-5, precipitate evacuation of staffs, 151-2, 195, numbers embarked, 181n; escapes from, 67n, 122n, 185-90, 312n, 313-15, 336n
GREEK AIR FORCE, 302
GREEK ARMY, 89, 90-1, 93, 94, 95, 102, 104, 105, 110, 132, 143, 517n; in Albania, 1-2, 5, 25, 41, 112, 192, supply of, 29-30, 35, 40; cooperation with Yugoslav

INDEX 575

GREEK ARMY—*continued*
Army, 3, 40; strength and dispositions, 10-11, 13, 28; British estimates of, 17, 33-4, 60n, 78, 131; equipment, 34, 42, 53, 54; difficulties of cooperation with, 41-2, 66, 77-9, 81, 194-5; in eastern Macedonia, 45-6, 52; effect of defeats on, 111-12, 131; surrenders in Epirus, 133, 142, 195; capitulates to Germans, 153; in Crete, 205, 206, 227, 247, 254, 279, 283, 284, 285, 287, 291, 293, 304; strength, 203, 207, 212-13, 214, 219, 241n, organisation of, 212-13, 224n, at Retimo, 263-4, 265, 267, 269, 277, strength and equipment, 256n
—ARMIES: *Central Macedonian*, 36, 44, 46, 58, 65, 72, 76, 78, 81, 90, 92; *Eastern Macedonian*, 10, 39-40, 42, 45; *Epirus*, 40, 54, 66, 77, 79, 81, 83, 92, 111-12, 131, 133, 142; *Western Macedonian*, 40, 43, 66, 76, 77, 79, 80, 83, 90n, 91, 93
—CORPS: *III*, 58, 92
—DIVISIONS: *Cavalry*, 43, 46, 48, 54, 58, 65, 66, 78, 80, 92. *Infantry:* 5th (Cretan), 203, 212; 7th, 5n, 10, 13, 39, 40; 9th, 80, 83, 92; 10th, 80, 83, 92; 11th, 54, 83; 12th, 5n, 10, 13, 27, 33, 34n, 36, 43, 44, 45, 46, 54, 65, 66, 68, 77, 78, 80, 92; 13th, 43, 80, 83, 92; 14th, 5n, 10, 13, 39, 40; 18th, 5n, 10, 13, 39, 40; 19th, 5n, 13, 33, 34, 36, 40, 41, 42; 20th, 5n, 13, 33, 34n, 36, 44, 46, 47, 57, 58, 65, 66, 77, 78, 80, 83, 92
—BRIGADES: *21 Greek*, 43, 48, 65, 66; *Dodecanese Regiment*, 47, 54, 58, 60, 66, 71; *Evros*, 39; *Nestos*, 39-40, 46n
—BATTALIONS: *1st*, 218, 219, 240; *2nd*, 219, 226, 238, 242; *3rd Recruit*, 280n; *4th*, 257, 258, 260, 272; *6th*, 217, 218, 224; *7th Recruit*, 280n; *8th*, 218, 224, 225, 244, 246, *Reserve Officers' College Bn*, 149
GREEK GOVERNMENT, suggests evacuation of Lustre Force, 131, 143; Venizelist party, 131-2; weaknesses of, 191-2, 203, 213; transferred to Crete, 150, 153, 207, 214-15, evacuated to Egypt, 226; under German occupation, 142n
GREEK NAVY, 312
GREEKS, THE, 14, 17, 31, 67n, 133n, 139, 155, 164, 176, 178, 185, 186-7, 189, 308, 312, 315
GREEN, Lt-Col C. H., 31n, 186, 190
GREEN, Pte F. W. J., 268
GREEN, Pte J. B., 308
GREEN HILL (Map p. 410), 389
GREENWAY, Capt G. J., 266, 312n
GREIFFENBERG, Maj-Gen von, 49n, 71, 142
GREVENA (Map p. 34; Sketches pp. 55, 78), 47, 58, 69, 76, 77, 79, 80, 81, 83, 87, 90, 91, 92, 93, 95, 102, 103, 110, 126, 128, 158, 184
Greyhound, British destroyer, 239, 318
GRIEVE, Capt B. R., 110, 111, 171
Griffin, British destroyer, 170n, 179
Grimsby, British sloop, 170n
GROUNDWATER, Pte M., 406, 455
GROVES, Lt M. D., 355, 370
GUEDENEY, FORT (Sketch p. 421), 421
Guepard, French destroyer, 363
GUINN, Lt-Col H. G., 137, 138
GULLETT, Hon Sir Henry, 548n, 559
GURNES (Sketch p. 288), 284, 285, 292, 293

HABBANIYA (Sketch p. 199), Iraqi attack on, 200-201
HABBOUCH (Sketch p, 334), 352
HABIL, JEBEL (Sketch p. 509), 510
HACKETT, Brig J. W., 407
HADDY, Lt A. C., 361, 362n
HADWELL, Pte J. M., 314
HAIFA (Map p. 339), 67n, 189, 198, 200, 202, 336, 419, 440, 467n
HAIG, Lt-Cdr R. A., 254, 271, 273
HAINING, Gen Sir Robert, 321n
HALDER, General Franz, 202
HALFAYA PASS, 197
HALIFAX, Rt Hon Earl, 321n
HALL, Maj K. S., 459
HALLIDAY, Capt G. H., 235
HAMA (Sketch p. 516), 516
HAMADAN (Sketch p. 533), 533
HAMILTON, Maj H. M., 449, 450
HAMMER, Brig H. H., 117, 153
HAMMON, Capt J. D. C., 390
HAMRA, EL (Map p. 482), 484
HANITA (Sketch p. 348), 346
HANN, L-Sgt J. E., 450
HANSEN, Major, 331

HANSEN, Pte I., 308, 309
HARAM, EL (Sketch p. 462), 461, 462, 470, 472, 482
HARANT, Captain, 426-7
HARET JENDAL (Sketches pp. 504, 506), 507
HARGEST, Brig J., 99, 100, 213, 224, 232, 235, 236, 237, 238, 249, 250, 253, 296, 299, 301, 302, 304
HARKNESS, Capt J. B., 186
HARLEY, Lt K. N., 473
HARLOCK, Brig H. G. F., 173, 178, 180, 181
HARPER, Maj C. H. D., 351
HARPER, Lt T., 385, 487
HART, Capt Liddell, 227n
HARTMANN, General, 50, 51, 52
HASBANI RIVER (Sketch p. 353), 353
HASBAYA (Map p. 386; Sketch p. 343), 343, 344, 352, 372, 395, 396, 412, 449
HASROUT (Sketches pp. 462, 475), 461, 464, 475, 476
HASSANIYE (Sketch p. 377), 378, 382
HASSETCHE (Sketch p. 478), 479
Hasty, British destroyer, 164, 180
HAURAN (Sketch p. 334), 338, 377
Havock, British destroyer, 164, 177, 179, 181
HAWAII, 549
HAYES, Maj P. B., 138
HEAGNEY, Maj B. S., 274
HEARMAN. Maj J. M., 361, 362, 473, 485, 487, 488
HEBBARIYE (Map p. 386; Sketch p. 396), 371, 373 395, 396, 403
HEIDRICH, Colonel, 230, 233, 240, 254
HEILMANN, Major, 242, 243
HEJAZ RAILWAY, 344
HELE, Capt I. H. T., 559
Hellas, Greek yacht, 161
HELLENIC STATE RAILWAYS, 29
HELY, Brig A. F., 243n, 250
HENDERSON, Cpl G. F., 346
HENDERSON, L-Sgt N. F., 447
HENDRY, Lt-Col J. G., 108, 113, 114, 116, 119, 120, 139
HENRY, Capt R. L., 364n, 379n, 483n
HERAKLION (Map p. 282; Sketches pp. 203, 208), 186, 203, 205, 208, 211, 212, 215, 220, 232-3, 238, 239, 241, 247, 255, 258, 263, 273, 296, 298, 310, 312; population, 202, 279; garrison, 213, 214, 279, 280n, dispositions and strength, 218-19, reinforcement of, 243, 244, 287, 288; airfield at, 227. 229, 279, 280; German plan for capture, 228-9; defence of, 281-94; German account, 284-6, 292-3
Hereward, British destroyer, 173n, 174, 175, 180, 292, 318
HERINGTON, J., 391n
Hermes, British aircraft carrier, 532
HERMON, MOUNT, 333, 374, 390, 393, 395, 421, 432, 443, 477
Hero, British destroyer, 172, 173n, 174, 175, 180, 181, 226n, 251n
HERODOTUS, 95n, 99n
HERRING, Lt-Gen Sir Edmund, 36n, 44, 146; becomes G.O.C., 6th Division, 544
HERRON, Lt A. A., 267
HEUGH, Maj H., 74
HEYWOOD, Maj-Gen T. G. G., 12, 132n
HICKEY, Pte J. H., 487
HICKS, Cpl L. R., 355
HICKSON, Sgt D. R., 425
HIDDINS, Cpl A. J., 118
HIJJANE (Sketch p. 393), 412
HILDEBRANDT, Lt C. W., 434, 436, 437, 438
HILL, WO2, 122n
HILL "A" (Map p. 258), 256, 257, 259-60, 261, 263, 265, 266, 267, 275, 276
HILL "B" (Map p. 258), 256, 257, 258, 260, 263, 266, 272
HILL "C" (Map p. 258), 256
HILL "D" (Map p. 258), 256, 257, 261, 267, 273
HILL 104 (Map p. 482), 494
HILL 107 (Map p. 218), 223, 230, 233, 236
HILL 127 (Sketch p. 381), 384
HILL 143 (Map p. 482), 470
HILL 168 (Map p. 482), 485
HILL 182, *see* A.M.E.S. RIDGE
HILL 225 (Map p. 482), 494, 495
HILL 230 (Sketch p. 500), 500
HILL 250 (Map p. 482), 483
HILL 296, *see* APEX HILL
HILL 335 (Map p. 482), 493
HILL 394 (Map p. 482), 470, 471, 483, 491, 492n

576   INDEX

HILL 498 (Map p. 482), 491, 496
HILL 512 (Map p. 482), 484, 493, 496
HILL 560 (Map p. 482), 484, 492, 496-7
HILL 567 (Map p. 482), 489, 490
HILL 569 (Map p. 482), 491, 498, 511
HILL 781 (Sketch p. 462), 464
HILL 814 (Sketch p. 462), 476
HILL 832 (Sketch p. 462), 461, 462, 475, 476
HILL 882 (Sketch p. 75), 86
HILL 892 (Sketch p. 296), 307
HILL 903 (Sketch p. 500), 503
HILL 1001 (Map p. 66), 48, 57, 62, 63
HILL 1054 (Sketch p. 504), 505, 506, 507
HILL 1066 (Map p. 410), 465
HILL 1069 (Sketch p. 506), 506
HILL 1115 (Map p. 410), 477
HILL 1199 (Map p. 410), 405
HILL 1203 (Sketch p. 506), 506
HILL 1284 (Map p. 410), 405, 453-9, 464
HILL 1332 (Map p. 410), 405, 409, 411, 453-6, 464, 465
HILL 1377 (Map p. 410), 411, 452, 454, 456, 465
HILL 1628 (Greece), 85
HILL-GRIFFITHS, Capt K., 139
HIMMLER, Heinrich, 57n
HINGSTON, W. G., 416n
HIPWELL, Pte R. J., 313n
HIPWORTH, Maj J. A., 280n
HITLER, Adolf, 1, 14, 57n, 182, 227n, 523, 524, 530; orders invasion of Greece, 6, issues directive, 48-9; relations with Yugoslavia, 24, 192; dissuaded from attacking Cyprus, 318; relations with Vichy, 324, 325, 329-30, 331; fixes date for invasion of Russia, 330
HODDINOTT, Capt F. J., 121, 432, 438
HODGE, Maj F. W., 397, 399
HOLLAND, 56, 197, 227n
HOLMES, Sgt A. R., 349
HOLT, Hon H. E., 537
HOMS (Map p. 339; Sketch p. 478), 338, 415, 428, 440, 442, 478, 509, 510, 515, 517, 519, 535
HONNER, Lt-Col R., 134n, 157, 158, 260, 264, 266, 267, 268-9, 272, 273, 274, 275, 309
Hood, British battle cruiser, 318
HOOPER, Maj G. F. R., 261, 272, 310
HOPKINS, Harry L., 8n
HOPKINS, L-Cpl N. H., see F. W. MCVICAR
HOPKINS, Maj-Gen R. N. L., 553
HOPKINSON, Maj W., 365
HORLEY, Capt D. G., 349, 350, 362, 363, 364, 365, 366, 380, 382
HORNE, Pte H. R., 308-9
HORSES, use by "Kelly Gang", 404, 447
HOSKING, Lt C. G. S., 312-13
Hotspur, British destroyer, 179, 181, 292, 305
HOUGHTON, Captain, 402, 403
HOURANI, A. H., 9
HOUSSANIYE (Sketch p. 416), 429
HOUSTON, Capt J. R., 354, 355, 390, 405, 406, 411
HOUSTON, Lt R. G., 449, 450
HOVENDENE, Lt-Col H. E., 558n
HOWARD, Lt-Col F. J., 559, 560
HOWDEN, Lt-Col W. S., 351, 378
HOWLETT, Lt L. F., 291n
HOYER, Sgt-Major, 255
HOYSTED, Sgt A. R., 431
HUGHES, Lt, 103
HUGHES, Col C. E., 186, 188
HULA, LAKE (Sketch p. 334), 337n, 343
HULL, Cordell, 330n
HULL, Capt R. D., 312n
HUMBLEY, Maj A. S., 398-9
HUNGARY, 2, 48, 50
HUNTER, Lt A., 167
HURFORD, Lt W. C., 443
HURLEY, Capt F. J. F., 560
HURLEY, Brig G. E. W., 150n
HURRELL, Capt L. T., 507, 508
HUTCHINSON, Sgt S. M., 271
HUTCHISON, Lt-Col I., 422, 424, 425, 428, 431, 432, 433, 436n, 437, 438, 439, 493, 504, 505
HUTSON, Brig H. P. W., 30n
HUTTON, Lt-Cdr P. C., 164n
Hyacinth, British sloop, 161, 179
HYLES, Capt J. H., 89

IBELES SAKI (Map p. 386; Sketch p. 367), 372, 373n, 386, 387, 395, 397, 398-9, 446, 447-9

IDA, MOUNT, 279
IERAPETRA (Sketch p. 203), 203
IKINGI MARYUT, 216
Ilex, British destroyer, 413
IMBROS ISLAND, 315
Imperial, British destroyer, 292, 318
IMPERIAL WAR GRAVES COMMISSION, 186
IMSAR (Sketch p. 367), 366, 367
IMVROS (Sketch p. 296), 297, 300, 307
INDIA, 199, 200, 215, 333, 523, 533n, 544, 551, 555
INDIAN ARMY, 180, 528; strength in Syrian campaign, 526; estimated build-up in Middle East, 541, value in, 551, 552; cooperation with British Army, 552
—DIVISIONS: 4th, 320, 341, 531; 5th, 320, 441, 531, 533n; 6th, 533n; 8th, 532; 10th, 199, 201, 440, 441, 478-80, 515, 532, 535
—BRIGADES: 2nd Armd, 532; 5th Inf, 334, 338, 342, 344; in Syria, 356-7, 373, 375, 391, 393, 403, 407, 414, 415, 416-17, 418, 419, 420-1, 424, 430, 439, 477, 529, 535; 17th Inf, 478; 20th Inf, 479; 21st Inf, 201, 479; 24th Inf, 478; 25th Inf, 201
—REGIMENTS: 3/10th Baluch, 532; 4/13th Frontier Force, 479; 2/4th Gurkha, 479; 13th Lancers, 479; 3/1st Punjab, 338n, in Syria, 356-7, 394, 403, 415, 417, 418, casualties, 430n; 4/6th Rajputana Rifles, 338n; in Syria, 356-7, 394, 403, 415, 416, casualties, 430n
INDIAN OCEAN, 198, 555
INDO-CHINA, 545
INGLIS, Maj-Gen L. M., 217, 219n, 225, 234, 235, 242, 244, 245, 246, 248, 249, 251
INGRAM, Sgt L. S., 147
INKPEN, Capt F. M. B., 380
INNSARIYE (Sketches pp. 367, 376), 367, 375
INTELLIGENCE, British, of German strength in Balkans, 37, and scale of attack in Crete, 205, 207, 208-9, 210, 213, 219, 228, 231; of Vichy strength in Syria, 325, 337-8; Joint Intelligence Committee, 207; German, in Greece, 24n, 70-1, 93; in Crete, 228, 284, 286, 293; in Syria, 330
IRAN, see PERSIA
IRAQ, 326, 327, 340, 391, 412, 414, 467, 523, 524, 531, 533n, 534, 535n, 555; British policy in, 197-8; relations with Germany, 198-9, German aid to, 201-2, 330, 331, 332, 524; campaign in, 199-201; advance into Syria from, 440, 441, 478-80; relations with Persia, 532
IRAQI ARMY, 329; strength of, 198; at Habbaniya, 199-201, 202
IRBID (Sketch p. 357), 391
IRELAND, 541
IRVINE, Cpl L. J., 188
IRWIN, Lt W., 63
ISAACHSEN, Lt-Col O. C., 366, 378, 383, 384
Isis, British destroyer, 179, 181, 413
ISKANDAROUN (Sketch p. 343), 342, 346-7, 350, 351, 360
ITALIAN AIR FORCE, 31, 201; in Albania, 5n, 37; strength in Mediterranean, 320; and use of Syrian airfields, 329, 330
ITALIAN ARMY, 14, 321n, 551, 555; in Albania, 1-2, 4, 5, 25, 27, 58; in Abyssinia, 7, 197, 531; cooperation with German Army in Balkans campaign, 50-1, 54, 70, 94, 132, 133n, 195; in Libya, 197, 530; in Crete, 293n
ITALIAN NAVY, 52, 197, 292n, 310; at Matapan, 23
ITALY, 11n, 15, 25, 48, 201, 310, 524, 533, 562; invades Greece, 1, 191; and German, 48; relations with France, 329-30; influence in Persia, 532

JABOOR, Lt-Col R. F., 218n
Jackal, British destroyer, 305
JACKSON, Pte A., 476n
JACKSON, Lt-Col D. A. C., 155, 157, 264, 265, 266, 269, 270, 271, 312
JACKSON, Lt-Col D. R., 179, 185-6, 190
JACOB, Lt, 127
JADRA (Sketch p. 462), 461
JAGER, Gnr C. H., 313n
Jaguar, British destroyer, 298
JAIS, Colonel, 159, 254, 255
JAMIESON, L-Sgt R. T., 472
JAMLIYE (Sketch p. 385), 386
JANKOVIC, General, 26-7
Janus, British destroyer, 363
JAPAN, 15, 17, 25, 549-50, 551, 552, 555, 562
JAVA, 550

INDEX

JDAIDET ARTOUZ (Sketch p. 393), 403
JEBEL DRUSE, 323, 324, 327, 333, 374, 394, 412, 467n, 510, 534
JEFFERSON, Lt M. F., 444
JEFFREY, Gp Capt P., 391
JENKINS, Capt C. H., 138n
JENNEQUIN, General, 331, 334; arrest of, 520, 521
JEREINE (Sketch p. 343), 342
JERME (Sketch p. 367), 389, 390, 401, 408, 459n
JERUSALEM. 328, 336, 340, 413, 441, 511, 519, 521, 527, 546, 548, 560; Grand Mufti of, 198, 201
JESS, Lt-Gen Sir Carl, 537
JEWS, 186, 304, 337, 346, 348
JEZZINE (Map p. 410; Sketch p. 334), 340, 385n, 393, 400, 401, 402n, 414, 446, 461, 467, 557n; advance to, 387, 388-90; French counter-attack, 404-5; operations round, 409-12, 464-5, 477, 505-10; reinforcement of, 412-13, 452-3
JISR ABOU ZEBLE (Sketch p. 353), 353
JISR BENNT JACUB (Sketch p. 334), 337n, 400, 412
JLEILIYE (Sketch p. 475), 475
JOCK COLUMNS, 536
JOHNS, Lt R. D., 385
JOHNSON, Capt A. M., 487n
JOHNSON, Lt A. T., 505
JOHNSON, Capt C. M., 121, 122, 127
JOHNSON, Pte H. C., 266
JOHNSON, Capt I., 349, 360, 361, 362
JOHNSON, Maj R. L., 375, 378
JOHNSON, Capt S. H., 222
JOHNSTON, Cpl H. H., 261
JOHNSTON, Brig W. W. S., 34n
JOHNSTONE, Cpl N. M., 281n, 292
JONES, Lt-Col J. S., 161, 162, 166, 167
JONES, Brig L. B., 356, 393, 415, 417
JORDAN RIVER (Sketch p. 357), 337n, 338, 344, 358, 400 401, 402n
JORDAN VALLEY, 342, 401, 419
JOSE, Lt R., 384
JUBB, Tpr N., 350
JUDEAN HILLS, 474
JUFFA (Sketch p. 440), 441
JULIS, 419, 424, 550
Juno, British destroyer, 233, 239, 318

KABOUN (Sketch p. 416), 426
KADEM (Sketch p. 416), 415, 427
KAFR BADDA (Sketch p. 361), 365, 366-7
KAFR CHEBAA, *see* CHEBAA
KAFR EL AOUAMID (Sketch p. 416), 429
KAFR HAMMAM, 447
KAFR HOUN (Map p. 410), 388, 389, 409, 459n
KAFR MATTA (Sketch p. 500), 496, 503, 505
KAFR MAYA (Sketch p. 462), 461, 463
KAFR MECHKI (Sketch p. 334), 344
KAFR NAFFAKH (Sketch p. 357), 356
KAFR ROUMMANE (Map p. 386), 447
KAFR SIR (Sketch p. 343), 343, 351, 366, 367
KAFR SUSS (Sketch p. 416), 426
KAFR TIBNITE (Map p. 386; Sketch p. 353), 354
KALABAKA (Map p. 34; Sketch p. 78), 76, 79, 81, 90-2, 93, 97, 99, 102-4, 109-11, 122, 125-6, 128, 133, 142, 158
Kalamara, Greek yacht, 186
KALAMATA (Sketch p. 145), 164, 168, 169, 184, 185, 188, 189; embarkations from, 152, 162, 163, 165, 171-5, total embarked, 181n; action at, 178, 179-81
KALAVRITA (Sketch p. 145), 169
KALGOORLIE, 362
KALIVES (Map p. 218), 226n, 253, 295
KALLIDROMON MOUNTAINS, 189
KALLIPEVKE (Sketch p. 124), 126
KALOTHRONION (Sketch p. 156), 155
KAMECHLIE (Sketch p. 478), 479
Kandahar, British destroyer, 170, 180, 302
Kanimbla, Australian transport, 532
KARACHI, 199
KARACOL (Map p. 482; Sketch p. 500), 502
KARASSOS, General, 46, 47, 54, 58
KARATSOS (Map p. 218; Sketch p. 245), 224, 225, 230, 246, 254
KARDITSA (Sketch p. 159), 126, 158
KARITSA (Sketch p. 187), 185
KARPERON, 102
KARYA (Sketch p. 84), 99
Kashmir, British destroyer, 239, 318

KASO STRAIT (Sketch p. 203), 227, 292
KASTANIA (Sketch p. 75), 86
KASTELLI (Sketch p. 203), 219, 227, 229, 240
KASTORIA (Sketch p. 78), 40, 76, 77, 92, 93, 94
KATEKAR, Maj H. J., 472, 494, 495
KATERINI (Map p. 34; Sketches pp. 84, 101), 33-4, 35, 36-7, 40, 44, 70, 71, 72, 84, 98, 99, 100, 102, 106, 122, 123, 184
KATO DHIO VOUNA (Sketch p. 147), 158
KATO NEVROKOP (Sketch p. 45), 39
KAWAKJI, FAWZI EL, 441, 479
KAY, Col W. E., 161
KEA ISLAND (Sketch p. 145), 170
KEIME, Colonel, 412, 429
KEITEL, Field Marshal Wilhelm, 331
KEITH, Major, 300
KELB, JEBEL EL (Sketch p. 393), 393, 394, 407, 420
KELLI (Map p. 66), 57, 71
Kelly, British destroyer, 239, 318
KELLY, Lt C. C., 355
KELLY, Maj S. J., 150n
"KELLY GANG", 404n, 447
KELSALL, Capt D. V. C., 109
Kelvin, British destroyer, 302
KENALI (Sketch p. 10), 26
KENDALL, Maj-Gen R., 153, 545
KENNEDY, Capt J., 402, 403
KENTWELL, Cpl R. N., 119
KENYA, 25n
KEPHISSIA (Sketch p. 175), 169, 182
KERASIA (Sketch p. 55), 54, 58, 75
KERATES (Sketch p. 296), 297
KERKINITIS, LAKE, 40
KERMANSHAH (Sketch p. 533), 533
KERR, Maj R. J. L., 475
KESTEVEN, Lt K. L., 287, 289
KEY, Lt-Col A. S., 65n
KEYES, Lt-Col G. C. T., VC, 360, 364
KHALDE (Map p. 482; Sketch p. 500), 480, 503
KHALKIS (Map p. 34), 141, 148
KHANAQIN (Sketch p. 533), 532
KHAN DEINOUN (Sketch p. 374), 373-4, 418, 419
KHAN SAADA (Sketch p. 377), 377, 378
KHARAT, MOUNT (Map p. 410), 453, 455, 456, 458, 459, 460, 464, 474, 477
KHARKOV, 549
Khedive Ismail, Egyptian transport, 174
KHEIBE (Map p. 386), 373, 448-9
KHEURBET EL BIAR (Map p. 482), 480, 493, 497
KHIAM (Map p. 386; Sketches pp. 343, 396), 344, 352, 353-4, 358, 368, 370, 371, 373n, 387, 395, 397, 399, 400, 404, 412, 447, 449
KHIRBE (Map p. 386; Sketch p. 343), 354-6, 358, 368, 370-1, 386, 408n, 412
KHOUDESION (Sketch p. 288), 291
KHYBER PASS, 333
KIELY, Capt V. A., 259
KIFISOKHORI (Sketch p. 147), 125n
KILKIS (Sketch p. 45), 42
KILLALEA, Sgt H., 136n
KILLEARN, Rt Hon Lord, 321, 358
KILLEN, Tpr T. D., 377
KILLEY, Capt G. H., 263
Kimberley, British destroyer, 176, 180, 181, 312, 350
KING, Capt E. H., 118, 186
KING, Admiral E. L. S., 238, 302, 305, 335, 363
KING, Maj-Gen R., 92, 125, 149, 158, 164, 492, 493, 499, 502, 503, 504
Kingston, British destroyer, 170, 176, 180
KINGSTONE, Brig J. J., 440, 441
Kipling, British destroyer, 239
KIPPENBERGER, Maj-Gen Sir Howard, 109, 122, 123, 213, 217, 224, 225, 226, 237, 245-6, 248, 251, 252n, 536n
KIRIANNA (Map p. 258), 256
KIRK, Capt V. D., 236
KIRKBRIDE, Sir Alec, 324
KIRKUK (Sketches pp. 198, 533), 199, 440, 532
KISAMOS BAY (Sketch p. 203), 227, 229
KISWE (Sketches pp. 334, 374), 338, 358, 374, 390-1, 393-4, 402, 403, 412, 418, 427, 429
KITHERA ISLAND (Sketch p. 145), 179, 181n
KLADHISOS CREEK (Map p. 218), 251
KLEIDI (Maps pp. 34, 66), 46, 61, 65, 71
KLEIST, Field Marshal Ewald von, 49, 50, 51, 70, 71
KLISOURA PASS (Map p. 34; Sketch p. 55), 43, 65, 66, 71, 76, 77, 78, 80, 83, 92, 93

578　　　　　　　　　　INDEX

KNIMIS, CAPE (Sketch p. 147), 149, 155
KNOSSOS (Map p. 282; Sketch p. 288), 279, 284, 288, 289, 290, 291, 293
KNOX, Maj D. W. R., 153
KOKKINIA (Sketch p. 175), 182
KOKKINOPLOS (Sketch p. 84). 101, 109
KOMITADHES (Sketch p. 296), 297, 299, 302, 304, 305, 306, 307
KOREA, 528n
KORITZA (Map p. 34), 46, 66
KORYZIS, Alexander, 5-6, 8, 9, 12, 104, 112
KOSCIUSKO, MOUNT, 547, 548
KOTULAS, General, 36, 37, 43, 46
KOULOURI (Sketch p. 127), 127
KOZANI (Maps pp. 34, 38), 30, 34, 36, 42, 47, 55, 65, 68, 69, 70, 71, 72, 75, 76, 77, 81, 86, 87, 94
KRAKAU, Colonel, 246, 247, 254, 255
KRAMDECH (Map p. 482), 489
KRAMME, Pte J. H., 494
KRIEKOUKI, see ERITHRAI
KRISTOS (Map p 218), 249
KRIVA PALANKA (Sketch p. 4), 52
KROH, Major, 275, 276, 277
KTENI (Sketch p. 75), 76
KUEBLER, General, 49, 50
KUHN, General, 71
KUMANOVO (Sketch p. 4), 52
KUNEITRA (Map p. 339; Sketches pp. 334, 357), 337n, 338, 352, 356, 358, 391, 393, 400, 415, 418, 419, 421, 429, 439n, 467; French counter-attack, 394-5, 401-3, 412; British recapture, 406-7
KUMNIG, Pte, 255
KYFFIN, Capt P. J., 346, 347, 378, 455

LABIYE, EL (Map p. 482), 470, 471, 472, 482, 491
LABOUNA (Sketch p. 343), 342, 348
LACEY, Lt A. R., 114
LAMB, Lt-Col D. J., 107, 108, 119, 120, 121, 122, 138, 153, 419, 420, 421, 422, 423, 426
LAMIA (Map p. 34; Sketch p. 78), 29, 80, 82, 92, 93, 104, 107, 108, 111, 112, 122, 125n, 128, 129, 134, 139, 140, 142, 143, 146, 149, 158, 184, 186, 189; rearguard at, 136-8, 141
LAMPSON, Sir Miles, see KILLEARN
LANDALE, Maj W. G. A., 454, 455, 456
LANE, Cpl P. A., 67n
LANG, Lt-Col J. T., 445
LANGLANDS, Lt E. R., 460
LANGRIDGE, Capt B. D. N., 365
LAPTHORNE, Lt H. D., 355
LARGE, Brig D. T. M., 164n
LARISA (Map p. 34; Sketch p. 96), 11, 27, 29, 30, 35, 36, 40, 41, 66, 76, 79, 82, 83, 90n, 92, 94, 95, 97, 98, 99, 103, 104n, 105, 106, 107, 108, 109n, 110, 111, 114, 119, 120, 121, 122, 123, 125, 126, 127, 128, 129, 133, 134, 135, 139, 142, 143, 146, 158, 186, 188
LASCARS, 178, 180
LATAKIA (Map p. 339; Sketch p. 516), 323, 514, 534
LATHAM, Brig H. B., 181n
LAUSANNE, TREATY OF, 323
LAVA (Sketch p. 73), 86, 102
LAVAL, Pierre, 325
LAVARACK, Lt-Gen Sir John, 335, 338n, 550, 555; warned to prepare for move of 7 Div to Palestine, 326, 327; and plan for invasion of Syria, 336, 337, 340-1; warned of impending appointment to I Corps, 340, assumes command, 413-14; estimate of, 341; in Syrian campaign, 368, 370, 386, 387, 390n, 395, 403, 431, 460, 477, 515, orders to meet threat of French counter-attack, 400-1, approves Berryman's policy at Merdjayoun, 404, 446, 449, reinforces Jezzine, 412-13, proposes diversion of main effort to Damascus front, 418-19, presses Wavell for tanks, 430n, ordered to concentrate on drive to Beirut, 467-9, conduct of campaign, 526-7; relations with Free French, 468-9, 516-19; and Syrian armistice, 511-13, 514; arrest of French generals, 520-1; and Press censorship, 525; recommended as commander of "Australian Corps", 340-1, 529; experience, 554
LAWLEY, Sgt R. H., 349
LAWRENCE, T. E., 356
LAWRY Lt P. C., 267
LAYBOURNE-SMITH, Maj G., 300, 304, 305n
LAYCOCK, Maj-Gen R. E., 253
LEAGUE OF NATIONS, 323, 324

LEASK, Capt J. C., 499
LEAVE, 31-2, 559
"LEAVING", landing barge, 309
LEBANESE, THE, 325
LEBANON, THE, 202, 326, 327, 333, 337, 379, 413, 452, 478, 514, 515, 519, 521, 544, 548; history and geography of, 323-4, 333
LEBANON MOUNTAINS, 333, 343, 400, 405, 461, 467, 470, 474, 534, 548
LE BRUN, Sgt K. W., 458
Le Chevalier Paul, French destroyer, 413
LECKIE, Col D. F., 223, 236
LECOULTEUX, Colonel, 412
LEE, Lt-Col A. J., 384, 483, 484, 496, 497
LEE, Air Vice-Marshal A. S. G., 11n, 195n
LEE, Brig E. A., 34n, 35, 43, 44, 82, 90, 97, 111, 135, 136, 137, 138, 153, 161, 162, 163, 168, 177, 179
LEE, Sgt J. P., 310
LEE, Lt V., 269
LEES, Sgt J. H., 147
LEGENTILHOMME, General Paul, 338, 373, 390, 391, 393, 417, 418, 427, 468-9, 517
LEGGE, Pte A. B., 308
LEMNOS ISLAND (Sketch p. 4), 52
LEND-LEASE, 530
Le Nevez, WO2 R., 139
LENINGRAD, 530
LEPTOKARIA (Sketch p. 85), 67n, 126
LERGESSNER, Capt E. T., 243, 261n, 265, 266n, 267, 275
LESKOVIKI (Map p. 34), 54
LEVADHION (Map p. 34; Sketch p. 84), 30, 98, 100
LEVADIA (Sketch p. 147), 136n, 139, 143, 149, 151, 158
LEVANT, 70, 322, 323; German plans and policy in, 331, 523-4
LEVENTES (Sketch p. 73), 73, 74
LEWINGTON, Capt A. J. M., 355
LIAISON, 553; with Free French, 468-9, 525; with Greeks, 41-2, 66, 77-9, 81, 194-5, 205, 207; with navy, 365, 379n
LIBYA, 32, 37, 60, 107, 112, 132, 193, 321n, 388, 439n, 474, 529, 530, 536n
LILLINGSTON, Lt-Col E. G. G., 68, 161, 166, 167
LIMB, Lt T. M., 371
LIMOS, D. G., 185
LIST, Field Marshal, 48, 49, 50, 51, 70, 71, 94, 128, 142, 165, 184, 195
LISTER, Lt-Col M. D. B., 171
LITANI RIVER (Sketches pp. 343, 361), 333, 342, 343, 344, 350, 351, 352, 354, 368, 370, 375, 387, 388, 395, 401, 408, 443, 446, 447; crossing of, 360-6, 367, 374
LITANI VALLEY, 355, 393, 405, 409
LJUBLJANA (Sketch p. 51), 94
LLOYD, Maj-Gen W. L., 338n, 356, 373, 375, 391, 393, 394, 403, 407, 412, 417-18, 420-1, 422, 424, 428, 429, 430, 468; estimate of, 342, 415
LOCHHEAD, WO2 J. A., 457, 458
LOFOI (Map p. 66), 53, 57
LOGAN, Lt-Col E. P., 318
LOHR, General A., 227, 317, 318
LOMAX, Maj-Gen C. E. N., 430, 431, 432, 433, 438, 439n
LONDON, 2, 3, 7, 14 et seq, 21, 131, 192, 194, 197, 204, 207, 210n, 211, 220, 254, 320, 321, 326, 327, 328, 391, 478, 524, 525, 538, 540, 541, 555
LONGMORE, Air Chief Marshal Sir Arthur, 2-3, 8, 9, 11n, 220, 298n, 322
LONGOS (Sketch p. 147), 139, 141
LONGWORTH, Maj L. E., 364
LOUCH, Brig T. S., 134, 155
LOUTRO (Sketch p. 296), 304
LOUTSA (Sketch p. 175), 176
LOVE, Lt-Col J. P., 62n
LOVE, Lt J. T., 113, 114
LOVEGROVE, Maj E. P., 561n
LOVELL, Lt-Col D. J. H., 153
LOVELL, Col S. H., 521
LOVERIDGE, Col N. B., 36n
LOVETT, Lt H. I., 115
LOWEN, Lt-Col I. H., 79
LUCAS, Capt L., 382
LUCAS, Brig L. C., 36n, 76n, 88, 99
LUFF, Pte S. P. C., 390
LUFTWAFFE, see GERMAN AIR FORCE
LUNEBERG, 219
LUNN, Maj H. T., 234, 235, 306

INDEX

Lupo, Italian destroyer, 233
LUXTON, Lt-Col L., 150n
LUXTON, Lt-Col T., 62, 136
LYNCH, Lt-Col R. J., 245
LYON, Cpl F. G., 108
LYTTLETON, Capt Rt Hon Oliver, 516, 518, 519, 525, 531

MAAMERIYE (Sketch p. 367), 378
MAANI. JEBEL (Sketch p. 393), 391
MACARTHUR-ONSLOW, Brig D., 388, 396, 397, 399, 443
MACARTNEY, Maj R. R., 308
MACAULAY, Capt T. B., 463, 505, 506
MCCAFFREY, Lt J., 138
MCCARTY, Lt-Col J., 62, 63, 88, 89
MCCASKILL, Capt D. M., 157, 266, 267
MCCONNEL, Maj-Gen D. F., 548
MCCONNELL, L-Cpl R. D., 456
MCCULLOUGH, Capt K., 362, 364, 380
MCDERMID, Pte G. R. W., 268
MCDERMOTT, Lt J. L., see J. L. PERRY
MCDONALD, Dvr. 136n
MACDONALD, Col A. B., 342, 343, 349, 351, 360, 362, 363, 365, 380, 473, 485, 487, 488
MCDONALD, Pte C. T., 270n
MACDONALD, Capt G. G., 384
MCDONALD, Lt-Col H. H., 60, 61
MACDONALD, Capt J. E., 423, 424n
MCDONALD, Cpl R., 310
MCDONNELL, Maj A. J. L., 558n
MACDOUGAL, Lt B. H., 423, 424, 431, 498
MACDUFF, Maj A. P., 178, 180
MCEACHERN, Sgt J. C., 477n
MACEDONIA, 5, 6, 8, 10, 11, 12, 13, 24, 25, 29, 35, 45, 46, 48, 99n, 184
MACFARLANE, Maj C. W., 137, 138
MCGAVIN, Capt A. S. D. J., 465, 495
MCGEOCH, Lt B. de B., 251, 252, 277n
MCGRATH, Brig P. S., 341n
MCGREGOR, Maj W. R., 120, 422, 428, 431
MACHMOUCHE (Map p. 410), 452
MACHRHARA (Map p. 410; Sketches pp. 334, 462), 340, 405, 411, 465
MACKAY, Pte H., 498n
MACKAY, Lt-Gen Sir Iven, 206, 211, 341; in Greece, 36, 43, 46, 47, 54, 56, 58, 62, 64, 65, 66, 69-70, 72, 74, 76, 87, 98-9, 104n, 108, 109, 110, 111, 125, 134, 136, 138, 139, 140-1, 143, 145, 149, 150, 152; reconnoitres Veria Pass, 37; assumes command at Vevi, 44-5, orders withdrawal, 58-9; and Greek discipline, 60n; under air attack, 129, 135, efficacy of, 547n; embarks from Greece, 166; recalled to Australia as GOC Home Forces, 544, 549
MACKENZIE, Cpl J. R., 349n
MACKENZIE, Maj R. B., 365, 381
MCKERROW, Capt I., 258
MACKINNON, Maj A. S., 422
MACKINNON, Maj W. A., 488-9
MACKY, Lt-Col N. L., 95, 96, 97, 106, 115
MCLAREN, Pte I. A., 313n
MACLEAN, Col F. W., 150n, 171, 178
MCLENNAN, Sgt T. A. L., 458
MACMEIKAN, Capt T. K. L., 487, 502
MCNAB, Brig G. A. C., 310
MCNAUGHT, Lt-Col G. C., 217n
MCPHEE, Lt-Col D. R., 375, 376
MCPHERSON, Lt K. J., 118
MCPHERSON, Maj R. E., 156
MACPHERSON, Lt W. N., 383, 384, 483
MCQUARRIE, Pte D. N., 312
MACQUEEN, Cpl A. A., 114
MCROBBIE, Lt A. F., 155, 157
MCVICAR, L-Cpl F. W., 368
MCWILLIAM, Sgt, 310
MADANI, JEBEL (Sketch p. 393), 393, 403, 415, 417n
MADDERN, Maj R., 88
MADIGAN, Capt E. B., 486, 489
MAGINOT LINE, 52, 537
MAIR, Sgt J. S., 429
MAITLAND, Capt F. J. V., 433, 437
MAJDAL, EL, 419
MAKRIKHORI (Map p. 106; Sketch p. 127), 107, 115, 116, 117, 127
MALARIA, in Syria, 526
MALAYA, 7, 199, 202, 541, 547, 549; A.I.F. strength in, 540

MALEME (Map p. 218; Sketch p. 203), 203, 205, 208, 211n, 214, 220, 247, 287, 312; strength and dispositions, 213, 217-19; see also MALEME-SUDA
MALEME-SUDA (Map p. 218; Sketches pp. 229, 245, 252), fight for the airfield, 221-3, 225, 226, 231-2, 234, 235-8, 241; operations round Galatas, 224-6, 237, 242, 243-6, 247, round Canea, 226, 238, 242, 247-9, 250, 251; German account, 227-31, 233-4, 239-40, 243, 244, 254-5; reinforcement of garrison, 241, 243, 244, 251n; at 42nd Street, 249-53, 254-5
MALIKIYA, EL (Sketches pp. 343, 348), 342, 349
MALLIA (Sketch p. 288), 288
MALTA, 26, 320, 531
MANDER-JONES, Lt-Col E., 150n
MANDRA (Sketch p. 145), 151
MANIADAKIS, M., 132
MANN, Capt G. W., 262, 264
MANN, Lt J. G., 292n
MANN, Lt W. R., 166, 167
MANPOWER, available for A.I.F., 537, 540, 541-2
MARAT, MOUNT (Map p. 410), 477
MARATHON (Sketches pp. 145, 175), 144, 145, 149, 163, 164, 168, 170
MAR ELIAS (Sketch p. 381), 385
"MARITA", OPERATION, 48
MARKHAM VALLEY, 291n
MARKOPOULON (Sketch p. 175), 170, 176
MAR MIKHAIL (Map p. 482), 486, 501
MARSA BREGA, 234
MARSDEN, Capt E. C. H., 382
MARSEILLES, 325
MARSHALL, Maj E. S., 373, 404
MARSHALL, Pte G., 301
MARSHALL, Cpl G. E. D., 372
MARSHALL, Maj H. C. D., 234, 235, 306, 307
MARSON, Lt-Col R. H., 443, 444, 445, 463, 475, 476, 505, 506, 507
MARTEL, Lt-Gen Sir Giffard, 14n
MARTIN, Cpl A. K. M., 483
MARTIN, Sgt B. S., 371
MARTIN, Lt E. T., 503
MARTIN, WO2 F. L., 486n
MARTIN, Brig J. E. G., 555
MARTINET, Capt, 426
MASON, Lt, 266
MATAPAN, BATTLE OF, 23, 36
MATHER, Lt-Col C. H., 204
MATTHEW, Lt D. H., 499
MAVRODENDRI (Sketch p. 55), 69
MAVROLITHOS (Sketch p. 127), 127
MAVRONERI RIVER, 100
MAVROPIYE (Sketch p. 68), 69
MAXWELL-HYSLOP, Lt-Col R., 558n
MAYBERRY, Lt-Col W. M., 398, 400, 404
MAYRHOFER, Capt M., 265n
MAZAR, JEBEL (Sketches pp. 416, 509), 467, 474, 513; advance to, 429-32; operations at, 432-40, 509-10; casualties at, 438n, 510
MAZARAKIS, General, 131, 132
MAZBOUD (Sketch p. 462), 463
MAZRAAT ECH CHOUF, capture of, 505-7
MAZRAAT ED DAHR (Sketch p. 475), 475
MAZRAAT ISLAMIYE (Map p. 386), 447
MAZRAAT KOUFRA (Sketch p. 367), 390
MDOUKA (Sketch p. 413), 510
MEDITERRANEAN FLEET, see BRITISH NAVY
MEDITERRANEAN SEA, 21, 197, 201, 202, 206, 318, 330, 524, 562; British air strength in, 17n; 320; effect of Matapan, 23; German air strength in, 207, 320
MEECHAM, Capt N. B. G., 362
MEECHAM, Lt R. N. G., 362n
MEGARA (Sketches pp. 145, 175), 144, 150, 153, 161, 162, 167, 228; embarkations from, 152, 163-4, 211, total, 181n
MEG KHORAFIA (Map p. 218), 226n, 277
MEINDL, General, 228, 230
MELBOURNE, 560
MELVAINE, Pte M. V. C., 434
MELVILLE, Cpl A. H., 106
MENEXES PASS, 123, 124
MENZIES, Rt Hon R. G., 340, 537, 539; visits Middle East, 7-8, 14, 18; views on Greek expedition, 11n, 14-15; functioning of British War Cabinet, 15, 194; requests re-examination of Greek plan, 16-17, 19; raises question of leadership of Lustre Force, 21-2, and appointment of Blamey to higher

580   INDEX

MENZIES, Rt. Hon. R. G.—*continued*
    command, 151; proposes formation of Anzac Corps, 70n; defence of Cyprus, 318; and invasion of Syria, 328-9; expansion of A.I.F., 540-41; resigns Prime Ministership, 542n
MERDJAYOUN (Map p. 386; Sketches pp. 334, 343), 337, 338, 340, 343, 344, 352, 353, 367-8, 389n, 393, 402n, 413, 414, 418, 429, 430, 442, 452, 460, 461, 463, 467, 477, 502, 509, 510, 535; patrols at, 368-70; capture of, 386-7; operations round, 387-8, 403-4, 408-9, 431, 443-6, 446-9, 449-51; strength and dispositions, 395-7, 404, reinforcement of, 400-401, 405; French counter-attack, 397-400, 412; casualties, 409, 446, 451n, 468
MERSA MATRUH (Sketch p. 298), 30, 216, 310, 311, 313, 320, 334n, 335, 336, 548
METAXAS, General J., 3, 4, 5, 132; government of, 203n
METAXAS LINE, 3, 4, 13, 26, 51, 52
METSOVON (Map p. 34; Sketch p. 78), 54, 76, 79, 83, 93, 102, 128, 142
METSUDAT (Map p. 386; Sketch p. 353), 352
METULLA (Sketches pp. 334, 343), 336, 338, 343, 354, 368, 398, 399, 400, 402n, 412
MEZZE (Sketch p. 416), 407, 412, 415, 419, 420-21, 429, 439n, 468, 545; action at, 416-18, 426-7
MIDDLE EAST, 1, 15, 200, 530, 536-7, 542, 543, 549, 550, 551, 556, 560, 561, 562; British strength in, 8, 17, 323, 531, 540, strategy in, 533, 534; extent of British reinforcement of, 541; appointment of political authority to, 321, 326, 516, 525, 531; conduct of campaigns in, 552-5
MIDDLE EAST DEFENCE COMMITTEE, 531
MIDDLE EAST WAR COUNCIL, 531
MIKROVALTON (Sketch p. 75), 75, 89
MILES, Brig R., 106n, 154, 155, 169-70
MILES, Capt W. N., 444, 476
MILITIA, 543, 552; establishment of, 541; strength on full-time duty, 543n; response to Munich crisis, 551; and officering of A.I.F., 555-6, 557, 558
MILLAR, Capt D. H., 89, 283n
MILLARD, Lt-Col A. B., 370, 371, 447
MILLER, Lt-Col J., 179, 190
MILLER, Maj W. V., 235, 251-2
MILLROY, Maj A. J., 506
MILLS, Maj E. D., 547
MILLS, Lt-Col T., 349, 350, 351, 366, 377, 381, 382, 461, 501
MILOI (Sketch p. 145), 162, 164, 165, 167, 177
MILOS ISLAND (Sketch p. 187), 181, 233, 238
MITCHELL, Col J. W., 60, 61
MITCHELL, Capt T. W., 547
MITCHELL, Maj W. H., 475
MITROVICA (Sketch p. 51), 71
MITTELHAUSER, General, 323
MIYEOUMIYE (Sketch p. 381), capture of, 382-4
MOLLOY, Col A. D., 36n
MOLONEY, Lt B. W., 362
MOLOS (Sketch p. 147), 140, 141, 152; rearguard at, 148-9, 153-5, 158-9
MOLOTOV, V. M., 48, 538
MONAGHAN, Brig R. F., 344, 352, 353, 373, 395, 396, 397, 403, 404, 449n, 450, 474, 475, 501, 502
MONASH, General Sir John, 542n
MONASTIR (Map p. 34; Sketch p. 4), 3, 27, 29, 34, 35, 43, 47, 52, 70, 80, 158
"MONCOLUMN", *see* A.I.F. (2/33rd Battalion)
MONEMVASIA (Sketch p. 145), 168, 175; embarkations from, 163, 177, 179, total, 181n
MONTAGNE, Robert, 323n
MONTOIRE, 329
MOONEY, Cpl F. J., 476n
MOORE, Maj Brooke, 182
MOORE, Capt R. McC., 118
MORE, Lt-Col G. R. M., 360, 364
MORETTI, L-Cpl F., 362
MORGAN, WO2 W., 425
MORHEUR, EL (Sketch p. 353), 352
MORIARTY, Capt O. B., 261, 263, 276
MORISH, Lt J. C., 310
MORRIS, Capt C., 397n
MORRIS, Pte J., 383
MORRIS, Lt J. I., 137
MORRISON, Lt-Col S. A., 388
MORSE, Vice-Admiral Sir Anthony, 247, 301, 302
MORSHEAD, Lt-Gen Sir Leslie, 555
MORTIMER, Cpl W. A., 310

MORTIMORE, Lt H. E., 458
MOSCOW, 48, 530, 549
MOSKHOKORI (Sketch p. 73), 85
MOSUL (Sketch p. 198), 201, 440, 478, 479
MOTEN, Brig M. J., 343, 347, 351, 375, 376, 377, 378, 382, 384, 385, 471, 483, 484, 496, 497
MOTT, Capt M. L., 495
MOUADAMMIYE (Sketch p. 416), 415, 417n, 419
MOUKELBE (Sketch p. 393), 393, 394
MOUMSIYE (Sketch p. 395), 407
MOUNT, Dvr A. E., 429n
MOUNTBATTEN, Admiral Rt Hon Earl, 239
MOUNTJOY, Sgt, 436, 438
MOURHIRA, EL (Map p. 482), 472, 480, 490
MOURNIES (Map p. 218), 226, 230, 238, 243n, 248, 250
MTERIATE (Sketch p. 462), 463
MTOULLE, EL (Sketches pp. 462, 475), 461, 475, 476, 477, 506
MUCKLOW, Sgt C. W., 507
MUIR, Lt-Col R. A. C., 464
MULES, in Greece, 72, 73; in Syria, 490, 491n, 492, 498
MULLIGHAN, Lt T. D., 471, 494
MUNICH, 192, 551
MUR, RIVER (Sketch p. 51), 51
MURCHISON, Lt-Col A. C., 107, 114, 116, 117n, 119, 120, 127, 432, 433, 434, 435, 436, 437, 438, 439, 493, 504
MURDOCH, Capt M. H., 423, 424, 426, 430, 431, 498
MURPHY, Pte A. D., 62
MURPHY, Gnr K., 313n
MURPHY, S-Sgt R. P., 363
MURRAY, Lt-Col A. T., 356
MURRAY, Maj J. D., 275
MURRAY, Maj-Gen J. J., 549
MYTILENE ISLAND (Sketches pp. 4, 187), 52, 186, 188
MZERIB (Sketch p. 413), 419

NAAME, EN (Map p. 482), 481, 498, 499, 500
NABATIYE ET TAHTA (Sketch p. 343), 343, 344, 352, 398
NAGLE, Maj J. F., 399
NAGRAT, WADI (Map p. 410), 464, 475, 477
Naiad, British cruiser, 227, 238, 239
NAISMITH, Sgt A. K., 106
NAJHA (Sketch p. 374), 373
Napier, Australian destroyer, 302
NAQOURA (Sketch p. 348), 347-8
NAQOURA, RAS EN (Sketch p. 334), 342, 346
NASH, Rt Hon W., 70n
NASICE (Sketch p. 51), 71
NASON, Capt C. H. T., 450, 502
NAVPAKTOS (Sketch p. 145), 149
NAVPLION (Sketch p. 145), 144, 150, 153, 168, 178, 179, 184, 185; embarkations from, 152, 160-61, 170, 171, 181
NAZARETH, 340, 365, 398, 414
NAZISM, 191, 517
NEA ALIKARNASSOS (Map p. 282), 279, 281
NEAME, Lt-Gen Sir Philip, VC, 14n, 21
NEAPOLIS, 76n, 92, 313
NEBEK (Sketch p. 478), 442, 465-6, 469, 478, 535
NELSON. Maj St E. D., 252
NEO KHORION (Map p. 218; Sketch p. 296), 235, 253, 295
NESTOS RIVER (Sketches pp. 4, 39), 3, 10, 25, 26, 39
NETHERLANDS EAST INDIES, reinforcement of, 549, 550
NEVROKOP (Sketch p. 45), 52
NEW GUINEA, 189, 190, 526n
NEWTON, Maj T. H., 510
NEW ZEALAND, consultation with Great Britain about Greek campaign, 14-15, 16-17, 18n, 20, 194; and Crete campaign 208, 209, 210; and Anzac Corps proposals, 70n, 540-1, 544; forms Armoured brigade, 539
NEW ZEALAND ARMY, 69; establishment of Overseas force, 541n; cooperation with British Army, 552
—ARMY HEADQUARTERS, 541
NEW ZEALAND DIVISION, 7, 15, 17, 18n, 23, 27, 30, 32-3, 317, 320; in Greece, 34, 35, 36, 37n, 40, 43, 44, 46, 47, 56, 58, 70, 71, 72, 82, 83, 93, 99, 108-9, 139, 140-2, 143, 144-5, 150n, 151, 153, 168-9, strength and losses, 182-3; in Crete, 208, 210, 217, 218-19, 221, 225, 226, 232, 234, 242, 243n, 244, 247, 248, 250, 301, 312, staff of, 211, strength, 213-14, 241n, 315, 316, losses, 315n, 316; and Anzac Corps proposals, 70n, 341, 539, 540-2

INDEX 581

NEW ZEALAND DIVISION—*continued*
—ARTILLERY, 72, 216; *Regiments*: 4th Field, 33*n*; in Greece, 97, 106*n*, 107*n*, 123, 149, losses, 183*n*; losses in Crete, 315*n*; 5th Field, 33*n*; in Greece, 84, 123, 141, 154, losses, 183*n*; losses in Crete, 315*n*; 6th Field, 33*n*; in Greece, 75, 86, losses, 183*n*; 27th Bty, in Crete, 223, 231, 242; 7th Anti-Tank, 33*n*, in Greece, 107*n*, losses, 183*n*
—CAVALRY: *Div Cav Regt*, 33*n*, in Greece, 35, 36, 42, 53, 72, 102, 119, 122-3, 133, 162, 163, 165, 167, 169, 176, losses, 183*n*; in Crete, 218, 224, 226, 232, losses, 315*n*
—ENGINEERS, 165; *6 Fd Coy*, 165; *19 Army Troops Coy*, 83-4. NZE *Composite Inf Unit*, in Crete, 218, 223-4, 232, 241*n*, 242
—INFANTRY: *Brigades*: 4th, 34; in Greece, 36, 37, 43-4, 47, 54, 56, 66*n*, 74-5, 76, 82, 85, 86, 87, 99, 122, 140, 144, 148, 152, 162, 163, 165, 167, 168-9, 170, 175-6, 177, 181*n*; in Crete, 211, 213, 217, 218, 219, 225, 232, 236, 237, 242, 244, 246, 248-9, 251, 295, 297-8, 299, 301, 304; 5th, 34; in Greece, 36, 37, 44, 56, 74*n*, 82, 84, 99, 100-2, 109, 140, 141, 145, 148, 149, 152, 160, 170, 181*n*; in Crete, 208, 211, 213, 218, 222-4, 225, 231, 232, 236, 237, 242, 243, 244, 246, 247, 248, 249, 250-1, 253, 255, 295-6, 299, 301, 302, 304, 305; 6th, 34; in Greece, 36, 37, 42, 44, 47, 56, 74*n*, 81, 82, 84, 85, 99, 102, 109, 123-5, 128, 133, 141, 145, 148-9, 152, 154-5, 162, 163, 168, 175, 177, 179, 181*n*; arrives Crete, 208, 211; in Egypt, 217*n*; 9th, 217; 10th, formation, 217; in Crete, 218, 224-6, 237, 242
Battalions: 4th, see 4th Bde; 18th, 33*n*; in Greece, 86, 109, 176, casualties, 183*n*; in Crete, 211, 213*n*, 214, 219, 225, 241*n*, 242, 244-5, 248, 302, casualties, 315*n*; 19th, 33*n*; in Greece, 86, 87, 102, 109, 165, 176, casualties, 183*n*; in Crete, 211, 213*n*, 218, 219, 224, 225-6, 232, 237, 241*n*, 247, 248, 251, 252, 292, 302, casualties, 315*n*; 20th, 33*n*; in Greece, 86, 87, 102, 109, 176, casualties, 183*n*; in Crete, 211, 213*n*, 217, 232, 234, 235, 236, 241*n*, 245, 246, 247, 248, 251, 301, 302, 304, 305, casualties, 315*n*; 21st, 33*n*; in Greece, 37*n*, 47, 134, 149*n*, 185, 188; at Platamon, 47, 56, 94, 95-6, 97, 126, at Pinios, 97, 100, 106, 107, 108, 114-15, 117, 118, 119, 122, casualties, 183*n*; in Crete, 211, 213*n*, 218, 222, 223, 231, 236, 241*n*, 242, 247, 248, 251-2, 295, 301, 304, 305, casualties, 315*n*; 22nd, 33*n*; in Greece, 84, 100, 140, 141, 148, 149, 163, 165, casualties, 183*n*; in Crete, 211, 213*n*, 218, 221-3, 224, 230, 231, 241*n*, 242, 248, 251, 295, 304, 305; casualties, 315*n*; 23rd, 33*n*; in Greece, 84, 100, 101, 109, 140, 141, 149, casualties, 183*n*; in Crete, 211, 213*n*, 218, 223, 231, 236, 238, 241*n*, 242, 246, 248, 295, 297, 299, 304, 305; casualties, 315*n*; 24th, 33*n*; in Greece, 84, 99*n*, 123, 124, 125, 141, 148, 153, 154, 168, casualties, 183*n*; 25th, 33*n*; in Greece, 99*n*, 123, 125, 133, 138*n*, 141, 148, 153, 154, 168, casualties, 183*n*; 26th, 33*n*; in Greece, 74, 75, 88, 89, 99*n*, 123, 125, 141, 148, 153, 154, 167, 168, 177, casualties, 183*n*; 27th (MG), 33*n*; in Greece, 35, 43, 44, 48, 56, 59, 60, 63, 67, 68, 69, 141, casualties, 183*n*; in Crete, 213*n*, casualties, 315*n*; 28th (Maori), 33*n*; in Greece, 37*n*, 84, 100-1, 141, 149*n*, 163, 165, casualties, 183*n*; in Crete, 211, 213*n*, 218, 223, 224, 231, 232, 235-6, 238, 241*n*, 242, 247, 248, 251-2, 295, 301-2, 304, 305, casualties, 315*n*; NZ Composite Bn, in Crete, 218, 224, 226, 230, 241*n*, 243, 245, 250; NZ Reinforcement Bn, 143, 171, 178, 180
—KIWI CONCERT PARTY, 246
—MEDICAL: *6 Fd Amb*, 225; *Nurses*, evacuation from Greece, 150
—SERVICE CORPS, 242; *Petrol Coy*, in Crete, 224, 225, 237; *Div Supply Column*, 136*n*
NEW ZEALAND CABINET DEFENCE COMMITTEE, 70*n*
NEW ZEALAND WAR HISTORY SECTION, 114*n*
NICHOLLS, Maj F. J., 471, 484, 489, 490, 492, 494, 496, 497
NICOL, Pte H., 312
NIHA (Sketch p. 506), 505, 507
NIHA, JEBEL (Map p. 410), 405
NIKAIA (Sketch p. 124), 128, 129
NILE DELTA, 335*n*
NIMFAION (Map p. 66), 43
NIMPHAEA (Sketch p. 45), 39, 40
NISH (Sketch p. 4), 51, 94, 158
NIXON, H. H. A., *see* J. H. SPENCE

Nizam, Australian destroyer, 251*n*, 302
NOLAN, Maj R. K. J., 110
NOONAN, Maj B. S., 348, 378, 493, 495, 500, 501, 502
NORCOTT, Cpl H. A., 426
NORRIS, Pte F. A., 372
NORRIS, Maj-Gen F. K., 341*n*, 464*n*
NORTH AFRICA, 1, 2, 3, 6, 7, 9, 39, 50, 197, 202, 220, 308, 320, 325, 330, 331, 531, 533, 537, 554, 555; *see also* WESTERN DESERT
NORTHCOTT, Lt-Gen Sir John, 539*n*
NORWAY, 523
Nubian, British destroyer, 180
NUGENT, Sgt H., 308
NURSES, embarkation from Greece, 150, 164
NYE, Lt C. C. P., 505

OAKES, Lt-Col T. H. E., 150*n*, 177*n*
O'BRIEN, Maj-Gen J. W. A., 387, 397*n*, 401, 487*n*, 502
O'BRIEN, Pte L. C., 362
OCHRID, LAKE (Map p. 34), 43*n*, 51, 54
O'CONNOR, General Sir Richard, 21, 193, 197, 527
O'DAY, Maj G., 457, 458, 459
ODESSA, 530
OFFICERS, *A.I.F.*, return to Australia, 549; selection for senior commands, 554-5; O.C.T.U. graduates, 555-6; commissioning from ranks, 556-8. *French*, arrest of, 520
OIL, 6, 8, 15, 48, 197, 198, 200, 202, 227*n*, 530, 532, 534
OITI (Sketches pp. 147, 156), 141
OITI, MOUNT, 189
OLDFIELD, Lt T. C., 59
OLIVE OIL FACTORY (Map p. 258; Sketch p. 262), 256, 258, 263, 264, 266, 267, 276, 277
O'LOUGHLIN, Lt-Col B. J., 36*n*, 150*n*, 160, 171, 178, 179*n*
O'LOUGHLIN, Lt C. E., 486
OLYMPUS, MOUNT (Map p. 34; Sketch p. 93), 3, 10, 29, 32, 35, 43, 46, 47, 54, 56, 68, 72, 85, 94, 97, 98, 99, 101, 113, 126, 158
OLYMPUS-ALIAKMON LINE (Sketch p. 55), 40, 43, 93; withdrawal to, 46, 56, 58, 68, 72-6, effect on Greek Army, 65, 76-9; decision to withdraw from, 80, 87, 194-5; dispositions on, 83-4
OLYMPUS PASS (Sketch p. 84), 36, 37, 40, 44, 58, 82, 83, 84, 94, 95, 99, 128; withdrawal from, 100-102; rearguard in, 122-3, 126
O'NEILL, Capt J. H., 349
ONSLOW, Brig D. M., *see* MACARTHUR-ONSLOW
Orion, British cruiser, 23, 170, 233, 291, 292
OSBORNE, WO2 W. J., 464
OSSA, MOUNT (Sketch p. 127), 99*n*, 114, 115, 122, 185
OSWELL, Lt J. L., 370, 371
OTHRYS, MOUNT, 139
OTT, General, 50
OTTOMAN EMPIRE, 322
OUARDANIYE, EL (Sketch p. 462), 461
OUASTA, EL (Sketch p. 367), 367
OVERSBY, Lt T., 486*n*
OWEN STANLEY MOUNTAINS, 190
OXLEY-BOYLE, Brig R. F. C., 438

PACKARD, Maj-Gen C. D., 150
PAGE, Col J. R., 75
PAINE, Brig D. D., 34*n*
PALAIRET, Sir Michael, 112, 131
PALAMAS (Sketch p. 124), 125
PALANDRI, Maj J. D., 265*n*
PALESTINE, 32, 201, 202, 216, 317, 320, 321, 324, 326, 327, 328, 333, 334*n*, 335, 336, 349, 401, 406, 413, 419, 424, 447, 451, 467*n*, 470, 532, 537, 550, 553, 559, 561, 562
PALESTINE POLICE, 340, 406
PALESTINIANS, THE, in Greece, 165, 178, 180, strength and losses, 182-3; in Crete, 213, 253, 304
PALIOKHORION (Sketch p. 156), 159
PALMYRA (Map p. 339; Sketches pp. 440, 466), 322, 338, 479, 511, 512, 515, 536, operations at, 440-41, 442, 466, 477, 528
PANDELEIMON (Map p. 66), 57
PAPAGOS, Field Marshal A., 4*n*, 6*n*, 15, 16, 33, 35, 39, 42, 44, 46, 54, 104, 112, 131, 132*n*; estimates force required to defend Greece, 3, 28; orders offensive in Albania, 5, 40, halts offensive, 43; at Athens Conference, 10-11; and defence of Eastern Macedonia, 12, 13, 24, 25, 26, 34, 194; discussions with Yugoslavs, 27; criticises failure to cover Greek

INDEX

PAPAGOS, Field Marshal A.—*continued*
  withdrawal from Florina Valley, 65, 66; misunderstandings with W Group, 76-9, 92-3; orders dismissal of Tsolakoglou, 133; resigns, 153; and British aid to Greece, 191, 193
PAPPAS, Colonel, 58
PARAMYTHIA (Map p. 34), 23
PARAPOTAMOS (Sketch p. 127), 113, 116, 127
PARATROOPS, GERMAN, *see* GERMAN AIR FORCE
PARBURY, Lt-Col P. K., 119n, 421, 422, 423, 424, 425, 428, 430, 439, 498, 504
PARIS, 329
PARK, Capt E. N., 313n
PARKES, Capt H. K., 154
PARKINSON, C. N., 402n
PARKINSON, Maj-Gen G. B., 106, 117, 118
PARNASSUS, MOUNT, 32
PARRINGTON, Brig L., 152, 171, 172, 179, 181
PATRAS (Sketch p. 145), 149, 166, 169, 183
PATROLS, Aust, at Merdjayoun, 368-70; Damascus area, 429, 477n; at Jezzine, 464-5; at Damour, 470-73
PAUL, Prince, of Yugoslavia, 11, 24, 25, 51
PAULEY, Cpl W. H., 268
PAXTON, Maj R., 558n
PEACH, Maj C. N. B., 400, 404
PEAKE, Lt-Col F. G., 324n
Pearleaf, British oiler, 532
PEDDER, Lt-Col R. R. N., 342, 364, 365
PEELER, S-Sgt W., VC, 451
PEIRCE, Lt D. C., 85, 186-7
PELOPONNESE, 80, 112, 143, 151, 153, 162, 163, 165, 168, 169, 177, 179, 182, 183-4, 188, 192, 313, 317
PEMBERTON, Major, 171
PEMBERTON, Capt J. M., 409
PERDIKA (Maps pp. 34, 66), 43, 47, 54, 58
PERESITCH, Colonel, 24, 25
PERIVOLIA (Retimo area: Map p. 258; Sketch p. 270), 256, 259, 260, 262; operations round, 263-71, 272, 273, 274, 275, 276, 277, 278
PERIVOLIA (Suda Bay area: Map p. 218; Sketch p. 245), 226, 230, 234, 242, 248, 254
PERRY, Lt J. L., 422
PERSIA, 198, 200, 201, 202, 534; German plan to invade, 530; Anglo-Soviet advance in, 531-3
PERSIAN AIR FORCE, strength, 532
PERSIAN ARMY, strength and dispositions, 532; surrenders, 533
PERSIAN GULF (Sketch p. 533), 330, 530, 532, 534, 535
Perth, Australian cruiser, at Matapan, 23; evacuation of Greece, 170, 180; Crete, 227, 238, 298, 300; Syria, 488n
PESHAWAR, 333
PETAIN, Marshal, 323, 332, 517; relations with Germany, 324-5, 329, 330; agrees to cessation of fighting in Syria, 511
PETER, King, of Yugoslavia, 24, 25
PETRAIS (Map p. 66), 71
PETRANA (Sketch p. 75), 86
PETRON, LAKE (Map p. 66), 35, 47, 57, 60n
PHALERON, Greek airfield, 228
PHARSALA (Sketch p. 78), 46, 67n, 81, 82, 93, 105, 106, 109, 111, 126, 128, 129, 130
PHILIPPINE ISLANDS, 549
PHILLIPS, Sgt A. M., 362
PHILLIPS, Maj J. F., 166, 167
Phoebe, British cruiser, evacuation of Greece, 161, 173n, 180, of Crete, 298, 303n, 305
PIERIA MOUNTAINS (Map p. 38), 36, 40
PIGI (Map p. 258), 256, 257, 262
PIGI, WADI (Map p. 258), 256, 257, 258, 259
PIMPLE, THE (Merdjayoun), 447, 448, 449
PINDUS MOUNTAINS (Map p. 34), 29, 77, 78, 79, 80, 92, 94, 128
PINIOS GORGE (Map p. 106; Sketch p. 127), 67n, 95n, 128, 336; reinforcement of, 96-8, 111n; dispositions, 106-8; engagement in, 113-22; German account, 126-7; escapes from, 185, 186
PINIOS RIVER, 99, 102, 105, 110, 125, 126, 129
PINK HILL (Sketch p. 245), 230
PIRAEUS (Map p. 34; Sketch p. 82), 13, 14, 23, 24n, 30, 31, 32, 79, 144n, 160, 161, 181n, 292; capacity of port, 29; German bombing of, 40
PIRGOS (Map p. 218), 222, 223, 229,232, 233, 236, 239, 240
PISODERION PASS (Map p. 34; Sketches pp. 55, 78), 43, 46, 54, 58, 66, 71, 76, 83

PITCAIRN, Lt-Col A. A., 281
PITSIKAS, General, 92, 133, 142
PLAKIAS BAY (Sketch p. 203), 272, 303
PLANT, Maj-Gen E. C. P., commands A.I.F. Rear Echelon, 22, 25th Brigade, 459; at Jezzine, 460, 461 477, 480, 505; arrest of French generals, 520, 521; returns to Australia, 549
PLANTARD, Colonel, 426
PLATAMON (Sketches pp. 55, 84), 47, 56, 100; demolitions at, 83-4; action at, 95-6, 97, 126
PLATANES (Map p. 258), 256, 264, 265, 272
PLATANES, WADI, 264, 273, 274, 275
PLATANIAS (Map p. 218), 229, 233, 235; New Zealand withdrawal, 242
PLATANIAS RIVER, 232n, 237, 242
PLATT, Gen Sir William, 21
PLIMMER, Lt-Col J. R. L., 225
PLYTRA (Sketch p. 145), 163
POINT 212 (Map p. 482), 480
POINT 278 (Map p. 482), 497
Pola, Italian cruiser, 23
POLAND, 45, 57n, 530
POLISH BRIGADE, 7, 9, 37, 197
POLLARD, Col R. G., 341n, 464n, 508
POOLE, Lt-Cdr F. G., 312
"PORTCOLUMN", *see* A.I.F. (2/31st Battalion)
PORTER, Maj-Gen S. H. W. C., 344, 352, 355, 368, 370, 386, 389, 390, 405, 411, 454, 459, 464
PORTO RAFTI (Sketches pp. 145, 175), 144, 150, 169, 177, 232n; embarkations from, 160, 170, 176, total, 181n
PORT SAID, 188, 360
POTTS, Brig A. W., 349, 351, 485, 548
POUND, Admiral of the Fleet Sir Dudley, 20
POWELL, Cpl R., 73n
PRASSAS (Map p. 282), 284
PRATT, L-Cpl V. G., 444
PRESPA, LAKE (Map p. 34), 43n
PRESS CENSORSHIP, in Middle East, 525, 526
PREVALI (Sketch p. 203), 312
PREVALI, ABBOT OF, 312n
PRIDHAM-WIPPELL, Admiral Sir Henry, 23, 163, 170, 174, 181
PRILEP (Sketch p. 10), 52, 80
PRIOR, Brig C. E., 36n, 143, 150
PRISON CAMPS, German, 188-9, 313-14
PRISONERS, Australian, in Greece, 67n, 71, 183, in Crete, 315n, 316, in Syria, 409, 422-3, 427, 438n, repatriation, 519-21; British, in Greece, 183, 188-9 in Crete, 293, 307, 315n, 316, in Syria, 412, 510, 526, repatriation, 515, 519-21; French, in Syria, 347, 363-4, 365, 377, 379n, 386, 407 409, 424, 448, 486, repatriation, 515, 519-21; German, in Greece, 160n, in Crete, 260, 262, 267, 275, 293, 316n; Greek, in Crete, 307, 316; Indian, in Syria, 426n, repatriation, 519-21; Italian, in Greece, 188-9, in Crete, 207, 215, 296, 316; New Zealand, in Greece, 183, in Crete, 315n, 316
PRISON VALLEY, 233
PROASTEION, rearguard at, 68-9, 76
PROSILION (Sketch p. 75), 86, 87, 102
PROUD, Pte F. W., 268
PTOLEMAIS (Map p. 34; Sketch p. 55), 65, 72, 74; rearguard at, 59, 68-9, German account, 71
PUBLIC RELATIONS, in Middle East, 525, 560-62
PUGH, Pte H. B. A., 450
PULVER, Brig B. W., 36n
PUMPHREY, Lt J. L., 176
PURVES, Pte P. C., 138n
PUTTICK, Lt-Gen Sir Edward, 86, 87, 102, 169, 170, 218, 221, 225, 231, 232, 237, 238, 242, 246, 247, 248, 251, 300; commands NZ Div in Crete, 211; orders withdrawal of NZ Div to 42nd Street, 249-50

QARAOUN (Sketch p. 334), 344
QARQAFE, EL (Map p. 482), 493
QASMIYE (Sketch p. 367), 367
QASSOUBA, WADI (Map p. 482), 490
QATANA (Sketch p. 416), 429, 430, 432, 477
QLEAA (Map p. 386; Sketch p. 396), 371, 398 *et seq*, 404, 408
QUILLIAM, Col C. D., 177
QUINAN, General Sir Edward, 200, 478, 532, 533

RACHAYA EL FOKHAR (Map p. 386; Sketch p. 396), 373, 396, 397, 403, 404, 447

INDEX

RAFINA (Sketches pp. 145, 175), 144, 149n, 150, 169; embarkations from, 163, 170, 176-7, total embarked, 181n
RAHN, R., 201, 330, 331, 358, 511
RAKKA (Sketch p. 478), 479
RAMA, ER, see ER RAMA
RAMCKE, Colonel, 240, 243, 254, 255
RAMIET (Sketch p. 343), 342
RASHEIYA (Sketch p. 334), 340
RASHID ALI, 198, 199, 201, 524
RAS NEBI YOUNES (Sketches pp. 385, 462), 385
RATTLING BRIDGE (Map p. 282), 286
RAU, Brig W. L., 376
RAWLINGS, Admiral Sir Bernard, 239
RAYAK (Map p. 339), 326, 327, 333, 338, 340, 352, 391, 511, 546; airfield, 322, 344, 431
RECRUITING, A.I.F., 541, 542, 549
REDDISH, Brig J., 411
REDDY, Maj L. G., 88, 135
REDPATH, WO2 J. A., 313
RED SEA, 320
REES, N., 186
REFUGE POINT (Retimo), 258, 275, 276
REID, Lt R. J. C., 486n, 487
REINFORCEMENTS, A.I.F., 470; estimated number required for Anzac Army, 540; maintenance of, 541-4; quality of, 556, 557
REINHARD, General, 49, 50, 71
REINHARDT, General, 49
REITER, Lt F. A., 252
REMEICHE (Sketch p. 343), 342
RETIMO (Map p. 258; Sketch p. 203), 203, 205, 212, 220, 232, 233, 234, 238, 239, 240, 241, 242-3, 244, 247, 254, 255, 279, 293, 297; population, 202; garrison, 213, 219, 256-7, dispositions of, 218-19, 257-8; operations at, 259-74, 275, 277-8; German account, 227-9, 243, 275-77, casualties at, 275; escapes from, 278, 309-10, 311, 312
REZANIYE, ER (Map p. 482; Sketch p. 462), 461, 471, 490, 491
RHADJAR (Sketch p. 353), 353
RHARIFE (Sketches pp. 462, 475), 505, 506; advance to, 460, 461, 474, 475-6, 477, casualties, 476n
RHAZIYE (Sketch p. 381), 379
RHODEN, Lt-Col P. E., 489, 490
RHODES, 4, 6, 7, 16, 197, 207
RHODOPOLES (Sketch p. 45), 52
RICE, Maj D. G., 483, 484
RICHARDS, Lt G. T. E., 166
RICHARDS, Pte H., 309
RICHTHOFEN, General von, 227
RICKARD, Lt-Col A. L., 400, 448
RIDDELL, Maj J., 547
RIHANE (Sketch p. 367), 388
RINGEL, Maj-Gen, 233, 239, 240, 243, 297, 317n
RISSON, Maj-Gen R. J. H., 341n
RIZA SHAH, 532
RMAILE (Sketch p. 462), 460
ROATTA, General, 50
ROBERTS, Lt F. E., 268
ROBERTSON, Maj A. C., 446, 476
ROBERTSON, Cpl M. R. S., 445
ROBERTSON, Lt-Col W. T., 59, 60
ROBINSON, Maj A., 485, 486, 489
ROBSON, Lt-Col E. M., 389, 409, 411, 454, 455, 464
RODONA (Map p. 66), 59, 60, 61, 62
ROGERS, Cpl B. M., 270n
ROGERS, Cpl D. R., 270n
ROGERS, Brig J. D., 34n, 150, 164n, 469, 546, 561
ROGERS, Lt T. L., 261-2
ROLFE, Capt C. B. N., 135n, 283
ROMMEL, Field Marshal Erwin, 523
ROOSEVELT, Franklin D., 8n, 329, 530, 531
ROSE, Lt R. N., 486
ROSH PINNA, 343, 398, 400, 418, 420
ROSS, Pte C. F., 488
ROSTOV, 530
ROUMANE, ER (Map p. 482), 480, 484, 496, 497
ROUTE "A" (Map p. 386), 344, 388, 396, 398, 399, 412, 446, 449
ROUTE "B" (Map p. 386), 344, 352, 388, 396, 397, 412, 446, 449
ROWELL, Maj F. A., 498, 499, 500
ROWELL, Lt-Gen Sir Sydney, 211; in Greece, 34, 74, 79, 97, 98, 129, 141, 149, presses for withdrawal of NZ Division to Olympus passes, 40, protests at evacuation of Anzac Corps headquarters, 151;

ROWELL, Lt-Gen Sir Sydney—*continued*
 proposes that I Aust Corps should control operations in Syria from outset, 340, 527, in Syria, 418, 420; returns to Australia, 549
ROYAL, Maj R., 295
ROYAL AIR FORCE, see BRITISH AIR FORCE
ROYAL PERIVOLIANS, see NEW ZEALAND COMPOSITE BATTALION
ROYCE, Maj G. E., 269
RUDD, Lt L. K., 348, 379, 384
RUDEL, Judge, 240
RUMANIA, 2, 11n, 15, 49; German air strength in, 18n; oilfields, 6, 8, 15, 48, 197, 227n
RUPEL PASS (Sketch p. 45), 34, 45, 52, 80
RUSES, Aust, in Crete, 260, 264, in Syria, 345, 459-60; British, in Crete, 283-4, in Syria, 336; French, in Syria, 496; German, in Greece, 56; in Crete, 286n, 301n
RUSSELL, Sgt D. H., 64n
RUSSELL, Lt-Col J. T., 245
RUSSELL, Col R. H., 170
RUSSELL, Maj W. B., 453n, 454, 456, 459, 489, 490, 557n
RUSSIA, 11, 188, 189, 318, 320, 534, 538; German plan to invade, 6, 48, 330, effect of Greek campaign on plan, 192-3: invasion of, 441, 523, 524, 530, 549; relations with Iraq, 201n; and Persia, 530-33
RUTBA (Sketch p. 198), 200, 201
RYAN, Pte A., 362
RYAN, Lt-Col J. J., 265n, 269, 270n, 310
RYAN, Maj W. H., 214, 226
RYMNION (Sketch p. 75), 75, 87
RYRIE, Maj E. J., 502

SAADIYATE, ES (Map p. 482; Sketch p. 462), 461, 462, 469, 470
SABBURA (Sketch p. 416), 430
SADLEIR, Cpl J. C., 365
SAGRET FELLAH, WADI (Map p. 410), 465
SAHL ES SAHRA (Sketch p. 416), 439
ST GEORGE, CHURCH OF (Map p. 258; Sketch p. 270), 264, 265, 266, 269, 271
ST JOHN'S HILL, 242n
SAKHET EZ ZEITOUN (Sketch p. 381), 380
SAKIYE, ES (Sketch p. 377), 376, 377
SALHIYE (Sketch p. 385), 386
SALISBURY-JONES, Maj-Gen A. G., 212
SALOM, Lt A. L., 487
SALONIKA (Sketches pp. 4, 39), 2, 11, 29, 37, 40, 41, 67n, 182, 184, 188, 313, 315, 511, 521; value in event of Yugoslav cooperation, 3, 8, 9, 10, 13, 24, 26, 34, 194, cost of decision to defend, 46; proposed as port of disembarkation of Lustre Force, 12; German occupation of, 52, 94
SALUM, 197
SALVATION ARMY, 559
Salween, British transport, 170, 174
SAMAKH (Sketch p. 413), 419
SAMARIA, 467n
SAMOTHRACE ISLAND (Sketch p. 4), 52
SAMPSON, Maj R. G., 87
SAMSON, Lt-Col B. E. G., 494, 499
SANAMEIN (Sketch p. 374), 412
SANDOVER, Brig R. L., 155, 156, 157, 158, 257, 260, 264, 265, 266, 267, 269, 270n, 271, 272, 273, 274, 275, 278, 309, 310, 312, 556n
SANTI, Bdr E. W., 154
SARAFAND (Palestine), 336
SARAFEND (Sketch p. 377), 377
SARAFIS, General, 132n, 191-2, 203n
SARAJEVO (Sketch p. 4), 94
SARGENT, Capt A. H., 289
SARRAIL, General, 324
SARRAIL, FORT (Sketch p. 421), 421, 422, 423, 426, 427
SASSA (Sketches pp. 374, 395), 391, 394, 412
SATANIQ, WADI (Sketch p. 381), 379, 380, 382, 383
SAVAGE, Lt B. M., 262, 263
SAVAGE, Rt Hon M. J., 70n
SAVAGE, Col R. W., 547, 548
SAVE RIVER (Sketch p. 51), 50, 51
SAVIGE, Capt J. R., 235
SAVIGE, Lt-Gen Sir Stanley, in Greece, 79, 82, 90, 96, 122, 125, 134, 135, 141-2, 145, 148n, 150, 153, 161, 171, 172-3; meets Tsolakoglou, 91-2; misunderstanding with I Armd Bde, 103, 104, 110-11; in Syria, 439n, 467, 474, 491, 493, 499, 502, 503, 504;

584　　　　　　　　INDEX

SAVIGE, Li-Gen Sir Stanley—*continued*
　arrest of French officers, 520-21; returns to Australia, 549
SAXBY, Col N. H. W., 545
SCARPANTO, 520, 521
SCHAETTE, Major, 240
SCHERBER, Major, 229
SCHIRMER, Capt, 285
SCHULZ, Major, 285, 293
SCHUSTER, Admiral, 228
SCOTT, Lt H. H., 270
SCOTT ORR, Pte W., 425
SEBA BIYAR (Sketch p. 466), 466
SEBLINE (Sketches pp. 385, 462), 386, 460, 461, 463
SECOMBE, Lt-Gen V. C., 341*n*
SELINO KASTELLI (Sketch p. 203), 230
SERBIA, *see* YUGOSLAVIA
SERRAI (Sketch p. 45), 52
SERVIA (Map p. 34; Sketch p. 75), 27, 30, 32, 36, 44, 46, 54, 56, 65, 80, 99, 160*n*, 178; withdrawal to, 72-4, dispositions at, 74-6; action at, 86-7, 93, 101-2, 109, 126; withdrawal from, 82, 106, 107, 109; rearguard at, 122-3
SEYAR, Es (Map p. 482; Sketch p. 462), 461, 469, 470
SFAKIA (Sketches pp. 203, 296), 203, 247, 249, 271, 273, 317*n*; withdrawal to, 253-4, 255, 295-7, 298-9; rearguard at, 299, 300-1, 304; embarkations from, 295, 297-8, 299-300, 301-3, 305-6; surrender at, 307; German account, 297, 307; escapes from, 307-9
SHAHABAD (Sketch p. 533), 533
SHAIBA (Sketch p. 198), 200
SHANNON, Cpl T. A., 501
SHEDDEN, Sir Frederick, proposes Blamey for higher command, 21, 151
SHEIKH MANSOUR, JEBEL (Sketch p. 413), 510
SHEIKH MESKINE (Sketches pp. 334, 395), 338, 344, 356-7, 358, 373, 391, 394, 402, 407, 412, 467*n*
SHEPPARD, Col A. W., 150*n*, 160, 170
SHEPPARD, Lt R., 406, 507, 508, 509
SHERWOOD, R. E., 8*n*
SHIPPING, British losses, 175, 318
SHREEVE, Pte R. H., 274
SIATISTA PASS (Map p. 34; Sketches pp. 55, 78), 46, 54, 65, 66, 76, 77, 78, 89
SICILY, 23, 202; withdrawal of German aircraft, 531; proposed invasion, 553*n*
SICKLEN, Pte W. A., 315
SIDI BARRANI, 308, 309, 312
SIDON (Map p. 339; Sketches pp. 376, 377, 381), 333, 340, 363, 389, 393, 405, 413, 414, 419, 432, 447, 461, 467, 470; advance to, 375-86
SIKOURION (Sketch p. 101), 107, 119, 122, 186
SILVERMAN, Lt-Col J. S., 378
SIMOVIC, General, 25
SIMPSON, Lt, 260*n*
SIMPSON, Maj-Gen C. H., 34*n*
SIMPSON, Lt-Col C. L., 60
SIMPSON, Col J. T., 34*n*
SIMPSON, Brig N. W., 341*n*
SIMS, Maj C. A. W., 472, 482, 497
SINAI DESERT, 548
SINCLAIR, Capt R. B., 222
SIN KARES (Sketch p. 296), 299
SITARIA (Map p. 66), 53
SITIA (Sketch p. 203), 227
SKALA LEPTOKARIAS (Sketch p. 84), 99
SKAMNOS (Sketch p. 156), 159
SKERRETT, Sgt C. J., 67*n*
SKHIMATARION (Sketch p. 145), 169
SKIATHOS ISLAND (Sketch p. 187), 67*n*, 185, 188
SKINES, 313
SKIPPER, Capt J. W., 472
SKI TROOPS, in Syria, 547-8
SKOPELOS ISLAND (Sketch p. 187), 186, 188
SKOPLJE (Sketch p. 4), 51, 52, 94; capture of, 42
SKOTEINA (Sketch p. 73), 84, 100
SKOULAS, General, 207, 254
SKYROS ISLAND (Sketch p. 187), 67*n*, 186, 189
Slamat, British transport, 171, 181*n*
SLESSOR, K., 560
SLIM, Field Marshal Sir William, 441, 478, 479, 532, 533
SMALLWOOD, Cpl R. G., 258
SMART, Air Vice-Marshal H. G., 200
SMEAL, Cpl D. G., 73, 74
SMITH, Lt-Gen Sir Arthur, 212, 523; visits Athens, 24; favours invasion of Syria, 524

SMITH, WO2 C. R. F., 425-6
SMITH, G. A., 333*n*
SMITH, L-Sgt H. V., 384
SMITH, Lt S., 63
SMITH, Sgt W. R. D., 457, 458
SMUTS, Field Marshal Rt Hon J. C., 554
SMYRNA (Sketch p. 187), 67*n*, 188, 189
SNOOK, Maj R. J. B., 283
SOFIA (Sketch p. 4), 51, 158
SOMME, 536*n*
SOTIR (Sketch p. 67), 61, 65, 74; rearguard at, 59, 66-8
SOUEIDA (Map p. 339), 358, 517, 519
SOUMPASI (Sketch p. 124), 90*n*, 92, 109*n*, 128
SOUQ WADI BARADA (Sketch p. 416), 429
SOUTH AFRICAN AIR FORCE, 310
SOUTH AFRICAN ARMY, 554, 561, 562; strength in Middle East, 541; cooperation with British Army, 552. 1st *South African Div*, 320, 531
SOUTHWORTH, Lt W. G., 115, 118, 236*n*
SPAIN, 19
SPEARS, Maj-Gen Sir Edward, 321, 328, 518, 519*n*; A.I.F. discipline, 545
SPEARS MISSION, 518*n*, 519, 547
SPECKMAN, Brig C. R., 341*n*
SPENCE, Cpl J. H., 433
SPENDER, Hon Sir Percy, 17, 18, 20, 340
SPERKHIOS RIVER (Sketch p. 147), 140, 146, 147, 149, 156
SPRY, Col C. C. F., 150*n*, 163
SRIFA (Sketches pp. 343, 367), 343, 366
STABLE, Maj N. S., 507, 508
STAFF CORPS, 341, 558
STALEY, Cpl E. R., 378, 557*n*
STALIN, Marshal Joseph, 524
STALOS (Map p. 218), 240, 242, 243
STANTON, Lt C., 262*n*
STANTON, Lt-Col F. A., 436*n*, 505*n*
STAPLEDON, Lt H. D., 486
STAVROMENOS (Map p. 258), 256, 265, 267
STEADMAN, L-Cpl J. P., 116
STEEL, Pte E., 67*n*
STEELE, Maj-Gen Sir Clive, 34*n*, 99, 128, 129*n*, 134, 135, 149
STEIERMARK PROVINCE, 50
STENZLER, Major, 230
STEPHANIDES, Lt T., 239*n*, 253-4
STEVENS, Maj-Gen J. E. S., estimate of, 341; in Syria, 345, 348, 351, 360, 364, 365, 366, 375-6, 378, 379, 380, 382, 384, 385, 387, 460, 461, 462-3, 475, 480, 484, 485, 490, 491, 499, 502, 503, 548, problems of, 342-4, ordered to halt coastal advance, 412-13, policy at Damour, 469-71, 473-4
STEVENSON, WO2 E. J., 167
STEVENSON, Brig J. R., 424, 425, 426, 428, 429, 430, 431, 432, 433, 438, 439, 492, 493, 498, 520, 521
STEWART, Hon Sir Frederick, 512
STEWART, Capt G. F., 366, 382
STEWART, Col K. L., 97*n*, 208, 210, 237
STILIS (Map p. 34), 29
STILOS (Map p. 218; Sketch p. 296), 249, 251, 253, 255, 295, 297
STOGDALE, Bdr G. E. D., 547
STONEHAM, Lt A. C., 270*n*
STOVIN, WO1 R. C., 114, 116
STRINGER, Lt J. R., 443
STRUMA RIVER (Map p. 34), 10, 26, 27, 39, 40, 42, 45
STRUMICA (Sketch p. 39), 41, 52
STRUTT, Brig H. W., 64, 232, 242
Stuart, Aust destroyer, 23, 161, 170, 298
STUDENT, General Kurt, 219*n*, 227, 228, 233, 247, 284, 292
STUMME, General, 50, 51, 52, 70, 93, 94, 126, 128, 142
STURDEE, Lt-Gen Sir Vernon, size of A.I.F., 537, maintenance of, 541, 542, 543; return of officers from Middle East, 549
STURM, Colonel, 167, 263, 275, 276
SUBLET, Lt-Col F. H., 361, 362, 363, 364, 367
SUDA (Map p. 218; Sketch p. 296), 218, 226*n*, 241, 242, 243, 247, 250, 251, 253, 255, 265, 277, 278, 280*n*, 284, 287, 296, 307*n*; *see also* MALEME-SUDA
SUDA BAY (Map p. 218; Sketch p. 296), 170*n*, 174, 179, 202, 203, 205, 206, 208, 211, 212, 226, 228, 229, 230, 235, 237, 241, 243, 244, 249, 250, 251, 255, 263, 270*n*, 280, 287, 295, 317; garrison of, 213, dispositions, 218-19; air attacks on, 217, 219-20, 239

INDEX 585

SUDAN, 21
SUDETENLAND, 57n
SUEZ CANAL, 330, 385n, 534; mining of, 15-16; German threat to, 530
SUKHNA (Sketch p. 466), 466
SUMMONS, Lt W. I., 409
SUSSMAN, General, 228, 229, 230
SUTHERLAND, Brig R. B., 36n, 47, 138, 143
SWANSON, WO L. R., 289
SWEET, Lt-Col H. G., 181
SWEETAPPLE, Lt A. M., 354
SWINTON, Capt C. N., 85, 117
SYDNEY, 512
SYMINGTON, Maj N. M., 351n
SYMINGTON, Maj W. G., 362
SYMMONS, Pte F. W., 266
SYN AMMONDARI (Sketch p. 296), 296
SYN TOMAI (Sketch p. 124), 111, 125, 134n
SYRIA, 188, 190, 198, 202, 208, 315, 320, 530, 531, 532, 537, 542n, 553, 554, 555; German influence and aid in, 201, 325, 327, 329-30, 331; French strength in, 321, 333-4, 524-5; proposed Free French advance into, 322, 326, 327; British decision to occupy, 327-8, 331, plan of invasion, 334-44; Italian Armistice Commission in, 329, 332; campaign in, 345-514, conduct of operations in, 467-9, 523-9, advance from Iraq, 478-80; Armistice, 511-14, administration of, 515-22; strength of national contingents participating in campaign, 525-6, casualties, 526; defence and occupation of, 519, 534-6, 544-9, 550
SYRIANS, THE, 324, 325, 516, 517, 518, 521-2

TACTICS, Aust, under air attack, 235; at Retimo, 274; at Jezzine, 389-90; on Jebel Mazar, 434; 439-40; British, in Middle East, criticism of, 536-7; French, in Syria, 355, 367; German, in Greece, 59, 60, 87n, 130, in Crete, 293; Greek, 42
TANAGRA, Greek airfield, 228
TANKS, Aust, in Syria, 461, 501-2; British, fitted with Australian tracks, 7, 104; in Greece, strength, 30n, 166, losses, 69, 90, 141; reinforcement of Middle East with, 202; in Crete, strength, 202, 215, 218, 219, 258; strength in Middle East, 321n; in Syria, 430n; losses in Western Desert offensive, 523; French, in Syria, 344, strength, 358, 527; German, in Greece, 117, 118, 119, 120, 123, 124, 154; strength at Pinios, 126; losses, 69, 159; strength in Crete, 228
TANNER, Lt R. R., 108, 188
TATOI (Sketch p. 175), 148, 162; rearguard at, 169
TAURUS MOUNTAINS (Sketch p. 533), 530, 534, 544, 547
TAVRONITIS RIVER (Map p. 218), 221, 222, 223, 226, 229, 230
TAYLOR, Pte A. H., 309
TAYLOR, WO2 D. R., 106, 135-6
TEDDER, Marshal of the R.A.F. Lord, 298, 322, 327, 335, 531
TEHRAN (Sketch p. 533), 532
TEL ABIAD (Sketch p. 478), 479
TEL AVIV, 547n, 559
TEL EL KEBIR, 216
TEMPE (Map p. 106; Sketch p. 127), 97, 99, 106, 107, 115, 119, 121, 122, 127, 134, 185, 236n
THASOS ISLAND (Sketch p. 4), 52
THEBES (Map p. 34), 139, 141, 142, 143, 144, 169
THEODORA (Sketch p. 145), 144, 152
THERMOPYLAE LINE (Sketches pp. 82, 147), 160, 183, 191, 195; withdrawal to, 80-81, 82-3, 85, 90, 93, 98-9, 101, 103, 104, 105-6, 108-11, 112, 113, 128-30, 133-9; British hopes of prolonged defence on, 131-2; dispositions, 139-42, 148-9; engagement at, 145-7, 153-9, 183, 184; see also BRALLOS PASS; MOLOS
THESSALY, 29, 32, 37, 82, 95, 99n, 105, 106, 111, 136, 142, 184
THOM, Cpl J. G., 116
THOMAS, Maj C. C., 389, 411n
THOMAS, Maj H. W., 306
THOMAS, Sgt J. V., 547
THOMAS, Lt S. E., 483, 497
THOMPSON, Lt N. O., 264
THOMPSON, Capt R. V., 455
THOMSON, Lt A. W., 494
THOMSON, Capt C. L., 405, 409, 411
THRACE, 10, 11, 13, 14, 39-40, 45-6, 51
Thresher, British submarine, 312

Thurland Castle, British transport, 164
TIARKS, Brig J. G. E., 441n, 510
TIBERIAS, LAKE, 338, 535-6
TIBNINE (Sketches pp. 343, 348), 342, 343, 350, 351
TIDBURY, Brig O. H., 204
TILNEY, Capt W. W., 448, 507
TIMBAKION (Sketches pp. 203, 288), 203, 215, 219, 238, 241, 243, 244, 287, 288, 290, 303, 311
TIPTON, WO1 L. E., 500
TIRANA (Map p. 34; Sketch p. 39), 27, 40
TIRNAVOS (Map p. 34; Sketches pp. 101, 124), 41, 81, 82, 105, 106n, 110, 113, 122, 125
TOBRUK, 2, 9, 30, 37, 132, 159, 188, 197, 216, 320, 326, 335, 470, 523, 537, 544, 549, 553, 555n
TOCRA, 30
TODD, Brig G. H. N., 388, 395, 397, 398
TOLOS (Sketch p. 145), 150, 178; embarkations from, 152, 160, 161, 170-71, total embarked, 181; rearguard at, 179; escapes from, 185
TOMLINSON, Lt-Col P. A., 290, 291
TOPFER, Lt G. H. G., 450
TOPOLIA, Greek airfield, 228
Torbay, British submarine, 312
TORR, Brig A. G., 217
TOULON, 521
TOUMAT, MOUNT (Map p. 410; Sketch p. 462), 405, 465, 474
TRAINING, Aust, 474, 547, 553, 557, of Ski troops,, 548; Greek, 212-13
TRANSJORDAN, 198, 199, 324, 326, 333, 338, 391n, 413, 440, 534
TRANSPORT: motor, destruction in Greece, 164, 172, 173, of Creforce, 241n. Greek, 34, 72-3
TRAVERS, Maj B. H., 36n, 66n
TRAVERS, Gnr F. D., 313n
TRAVERS, Capt W. H., 259, 263
TREACY, Capt M. A., 489, 490
TRELOAR, Lt A., 379n
TRELOAR, Lt-Col J. L., 559, 560
TRETHOWAN, Capt J. M., 300
TRIKKALA (Sketches pp. 78, 124), 40, 76, 82, 91, 110, 125, 126
TRIPARTITE PACT, 25
TRIPOLI (Syria; Map p. 339; Sketch p. 535), 200n, 338, 374, 440, 478, 514, 517, 519, 521, 534, 548, 550; fortress at, 534, 535-6
TRIPOLI (Tripolitania), 6, 16, 193, 321, 551; naval bombardment of, 202
TRIPOLIS (Sketch p. 145), 162, 163, 164, 165, 167, 168, 175, 177, 179, 184
TRIPOLITANIA, 30, 193
TRIPPIER, Maj A. W., 69
TROUSDALE, Lt-Col A. C., 185
TRUSKETT, Sig W. J., 136
TSARITSANI (Map p. 34), 35
TSIKALARIA (Map p. 218), 249
TSIOTION (Sketch p. 124), 125
TSOLAKOGLOU, General, 90n, 91-2, 94, 111, 133, 142, 143
TSOUDEROS, M., 207, 214
TUNISIA, 202
TURKEY, 5, 14, 17, 24, 48, 50, 67n, 122n, 139, 185, 186, 188, 189, 190, 198, 200, 313, 315, 323, 531, 533, 534, 535, 537; and Balkan front, 6, 8, 11-12, 15, 16, 25, 191-2; signs pact with Germany, 327n; German plan for invasion of, 530; relations with Persia, 532; and proposed employment of A.I.F. in, 544
TURKISH AIR FORCE, 11n
TURLE, Rear-Admiral C. E., 112, 131, 207
TURNU MAGURELE (Sketch p. 4), 49
TYRE (Sketches pp. 334, 343), 333, 342, 379, 400; advance to, 345-52
TYRRELL, Capt W. A., 173
TYSON, Maj J. T., 165, 166, 167

UKRAINE, 538
Ulster Prince, British transport, 160-61, 171
UNITED STATES, 318, 512, 513, 538, 558; and Greek campaign, 15, 19, 191, 192; relations with France, 325, 328-9, 330, 331; Lend-Lease aid, 530
UNITED STATES ARMY, 526n, 528n
UPHAM, Capt C. H., VC and bar, 236, 245, 301
UREN, L-Cpl J. W., 457
UTZ, Colonel, 240, 243, 246, 254

VAFIOPULOUS, Cpl C., 455

Valiant, British battleship, 239
VALLIER, FORT (Sketch p. 421), 421, 422, 426, 428
Valmy, French destroyer, 363
VALONA (Sketch p. 2), 5, 23, 27, 40
VAMOS (Map p. 218), 277
VAN DEVENTER, Col D. J. C. B., 554
VAPP, Cpl C., *see* VAFIOPULOUS
VARDAR RIVER, *see* AXIOS RIVER
VASEY, Maj-Gen G. A., in Greece, 67, 68, 71, 75, 76, 79, 88, 102, 163; at Vevi, 44, 57, 60, 61, 62, 64-5; at Brallos, 138, 140, 141, 142, 145, 148, 156, 157, 158, orders at, 143; in Crete, 212, 213, 218, 219, 232, 234, 235, 236, 238, 242, 248, 249, 251, 253, 296, 298, 299, 300, 301, 303, 304, commands AIF, 211, requests allotment of command, 234, orders withdrawal 19th Brigade to 42nd Street, 249-50; embarks, 305-6; returns to Australia, 549
VATERON (Sketch p. 55), 58
VEGORRITIS, LAKE (Maps pp. 38, 66), 35, 43, 47, 57, 65, 66
VELEMISTION (Sketch p. 101), 103
VELES (Sketch p. 45), 42, 51
VELVENDOS (Sketch p. 73), 73, 85
Vendetta, British destroyer, 164
VENETIKOS RIVER (Map p. 34; Sketch p. 4), 4, 46, 77, 79, 81, 83, 89, 103, 128
VERDILHAC, General de, 334, 374, 412, 510, 511, 513, 514, 515, 520
VERIA PASS (Maps pp. 34, 38; Sketch p. 10), 10, 30, 33, 34, 35, 36, 37, 41-2, 46, 94, 108; withdrawal from, 54, 58, 73-4, 85
VERMION MOUNTAINS (Map p. 38), 3, 35, 36, 43, 46, 54, 66, 77, 78
VERMION-OLYMPUS LINE (Map p. 38; Sketch p. 4), 4, 26, 40, 43; proposed withdrawal of Greek forces to, 11, 12, 13, 25, 26, 194; reconnaissances of, 27, 33; dispositions on, 33-4, 37
VERNACOS, Lt-Cdr, 313
VEVI (Map p. 66; Sketch p. 59), 43, 44, 46, 47, 53, 88, 89; Allied dispositions at, 48; rearguard at, 56-8, 59-66, 67n; losses at, 64; German account, 71
VIAL, Lt-Col R. R., 76, 153, 173, 181
VICTORIA, railway system, 29n
VIENNA, 50
VIETINGHOFF, General von, 49, 50, 71
VILLA ARIADNE, 290
VITSILOKOUMOS (Sketch p. 303), 299
Vittorio Veneto, Italian battleship, 23
VLACHOS, George, 14
VLAKHERONITISSA (Map p. 218), 223
VLASTI PASS (Sketch p. 78), 65, 76
VOLOS (Map p. 34; Sketch p. 82), 29, 44n, 67n, 82, 108, 109, 122, 125, 129n, 136, 139, 142, 144n; rearguard at, 133-4
VON BIBRA, Pte K. C., 455, 456n, 557n
Voyager, British destroyer, 161
VRISES (Sketch p. 296), 296
VUKOVAR (Sketch p. 51), 51
VUTRINTO, LAKE (Sketch p. 78), 77

WAIN, Col W. J., 380
WALKER, Col A. S., 182n
WALKER, Pte C. M., 455, 456n, 557n
WALKER, Maj E. S., 116
WALKER, Maj K. R., 308
WALKER, Lt-Col T. G., 135, 172, 234, 236, 251, 252, 255, 297, 304, 306, 307
WALLER, Capt H. M. L., 23, 170
WALLER, Cpl L. L., 464
WALLER, Brig R. P., 69, 89-90, 155n
WALSH, L-Sgt B. W., 361
WARBURTON, Sgt C. H., 450
WAR CORRESPONDENTS, 559-62
WARDLE, Lt-Col M. K., 556, 557n
WARDLEY, Lt W. J., 346, 347
Warsaw, Polish merchantman, 67n
Warspite, British battleship, 239
WASHINGTON, 328
Waterhen, British destroyer, 164
WATKINS, Lt-Cdr G. R. G., 177
WATSON, Maj G. C., 113, 114, 127
WATTS, Capt R. H., 366
WAVELL, Field Marshal Rt Hon Earl, 6, 21, 24, 83, 197, 202, 212, 325, 335, 337, 470, 527, 536, 556, 557, 560; visits Athens, 2-3, 12-13; Chiefs of Staffs instructions to, 4-5, 16, 391; selects force for Greece, 7; views on Greek expedition, 8, 9, 11, 15,

WAVELL, Field Marshal Rt Hon Earl—*continued*
193; at Athens Conference, 10n, 11; discussions with Australian Prime Minister, 8, 14, 19, and Blamey, 18, 20; retains Polish Brigade in Egypt, 37, 39; and embarkation from Greece, 104-5, 112, 113, 131-2, 133, 143, 169; recommends Blamey as Deputy C-in-C Middle East, 151; extension of command to Iraq, 201; and defence of Crete, 205, 206, 207-8, 209-10, 215, 228, 241; visits Crete, 208-9; Freyberg's messages to, 220, 227, 241, 247; and evacuation of Crete, 254, 298, 300, 302; strength in Middle East, 320-1, requests appointment of political authority, 321, 322, 525, 531; and invasion of Syria, 322, 326, 327-8, 333, 336, reinforces invading force, 391-2; on value of tanks in Syria, 430n; and advance from Iraq into Syria, 440, 442; suggests resumption of offensive in Syria, 449; becomes C-in-C India, 523, estimate of, 523-4, 555; orders advance into Persia, 532; and Anzac Corps proposals, 539, 541
WAYTE, Pte J. J., 354
WEBB, L-Cpl T., 353
WEICHS, Field Marshal Maximilian von, 49, 51, 94
WEIR, Capt S. I., 135
WELD, Maj-Gen C. J., 479
WELLINGTON (N.Z.), 20, 541
WELLINGTON, Col N. F., 401, 443, 448, 449
WELLMAN, Col L. J., 36n
WELLS, Lt-Gen H., 34, 54, 103, 137, 143
WELSH, L-Cpl I. D., 313-15
WEST, Cpl H., 62
WEST, Maj N. P., 88
WEST AFRICA, 320, 327
WESTERN DESERT, 65, 320, 326, 327, 341, 342, 392, 430n, 529, 530, 536, 537, 553, 554, 555, 560, 562; allotment of armour in, 21; British offensive in, 523, 524; reinforcement of, 531; Eighth Army offensive, 549
WESTON, Lt-Gen E. C., 206, 207, 211n, 213, 218, 219, 226, 234, 238, 243n, 248, 249, 250, 251, 253, 297, 298, 301, 302, 303, 307; assumes command in Crete, 204, problems of, 205; placed in command western sector of Crete, 295; orders surrender at Sfakia, 305
WEYGAND, General, 321n, 323, 324, 325, 330
WEYGAND, FORT (Sketch p. 421), 421, 423, 425-6, 427
WHEAT HILL (Sketch p. 245), 245
WHITE, Lt A. E. D., 443, 445, 463
WHITE, General Sir Brudenell, 542n, 559
WHITE, Maj D. A. H., 375, 376, 482, 483, 497
WHITE, Pte R. G., 268
WHITE, L-Cpl R. S., 501
WHITTAKER, Lt R. K., 455
WHITTLE, Lt J. S., 262
WHYTE, Pte A., 271
WIECK, Cpl S., 363, 488
WIEDEMANN, Capt, 275, 276, 277
WIENER NEUSTADT, 50
WILLIAMS, Maj D. E., 433, 434, 436, 438
WILLIAMS, Cpl J., 445
WILLIAMS, Lt T. H., 134
WILLMOTT, Lt R., 261n, 262
WILLOUGHBY, Cpl T. R., 268, 269
WILLS, Brig K. A., 150n
WILMOT, C., 197n
WILSON, Field Marshal Lord, 13, 29, 204, 210, 325, 532; selected to command expedition to Greece, 9, 11; arrives Athens, 21; staff, 22; staff talks with Yugoslavs, 24-5, 27, with Papagos, 25; requests staff to reconnoitre lines of withdrawal, 28; in Greece, 37, 41, 68, 83, 87, 102, 103, 104, 113, 129n 139, 140, 141, 148, 149, 150, 155, 163, 164, 165, 167; and Doiran-Nestos line, 25, 34; assumes command of Allied forces in Central Macedonia, 35-6; and withdrawal to Olympus-Aliakmon line, 40, 43, 46, 54-5, 58; withdraws Armoured Brigade from Axios plain, 42; problems of command, 44, 65-6; misunderstandings with Papagos, 76-9, 92-3, 194; and withdrawal to Thermopylae, 80, 81-2; orders withdrawal of Armoured Brigade to Kalabaka, 90; and embarkation from Greece, 112, 131-2, 133, 143-5, 151, 152, 169, embarks, 168; assumes command in Crete, 206-7; appointed commander British Troops in Palestine and Transjordan, 208; ordered to plan for advance into Syria, 326, confers with de Gaulle, 328, plans advance, 336-8, 340, 344; in Syrian campaign, 391, 400, 402, 403, 406, 413, 467, 478, orders concentration on advance

INDEX

WILSON, Field Marshal Lord—*continued*
to Beirut, 414, 467-8, agrees to diversion of main effort to Damascus area, 418; and Syrian Armistice, 511, 512, 513-14, administration of, 515, 517, 518, 519; conduct of Syrian campaign, 526-7; and defence of Syria, 532, 534; commands Ninth Army, 544; on A.I.F. discipline, 546
WILSON, Lt-Col B., 457*n*
WILSON, Pte B. G., 457*n*
WILSON, Pte C. R., 457*n*
WILSON, Lt-Col E. H., 561
WILSON, Col J. G., 125-6
WILSON, Capt R., 438
WILSON, Pte R. I., 348
WILSON, Pte R. J., 362
WILSON, WO2 W. J., 457, 458
WILTON, Col J. G. N., 408
"WINDY CORNER" (Map p. 386), 396, 397, 400
WISSHAUPT, Ernst, 52*n*
WITHY, Lt-Col C. B., 444, 461, 462, 463, 474, 476, 505
WITTMAN, Lt-Col, 277
WOOD, Capt F. H., 297*n*
WOOD, Capt S. F., 155, 156, 157, 269-70
WOODHILL, Capt P. J., 173, 181
WOODWARD, Maj-Gen E. W., 34*n*
WOOLFORD, Capt H. B., 459*n*
WOORE, Maj T. G., 375
WOOTTEN, Maj-Gen G. F., 555
WRAY, Maj C. H. W., 382
WREN, Capt E. D., 62, 63*n*
WRIGHT, Maj H. E., 352
WRIGLEY, Brig H., 161
Wryneck, British destroyer, 171
WYNTER, Lt-Gen H. D., 552*n*; invalided to Australia, 555

XAMOUDHOKHORI (Map p. 218), 223, 236
XINIA (Sketch p. 136), 137

XINON NERON (Map p. 66; Sketch p. 67), 47, 63, 71

YAFOUR (Sketches pp. 416, 509), 430, 432, 433, 438, 439
YAFOUR, COL DE (Sketch p. 416), 433, 439
YANNINA (Sketches pp. 78, 159), 80, 112, 128, 131, 133, 142, 149, 158, 183, 184
YANNINA, BISHOP OF, 104, 133
YANTA (Sketch p. 413), 510
YAROUN (Sketches pp. 343, 348), 342, 349
YERATE (Map p. 482), 473, 485, 487*n*, 488
York, British cruiser, 23, 239
YOUHMOUR (Sketch p. 334), 344
YOUNG, Cpl J. T., 273
Y.M.C.A., 559
YUGOSLAV AIR FORCE, 51
YUGOSLAV ARMY, 37, 39, 51, 53, 70, 86, 89, 152, 173; value of Salonika to, 10; Staff talks with, 24-5, 26-7; estimated value of, 26, 27; cooperation with Greek Army, 40, 41, 43; collapse of, 42, 52, 71
YUGOSLAVIA, 6, 11, 14, 16, 17, 27, 29, 34, 35, 41, 43, 46, 80, 112, 158, 173*n*, 184, 497; relations with Germany, 3, 12; with Britain and Greece, 3, 8, 13, 15, 24-5, 26-7, 28, 191, 192-3, 194; *coup d'etat* in, 25, 48, 194; German invasion of, 39, 49, 50-52, 70, 71, 94; surrender of, 94
YUGOSLAVS, THE, 165, 171, 178, 180

ZAGARI, 187
ZAGREB (Sketch p. 51), 50, 71, 94
ZAHARANI, WADI (Sketch p. 377), 378, 379
ZAHLE (Sketch p. 334), 344, 388, 405, 431, 535
ZAMALKA (Sketch p. 416), 426
Zara, Italian cruiser, 23
ZARKOS (Sketch p. 124), 82, 99, 102, 110, 111, 125
ZEBEDANI (Sketch p. 334), 535
ZEINI, WADI (Sketch p. 462), 460-61
ZHALTA (Map p. 410), 389, 390
ZOUADE, WADI (Map p. 482), 492

www.ingramcontent.com/pod-product-compliance
Lightning Source LLC
Chambersburg PA
CBHW050522300426
44113CB00012B/1921